World Travel Atlas
5th edition

ISBN: 0 946393 95 8

©1998 Columbus Press Limited

Columbus Press Limited, Columbus House, 28 Charles Square, London N1 6HT.
Tel: +44 (0) 171 417 0700. Fax: +44 (0) 171 417 0710. E-Mail: booksales@colguide.demon.co.uk.

Editor
Mike Taylor of the University of Brighton

Specialist Cartography
David Burles

General Cartography
AND Map Graphics

Additional Research
Kate Meere, Nonke Beyer, Nick Ryan, Barbara Bentele, Nick Dent, Pedro Machado, Tony Peisley, Patrick Thorne

Front Cover Design
Warren Evans

Statistics Design
Gavin Crosswell

Index Design
Daniel Josty

Regional Booksales Managers
Peter Korniczky, Martin Newman, Henry Wallis

German Booksales (Columbus Press, 38018 Braunschweig)
Gunter Knop, Michael Knop

United States Booksales (SF Communications, Roanoke, VA 24018)
David Frank, Amanda Betley

Production Director
Brian Quinn

Publisher
Stephen Collins

Printed and Bound in the United Kingdom by
Thanet Press Ltd, Margate

Colour Reproduction by
Kingswood-Steele, London N1

Cartography on Pages 1-46
Maps supplied by ICA Bokförlag, AB, Sweden © 1997/8, and designed and produced by AND Map Graphics Ltd, Finchampstead, Berkshire, United Kingdom

Information for Skiing Maps on Pages 70 & 116 supplied by
Snow-Hunter, Inverness

The publishers would like to thank all the tourist offices, embassies, airlines, cruise and ferry operators, sporting bodies and other organisations and individuals who assisted in the preparation of this edition, with particular thanks to UNESCO, the World Tourism Organisation, the British Tourism Authority, the English Tourist Board, the World Health Organisation, the Travel Industry Association of America, the Automobile Association, the Royal Automobile Club, the Tidy Britain Group and the National Maritime Museum.

Whilst every effort is made by the publishers to ensure the accuracy of the information contained in this edition of the World Travel Atlas, the publishers accept no responsibility for any loss occasioned to any person acting or refraining from acting as a result of the material contained in this publication or liability for any financial or other agreements which may be entered into with any organisations or individuals listed in the text.

Copies of the Teachers' Supplement to the World Travel Atlas, which names all the features marked in the Outline Maps on pages X1 to X16, are also available. Contact the publishers at the above address for details.

CONTENTS

STATISTICS — IV-VIII

World — iv-v
United States — vi
United Kingdom — vii
Countries A-Z — viii

GENERAL REFERENCE MAPS — 1-46

Key and Introduction — 1
World Political — 2-3
Europe — 4
Benelux and the Surrounding Area — 5
British Isles — 6-7
Germany — 8-9
France — 10
Spain and Portugal — 11
Italy — 12
Central Europe — 13
The Balkans — 14
Greece and Turkey — 15
Scandinavia — 16
European Russia — 17
Middle East — 18
Africa — 19
Northwest Africa — 20
Northeast Africa — 21
West Africa — 22
Central Africa — 23
Southern Africa — 24
Asia — 25
Northwest Asia — 26
Northeast Asia — 27
South Asia — 28
East Asia — 29
Japan and Korea — 30
South-East Asia — 31
Malaysia and Indonesia — 32
Oceania — 33
Australia — 34
New Zealand and New Guinea — 35
North America — 36
Central America — 37
Canada — 38-39
United States of America — 40-41
South America — 42
Northern South America — 43
Central South America — 44
Eastern Brazil and Southern South America — 45
Polar Regions — 46

SPECIALIST MAPS — 47-136

Key and Introduction — 47

World — 48-64

Climate — 48
Time — 49
Health — 50
National Income — 51
Tourism — 51
Sport — 52
Driving — 53
Airports — 54-56
IATA Areas — 54-56
International Flight Times — 57
Cruising — 58-59
UNESCO Natural Heritage Sites — 60-61
UNESCO Cultural Heritage Sites — 62-64

Europe — 65-97

Climate — 65
Railways — 66-67
Ferries — 66-67
Blue Flag Beaches — 68-69
Skiing — 70
Historical — 71
National Parks — 72
Leisure Parks — 73
United Kingdom — 74
United Kingdom Beaches — 75
United Kingdom National Parks — 75
United Kingdom Motorways — 76
United Kingdom Airports — 76-77
United Kingdom Ferries — 78
Ireland — 79
Benelux — 80
Germany — 81-82
German Spas — 83
France — 84-85
Spain — 86-87
Portugal — 88
Switzerland — 89
Austria — 89
Italy — 90-91
Greece — 92-93
Turkey — 92-93
Malta — 93
Cyprus — 93
Scandinavia — 94-95
Central Europe — 96-97
The Former Soviet Union — 96-97

Africa 99-103

Climate	99
Languages	100
South Africa	100
Morocco	101
Egypt	101
Tunisia	101
Kenya	101
Tanzania	102
Zimbabwe	102
Parks and Game Reserves	102-103

Asia 98 & 104-112

The Holy Land	98
Ancient Trade Routes	98
South and East Asia Climate	104
India	105-106
Sri Lanka	106
Maldives	106
Seychelles	106
China	107
Hong Kong & Macau	107
Malaysia	108
Singapore	108
Vietnam	108
Thailand	109
Indonesia	110
Australia	111-112
New Zealand	112

The Americas 113-127

North America Climate	113
North America Railways	114-115
North America Airports	114-115
North America Skiing	116
United States of America	117-119
United States National Parks	120-121
United States Theme Parks	120-121
Canada	122-123
Mexico	123
Caribbean Languages	124
Bahamas	124
Jamaica	124
Cuba	124
Puerto Rico	125
Antigua	125
St Kitts and Nevis	125
Barbados	125
St Lucia	125
Trinidad and Tobago	125
South America Climate	126
South America	127

Relief Maps 128-136

World	128
Europe	129
Africa	130
Asia	131
North America	132
South America	133
Australia and New Zealand	134
Polar Regions	135
The Earth from Space	136

APPENDICES 137-140

1. Geographical Definitions	137
2. US States	138
3. Canadian Provinces and Territories	138
4. Australian States and Territories	138
5. French Départements	138
6. World's Major Urban Areas	139
7. World's Longest Rivers	139
8. World's Highest and Lowest Points	139
9. Conversion Chart	139
10. International Glossary	139-140

INDEX 141-184

OUTLINE MAPS X1-X16

World	X1
Europe and the Mediterranean	X2
The Former Soviet Union	X2
British Isles	X3
Netherlands	X4
Belgium and Luxembourg	X4
Germany	X5
France	X6
Spain	X7
Portugal	X7
Switzerland	X8
Austria	X8
Italy	X9
Greece and Turkey	X10
Malta and Cyprus	X11
Scandinavia	X11
Africa	X12
India	X13
China	X13
Australia	X14
Canada	X14
United States of America	X15
Mexico	X15
The Caribbean	X16

WORLDWIDE

Figures 1a-e
TOURISM PAYMENTS – RECEIPTS AND EXPENDITURE

Figure 1a **US tourism payments**
Source: World Tourism Organization 1995 statistics

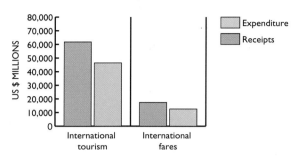

Figure 1b **Canada tourism payments**
Source: World Tourism Organization 1996 statistics

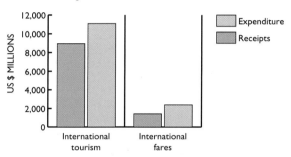

Figure 1c **UK tourism payments**
Source: World Tourism Organization 1995 statistics

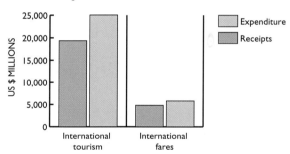

Figure 1d **Germany tourism payments**
Source: World Tourism Organization 1996 statistics

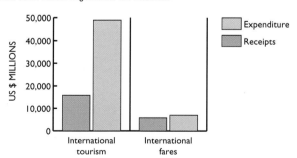

Figure 1e **Japan tourism payments**
Source: World Tourism Organization 1996 statistics

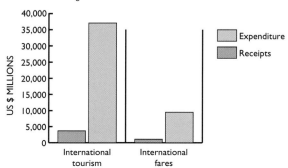

Figure 2 **TOURIST ARRIVALS BY REGION (1996)**
Source: World Tourism Organization

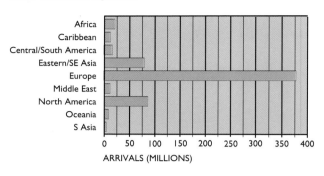

Figure 3 **TOURIST ARRIVALS BY REGION % CHANGE 96/95**
Source: World Tourism Organization

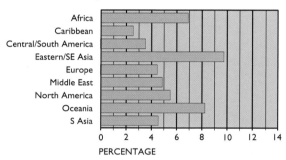

Figure 4
THE TOP 50 AIRPORTS
Source: Annual Airport Traffic Statistics, Airports Council International (ACI), 1996

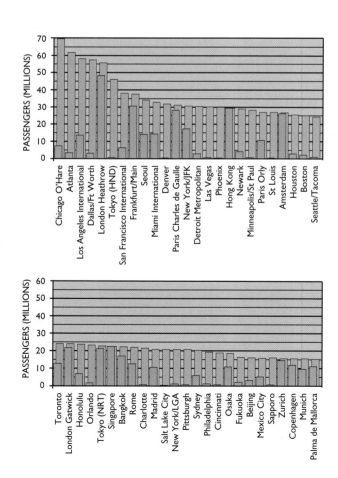

WORLDWIDE

Figures 6a-j
WORLDWIDE DESTINATIONS – WHO GOES WHERE

Figure 6a United States – destinations by region, 1996
Source: World Tourism Organization

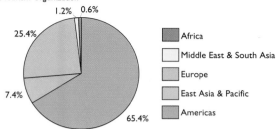

Figure 6b Canada – destinations by region, 1996
Source: World Tourism Organization

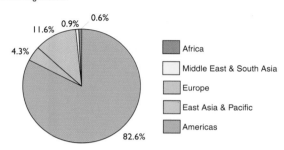

Figure 6c United Kingdom – destinations by region, 1996
Source: World Tourism Organization

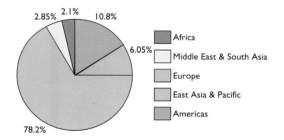

Figure 6d Germany – destinations by region, 1996
Source: World Tourism Organization

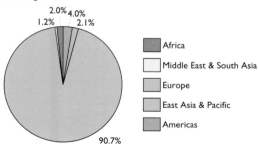

Figure 6e Japan – destinations by region, 1996
Source: World Tourism Organization

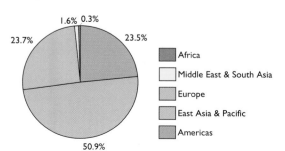

Figure 6f Australia – destinations by region, 1995
Source: World Tourism Organization

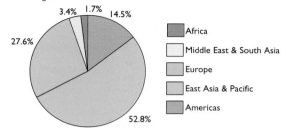

Figure 6g Netherlands – destinations by region, 1995
Source: World Tourism Organization

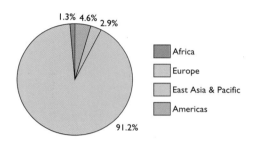

Figure 6h France – destinations by region, 1996
Source: World Tourism Organization

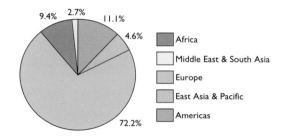

Figure 6i Spain – destinations by region, 1995
Source: World Tourism Organization

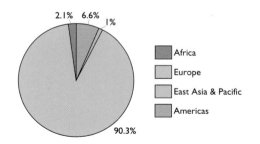

Figure 6j Sweden – destinations by region, 1995
Source: World Tourism Organization

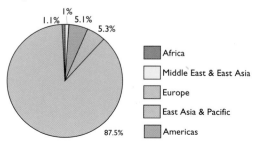

USA

Figure 7
DOMESTIC TRAVEL – EXPENDITURE BY STATE, 1994
Source: Travel Industry Association of America

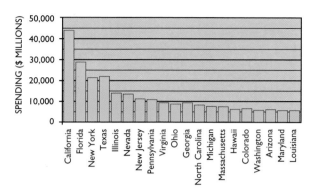

Figure 8
DOMESTIC TRAVEL – EMPLOYMENT BY STATE, 1994
Source: Travel Industry Association of America

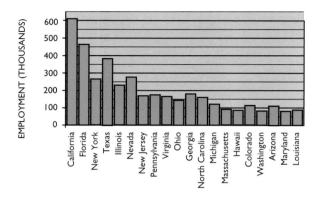

Figure 9
INTERNATIONAL VISITORS TO THE USA, 1996
Source: International Trade Administration Tourism Industries

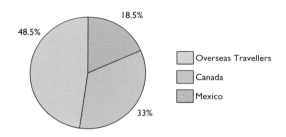

Figure 10
OVERSEAS VISITORS TO THE USA, 1996
Source: International Trade Administration Tourism Industries

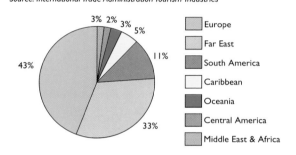

Figure 11
TOP STATES VISITED BY OVERSEAS TRAVELLERS TO THE U.S. 1995
Source: Survey of International Air Travelers to the United States (In-Flight Survey)

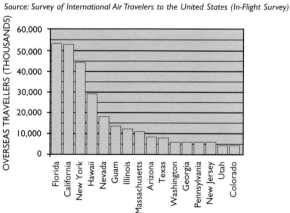

Figure 12
ARRIVALS BY MODES OF TRANSPORT, 1995
Source: World Tourism Organization

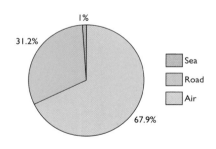

Figure 13
TOP CITIES VISITED BY OVERSEAS TRAVELLERS TO THE U.S. 1995
Source: Survey of International Air Travelers to the United States (In-Flight Survey)

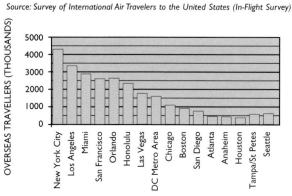

Figure 14
US TOURISM RECEIPTS
Source: World Tourism Organization

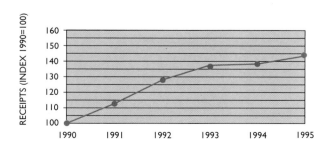

UNITED KINGDOM

Figure 14
OVERSEAS VISITS TO THE UK BY AREA OF RESIDENCE, 1996
Source: British Tourist Authority 1997

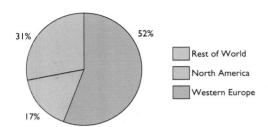

Rest of World
North America
Western Europe

Figure 15
OVERSEAS VISITS TO THE UK BY PURPOSE OF VISIT, 1995
Source: British Tourist Authority 1996

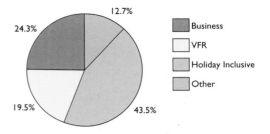

Business
VFR
Holiday Inclusive
Other

Figure 16
TOP FIVE COUNTRIES OF ORIGIN OF VISITORS TO UK
Source: British Tourist Authority 1997

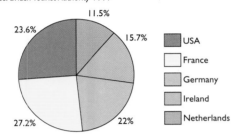

USA
France
Germany
Ireland
Netherlands

Figure 17
ENGLAND – TYPES OF LOCATION
Source: British Tourist Authority/English Tourist Board 1996

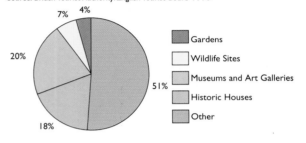

Gardens
Wildlife Sites
Museums and Art Galleries
Historic Houses
Other

Figure 18
VISITS TO TOP TWENTY ATTRACTIONS CHARGING ADMISSIONS
Source: Statistics supplied to British Tourist Authority/English Tourist Board 1997

Chester Zoo
Roman Baths and Pump Room, Bath
Drayton Manor Park, Staffordshire
Kew Gardens, London
St Paul's Cathedral, London
London Zoo
Windemere Lake Cruises, Cumbria
Thorpe Park, Surrey
Flamingo Land, Yorkshire
Edinburgh Castle
Blackpool Tower
Windsor Castle, Berkshire
Legoland, Windsor
Science Museum, London
Natural History Museum, London
Chessington World of Adventures
Canterbury Cathedral
Tower of London
Madame Tussauds, London
Alton Towers, Staffordshire

0 0.5 1 1.5 2 2.5 3
VISITS (MILLIONS)

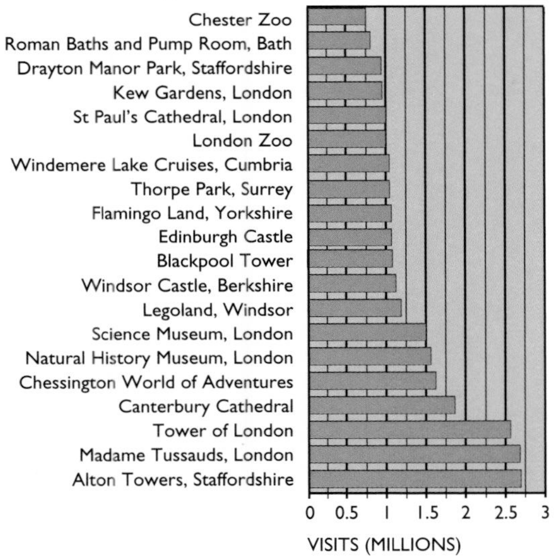

Figure 19
DISTRIBUTION OF OVERSEAS TOURISM, 1996
Source: Statistics supplied to British Tourist Authority/English Tourist Board 1997

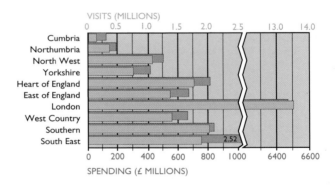

VISITS (MILLIONS)
0 0.5 1.0 1.5 2.0 2.5 13.0 14.0

Cumbria
Northumbria
North West
Yorkshire
Heart of England
East of England
London
West Country
Southern
South East

2.52

0 200 400 600 800 1000 6400 6600
SPENDING (£ MILLIONS)

Figure 20
OVERSEAS SPENDING IN THE UK, 1985-1995
Source: Statistics supplied to British Tourist Authority/English Tourist Board 1996

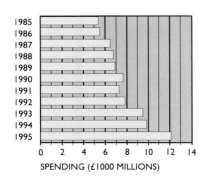

1985
1986
1987
1988
1989
1990
1991
1992
1993
1994
1995

0 2 4 6 8 10 12 14
SPENDING (£1000 MILLIONS)

Figure 21
TOURISM SPENDING BREAKDOWN, 1996
Source: Statistics supplied to British Tourist Authority/English Tourist Board 1997

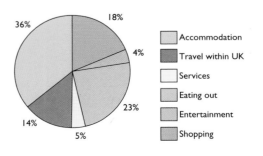

Accommodation
Travel within UK
Services
Eating out
Entertainment
Shopping

COUNTRIES A-Z

The list below gives information on all the world's independent states. Many countries have dependencies, overseas possessions, colonies, offshore island groups etc and with the exception of a few common-sense exceptions (such as Réunion and Gibraltar), these have not been listed. The matter of defining what is and what is not a state is by no means clear-cut, but no political or other subjective stance has been adopted. For more information on states and territories worldwide, please consult the relevant pages of your *World Travel Guide*.

Some **Country** names have been shortened for reasons of space. **Area** is given in 1,000s of square kilometres, **Population** in 1,000s and **Population Density** as the latter divided by the former. Population figures are based on the most up-to-date information available (usually census returns or official estimates), some being as recent as 1996. In general, refugees are not included. Please see the notes at the foot of the chart regarding **Capitals**, as some countries have more than one, or are in the process of changing over from one to another.

Country	Area	Pop.	Pop. Den.	Capital
Afghanistan	652	17,080	28.5	Kabul
Albania	28.7	3,363	117	Tirana
Algeria	2,382	26,581	11.2	Algiers
American Samoa	0.19	53	272.1	Pago Pago
Andorra	0.47	65	130.6	Andorra la Vella
Angola	1,247	10,609	8.5	Luanda
Anguilla	0.1	10.3	107.3	The Valley
Antigua & Barbuda	0.4	64.1	145.3	St John's
Argentina	2,767	34,180	12.4	Buenos Aires
Armenia	29.8	3,754	126	Yerevan
Aruba	0.19	80	416.2	Oranjestad
Australia	7,682	17,657	2.3	Canberra
Austria	84	8,031	95	Vienna
Azerbaijan	87	7,499	86.6	Baku
Bahamas	14	269	19.3	Nassau
Bahrain	0.7	568	817	Manama
Bangladesh	148	117,787	798	Dhaka
Barbados	0.4	264	614.0	Bridgetown
Belarus	208	10,297	49.6	Minsk
Belgium	31	10,101	330.9	Brussels
Belize	23	209	9.1	Belmopan
Benin	113	5,215	46.3	Porto Novo
Bermuda	0.05	59.5	1124	Hamilton
Bhutan	47	600	12.9	Thimphu
Bolivia	1,085	7,237	6.6	La Paz [1]
				Sucre [1]
Bonaire	0.3	10.2	35.4	Kralendijk
Bosnia-Herzegovina	51	3,527	69	Sarajevo
Botswana	582	1,450	2.5	Gaborone
Brazil	8,512	155,822	18.3	Brasília
British Virgin Is.	0.2	19	124.2	Road Town
Brunei	6	284.5	49.3	Bandar Seri Begawan
Bulgaria	111	8,427	75.9	Sofia
Burkina Faso	274	9,889	36.1	Ouagadougou
Burundi	28	6,134	220.4	Bujumbura
Cambodia	181	9,568	52.9	Phnom Penh
Cameroon	475	11,540	24.3	Yaoundé
Canada	9,958	29,248	2.9	Ottawa
Cape Verde	4	341	84.7	Praia
Cayman Is.	0.2	32	123.5	George Town
Central African Rep.	623	2,463	4	Bangui
Chad	1,284	6,214	4.9	Ndjaména
Chile	757	14,210	18.8	Santiago
China, People's Rep. [2]	9,572	1,204,690	125.8	Beijing (Peking)
Colombia	1,142	34,520	30.2	Bogotá
Comoro Is.	2	484	259.9	Moroni
Congo	342	1,843	5.4	Brazzaville
Congo, Dem. Rep [3]	2,345	36,672	15.6	Kinshasa
Cook Is.	0.2	19	80	Avarua
Costa Rica	51	3,500	68.5	San José
Côte d'Ivoire	322	13,695	42.5	Yamoussoukro [4]
				Abidjan [4]
Croatia	57	4,779	84.4	Zagreb
Cuba	111	10,901	98.3	Havana
Curaçao	0.4	144	324.5	Willemstad
Cyprus	9	730	78.9	Nicosia
Czech Rep.	79	10,333	131.0	Prague
Denmark	43	5,216	121	Copenhagen
Djibouti	23	520	22.4	Djibouti
Dominica	0.7	71	94.9	Roseau
Dominican Rep.	48	7,769	160.4	Santo Domingo
Ecuador	272	11,460	42.1	Quito
Egypt	998	57,851	58	Cairo
El Salvador	21	5,048	239.9	San Salvador
Equatorial Guinea	28	356	12.7	Malabo
Eritrea	121	3,436	28.4	Asmara
Estonia	45	1,476	33	Tallinn
Ethiopia	1,133	56,677	50.0	Addis Ababa
Falkland Is.	12	2	0.2	Stanley
Fiji	18	797	42.6	Suva
Finland	338	5,098	15.1	Helsinki
France	544	57,903	106.4	Paris
French Guiana	91	114	1.3	Cayenne
French Polynesia	4	212	50.9	Papeete
Gabon	268	1,011	3.8	Libreville
Gambia, The	11	1,038	91.9	Banjul
Georgia	70	5,471	78.5	Tbilisi
Germany	357	81,338	227.9	Berlin [5]
				Bonn [5]
Ghana	239	17,000	71.3	Accra
Gibraltar	0.007	28	4319.2	Gibraltar
Greece	132	10,368	78.5	Athens
Greenland	2,176	55	0.03	Nuuk
Grenada	0.3	95	276.9	St George's
Guadeloupe	2	387	217.4	Basse-Terre [6]
				Pointe-à-Pitre [6]
Guam	0.5	146	265.9	Agaña
Guatemala	109	10,322	97.5	Guatemala City
Guinea Rep.	246	5,600	22.8	Conakry
Guinea-Bissau	36	1050	26.1	Bissau
Guyana	215	738	3.4	Georgetown
Haiti	28	7,041	253.7	Port-au-Prince
Honduras	112	5,770	51.5	Tegucigalpa
Hungary	93	10,277	110.5	Budapest
Iceland	103	268	2.6	Reykjavík
India	3,287	920,000	279.9	New Delhi
Indonesia	1,904	194,440	102	Jakarta
Iran	1,648	59,778	36.3	Tehran
Iraq	438	17,903	40.8	Baghdad
Ireland	70	3,582	52.0	Dublin
Israel	22	5,462	249.4	Jerusalem
Italy	301	57,269	190.1	Rome
Jamaica	11	2,374	216	Kingston
Japan	378	125,200	331.4	Tokyo
Jordan	98	5,198	53.2	Amman
Kazakhstan	2,717	16,763	6.2	Akmola [7]
Kenya	580	29,292	50.5	Nairobi
Kiribati	1	78	96	Bairiki
Korea, DPR (N)	121	23,483	194.8	Pyongyang
Korea, Rep. (S)	99	44,850	451.3	Seoul
Kuwait	18	1,576	88.4	Kuwait City
Kyrgyzstan	199	4,476	22.6	Bishkek
Laos	237	4,581	19.3	Vientiane
Latvia	65	2,530	39.2	Riga
Lebanon	10	2,745	262.6	Beirut
Lesotho	30	1,700	56	Maseru
Liberia	98	2,700	27.6	Monrovia
Libya	1,776	4,899	2.8	Tripoli
Liechtenstein	0.2	31	191	Vaduz
Lithuania	65	3,717	56.9	Vilnius
Luxembourg	3	407	157.2	Luxembourg-Ville
Macau	0.02	400	20,250	Macau
Macedonia (FYR)	26	1,937	75.3	Skopje
Madagascar	587	12,092	20.6	Antananarivo
Malawi	118	10,033	84.7	Lilongwe
Malaysia	330	20,103	61	Kuala Lumpur
Maldives	0.3	245	821	Malé
Mali	1,240	8,156	6.6	Bamako
Malta	0.3	369	1169	Valletta
Marshall Is.	0.2	52	287	Majuro
Martinique	1	371	328.7	Fort-de-France
Mauritania	1,031	2,211	2.1	Nouakchott
Mauritius	2	1,113	565.1	Port Louis
Mayotte	0.4	94	252.4	Dzaoudzi
Mexico	1,958	93,008	47.5	Mexico City
Micronesia, Fed. States	0.7	105	149.6	Pohnpei
Moldova	34	4,350	129.1	Chisinău
Monaco	0.002	30	15,370	Monaco-Ville
Mongolia	1,567	2,317	1.5	Ulan Bator
Montserrat	0.1	11	103.7	Plymouth [8]
Morocco	711 [9]	26,024 [9]	36.7 [9]	Rabat
Mozambique	799	17,423	21.8	Maputo
Myanmar	677	41,550	61.4	Yangon [10]
Namibia	824	1,500	1.8	Windhoek
Nauru	0.02	10	465.7	Yaren District
Nepal	147	19,280	131	Kathmandu
Netherlands	34	15,385	453	Amsterdam
New Caledonia	19	183	9.6	Nouméa
New Zealand	271	3,592	13.3	Wellington
Nicaragua	120	4,500	37.4	Managua
Niger	1,267	8,361	6.6	Niamey
Nigeria	924	88,515	95.8	Abuja [11]
Niue	0.3	2	8.8	Alofi
N. Mariana Is.	0.5	53	115.8	Saipan
Norway	324	4,348	13.4	Oslo
Oman	310	2,096	6.8	Muscat
Palau	0.5	17	34	Koror
Pakistan	796	126,610	159	Islamabad
Panama	76	2,631	34.8	Panama City
Papua New Guinea	463	3,997	8.6	Port Moresby
Paraguay	407	4,642	11.4	Asunción
Peru	1,285	23,088	18	Lima
Philippines	300	67,038	223.5	Manila
Poland	313	38,609	123.4	Warsaw
Portugal	92	9,902	107.3	Lisbon
Puerto Rico	9	3,720	415.2	San Juan
Qatar	11	593	51.8	Doha
Réunion	3	642	255.7	Saint-Denis
Romania	238	22,731	95.4	Bucharest
Russian Federation	17,075	148,100	8.7	Moscow
Rwanda	26	7,165	272	Kigali
Saba	0.01	1	86.9	The Bottom
St Eustatius	0.02	2	87.6	Oranjestad
St Kitts & Nevis	0.3	44	166.9	Basseterre
St Lucia	0.6	140	227	Castries
St Maarten	0.03	32	947.7	Philipsburg
St Vincent & the Gren.	0.4	111	285	Kingstown
Samoa [12]	3	164	57.9	Apia
San Marino	0.06	25	414	San Marino
São Tomé e Príncipe	1	125	124.9	São Tomé
Saudi Arabia	2,240	16,929	7.6	Riyadh
Senegal	197	8,152	41.4	Dakar
Seychelles	0.5	74	163	Victoria
Sierra Leone	72	4,509	62.9	Freetown
Singapore	0.6	2,986	4612.4	Singapore
Slovak Rep.	49	5,368	109.5	Bratislava
Slovenia	20	1,989	98.2	Ljubljana
Solomon Is.	28	366	13.3	Honiara
Somalia	638	7,114	11.2	Mogadishu
South Africa	1,219	41,245	33.8	Pretoria [13]
				Cape Town [13]
				Bloemfontein [13]
Spain	505	39,188	78.4	Madrid
Sri Lanka	66	18,000	274.3	Colombo
Sudan	2,506	24,940	10	Khartoum
Suriname	163	418	2.6	Paramaribo
Swaziland	17	879	50.6	Mbabane
Sweden	450	8,839	19.6	Stockholm
Switzerland	41	7,019	170	Bern
Syria	185	15,000	81	Damascus
Taiwan	36	21,126	586.8	Taipei
Tajikistan	143	5,751	40.2	Dushanbe
Tanzania	945	30,340	32.1	Dodoma
Thailand	513	60,000	115.2	Bangkok
Togo	57	3,928	69.2	Lomé
Tonga	0.7	98	131	Nuku'alofa
Trinidad & Tobago	5	1,250	243.7	Port of Spain
Tunisia	164	8,947	57.9	Tunis
Turkey	779	61,644	79.1	Ankara
Turkmenistan	488	4,483	9.2	Ashgabat
Turks & Caicos Is.	0.4	14	32.6	Cockburn Town
Tuvalu	0.03	9	346	Funafuti
Uganda	241	16,671	69.1	Kampala
Ukraine	604	51,728	85.7	Kyyiv (Kiev)
United Arab Emirates	78	2,378	30.6	Abu Dhabi
United Kingdom	242	58,394	241.5	London
United States	9,809	264,648	27	Washington DC
US Virgin Is.	0.3	102	293.3	Charlotte Amalie
Uruguay	176	3,167	18	Montevideo
Uzbekistan	447	22,098	49.4	Tashkent
Vanuatu	12	165	13.5	Port Vila
Vatican City	0.0004	0.8	1741	Vatican City
Venezuela	912	21,377	23.4	Caracas
Vietnam	331	70,983	214.4	Hanoi
Yemen	537	14,561	27.1	San'a
Yugoslavia	102	10,482	102.6	Belgrade
Zambia	753	8,210	10.9	Lusaka
Zimbabwe	391	11,215	28.7	Harare

Notes:

1. *La Paz (administrative), Sucre (legislative).*
2. *Including Hong Kong.*
3. *Formerly Zaïre.*
4. *Yamoussoukro (administrative), Abidjan (commercial).*
5. *Berlin is the capital and Bonn the administrative capital. Berlin will also become an administrative capital by 2002.*
6. *Basse-Terre (administrative), Pointe-à-Pitre (commercial).*
7. *The former capital was Almaty (Alma Ata).*
8. *Plymouth was destroyed during the recent volcanic activity. Discussions are currently being held concerning the site and name of the new capital.*
9. *Including the area of Western Sahara.*
10. *Formerly known as Rangoon.*
11. *The former capital was Lagos.*
12. *Formerly known as Western Samoa.*
13. *Pretoria (administrative), Cape Town (legislative), Bloemfontein (judicial). This arrangement is currently under review.*

GENERAL MAP SECTION

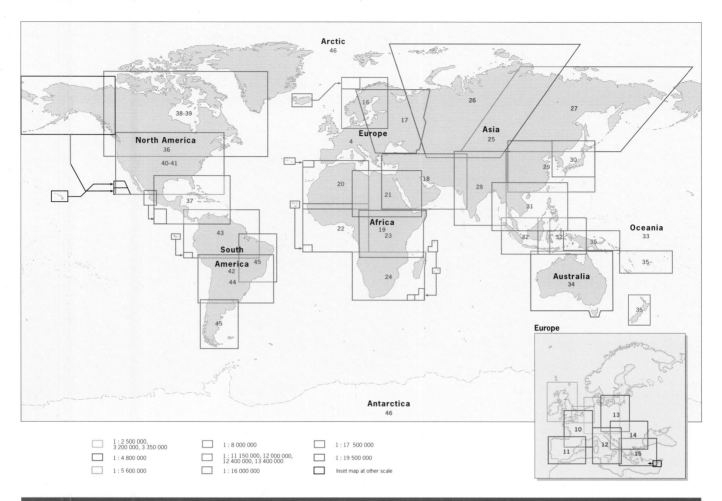

▢	1 : 2 500 000, 3 200 000, 3 350 000	▢	1 : 8 000 000	▢	1 : 17 500 000
▢	1 : 4 800 000	▢	1 : 11 150 000, 12 000 000, 12 400 000, 13 400 000	▢	1 : 19 500 000
▢	1 : 5 600 000	▢	1 : 16 000 000	▢	Inset map at other scale

KEY TO MAP SYMBOLS

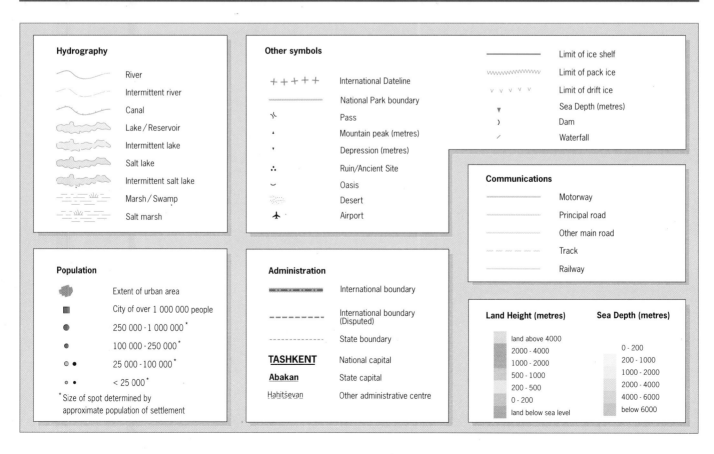

Hydrography

River
Intermittent river
Canal
Lake / Reservoir
Intermittent lake
Salt lake
Intermittent salt lake
Marsh / Swamp
Salt marsh

Population

Extent of urban area
City of over 1 000 000 people
250 000 - 1 000 000 *
100 000 - 250 000 *
25 000 - 100 000 *
< 25 000 *

* Size of spot determined by
approximate population of settlement

Other symbols

+ + + + +   International Dateline
National Park boundary
Pass
Mountain peak (metres)
Depression (metres)
Ruin/Ancient Site
Oasis
Desert
Airport

Administration

International boundary
International boundary
(Disputed)
State boundary
TASHKENT   National capital
Abakan   State capital
Hahitševan   Other administrative centre

Limit of ice shelf
Limit of pack ice
Limit of drift ice
Sea Depth (metres)
Dam
Waterfall

Communications

Motorway
Principal road
Other main road
Track
Railway

Land Height (metres)

land above 4000
2000 - 4000
1000 - 2000
500 - 1000
200 - 500
0 - 200
land below sea level

Sea Depth (metres)

0 - 200
200 - 1000
1000 - 2000
2000 - 4000
4000 - 6000
below 6000

WORLD - POLITICAL

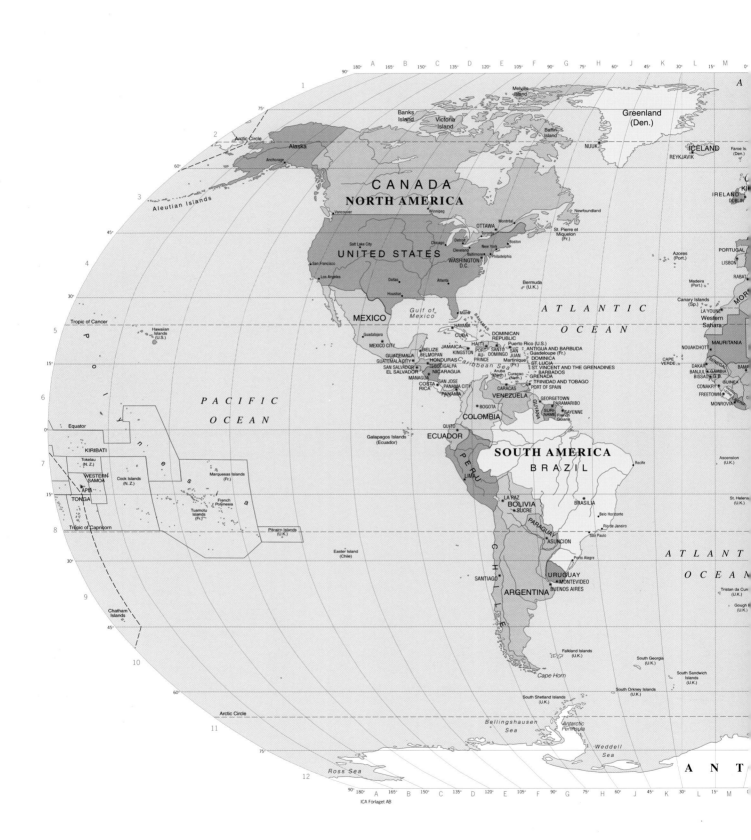

ICA Förlaget AB

WORLD - POLITICAL

ALB. - Albania
AR. - Armenia
AZ. - Azerbaijan
B. - Burundi
B.H. - Bosnia-Herzegovina
BEL. - Belgium
BH. - Bhutan
BULG. - Bulgaria
CR. - Czech Republic
CZ. - Croatia
EQ.G. - Equatorial Guinea
G.B. - Guinea-Bissau
GE. - Georgia
HGY. - Hungary
L. - Lesotho
LEB. - Lebanon
LIE. - Liechtenstein
LUX. - Luxembourg
MA. - Former Yugoslav Republic of Macedonia
NETH. - The Netherlands
R. - Rwanda
S. - Swaziland
SL. - Slovenia
SLO. - Slovak Republic
U.A.E. - United Arab Emirates
YUG. - Federal Republic of Yugoslavia

Robinson Projection

| 0 | 1000 | 2000 | 3000 km |
| 0 | 1000 | 2000 | 3000 miles |

EUROPE

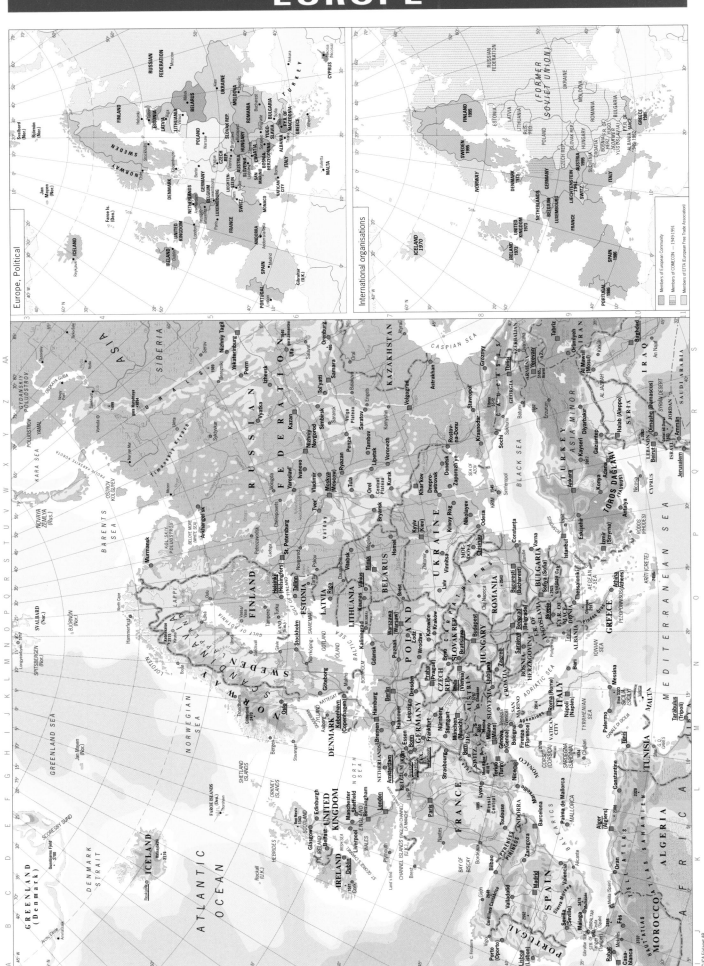

Europe, Political

International organisations

Members of European Community
Members of COMECON — 1949-1991
Members of EFTA (European Free Trade Association)

© ICA Förlaget AB

BENELUX AND SURROUNDING AREA

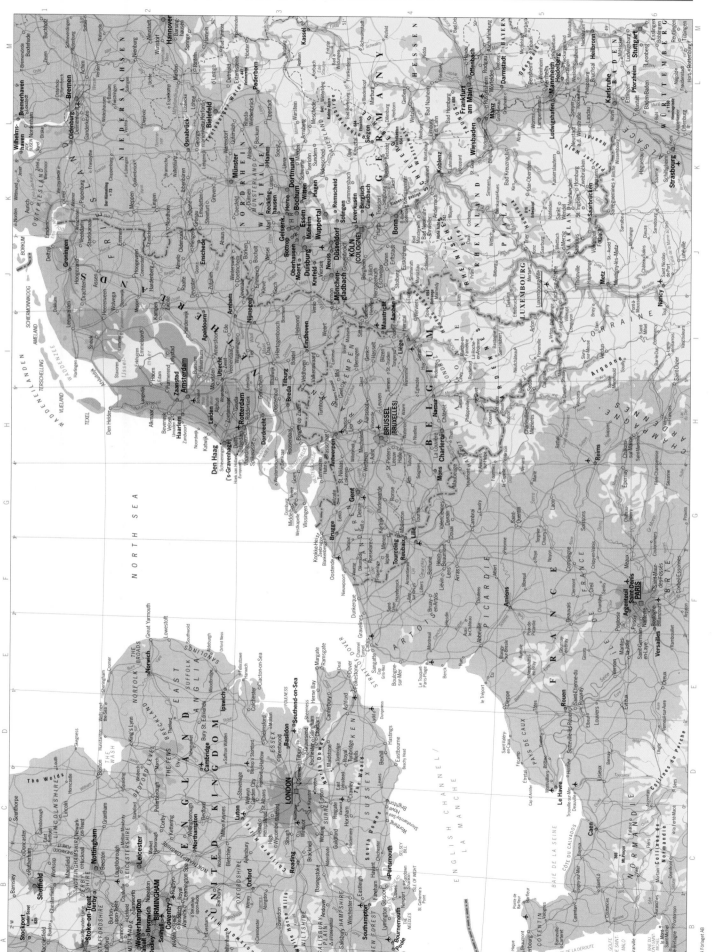

Scale 1 : 3 200 000

0   25   50   100 km

0   25   50 miles

© ICA Förlaget AB

BRITISH ISLES

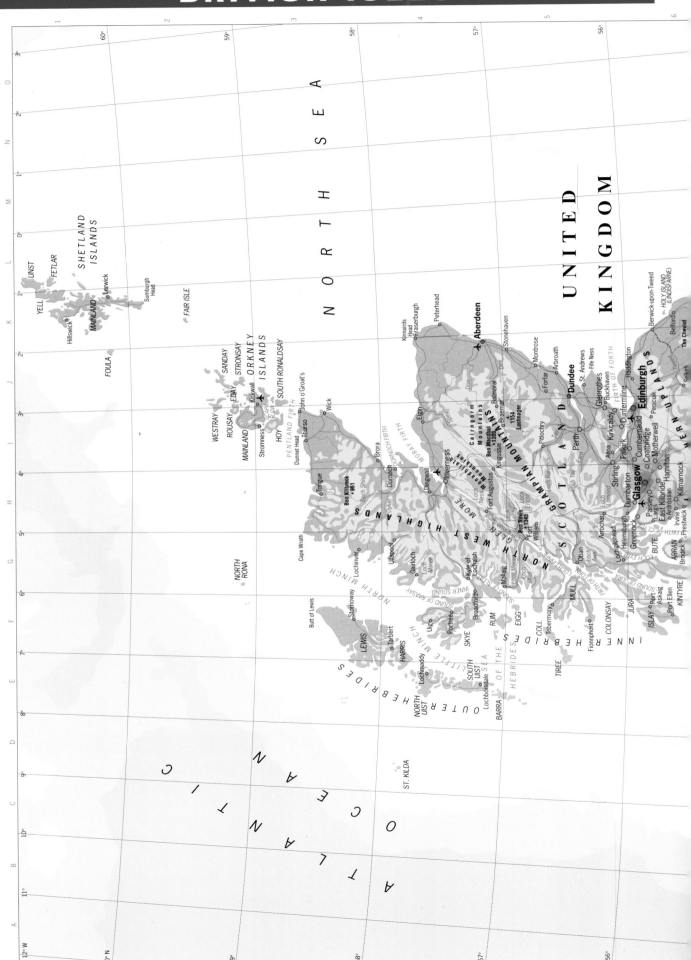

BRITISH ISLES

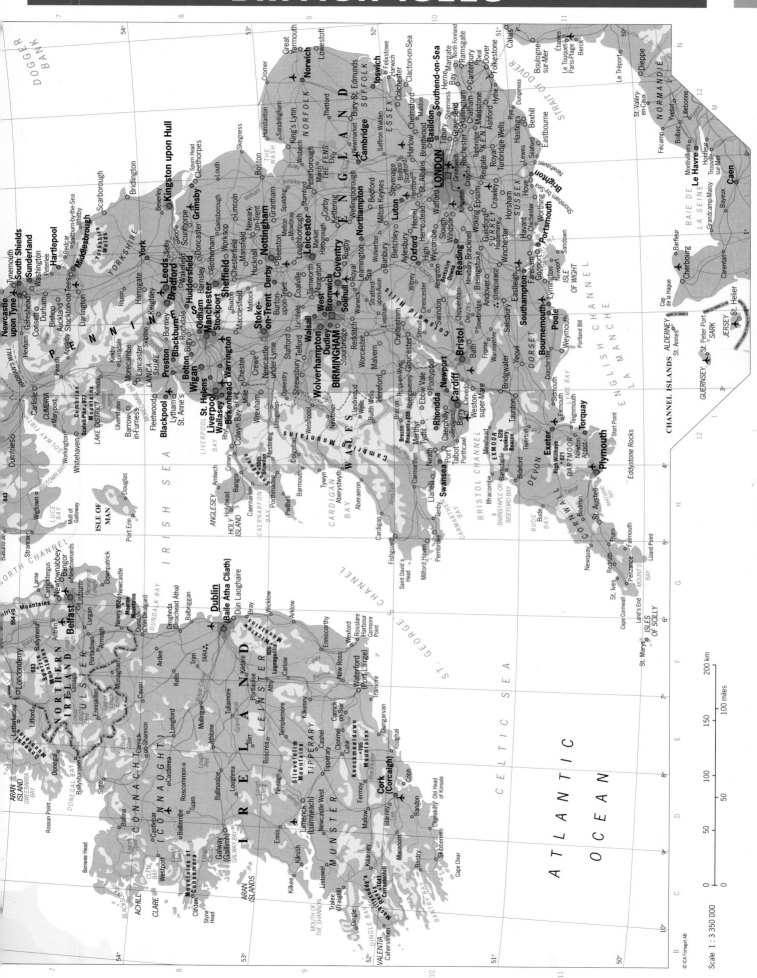

Scale 1 : 3 350 000

© ICA Förlaget AB

GERMANY

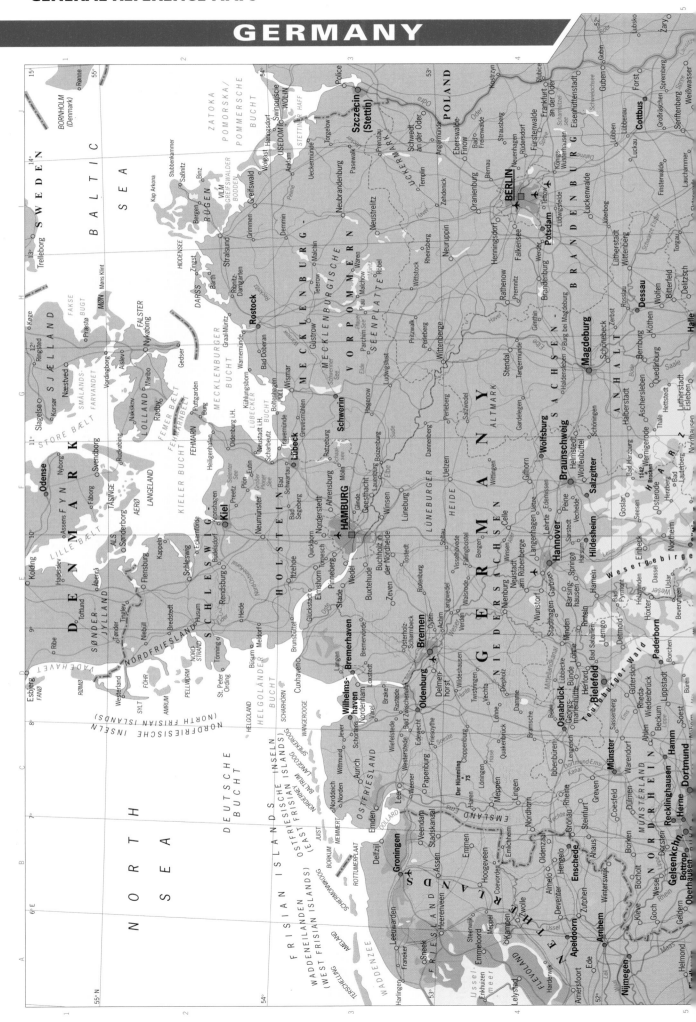

GERMANY

Scale 1 : 2 500 000

0   50   100   150 km

0   50   100 miles

© ICA Förlaget AB

FRANCE

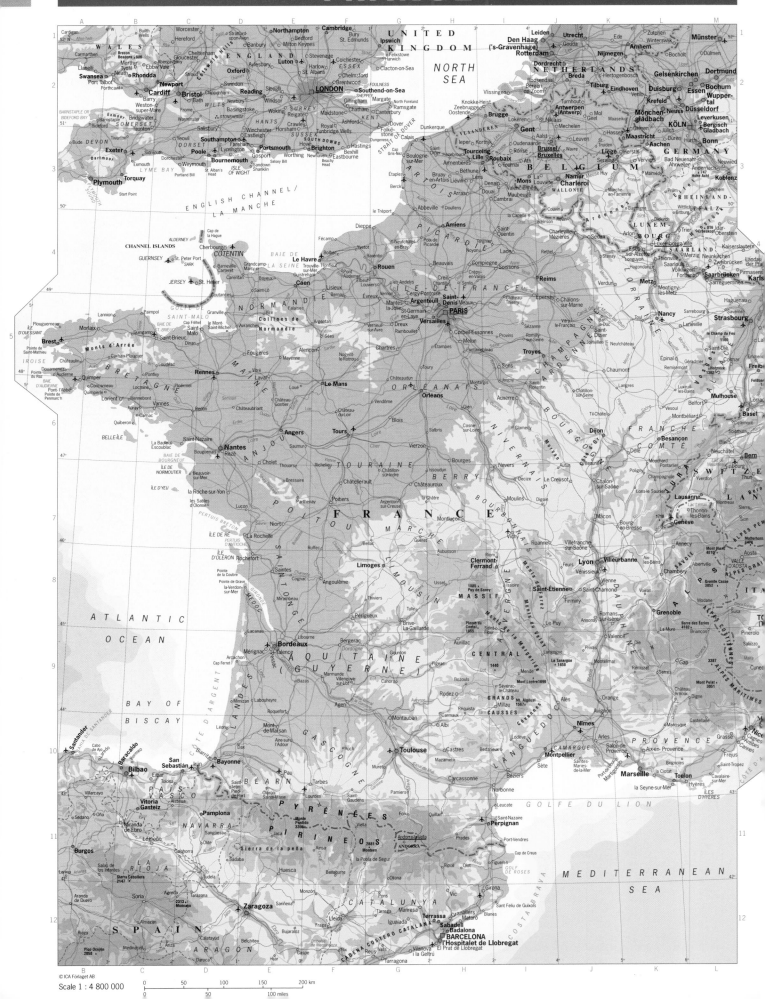

© ICA Förlaget AB

Scale 1 : 4 800 000

0   50   100   150   200 km

0   50   100 miles

SPAIN AND PORTUGAL

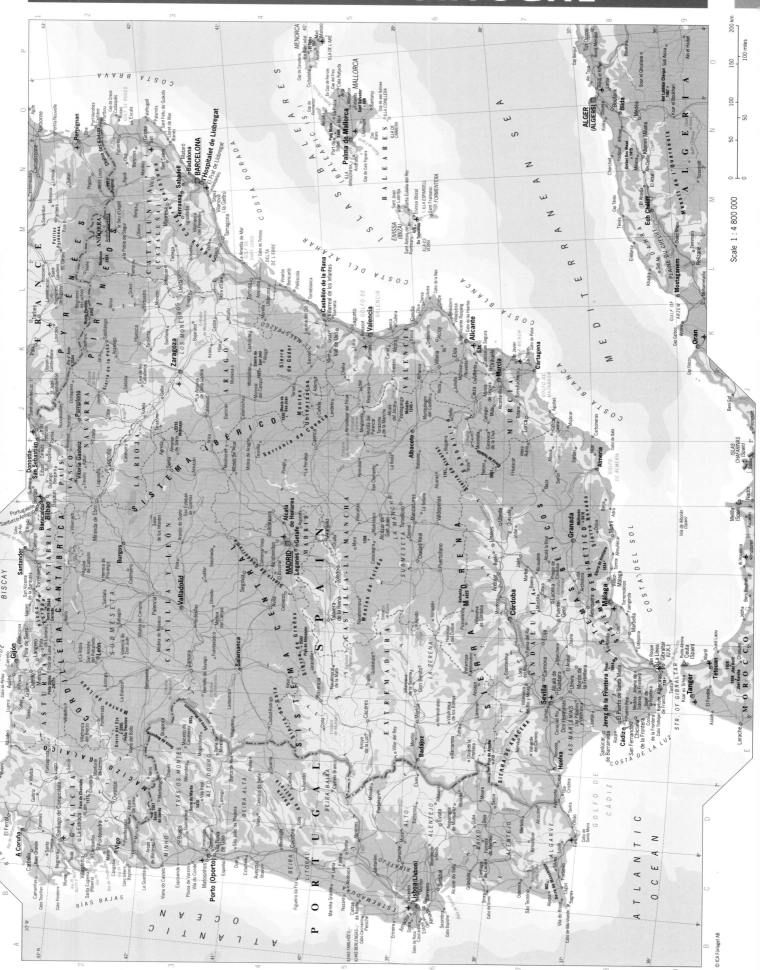

Scale 1 : 4 800 000

© ICA Förlaget AB

ITALY

Scale 1 : 4 800 000

0   50   100   150   200 km

CENTRAL EUROPE

Scale 1 : 4 800 000

```
0    50    100    150    200 km
0         50        100 miles
```

THE BALKANS

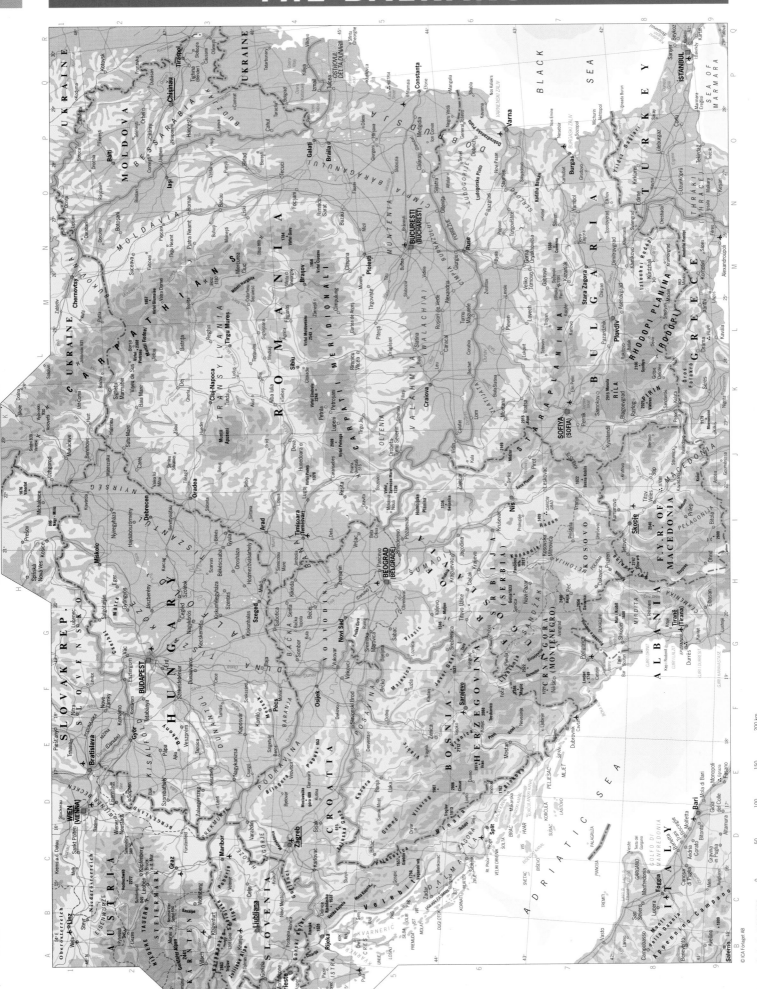

GREECE AND TURKEY

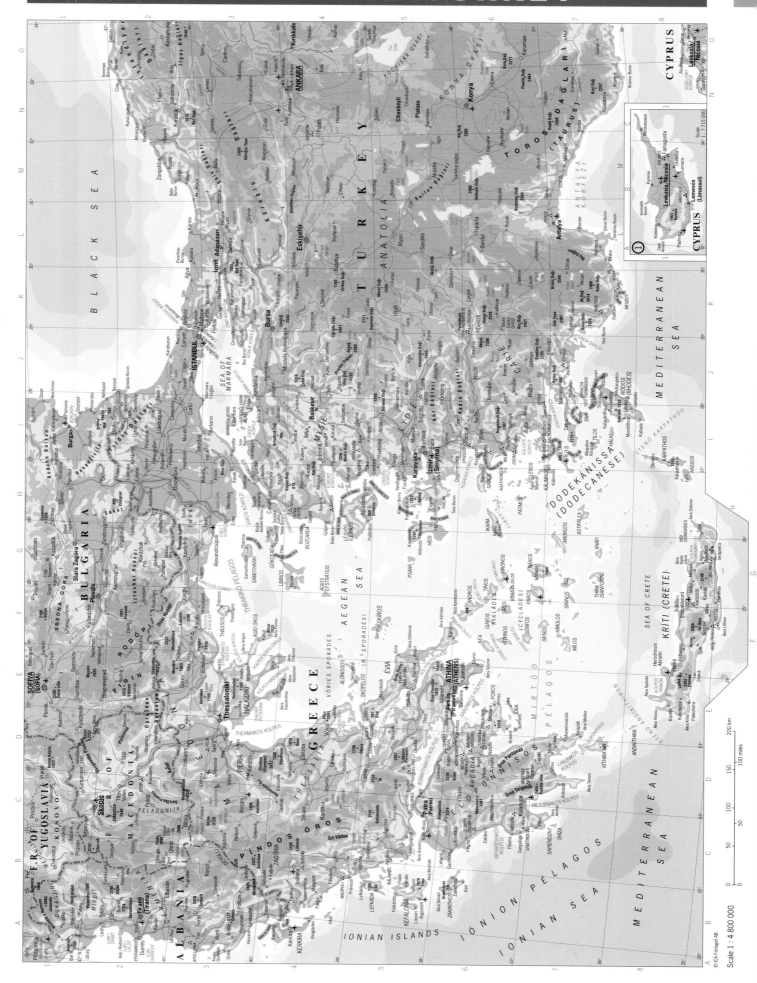

Scale 1 : 4 800 000

SCANDINAVIA

DENMARK STRAIT

ICELAND

VATNAJÖKULL

ATLANTIC OCEAN

NORWEGIAN SEA

N O R W A Y

S W E D E N

F I N L A N D

R U S S I A N   F E D.

LAPPLAND

FINNMARK

TROMS

NORDLAND

VÄSTER-BOTTEN

NORR-BOTTEN

OULU

LAPPI

KUOPIO

POHJOIS-KARJALA

KESKI-SUOMI

MIKKELI

TURUN JA PORI

HÄME

KYMI

UUDENMAA

VÄSTER-NORRLAND

JÄMTLAND

GÄVLEBORG

DALARNA

VÄRMLAND

VÄSTMANLAND

UPPSALA

SÖDERMAN-LAND

ÖSTERGÖTLAND

SKARABORG

ÄLVSBORG

GÖTEBORG OCH BOHUS

HALLAND

JÖNKÖPING

KRONOBERG

KALMAR

BLEKINGE

SKÅNE

GOTLAND

ÖLAND

GULF OF BOTHNIA

ÅLAND (AHVENANMAA)

GULF OF FINLAND

ESTONIA

LATVIA

LITHUANIA

BELARUS

GERMANY

POLAND

DENMARK

JYLLAND

SKAGERRAK

KATTEGAT

BALTIC SEA

NORTH SEA

BARENTS SEA

Murmansk

Oslo
Stockholm
Helsinki (Helsingfors)
Tallinn
Riga
Vilnius
MENSK (MINSK)
København (Copenhagen)
Malmö
Göteborg
Bergen
Trondheim
HAMBURG
Kiel
Rostock
Gdańsk
Gdynia
Kaliningrad
Kaunas
Klaipėda
Liepāja
Tartu
Pskov
Daugavpils
Tampere (Tammerfors)
Turku (Åbo)
Espoo (Esbo)
Vantaa (Vanda)
Uppsala
Västerås
Örebro
Eskilstuna
Norrköping
Linköping
Jönköping
Borås
Helsingborg
Odense
Aalborg
Århus
Reykjavík

© ICA Förlaget AB

Scale 1 : 8 000 000
0   100   200   300 km

EUROPEAN RUSSIA

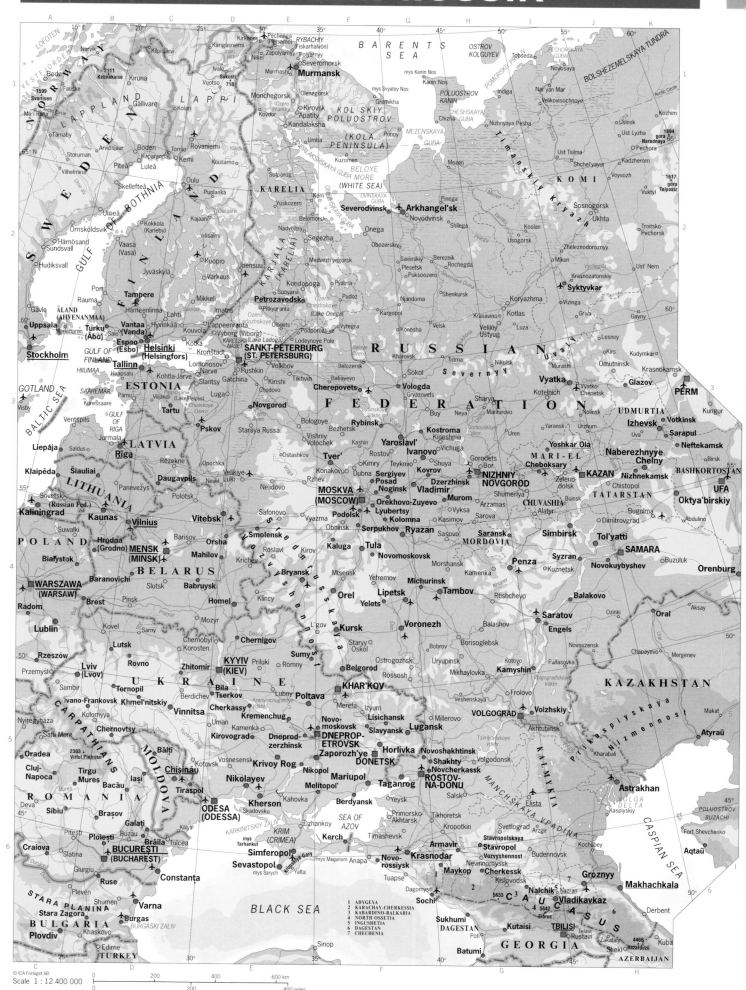

© ICA Förlaget AB

Scale 1 : 12 400 000

0 200 400 600 km

0 200 400 miles

MIDDLE EAST

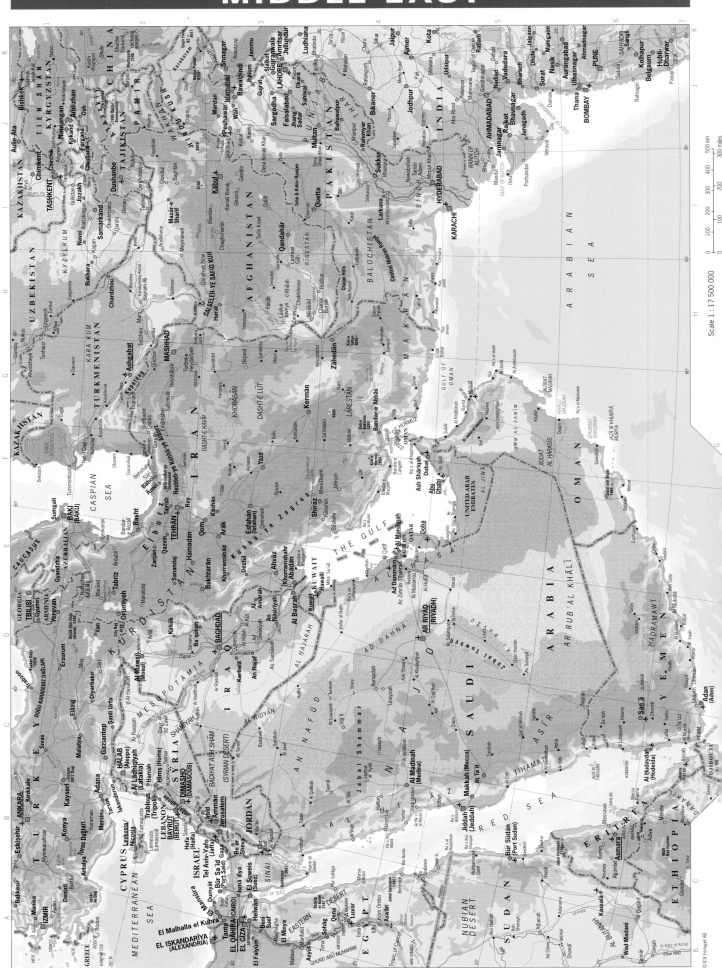

Scale 1 : 17 500 000

AFRICA

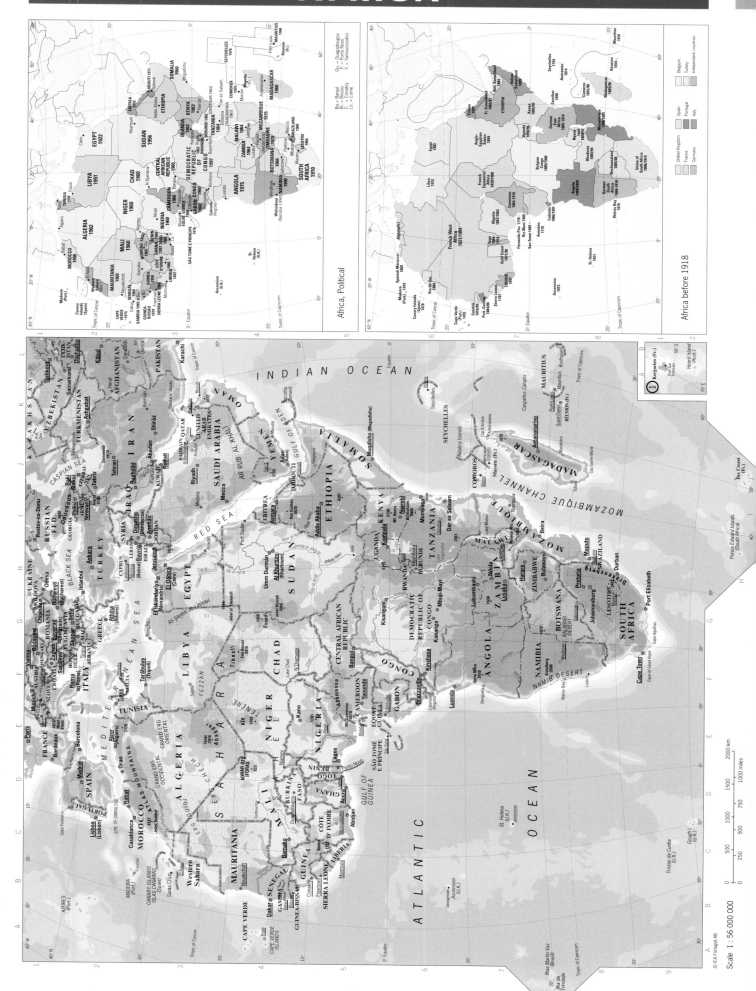

Africa, Political

Africa before 1918

Scale 1 : 56 000 000

© ICA Förlaget AB

NORTHWEST AFRICA

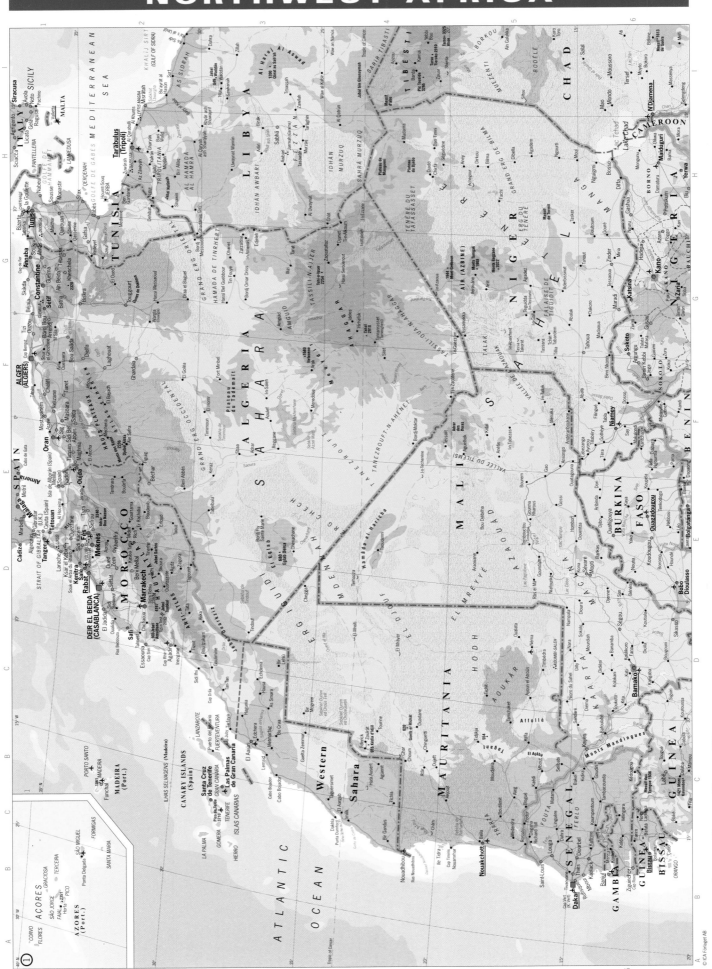

NORTHEAST AFRICA

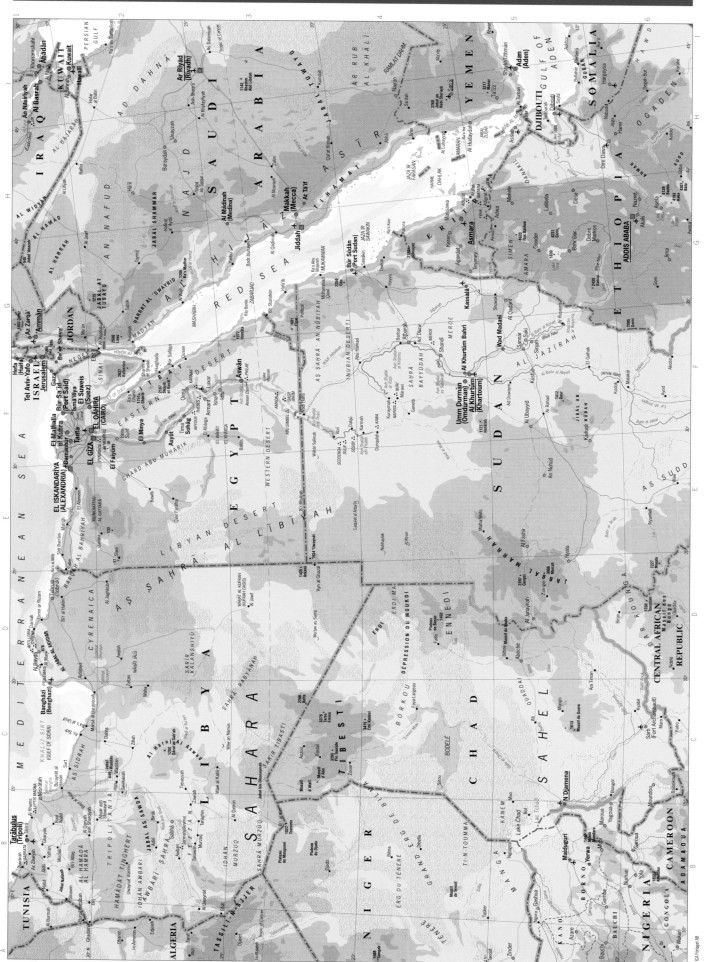

Scale 1:16 000 000

0   200   400   600 km

©CA Förlaget AB

WEST AFRICA

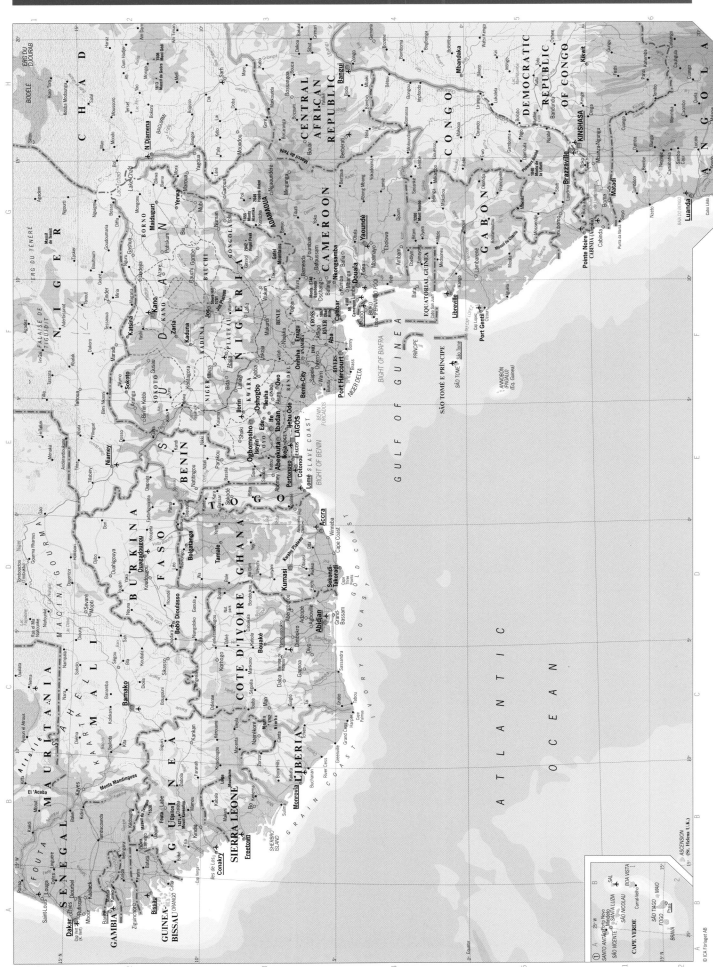

Scale 1 : 16,000,000

© ICA Förlaget AB

CENTRAL AFRICA

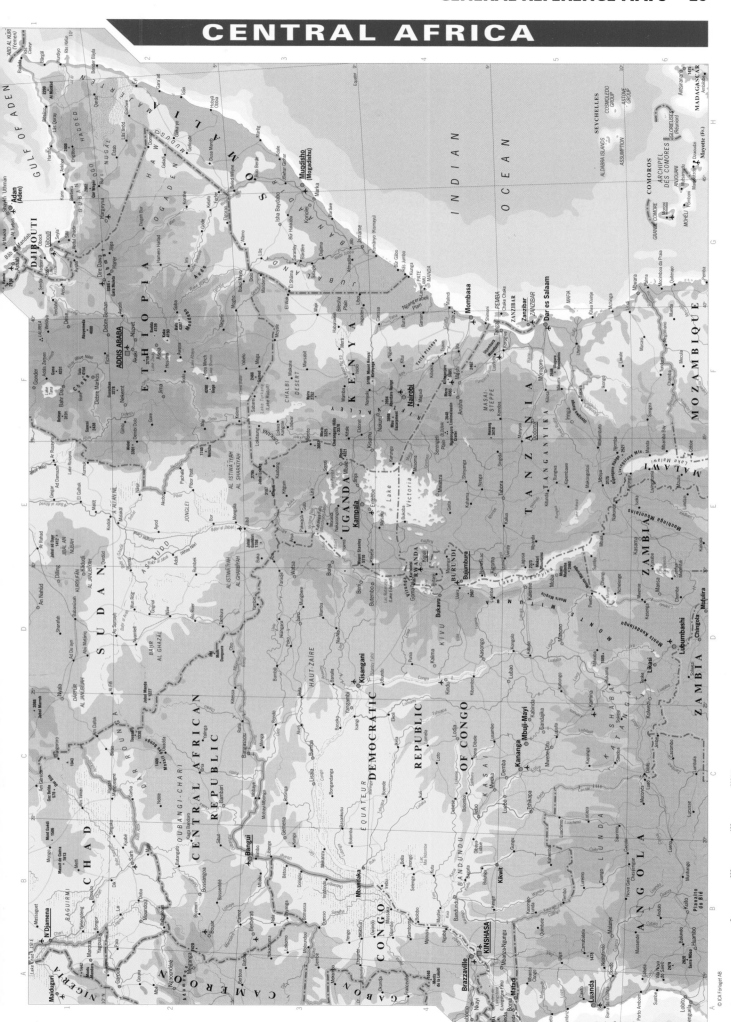

Scale 1 : 16 000 000

© ICA Förlaget AB

SOUTHERN AFRICA

ASIA

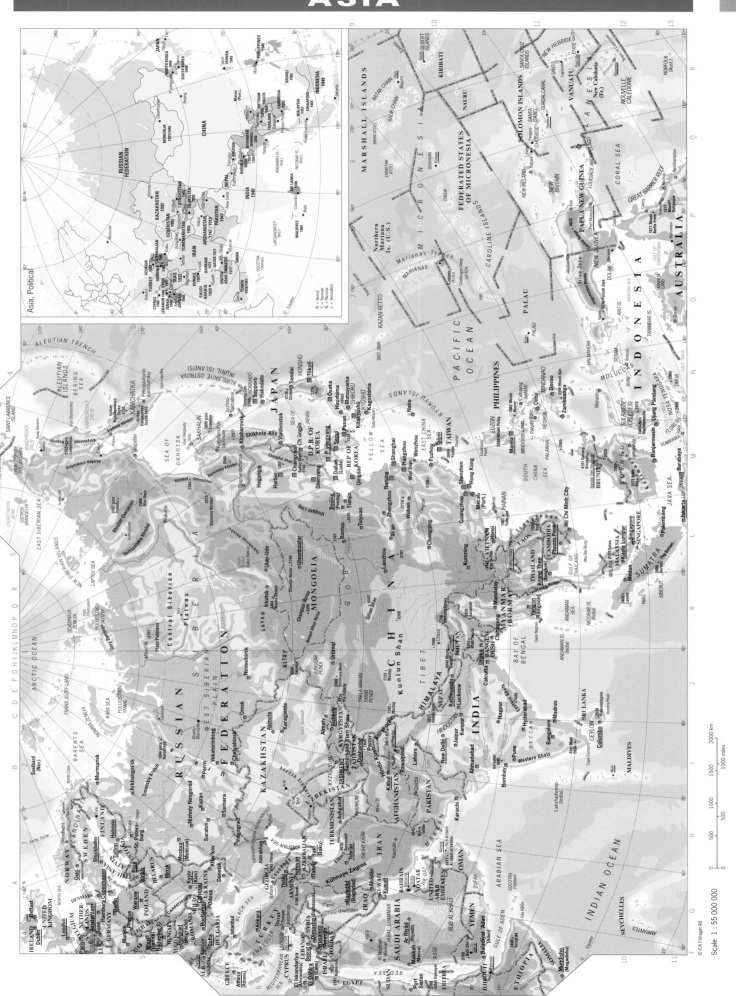

Asia, Political

Scale 1:55 000 000

© ICA Förlaget AB

N. W.

ASIA

ARCTIC OCEAN

BARENTS SEA

NORWAY

KARA SEA

LAPTEV SEA

SIBERIA

RUSSIAN FEDERATION

KAZAKHSTAN

CASPIAN SEA

MONGOLIA

UZBEKISTAN

TURKMENISTAN

TAJIKISTAN

KYRGYZSTAN

CHINA

IRAN

AFGHANISTAN

INDIA

TIBET

© ICA Förlaget AB

Scale 1 : 19 150 000

0   200   400   600 km

0   200   400 miles

NORTHEAST ASIA

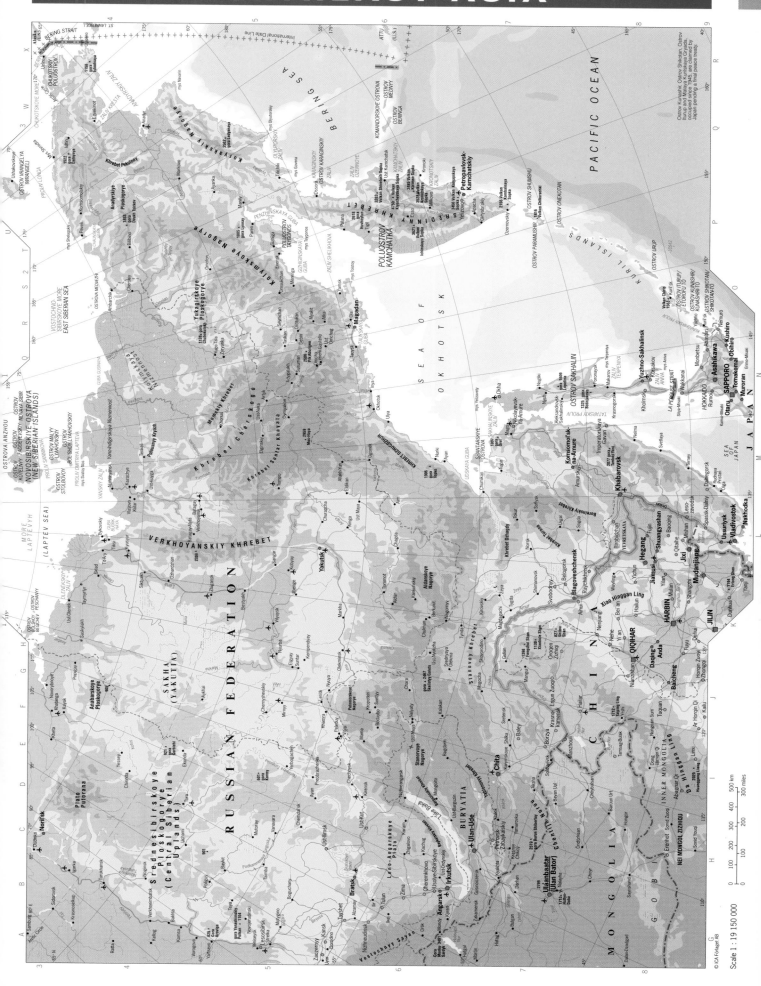

Scale 1 : 19 150 000

SOUTH ASIA

© ICA Förlaget AB

Scale 1 : 16 000 000

0   200   400   600 km

0   200   400 miles

EAST ASIA

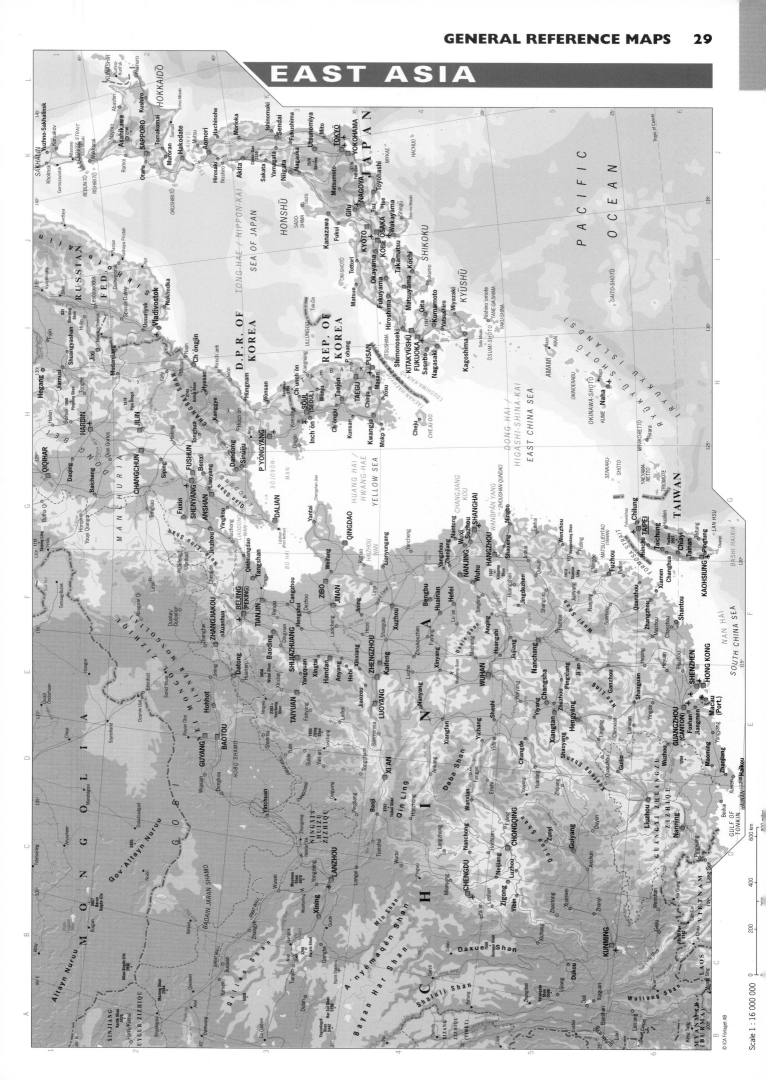

Scale 1 : 16 000 000

© ICA Förlaget AB

JAPAN AND KOREA

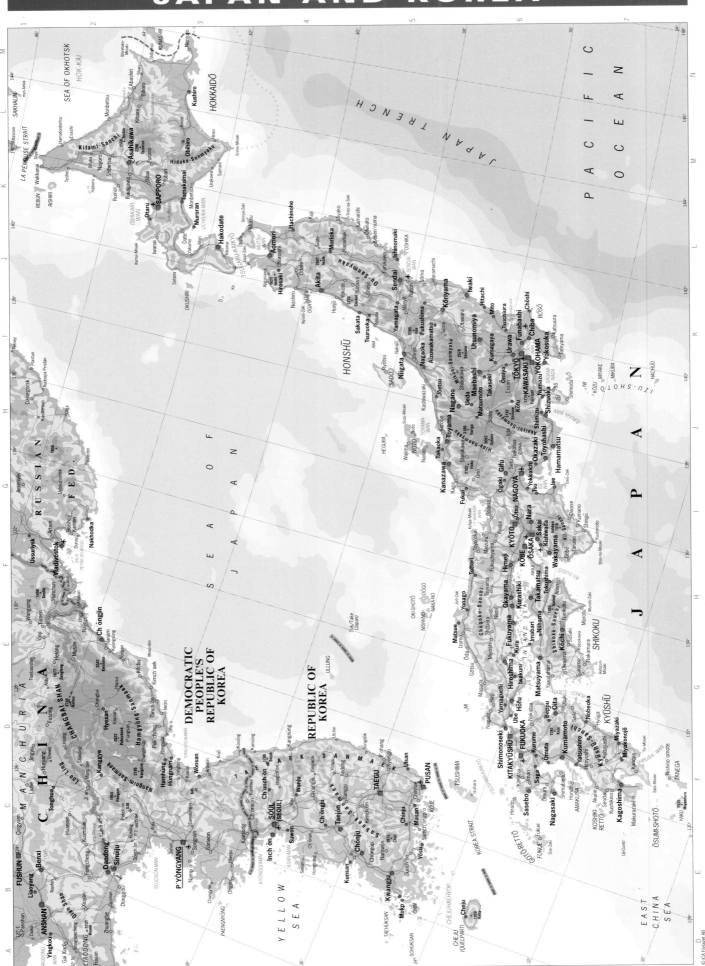

SOUTH-EAST ASIA

Scale 1 : 16 000 000

© ICA Förlaget AB

MALAYSIA AND INDONESIA

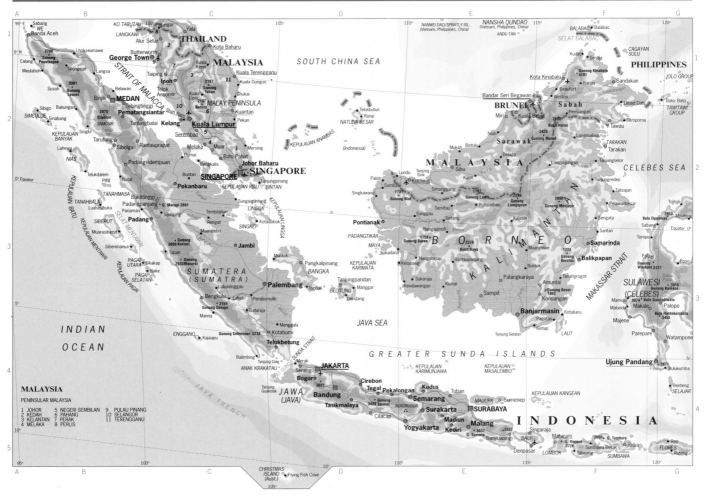

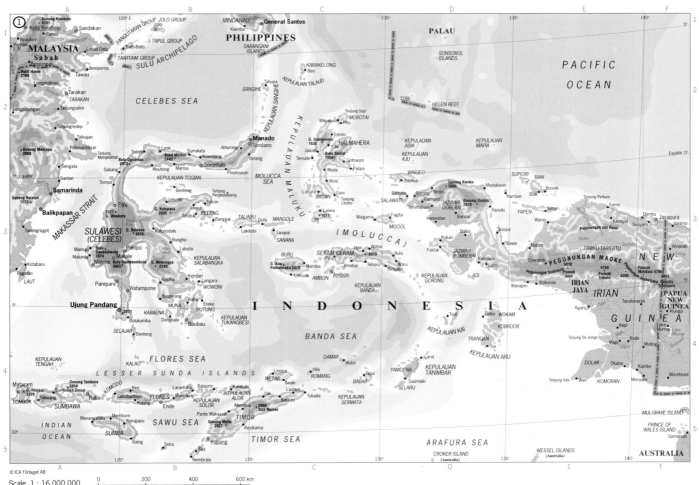

MALAYSIA

PENINSULAR MALAYSIA

1 JOHOR   5 NEGERI SEMBILAN   9 PULAU PINANG
2 KEDAH   6 PAHANG   10 SELANGOR
3 KELANTAN   7 PERAK   11 TERENGGANU
4 MELAKA   8 PERLIS

© ICA Förlaget AB

Scale 1 : 16 000 000

0   200   400   600 km

OCEANIA

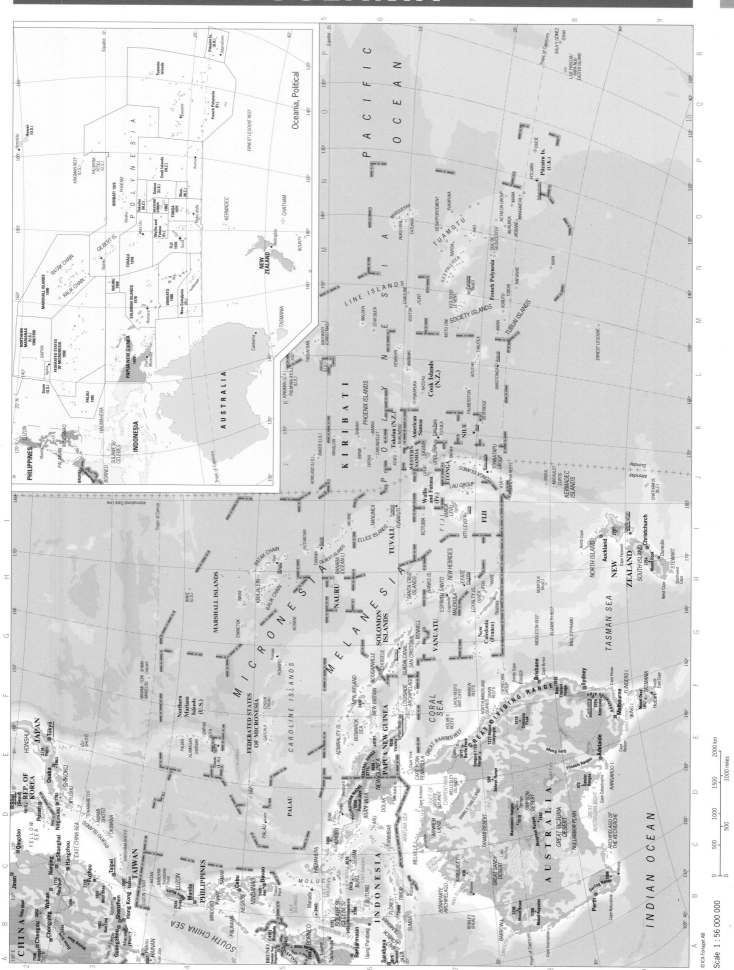

Oceania, Political

Scale 1 : 56 000 000

AUSTRALIA

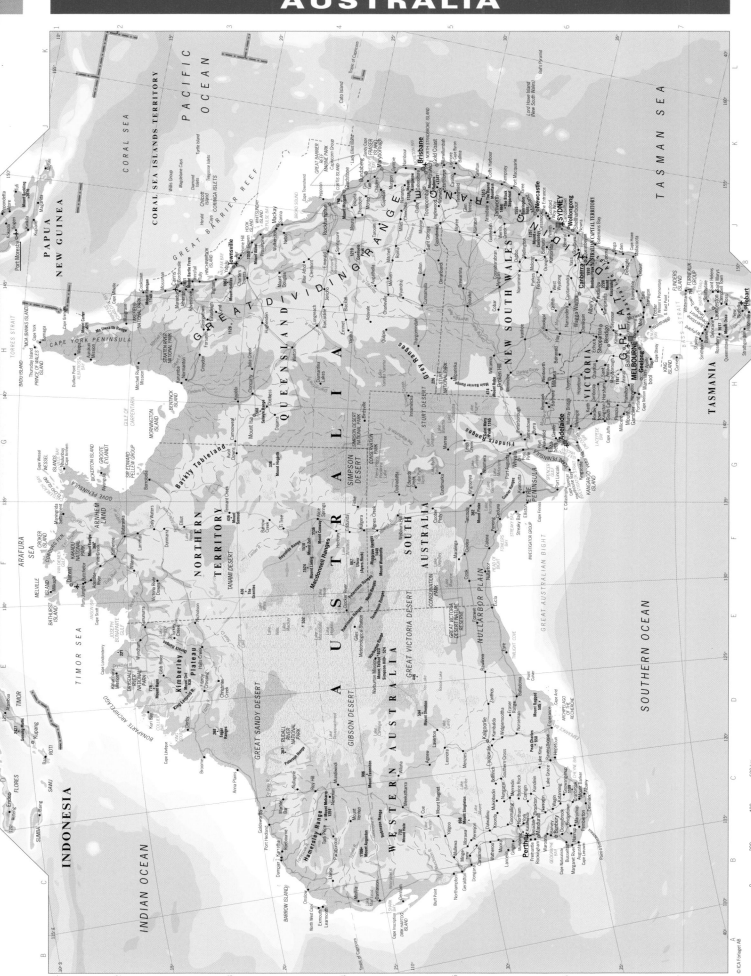

NEW ZEALAND AND NEW GUINEA

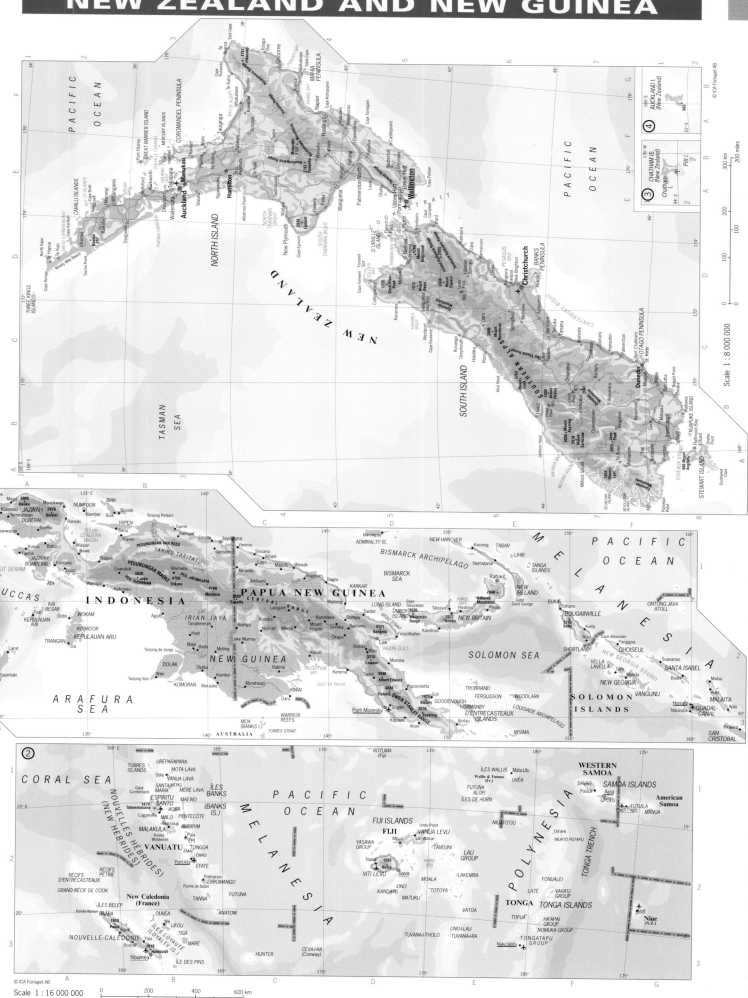

Scale 1 : 8 000 000

Scale 1 : 16 000 000

© ICA Förlaget AB

NORTH AMERICA

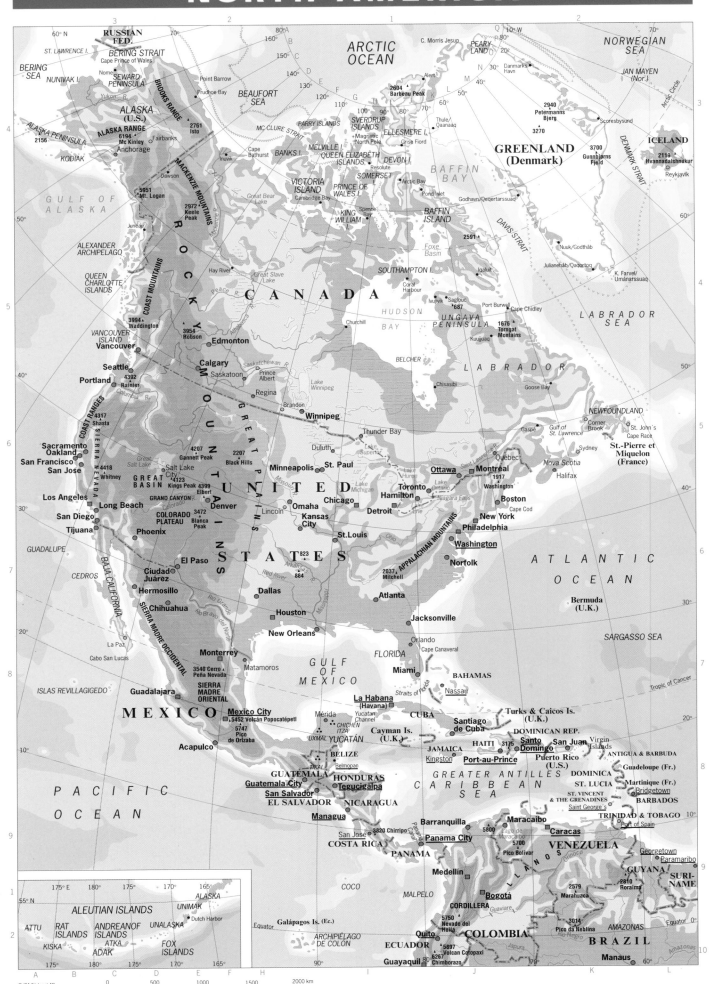

© ICA Förlaget AB

Scale 1 : 36 000 000

CENTRAL AMERICA

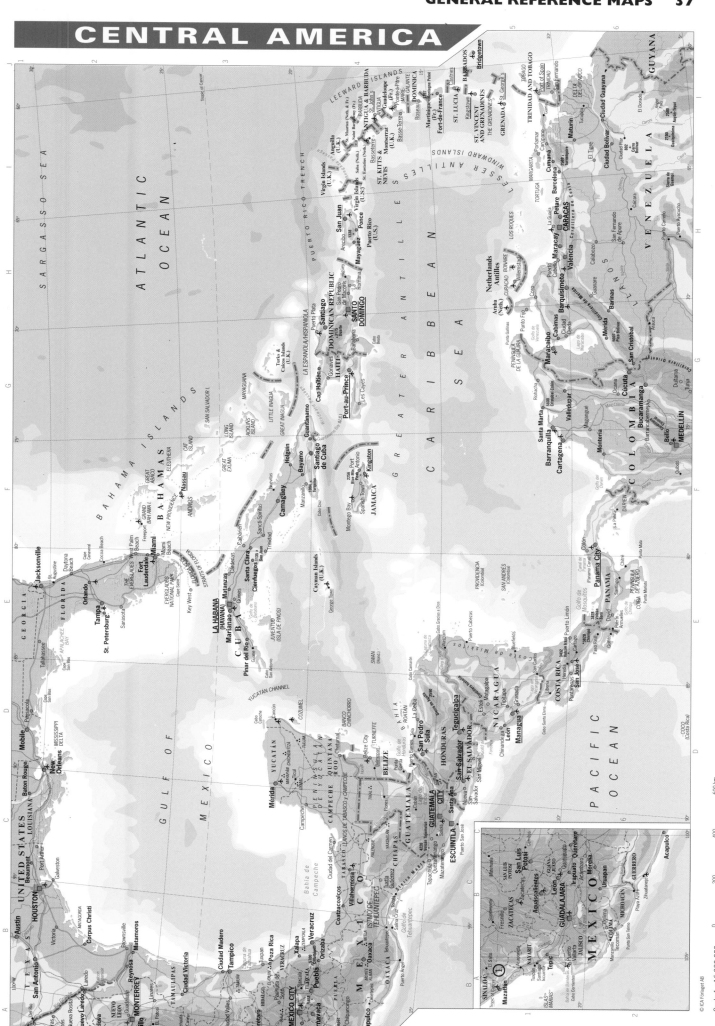

Scale 1 : 16 000 000

© ICA Förlaget AB

CANADA

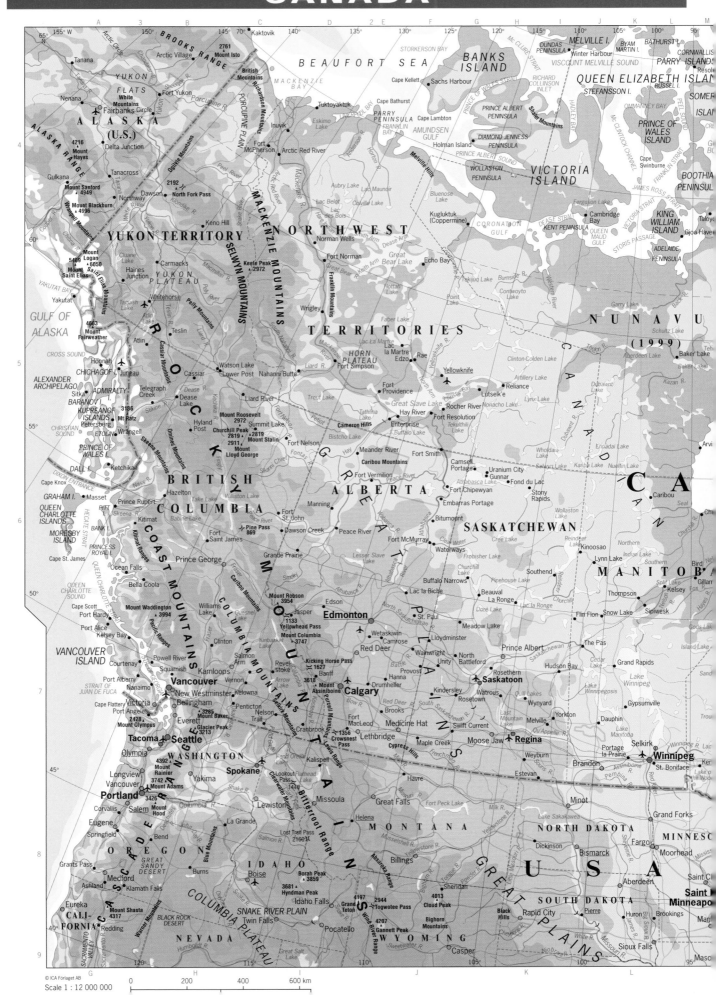

Scale 1 : 12 000 000

© ICA Förlaget AB

0   200   400   600 km

CANADA

UNITED STATES

A B C D E F

2200 Golden Winde
VANCOUVER ISLAND
Vancouver
New Westminster
Kamloops
Red Deer
Prince Albert
Saskatoon
BRITISH COLUMBIA
ALBERTA
SASKATCHEWAN
Banff
Calgary
Yorkton
Strait of Juan de Fuca
Cape Flattery
Victoria
Port Angeles
Bellingham
Mount Vernon
Kelowna
Lethbridge
Medicine Hat
Cypress Hills
Moose Jaw
Regina
Weyburn
2428 Oak Harbor
Everett
Bremerton
Mount Olympus
Bellevue
Aberdeen
Seattle
Tacoma
Olympia
WASHINGTON
Spokane
Coeur d'Alene
Libby
Kalispell
Shelby
Havre
Glasgow
Malta
Fort Peck Lake
Wolf Point
Williston
Estevan
Brar
Minc
Astoria
Longview
4392 Mount Rainier
Ellensburg
Moses Lake
Grand Coulee Dam
Grand Coulee
Lookout Pass 1440
Missoula
Helena
Great Falls
Lewistown
Glendive
NORTH DAKOTA
Dickinson
Mandan
Lake Sakakawea
Portland
Oregon City
Salem
Yakima
Richland
Kennewick
Walla Walla
Pullman
Moscow
Lewiston
Clearwater Mountains
Anaconda
Butte
Bozeman
Livingston
Billings
Miles City
Buffalo
Mobridge
Lake Oahe
Corvallis
Albany
3426 Mt. Hood
The Dalles
Pendleton
La Grande
Baker
Blue Mountains
HELLS CANYON
Lost Trail Pass 2160
Dillon
Yellowstone River
MONTANA
Sheridan
Gillette
Rapid City
SOU
Bend
OREGON
Burns
GREAT SANDY DESERT
IDAHO
3859 Borah Peak
Bighorn Mountains
4013 Cloud Peak
Black Hills
2207 Harney Peak
Eugene
Springfield
Roseburg
Coos Bay
Cape Blanco
Grants Pass
Medford
Ashland
Klamath Falls
HARNEY BASIN
COLUMBIA PLATEAU
Caldwell
Nampa
Boise
Snake River
Gooding
Idaho Falls
Rexburg
Jackson
4197 Grand Teton
Powell
4207 Gannett Peak
Riverton
WYOMING
Newcastle
Casper
Hot Springs
Chadron
Sand Hills
NEBRAS
Cape Mendocino
Eureka
4317 Mount Shasta
Alturas
Lakeview
Altamont
Twin Falls
Pocatello
2301 South Pass
Rawlins
Laramie
Cheyenne
Scottsbluff
Valenti
Redding
Red Bluff
Ukiah
BLACK ROCK DESERT
2966 Granite Peak
Winnemucca
Elko
Wells
Brigham
Logan
Ogden
Green River
Rock Springs
Laramie Mountains
Fort Collins
Greeley
Sterling
McCook
North P
Santa Rosa
Sacramento
Vallejo
Berkeley
Oakland
Stockton
San Francisco
San Jose
Marysville
Yuba City
Sparks
Battle Mountain
GREAT BASIN
GREAT SALT LAKE
Great Salt Lake
GREAT SALT LAKE DESERT
Salt Lake City
Tooele
Provo
Orem
Nephi
Vernal
Craig
Steamboat Springs
4345 Longs Peak
Longmont
Boulder
Aurora
Denver
UNI
Carson City
Austin
NEVADA
Hawthorne
Tonopah
UTAH
Ely
Richfield
Price
Glenwood Springs
Grand Junction
Aspen
4399 Mount Elbert
Montrose
Colorado Springs
Pueblo
Lamar
Arkansas River
Monterey
SAN JOAQUIN VALLEY
Fresno
Madera
Merced
4342 White Mountain Peak
3710 Delano Peak
Cedar City
Moab
COLORADO
Durango
4372 Blanca Peak
Garden City
Dodge
Liberal
San Luis Obispo
Santa Maria
Santa Barbara
Oxnard
Hanford
4418 Mount Whitney
Porterville
Delano
Bakersfield
Lancaster
DEATH VALLEY
CALIFORNIA
MOJAVE DESERT
Barstow
St. George
Lake Powell
Page
GRAND CANYON
Tuba City
Shiprock
Farmington
Chinle
Raton
4011 Wheeler Peak
Clayton
Guymon
Dalhart
Dumas
Borger
Pampa
LOS ANGELES
Long Beach
Pasadena
San Bernardino
Riverside
Santa Ana
3506
Newport Beach
Oceanside
CHANNEL ISLANDS
Salton Sea
Las Vegas
Lake Mead
Hoover Dam
Boulder City
Henderson
Kingman
Lake Havasu City
3951 Humphreys Peak
Flagstaff
Winslow
Holbrook
Gallup
Los Alamos
Rio Rancho
Santa Fe
Belen
Albuquerque
STA
Amarillo
Hereford
San Diego
Escondido
Brawley
Tijuana
Mexicali
Yuma
San Luis Río Colorado
ARIZONA
Phoenix
Scottsdale
Mesa
Prescott
St. Johns
3476 Baldy Peak
Casa Grande
Tucson
Clifton
Silver City
Socorro
NEW MEXICO
Clovis
Portales
Lubbock
Wichita Fa
Ensenada
3088 Encantada
Nogales
Green Valley
Nogales
Douglas
Agua Prieta
Deming
Las Cruces
Sierra Blanca Peak
Roswell
Artesia
Hobbs
LLANO ESTACADO
Lamesa
Snyder
Abilene
San Quintin
Rosario de Arriba
SONORA
Caborca
Magdalena
1646 Viejo
El Paso
Ciudad Juárez
Van Horn
Carlsbad
Pecos River
Sweetwater
Midland
Big Spring
Odessa
San Angelo
TEXAS
Punta Prieta
BAJA CALIFORNIA
GOLFO DE CALIFORNIA
TIBURON
Hermosillo
Nuevo Casas Grandes
El Sueco
Alpine
Fort Stockton
Colorado R.
Junction
EDWARDS PLATEAU
Del Rio
San Antonio
Uvalde
Punta Eugenia
Guerrero Negro
Guaymas
Empalme
Ciudad Obregón
Santa Rosalía
SIERRA MADRE OCCIDENTAL
Madera
2978
2955
Puerto de Lajas
Chihuahua
CHIHUAHUA
Ciudad Delicias
Ciudad Camargo
Hidalgo del Parral
3659
3315
Ojinaga
Presidio
Rio Grande
2385 Emory Peak
2896
Ciudad Acuña
Piedras Negras
Eagle Pass
Nueva Rosita
BOLSÓN DE MAPIMÍ
BAJA CALIFORNIA SUR
CARMEN
CERRALVO
Huatabampo
Navojoa
Álamos
3992 Mohinora
Agua Caliente
ALTIPLANICIE MEXICANA
MEXICO
COAHUILA
Nuevo Laredo
Monclova
Reynosa
NUEVO LEÓN
MONTERREY
Cabo San Lázaro
SAN JOSÉ
Los Mochis
Guasave
Guamúchil
Culiacán
4054 Peña Nevada
Gómez Palacio
Torreón
Saltillo
Linares
SIERRA MAD
Ciudad Victor
San José del Cabo
Cabo San Lucas
2164 Las Casitas
SINALOA
Durango
El Salto
DURANGO
ZACATECAS
Fresnillo de Gonzáles Echeverría
Zacatecas
SAN LUIS POTOSÍ
ORIENTA
Ciudad
Mazatlán
NAYARIT
La Paz

HAWAII inset
KAUAI
NIIHAU
Waimea
KAUAI CHANNEL
OAHU
Wahiawa
Kaneohe
Honolulu
MOLOKAI
Kahului
MAUI
LANAI
KAHOOLAWE
HAWAII
Mauna Kea 4205
Hilo
Kailua Kona
Mauna Loa 4170
PACIFIC OCEAN
ALENUIHAHA CHANNEL
KAIWI CHANNEL

ALASKA inset
Arctic Circle
CHUKCHI SEA
Prudhoe Bay
Mackenzie
Mt Isto 2761
RUSSIAN FED.
BERING STRAIT
ST. LAWRENCE I.
Nome
NORTON SOUND
NUNIVAK I.
U.S.A. ALASKA
Fairbanks
Yukon
Mt McKinley 6194
CANADA
4317 Mt Wrangell
6050 Mt Logan
Bethel
Anchorage
Juneau
BRISTOL BAY
KENAI PEN.
KODIAK I.
ALASKA PENINSULA
BERING SEA
GULF OF ALASKA
ALEUTIAN ISLANDS
PACIFIC OCEAN

© ICA Förlaget AB
Scale 1 : 13 400 000
0 200 400 600 km
0 200 400 miles

UNITED STATES

SOUTH AMERICA

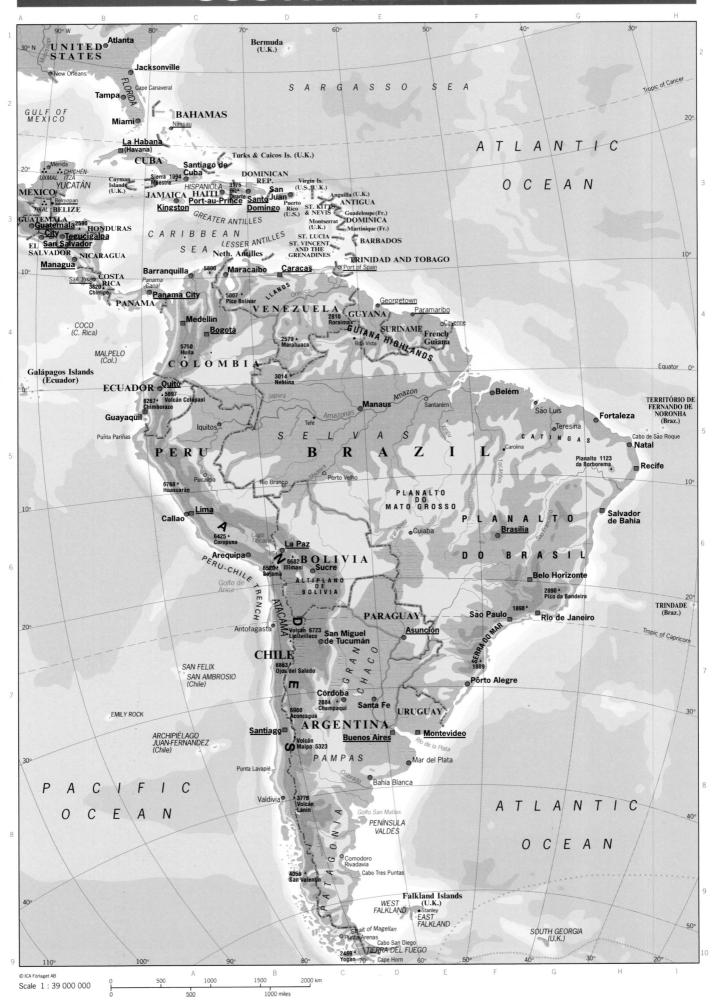

Scale 1 : 39 000 000

NORTHERN SOUTH AMERICA

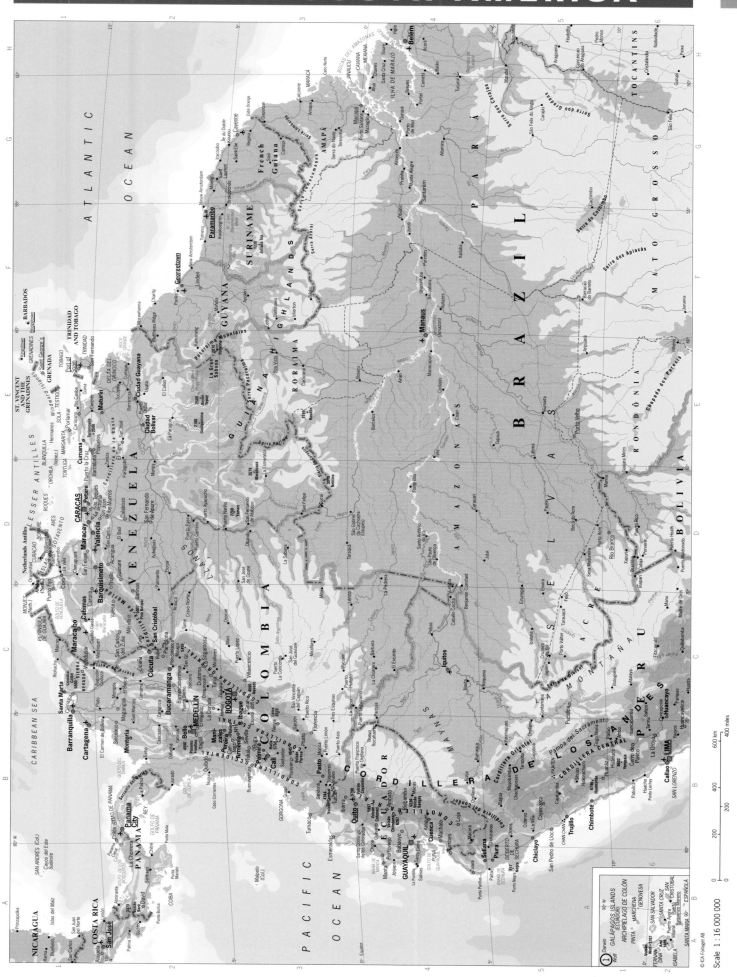

Scale 1 : 16 000 000

© ICA Förlaget AB

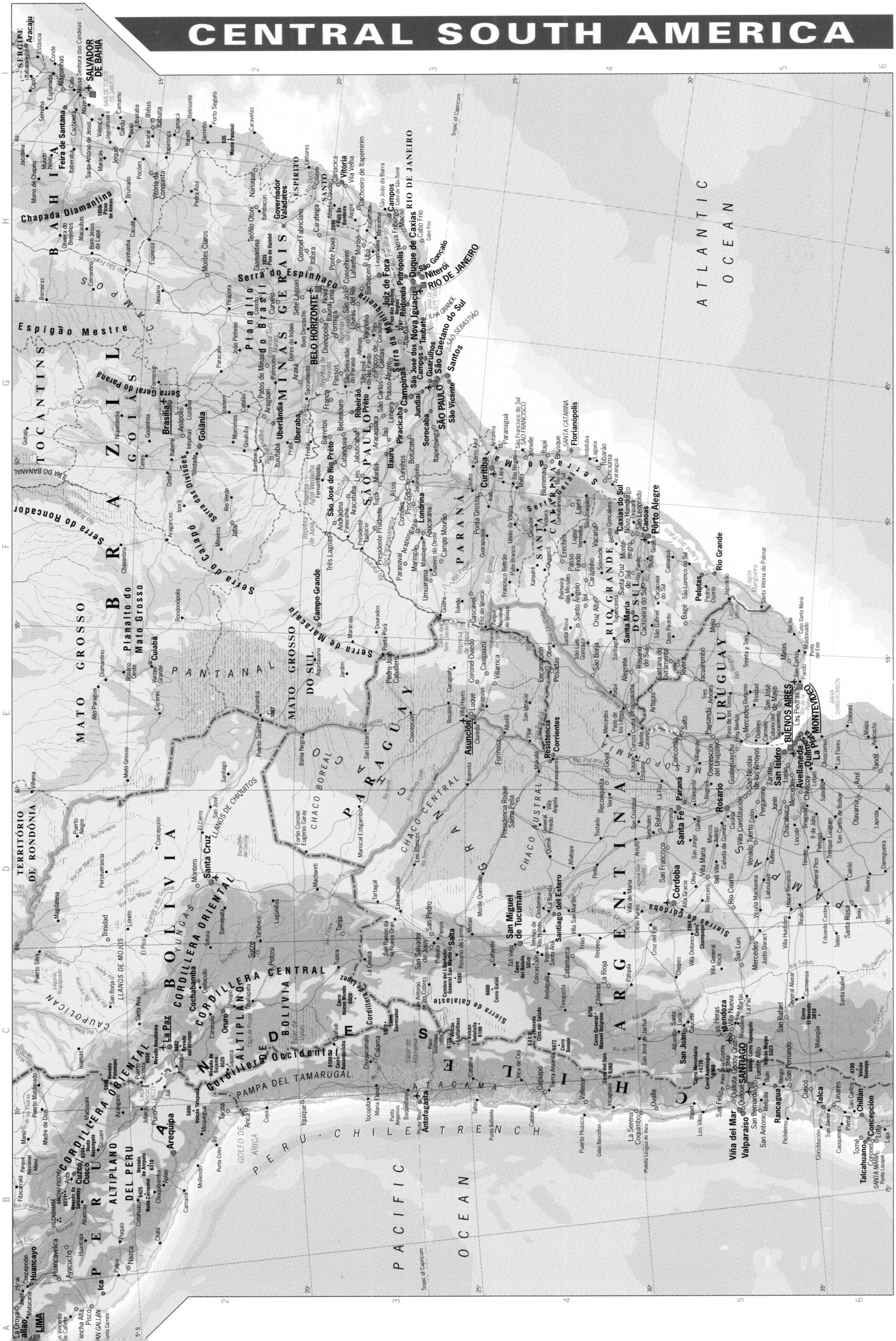

CENTRAL SOUTH AMERICA

BRAZIL

BAHIA

Chapada Diamantina

Espigão Mestre

TOCANTINS

GOIÁS

MINAS GERAIS

Serra do Espinhaço

Planalto do Brasil

BELO HORIZONTE

ESPÍRITO SANTO

Vitória

RIO DE JANEIRO

RIO DE JANEIRO
Niterói
Duque de Caxias

Juiz de Fora

ATLANTIC OCEAN

Brasília

Goiânia

SÃO PAULO

SÃO PAULO
São Vicente
Santos
São Caetano do Sul
Guarulhos
Campinas
Sorocaba
Jundiaí
Piracicaba

PARANÁ

Curitiba

MATO GROSSO

Planalto do Mato Grosso

MATO GROSSO DO SUL

PANTANAL

Campo Grande

Cuiabá

SANTA CATARINA

Florianópolis

RIO GRANDE DO SUL

Caxias do Sul
Canoas
Porto Alegre

Rio Grande
Pelotas

URUGUAY

MONTEVIDEO

PERU

LIMA

Arequipa

Cuzco

ALTIPLANO DEL PERU

CORDILLERA ORIENTAL

BOLIVIA

La Paz
Cochabamba
Oruro
Santa Cruz
Sucre
Potosí

CORDILLERA CENTRAL

ALTIPLANO DE BOLIVIA

CORDILLERA OCCIDENTAL

PAMPA DEL TAMARUGAL

ATACAMA

PARAGUAY

Asunción

CHACO CENTRAL

CHACO AUSTRAL

CHACO BOREAL

Resistencia
Corrientes

ARGENTINA

Córdoba

San Miguel de Tucumán
Santiago del Estero
Salta

Santa Fe
Paraná
Rosario

BUENOS AIRES
La Plata
Avellaneda
San Isidro
Quilmes

Mendoza
San Juan

CHILE

SANTIAGO
Viña del Mar
Valparaíso
Rancagua
Talca
Chillán
Concepción
Talcahuano

PACIFIC OCEAN

PERU-CHILE TRENCH

© ICA för laget AB

600 km

EAST BRAZIL AND SOUTHERN SOUTH AMERICA

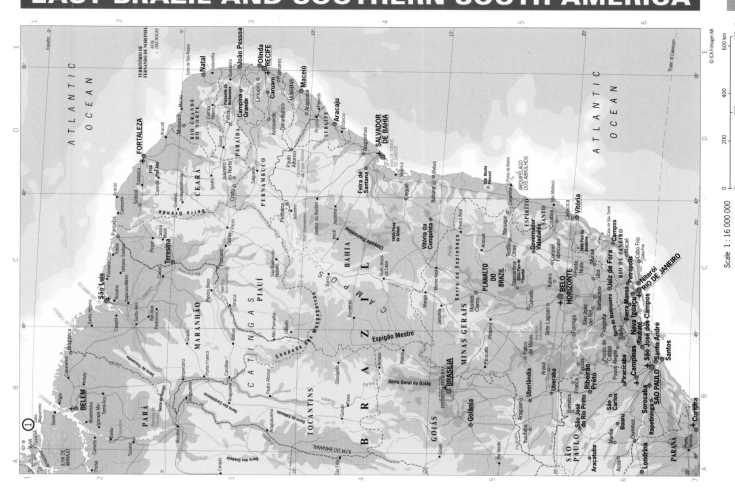

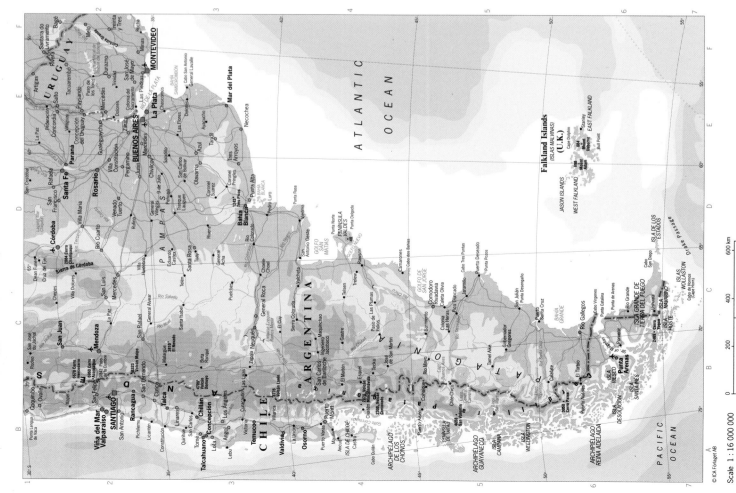

POLAR REGIONS

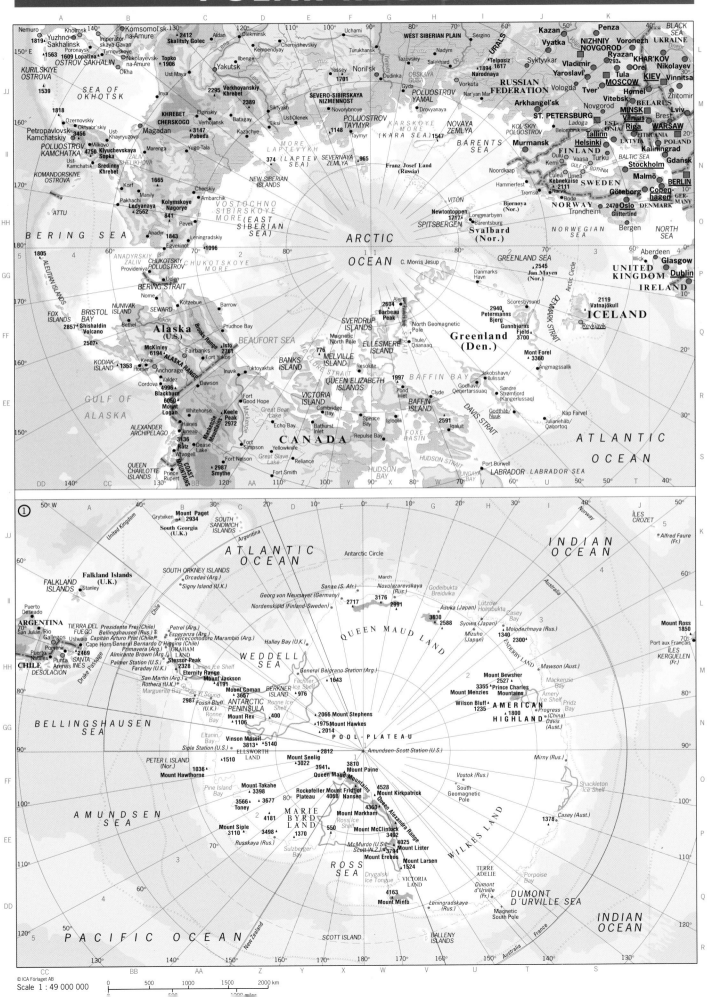

Scale 1 : 49 000 000

SPECIALIST MAP SECTION

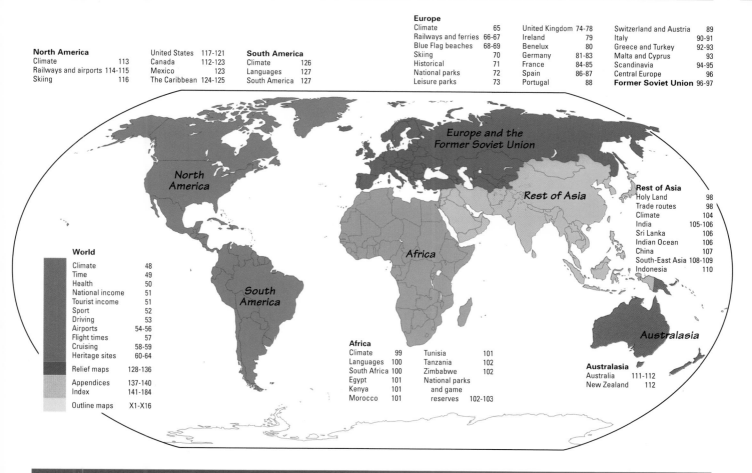

North America
Climate   113
Railways and airports 114-115
Skiing   116

United States   117-121
Canada   122-123
Mexico   123
The Caribbean   124-125

South America
Climate   126
Languages   127
South America   127

Europe
Climate   65
Railways and ferries 66-67
Blue Flag beaches   68-69
Skiing   70
Historical   71
National parks   72
Leisure parks   73

United Kingdom 74-78
Ireland   79
Benelux   80
Germany   81-83
France   84-85
Spain   86-87
Portugal   88

Switzerland and Austria   89
Italy   90-91
Greece and Turkey   92-93
Malta and Cyprus   93
Scandinavia   94-95
Central Europe   96
Former Soviet Union 96-97

World
Climate   48
Time   49
Health   50
National income 51
Tourist income   51
Sport   52
Driving   53
Airports   54-56
Flight times   57
Cruising   58-59
Heritage sites 60-64

Relief maps   128-136

Appendices   137-140
Index   141-184
Outline maps   X1-X16

Rest of Asia
Holy Land   98
Trade routes   98
Climate   104
India   105-106
Sri Lanka   106
Indian Ocean   106
China   107
South-East Asia 108-109
Indonesia   110

Africa
Climate   99
Languages   100
South Africa   100
Egypt   101
Kenya   101
Morocco   101

Tunisia   101
Tanzania   102
Zimbabwe   102
National parks
  and game
  reserves   102-103

Australasia
Australia   111-112
New Zealand   112

KEY TO MAP SYMBOLS

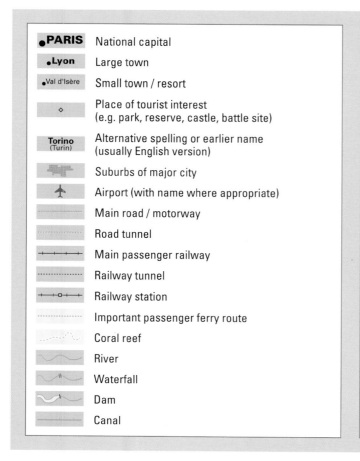

●**PARIS**	National capital
●**Lyon**	Large town
●Val d'Isère	Small town / resort
◇	Place of tourist interest (e.g. park, reserve, castle, battle site)
Torino (Turin)	Alternative spelling or earlier name (usually English version)
	Suburbs of major city
✈	Airport (with name where appropriate)
	Main road / motorway
	Road tunnel
─┼─┼─	Main passenger railway
	Railway tunnel
─┼─□─┼─	Railway station
	Important passenger ferry route
	Coral reef
	River
	Waterfall
	Dam
	Canal

△	Mountain peak, with altitude in metres
▽	Land depression, with altitude in metres
=	Pass, with altitude in metres; canyon
─·─··─	International boundary
─ ─ ─	International boundary (disputed)
	Internal administrative boundary
ISÈRE	Internal administrative name
ANJOU	Large area of tourist interest / physical region
FORÊT DE ST-GERMAIN	Small area of tourist interest / physical region
	National Park / Reserve boundary
(Below sea level)	*Land altitude tints*

Major tourist attractions:

⚑ **Leisure park**
Members of IAAPA (International Association of Amusement Parks and Attractions)

⚑ **Zoo / animal park**
Members of appropriate national or international association or federation, open to the public for at least 6 months of the year and charging an admission fee

⚑ **Aquarium**
Similar criteria to zoos (above)

Major sporting venues:

⚑ **Formula One**
Racecourses which have held a Formula One race since 1990

⚑ **Golf**
Courses where one of the four 'majors' (British Open, US Open, US Masters and US PGA Championship) or the Ryder Cup has been held since 1980

⚑ **Horse racing**
Major horse racecourses

⚑ **Tennis**
'Grand Slam' venues (see p52), ATP (Association of Tennis Professionals) and WTA (Women's Tennis Association) tour venues

CLIMATE

Climate Legend

Polar: no warm season (warmest month below 10°C)
Ice cap (perpetual frost: all months below 0°C) and tundra (warmest month between 0°C and 10°C)

Cooler humid: rainy climates with severe winters
Subarctic (less than four months over 10°C), continental cool summer (coldest month below 0°C, warmest month above 10°C) and continental warm summer (warmest month above 22°C)

Warmer humid: rainy climates with mild winters (coolest month between 0°C and 18°C, warmest month above 10°C)
Marine west coast (warmest month below 22°C), humid subtropical (warmest month above 22°C) and mediterranean (dry season in summer)

Dry Steppe/semi-arid and desert/arid

Tropical humid: rainy climates with no winter (coolest month above 18°C)
Savanna (dry season in either summer or winter) and rainforest (constantly moist or monsoon rain with only a short dry season)

HOURS OF DAYLIGHT AND THE SEASONS

Northern hemisphere

Southern hemisphere

Hours of daylight

Latitude:
Equator
20°
40°
60°
80°

1 Vernal equinox
2 Summer solstice (longest day)
3 Autumnal equinox
4 Winter solstice (shortest day)

Excludes twilight, which lasts approximately 20 minutes before sunrise and 20 minutes after sunset at the Equator. This time increases to 30 minutes at 30 N or S and 40 minutes at 50 N or S.

Dates are approximate

	Northern hemisphere	Southern hemisphere
1	21 Mar	23 Sep
2	21 Jun	21 Dec
3	23 Sep	21 Mar
4	21 Dec	21 Jun

WINTER — SPRING — SUMMER — AUTUMN (FALL)
Jan Feb Mar Apr May Jun Jul Aug Sep Oct Nov Dec

SUMMER — AUTUMN (FALL) — WINTER — SPRING
Jan Feb Mar Apr May Jun Jul Aug Sep Oct Nov Dec

TEMPERATURE CONVERSION

°Celsius	-10	0	10	20	30	40
°Fahrenheit	14	32	50	68	86	104

RAINFALL CONVERSION

Millimetres	102	203	305	406	508	610
Inches	4	8	12	16	20	24

The Tropics of Cancer and Capricorn are lines of latitude, 23° 28' N and S, where the sun appears directly overhead during the summer solstice in the respective northern and southern hemispheres.

The Arctic Circle marks the northernmost point at which the sun can be seen during the winter solstice. Positioned at 66° 30' N.

The Antarctic Circle marks the southernmost point at which the sun can be seen during the winter solstice. Positioned at 66° 30' S.

TIME

SUNDAY
INTERNATIONAL
DATE LINE
MONDAY

+12

+13

+12

+12

+12½ ·4

+11

+12

+11

+11

+11½

+10

+12

+10

+10

+10½

+12

+9

+10

+9

+10

+9½

+8

+9

+8

+9½

+8

+7

+8

+7

+8

+7

+6½ ·2

+5 ¾ ·4

+6

+6¼ ·2

+6

+5½

+5

+5

+5

HOURS AHEAD OF GMT

+4½

+5

+4

+3½ ·2

+4

+4

+4

+3

+3

+3

+3

+3

+2

+2

+2

CENTRAL
EUROPEAN
TIME
+1

+1

+1

GMT

GMT

GMT

GMT

GMT

GMT

GREENWICH
MEAN TIME
(GMT)

-1

-1

-2

-2

HOURS BEHIND GMT

No standard time
legally adopted

NEWFOUNDLAND
STANDARD
TIME

ATLANTIC
STANDARD
TIME
-4

-3½

-3

-3

-3

-4

-4

-4

-4

EASTERN
STANDARD
TIME
-5

-5

-5

-5

-6

CENTRAL
STANDARD
TIME
-6

MOUNTAIN
STANDARD
TIME
-7

-6

PACIFIC
STANDARD
TIME
-8

-7

-9

-9

ALASKA
STANDARD
TIME
-9

-10

+14

+13

-10

-11

ALEUTIAN/
HAWAII
STANDARD
TIME
-10

SUNDAY
INTERNATIONAL
DATE LINE
MONDAY

The term GMT (Greenwich Mean Time) has
been generally replaced by UTC (Universal
Time Co-ordinate), although the times are
the same and it is still known as GMT in the
UK and USA. UTC is used throughout the
world for marine and airline navigation.

COUNTRIES WITH DAYLIGHT SAVING (clocks put forward one hour)
29 March 1998 – 24 October 1998, except where indicated

Albania
Andorra
Australia (Australian Capital
Territory, New South Wales,
South Australia and Victoria)
25 October 1998 – 27 March 1999
Australia (Tasmania)
4 October 1998 – 27 March 1999
Austria
Bahamas
5 April 1998 – 24 October 1998
Belarus
Belgium
Bermuda
5 April 1998 – 24 October 1998
Bosnia-Herzegovina

Brazil (except northeast states,
Acre, Amapá, Amazonas, east
Pará and west Pará)
4 October 1998 – 20 February 1999
Bulgaria
Canada (except eastern Québec,
western Ontario and
Saskatchewan)
5 April 1998 – 24 October 1998
Chile
11 October 1998 – 13 March 1999
Croatia
Cuba
5 April 1998 – 3 October 1998
Cyprus
Czech Republic

Denmark
Easter Island
11 October 1998 – 13 March 1999
Egypt
26 March 1998 – 24 September 1998
Estonia
Falkland Is
13 September 1998 – 17 April 1999
Finland
France
Georgia
Germany
Gibraltar
Greece
Greenland (except Thule and east
Greenland)

Haiti
5 April 1998 – 24 October 1998
Hungary
Iran
21 March 1998 – 23 September 1998
Iraq
1 April 1998 – 30 September 1998
Ireland
Israel
April – September 1998 (exact dates
unavailable at time of going to press)
Italy
Jordan
2 April – 1 October 1998 (provisional)
Kazakhstan
Kyrgyzstan
12 April 1998 – 26 September 1998

Latvia
29 March 1998 – 26 September 1998
Lebanon
26 April 1998 – 26 September 1998
Liechtenstein
Lithuania
Luxembourg
Macedonia, Former Yugoslav
Republic of
Malta
29 March 1998 – 26 September 1998
Mexico (Baja California only)
5 April 1998 – 24 October 1998
Moldova
Monaco
Mongolia
29 March 1998 – 26 September 1998

Netherlands
New Zealand
4 October 1998 – 20 March 1999
Norway
Paraguay
October 1998 – February 1999 (exact
dates unavailable at time of going to
press)
Poland
Portugal
Romania
29 March 1998 – 26 September 1998
Russian Federation
5 April 1998 – 24 October 1998
San Marino
Slovak Republic

Slovenia
Spain
Sweden
Switzerland
Syria
1 April 1998 – 30 September 1998
Turkey
Turks & Caicos Is
5 April 1998 – 24 October 1998
Ukraine
United Kingdom
United States (except Arizona,
Hawaii and Indiana)
5 April 1998 – 24 October 1998
Yugoslavia, Fed. Republic of

HEALTH

MALARIA

The main antimalarial drugs and their side-effects

Chloroquine (CHL). Usually well tolerated. The few people who may experience uncomfortable side-effects, such as gastrointestinal disturbance, may tolerate it better by taking the drug with meals and in divided twice-weekly doses.

Chloroquine + proguanil (C+P). Often causes gastrointestinal upsets (see above).

Mefloquine (MEF). Usually well tolerated. Mild side-effects such as dizziness or gastrointestinal effects may occur for a while during early prophylaxis, but spontaneously resolve. If these side-effects are unacceptable, C+P or DOX can be used instead. Major neurological and psychiatric disorders occur in about one in 10,000 users.

Doxycycline (DOX). Side-effects common. Tablets should always be taken with plenty of fluid, and never taken just prior to lying down.

All prophylactic regimens should begin at least one week before travel, in order to deal with possible side-effects before departure, which can occasionally be severe. Special caution should be exercised by pregnant women. All drugs should be continued for four weeks after the last possible exposure to infection.

In many countries of the Americas and South-East Asia (for example, China, Indonesia, Malaysia, Mexico, Myanmar and Philippines), malaria is largely confined to rural areas not visited by most travellers. Any travel to these areas is most often during day-time when there is minimal risk of exposure. Chemoprophylaxis is recommended only for those travellers who will be exposed outdoors during the evening or night-time in rural areas. Although chemoprophylaxis is not recommended in areas with very limited risk, travellers should be advised to use insect repellents and other personal protection measures.

Travellers are reminded that protection from biting mosquitoes is the first line of defence against malaria, and no antimalarial prophylactic regimen gives complete protection.

Malaria zones:

A Risk generally low and seasonal, no risk in many areas (for example urban areas). *Plasmodium falciparum* absent or sensitive to chloroquine.

Recommended prophylaxis:
Chloroquine, or (in case of very low risk), no prophylaxis, with chloroquine as a stand-by when prompt medical attention unavailable.

B Low risk in most areas. Chloroquine alone will protect against *P. vivax*. Chloroquine with proguanil will give some protection against *P. falciparum* and may alleviate the disease if it occurs despite prophylaxis.

Recommended prophylaxis:
Chloroquine + proguanil *or* chloroquine alone (if proguanil unavailable) *or* (in the case of very low risk), no prophylaxis.

C In Africa, risk high except in some high-altitude areas. In Asia and America, risk low in most areas except in the Amazon basin (colonisation and mining areas), where the risk is high. Resistance to sulfadoxine-pyrimethamine is common in Asia, but variable in America. It is effective in most of Africa.

Recommended prophylaxis:
Mefloquine *or* chloroquine + proguanil, except in the border areas Cambodia/Myanmar/Thailand, where doxycycline is recommended.

This page is based on information supplied by the World Health Organisation (WHO). In all cases, travellers should seek up-to-date medical advice before departure regarding recent developments and further health requirements.
The Columbus Press World Travel Health Guide contains detailed information on health risks, vaccination requirements and medical facilities for every country in the world. For more information, call +44 (0) 171 0700.

Areas where malaria transmission occurs

☐ Areas with limited risk

☐ Areas in which malaria has disappeared, been eradicated or never existed

YELLOW FEVER

SUDAN

The yellow fever endemic zones cover areas of Africa and South America. Countries named in red type are either fully within a zone or have part of their area affected by it. Countries only partially within the yellow fever zones are:

Africa: southern parts of Mali, Niger, Chad and Sudan; all of Somalia except the northwest; far west of Zambia; all of Democratic Republic of Congo except the far south are regarded as endemic zones.

South America: all of Colombia except the southwest; eastern parts of Ecuador, Peru, Bolivia except the west; all of Brazil except the eastern coastal states are regarded as endemic zones.

NIGER

Countries marked with a box require a yellow fever vaccination certificate *of vaccination against yellow fever* from *all* travellers, whether they are arriving from an infected area or not.

Due to the risks involved, pregnant women and children under one year of age (or in some cases six to nine months of age) usually do not require a yellow fever certificate. However, those travelling with children should seek advice before entering the country by contacting the relevant embassies or telephoning the Travellers Healthline on 0891 224100 (in UK only).

EGYPT

All countries where yellow fever is endemic (marked in red type: see left) also require the certificate if travelling from an endemic area, with the exception of Colombia, Panama, Venezuela and Zambia, where no certificate is required.

Countries marked with an asterisk (*) require yellow fever certificates from those arriving from non-infected countries if they are staying for more than two weeks. Travellers should seek advice as above before entering the country by contacting the relevant embassies or telephoning the Travellers Healthline on 0891 224100 (in UK only).

CHAD

A dashed box indicates the country recommends yellow fever vaccinations for all travellers, but this is not a condition of entry.

NATIONAL INCOME

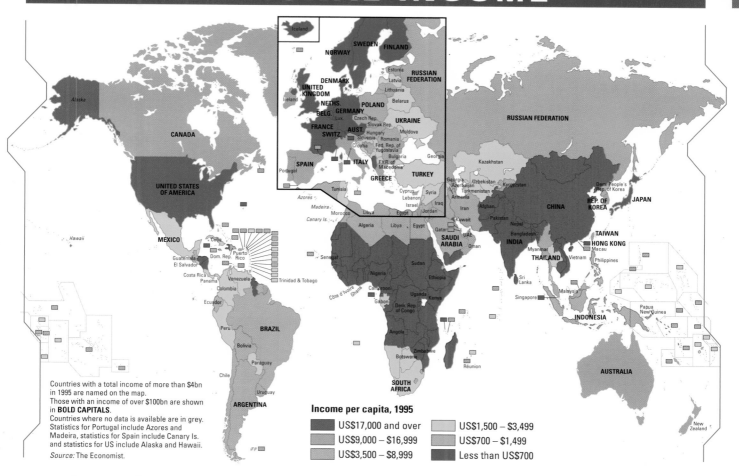

Countries with a total income of more than $4bn in 1995 are named on the map.
Those with an income of over $100bn are shown in **BOLD CAPITALS**.
Countries where no data is available are in grey.
Statistics for Portugal include Azores and Madeira, statistics for Spain include Canary Is. and statistics for US include Alaska and Hawaii.

Source: The Economist.

Income per capita, 1995

- US$17,000 and over
- US$9,000 – $16,999
- US$3,500 – $8,999
- US$1,500 – $3,499
- US$700 – $1,499
- Less than US$700

INCOME FROM TOURISM

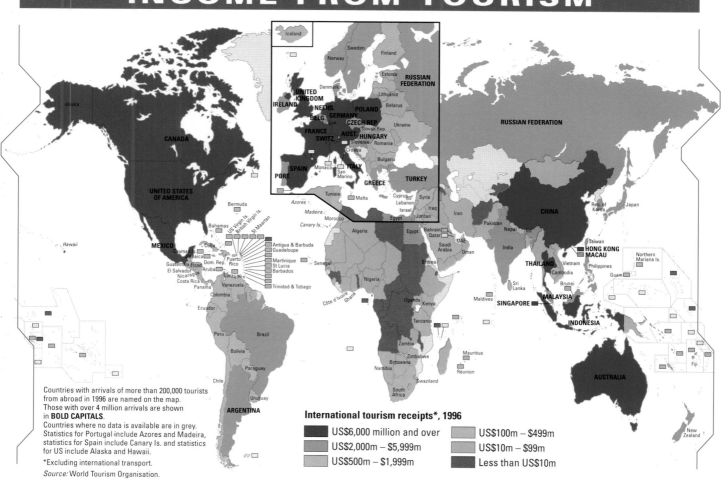

Countries with arrivals of more than 200,000 tourists from abroad in 1996 are named on the map.
Those with over 4 million arrivals are shown in **BOLD CAPITALS**.
Countries where no data is available are in grey.
Statistics for Portugal include Azores and Madeira, statistics for Spain include Canary Is. and statistics for US include Alaska and Hawaii.

*Excluding international transport.

Source: World Tourism Organisation.

International tourism receipts*, 1996

- US$6,000 million and over
- US$2,000m – $5,999m
- US$500m – $1,999m
- US$100m – $499m
- US$10m – $99m
- Less than US$10m

SPORT

SUMMER OLYMPICS

Shown on map: dates and venues of all Olympic Games

The first modern Olympic Games, founded by Frenchman Baron de Coubertin, were held at Athens in 1896. They are held every four years. An extra Olympics were held in 1906 to celebrate the tenth anniversary of the 1896 games. The next Olympic Games are due to be held at Sydney in the year 2000 and at Athens in 2004.

WINTER OLYMPICS

Shown on map: dates and venues of all Winter Olympics

The first separate Winter Games took place in 1924 at Chamonix, France. The games originally took place in the same year as the Summer Olympics, but beginning in 1994, are now held in between the Summer Games. The next Winter Olympics are due to be held at Salt Lake City, Utah in 2002.

COMMONWEALTH GAMES

Shown on map: dates and venues of all Games

Originally the British Empire Games and first held in 1930 at Hamilton, Ontario. Renamed the British Empire and Commonwealth Games in 1954, the British Commonwealth Games in 1970 and the Commonwealth Games in 1978. Held every four years, the next games are due to be held at Kuala Lumpur, Malaysia in 1998.

WORLD ATHLETICS CHAMPIONSHIPS

Shown on map: dates and venues of all Championships

The World Athletics Championships were first held in Helsinki in 1983, and at four-year intervals until 1991. They are now held every two years. The next championships are due to be held at Valencia, Spain in 1999.

FOOTBALL WORLD CUP

Shown on map: all World Cups, indicating date and country, and venue for the final

Association Football's premier event. Brazil kept the Jules Rimet Trophy after winning it for the third time in 1970. The teams now compete for the FIFA World Cup. Held every four years, the next competition is in France in 1998. Japan and the Republic of Korea are due to co-host the event in 2002.

CRICKET WORLD CUP

Shown on map: all World Cups, indicating date and country, and venue for the final

The venue of the first Cricket World Cup in 1975 was England. Played every 4-5 years, it was not until 1987 that the competition was held outside England, but the next World Cup in 1999 will again see England as host.

RUGBY UNION WORLD CUP

Shown on map: all World Cups, indicating date and country, and venue for the final

The first Rugby Union World Cup was held 1987 and is now held every four years, with the next competition in Wales in 1999.

GOLF

Shown on map: starting dates and venues of the four majors for the 1998 season

The four major tournaments are the British Open, the US Open, the US PGA Championship and the US Masters. The leading international team tournament is the Ryder Cup, held every two years and next due to be contested in 1999.

HORSE RACING

Shown on map: dates and venues of major horse races in the 1998 calendar

The five English Classics are the 1000 and 2000 Guineas at Newmarket, The Oaks and The Derby at Epsom and the St Leger at Doncaster. Among the world's richest races are the Dubai World Cup and the Japan Cup. Steeplechasing's most famous race is the Grand National, held at Aintree near Liverpool.

MOTOR RACING

Shown on map: dates and venues for the F1 1998 season; dates of the Indianapolis 500 and Le Mans for 1998

The Formula One season begins in Melbourne on 8th March and finishes in Suzuka, Japan on 1st November. The Indianapolis 500 was first raced in 1911 and is held annually as part of the Memorial Day celebrations. The Le Mans 24-Hour Race is the world's greatest endurance motor race.

TENNIS

Shown on map: starting dates and venues of the four Grand Slam tournaments, the Grand Slam Cup and the Hopman Cup for 1998

The four Grand Slam tournaments are the Australian Open, the French Open, Wimbledon and the US Open. The leading international team tournament, the Davis Cup is held at various venues throughout the year. The ATP (Association of Tennis Professionals) and the WTA (Women's Tennis Association) co-ordinate annual 'tours' for men and women players respectively where players can gain ranking points.

Motor racing in Europe

Imola	26 APR 1998	*San Marino Grand Prix*
Barcelona	10 MAY 1998	*Spanish Grand Prix*
Monte Carlo	24 MAY 1998	*Monaco Grand Prix*
Le Mans	6 JUN 1998	*Le Mans 24-Hour Race*
Silverstone	12 JUL 1998	*British Grand Prix*
Spielberg	26 JUL 1998	*Austrian Grand Prix*
Hockenheim	2 AUG 1998	*German Grand Prix*
Budapest	16 AUG 1998	*Hungarian Grand Prix*
Spa-Francorchamps	30 AUG 1998	*Belgian Grand Prix*
Monza	13 SEP 1998	*Italian Grand Prix*
Nürburgring	27 SEP 1998	*Luxembourg Grand Prix*
Estoril	11 OCT 1998	*Portuguese Grand Prix*

Horse racing in Europe

Aintree	4 APR 1998	*Grand National*
Newmarket	2-3 MAY 1998	*2000 & 1000 Guineas*
Epsom	5-6 JUN 1998	*The Oaks & The Derby*
Ascot	16-19 JUN 1998	*Royal Ascot*
The Curragh	27-28 JUN 1998	*Irish Derby*
Doncaster	12 SEP 1998	*St Leger*
Longchamp, Paris	4 OCT 1998	*Prix de l'Arc de Triomphe*

Details of all events for the forthcoming season may be subject to change at short notice

Legend:
- Summer Olympics
- Winter Olympics
- Commonwealth Games
- World Athletics Championships
- Football World Cup
- Rugby Union World Cup
- Cricket World Cup
- Tennis
- Golf
- Horse racing
- Motor racing

Map labels:

SUNDAY INTERNATIONAL DATE LINE MONDAY

NEW ZEALAND — Auckland 1950, Final: Auckland 1987, Christchurch 1974

Brisbane 1982, Sydney 2000, 22 NOV 1998, 3 NOV 1998, *Japan Cup*, Melbourne 1938, 8 MAR 1998, Final: Melbourne 1956, *Australian Grand Prix*, 13 JAN 1998, *Australian Open*, Perth 1962, 4 JAN 1998, *Hopman Cup*

AUSTRALIA & NEW ZEALAND 1992, Final: Melbourne
(Equestrian events held in Stockholm due to Australian quarantine regulations)

Sapporo 1972, Nagano 1998, Tokyo 1964, 1991, Suzuka 1 NOV 1998, *Japanese Grand Prix*, Seoul 1988, JAPAN & REP. OF KOREA 2002, Hong Kong 13 DEC 1998, *Hong Kong International Races*, Kuala Lumpur 1998

INDIA & PAKISTAN 1987, Final: Calcutta, India, INDIA, PAKISTAN & SRI LANKA 1996, Final: Lahore, Pakistan, Dubai 28 MAR 1998, *Dubai World Cup*

Moscow 1980, Helsinki 1952, 1983, Final: Stockholm, SWEDEN 1958, Stockholm 1912, Gothenburg 1995, Oslo 1952, Lillehammer 1994, Berlin 1936, Amsterdam 1928, Antwerp 1920, GERMANY 1974, Final: Munich, Munich 1972, 22 SEP 1998, *Grand Slam Cup*, Stuttgart 1993, Cortina 1956, SWITZ. 1954, Final: Bern, ITALY 1934, Final: Rome, Rome 1960, Innsbruck 1964, 1976, Sarajevo 1984, Athens 1896, 1906, 2004, Garmisch Partenkirchen 1936, St Moritz 1928, 1948, Chamonix 1924

ENGLAND 1966, 1991, Final: London 1979, 1983, 1975, London, Edinburgh 1970, 1986, FRANCE 1938, 1998, Final: Paris, WALES 1999, Final: Cardiff, Cardiff 1958, Grenoble 1968, Albertville 1992, SPAIN 1982, Final: Madrid, Barcelona 1992, Valencia 1999

Royal Birkdale, Southport 16 JUL 1998, *British Open*, London 1908, 1934, 1948, 22 JUN 1998, All-England Championships (Wimbledon), Paris 1900, 1924, 25 MAY 1998, *French Open*

Edmonton 1978, Calgary 1988, Vancouver, Victoria 1994, Sahalee, Seattle 13 AUG 1998, *US PGA Championship*, Squaw Valley 1960, Salt Lake City 2002, Olympic Club, San Francisco 18 JUN 1998, *US Open*, Los Angeles 1932, 1984

Montreal 1976, 7 JUN 1998, *Canadian Grand Prix*, Lake Placid 1932, 1980, Hamilton 1930, New York 6 JUN 1998, Belmont Stakes*, US Open 31 AUG 1998, Pimlico, Baltimore 16 MAY 1998, Preakness Stakes*, Indianapolis 500 24 MAY 1998, Louisville 2 MAY 1998, Kentucky Derby*, Augusta 9 APR 1998, *US Masters*, Atlanta 1996, St Louis 1904, UNITED STATES 1994, Final: Los Angeles, Kingston 1966

*The Three Triple Crown races

MEXICO 1970, 1986, Finals: Mexico City, Mexico City 1968

SOUTH AFRICA 1995, Final: Johannesburg, BRAZIL 1950, Final: Rio de Janeiro, São Paulo 29 MAR 1998, *Brazilian Grand Prix*, URUGUAY 1930, Final: Montevideo, Buenos Aires, ARGENTINA 1978, Final: Buenos Aires, 12 APR 1998, *Argentine Grand Prix*, CHILE 1962, Final: Santiago

SUNDAY INTERNATIONAL DATE LINE MONDAY

DRIVING

Speed limits in selected countries of North America and Europe (kilometres per hour)†

	Built-up areas	Other roads outside built-up areas	'Motorways'
Russian Federation	60	110	110
Spain and Portugal	50 (60 in Portugal)	90 – 100	120
Germany and Austria	50	100 – 130 (100 in Austria)	130 (Germany: recommended only)
Italy	50	90 – 110	130
France, Belgium & Netherlands	50	90 (80 in Neths.)	100 – 120 (100-120 in Neths., 110 in France, 120 in Belgium)
UK and Ireland	48 (30mph)	96 (60-70mph)	112 (70mph)

Canada

50

80 – 110

Newfoundland and Saskatchewan: as posted

Speed limit varies according to province: 80kph in New Brunswick*, Newfoundland* and Saskatchewan (*100kph on Trans-Canada Highway); 90kph in British Columbia, Manitoba, NW Territories, Prince Edward I. and Yukon† (*100kph on Alaska Highway); between 80-100kph in Nova Scotia; 90-100kph in Ontario and Québec; 110kph in Alberta.

United States

40 – 48 (25mph)(30mph)

90 – 120 (55mph)(75mph)

The maximum speed limit on rural interstate highways varies from state to state. In general the busier eastern states have lower limits, usually 65mph, while the central and western states have higher limits.
See map inset above.

US rural interstate highway speed limits:

- 80kph (50mph)
- 90kph (55mph)
- 105kph (65mph)
- 112/120kph (70/75mph)
- No speed limit

1000 km
500 miles

ALASKA
HAWAII

Key

- **Countries where traffic drives on the right †**
- **Countries where traffic drives on the left †**

International distinguishing signs

These signs signify the country of registration of the vehicle. The standardisation of signs has been under consideration for some time, but no final agreement has been reached. The signs shown here are based on information supplied by the United Nations. Those marked with an asterisk (*) are not included in the United Nations' list of signs established according to the 1918 or the 1968 Convention on Road Traffic.

The following maximum speed limit regulations are for private cars only. Speed limits for mopeds, motorcycles, scooters, agricultural tractors, cars with trailers or caravans, vehicles towing another vehicle, minibuses, buses, coaches, trucks, camper vans, mobile homes, heavy goods vehicles and recently qualified drivers often vary from those shown.

† Information supplied by the RAC.

SUNDAY
INTERNATIONAL
DATE LINE
MONDAY

AIRPORTS

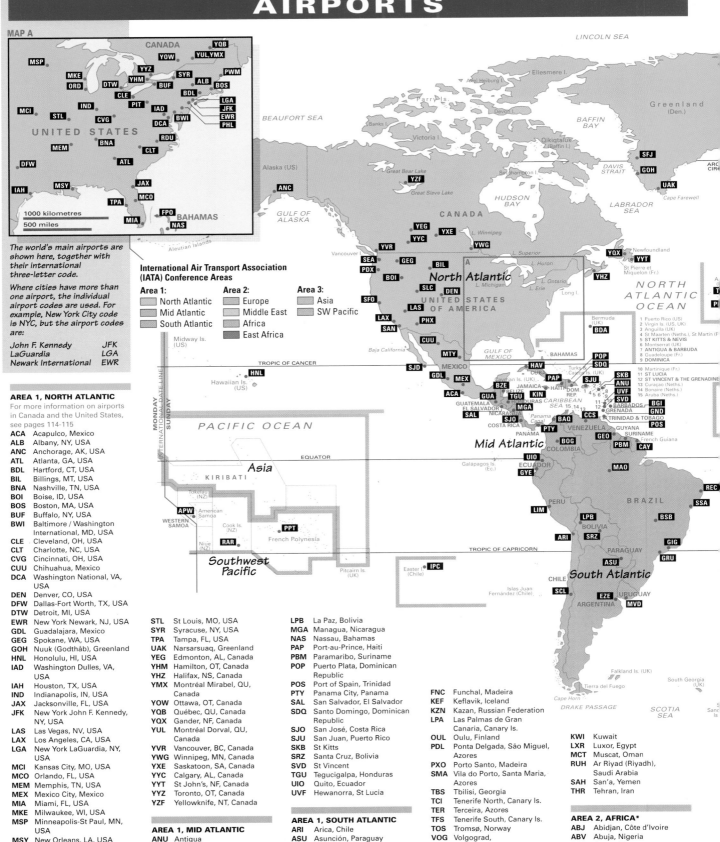

MAP A

The world's main airports are shown here, together with their international three-letter code.

Where cities have more than one airport, the individual airport codes are used. For example, New York City code is NYC, but the airport codes are:

John F. Kennedy	JFK
LaGuardia	LGA
Newark International	EWR

International Air Transport Association (IATA) Conference Areas

Area 1:	Area 2:	Area 3:
North Atlantic	Europe	Asia
Mid Atlantic	Middle East	SW Pacific
South Atlantic	Africa	
	East Africa	

AREA 1, NORTH ATLANTIC

For more information on airports in Canada and the United States, see pages 114-115

ACA	Acapulco, Mexico
ALB	Albany, NY, USA
ANC	Anchorage, AK, USA
ATL	Atlanta, GA, USA
BDL	Hartford, CT, USA
BIL	Billings, MT, USA
BNA	Nashville, TN, USA
BOI	Boise, ID, USA
BOS	Boston, MA, USA
BUF	Buffalo, NY, USA
BWI	Baltimore / Washington International, MD, USA
CLE	Cleveland, OH, USA
CLT	Charlotte, NC, USA
CVG	Cincinnati, OH, USA
CUU	Chihuahua, Mexico
DCA	Washington National, VA, USA
DEN	Denver, CO, USA
DFW	Dallas-Fort Worth, TX, USA
DTW	Detroit, MI, USA
EWR	New York Newark, NJ, USA
GDL	Guadalajara, Mexico
GEG	Spokane, WA, USA
GOH	Nuuk (Godthåb), Greenland
HNL	Honolulu, HI, USA
IAD	Washington Dulles, VA, USA
IAH	Houston, TX, USA
IND	Indianapolis, IN, USA
JAX	Jacksonville, FL, USA
JFK	New York John F. Kennedy, NY, USA
LAS	Las Vegas, NV, USA
LAX	Los Angeles, CA, USA
LGA	New York LaGuardia, NY, USA
MCI	Kansas City, MO, USA
MCO	Orlando, FL, USA
MEM	Memphis, TN, USA
MEX	Mexico City, Mexico
MIA	Miami, FL, USA
MKE	Milwaukee, WI, USA
MSP	Minneapolis-St Paul, MN, USA
MSY	New Orleans, LA, USA
MTY	Monterrey, Mexico
ORD	Chicago, IL, USA
PDX	Portland, OR, USA
PHL	Philadelphia, PA, USA
PHX	Phoenix, AZ, USA
PIT	Pittsburgh, PA, USA
PWM	Portland, ME, USA
RDU	Raleigh-Durham, NC, USA
SAN	San Diego, CA, USA
SEA	Seattle, WA, USA
SFJ	Søndre Strømfjord, Greenland
SFO	San Francisco, CA, USA
SJD	San José del Cabo, Mexico
SLC	Salt Lake City, UT, USA

STL	St Louis, MO, USA
SYR	Syracuse, NY, USA
TPA	Tampa, FL, USA
UAK	Narsarsuaq, Greenland
YEG	Edmonton, AL, Canada
YHM	Hamilton, OT, Canada
YHZ	Halifax, NS, Canada
YMX	Montréal Mirabel, QU, Canada
YOW	Ottawa, OT, Canada
YQB	Québec, QU, Canada
YQX	Gander, NF, Canada
YUL	Montréal Dorval, QU, Canada
YVR	Vancouver, BC, Canada
YWG	Winnipeg, MN, Canada
YXE	Saskatoon, SA, Canada
YYC	Calgary, AL, Canada
YYT	St John's, NF, Canada
YYZ	Toronto, OT, Canada
YZF	Yellowknife, NT, Canada

AREA 1, MID ATLANTIC

ANU	Antigua
BAQ	Barranquilla, Colombia
BDA	Bermuda
BGI	Barbados
BOG	Bogotá, Colombia
BZE	Belize City, Belize
CAY	Cayenne, French Guiana
CCS	Caracas, Venezuela
FPO	Freeport, Bahamas
GEO	Georgetown, Guyana
GND	Grenada
GUA	Guatemala City, Guatemala
GYE	Guayaquil, Ecuador
HAV	La Habana (Havana), Cuba
KIN	Kingston, Jamaica
LIM	Lima, Peru

LPB	La Paz, Bolivia
MGA	Managua, Nicaragua
NAS	Nassau, Bahamas
PAP	Port-au-Prince, Haiti
PBM	Paramaribo, Suriname
POP	Puerto Plata, Dominican Republic
POS	Port of Spain, Trinidad
PTY	Panama City, Panama
SAL	San Salvador, El Salvador
SDQ	Santo Domingo, Dominican Republic
SJO	San José, Costa Rica
SJU	San Juan, Puerto Rico
SKB	St Kitts
SRZ	Santa Cruz, Bolivia
SVD	St Vincent
TGU	Tegucigalpa, Honduras
UIO	Quito, Ecuador
UVF	Hewanorra, St Lucia

AREA 1, SOUTH ATLANTIC

ARI	Arica, Chile
ASU	Asunción, Paraguay
BSB	Brasília, Brazil
EZE	Buenos Aires, Argentina
GIG	Rio de Janeiro, Brazil
GRU	São Paulo, Brazil
IPC	Easter Island
MAO	Manaus, Brazil
MVD	Montevideo, Uruguay
REC	Recife, Brazil
SCL	Santiago, Chile
SSA	Salvador, Brazil

AREA 2, EUROPE*

BAK	Baki (Baku), Azerbaijan
EVN	Yerevan, Armenia

FNC	Funchal, Madeira
KEF	Keflavik, Iceland
KZN	Kazan, Russian Federation
LPA	Las Palmas de Gran Canaria, Canary Is.
OUL	Oulu, Finland
PDL	Ponta Delgada, São Miguel, Azores
PXO	Porto Santo, Madeira
SMA	Vila do Porto, Santa Maria, Azores
TBS	Tbilisi, Georgia
TCI	Tenerife North, Canary Is.
TER	Terceira, Azores
TFS	Tenerife South, Canary Is.
TOS	Tromsø, Norway
VOG	Volgograd, Russian Federation

AREA 2, MIDDLE EAST*

ADE	Adan (Aden), Yemen
AUH	Abu Dhabi, UAE
BAH	Bahrain
BGW	Baghdad, Iraq
DHA	Dhahran, Saudi Arabia
DOH	Doha, Qatar
DXB	Dubai, UAE
JED	Jiddah (Jeddah), Saudi Arabia
KRT	Al Khurtum (Khartoum), Sudan

KWI	Kuwait
LXR	Luxor, Egypt
MCT	Muscat, Oman
RUH	Ar Riyad (Riyadh), Saudi Arabia
SAH	San'a, Yemen
THR	Tehran, Iran

AREA 2, AFRICA*

ABJ	Abidjan, Côte d'Ivoire
ABV	Abuja, Nigeria
ACC	Accra, Ghana
ADD	Addis Ababa, Ethiopia
ASM	Asmara, Eritrea
BEW	Beira, Mozambique
BGF	Bangui, Central African Rep.
BJL	Banjul, The Gambia
BJM	Bujumbura, Burundi
BKO	Bamako, Mali
BZV	Brazzaville, Congo
CKY	Conakry, Guinea
COO	Cotonou, Benin
CPT	Cape Town, South Africa
DKR	Dakar, Senegal
DLA	Douala, Cameroon
DUR	Durban, South Africa

AIRPORTS

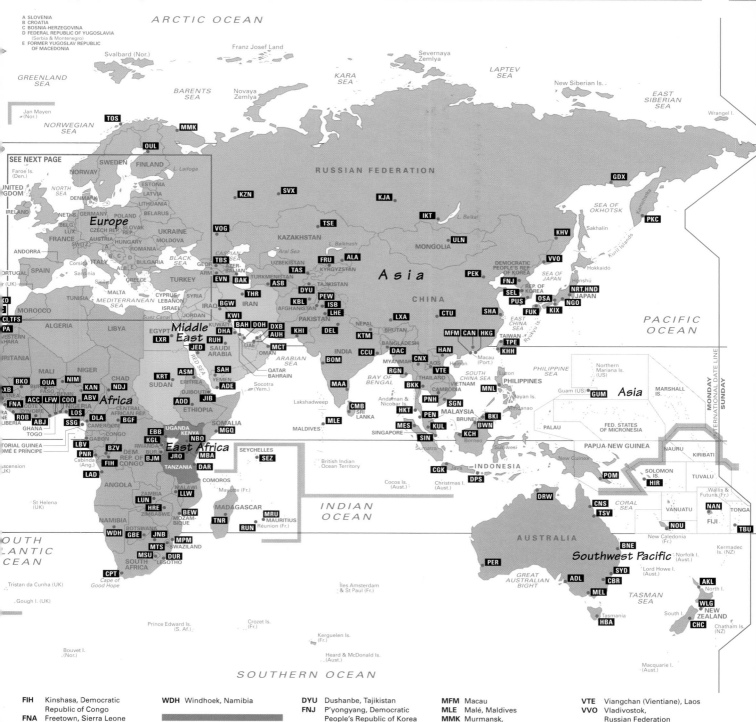

A SLOVENIA
B CROATIA
C BOSNIA-HERZEGOVINA
D FEDERAL REPUBLIC OF YUGOSLAVIA
   (Serbia & Montenegro)
E FORMER YUGOSLAV REPUBLIC
   OF MACEDONIA

FIH	Kinshasa, Democratic Republic of Congo	**WDH**	Windhoek, Namibia	**DYU**	Dushanbe, Tajikistan	**MFM**	Macau
FNA	Freetown, Sierra Leone			**FNJ**	P'yongyang, Democratic People's Republic of Korea	**MLE**	Malé, Maldives
GBE	Gaborone, Botswana	**AREA 2, EAST AFRICA**		**FRU**	Bishkek, Kyrgyzstan	**MMK**	Murmansk, Russian Federation
HRE	Harare, Zimbabwe	**DAR**	Dar es Salaam, Tanzania	**FUK**	Fukuoka, Japan	**MNL**	Manila, the Philippines
JIB	Djibouti	**EBB**	Entebbe, Uganda	**GDX**	Magadan, Russian Federation	**NGO**	Nagoya, Japan
JNB	Johannesburg, South Africa	**JRO**	Kilimanjaro, Tanzania	**GUM**	Guam	**NRT**	Tokyo Narita, Japan
KAN	Kano, Nigeria	**MBA**	Mombasa, Kenya	**HAN**	Hanoi, Vietnam	**OSA**	Osaka, Japan
KGL	Kigali, Rwanda	**NBO**	Nairobi, Kenya	**HKG**	Hong Kong, China	**PEK**	Beijing (Peking), China
MGQ	Muqdisho (Mogadishu), Somalia			**HKT**	Phuket, Thailand	**PEN**	Pinang (Penang), Malaysia
MPM	Maputo, Mozambique	**AREA 3, ASIA**		**HND**	Tokyo Haneda, Japan	**PEW**	Peshawar, Pakistan
MRU	Mauritius	**ALA**	Almaty, Kazakhstan	**IKT**	Irkutsk, Russian Federation	**PKC**	Petropavlovsk Kamchatskiy, Russian Federation
MSU	Maseru, Lesotho	**ASB**	Ashgabat, Turkmenistan	**ISB**	Islamabad, Pakistan	**PNH**	Phnom Penh, Cambodia
MTS	Manzini, Swaziland	**BKI**	Kota Kinabalu, Malaysia	**KBL**	Kabul, Afghanistan	**POM**	Port Moresby, Papua New Guinea
NDB	Nouadhibou, Mauritania	**BKK**	Krung Thep (Bangkok), Thailand	**KCH**	Kuching, Malaysia	**PUS**	Pusan, Rep. of Korea
NDJ	N'Djamena, Chad	**BOM**	Bombay, India	**KHH**	Kaohsiung, Taiwan	**RGN**	Yangon (Rangoon), Myanmar
NIM	Niamey, Niger	**BWN**	Bandar Seri Begawan, Brunei	**KHI**	Karachi, Pakistan	**SEL**	Soul (Seoul), Rep. of Korea
NKC	Nouakchott, Mauritania	**CAN**	Guangzhou (Canton), China	**KHV**	Khabarovsk, Russian Federation	**SGN**	Ho Chi Minh City, Vietnam
OUA	Ouagadougou, Burkina Faso	**CCU**	Calcutta, India	**KIX**	Kansai, Japan	**SHA**	Shanghai, China
OXB	Bissau, Guinea-Bissau	**CGK**	Jakarta, Indonesia	**KJA**	Krasnoyarsk, Russian Federation	**SIN**	Singapore
PNR	Pointe-Noire, Congo	**CMB**	Colombo, Sri Lanka	**KTM**	Kathmandu, Nepal	**SVX**	Yekaterinburg, Russian Federation
ROB	Monrovia, Liberia	**CNX**	Chiang Mai, Thailand	**KUL**	Kuala Lumpur, Malaysia	**TAS**	Tashkent, Uzbekistan
RUN	Réunion	**CTU**	Chengdu, China	**LHE**	Lahore, Pakistan	**TPE**	Taipei, Taiwan
SEZ	Mahé, Seychelles	**DAC**	Dhaka, Bangladesh	**LXA**	Lhasa, China	**TSE**	Akmola, Kazakhstan
SID	Sal, Cape Verde	**DEL**	Delhi, India	**MAA**	Madras, India	**ULN**	Ulaanbaatar (Ulan Bator), Mongolia
SSG	Malabo, Equatorial Guinea	**DPS**	Denpasar, Bali, Indonesia	**MES**	Medan, Indonesia	
TNR	Antananarivo, Madagascar					

VTE	Viangchan (Vientiane), Laos
VVO	Vladivostok, Russian Federation
AREA 3, SOUTHWEST PACIFIC	
ADL	Adelaide, Australia
AKL	Auckland, New Zealand
APW	Apia, Western Samoa
BNE	Brisbane, Australia
CBR	Canberra, Australia
CHC	Christchurch, New Zealand
CNS	Cairns, Australia
DRW	Darwin, Australia
HBA	Hobart, Tasmania, Australia
HIR	Honiara, Solomon Is.
MEL	Melbourne, Australia
NAN	Nadi, Fiji
NOU	Nouméa, New Caledonia
PER	Perth, Australia
PPT	Papeete, Tahiti, French Polynesia
RAR	Rarotonga, Cook Is.
SYD	Sydney, Australia
TBU	Tongatapu, Tonga
TSV	Townsville, Australia
WLG	Wellington, New Zealand
*	See next page for other airports in these areas

AIRPORTS

See previous page for key to area colours.

Where cities have more than one airport, the individual airport codes are used. For example, Berlin city code is BER, but the airport codes are:

Schönefeld   SXF
Tegel   TXL

AREA 2, EUROPE

For more information on airports in the UK, see pages 76–77.

AAE	Annaba, Algeria
AAR	Århus, Denmark
ABZ	Aberdeen, Scotland
AGA	Agadir, Morocco
AGB	Augsburg, Germany
AGP	Málaga, Spain
AJA	Ajaccio, France
ALC	Alicante, Spain
ALG	Alger (Algiers), Algeria
AMS	Amsterdam, The Netherlands
ANR	Antwerpen (Antwerp), Belgium
ARN	Stockholm, Sweden
ATH	Athína (Athens), Greece
AXD	Alexandroúpoli, Greece
AYT	Antalya, Turkey
BCN	Barcelona, Spain
BEG	Beograd (Belgrade), Federal Republic of Yugoslavia
BFS	Belfast, Northern Ireland
BGO	Bergen, Norway
BHX	Birmingham, England
BIO	Bilbao, Spain
BLQ	Bologna, Italy
BOD	Bordeaux, France
BOJ	Burgas, Bulgaria
BRE	Bremen, Germany
BRN	Bern (Berne), Switzerland
BRU	Bruxelles (Brussel/Brussels), Belgium
BSL	Basel (Basle), Switzerland
BTS	Bratislava, Slovak Republic

BUD	Budapest, Hungary
CAG	Cágliari, Italy
CDG	Paris Charles de Gaulle, France
CFE	Clermont-Ferrand, France
CFU	Kérkira (Corfu), Greece
CGN	Köln (Cologne) / Bonn, Germany
CHQ	Haniá (Canea), Greece
CMN	Deir el Beida (Casablanca), Morocco
CND	Constanta, Romania
CPH	København (Copenhagen), Denmark
CTA	Catánia, Italy
CWL	Cardiff, Wales
CZL	Constantine, Algeria
DBV	Dubrovnik, Croatia
DJE	Jerba, Tunisia
DLM	Dalaman, Turkey
DME	Moskva (Moscow) Domodedovo, Russian Fed.
DRS	Dresden, Germany
DUB	Dublin, Ireland
DUS	Düsseldorf, Germany
EDI	Edinburgh, Scotland
EIN	Eindhoven, The Netherlands
ENS	Enschede, The Netherlands
ESB	Ankara, Turkey
FAE	Vágar, Faroe Islands
FAO	Faro, Portugal
FBU	Oslo, Norway
FCO	Roma (Rome), Italy
FEZ	Fès, Morocco
FRA	Frankfurt am Main, Germany
GDN	Gdansk, Poland
GIB	Gibraltar
GLA	Glasgow, Scotland
GOA	Génova (Genoa), Italy
GOT	Göteborg (Gothenburg), Sweden
GRO	Girona, Spain
GRQ	Groningen, The Netherlands
GVA	Genève (Geneva), Switz.
HAJ	Hannover, Germany
HAM	Hamburg, Germany

HEL	Helsinki (Helsingfors), Finland
HER	Iráklio (Herakleion), Greece
IBZ	Eivissa (Ibiza), Spain
INN	Innsbruck, Austria
IOA	Ioánina, Greece
IST	Istanbul, Turkey
IZM	Izmir (Smyrna), Turkey
JKG	Jönköping, Sweden
JMK	Míkonos, Greece
JSI	Skíathos, Greece
JTR	Thíra, Greece
KBP	Kyyiv (Kiev), Ukraine
KGS	Kos (Cos), Greece
KIV	Chisinau (Kishinev), Moldova
KLU	Klagenfurt, Austria
KRK	Kraków (Cracow), Poland
KRS	Kristiansand, Norway
LCY	London City, England
LDE	Lourdes, France
LED	Sankt-Peterburg (St Petersburg), Russian Fed.
LEH	Le Havre, France
LEJ	Leipzig/Halle, Germany
LGG	Liège, Belgium
LGW	London Gatwick, England
LHR	London Heathrow, England
LIL	Lille, France
LIN	Milano (Milan) Linate, Italy
LIS	Lisboa (Lisbon), Portugal
LJU	Ljubljana, Slovenia
LNZ	Linz, Austria
LTN	London Luton, England
LUX	Luxembourg
LWO	Lviv (Lvov), Ukraine
LYS	Lyon, France
MAD	Madrid, Spain
MAH	Maó (Mahón), Spain
MAN	Manchester, England
MGL	Mönchengladbach, Germany
MIR	Monastir, Tunisia
MLA	Malta
MMX	Malmö, Sweden
MRS	Marseille, France
MSQ	Mensk (Minsk), Belarus
MST	Maastricht, The Netherlands

MUC	München (Munich), Germany
MXP	Milano (Milan) Malpensa, Italy
NAP	Nápoli (Naples), Italy
NCE	Nice, France
NCL	Newcastle, England
NOC	Knock, Ireland
NTE	Nantes, France
NUE	Nürnberg (Nuremberg), Germany
NYO	Nyköping, Sweden
ODS	Odesa (Odessa), Ukraine
OPO	Porto (Oporto), Portugal
ORK	Cork, Ireland
ORN	Oran, Algeria
ORY	Paris Orly, France
OST	Oostende (Ostend), Belgium
OTP	Bucuresti (Bucharest), Romania
PAS	Páros, Greece
PMI	Palma de Mallorca, Spain
PMO	Palermo, Italy
PRG	Praha (Prague), Czech Rep.
PSA	Pisa, Italy
RAK	Marrakech, Morocco
RBA	Rabat, Morocco
REU	Reus, Spain
RHO	Ródos (Rhodes), Greece
RIX	Riga, Latvia
RNS	Reims, France
ROV	Rostov-na-Donu, Russian Fed.
RTM	Rotterdam, The Netherlands
SCN	Saarbrücken, Germany
SCQ	Santiago de Compostela, Spain
SDL	Sundsvall, Sweden
SFA	Sfax, Tunisia
SIP	Simferopol, Ukraine
SJJ	Sarajevo, Bosnia-Herz.
SKG	Thessaloniki (Salonika), Greece
SKP	Skopje, FYR of Macedonia
SNN	Shannon, Ireland
SOF	Sofiya (Sofia), Bulgaria
STN	London Stansted, England
STR	Stuttgart, Germany

SVG	Stavanger, Norway
SVO	Moskva (Moscow) Sheremetyevo, Russian Fed.
SVQ	Sevilla (Seville), Spain
SXF	Berlin Schönefeld, Germany
SZG	Salzburg, Austria
TIA	Tiranë (Tirana), Albania
TKU	Turku (Åbo), Finland
TLL	Tallinn, Estonia
TLS	Toulouse, France
TMP	Tampere, Finland
TNG	Tanger (Tangier), Morocco
TOE	Tozeur, Tunisia
TRD	Trondheim, Norway
TRN	Torino (Turin), Italy
TSR	Timisoara, Romania
TUN	Tunis, Tunisia
TXL	Berlin Tegel, Germany
VAA	Vaasa (Vasa), Finland
VAR	Varna, Bulgaria
VCE	Venézia (Venice), Italy
VIE	Wien (Vienna), Austria
VKO	Moskva (Moscow) Vnukovo, Russian Fed.
VLC	Valencia, Spain
VNO	Vilnius, Lithuania
WAW	Warszawa (Warsaw), Poland
ZAG	Zagreb, Croatia
ZRH	Zürich, Switzerland

AREA 2, MIDDLE EAST

ALP	Halab (Aleppo), Syria
ALY	El Iskandarîya (Alexandria), Egypt
AMM	Amman, Jordan
BEY	Bayrut (Beirut), Lebanon
CAI	El Qâhira (Cairo), Egypt
DAM	Dimashq (Damascus), Syria
LCA	Larnaca, Cyprus
PFO	Paphos, Cyprus
TLV	Tel Aviv-Yafo, Israel

AREA 2, AFRICA

TIP	Tarabulus (Tripoli), Libya

FLIGHT TIMES

Average flight times from London, New York and Singapore to other major destinations. Hours do not include stopover time, when necessary, from one destination to another.

Less than 2 hours
2 hours – 4 hours 59 mins
5 hours – 8 hours 59 mins
9 hours – 14 hours 59 mins
15 hours – 24 hours 59 mins
25 hours and over

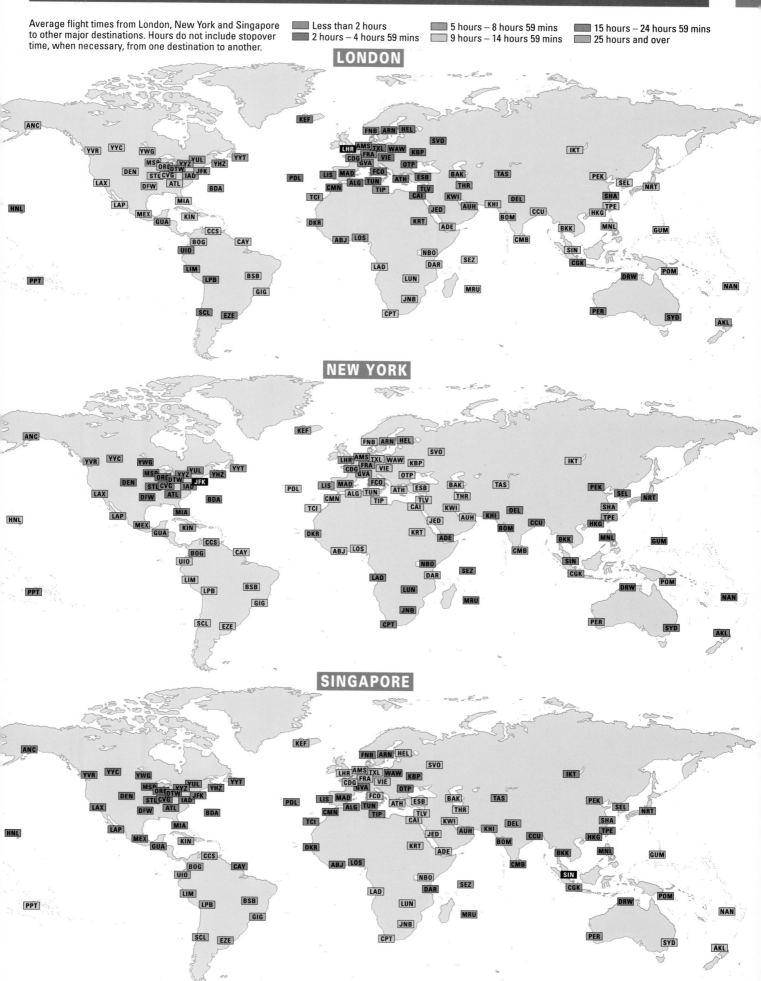

LONDON

NEW YORK

SINGAPORE

CRUISING

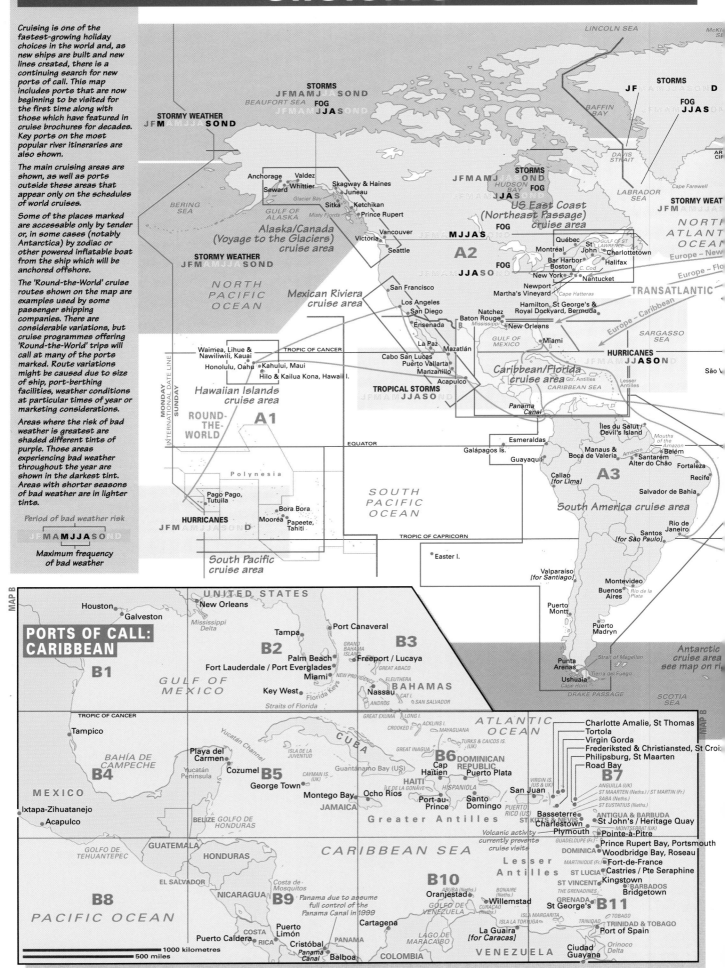

Cruising is one of the fastest-growing holiday choices in the world and, as new ships are built and new lines created, there is a continuing search for new ports of call. This map includes ports that are now beginning to be visited for the first time along with those which have featured in cruise brochures for decades. Key ports on the most popular river itineraries are also shown.

The main cruising areas are shown, as well as ports outside these areas that appear only on the schedules of world cruises.

Some of the places marked are accessable only by tender or, in some cases (notably Antarctica) by zodiac or other powered inflatable boat from the ship which will be anchored offshore.

The 'Round-the-World' cruise routes shown on the map are examples used by some passenger shipping companies. There are considerable variations, but cruise programmes offering 'Round-the-World' trips will call at many of the ports marked. Route variations might be caused due to size of ship, port-berthing facilities, weather conditions at particular times of year or marketing considerations.

Areas where the risk of bad weather is greatest are shaded different tints of purple. Those areas experiencing bad weather throughout the year are shown in the darkest tint. Areas with shorter seasons of bad weather are in lighter tints.

Period of bad weather risk

JFMA**MJJAS**OND

Maximum frequency of bad weather

PORTS OF CALL: CARIBBEAN

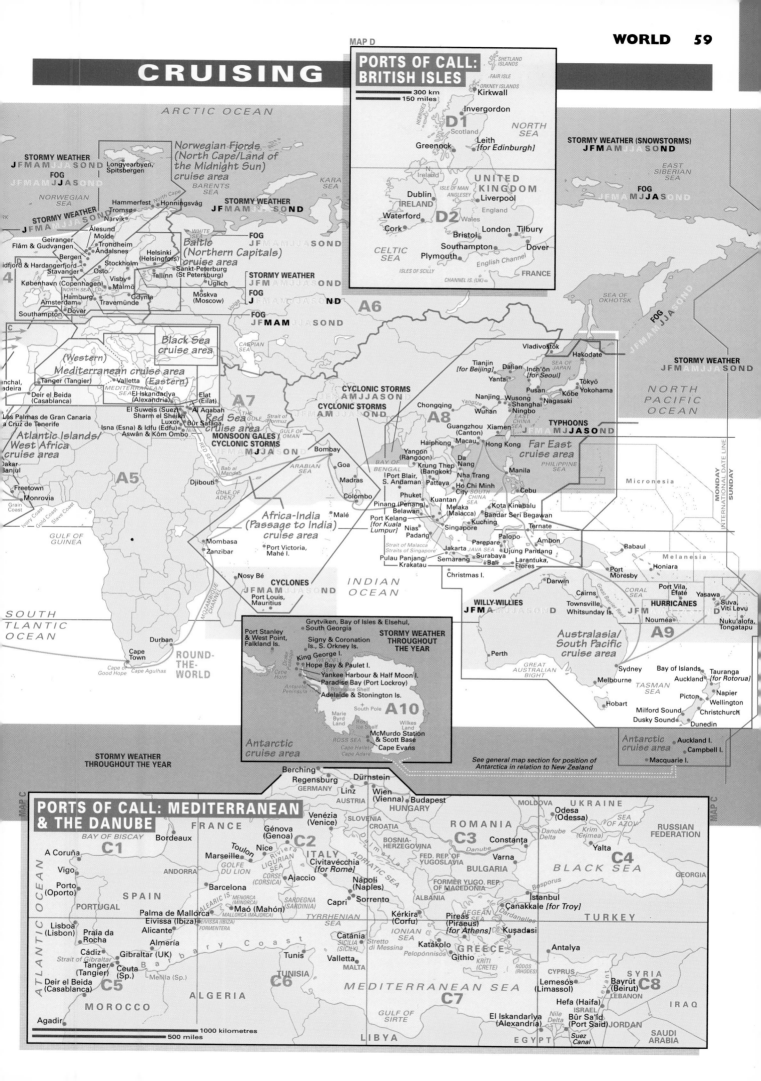

UNESCO NATURAL HERITAGE SITES

All properties which belong to the UNESCO World Heritage List are considered to be of world importance either because of their natural features or their significant man-made contribution to world culture. Sites for consideration of heritage status are submitted by the appropriate government ministry. UNESCO then considers each proposal under strict criteria and designates sites where appropriate.

Some countries are not signatories to the convention, and so the UNESCO list is not fully comprehensive worldwide.

There are two main categories of property: natural and cultural.

NATURAL SITES.
(i) Natural features: physical and biological formations of scientific importance;
(ii) Geological and physiographical formations: delineated areas which constitute the habitat of threatened species of animals or plants;
(iii) Natural sites: areas of universal value in terms of natural beauty and conservation.

Properties named in red are included on the list of World Heritage in Danger.

For further information, contact:

The World Heritage Centre, UNESCO, 7 place de Fontenoy, 75352 Paris 07, France.

Tel: +33 1 45 68 10 00.

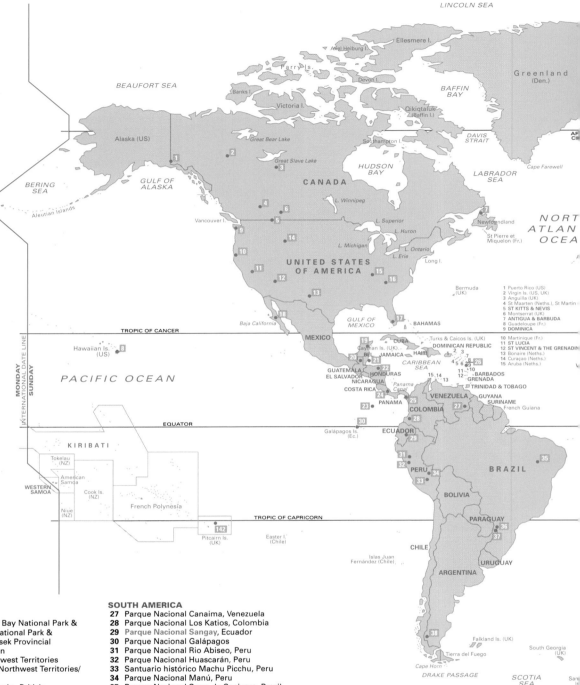

1 Puerto Rico (US)
2 Virgin Is. (US, UK)
3 Anguilla (UK)
4 St Maarten (Neths.), St Martin (Fr.)
5 ST KITTS & NEVIS
6 Montserrat (UK)
7 ANTIGUA & BARBUDA
8 Guadeloupe (Fr.)
9 DOMINICA
10 Martinique (Fr.)
11 ST LUCIA
12 ST VINCENT & THE GRENADINES
13 Bonaire (Neths.)
14 Curaçao (Neths.)
15 Aruba (Neths.)

CANADA & UNITED STATES

1 Kluane National Park, Glacier Bay National Park & Preserve, Wrangell-St Elias National Park & Preserve and Tatshenshini-Alsek Provincial Wilderness Park, Alaska/Yukon
2 Nahanni National Park, Northwest Territories
3 Wood Buffalo National Park, Northwest Territories/Alberta
4 Canadian Rocky Mountains Parks, British Columbia/Alberta
5 Waterton-Glacier International Peace Park, Alberta/Montana
6 Dinosaur Provincial Park, Alberta
7 Gros Morne National Park, Newfoundland
8 Hawaii Volcanoes National Park, Hawaii
9 Olympic National Park, Washington
10 Redwood National Park, California
11 Yosemite National Park, California
12 Grand Canyon National Park, Arizona
13 Carlsbad Caverns National Park, New Mexico
14 Yellowstone National Park, Wyoming
15 Mammoth Cave National Park, Kentucky
16 Great Smoky Mountains National Park, Tennessee/North Carolina
17 Everglades National Park, Florida

MEXICO, CENTRAL AMERICA & CARIBBEAN

18 El Vizcaíno whale sanctuary, Mexico
19 Reserva de la Biósfera Sian Ka'an, Mexico
20 Parque Nacional Tikal, Guatemala
21 Barrier Reef Reserve System, Belize
22 Reserva de la Biósfera Río Platano, Honduras
23 Parque Nacional Isla del Coco, Costa Rica
24 Cordillera de Talamanca and Parque Internacional La Amistad, Costa Rica/Panama
25 Parque Nacional del Darién, Panama
26 Morne Trois Pitons National Park, Dominica

SOUTH AMERICA

27 Parque Nacional Canaima, Venezuela
28 Parque Nacional Los Katios, Colombia
29 Parque Nacional Sangay, Ecuador
30 Parque Nacional Galápagos
31 Parque Nacional Rio Abiseo, Peru
32 Parque Nacional Huascarán, Peru
33 Santuario histórico Machu Picchu, Peru
34 Parque Nacional Manú, Peru
35 Parque Nacional Serra da Capivara, Brazil
36 Parque Nacional do Iguaçu, Brazil
37 Parque Nacional de Iguazu, Argentina
38 Parque Nacional Los Glaciares, Argentina

EUROPE (including Atlantic islands and Turkey)

39 Lapponian area, Sweden
40 St Kilda, Scotland
41 Giant's Causeway and its coast, Northern Ireland
42 Messel Pit fossil site, Germany
43 Mont-St Michel and its bay, France
44 Paris: banks of the Seine, France
45 Golfe de Girolata, Golfe de Porto, les Calanche and Réserve Naturelle Scandola, Corsica, France
46 Monte Perdido, France/Spain
47 Parque Nacional Coto de Doñana, Spain
48 Parque Nacional de Garajonay, Gomera, Canary Is.
49 Bialowieza National Park & Beloveshskaya Pushcha, Poland/Belarus
50 Aggtelek Caves and the Slovak karst, Hungary/Slovak Republic
51 Skocjan Caves, Slovenia
52 Plitvice Lakes National Park, Croatia
53 Durmitor National Park, Federal Republic of Yugoslavia
54 Kotor and its gulf, Federal Republic of Yugoslavia
55 Ohrid Lake and its region, Former Yugoslav Republic of Macedonia
56 Danube Delta, Romania

57 Srebarna Nature Reserve, Bulgaria
58 Pirin National Park, Bulgaria
59 Metéora, Greece
60 Olimbía (Olympia): archaeological site, Greece
61 Áthos, Greece
62 Hierapolis-Pamukkale, Turkey
63 Göreme National Park and Cappadocia rock sites, Turkey

FORMER SOVIET UNION

64 Komi virgin forests, Russian Federation
65 Lake Baikal, Russian Federation
66 Kamchatka volcanoes, Russian Federation

AFRICA

67 Ichkeul National Park, Tunisia
68 Tassili n'Ajjer, Algeria
69 Bandiagara Cliffs: Land of the Dogon, Mali
70 Banc d'Arguin National Park, Mauritania
71 Parc National des Oiseaux du Djoudj (Djoudj National Bird Sanctuary), Senegal
72 Parc National du Niokolo Koba, Senegal
73 Réserve du Monts Nimba, Guinea/Côte d'Ivoire
74 Parc National de la Comoé, Côte d'Ivoire
75 Parc National de Taï, Côte d'Ivoire
76 Parc National du "W", Niger
77 Réserve du Air and Réserve du Ténéré, Niger

UNESCO NATURAL HERITAGE SITES

A SLOVENIA
B CROATIA
C BOSNIA-HERZEGOVINA
D FEDERAL REPUBLIC OF YUGOSLAVIA
  (Serbia & Montenegro)
E FORMER YUGOSLAV REPUBLIC
  OF MACEDONIA

78 Simien National Park, Ethiopia
79 Parc National de Manovo-Gounda St Floris, Central African Republic
80 Réserve du Dja, Cameroon
81 Parc National de la Salonga, Dem. Rep. of Congo
82 Parc National de la Garamba, Dem. Rep. of Congo
83 Réserve de Okapi, Dem. Rep. of Congo
84 Parc National des Virunga, Dem. Rep. of Congo
85 Parc National du Kahuzi-Biega, Dem. Rep. of Congo
86 Ruwenzori Mountains National Park, Uganda
87 Bwindi Impenetrable National Park, Uganda
88 Sibiloi and Central Island National Parks, Kenya
89 Mount Kenya National Park and forest, Kenya
90 Serengeti National Park, Tanzania
91 Ngorongoro Conservation Area, Tanzania
92 Kilimanjaro National Park, Tanzania
93 Selous Game Reserve, Tanzania
94 Lake Malawi National Park, Malawi
95 Victoria Falls (Mosi-oa-Tunya), Zambia/Zimbabwe
96 Mana Pools National Park and Sapi & Chewore safari areas, Zimbabwe
97 Ilha da Moçambique, Mozambique
98 Réserve du Tsingy Bemaraha, Madagascar
99 Aldabra Atoll, Seychelles
100 Vallée de Mai Nature Reserve, Seychelles
101 Gough Island Wildlife Reserve

MIDDLE EAST
102 Arabian Oryx Sanctuary, Oman

SOUTH, EAST & SE ASIA
103 Sagarmatha National Park, Nepal
104 Royal Chitwan National Park, Nepal
105 Nanda Devi National Park, India
106 Keoladeo National Park, India
107 Manas Wildlife Sanctuary, India
108 Kaziranga National Park, India
109 Sundarbans National Park, India
110 Sundarbans, Bangladesh
111 Dambulla Golden Rock Temple, Sri Lanka
112 Sinharaja Forest Reserve, Sri Lanka
113 Tai Shan, Shandong, China
114 Huang Shan, Anhui, China
115 Jiuzhaigou Valley Scenic and Historic Interest Area, Sichuan, China
116 Huanglong Scenic and Historic Interest Area, Sichuan, China
117 Emei Shan and Leshan Giant Buddha, Sichuan, China
118 Wulingyuan Scenic and Historic Interest Area, Hunan, China
119 Yakushima, Japan
120 Shirakami-Sanchi, Japan
121 Ha Long Bay, Vietnam

122 Sukhothai and its region: historic towns, Thailand
123 Thung Yai-Huai Kha Khaeng Wildlife Sanctuaries, Thailand
124 Tubbataha Reef Marine Park, Philippines
125 Ujung Kulon National Park and Krakatau Nature Reserve, Indonesia
126 Komodo National Park, Indonesia

AUSTRALASIA & PACIFIC
127 Shark Bay, Australia
128 Kakadu National Park, Australia
129 Queensland wet tropics, Australia
130 Central eastern rainforest reserves, Australia
131 Great Barrier Reef, Australia
132 Uluru-Kata Tjuta National Park, Australia
133 Naracoorte & Riversleigh: fossil mammal sites, Australia
134 Willandra Lakes region, Australia
135 Fraser Island, Australia
136 Tasmanian wilderness, Australia
137 Lord Howe island group, Australia
138 Heard and McDonald Islands
139 Macquarie Island
140 Tongariro National Park, New Zealand
141 Te Wahipounamu-Southwest New Zealand
142 Fiordland National Park, New Zealand
143 Henderson Island

UNESCO CULTURAL HERITAGE SITES

All properties which belong to the UNESCO World Heritage List are considered to be of world importance either because of their natural features or their significant man-made contribution to world culture. Sites for consideration of heritage status are submitted by the appropriate government ministry. UNESCO then considers each proposal under strict criteria and designates sites where appropriate.

Some countries are not signatories to the convention, and so the UNESCO list is not fully comprehensive worldwide.

There are two main categories of property: natural and cultural.

CULTURAL SITES.
(i) Monuments: including sculptures, memorial stones, obelisks, cave paintings and inscriptions;
(ii) Groups of buildings: these can be separated or connected but are usually set in a unique landscape;
(iii) Sites of anthropological or archaeological importance.

Properties named in red are included on the list of World Heritage in Danger.

The Organization of World Heritage Cities (OWHC) was established in 1993, based on the idea that cultural and historic sites within cities experience particular pressures and require a more dynamic style of management than other sites. Most of these cities contain one or more UNESCO Cultural Heritage Sites, but this is not an essential requirement for membership of the OWHC.

World Heritage Cities are named on the map.

For further information, contact:

The World Heritage Centre,
UNESCO,
7 place de Fontenoy,
75352 Paris 07,
France.

Tel: +33 1 45 68 10 00.

CANADA & UNITED STATES
1 Anthony Island, British Columbia
2 Head-Smashed-In Buffalo Jump, Alberta
3 Québec: historic area
4 Lunenburg: old city, Nova Scotia
5 L'Anse aux Meadows Historic Park, Newfoundland
6 Mesa Verde National Park, Colorado
7 Chaco Culture National Historical Park, New Mexico
8 Pueblo de Taos, New Mexico
9 Cahokia Mounds State Historic Site, Illinois
10 Charlottesville: Monticello and University of Virginia, Virginia
11 Philadelphia: Independence Hall, Pennsylvania
12 Statue of Liberty, New Jersey

MEXICO, CENTRAL AMERICA & CARIBBEAN
13 Sierra de la San Francisco: rock paintings, Mexico
14 Zacatecas: historic centre, Mexico
15 Guanajuato: historic town and adjacent mines, Mexico
16 Querétaro: historic monuments, Mexico
17 Teotihuacan: pre-Hispanic city, Mexico
18 El Tajín: pre-Hispanic city, Mexico
19 Guadalajara: Hospicio Cabañas, Mexico
20 Morelia: historic centre, Mexico
21 Mexico City: historic centre and Xochimilco, Mexico

22 Popocatépetl: monasteries, Mexico
23 Puebla: historic centre, Mexico
24 Oaxaca: historic centre and Monte Albán: archaeological site, Mexico
25 Palenque: pre-Hispanic city and National Park, Mexico
26 Uxmal: pre-Hispanic city, Mexico
27 Chichén Itzá: pre-Hispanic city, Mexico
28 Antigua, Guatemala
29 Quiriguá: archaeological park and ruins, Guatemala
30 Copán: Maya site, Honduras
31 Joya de Cerén: archaeological site, El Salvador
32 Portobelo and San Lorenzo: fortifications, Panama
33 Panama City: historic district and the Salón Bolívar, Panama
34 La Habana (Havana): old town and its fortifications, Cuba
35 Trinidad and Valley de los Ingenios, Cuba
36 Santiago de Cuba: San Pedro de la Roca Castle, Cuba
37 Citadel, Sans-Souci and Ramiers Historic Park, Haiti
38 Santo Domingo: colonial city, Dominican Republic
39 La Fortaleza and San Juan: historic sites, Puerto Rico
40 Willemstad: historic area, inner city and harbour, Curaçao

SOUTH AMERICA
41 Coro: town and its port, Venezuela
42 Cartagena: port, fortress and monuments, Colombia
43 Mompós: historic centre, Colombia
44 Parque Arqueológico Nacional Tierradentro, Colombia
45 Parque Arqueológico San Agustín, Colombia
46 Quito: old city, Ecuador
47 Chan Chan: archaeological area, Peru

48 Chavin: archaeological site, Peru
49 Lima: historic centre, Peru
50 Santuario histórico Machu Picchu, Peru
51 Cuzco: old city, Peru
52 Nazca: geoglyphs and Pampas de Juma, Peru
53 Potosí, Bolivia
54 Sucre: historic city, Bolivia
55 Chiquitos Jesuit missions, Bolivia
56 Jesús and Trinidad: Jesuit missions, Paraguay
57 Brasília, Brazil
58 Parque Nacional Serra da Capivara, Brazil
59 São Luís: historic centre, Brazil
60 Olinda: historic centre, Brazil
61 Salvador de Bahia: historic centre, Brazil
62 Ouro Prêto: historic town, Brazil
63 Congonhas: Sanctuary of Bom Jesus, Brazil
64 São Miguel: Jesuit mission ruins, Brazil; Loreto, San Ignacio Miní, Santa Ana & Santa Maria Mayor: Guaraní Jesuit missions, Argentina
65 Colonia del Sacramento: historic quarter, Uruguay
66 Parque Nacional Rapa Nui, Easter Island

EUROPE* (including Atlantic islands)
67 Angra do Heroísmo: central area, Azores
68 Urnes: stave church, Norway
69 Røros: mining town, Norway
70 Alta: rock drawings, Norway
71 Lapponian area, Sweden
72 Luleå: Gammelstad church town, Sweden
73 Rauma: old town, Finland
74 Petäjävesi: old church, Finland
75 Verla: groundwood and board mill, Finland

FORMER SOVIET UNION*
76 Solovetskiye Ostrova: cultural and historic ensemble, Russian Federation
77 Khizi Pogost, Russian Federation

78 Mtskheta: historic church, Georgia
79 Haghpat: monastery, Armenia
80 Itchan Kala, Uzbekistan
81 Bukhara: historic centre, Uzbekistan

AFRICA*
82 Thebes: ancient city and necropolis, Egypt
83 Abu Simbel to Philae: Nubian monuments, Egypt
84 Aksum: archaeological site, Ethiopia
85 Fasil Ghebbi & Gonder monuments, Ethiopia
86 Lalibela: rock-hewn churches, Ethiopia
87 Awash Lower Valley, Ethiopia
88 Tiya: carved steles, Ethiopia
89 Omo Lower Valley, Ethiopia
90 Tadrart Acacus: rock-art sites, Libya
91 Tassili n'Ajjer, Algeria
92 Chinguetti, Ouadane, Oualata and Tichitt: trading and religious centres, Mauritania
93 Timbuktu, Mali
94 Djenne: old towns, Mali
95 Île de Gorée, Senegal
96 Ashante traditional buildings, Ghana
97 Accra and Volta areas: forts and castles, Ghana
98 Abomey: royal palaces, Benin

Map labels: LINCOLN SEA, Ellesmere I., Axel Heiberg I., Greenland (Den.), Parry Is., Devon I., BAFFIN BAY, Banks I., Victoria I., Qikiqtaluk (Baffin I.), NORTH ATLANTIC OCEAN, BEAUFORT SEA, Great Bear Lake, Southampton I., DAVIS STRAIT, Alaska (US), Great Slave Lake, HUDSON BAY, Newfoundland, Cape Farewell, Aleutian Islands, L. Winnipeg, CANADA, Québec, Lunenburg, St Pierre et Miquelon (Fr.), LABRADOR SEA, Angra Heroísm, BERING SEA, GULF OF ALASKA, Vancouver I., L. Superior, L. Huron, L. Michigan, UNITED STATES OF AMERICA, L. Ontario, L. Erie, Long I., Bermuda (UK), TROPIC OF CANCER, GULF OF MEXICO, Baja California, MEXICO, La Habana (Havana), BAHAMAS, HAITI, CUBA, Turks & Caicos Is. (UK), Zacatecas, Cayman Is. (UK), JAMAICA, Santo Domingo, San Juan, MONDAY INTERNATIONAL DATE LINE SUNDAY, Hawaiian Is. (US), PACIFIC OCEAN, EQUATOR, KIRIBATI, Tokelau (NZ), American Samoa, WESTERN SAMOA, Cook Is. (NZ), Niue (NZ), French Polynesia, GUATEMALA, HONDURAS, EL SALVADOR, NICARAGUA, COSTA RICA, PANAMA, La Vela, Coro, Cartagena, Mompós, COLOMBIA, VENEZUELA, GUYANA, SURINAME, French Guiana, TRINIDAD & TOBAGO, GRENADA, BARBADOS, Quito, ECUADOR, Galápagos Is. (Ec.), PERU, Lima, Cuzco, BRAZIL, Olin, Salvado de Bahia, BOLIVIA, Sucre, Potosí, Brasília, Ouro Prêto, PARAGUAY, TROPIC OF CAPRICORN, Pitcairn Is. (UK), Easter I. (Chile), Islas Juan Fernández (Chile), CHILE, ARGENTINA, URUGUAY, Colonia del Sacramento, Falkland Is. (UK), South Georgia (UK), Tierra del Fuego, Cape Horn, DRAKE PASSAGE, SCOTIA SEA

1 DOMINICAN REPUBLIC
2 Puerto Rico (US)
3 Virgin Is. (US, UK)
4 Anguilla (UK)
5 St Maarten (Neths.), St Martin (Fr.)
6 ST KITTS & NEVIS
7 Montserrat (UK)
8 ANTIGUA & BARBUDA
9 Guadeloupe (Fr.)
10 DOMINICA
11 Martinique (Fr.)
12 ST LUCIA
13 ST VINCENT & THE GRENADINES
14 Bonaire (Neths.)
15 Curaçao (Neths.)
16 Aruba (Neths.)

MAP A: Guanajuato, Querétaro, Morelia, MEXICO, Mexico City, Puebla, Oaxaca, BAHÍA DE CAMPECHE, Yucatán Peninsula, PACIFIC OCEAN, GUATEMALA, Antigua, EL SALVADOR, HONDURAS, BELIZE, NICARAG., 1000 km, 500 miles

UNESCO CULTURAL HERITAGE SITES

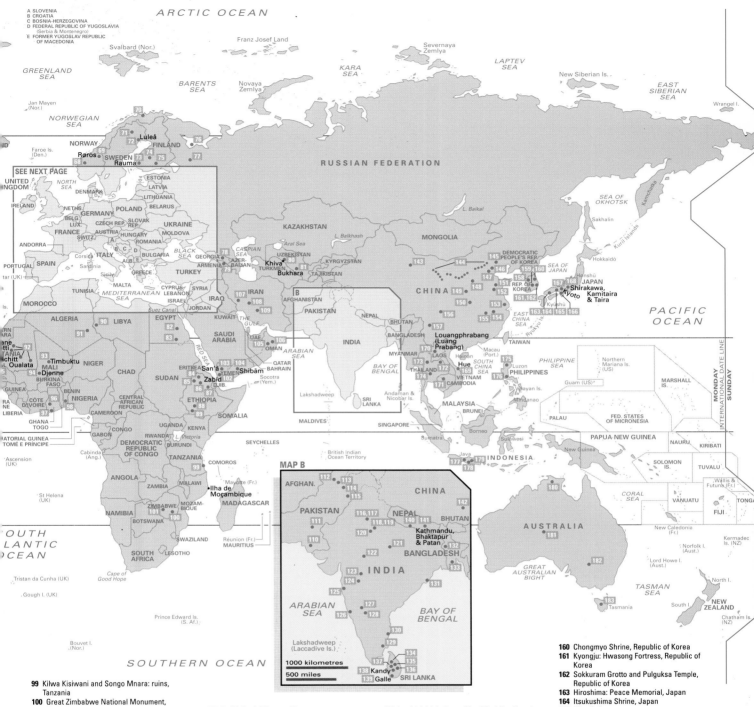

A SLOVENIA
B CROATIA
C BOSNIA-HERZEGOVINA
D FEDERAL REPUBLIC OF YUGOSLAVIA
   (Serbia & Montenegro)
E FORMER YUGOSLAV REPUBLIC
   OF MACEDONIA

MAP B

1000 kilometres
500 miles

99 Kilwa Kisiwani and Songo Mnara: ruins,
   Tanzania
100 Great Zimbabwe National Monument,
   Zimbabwe
101 Khami Ruins National Monument,
   Zimbabwe

MIDDLE EAST*
102 Zabid: historic town, Yemen
103 San'a: old city, Yemen
104 Shibam: old walled city, Yemen
105 Bahla: fort, Oman
106 Bat, Al-Khutm and Al-Ayn: archaeolgical
   sites, Oman
107 Tchogha Zanbil: ziggurat and complex,
   Iran
108 Esfahan (Isfahan): Meidam Emam, Iran
109 Persepolis: ancient city, Iran

SOUTH, EAST & SE ASIA
110 Thatta: historical monuments, Pakistan
111 Mohenjodaro: archaeological site,
   Pakistan
112 Takht-i-Bakhi: Buddhist ruins;
   Sahr-i-Bahlol: remains of city, Pakistan
113 Taxila: archaeological site, Pakistan
114 Rohtas: fort, Pakistan
115 Lahore: fort and Shalimar Gardens,
   Pakistan
116 Delhi: Humayun's Tomb, India

117 Delhi: Qutb Minar and its monuments,
   India
118 Agra Fort, India
119 Taj Mahal, Agra, India
120 Fatehpur Sikri: Mongol city, India
121 Khajuraho: group of monuments, India
122 Sanchi: Buddhist monastery, India
123 Ajanta Caves, India
124 Ellora Caves, India
125 Elephanta Caves, India
126 Goa: churches and convents, India
127 Pattadakal: group of monuments, India
128 Hampi: group of monuments, India
129 Thanjavur: Brihadisvara Temple, India
130 Mahabalipuram: group of monuments,
   India
131 Konarak: Sun Temple, India
132 Paharpur: ruins of the Buddhist Vihara,
   Bangladesh
133 Bagerhat: historic city, Bangladesh
134 Anuradhapura: sacred city, Sri Lanka
135 Sigiriya: ancient city, Sri Lanka
136 Polonnaruwa: ancient city, Sri Lanka
137 Dambulla Golden Rock Temple, Sri Lanka
138 Kandy: sacred city, Sri Lanka
139 Galle: old town and its fortifications, Sri
   Lanka

140 Lumbini: birthplace of Lord Buddha, Nepal
141 Kathmandu Valley, Nepal
142 Lhasa: Potala Palace, Tibet, China
143 Mogao Caves, Gansu, China
144 Great Wall, China
145 Chengde: mountain resort and outlying
   temples, Hebei, China
146 Beijing (Peking): Imperial Palace of the
   Ming and Qing Dynasties, China
147 Zhoukoudian: Peking Man site, China
148 Pingyao: ancient city, Shanxi, China
149 Xi'an area: Mausoleum of the first Qin
   Emperor, Shaanxi, China
150 Wudangshan: ancient building complex,
   Hubei, China
151 Tai Shan, Shandong, China
152 Qufu: temple & cemetery of Confucius and
   Kong family mansion, Shandong, China
153 Suzhou: classical gardens, Jiangsu, China
154 Huang Shan, Anhui, China
155 Lu Shan, Jiangxi, China
156 Emei Shan and Leshan Giant Buddha,
   Sichuan, China
157 Lijiang: old town, Yunnan, China
158 Seoul: Ch'angdokkung Palace Complex,
   Republic of Korea
159 Haeinsa Temple, Republic of Korea

160 Chongmyo Shrine, Republic of Korea
161 Kyongju: Hwasong Fortress, Republic of
   Korea
162 Sokkuram Grotto and Pulguksa Temple,
   Republic of Korea
163 Hiroshima: Peace Memorial, Japan
164 Itsukushima Shrine, Japan
165 Himeji, Japan
166 Horyuji: Buddhist monuments, Japan
167 Kyoto: ancient city monuments, Japan
168 Shirakawa-Go and Gokayama: historic
   villages, Japan
169 Hue: monuments complex, Vietnam
170 Louangphrabang (Luang Prabang), Laos
171 Angkor, Cambodia
172 Ban Chiang: archaeological site, Thailand
173 Sukhothai and its region: historic towns,
   Thailand
174 Ayutthaya and its region: historic towns,
   Thailand
175 Cordillera Central: rice terraces, the
   Philippines
176 Manila: Baroque churches, the Philippines
177 Borobudur: temple compound, Indonesia
178 Prambanan: temple compound, Indonesia
179 Sangiran: early man site, Indonesia

AUSTRALASIA & PACIFIC
180 Kakadu National Park, Australia
181 Uluru-Kata Tjuta National Park, Australia
182 Willandra Lakes region, Australia
183 Tasmanian wilderness, Australia

* See next page for other sites in these areas

UNESCO

UNESCO CULTURAL HERITAGE SITES

Cities named on the map are members of the Organization of World Heritage Cities (OWHC). See previous page for explanation.
THE SEVEN WONDERS OF THE ANCIENT WORLD
A Statue of Zeus, Olympia 9-metre statue of the Greek god covered in gold and ivory
B Temple of Artemis, Ephesus Marble temple in honour of goddess of hunting and the moon
C Mausoleum, Halikarnassos Tomb of Mausolus built by his widow
D Colossus of Rhodes 32-metre high bronze statue of the sun god Helios
E Pharos of Alexandria World's first known lighthouse, 122 metres high
F Egyptian Pyramids Oldest of the ancient wonders and the only one surviving today
G Hanging Gardens of Babylon Series of terraces of trees and flowers along the banks of the Euphrates
NORWAY
SWEDEN
FIN.
ESTONIA
LATVIA
LITHUANIA
RUSSIAN FEDERATION
BELARUS
UKRAINE
MOLDOVA
ROMANIA
BULGARIA
TURKEY
GEORGIA
UNITED KINGDOM
IRELAND
DENMARK
NETHERLANDS
BELGIUM
GERMANY
POLAND
CZECH REP.
SLOVAK REP.
AUSTRIA
HUNGARY
SWITZ.
LIECH.
FRANCE
SLOVENIA
CROATIA
BOSNIA-HERZEGOVINA
FED. REP. OF YUGO.
FORMER YUGO. REP. OF MACEDONIA
ALBANIA
GREECE
ITALY
MONACO
ANDORRA
SPAIN
PORTUGAL
MOROCCO
ALGERIA
TUNISIA
LIBYA
EGYPT
CYPRUS
SYRIA
LEBANON
ISRAEL
JORDAN
IRAQ
SAUDI ARABIA
NORTH SEA
CELTIC SEA
BAY OF BISCAY
ATLANTIC OCEAN
BALTIC SEA
BLACK SEA
MEDITERRANEAN SEA
TYRRHENIAN SEA
IONIAN SEA
AEGEAN SEA
ADRIATIC SEA
GULF OF FINLAND
GULF OF SIRTE
Bergen
Edinburgh
Bath
Lübeck
Potsdam
Goslar
Quedlinburg
Bamberg
Luxembourg-Ville
Paris
Nancy
Strasbourg
Mont-St Michel
Bern (Berne)
Capriate San Gervasio
Vicenza
Ferrara
Venézia (Venice)
Firenze (Florence)
San Gimignano
Siena
Pienza
Roma (Rome) & Vatican City
Nápoli (Naples)
Matera
Split
Dubrovnik
Kotor
Ohrid
Salzburg
Český Krumlov
Telč
Kutná Hora
Praha (Prague)
Kraków (Cracow)
Warszawa (Warsaw)
Zamość
Banská Štiavnica
Budapest
Biertan
Nesebûr (Nessebar)
Istanbul
Safranbolu
Visby
Vilnius
St Petersburg
Novgorod
Moskva (Moscow)
Santiago de Compostela
Salamanca
Segovia
Porto (Oporto)
Ávila
Toledo
Cuenca
Cáceres
Mérida
Sintra
Évora
Córdoba
Granada
Alger (Algiers)
Tunis
Sousse
Qairouan (Kairouan)
Valletta
Fès
Meknès
Marrakech
Ghardaya
Ghadāmis
Ródos (Rhodes)
Halab (Aleppo)
Bosra
Dimashq (Damascus)
Jerusalem
El Qâhira (Cairo)
1000 kilometres
500 miles

Properties named in red are included on the list of World Heritage in Danger.

EUROPE (including Turkey)

1 Bergen: Bryggen area, Norway
2 Tanum: rock carvings, Sweden
3 Engelsberg: ironworks, Sweden
4 Birka and Hovgården: archaeological sites, Sweden
5 Drottningholm Palace, Sweden
6 Stockholm: Skogskyrkogarden, Sweden
7 Visby: Hanseatic town and former Viking site, Sweden
8 Helsinki (Helsingfors): Suomenlinna Fortress, Finland
9 Jelling: mounds, runic stones and church, Denmark
10 Roskilde: cathedral, Denmark
11 Skellig Michael: monastic complex, Ireland
12 Brú Na Bóinne: archaeological ensemble at the bend of the Boyne, Ireland
13 Edinburgh: old and new towns, Scotland
14 Castles and town walls of King Edward, northwest Wales
15 Hadrian's Wall, England
16 Durham: castle and cathedral, England
17 Studley Royal Park and Fountains Abbey ruins, England
18 Ironbridge Gorge, England
19 Bath, England
20 Stonehenge, Avebury and associated megalithic sites, England
21 Blenheim Palace, England
22 London: Tower of London, England
23 London: Westminster Palace, Abbey of Westminster and St Margaret's Church, England
24 London: Maritime Greenwich, England
25 Canterbury: cathedral, St Augustine's Abbey and St Martin's Church, England
26 Schokland: prehistoric settlements, The Netherlands
27 Amsterdam: defence line, The Netherlands
28 Kinderdijk-Elshout: mill network, The Netherlands
29 Luxembourg-Ville: old quarters and fortifications
30 Lübeck: Hanseatic city, Germany
31 Berlin and Potsdam: palaces and parks, Germany
32 Eisleben and Wittenberg: Luther memorials, Germany
33 Dessau and Weimar: Bauhaus buildings, Germany
34 Quedlinburg: Collegiate church, castle and old town, Germany
35 Goslar: historic town and Rammelsberg mines, Germany
36 Hildesheim: St Mary's Cathedral and St Michael's Church, Germany
37 Aachen (Aix-la-Chapelle): cathedral, Germany
38 Köln (Cologne): cathedral, Germany
39 Brühl: Augustusburg and Falkenlust Castles, Germany
40 Trier: Roman monuments, cathedral and Liebfrauen Church, Germany
41 Völklingen: ironworks, Germany
42 Maulbronn: Cistercian monastery complex, Germany
43 Speyer: cathedral, Germany
44 Lorsch: abbey and Altenmünster, Germany
45 Würzburg: Residence with the Court Gardens and Residence Square, Germany
46 Bamberg, Germany
47 Wies: pilgrimage church, Germany
48 Mont-St Michel and its bay, France
49 Amiens: cathedral, France
50 Reims: Notre-Dame Cathedral, former Abbey of St Remi and Tau Palace, France
51 Nancy: Place Stanislas, Place de la Carrière and Place d'Alliance, France
52 Strasbourg: Grand Île, France
53 Arc-et-Senans: royal saltworks, France
54 Fontenay: Cistercian abbey, France
55 Vézelay: basilica and hill, France
56 Bourges: cathedral, France
57 Fontainebleau: palace and park, France
58 Paris: banks of the Seine, France
59 Versailles: palace and park, France
60 Chartres: cathedral, France
61 Chambord: château and estate, France
62 St Savin-sur-Gartempe: church, France
63 Vézère Valley: Lascaux and other decorated grottoes, France
64 Canal du Midi, France
65 Remoulins: Pont du Gard Roman aqueduct, France
66 Orange: Roman theatre and its surroundings and the triumphal arch, France
67 Avignon: historic centre, France
68 Arles: Roman and Romanesque monuments, France
69 Carcassonne: historic fortified city, France
70 Barcelona: Parque & Palacio Güell and Casa Milá, Spain
71 Barcelona: Palau de la Música Catalaña and the Hospital de Sant Pau, Spain
72 Poblet: monastery, Spain
73 Valencia: La Lonja de la Sada, Spain
74 Teruel: Mujedar architecture, Spain
75 Cuenca: historic walled town, Spain
76 San Millán and Suso: monasteries, Spain
77 Burgos: cathedral, Spain
78 Las Médulas, Spain
79 Camino de Santiago: The Way of St James pilgrimage route, Spain
80 Altamira Cave, Spain
81 Asturias: churches of the Asturias Kingdom, Spain
82 Santiago de Compostela: old town, Spain
83 Salamanca: old city, Spain
84 Ávila: old town with extra-muros churches, Spain
85 Segovia: old town and aqueduct, Spain
86 El Escorial: monastery, Spain
87 Toledo: historic city, Spain
88 Guadalupe: Royal Monastery of Santa Maria, Spain
89 Cáceres: old town, Spain
90 Mérida: archaeological ensemble, Spain
91 Sevilla (Seville): cathedral, Alcazar and Archivo de Indias, Spain
92 Córdoba: mosque and historic centre, Spain
93 Granada: Alhambra, Generalife & Albaicín quarter, Spain
94 Porto (Oporto): historic centre, Portugal
95 Tomar: Convent of Christ, Portugal
96 Batalha: monastery, Portugal
97 Alcobaça: monastery, Portugal
98 Sintra: historic city, Portugal
99 Lisboa (Lisbon): Monastery of the Hieronymites and Tower of Belém, Portugal
100 Évora: historic centre, Portugal
101 Bern (Berne): old city, Switzerland
102 St Gallen: convent, Switzerland
103 Müstaír: Benedictine Convent of St John, Switzerland
104 Salzburg: historic centre, Austria
105 Hallstadt-Dachstein-Salzkammergut: cultural landscape, Austria
106 Wien (Vienna): Schönbrunn Palace and Gardens, Austria
107 Torino (Turin): Residences of the Royal House of Savoy, Italy
108 Milano (Milan): Church and Dominican Convent of Santa Maria delle Grazie with "The Last Supper" by Leonardo da Vinci, Italy
109 Crespi d'Adda, Italy
110 Val Camónica: rock drawings, Italy
111 Vicenza: city and the Palladian Villas of the Veneto, Italy
112 Pádova (Padua): botanical garden, Italy
113 Venézia (Venice) and its lagoon, Italy
114 Ferrara, Renaissance city, Italy
115 Ravenna: early Christian monuments and mosaics, Italy
116 Modena: cathedral, Torre Civica and Piazza Grande, Italy
117 Firenze (Florence): historic centre, Italy
118 Portovénere, Cinque Terre, Ísola Palmária, Ísola del Tino and Ísola del Tinetto, Italy
119 Pisa: Piazza del Duomo, Italy
120 San Gimignano: historic centre, Italy
121 Siena: historic centre, Italy
122 Pienza: historic centre, Italy
123 Vatican City
124 Roma (Rome): historic centre, incl. extraterritorial properties of the Holy See & San Paolo fuori le Mura, Italy
125 Caserta: Royal Palace with park, Vanvitelli Aqueduct and San Leucio complex, Italy
126 Nápoli (Naples): historic centre, Italy
127 Herculaneum, Pompei and Torre Annunziata: archaeological areas, Italy
128 Costiera Amalfitana, Italy
129 Matera: I Sassi di Matera, Italy
130 Alberobello: Trulli houses, Italy
131 Castel del Monte: medieval castle, Italy
132 Villa Romana del Casale, Italy
133 Agrigento: archaeological area, Sicily, Italy
134 Su Nuraxi di Barúmini, Sardinia, Italy
135 Malbork: Teutonic castle, Poland
136 Torun: medieval town, Poland
137 Warszawa (Warsaw): historic centre, Poland
138 Zamosc: old city, Poland
139 Wieliczka: salt mines, Poland
140 Kraków (Cracow): historic centre, Poland
141 Oswiecim (Auschwitz): concentration camp, Poland
142 Praha (Prague): historic centre, Czech Republic
143 Kutná Hora: historical centre, Church of Santa Barbara and Cathedral of Our Lady at Sedlec, Czech Republic
144 Zelená Hora: St John of Nepomuk, Czech Republic
145 Cesky Krumlov: historic centre, Czech Republic
146 Telc: historic centre, Czech Republic
147 Lednice-Valtice: cultural landscape, Czech Republic
148 Banská Stiavnica, Slovak Republic
149 Vlkolínec, Slovak Republic
150 Spisské Pohradie: Spissky Hrad and associated monuments, Slovak Republic
151 Hollokö: traditional village, Hungary
152 Budapest: including the banks of the Danube and Buda Castle area, Hungary
153 Pannonhalma: Millenary Benedictine Abbey and its natural environment, Hungary
154 Porec: Episcopal complex, Croatia
155 Trogir: historic city, Croatia
156 Split: historic centre with Diocletian Palace, Croatia
157 Dubrovnik: old city, Croatia
158 Kotor and its gulf, Fed. Rep. of Yugoslavia
159 Stari Ras and Sopocani Monastery, Fed. Rep. of Yugoslavia
160 Studenica: monastery, Fed. Rep. of Yugoslavia
161 Ohrid Lake and its region, F.Y.R. of Macedonia
162 Butrinti (Buthrotum): archaeological site, Albania
163 Horezu: monastery, Romania
164 Biertan: town and fortified church, Romania
165 Moldavia churches, Romania
166 Boyana: church, Bulgaria
167 Sveshtari: Thracian tomb, Bulgaria
168 Ivanovo: rock-hewn churches, Bulgaria
169 Madara: horseman stone relief, Bulgaria
170 Nesebur (Nessebar): ancient city, Bulgaria
171 Kazanluk: Thracian tomb, Bulgaria
172 Rila: monastery, Bulgaria
173 Áthos, Greece
174 Thessaloníki (Salonika): Palaeochristian and Byzantine monuments, Greece
175 Vergina: archaeological site, Greece
176 Metéora, Greece
177 Delfí (Delphi): archaeological site, Greece
178 Olimbía (Olympía): archaeological site, Greece
179 Bassae: Temple of Apollo Epicurius, Greece
180 Místrás, Greece
181 Epídavros (Epidaurus): archaeological site, Greece
182 Athína (Athens): Acropolis, Greece
183 Híos (Chios): Daphni, Hossios, Luckas and Néa Moni monasteries, Greece
184 Sámos: Pythagoreion and Heraion, Greece
185 Dílos, Greece
186 Ródos (Rhodes): medieval city, Greece
187 Xanthos-Letoon, Turkey
188 Hierapolis-Pamukkale, Turkey
189 Istanbul: historic areas, Turkey
190 Safranbolu, Turkey
191 Hattusha: Hittite city, Turkey
192 Göreme National Park and Cappadocia rock sites, Turkey
193 Divrigi: Great Mosque and hospital, Turkey
194 Nemrut Dag: archaeological site, Turkey
195 Ggantija: megalithic temples, Malta
196 Hal Saflieni Hypogeum, Malta
197 Valletta: old city, Malta
198 Paphos: archaeological site, Cyprus
199 Troödos region: painted churches, Cyprus

FORMER SOVIET UNION

200 Tallinn: historic centre, Estonia
201 Riga: historic centre, Latvia
202 Vilnius: old city, Lithuania
203 Kyyiv (Kiev): St Sophia Cathedral, related monastic buildings and Lavra of Kyyiv-Pechersk, Ukraine
204 Sankt-Peterburg (St Petersburg): historic centre and related monuments, Russian Fed.
205 Novgorod: historic monuments and surroundings, Russian Fed.
206 Moskva (Moscow): Kremlin & Red Square, Russian Fed.
207 Moskva (Moscow): Church of the Ascension at Kolomenskoye, Russian Fed.
208 Sergiyev Posad: architectural ensemble of the Trinity Sergius Lavra, Russian Fed.
209 Vladimir and Suzdal: White Monuments, Russian Fed.
210 Upper Svaneti area, Georgia
211 Kutaisi: Bagrati Cathedral and Gelati Monastery, Georgia

AFRICA

212 Tétouan: medina, Morocco
213 Fès: medina, Morocco
214 Volubilis: archaeological site, Morocco
215 Meknès: historic city, Morocco
216 Marrakech: medina, Morocco
217 Aït Benhaddou: fortified village, Morocco
218 Tipasa: archaeological site, Algeria
219 Alger (Algiers): Kasbah, Algeria
220 Benî Hammâd: Al Qal'a, Algeria
221 Djemila: Roman ruins, Algeria
222 Timgad: Roman ruins, Algeria
223 M'Zab Valley, Algeria
224 Dougga, Tunisia
225 Tunis: medina, Tunisia
226 Carthage: archaeological site, Tunisia
227 Kerkouane: Punic town and its necropolis, Tunisia
228 Sousse: medina, Tunisia
229 El Jem: amphitheatre, Tunisia
230 Qairouan (Kairouan), Tunisia
231 Ghadamis: old town, Libya
232 Sabratha: archaeological site, Libya
233 Leptis Magna: archaeological site, Libya
234 Cyrene: archaeological site, Libya
235 Abu Mena: Christian ruins, Egypt
236 El Qâhira (Cairo): Islamic city, Egypt
237 Memphis: Pyramid fields from Giza to Dahshur and its necropolis, Egypt

MIDDLE EAST

238 Halab: ancient city of Aleppo, Syria
239 Tadmur: archaeological site of Palmyra, Syria
240 Dimashq (Damascus): ancient city, Syria
241 Bosra: ancient city, Syria
242 Anjar: archaeological site, Lebanon
243 Baalbek, Lebanon
244 Byblos, Lebanon
245 Soûr: archaeological site of Tyre, Lebanon
246 Jerusalem: old city and its walls (proposed by Jordan)
247 Qasr Amra, Jordan
248 Petra, Jordan
249 Hatra, Iraq

TEMPERATURE CONVERSION

°Celsius	−10	0	10	20	30	40
°Fahrenheit	14	32	50	68	86	104

RAINFALL CONVERSION

Millimetres	102	203	305	406	508	610
Inches	4	8	12	16	20	24

CLIMATE

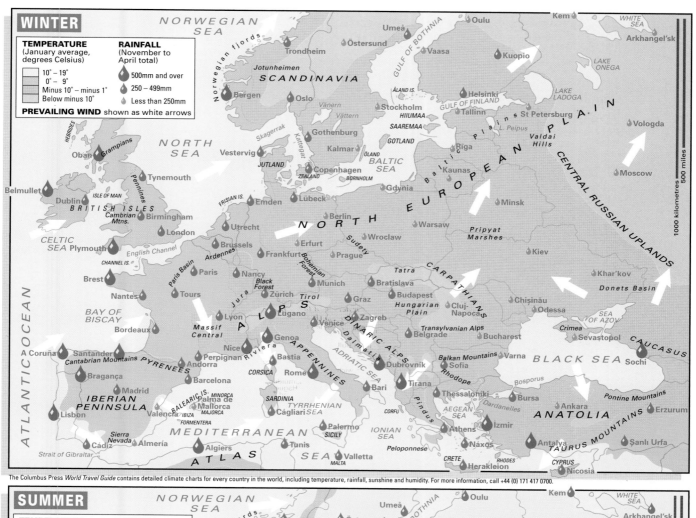

The Columbus Press *World Travel Guide* contains detailed climate charts for every country in the world, including temperature, rainfall, sunshine and humidity. For more information, call +44 (0) 171 417 0700.

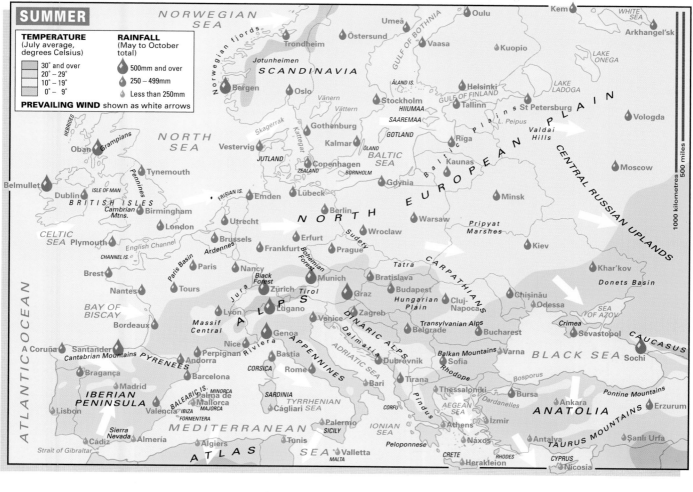

RAILWAYS AND FERRIES

This map shows principal rail and shipping routes in Europe. Some of the railways marked have limited services but are included because of their significance (such as connection to resort or international crossing).

A number of European rail passes are available, offering free travel on many rail and ferry services.

The Eurailpass is valid for first-class rail travel in the countries shown on the map. For those under 26, the Eurail Youthpass is valid in the same countries for second-class rail travel. The pass is not available to European residents or to visitors from Algeria, Morocco, Tunisia, Turkey or the former Soviet Union.

European residents are eligible for the Inter-Rail pass, offering train travel in the area shown on the map, excluding the country of issue. Passes are available for one or more zones within the validity area.

RAILWAYS:

———— Dedicated high-speed rail line
———— Other railway
·········· Direct Eurostar services (excluding seasonal services)

SHIPPING SERVICES (with average shortest journey times):
Times may vary depending on the operator, vessel and weather conditions. Night sailings usually take longer.

———— 3 hours or less
– – – – 3 hours 1 min – 10 hours
— — — 10 hours 1 min – 20 hours
= = = = Over 20 hours

Pecked lines are used to identify individual routes and do not represent a different type of service.

EURAILPASS AND INTER-RAIL PASS:

▭ Inter-Rail pass **and** Eurailpass valid in these countries
▭ Inter-Rail pass valid, Eurailpass not valid

CHANNEL TUNNEL
Eurostar: Direct railway services between London (Waterloo International) and Paris (Gare du Nord), Disneyland Paris and Brussels (Gare du Midi / Zuidstation) via Ashford International, Calais-Fréthun and Lille-Europe. Services from Scotland and the north of England are planned.
Le Shuttle: Cars, coaches and motorcycles, together with their passengers, are carried on shuttles operating 24 hours a day throughout the year. Loading/unloading takes place at the Folkestone and Calais terminals.

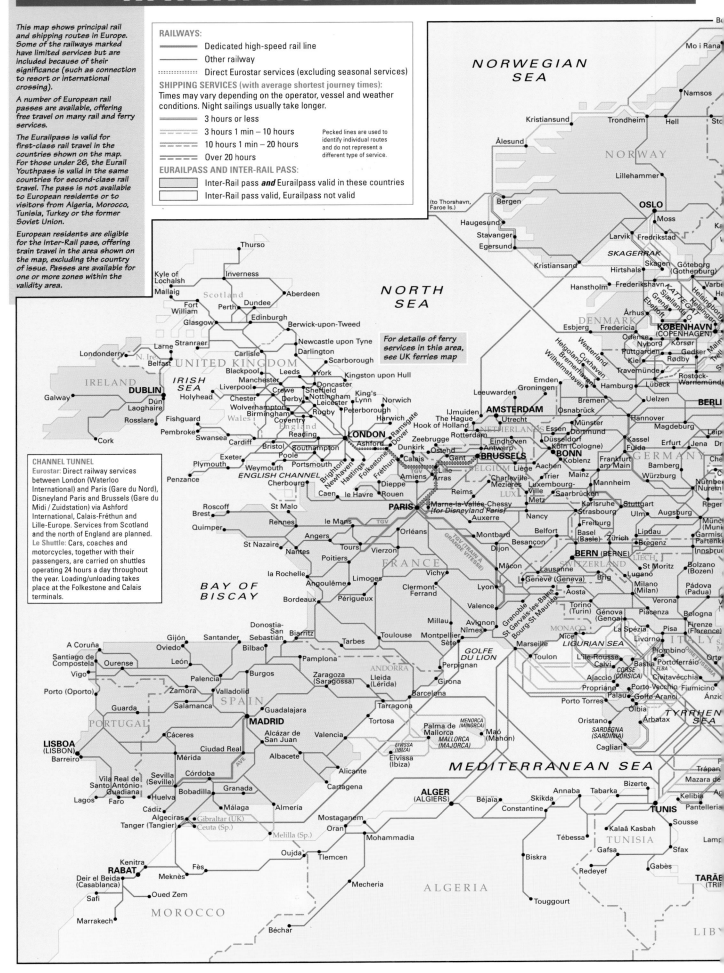

RAILWAYS AND FERRIES

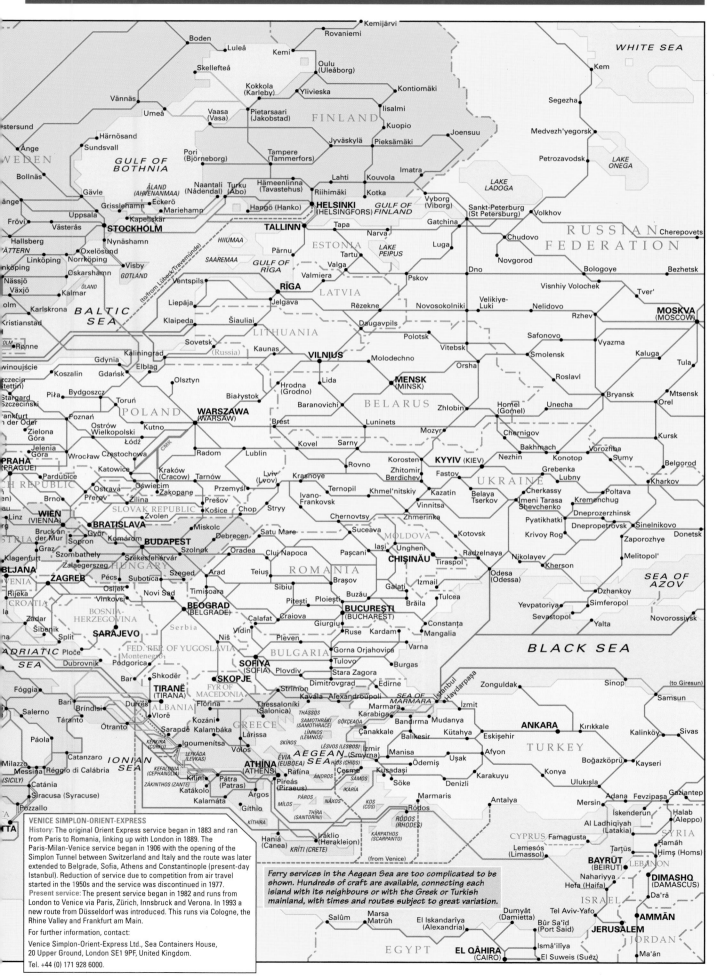

VENICE SIMPLON-ORIENT-EXPRESS

History: The original Orient Express service began in 1883 and ran from Paris to Romania, linking up with London in 1889. The Paris-Milan-Venice service began in 1906 with the opening of the Simplon Tunnel between Switzerland and Italy and the route was later extended to Belgrade, Sofia, Athens and Constantinople (present-day Istanbul). Reduction of service due to competition from air travel started in the 1950s and the service was discontinued in 1977.

Present service: The present service began in 1982 and runs from London to Venice via Paris, Zürich, Innsbruck and Verona. In 1993 a new route from Düsseldorf was introduced. This runs via Cologne, the Rhine Valley and Frankfurt am Main.

For further information, contact:

Venice Simplon-Orient-Express Ltd., Sea Containers House, 20 Upper Ground, London SE1 9PF, United Kingdom. Tel. +44 (0) 171 928 6000.

Ferry services in the Aegean Sea are too complicated to be shown. Hundreds of craft are available, connecting each island with its neighbours or with the Greek or Turkish mainland, with times and routes subject to great variation.

BLUE FLAG BEACHES

The European Blue Flag Campaign is an environmental awareness raising activity by the Foundation for Environmental Education in Europe (FEEE).

To qualify for a Blue Flag, a beach has to fulfil a number of strict criteria regarding water quality (compliance with the EU Bathing Water Directive), environment, education and information, beach area management and safety. The Blue Flag is awarded annually and is valid for one year.

1,809 resort beaches in 16 countries have been awarded Blue Flags for 1997. In addition, Blue Flags, based on slightly different criteria, have been awarded to 502 marinas in 15 countries.

For further information, contact any of the national Blue Flag operator organizations.

Countries where the Blue Flag Campaign is fully operational
Countries where the Blue Flag Campaign is partially operational (pilot schemes in operation)

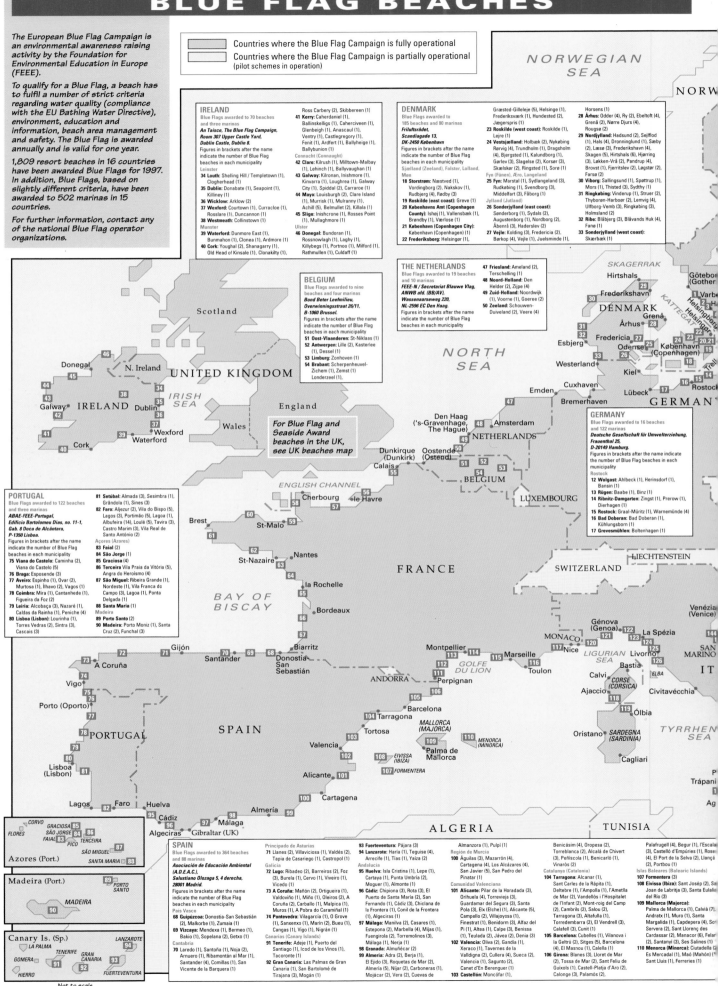

IRELAND
Blue Flags awarded to 70 beaches and three marinas
An Taisce, The Blue Flag Campaign, Room 307 Upper Castle Yard, Dublin Castle, Dublin 8.
Figures in brackets after the name indicate the number of Blue Flag beaches in each municipality
Leinster
34 **Louth:** Shelling Hill / Templetown (1), Clogherhead (1)
35 **Dublin:** Donabate (1), Seapoint (1), Killiney (1)
36 **Wicklow:** Arklow (2)
37 **Wexford:** Courtown (1), Curracloe (1), Rosslare (1), Duncannon (1)
38 **Westmeath:** Collinstown (1)
Munster
39 **Waterford:** Dunmore East (1), Bunmahon (1), Clonea (1), Ardmore (1)
40 **Cork:** Youghal (2), Shanagarry (1), Old Head of Kinsale (1), Clonakilty (1),

Ross Carbery (2), Skibbereen (1)
41 **Kerry:** Caherdaniel (1), Ballinskelligs (1), Caherciveen (1), Glenbeigh (1), Anascaul (1), Ventry (1), Castlegregory (1), Fenit (1), Ardfert (1), Ballyheige (1), Ballybunion (1)
Connacht (Connaught)
42 **Clare:** Kilrush (1), Milltown-Malbay (1), Lehinch (1), Ballyvaughan (1)
43 **Galway:** Kilronan, Inishmore (1), Kinvarra (1), Loughrea (1), Galway City (1), Spiddal (2), Carraroe (1)
44 **Mayo:** Louisburgh (2), Clare Island (1), Murrisk (1), Mulranny (1), Achill (3), Belmullet (2), Killala (1)
45 **Sligo:** Inishcrone (1), Rosses Point (1), Mullaghmore (1)
Ulster
46 **Donegal:** Bundoran (1), Rossnowlagh (1), Laghy (1), Killybegs (1), Portnoo (1), Milford (1), Rathmullen (1), Culdaff (1)

BELGIUM
Blue Flags awarded to nine beaches and four marinas
Bond Beter Leefmilieu, Overwinningsstraat 26/11, B-1060 Brussel.
Figures in brackets after the name indicate the number of Blue Flag beaches in each municipality
51 **Oost-Vlaanderen:** St-Niklaas (1)
52 **Antwerpen:** Lille (2), Kasterlee (1), Dessel (1)
53 **Limburg:** Zonhoven (1)
54 **Brabant:** Scherpenheuvel-Zichem (1), Zemst (1), Londerzeel (1)

DENMARK
Blue Flags awarded to 185 beaches and 80 marinas
Friluftsrådet, Scandiagade 13, DK-2450 København
Figures in brackets after the name indicate the number of Blue Flag beaches in each municipality
Sjælland (Zeeland), Falster, Lolland, Møn
18 **Storstrøm:** Næstved (1), Vordingborg (2), Nakskov (1), Rudbjerg (4), Rødby (3)
19 **Roskilde (east coast):** Greve (1)
20 **Københavns Amt (Copenhagen County):** Ishøj (1), Vallensbæk (1), Brøndby (1), Værløse (1)
21 **København (Copenhagen City):** København (Copenhagen) (1)
22 **Frederiksborg:** Helsingør (1),

Græsted-Gilleleje (5), Helsinge (1), Frederiksværk (1), Hundested (2), Jægerspris (1)
23 **Roskilde (west coast):** Roskilde (1), Lejre (1)
24 **Vestsjælland:** Holbæk (2), Nykøbing Rørvig (1), Trundholm (1), Dragsholm (4), Bjergsted (1), Kalundborg (1), Gørlev (3), Slagelse (2), Korsør (3), Skælskør (2), Ringsted (1), Sorø (1)
Fyn (Fünen), Æro, Langeland
25 **Fyn:** Marstal (1), Sydlangeland (3), Rudkøbing (1), Svendborg (3), Middelfart (3), Fåborg (1)
Jylland (Jutland)
26 **Sønderjylland (east coast):** Sønderborg (1), Sydals (2), Augustenborg (1), Nordborg (2), Åbenrå (3), Haderslev (1)
27 **Vejle:** Kolding (3), Fredericia (2), Børkop (1), Vejle (1), Juelsminde (1)

Horsens (1)
28 **Århus:** Odder (4), Ry (2), Ebeltoft (4), Grenå (1), Nørre Djurs (4), Rougsø (2)
29 **Nordjylland:** Hadsund (2), Sejlflod (1), Hals (4), Dronninglund (1), Sæby (2), Læsø (3), Frederikshavn (4), Skagen (5), Hirtshals (6), Hjørring (3), Løkken-Vrå (2), Pandrup (4), Brovst (1), Fjerritslev (2), Løgstør (2), Farsø (2)
30 **Viborg:** Sallingsund (1), Spøttrup (1), Mors (1), Thisted (3), Sydthy (1)
31 **Ringkøbing:** Vinderup (1), Struer (2), Thyborøn-Harboør (2), Lemvig (4), Ulfborg-Vemb (3), Ringkøbing (3), Holmsland (2)
32 **Ribe:** Blåbjerg (3), Blåvands Huk (4), Fanø (1)
33 **Sønderjylland (west coast):** Skærbæk (1)

THE NETHERLANDS
Blue Flags awarded to 19 beaches and 10 marinas
FEEE-N / Secretariat Blauwe Vlag, ANWB afd. (BB/AV), Wassenaarseweg 220, NL-2596 EC Den Haag.
Figures in brackets after the name indicate the number of Blue Flag beaches in each municipality
47 **Friesland:** Ameland (2), Terschelling (1)
48 **Noord-Holland:** Den Helder (2), Zijpe (4)
49 **Zuid-Holland:** Noordwijk (1), Voorne (1), Goeree (2)
50 **Zeeland:** Schouwen-Duiveland (2), Veere (4)

GERMANY
Blue Flags awarded to 16 beaches and 122 marinas
Deutsche Gesellschaft für Umwelterziehung, Frauenthal 25, D-20149 Hamburg.
Figures in brackets after the name indicate the number of Blue Flag beaches in each municipality
Rostock
12 **Wolgast:** Ahlbeck (1), Herinsdorf (1), Bansin (1)
13 **Rügen:** Baabe (1), Binz (1)
14 **Ribnitz-Damgarten:** Zingst (1), Prerow (1), Dierhagen (1)
15 **Rostock:** Graal-Müritz (1), Warnemünde (4)
16 **Bad Doberan:** Bad Doberan (1), Kühlungsborn (1)
17 **Grevesmühlen:** Boltenhagen (1)

PORTUGAL
Blue Flags awarded to 122 beaches and three marinas
ABAE-FEEE-Portugal, Edifício Bartolomeu Dias, no. 11-1, Gab. 8 Doca de Alcântara, P-1350 Lisboa.
Figures in brackets after the name indicate the number of Blue Flag beaches in each municipality
75 **Viana do Castelo:** Caminha (2), Viana do Castelo (5)
76 **Braga:** Esposende (3)
77 **Aveiro:** Espinho (1), Ovar (2), Murtosa (1), Ílhavo (2), Vagos (1)
78 **Coimbra:** Mira (1), Cantanhede (1), Figueira da Foz (2)
79 **Leiria:** Alcobaça (3), Nazaré (1), Caldas da Rainha (1), Peniche (4)
80 **Lisboa (Lisbon):** Lourinha (1), Torres Vedras (2), Sintra (3), Cascais (3)

81 **Setúbal:** Almada (3), Sesimbra (1), Grândola (3), Sines (3)
82 **Faro:** Aljezur (2), Vila do Bispo (5), Lagos (3), Portimão (5), Lagoa (1), Albufeira (14), Loulé (5), Tavira (3), Castro Marim (3), Vila Real de Santo António (1)
Açores (Azores)
83 **Faial** (2)
84 **São Jorge** (1)
85 **Graciosa** (4)
86 **Terceira** Vila Praia da Vitória (5), Angra do Heroísmo (4)
87 **São Miguel:** Ribeira Grande (1), Nordeste (1), Vila Franca do Campo (1), Lagoa (1), Ponta Delgada (1)
88 **Santa Maria** (1)
Madeira
89 **Porto Santo** (2)
90 **Madeira:** Porto Moniz (1), Santa Cruz (2), Funchal (3)

For Blue Flag and Seaside Award beaches in the UK, see UK beaches map

SPAIN
Blue Flags awarded to 364 beaches and 88 marinas
Asociación de Educación Ambiental (A.D.E.A.C.), Salustiano Olozaga 5, 4 derecha, 28001 Madrid.
Figures in brackets after the name indicate the number of Blue Flag beaches in each municipality
País Vasco
68 **Guipúzcoa:** Donostia-San Sebastián (2), Malkorbe (1), Zumaia (1)
69 **Vizcaya:** Mendexa (1), Bermeo (1), Bakio (1), Sopelana (1), Getxo (1)
Cantabria
70 **Cantabria:** Laredo (1), Santoña (1), Noja (2), Arnuero (1), Ribamontán al Mar (1), Santander (1), Comillas (1), San Vicente de la Barquera (1)
Galicia
72 **Lugo:** Ribadeo (2), Barreiros (2), Foz (3), Burela (1), Cervo (1), Viveiro (1), Vicedo (1)
73 **A Coruña:** Mañón (2), Ortigueira (1), Valdoviño (1), Miño (1), Oleiros (2), A Coruña (2), Carballo (1), Malpica (1), Muros (1), A Pobra do Caramiñal (1)
74 **Pontevedra:** Vilagarcía (1), O Grove (1), Sanxenxo (1), Marín (2), Bueu (1), Cangas (2), Vigo (1), Nigrán (2)
Principado de Asturias
71 **Llanes** (2), Villaviciosa (1), Valdés (1), Tapia de Casariego (1), Castropol (1)
Canarias (Canary Islands)
91 **Tenerife:** Adeje (1), Puerto del Santiago (1), Icod de los Vinos (1), Tacoronte (1)
92 **Gran Canaria:** Las Palmas de Gran Canaria (1), San Bartolomé de Tirajana (4), Mogán (1)
93 **Fuerteventura:** Pájara (3)
94 **Lanzarote:** Haría (1), Teguise (4), Arrecife (1), Tías (1), Yaiza (2)
Andalucía
95 **Huelva:** Isla Cristina (1), Lepe (1), Cartaya (1), Punta Umbría (2), Moguer (1), Almonte (1)
96 **Cádiz:** Chipiona (3), Rota (3), El Puerto de Santa María (2), San Fernando (1), Cádiz (3), Chiclana de la Frontera (2), Conil de la Frontera (1), Algeciras (1)
97 **Málaga:** Manilva (2), Casares (1), Estepona (2), Marbella (4), Mijas (1), Fuengirola (2), Torremolinos (3), Málaga (2), Nerja (1)
98 **Granada:** Almuñécar (2)
99 **Almería:** Adra (3), Berja (1), El Ejido (3), Roquetas de Mar (2), Almería (5), Níjar (2), Carboneras (1), Mojácar (2), Vera (2), Cuevas de

Almanzora (1), Pulpí (1)
Región de Murcia
100 **Águilas** (3), Mazarrón (4), Cartagena (4), Los Alcázares (4), San Javier (3), San Pedro del Pinatar (1)
Comunidad Valenciana
101 **Alicante:** Pilar de la Horadada (2), Orihuela (4), Torrevieja (3), Guardamar del Segura (3), Santa Pola (3), Elx (Elche) (1), Alicante (5), Campello (2), Villajoyosa (1), Finestrat (1), Benidorm (3), Alfaz del Pi (1), Altea (1), Calpe (3), Benissa (1), Teulada (2), Jávea (2), Denia (3)
102 **Valencia:** Oliva (2), Gandia (1), Xeraco (1), Tavernes de la Valldigna (2), Cullera (4), Sueca (2), Valencia (1), Sagunto (2), Canet d'En Berenguer (1)
103 **Castellón:** Moncófar (1),

Benicàsim (4), Oropesa (2), Torreblanca (2), Alcalá de Chivert (3), Peñíscola (1), Benicarló (1), Vinaròs (2)
Catalunya (Catalonia)
104 **Tarragona:** Alcanar (1), Sant Carles de la Rápita (1), Deltebre (1), l'Ampolla (1), l'Ametlla de Mar (2), Vandellòs i l'Hospitalet de l'Infant (2), Mont-roig del Camp (2), Cambrils (2), Salou (2), Tarragona (3), Altafulla (1), Torredembarra (2), El Vendrell (3), Calafell (2), Cunit (1)
105 **Barcelona:** Cubelles (1), Vilanova i la Geltrú (1), Sitges (5), Barcelona (4), El Masnou (1), Calella (1)
106 **Girona:** Blanes (3), Lloret de Mar (2), Tossa de Mar (2), Sant Feliu de Guíxols (1), Castell-Platja d'Aro (2), Calonge (3), Palamós (2),

Palafrugell (4), Begur (1), l'Escala (3), Castelló d'Empúries (3), Roses (4), El Port de la Selva (2), Llançà (2), Portbou (1)
Islas Baleares (Balearic Islands)
107 **Formentera** (2)
108 **Eivissa (Ibiza):** Sant Josép (2), Sant Joan de Labritja (3), Santa Eulalia del Río (3)
109 **Mallorca (Majorca):** Palma de Mallorca (1), Calvià (7), Andratx (1), Muro (1), Santa Margalida (1), Capdepera (4), Son Servera (2), Sant Llorenç des Cardassar (2), Manacor (6), Felanitx (2), Santanyí (3), Ses Salines (1)
110 **Menorca (Minorca):** Ciutadella (2), Es Mercadal (1), Maó (Mahón) (4), Sant Lluís (1), Ferreries (1)

Azores (Port.)

Madeira (Port.)

Canary Is. (Sp.)

Not to scale

BLUE FLAG BEACHES

SKIING

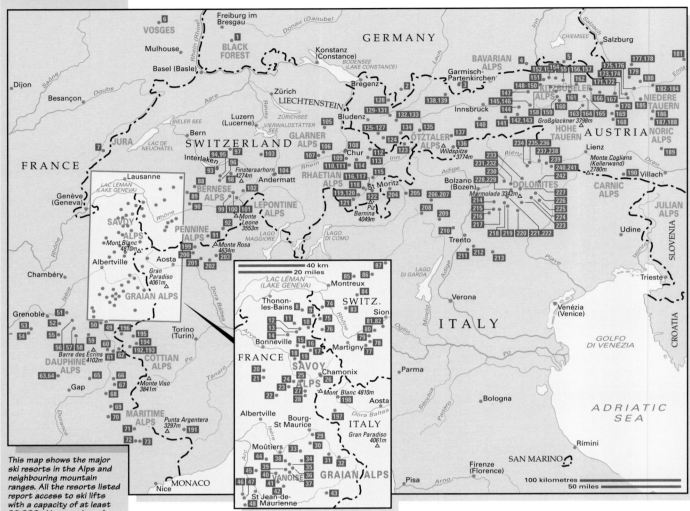

This map shows the major ski resorts in the Alps and neighbouring mountain ranges. All the resorts listed report access to ski lifts with a capacity of at least 20,000 skiers per hour (as at September 1997), with the exception of those marked with an asterisk (*), which are included because of their significance.

Resorts based on traditional villages are shown in normal type, modern-style purpose-built resorts in bold italics.

The classifications reflect skiing accessible from resorts which may also include terrain accessed from neighbouring resorts.

Data compiled by Snow-Hunter Ltd., all rights reserved.
Fax: +44 (0) 1463 741273.
email: patrick@snowhunt. demon.co.uk

Resort altitude:
□ 1,500 metres or above
□ 1,000 – 1,499 metres
No black square: under 1,000 metres

Skier uplift:
■ 100,000 skiers per hour or more
■ 50,000 – 99,999 skiers per hour
■ 30,000 – 49,999 skiers per hour
No colour: Less than 30,000

Altitude at top of highest ski run:
○ 3,000 metres or above
○ 2,000 – 2,999 metres
No black circle: under 2,000 metres

Maximum vertical drop:
● 2,000 metres or more
● 1,500 – 1,999 metres
● 1,000 – 1,499 metres
No colour: Less than 1,000 metres

Germany
1 Feldberg
2 Oberstdorf
3 Garmisch-Partenkirchen
4 Bayrischzell
5 Reit im Winkl

France
6 la Bresse-Hohneck
7 Métabief / le Mont d'Or
8 Abondance
9 Châtel
10 *Avoriaz*
11 St Jean-d'Aulps
12 Morzine
13 les Gets
14 *le Praz de Lys*
15 Morillon les Essert
16 Samoëns
17 Sixt
18 les Carroz
19 *Flaine*
20 le Grand-Bornand
21 la Clusaz
22 Notre-Dame-de-Bellecombe
23 Megève
24 Combloux
25 St Gervais / *le Bettex*
26 Chamonix-Mont Blanc
27 St Nicolas-de-Véroce
28 les Contamines-Montjoie*
29 *les Arcs*
30 Peisey-Nancroix-Vallandry
31 *Tignes*
32 Val d'Isère
33 *la Plagne / les Coches /* Montchavin / Plagne Montalbert
34 Champagny-en-Vanoise
35 *la Tania*
36 Courchevel
37 *la Rosière*
38 Brides-les-Bains
39 Méribel
40 St Martin-de-Belleville
41 *les Menuires*
42 *Val Thorens*
43 Val Cenis
44 *Valmorel*
45 *St François-Longchamp*
46 la Toussuire
47 le Corbier
48 St Jean d'Arves
49 Valmeinier
50 Valloire
51 *les Sept Laux*

52 Chamrousse
53 Villard-de-Lans / *Cote 2000*
54 Corrençon-en-Vercors
55 *Alpe du Grand Serre*
56 Vaujany / Oz-en-Oisans
57 *Alpe d'Huez* / Auris-en-Oisans / Villard-Reculas
58 *les Deux Alpes*
59 *la Grave*
60 Serre-Chevalier
61 Briançon
62 la Joue du Loup
63 *Superdévoluy*
64 *Superdévoluy*
65 *Orcières-Merlette*
66 *Risoul*
67 Vars
68 *les Orres*
69 *Pra-Loup*
70 *la Foux-d'Allos*
71 Auron / St Étienne-de-Tinée
72 Valberg
73 Beuil-les-Launes

Switzerland
74 Torgon
75 Morgins
76 Champéry-Planachaux / Val-d'Illiez / Les Crosets
77 Le Châble / Bruson
78 Verbier
79 La Tzoumas (Mayens-de-Riddes)
80 Nendaz
81 Mayens-de-l'Ours
82 Veysonnaz / Les Collons
83 Villars-sur-Ollon / Gryon
84 Les Diablerets
85 Château-d'Oex*
86 Gstaad-Saanenland
87 Zweisimmen
88 Adelboden
89 Lenk
90 Crans-Montana
91 Zermatt
92 Saas Fee
93 Interlaken / Wilderswil bei Interlaken
94 Lauterbrunnen
95 Wengen
96 Mürren* / Stechelberg*
97 Grindelwald
98 Riederalp
99 Bettmeralp
100 Mörel-Breiten

101 Fiesch
102 Sörenberg
103 Engelberg
104 Andermatt*
105 Flumserberg
106 Flims
107 Laax
108 Chur*
109 Churwalden
110 Lenzerheide-Valbella
111 Parpan
112 Klosters / Fideris
113 Davos
114 Arosa
115 La-Punt-Chaumes-ch.
116 Celerina
117 Samedan
118 St Moritz
119 Sils-Maria*
120 Silvaplana-Surlej*
121 Maloja
122 Pontresina*
123 Samnaun

Austria
124 Partenen
125 Gaschurn
126 Gortipohl
127 St Gallenkirch
128 Kleinwalsertal (Hirschegg / Mittelberg / Riezlern)
129 Lech / Oberlech
130 Zug
131 Zürs
132 St Anton am Arlberg / St Jakob am Arlberg
133 St Christoph am Arlberg
134 Ischgl / Silvretta
135 Serfaus
136 Obergurgl / Hochgurgl
137 Sölden
138 Lermoos*
139 Ehrwald
140 Neustift im Stubaital
141 Hintertux
142 Finkenberg
143 Mayrhofen
144 Zell am Ziller
145 Gerlos
146 Königsleiten
147 Wildschönau [Auffach / Mühltal / Niederau / Oberau / Thierbach]
148 Brixen im Thale
149 Hopfgarten im Brixental

150 Westendorf*
151 Söll
152 Scheffau
153 Ellmau / Going
154 St Johann in Tirol
155 Fieberbrunn*
156 Kirchberg in Tirol / Aschau in Tirol
157 Kitzbühel
158 Aurach
159 Jochberg / Pass Thurn
160 Mittersill / Pass Thurn
161 Saalbach Hinterglemm
162 Leogang
163 Kaprun
164 Zell am See
165 Maria Alm
166 Dienten am Hochkönig
167 St Johann im Pongau
168 Badgastein
169 Bad Hofgastein
170 Großarl
171 Flachauwinkel
172 Kleinarl
173 Flachau
174 Wagrain
175 Altenmarkt-Zauchensee
176 Radstadt
177 Gosau
178 Rußbach
179 Annaberg
180 Filzmoos
181 Tauplitz
182 Haus in Ennstal*
183 Ramsau am Dachstein*
184 Schladming
185 Obertauern
186 Mauterndorf / Mariapfarr
187 St Margarethen im Lungau
188 St Michael im Lungau
189 Bad Kleinkirchheim
190 Karnische Skiregion

Italy
191 Limone Piemonte
192 *San Sicário* / Cesana
193 *Clavière*
194 *Sestriere*
195 Sàuze d'Oulx
196 Bardonecchia
197 la Thuile
198 Courmayeur*
199 *Breuil-Cervinia*
200 Valtournenche
201 Champoluc / Antagnod
202 Gressoney-la-Trinité /

203 Gressoney-St Jean
204 Alagna-Valsésia
205 Livigno
206 Bormio*
207 *Folgárida*
208 *Marilléva*
209 Passo Tonale
210 Madonna di Campíglio
211 Andalo
212 Folgária
213 Lavarone / Luserna
214 Asiago / Canove
215 *Obereggen*
216 Alpe di Pampeago / Tésero
217 Cavalese*
218 Predazzo
219 Moena di Fassa
220 San Martino di Castrozza / *Passo Rolle*
221 Pozza di Fassa*
222 Vigo di Fassa*
223 Falcade
224 Alleghe
225 Zoldo Alto / Valzoldana
226 Selva di Cadore
227 Arabba
228 Campitello di Fassa*
229 Canazei*
230 Ortisei (St Ulrich)
231 Santa Cristina / Pranauron
232 Selva Gardena (Wolkenstein)
233 Alta Badia [Colfosco / Corvara / la Villa (Stern) / San Cassiano (St Kassian) / Pedráces / San Leonardo (St Leonhard)]
234 San Vigilio di Marebbe
235 Riscone (Reischach)
236 Valdàora (Olang)
237 Dobiacco (Toblach)
238 Villabassa (Niederdorf)
239 San Cándido (Innichen)
240 Sesto (Sexten)
241 Versciaco (Vierschach)
242 Cortina

The World Ski and Snowboarding Guide, published by Columbus Press, is a comprehensive guide to the world's ski resorts. For more information, call +44 (0) 171 417 0700.

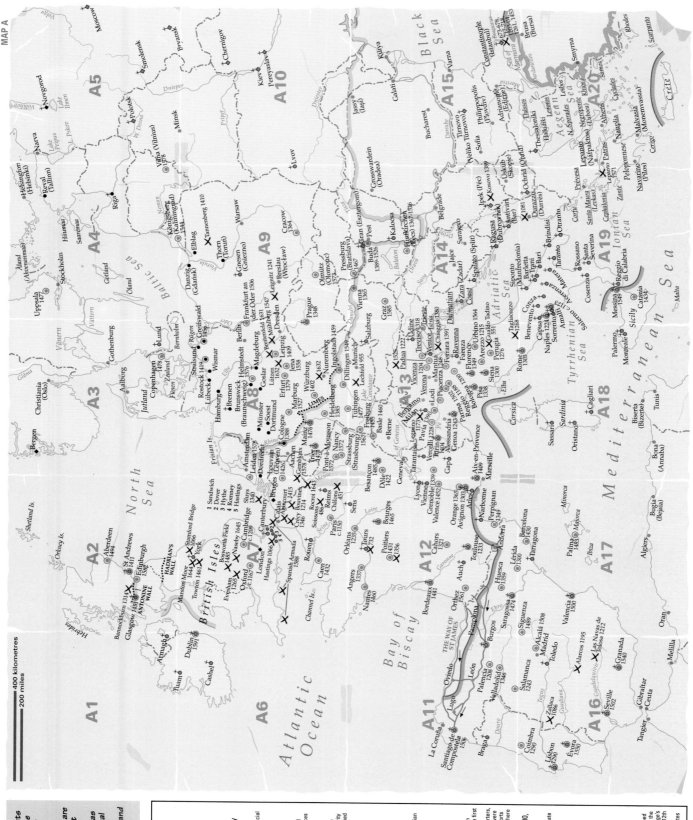

HISTORICAL

NATIONAL PARKS

Europe has a large variety of scenery, habitats and fauna, and most countries have set aside areas of natural beauty in order to preserve the landscape and wildlife. This map shows the most important areas designated as National Parks throughout Europe except for the former Soviet Union, but including the Baltic states. The best period for visiting each park is shown in blue (no date: all year / information not available).

Iceland
1 Jökulsárgljúfur
Spectacular gorges
2 Skaftafell
Glacial country with icecap & sand plain

Norway
3 Øvre Pasvik May-Sep
Forest & tundra
4 Stabbursdalen May-Oct
Arctic landscape with tundra, lakes, gravel plains & forest
5 Øvre Anarjokka May-Sep
Undulating tundra with woodland & lakes
6 Reisa May-Oct
Mixed mountain country
7 Øvre Dividal May-Sep
Mountainous country with tundra & woodland
8 Ånderdalen May-Sep
Mixed mountain country
9 Saltfjellet-Svartisen May-Sep Varied landscape; fjords, mountains & glacier
10 Børgefjell May-Oct
Remote mountain area with varied habitats
11 Gressåmoen May-Oct
Mountainous country & spruce forest
12 Dovrefjell May-Aug
Mountainous tundra & permanent snowfields; famous for its flora
13 Rondane May-Sep
Mountain country with varied landscapes
14 Jotunheimen May-Sep
Mountainous area with tundra, bogs & forest
15 Hardangervidda
May-Oct Large mountain plateau, a popular walking area

Sweden
16 Vadvetjåkka May-Sep
Mountainous country
17 Abisko May-Sep
Mountain & forest with tundra, lakes & rivers
18 Muddus May-Sep
Forest, tundra & bog
19 Padjelanta, Sarek and Stora Sjöfallet May-Sep
3 parks protect Europe's largest wilderness area; mixed landscape
20 Pieljekaise May-Sep
Wooded mountainous country with tundra, open water & bogs
21 Skuleskogen Apr-Oct
Forested hill country
22 Töfsingdalen May-Oct
Woodland, tundra & bog
23 Sånfjället May-Oct
Woodland, tundra & bog
24 Hamra May-Oct
Woodland, tundra & bog, noted for its insects
25 Garphyttan Apr-Oct
Forest & meadows
26 Tiveden May-Oct
Hilly forest, lakes & bogs
27 Store Mosse Apr-Jul
Predominantly boggy, with lakes & forest

Finland
28 Pallas-Ounastunturi
May-Sep Upland plateau & taiga, with lakes, tundra, gorges & forest
29 Lemmenjoki May-Sep
Wilderness mountain area; gold rush in 1940's
30 Urho Kekkonen May-Sep
Large wilderness area; fells and pine moors
31 Pyhätunturi May-Sep
Mountainous area with tundra, bogs & forest
32 Oulanka May-Sep
Varied tundra landscape
33 Petkeljärvi May-Sep
Typical Finnish lakeland scenery, with lakes, bogs, forest & moorland
34 Linnansaari May-Sep
Mainly lake with some islands
35 Pyhä-Häkki May-Sep
Mainly forest & bog
36 Liesjärvi May-Sep
Lakes, previously cultivated land & forest

37 Saaristomeri May-Sep
Extensive island group with mixed habitats

Ireland
38 Glenveagh Apr-Jul
Mixed upland area
39 Connemara Apr-Sep
Typical western Ireland mountain area
40 Killarney May-Oct
Ancient woodland with moorland, lakes, bogs, wetland & mountains
41 Wicklow Mountains
May-Aug Partly wooded mountains with upland moorland & grassland

United Kingdom
42 Northumberland Apr-Oct
Mainly upland grassy moorland; Hadrian's Wall in the south
43 Lake District Apr-Nov
Mountain & lakeland; very popular all year
44 Yorkshire Dales May-Jul
Varied upland country
45 North York Moors
Apr-Sep Hilly uplands with heather moorland
46 Peak District May-Jul
Limestone in the south, with many caves; high peat moors in the north
47 Snowdonia May-Aug
Mountain country with lakes, moorland, grassland & woodland
48 Pembrokeshire Coast
Apr-Jul Scenic coastline; varied seabird habitats
49 Brecon Beacons
May-Oct Mainly grass-covered mountain area
50 Exmoor May-Jul
High heather moorland & wooded valleys, with dramatic coastline
51 Dartmoor May-Sep
Granite uplands with heather & grassland

Netherlands
52 Dwingelderveld
May-Sep Heathland, fen & woodland with lakes
53 De Hoge Veluwe Apr-Oct
Variety of habitats: heathland, dunes, fens, wet heath & woodland
54 Veluwezoom Apr-Oct
Heath & mixed woodland

Germany
55 Niedersächsisches
Wattenmeer
East Frisian Islands; mudflats & saltmarsh
56 Hamburgisches W'meer
Mudflats & saltmarsh
57 Schleswig-Holsteinisches W'meer
Mudflats & saltmarsh
58 Vorpommersche
Boddenlandschaft
Mudflats & saltmarsh with dunes, lagoons, lakes & woodland
59 Jasmund May-Nov
Varied landscape with cliffs, lakes & woodland
60 Müritz Apr-Nov
Woodland & lakes with heath, marsh & pasture
61 Unteres Odertal
Apr-Jun, Sep-Nov
Floodplain of the Oder; park shared with Poland
62 Sächsische Schweiz
Apr-Oct Numerous rock towers; lower slopes wooded; deep valleys
63 Hoch Harz May-Oct
Wooded mountains with moorland, bogs & lakes; affected by acid rain
64 Bayerischer Wald
May-Aug
Wooded mountain area
65 Berchtesgaden May-Sep
Mountain landscape with Alpine pastures, small glaciers, cliffs, lakes & varied woodland

France
66 Vanoise Jun-Sep
High mountain scenery
67 Ecrins Apr-Sep
High mountain scenery with many glaciers

68 Mercantour Apr-Sep
Some of the best parts of the Maritime Alps
69 Port-Cros Mar-Sep
Small wooded island
70 Cévennes May-Sep
Varied mountain & forest with bogs & moors
71 Pyrénées Occidentales
May-Sep, Oct-Jul
Diverse mountain landscape; snowfields, pastures & woodland

Spain
72 Ordesa May-Jul
Spectacular mountain & gorge scenery; forests & Alpine pastures
73 Covadonga May-Sep
Mountain area with mixed woodlands, pasture & glacial lakes
74 Tablas de Daimiel
Apr-Jul Small wetland
75 Coto de Doñana Feb-Jun
Guadalquivir delta; important wildlife site
76 Caldera de Taburiente
Volcanic landscape
77 Garajonay
Heavily wooded area
78 Cañadas del Teide
Volcanic landscape
79 Timanfaya
Volcanic landscape

Portugal
80 Peneda-Gerês Apr-Oct
Mountain & forest area; cliffs & rock formations

Switzerland
81 The Swiss National Park
May-Oct Strictly controlled mountainous area; forests, pastures, lakes, cliffs & snowfields

Austria
82 Hohe Tauern May-Sep
High Alpine scenery; forests in lower areas
83 Nockberge Apr-Oct
Forested mountain area with bogs & moors

Italy
84 Stelvio Apr-Oct
Typical Alpine scenery & Italy's largest glacier
85 Gran Paradiso Apr-Oct
High Alpine country; famous for the Ibex
86 Abruzzo Apr-Oct
Wooded mountainous area
87 Circeo Mar-Jun
Coastal marsh & rocky promontory near Rome
88 Calàbria Apr-Jul
Three areas of wooded mountainous landscape

Poland
89 Woliński Apr-Oct
Woodland, lakes and sea cliffs; white-tailed sea eagle the main attraction
90 Słowiński Apr-Jul
Coastal landscape with shifting sand dunes
91 Kampinoski May-Jul
Varied landscape close to Warsaw
92 Mazurski and Wigierski
Numerous lakes and extensive forests
93 Biebrzanski Apr-Jul
Central Europe's largest area of natural peat bogs
94 Białowieski Apr-Jul
Europe's largest original lowland forest; European bison the main attraction

95 Bieszczadzki May-Sep
Remote wooded mtn area in E. Carpathians
96 Babiogórski, Tatrzanski, Gorczanski & Pieninski
May-Oct Four parks in the spectacular High Tatra mountains
97 Ojcowski May-Sep
Hilly landscape with many rock pinnacles
98 Gory Stolowe and Karkonoski May-Sep
Dramatic mountain scenery of the Sudeten Mountains

Czech Republic
99 Krkonose May-Oct
Wooded mountain area with Alpine pastures, meadows, bogs & lakes

Slovak Republic
100 Vysoké Tatry May-Oct
Spectacular mountain area with forests, lakes, grassland & bogs
101 Nizke Tatry Apr-Jul
Mountainous country with varied woodland, pastures, bogs & lakes
102 Pieninsky May-Oct
Limestone mountains with mixed forests

Hungary
103 Aggtelek Apr-Oct
Important karst scenery
104 Bukk Apr-Jul
Hilly forested region
105 Hortobágyi
Varied steppe landscape good for birdwatching
106 Kiskunság Apr-Jul
Wide range of lowland habitats

Slovenia
107 Triglav
Limestone mountain scenery & mixed forest

Croatia
108 Risnjak
Limestone mountain scenery & mixed forest
109 Plitvice Lakes
Scenic lakes linked by waterfalls
110 Paklenica
Limestone peaks, gorges & mixed forest
111 Kornati
Limestone islands with karst scenery
112 Krka
Follows the Krka river; lakes, dams, gorges, falls & woodland
113 Mljet
Western part of island

Bosnia-Herzegovina
114 Sutjeska
Wooded mountainous area; mixed landscape & reserve of virgin forest

Federal Republic of Yugoslavia
115 Fruska Gora
Wooded hilly valley
116 Djerdap
Gorge of the Danube; dam has created a long thin lake
117 Tara
Mixed upland scenery
118 Durmitor
Mountain area in the west, Tara Gorge in east; mixed landscape & karst

119 Biogradska Gora
Mountain area with high grasslands & five lakes
120 Lovcen
Wooded limestone mountains
121 Skadarsko jezero
Yugoslav part of Lake Scutari

Former Yugoslav Rep. of Macedonia
122 Mavrovo
Mountain area, partly wooded
123 Galicica
S. end of Dinaric Alps; mostly natural forest
124 Pelister
Wooded mountain area with Alpine pastures

Albania
125 Dajtit, Lura and Thethi
Three separate parks; forested mountain areas
126 Divjaka
Dunes & coastal woodland
127 Llogara
Woodland & pastures
128 Tomorri
Mountainous landscape with forests & pastures

Romania
129 Retezat May-Sep
Mountain country with extensive forests

Bulgaria
130 Rusenski Lom May-Oct
Deciduous woodland
131 Vitosa May-Oct
Varied mountain area
132 Pirin Apr-Oct
High mountains; forest & mixed landscape

Greece
133 Préspa Apr-Jul
Shallow lakes with reed- & sedge-beds
134 Ólimbos (Olympus)
Apr-Oct Mountain area with maquis & forest
135 Pindos May-Oct
Wooded mountain area
136 Víkos-Aóos May-Jun
Wooded mountain area; Víkos & Aóos gorges
137 Aínos Mar-Jul
Area around Mt Aínos
138 Iti Óros May-Oct
Wooded mountain area
139 Parnassós Apr-Nov
Wilderness mountain area; mixed habitats
140 Párnitha Apr-Jul
Limestone area; maquis
141 Soúnion Mar-May
Typical Greek coast

Turkey
142 Manyas-Kuscenneti
Part of large lake

Estonia
143 Lahemaa
Wooded area & scenic coast

Latvia
144 Gauja
River & gorge scenery

Lithuania
145 Zemaitija
Lakeland area
146 Aukstaitija (Ignalina)
Forest & lakes; great diversity of wildlife
147 Trakai
Five lakes with Trakai Castle as centrepiece
148 Dzukija
Confluence of Nemunas & Merkys rivers

LEISURE PARKS

This map shows major theme parks and amusement parks in Europe. Most of those shown are members of either the International Association of Amusement Parks and Attractions (IAAPA) or the European Federation of Amusement and Leisure Parks ('Europark'). Many parks which primarily attract visitors from the local area are excluded for reasons of space. A number of zoos, waterparks and museums are also members of IAAPA or Europark.

For more information, contact:

IAAPA,
1448 Duke Street,
Alexandria,
Virginia 22314,
USA.

Tel. +1 703 836 4800.

Europark,
Floralaan West 143,
NL-5644 BH Eindhoven,
The Netherlands.

Tel. +31 40 212 8526.

EUROPE'S MOST POPULAR PARKS IN 1996
Number of visitors (world ranking in brackets)
Disneyland Paris France: 11.7 million (4th)
Blackpool Pleasure Beach UK: 7.5 million (9th)
Tivoli Denmark: 3.1 million (25th)
De Efteling The Netherlands: 3.0 million (28th)
Alton Towers UK: 2.7 million (=35th)
Port Aventura Spain: 2.7 million (=35th)
Europa-Park Germany: 2.5 million (38th)
Liseberg Sweden: 2.4 million (=40th)
Gardaland Italy: 2.4 million (=40th)
Dyrehavsbakken Denmark: 2.1 million (49th)
Source: Amusement Business

Norway
1 Kristiansand Dyrepark
Combined animal park and entertainment park
2 Telemark Sommarland, Bø
Combined theme park and waterpark
3 Lunds Tivoli, Oslo
Amusement park
4 TusenFryd & VikingLandet, Vinterbru
Theme park with many rides and large Viking Land

Sweden
5 Liseberg, Gothenburg
Large theme park with convention facilities, exhibition hall and sports stadium
6 Parken Zoo i Eskilstuna
Theme park, waterpark and zoo
7 Gröna Lunds Tivoli, Stockholm
Amusement park in the centre of Stockholm
8 Furuviksparken, Gavle
Amusement park and zoo
9 Jamtli Historieland, Östersund
Historical theme park

Finland
10 Wasalandia, Vaasa
Amusement park; Tropical Bath Tropiclandia nearby
11 Tampereen Sarkanniemi Oy, Tampere
City-centre amusement park and entertainment centre; also includes an art museum
12 Linnanmaki, Helsinki
Finland's most popular amusement park

Denmark
13 Jesperhus Blomsterpark, Nykøbing, Mors
Amusement park, family entertainment centre and zoo
14 Fårup Aquapark & Sommerland, Saltum
Amusement park with 30 activities and Scandinavia's largest waterpark
15 Djurs Sommerland, Nimtofte
Amusement park with more than 50 activities in six attractions: Summerland, Waterland, Africa Land, Mexico Land, Cowboy Village and Lillensland
16 Legoland, Billund
Theme park based on Lego toy products; 22 family rides plus 75,000 square metres of Lego brick replicas of world monuments
17 Dyrehavsbakken ('Bakken'), Klampenborg
The world's oldest amusement park, with 24 rides
18 Tivoli, Copenhagen
Large amusement park

Ireland
19 Perks Pleasure Park, Youghal
Major rides include Vampire Ghost Train, Trabant and a giant big wheel supported by Perkie Bear
20 Clara Lara Fun Park, Wicklow
Park and amusement centre including Aqua Shuttle and Pirate Galleon plus a junior playground

United Kingdom
21 Barry's Amusement Park, Portrush
Star rides include Looping Dipper and Music Express
22 Blackpool Pleasure Beach
150 attractions including The Avalanche, Blackhole, Tagada, Nicky's Circus Ride, Beaver Creek, Believe It Or Not, Haunted Crypt, five wooden rollercoasters and a bobsleigh run
23 Camelot Theme Park, Chorley, Lancashire
A medieval world with over 100 attractions and rides including Excalibur, a 360° rotation swing ride
24 Lightwater Valley, Ripon
Theme park with unique attractions including the world's first suspended hang-glider ride and the world's longest rollercoaster
25 Flamingo Land, Malton
Popular holiday village and zoo with many rides in 150 hectares
26 Alton Towers, near Stoke-on-Trent
One of the UK's most popular theme parks with 125 rides and attractions including Nemesis and Storyland Land theme park
27 Gullivers Kingdom, Matlock Bath
Family theme park with over 40 rides, hot-air balloon flights and chair lift
28 American Adventure, Ilkeston
Theme park with Nightmare Niagara log flume
29 Magical World of Fantasy Island, Ingoldmells
Themed indoor family resort; based on Jules Verne
30 Drayton Manor Park, Tamworth
Theme park and zoo; 50 rides and attractions including Paratower, Jungle Cruise, Pirate's Adventure, Splash Canyon and The Haunting
31 Pleasurewood Hills, Lowestoft
East Anglia's no.1 theme park with 50 rides including Cannonball Express rollercoaster and the Log Flume
32 Oakwood Adventure, Narberth
Amusement park with over 40 attractions including Megafobia rollercoaster, Snake River Falls flume and a bobsleigh run
33 Barry Island Pleasure Beach, Barry
50 rides and attractions including Cyclone rollercoaster and African Experience ride
34 Legoland, Windsor
Children's theme park divided into five areas: The Beginning, The Imaginative Centre, Miniland, Duplo Gardens & Lego Traffic, My Town & The Wild Woods
35 Thorpe Park, Chertsey
Theme park with many rides including Canada Creek, Carousel Kingdom, A Drive in the Country, Flying Fish, Depth Charge and No Way Out, a backwards dark ride
36 Chessington World of Adventures
Zoo and amusement park with rides including Dragon River and Rameses Revenge
37 Fun Acres, Southsea
Seaside park with boat trips and 10 major rides
38 Harbour Park, Littlehampton
Seaside amusement park

The Netherlands
39 Ponypark, Slagharen
Theme park with over 40 rides
40 Avonturenpark Hellendoorn
Amusement park with many rides and animal attractions
41 Walibi Flevo, Dronten
Family amusement park with El Condor rollercoaster and Crazy River water flume
42 Zeedierenpark Harderwijk
Europe's largest marine park, with a research dept.
43 Duinrell, Wassenaar
Theme park close to the beach with over 50 rides and attractions, including Splash and Waterspin
44 Familiepark Drievliet, Rijswijk
More than 20 major attractions, including The Coppermine rollercoaster
45 De Efteling, Kaatsheuvel
Family leisure park with a full range of attractions including a golf course, Dreamflight dark ride, Fata Morgana, Inca City and two rollercoasters

Belgium
46 Meli Park, De Panne
Attractions and rides plus a bird and animal park
47 Bellewaerde Park, Ypres
Exotic animals on display and over 30 rides in four theme areas: Jungle, Western, Mexico and Orient
48 Action Planet, Antwerp
Indoor adventure sports park
49 Bobbejaanland, Lichtaart
Amusement and theme park with 45 major rides, including The Revolution and Arcade 2000; also includes Kinderland, a covered children's play area with 20 rides

50 Walibi, Wavre
Amusement park and waterpark with 40 rides including Rapid River, Shuttle Loop, Corkscrew and Jumbo Jet

Germany
51 Familien-Freizeitpark Tolk-Schau, Tolk
Amusement park situated in a scenic landscape
52 Hansapark, Neustadt in Holstein
Theme park with rides and attractions including an Aqua Stadium, a water circus and Adventureland
53 Ferienzentrum Schloß Dankern, Haren
Family entertainment centre with many water facilities
54 Heide-Park, Soltau
Amusement park with 36 major rides including a rapids ride, two monorails, a looping rollercoaster with four 360° turns and a bobsleigh ride
55 Serengeti Safaripark, Hodenhagen
Animal park with leisure attractions
56 Dinosaurier Park Münchehagen, Rehburg-Loccum
Dinosaur park
57 Warner Brothers Movie World, Bottrop
A unique movie theme park
58 Hollywood-Park, Stukenbrock
Combined safari park and amusement park, with attractions including Hollywood Theatre, a circus and a western show, a monkey area, Disco Round, Flying Carpet, a steam carousel and rollercoasters
59 Fort Fun Abenteuerland, Bestwig
Amusement park with a Western town
60 Panoramapark Sauerland, Kirchhundem
Wild animal park and amusement park with its own 500-kilowatt windpower station
61 Phantasialand, Brühl
Theme park divided into five areas: China Town, Old Berlin, Mexico, Petite Paris and Future World; many rides including Colorado Adventure and Michael Jackson Thrill Ride
62 Eifelpark, Gondorf bei Bitburg
Wild animal park and amusement park, includes the Eifel Domino
63 Holiday-Park, Haßloch
Theme park with many attractions including Thunder River, The Barrels of the Devil, Lilliput-Express, Aquascope, Stormship, a 180° cinema, Falkenstein Castle, Pfalz village and a looping rollercoaster
64 Erlebnispark Tripsdrill, Cleebronn
Germany's oldest amusement park
65 Freizeit-Land, Geiselwind
Theme park with many attractions including Cinema 2000, a Viking ship, a space adventure area, prehistoric world, Enterprise ride, Shuttle ride and a rollercoaster
66 Freizeit-und Miniaturpark Allgäu, Weitnau
Adventure park with many miniature buildings and trains; includes a large children's park with Nautic Jet, Luna Loop and Butterfly
67 Europa-Park, Rust
Large theme park with many rides

France
68 Mirapolis, Cergy-Pontoise
Large amusement park with activities related to legends and epics, includes Gargantua statue
69 La Mer de Sable, Ermenonville
Amusement park developed into themed areas: China, Wild West and Morocco; includes Babagattau Village
70 Parc Astérix, Plailly
Theme park based on comic strip hero Asterix with star rides Descent of the Styx, Big Splash and Goudume
71 Jardin d'Acclimation, Paris
Amusement park with family rides and a zoo
72 Parc Floral, Paris
Amusement park set within a large garden area
73 Disneyland Paris, Marne-la-Vallée
Divided into five 'lands': Main Street USA, Frontierland, Adventureland, Fantasyland and Discoveryland; rides include Space Mountain and Raiders of The Lost Ark
74 Futuroscope, Poitiers
Advanced visual-image technology in cinemas and leisure complexes; Showscan has a double-3D screen

Spain
75 Parque de Atracciones Tibidabo, Barcelona
Urban amusement park, founded 1899, renovated 1988
76 Port Aventura, Salou
Spain's largest theme park with five areas: Mediterrania, Polynesia, China, Mexico and Far West
77 Txiki Park, Pamplona
Family entertainment centre designed for children
78 Parque de Atracciones Casa de Campo, Madrid
Urban amusement park, Madrid's principal entertainment centre
79 Sioux City, San Agustín
Theme park with stage shows and concerts

Portugal
80 Zoomarine, Albufeira
Zoo and marine theme park

Switzerland
81 Conny-Land, Lipperswil
Amusement park with underwater and animal shows

Austria
82 Safari- und Abenteuerpark, Gänserndorf
Adventure park and drive-through safari park

Italy
83 Gardaland, Castelnuovo del Garda
Large amusement park with 25 different attractions, eleven entertainments and four themed villages
84 Fiabilandia, Rimini
Amusement park and funfair
85 Luneur, Rome
Amusement park and funfair
86 Edenlandia, Naples
Amusement/theme park

Turkey
87 Tatilya Turizm, Avcilar, Istanbul
World's fourth largest indoor entertainment centre

UNITED KINGDOM

See pages 6-7 for general map

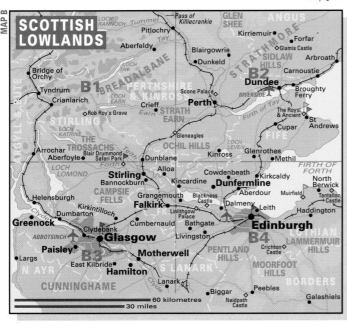

SCOTTISH LOWLANDS

Pass of Killiecrankie, GLEN SHEE, ANGUS, STRATHMORE, SIDLAW HILLS, Pitlochry, Kirriemuir, Forfar, Aberfeldy, Blairgowrie, Arbroath, Glamis Castle, Dunkeld, Carnoustie, **B1**, BREADALBANE, PERTHSHIRE & KINROSS, STRATH EARN, Scone Palace, Broughty Ferry, **Dundee**, RIVERSIDE Dr., Tyndrum, Crianlarich, Crieff, **Perth**, Firth of Tay, The Royal & Ancient, St Andrews, Arrochar, Blair Drummond Safari Park, Gleneagles, Kinross, Cupar, Aberfoyle, Dunblane, FIFE, Glenrothes, LOCH LEVEN, Kincardine, Cowdenbeath, Kirkcaldy, North Berwick, STIRLING, Alloa, **Dunfermline**, Aberdour, Muirfield, Tantallon Castle, Helensburgh, Bannockburn, Grangemouth, Blackness Castle, Dalmeny, Leith, Haddington, Greenock, Cumbernauld, Linlithgow Palace, **Edinburgh**, LOTHIAN, LAMMERMUIR HILLS, Paisley, **Glasgow**, Motherwell, Bathgate, Livingston, **B4**, Crichton Castle, Largs, East Kilbride, Hamilton, Lanark, Biggar, Peebles, Galashiels, MOORFOOT HILLS, BORDERS, Neidpath Castle

60 kilometres
30 miles

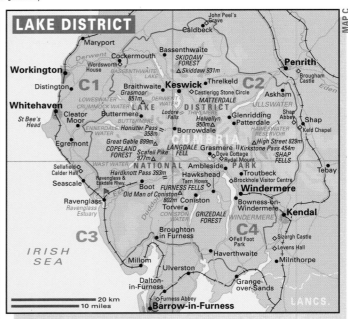

LAKE DISTRICT

John Peel's Grave, Caldbeck, Maryport, Derwent, Cockermouth, Bassenthwaite, SKIDDAW FOREST, **Penrith**, Workington, Wordsworth House, Skiddaw 931m, Threlkeld, Brougham Castle, **C1**, Distington, Braithwaite, Grasmoor 851m, **Keswick**, Castlerigg Stone Circle, Askham, **C2**, MATTERDALE, ULLSWATER, Whitehaven, St Bee's Head, Cleator Moor, Buttermere, Lodore Falls, Helvellyn 950m, Glenridding, Patterdale, Shap Abbey, Shap, Keld Chapel, Egremont, Great Gable 899m, Honister Pass 358m, Borrowdale, LANGDALE FELL, Kirkstone Pass 454m, Scafell Pike 977m, Grasmere, Rydal Mount, SHAP FELLS, Sellafield, Calder Hall, Ambleside, Troutbeck, Tebay, Seascale, Ravenglass & Eskdale Rlwy., Tarn Hows, Hawkshead, Brockhole Visitor Centre, **Windermere**, Ravenglass, Boot, FURNESS FELLS, Bowness-on-Windermere, Old Man of Coniston 802m, Coniston, Ravenglass Estuary, Torver, GRIZEDALE FOREST, **Kendal**, Sizergh Castle, Broughton in Furness, Fell Foot Park, Levens Hall, **IRISH SEA**, **C3**, Millom, Haverthwaite, Milnthorpe, Ulverston, Dalton-in-Furness, Grange-over-Sands, Furness Abbey, **Barrow-in-Furness**, LANCS.

20 km
10 miles

HEART OF ENGLAND

VALE OF TRENT, Loughborough, CHARNWOOD FOREST, STAFFS, Boscobel House, **Shrewsbury**, THE WREKIN, Telford, Lichfield, Tamworth, Welshpool, Ironbridge, CANNOCK CHASE, Drayton Manor Park, Twycross, **Leicester**, SHROPSHIRE HILLS, Severn Gorge, Walsall, The Belfry, Bosworth Field, **D2**, Montgomery, WENLOCK EDGE, Bridgnorth, **Wolverhampton**, West Bromwich, BLACK COUNTRY, Dudley, Nuneaton, THE LONG MYND, **D1**, Ludlow, WYRE FOREST, **Birmingham**, National Exhibition Centre, ELMDON, Rugby, CLUN FOREST, West Midland Safari Park, Kidderminster, **Coventry**, RADNOR FOREST, THE MARCHES, Leominster, Stourport, Royal Leamington Spa, BAGINTON, National Agricultural Centre, TEME VALLEY, Warwick, WARWICKSHIRE, NORTHANTS, Hay-on-Wye, HEREFORD & WORCESTER, **Worcester**, Ragley Hall, Charlecote Park, Stratford-upon-Avon, GOLDEN VALLEY, MALVERN HILLS, Great Malvern, Evesham, Hidcote Manor, Banbury, **Hereford**, Ledbury, VALE OF EVESHAM, Snowshill Manor, Broadway, Moreton-in-Marsh, BLACK MOUNTAINS, Ross-on-Wye, Goodrich, National Birds of Prey Centre, Tewkesbury, Cheltenham, Stow-on-the-Wold, Bourton-on-the-Water, Blenheim Palace, Abergavenny, Symond's Yat, STAVERTON, Chedworth Roman Villa, Cotswold Wildlife Park, OXFORDSHIRE, **D3**, Monmouth, FOREST OF DEAN, **Gloucester**, COTSWOLD HILLS, **D4**, Raglan Castle, WYE VALLEY, Slimbridge, Stroud, Cirencester, **Oxford**, Tintern Abbey, MON VALLEY, GLOUCESTERSHIRE, BRIZE NORTON, Thames, Chepstow, Nailsworth, Malmesbury, Abingdon, Great Coxwell Barn, Didcot, **Newport**

60 kilometres
30 miles

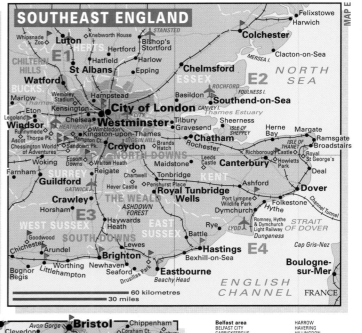

SOUTHEAST ENGLAND

Felixstowe, Harwich, STANSTED, Whipsnade Zoo, **Luton**, Knebworth House, Bishop's Stortford, **Colchester**, HERTS, Hertford, Clacton-on-Sea, CHILTERN HILLS, **E1**, Hatfield, Harlow, Epping, **Chelmsford**, MERSEA I., **E2**, NORTH SEA, **St Albans**, **Watford**, BUCKS., ESSEX, ROCHFORD, FOULNESS I., Marlow, Wembley Stadium, Hampstead, Basildon, **Southend-on-Sea**, Eton, Kensington, **City of London**, CANVEY I., Thames Estuary, Legoland, Chelsea, **Westminster**, Tilbury, Sheerness, Herne Bay, Margate, Ascot, Thorpe Pk., Kingston-upon-Thames, Gravesend, ISLE OF SHEPPEY, Ramsgate, Broadstairs, **Windsor**, Runnymede, HEATHROW, Hampton Ct., Brands Hatch, **Chatham**, ISLE OF THANET, Royal St George's, Chessington World of Adventures, **Croydon**, Rochester, **Canterbury**, Howletts Park, Deal, **Guildford**, Sandown Pk., Epsom Downs, Walton Heath, Leeds Castle, Maidstone, NORTH DOWNS, Woking, Richborough, Farnham, Reigate, Chartwell, Tonbridge, Ashford, **Dover**, **Crawley**, Hever Castle, Penshurst Place, **Royal Tunbridge Wells**, Hythe, Folkestone, Channel Tunnel, Horsham, GATWICK, THE WEALD, ASHDOWN FOREST, Romney, Hythe & Dymchurch Light Railway, Dymchurch, Port Lympne Wildlife Park, STRAIT OF DOVER, **E3**, WEST SUSSEX, Haywards Heath, SOUTH DOWNS, Rye, Dungeness, Cap Gris-Nez, Chichester, Arundel, Lewes, Battle, **Hastings**, Goodwood, KENT, EAST SUSSEX, **E4**, Bognor Regis, Littlehampton, Worthing, Newhaven, **Brighton**, Bexhill-on-Sea, **Boulogne-sur-Mer**, Seaford, **Eastbourne**, Drusillas Park, Beachy Head, **ENGLISH CHANNEL**, FRANCE

60 kilometres
30 miles

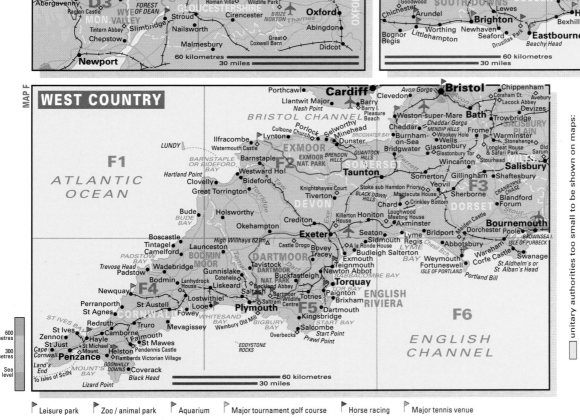

WEST COUNTRY

Porthcawl, **Cardiff**, Chippenham, Clevedon, Avon Gorge, **Bristol**, Corsham Ct., Avebury, Llantwit Major, Barry, Barry I. Pleasure Beach, Lacock Abbey, Devizes, Nash Point, **Bath**, BRISTOL CHANNEL, Weston-super-Mare, SALISBURY PLAIN, Trowbridge, Cheddar Gorge, MENDIP HILLS, Frome, Warminster, Ilfracombe, Lynton, Porlock, Selworthy, Minehead, Wookey Hole, Wells, Longleat House & Safari Park, Old Sarum, LUNDY, Watermouth Castle, Culbone Church, Dunster, EXMOOR, BRIDGWATER BAY, Burnham-on-Sea, Glastonbury, Stonehenge, Stourhead, **F1**, Barnstaple, EXMOOR NAT. PARK, BRENDON HILLS, QUANTOCK HILLS, Bridgwater, Glastonbury Tor, Wincanton, **Salisbury**, Hartland Point, Westward Ho!, Bideford, Knightshayes Court, SOMERSET, Somerton, Yeovil, Shaftesbury, CRANBORNE CHASE, Clovelly, Great Torrington, Tiverton, BLACK DOWN HILLS, Stoke sub Hamdon Priory, Montacute House, Sherborne, Blandford Forum, **F3**, ATLANTIC OCEAN, Bude, BUDE BAY, Holsworthy, Crediton, Killerton House, Honiton, Chard, Crinkley Bottom, Loughwood Meeting House, Axminster, DORSET, Boscastle, Okehampton, DEVON, Seaton, Bridport, Maiden Castle, **Bournemouth**, Tintagel, Camelford, High Willhays 621m, Castle Drogo, Bovey Tracey, A la Ronde House, Lyme Regis, Dorchester, Poole, ISLE OF PURBECK, Wadebridge, Bodmin, DARTMOOR, Budleigh Salterton, Exmouth, LYME BAY, Abbotsbury, Wareham, Corfe Castle, Swanage, **F4**, Launceston, DARTMOOR NAT. PARK, Buckfastleigh, **Exeter**, Teignmouth, Newton Abbot, Weymouth, Fortuneswell, St Aldhelm's or St Alban's Head, Newquay, Perranporth, St Agnes, Gunnislake, Lanhydrock House, Liskeard, Buckland Abbey, **Torquay**, TORBAY, BABBACOMBE BAY, Portland Bill, ISLE OF PORTLAND, St Austell, Lostwithiel, Saltash, Paignton, Brixham, ENGLISH RIVIERA, Redruth, Camborne, Truro, Mevagissey, Looe, Fowey, Dartmouth, Saltram House, Totnes, **F5**, **Plymouth**, Kingsbridge, START BAY, Zennor, St Ives, Hayle, St Michael's Mount, Helston, Wembury Old Mill, Salcombe, Overbecks, Start Point, Prawle Point, St Just, Pendennis Castle, Flambards Victorian Village, EDDYSTONE ROCKS, BIGBURY BAY, **F6**, Cape Cornwall, Land's End, To Isles of Scilly, **Penzance**, GOONHILLY DOWNS, Coverack, Black Head, Lizard Point, MOUNT'S BAY, **ENGLISH CHANNEL**

ST IVES BAY, PADSTOW BAY, TREVOSE HEAD, CORNWALL, WHITSAND BAY

600 metres
300 metres
Sea level

60 kilometres
30 miles

---

unitary authorities too small to be shown on maps:

Belfast area
BELFAST CITY
CARRICKFERGUS
CASTLEREAGH
NEWTOWNABBEY
NORTH DOWN
Birmingham and Coventry
BIRMINGHAM
COVENTRY
DUDLEY
SANDWELL
SOLIHULL
WALSALL
WOLVERHAMPTON
Bristol area
BATH AND NORTH EAST SOMERSET
BRISTOL
NORTH WEST SOMERSET
SOUTH GLOUCESTERSHIRE
Edinburgh area
EAST LOTHIAN
EDINBURGH
MIDLOTHIAN
WEST LOTHIAN
Glasgow area
DUMBARTON AND CLYDEBANK
EAST DUNBARTONSHIRE
EAST RENFREWSHIRE
GLASGOW
INVERCLYDE
NORTH LANARKSHIRE
RENFREWSHIRE
Leeds and Huddersfield
BRADFORD
CALDERDALE
KIRKLEES
LEEDS
WAKEFIELD
Liverpool area
KNOWSLEY
LIVERPOOL
ST HELENS
SEFTON
WIRRAL
Greater London
BARKING AND DAGENHAM
BARNET
BEXLEY
BRENT
BROMLEY
CAMDEN
CITY OF LONDON
CROYDON
EALING
ENFIELD
GREENWICH
HACKNEY
HAMMERSMITH AND FULHAM
HARINGEY

HARROW
HAVERING
HILLINGDON
HOUNSLOW
ISLINGTON
KENSINGTON AND CHELSEA
KINGSTON-UPON-THAMES
LAMBETH
LEWISHAM
MERTON
NEWHAM
REDBRIDGE
RICHMOND UPON THAMES
SOUTHWARK
SUTTON
TOWER HAMLETS
WALTHAM FOREST
WANDSWORTH
WESTMINSTER
Manchester area
BOLTON
BURY
MANCHESTER
OLDHAM
ROCHDALE
SALFORD
STOCKPORT
TAMESIDE
TRAFFORD
WIGAN
Middlesbrough area
HARTLEPOOL
MIDDLESBROUGH
REDCAR
STOCKTON-ON-TEES
Newcastle upon Tyne and Sunderland
GATESHEAD
NEWCASTLE UPON TYNE
NORTH TYNESIDE
SOUTH TYNESIDE
SUNDERLAND
Sheffield and Doncaster
BARNSLEY
DONCASTER
ROTHERHAM
SHEFFIELD
South Wales
BLAENAU GWENT
BRIDGEND
CAERPHILLY
CARDIFF
MERTHYR TYDFIL
MONMOUTHSHIRE
NEATH AND PORT TALBOT
NEWPORT
RHONDDA CYNON TAFF
SWANSEA
TORFAEN
VALE OF GLAMORGAN

▶ Leisure park   ▶ Zoo / animal park   ▶ Aquarium   ▶ Major tournament golf course   ▶ Horse racing   ▶ Major tennis venue

UK BEACHES AND NATIONAL PARKS

The European Blue Flag Campaign is an environmental awareness raising activity by the Foundation for Environmental Education in Europe (FEEE).

To qualify for a Blue Flag, a beach has to fulfil a number of strict criteria regarding water quality (compliance with the EU Bathing Water Directive), environment, education and information, beach area management and safety. The Blue Flag is awarded annually and is valid for one year.

38 UK resort beaches were awarded Blue Flags for 1997.

For further information, contact:

Tidy Britain Group,
Seymour House,
Muspole Street,
Norwich, NR3 1DJ.

Tel. +44 (0) 1603 766076.

Ten of the most beautiful expanses of country in England and Wales have been awarded National Park status by Parliament in recognition of their scenic importance and use for open-air recreation.

For further information, contact:

The Countryside Commission,
John Dower House,
Crescent Place,
Cheltenham, GL50 3RA.

Tel. +44 (0) 1242 521381.

The Seaside Award is awarded annually by the Tidy Britain Group to resort and rural beaches in the UK and Channel Is.

Resort beaches: busy beaches in or close to towns are assessed on 29 criteria including general cleanliness, water quality, safety provisions, beach facilities and provision for the disabled.

Rural beaches: situated in more remote locations, they are assessed on 13 similar key issues but are not expected to maintain the same standard of supervision or facilities as resort beaches.

224 beaches qualified for the Award for 1997.

1997 European Blue Flag:
○ Blue Flag beach

1997 Seaside Award:
● Resort beach
● Rural beach

Water quality results for the current season are updated weekly and are displayed at all Award beaches.

Beach character:
s Sandy
h Shingle
r Rocky
m Mud flats

Scotland
s 1 Troon South
s 2 Dornoch
sr 3 Nairn Central
s 4 Inverboyndie
s 5 Fraserburgh
s 6 Water of Philorth
s 7 Cruden Bay
s 8 Balmedie
s 9 St Andrews West Sands
s 10 Kingsbarns
s 11 Elie
sr 12 Aberdour: Silver Sands
s 13 Gullane Bents
s 14 Belhaven Bay

Northumbria
sr 15 Bamburgh
sr 16 Seahouses North: St Aidans
sr 17 Beadnell Bay
sr 18 Low Newton
s 19 Warkworth
sr 20 Amble Links
sr 21 Tynemouth: Cullercoats
s 22 Tynemouth: Longsands South
sh 23 South Shields: Sandhaven
sh 24 Whitburn North: Seaburn
sh 25 Whitburn South: Roker
sh 26 Seaton Carew: Foreshore

Yorkshire
sr 27 Runswick Bay
s 28 Sandsend
sh 29 Whitby: West Cliff
sr 30 Robin Hood's Bay
sh 31 Scarborough: North Bay
s 32 Filey
sh 33 Flamborough: South Landing
s 34 Bridlington North
s 35 Bridlington South

East Midlands
s 36 Mablethorpe Central
s 37 Skegness: Tower Esplanade

East Anglia
shm 38 Snettisham
sh 39 Heacham North
s 40 Hunstanton
s 41 Wells-next-the-Sea
h 42 Sheringham
sh 43 Cromer
s 44 Mundesley
s 45 Great Yarmouth Central
s 46 Great Yarmouth: Gorleston
s 47 Lowestoft: Gunton
s 48 Lowestoft South
s 49 Kessingland
s 50 Southwold
s 51 Sizewell
s 52 Thorpeness
s 53 Aldeburgh
s 54 Dovercourt
s 55 Brightlingsea
shm 56 Shoeburyness East
shm 57 Southend-on-Sea: Leigh Bell Wharf
s 58 Southend-on-Sea: Three Shells

South East England
shm 59 Sheerness: Beach Street
hm 60 Sheerness: Minster Leas
sm 61 Leysdown-on-Sea: Grove Ave.
s 62 Birchington: Minnis Bay
sh 63 Margate: Main Sands
sh 64 Broadstairs: Joss Bay
sh 65 Ramsgate: Main Sands
sh 66 Dymchurch
sh 67 Greatstone-on-Sea: Romney Sands
s 68 Camber
h 69 Winchelsea
h 70 Pevensey
sh 71 Pevensey Bay
sh 72 Eastbourne: Pier to Wish Tower
hr 73 Birling Gap
s 74 Cuckmere Haven
s 75 Worthing Town
s 76 Littlehampton
s 77 Bognor Regis
s 78 West Wittering

Southern England
sh 79 Hayling Island West
s 80 Hill Head
shm 81 Lepe Country Park
sh 82 Christchurch: Friar's Cliff
sh 83 Christchurch: Highcliffe Castle
s 84 Bournemouth: Fisherman's Walk
s 85 Bournemouth: Durley
s 86 Poole: Sandbanks
s 87 Swanage Central

Isle of Wight
sh 88 Totland Bay
sh 89 Colwell Bay
sh 90 Gurnard
sh 91 Cowes West
sh 92 Cowes East
sh 93 Springvale
sh 94 Seagrove Bay

sh 95 St Helens: Duver
s 96 Yaverland
s 97 Sandown
sh 98 Shanklin

West Country
sh 99 Weymouth Central
sm 100 Dawlish Warren
s 101 Dawlish: Coryton Cove
s 102 Teignmouth Town
s 103 Shaldon: Ness Cove
○ sh 104 Torquay: Oddicombe
○ s 105 Torquay: Redgate
○ h 106 Tor Bay: Meadfoot
○ s 107 Tor Bay: Corbyn Head
s 108 Tor Bay: Paignton
○ s 109 Tor Bay: Goodrington South Sands
s 110 Tor Bay: Broadsands
○ h 111 Tor Bay: Breakwater, Shoalstone
sh 112 Blackpool Sands
s 113 Strete Gate
h 114 Torcross
h 115 Beesands
sr 116 Salcombe: North Sands
s 117 Inner Hope: Hope Cove
s 118 Outer Hope: Mouthwell
s 119 Thurlestone: South Milton Sands
s 120 Bantham
s 121 Challaborough
s 122 St Austell: Porthpean
○ s 123 Sennen Cove
○ s 124 St Ives: Porthmeor Sands
○ s 125 St Ives: Porthminster
s 126 St Merryn: Treyarnon Bay
s 127 St Merryn: Constantine Bay
s 128 St Merryn: Harlyn Bay
s 129 Polzeath
shr 130 Bude: Widemouth Bay
s 131 Bude: Crooklets
shr 132 Bude: Sandymouth
s 133 Bude: Summerleaze
s 134 Croyde Bay
s 135 Woolacombe
s 136 Burnham-on-Sea
s 137 Weston-super-Mare

Wales
s 138 Southerndown
○ s 139 Porthcawl: Rest Bay
s 140 Caswell Bay
s 141 Oxwich Bay
○ s 142 Port-Eynon
s 143 Rhossili/Llangennith
s 144 Pembrey: Cefn Sidan
shr 145 Amroth
s 146 Saundersfoot: Wiseman's Bridge
s 147 Saundersfoot: Coppet Hall
○ s 148 Tenby North
s 149 Tenby South
s 150 Lydstep
s 151 Skrinkle
s 152 Manorbier
s 153 Freshwater East
s 154 Barafundle Bay
s 155 Bosherston: Broadhaven
shr 156 West Angle Bay
shr 157 Milford Haven: Gelliswick
sh 158 Dale
shr 159 Marloes
h 160 Martin's Haven
sr 161 St Brides Haven
s 162 Broad Haven
shr 163 Nolton Haven
sh 164 Newgale
s 165 St David's: Caerfai
○ s 166 St David's: Whitesands
s 167 Abereiddy
sr 168 Cwm-yr-Eglwys
s 169 Newport Sands
s 170 St Dogmaels: Poppit Sands
s 171 Mwnt
s 172 Aberporth: Traeth y Dyffryn
s 173 Tresaith
s 174 Penbryn
s 175 Llangrannog
sr 176 Llangrannog: Cilborth
s 177 Cwmtydu
s 178 New Quay: Traethgwyn
s 179 New Quay: Traeth yr Harbwr
s 180 New Quay: Traeth y Dolau
s 181 Aberaeron South
r 182 Llanrhystud
○ s 183 Aberystwyth North
s 184 Llangrawen: Clarach
s 185 Borth
○ sh 186 Tywyn
○ s 187 Fairbourne
○ s 188 Barmouth: Abermaw
s 189 Llandanwg
sh 190 Criccieth
s 191 Pwllheli: Marian y De
sh 192 Abersoch
sh 193 Aberdaron
s 194 Dinas Dinlle
s 195 Llanfairfechan
s 196 Penmaenmawr
s 197 Llandudno: North Shore
h 198 Pensarn
s 199 Rhyl
s 200 Talacre

Anglesey
s 201 Newborough: Llanddwyn
s 202 Aberffraw: Traeth Mawr
s 203 Llanfaelog: Porth Nobla
s 204 Rhosneigr: Traeth Crigyll
s 205 Holy Island: Traeth Llydan
s 206 Holy Island: Borth Wen
s 207 Holy Island: Treaddur Bay
s 208 Holy Island: Porth Dafarch
s 209 Llanfachraeth: Porth Tywyn Mawr
s 210 Cemaes Bay
s 211 Llanelian: Porth Eilian
h 212 Moelfre
s 213 Moelfre: Traeth Lligwy
s 214 Benllech
s 215 Llanddona
s 216 Beaumaris

North West
sr 217 Formby: Lifeboat Road
s 218 Ainsdale

Northern Ireland
s 219 Benone Strand
s 220 Portstewart Strand
s 221 Portrush West Bay Strand
s 222 Portrush East Bay Strand
s 223 Ballycastle
sh 224 Waterfoot
s 225 Crawfordsburn
s 226 Helen's Bay
s 227 Tyrella
sh 228 Cranfield West

Channel Islands
Guernsey
sr 229 L'Erée
s 230 Vazon Bay
s 231 Port Soif Bay
s 232 Pembre/L'Ancresse
sr 233 Portelet Bay

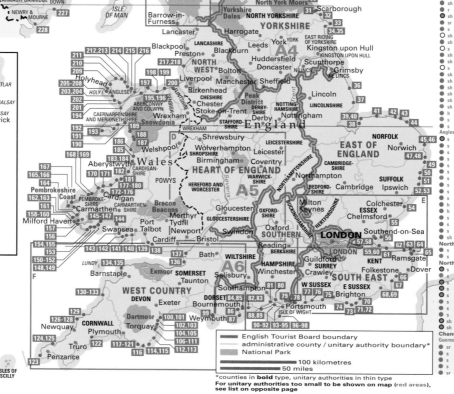

English Tourist Board boundary
administrative county / unitary authority boundary*
National Park

├─── 100 kilometres
└─── 50 miles

*counties in **bold** type, unitary authorities in thin type
For unitary authorities too small to be shown on map (red areas),
see list on opposite page

UK MOTORWAYS AND AIRPORTS

During the last few years regional UK airports have developed an international route network which supplements the London hub and this map aims to highlight the wide choice of destinations available.

All scheduled passenger flights to international destinations, licensed as at October 1997, are listed. Periods of operation or service are not indicated. Commercial or other considerations may result in services being suspended or withdrawn at short notice. Please check with the appropriate airport and/or airline to confirm details of flights. During the summer period many airlines expand their services, with charter flights and more scheduled services to holiday destinations.

Domestic routes within the UK (England, Wales, Scotland and Northern Ireland) have not been included, but flights to the Isle of Man and the Channel Islands are shown.

Where cities have more than one airport, the individual airport codes are used. For example, London city code is LON, but the airport codes are:

Biggin Hill	BQH
City	LCY
Gatwick	LGW
Heathrow	LHR
Luton	LTN
Stansted	STN

ABZ Aberdeen
Flights to six destinations

Channel Islands: Jersey	JER
France: Nice	NCE
France: Paris	CDG
Netherlands: Amsterdam	AMS
Norway: Bergen	BGO
Norway: Haugesund	HAU

BHX Birmingham
Flights to 30 destinations

Belgium: Brussels	BRU
Canada: Toronto	YYZ
Channel Islands: Guernsey	GCI
Channel Islands: Jersey	JER
Cyprus: Larnaca	LCA
Denmark: Billund	BLL
Denmark: Copenhagen	CPH
France: Lyon	LYS
France: Paris	CDG
Germany: Berlin	TXL
Germany: Düsseldorf	DUS
Germany: Frankfurt a. Main	FRA
Germany: Hannover	HAJ
Germany: Munich	MUC
Germany: Stuttgart	STR
Ireland: Cork	ORK
Ireland: Dublin	DUB
Ireland: Knock	NOC
Isle of Man	IOM
Italy: Milan	LIN
Malta	MLA
Netherlands: Amsterdam	AMS
Netherlands: Eindhoven	EIN
Spain: Barcelona	BCN
Switzerland: Basle	BSL
Switzerland: Zürich	ZRH
Turkmenistan: Ashgabat	ASB
USA: Chicago	ORD
USA: New York Newark	EWR
USA: New York JF Kennedy	JFK

BLK Blackpool
Flights to two destinations

| Channel Islands: Jersey | JER |
| Isle of Man | IOM |

BOH Bournemouth
Flights to one destination

| Ireland: Dublin | DUB |

BRS Bristol
Flights to seven destinations

Belgium: Brussels	BRU
Channel Islands: Guernsey	GCI
Channel Islands: Jersey	JER
France: Paris	CDG
Ireland: Cork	ORK
Ireland: Dublin	DUB
Netherlands: Amsterdam	AMS

BZZ Brize Norton
Flights to one destination

| Falkland Islands | MPN |

CBG Cambridge
Flights to one destination

| Netherlands: Amsterdam | AMS |

CWL Cardiff
Flights to seven destinations

Belgium: Brussels	BRU
Channel Islands: Guernsey	GCI
Channel Islands: Jersey	JER
France: Paris	CDG
Ireland: Dublin	DUB
Isle of Man	IOM
Netherlands: Amsterdam	AMS

EDI Edinburgh
Flights to 14 destinations

Belgium: Brussels	BRU
Channel Islands: Guernsey	GCI
Channel Islands: Jersey	JER
Denmark: Copenhagen	CPH
France: Nice	NCE
France: Paris	CDG
Germany: Düsseldorf	DUS
Germany: Frankfurt a. Main	FRA
Germany: Munich	MUC
Ireland: Dublin	DUB
Netherlands: Amsterdam	AMS
Spain: Palma de Mallorca	PMI
Sweden: Stockholm	ARN
Switzerland: Zürich	ZRH

EMA East Midlands
Flights to nine destinations

Belgium: Brussels	BRU
Channel Islands: Guernsey	GCI
Channel Islands: Jersey	JER
France: Nice	NCE
France: Paris	CDG
Ireland: Dublin	DUB
Netherlands: Amsterdam	AMS
Spain: Málaga	AGP
Spain: Palma de Mallorca	PMI

EXT Exeter
Flights to three destinations

Channel Islands: Guernsey	GCI
Channel Islands: Jersey	JER
Ireland: Dublin	DUB

GLA Glasgow
Flights to 18 destinations

Belgium: Brussels	BRU
Canada: Toronto	YYZ
Channel Islands: Guernsey	GCI
Channel Islands: Jersey	JER
Denmark: Copenhagen	CPH
France: Nice	NCE
France: Paris	CDG
Germany: Frankfurt a. Main	FRA
Germany: Hannover	HAJ
Ireland: Donegal	CFN
Ireland: Dublin	DUB
Isle of Man	IOM
Malta	MLA
Netherlands: Amsterdam	AMS
Spain: Palma de Mallorca	PMI
USA: Boston	BOS
USA: Chicago	ORD
USA: New York	JFK

HUY Humberside
Flights to two destinations

| Channel Islands: Jersey | JER |
| Netherlands: Amsterdam | AMS |

INV Inverness
Flights to one destination

| Netherlands: Amsterdam | AMS |

LBA Leeds / Bradford
Flights to eight destinations

Belgium: Brussels	BRU
Channel Islands: Guernsey	GCI
Channel Islands: Jersey	JER
France: Paris	CDG
Germany: Düsseldorf	DUS
Ireland: Dublin	DUB
Isle of Man	IOM
Netherlands: Amsterdam	AMS

LPL Liverpool
Flights to three destinations

Channel Islands: Jersey	JER
Ireland: Dublin	DUB
Isle of Man	IOM

MAN Manchester
Flights to 56 destinations

Austria: Vienna	VIE
Belgium: Brussels	BRU
Canada: Toronto	YYZ
Channel Islands: Guernsey	GCI
Channel Islands: Jersey	JER
China: Hong Kong	HKG
Cyprus: Larnaca	LCA
Czech Republic: Prague	PRG
Denmark: Billund	BLL
Denmark: Copenhagen	CPH
Finland: Helsinki	HEL
France: Paris	CDG
Germany: Berlin	TXL
Germany: Düsseldorf	DUS
Germany: Frankfurt a. Main	FRA
Germany: Hamburg	HAM
Germany: Hannover	HAJ
Germany: Munich	MUC
Gibraltar	GIB
India: Bombay	BOM
India: Delhi	DEL
Ireland: Cork	ORK
Ireland: Dublin	DUB
Ireland: Knock	NOC
Isle of Man	IOM
Israel: Tel Aviv-Yafo	TLV
Italy: Milan	LIN
Italy: Rome	FCO
Luxembourg	LUX
Malta	MLA
Mauritius	MRU
Netherlands: Amsterdam	AMS
Netherlands: Eindhoven	EIN
Netherlands: Rotterdam	RTM
Norway: Oslo	FBU
Pakistan: Islamabad	ISB
Pakistan: Karachi	KHI
Pakistan: Lahore	LHE
Poland: Warsaw	WAW
Portugal: Lisbon	LIS
Portugal: Oporto	OPO
Singapore	SIN
Spain: Barcelona	BCN
Spain: Madrid	MAD
Sweden: Stockholm	ARN
Switzerland: Basle	BSL
Switzerland: Geneva	GVA
Switzerland: Zürich	ZRH
Turkey: Istanbul	IST
UAE: Dubai	DXB
USA: Atlanta	ATL
USA: Chicago	CHI
USA: New York Newark	EWR
USA: New York JF Kennedy	JFK
USA: Orlando	MCO
Uzbekistan: Tashkent	TAS

MME Teesside
Flights to two destinations

| Channel Islands: Jersey | JER |
| Netherlands: Amsterdam | AMS |

NCL Newcastle
Flights to 12 destinations

Belgium: Brussels	BRU
Channel Islands: Guernsey	GCI
Channel Islands: Jersey	JER
Denmark: Copenhagen	CPH
France: Paris	CDG
Germany: Düsseldorf	DUS
Ireland: Dublin	DUB
Isle of Man	IOM
Netherlands: Amsterdam	AMS
Norway: Bergen	BGO
Norway: Oslo	FBU
Norway: Stavanger	SVG

PIK Glasgow Prestwick
Flights to two destinations

| Ireland: Dublin | DUB |
| USA: Orlando | MCO |

PLH Plymouth
Flights to four destinations

Channel Islands: Guernsey	GCI
Channel Islands: Jersey	JER
France: Paris	CDG
Ireland: Cork	ORK

SOU Southampton
Flights to seven destinations

Belgium: Brussels	BRU
Channel Islands: Alderney	ACI
Channel Islands: Guernsey	GCI
Channel Islands: Jersey	JER
France: Le Havre	LEH
France: Paris	CDG
Netherlands: Amsterdam	AMS

BFS Belfast International
Flights to five destinations

Channel Islands: Jersey	JER
France: Nice	NCE
France: Paris	CDG
Netherlands: Amsterdam	AMS
Spain: Palma de Mallorca	PMI

BHD Belfast City
Flights to four destinations

Channel Islands: Jersey	JER
France: Paris	CDG
Germany: Düsseldorf	DUS
Isle of Man	IOM

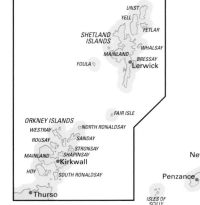

Map: UK Motorways and Airports

motorway

100 km
50 miles

LONDON AIRPORTS AND CONNECTIONS

This diagram shows principal public transport connections to London's airports from central London and links between airports.

It is not drawn to scale. Connections are shown as simple lines to improve legibility.

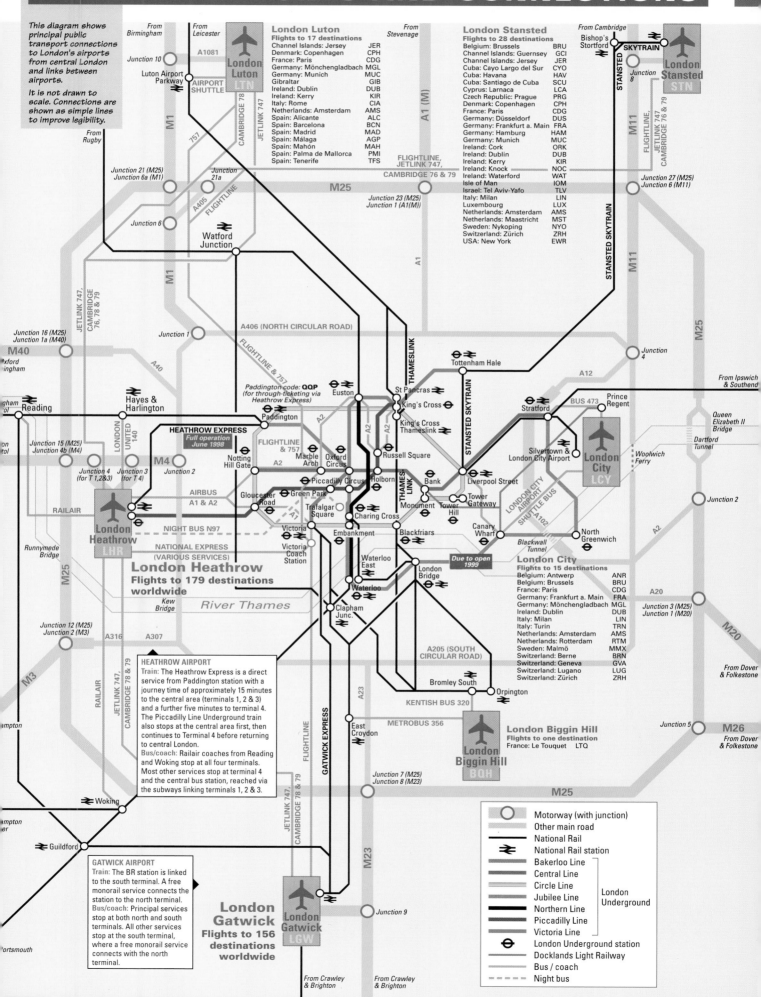

London Luton
Flights to 17 destinations

Channel Islands: Jersey	JER	
Denmark: Copenhagen	CPH	
France: Paris	CDG	
Germany: Mönchengladbach	MGL	
Germany: Munich	MUC	
Gibraltar	GIB	
Ireland: Dublin	DUB	
Ireland: Kerry	KIR	
Italy: Rome	CIA	
Netherlands: Amsterdam	AMS	
Spain: Alicante	ALC	
Spain: Barcelona	BCN	
Spain: Madrid	MAD	
Spain: Málaga	AGP	
Spain: Mahón	MAH	
Spain: Palma de Mallorca	PMI	
Spain: Tenerife	TFS	

London Stansted
Flights to 28 destinations

Belgium: Brussels	BRU
Channel Islands: Guernsey	GCI
Channel Islands: Jersey	JER
Cuba: Cayo Largo del Sur	CYO
Cuba: Havana	HAV
Cuba: Santiago de Cuba	SCU
Cyprus: Larnaca	LCA
Czech Republic: Prague	PRG
Denmark: Copenhagen	CPH
France: Paris	CDG
Germany: Düsseldorf	DUS
Germany: Frankfurt a. Main	FRA
Germany: Hamburg	HAM
Germany: Munich	MUC
Ireland: Cork	ORK
Ireland: Dublin	DUB
Ireland: Kerry	KIR
Ireland: Knock	NOC
Ireland: Waterford	WAT
Isle of Man	IOM
Israel: Tel Aviv-Yafo	TLV
Italy: Milan	LIN
Luxembourg	LUX
Netherlands: Amsterdam	AMS
Netherlands: Maastricht	MST
Sweden: Nykoping	NYO
Switzerland: Zürich	ZRH
USA: New York	EWR

London Heathrow
Flights to 179 destinations worldwide

HEATHROW AIRPORT
Train: The Heathrow Express is a direct service from Paddington station with a journey time of approximately 15 minutes to the central area (terminals 1, 2 & 3) and a further five minutes to terminal 4. The Piccadilly Line Underground train also stops at the central area first, then continues to Terminal 4 before returning to central London.
Bus/coach: Railair coaches from Reading and Woking stop at all four terminals. Most other services stop at terminal 4 and the central bus station, reached via the subways linking terminals 1, 2 & 3.

HEATHROW EXPRESS
Full operation June 1998

London City
Flights to 15 destinations

Belgium: Antwerp	ANR
Belgium: Brussels	BRU
France: Paris	CDG
Germany: Frankfurt a. Main	FRA
Germany: Mönchengladbach	MGL
Ireland: Dublin	DUB
Italy: Milan	LIN
Italy: Turin	TRN
Netherlands: Amsterdam	AMS
Netherlands: Rotterdam	RTM
Sweden: Malmö	MMX
Switzerland: Berne	BRN
Switzerland: Geneva	GVA
Switzerland: Lugano	LUG
Switzerland: Zürich	ZRH

London Biggin Hill
Flights to one destination
France: Le Touquet   LTQ

GATWICK AIRPORT
Train: The BR station is linked to the south terminal. A free monorail service connects the station to the north terminal.
Bus/coach: Principal services stop at both north and south terminals. All other services stop at the south terminal, where a free monorail service connects with the north terminal.

London Gatwick
Flights to 156 destinations worldwide

Paddington code: **QQP**
(for through-ticketing via Heathrow Express)

Due to open 1999

Legend

Motorway (with junction)	
Other main road	
National Rail	
National Rail station	
Bakerloo Line	
Central Line	
Circle Line	London
Jubilee Line	Underground
Northern Line	
Piccadilly Line	
Victoria Line	
London Underground station	
Docklands Light Railway	
Bus / coach	
Night bus	

UK FERRIES

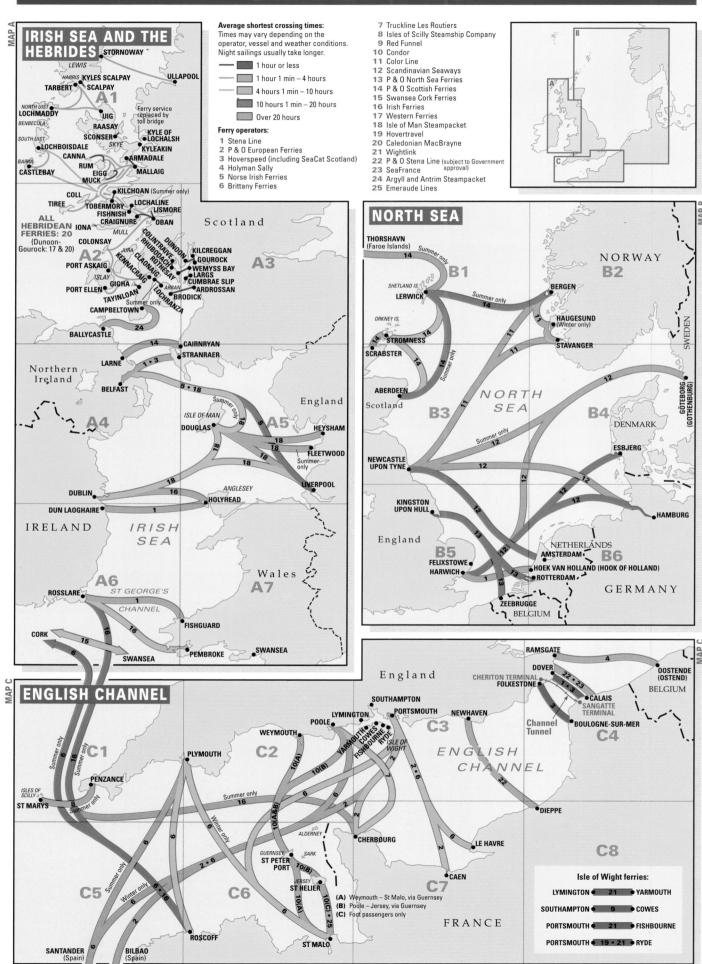

IRISH SEA AND THE HEBRIDES

STORNOWAY
LEWIS
HARRIS KYLES SCALPAY
TARBERT SCALPAY
ULLAPOOL
NORTH UIST
LOCHMADDY UIG
BENBECULA RAASAY
SOUTH UIST SCONSER
KYLE OF LOCHALSH
LOCHBOISDALE SKYE
KYLEAKIN
Ferry service replaced by toll bridge
BARRA CANNA
RUM ARMADALE
CASTLEBAY EIGG MALLAIG
MUCK
COLL KILCHOAN (Summer only)
TIREE TOBERMORY LOCHALINE
FISHNISH LISMORE
ALL HEBRIDEAN FERRIES: 20 CRAIGNURE OBAN
(Dunoon-Gourock: 17 & 20) IONA MULL
COLONSAY DUNOON
COLINTRAIVE KILCREGGAN
RHUBODACH GOUROCK
PORT ASKAIG JURA CLADNAIG ROTHESAY WEMYSS BAY
ISLAY KENNACRAIG LARGS
GIGHA CUMBRAE SLIP
PORT ELLEN TAYINLOAN ARRAN ARDROSSAN
LOCHRANZA BRODICK
CAMPBELTOWN Summer only
24
BALLYCASTLE CAIRNRYAN
14 STRANRAER
Northern Ireland LARNE
1 • 3
BELFAST
5 • 18
A4 Summer only
ISLE OF MAN HEYSHAM
DOUGLAS 18
18 FLEETWOOD
18 18 Summer only
18
DUBLIN 18 LIVERPOOL
16 ANGLESEY
DUN LAOGHAIRE HOLYHEAD
1
IRELAND IRISH SEA Wales

Scotland

A1 A2 A3 A5 A6 A7

England

ROSSLARE
ST GEORGE'S CHANNEL
1
CORK 16 16
15 FISHGUARD
6
SWANSEA PEMBROKE SWANSEA

Average shortest crossing times:
Times may vary depending on the operator, vessel and weather conditions. Night sailings usually take longer.

— 1 hour or less
— 1 hour 1 min – 4 hours
— 4 hours 1 min – 10 hours
— 10 hours 1 min – 20 hours
— Over 20 hours

Ferry operators:
1 Stena Line
2 P & O European Ferries
3 Hoverspeed (including SeaCat Scotland)
4 Holyman Sally
5 Norse Irish Ferries
6 Brittany Ferries
7 Truckline Les Routiers
8 Isles of Scilly Steamship Company
9 Red Funnel
10 Condor
11 Color Line
12 Scandinavian Seaways
13 P & O North Sea Ferries
14 P & O Scottish Ferries
15 Swansea Cork Ferries
16 Irish Ferries
17 Western Ferries
18 Isle of Man Steampacket
19 Hovertravel
20 Caledonian MacBrayne
21 Wightlink
22 P & O Stena Line (subject to Government approval)
23 SeaFrance
24 Argyll and Antrim Steampacket
25 Emeraude Lines

NORTH SEA

THORSHAVN (Faroe Islands) Summer only
14
SHETLAND IS. Summer only
LERWICK 14
ORKNEY IS. 11
STROMNESS 14 HAUGESUND (Winter only)
SCRABSTER 14 Summer only STAVANGER
14 14
ABERDEEN 14
Scotland 11
B3 NORTH SEA
11 12
Summer only
12
NEWCASTLE UPON TYNE 12 12
12 12
KINGSTON UPON HULL 12 12
12
England 12 13
FELIXSTOWE NETHERLANDS
HARWICH AMSTERDAM B6
1 HOEK VAN HOLLAND (HOOK OF HOLLAND)
13 ROTTERDAM
ZEEBRUGGE GERMANY
BELGIUM

NORWAY
B1 B2
BERGEN
HAUGESUND
STAVANGER
B4
DENMARK
ESBJERG
HAMBURG
B5

GÖTEBORG (GOTHENBURG) SWEDEN

ENGLISH CHANNEL

England
RAMSGATE 4
DOVER 22 • 23
CHERITON TERMINAL 1 • 3 OOSTENDE (OSTEND)
FOLKESTONE 3 CALAIS BELGIUM
SANGATTE TERMINAL
Channel Tunnel BOULOGNE-SUR-MER C4
SOUTHAMPTON
LYMINGTON PORTSMOUTH NEWHAVEN C3
POOLE
WEYMOUTH YARMOUTH COWES RYDE
FISHBOURNE ISLE OF WIGHT
PLYMOUTH 2 ENGLISH CHANNEL
C2 10(A) 7 2 • 6 22
10(B) 2
Summer only 16 2 DIEPPE
ISLES OF SCILLY 8 2
ST MARYS PENZANCE 6 CHERBOURG 6 LE HAVRE
Summer only 10(A&B) 2
6 Winter only 6 2
C5 ALDERNEY CAEN
Summer only GUERNSEY SARK C7
Winter only ST PETER PORT 10(B)
6 • 16 JERSEY
2 • 6 ST HELIER
2 10(A) 10(C) • 25
ROSCOFF ST MALO
SANTANDER (Spain) BILBAO (Spain) FRANCE
6 6

C1 C6 C8

(A) Weymouth – St Malo, via Guernsey
(B) Poole – Jersey, via Guernsey
(C) Foot passengers only

Isle of Wight ferries:
LYMINGTON ●—21—● YARMOUTH
SOUTHAMPTON ●—9—● COWES
PORTSMOUTH ●—21—● FISHBOURNE
PORTSMOUTH ●—19 • 21—● RYDE

IRELAND

See page 7 for general map

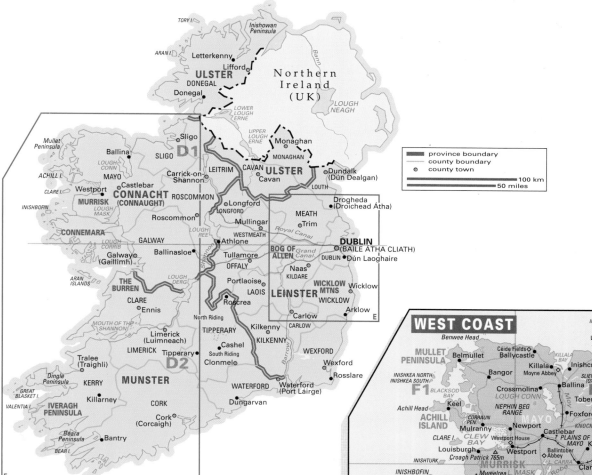

WEST COAST

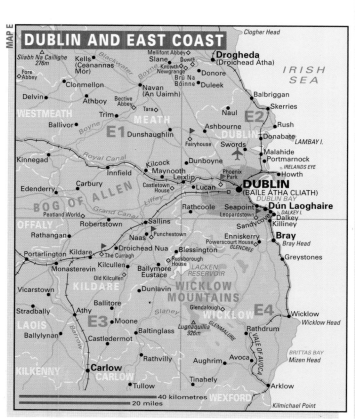

DUBLIN AND EAST COAST

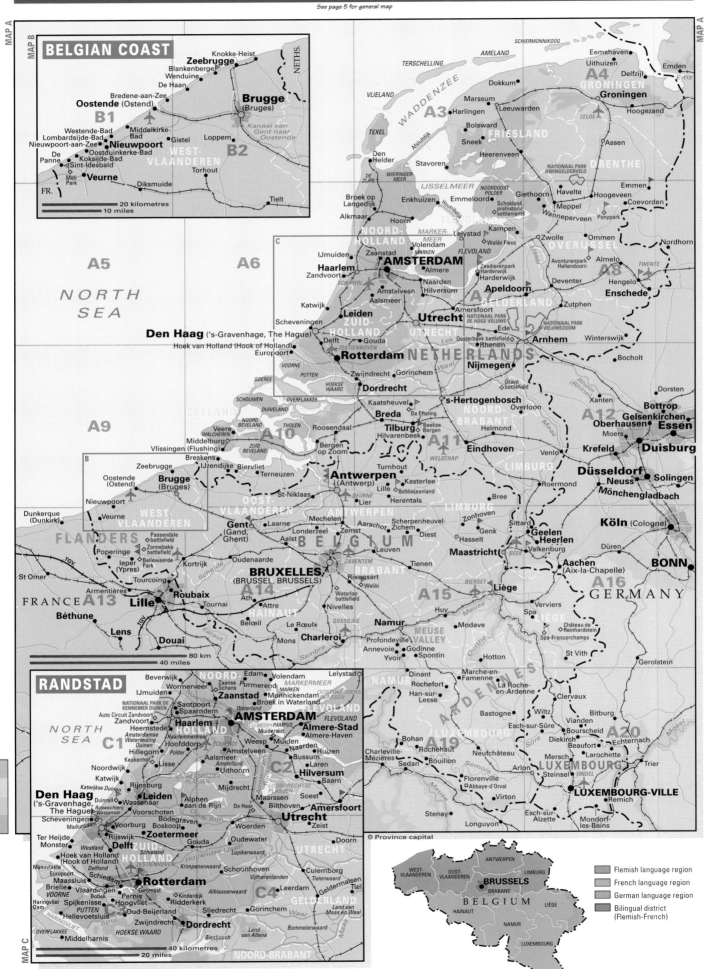

BENELUX

See page 5 for general map

BELGIUM   **NETHERLANDS**   **LUXEMBOURG**

BELGIAN COAST

Knokke-Heist
Zeebrugge
Blankenberge
Wenduine
De Haan
Bredene-aan-Zee
Oostende (Ostend)
Brugge (Bruges)
Middelkirke-Bad
Gistel
Loppem
Westende-Bad
Lombardsijde-Bad
Nieuwpoort-aan-Zee
Nieuwpoort
Oostduinkerke-Bad
De Panne
Koksijde-Bad
Sint-Idesbald
WEST-VLAANDEREN
Torhout
Veurne
Meli Park
Diksmuide
Tielt

20 kilometres
10 miles

MAP A **MAP A** **MAP B**

NETHS.

SCHIERMONNIKOOG
AMELAND
TERSCHELLING
Eemshaven
Uithuizen
Delfzijl
Emden
Emden
VLIELAND
Dokkum
Marssum
GRONINGEN
Groningen
Hoogezand
WADDENZEE
Harlingen
Leeuwarden
TEXEL
Bolsward
Sneek
FRIESLAND
Heerenveen
EELDE
Assen
DRENTHE
Den Helder
Stavoren
NATIONAAL PARK
DWINGELDERVELD
Emmen
DE ZIJPE
WIERINGER-
MEER
IJSSELMEER
Meppel
Hoogeveen
Coevorden
Broek op
Langedijk
Enkhuizen
Emmeloord
NOORDOOST
POLDER
Giethoorn
Havelte
Wanneperveen
Nordhorn
Alkmaar
Hoorn
Kampen
Zwolle
Ommen
Schokland prehistoric
settlements
Ponypark
NOORD-
HOLLAND
Volendam
Zaanstad
MARKER-
MEER
Lelystad
Walibi Flevo
OVERIJSSEL
A5 **A6**
AMSTERDAM
Almere
FLEVOLAND
Zeedierenpark
Harderwijk
Avonturenpark
Hellendoorn
Almelo
A8
IJmuiden
Zaandstad
TWENTE
Haarlem
Zandvoort
SCHIPHOL
Naarden
Hilversum
Apeldoorn
Deventer
Hengelo
Enschede
Amstelveen
Aalsmeer
GELDERLAND
Zutphen
NORTH
SEA
Katwijk
A7
Amersfoort
NATIONAAL PARK
DE HOGE VELUWE
Scheveningen
Leiden
UTRECHT
Ede
Oosterbeek battlefield
NATIONAAL PARK
VELUWEZOOM
A9
Utrecht
Rhenen
Arnhem
Winterswijk
Den Haag ('s-Gravenhage, The Hague)
Delft
Gouda
Lek
IJssel
Hoek van Holland (Hook of Holland)
Europoort
NETHERLANDS
Rotterdam
Nijmegen
Bocholt
VOORNE
PUTTEN
Zwijndrecht
Gorinchem
Grave
battlefield
Rhein (Rhine)
Dorsten
HOEKSE
WAARD
Dordrecht
A12
GOEREE
SCHOUWEN
OVERFLAKKEE
DUIVELAND
Kaatsheuvel
s-Hertogenbosch
Overloon
Xanten
Bottrop
Gelsenkirchen
ZEELAND
Veere
NOORD
BEVELAND
THOLEN
Roosendaal
Breda
De Efteling
NOORD-
BRABANT
Helmond
Moers
Oberhausen
Essen
WALCHEREN
Tilburg
Beekse
Bergen
Maas
A11
Venlo
Krefeld
Duisburg
Middelburg
ZUID
BEVELAND
Bergen
op Zoom
Hilvarenbeek
Eindhoven
WELSCHAP
Düsseldorf
Solingen
Vlissingen (Flushing)
Breskens
IJzendijke
Biervliet
Turnhout
Kasterlee
Lille
Bobbejaanland
Herentals
Roermond
Bree
LIMBURG
Neuss
Mönchengladbach
Zeebrugge
Brugge (Bruges)
Terneuzen
Antwerpen (Antwerp)
DEURNE
A10
Köln (Cologne)
Oostende (Ostend)
Nieuwpoort
St-Niklaas
Lier
Zonhoven
Genk
Sittard
Veurne
WEST-VLAANDEREN
OOST-VLAANDEREN
ANTWERPEN
Aarschot
Scherpenheuvel-
Zichem
Hasselt
Geleen
Heerlen
Düren
Dunkerque (Dunkirk)
Mechelen
LIMBURG
Valkenburg
Aachen (Aix-la-Chapelle)
FLANDERS
Passchendaele
battlefield
Gent (Gand, Ghent)
Laarne
Londerzeel
Zemst
Diest
Maastricht
BEER
BONN
Poperinge
Zonnebeke
battlefield
Bellewaerde
Park
Oudenaarde
Aalst
BRABANT
Leuven
Tienen
Ieper (Ypres)
Kortrijk
ZAVENTEM
GERMANY
St Omer
Tourcoing
BRUXELLES (BRUSSEL, BRUSSELS)
Rixensart
Walibi
BIERSET
Spa
Verviers
A13
Armentières
Roubaix
A14
Ath
Attre
Waterloo
battlefield
Nivelles
A15
Liège
Château de
Reinhardstein
Spa-Francorchamps
France
Lille
Tournai
Beloeil
Le Rœulx
GOSSELIES
Huy
Modave
LIÈGE
St Vith
Béthune
HAINAUT
Namur
Profondeville
Meuse
Gerolstein
Lens
Mons
Charleroi
Annevoie
Godinne
Spontin
MEUSE
VALLEY
Hotton
Douai
Sambre
Yvoir
Ourthe
Amblève
80 km
40 miles

RANDSTAD

NOORD-
Edam
Volendam
Lelystad
Beverwijk
Wormerveer
Purmerend
MARKERMEER
NAMUR
Dinant
Rochefort
Marche-en-
Famenne
La Roche-
en-Ardenne
Clervaux
IJmuiden
Zaanse
Schans
Monnickendam
Broek in Waterland
OOSTVAARDERS
PLASSEN
Han-sur-
Lesse
Bastogne
Wiltz
Bitburg
Zaanstad
Waterland
FLEVOLAND
Vianden
Auto Circuit
Kennemerduin
Santpoort
Spaarndam
AMSTERDAM
Muiderslot
Esch-sur-Sûre
Bourscheid
NATIONAAL PARK
DE KENNEMER DUINEN
Hoofddorp
PAMPUS
Almere-Stad
Bohan
Rochehaut
Neufchâteau
Beaufort
Diekirch
Echternach
NORTH
SEA
Zandvoort
Heemstede
Haarlem
Amsterdamse
Waterleiding
Duinen
Polder
Weesp
Muiden
Almere-Haven
C1
Naarden
Bussum
Charleville-
Mézières
Sedan
Bouillon
LUXEMBOURG
Mersch
Larochette
Hillegom
Keukenhof
Amstelveen
Uithoorn
Hilversum
Laren
Arlon
LUXEMBOURG
Trier
Noordwijk
Lisse
Aalsmeer
WESTEINDER
PLASSEN
Baarn
Florenville
Abbaye-d'Orval
Steinsel
FINDEL
Katwijk
Rijnsburg
Mijdrecht
LOOSDRECHTSE
PLASSEN
Amersfoort
Virton
LUXEMBOURG-VILLE
Remich
Den Haag ('s-Gravenhage, The Hague)
Leiden
Alphen aan de Rijn
Maarssen
Soest
Bilthoven
Stenay
Longuyon
Esch-sur-
Alzette
Mondorf-
les-Bains
Scheveningen
Madurodam
Voorschoten
Duinrell
Wassenaar
Boswachterij
Wassenaar
De Haar
Utrecht
Zeist
Ter Heijde
Monster
Rijswijk
Voorburg
Bodegraven
Boskoop
Woerden
Oudewater
Doorn
© Province capital
Westland
Zoetermeer
Delft
Gouda
ZUID-
HOLLAND
Schieland
Lopikerwaard
Hollandse IJssel
UTRECHT
Hoek van Holland (Hook of Holland)
ZESTIENHOVEN
C4
Schoonhoven
Vijfherenlanden
Culemborg
Maasvlakte
Europoort
Schiedam
Rotterdam
Euromast
Kinderdijk
Vlaardingen
Pernis
Hoogvliet
Ridderkerk
Krimpenerwaard
GELDERLAND
Leerdam
Gelderr malsen
Tiel
Maassluis
Brielle
Vlaardingen
Sliedrecht
Alblasserwaard
Haringvliet
Dam
Spijkenisse
Oud-Beijerland
Zwijndrecht
Gorinchem
Land van Maas en Waal
Bommelerwaard
Hellevoetsluis
VOORNE
PUTTEN
HOEKSE WAARD
Dordrecht
Biesbosch
Land
van Altena
Waal
OVERFLAKKEE
Middelharnis
40 kilometres
20 miles

400
metres
200
metres
Sea
level

MAP C

NOORD-BRABANT

◆ Leisure park   ▲ Zoo / animal park   ▲ Aquarium   ◆ Formula One   ■ Major tennis venue

WEST-
VLAANDEREN
ANTWERPEN
LIMBURG
OOST-
VLAANDEREN
BRUSSELS
BRABANT
BELGIUM
HAINAUT
LIÈGE
NAMUR
LUXEMBOURG

Flemish language region
French language region
German language region
Bilingual district (Flemish-French)

GERMANY

See pages 8-9 for general map

Land boundary
● Land capital

100 km
50 miles

RUHRGEBIET

MAP E

30 km
15 miles

BERLIN

MAP F

20 km
10 miles

1000 metres
500 metres
Sea level

▶ Leisure park   ▶ Zoo / animal park   ▶ Aquarium   ▶ Major tennis venue

GERMANY

See pages 8-9 for general map

Germany has a well-developed network of tourist routes passing through areas of scenic or historic interest. Some of the most well-known are:

Romantische Straße (Romantic Road). Established in 1950, it runs for 350 kilometres from northern Bavaria to the Bavarian Alps. See panel for the route.

Straße der Kaiser und Könige (Route of Emperors and Kings). One of Germany's oldest transit routes, running from Frankfurt am Main in the west, following the Main and Danube rivers, to Passau on the Austrian border and continuing to Vienna.

Weinstraße (Wine Road). Germany's oldest designated tourist route, passing through vineyards of the Pfalz.

Mosel Weinstraße (Mosel Wine Road). Follows the Mosel from Trier to Koblenz. Boat cruises are popular along this stretch of river.

Deutsche Märchenstraße (German Fairy-Tale Road). This route runs from Bremen to the River Main through many places connected with fairy tales.

Burgenstraße (Castle Road). Passes many fortifications in the Neckar valley between Mannheim and Heilbronn, then continues east to Nuremburg.

Schwarzwald-Hochstraße (Black Forest Highway). One of Germany's most famous roads, linking Baden-Baden with Freudenstadt.

ROMANTIC ROAD

- **Würzburg**
- Tauberbischofsheim
- Bad Mergentheim
- Weikersheim
- Röttingen
- Creglingen
- **Rothenburg ob der Tauber**
- Schillingsfürst
- Feuchtwangen
- Dinkelsbühl
- Wallerstein
- **Nördlingen im Ries**
- Harburg
- **Donauwörth**
- **Augsburg**
- Friedberg
- **Landsberg am Lech**
- Hohenfurch
- Schongau
- Peiting
- Rottenbuch
- Wildsteig
- Wieskirche
- Steingaden
- Schwangau
- **Füssen**

Diagrammatic only: not to scale

RHINE AND BLACK FOREST

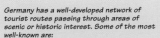

RHINE GORGE AND MOSEL

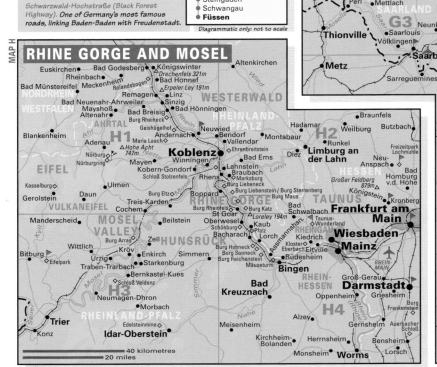

40 kilometres
20 miles

80 km
40 miles

SOUTHERN BAVARIA

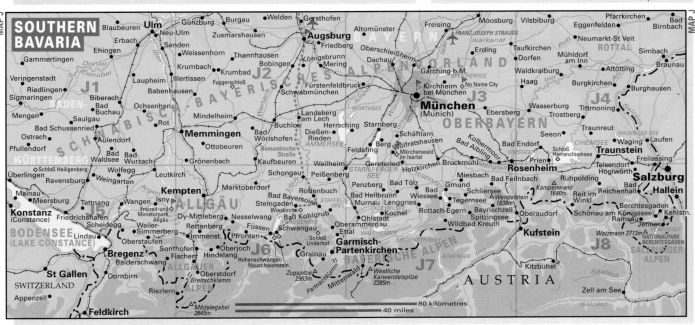

80 kilometres
40 miles

1000 metres
500 metres
Sea level

▶ Leisure park   ▶ Zoo / animal park   ▶ Aquarium   ▶ Formula One   ▶ Major tennis venue

GERMAN SPAS

Spa holidays are first and foremost to improve or restore one's health, but patients also have a chance to meet people and get to know a different culture. There are nearly 400 recognised spa institutions in Germany which are grouped according to the requirements shown on this page.

For further information, contact:

Deutscher Bäderverband e.V.
Schumannstraße 111, D-53113 Bonn.
Tel. +49 (0) 228 262010

All registered spas satisfy a number of basic criteria regarding the treatment facilities (including facilities for treating specific conditions); scientific assessment of the main treatment areas and contraindications (with the exception of seaside spas); suitability of climate and good air quality.

The spas are categorised as follows, depending on the following points. Some spas of the same type have been grouped together.

- **Spa**
- **Seaside spa** (located within 2 kilometres of the seashore)
- **Seaside health spa** (located within 2 km of the seashore and scientific proof of a therapeutically suitable climate)
- ☐ **Kneipp health spa** (scientific proof of a therapeutically suitable climate)
- ☐ **Kneipp spa** (ten years of establishment as a Kneipp health spa with no complaints during that period)
- **Climatic spa** (scientific proof of a therapeutically suitable climate which is constantly monitored by meteorological stations and scientific proof of a specific air quality)
- **Town with spa facilities**

Schleswig-Holstein
1 Helgoland
2 Sylt: Hörnum / Kampen / Keitum (Sylt-Ost) / List / Rantum
2 Sylt: Wenningstedt / Westerland
3 Amrum: Nebel / Norddorf / Wittdün
4 Föhr: Nieblum / Utersum / Wyk
5 Pellworm
6 Nordstrand
7 St Peter Ording
8 Büsum
9 Friedrichskoog
10 Glücksburg
11 Gelting
12 Schönhagen
13 Damp
14 Eckernförde
15 Strande
16 Heikendorf
17 Laboe
18 Schönberg
19 Hohwacht
20 Weißenhaus
21 Heiligenhafen
22 Burg
23 Großenbrode
24 Dahme / Kellenhusen
25 Grömitz
26 Neustadt / Sierksdorf
27 Scharbeutz-Haffkrug
28 Timmendorf-Niendorf
29 Travemünde
30 Bad Schwartau
31 Bad Malente-Gremsmühlen
32 Eutin
33 Bad Bramstedt
34 Bad Segeberg
35 Mölln

Niedersachsen
36 Borkum
37 Juist
38 Norderney
39 Baltrum
40 Langeoog
41 Spiekeroog
42 Wangerooge
43 Norden
44 Dornum: Dornumersiel / Neßmersiel
45 Esens-Bensersiel
46 Neuharlingersiel
47 Carolinensiel
48 Horumersiel
49 Wilhelmshaven
50 Dangast
51 Bad Zwischenahn
52 Butjadingen: Burhave / Eckwarden / Tossens
53 Wursten: Dorum / Wremen
54 Cuxhaven
55 Neuhaus
56 Bad Bederkesa
57 Lüneburg
58 Bad Bevensen
59 Bodenteich
60 Soltau
61 Fallingbostel
62 Blenhorst
63 Bad Bentheim
64 Bad Iburg
65 Bad Laer / Bad Rothenfelde
66 Melle
67 Bad Essen
68 Bad Eilsen
69 Bad Nenndorf
70 Bad Münder
71 Bad Pyrmont
72 Salzhemmendorf
73 Bad Salzdetfurth
74 Bad Gandersheim
75 Bad Grund
76 Salzgitter-Bad

77 Hahnenklee
78 Bad Harzburg
79 Oberharz: Altenau / Buntenbock / Clausthal-Zellerfeld / Schulenberg / Wildemann
80 St Andreasberg / Braunlage
81 Hohegeiß / Wieda
82 Bad Lauterberg
83 Bad Sachsa

Nordrhein-Westfalen
84 Steinbeck
85 Randringhausen / Hüllhorst
86 Preußisch-Oldendorf
87 Levern
88 Rothenuffeln
89 Hopfenberg
90 Minden
91 Porta Westfalica
92 Vlotho: Bad Seebruch / Bad Senkelteich
93 Bad Salzuflen
94 Bad Oeynhausen / Wulferdingsen
95 Hiddesen
96 Bad Lippspringe
97 Bad Meinberg
98 Schieder
99 Bad Driburg / Bad Hermannsborn
100 Bruchhausen
101 Germete
102 Wünnenberg
103 Westernkotten
104 Bad Sassendorf
105 Bad Waldliesborn
106 Hamm
107 Ennepetal
108 Olsberg
109 Winterberg
110 Bad Fredeburg
111 Bad Berleburg
112 Bad Laasphe
113 Eckenhagen
114 Nümbrecht
115 Bad Honnef
116 Bad Münstereifel
117 Gemünd
118 Aachen

Hessen
119 Bad Karlshafen
120 Willingen: Usseln / Schwalefeld
121 Arolsen
122 Naumburg
123 Kassel-Wilhelmshöhe
124 Bad Emstal
125 Bad Wildungen
126 Bad Zwesten
127 Gladenbach
128 Bad Endbach
129 Witzenhausen
130 Bad Sooden
131 Bad Hersfeld
132 Neukirchen
133 Gersfeld
134 Bad Salzschlirf
135 Herbstein
136 Bad Soden-Salmünster
137 Bad Orb
138 Bad Salzhausen
139 Bad Nauheim
140 Bad Camberg
141 Schlangenbad / Bad Schwalbach
142 Wiesbaden
143 Königstein
144 Bad Soden
145 Bad Homburg
146 Bad Vilbel
147 Bad König
148 Lindenfels
149 Grasellenbach

Rheinland-Pfalz
150 Bodendorf / Bad Breisig / Bad Neuenahr
151 Bad Hönningen
152 Rengsdorf / Ehlscheid
153 Bad Marienberg
154 Vallendar
155 Bad Ems / Lahnstein
156 Boppard
157 Bad Bertrich
158 Daun
159 Kyllburg
160 Manderscheid
161 Traben-Trarbach
162 Bad Sobernheim
163 Bad Münster am Stein
164 Bad Kreuznach
165 Bad Dürkheim
166 Bad Bergzabern

Saarland
167 Weiskirchen
168 Nonnweiler
169 Blieskastel

Baden-Württemberg
170 Eberbach
171 Bad Mergentheim
172 Bad Schönborn
173 Bad Rappenau / Bad Wimpfen
174 Schwäbisch Hall
175 Hoheneck
176 Stuttgart: St Berg / St Bad Cannstadt / Leutze
177 Bad Liebenzell
178 Schömberg
179 Waldbronn
180 Dobel / Bad Herrenalb
181 Baden-Baden / Gaggenau
182 Bad Teinach
183 Bad Wildbad
184 Sasbachwalden
185 Baiersbronn
186 Freudenstadt
187 Bad Peterstal
188 Bad Rippoldsau
189 Bad Imnau
190 Bad Niedernau
191 Sebastiansweiler
192 Beuren / Bad Urach
193 Bad Boll
194 Bad Ditzenbach / Bad Überkingen
195 Freiburg im Breisgau
196 Waldkirch
197 Schönwald / Triberg
198 Königsfeld
199 Villingen
200 Bad Dürrheim
201 Bad Krozingen
202 Badenweiler
203 Bad Bellingen
204 Bad Säckingen
205 Todtmoos
206 St Blasien
207 Höchenschwand
208 Schluchsee
209 Hinterzarten / Lenzkirch / Titisee
210 Friedenweiler
211 Radolfzell
212 Überlingen
213 Aulendorf
214 Bad Buchau / Saulgau
215 Biberach-Jordanbad
216 Bad Schussenried / Bad Waldsee
217 Bad Wurzach
218 Isny

Bayern
219 Bad Brückenau
220 Bad Bocklet / Bad Kissingen
221 Bad Neustadt
222 Bad Königshofen
223 Rodach

224 Staffelstein
225 Bad Steben
226 Bad Berneck
227 Bischofsgrün
228 Bad Alexandersbad
229 Bad Windsheim
230 Bad Gögging
231 Bad Abbach
232 Kötzting
233 Bodenmais
234 Krumbad
235 Bad Wörishofen
236 Ottobeuren
237 Grönenbach
238 Weiler-Simmerberg
239 Scheidegg
240 Oberstaufen
241 Fischen
242 Oberstdorf
243 Hindelang
244 Füssen: Bad Faulenberg / Hopfen am See / Weißensee
245 Schwangau
246 Garmisch-Partenkirchen
247 Oy-Mittelberg
248 Bad Bayersoien
249 Bad Kohlgrub
250 Murnau
251 Bad Heilbrunn
252 Bad Tölz
253 Bad Wiessee
254 Bad Aibling
255 Bad Endorf
256 Prien
257 Wildbad
258 Rottach-Egern / Tegernsee
259 Bayrischzell
260 Bad Feilnbach
261 Bad Reichenhall: Bayerisch Gmain / Karlstein-Nonn
262 Berchtesgaden: Bischofswiesen / Königssee / Markschellenberg / Oberau / Ramsau / Schönau
263 Bad Birnbach / Bad Griesbach
264 Bad Füssing
265 Kellberg

Mecklenburg-Vorpommern
266 Boltenhagen
267 Rerik
268 Kühlungsborn
269 Heiligendamm
270 Nienhagen / Warnemünde
271 Bad Doberan
272 Bad Sülze
273 Graal-Müritz
274 Dierhagen
275 Ahrenshoop / Wustrow
276 Prerow
277 Zingst
278 Hiddensee: Grieben / Neuendorf / Plogshagen / Vitte
279 Rügen: Binz
280 Rügen: Baabe / Göhren / Sellin
281 Rügen: Thießow
282 Lubmin
283 Usedom: Zempin / Zinnowitz
284 Usedom: Kölpinsee / Koserow / Ückeritz
285 Usedom: Ahlbeck / Bansin / Heringsdorf
286 Kurort Krakow am See

Brandenburg
287 Bad Wilsnack
288 Bad Freienwalde
289 Buckow
290 Bad Saarow
291 Bad Liebenwerda

Sachsen-Anhalt
292 Bad Schmiedeberg
293 Salzelmen
294 Blankenburg
295 Bad Suderode
296 Bad Kösen

Thüringen
297 Heilbad Heiligenstadt
298 Bad Frankenhausen
299 Bad Tennstedt
300 Bad Langensalza
301 Tabarz
302 Friedrichroda
303 Bad Liebenstein
304 Bad Salzungen
305 Bad Colberg
306 Stützerbach
307 Masserberg
308 Moorbad Lobenstein
309 Bad Berka
310 Bad Sulza
311 Bad Klosterlausnitz

Sachsen
312 Bad Düben
313 Bad Lausick
314 Schlema
315 Bad Elster
316 Bad Brambach
317 Kurort Oberwiesenthal
318 Bad Gottleuba
319 Berggießhübel
320 Bad Schandau
321 Bad Muskau

Land boundary

100 km
50 miles

FRANCE

See page 10 for general map

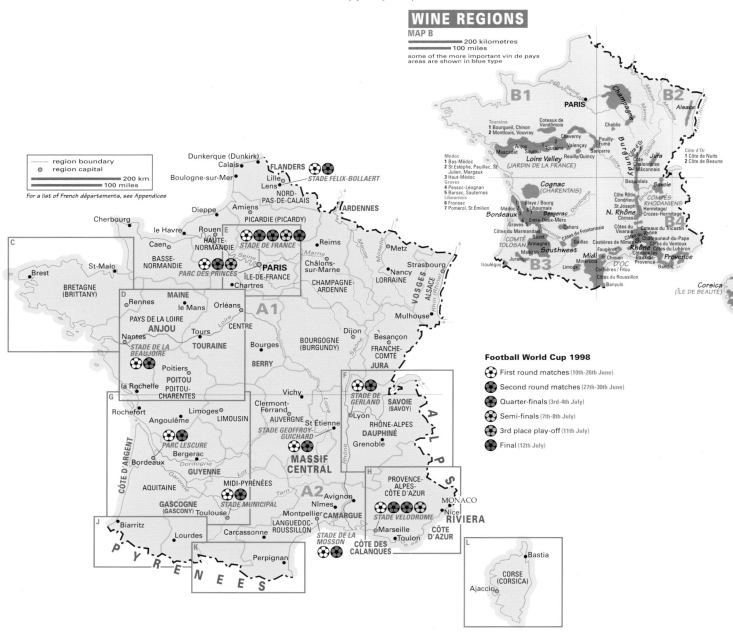

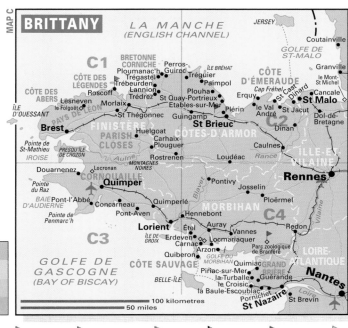

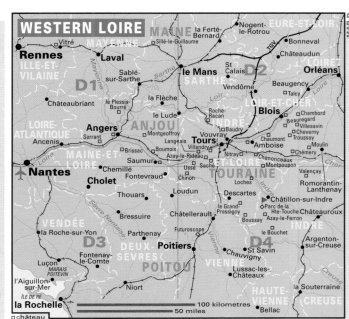

FRANCE

See page 10 for general map

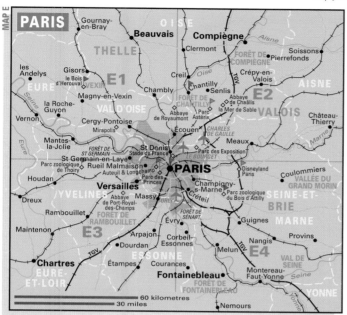

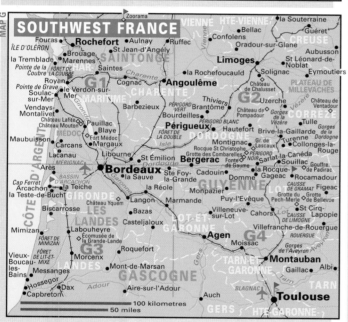

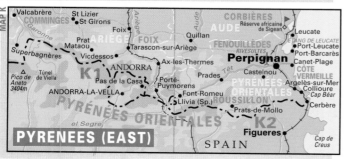

▶ Leisure park   ▶ Zoo / animal park   ▶ Aquarium   ▶ Formula One   ▶ Horse racing   ▶ Major tennis venue

SPAIN

See page 11 for general map

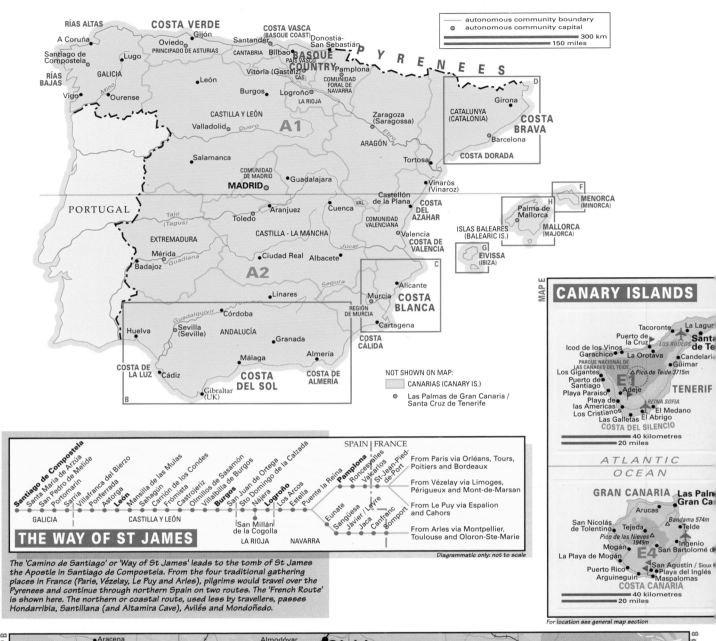

SPAIN

See page 11 for general map

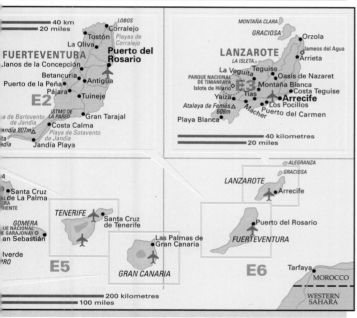

▷ Leisure park   ▷ Zoo / animal park   ▷ Aquarium   ▷ Formula One   ▷ Major tournament golf course   ▷ Major tennis venue

PORTUGAL

See page 11 for general map

district boundary
○ district capital
100 km
50 miles

COSTA VERDE
SERRA DA PENEDA
Monção
Viana do Castelo
VIANA DO CASTELO
Viana do Castelo
SERRA DO GERÊS
Bragança
Braga
BRAGA
Braga
TRAS OS MONTES
VILA REAL
Vila Real
BRAGANÇA
Póvoa de Varzim
PORTO
Porto (Oporto)
A1
Douro
MONTANHÃS
Espinho
AVEIRO
VISEU
GUARDA
Aveiro
Viseu
Guarda
SERRA DA ESTRELA
COSTA DE PRATA
Figueira da Foz
Coimbra
COIMBRA
Covilhã
CASTELO BRANCO
Leiria
LEIRIA
Castelo Branco
Fátima
Nazaré
Tejo (Tagus)
SANTARÉM
A2
Portalegre
PORTALEGRE
Peniche
Santarém
RIBATEJO
LISBOA
D
LISBOA (LISBON)
Elvas
COSTA DO ESTORIL
ÉVORA
Setúbal
Évora
BARRAGEM DE ALQUEVA
COSTA DE LISBOA
PLANÍCIES
COSTA DA GALÉ
SETÚBAL
Beja
Moura
Sines
BEJA
A3
COSTA DOURADA
Odemira
E
Guadiana
Portimão
FARO
Faro
ALGARVE

AUTONOMOUS REGIONS (NOT SHOWN ON MAP):
☐ AÇORES (AZORES)   ☐ MADEIRA
○ Ponta Delgada   ○ Funchal

AZORES

200 kilometres
100 miles

CORVO
Santa Cruz das Flores
FLORES
ATLANTIC OCEAN
Santa Cruz da Graciosa
GRACIOSA
TERCEIRA
B1
FAIAL
Horta
Calheta
SÃO JORGE
Angra do Heroísmo
20 km
10 miles
Lajes do Pico
PICO
B2
SÃO MIGUEL
SÃO MIGUEL
Ponta da Ferraria
Ribeira Grande
Pico da Vara 1105m△
Nordeste
Ponta Delgada
FORMIGAS
Caldeiras das Sete Cidades
Lagoa
Furnas
Ponta do Arnel
Ponta Delgada
Povoação
Vila Franca do Campo
SANTA MARIA
Vila do Porto

MAP B
For location see general map section

MADEIRA

ATLANTIC OCEAN
Porto Moniz
São Jorge
Santana
Seixal
Boaventura
Faial
C2
São Vicente
Porto da Cruz
BAIA DE ZARCO
Ponta do Pargo
PAUL DA SERRA
Pico Ruivo 1862m△
Portela
Ponta do Castelo
Prazeres
C1
Pico de Arieiro 1818m△
Canical
ILHÉU DE AGOSTINHO
Calheta
Curral das Freiras
Santo da Serra
Prainha
Machico
ILHÉU DE FORA
Ponta do Sol
Terreiro da Luta
Agua de Pena
Santa Cruz
Cabo Girão
Quinta do Palheiro Ferreiro
Caniço
Câmara de Lobos
Funchal

30 kilometres
15 miles

MAP C
For location see general map section

LISBON

Alenquer
Vila Franca de Xira
Benavente
Coruche
Ericeira
Mafra
LISBOA
Tejo (Tagus)
Sorraia
ATLANTIC OCEAN
PORTELA DE SACAVÉM
RESERVA NATURAL DO ESTUÁRIO DO TEJO
SANTARÉM
Praia das Macas
Praia Grande
Colares
Infantado
Cabo da Roca
SERRA Sintra DE SINTRA
Amadora
Alcochete
Malveira da Serra
Queluz
LISBOA (LISBON)
D2
Guincho
D1
Estoril
Belém
Montijo
SETÚBAL
Cabo Raso
Cascais
Praia Parede
Carcavelos
Almada
Barreiro
Aguas de Moura
COSTA DO ESTORIL
Costa da Caparica
Seixal
Santo Estevão
COSTA AZUL (COSTA DO SOL)
Vila Nogueira de Azeitão
Palmela
Marateca
LAGOA DE ALBUFEIRA
Outão
Setúbal
Sado
Sesimbra
SERRA DA ARRÁBIDA
Tróia
Portinão da Arrábida
COSTA BELA
Cabo Espichel

30 kilometres
15 miles

MAP D

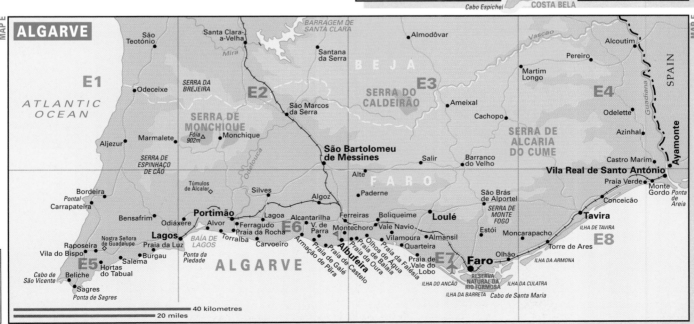

MAP E

ALGARVE

BARRAGEM DE SANTA CLARA
São Teotónio
Santa Clara-a-Velha
Almodôvar
Vascao
Alcoutim
E1
Odeceixe
SERRA DA BREJEIRA
Santana da Serra
BEJA
Pereiro
Martim Longo
ATLANTIC OCEAN
E2
SERRA DO CALDEIRÃO
E3
E4
Aljezur
Marmalete
SERRA DE MONCHIQUE
São Marcos da Serra
Ameixal
Odelette
Fóia 902m△
Monchique
Cachopo
Azinhal
SERRA DE ESPINHAÇO DE CÃO
São Bartolomeu de Messines
Salir
Barranco do Velho
SERRA DE ALCARIA DO CUME
Castro Marim
Bordeira
Túmulos de Alcalar
Alte
FARO
Vila Real de Santo António
Pontal Carrapateira
Silves
Algoz
Paderne
São Brás de Alportel
Praia Verde
Bensafrim
Lagoa
Alcantarilha
Ferreiras
Boliqueime
Loulé
SERRA DE MONTE FOGO
Monte Gordo
Odiáxere
Portimão
V. de Parra
Montechoro
Vale Navio
Estói
Moncarapacho
Conceição
Alvor
E6
Praia da Rocha
Vilamoura
Almansil
Tavira
Lagos
Ferragudo
Torralba
Carvoeiro
Quarteira
Torre de Ares
E8
Raposeira
Nostra Señora de Guadelupe
BAÍA DE LAGOS
Praia da Luz
Praia de Agua
Praia de Falesia
Olhão
ILHA DE TAVIRA
Vila do Bispo
Salema
Burgau
Ponta da Piedade
Armação de Pera
Albufeira
Praia de Vale do Lobo
ILHA DA ARMONA
E5
Hortas do Tabual
Praia de Castelo
Faro
Cabo de São Vicente
Beliche
Praia de Galé
E7
ILHA DO ANCÃO
Sagres
ALGARVE
RESERVA NATURAL DA RIA FORMOSA
ILHA DA CULATRA
Ponta de Sagres
ILHA DA BARRETA
Cabo de Santa Maria

SPAIN
Guadiana
Ayamonte
Odelette
Castro Marim
Monte Gordo Ponta de Areia

500 metres
200 metres
Sea level

40 kilometres
20 miles

▶ Leisure park   ▶ Zoo / animal park   ▶ Aquarium   ▶ Formula One   ▶ Major tennis venue

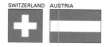

SWITZERLAND AND AUSTRIA

See pages 9, 10, 12 & 13 for general maps

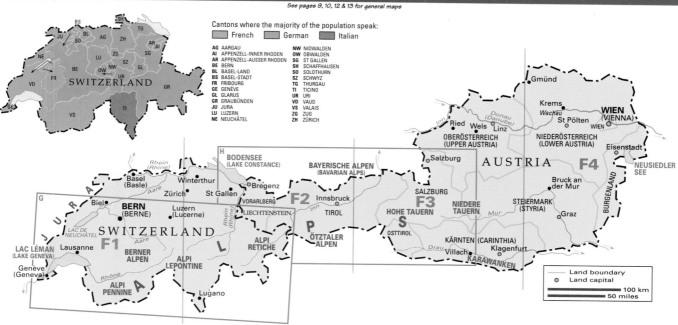

ITALY

See page 12 for general map

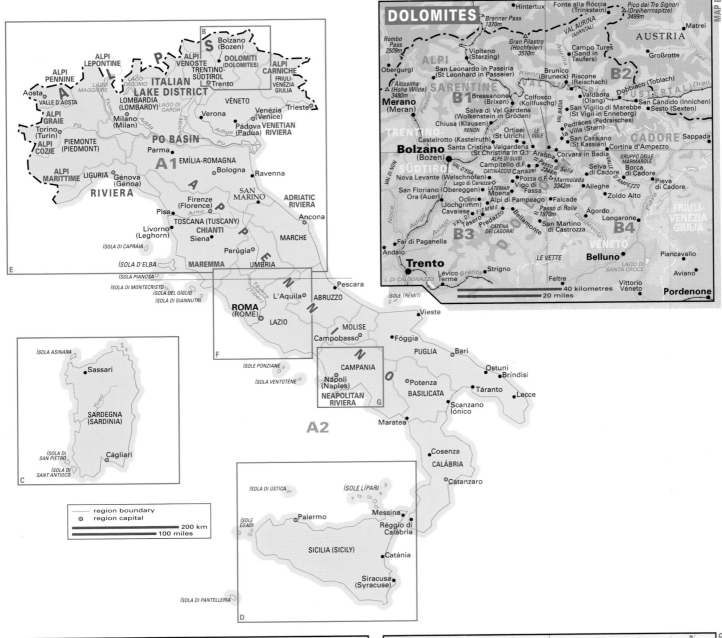

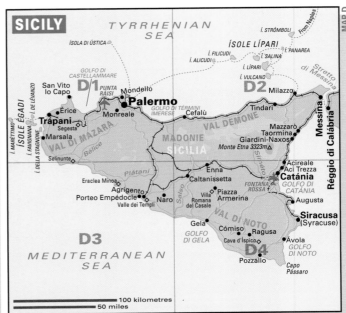

ITALY

See page 12 for general map

NORTH ITALY

LIECHTENSTEIN

BERN
SWITZERLAND
AUSTRIA

Lausanne
Montreux
Lausanne

LAC DE NEUCHÂTEL
LAC LÉMAN
Sion
Montreux

Chamonix
Mont Blanc 4810m
Matterhorn 4478m
Monte Rosa 4634m
Breuil-Cervinia
Courmayeur
la Thuile
Col du Grand St Bernard 2473m
Aosta
Col du Petit St Bernard 2188m
PARCO NAZIONALE DEL GRAN PARADISO
Gran Paradiso 4061m

Luzern
VIERWALD-STÄTTER SEE
Andermatt
Chur
Davos
ALPI LEPONTINE
Bellinzona
Locarno
Domodóssola
Macugnaga
Valtournenche
Gressoney-la-Trinité
Chamois
Orta
Arona

ALPI PENNINE
LAGO MAGGIORE

Stélvio (Stilfs)
Solda (Sulden)
PARCO NAZIONALE DELLO STELVIO

Bormio
Sta Catarina Valfurva
Madésimo
San Mamete
Sondrio
Tirano
Chiesa
Aprica
Ponte di Legno
Passo del Tonale 1883m
VAL CAMONICA

Menaggio
Bellágio
Cadenábbia / Tremezzo
Fóppolo
Como
Lecco
LAGO DI COMO
Cernóbbio
Bérgamo
Capriate
San Gervasio

Brenner Pass 1370m
Vipiteno (Sterzing)
Campo Tures (Sand in Taufers)
Brunico (Bruneck)
Merano (Meran)
Bressanone (Brixen)
Cortina d'Ampezzo
Bolzano (Bozen)

ALPI VENOSTE
DOLOMITI
Marmolada 3342m
Predazzo
San Martino di Castrozza
TRENTINO-SUDTIROL
Madonna di Campiglio
BRENTA
Trento

Lienz
Monte Coglians (Kellerwand) 2780m
Ravascletto
ALPI CARNICHE
Sella Nevea

Spittal
Villach
SLOVENIA

Belluno
Feltre
Vittorio Véneto
Rovereto
Riva del Garda
Malcésine
Bassano di Grappa
Montebelluna
Pordenone
Udine
Gorizia
Palmanova
Aquileia

Monza
Milano (Milan)
Novara
Vercelli
Vigévano
Certosa di Pavia
Pavia
Lodi
Crema
Bréscia
Salò
Desenzano
Sirmione
Gardone Riviera
Bardolino
VALPOLICELLA
Soave
Verona
Vicenza
Cittadella
Treviso
Mestre
MARCO POLO
Venézia (Venice)
Lido di Jésolo
Caorle
Bibione
Lignano
Grado
Trieste
Koper
CROATIA

Torino (Turin)
Chivasso
Asti
Alessándria
Tortona
Piacenza
Cremona
Mantova (Mantua)
Ásola
Montagnana
Pádova (Padua)
Abano
Montegrotto
Strà
Legnano
Rovigo
POLESINE
Chióggia
LAGUNA VENETA
RIVIERA
GOLFO DI VENÉZIA
Pula

Novara
Biella
Ivrea
ALPI GRAIE
Bardonécchia
Sáuze d'Oulx
Sestriere
Clavière
ALPI COZIE
Pinerolo
Monte Viso 3841m
Cúneo
Mondovi
Frabosa
Limone Piemonte
Ormea
Punta Argentera 3297m
ALPI MARITTIME

Casale Monferrato
COLLINE DEL PO
BARBARESCO
Acqui Terme
Alba
BAROLO
PIEMONTE

Fidenza
Salsomaggiore
Parma
Miróndola
Cento
Modena
Réggio nell' Emília
G. MARCONI
Bologna
Ímola
EMILIA-ROMAGNA

Ferrara
Pómposa Abbazia
Porto Garibaldi
LIDI DI COMACCHIO
ADRIATIC SEA

Génova (Genoa)
CRISTÓFO COLOMBO
LIGURIA
Rapallo
Sta Margherita Ligure
Chiávari
Lavagna
Portofino
Sestri Levante
Monéglia
Levanto
Cinque Terre
Portovénere
Lérici
La Spézia
Sarzana
Carrara
Marina di Massa
Forte dei Marmi

Ravenna
Milano Maríttima
Cérvia
Cesenático
Forli
Faenza

RIVIERA DI LEVANTE
RIVIERA DI PONENTE
Pontrémoli
Sécchia
APPENNINO

Rímini
Riccione
Misano Adriático
Gabicce Mare
Pésaro
Fano
Cattólica
San Leo
SAN MARINO
ADRIATIC RIVIERA

MONACO
Nice
Cannes
Tággia
Bussana
San Remo
Ospedaletti
Bordighera
Ventimiglia
Imperia
Diano Marina
Alássio
Albenga
Laigueglia
Noli
Pietra Lígure
Spotorno
Savona

RIVIERA DI PONENTE
GOLFO DI GENOVA

Pistóia
Montecatini
Lucca
Prato
Fiésole
Firenze (Florence)
GALILEO GALILEI
San Gimignano
Arno
Arezzo

Urbino
Senigállia
Corinaldo
Ancona
Sirolo
Loreto
Porto Recanati
Jesi
Grotta di Frasassi
MARCHE
Matélica
Civitanova Marche
CONERO
Porto Potenza Picena
Cupra Maríttima
San Benedetto del Tronto

Livorno (Leghorn)
Tirrénia
ÍSOLA DI GORGONA
Querciarella
Castiglioncello
Rosignano Maríttimo
Volterra
Monteriggioni
Siena
CHIANTI
TOSCANA
Cortona
Città di Castello
Gúbbio
Perúgia
Assisi
Spello
Foligno
Montefalco
UMBRIA

Marina di Pietrasanta
Lido de Camaiore
Viaréggio
Pisa

Castagneto Carducci
San Vincenzo
Piombino
Río Marina
Porto Azzurro
ÍSOLA D'ELBA
ÍSOLA DI CAPRAIA

Massa Maríttima
Follónica
Grosseto
MAREMMA
San Galgano
Pienza
Montepulciano
Castiglione della Pescáia
Castiglione del Lago
Abbazia di Monte Oliveto Maggiore
Chiusi
Todi
Acquasanta
Ascoli Piceno
Giulianova
ABRUZZO

LAGO TRASIMENO
Chiusi
Orvieto
DIRETTISSIMA
Tévere (Tiber)
Spoleto

LIGURIAN SEA
CORSE (France)

100 kilometres
50 miles

FRANCE

ROME

Orvieto
Bolsena
Spoleto
Acquasparta
Amélia
Terni
Teramo
LAGO DI BOLSENA
UMBRIA
Orte
MONTI RIETINI
GRAN SASSO D'ITALIA
Corno Grande 2912m
Rieti
LAGO DI CAMPOTOSTO

Capodimonte
Villa Lante
Tuscánia
Viterbo
Vetralla
Tarquinia
MONTI CIMINI
LAGO DI VICO
SABINA
L'Áquila
ABRUZZO

Civitavécchia
Tolfa
Santa Marinella
Capo Linaro
Cervéteri
Ladispoli
MONTI DELLA TOLFA
Civita Castellana
LAGO DI BRACCIANO
Bracciano
Campo Felice
Rocca di Cámbio
Celano
Avezzano
Tagliacozzo
MONTI SIMBRUINI
PIANA DEL FUCINO
Sulmona
Pópoli

VATICAN CITY
ROMA (ROME)
LEONARDO DA VINCI
Fiumicino
Ostia
CIAMPINO
Frascati
Palestrina
Anagni
Sora
Villa Adriana (Hadrian)
Tívoli
CASTELLI ROMANI
Rocca di Papa
Albano Laziále
Castel Gandolfo
Genzano di Roma
Velletri
LAGO DI NEMI
LAZIO
AGRO ROMANO
PARCO NAZIONALE D'ABRUZZO

Aprilia
Ánzio
Nettuno
Torre Astura
Latina
Frosinone
Ceccano
Abbazia di Casamari
Abbazia di Fossanova
Abbazia di Montecassino

F1 F2 F3 F4

Priverno
MONTI LEPINI
MONTI AUSONI
Fondi
Sperlonga
Formia
MONTI AURUNCI
GOLFO DI GAETA
Terracina
Sabáudia
Faro di Santa Eufémia
San Felice Circèo
PARCO NAZIONALE DEL CIRCEO
LAGO DI SABÁUDIA
Villa di Tibério
Gaeta

TYRRHENIAN SEA

80 kilometres
40 miles

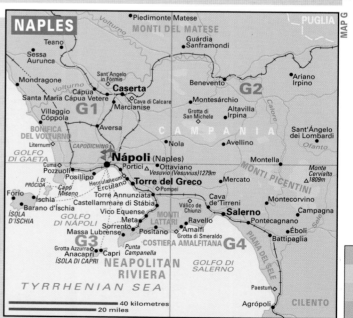

NAPLES

Piedimonte Matese
MONTI DEL MATESE
PUGLIA
Teano
Sessa Aurunca
Guárdia Sanframondi
Benevento
Ariano Irpino

Mondragone
Sant'Angelo in Fórmis
Cápua
Caserta
Santa Maria Cápua Vetere
Marcianise
Cava di Calcare
Montesárchio
Altavilla Irpina
Sant'Angelo dei Lombardi
CAMPANIA

Villaggio Cóppola
BONIFICA DEL VOLTURNO
Aversa
Grotta di San Michele
Nola
Avellino
Montella

Liternum
GOLFO DI GAETA
CAPODICHINO
Nápoli (Naples)
Portici
Ottaviano
Vesuvio (Vesuvius) 1279m
Mercato
Monte Cervialto 1809m
MONTI PICENTINI

Cuma
Pozzuoli
Posíllipo
Capo Miseno
Herculaneum Erculano
Torre del Greco
Pompei
Torre Annunziata
Castellammare di Stábia
Salerno
Pontecagnano
Corcovino
Campagna
MONTI LATTARI

Fório
Ischia
Barano d'Ischia
ÍSOLA D'ISCHIA
PRÓCIDA
Sorrento
Vico Equense
Meta
Massa Lubrense
Positano
Amalfi
Ravello
Válico de Chiunzi
Cava de' Tirreni
Montecorvino
Éboli
Battipaglia
PIANA DEL SELE

Grotta Azzurra
Anacapri
Capri
Punta Campanella
ÍSOLA DI CAPRI
NEAPOLITAN RIVIERA
COSTIERA AMALFITANA
Grotta di Smeraldo
GOLFO DI SALERNO

G1 G2 G3 G4

GOLFO DI NÁPOLI
TYRRHENIAN SEA
Paestum
Agrópoli
CILENTO

2000 metres
1000 metres
Sea level

▶ Leisure park   ▶ Zoo / animal park   ▶ Aquarium   ▶ Formula One   ▶ Major tennis venue

GREECE AND TURKEY

See page 15 for general map

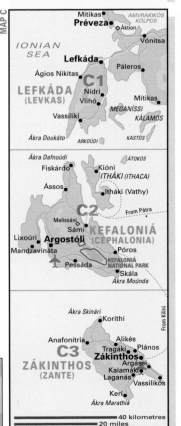

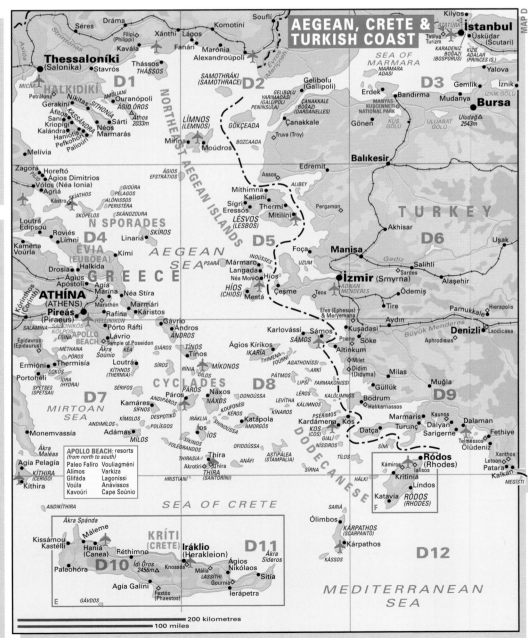

GREECE AND TURKEY

See page 15 for general map

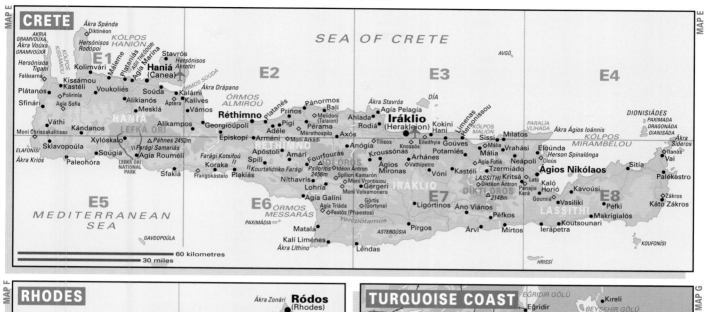

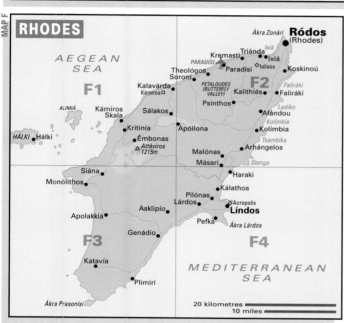

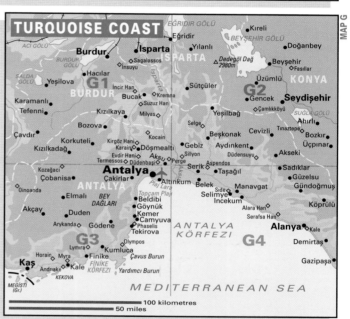

MALTA

See page 12 for general map

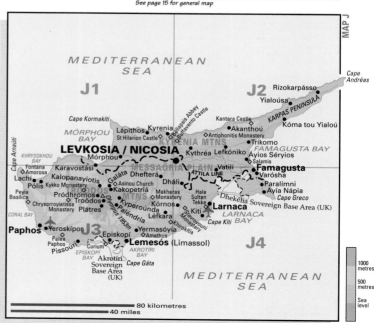

CYPRUS

See page 15 for general map

NORWAY

SCANDINAVIA

See page 16 for general map

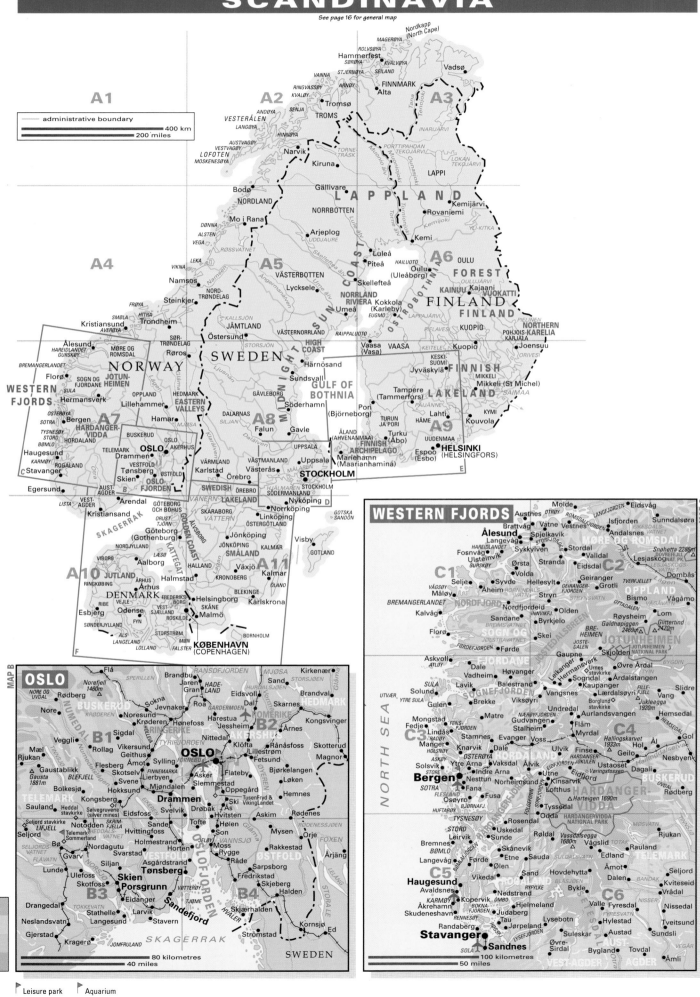

SCANDINAVIA

See page 16 for general map

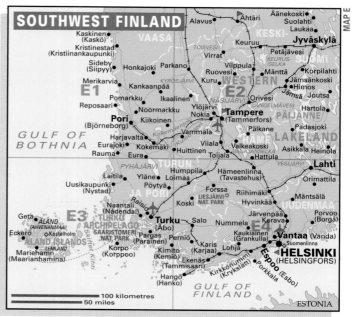

▼ Leisure park   ◿ Zoo / animal park   ▲ Aquarium   ▶ Major tennis venue

CZECH REPUBLIC

CENTRAL EUROPE AND...

See pages 13 & 14 for general maps

boundary of the Former Soviet Union
Russian Federation
Republic within the Russian Federation
Capital of Republic within the Russian Federation

OSTROV GREEM BELL
OSTROV USHAKOVA
OSTROV KOMSOMOLETS
OS OKTYA REVO
OSTROV PIONER

ZEMLYA GEORGA
ZEMLYA VILCHEKA
ZEMLYA FRANTSA-IOSIFA
(FRANZ JOSEF LAND)

NOVAYA ZEMLYA

OSTROV BELYY
POLUOSTROV YAMAL (YAMAL PENINSULA)
GYDANSKIY POLUOSTROV (GYDAN PENINSULA)
OSTROV VAYGACH
OSTROV KOLGUYEV
OBSKAYA GUBA (OB ESTUARY)

Murmansk
KOLSKIY POLUOSTROV (KOLA PENINSULA)
WHITE SEA
KARELIA
Vorkuta
Noril'sk

Arkhangel'sk
KOMI
TYUMEN
ZAPADNO SIBIRSKOYE RAVNINA (WEST SIBERIAN PLAIN)
A4
RUSSIA

LAKE ONEGA
Khizi Pogost
Petrozavodsk
Kotlas
Syktyvkar
Surgut

VALAAM
LAKE LADOGA

TALLINN
HIIUMAA
SAAREMAA
ESTONIA
Sankt-Peterburg (St Petersburg)
Novgorod
E
A2
Perm
Yekaterinburg
Krasnoyarsk

BALTIC REPUBLICS
RIGA
LATVIA
Yaroslavl'
Tver'
Nizhniy Novgorod
MARI-EL
Yoshkar-Ola
UDMURTIA
Izhevsk
URAL MOUNTAINS
A3
Chelyabinsk
Omsk
Novosibirsk
Tay

LITHUANIA
A1
Polotsk
GOLDEN RING
Cheboksary
CHUVASHIA
Kazan
TATARSTAN
Ufa
BASHKORTOSTAN
Irtysh
Ob
Gorno-Altaysk
KHAKASSIA
Abakan
Kyzyl
TUV

Kaliningrad (Russian Fed.)
VILNIUS
MENSK (MINSK)
Smolensk
MOSKVA (MOSCOW)
Saransk
MORDOVIA
Simbirsk
Samara
CITIES OF THE VOLGA
Orenburg
AKMOLA
Pavlodar
Semey
ALTAY
Yenis
TUV

Brest
BELARUS
Bryansk
Voronezh
Saratov
TURGAY BASIN
Karaganda
Uskemen

KYYIV (KIEV)
Lviv (Lvov)
UKRAINE
Dnepr
Don
Volga
Volgograd
KIRGIZ STEPPE
KAZAKHSTAN
LAKE BALKHASH
Taldy-Kurgan

CHISINAU
MOLDOVA
Odesa (Odessa)
DONETS BASIN
Rostov-na-Donu
Elista
KALMYKIA
VOLGA DELTA
Astrakhan
Atyraū
Ural
ARAL SEA
Baikonur Cosmodrome
Kzyl-Orda
TIEN SHAN

SEA OF AZOV
CRIMEA
Sevastopol
Yalta
RUSSIAN BLACK SEA COAST
USTYURT PLATEAU
Syr Darya
FERGANA BASIN
Aulie-Ata
Almaty
BISHKEK

MAP B
BLACK SEA
BOSPORUS
Dagomys
Sochi
Sukhumi
CAUCASUS MTNS
GEORGIA
CASPIAN SEA
UZBEKISTAN
Nukus
Khiva
Chimkent
Bukhara
Samarkand
TASHKENT
KYRGYZSTAN

ARMENIA
TBILISI
BAKI (BAKU)
TURKMENISTAN
Türkmenbashi
Amu Darya
TAJIKISTAN
PAMIR
DUSHANBE

YEREVAN
AZERBAIJAN
ASHGABAT
Mary

Russian Republics in the Caucasus
1 Adygeya (capital: Maykop)
2 Karachay-Cherkessia (Cherkessk)
3 Kabardino-Balkaria (Nalchik)
4 North Ossetia (Vladikavkaz)
5 Ingushetia (Nazran)
6 Chechenia (Groznyy)
7 Dagestan (Makhachkala)

CENTRAL EUROPE

BALTIC COAST
Gdynia
POMERANIA
Gdańsk
Kętrzyn
MASURIA
Szczecin (Stettin)
Poznań
Wisła (Vistula)
WARSZAWA (WARSAW)
POLAND
B1
Łódź
Lublin
Odra (Oder)
Wrocław
Częstochowa
SILESIA
PRAHA (PRAGUE)
SUDETY
C
Plzeň (Pilsen)
CZECH REPUBLIC
BOHEMIA
Ostrava
Kraków (Cracow)
Oświęcim (Auschwitz)
Zakopane
MORAVIA
Brno
TATRY
Levoča
Košice
SLOVAK REPUBLIC
Nitra
CARPATHIANS

BRATISLAVA
BUDAPEST
Miskolc
Tokaj
Debrecen
BUKOVINA
HUNGARY
HUNGARIAN PLAIN
Pécs
Szeged
ROMANIA
MOLDAVIA
DANUBE DELTA
D

JULIAN ALPS
Bled
LAKE BALATON
Sibiu
Brasov
Sinaia
TRANSYLVANIAN ALPS
BUCUREŞTI (BUCHAREST)

LJUBLJANA
ZAGREB
SLOVENIA
CROATIA
BEOGRAD (BELGRADE)
WALACHIA
BLACK SEA COAST
Constanța

Portorož
ISTRA (ISTRIA)
Rijeka
Zadar
DINARIC ALPS
BOSNIA-HERZEGOVINA
SARAJEVO
B2
FEDERAL REPUBLIC OF YUGOSLAVIA
SOFIYA (SOFIA)
Varna
Burgas

Split
Makarska
DALMATIA
DALMATIAN COAST
Dubrovnik
Kotor
Podgorica
Priština
BULGARIA
RILA
RHODOPE
Plovdiv
Borovets

TIRANË (TIRANA)
SKOPJE
Pamporovo
ALBANIA
Ohrid
FORMER YUGOSLAV REPUBLIC OF MACEDONIA
Vlorë
Gjirokastër

400 km
200 miles

BOHEMIA

Dresden
Freiberg
Rumburk
Zittau
POLAND
Jelenia Gora
Frýdlant
Liberec
Harrachov
Sněžka 1602m
KRKONOŠE NAT. PARK
Jánské Lázně

Chemnitz
Greiz
ČESKÉ ŠVÝCARSKO (BOHEMIAN SWITZERLAND)
Benešov
Děčín
Jablonné v Podještědí
Turnov
Trutnov
Ratibořice

Zwickau
Aue
Teplice
Ústí nad Labem
Česká Lípa
Mnichovo Hradiště
Sobotka
MAP C

Plauen
KRUŠNÉ HORY
C1
Litvínov
Most
Terezín
Kokořín
Mělník
Mladá Boleslav
C2

Klingenthal
Klínovec 1244m
Chomutov
Louny
Lovosice
Poděbrady
Hradec Králové

Jáchymov
Kadaň
Žatec
ZAHRADA ČECH (GARDEN OF BOHEMIA)
Přerov nad Labem
Kolín

Ostrov
Ohře
Kladno
Lidice
PRAHA (PRAGUE)
Kutná Hora
Pardubice

Karlovy Vary (Karlsbad)
CZECH
Křivoklát
Vyšehrad
Kačina
Čáslav

Františkovy Lázně
Sokolov
Loket
Teplá
Plasy
KŘIVOKLÁTSKO
VRCHOVINA
Kouřim
Sázava
Český Šternberk
Lichnice

Cheb
Mariánské Lázně (Marienbad)
Hořovice
REPUBLIC
Havlíčkův Brod
Přibyslav

Marktredwitz
SLAVKOVSKÝ LES
Berounka
Rokycany
Příbram
Chýnovské jeskyně
Kalište
Lipnice nad Sázavou

Bor
Kladruby
Radbuza
Plzeň (Pilsen)
Orlík
Milevsko
Kámen
Pelhřimov
Jihlava

Weiden
Mže
Švihov
Blatna
Zvíkov
Písek
Červená Lhota
Telč
Třebíč

Klenčí pod Čerchovem
Domažlice
Klatovy
Tábor
Bechyně
Jindřichův Hradec
Slavonice

GERMANY
Cham
Sušice
Rabi
Strakonice
Vimperk
Prachatice
ČESKÉ BUDĚJOVICE
C4
Raabs
Znojmo

Regensburg
Železná Ruda
ŠUMAVA
Kratochvíle
Hluboká
Trebon
Zlatá Koruna
Gmünd
Retz

Straubing
Deggendorf
Volary
LIPENSKÉ PŘEHRADNÍ
Český Krumlov
Rožmberk

C3
Plechý 1378m
Vyšší Brod

Landshut
Passau
Freistadt
AUSTRIA
Krems

Isar
Donau (Danube)

100 kilometres
50 miles

► Zoo / animal park   ▷ Major tennis venue

...THE FORMER SOVIET UNION

See pages 16, 17, 26 & 27 for general maps

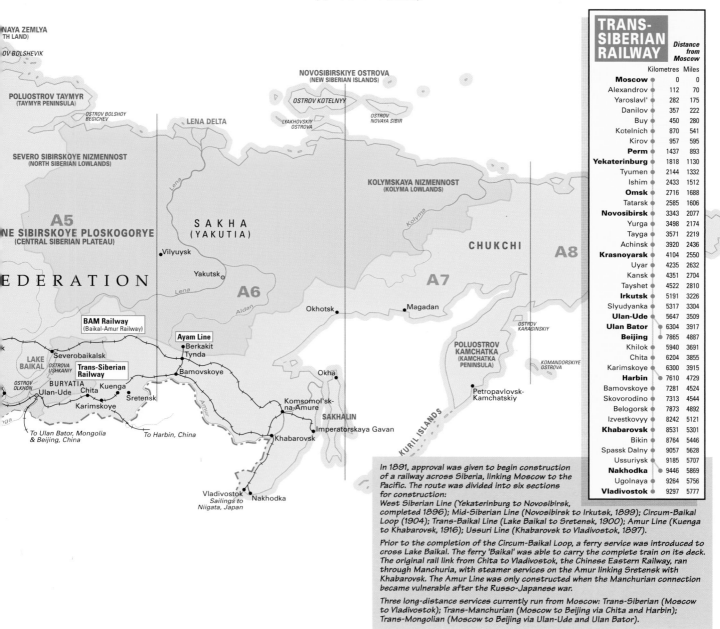

TRANS-SIBERIAN RAILWAY

	Distance from Moscow	
	Kilometres	Miles
Moscow	0	0
Alexandrov	112	70
Yaroslavl'	282	175
Danilov	357	222
Buy	450	280
Kotelnich	870	541
Kirov	957	595
Perm	1437	893
Yekaterinburg	1818	1130
Tyumen	2144	1332
Ishim	2433	1512
Omsk	2716	1688
Tatarsk	2585	1606
Novosibirsk	3343	2077
Yurga	3498	2174
Tayga	3571	2219
Achinsk	3920	2436
Krasnoyarsk	4104	2550
Uyar	4235	2632
Kansk	4351	2704
Tayshet	4522	2810
Irkutsk	5191	3226
Slyudyanka	5317	3304
Ulan-Ude	5647	3509
Ulan Bator	6304	3917
Beijing	7865	4887
Khilok	5940	3691
Chita	6204	3855
Karimskoye	6300	3915
Harbin	7610	4729
Bamovskoye	7281	4524
Skovorodino	7313	4544
Belogorsk	7873	4892
Izvestkovyy	8242	5121
Khabarovsk	8531	5301
Bikin	8764	5446
Spassk Dalny	9057	5628
Ussuriysk	9185	5707
Nakhodka	9446	5869
Ugolnaya	9264	5756
Vladivostok	9297	5777

In 1891, approval was given to begin construction of a railway across Siberia, linking Moscow to the Pacific. The route was divided into six sections for construction:

West Siberian Line (Yekaterinburg to Novosibirsk, completed 1896); Mid-Siberian Line (Novosibirsk to Irkutsk, 1899); Circum-Baikal Loop (1904); Trans-Baikal Line (Lake Baikal to Sretensk, 1900); Amur Line (Kuenga to Khabarovsk, 1916); Ussuri Line (Khabarovsk to Vladivostok, 1897).

Prior to the completion of the Circum-Baikal Loop, a ferry service was introduced to cross Lake Baikal. The ferry 'Baikal' was able to carry the complete train on its deck. The original rail link from Chita to Vladivostok, the Chinese Eastern Railway, ran through Manchuria, with steamer services on the Amur linking Sretensk with Khabarovsk. The Amur Line was only constructed when the Manchurian connection became vulnerable after the Russo-Japanese war.

Three long-distance services currently run from Moscow: Trans-Siberian (Moscow to Vladivostok); Trans-Manchurian (Moscow to Beijing via Chita and Harbin); Trans-Mongolian (Moscow to Beijing via Ulan-Ude and Ulan Bator).

ROMANIAN AND BULGARIAN COAST

200 kilometres
100 miles

MOSCOW AND ST PETERSBURG

200 kilometres
100 miles

1000 metres
500 metres
Sea level

▶ Zoo / animal park   ▶ Aquarium   ▶ Major tennis venue

THE HOLY LAND AND CENTRAL ASIA

See pages 18, 26 & 29 for general maps

Crucible of ancient civilizations, harsh landscape of the Prophets of the Old Testament revered by Jew, Muslim and Christian alike, and dramatic setting for the story of Christ from his birth in Bethlehem to his crucifixion outside Jerusalem, the Holy Land is a region of monumental and complex significance - as Promised Land, place of pilgrimage and miracles and the setting for the rise and fall of empires and kingdoms.

No city symbolises this rich heritage more than Jerusalem. As the site of the ancient Temples of Judaism, so central to the ancient Jewish state, Jerusalem is the region's spiritual heart. For Christians, Jerusalem is the site of the Crucifixion, the culmination of the life of Christ. The city is also an integral part of the sacred geography of Islam, which also reveres the Old Testament Patriarchs, and is the third most sacred site in Islam after Mecca and Medina. In addition to sites of great spiritual significance, the Holy Land contains archaeological and architectural sites of immense importance.

Since the proclamation of the state of Israel in 1948, the politics of the area have been dominated by conflict between Israel and surrounding Arab states. Recent developments have offered some hope of future peace, which should herald a significant rise in the number of visitors to the region.

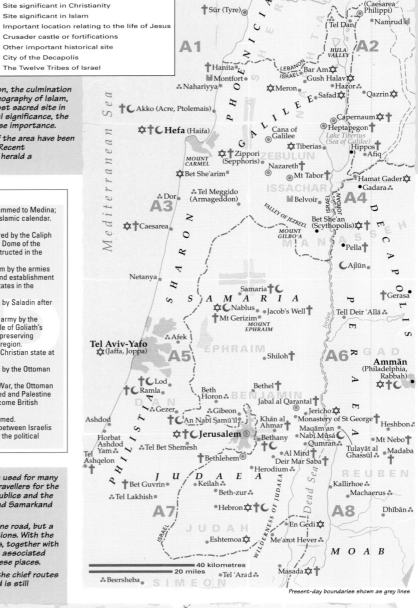

THE HOLY LAND

✡	Site significant in Judaism
†	Site significant in Christianity
☾	Site significant in Islam
☽	Important location relating to the life of Jesus
🏰	Crusader castle or fortifications
⚜	Other important historical site
●	City of the Decapolis
	The Twelve Tribes of Israel

PRINCIPAL DATES IN THE HISTORY OF THE HOLY LAND

1600	Abraham, the first of the Patriarchs, migrates from Ur in Mesopotamia to Palestine.
1250	Jews released from captivity in Egypt by Moses.
1006-966	Under the reign of David, Jerusalem becomes the religious and political capital of the ancient Jewish state.
966-926	Reign of Solomon: the golden age for the ancient Jewish state, which was divided after his death into the Kingdoms of Israel and Judah.
587	Conquest and destruction of Jerusalem by Babylon.
332	Capture of Palestine by Alexander the Great.
63	Palestine becomes part of the Roman Empire.
39-4	Reign of Herod the Great.
6*	Birth of Jesus Christ.
29*	Crucifixion of Christ outside Jerusalem.
66-70	Jewish revolt against Roman rule, culminating in the razing of the Temple in AD70.
133	Jewish revolt suppressed, leading to the forced emigration of Jews to locations throughout the Roman Empire (diaspora).
570	Birth of Mohammed in Mecca.

622	Hegira: flight of Mohammed to Medina; the beginning of the Islamic calendar.
633	Death of Mohammed.
638	Jerusalem is conquered by the Caliph Omar, after which the Dome of the Rock Mosque is constructed in the city.
1100	Conquest of Jerusalem by the armies of the First Crusade and establishment of several Christian states in the region.
1187	Capture of Jerusalem by Saladin after the Battle of Hattin.
1260	Defeat of the Mongol army by the Mamaluks at the Battle of Goliath's Well (Ain Jalut), thus preserving Islamic control in the region.
1291	Overthrow of the last Christian state at Acre.
1517	Capture of Jerusalem by the Ottoman Turks.
1920	After the First World War, the Ottoman Empire is dismembered and Palestine and Trans-Jordan become British Protectorates.
1948	State of Israel proclaimed.
1990s	Ongoing peace talks between Israelis and Palestinians over the political future of the region.

* The exact dates of Christ's birth and death are not known with certainty

The ancient trade routes between Europe and the Far East have been used for many centuries, but the Central Asian region has been virtually closed to travellers for the last 70 years. With the recent independence of the former Soviet republics and the opening up of tourism in China, fabled cities like Bukhara, Kashgar and Samarkand are now once again accessible to travellers and tourists.

The famous Silk Road, once linking China with Europe, is in fact not one road, but a number of different routes depending on the season and local conditions. With the opening of the borders between China and the Central Asian republics, together with improved road and rail links, it is possible to visit many ancient sites associated with the Silk Road and package tours are available linking many of these places.

The modern Karakoram Highway crosses the Khunjerab Pass, one of the chief routes over the Himalayas between Jammu and Kashmir and China. The road is still vulnerable to closure along its 1200 km length.

Present-day boundaries shown as grey lines

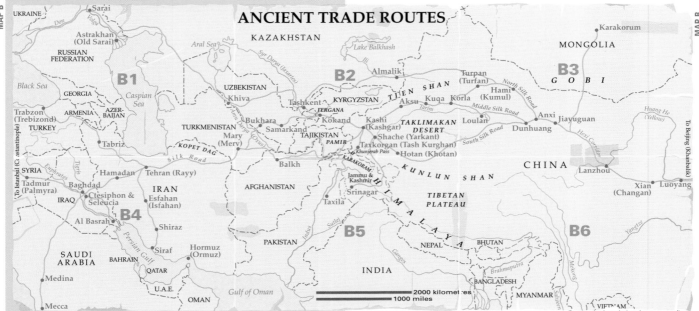

ANCIENT TRADE ROUTES

Present-day boundaries shown as grey lines

CLIMATE

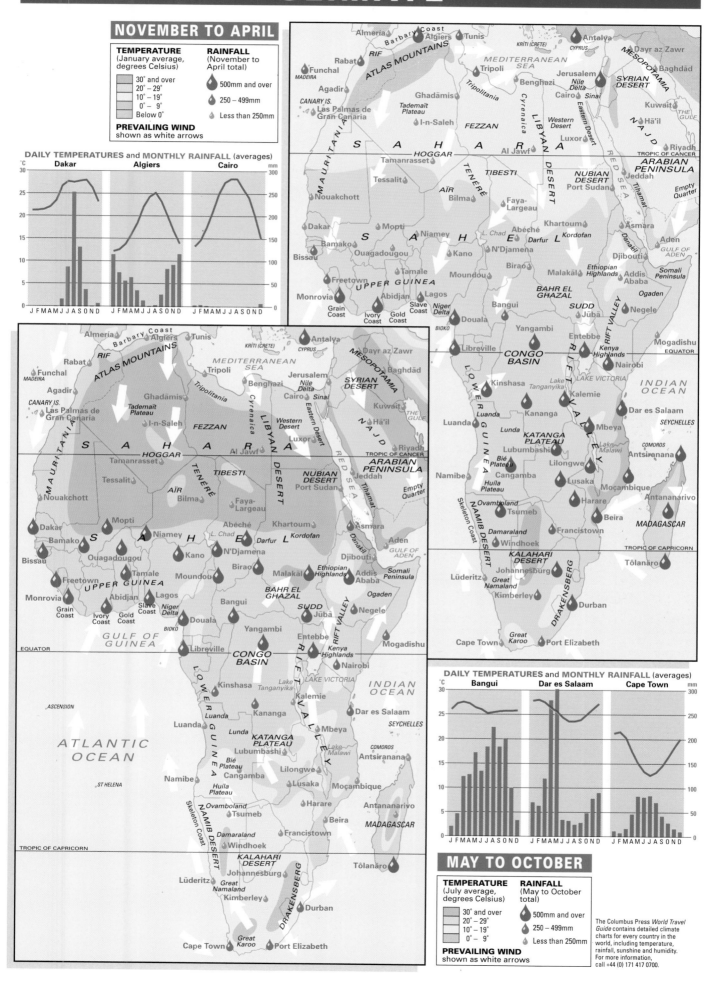

TEMPERATURE CONVERSION

°Celsius	−10	0	10	20	30	40
°Fahrenheit	14	32	50	68	86	104

RAINFALL CONVERSION

Millimetres	102	203	305	406	508	610
Inches	4	8	12	16	20	24

NOVEMBER TO APRIL

TEMPERATURE
(January average, degrees Celsius)

- 30° and over
- 20° – 29°
- 10° – 19°
- 0° – 9°
- Below 0°

RAINFALL
(November to April total)

- 500mm and over
- 250 – 499mm
- Less than 250mm

PREVAILING WIND
shown as white arrows

DAILY TEMPERATURES and MONTHLY RAINFALL (averages)

Dakar   Algiers   Cairo

DAILY TEMPERATURES and MONTHLY RAINFALL (averages)

Bangui   Dar es Salaam   Cape Town

MAY TO OCTOBER

TEMPERATURE
(July average, degrees Celsius)

- 30° and over
- 20° – 29°
- 10° – 19°
- 0° – 9°

RAINFALL
(May to October total)

- 500mm and over
- 250 – 499mm
- Less than 250mm

PREVAILING WIND
shown as white arrows

The Columbus Press *World Travel Guide* contains detailed climate charts for every country in the world, including temperature, rainfall, sunshine and humidity. For more information, call +44 (0) 171 417 0700.

AFRICA

See page 19 for general map

OFFICIAL LANGUAGES
(Numbers refer to the notes below)

- Arabic
- English
- French
- Portuguese
- Spanish
- Other

1. French is widely spoken by black communities in the south.
2. French is widely spoken throughout the country, except in the north where Spanish is more predominant. Berber is spoken by a large minority.
3. French is used for most official and business transactions. Berber is spoken by a large minority.
4. French is used for most business transactions. English is spoken in major cities and resorts. Berber is spoken by a large minority.
5. English is normally understood in hotels, restaurants and shops.
6. English and French are widely spoken in urban centres.
7. English is widely spoken throughout the country.
8. The official languages are Arabic and Tigrinya. English and Italian are the most common foreign languages.
9. The official language is Ahmaric, and English is widely understood. Italian and French are still widely spoken.
10. The official languages are Arabic and Somali. Some English and Italian are also spoken.
11. The official languages are English and Swahili.
12. The official languages are English, French and Kinyarwanda.
13. The official languages are French and Kirundi
14. Chichewa is widely spoken and is regarded as the national language by Malawi's largest eth group, the Chewa.
15. The official languages are English, Ndebele a Shona.
16. The official languages are Afrikaans, English, Ndebele, Pedi, Sesotho, Siswati, Tsonga, Tsw Venda, Xhosa and Zulu.
17. The official languages are English and Siswati
18. The official languages are English and Sesotho
19. The official languages are English, French and Comorian (a blend of Arabic and Swahili).
20. The official language is Creole, but English an French are widely spoken.
21. The official languages are French and Malaga Very little English is spoken.

SOUTH AFRICA

See page 24 for general map

- province boundary
- province capital

600 km
300 miles

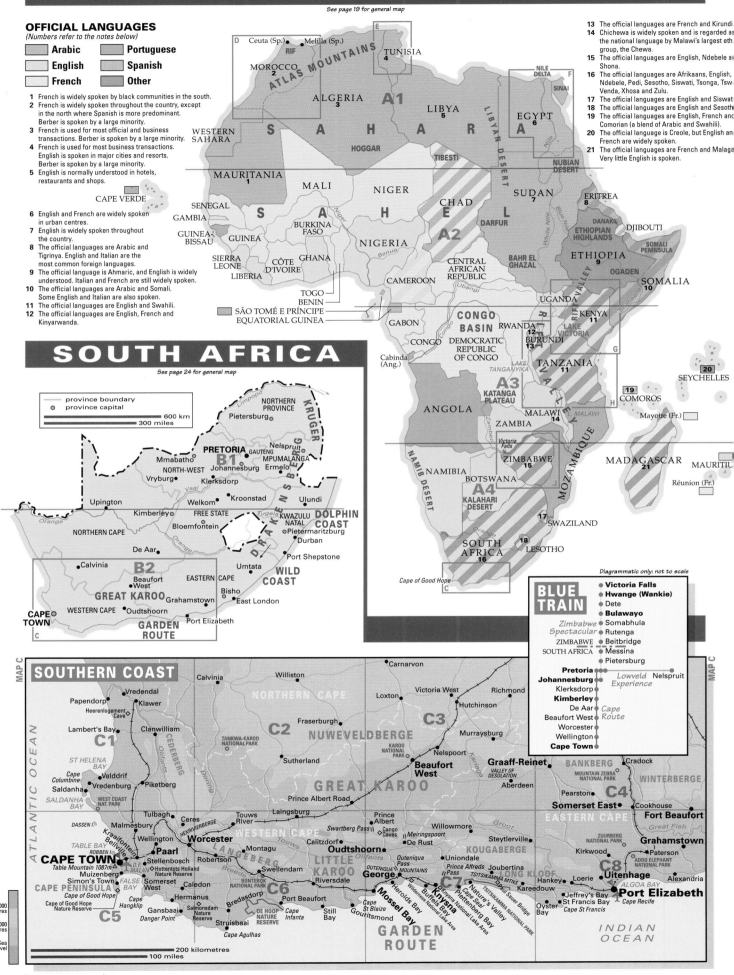

MOROCCO   TUNISIA   EGYPT   KENYA

AFRICA

See pages 20-23 for general maps

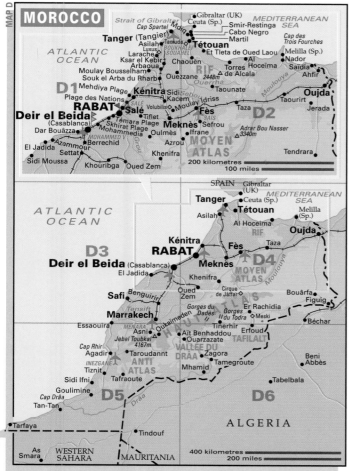

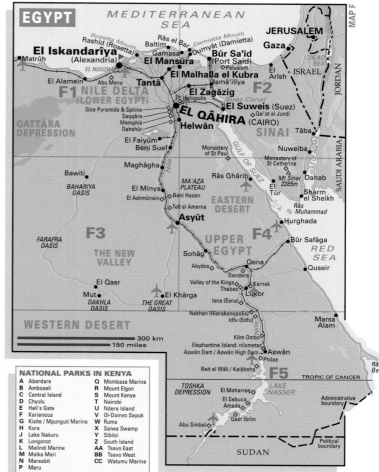

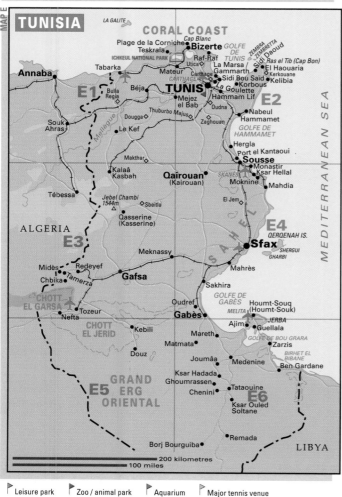

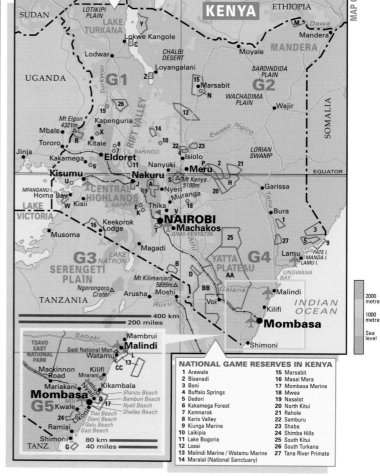

NATIONAL PARKS IN KENYA

A	Aberdare	Q	Mombasa Marine
B	Amboseli	R	Mount Elgon
C	Central Island	S	Mount Kenya
D	Chyulu	T	Nairobi
E	Hell's Gate	U	Ndere Island
F	Karianous	V	Ol-Doinyo Sapuk
G	Kisite / Mpunguti Marine	W	Ruma
H	Kora	X	Saiwa Swamp
J	Lake Nakuru	Y	Sibiloi
K	Longonot	Z	South Island
L	Malindi Marine	AA	Tsavo East
M	Malka Mari	BB	Tsavo West
N	Marsabit	CC	Watamu Marine
P	Meru		

NATIONAL GAME RESERVES IN KENYA

1	Arawale	15	Marsabit
2	Bisanadi	16	Masai Mara
3	Boni	17	Mombasa Marine
4	Buffalo Springs	18	Mwea
5	Dodori	19	Nasalot
6	Kakamega Forest	20	North Kitui
7	Kamnarok	21	Rahole
8	Kerio Valley	22	Samburu
9	Kiunga Marine	23	Shaba
10	Laikipia	24	Shimba Hills
11	Lake Bogoria	25	South Kitui
12	Losai	26	South Turkana
13	Malindi Marine / Watamu Marine	27	Tana River Primate
14	Maralal (National Sanctuary)		

2000 metres
1000 metres
Sea level

▲ Leisure park   ▲ Zoo / animal park   ▲ Aquarium   ▲ Major tennis venue

TANZANIA   ZIMBABWE

AFRICA

See pages 20-23 for general maps

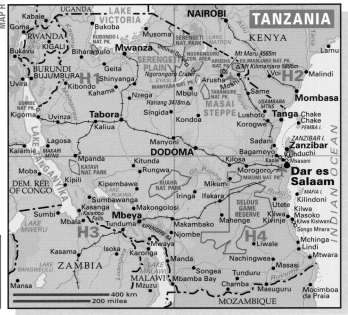

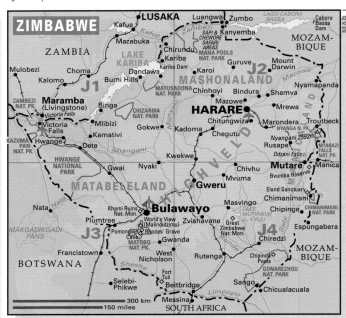

▶ Zoo / animal park

Africa is a prime destination for wildlife holidays: its national parks, game reserves and wildlife sanctuaries feature prominently in package holidays and tourist itineraries to the continent. Many parks, such as the Masai Mara, Serengeti and Kruger, are well-known throughout the world and some have been recognised by both UNESCO and the WWF for their unique and important character (UNESCO's World Heritage list is featured elsewhere in this atlas).

The area of Africa south of the Sahara is featured here. Although there are areas of wildlife interest in northern Africa, particularly on the Mediterranean coast, these are generally on a much smaller scale and do not usually provide the primary motivation for travel to these countries.

The map and table features the major parks and reserves used by tour operators and visited by overseas tourists. Some lesser-known parks are also included to give a broader geographical spread; access to many of these may be difficult due to poor infrastructure or political problems.

The table lists the major species most likely to be seen while visiting each park or those animals for which the park is famous, according to independent reports and government literature. Quality of information varies considerably from country to country and the following table should be regarded as a rough guide only; in some cases no species information is currently available. Poaching is a serious problem in some countries, particularly where wildlife tourism is less developed.

	COUNTRY	PARK/RESERVE	ELEPHANT	RHINOCEROS	HIPPOPOTAMUS	BUFFALO	ZEBRA	GIRAFFE	ANTELOPE	LION	LEOPARD	CHEETAH	HYENA	WARTHOG	GORILLA	CHIMPANZEE	MONKEY
1	Mauritania	Banc d'Arguin National Park						MIGRATING BIRDS									
2	Mali	Lac Faguibine						MIGRATING BIRDS									
3	Niger	Parc National du "W"															
4	Niger	Réserve du Aïr															
5	Niger	Réserve du Ténéré															
6	Senegal	Parc National des Oiseaux du Djoudj						MIGRATING BIRDS									
7	Senegal	Parc National de la Langue de Barbarie						WATERFOWL (FLAMINGOS ETC)									
8	Senegal	Parc National du Delta du Saloum						SMALL MAMMALS & MIGRATING BIRDS									
9	Senegal	Parc National de Basse-Casamance															
10	Senegal	Parc National de Niokolo Koba															
11	The Gambia	Abuko Nature Reserve						BUDGERIGARS									
12	The Gambia	Kiang West National Park															
13	Sierra Leone	Outamba-Kilimi National Park															
14	Sierra Leone	Mount Bintumani															
15	Sierra Leone	Mamunta-Mayoso Wildlife Sanctuary						BIRDS & SMALL MAMMALS									
16	Sierra Leone	Gola Forest Reserve						BUDGERIGARS									
17	Sierra Leone	Tiwai Island Wildlife Sanctuary						BUTTERFLIES & BUDGERIGARS									
18	Liberia	Sapo National Park															
19	Côte d'Ivoire	Parc National de Taï															
20	Côte d'Ivoire	Parc National de la Marahoué															
21	Côte d'Ivoire	Parc National de la Comoé															
22	Ghana	Mole National Park															
23	Ghana	Bui National Park															
24	Ghana	Kujani Game Reserve															
25	Ghana	Owabi Wildlife Sanctuary						BIRDS & SMALL MAMMALS									
26	Ghana	Bia National Park															
27	Ghana	Kakum Nature Park															
28	Burkina Faso	Parc National d'Arly															
29	Togo	Parc National de la Kéran															
30	Togo	Parc National de Fazao-Malfakassa															
31	Benin	Parc National de la Pendjari															
32	Nigeria	Kamuku Wildlife Reserve						BUDGERIGARS									
33	Nigeria	Hadejia-Nguru Wetlands						WETLAND BIRDS									
34	Nigeria	Yankari National Park															
35	Nigeria	Gashaka Game Reserve															
36	Nigeria	Okomo Sanctuary															
37	Nigeria	Cross River National Park															
38	Cameroon	Parc National du Korup						BUDGERIGARS & RAINFOREST BIRDS									
39	Cameroon	Réserve du Dja															
40	Cameroon	Parc National de la Bénoué															
41	Cameroon	Parc National de Bouba Ndjida															
42	Cameroon	Parc National de Waza															
43	Chad	Parc National de Zakouma				(Widespread poaching; greatly depleted stocks)											
44	Central African Rep.	Parc National Manovo-Gounda-St Floris															
45	Central African Rep.	Parc National du Bamingui-Bangoran															
46	Central African Rep.	Réserve du Dzanga-Sangha															
47	Gabon	Réserve de Lopé															
48	Gabon	Parc National de l'Okanda						OKAPI									
49	Gabon	Réserve d'Iguéla															

	COUNTRY	PARK/RESERVE	ELEPHANT	RHINOCEROS	HIPPOPOTAMUS	BUFFALO	ZEBRA	GIRAFFE	ANTELOPE	LION	LEOPARD	CHEETAH	HYENA	WARTHOG	GORILLA	CHIMPANZEE	MONKEY
50	Gabon	Réserve de Petit-Loango						LEATHERBACK SEA TURTLE									
51	Gabon	Réserve de la Moukalaba						LEATHERBACK SEA TURTLE									
52	Gabon	Réserve de Ndendé															
53	Congo, Dem. Rep.	Parc National de la Salonga															
54	Congo, Dem. Rep.	Parc National de la Garamba															
55	Congo, Dem. Rep.	Réserve du Okapi						OKAPI									
56	Congo, Dem. Rep.	Parc National des Virunga															
57	Congo, Dem. Rep.	Parc National de la Maiko															
58	Congo, Dem. Rep.	Parc National du Kahuzi-Biega															
59	Congo, Dem. Rep.	Parc National de l'Upemba															
60	Congo, Dem. Rep.	Parc National de Kundelungu															
61	Sudan	Dinder National Park						(Data unavailable)									
62	Ethiopia	Simien National Park						(Data unavailable)									
63	Ethiopia	Awash National Park						(Data unavailable)									
64	Ethiopia	Langano & Shala-Abiyata Lakes Nat. Pk.						(Data unavailable)									
65	Ethiopia	Bale Mountains National Park						(Data unavailable)									
66	Ethiopia	Omo and Mago National Parks						(Data unavailable)									
67	Somalia	Hargeysa National Park						(Data unavailable)									
68	Somalia	Kismayo National Park						(Data unavailable)									
69	Uganda	Ruwenzori National Park															
70	Uganda	Queen Elizabeth National Park															
71	Uganda	Bwindi Impenetrable National Park															
72	Rwanda	Parc des Volcans															
73	Rwanda	Parc National de l'Akagera						BIRDLIFE									
74	Kenya	Sibiloi National Park															
75	Kenya	Marsabit National Park															
76	Kenya	Mount Elgon National Park															
77	Kenya	Samburu National Reserve															
78	Kenya	Meru National Park															
79	Kenya	Mount Kenya National Park															
80	Kenya	Aberdare National Park															
81	Kenya	Lake Nakuru National Park						FLAMINGOS									
82	Kenya	Masai Mara National Reserve															
83	Kenya	Nairobi National Park															
84	Kenya	Amboseli National Park															
85	Kenya	Tsavo National Park															
86	Kenya	Shimba Hills National Reserve						SABLE ANTELOPE									
87	Tanzania	Rubondo Island National Park						WETLAND BIRDS									
88	Tanzania	Serengeti National Park															
89	Tanzania	Ngorongoro Conservation Area															
90	Tanzania	Kilimanjaro National Park															
91	Tanzania	Arusha National Park															
92	Tanzania	Tarangire National Park															
93	Tanzania	Gombe National Park															
94	Tanzania	Ruaha National Park															
95	Tanzania	Selous Game Reserve															
96	Malawi	Nyika National Park						BUTTERFLIES & BIRDS									
97	Malawi	Kasungu National Park															
98	Malawi	Lake Malawi National Park															

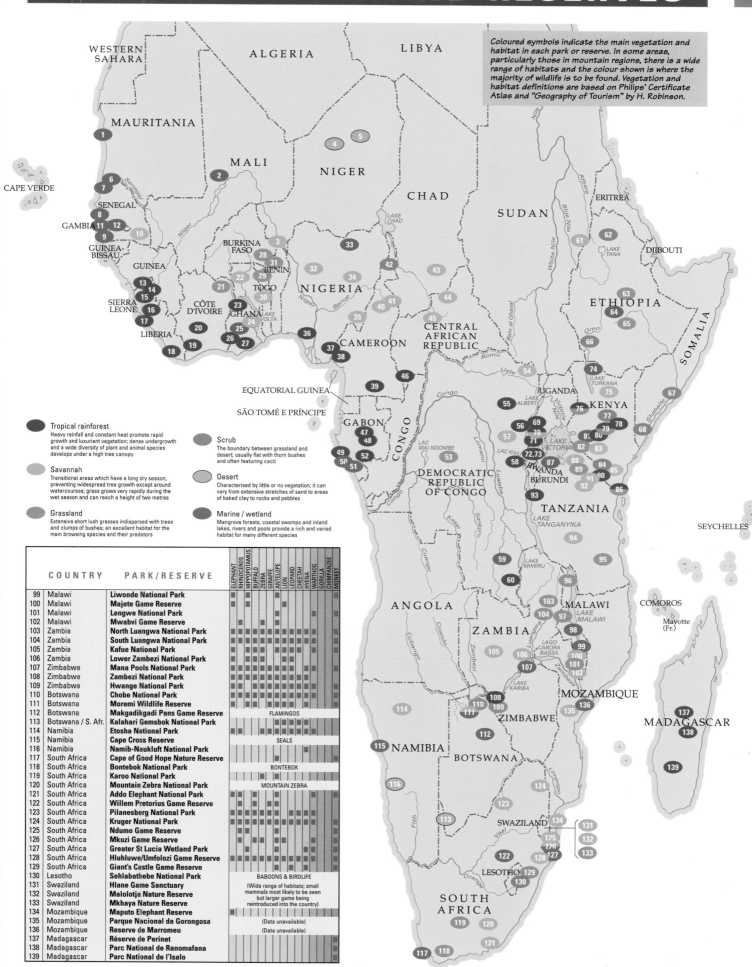

WILDLIFE PARKS AND RESERVES

Coloured symbols indicate the main vegetation and habitat in each park or reserve. In some areas, particularly those in mountain regions, there is a wide range of habitats and the colour shown is where the majority of wildlife is to be found. Vegetation and habitat definitions are based on Philips' Certificate Atlas and "Geography of Tourism" by H. Robinson.

Tropical rainforest
Heavy rainfall and constant heat promote rapid growth and luxuriant vegetation; dense undergrowth and a wide diversity of plant and animal species develops under a high tree canopy

Savannah
Transitional areas which have a long dry season, preventing widespread tree growth except around watercourses; grass grows very rapidly during the wet season and can reach a height of two metres

Grassland
Extensive short lush grasses indispersed with trees and clumps of bushes; an excellent habitat for the main browsing species and their predators

Scrub
The boundary between grassland and desert; usually flat with thorn bushes and often featuring cacti

Desert
Characterised by little or no vegetation; it can vary from extensive stretches of sand to areas of baked clay to rocks and pebbles

Marine / wetland
Mangrove forests, coastal swamps and inland lakes, rivers and pools provide a rich and varied habitat for many different species

	COUNTRY	PARK/RESERVE
99	Malawi	Liwonde National Park
100	Malawi	Majete Game Reserve
101	Malawi	Lengwe National Park
102	Malawi	Mwabvi Game Reserve
103	Zambia	North Luangwa National Park
104	Zambia	South Luangwa National Park
105	Zambia	Kafue National Park
106	Zambia	Lower Zambezi National Park
107	Zimbabwe	Mana Pools National Park
108	Zimbabwe	Zambezi National Park
109	Zimbabwe	Hwange National Park
110	Botswana	Chobe National Park
111	Botswana	Moremi Wildlife Reserve
112	Botswana	Makgadikgadi Pans Game Reserve
113	Botswana / S. Afr.	Kalahari Gemsbok National Park
114	Namibia	Etosha National Park
115	Namibia	Cape Cross Reserve
116	Namibia	Namib-Naukluft National Park
117	South Africa	Cape of Good Hope Nature Reserve
118	South Africa	Bontebok National Park
119	South Africa	Karoo National Park
120	South Africa	Mountain Zebra National Park
121	South Africa	Addo Elephant National Park
122	South Africa	Willem Pretorius Game Reserve
123	South Africa	Pilanesberg National Park
124	South Africa	Kruger National Park
125	South Africa	Ndumo Game Reserve
126	South Africa	Mkuzi Game Reserve
127	South Africa	Greater St Lucia Wetland Park
128	South Africa	Hluhluwe/Umfolozi Game Reserve
129	South Africa	Giant's Castle Game Reserve
130	Lesotho	Sehlabathebe National Park
131	Swaziland	Hlane Game Sanctuary
132	Swaziland	Malolotja Nature Reserve
133	Swaziland	Mkhaya Nature Reserve
134	Mozambique	Maputo Elephant Reserve
135	Mozambique	Parque Nacional da Gorongosa
136	Mozambique	Reserve de Marromeu
137	Madagascar	Réserve de Perinet
138	Madagascar	Parc National de Ranomafana
139	Madagascar	Parc National de l'Isalo

Column headings (animal symbols): ELEPHANT, RHINOCEROS, HIPPOPOTAMUS, BUFFALO, ZEBRA, GIRAFFE, ANTELOPE, LION, LEOPARD, CHEETAH, HYENA, WARTHOG, GORILLA, CHIMPANZEE, MONKEY

FLAMINGOS
SEALS
BONTEBOK
MOUNTAIN ZEBRA
BABOONS & BIRDLIFE
(Wide range of habitats; small mammals most likely to be seen but larger game being reintroduced into the country)
(Data unavailable)
(Data unavailable)

CLIMATE

TEMPERATURE CONVERSION

°Celsius	−10	0	10	20	30	40
°Fahrenheit	14	32	50	68	86	104

RAINFALL CONVERSION

Millimetres	102	203	305	406	508	610
Inches	4	8	12	16	20	24

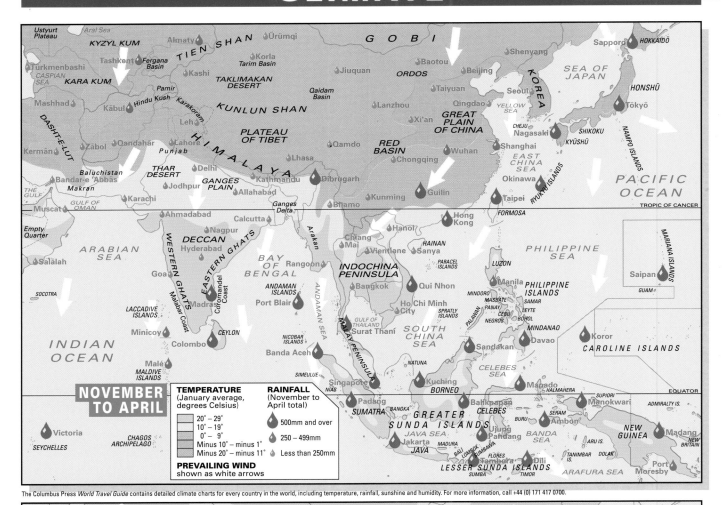

NOVEMBER TO APRIL

TEMPERATURE
(January average, degrees Celsius)
- 20° – 29°
- 10° – 19°
- 0° – 9°
- Minus 10° – minus 1°
- Minus 20° – minus 11°

RAINFALL
(November to April total)
- 500mm and over
- 250 – 499mm
- Less than 250mm

PREVAILING WIND
shown as white arrows

The Columbus Press *World Travel Guide* contains detailed climate charts for every country in the world, including temperature, rainfall, sunshine and humidity. For more information, call +44 (0) 171 417 0700.

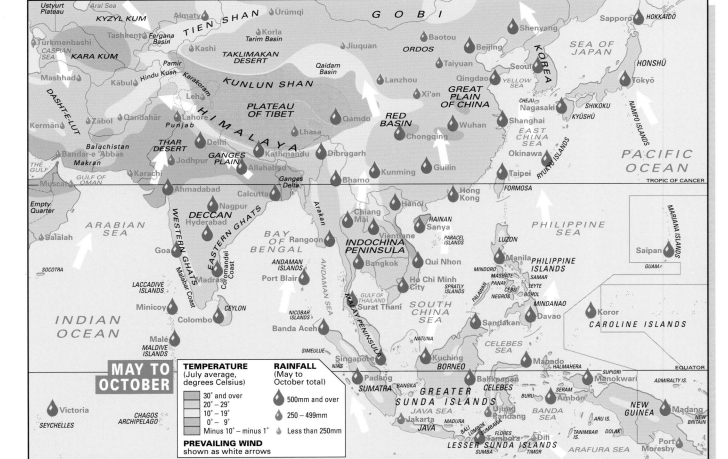

MAY TO OCTOBER

TEMPERATURE
(July average, degrees Celsius)
- 30° and over
- 20° – 29°
- 10° – 19°
- 0° – 9°
- Minus 10° – minus 1°

RAINFALL
(May to October total)
- 500mm and over
- 250 – 499mm
- Less than 250mm

PREVAILING WIND
shown as white arrows

INDIA

See page 28 for general map

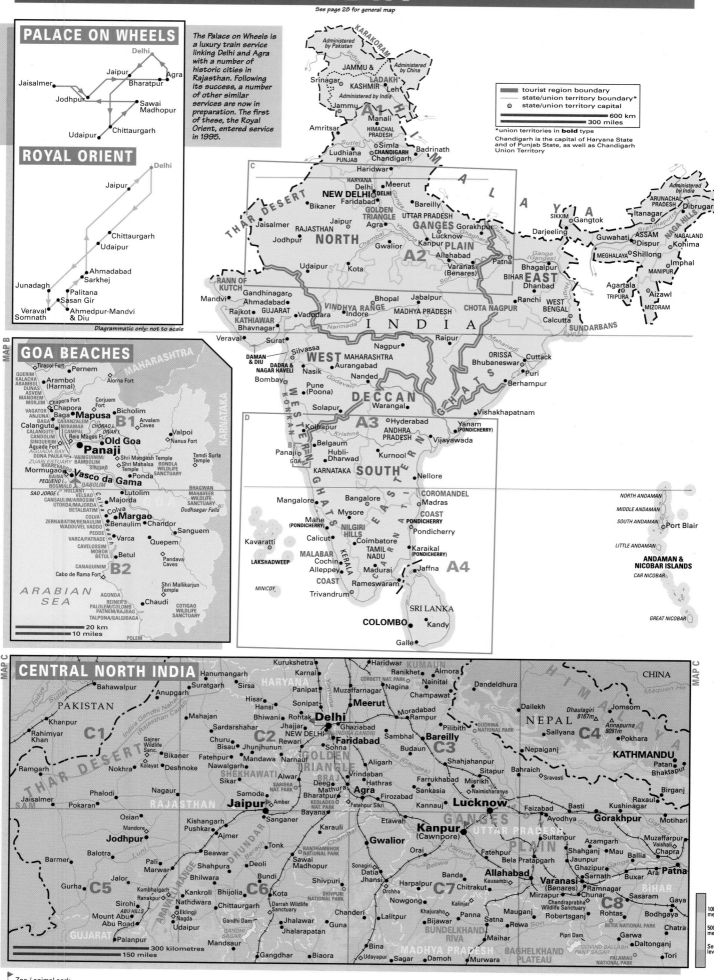

INDIA AND SRI LANKA

See page 28 for general map

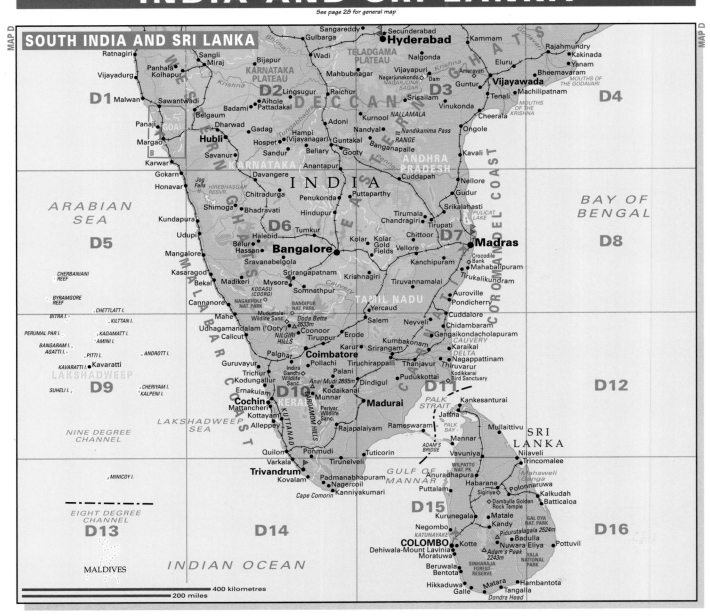

MALDIVES

See page 28 for general map

SEYCHELLES

See page 24 for general map

▶ Leisure park ▶ Zoo / animal park ▶ Major tennis venue

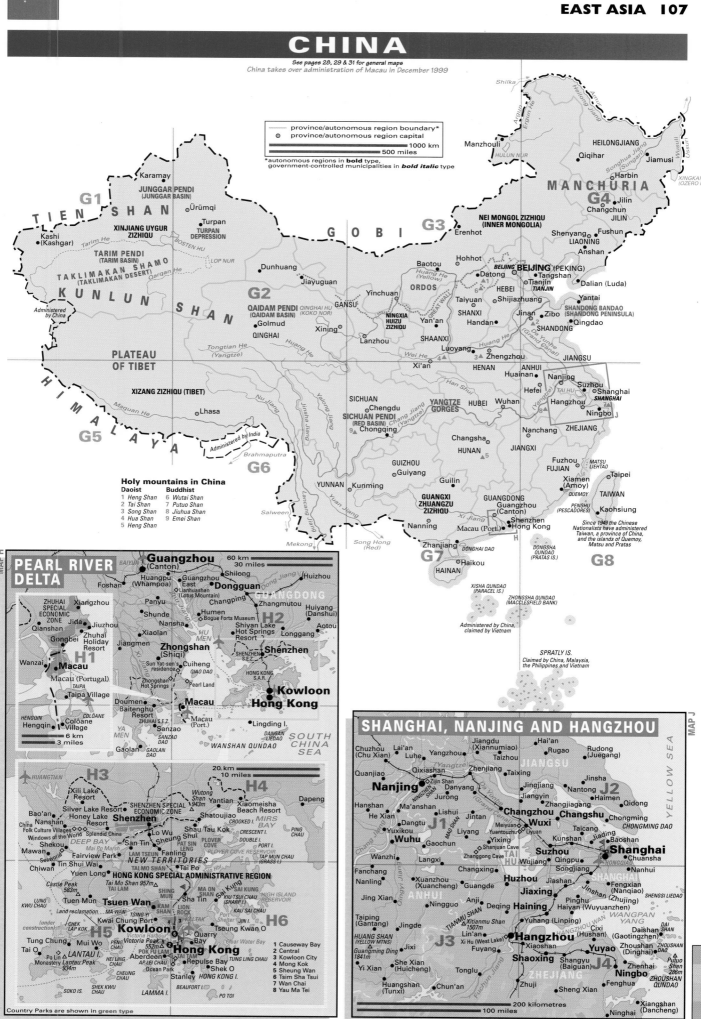

CHINA

See pages 28, 29 & 31 for general maps
China takes over administration of Macau in December 1999

province/autonomous region boundary*
province/autonomous region capital

1000 km
500 miles

*autonomous regions in **bold** type,
government-controlled municipalities in ***bold italic*** type

Holy mountains in China

Daoist	Buddhist
1 Heng Shan	6 Wutai Shan
2 Tai Shan	7 Putuo Shan
3 Song Shan	8 Jiuhua Shan
4 Hua Shan	9 Emei Shan
5 Heng Shan	

Since 1949 the Chinese
Nationalists have administered
Taiwan, a province of China,
and the islands of Quemoy,
Matsu and Pratas

Administered by China,
claimed by Vietnam

SPRATLY IS.
*Claimed by China, Malaysia,
the Philippines and Vietnam*

PEARL RIVER DELTA

60 km
30 miles

6 km
3 miles

20 km
10 miles

Country Parks are shown in green type

SHANGHAI, NANJING AND HANGZHOU

200 kilometres
100 miles

1000 metres
500 metres
Sea level

Leisure park   Zoo / animal park   Horse racing   Major tennis venue

1 Causeway Bay
2 Central
3 Kowloon City
4 Mong Kok
5 Sheung Wan
6 Tsim Sha Tsui
7 Wan Chai
8 Yau Ma Tei

INDOCHINA

See page 31 for general map

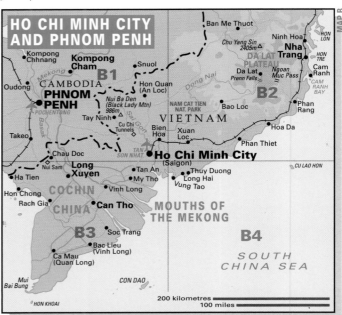

HO CHI MINH CITY AND PHNOM PENH

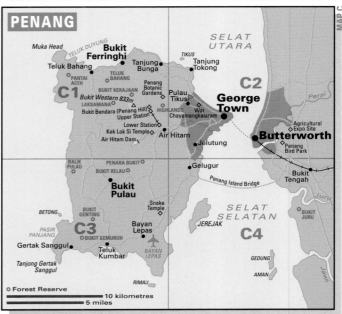

PENANG

KUALA LUMPUR

SINGAPORE

THAILAND

See page 31 for general map

NORTHERN HILLS

F1

Chiang Rai
Mae Hong Son
Chiang Mai
Nan
Lampang
Tak
Phitsanulok

CENTRAL PLAINS
F2

Nong Khai
Ban Chiang
Udon Thani
Nakhon Phanom
Sakon Nakhon
Khon Kaen
Mukdahan

KORAT PLATEAU

Nakhon Sawan
Phimai
Lop Buri
Nakhon Ratchasima (Khorat)
Phanom Rung
Ayutthaya
Ubon Ratchathani

KRUNG THEP (BANGKOK)
Ratchaburi
Chon Buri
Petchaburi
Pattaya
Hua Hin
KO SAMET
Chanthaburi
KO CHANG
KO KUT

Prachuap Khiri Khan

F3

Chumphon
ISTHMUS OF KRA
KO TAO
KO SURIN
KO PHANGAN
KO SAMUI
KO PHRA THONG
Don Sak
Surat Thani
Nakhon Si Thammarat
K
KO PHUKET
Phuket
KO LANTA
Trang
THALE LUANG
PENINSULAR THAILAND
F4
Songkhla
Hat Yai
KO TARUTAO
Sadao
Narithiwat

200 km
100 miles

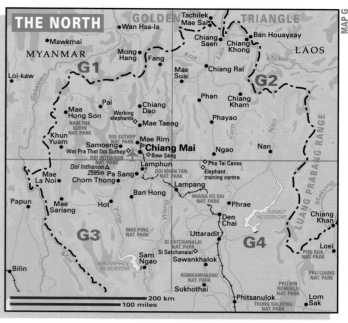

THE NORTH

GOLDEN TRIANGLE

G

Tachilek
Mae Sai
Wan Hsa-la
Mawkmai
Chiang Saen
Ban Houayxay
MYANMAR
Mong Hang
Fang
Chiang Khong
LAOS
G1
Loi-kaw
Mae Hong Son
Pai
Chiang Dao
Mae Suai
Chiang Rai
G2
Khun Yuam
Working elephants
Mae Taeng
Phan
Chiang Kham
Mae Rim
Phayao
Samoeng
Chiang Mai
Wat Pra That Doi Suthep
Baw Sang
Ngao
Nan
Doi Inthanon 2595m
Lamphun
Pha Tai Caves
Mae La Noi
Pa Sang
Elephant training centre
Chom Thong
Ban Hong
Lampang
Papun
Hot
Phrae
Chiang Khan
Mae Sariang
Den Chai
G3
Uttaradit
G4
Loei
Bilin
Sam Ngao
Si Satchanalai
Sawankhalok
Sukhothai
Phitsanulok
Lom Sak

200 km
100 miles

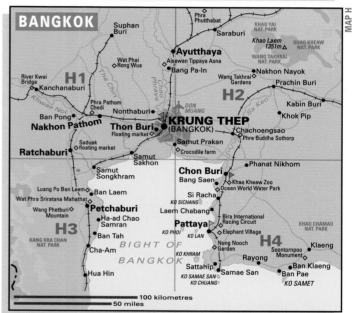

BANGKOK

Suphan Buri
Phra Phutthabat
Saraburi
Khao Laem 1351m
H
Wat Phai Rong Wua
Ayutthaya
Aisawan Tippaya Asna
Bang Pa-In
Wang Takhrai Gardens
Nakhon Nayok
River Kwai Bridge
H1
Kanchanaburi
Phra Pathom Chedi
Nonthaburi
H2
Prachin Buri
Ban Pong
Kabin Buri
Khok Pip
Nakhon Pathom
Thon Buri
KRUNG THEP (BANGKOK)
Chachoengsao
Phra Buddha Sothorp
Saduak floating market
Floating market
Samut Prakan
Crocodile farm
Ratchaburi
Samut Sakhon
Phanat Nikhom
Samut Songkhram
Chon Buri
Luang Po Ban Laem
Ban Laem
Bang Saen
Khao Kheaw Zoo
Ocean World Water Park
Wat Phra Sriratana Mahathat
Si Racha
KO SICHANG
Wang Phetburi Mountain
Laem Chabang
Petchaburi
Bira International Racing Circuit
H3
Ha-ad Chao Samran
Pattaya
Elephant Village
KO PHOI
KO LAN
Ban Tah
H4
Cha-Am
Nong Nooch Garden
Soontornpoo Monument
Klaeng
KO KHRAM
Rayong
Hua Hin
Sattahip
Samae San
Ban Pae
KO SAMAE SAN
KO CHUANG
Ban Klaeng
KO SAMET
BIGHT OF BANGKOK

100 kilometres
50 miles

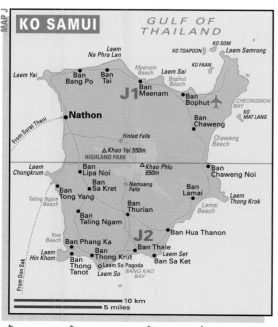

KO SAMUI

GULF OF THAILAND

Laem Na Phra Lan
KO SOM
KO TOAPOON
Laem Samrong
Laem Yai
KO FAAN
Laem Sai
Maenam Beach
Ban Bang Po
Ban Tai
J1
Ban Maenam
Bophut Beach
Ban Bophut
CHEONGMON BAY
From Surat Thani
Nathon
Ban Chaweng
KO MAT LANG
Hinlad Falls
Chaweng Beach
△Khao Yai 550m
HIGHLAND PARK
Laem Chongkrum
Ban Lipa Noi
△Khao Phlu 650m
Ban Chaweng Noi
Namuang Falls
Ban Sa Kret
Ban Lamai
Taling Ngam Beach
Ban Tong Yang
Ban Thurian
Lamai Beach
Laem Thong Krok
Yow Beach
Ban Taling Ngam
J2
Ban Hua Thanon
From Don Sak
Ban Phang Ka
Ban Thale
Laem Set
Laem Hin Khom
Ban Thong Tanot
Ban Thong Krut
Ban Sa Ket
Laem So Pagoda
Laem So
BANG KAO BAY

10 km
5 miles

EASTERN & ORIENTAL EXPRESS

	Distance from Bangkok	
	Kilometres	Miles
Chiang Mai	751	467
Bangkok	0	0
Hua Hin	229	142
Hat Yai	945	587
Butterworth	1161	721
Kuala Lumpur	1552	964
Singapore	1946	1209

The Eastern & Oriental Express is a luxury train service connecting Thailand, Malaysia and Singapore. The journey takes two days. An overnight service to Chiang Mai is also available.

For further information, contact:

Venice-Simplon-Orient-Express Ltd., Sea Containers House, 20 Upper Ground, London SE1 9PF, United Kingdom. Tel. +44 (0) 171 928 6000.

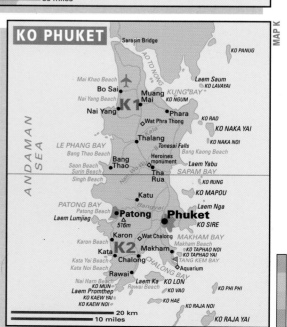

KO PHUKET

Sarasin Bridge
KO PANUG
AO TO NONG
Mai Khao Beach
Bo Sai
Muang Mai
KUNG BAY
KO NGUM
Nai Yang Beach
K1
Laem Saum
KO LAVAYAI
Nai Yang
Phara
Wat Phra Thong
KO RAD
KO NAKA YAI
Thalang
KO NAKA NOI
ANDAMAN SEA
LE PHANG BAY
Tonesai Falls
Bang Kaong Beach
Bang Thao Beach
Heroines monument
Laem Yabu
Saon Beach
Bang Thao
SAPAM BAY
Surin Beach
Tha Rua
KO RUNG
Singh Beach
Katu
KO MAPOU
PATONG BAY
Bangyai
KO NGA
Patong Beach
Patong
△516m
Phuket
KO SIRE
Laem Lumjiag
Karon
Wat Chalong
MAKHAM BAY
Karon Beach
Kata
Makham
Makham Beach
K2
KO TAPHAO NOI
KO TAPHAO YAI
Kata Yai Beach
Chalong
TANG KEM BAY
Kata Noi Beach
CHALONG BAY
Rawai
Aquarium
Nai Harn Beach
Laem Ka
KO LON
Laem Promthep
KO MUN
KO PHI PHI
Laem Ka
KO KAEW YAI
KO VAO
KO KAEW NOI
KO HAE
KO RAJA NOI
KO RAJA YAI

20 km
10 miles

1000 metres
500 metres
Sea level

▶ Leisure park   ▶ Zoo / animal park   ▶ Aquarium   ▶ Major tennis venue

INDONESIA

See page 32 for general maps

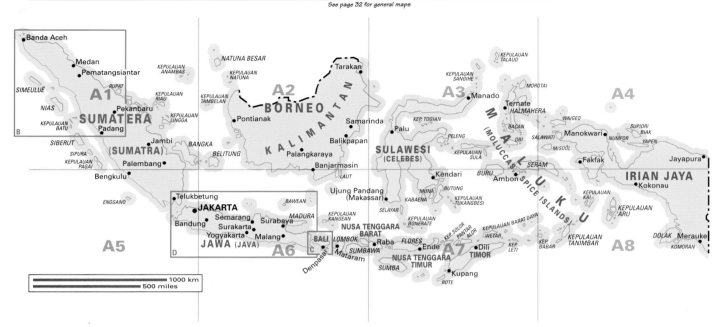

Banda Aceh · Medan · Pematangsiantar · Pekanbaru · Padang · SUMATERA (SUMATRA) · SIMEULUË · NIAS · KEPULAUAN BATU · SIBERUT · SIPURA · KEPULAUAN PAGAI · Jambi · BANGKA · BELITUNG · Palembang · Bengkulu · ENGGANO · A1 · A5 · KEPULAUAN ANAMBAS · KEPULAUAN NATUNA · NATUNA BESAR · KEPULAUAN RIAU · KEPULAUAN TAMBELAN · KEPULAUAN LINGGA · Pontianak · A2 · BORNEO · KALIMANTAN · Tarakan · Samarinda · Balikpapan · Palangkaraya · Banjarmasin · LAUT · Telukbetung · JAKARTA · Bandung · Semarang · Surakarta · Surabaya · Yogyakarta · Malang · MADURA · BAWEAN · JAWA (JAVA) · A6 · BALI · Denpasar · Mataram · Lombok · Raba · Sumbawa · NUSA TENGGARA BARAT · NUSA TENGGARA TIMUR · SUMBA · ROTE · Kupang · Ende · FLORES · Dili · TIMOR · A7 · KEPULAUAN SANGIHE · KEPULAUAN TALAUD · Manado · Ternate · HALMAHERA · MOROTAI · SULAWESI (CELEBES) · Palu · KEP. TOGIAN · PELENG · BACAN · OBI · SALAWATI · MISOOL · SERAM · BURU · Ambon · Ujung Pandang (Makassar) · Kendari · MUNA · BUTUNG · KABAENA · SELAYAR · KEPULAUAN TUKANGBESI · KEPULAUAN BONERATE · KEP. SOLOR · PANTAR · ALOR · WETAR · KEP. LETI · KEP. BABAR · KEPULAUAN BARAT DAYA · KEPULAUAN TANIMBAR · A3 · WAIGEO · SUPIORI · BIAK · NUMFOR · YAPEN · Manokwari · Fakfak · KEPULAUAN KAI · KEPULAUAN ARU · A4 · IRIAN JAYA · Jayapura · Kokonau · DOLAK · Merauke · KOMORAN · A8 · M A L U K U (MOLUCCAS) SPICE ISLANDS

1000 km
500 miles

NORTHERN SUMATRA

Sabang · BREUEH · WE · Banda Aceh · Lho-Nga Beach · Meureudu · Bireuen · Lhokseumawe · Gunung Peuetsagoe 2780m · Gunung Geureudong 2855m · Calang · Takingeun · DANAU LAUTTAWAR · Langsa · B1 · ACEH · Meulaboh · Gunung Leuser 3381m · Blangkerejen · Pangkalanbrandan · Susoh · Orang-utan rehabilitation centre · Belawan · Binjai · Medan · Tapaktuan · Brastagi · POLONIA · Tebingtinggi · Sibigo · Bakungan · Kabanjahe · Karo Batak Villages · Pematangsiantar · G. Siluatan 2475m · Prapat · Tuk Tuk · Tanjungbalai · Labuhanbilik · Sinabang · Singkil · Tarutung · SAMOSIR · LAKE TOBA · SUMATERA UTARA · Rantauprapat · Bagansiapiapi · Lahewa · Gunungsitoli · Sibolga · MUSALA · Padanglawas · Dumai · RUPAT · INDIAN OCEAN · NIAS · B3 · Hilisimaetano · Telukdalem · Bawamataluo · Hutanopan · Natal · Padangsidempuan · B4 · RIAU · Siak Kecil Reserve · Pekanbaru · EQUATOR · KEPULAUAN BANYAK · KEPULAUAN BATU · TANAHMASA · TANAHBALA · Luahasibuka · DANAU MANINJAU · Bukittinggi · Payakumbuh · Gunung Merapi 2891m · Padangpanjang · Batusangkar · Sijunjung · DANAU SINGKARAK · Pariaman · Solok · BARAT · Rimbo Panti Reserve · Muaro Takus · Lemba Harau Reserve · SUMATERA BARAT · Padang · Georgetown · PINANG · Taiping · Ipoh · MALAYSIA · B2 · STRAIT OF MALACCA · KUALA LUMPUR · Kelang

300 kilometres
150 miles

MAP B

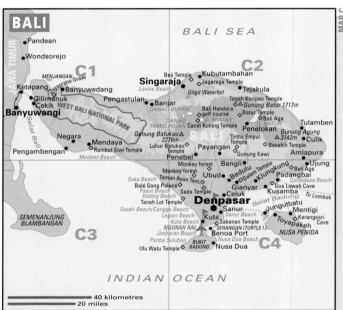

BALI

BALI SEA · Pandean · Wondsorejo · JAWA TIMUR · Ketapang · MENJANGAN · Jayaprana Grave · Banyuwedang · Gilimanuk · Cekik · Pengastulan · Banjar · Lovina Beach · C1 · Singaraja · Jagaraga Temple · Gitgit Waterfall · Tegeh Koripan Temple · Tejakula · C2 · Beji Temple · Kubutambahan · Banyuwangi · WEST BALI NATIONAL PARK · DANAU BUYAN · Bali Handara golf course · Gunung Batur 1717m · Batur Temple · Tulamben · DANAU TAMBLINGAN · Candi Kuning Temple · Bali Aga · DANAU BRATAN · Negara · Mendaya · Rambut Siwi Temple · Gunung Batukau 2276m · Luhur Batukau Temple · Penebel · Payangan · Tirtha Empul · Gunung Kawi · G. BATUR 3142m · Gunung Agung 3142m · Culik · Besakih Temple · Amlapura · Pengambengan · Medewi Beach · Monkey forest · Ubud · Bedulu · Bangli · Gianyar · Klungkung · Ujung · BALI AGA · Soka Beach · Taman Ayun Tem. · Dalem Temple · Padangbai · Candidasa Beach · Balé Gong Palace · Sada Temple · Celuk · Kusamba · Goa Lawah Cave · Pasut Beach · Kerangasari · Klating Beach · Denpasar · Sanur · SELAT BADUNG · Jungutbatu · Tanah Lot Temple · Seseh Beach/Canggu Beach · Legian Beach · Kuta · Sakenan Temple · Toyapakeh · Mentigi · Kuta Beach · NGURAH RAI · SERANGAN (TURTLE I.) · Benoa Port · NUSA PENIDA · C4 · Jimbaran Beach · Pantai Suluban · Nusa Dua Beach · Benoa · BUKIT BADUNG · Ulu Watu Temple · Nusa Dua · SEMENANJUNG BLAMBANGAN · C3 · To Lombok · Selat Bali · INDIAN OCEAN

40 kilometres
20 miles

MAP C

JAVA

JAVA SEA · Telukbetung · Panjang · LEGUNDI · Bakauheni · D1 · SOEKARNO-HATTA · SEBUKU · SEBESI · Merak · Banten · Jaya Ancol Dreamland · Bekasi · Karawang · Krakatau 813m · Anyer · Serang · JAKARTA · HALIM PERDANA KUSUMA · Karang · Purwakarta · Subang · Kandanghaur · Indramayu · Jatibarang · Carita · Labuhan · Rangkasbitung · Bogor · JAWA BARAT · Cianjur · Jatiwangi · D2 · Cirebon · PANAITAN · Gunung Pangrango 3022m · G. Tangkuban Berahu 2076m · Majalengka · Brebes · Tegal · Pekalongan · Weleri · Tanjung Guakolak · DELI · TINJIL · Pelabuhanratu · Sukabumi · Cimahi · Bandung · G. Cirema 3078m · Ciledug · Pemalang · G. Slamet 3428m · JAWA TENGAH · Semarang · Demak · Kudus · Jepara · Tayu · Rembang · D3 · Tuban · MADURA · Ambunten · Sumenep · Bangkalan · Sampang · Pamekasan · Genteng · Garut · Tasikmalaya · Ciamis · Banjar · Purwokerto · Purbolinggo · Wonosobo · G. Sumbing 3371m · DIENG PLATEAU · Temanggung · Bandungan · Purwodadi · Cepu · Bojonegoro · Gresik · Surabaya · SELAT MADURA · PUTERAN · SAPUDI · RAAS · GENTENG · Sindangbarang · Pangandaran · Kroya · Banyumas · Kebumen · Magelang · G. Merbabu 3142m · Salatiga · Solo · Mojokerto · Trowulan · Bangil · Pameungpeuk · Cijulang · Cilacap · Jatijajar Caves · Kaliurang · Candi Sukuh Tem. · Prambanan · Surakarta (Solo) · Jombang · Kertosono · Madiun · G. Lawu 3265m · Pasuruan · Probolinggo · Pasirputih · Situbondo · Yogyakarta · Parangtritis · Tawangmangu · Kediri · Tulungagung · G. Arjuna 3339m · Malang · G. Argopuro 3088m · Lawang · Bondowoso · G. Bromo 2329m · Jember · D8 · Pacitan · Blitar · G. Lawu · G. Semeru 3637m · Lumajang · G. Raung 3332m · Banyuwangi · BALI · Ketapang · Brantas · D5 · D6 · D7 · INDIAN OCEAN · SEMPU · BARUNG · Semenanjung Blambangan · KEPULAUAN KARIMUNJAWA · BAWEAN · KEPULAUAN MASALEMBO · D4 · Lamongan

MAP D

200 kilometres
100 miles

1000 metres · 500 metres · Sea level

▶ Leisure park ▶ Zoo / animal park ▶ Major tennis venue

AUSTRALIA

See page 34 for general map

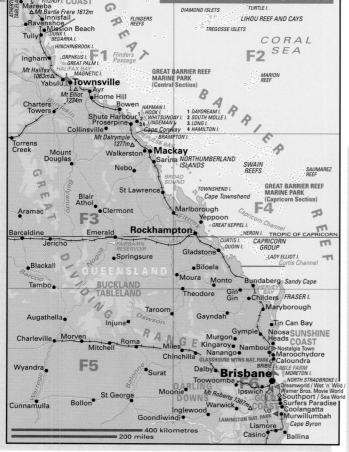

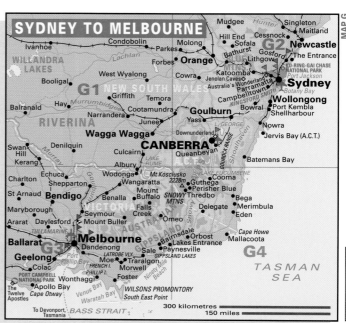

AUSTRALIA
See page 34 for general map

THE RED CENTRE

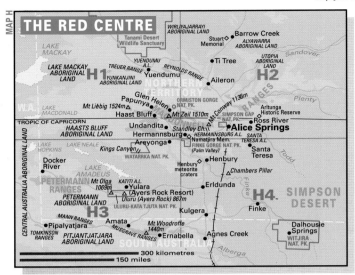

Tanami Desert Wildlife Sanctuary
WIRLIYAJARRAYI ABORIGINAL LAND
Stuart Memorial
Barrow Creek
ALYAWARRA ABORIGINAL LAND
Sandover
LAKE MACKAY
YUENDUMU
Ti Tree
UTOPIA ABORIGINAL LAND
LAKE MACKAY ABORIGINAL LAND
H1
TREUER RANGE
REYNOLDS RANGE
YUNKANJINI ABORIGINAL LAND
Aileron
H2
NORTHERN TERRITORY
Plenty
W.A.
LAKE MACDONALD
Glen Helen
Papunya
Mt Liebig 1524m
ORMISTON GORGE NAT. PK.
Mt Zeil 1510m
Mt Conway 1136m
SIMPSON GAP NAT. PK.
Arltunga Historic Reserve
RANGES
Haast Bluff
Alice Springs
Ross River
TROPIC OF CAPRICORN
HAASTS BLUFF ABORIGINAL LAND
Undandita
Standley Chm.
HERMANNSBURG A.L.
SANTA TERESA A.L.
LAKE HOPKINS
Hermannsburg
Namatjira Mem.
Santa Teresa
Areyonga
FINKE GORGE NAT. PK. (Palm Valley)
LAKE NEALE
Kings Canyon
Henbury
Todd
WATARRKA NAT. PK.
Docker River
Henbury meteorite craters
Erldunda
LAKE AMADEUS
Mt Olga 1069m
KATITI A.L.
Yulara
Uluru (Ayers Rock Resort)
Uluru (Ayers Rock) 867m
Kulgera
Chambers Pillar
H4
PETERMANN RANGES
ULURU-KATA TJUTA NAT. PK.
Finke
SIMPSON DESERT
PETERMANN ABORIGINAL LAND
H3
MANN RANGES
Amata
Mt Woodroffe 1440m
Dalhousie Springs
CENTRAL AUSTRALIA ABORIGINAL LAND
Pipalyatjara
MUSGRAVE RANGES
Ernabella
Agnes Creek
WITJIRA NAT. PK.
TOMKINSON RANGES
PITJANTJATJARA ABORIGINAL LAND
SOUTH AUSTRALIA
Alberga

300 kilometres
150 miles

LONG-DISTANCE RAIL SERVICES

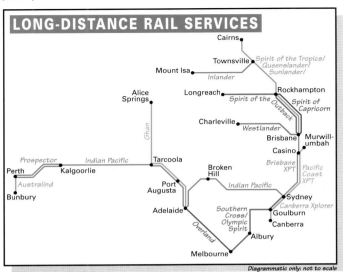

Cairns
Townsville
Spirit of the Tropics/ Queenslander/ Sunlander
Mount Isa
Inlander
Longreach
Rockhampton
Alice Springs
Spirit of the Outback
Spirit of Capricorn
Charleville
Westlander
Brisbane
Murwillumbah
Casino
Ghan
Prospector
Indian Pacific
Tarcoola
Broken Hill
Brisbane XPT
Perth
Kalgoorlie
Pacific Coast XPT
Australind
Bunbury
Port Augusta
Indian Pacific
Sydney
Canberra Xplorer
Adelaide
Southern Cross/ Olympic Spirit
Goulburn
Canberra
Overland
Albury
Melbourne

Diagrammatic only: not to scale

NEW ZEALAND
See page 35 for general map

CENTRAL NORTH ISLAND

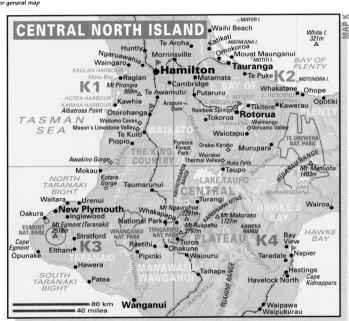

MAYOR I.
MATAKANA I.
White I. 321m
MAP K
Waihi Beach
Te Aroha
Katikati
Omokoroa
Mount Maunganui
Huntly
Morrinsville
Ngaruawahia
Waingaro
MOTITI I.
BAY OF PLENTY
Hamilton
Tauranga
RAGLAN HARBOUR
Manu Bay
Raglan
Mt Pirongia 959m
Matamata
Te Puke
K2
MOTUHORA I.
K1
Cambridge
Te Awamutu
Putaruru
L. ROTOEHU
Whakatane
Ohope
AOTEA HARBOUR
KAWHIA HARBOUR
Kawhia
Albatross Point
Arapuni Dam
Rainbow Springs
L. ROTOITI
L. ROTOMA
Tikitere
Kawerau
Opotiki
Otorohanga
Tokoroa
Rotorua
TASMAN SEA
Waitomo Caves
Waimangu Volcanic Valley
TE UREWERA NAT. PARK
Mason's Limestone Valley
Te Kuiti
WAIKATO
Waiotapu
Piopio
THE KING COUNTRY
Pureora Forest Park
Orakei Korako
Murupara
Mokau
Kotare Gorge
Awakino Gorge
Wairakei Thermal Valley
Huka Falls
LAKE TAUPO
HUIARAU RANGE
Mt Manuoha 1403m
NORTH TARANAKI BIGHT
Waitara
Urenui
Taumarunui
Taupo
CENTRAL
Rangitaiki
HAULIHUNGAROA RANGE
KAIMANAWA MTNS.
WAIKAREMOANA
Wairoa
Oakura
New Plymouth
Inglewood
Whakapapa
Mt Ngauruhoe 2291m
National Park
Turangi
KAWEKA RANGE
HAWKE'S BAY
EGMONT NAT. PARK
Mt Egmont (Taranaki) 2518m
Stratford
Mt Ruapehu 2797m
TONGARIRO NAT. PARK
Mt Makorako 1727m
PLATEAU
Bay View
Cape Egmont
Eltham
K3
Turoa
Ohakune
Raetihi
Waiouru
Taradale
Napier
Opunake
TARANAKI
Hawera
Pipiriki
Taihape
Havelock North
Hastings
Cape Kidnappers
Patea
MANAWATU WANGANUI
RUAHINE RANGE
HAWKE BAY
SOUTH TARANAKI BIGHT
Rangitikei
Waipawa
K4
Waipukurau

80 km
40 miles
Wanganui

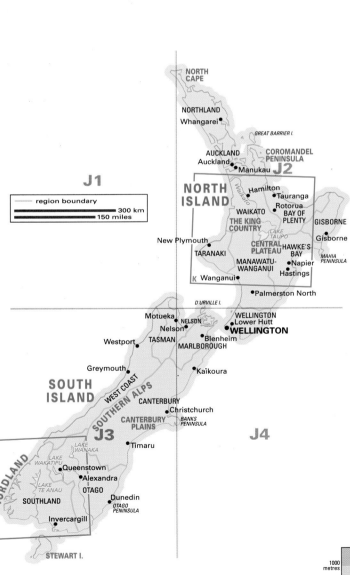

NORTH CAPE
NORTHLAND
Whangarei
GREAT BARRIER I.
AUCKLAND
Auckland
Manukau
COROMANDEL PENINSULA
J2
J1
region boundary
300 km
150 miles
NORTH ISLAND
Waikato
Hamilton
Tauranga
Rotorua
BAY OF PLENTY
WAIKATO
THE KING COUNTRY
GISBORNE
Gisborne
CENTRAL PLATEAU
HAWKE'S BAY
LAKE TAUPO
New Plymouth
TARANAKI
MANAWATU-WANGANUI
Napier
K
Wanganui
Hastings
MAHIA PENINSULA
Palmerston North
D'URVILLE I.
Motueka
NELSON
WELLINGTON
Lower Hutt
Nelson
WELLINGTON
TASMAN
Blenheim
Westport
MARLBOROUGH
Greymouth
Kaikoura
SOUTH ISLAND
WEST COAST
SOUTHERN ALPS
CANTERBURY
J4
CANTERBURY PLAINS
Christchurch
BANKS PENINSULA
J3
LAKE WANAKA
Timaru
FIORDLAND
LAKE WAKATIPU
Queenstown
Alexandra
LAKE TE ANAU
OTAGO
Dunedin
SOUTHLAND
OTAGO PENINSULA
L
Invercargill
STEWART I.

SOUTHLAND

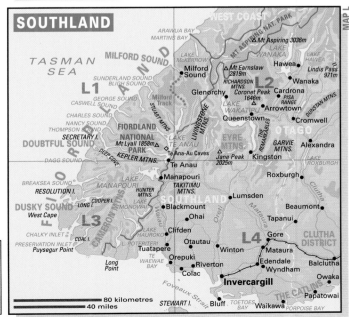

WEST COAST
MT ASPIRING NAT. PARK
ARAWATA BAY
MARTINS BAY
Mt Aspiring 3036m
LAKE WANAKA
TASMAN SEA
MILFORD SOUND
Hawea
LAKE HAWEA
Lindis Pass 971m
LAKE McKERROW
Mt Earnslaw 2819m
SUNDERLAND SOUND
BLIGH SOUND
Milford Sound
RICHARDSON MTNS.
Wanaka
L1
GEORGE SOUND
Coronet Peak 1646m
L2
CASWELL SOUND
Glenorchy
PISA RANGE
Cardrona
CHARLES SOUND
Milford Track
DUNSTAN MTNS.
NANCY SOUND
FIORDLAND
LIVINGSTONE MTNS.
Arrowtown
THOMPSON SOUND
SECRETARY I.
NATIONAL
Mt Lyall 1858m
Te Ana-Au Caves
Queenstown
Cromwell
DOUBTFUL SOUND
PARK
LAKE TE ANAU
EYRE MTNS.
OTAGO
DEEP COVE
KEPLER MTNS.
Jane Peak 2025m
THE REMARKABLES
LAKE ROXBURGH
DAGG SOUND
Te Anau
GARVIE MTNS.
Alexandra
Kingston
BREAKSEA SOUND
LAKE MANAPOURI
TAKITIMU MTNS.
Roxburgh
RESOLUTION I.
Manapouri
HUNTER MTNS.
SOUTHLAND
DUSKY SOUND
LONG I.
COOPER I.
Lumsden
Beaumont
Clutha
West Cape
LAKE MONOWAI
Blackmount
CHALKY INLET
COAL I.
Ohai
Tapanui
CLUTHA DISTRICT
PRESERVATION INLET
LAKE HAUROKO
Clifden
Otautau
L3
Gore
Puysegur Point
L. ROTEITIPOU
Tuatapere
Orepuki
Winton
Mataura
Edendale
L4
Long Point
WAEWAE BAY
Riverton
Colac
Mataura
Wyndham
Owaka
Invercargill
Bluff
FOVEAUX STRAIT
STEWART I.
TOETOES BAY
Waikawa
Balclutha
THE CATLINS
PORPOISE BAY
Papatowai

80 kilometres
40 miles

1000 metres
500 metres
Sea level

▶ Zoo / animal park   ▶ Aquarium

TEMPERATURE CONVERSION

°Celsius	−10	0	10	20	30	40
°Fahrenheit	14	32	50	68	86	104

RAINFALL CONVERSION

Millimetres	102	203	305	406	508	610
Inches	4	8	12	16	20	24

CLIMATE

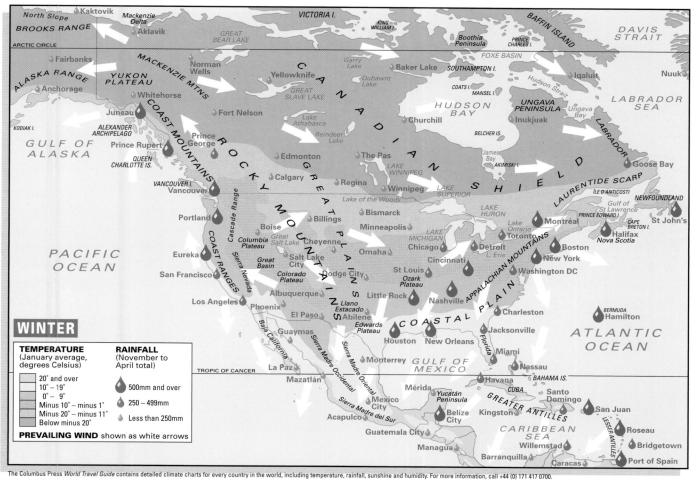

WINTER

TEMPERATURE
(January average, degrees Celsius)

- 20° and over
- 10° – 19°
- 0° – 9°
- Minus 10° – minus 1°
- Minus 20° – minus 11°
- Below minus 20°

RAINFALL
(November to April total)

- 500mm and over
- 250 – 499mm
- Less than 250mm

PREVAILING WIND shown as white arrows

The Columbus Press *World Travel Guide* contains detailed climate charts for every country in the world, including temperature, rainfall, sunshine and humidity. For more information, call +44 (0) 171 417 0700.

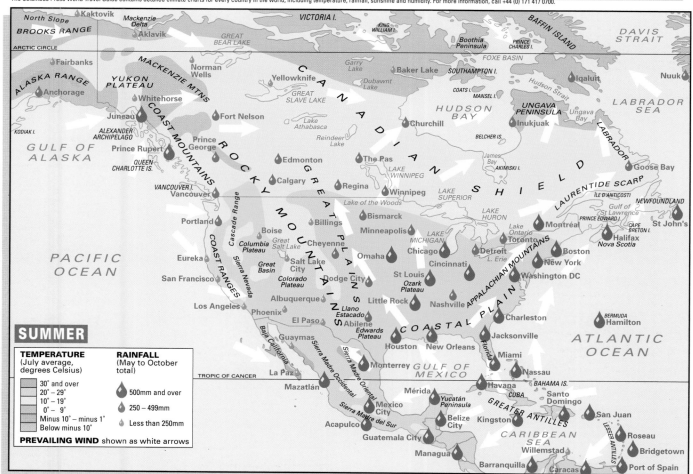

SUMMER

TEMPERATURE
(July average, degrees Celsius)

- 30° and over
- 20° – 29°
- 10° – 19°
- 0° – 9°
- Minus 10° – minus 1°
- Below minus 10°

RAINFALL
(May to October total)

- 500mm and over
- 250 – 499mm
- Less than 250mm

PREVAILING WIND shown as white arrows

RAILWAYS AND AIRPORTS

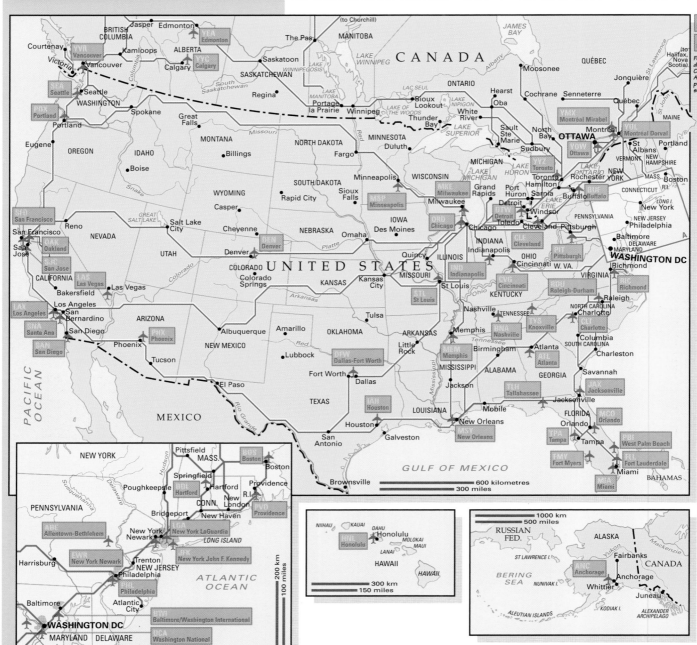

AIR: This map shows the major US and Canadian airports with international direct flights. Deregulation of the route licencing system has seen the rapid growth of these routes, avoiding the traditional gateways of New York and Toronto. North American airlines have developed, for marketing and economic reasons, regional hubs where passengers can make convenient inter-flight connections. The table opposite provides a comprehensive guide to the countries which these airports offer direct flights to or from.

All scheduled passenger flights to international destinations, licensed as at October 1997, are included. Periods of operation or service are not indicated. Commercial or other considerations may result in services being suspended or withdrawn at short notice. Please check with the appropriate airport and/or airline to confirm details of flights. During the summer period many airlines expand their services, with charter flights and more scheduled services to holiday destinations.

Flights between the US and Canada have not been included in the list. Airports operating flights solely between Canada, the United States and Mexico (for example San Antonio airport) are also not shown.

Where cities have more than one airport, the individual airport code is used. For example, New York City code is NYC, but the airport codes are:

John F. Kennedy	JFK
LaGuardia	LGA
Newark International	EWR

RAIL: The map also shows the main passenger routes in the US and Canada. The transcontinental services are provided by Amtrak in the US and by VIA Rail in Canada. Services on these routes vary considerably in terms of times and days of operation so details should be obtained from the appropriate rail companies. The principal long-distance services are shown on the right.

These routes are supplemented by interurban and suburban rail services and in addition there is a comprehensive network of long-distance buses.

LONG-DISTANCE RAIL SERVICES

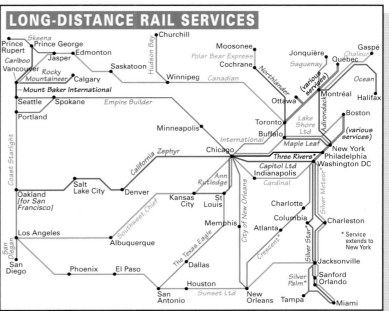

Diagrammatic only: not to scale

AIRPORTS

CANADA · UNITED STATES

This table shows the number of airports in each country with direct connections from individual US or Canadian airports, licensed as of October 1997. Code-sharing routes (where passengers need to change aircraft) are not included. In general, at least one route is to the international airport/s serving the country's capital (see page viii). Figures are in red where this is NOT the case.

The columns of the table list individual airports. Under **CANADA**: YEA Edmonton, YHZ Halifax, YMX Montréal Mirabel, YOW Ottawa, YUL Montréal Dorval, YVR Vancouver, YYC Calgary, YYT St John's, YYZ Toronto. Under **UNITED STATES**: ABE Allentown-Bethlehem, ANC Anchorage, ATL Atlanta, BDL Hartford, BNA Nashville, BOS Boston, BUF Buffalo, BWI Baltimore / Washington Int., CLE Cleveland, CLT Charlotte, CVG Cincinnati, DCA Washington National, DEN Denver, DFW Dallas-Fort Worth, DTW Detroit, EWR New York Newark, FLL Fort Lauderdale, FMY Fort Myers, HNL Honolulu, IAD Washington Dulles, IAH Houston, IND Indianapolis, JAX Jacksonville, JFK New York John F. Kennedy, LAS Las Vegas, LAX Los Angeles, LGA New York LaGuardia, MCO Orlando, MEM Memphis, MIA Miami, MKE Milwaukee, MSP Minneapolis, MSY New Orleans, OAK Oakland, ORD Chicago, PBI West Palm Beach, PDX Portland, PHL Philadelphia, PHX Phoenix, PIT Pittsburgh, PVD Providence, RDU Raleigh-Durham, RIC Richmond, SAN San Diego, SEA Seattle, SFO San Francisco, SJC San Jose, SNA Santa Ana, STL St Louis, TLH Tallahassee, TPA Tampa, TYS Knoxville.

IATA AREAS

AREA 1, NORTH ATLANTIC

Mexico — Canada: Montréal Dorval 1, Calgary 3, Toronto 2. United States: ABE 3, ANC 3, ATL 1, BDL 1, BNA 3, BWI 1, CLT 2, CVG 1, DEN 5, DFW 9, DTW 4, EWR 2, IAH 2, JFK 12, LAS 1, LGA 3, MCO 4, MEM 23, MIA 2, MKE 2, MSP 1, MSY 5, OAK 3, ORD 2, PHL 2, PHX 2, PIT 8, SAN 4, SEA 2, SFO 10, STL 3, SAN 4, SJC 3, SNA 7, TPA 3, and others 1 1 2.

AREA 1, MID ATLANTIC

Country	YYZ	Selected US connections
Antigua & Barbuda	1	ATL 1; EWR 1; JFK 1; MIA 1
Aruba	1	ATL 1; BWI 1; BOS 1; CLT 1; EWR 1; IAD 1; JFK 1; LGA 1; MIA 9; PHL 1; TPA 3
Bahamas	1	ANC 1; ATL 1; BWI 1; BOS 1; CLE 1; CLT 1; DFW 1; EWR 1 11; FLL 1; JFK 1 1; LGA 1 5; MIA 9; PHL 1 5; TPA 1 2; STL 3 4 1
Barbados	1	ATL 1; EWR 1; JFK 1; MIA 1; PBI 1
Belize		DFW 1; MIA 1; MSP 1
Bermuda (YHZ 1)	1	ATL 1; BDL 1; BOS 1; BWI 1; CLT 1; EWR 1; JFK 1; LAS 1 1; MIA 1; PHL 1; PIT 1
Bolivia		MIA 2
Bonaire		ATL 1; BWI 1; EWR 1; MIA 1; TYS 1
Cayman Is.		ATL 1; BNA 1; DTW 1 1; DFW 1; IAH 1; JFK 1 1 1; MIA 2
Colombia		BDL 1; EWR 1; JFK 1; LAX 1; MIA 5; SJC 1
Costa Rica	1	DFW 1; IAH 1 1; JFK 1 1 1; MIA 1; ORD 1; TLH 1
Cuba (YUL 2)	3	MIA 2; SFO 1 1
Curaçao		ATL 1; BWI 1; EWR 1; MIA 1; TYS 1
Dominican Republic		ATL 3; BDL 1; EWR 1; JFK 2; MIA 4
Ecuador		EWR 1; MIA 1
El Salvador		DCA 1; DFW 1; IAH 1 1; JFK 1; LAX 1; MIA 1; ORD 1; SEA 1
French Guiana		MIA 1
Grenada		EWR 1; JFK 1; MIA 1
Guadeloupe (YUL 1, YVR 1)		MIA 1
Guatemala		BNA 1; DFW 1; IAH 1 1; JFK 1; LAX 1; MIA 1; PDX 1; SEA 1
Guyana		EWR 1; JFK 1; MIA 1
Haiti (YUL 1, YVR 1)		EWR 1; JFK 1; MIA 1
Honduras		BOS 1; IAH 4; JFK 1 4; MIA 4; MSP 4; MSY 1
Jamaica	2	ATL 2; BOS 1; CLT 1; JFK 1 2 2; MIA 2; LAS 2 1 1; ORD 2 1 1; PHX 1; PHL 1 2; SFO 1 1
Martinique		MIA 1
Nicaragua		BNA 1; DEN 1; IAH 1; MIA 1
Panama		DEN 1; IAH 1; JFK 1 1 1 1; LAX 1; MIA 1; ORD 1; TPA 1
Peru		ATL 1; DFW 1; JFK 1; MIA 1
Puerto Rico	1	ABE 1 1; ATL 1 1 1; BDL 1 1; BOS 1 1; DFW 1 1 1 1; HNL 1; JFK 2 1 1; LAS 1 1 1; MIA 1; PBI 1; PHL 1; PVD 1 1; SEA 2 1 1; STL 1 1; TPA 1
St Lucia	1	JFK 2; MIA 1; PBI 1
St Maarten		CLT 1; MIA 1; SEA 1
Trinidad & Tobago	1	EWR 1; MIA 1
Turks & Caicos Is.		MIA 1
Venezuela		JFK 1; MIA 4; OAK 1 1; SAN 1

AREA 1, SOUTH ATLANTIC

Country	YYZ	Selected US connections
Argentina	1	EWR 1; IAH 1; JFK 1; MIA 1
Brazil	1	ANC 2; DCA 2; DFW 2; EWR 1 2; IAH 2; JFK 4 3 7 9; MIA 1
Chile		EWR 1; JFK 1; LAX 1; MIA 1
Paraguay		MIA 1
Uruguay		JFK 1; MIA 1

AREA 2, EUROPE

Country	Canada	Selected US connections
Austria		ATL 1; JFK 1; MIA 1
Azores		BOS 1
Belgium		ATL 1; BOS 1; JFK 1; LGA 1 1; MIA 1 1
Bulgaria		JFK 1
Czech Republic (YHZ 1, YOW 1)	YYZ 1	JFK 1
Denmark		JFK 1; PHL 1
Finland		JFK 1; SEA 1
France (YHZ 1, YUL 1, YVR 1)	YYZ 1	ANC 1; ATL 1; CVG 1; DCA 1 1 1; EWR 1 1; JFK 3; LAX 2; MIA 1 2; PBI 1; SFO 2; SJC 1
Germany* (YEA 1, YHZ 1, YUL 1, YVR 1, YYC 1)	YYZ 1	ABE 2 3; ATL 1; DCA 2 1; DEN 1 1 3; DTW 2 2; IAH 1 1; JFK 3 2 1; LAX 3; LGA 3; MIA 1; ORD 3; PHL 1 2 1 1; SFO 3; SJC 1; TLH 2
Greece		ATL 1; JFK 1; MIA 1
Hungary (YEA 1)		ATL 1; JFK 1
Iceland		BDL 1; BWI 1; JFK 1; MIA 1
Ireland		ANC 2; ATL 1; EWR 2; IAH 1; JFK 2; ORD 1; PHL 2
Italy (YHZ 1, YUL 1)	YYZ 1	ANC 2; ATL 1; DFW 1; EWR 2; IAH 2; JFK 2; MIA 1; ORD 2; PHL 2
Luxembourg		ATL 1; BDL 1; JFK 1; MIA 1
Malta		ATL 1; JFK 1
Morocco (YHZ 1)		JFK 1
Netherlands (YHZ 1, YUL 1, YVR 1)	YYZ 1	ATL 1; BWI 1; CLE 1; DTW 1; IAH 1; JFK 1; LGA 1 1 1; MIA 1; ORD 1 1; SFO 1; SJC 1 1
Norway		JFK 1
Poland (YUL 1)		JFK 1; ORD 1
Portugal		EWR 2; JFK 1
Romania		EWR 2; JFK 1; ORD 2
Russian Fed. (Europe) (YEA 1)		DCA 1; JFK 1; MIA 1; SEA 1 1
Spain (YEA 1, YUL 1)		ANC 2; JFK 2; LAX 1; MIA 1; PBI 1; SJC 1 1
Sweden		JFK 1; ORD 1
Switzerland (YMX 1, YOW 1, YUL 1, YVR 1, YYZ 1)		ATL 1; BOS 1; DCA 1; JFK 1; MIA 1; ORD 1
Turkey		JFK 1
Ukraine		DCA 1 1; JFK 1
United Kingdom (YEA 1, YHZ 1, YMX 1, YOW 1, YUL 1, YVR 1, YYC 1, YYT 1, YYZ 4)		ANC 2; ATL 3; BWI 1 1; DCA 1 1 2 5 1; DFW 1; EWR 6; IAH 2; JFK 6; LAX 3; MIA 2; ORD 4; PHL 2; SEA 2 1; SFO 1; STL 1

AREA 2, MIDDLE EAST

Country	Canada	Selected US connections
Israel (YHZ 1)		ATL 1; JFK 1; MIA 1
Jordan (YHZ 1)		DFW 1; MIA 1; ORD 1
Kuwait		MIA 1; ORD 1
Saudi Arabia		DCA 3; DFW 2; IAH 3

AREA 2, AFRICA

Country	Selected US connections
Côte d'Ivoire	JFK 1
Egypt	JFK 1; LAX 1
Ghana	JFK 1
Senegal	JFK 1
South Africa†	JFK 1; MIA 1

AREA 3, ASIA

Country	Canada	Selected US connections
Bangladesh		JFK 1
China	YOW 3, YYZ 1	DFW 1; JFK 3 3; SFO 1; SEA 1; STL 1 3
Guam		SFO 1
India (YHZ 1, YOW 1, YUL 1, YVR 1, YYZ 2)		DFW 1; JFK 2; LAX 1
Indonesia		HNL 2; HNL 3
Japan (YOW 2, YUL 1, YYZ 2)		ANC 1; DFW 1 2; HNL 7 1; JFK 1 2; LAX 2; ORD 2; SEA 1 2; SFO 1; STL 1 2 1
Kiribati (E)		HNL 1
Korea, Republic of (YHZ 1, YVR 1, YYC 1, YYZ 1)		ANC 1 1; ATL 1; HNL 1 1 1; JFK 1; LAX 1; ORD 1; SEA 1; SFO 1; STL 1 1
Malaysia	YYC 1	JFK 1
Marshall Is.		HNL 2
Micronesia, Fed. States		HNL 3
Pakistan	YYZ 2	JFK 3
Philippines	YVR 1	JFK 1; SFO 1
Russian Fed. (Asia)		ANC 4; SEA 4 1
Singapore	YVR 1	JFK 1; LAX 1; MIA 1; SFO 1
Taiwan (YVR 1)		DFW 1 1; JFK 1; LAX 1; SFO 1; SEA 1 1
Thailand (YVR 1)		JFK 1; TPA 1
Uzbekistan		JFK 1

AREA 3, SOUTHWEST PACIFIC

Country	Canada	Selected US connections
American Samoa		HNL 1
Australia		HNL 1; LAX 2; SEA 1
Cook Is.		HNL 1
Fiji	YYZ 1	HNL 1; LAX 1
French Polynesia (SW)		HNL 1
Kiribati (W)		HNL 1
New Zealand		HNL 1; LAX 1
Tonga		HNL 1
Western Samoa		HNL 1

For the purposes of this table: *Bonn is regarded as Germany's sole capital. †Pretoria is regarded as South Africa's sole capital.

CANADA UNITED STATES

SKIING

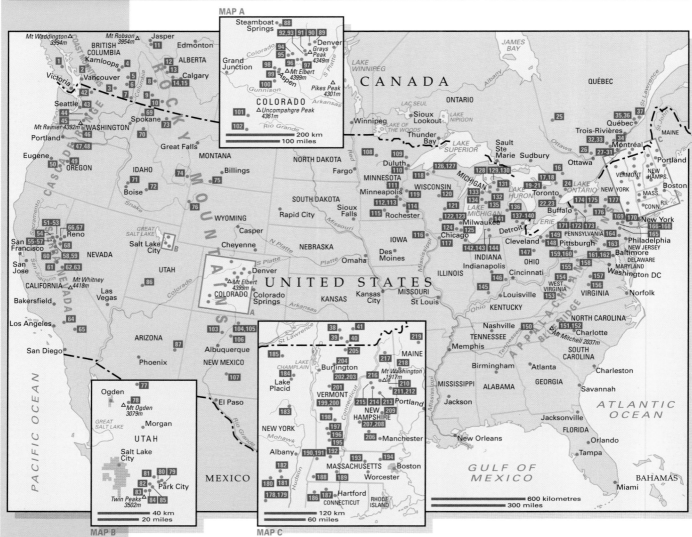

This map shows the major US and Canadian ski resorts (excluding Alaska). All the resorts listed report access to ski lifts with a capacity of at least 6,000 skiers per hour (as at September 1997), with the exception of those marked with an asterisk (*), which are included because of their significance.

Resorts without slopeside accommodation are shown in italics.

Data compiled by Snow-Hunter Ltd., all rights reserved.
Fax: +44 (0) 1463 741273.
email: patrick@snowhunt.demon.co.uk

Resort altitude:
□ 2,500 metres or above
□ 500 – 2,499 metres
No black square: under 500 metres

Skier uplift:
■ 40,000 skiers per hour or more
■ 25,000 – 39,999 skiers per hour
■ 10,000 – 24,999 skiers per hour
No colour: Less than 10,000

Altitude at top of highest ski run:
● 3,000 metres or above
○ 1,000 – 2,999 metres
No black circle: under 1,000 metres

Maximum vertical drop:
● 1,000 metres or more
● 750 – 999 metres
● 500 – 749 metres
No colour: Less than 500 metres

Canada
British Columbia
1 Mount Washington
2 Whistler & Blackcomb
3 Apex
4 Sun Peaks (formerly Tod Mountain)
5 Silver Star
6 Big White
7 Red Mountain
8 Panorama
9 Kimberley
10 Fernie Snow Valley
Alberta
11 Marmot Basin (Jasper)
12 Lake Louise (Banff)
13 Sunshine Village (Banff)
14 Fortress Mountain
15 Nakiska
Ontario
16 Sir Sam's
17 Mount St Louis / Moonstone
18 Ski Snow Valley
19 Beaver Valley
20 Blue Mountain
21 Talisman
22 Caledon
23 Glen Eden
24 Ski Dagmar
Québec
25 Mont Video
26 Edelweiss Valley
27 Mont Gabriel
28 Mont Olympia
29 Mont Ste Sauveur
30 Ski le Chantecler
31 Ski Morin Heights
32 Mont Blanc
33 Tremblant
34 Val St Come
35 Mont Ste Anne
36 Le Relais
37 Stoneham
38 Bromont
39 Mont Sutton
40 Owl's Head
41 Mont Orford

United States
Washington
42 Mount Baker
43 Stevens Pass
44 The Pass [Alpental / Hyak / Ski Acres / Snoqualmie]
45 Crystal Mountain
46 White Pass Village
Oregon
47 Mount Hood Meadows
48 Timberline
49 Mount Bachelor
50 Willamette Pass
California
51 Donner Ski Ranch
52 Northstar-at-Tahoe
53 Sugar Bowl
54 Boreal
55 Alpine Meadows
56 Homewood
57 Squaw Valley (Squaw Creek)
58 Sierra-at-Tahoe
59 Kirkwood
60 Bear Valley
61 Dodge Ridge
62 June Mountain
63 Mammoth Mountain
64 Mountain High
65 Snow Summit
Nevada
66 Diamond Peak
67 Mount Rose
68 Heavenly
Idaho
69 Schweitzer Mountain
70 Silver Mountain
71 Bogus Basin
72 Sun Valley
Montana
73 Big Mountain
74 Big Sky
75 Red Lodge Mountain
Wyoming
76 Jackson Hole, Teton
Utah
77 Powder Mountain
78 Snowbasin
79 Deer Valley
80 Park City
81 The Canyons (formerly Wolf Mountain and Park West)
82 Solitude
83 Snowbird
84 Alta
85 Brighton
86 Brian Head
Arizona
87 Sunrise Park
Colorado
88 Steamboat
89 Eldora Mountain
90 Winter Park (Mary Jane)
91 Loveland
92 Arapahoe Basin
93 Keystone
94 Vail
95 Beaver Creek
96 Copper Mountain
97 Breckenridge
98 Snowmass
99 Aspen
100 Crested Butte
101 Telluride
102 Purgatory
New Mexico
103 Pajarito Mountain
104 Red River
105 Taos
106 Santa Fe
107 Ski Apache
Minnesota
108 Buena Vista
109 Giants Ridge
110 Spirit Mountain
111 Wild Mountain
112 Afton Alps
113 Buck Hill
114 Welch Village
115 Mount Kato
Iowa
116 Sundown Mountain
Illinois
117 Chestnut Mountain
Wisconsin
118 Whitecap Mountains
119 Trollhaugen
120 Rib Mountain
121 Nordic Mountain
122 Cascade Mountain
123 Devils Head
124 Alpine Valley
125 Wilmot Mountain
Michigan
126 Big Powderhorn Mountain
127 Indianhead Mountain & Bear Creek
128 Boyne Mountain
129 Boyne Highlands
130 Nub's Nob
131 Treetops / Sylvan
132 Shanty Creek / Schuss Mountain
133 Caberfae Peaks
134 Sugar Loaf
135 Crystal Mountain
136 Brintz Apple Mountain
137 Alpine Valley
138 Mount Brighton
139 Mount Holly
140 Pine Knob
141 Cannonsburg
142 Bittersweet
143 Timber Ridge
144 Swiss Valley
Indiana
145 Paoli Peaks
146 Perfect North Slopes
Ohio
147 Snow Trails
148 Boston Mills / Brandywine
149 Alpine Valley
Tennessee
150 Ober Gatlinburg
North Carolina
151 Ski Beech Mountain
152 Sugar Mountain
West Virginia
153 Winterplace
154 Snowshoe
155 Canaan Valley
Virginia
156 Wintergreen
157 Massanutten
Maryland
158 Wisp
Pennsylvania
159 Hidden Valley
160 Seven Springs
161 Ski Liberty
162 Whitetail
163 Ski Roundtop
164 Doe Mountain
165 Blue Mountain
166 Big Boulder
167 Camelback
168 Jack Frost
169 Shawnee Mountain
New Jersey
170 Vernon Valley
New York
171 Peek'n Peak
172 Holiday Valley
173 Kissing Bridge
174 Swain
175 Bristol Mountain
176 Greek Peak
177 Labrador Mountain
178 Big Vanilla at Davos
179 Holiday Mountain
180 Belleayre
181 Hunter Mountain
182 Ski Windham
183 Gore Mountain
184 Whiteface Mountain
185 Titus Mountain
Connecticut
186 Mohawk Mountain
187 Ski Sundown
Massachusetts
188 Butternut Basin
189 Mount Tom
190 Brodie
191 Jiminy Peak
192 Berkshire East
193 Wachusett Mountain
194 Nashoba Valley
Vermont
195 Mount Snow (Haystack / Carinthia)
196 Stratton
197 Bromley Mountain
198 Okemo Mountain
199 Killington
200 Pico
201 Sugarbush
202 Bolton Valley
203 Stowe (Mount Mansfield)
204 Smugglers' Notch
205 Jay Peak
New Hampshire
206 Pats Peak
207 King Ridge
208 Mount Sunapee
209 Gunstock
210 Wildcat
211 Attitash-Bear Peak
212 Cranmore
213 Waterville Valley
214 Loon
215 Cannon
216 Bretton Woods
217 The Balsams*
Maine
218 Sunday River
219 Sugarloaf USA

The World Ski and Snowboarding Guide, published by Columbus Press, is a comprehensive guide to the world's ski resorts. For more information, call +44 (0) 171 417 0700.

UNITED STATES

See pages 40-41 for general map

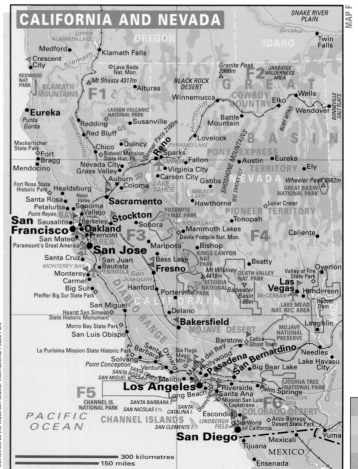
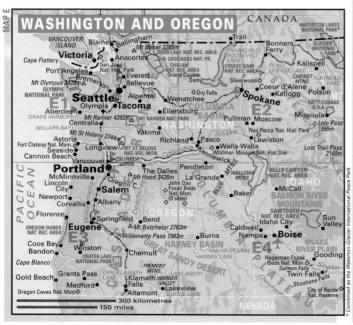

▶ Leisure park ▶ Zoo / animal park ▶ Aquarium ▶ Major tournament golf course ▶ Major tennis venue

UNITED STATES

See pages 40-41 for general map

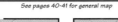

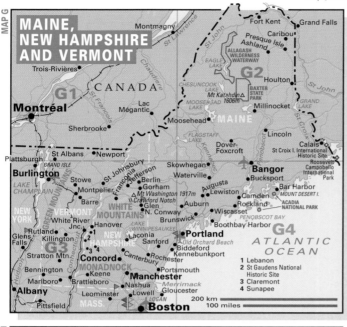

MAINE, NEW HAMPSHIRE AND VERMONT

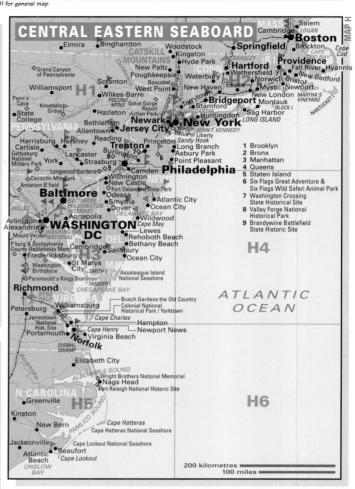

CENTRAL EASTERN SEABOARD

1 Brooklyn
2 Bronx
3 Manhattan
4 Queens
5 Staten Island
6 Six Flags Great Adventure & Six Flags Wild Safari Animal Park
7 Washington Crossing State Historical Site
8 Valley Forge National Historical Park
9 Brandywine Battlefield State Historic Site

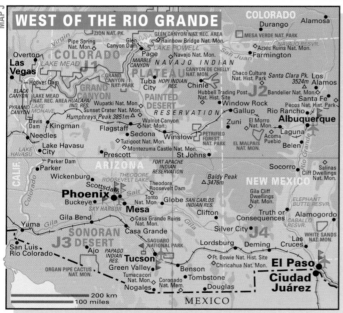

WEST OF THE RIO GRANDE

LOUISIANA

INCOME FROM TOURISM

Total spent in each state by domestic and foreign tourists and travellers, 1994

$20,000 million and over*
$10,000m – $19,999m
$5,000m – $9,999m
$2,000m – $4,999m
Less than $2,000m

*Actual figure on map

EMPLOYMENT IN TOURISM

Employment generated by travel and tourism as a percentage of total state employment, 1994

7.0% and over*
5.0% – 6.9%
3.0% – 4.9%
Less than 3.0%

*Actual figure on map

Source: Travel Industry Association of America

Leisure park   Zoo / animal park   Aquarium   Major tournament golf course   Horse racing   Major tennis venue

UNITED STATES

See pages 40-41 for general map

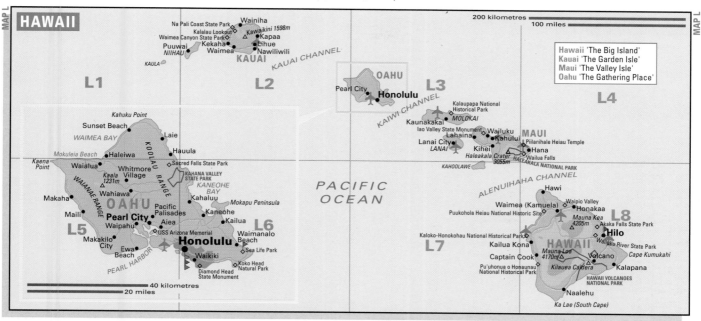

HAWAII

L1 L2 L3 L4

L5 L6 L7 L8

Hawaii 'The Big Island'
Kauai 'The Garden Isle'
Maui 'The Valley Isle'
Oahu 'The Gathering Place'

200 kilometres
100 miles

PACIFIC OCEAN

OAHU (detail)

Kahuku Point
Sunset Beach
Laie
Hauula
Waialua Whitmore Village
Haleiwa
Mokuleia Beach
WAIMEA BAY
Kaena Point
Waianae
Wahiawa Kaala 1231m
Makaha
Pacific Palisades
Kahaluu
Kaneohe
Kailua
KOOLAU RANGE
Maili
WAIANAE RANGE
Makakilo City
OAHU
Pearl City
Waipahu
Aiea
KANEOHE BAY
Mokapu Peninsula
Ewa Beach
Honolulu
USS Arizona Memorial
Waikiki
Diamond Head State Monument
Koko Head Natural Park
Sea Life Park
Waimanalo Beach
PEARL HARBOR

40 kilometres
20 miles

Na Pali Coast State Park
Wainiha
Kalalau Lookout Kawaikini 1598m
Waimea Canyon State Park Kapaa
Puuwai Kekaha Lihue
NIIHAU Waimea Nawiliwili
KAUAI
KAULA
KAUAI CHANNEL

Pearl City
Honolulu
OAHU
KAIWI CHANNEL

Kalaupapa National Historical Park
Kaunakakai MOLOKAI
Iao Valley State Monument Wailuku
Lahaina Kahului
Lanai City MAUI
LANAI Kihei Pailanihale Heiau Temple
Hana
Haleakala Crater 3055m Wailua Falls
KAHOOLAWE HALEAKALA NATIONAL PARK
ALENUIHAHA CHANNEL

Hawi
Waipio Valley
Waimea (Kamuela) Honakaa
Puukohola Heiau National Historic Site
Mauna Kea 4205m Akaka Falls State Park
Kaloko-Honokohau National Historical Park
Kailua Kona
HAWAII Wailuku River State Park
Captain Cook Mauna Loa 4170m Cape Kumukahi
Pu'uhonua o Honaunau National Historical Park Volcano Kalapana
Kilauea Caldera
HAWAII VOLCANOES NATIONAL PARK
Naalehu
Ka Lae (South Cape)

MAP L   MAP L
MAP M   MAP M
MAP N

FLORIDA

Enterprise Tifton
MISS. Mobile ALABAMA Dothan GEORGIA Waycross
Escambia
De Funiak Springs 105m Bainbridge Fernandina Beach
Milton Florida Caverns State Park Valdosta Timucuan Ecological and Historic Preserve
Pensacola Fort Walton Beach Marianna SUWANNEE Fort Caroline National Memorial
Biloxi Pascagoula Destin Seaside OKEFENOKEE SWAMP Jacksonville
MOBILE BAY Fort Pickens M2 Tallahassee M3 Castillo de San Marcos National Monument
M1 SANTA ROSA I. Panama City Fort Gadsden State Historic Site Lake City St Augustine
GULF OF MEXICO Cape San Blas Apalachicola Gainesville Fort Matanzas National Monument
DOG I. Marineland of Florida
ST VINCENT I. ST GEORGE I. Palatka M4
Cedar Keys National Wildlife Refuge Ormond Beach
Florida's Silver Springs Daytona Beach
Homossassa Springs State Wildlife Park Ocala DeLand
Weeki Wachee Spring Lake Monroe ATLANTIC OCEAN
Spring Hill Sanford Canaveral National Seashore
FLORIDA Titusville Merritt I. National Wildlife Refuge
Universal Studios Florida Orlando John F. Kennedy Space Center
Tarpon Springs Walt Disney World Port Canaveral
Busch Gardens Sea World of Florida LAKE APOPKA Cape Canaveral
Spongeorama Kissimmee Cocoa Beach
Clearwater Tampa Bay Lakeland Winter Haven Melbourne
ANCLOTE KEYS M5 Florida's Cypress Gardens
SAND KEY Tampa Bok Tower Gardens Lake Wales
St Petersburg TAMPA BAY M6
De Soto National Memorial Fort Pierce
Bradenton Highlands Hammock State Recreation Area
LONGBOAT KEY Sarasota Myakka River State Park
SIESTA KEY
Port Charlotte LAKE OKEECHOBEE
CHARLOTTE HARBOR Fort Myers Belle Glade PGA National
Cape Coral West Palm Beach
JN 'Ding' Darling National Wildlife Refuge PINE I. Palm Beach
CAPTIVA I. Boynton Beach
SANIBEL I. Bonita Springs Delray Beach
Naples Coral Springs Pompano Beach
BIG CYPRESS SWAMP Boca Raton Fort Lauderdale
MARCO I. BIG CYPRESS NATIONAL PRESERVE Dania
GULF OF MEXICO TEN THOUSAND ISLANDS Hollywood Gulfstream Park
Miami Hialeah Miami Beach
EVERGLADES Coral Gables Key Biscayne
M7 Miami Seaquarium
EVERGLADES NATIONAL PARK Florida City Bill Baggs Cape Florida State Recreation Area
Cape Sable Homestead BISCAYNE NATIONAL PARK
Bahia Honda State Recreation Area Key Largo John Pennekamp Coral Reef State Park
Key Deer National Wildlife Refuge Islamorada
Great White Heron National Wildlife Refuge M8
Fort Jefferson PINE KEYS Marathon
DRY TORTUGAS NATIONAL PARK BIG PINE KEY
Key West Looe Key National Marine Sanctuary
FLORIDA KEYS

2000 metres
1000 metres
Sea level

EAST TEXAS

OKLAHOMA
Waurika LAKE TEXOMA ARK.
Wichita Falls Ardmore Hugo
Bowie Durant Denison Dam Paris Fulton
Olney Decatur Denton Sherman Eisenhower Birthplace State Hist. Site
Graham LAKE ARROWHEAD McKinney Greenville Sulphur Springs De Kalb Texarkana
N1 Lewisville Plano LAVON LAKE Mount Pleasant Atlanta
Mineral Wells Fort Worth Six Flags over Texas Dallas LAKE TAWAKONI Jefferson
Weatherford Arlington Grand Prairie Terrell Mineola Longview N2 Marshall Shreveport
Cisco Cleburne Waxahachie SABINE Tyler Kilgore Henderson LOUISIANA
Stephenville Hillsboro Corsicana Jacksonville Timpson
Brownwood Texas Safari Wildlife Park TEXAS Waco Palestine Rusk Nacogdoches TOLEDO BEND RESERVOIR
Goldthwaite Marlin Buffalo Crockett San Augustine
San Saba Copperas Cove Fort Hood Temple Hearne SAM RAYBURN RESERVOIR Lufkin Jasper
Lampasas Llano Georgetown College Station Navasota LAKE LIVINGSTON N4 Woodville Kirbyville
Fredericksburg Taylor Brenham Huntsville Livingston BIG THICKET NAT. PRES.
Lyndon B. Johnson Nat. Hist. Pk. Austin Bastrop Conroe Cleveland
Six Flags Fiesta Texas San Marcos Lockhart Liberty Beaumont Orange
New Braunfels Columbus Houston Baytown Port Arthur
Sea World of Texas Seguin Six Flags AstroWorld & WaterWorld Pasadena High Island
San Antonio San Antonio Missions Nat. Hist. Park Rosenberg Texas City Johnson Space Center GALVESTON BAY
Yoakum Galveston GALVESTON I.
Floresville El Campo Bay City Freeport
Victoria Matagorda
Beeville Port Lavaca MATAGORDA PENINSULA
N5 Refugio Port O'Connor N6
Freer Rockport COPANO BAY MATAGORDA I.
Corpus Christi SAN ANTONIO BAY
Alice Port Aransas GULF OF MEXICO
Kingsville CORPUS CHRISTI BAY
Hebbronville Padre I. National Seashore
Falfurrias BAFFIN BAY PADRE ISLAND

BALCONES ESCARPMENT
COASTAL PLAIN

200 kilometres
100 miles

▶ Leisure park   ▶ Zoo / animal park   ▶ Aquarium   ▶ Major tournament golf course

▶ Horse racing   ▶ Major tennis venue

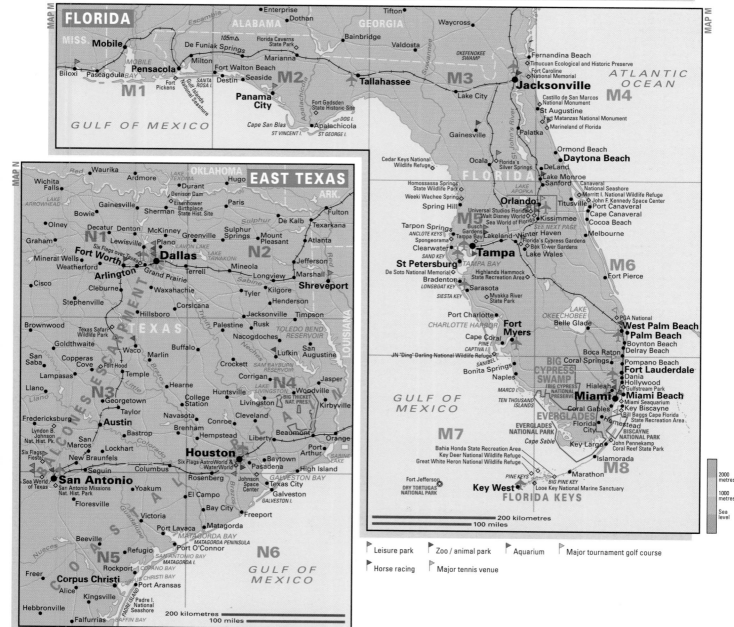

US NATIONAL PARKS...

National Park Service:

- ● National Park / Preserve
- ○ National Memorial
- ■ National Monument
- ● National Recreation Area / Seashore / Lakeshore
- ■ National Battlefield / Battlefield Park / Battlefield Site / Military Park
- ○ National Historic Site / Historical Park
- ● Theme park

The National Park Service is responsible for over 360 sites set aside to preserve the natural, historical and cultural heritage of the United States. For further information, contact:

National Park Service, 1849 C Street Northwest, Washington DC, 20240.

Tel. +1 202 208 4747.

The map also shows some of the more well-known theme parks, from Disneyland in California to Sea World of Florida. For further information, contact:

International Association of Amusement Parks and Attractions (IAAPA), 1448 Duke Street, Alexandria, Virginia 22314.

Tel. +1 703 836 4800.

TOP US THEME PARKS IN 1996
Number of visitors in millions
(world ranking in brackets)
Disneyland CA: 15.0 (2nd)
Magic Kingdom FL: 13.8 (3rd)
EPCOT Center FL: 11.2 (5th)
Disney-MGM Studios FL: 10.0 (6th)
Universal Studios FL: 8.4 (7th)
Universal Studios CA: 5.4 (11th)
Sea World FL: 5.1 (13th)
Busch Gardens FL: 4.2 (14th)
Six Flags NJ: 4.0 (16th)
Sea World CA: 3.9 (17th)
Kings Island OH: 3.6 (19th)
Berry Farm CA: 3.6 (20th)
Cedar Point OH: 3.5 (21st)
Santa Cruz Beach CA: 3.2 (=23rd)
Six Flags TX: 3.1 (=25th)
Six Flags IL: 3.0 (28th)
Camp Snoopy MN: 2.6 (37th)
Great America CA: 2.5 (=38th)
Kings Dominion VA: 2.4 (=40th)
AstroWorld TX: 2.4 (=40th)
Circus Circus NV: 2.3 (45th)
Six Flags GA: 2.2 (=46th)
Busch Gardens VA: 2.2 (=46th)
Six Flags Fiesta TX: 2.1 (=49th)
Dollywood TN: 2.1 (=49th)
Hersheypark PA: 2.1 (=49th)
Source: Amusement Business

Alaska
1 Cape Krusenstern National Monument
2 Noatak National Preserve
3 Gates of the Arctic National Park and Preserve
4 Kobuk Valley National Park
5 Bering Land Bridge National Preserve
6 Yukon-Charley Rivers National Preserve
7 Denali National Park and Preserve
8 Lake Clark National Park and Preserve
9 Katmai National Park and Preserve
10 Aniachak National Monument and Preserve
11 Kenai Fjords National Park
12 Wrangell-St Elias National Park and Preserve
13 Glacier Bay National Park and Preserve
14 Sitka National Historic Park
15 Klondike Gold Rush National Historical Park

Hawaii
16 USS Arizona Memorial
17 Kalaupapa National Historical Park
18 Haleakala National Park
19 Puukohola Heiau National Historic Site
20 Kaloko-Honokohau National Historical Park
21 Pu'uhonua o Honaunau National Historical Park
22 Hawaii Volcanoes National Park

Washington
23 San Juan Island National Historical Park
24 Olympic National Park
25 Ebey's Landing National Historical Reserve
26 North Cascades National Park
27 Ross Lake National Recreation Area
28 Lake Chelan National Recreation Area
29 Coulee Dam National Recreation Area
30 Whitman Mission National Historic Site
31 Mount Rainier National Park
32 Fort Vancouver National Historic Site

Oregon
33 Fort Clatsop National Memorial
34 McLoughlin House National Historic Site
35 John Day Fossil Beds National Monument
36 Crater Lake National Park
37 Oregon Caves National Monument

California
38 Redwood National Park
39 Lava Beds National Monument
40 Whiskeytown-Shasta-Trinity National Recreation Area
41 Lassen Volcanic National Park
42 Point Reyes National Seashore
43 Muir Woods National Monument
44 Fort Point National Historic Site
45 Golden Gate National Recreation Area
46 San Francisco Maritime National Historical Park
47 Port Chicago Naval Magazine National Memorial
48 John Muir National Historic Site
49 Eugene O'Neill National Historic Site
50 Pinnacles National Monument
51 Yosemite National Park
52 Devils Postpile National Monument
53 Sequoia and Kings Canyon National Parks
54 Manzanar National Historic Site
55 Death Valley National Park
56 Channel Islands National Park
57 Santa Monica Mountains National Recreation Area
58 Cabrillo National Monument
59 Joshua Tree National Park
60 Mojave National Preserve

Nevada
61 Lake Mead National Recreation Area
62 Great Basin National Park

Idaho
63 City of Rocks National Reserve
64 Hagerman Fossil Beds National Monument
65 Craters of the Moon National Monument
66 Nez Perce National Historical Park

Montana
67 Glacier National Park
68 Grant-Kohrs Ranch National Historic Site
69 Big Hole National Battlefield
70 Bighorn Canyon National Recreation Area
71 Little Bighorn Battlefield National Monument

Wyoming
72 Devils Tower National Monument
73 Fort Laramie National Historic Site
74 Yellowstone National Park
75 John D. Rockefeller, Jr. Memorial Parkway
76 Grand Teton National Park
77 Fossil Butte National Monument

Utah
78 Golden Spike National Historic Site
79 Timpanogos Cave National Monument
80 Zion National Park
81 Cedar Breaks National Monument
82 Bryce Canyon National Park
83 Capitol Reef National Park
84 Rainbow Bridge National Monument
85 Natural Bridges National Monument
86 Canyonlands National Park
87 Arches National Park

Colorado
88 Dinosaur National Monument
89 Rocky Mountain National Park
90 Colorado National Monument
91 Black Canyon of the Gunnison National Monument
92 Curecanti National Recreation Area

93 Florissant Fossil Beds National Monument
94 Hovenweep National Monument
95 Yucca House National Monument
96 Mesa Verde National Park
97 Great Sand Dunes National Monument
98 Bent's Old Fort National Historic Site

Arizona
99 Pipe Spring National Monument
100 Grand Canyon National Park
101 Glen Canyon National Recreation Area (also in Utah)
102 Navajo National Monument
103 Canyon de Chelly National Monument
104 Hubbell Trading Post National Historic Site
105 Wupatki National Monument
106 Sunset Crater National Monument
107 Walnut Canyon National Monument
108 Tuzigoot National Monument
109 Montezuma Castle National Monument
110 Petrified Forest National Park
111 Tonto National Monument
112 Hohokam Pima National Monument
113 Casa Grande Ruins National Monument
114 Organ Pipe Cactus National Monument
115 Tumacacori National Historical Park
116 Coronado National Memorial
117 Saguaro National Park
118 Fort Bowie National Historic Site
119 Chiricahua National Monument

New Mexico
120 Gila Cliff Dwellings National Monument
121 White Sands National Monument
122 Carlsbad Caverns National Park
123 Salinas Pueblo Missions National Monument
124 Aztec Ruins National Monument
125 Chaco Culture National Historical Park
126 El Morro National Monument
127 El Malpais National Monument
128 Petroglyph National Monument
129 Bandelier National Monument
130 Pecos National Historical Park
131 Fort Union National Monument
132 Capulin Volcano National Monument

Texas
133 Lake Meredith National Recreation Area
134 Alibates Flint Quarries National Monument

135 Chamizal National Memorial
136 Guadalupe Mountains National Park
137 Fort Davis National Historic Site
138 Big Bend National Park
139 Amistad National Recreation Area
140 Lyndon B. Johnson National Historical Park
141 San Antonio Missions National Historical Park
142 Palo Alto Battlefield National Historic Site
143 Padre Island National Seashore
144 Big Thicket National Preserve

Oklahoma
145 Chickasaw National Recreation Area

North Dakota
146 International Peace Garden
147 Fort Union Trading Post National Historic Site
148 Theodore Roosevelt National Park (North and South Units)
149 Knife River Indian Villages National Historic Site

South Dakota
150 Jewel Cave National Monument
151 Mount Rushmore National Memorial
152 Wind Cave National Park
153 Badlands National Park

Minnesota
154 Pipestone National Monument
155 Voyageurs National Park
156 Grand Portage National Monument

Wisconsin
157 Apostle Islands National Lakeshore
158 Ice Age National Scientific Reserve

Michigan
159 Isle Royale National Park
160 Keweenaw National Historical Park
161 Pictured Rocks National Lakeshore
162 Father Marquette National Memorial and Museum
163 Sleeping Bear Dunes National Lakeshore

Nebraska
164 Agate Fossil Beds National Monument
165 Scotts Bluff National Monument
166 Chimney Rock National Historic Site
167 Homestead National Monument of America

Iowa
168 Effigy Mounds National Monument
169 Herbert Hoover National Historic Site

Kansas
170 Fort Larned National Historic Site

171 Brown v. Board of Education National Historic Site
172 Fort Scott National Historic Site

Missouri
173 Harry S. Truman National Historic Site
174 George Washington Carver National Monument
175 Wilson's Creek National Battlefield
176 Ulysses S. Grant National Historic Site
177 Jefferson National Expansion Memorial

Illinois
178 Lincoln Home National Historic Site
179 Illinois and Michigan Canal National Heritage Corridor
180 Chicago Portage National Historic Site

Indiana
181 Indiana Dunes National Lakeshore
182 George Rogers Clark National Historical Park
183 Lincoln Boyhood National Memorial

Ohio
184 William Howard Taft National Historic Site
185 Dayton Aviation National Historical Park
186 Hopewell Culture National Historical Park
187 Perry's Victory and International Peace Memorial
188 James A. Garfield National Historic Site
189 David Berger National Memorial
190 Cuyahoga Valley National Recreation Area

Arkansas
191 Pea Ridge National Military Park
192 Fort Smith National Historic Site
193 Hot Springs National Park
194 Arkansas Post National Memorial

Louisiana
195 Poverty Point National Monument
196 Cane River Creole National Historical Park and National Heritage Area
197 New Orleans Jazz National Historical Park
198 Jean Lafitte National Historical Park

Mississippi
199 Natchez National Historical Park
200 Vicksburg National Military Park
201 Natchez Trace Parkway (also in Alabama and Tennessee)
202 Tupelo National Battlefield
203 Brices Cross Roads National Battlefield Site

Alabama
204 Tuskegee Institute National Historic Site
205 Horseshoe Bend National Military Park

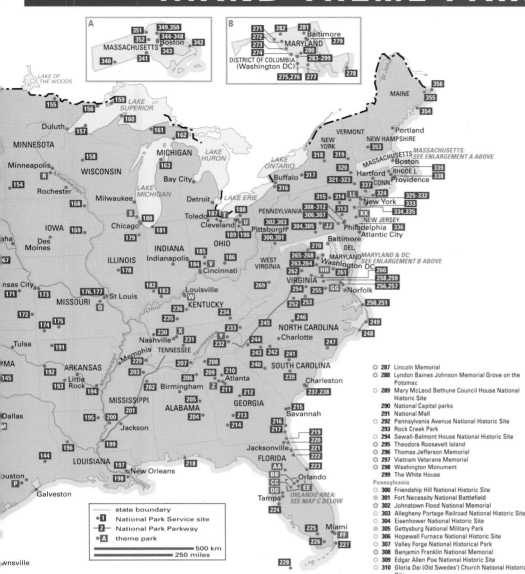

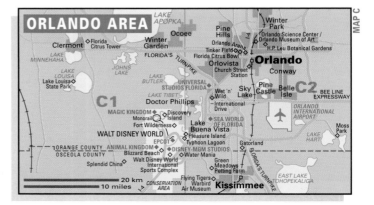

...AND THEME PARKS

A
MASSACHUSETTS
351 349,350
352 344-348 342
340 341 Boston 343

B
271 282 281
272 Baltimore
273 MARYLAND 279
274 280
DISTRICT OF COLUMBIA 283-299
(Washington DC)
275,276 277 278

Map labels (main map):

LAKE OF THE WOODS
159 LAKE SUPERIOR
155 156 160
Duluth 157 161 162 356
MINNESOTA 158 MAINE 355 354
Minneapolis R MICHIGAN LAKE HURON 163 Portland
Rochester 154 WISCONSIN VERMONT 353 NEW HAMPSHIRE
Mississippi Bay City NEW YORK 318 319 MASSACHUSETTS: SEE ENLARGEMENT A ABOVE
Milwaukee 168 LAKE MICHIGAN 320 Boston
Des Moines S LAKE ONTARIO Buffalo 317 321-323 Hartford RHODE I. 339
IOWA 169 180 Detroit LAKE ERIE 316 CONN. 337 Providence 338
Chicago 179 Toledo 187 188 PENNSYLVANIA 315 314 LL 324 325-332
INDIANA 181 Cleveland 189 190 308-312 313 New York 333
67 185 Indianapolis 184 Pittsburgh 306,307 KK 334,335
Kansas City 173 OHIO 186 304,305 302,303 JJ NEW JERSEY 336
176,177 V WEST VIRGINIA 300,301 Baltimore 270 Atlantic City
St Louis 182 183 Cincinnati DEL.
MISSOURI Louisville 265-268 263,264 MARYLAND & DC: SEE ENLARGEMENT B ABOVE
172 Q 236 W KENTUCKY 234 262 Washington DC 260
174 175 235 VIRGINIA HH 261 258,259
Nashville 230 X 231 269 254 255 GG Norfolk 256,257
Tulsa 191 232 233 244 245 252 253 250,251
ARKANSAS 229 Y 208 210 NORTH CAROLINA 246 249 248
Memphis 203 207 209 243 242 240 Charlotte 247
145 192 202 206 239 SOUTH CAROLINA 237,238
Little Rock 193 194 Birmingham Z 211 212 Charleston
MISSISSIPPI 205 GEORGIA 215
195 200 201 Atlanta 213 214 Savannah
MA 204 216 217 219
196 199 JOHNS 220
144 LOUISIANA 197 218 FLORIDA 221 222
New Orleans AA 223
Jackson BB Orlando
Dallas CC DD EE ORLANDO AREA: SEE MAP C BELOW
Galveston 198 Tampa 224
P 225 Miami
Houston 226 FF 227
ownsville 228

Legend:
— state boundary
• 1 National Park Service site
2 National Park Parkway
• A theme park

500 km
250 miles

Listings (right columns)

○ 330 St Paul's Church National Historic Site
● 331 Statue of Liberty National Monument
○ 332 Theodore Roosevelt Birthplace National Historic Site
● 333 Fire Island National Seashore
New Jersey
○ 334 Edison National Historical Site
○ 335 Morristown National Historical Park
336 Pinelands National Reserve
Connecticut
○ 337 Weir Farm National Historic Site
Rhode Island
○ 338 Touro Synagogue National Historic Site
● 339 Roger Williams National Memorial
Massachusetts
○ 340 Springfield Armory National Historic Site
341 Blackstone River Valley National Heritage Corridor
○ 342 Cape Cod National Seashore
○ 343 Adams National Historic Site
○ 344 Boston African American National Historical Site
○ 345 Boston National Historical Park
○ 346 Frederick Law Olmsted National Historic Site
○ 347 John F. Kennedy National Historic Site
○ 348 Longfellow National Historic Site
○ 349 Saugus Iron Works National Historic Site
○ 350 Salem Maritime National Historic Site
○ 351 Lowell National Historical Park
○ 352 Minute Man National Historical Park
New Hampshire
○ 353 St-Gaudens National Historic Site
Maine
○ 354 Acadia National Park
○ 355 St Croix Island International Historic Site
Canada
New Brunswick
356 Roosevelt Campobello International Park
(Not shown on map):
Puerto Rico
○ San Juan National Historic Site
US Virgin Islands
● Buck Island Reef National Monument
○ Christiansted National Historic Site
○ Salt River Bay National Historical Park and Ecological Preserve
● Virgin Islands National Park
American Samoa
● The National Park of American Samoa
Northern Mariana Islands
American Memorial Park
○ War in the Pacific National Historical Park

THEME PARKS
● A Marine World Africa USA, Vallejo, California
● B Paramount's Great America, Santa Clara, California
● C Santa Cruz Beach Boardwalk, Santa Cruz, California
● D Six Flags Magic Mountain, Valencia, California
● E Universal Studios Hollywood, Universal City, Los Angeles, California
● F Raging Waters, San Dimas, Los Angeles, California
● G Knott's Berry Farm, Buena Park, Los Angeles, California
● H Disneyland, Anaheim, Los Angeles, California
● J Sea World of California, San Diego, California
● K Circus Circus, Las Vegas, Nevada
● L Six Flags over Texas, Arlington, Texas
● M Fair Park, Dallas, Texas
● N Six Flags Fiesta, San Antonio, Texas
● O Sea World of Texas, San Antonio, Texas
● P Six Flags AstroWorld / Six Flags WaterWorld, Houston, Texas
● Q Six Flags over Mid-America, Eureka, Missouri
● R Knott's Camp Snoopy, Bloomington, Minnesota
● S Six Flags Great America, Gurnee, Illinois
● T Cedar Point, Sandusky, Ohio
● U Sea World of Ohio, Aurora, Ohio
● V Paramount's Kings Island, Kings Mills, Ohio
● W Kentucky Kingdom – The Thrill Park, Louisville, Kentucky
● X Opryland USA, Nashville, Tennessee
● Y Dollywood, Pigeon Forge, Tennessee
● Z Six Flags over Georgia, Atlanta, Georgia
● AA Florida's Silver Springs, Silver Springs, Florida
● BB Universal Studios Florida, Orlando, Florida
● CC Walt Disney World Resort Complex (including the Magic Kingdom theme park, EPCOT Center, Disney-MGM Studios theme park, Fort Wilderness recreation area), Lake Buena Vista, Florida
● DD Busch Gardens Tampa Bay, Florida
● EE Sea World of Florida, Orlando, Florida
● FF Miami Seaquarium, Miami, Florida
● HH Paramount's Kings Dominion, Doswell, Virginia
● GG Busch Gardens the Old Country, Williamsburg, Virginia
● JJ Hersheypark, Hershey, Pennsylvania
● KK Six Flags Great Adventure, Jackson, New Jersey
● LL Great Gorge Resort Action Park, McAfee, New Jersey

Middle column listings

○ 287 Lincoln Memorial
○ 288 Lyndon Baines Johnson Memorial Grove on the Potomac
○ 289 Mary McLeod Bethune Council House National Historic Site
○ 290 National Capital parks
○ 291 National Mall
○ 292 Pennsylvania Avenue National Historic Site
○ 293 Rock Creek Park
○ 294 Sewall-Belmont House National Historic Site
○ 295 Theodore Roosevelt Island
○ 296 Thomas Jefferson Memorial
○ 297 Vietnam Veterans Memorial
○ 298 Washington Monument
○ 299 The White House
Pennsylvania
○ 300 Friendship Hill National Historic Site
● 301 Fort Necessity National Battlefield
○ 302 Johnstown Flood National Memorial
○ 303 Allegheny Portage Railroad National Historic Site
○ 304 Eisenhower National Historic Site
○ 305 Gettysburg National Military Park
○ 306 Hopewell Furnace National Historic Site
○ 307 Valley Forge National Historical Park
● 308 Benjamin Franklin National Memorial
○ 309 Edgar Allen Poe National Historic Site
○ 310 Gloria Dei (Old Swedes') Church National Historic Site
○ 311 Independence National Historical Park
● 312 Thaddeus Kosciuszko National Memorial
313 Delaware and Lehigh Navigation Canal National Heritage Corridor
○ 314 Delaware Water Gap National Recreation Area
○ 315 Steamtown National Historic Site
New York
○ 316 Theodore Roosevelt Inaugural National Historic Site
○ 317 Women's Rights National Historical Park
● 318 Fort Stanwix National Monument
○ 319 Saratoga National Historical Park
○ 320 Martin Van Buren National Historic Site
○ 321 Eleanor Roosevelt National Historic Site
○ 322 Vanderbilt Mansion National Historic Site
○ 323 Home of Franklin Delano Roosevelt National Historic Site
○ 324 Sagamore Hill National Historic Site
● 325 Castle Clinton National Monument
○ 326 Federal Hall National Memorial
○ 327 Gateway National Recreation Area (also in New Jersey)
○ 328 General Grant National Memorial
○ 329 Hamilton Grange National Memorial

Bottom left listings

● 206 Little River Canyon National Preserve
● 207 Russell Cave National Monument
Georgia
● 208 Chickamauga and Chattanooga National Military Park
○ 209 Kennesaw Mountain National Battlefield Park
○ 210 Chattahoochee River National Recreation Area
○ 211 Martin Luther King Jr. National Historic Site
● 212 Ocmulgee National Monument
○ 213 Andersonville National Historic Site
○ 214 Jimmy Carter National Historic Site
● 215 Fort Pulaski National Monument
● 216 Fort Frederica National Monument
○ 217 Cumberland Island National Seashore
Florida
○ 218 Gulf Islands National Seashore (also in Mississippi)
○ 219 Timucuan Ecological and Historic Preserve
○ 220 Fort Caroline National Memorial
● 221 Castillo de San Marcos National Monument
● 222 Fort Matanzas National Monument
○ 223 Canaveral National Seashore
○ 224 De Soto National Memorial
● 225 Big Cypress National Preserve
● 226 Everglades National Park
● 227 Biscayne National Park
● 228 Dry Tortugas National Park
Tennessee
● 229 Shiloh National Military Park
○ 230 Fort Donelson National Battlefield
○ 231 Stones River National Battlefield and Cemetery
● 232 Great Smoky Mountains National Park (also in North Carolina)
○ 233 Andrew Johnson National Historic Site
Kentucky
○ 234 Cumberland Gap National Historical Park
○ 235 Mammoth Cave National Park
○ 236 Abraham Lincoln Birthplace National Historic Site
South Carolina
○ 237 Fort Sumter National Monument
○ 238 Charles Pinckney National Historic Site
● 239 Congaree Swamp National Monument
○ 240 Ninety Six National Historic Site
241 Historic Camden
● 242 Kings Mountain National Military Park
○ 243 Cowpens National Battlefield
North Carolina
○ 244 Carl Sandburg Home National Historic Site
245 Blue Ridge Parkway (also in Virginia)

Bottom middle listings

○ 246 Guilford Courthouse National Military Park
● 247 Moores Creek National Battlefield
○ 248 Cape Lookout National Seashore
○ 249 Cape Hatteras National Seashore
● 250 Fort Raleigh National Historic Site
○ 251 Wright Brothers National Memorial
Virginia
○ 252 Booker T. Washington National Monument
○ 253 Red Hill Patrick Henry National Memorial
○ 254 Appomattox Court House National Historical Park
● 255 Petersburg National Battlefield
○ 256 Jamestown National Historic Site
○ 257 Colonial National Historical Park
○ 258 Maggie L. Walker National Historic Site
● 259 Richmond National Battlefield Park
○ 260 Green Springs Historic District
● 261 George Washington Birthplace National Monument
○ 262 Shenandoah National Park
○ 263 Fredericksburg and Spotsylvania County Battlefields Memorial
○ 264 Prince William Forest Park
● 265 Manassas National Battlefield Park
266 Wolf Trap Farm Park for the Performing Arts
267 George Washington Memorial Parkway
● 268 Arlington House, The Robert E. Lee Memorial
West Virginia
○ 269 Gauley River National Recreation Area
○ 270 Harpers Ferry National Historical Park
Maryland
○ 271 Antietam National Battlefield
● 272 Monocacy National Battlefield
○ 273 Chesapeake and Ohio Canal National Historical Park
○ 274 Clara Barton National Historic Site
○ 275 Fort Washington Park
○ 276 Piscataway Park
○ 277 Thomas Stone National Historic Site
● 278 Assateague Island National Seashore
● 279 Fort McHenry National Monument and Historic Shrine
280 Greenbelt Park
● 281 Hampton National Historic Site
● 282 Catoctin Mountain Park
District of Columbia
○ 283 Constitution Gardens
○ 284 Ford's Theatre National Historic Site
○ 285 Frederick Douglass National Historic Site
○ 286 Korea War Veterans Memorial

Orlando Area inset map (Map C)

ORLANDO AREA
LAKE APOPKA
Winter Park
Clermont
Florida Citrus Tower
Ocoee
Pine Hills
Orlando Science Center / Orlando Museum of Art
LAKE MINNEHAHA
Winter Garden
FLORIDA'S TURNPIKE
Orlando Arena
Tinker Field
H.P. Leu Botanical Gardens
LAKE LOUISA
JOHNS LAKE
LAKE BUTLER
Florida Citrus Bowl
Orlovista
Church Street Station
Orlando
Lake Louisa State Park
UNIVERSAL STUDIOS FLORIDA
LAKE TIBET
Wet 'n' Wild
Sky Lake
Pine Castle
Belle Isle
Conway
C1
Doctor Phillips
International Drive
C2
BEE LINE EXPRESSWAY
MAGIC KINGDOM
Discovery Island
Monorail
Fort Wilderness
SEA WORLD OF FLORIDA
ORLANDO INTERNATIONAL AIRPORT
WALT DISNEY WORLD
Lake Buena Vista
Pleasure Island
LAKE HART
Moss Park
EPCOT
Typhoon Lagoon
ORANGE COUNTY
OSCEOLA COUNTY
ANIMAL KINGDOM
Blizzard Beach
DISNEY-MGM STUDIOS
Water Mania
Gatorland
Splendid China
Walt Disney World International Sports Complex
Green Meadows Petting Farm
EAST LAKE TOHOPEKALIGA
FLORIDA'S TURNPIKE
20 km
10 miles
CONSERVATION AREA
Flying Tigers Warbird Air Museum
Kissimmee
MAP C

CANADA

See pages 38-39 for general map

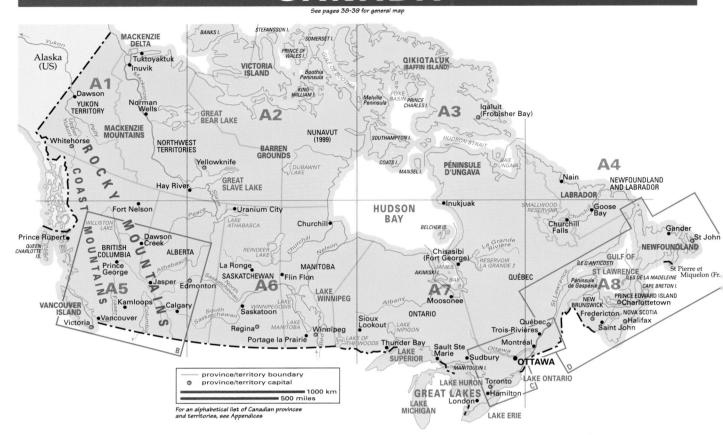

Alaska (US)

MACKENZIE DELTA

BANKS I.
STEFANSSON I.
SOMERSET I.
PRINCE OF WALES I.
Boothia Peninsula
GULF OF BOOTHIA

QIKIQTALUK (BAFFIN ISLAND)

A1
Dawson
Tuktoyaktuk
Inuvik
YUKON TERRITORY
Norman Wells
Whitehorse
MACKENZIE MOUNTAINS

VICTORIA ISLAND
King William I.

A2
GREAT BEAR LAKE
NORTHWEST TERRITORIES
Yellowknife
Hay River
GREAT SLAVE LAKE
NUNAVUT (1999)
BARREN GROUNDS
DUBAWNT LAKE

Melville Peninsula
FOXE BASIN
PRINCE CHARLES I.

A3
Iqaluit (Frobisher Bay)
SOUTHAMPTON I.
COATS I.
MANSEL I.
PÉNINSULE D'UNGAVA
BAIE D'UNGAVA

A4
Nain
NEWFOUNDLAND AND LABRADOR
LABRADOR
Goose Bay
Churchill Falls
SMALLWOOD RESERVOIR
Gander
St John
NEWFOUNDLAND

Prince Rupert
QUEEN CHARLOTTE IS.
BRITISH COLUMBIA
Fort Nelson
WILLISTON LAKE
Dawson Creek
Prince George
ALBERTA
Jasper
Kamloops

ROCKY MOUNTAINS
COAST MOUNTAINS

LAKE ATHABASCA
Uranium City
REINDEER LAKE
La Ronge
SASKATCHEWAN
Flin Flon
Churchill
HUDSON BAY
BELCHER IS.
Inukjuak
Chisasibi (Fort George)
La Grande Rivière
RÉSERVOIR LA GRANDE 2
JAMES BAY
AKIMISKI I.
QUÉBEC

GULF OF ST LAWRENCE
ÎLE D'ANTICOSTI
ÎLES DE LA MADELEINE
CAPE BRETON I.
St Pierre et Miquelon (Fr.)
Péninsule de Gaspésie

A5
VANCOUVER ISLAND
Victoria
Vancouver
Prince George
Edmonton
Calgary

A6
MANITOBA
LAKE WINNIPEG
Saskatoon
Regina
Winnipeg
Portage la Prairie
LAKE MANITOBA
LAKE WINNIPEGOSIS
Sioux Lookout

A7
Moosonee
ONTARIO
Albany
LAKE NIPIGON
Thunder Bay
LAKE SUPERIOR

A8
NEW BRUNSWICK
Fredericton
Québec
Trois-Rivières
Montréal
OTTAWA
LAKE ONTARIO
PRINCE EDWARD ISLAND
Charlottetown
NOVA SCOTIA
Halifax
Saint John

Sault Ste Marie
Sudbury
MANITOULIN I.
GREAT LAKES
LAKE HURON
LAKE MICHIGAN
Toronto
Hamilton
London
LAKE ERIE

province/territory boundary
province/territory capital

1000 km
500 miles

For an alphabetical list of Canadian provinces and territories, see Appendices

TORONTO TO QUÉBEC

MAP B

Sturgeon Falls
Témiskaming
North Bay
Mattawa
B1
LAKE NIPISSING
GRUNDY LAKE PROV. PARK
ALGONQUIN PROVINCIAL PARK
Parry Sound
Huntsville

LA VÉRENDRYE PROVINCIAL RESERVE
RÉSERVOIR BASKATONG
Mercier Dam
QUÉBEC
Maniwaki
Mont-Laurier
B2
Ottawa
Gatineau
Pembroke
GATINEAU PARK
Barrys Bay
Arnprior
Ottawa

ST MAURICE PROV. RESERVE
ROUGE-MATAWAN PROVINCIAL RESERVE
MONT-TREMBLANT PROVINCIAL PARK
MASTIGOUCHE PROV. RES.
LA MAURICIE NAT. PK.
Shawinigan
Ste Agathe-des-Monts
PAPINEAU-LABELLE PROV. RESERVE
Ste Sauveur-des-Monts
B3
Joliette
Lachute

Québec
Ste Foy
Lévis
ST LAWRENCE
Trois-Rivières
Cap-de-la-Madeleine
Drummondville
B4
Lac St Pierre
FRONTENAC PROV. PARK
Lac Mégantic
MONT-MEGANTIC PROV. PARK

GEORGIAN BAY
GEORGIAN BAY ISLANDS NATIONAL PARK
Santa's Village
Penetanguishene
Midland
NATTAWASAGA BAY
Collingwood
Barrie
B5
ONTARIO
Gravenhurst
Washago
HALIBURTON HIGHLANDS
Bancroft
BON ECHO PROV. PARK
Kaladar
B6
Perth
Carleton Place
Upper Canada Village
Cornwall
B7
OTTAWA
Hull
ST LAWRENCE
Brockville
Ogdensburg
ST LAWRENCE IS. NATIONAL PARK
UPLANDS
Valleyfield
MIRABEL
DORVAL
Montréal
St Hyacinthe
YAMASKA PROV. PARK
MONT-ST BRUNO PROV. PARK
Fort Chambly
St Jean
Granby
MONT-ORFORD PROVINCIAL PARK
Sherbrooke
B8
Fort Lennox
St Albans
LAKE CHAMPLAIN
Newport

Orangeville
Canada's Wonderland
Paramount Canada's Wonderland
Brampton
Africa's Lion Safari
Kitchener
LESTER B. PEARSON
Mississauga
Centreville
Toronto
Whitby
Oshawa
Magic Hill Farm
Newmarket
Port Hope
Trenton
Belleville
Picton
Point Petre
LAKE ONTARIO
Watertown
UNITED STATES
Lindsay
Peterborough
Kingston
LAKE SIMCOE

Burlington
St Catharines
Hamilton
B9
Fort George
Waterport
Oswego
Brantford
Niagara Falls
Niagara Falls
Dunnville
Fort Erie
Buffalo
WELLAND CANAL
Long Point
LAKE ERIE
FINGER LAKES
Rochester
B10
ONEIDA LAKE
Rome
Syracuse
Auburn
CANADAIGUA LAKE
SKANEATELES LAKE
OWASCO LAKE
SENECA LAKE
CAYUGA LAKE
Erie Canal

2000 metres
1000 metres
Sea level

▶ Leisure park   ▶ Zoo / animal park   ▶ Aquarium   ▶ Formula One   ▶ Major tennis venue

200 kilometres
100 miles

SW CANADA

MAP C

WILLISTON LAKE
Fort St John
Alaska Highway
W.A.C. Bennett Dam
Dawson Creek
Peace River
C1
Hazelton
Skeena
Houston
Nechako
Vanderhoof
Prince George
Grande Prairie
LESSER SLAVE LAKE
Slave Lake
C2
ALBERTA
Edson
Edmonton
ELK ISLAND NATIONAL PARK
TWEEDSMUIR PROV. PARK
BOWRON LAKE PROV. PARK
Quesnel
Barkerville
WELLS GRAY PROV. PARK & RECREATION AREA
Mt Robson 3954m
MOUNT ROBSON PROV. PARK
JASPER NATIONAL PARK
Jasper
Yellowhead Pass 1133m
COLUMBIA ICEFIELD
Mt Columbia 3747m
HAMBER PROV. PARK
North Saskatchewan
Red Deer
Drumheller
BANFF NAT. PARK
Kicking Horse Pass 1627m
Lake Louise
C4
Calgary
Calaway Park
Banff
MT ASSINIBOINE PROV. PARK
Radium Hot Springs
Fairmont Hot Springs
Fort Macleod
Fort Steele
WATERTON LAKES NATIONAL PARK
Cranbrooke
Bonners Ferry

BRITISH COLUMBIA
Williams Lake
Mt Waddington 3994m
C3
Bear Cove
Lillooet
Whistler
GARIBALDI PROV. PARK
VANCOUVER ISLAND
STRATHCONA PROV. PARK
Courtenay
Paradise Sea-Side Resort
Port Alberni
PACIFIC RIM NATIONAL PARK RESERVE
Nanaimo
Duncan
Vancouver
Hope
Dinotown
Kamloops
Revelstoke
MT REVELSTOKE NAT. PARK
GLACIER NAT. PARK
YOHO NAT. PARK
KOOTENAY NAT. PARK
Kelowna
Penticton
Trail
CASCADE MTNS.
UNITED STATES
GLACIER NATIONAL PARK

PACIFIC OCEAN
Victoria
Fort Rod Hill
Anacortes
From Seattle
Str. of Juan de Fuca

400 kilometres
200 miles

Combined as the Waterton-Glacier International Peace Park

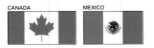

CANADA

See pages 38-39 for general map

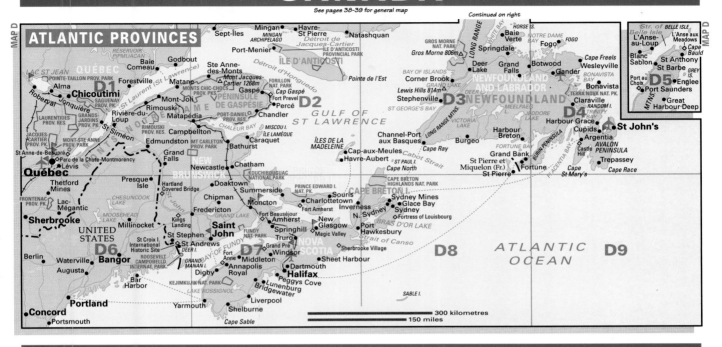

MEXICO

See page 37 for general map

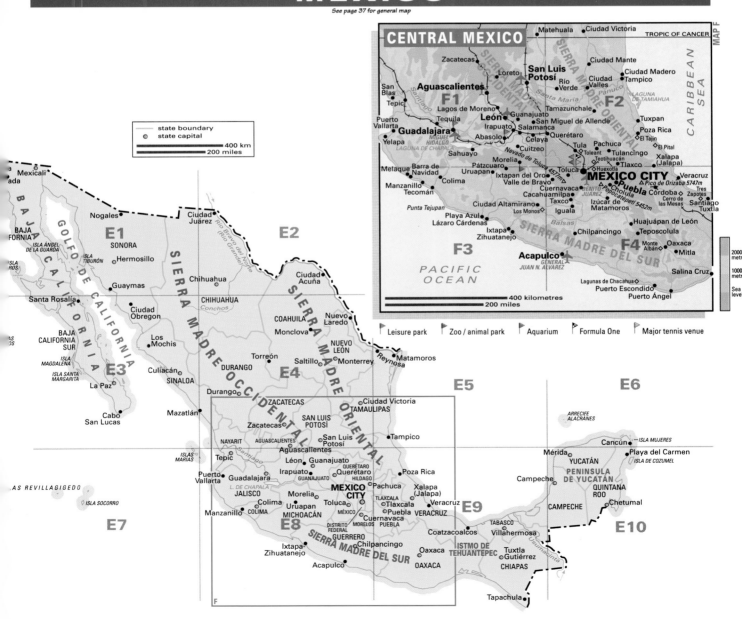

BAHAMAS   JAMAICA   CUBA

THE CARIBBEAN

See page 37 for general map

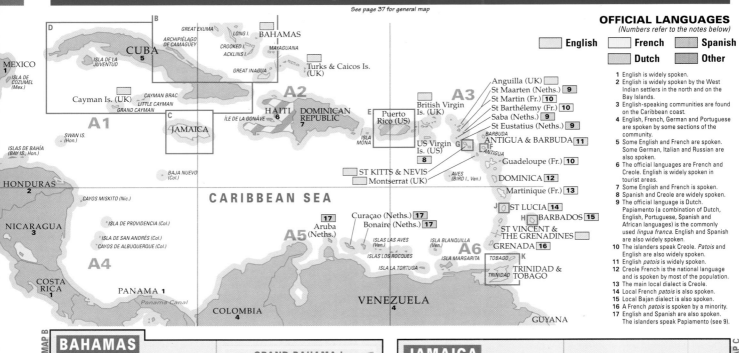

OFFICIAL LANGUAGES
(Numbers refer to the notes below)

English   French   Spanish   Dutch   Other

1 English is widely spoken.
2 English is widely spoken by the West Indian settlers in the north and on the Bay Islands.
3 English-speaking communities are found on the Caribbean coast.
4 English, French, German and Portuguese are spoken by some sections of the community.
5 Some English and French are spoken. Some German, Italian and Russian are also spoken.
6 The official languages are French and Creole. English is widely spoken in tourist areas.
7 Some English and French is spoken.
8 Spanish and Creole are widely spoken.
9 The official language is Dutch. Papiamento (a combination of Dutch, English, Portuguese, Spanish and African languages) is the commonly used lingua franca. English and Spanish are also widely spoken.
10 The islanders speak Creole. Patois and English are also widely spoken.
11 English patois is widely spoken.
12 Creole French is the national language and is spoken by most of the population.
13 The main local dialect is Creole.
14 Local French patois is also spoken.
15 Local Bajan dialect is also spoken.
16 A French patois is spoken by a minority.
17 English and Spanish are also spoken. The islanders speak Papiamento (see 9).

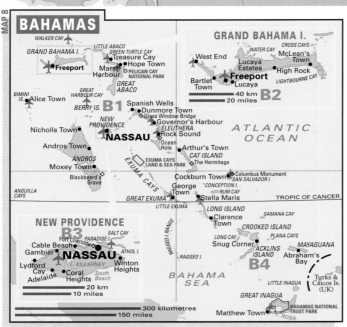

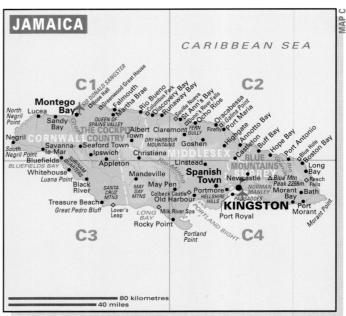

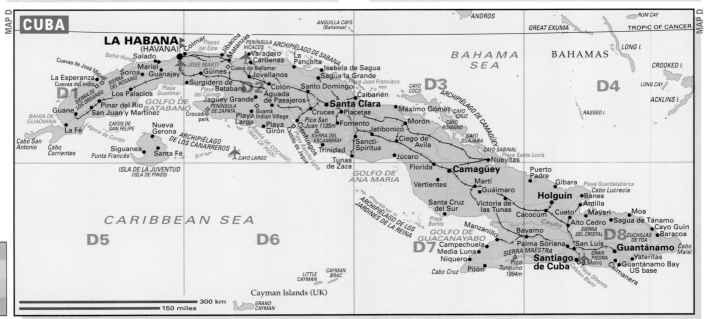

▶ Zoo / animal park   ▶ Aquarium

THE CARIBBEAN

See page 37 for general map

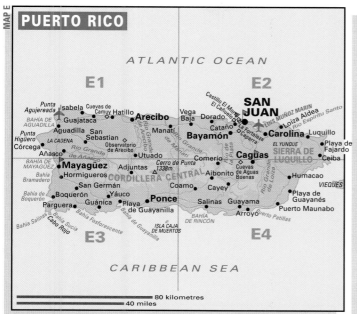

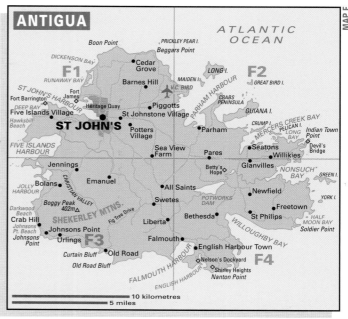

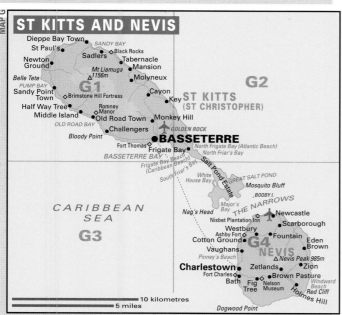

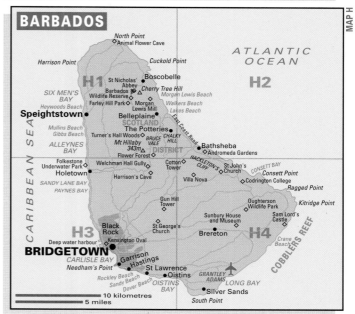

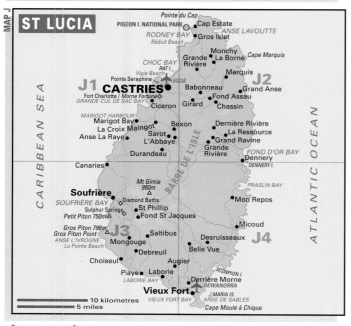

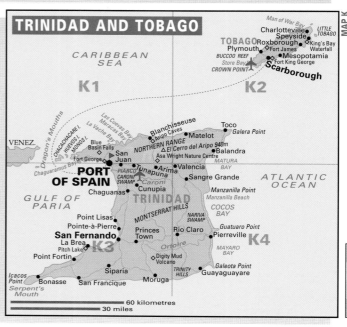

▶ Leisure park ▶ Zoo / animal park

CLIMATE

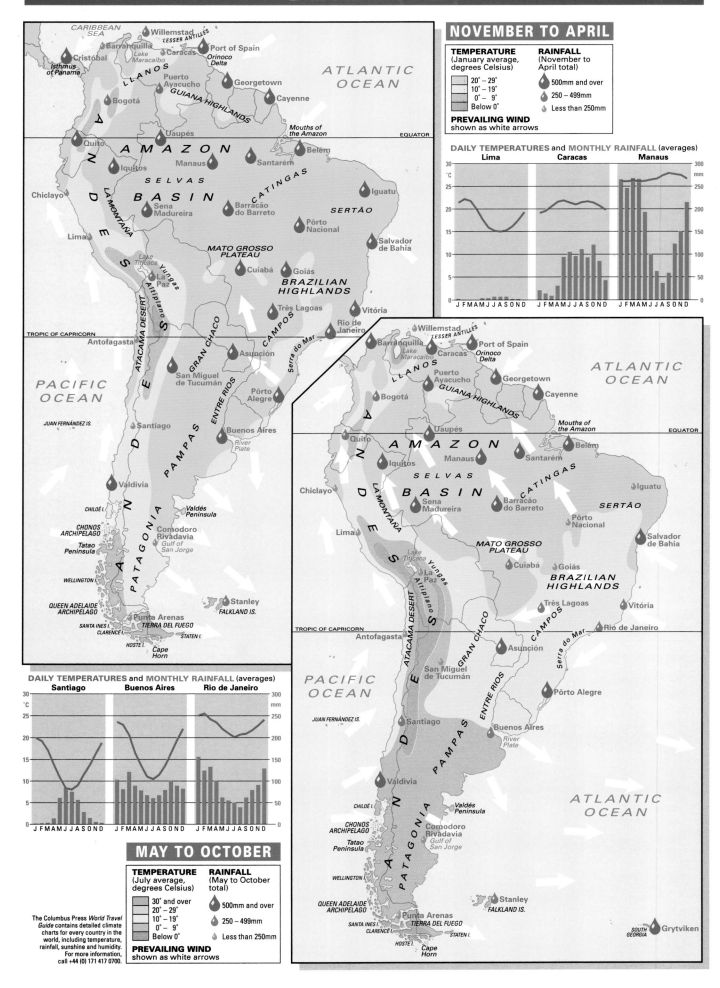

The Columbus Press *World Travel Guide* contains detailed climate charts for every country in the world, including temperature, rainfall, sunshine and humidity. For more information, call +44 (0) 171 417 0700.

TEMPERATURE CONVERSION

Celsius	−10	0	10	20	30	40
Fahrenheit	14	32	50	68	86	104

RAINFALL CONVERSION

Millimetres	102	203	305	406	508	610
Inches	4	8	12	16	20	24

NOVEMBER TO APRIL

TEMPERATURE
(January average, degrees Celsius)

- 20° – 29°
- 10° – 19°
- 0° – 9°
- Below 0°

RAINFALL
(November to April total)

- 500mm and over
- 250 – 499mm
- Less than 250mm

PREVAILING WIND
shown as white arrows

DAILY TEMPERATURES and MONTHLY RAINFALL (averages)

Lima   Caracas   Manaus

MAY TO OCTOBER

TEMPERATURE
(July average, degrees Celsius)

- 30° and over
- 20° – 29°
- 10° – 19°
- 0° – 9°
- Below 0°

RAINFALL
(May to October total)

- 500mm and over
- 250 – 499mm
- Less than 250mm

PREVAILING WIND
shown as white arrows

DAILY TEMPERATURES and MONTHLY RAINFALL (averages)

Santiago   Buenos Aires   Rio de Janeiro

ARGENTINA BRAZIL PERU URUGUAY

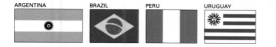

SOUTH AMERICA

See pages 43-45 for general maps

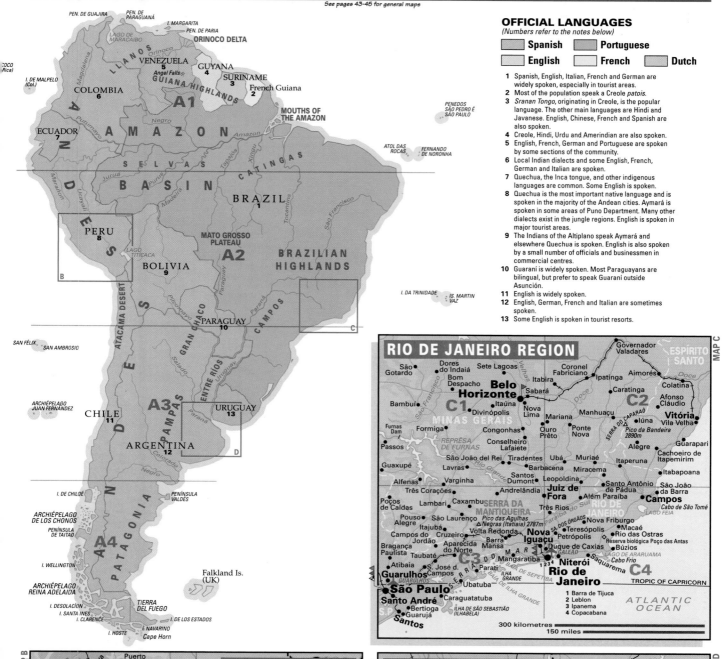

OFFICIAL LANGUAGES
(Numbers refer to the notes below)

- Spanish
- Portuguese
- English
- French
- Dutch

1 Spanish, English, Italian, French and German are widely spoken, especially in tourist areas.
2 Most of the population speak a Creole *patois*.
3 *Sranan Tongo*, originating in Creole, is the popular language. The other main languages are Hindi and Javanese. English, Chinese, French and Spanish are also spoken.
4 Creole, Hindi, Urdu and Amerindian are also spoken.
5 English, French, German and Portuguese are spoken by some sections of the community.
6 Local Indian dialects and some English, French, German and Italian are spoken.
7 Quechua, the Inca tongue, and other indigenous languages are common. Some English is spoken.
8 Quechua is the most important native language and is spoken in the majority of the Andean cities. Aymará is spoken in some areas of Puno Department. Many other dialects exist in the jungle regions. English is spoken in major tourist areas.
9 The Indians of the Altiplano speak Aymará and elsewhere Quechua is spoken. English is also spoken by a small number of officials and businessmen in commercial centres.
10 Guaraní is widely spoken. Most Paraguayans are bilingual, but prefer to speak Guaraní outside Asunción.
11 English is widely spoken.
12 English, German, French and Italian are sometimes spoken.
13 Some English is spoken in tourist resorts.

RIO DE JANEIRO REGION

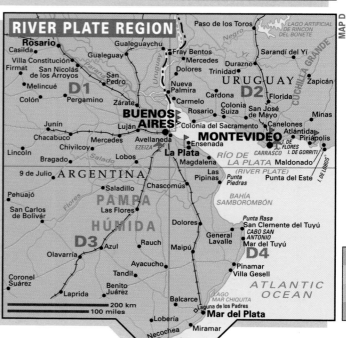

SOUTHERN PERU

RIVER PLATE REGION

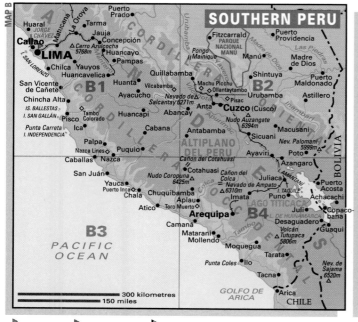

▶ Leisure park   ▶ Zoo / animal park   ▶ Formula One

WORLD

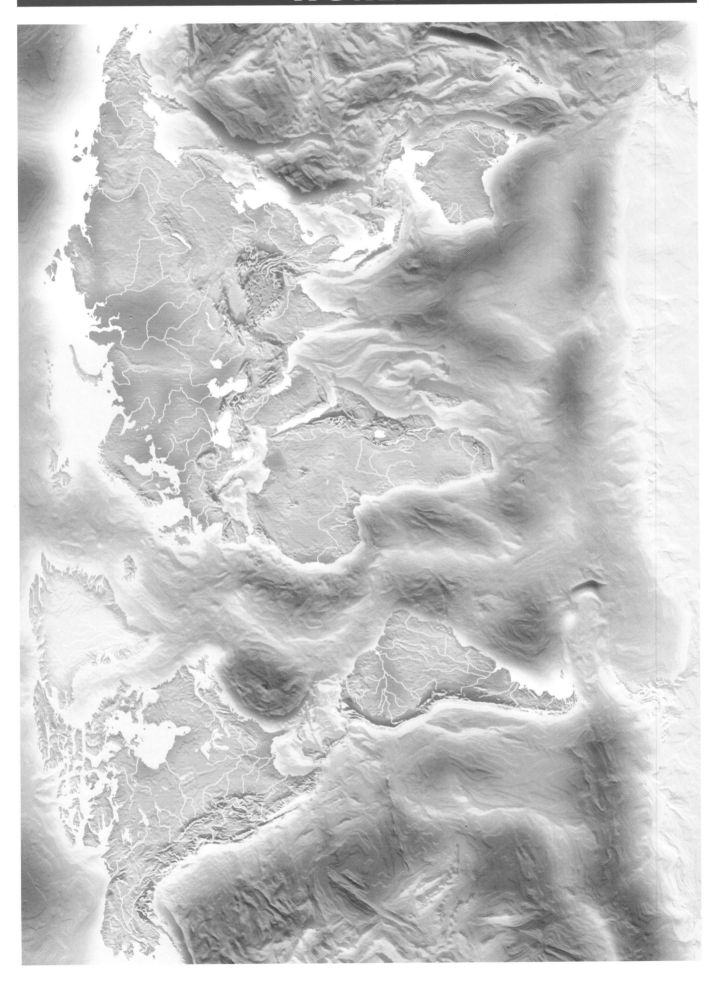

EUROPE

The British Isles

The Alps

AFRICA

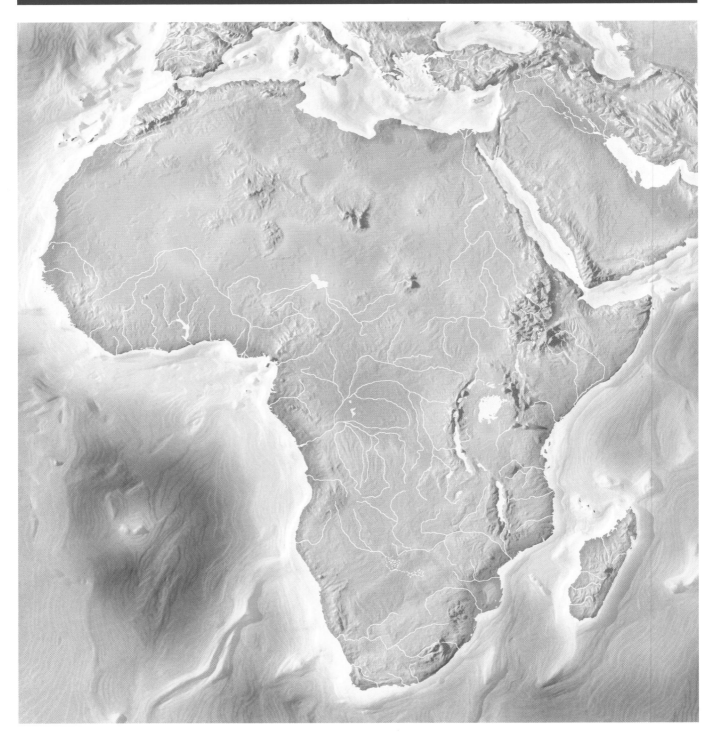

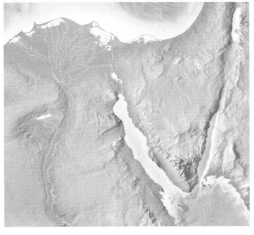

Nile Delta, Sinai
and the Suez Canal

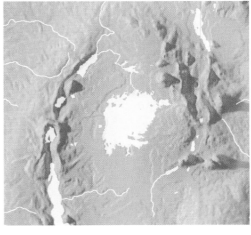

Lake Victoria region

ASIA

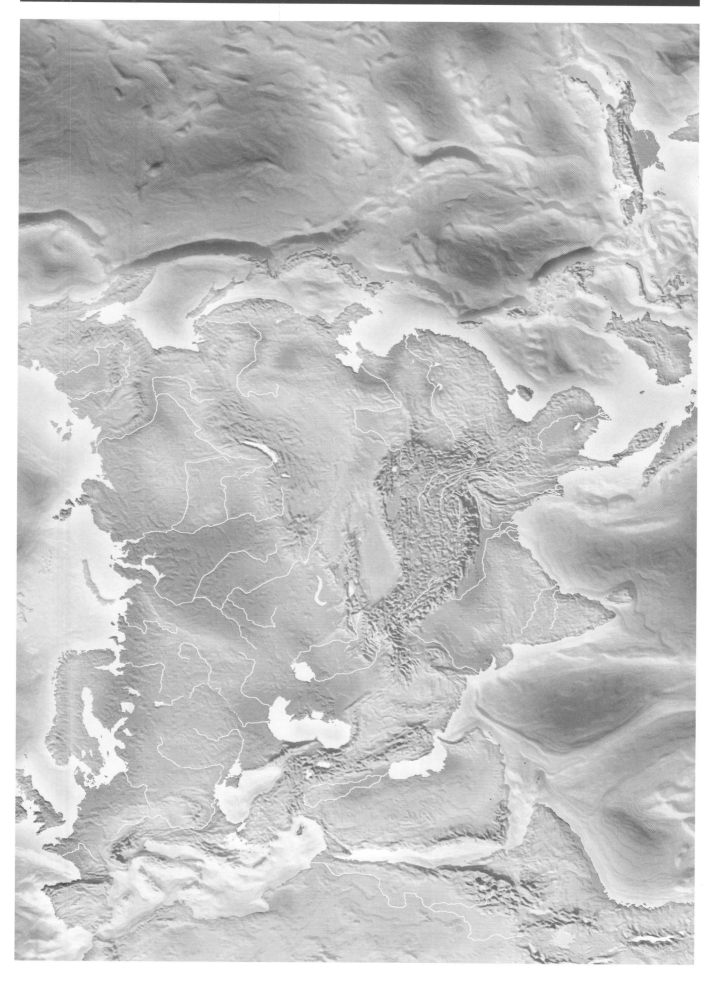

NORTH AMERICA

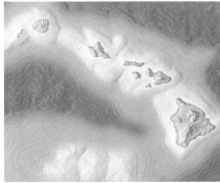

Hawaii

Panama and the Panama Canal

Northern Caribbean

SOUTH AMERICA

AUSTRALIA AND NEW ZEALAND

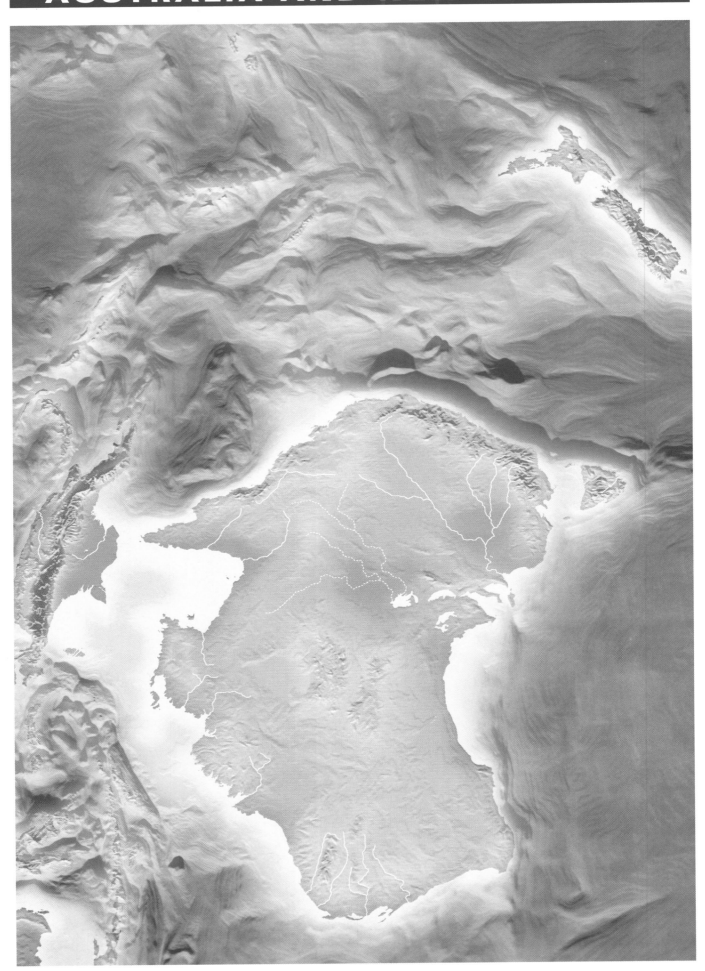

POLAR REGIONS

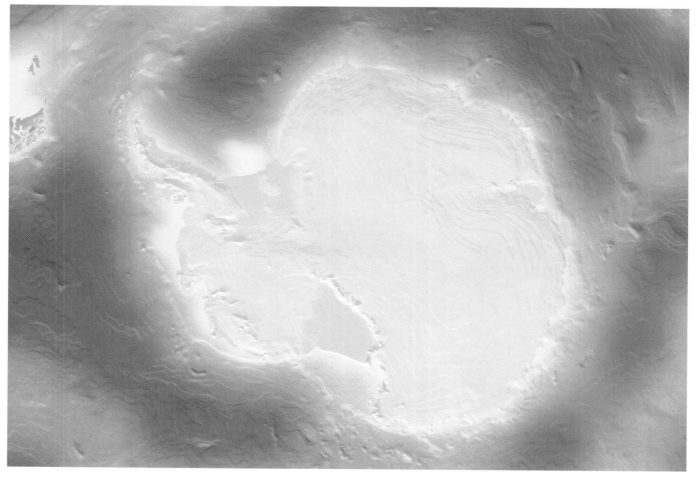

EARTH FROM SPACE

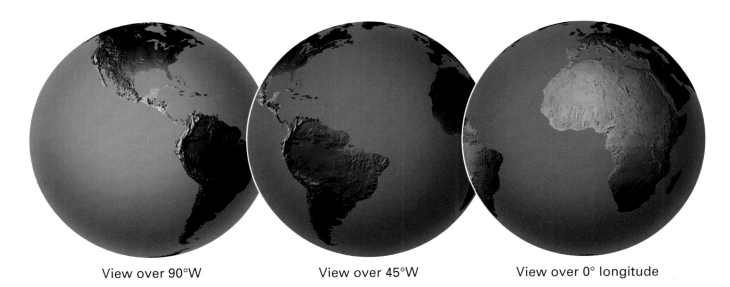

View over 90°W

View over 45°W

View over 0° longitude

PACIFIC OCEAN

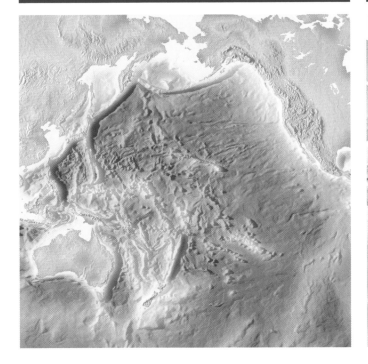

ATLANTIC OCEAN

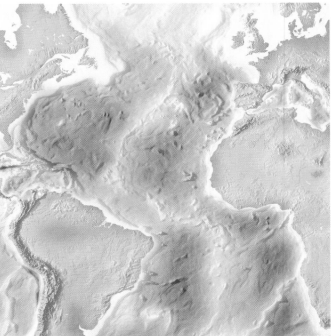

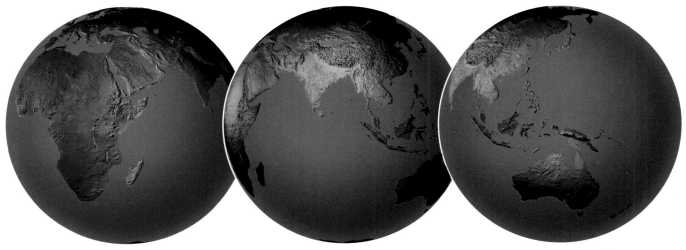

View over 45°E

View over 90°E

View over 135°E

APPENDICES

1: GEOGRAPHICAL DEFINITIONS

The following list includes names and abbreviations which appear in this atlas, together with other terms that are commonly used in the travel industry. Various authorities differ on the exact definitions of some of these entries; the definitions given here are those which are generally understood within the travel trade.

Arabian Peninsula
Geographical region comprising: Bahrain, Kuwait, Oman, Qatar, Saudi Arabia, United Arab Emirates, Yemen.

ASEAN (Association of South-East Asian Nations)
Regional organisation comprising the following member countries: Brunei, Indonesia, Laos, Malaysia, Myanmar, the Philippines, Singapore, Thailand, Vietnam.

Australasia
Geographical region comprising: Australia, New Caledonia, New Zealand, Solomon Islands, Vanuatu and the island of New Guinea including all of Papua New Guinea. Often described as equivalent to all of Oceania between the Equator and 47°S. The term is not commonly used, especially in Australia and New Zealand because of confusion with Australia.

Bahama Islands
Group of islands in the Atlantic Ocean comprising the Commonwealth of the Bahamas and the Turks and Caicos Islands.

Balkans, The
The Balkan Peninsula, which is bordered by the Adriatic and Ionian Seas to the west, the Aegean and Black Seas to the east and the Mediterranean Sea to the south. The countries occupying this peninsula are described as Balkan states: Albania, Bosnia-Herzegovina, Bulgaria, Croatia, Greece, Former Yugoslav Republic of Macedonia, Romania, Slovenia, Federal Republic of Yugoslavia and the European part of Turkey.

Borneo
Island in the Malay Archipelago divided between Brunei, Indonesia (the provinces of Central, East, South and West Kalimantan) and Malaysia (the states of Sabah and Sarawak).

British Isles
Geographical region comprising: United Kingdom, Republic of Ireland, Isle of Man, Channel Islands.

Caribbean
General tourist destination term used to describe the West Indies.

Caroline Islands
Archipelago in the west Pacific Ocean. Islands comprise the Federated States of Micronesia and Palau.

Celebes
Island in the Malay Archipelago called Sulawesi in Indonesian.

Central America
Geographical region comprising: Belize, Costa Rica, El Salvador, Guatemala, Honduras, Nicaragua, Panama. Usually considered part of the North American continent.

Ceylon
Island off the southeast coast of India, officially Sri Lanka.

Channel Islands
Group of islands comprising Jersey, Guernsey, Alderney, Sark and Herm, situated off the northwest coast of France. They are possessions of the British Crown and not officially part of the United Kingdom.

CIS (Commonwealth of Independent States)
Countries of the former Soviet Union with the exception of Estonia, Latvia and Lithuania.

Commonwealth, The
Free association of sovereign independent states comprising the following countries: Antigua and Barbuda, Australia, Bahamas, Bangladesh, Barbados, Belize, Botswana, Brunei, Cameroon, Canada, Cyprus, Dominica, Fiji, The Gambia, Ghana, Grenada, Guyana, India, Jamaica, Kenya, Kiribati, Lesotho, Malawi, Malaysia, Maldives, Malta, Mauritius, Mozambique, Namibia, Nauru, New Zealand, Pakistan, Papua New Guinea, St Kitts and Nevis, St Lucia, St Vincent and the Grenadines, Seychelles, Sierra Leone, Singapore, Solomon Islands, South Africa, Sri Lanka, Swaziland, Tanzania, Tonga, Trinidad and Tobago, Tuvalu, Uganda, United Kingdom, Vanuatu, Western Samoa, Zambia, Zimbabwe. Dependencies and associated states of Australia, New Zealand and the UK are also members. Nigeria's membership was suspended in November 1995. Fiji was re-admitted in October 1997 after a period of suspension.

East Indies
General geographical term sometimes applied loosely to India, Indochina and the Malay Archipelago. Often used as alternative to the Malay Archipelago or the Republic of Indonesia itself. The term is rarely used.

EU (European Union)
Regional organisation comprising the following member countries: Austria, Belgium, Denmark, Finland, France, Germany, Greece, Ireland, Italy, Luxembourg, The Netherlands, Portugal, Spain, Sweden, United Kingdom.

Europe
Continent. Northern boundary formed by Arctic Ocean. Eastern boundary formed by Ural Mountains, Ural river and Caspian Sea. Southern boundary formed by Caucasus Mountains, Black Sea, Bosporus, Aegean Sea and Mediterranean Sea. Western boundary formed by Atlantic Ocean. Includes Iceland, Svalbard and area of Turkey west of the Bosporus.

Far East
General geographical term describing east and South-East Asia: Brunei, Cambodia, China, Indonesia, Japan, Democratic People's Republic of Korea (North Korea), Republic of Korea (South Korea), Laos, Malaysia, Myanmar, the Philippines, Singapore, Taiwan, Thailand, Vietnam. Sometimes extended to include Mongolia and the eastern Siberian region of the Russian Federation.

FEEE (Foundation for Environmental Education in Europe)
A network of organisations working to promote environmental education in Europe. The FEEE's Blue Flag Campaign for beaches and marinas is presently operating in the following countries: Belgium, Bulgaria, Cyprus, Denmark, Estonia, Finland, France, Germany, Greece, Ireland, Italy, The Netherlands, Portugal, Slovenia, Spain, Sweden, Turkey, United Kingdom.

Formosa
Island off the southeast coast of the People's Republic of China, known variously as the Republic of China or Taiwan.

Franc Zone
Countries whose currencies are linked with the French franc at a fixed exchange rate. Each country has its own central issuing bank and its currency is freely covertible into French francs. Members are Benin, Burkina Faso, Cameroon, Central African Republic, Chad, Comoros, Congo, Côte d'Ivoire, Equatorial Guinea, Gabon, Guinea-Bissau, Mali, Niger, Senegal, Togo.

FSU (Former Soviet Union)
Armenia, Azerbaijan, Belarus, Estonia, Georgia, Kazakhstan, Kyrgyzstan, Latvia, Lithuania, Moldova, Russian Federation, Tajikistan, Turkmenistan, Ukraine, Uzbekistan.

Great Britain
Geographical region comprising: England, Scotland, Wales.

Greater Antilles
Group of Caribbean islands comprising: Cayman Islands, Cuba, Hispaniola, Jamaica, Puerto Rico.

Hispaniola
Island in the Greater Antilles divided between the Dominican Republic and Haiti.

IATA (International Air Transport Association)
An association which acts as a governing body of the major airlines, responsible for establishing fare levels and for rules and regulations concerning international passenger and cargo services. It has over 100 tariff members and a further 100 trade associate airlines.

Iberia
Peninsula in southwest Europe occupied by Spain, Portugal, Andorra and Gibraltar.

Indochina
Geographical region comprising: Cambodia, Laos, Malaysia (Peninsular), Myanmar, Singapore, Thailand, Vietnam.

Lesser Antilles
Group of Caribbean islands comprising: Virgin Islands, Leeward Islands, Windward Islands, Aruba, Barbados, Bonaire, Curaçao, Trinidad and Tobago. Also includes the chain of small Venezuelan islands east of Bonaire.

Leeward Islands
Group of Caribbean islands comprising: Anguilla, Antigua and Barbuda, Dominica, Guadeloupe, Montserrat, Saba, St Eustatius, St Kitts and Nevis, St Maarten/St Martin.

Low Countries
Geographical region comprising: Belgium, Luxembourg, The Netherlands.

Maghreb
Arabic name for northwest Africa and, during the Moorish period, Spain. Algeria, Morocco and Tunisia are described as Maghreb countries.

Malay Archipelago
The largest island group in the world, off the southeast coast of Asia and between the Indian and Pacific Oceans. Major islands include Borneo, Sulawesi (Celebes), Jawa (Java), New Guinea and Sumatera (Sumatra). Countries within this archipelago: Brunei, Indonesia, Malaysia (East), Papua New Guinea, the Philippines.

Mediterranean
General tourist destination term used to describe the islands of the Mediterranean Sea and the countries bordering it.

Melanesia
Collective name for the islands in the southwest Pacific Ocean, south of the Equator and northeast of Australia. Includes: Fiji, Nauru, New Caledonia, Papua New Guinea (excluding New Guinea mainland), Solomon Islands, Vanuatu.

Micronesia
Collective name for the islands in the west Pacific Ocean, north of the Equator and east of the Philippines. Includes: Guam, Kiribati (west), Marshall Islands, Federated States of Micronesia, Northern Mariana Islands, Palau.

Middle East
General geographical term describing a loosely defined area comprising: countries of the Arabian Peninsula, Egypt, Iran, Iraq, Israel, Jordan, Lebanon, Syria. Usually extended to include Algeria, Cyprus, Libya, Morocco, Sudan, Tunisia and Turkey.

NAFTA (North American Free Trade Agreement)
Regional organisation comprising: Canada, Mexico, USA.

Near East
Rarely used general geographical term describing an area of SW Asia: the Arabian Peninsula, Cyprus, Israel, Jordan, Lebanon, Syria, Turkey. Usually extended to Egypt and Sudan.

Netherlands Antilles
Islands of the West Indies administered by The Netherlands, comprising: Bonaire, Curaçao, Saba, St Eustatius, St Maarten. Aruba, formerly part of the Netherlands Antilles is now administered from The Netherlands separately.

New Guinea
Island in the Malay Archipelago divided between Papua New Guinea and the Indonesian province of Irian Jaya.

North America
Continent comprising: Bermuda, Canada, Mexico, USA, West Indies. Generally considered to include Central America and Greenland.

Oceania
General geographical term describing the islands of the central and south Pacific Ocean, including Melanesia, Micronesia and Polynesia. Sometimes extended to include Australia, New Zealand and the Malay Archipelago.

OECD (Organisation for Economic Cooperation and Development)
International organisation comprising the following member countries: Australia, Austria, Belgium, Canada, Czech Republic, Denmark, Finland, France, Germany, Greece, Hungary, Iceland, Ireland, Italy, Japan, Republic of Korea, Luxembourg, Mexico, The Netherlands, New Zealand, Norway, Poland, Portugal, Spain, Sweden, Switzerland, Turkey, United Kingdom, USA.

OPEC (Organisation of the Petroleum Exporting Countries)
International organisation comprising the following member countries: Algeria, Indonesia, Iran, Iraq, Kuwait, Libya, Nigeria, Qatar, Saudi Arabia, United Arab Emirates, Venezuela.

Polynesia
Collective name for the islands of the central and south Pacific Ocean. Includes: American Samoa, Cook Islands, Easter Island, French Polynesia, Hawaii, Kiribati (east), New Zealand, Niue, Pitcairn Islands, Tokelau, Tonga, Tuvalu, Wallis and Futuna, Western Samoa.

Scandinavia
Geographical region comprising: Denmark, Norway, Sweden. Often extended to include Finland and Iceland.

Schengen Agreement
Agreement of European Union states with the intention of facilitating movement between member countries. Established in March 1995, all EU countries except for Ireland and the UK are members. The agreement is implemented in Austria, Belgium, France, Germany, Italy, Luxembourg, The Netherlands, Portugal, Spain. For further details, please refer to the Columbus Press *World Travel Guide*.

South America
Continent comprising: countries on mainland south of Panama, Falkland Islands, Galapagos Islands.

Ulster
Geographical region comprising Northern Ireland plus the counties of Cavan, Donegal and Monaghan in the Republic of Ireland. It is often used (incorrectly) as an unofficial term to describe Northern Ireland.

UNESCO (United Nations Educational, Scientific and Cultural Organisation)
Specialized agency of the United Nations. Its purpose is to contribute to peace and security by promoting collaboration among the nations through education, science and culture.

United Kingdom
Country comprising Great Britain and Northern Ireland (the Isle of Man and the Channel Islands are Crown dependencies and not officially part of the UK).

United Nations
International organisation. Every state in the world is a member with the exception of Kiribati, Nauru, Switzerland, Taiwan, Tonga, Tuvalu and the Vatican City.

West Indies
Islands enclosing the Caribbean Sea, divided into the following groups: Bahama Islands, Greater Antilles, Lesser Antilles.

Windward Islands
Group of Caribbean islands comprising: Grenada, Martinique, St Lucia, St Vincent and the Grenadines.

WWF (World-Wide Fund For Nature / World Wildlife Fund)
One of the world's largest private international nature conservation organisations. Its aim is to conserve nature by preserving genetic, species and ecosystem diversity.

APPENDICES

2: US STATES

ISO abbreviation*	Name	Nickname	Date of admission to the Union	State capital
AK	Alaska	Last Frontier	3rd Jan 1959	Juneau
AL	Alabama	Yellowhammer State	14th Dec 1819	Montgomery
AR	Arkansas	The Natural State	15th June 1836	Little Rock
AZ	Arizona	Grand Canyon State	14th Feb 1912	Phoenix
CA	California	Golden State	9th Sept 1850	Sacramento
CO	Colorado	Centennial State	1st Aug 1876	Denver
CT	Connecticut	Constitution State	9th Jan 1788 †	Hartford
DC	District of Columbia	(Federal District, coextensive with the city of Washington)		
DE	Delaware	Diamond State	7th Dec 1787 †	Dover
FL	Florida	Sunshine State	3rd Mar 1845	Tallahassee
GA	Georgia	Peach State	2nd Jan 1788 †	Atlanta
HI	Hawaii	Aloha State	21st Aug 1959	Honolulu
IA	Iowa	Hawkeye State	28th Dec 1846	Des Moines
ID	Idaho	Gem State	3rd July 1890	Boise
IL	Illinois	Land of Lincoln	3rd Dec 1818	Springfield
IN	Indiana	Hoosier State	11th Dec 1816	Indianapolis
KS	Kansas	Sunflower State	29th Jan 1861	Topeka
KY	Kentucky	Bluegrass State	1st June 1792	Frankfort
LA	Louisiana	Pelican State	30th Apr 1812	Baton Rouge
MA	Massachusetts	Bay State	6th Feb 1788 †	Boston
MD	Maryland	Old Line State	28th Apr 1788 †	Annapolis
ME	Maine	Pine Tree State	15th Mar 1820	Augusta
MI	Michigan	Great Lakes State	26th Jan 1837	Lansing
MN	Minnesota	North Star State	11th May 1858	St Paul
MO	Missouri	Show Me State	10th Aug 1821	Jefferson City
MS	Mississippi	Magnolia State	10th Dec 1817	Jackson
MT	Montana	Treasure State	8th Nov 1889	Helena
NC	North Carolina	Tar Heel State	21st Nov 1789 †	Raleigh
ND	North Dakota	Peace Garden State	2nd Nov 1889	Bismarck
NE	Nebraska	Cornhusker State	1st Mar 1867	Lincoln
NH	New Hampshire	Granite State	21st June 1788 †	Concord
NJ	New Jersey	Garden State	18th Dec 1787 †	Trenton
NM	New Mexico	Land of Enchantment	6th Jan 1912	Santa Fe
NV	Nevada	Silver State	31st Oct 1864	Carson City
NY	New York	Empire State	26th July 1788 †	Albany
OH	Ohio	Buckeye State	1st Mar 1803	Columbus
OK	Oklahoma	Sooner State	16th Nov 1907	Oklahoma City
OR	Oregon	Beaver State	14th Feb 1859	Salem
PA	Pennsylvania	Keystone State	12th Dec 1787 †	Harrisburg
RI	Rhode Island	The Ocean State	29th May 1790 †	Providence
SC	South Carolina	Palmetto State	23rd May 1788 †	Columbia
SD	South Dakota	Mount Rushmore State	2nd Nov 1889	Pierre
TN	Tennessee	Volunteer State	1st June 1796	Nashville
TX	Texas	Lone Star State	29th Dec 1845	Austin
UT	Utah	Beehive State	4th Jan 1896	Salt Lake City
VA	Virginia	The Old Dominion State	25th June 1788 †	Richmond
VT	Vermont	Green Mountain State	4th Mar 1791	Montpelier
WA	Washington	Evergreen State	11th Nov 1889	Olympia
WI	Wisconsin	Badger State	29th May 1848	Madison
WV	West Virginia	Mountain State	20th June 1863	Charleston
WY	Wyoming	Equality State / Cowboy State	10th July 1890	Cheyenne

International Standards Organisation. † Original thirteen states: date of ratification of the Constitution.

3: CANADIAN PROVINCES AND TERRITORIES

ISO abbrev.	Name	Language*	Date of entry to the Dominion	Province/territory capital
AL	Alberta	English	1st Sept 1905	Edmonton
BC	British Columbia	English	20th July 1871	Victoria
MN	Manitoba	English	15th July 1870	Winnipeg
NB	New Brunswick	English †	1st July 1867	Fredericton
NF	Newfoundland and Labrador	English	31st March 1949	St John's
NS	Nova Scotia	English	1st July 1867	Halifax
NT	Northwest Territories	English	1870	Yellowknife
NU	Nunavut (territory)	Inuktitut **	(to be established on 1st April 1999)	Iqaluit
OT	Ontario	English	1st July 1867	Toronto
PE	Prince Edward Island	English	1st July 1873	Charlottetown
QU	Québec	French	1st July 1867	Québec
SA	Saskatchewan	English	1st Sept 1905	Regina
YT	Yukon Territory	English	13th June 1898	Whitehorse

*Although Canada is officially bilingual (English & French), this column indicates the most commonly-spoken language in each region. † Approx. 35% of the population are French-speaking. ** The language of the Inuit.*

4: AUSTRALIAN STATES AND TERRITORIES

ISO abbrev.	Name	Nickname	Date of granting of responsible gov't	State/territory capital
AC	Australian Capital Territory	Nation's Capital	1911 *	Canberra
CL	Coral Sea Territory	(External Territory bordering the Queensland coast and Gt. Barrier Reef)		
NS	New South Wales	Premier State	1788 †	Sydney
NT	Northern Territory	Outback Australia	1911 **	Darwin
QL	Queensland	Sunshine State	1859	Brisbane
SA	South Australia	Festival State	1856	Adelaide
TS	Tasmania	Holiday Isle	1856	Hobart
VI	Victoria	Garden State	1855	Melbourne
WA	Western Australia	State of Excitement	1890	Perth

*Canberra became the seat of the Australian government on 9th May 1927. † Date of first settlement: New South Wales originally covered the whole island with the exception of Western Australia. ** Transferred to Commonwealth from South Australia in 1911, self-government within the Commonwealth granted 1978.*

5: FRENCH DÉPARTEMENTS

Dept. no.	Name	Département capital	Region
01	Ain	Bourg-en-Bresse	Rhône-Alpes
02	Aisne	Laon	Picardie
03	Allier	Moulins	Auvergne
04	Alpes-de-Haute-Provence	Digne	Provence-Alpes-Côte d'Azur
05	Hautes-Alpes	Gap	Provence-Alpes-Côte d'Azur
06	Alpes-Maritimes	Nice	Provence-Alpes-Côte d'Azur
07	Ardèche	Privas	Rhône-Alpes
08	Ardennes	Charleville-Mézières	Champagne-Ardenne
09	Ariège	Foix	Midi-Pyrénées
10	Aube	Troyes	Champagne-Ardenne
11	Aude	Carcassonne	Languedoc-Roussillon
12	Aveyron	Rodez	Midi-Pyrénées
13	Bouches-du-Rhône	Marseille	Provence-Alpes-Côte d'Azur
14	Calvados	Caen	Basse-Normandie
15	Cantal	Aurillac	Auvergne
16	Charente	Angoulême	Poitou-Charentes
17	Charente-Maritime	La Rochelle	Poitou-Charentes
18	Cher	Bourges	Centre
19	Corrèze	Tulle	Limousin
20 [2A]	Corse-du-Sud	Ajaccio	Corse
20 [2B]	Haute-Corse	Bastia	Corse
21	Côte-d'Or	Dijon	Bourgogne
22	Côtes-d'Armor	St Brieuc	Bretagne
23	Creuse	Guéret	Limousin
24	Dordogne	Périgueux	Aquitaine
25	Doubs	Besançon	Franche-Comté
26	Drôme	Valence	Rhône-Alpes
27	Eure	Évreux	Haute-Normandie
28	Eure-et-Loir	Chartres	Centre
29	Finistère	Quimper	Bretagne
30	Gard	Nîmes	Languedoc-Roussillon
31	Haute-Garonne	Toulouse	Midi-Pyrénées
32	Gers	Auch	Midi-Pyrénées
33	Gironde	Bordeaux	Aquitaine
34	Hérault	Montpellier	Languedoc-Roussillon
35	Ille-et-Vilaine	Rennes	Bretagne
36	Indre	Châteauroux	Centre
37	Indre-et-Loire	Tours	Centre
38	Isère	Grenoble	Rhône-Alpes
39	Jura	Lons-le-Saunier	Franche-Comté
40	Landes	Mont-de-Marsan	Aquitaine
41	Loir-et-Cher	Blois	Centre
42	Loire	St Étienne	Rhône-Alpes
43	Haute-Loire	Le Puy	Auvergne
44	Loire-Atlantique	Nantes	Pays de la Loire
45	Loiret	Orléans	Centre
46	Lot	Cahors	Midi-Pyrénées
47	Lot-et-Garonne	Agen	Aquitaine
48	Lozère	Mende	Languedoc-Roussillon
49	Maine-et-Loire	Angers	Pays de la Loire
50	Manche	St Lô	Basse-Normandie
51	Marne	Châlons-sur-Marne	Champagne-Ardenne
52	Haute-Marne	Chaumont	Champagne-Ardenne
53	Mayenne	Laval	Pays de la Loire
54	Meurthe-et-Moselle	Nancy	Lorraine
55	Meuse	Bar-le-Duc	Lorraine
56	Morbihan	Vannes	Bretagne
57	Moselle	Metz	Lorraine
58	Nièvre	Nevers	Bourgogne
59	Nord	Lille	Nord-Pas-de-Calais
60	Oise	Beauvais	Picardie
61	Orne	Alençon	Basse-Normandie
62	Pas-de-Calais	Arras	Nord-Pas-de-Calais
63	Puy-de-Dôme	Clermont-Ferrand	Auvergne
64	Pyrénées-Atlantiques	Pau	Aquitaine
65	Hautes-Pyrénées	Tarbes	Midi-Pyrénées
66	Pyrénées-Orientales	Perpignan	Languedoc-Roussillon
67	Bas-Rhin	Strasbourg	Alsace
68	Haut-Rhin	Colmar	Alsace
69	Rhône	Lyon	Rhône-Alpes
70	Haute-Sâone	Vesoul	Franche-Comté
71	Saône-et-Loire	Mâcon	Bourgogne
72	Sarthe	Le Mans	Pays de la Loire
73	Savoie	Chambéry	Rhône-Alpes
74	Haute-Savoie	Annecy	Rhône-Alpes
75	Paris	Paris	Île-de-France
76	Seine-Maritime	Rouen	Haute-Normandie
77	Seine-et-Marne	Melun	Île-de-France
78	Yvelines (canton)	Versailles	Île-de-France
79	Deux-Sèvres	Niort	Poitou-Charentes
80	Somme	Amiens	Picardie
81	Tarn	Albi	Midi-Pyrénées
82	Tarn-et-Garonne	Montauban	Midi-Pyrénées
83	Var	Toulon	Provence-Alpes-Côte d'Azur
84	Vaucluse	Avignon	Provence-Alpes-Côte d'Azur
85	Vendée	La Roche-sur-Yon	Pays de la Loire
86	Vienne	Poitiers	Poitou-Charentes
87	Haute-Vienne	Limoges	Limousin
88	Vosges	Épinal	Lorraine
89	Yonne	Auxerre	Bourgogne
90	Territoire-de-Belfort	Belfort	Franche-Comté
91	Essonne (canton)	Évry	Île-de-France
92	Hauts-de-Seine (canton)	Nanterre	Île-de-France
93	Seine-St-Denis (canton)	Bobigny	Île-de-France
94	Val-de-Marne (canton)	Créteil	Île-de-France
95	Val-d'Oise (canton)	Cergy	Île-de-France

APPENDICES

6: THE WORLD'S MAJOR URBAN AREAS

This list shows the world's fifty largest urban agglomerations in 1995, according to the UN, with estimates of their population in 1995 and forecasts for the year 2000.

Urban agglomeration and country	Population ('000) 1995	2000
Tokyo-Yokohama-Kawasaki-Chiba, Japan	26,836	27,856
São Paulo, Brazil	16,417	17,803
New York-Jersey City-Newark, USA	16,329	16,640
Mexico City-Fed. Dist., Mexico	15,643	16,354
Bombay, India	15,093	18,121
Shanghai, China	15,082	17,213
Los Angeles-Long Beach, USA	12,410	13,148
Beijing, China	12,362	14,206
Calcutta, India	11,673	12,660
Seoul, Rep. of Korea	11,641	12,278
Jakarta, Indonesia	11,500	14,091
Buenos Aires, Argentina	10,990	11,378
Tianjin, China	10,687	12,369
Osaka-Kobe, Japan	10,601	10,601
Lagos, Nigeria	10,287	13,455
Rio de Janeiro, Brazil	9,888	10,213
Delhi, India	9,882	11,678
Karachi, Pakistan	9,863	12,079
Cairo, Egypt	9,656	10,731
Paris, France	9,469	9,551
Metro Manila, Philippines	9,280	10,801
Moscow, Russian Fed.	9,233	9,282
Dhaka, Bangladesh	7,832	10,193
Istanbul-Usküdar, Turkey	7,817	9,316
Lima-Callao, Peru	7,452	8,381
Greater London, United Kingdom	7,335	7,335
Chicago-Gary-Hammond, USA	6,846	6,962
Tehran, Iran	6,830	7,347
Bangkok, Thailand	6,566	7,320
Essen-Dortmund-Duisburg, Germany	6,481	6,518
Madras, India	5,906	6,561
Bogotá, Colombia	5,614	6,323
Hong Kong, China	5,574	5,712
Hyderabad, India	5,343	6,678
Shenyang, China	5,310	6,134
St Petersburg, Russian Fed.	5,111	5,111
Lahore, Pakistan	5,085	6,201
Santiago, Chile	5,065	5,439
Bangalore, India	4,749	5,527
Toronto, Canada	4,483	4,930
Baghdad, Iraq	4,478	5,068
Wuhan, China	4,399	5,101
Philadelphia-Camden, USA	4,304	4,413
Milan, Italy	4,251	4,251
Kinshasa, Dem. Rep. of Congo	4,214	5,121
Washington DC-Alexandria-Arlington, USA	4,111	4,474
Pusan, Rep. of Korea	4,082	4,244
Madrid, Spain	4,072	4,072
Guangzhou, China	4,056	4,676
Belo Horizonte, Brazil	3,899	4,429

7: THE WORLD'S LONGEST RIVERS

Lengths include the river plus the tributaries comprising the longest watercourse, shown to the nearest 10 km/miles. Local names are shown in square brackets: [ ].

River	Length: (km)	(miles)	Source(s) and outflow
Nile-Kagera-Ruvuvu-Luvironza	6,690	4,160	Lake Victoria region – Mediterranean Sea
Amazon-Ucayali-Tambo-Ene-Apurimac	6,570	4,080	Peruvian Andes – Atlantic Ocean
Mississippi-Missouri-Beaverhead-Red Rock	6,020	3,740	SW Montana – Gulf of Mexico
Chang Jiang (Yangtze)-[Jinsha-Tongtian-Tuotuo]	5,980	3,720	Tanggula Shan, China – East China Sea
Yenisey-Angara-Selenga-Ider	5,870	3,650	Western Mongolia – Kara Sea
Amur-Argun-Kerulen	5,780	3,590	Eastern Mongolia – Sea of Japan
Ob-Irtysh-[Ertix]	5,410	3,360	Altay Mountains, China – Kara Sea
Paraná-Rio Grande	4,880	3,030	Sa. da Mantiquera, Brazil – Atlantic Ocean
Huang He (Yellow)	4,840	3,010	Bayan Har Shan, China – Yellow Sea
Congo-Lualaba	4,630	2,880	Katanga Plat., Congo D.R. – Atlantic Ocean
Lena	4,400	2,730	Baikal Mtns, Russian Fed., – Laptev Sea
Mackenzie-Slave-Peace-Finlay	4,240	2,630	Omineca Mtns, BC, Canada– Beaufort Sea
Mekong-[Lancang-Za]	4,180	2,600	Tanggula Shan, China – South China Sea
Niger-[Joliba/Kworra]	4,100	2,550	Guinea/Sierra Leone bdr. – Gulf of Guinea

8: HIGHEST AND LOWEST

Name	Metres	Feet	Country
AFRICA			
Kilimanjaro (Kibo)	5,895	19,340	Tanzania
Lake Assal	–155	–509	Djibouti
ANTARCTICA			
Vinson Massif	5,140	16,860	Antarctica
(ice covered)	–2,538	–8,327	Antarctica
ASIA			
Everest (Qomolangma Feng/ Sagarmatha)	8,848	29,028	China-Nepal
Dead Sea	–395	–1,296	Israel-Jordan
AUSTRALASIA			
Cook	3,764	12,349	New Zealand
Lake Eyre	–16	–52	Australia
EUROPE			
Elbrus	5,642	18,510	Russian Fed.
Caspian Sea	–28	–92	Australia
NORTH AMERICA			
McKInley (Denali)	6,194	20,320	Alaska, USA
Death Valley	–86	–282	California, USA
SOUTH AMERICA			
Aconcagua	6,960	22,834	Argentina
Valdés Peninsula	–40	–131	Argentina

Name	Metres	Feet	Country
SOME OTHER SIGNIFICANT MOUNTAINS			
K2 (Godwin Austin/ Qogir Feng)	8,611	28,250	China-Kashmir
Kangchenjunga	8,586	28,170	India-Nepal
Makalu	8,463	27,766	China-Nepal
Dhaulagiri	8,167	26,795	Nepal
Nanga Parbat	8,126	26,660	Kashmir
Annapurna	8,091	26,545	Nepal
Xixabangma Feng (Gosainthan)	8,012	26,286	China
Qullai Kommunizm	7,495	24,590	Tajikistan
Ojos del Salado	6,863	22,516	Argentina-Chile
Huascarán	6,768	22,205	Peru
Logan	5,951	19,524	Yukon, Canada
Citlaltépetl (Orizaba)	5,700	18,701	Mexico
Damavand	5,670	18,602	Iran
Kenya (Kirinyaga)	5,199	17,057	Kenya
Ararat	5,165	16,946	Turkey
Mont Blanc	4,810	15,781	France-Italy
Ras Dashen	4,620	15,158	Ethiopia
Whitney	4,418	14,495	California, USA
Kinabalu	4,101	13,455	Malaysia
Fuji	3,776	12,388	Japan

9: CONVERSIONS

Kilometres: 0 10 20 30 40 50 60 70 80 90 100
Miles: 0 10 20 30 40 50 60

Metres: 0 100 200 300 400 500 600 700 800 900 1,000
Feet: 0 500 1,000 1,500 2,000 2,500 3,000

Millimetres: 0 10 20 30 40 50 60 70 80 90 100
Inches: 0 0.5 1.0 1.5 2.0 2.5 3.0 3.5 4.0

°Centigrade: -10 -5 0 5 10 15 20 25 30 35 40
°Fahrenheit: 20 30 32 40 50 60 70 80 90 100

Freezing point

10: INTERNATIONAL GLOSSARY

The following list provides the English equivalents for some of the most common words used in this atlas and other international atlases.

A		
Å, -å	Danish, Norwegian	Stream
Abar, Abyar	Arabic	Wells
Açude	Portuguese	Reservoir
Adalar	Turkish	Islands
Adasi	Turkish	Island
Agía, Ágios	Greek	Saint
Aiguille(s)	French	Peak(s)
Ain, Aïn	Arabic	Spring, well
-air	Indonesian	Stream
Ákra, Akrotírion	Greek	Cape, point
Ala-	Finnish	Lower
A'lá	Arabic	Upper
Alt-	German	Old
Alta, Alto	Italian, Portug., Spanish	Upper
Altiplanicie	Spain	High plain, mesa
Älv, -älven	Swedish	River
am, an	German	On, upon
Áno	Greek	Upper
Anse	French	Bay
Ao	Chinese, Thai	Bay
'Aqabat	Arabic	Pass
Arrecife	Spanish	Reef
Arroio / Arroyo	Portuguese / Spanish	Watercourse
Archipiélago	Spanish	Archipelago
Aust-	Norwegian	East, eastern
Austral	Spanish	Southern
'Ayn	Arabic	Spring, well
B		
Baai	Afrikaans	Bay
Bab	Arabic	Strait
Bach	German	Stream
Bad	German	Spa
Badiyat	Arabic	Desert
Bælt	Danish	Strait
Baharu	Malay	New
Bahía	Spanish	Bay
Bahiret	Arabic	Lagoon
Bahr	Arabic	Bay, canal, lake
Bahra / Bahrat	Arabic	Lagoon / Lake
Baía / Baie	Portuguese / French	Bay
Baixo	Portuguese	Lower
Baja, Bajo	Spanish	Lower
Bala	Persian	Upper
Ban	Cambodian, Laotian, Thai	Village
-bana	Japanese	Cape, point
Bañado	Spanish	Marshy land
Banc / Banco	French / Spanish	Sandbank
Bandao	Chinese	Peninsula
Bandar	Arabian, Malay, Persian	Inlet, port
-bando	Korean	Peninsula
Baraj, Baraji	Turkish	Dam
Barat	Indonesian, Malay	West, western
Barqa	Arabic	Hill
Barra	Portuguese	Sandbank
Barracão	Portuguese	Dam, weir
Barragem	Portuguese	Reservoir
Baruun	Mongolian	Western
Bas, Basse	French	Lower
Bassin	French	Basin
Batin, Batn	Arabic	Depression
Becken	German	Basin
Beek	Flemish	Stream
bei	German	At, near
Bei	Chinese	North, northern
Beinn, Ben	Gaelic	Mountain
Belogor'ye	Russian	Mountain
Bereg	Russian	Bank, shore
-berg	Norwegian, Swedish	Mountain
Berg(e)	German	Mountain(s)
Besar	Indonesian, Malay	Big, great
Bir, Bîr / Bi'ar	Arabic	Well / Wells
Birkat, Birket	Arabic	Pool, well
-bjerg	Danish	Hill
Boca	Portuguese, Spanish	Mouth
Bocche	Italian	Estuary, mouths
Bodden	German	Bay, gulf
Bogazi	Turkish	Strait
Bogen	Norwegian	Bay
Bois	French	Woods
Boloto	Russian	Bog, marsh
Bol'sh-aya, -iye, -oy, -oye	Russian	Big
-bong	Korean	Mountain
Boquerón	Spanish	Pass
Bor	Polish	Forest
-botn / -botten	Norwegian / Swedish	Valley floor
Bouche	French	Estuary, mouth
-bre, -breen	Norwegian	Glacier
Bredning	Danish	Bay
Bron	Afrikaans	Spring, well
-brønn	Norwegian	Spring, well
Bucht / Bugt	German / Danish	Bay
Buhayrat, Buheirat	Arabic	Lake
Bukhta	Russian	Bay
Bukit	Malay	Hill
Bukt, Bukten	Norwegian, Swedish	Bay
Bulag	Mongolian	Spring
Bulak	Russian, Uighur	Spring
Burg	German	Castle
Burun, Burnu	Turkish	Cape, point
Büyük	Turkish	Big
C		
Cabeço	Portuguese	Summit
Cabeza	Spanish	Summit
Cabo	Portuguese, Spanish	Cape, headland
Cachoeira	Portuguese	Waterfall
Cala / Caleta	Catalan / Spanish	Inlet
Cañada	Spanish	Ravine
Cañadón	Spanish	Gorge
Canal	Portuguese, Spanish	Channel
Cañe	Spanish	Stream
Cañon	Spanish	Canyon
Cap / Capo	Catalan, French / Italian	Cape, headland
Catarata	Spanish	Waterfall
Cayo(s)	Spanish	Islet(s), rock(s)
Cerro	Spanish	Hill, peak
Chaco	Spanish	Plain
Chaîne	French	Mountain chain
Chalb	Arabic	Watercourse
Chapada	Portuguese	Hills, uplands
Chebka	Arabic	Hill
-chedo	Korean	Archipelago
Chenal	French	Channel
Chiang	Thai	Town
-ch'on	Korean	River
Chong	Thai	Bay
Chott	Arabic	Marsh, salt lake
Chuluu	Mongolian	Mountain
Chute	French	Waterfall
Ci	Indonesian	Stream
Ciénaga	Spanish	Marshy lake
Cima / Cime	Italian / French	Summit
Città / Ciudad	Italian / Spanish	City, town
Co	Tibetan	Lake
Col	French	High pass
Collado	Spanish	Hill, saddle
Colle	Italian	Pass
Collina	Italian	Hill
Colline(s)	French	Hill(s)
Combe	French	Valley
Conca	Italian	Hollow
Cordillera	Spanish	Mountain chain
Corne / Corno	French / Italian	Peak
Costa	Italian, Portug., Spanish	Coast, shore
Côte	French	Coast, slope
Coteau(x)	French	Hill(s)
Cove	Catalan	Cave
Cuchilla	Spanish	Mountain chain
Cuenca	Spanish	River basin
Cueva	Spanish	Cave
Cun	Chinese	Village
D		
Da	Chinese	Big
Dag / Dagh	Turkish / Persian	Mountain
Daglar	Turkish	Mountain
-dake	Japanese	Peak
-dal	Afrikaans, Danish, Norwegian, Swedish	Valley
Danau	Indonesian	Lake
Dao	Chinese	Island
Darreh	Persian	Valley
Daryacheh	Persian	Lake
Dasht	Persian, Urdu	Desert
Davaa	Mongolian	Pass
Denizi	Turkish	Sea
Dhar	Arabic	Hills, mountain
-diep	Flemish	Channel
Djebel / Djibâl	Arabic	Mountain / Mtns
-do	Korean	Island
Dolina	Russian	Valley
Dolna / Dolní	Bulgarian / Czech	Lower
Dolny	Polish	Lower
Dong	Chinese	East, eastern
Dong	Thai	Mountain
-dong	Korean	Village
Donja, Donji	Serbo-Croat	Lower
Dorf	German	Village
-dorp	Afrikaans	Village
Dûr	Arabic	Mountains
Dzüün	Mongolian	East, eastern
E		
Eiland(en)	Afrikaans, Flemish	Island(s)
-elv, -elva	Norwegian	River
Embalse	Spanish	Reservoir
Embouchure	French	Estuary
Ensenada	Spanish	Bay
Erg	Arabian	Desert & dunes
Eski	Turkish	Old
Estero	Spanish	Inlet, estuary, swamp
Estrecho	Spanish	Strait
Estreito	Portuguese	Strait
Étang	French	Lake, lagoon
F		
Fajj	Arabic	Watercourse
Fels	German	Rock
Feng	Chinese	Peak
Fiume	Italian	River
-fjäll, -fjället	Swedish	Mountain
-fjärden	Swedish	Fjord
-fjell, -fjellet	Norwegian	Mountain
-fjord, -fjorden	Danish, Norwegian	Fjord, lagoon
Fleuve	French	River
Foce	Italian	River-mouth
-fonn	Norwegian	Glacier
Förde	German	Inlet
Forêt / Forst	French / German	Forest
-foss	Norwegian	Waterfall
Fuente	Spanish	Source, well
G		
-gan	Japanese	Rock
Gang	Chinese	Harbour
Garet	Arabic	Hill
Gardaneh	Persian	Pass
Gat	Flemish	Channel
-gata	Japanese	Inlet, lagoon
Gau	German	District
Gave	French	Torrent
-gawa	Japanese	River
Gebel	Arabic	Mountain
Gebergte	Afrikaans	Mountain range
Gebiet	German	District, region
Gebirge	German	Mountains
Gedigi	Turkish	Pass
Gezîret / Gezâir	Arabic	Island / Islands
Ghadfat	Arabic	Watercourse
Ghadir	Arabic	Well
Ghard	Arabic	Sand dunes
Ghubbat	Arabic	Bay
Gipfel	German	Peak
Gletscher	German	Glacier
Gobi	Mongolian	Desert
Gol	Mongolian	River
Göl, Gölü	Turkish	Lake
Golfe	French	Bay, gulf
Golfete	Spanish	Bay
Golfo	Italian, Spanish	Bay, gulf
Gora	Bulgarian	Forest
Gora / Góra	Russian, Serbo-Croat / Polish	Mountain
Górka	Polish	Hill
Gornja, Gornji	Serbo-Croat	Upper
Gory / Góry	Russian / Polish	Mountains
Goulet	French	Narrow entrance
Grabean	German	Ditch, trench
-grad	Bulgarian, Russian, Serbo-Croat	Town, castle
Grand, Grands	French	Big
Grat	German	Crest, ridge
Greben'	Russian	Ridge
-gród	Polish	Town, castle
Groot	Afrikaans	Big
Groß, -e, -en, -er	German	Big
Grotta / Grotte	Italian / French	Cave, grotto
Grund	German	Ground, valley
Gryada	Russian	Ridge
Guan	Chinese	Pass
Guba	Russian	Bay
Guelta	Arabic	Well
-gunto	Japanese	Island group
Gunung	Indonesian, Malay	Mountain
H		
Hadabat	Arabic	Plain
Hadh, Hadhat	Arabic	Sand dunes
-haehyop	Korean	Strait
Hafar	Arabic	Wells
Hafen	German	Harbour, port
Haff	German	Bay
Hai	Chinese	Sea
Halbinsel	German	Peninsula
-halvøya	Norwegian	Peninsula
Hamad-a, -et	Arabic	Plateau
Hammad-ah, -at	Arabic	Plain, rocky plat.
-hamn	Norwegian, Swedish	Harbour
Hamun	Persian	Marsh
-hanto	Japanese	Peninsula
Hardt	German	Wooded hills
Harrat	Arabic	Lava fields
Hassi / Hasy	Arabic	Well
-haug	Norwegian	Hill
Haut, -e	French	Upper
Hawr	Arabic	Lake
-havn	Danish, Norwegian	Harbour
Hazm	Arabic	Plateau
He	Chinese	River
-hede	Danish, Norwegian	Heath
-hegység	Hungarian	Mountains
-hei / Heide	Norwegian / German	Heath, moor
Hersónisos	Greek	Peninsula
Higashi-	Japanese	East, eastern
-hisar	Turkish	Castle
Hisn	Arabic	Fort
-hø	Norwegian	Peak
Hoch / Hoë	German / Afrikaans	High
Hoek	Flemish	Cape, point
Hög / -høg(d)	Swedish / Norwegian	High, height
Höhe, Hohen-	German	Height
Hoog	Flemish	High

APPENDICES

10: INTERNATIONAL GLOSSARY

Continued from previous page

-høoj	Danish	Hill
Hora / Hory	Czech	Mountain / Mtns.
Horn	German	Peak, summit
Horní	Czech	Upper
Hot	Mongolian	Town
-høy	Norwegian	Height
-hrad	Czech	Castle
Hu	Chinese	Lake
Hügel	German	Hill

I

Idd	Arabic	Well
Idhan	Arabic	Sand dunes
'Idwet	Arabic	Mountain
Île(s) / Ilha(s)	French / Portuguese	Island(s)
Illa, Illes	Catalan	Island, islands
im, in	German	In
Inférieur, -e	French	Lower
Insel(n)	German	Island(s)
Irmak	Turkish	Large river
'Irq	Arabic	Sand dunes
Isla(s) / Isle	Spanish / French	Island(s)
Islote	Spanish	Small island
Iso	Finnish	Big
Ísola, Isole	Italian	Island, islands
Istmo	Spanish	Isthmus

J

Jabal	Arabic	Mountain
-järvi	Finnish	Lake
-jaure, -javrre	Lappish	Lake
Jazirat / Jaza'ir	Arabic	Island / Islands
Jbel, Jebel	Arabic	Mountain
Jezero / Jezioro	Serbo-Croat / Polish	Lake
Jiang	Chinese	River
Jiao	Chinese	Point, reef
Jibal	Arabic	Mountains
-jima	Japanese	Island
-joki / -jokka	Finnish / Lappish	River
-jøkulen	Norwegian	Glacier
-jökull	Icelandic	Glacier
Jun	Arabic	Bay

K

Kaap	Afrikaans	Cape
-kai	Japanese	Sea, bay, inlet
Kali	Indonesian	River
Kamm	German	Crest, ridge
Kampung	Indonesian, Malay	Village
Kanaal / Kanal	Flemish / German, Russian	Canal
-kapp	Norwegian	Cape
Karif	Arabic	Well
Kathib	Arabic	Sand dunes
Káto	Greek	Lower
-kawa	Japanese	River
Kecil	Indonesian, Malay	Small
Kepulauan	Indonesian	Archipelago
Kereb	Arabic	Hill, ridge
Keski-	Finnish	Central, middle
Khalîg, Khalij	Arabic	Bay, gulf
Khao	Thai	Peak
Khashm	Arabic	Mountain
Khawr, Khor / Khowr	Arabic / Persian	Inlet
Khrebet	Russian	Mountain range
Kis-	Hungarian	Small
Kita-	Japanese	North, northern
Klamm	German	Ravine
Klein	Afrikaans, German	Small
Klint / Klit	Danish	Cliff / Dunes
Klong	Thai	Canal, creek
Kloof	Afrikaans	Gorge
Ko / Koh	Thai / Cambodian	Island
-ko	Japanese	Lake, inlet
Kólpos	Greek	Gulf
Koog	German	Polder
Kop / Kopf	Afrikaans / German	Hill
Körfezi	Turkish	Bay, gulf
Kotlina	Czech, Polish	Basin, depression
Kotlovina	Russian	Depression
-köy	Turkish	Village
Kraj	Czech, Polish, Serbo-Croat	Region
Kray	Russian	Region
Kreis	German	District
Kryazh	Russian	Ridge
Kuala	Malay	Estuary
Küçük	Turkish	Small
Kuduk	Russian	Spring, well
Kuh	Persian	Mountain
Kul'	Russian	Lake
Kûlet	Arabic	Hill
Kum	Russian	Sandy desert
-kundo	Korean	Island group
-kylä	Finnish	Village

L

Lac	French	Lake
Laem	Thai	Point
Lago	Italian, Portug., Spanish	Lake
Lagoa	Portuguese	Lagoon
Laguna	Spanish	Lagoon, lake
Lam	Thai	Stream
Län	Swedish	Province
Land	German	Province, area
Lande	French	Heath, sandy moor
Las / Les	Polish / Czech, Russian	Forest, wood
Laut	Indonesia	Sea
Lednik	Russian	Glacier
lès, lez	French	Beside, near
Liedao	Chinese	Island group
Lille	Danish, Norwegian	Small
Liman	Russian	Bay, gulf
Liman, Limani	Turkish	Harbour, port
Límni	Greek	Lake, lagoon
Ling	Chinese	Mountain range
Llano	Spanish	Plain, prairie
Loma	Spanish	Hill
-luoto	Finnish	Rocky island
-lyng	Danish	Heath

M

Macizo	Spanish	Massif
Madinat	Arabic	City, town
Mae Nam	Thai	River
Mala / Malé	Serbo-Croat / Czech	Small
Malaya, -oye, -yy	Russian	Small
-man	Korean	Bay
Manâqîr	Arabic	Hills
Mar	Portuguese, Spanish	Sea
Marais	French	Marsh, swamp
Mare	Italian / Romanian	Sea / Big
Marsá	Arabic	Anchorage, inlet
Marsch	German	Fen, marsh
Masabb	Arabic	Estuary
Mashâsh	Arabic	Well
Massif	French	Mountains, upland
Mayor	Spanish	Higher, larger
Meer	Afrikaans, Flemish, German	Lake, sea
Méga, Megál-a, -i, -o	Greek	Big
Menor	Portuguese, Spanish	Lesser, smaller
Mer	French	Sea
Mersa	Arabic	Anchorage, inlet
Mesa, Meseta	Spanish	Tableland
Mesto	Czech, Serbo-Croat	Town
Mezzo	Italian	Middle, mid-
Miasto	Polish	Town
Mic / Mikr-í, ón	Romanian / Greek	Small
Mina'	Arabic	Harbour, port
Minami-	Japanese	South, southern
Minqâr	Arabic	Hill
-misaki	Japanese	Cape, point
Mishâsh / Mushâsh	Arabic	Well
Miti	Greek	Cape
Mittel-, Mitten-	German	Central, middle
Mjesto	Serbo-Croat	Town
Monasterio / Moni	Spanish / Greek	Monastery
Mont / Monte	French / Italian, Portuguese, Spanish	Mountain
Montagne(s)	French	Mountain(s)
Monti	Italian	Mountains
Moor	German	Bog, moor, swamp
Moos	German	Bog, moss
More	Russian	Sea
Mörön	Mongolian	River
Morro	Portuguese	Hill, mountain
-mose	Danish	Bog, moor
Moyen, -ne	French	Middle, mid-
Muara	Indonesian	Estuary
Mudiriyat	Arabic	Province
Muntii	Romanian	Mountains
-myr	Norwegian, Swedish	Moor, swamp
Mys	Russian	Cape

N

na	Bulgarian, Russian, Serbo-Croat	On
nad	Czech, Polish, Russian	Above, over
-nada	Japanese	Gulf, sea
Nádrz	Czech	Reservoir
-naes	Danish	Cape, point
Nafud	Arabic	Desert, dune
Nagor'ye	Russian	Highland, uplands
Nagy-	Hungarian	Big, great
Nahr	Arabic	River
Nakhon	Thai	Town
Nam	Korean, Vietnamese	South, southern
Nam	Burmese, Thai, Vietnamese	River
Nan	Chinese	South, southern
Naqb	Arabic	Pass
Nasb	Arabic	Hill, mountain
Né-a, -on, -os	Greek	New
Neder-	Flemish	Lower
Nehri	Turkish	River
Nei	Chinese	Inner
-nes	Icelandic, Norwegian	Cape, point
Neu- / Neuf, Neuve	German / French	New
Nevado	Spanish	Peak
-ni	Korean	Village
Nieder-	German	Lower
Nieu	Afrikaans	New
Nieuw, -e, -en, -er	Flemish	New
Nishi	Japanese	West, western
-nísi	Greek	Island
Nizhn-eye, -iy, -iye, -yaya	Russian	Lower
Nízina / Nízni	Czech	Lowland / Lower
Nizmennost'	Russian	Lowland
Noord-	Flemish	North, northern
Nord	Danish, French, German	North, northern
Nordre, Nørre	Danish	Northern
Norra	Swedish	Northern
Norte	Portuguese, Spanish	North
Nos	Bulgarian, Russian	Point, spit
Nótios	Greek	Southern
Nou	Romanian	New
Nouv-eau, -elle	French	New
Nova	Italian	New
Nova, Novi	Bulgarian, Serbo-Croat	New
Nova, Novo	Portuguese	New
Nová, Nové, Novy	Czech	New
Nov-aya, -o, -oye, -yy, -yye	Russian	New
Nowa, Nowe, Nowy	Polish	New
Nudo	Spanish	Mountain
Nueva, Nuevo	Spanish	New
Nuruu	Mongolian	Mountains
Nusa	Indonesian	Island
Nuur	Mongolian	Lake
Ny-	Danish, Norweg., Swedish	New

O

-ö, -ön / -ø	Swedish / Danish	Island
-oaivi, -oaivve	Lappish	Hill, mountain
Ober-	German	Upper
Oblast'	Russian	Province
Occidental	Spanish	Western
-odde	Danish, Norwegian	Cape, point
Ogla, Oglet	Arabic	Well
Okrug	Russian	District
Ömnö-	Mongolian	South, southern
Onder	Flemish	Lower
Öndör-	Mongolian	Upper
-oog	German	Island
Oost, -er, -elijk	Flemish	East, eastern
Orasu	Romanian	Town
Oriental, -e	French, Romanian, Spanish	Eastern
Ormani	Turkish	Forest
Órmos	Greek	Bay
Óros / Óri	Greek	Mountain / Mtns.
Ost- / Øster-	German / Danish, Norweg.	East, eastern
Ostan	Persian	Province
Östra-	Swedish	East, eastern
Ostrov(a)	Russian	Island(s)
Otok / Otoci	Serbo-Croat	Island / Islands
Oud, -e, -en, -er	Flemish	Old
Oued	Arabic	Dry river-bed
Ovasi	Turkish	Plain
Over-	Danish, Flemish	Upper
Över-, Övre-	Norwegian, Swedish	Upper
-øy, -a	Norwegian	Island
Ozero, Ozera	Russian	Lake, lakes

P

-pää	Finnish	Hill
Palai-á, -ó, Palió	Greek	Old
Parbat	Urdu	Mountain
Parc	French	Park
Pas	French	Low pass, strait
Paso	Spanish	Pass, strait
Pass / Passo	Spanish / Italian	Pass
Pays	French	Region
Pegunungan	Indonesian	Mountain range
Peña(s)	Spanish	Cliff(s), rocks(s)
Pendi	Chinese	Basin
Penisola	Italian	Peninsula
Peñon	Spanish	Cliff
Pereval	Russian	Pass
Perv-o, -yy	Russian	First
Peski	Russian	Sands, desert
Petit, -e, -es	French	Little
Pic	French, Spanish	Peak, summit
Pico / Picacho	Portuguese, Spanish	Peak, summit
Pik	Russian	Peak, summit
Pingyuan	Chinese	Plain
Pizzo	Italian	Peak, summit
-plaat	Dutch	Sandbank, shoal
Plage	French	Beach
Plaine / Planicie	French / Spanish	Plain
Plaj(i)	Turkish	Beach(es)
Planalto	Portuguese	Plateau
Planina	Bulgarian, Serbo-Croat	Mountains
Platja / Playa	Catalan / Spanish	Beach
Plato	Afrikaans, Bulg., Russian	Plateau
Platte	German	Plateau, plain
Plosina	Czech	Tableland
Ploskogor'ye	Russian	Plateau
pod	Czech, Russian	Under
Pohor-í, -ie	Czech	Mountain range
Pointe	French	Cape, point
Poluostrov	Russian	Peninsula
Pólwysep	Polish	Peninsula
Pongo	Spanish	Water gap
Ponta, Pontal	Portuguese	Point
Portile	Romanian	Gate
Portillo	Spanish	Gap, pass
Porto	Catalan, Italian, Portug.	Harbour, port
Pradesh	Hindi	State
Praia	Portuguese	Beach, shore
près	French	Near
Presqu'île	French	Peninsula
Pri-	Russian	Near
Proliv	Russian	Strait
Protoka	Russian	Channel
Prusmyk	Czech	Pass
Przelecz	Polish	Pass
Pubu	Chinese	Waterfall
Pueblo	Spanish	Village
Puente	Spanish	Bridge
Puerta	Spanish	Narrow pass
Puerto	Spanish	Harbour, port
Puk-	Korean	North, northern
Pulau	Indonesian, Malay	Island
Puna	Spanish	Desert plateau
Punta	Catalan, Italian, Spanish	Cape, point
Puntjak	Indonesian	Mountain
Puy	French	Peak

Q

Qa	Arabic	Depression
Qalamat, Qalib	Arabic	Well
Qanat	Arabic, Persian	U'ground conduit
Qararat	Arabic	Depression
Qâret	Arabic	Hill
Qiao	Chinese	Bridge
Qiuling	Chinese	Hills
Qoz	Arabic	Hill
Qu	Tibetan	Stream
Quan	Chinese	Spring
Quedas	Portuguese	Rapids
Qulban	Arabic	Wells
Qum	Persian	Sand
Qundao	Chinese	Archipelago
Qûr, Qurayyat	Arabic	Hills
Qurnat	Arabic	Peak
Quwayrat / Qurûn	Arabic	Hill / Hills

R

Ramlat	Arabic	Sands
Râs / Ra's	Arabic / Arabic, Persian	Cape, point
Raso	Portuguese	Upland
Ravnina / Razlivy	Russian	Plain
Região	Portuguese	Region
Reprêsa	Portuguese	Dam
Reshteh	Persian	Mountain range
-retto	Japanese	Island chain
-rev	Norwegian	Cliff, reef
Ri	Tibetan	Mountain
-ri	Korean	Village
Ria / Ría	Portuguese / Spanish	River-mouth
Ribeirão	Portuguese	River
Ribeiro	Portuguese	Stream
Rio / Río	Portuguese / Spanish	River
Rivier / Rivière	Afrikaans / French	River
Rocher	French	Cliff, rock
Rocque	French	Rock
Rt	Serbo-Croat	Cape, point
Rücken	German	Ridge
Rud / Rudkhaneh	Persian	River
Rudohorie	Czech	Mountains

S

-saari	Finnish	Island
Sabkhat	Arabic	Salt-flat
Sagar, Sagara	Hindi	Lake
Sahl	Arabic	Plain
Sahra	Arabic	Desert
-saki	Japanese	Cape, point
Salada / Salar, Salina	Spanish	Salt lake / Salt pan
Salto	Portuguese, Spanish	Waterfall
-san	Japanese, Korean	Mountain
-sanchi	Japanese	Mountainous area
Saniyat	Arabic	Well
Sanmaek	Korean	Mountain range
-sanmyaku	Japanese	Mountain range
San	Italian, Portug., Spanish	Saint
Sankt / Sant	German / Catalan	Saint
Santa, Santo	Italian, Portug., Spanish	Saint
São	Portuguese	Saint
Satu	Romanian	Village
Schloß	German	Castle, mansion
Schutzgebeit	German	Reserve
Sebkra	Arabic	Salt-flat
See	German	Lake
-sehir	Turkish	Town
Selat	Indonesian	Channel, strait
Selatan	Indonesian, Malay	South, southern
-selkä	Finnish	Open water, ridge
Selo	Russian, Serbo-Croat	Village
Selva	Spanish	Forest, wood
-sen	Japanese	Mountain
Serra / Serrania	Catalan, Portug. / Span.	Mountain range
-seto	Japanese	Channel, strait
Sever-naya, -noye, -nyy, -o	Russian	North, northern
Sfîntu	Romanian	Saint
Shahr	Persian	Town
Sha'ib, -an	Arabic	Watercourse
Shamo	Chinese	Desert
Shan	Chinese	Mountain(s)
Shandi	Chinese	Mountainous area
Shang	Chinese	Upper
Shankou	Chinese	Pass
Shanmai	Chinese	Mountain range
Sharm	Arabic	Cove, inlet
Shatt	Arabic	River, river-mouth
-shima / -shoto	Japanese	Island / Island group
Shuiku	Chinese	Reservoir
Sierra	Spanish	Mountain range
Silsilesi	Turkish	Mountain range
Sint	Afrikaans, Flemish	Saint
-sjø / sjön	Norwegian / Swedish	Lake
Skala, Skaly	Czech	Cliff, rock
-skog	Norwegian	Woods
-slette	Norwegian	Plain
Sliabh, Slieve	Gaelic	Mountain, upland
Sloboda	Russian	Suburb, large village
Sø	Danish, Norwegian	Lake
Söder-, Södra	Swedish	Southern
Solonchak	Russian	Salt lake
Sommet	French	Peak, summit
Sønder-	Danish	Southern
Søndre	Danish, Norwegian	Southern
Sopka	Russian	Hill
Sør	Norwegian	Southern
sous	French	Under
Spitze	German	Peak
Sredn-a, -i	Bulgarian	Central, middle
Sredn-e, -eye, -iy, -yaya	Russian	Central, middle
-stad	Afrikaans, Norwegian, Swedish	Town
-stadt	German	Town
Stara, Stari	Serbo-Croat	Old
Stará, Staré	Czech	Old
Star-aya, oye, -yy, -yye	Russian	Old
Stausee	German	Reservoir
Stenó	Greek	Pass, strait
Step'	Russian	Steppe
Stít	Czech	Peak
Stor-, Stora / Store	Swedish / Danish	Big
Strand	Gaelic, German	Beach
-strand	Danish, Norweg., Swedish	Beach
Straße	German	Road
-strede	Norwegian	Passage, strait
Strelka	Russian	Spit
Stretto	Italian	Strait
Sud	French	South
Süd(er)	German	South (southern)
Suhul	Arabic	Plain
Suid	Afrikaans	South
-suido	Japanese	Channel, strait
Sul	Portuguese	South
sul, sull'	Italian	On
Sund	Swedish	Sound, strait
Sungai	Indonesian, Malay	River
-suo	Finnish	Marsh, swamp
Supérieur / Superior	French / Spanish	Upper
Sur	Spanish	South
sur	French	On
Sveti	Serbo-Croat	Saint
Szent-	Hungarian	Saint

T

-take	Japanese	Peak
Tal	German	Valley
Tall(ât)	Arabic	Hill(s)
Tang	Persian	Pass, strait
Tanjung	Indonesian, Malay	Cape, point
Taraq	Arabic	Hills
Tasek	Malay	Lake
Tau	Russian	Mountain(s)
Tekojärvi	Finnish	Reservoir
Tell	Arabic	Hill
Teluk	Indonesian	Bay
Tengah	Indonesian	Middle
Teniet	Arabic	Pass
Tepe, Tepesi	Turkish	Hill, peak
Tepeler, Tepeleri	Turkish	Hills, peaks
Terre / Tierra	French / Spanish	Land
Thale	Thai	Lake
Tilat	Arabic	Hill
Timur	Indonesian	East, eastern
-tind, -tinderne	Norwegain	Peak, peaks
Tir'at	Arabic	Canal
-tji	Indonesian	Stream
-to	Japanese	Island
-toge	Japanese	Pass
-tong	Korean	Village
Tonle	Cambodian	Lake
-topp	Norwegian	Peak
Torrente	Spanish	Rapids
Travesía	Spanish	Desert
Tulul	Arabic	Hills
Túnel	Spanish	Tunnel

U

über	German	Above
-udden	Swedish	Cape, point
Új-	Hungarian	New
Ujung	Indonesian	Cape, point
-umi	Japanese	Inlet
Unter-	German	Lower
'Uqlat	Arabic	Well
-ura	Japanese	Inlet
'Urayq	Arabic	Sand ridge
'Uruq	Arabic	Area of dunes
Ust'ye	Russian	Estuary
Utara	Indonesian	North, northern
Uttar	Hindi	Northern
Uul	Mongolian	Mountains
Uval	Russian	Hill
'Uyun	Arabic	Springs

V

-vaara(t)	Finnish	Hill(s)
-vaart	Flemish	Canal
-våg	Norwegian	Bay
Val, Vall	Italian, Spanish	Valley
Vale	Portuguese, Romanian	Valley
Valle / Vallée	Italian, Spanish / French	Valley
Vallon	French	Small valley
-vann	Norwegian	Lake
-város	Hungarian	Town
-varre	Norwegian	Mountain
Väster, Västra	Swedish	Western
-vatn	Icelandic, Norwegian	Lake
-vatnet	Norwegian	Lake
-vatten, vattnet	Swedish	Lake
Vaux	French	Valleys
Vecchio	Italian	Old
Vechi	Romanian	Old
Velha, Velho	Portuguese	Old
Velik-a, -i	Serbo-Croat	Big
Velik-aya, -iy, -iye	Russian	Big
Vel'k-á, -é, -y	Czech	Big
Verkhn-e, -eye, -iy, -yaya	Russian	Upper
-vesi	Finnish	Lake, water
Vester	Danish	Western
Vest, Vestre	Norwegian	West, western
-vidda	Norwegian	Plateau
Vieja, Viejo / Vieux	Spanish / French	Old
Vig / -vik	Danish / Norwegian	Bay
Vila	Portuguese	Small town
Ville	French	Town
Víztároló	Hungarian	Reservoir
Vodokhranilishche	Russian	Reservoir
Volcán	Spanish	Volcano
Vorota	Russian	Channel, strait
Vostochn-aya, -oye, -yy	Russian	Eastern
Vozvyshennost'	Russian	Uplands
Vpadina	Russian	Depression
Vrch(y)	Czech	Mountain(s)
Vrchovina	Czech	Mountainous area
Vysocina	Czech	Upland
Vysok-aya, -oye	Russian	Upper

W

Wad	Flemish	Sand-flat
Wâdi, Wadi	Arabic	Watercourse
Wahat	Arabic	Oasis
Wai	Chinese	Outer
Wald	German	Forest
Wan / -wan	Chinese / Japanese	Bay
Wand	German	Cliff
Wasser	German	Lake, water
Wes-	Afrikaans	West
West, Wester	Flemish, German	West
Wielk-a, -i, -ie, -o	Polish	Big
Wysok-a, -i, -ie	Polish	Upper

X

Xi	Chinese	Stream, west
Xia	Chinese	Gorge, lower
Xian	Chinese	County
Xiao	Chinese	Small
Xu	Chinese	Islet

Y

-yama	Japanese	Mountain(s)
Yang	Chinese	Ocean
Yarimadasi	Turkish	Peninsula
Yeni	Turkish	New
Yli-	Finnish	Upper
Ytre-	Norwegian	Outer
Ytter-	Norwegian, Swedish	Outer
Yuan	Chinese	Spring
Yugo-	Russian	Southern
Yunhe	Chinese	Canal
Yuzhn-aya, -o, -oye, -yy	Russian	South, southern

Z

-zaki	Japanese	Cape, point
Zalew	Polish	Bay, inlet, lagoon
Zaliv	Russian	Bay
-zan	Japanese	Mountain
Zapadn-aya, -o, -oye, -yy	Russian	West, western
Zatoka	Polish	Gulf
-zee	Flemish	Sea
Zemlya	Russian	Land
-zhen	Chinese	Town
Zhong	Chinese	Middle
Zhou	Chinese	Islet
Zui	Chinese	Point, spit
Zuid	Flemish	South
Zuid-elijk, er	Flemish	Southern

INDEX 141

A INDEX Alfred Faure [Base]

INDEX

A

This index lists all locations and features which appear throughout this atlas, with the exception of the following special-subject map pages:

- World climate
- World time
- World health
- World income
- World sport
- World driving
- World airports*
- World flight times
- Europe climate
- Europe rail and ferries
- UK airports*
- Africa climate
- Asia climate
- North America climate
- US and Canada rail and air*
- South America climate

Maps marked * include a list of locations on the page itself

GENERAL ABBREVIATIONS

(for Australian, Canadian and US state/province abbreviations, see previous page)

Arch.	Archaeological
Hist.	Historic/Historical
I.	Island, Ile and equivalents
Int.	International
Is.	Islands, Iles and equivalents
Mem.	Memorial
Mon.	Monument
Mt	Mount/Mont
Mtn	Mountain/Montagne
Mtns	Mountains/Monts
Nac.	Nacional
Nat.	National
Naz.	Nazionale
Prov.	Provincial
St	Saint/Sankt/Sint

(All 'St' entries are treated as if spelt 'Saint' and are located in the index accordingly)

Ste	Sainte
Vdkhr.	Vodokhranilishche

Hyphens have been removed in certain cases for consistency and ease of viewing. The correct form appears on the map pages.

The following names, which appear in bold, indicate the entry is featured in one of the special subject maps:

Beach	Beach map
Park	National Park or leisure park map
Ski	Ski map
Spa	Spa map
Heritage C	UNESCO cultural heritage map
Heritage N	UNESCO natural heritage map

The following abbreviations appear occasionally, particularly to distinguish features with the same name:

[Adm]	Administrative region
[Apt]	Airport
[Riv]	River

A • Norway 16 G3
A Coruña • Spain 11 C1
A Coruña **Beach** • Spain 68 [73]
A la Ronde House • United Kingdom 74 F5
A Pobra do Caramiñal **Beach** • Spain 68 [73]
A'ali an Nil • Sudan 23 E2
A'nyêmaqên Shan • China 29 B4
Aachen **Heritage C** • Germany 64 [37]
Aachen • Germany 82 G1
Aachen **Spa** • Germany 83 [118]
Aaiún, El • Western Sahara 20 C3
Aalborg • Denmark 95 F5
Aalborg Bugt • Denmark 95 F6
Aalen • Germany 9 F8
Aalsmeer • Netherlands 80 C2
Aalst • Belgium 80 A14
Äänekoski • Finland 95 E2
Aarau • Switzerland 9 D9
Aare • Switzerland 89 G2
Aargub, El • Western Sahara 20 B4
Aarschot • Belgium 5 H4
Aarschot • Belgium 80 A15
Aazanèn • Morocco 11 H9
Aba • Nigeria 22 F3
Aba • Dem. Rep. of Congo 23 E3
Abadan • Iran 18 E3
Abadeh • Iran 18 F3
Abadia, El • Algeria 11 M8
Abaetetuba • Brazil 45 (1) B2
Abagnar Qi • China 29 F2
Abakan • Russian Fed. 26 P7
Abakan [Riv] • Russian Fed. 26 P7
Abala • Niger 20 F6
Abalak • Niger 20 G5
Abancay • Peru 127 B2
Abano • Italy 91 E7
Abashiri • Japan 30 M2
Abasolo • Mexico 123 E1
Abau • Papua New Guinea 35 (1) D3
Abay • Ethiopia 21 G5
Abay • Kazakhstan 26 L8
Abaya, Lake • Ethiopia 23 F2
Abbeville • France 10 G3
Abbeville • LA, United States 118 K3
Abbeyfeale • Ireland 79 F6
Abbot, Mt • QL, Australia 34 I4
Abbotsbury • United Kingdom 74 F6
Abbotsinch [Apt] • United Kingdom 74 B3
Abd al Kuri • Yemen 18 F7
Abdul Ghadir • Somalia 23 G1
Abdulino • Russian Fed. 17 I4
Abe, Lake • Ethiopia 21 H5
Abéché • Chad 21 D5
Abengourou • Côte d'Ivoire 22 D3
Abenrå **Beach** • Denmark 68 [26]
Abenrå • Denmark 95 F13
Abensberg • Germany 9 G8
Abeokuta • Nigeria 22 E3
Aberaeron • United Kingdom 7 H9
Aberaeron **Beach** • United Kingdom 75 [181]
Aberconwy & Colwyn • United Kingdom 75 A4
Aberdare Nat. Park • Kenya 101 G3
Aberdare Nat. Park **Park** • Kenya 103 [80]
Aberdare Range • Kenya 23 F4
Aberdaron **Beach** • United Kingdom 75 [193]
Aberdeen • United Kingdom 6 J4
Aberdeen • SD, United States 41 G2
Aberdeen • South Africa 100 C3
Aberdeen • Hong Kong, China 107 H5
Aberdeen • WA, United States 117 E1
Aberdeen [Adm] • United Kingdom 75 A2
Aberdeen Lake • NU, Canada 38 L4
Aberdeenshire • United Kingdom 75 A1
Aberdour • United Kingdom 74 B4
Aberdour **Beach** • United Kingdom 75 [12]
Abereiddy **Beach** • United Kingdom 75 [167]
Aberfeldy • United Kingdom 74 B1
Aberffraw **Beach** • United Kingdom 75 [202]
Aberfoyle • United Kingdom 74 B1
Abergavenny • United Kingdom 74 D3
Aberporth **Beach** • United Kingdom 75 [172]
Abers, Côte des • France 84 C1
Abersoch **Beach** • United Kingdom 75 [192]
Abert, Lake • OR, United States 117 E3
Aberystwyth • United Kingdom 7 H9
Aberystwyth **Beach** • United Kingdom 75 [183]
Abez • Russian Fed. 26 J4
Abha • Saudi Arabia 18 D6
Abidjan • Côte d'Ivoire 22 D3
Abilene • TX, United States 40 G5
Abingdon • United Kingdom 74 D4
Abisko • Sweden 16 J2
Abisko Nat. Park **Park** • Sweden 72 [17]
Abitibi • OT, Canada 39 O6
Abo • Finland 95 E3
Abo, Massif d' • Chad 21 C3
Abomey • Benin 22 E3
Abomey **Heritage C** • Benin 63 [98]
Abondance **Ski** • France 70 [8]
Abong Mbang • Cameroon 22 G4
Abony • Hungary 13 I10
Aborigen, pik • Russian Fed. 27 O4
Abraham's Bay • Bahamas 124 B4
Abrántes • Portugal 11 C5
Abri • Sudan 21 F3
Abrolhos, Arquipelago dos • Brazil 45 (1) D5
Abruzzo • Italy 12 H6
Abruzzo, Parco Naz. d' **Park** • Italy 72 [86]
Abruzzo, Parco Naz. d' • Italy 91 F4
Absaroka Range • MT/WY, United States 38 I7
Abu Dhabi • United Arab Emirates 18 F5
Abu Hamad • Sudan 21 F4
Abu Hills • India 105 C5
Abu Libdah, Khashm • Saudi Arabia 21 I3
Abu Madd, Ra's • Saudi Arabia 18 C5
Abu Matariq • Sudan 23 D1
Abu Mena **Heritage C** • Egypt 64 [236]
Abu Mena • Egypt 101 F1
Abu Road • India 105 C5
Abu Shajarah, Ra's • Sudan 21 G3
Abu Simbel **Heritage C** • Egypt 63 [83]
Abu Simbel • Egypt 101 F5
Abuja • Nigeria 22 F3
Abuko Nature Reserve **Park** • Gambia 103 [11]
Abut Head • New Zealand 35 C6
Abuyemeda • Ethiopia 23 F1
Aby • Ostergötland, Sweden 95 D3
Aby • Kalmar, Sweden 95 F8
Abyad, Ar Ra's al • Saudi Arabia 18 C5
Abyar ash Shuwayrif • Libya 21 B2
Abybro • Denmark 95 F5
Abydos • Egypt 101 F4
Açaba, El • Mauritania 20 C5
Acadia Nat. Park • ME, United States 118 G4
Acadia Nat. Park **Park** • ME, United States 121 [354]
Acámbaro • Mexico 37 (1) B1
Acaponeta • Mexico 37 (1) A1
Acapulco • Mexico 123 E4
Acará • Brazil 43 H4
Acarai, Serra • Brazil 43 F3
Acaraú • Brazil 45 (1) C2
Acarigua • Venezuela 43 D2
Accra • Ghana 22 D3
Accra area **Heritage C** • Ghana 63 [97]
Aceh • Indonesia 110 B1
Acerenza • Italy 71 A19
Achacachi • Bolivia 127 B4
Achaguas • Venezuela 43 D2
Achegour • Niger 20 H5
Achern • Germany 9 D8
Achill **Beach** • Ireland 68 [44]
Achill Head • Ireland 79 F1
Achill I. • Ireland 79 F1
Achim • Germany 8 E3
Achinsk • Russian Fed. 26 P6
Achonry • Ireland 79 F2
Aci Gölü • Turkey 93 G1
Aci Trezza • Sicily, Italy 90 D4
Acireale • Sicily, Italy 90 D4
Acklins I. • Bahamas 124 B4
Acoma Pueblo • NM, United States 118 J2
Aconcagua, Cerro • Argentina/Chile 44 C5
Açores • Atlantic Ocean 20 (1) B2
Acquasanta • Italy 91 E12
Acquasparta • Italy 91 F1
Acqui Terme • Italy 91 E6
Acraman, Lake • SA, Australia 34 G6
Acre • Brazil 43 C5
Acre • Israel 98 A1
Acre [Riv] • Bolivia/Brazil 43 D6
Acropolis • Rhodes, Greece 93 F4
Acroverde • Brazil 45 (1) D3
Actaeon Group • French Polynesia 33 N8
Action Planet **Park** • Belgium 73 [48]
Ada • OK, United States 41 G5
Adair, Cape • NU, Canada 39 Q2
Adak • AK, United States 36 (1) C2
Adale • Somalia 23 H3
Adam, Mt • Falkland Is. 45 D6
Adam's Bridge • India/Sri Lanka 106 D11
Adam's Peak • Sri Lanka 106 D15
Adamandás **Beach** • Greece 69 [184]
Adamaoua • Cameroon 22 G3
Adámas • Greece 92 D7
Adámas • Greece 92 D7
Adams, Grantley [Apt] • Barbados 125 H4
Adams, Mt • WA, United States 38 G7
Adams Nat. Hist. Site **Park** • MA, United States 121 [343]
Adamstown • Pitcairn Is. 33 O8
Adan • Yemen 18 E7
Adana • Turkey 18 B2
Adapazari • Turkey 15 L3
Adarama • Sudan 18 B6
Adare • Ireland 79 F6
Adare, Cape • Antarctica 59 A10
Adavale • QL, Australia 34 H5
Adda • Italy 91 E2
Addis Ababa • Ethiopia 23 F2
Addis Zemen • Ethiopia 23 F1
Addo Elephant Nat. Park • South Africa 100 C8
Addo Elephant Nat. Park **Park** • South Africa 103 [121]
Addu Atoll • Maldives 106 E3
Adeje **Beach** • Tenerife, Canary Is. 68 [91]
Adeje • Tenerife, Canary Is. 86 E1
Adelaide • SA, Australia 34 G6
Adelaide • Bahamas 124 B3
Adelaide I. • Antarctica 59 A10
Adelaide Peninsula • NU, Canada 38 L3
Adelaide [Riv] • NT, Australia 34 F2
Adelaide River • NT, Australia 34 F2
Adelboden **Ski** • Switzerland 70 [88]
Adelboden • Switzerland 89 G6
Adéle **Beach** • Crete, Greece 69 [189]
Adéle • Crete, Greece 93 E2
Ademuz • Spain 11 J4
Aden • Yemen 18 E7
Aden, Gulf of • Africa/Asia 19 I4
Adenau • Germany 82 H1
Aderbissinat • Niger 20 G5
Adi • Indonesia 32 (1) D3
Adige • Italy 91 E7
Adigrat • Eritrea 21 G5
Adilabad • India 28 C5
Adiri • Libya 21 B2
Adirondack Mtns • NY, United States 41 L3
Adjuntas • Puerto Rico 125 E3
Admiralty I. • AK, United States 38 E5
Admiralty Inlet • NU, Canada 39 N2
Admiralty Is. • Papua New Guinea 35 (1) D1
Adok • Sudan 23 E2
Adoni • India 106 D2
Adour • France 85 J2
Adra **Beach** • Spain 68 [99]
Adra • Spain 86 B8
Adrano • Sicily, Italy 12 I11
Adrar • Algeria 20 E3
Adrar Bou Nasser • Morocco 101 D2
Adrar des Iforas • Mali 20 F5
Adriana, Villa • Italy 91 F1
Adrianople • Turkey 71 A15
Adriatic Coast • Croatia 96 B2
Adriatic Riviera • Italy 91 E12
Adriatic Sea • Europe 12 I5
Adula • Switzerland 12 D2
Adulis • Eritrea 21 G4
Adwa • Ethiopia 21 G5
Adygalakh • Russian Fed. 27 O4
Adygeya • Russian Fed. 17 G6
Adzopé • Côte d'Ivoire 22 D3
Aegean Coast • Turkey 92 A2
Aegean Coast • Turkey 92 A2
Aegean Sea • Greece/Turkey 92 D
Aegean Sea • Greece/Turkey 92 D
Ærø • Denmark 95 F14
Æroskøbing • Denmark 95 F14
Afafi, Massif d' • Chad 21 C3
Afándou **Beach** • Rhodes, Greece 69 [187]
Afándou • Rhodes, Greece 93 F2
Afek • Israel 98 A5
Afétes **Beach** • Greece 69 [165]
Affollé • Mauritania 20 C5
Affroun • Algeria 11 N8
Afghanistan • Asia 18 I3
Afif • Saudi Arabia 18 D5
Afikpo • Nigeria 22 F3
Afiq • Syria 98 A4
Afitos **Beach** • Greece 69 [169]
Afitos • Greece 92 D1
Afitos • Greece 92 D1
Aflou • Algeria 20 F2
Afmadow • Somalia 23 G3
Afonso Cláudio • Brazil 127 C2
Afore • Papua New Guinea 34 I1
Afragola • Italy 12 I8
Africa's Lion Safari • OT, Canada 122 B9
Africa-India cruise area • Indian Ocean 59 A5/8
Africains, Bancs • Seychelles 106 F2
Africana, Reserva • Majorca, Spain 87 H2
Afsluitdijk • Netherlands 80 A3
Afton Alps **Ski** • MN, United States 116 [112]
Afuá • Brazil 43 G4
Afyon • Turkey 15 L5
Afyonkarahisar • Turkey 18 B2
Agadem • Niger 20 H5
Agadez • Niger 20 G5
Agadir • Morocco 101 D5
Agadyr • Kazakhstan 26 L8
Agalega • Mauritius 24 (2) C3
Agalta, Sierra de • Honduras 37 D4
Agana • Guam 33 F4
Agano • Japan 30 J6
Agartala • India 28 F4
Agate Fossil Beds Nat. Mon. **Park** • NE, United States 120 [164]
Agathoníssi • Greece 92 D8
Agathoníssi • Greece 92 D8
Agats • Indonesia 32 (1) E4
Agatti I. • India 106 D9
Agboville • Côte d'Ivoire 22 D3
Agde • France 11 O1
Agdz • Morocco 20 D2
Agen • France 85 G4
Agger • Germany 81 E4
Agger Tange • Denmark 95 F5
Aggtelek Caves **Heritage N** • Hungary 61 [50]
Aggtelek Nat. Park **Park** • Hungary 72 [103]
Agía Fotiá • Crete, Greece 93 E7
Agía Galíni • Crete, Greece 93 E6
Agía Marína • Léros, Greece 15 H6
Agía Marína • Attica, Greece 92 D4
Agía Marína • Attica, Greece 92 D4
Agía Marína • Crete, Greece 93 E1
Agía Pelagía • Kíthira, Greece 92 D7
Agía Pelagía • Kíthira, Greece 92 D7
Agía Pelagía • Crete, Greece 93 E3
Agía Rouméli • Crete, Greece 93 E5
Agía Sofia • Crete, Greece 93 E1
Agía Triáda **Beach** • Greece 69 [168]
Agía Triáda • Crete, Greece 93 E6
Agiássos • Greece 15 H4
Agincourt • France 71 A7
Agio Oros • Greece 92 D1
Agio Oros • Greece 92 D1
Agios Apóstoli • Greece 92 D4
Agios Apóstoli • Greece 92 D4
Agios Dimitrios **Beach** • Greece 69 [165]
Agios Dimitrios • Greece 92 D4
Agios Dimitrios • Greece 92 D4
Agios Efstratios • Greece 92 D4
Agios Efstratios • Greece 92 D4
Agios Górdis • Corfu, Greece 92 B1
Agios Górdis • Corfu, Greece 92 B1
Agios Ioánnis **Beach** • Crete, Greece 69 [191]
Agios Ioánnis, Akra • Crete, Greece 93 E4
Agios Kírikos • Greece 92 D8
Agios Kírikos • Greece 92 D8
Agios Míronas • Crete, Greece 93 E7
Agios Nikitas • Greece 92 C1
Agios Nikitas • Greece 92 C1
Agios Nikólaos **Beach** • Halkidikí, Greece 69 [169]
Agios Nikólaos **Beach** • Crete, Greece 69 [191]
Agios Nikólaos • Crete, Greece 93 E8
Agios Stefanos • Corfu, Greece 92 B1
Agios Stefanos • Corfu, Greece 92 B1
Agiou Orous, Kólpos • Greece 15 E3
Agnes Creek • SA, Australia 112 H4
Agnew • WA, Australia 34 D5
Agnita • Romania 14 L4
Agonda Beach • Goa, India 105 B2
Agordat • Eritrea 21 G4
Agordo • Italy 90 B4
Agostinho, I. de • Madeira 88 C2
Agostóli • Greece 92 C2
Agostóli • Greece 92 C2
Agra **Heritage C** • India 63 [118-119]
Agra • India 105 C3
Agreda • Spain 11 J3
Agriá • Greece 92 D4
Agriá • Greece 92 D4
Agriates, Désert des • Corsica, France 85 L2
Agrigento **Heritage C** • Sicily, Italy 64 [134]
Agrigento • Sicily, Italy 90 D3
Agrínio • Greece 15 C5
Agro Romano • Italy 91 F1
Agrópoli • Italy 91 G4
Agua • Brazil 44 F2
Agua Caliente • Mexico 40 E6
Agua de Pena • Madeira 88 C2
Agua Prieta • Mexico 40 E5
Agua Vermelha, Représa • Brazil 44 F2
Aguada Bay • Goa, India 105 B1
Aguada de Pasajeros • Cuba 124 D2
Aguada Fort • Goa, India 105 B1
Aguadilla • Puerto Rico 125 E1
Aguadilla, Bahía de • Puerto Rico 125 E1
Aguadulce • Spain 86 B8
Aguas Buenas, Cuevas de • Puerto Rico 125 E4
Aguas de Moura • Portugal 88 D2
Aguascalientes • Mexico 123 E1
Agudo • Spain 11 G6
Agueda • Spain 11 E4
Aguelhok • Mali 20 F5
Agüenit • Western Sahara 20 C4
Aguilar de Campóo • Spain 11 G2
Aguilas • Spain 11 J7
Aguilas **Beach** • Spain 68 [100]
Agujereada, Punta • Puerto Rico 125 E1
Agulhas, Cape • South Africa 100 C6
Agulhas Negras, Pico das • Brazil 127 C3
Agung, Gunung • Bali, Indonesia 110 C2
Agva • Turkey 15 K2
Ahaggar • Algeria 20 G4
Aharnés • Greece 15 E5
Ahaus • Germany 8 B4
Aheim • Norway 94 C1
Ahelóos • Greece 15 C4
Ahfir • Morocco 101 D2
Ahirli • Turkey 93 G2
Ahlada **Beach** • Crete, Greece 69 [190]
Ahlada • Crete, Greece 93 E3
Ahládi **Beach** • Greece 69 [164]
Ahlbeck **Beach** • Germany 69 [12]
Ahlbeck **Spa** • Germany 83 [285]
Ahlen • Germany 8 C5
Ahmadabad • India 28 B4
Ahmadnagar • India 28 B5
Ahmar • Ethiopia 23 G2
Ahon, Tarso • Chad 20 I4
Ahr • Germany 82 H1
Ahrensburg • Germany 8 F3
Ahrenshoop **Spa** • Germany 83 [275]
Ahrntal • Italy 90 B2
Ahrtal • Germany 82 H1
Ahtäri • Finland 95 E2
Ahus • Sweden 95 F11
Ahvaz • Iran 18 E3
Ahvenanmaa • Finland 95 E3
Ahwar • Yemen 18 E7
Aibonito • Puerto Rico 125 E4
Aichach • Germany 9 G8
Aiea • HI, United States 119 L5
Aierbach • Germany 9 H6
Aigle, l' • France 5 D6
Aigóual, Mt • France 10 I9
Aigues • France 10 K9
Aiguillon sur Mer, l' • France 84 D3
Aiguillon-sur-Mer, l' **Beach** • France 68 [64]
Aihole • India 106 D2
Aihui • China 27 K6
Ailao Shan • China 31 C2
Aileron • NT, Australia 112 H2
Aim • Russian Fed. 27 L5
Aimorés • Brazil 127 C2
Ain [Adm] • France 85 F1
Aïn Beïda • Algeria 20 G1
Aïn Defla • Algeria 11 M8
Aïn el Hadjel • Algeria 11 O9
Aïn Galakka • Chad 20 I5
Aïn Ouessera • Algeria 20 F1
Ain [Riv] • France 10 K7
Aïn Sefra • Algeria 20 E2
Aïn Taya • Algeria 11 O8
Ainazi • Latvia 16 M8
Aínos Nat. Park **Park** • Greece 72 [137]
Aínsa • Spain 11 L2
Ainsdale **Beach** • United Kingdom 75 [218]
Aïr • Niger 20 G5
Air Force I. • NU, Canada 39 Q3
Air Hitam • Penang, Malaysia 108 C1
Air Hitam Dam • Penang, Malaysia 108 C1
Aïr, Réserve du **Heritage N** • Niger 61 [77]
Aïr, Réserve du **Park** • Niger 103 [4]
Airão • Brazil 43 E4
Aire • France 5 I5
Aire • United Kingdom 7 K8
Aire, Canal d' • France 5 F4
Aire, I. de l' • Minorca, Spain 87 F4
Aire-sur-l'Adour • France 85 G3
Aire-sur-la-Lys • France 5 F4
Airolo • Switzerland 89 G7
Aisawan Tippaya Asna • Thailand 109 H1
Aisch • Germany 9 F7
Aisne • France 10 I4
Aïssa, Djebel • Algeria 20 E2
Aït Benhaddou **Heritage C** • Morocco 64 [218]
Aït Benhaddou • Morocco 101 D5
Aitape • Papua New Guinea 35 (1) C1
Aitutaki • Cook Is. 33 K7
Aiud • Romania 14 K3
Aix-en-Provence • France 85 H3
Aix-la-Chapelle **Heritage C** • Germany 64 [37]
Aix-la-Chapelle • Germany 82 G1
Aix-les-Bains • France 85 F1
Aizawl • India 28 F4
Aizuwakamatsu • Japan 30 J6
Ajaccio • Corsica, France 85 L3
Ajaccio, Golfe d' • Corsica, France 85 L3
Ajanta Caves **Heritage C** • India 63 [123]
Ajdabiya • Libya 21 D1
Ajigasawa • Japan 30 K4
Ajim • Tunisia 101 E6
Ajka • Hungary 13 G10
Ajlun • Jordan 98 A4
Ajmer • India 105 C6
Ajo • AZ, United States 118 J3
Ajo, Cabo de • Spain 11 H1
Aju, Kepulauan • Indonesia 32 (1) D2
Ak Dag • Turkey 15 K7
Akagera, Parc nat. de l' **Park** • Rwanda 103 [73]
Akaishi-Sanmayaky • Japan 30 I7
Akaka Falls State Park • HI, United States 119 L8
Akaki • Ethiopia 23 F2
Akanthoú • Cyprus 93 J2
Akaroa • New Zealand 35 D6
Akayzi • Turkey 15 L3
Akbaytal • Tajikistan 26 L10
Akçakoca • Turkey 15 M2
Akçakoca **Beach** • Turkey 69 [209]
Akçay • Turkey 93 G3
Akçay [Riv] • Turkey 15 J6
Akdag • Izmir, Turkey 15 H5
Akdag • Kütahya, Turkey 15 J4
Akdag • Denizli, Turkey 15 K5
Aker • Sweden 95 D3
Akersberga • Sweden 95 D4
Akershus • Norway 94 B2
Aketi • Dem. Rep. of Congo 23 C3
Akhdar, Al Jabal al • Oman 18 G5
Akhdar, Al Jabal al • Libya 21 D1
Akhisar • Turkey 92 D6
Akhisar • Turkey 92 D6
Akhtopol • Bulgaria 97 D4
Akhtubinsk • Russian Fed. 17 H5
Akimiski • NU, Canada 39 O6
Akirkeby • Denmark 95 F16
Akita • Japan 30 K5
Akjoujt • Mauritania 20 C5
Akka • Morocco 20 D3
Akkajaure • Sweden 16 J3
Akko • Israel 98 A1
Akköy • Turkey 15 I6
Akmeqit • China 26 M10
Akmola • Kazakhstan 26 L7
Akobo • Sudan 23 E2
Akobo [Riv] • Ethiopia/Sudan 23 E2
Akola • India 28 C4
Akören • Turkey 15 N6
Akosombo Dam • Ghana 22 E3
Akpatok I. • NU, Canada 39 R4
Akranes • Iceland 16 (1) B2
Akrehamn • Norway 94 C5
Akritas, Akra • Greece 15 C7
Akron • OH, United States 41 J3
Akrotíri • Greece 92 D8
Akrotíri • Greece 92 D8
Akrotíri • Cyprus 93 J3
Akrotíri Bay • Cyprus 93 J3
Akrotíri, Hersónisos • Crete, Greece 93 E1
Aksai Chin • China 28 C1
Aksakal • Turkey 15 J3
Aksaray • Cyprus 15 O8
Aksay • Kazakhstan 17 I6
Aksayqin Hu • China 28 C1
Aksehir • Turkey 15 M5
Aksehir Gölü • Turkey 15 M5
Akseki • Turkey 93 G2
Aksha • Russian Fed. 27 H6
Aksoran • Kazakhstan 26 M8
Aksu • China 26 N9
Aksu • Turkey 93 G1
Aksu [Riv] • Turkey 93 G4
Aksum • Ethiopia 21 G5
Aksum **Heritage C** • Ethiopia 63 [84]
Aktau • Uzbekistan 26 J9
Aktion • Greece 92 C1
Aktion • Greece 92 C1
Aktöbe • Kazakhstan 26 I7
Aktogay • Kazakhstan 26 M8
Akune • Japan 30 F9
Akure • Nigeria 22 F3
Akureyri • Iceland 16 (1) D2
Al • Norway 94 C4
Al Hoceïma • Morocco 101 D2
Al Jaghbub • Libya 21 D2
Al Jahrah • Kuwait 21 I2
Al Khums • Libya 21 B1
Al Mird • Jordan 98 A8
Al Qaryah ash Sharqiyah • Libya 21 B1
Al Qatrun • Libya 21 B3
Al Uwaynat • Libya 21 B2
Al-Ayn **Heritage C** • Oman 63 [106]
Al-Khutm **Heritage C** • Oman 63 [106]
Ala Dag • Turkey 15 N6
Alabama • United States 41 I5
Alabama [Riv] • AL, United States 41 I5
Alaçam Daglari • Turkey 15 J4
Alaçati • Turkey 15 H5
Alacranes, Arrecife • Mexico 123 E6
Aladzha Manastir • Bulgaria 97 D4
Alagna-Valsésia **Ski** • Italy 70 [203]
Alagnon • France 10 I8
Alagoas • Brazil 45 (1) D3
Alagoinhas • Brazil 44 I1
Alaior • Minorca, Spain 87 F4
Alajuela • Costa Rica 43 A1
Alaköl • Kazakhstan 26 N8
Alakurtti • Russian Fed. 16 P3
Alam • QU, Canada 123 D1
Alamagan • Northern Mariana Is. 33 F4
Alamein, El • Egypt 101 F1
Alamo • Somalia 23 G3
Alamogordo • NM, United States 118 J4
Alamos • Mexico 40 E6
Alamosa • CO, United States 118 J2
Aland • Finland 95 E3
Aland [Adm] • Finland 95 E3
Alands Hav • Finland/Sweden 95 D2
Alantika, Mts • Cameroon 22 G3
Alanya **Beach** • Turkey 69 [197]
Alanya • Turkey 93 G4
Alaotra, Lac • Madagascar 24 H3
Alapayevsk • Russian Fed. 26 J6
Alapli • Turkey 15 M2
Alara Han • Turkey 93 G4
Alarcon, Embalse de • Spain 11 I5
Alarcos • Spain 71 A16
Alas • Indonesia 110 B1
Alasasua • Spain 11 I2
Alasehir • Turkey 92 D6
Alasehir • Turkey 92 D6
Alaska • United States 40 (2) F2
Alaska, Gulf of • AK, United States 36 B4
Alaska Highway • BC, Canada 122 C1
Alaska Peninsula • AK, United States 40 (2) F2
Alaska Range • AK, United States 36 B3
Alaska/Canada cruise area • N. America 58 A2
Alássio • Italy 91 E9
Alatri • Italy 12 H7
Alatyr • Russian Fed. 17 H3
Alavus • Finland 95 E2
Alayskiy • Kyrgyzstan 26 L10
Alazeya • Russian Fed. 27 P2
Alba • Italy 91 E5
Alba Iulia • Romania 14 K3
Albacete • Spain 11 J5
Albæk • Denmark 95 F6
Albæk Bugt • Denmark 95 F6
Albanel, Lac • QU, Canada 39 Q6
Albania • Europe 17 A2
Albano, Lago • Italy 91 F3
Albano Laziale • Italy 91 F3
Albany • WA, Australia 34 C6
Albany • OT, Canada 39 O6
Albany • GA, United States 41 J5
Albany • OR, United States 117 E3
Albany • NY, United States 118 G3
Albardón • Argentina 44 C5
Albatross Bay • QL, Australia 34 H2
Albatross Point • New Zealand 112 K1
Albéces, Chaine des • France 11 N2
Albemarle Sound • NC, United States 118 H5
Albena • Bulgaria 97 D4
Albenga • Italy 91 E9
Alberche • Spain 11 G4
Alberdi • Paraguay 44 E4
Alberga • SA, Australia 112 H4
Alberobello **Heritage C** • Italy 64 [131]
Albert • France 5 F4
Albert Edward • Papua New Guinea 35 (1) D2
Albert Kanaal • Belgium 5 H3
Albert, Lake • Uganda/Dem. Rep. of Congo 23 E3
Albert Lea • MN, United States 41 H3
Albert Nile • Uganda 23 E3
Albert Town • Jamaica 124 C1
Alberta • Canada 38 H5
Albertville • France 85 F2
Albi • France 85 G4
Albina, Ponta • Angola 24 A3
Alblasserwaard • Netherlands 80 C4
Alborán, I. de • Spain 11 H9
Alborz, Reshteh-ye Kuhha-ye • Iran 18 F2
Alboux • Spain 11 I7
Albufeira **Beach** • Portugal 68 [82]
Albufeira • Portugal 88 E6
Albufeira, Lagoa de • Portugal 88 D1
Albuquerque • NM, United States 118 J2
Albury • NS, Australia 111 G3
Alcácer do Sal • Portugal 11 C6
Alcalá de Chivert **Beach** • Spain 68 [103]
Alcalá de Guadaira • Spain 11 F7
Alcalá de Henares • Spain 11 H4
Alcalá del Júcar • Spain 11 J5
Alcalá la Real • Spain 86 B3
Alcalar, Túmulos de • Portugal 88 E6
Alcamo • Sicily, Italy 12 G11
Alcanar **Beach** • Spain 68 [104]
Alcañiz • Spain 11 K3
Alcántara, Embalse de • Spain 11 E5
Alcantarilha • Portugal 88 E6
Alcantarilla • Spain 11 J6
Alcaraz • Spain 11 I6
Alcaraz, Sierra de • Spain 11 I6
Alcaria do Cume, Serra de • Portugal 88 E4
Alcaudete • Spain 11 G7
Alcázar de San Juan • Spain 11 H5
Alcira • Spain 11 K5
Alcobaça • Portugal 11 C5
Alcobaça **Heritage C** • Portugal 64 [98]
Alcobaça **Beach** • Portugal 68 [79]
Alcobendas • Spain 11 H4
Alcochete • Portugal 88 D2
Alcolea del Pinar • Spain 11 I3
Alcoutim • Portugal 88 E4
Alcoy • Spain 87 C1
Alcúdia • Majorca, Spain 87 H2
Alcúdia, Badia d' • Majorca, Spain 87 H2
Aldabra Atoll **Heritage N** • Seychelles 61 [99]
Aldabra, Groupe d' • Seychelles 106 F3
Aldan • Russian Fed. 27 K5
Aldan [Riv] • Russian Fed. 27 L4
Aldanskoye Nagorye • Russian Fed. 27 K5
Aldeburgh • United Kingdom 5 E2
Aldeburgh **Beach** • United Kingdom 75 [53]
Alderney • Channel Is. 7 J12
Aldershot • United Kingdom 5 C3
Aleg • Mauritania 20 C5
Alegranza • Canary Is. 87 E6
Alegre • Brazil 127 C2
Alegrete • Brazil 44 E4
Aleksandrov • Russian Fed. 97 E4
Aleksandrovsk-Sakhalinskiy • Russian Fed. 27 N6
Aleksandrów Lodzki • Poland 13 I6
Alem • Sweden 95 F8
Além Paraíba • Brazil 127 C4
Alençon • France 10 F5
Alenhuihaha Channel • HI, United States 119 L8
Alenquer • Portugal 88 D2
Aleppo • Syria 18 C2
Aléria • Corsica, France 85 L4
Alert • NU, Canada 36 J1
Alès • France 10 J9
Ales stenar • Sweden 95 F15
Alessándra • Italy 91 E6
Alestrup • Denmark 95 F5
Alesund • Norway 94 C1
Aleutian Is. • AK, United States 36 (1) C2
Aleutian Trench • AK, United States 25 T5
Alexander Archipelago • AK, United States 38 D5
Alexander, Cape • Solomon Is. 35 (1) F2
Alexanderbaai • South Africa 24 B5
Alexandra • New Zealand 112 L2
Alexandria • Romania 97 D1
Alexandria • South Africa 100 C8
Alexandria • Egypt 101 F1
Alexandria • VA, United States 118 H3
Alexandria • LA, United States 118 K1
Alexandroúpoli **Beach** • Greece 69 [174]
Alexandroúpoli • Greece 92 D2
Alexandroúpoli • Greece 92 D2
Alexandrów Kujawski • Poland 13 H5
Aleysk • Russian Fed. 26 N7
Alf • Germany 5 K4
Alfambra • Spain 11 J4
Alfatar • Bulgaria 97 D1
Alfaz del Pi **Beach** • Spain 68 [101]
Alfaz del Pi • Spain 87 C2
Alfenas • Brazil 127 C1
Alfiós • Greece 15 C6
Alföld • Hungary 13 J11
Alfred Faure [Base] • Pacific Ocean 46 (1) K5

Algajola • Corsica, France 85 L1
Algarås • Sweden 95 F3
Algarve • Portugal ..... 88 E
Algeciras Beach • Spain ..... 68 [96]
Algeciras • Spain 86 B6
Algeciras, Bahía de • Spain 11 F8
Alger • Algeria 20 F1
Alger Heritage C • Algeria ..... 64 [220]
Algeria • Africa 20 F3
Alghero • Sardinia, Italy 90 C1
Algiers • Algeria 20 F1
Algiers Heritage C • Algeria ..... 64 [220]
Algoa Bay • South Africa 100 C8
Algodonales • Spain 86 B6
Algonquin Prov. Park • OT, Canada 122 B1
Algoz • Portugal 88 E6
Algutsrum • Sweden 95 F8
Alholm • Denmark 95 F14
Aliabad • Iran 18 G4
Aliaga • Spain 11 K4
Aliaga • Turkey 15 I5
Alibates Flint Quarries Nat. Mon. Park • TX, United States ..... 120 [134]
Alibey Beach • Turkey ..... 69 [208]
Alibey • Turkey 92 D5
Alibey • Turkey 92 D5
Alicante Beach • Spain ..... 68 [101]
Alicante • Spain 87 C1
Alice • TX, United States 119 N5
Alice, Punta • Italy 12 L9
Alice Springs • NT, Australia 112 H2
Alice Town • Bahamas 124 B1
Alicudi, I. • Italy 90 C2
Aligarh • India 105 C3
Alijos, Rocas • Mexico 123 E3
Alikampos • Crete, Greece 93 E2
Alikés • Greece 92 C3
Alikés • Greece 92 C3
Alikianós • Crete, Greece 93 E1
Alima • Congo 22 H5
Alimatha • Maldives 106 E1
Alimiá • Greece 93 F1
Alimnia • Greece 92 D9
Alimnia • Greece 92 D9
Alimos Beach • Greece ..... 69 [162]
Alimos • Greece 92 D7
Alimos • Greece 92 D7
Alingsås • Sweden 95 F3
Alivéri • Greece 15 F5
Aljezur Beach • Portugal ..... 68 [82]
Aljezur • Portugal 88 E1
Alkmaar • Netherlands 80 A7
All Saints • Antigua & Barbuda 125 F3
Allagash Wilderness Waterway • ME, United States 118 G2
Allahabad • India 105 C8
Allakh-Yun • Russian Fed. 27 M4
Allanmyo • Myanmar 28 G5
Alleghe Ski • Italy ..... 70 [224]
Alleghe • Italy 90 B4
Allegheny Mtns • VA/WV United States 41 J4
Allegheny Portage Railroad Nat. Hist. Site Park • PA, United States ..... 121 [303]
Allen • Philippines 29 H2
Allen, Bog of • Ireland 79 E1
Allen, Lough • Ireland 7 D7
Allentown • PA, United States 118 H1
Aleppey • India 106 D10
Aller • Germany 8 E4
Allerheiligen • Germany 82 G6
Alleynes Bay • Barbados 125 H1
Allgäu • Germany 82 J6
Allgäuer Alpen • Germany 82 J6
Allier • France 10 I7
Allihies • Ireland 79 F7
Allingåbro • Denmark 95 F10
Alloa • United Kingdom 74 B3
Alma-Ata • Kazakhstan 26 M9
Almada Beach • Portugal ..... 68 [81]
Almada • Portugal 88 D1
Almadén • Spain 11 E6
Almalık • Kazakhstan 98 B2
Almansa • Spain 11 J6
Almansil • Portugal 88 E7
Almanzor, Pico de • Spain 11 F4
Almanzora • Spain 11 I7
Almas, Picos de • Brazil 44 H1
Almaty • Kazakhstan 26 M9
Almazán • Spain 11 I3
Almeirim • Brazil 43 G4
Almelo • Netherlands 80 A9
Almenar de Soria • Spain 11 I3
Almendra, Embalse de • Spain 11 E3
Almendralejo • Spain 11 E6
Almere-Haven • Netherlands 80 C2
Almere-Stad • Netherlands 80 C2
Almería Beach • Spain ..... 68 [99]
Almería • Spain 86 B8
Almería, Costa de • Spain 86 B8
Almería, Golfo de • Spain 86 B8
Almerimar • Spain 86 B8
Almhult • Sweden 95 F11
Almijara, Sierra de • Spain 86 B7
Almirante • Panama 43 A2
Almirante Brown [Base] • Antarctica 46 (1) II3
Almirós Beach • Greece ..... 69 [165]
Almiroú, Ormos • Crete, Greece 93 E2
Almodóvar • Portugal 88 E3
Almodóvar del Pinar • Spain 11 J5
Almodóvar del Río • Spain 86 B2
Almonte Beach • Spain ..... 68 [95]
Almonte • Spain 86 B1
Almora • India 105 C3
Almsta • Sweden 95 D2
Almuñécar Beach • Spain ..... 68 [98]
Almuñécar • Spain 86 B7
Alofi • Wallis & Futuna 35 (2) E1
Alofi • Niue 35 (2) G2
Alónissos • Greece 92 D4
Alónissos • Greece 92 D4
Alor, Kepulauan • Indonesia 32 (1) B4
Alorna Fort • Goa, India 105 B1
Alotau • Papua New Guinea 35 (1) G3
Alpbach • Austria 89 H3
Alpe d'Huez Ski • France ..... 70 [57]
Alpe d'Huez • France 85 F3
Alpe di Pampeago Ski • Italy ..... 70 [215]
Alpe di Suisi • Italy 90 B3
Alpe du Grand Serre Ski • France ..... 70 [55]
Alpen • Germany 81 E1
Alpena • MI, United States 41 J3
Alpental Ski • WA, United States ..... 116 [44]
Alpental • WA, United States 117 E1
Alpes Cottiennes • France/Italy 10 L8
Alpes de Haute-Provence • France 85 H1
Alpes Graies • France/Italy 10 M8
Alpes Maritimes • France/Italy 10 L9
Alpes Maritimes [Adm] • France 85 H2
Alpes Pennines • France/Switzerland 10 M7
Alphen aan de Rijn • Netherlands 80 C1

Alphonse • Seychelles 106 F2
Alpi Bernina • Italy 89 G8
Alpi Carniche • Italy 91 E4
Alpi Cozie • France/Italy 91 E5
Alpi di Pampeago • Italy 90 B3
Alpi Graie • France/Italy 12 A3
Alpi Lepontine • Italy/Switzerland 89 G7
Alpi Marittime • France/Italy 12 B4
Alpi Orobie • Italy 89 G8
Alpi Pennine • Italy/Switzerland 89 G6
Alpi Retiche • Italy/Switzerland 89 G4
Alpi Sarentine • Italy 90 B1
Alpi Venoste • Italy 91 E3
Alpine • TX, United States 40 F5
Alpine Meadows Ski • CA, United States ..... 116 [55]
Alpine Valley Ski • WI, United States ..... 116 [124]
Alpine Valley Ski • MI, United States ..... 116 [137]
Alpine Valley Ski • OH, United States ..... 116 [149]
Alpirsbach • Germany 82 G6
Alps • Europe 4 L7
Alqueria Blanca • Majorca, Spain 87 H4
Alqueva, Barragem de • Portugal 88 E3
Als • Denmark 95 F13
Alsace • France 10 M5
Alsandak • Cyprus 15 C8
Alsfeld • Germany 82 G2
Alslev • Denmark 8 G2
Alsten • Norway 94 A5
Alt St Johann • Switzerland 89 G3
Alta • Norway 16 L1
Alta Heritage C • Norway ..... 63 [70]
Alta • UT, United States ..... 116 [84]
Alta Badia Ski • Italy ..... 70 [233]
Alta Gracia • Argentina 44 D5
Altaelva • Norway 16 L2
Altafulla Beach • Spain ..... 68 [104]
Altamira • Brazil 43 G4
Altamira Cave Heritage C • Spain ..... 64 [81]
Altamont • OR, United States 117 E3
Altamura • Italy 12 K8
Altas, Rías • Spain 11 C1
Altavilla Irpina • Italy 91 G2
Altay • Russian Fed. 26 O7
Altay • Mongolia 29 B1
Altayn Nuruu • Mongolia 29 A1
Altdorf bei Nürnberg • Germany 9 G7
Alte • Portugal 88 E7
Altea Beach • Spain ..... 68 [101]
Altea • Spain 87 C2
Altea • Germany 81 E4
Altenahr • Germany 82 H1
Altenau Spa • Germany ..... 83 [79]
Altenberg • Germany 9 H6
Altenkirchen • Germany 82 H2
Altenmarkt • Austria 89 H4
Altenmarkt-Zauchensee Ski • Austria ..... 70 [175]
Alter do Chão • Brazil 58 A3
Altet [Apt] • Spain 87 C1
Altevatnet • Norway 16 J2
Altinkum • Aydın, Turkey 92 D8
Altinkum • Aydın, Turkey 92 D8
Altinkum • Antalya, Turkey 93 G3
Altinoluk • Turkey 15 H4
Altissima, I' • Austria/Italy 90 B1
Altlandsberg • Germany 81 F2
Altmark • Germany 8 G4
Altnaharra • Germany 9 G8
Alto Alentejo • Portugal 11 D6
Alto Cedro • Cuba 124 D8
Alto Douro • Portugal 11 D3
Alto Paraguai • Brazil 44 E1
Alto Parnaíba • Brazil 45 (1) B3
Alto, Pico • Brazil 45 (1) D2
Altomünster • Germany 82 J3
Alton Towers Park • United Kingdom ..... 73 [25]
Altoona • PA, United States 41 K3
Altötting • Germany 82 J4
Altun-Shan • China 26 O10
Alturas • CA, United States 117 F1
Altus • OK, United States 40 G5
Alur Setar • Malaysia 32 C1
Alvängen • Sweden 95 F2
Alvarez, General Juan N. [Apt] • Mexico 123 E4
Alvdalen • Sweden 16 H6
Alvesta • Sweden 95 F7
Alvik • Norway 94 C3
Alvkarleby • Sweden 16 I6
Alvor • Portugal 88 E6
Alvsborg • Sweden 95 F7
Alwar • India 105 C2
Alyangula • NT, Australia 34 G2
Alyawarra Aboriginal Land • NT, Australia 112 H2
Alysbyn • Sweden 16 K4
Alytus • Lithuania 13 N3
Alz • Germany 82 J4
Alzamay • Russian Fed. 26 Q6
Am Dam • Chad 22 I2
Am Géréda • Chad 23 C1
Am Timan • Chad 21 D5
Amacon • France 10 J6
Amada • Egypt 101 F5
Amadeus, Lake • NT, Australia 112 H3
Amadjuak Lake • NU, Canada 39 D3
Amador • Portugal 88 D1
Amadror • Algeria 20 G3
Amager • Denmark 95 F11
Amahai • Indonesia 32 (1) C3
Amakusa • Japan 30 E8
Amal • Sweden 95 F3
Amalfi • Italy 91 G4
Amaliáda • Greece 15 C6
Amaliáda Beach • Greece ..... 69 [157]
Amami • Japan 29 H5
Amami-Shoto • Japan 31 H1
Aman • Malaysia 108 C4
Amanab • Papua New Guinea 35 (1) C1
Amänningen • Sweden 95 D1
Amantani, I. • Peru 127 B4
Amantea • Italy 12 K9
Amapá • Brazil 43 G3
Amapá [Adm] • Brazil 43 G3
Amara • Ethiopia 21 G5
Amarah, Al • Iraq 18 E3
Amaravati • India 106 D3
Amari • Crete, Greece 93 E4
Amarillo • TX, United States 40 F4
Amasra • Turkey 15 N2
Amata • SA, Australia 112 H3
Amathus • Cyprus 93 J3
Amazon • S. America 42 E5
Amazon, Mouths of the • Brazil 42 F3
Amazonas • Brazil 43 F4
Amazonas [Adm] • Brazil 43 D4
Ambala • India 28 C2

Ambam • Cameroon 22 G4
Ambanja • Madagascar 24 H2
Ambarchik • Russian Fed. 27 R3
Ambato • Ecuador 43 B4
Amber • India 105 C2
Amberg • Germany 9 G7
Ambérieu-en-Bugey • France 85 F1
Ambilobe • Madagascar 24 H2
Amble Links Beach • United Kingdom ..... 75 [20]
Ambleside • United Kingdom 74 C4
Amblève • Belgium 80 A15
Ambo • Peru 43 B6
Amboise • France 84 D2
Amboise [Château] • France 84 D2
Ambon • Indonesia 32 (1) C3
Ambon [I.] • Indonesia 32 (1) C3
Ambongo • Madagascar 24 H3
Amboseli Nat. Park • Kenya 101 G3
Amboseli Nat. Park Park • Kenya ..... 103 [84]
Ambre, Mt d' • Madagascar 24 H2
Ambriz • Angola 23 A5
Ambrym • Vanuatu 35 (2) B2
Ambunten • Indonesia 110 D4
Ambunti • Papua New Guinea 35 (1) C1
Amded • Algeria 20 F4
Amderma • Russian Fed. 26 J4
Amdo • China 28 F2
Ameixal • Portugal 88 E5
Ameland Beach • Netherlands ..... 68 [47]
Ameland • Netherlands 80 A3
Amélia • Italy 91 F1
Amendolara • Italy 12 L8
American Adventure Park • United Kingdom ..... 73 [27]
American Highland • Antarctica 46 (1) M2
American Samoa • Pacific Ocean 35 (2) F1
Amersfoort • Netherlands 80 C2
Amery Ice Shelf • Antarctica 46 (1) M3
Ames • IA, United States 41 H3
Ametlla de Mar, l' Beach • Spain ..... 68 [104]
Amfilohía • Greece 15 C5
Amga • Russian Fed. 27 L4
Amga [Riv] • Russian Fed. 27 L4
Amguema • Russian Fed. 27 U3
Amguid • Algeria 20 G3
Amguid [Adm] • Algeria 20 G3
Amherst • NS, Canada 123 D7
Amherst, Fort • PE, Canada 123 D7
Amiens • France 10 H4
Amiens Heritage C • France ..... 64 [49]
Amini I. • India 106 D9
Amistad Nat. Recreation Area Park • TX, United States ..... 120 [139]
Amitié Estate • Seychelles 106 F4
Amlapura • Bali, Indonesia 110 C2
Amli • Norway 94 C6
Amlwch • United Kingdom 7 H8
Amman • Jordan 18 B3
Ammarnäs • Sweden 16 I4
Ammassalik • Greenland 4 C3
Ammersee • Germany 82 J2
Amok-kang • China/D.P.R. of Korea 29 H2
Amok • China/D.P.R. of Korea 30 D4
Amol • Iran 18 F2
Amoliani • Greece 92 D1
Amoliani • Greece 92 D1
Amorbach • Germany 82 G8
Amorgós • Greece 92 D8
Amorgós • Greece 92 D8
Amorosa, Fontana • Cyprus 93 J3
Amot • Buskerud, Norway 94 B1
Amot • Telemark, Norway 94 B2
Amoy • China 107 G8
Ampato, Nevado de • Peru 127 B4
Amper • Germany 82 J3
Ampezzo, Valle l' Beach • Spain ..... 68 [104]
Amposta • Spain 11 L4
Amravati • India 28 C4
Amritsar • India 28 B2
Amroth Beach • United Kingdom ..... 75 [145]
Amrum • Germany 8 D2
Amstar Spa • Germany ..... 83 [3]
Amsittene, Jebel • Morocco 20 D2
Amstelveen • Netherlands 80 C2
Amsterdam Heritage C • Netherlands ..... 64 [27]
Amsterdam • Netherlands 80 C2
Amsterdam-Rijnkanaal • Netherlands 80 C2
Amsterdamse Waterleiding Duinen • Netherlands 80 C1
Amstetten • Austria 13 D9
Amu Darya • Turkmenistan 18 H2
Amundsen Gulf • NT, Canada 38 G2
Amundsen Sea • Pacific Ocean 46 (1) EE4
Amundsen-Scott Station [Basel] • Antarctica 46 (1) A1
Amuntai • Indonesia 32 F3
Amur • Russian Fed. 27 K6
Amurang • Indonesia 32 (1) B2
Amursk • Russian Fed. 27 M6
Amvrakikós Kólpos • Greece 15 B4
Amvrosiyivka • Ukraine 25 H5
An Loc • Vietnam 108 B1
An Nabi Samu'il • Jordan 98 A5
An Tan • Vietnam 31 D3
An Uaimh • Ireland 79 E1
Ana María, Golfo de • Cuba 124 D7
Anabar • Russian Fed. 27 J3
Anabarskiy Ploskogorye • Russian Fed. 26 S3
Anacapri Beach • Italy ..... 69 [127]
Anacapri • Italy 91 G3
Anaconda • MT, United States 40 D2
Anacortes • WA, United States 117 E1
Anadyr • Russian Fed. 27 U4
Anadyrskiy Zaliv • Russian Fed. 27 V4
Anadyrskoye Ploskogorye • Russian Fed. 27 T3
Anáfi • Greece 92 D8
Anáfi [I.] • Greece 92 D8
Anafonítria • Greece 92 C3
Anafonítria • Greece 92 C3
Anagni • Italy 91 F4
Anaheim • CA, United States 117 F6
Análalava • Madagascar 24 H2
Anambas, Kepulauan • Indonesia 32 F2
Anambra • Nigeria 22 F3
Anamur • Turkey 15 N4
Anamur Burun • Turkey 15 N4
Anan • Japan 30 H8
Anantapur • India 106 D2
Anantnag • Pakistan 18 K3
Anápolis • Brazil 44 G2
Anascaul Beach • Ireland ..... 68 [41]
Anascaul • Ireland 79 F4
Anatahan • S. America 36 (1) C2
Añasco • Puerto Rico 125 E1
Anatolia • Turkey 15 L5
Anatolia, Central • Turkey 92 A3
Anatolia, Central • Turkey 92 A3

Anatolia, Eastern • Turkey 92 A4
Anatolia, Eastern • Turkey 92 A4
Anatoliki Rodópi • Greece 15 G2
Anatom • Vanuatu 35 (2) B3
Anatuya • Argentina 44 D4
Anávissos • Greece 92 D7
Anávissos • Greece 92 D7
Anazah, Jabal • Saudi Arabia 21 G1
Anbyon • D.P.R. of Korea 30 D5
Ancão, I. do • Portugal 88 E7
Ancenis • France 84 D1
Anchorage • AK, United States 40 (2) G2
Anclote Keys • FL, United States 119 M5
Ancohuma, Nevado • Bolivia 44 C2
Ancona • Italy 91 E12
Ancud • Chile 45 B4
Anda • China 27 K7
Andalgalá • Argentina 44 C4
Andalo Ski • Italy ..... 70 [210]
Andalo • Italy 90 B3
Andalsnes • Norway 94 C2
Ambre, Mt d' • Madagascar 24 H2
Andaman Is. • India 28 F6
Andaman Sea • India/Myanmar 31 B4
Andara • Namibia 24 C3
Andelys, les • France 85 E1
Andenes • Norway 16 I2
Andenne • Belgium 5 I4
Andéranboukane • Mali 20 F5
Anderdalen Nat. Park Park • Norway ..... 72 [8]
Andermatt Ski • Switzerland ..... 70 [104]
Andermatt • Switzerland 89 G3
Andernach • Germany 82 H1
Anderson • NT, Canada 38 F3
Anderson • IN, United States 41 I3
Anderson • SC, United States 41 J5
Andersonville Nat. Hist. Site Park • GA, United States ..... 121 [213]
Andes • S. America 42 C4
Andhra Pradesh • India 106 D3
Andikíthira • Greece 92 D10
Andíparos • Greece 92 D7
Andíparos • Greece 92 D7
Andirlangar • China 28 D1
Andizhan • Uzbekistan 18 J1
Andkhvoy • Afghanistan 18 I2
Andong • Rep. of Korea 30 E6
Andorra Beach • Andorra ..... 68 [121]
Andorra • Europe 85 K1
Andorra la Vella • Andorra 7 K10
Andøya • Norway 16 H2
Andradina • Brazil 44 F3
Andratx Beach • Majorca, Spain ..... 68 [109]
Andratx • Majorca, Spain 87 H1
Andreanov Is. • AK, United States 36 (1) C2
Andréas, Cape • Cyprus 93 J2
Andrelândia • Brazil 127 C3
Andrespol • Poland 13 I6
Andria • Italy 12 K8
Andríake • Turkey 93 G3
Androka • Madagascar 24 G5
Andromeda Gardens • Barbados 125 H2
Andros • Greece 92 D7
Andros • Greece 92 D7
Andros • Bahamas 124 B1
Andros [I.] • Greece 92 D7
Andros [I.] • Greece 92 D7
Andros Town • Bahamas 124 B1
Andújar • Spain 11 G6
Andulo • Angola 23 B6
Andutan • South China Sea 31 E5
Aneby • Sweden 95 F7
Anefis • Mali 20 F5
Anegada Passage • West Indies 37 I4
Aneto, Pico de • Spain 11 L2
Anga • Niger 20 H5
Angaga • Maldives 106 E1
Angamos, Punta • Chile 44 B3
Angara • Russian Fed. 27 E5
Angarsk • Russian Fed. 27 F6
Ange • Sweden 16 H5
Angel de la Guarda, I. • Mexico 123 E1
Angel Falls • Venezuela 43 E2
Angeles • Philippines 31 G3
Angelholm • Sweden 95 F11
Angermanälven • Sweden 16 I5
Angermünde • Germany 8 I3
Angers • France 84 D1
Angers [Château] • France 84 D1
Angkor • Cambodia 31 C4
Angkor Heritage C • Cambodia ..... 63 [171]
Anglem, Mt • New Zealand 35 A8
Anglesberg • Sweden 95 D1
Anglesey • United Kingdom 7 H8
Angmagssalik • Greenland 39 X3
Angoche • Mozambique 24 F3
Angol • Chile 45 B3
Angola • Africa 24 B2
Angoram • Papua New Guinea 35 (1) C1
Angoulême • France 85 G1
Angra do Heroísmo Heritage C • Azores ..... 62 [67]
Angra do Heroísmo Beach • Azores ..... 68 [86]
Angra do Heroísmo • Azores 88 B2
Angren • Uzbekistan 18 J1
Anguilla • West Indies 37 I4
Anguilla Cays • Bahamas 124 B3
Angus • United Kingdom 74 B2
Anholt • Denmark 95 F6
Anhui • China 107 G6
Aniachak Nat. Mon. & Preserve Park • AK, United States ..... 120 [10]
Anie, Pic d' • France/Spain 11 K2
Animal Flower Cave • Barbados 125 H1
Animal Kingdom • FL, United States 121 C1
Anina • Romania 13 I9
Aníva, Mys • Russian Fed. 27 N7
Aniva, Zaliv • Russian Fed. 27 N7
Anjar Heritage C • Lebanon ..... 64 [243]
Anji • China 107 J3
Anjou • France 84 D1
Anjouan • Comoros 24 G2
Anju • D.P.R. of Korea 30 C5
Anjuna Beach • Goa, India 105 B1
Ankang • China 29 D4
Ankara • Turkey 15 M3
Ankara • Turkey 15 M3
Ankara-Altindag • Turkey 15 N3
Ankara-Çankaya • Turkey 15 N3
Ankara-Yenimahalle • Turkey 15 O4
Ankaratra • Madagascar 24 H3
Ankarsrum • Sweden 95 F8
Ankhor • Somalia 23 H1
Anklam • Germany 8 I3
Ankober • Ethiopia 21 G5
Ann Arbor • MI, United States 41 J3
Anna Plains • WA, Australia 34 D3
Annaba • Algeria 101 E1
Annaberg Ski • Austria ..... 70 [179]
Annaberg-Buchholz • Germany 9 I6
Annam • Vietnam 31 C3

Annapolis • MD, United States 118 H3
Annapolis Royal • NS, Canada 123 D7
Annapurna • Nepal 28 D3
Anne, Fort • NS, Canada 123 D7
Annecy • France 85 F1
Annevoie • Belgium 80 A15
Anniston • AL, United States 41 I5
Annobón • Gabon 22 F5
Annonay • France 85 F3
Annotto Bay • Jamaica 124 C2
Annweiler • Germany 82 G6
Ano Merá Beach • Greece ..... 69 [281]
Ano Síros Beach • Greece ..... 69 [180]
Ano Viános • Crete, Greece 93 E7
Anógia • Crete, Greece 93 E6
Anópolis Beach • Crete, Greece ..... 69 [190]
Anópolis • Crete, Greece 29 F4
Ansbach • Germany 9 F7
Anse Boileau Bay • Seychelles 106 F1
Anse l'Ivrogne • St Lucia 125 J3
Anse la Raye • St Lucia 125 J1
Anse la Sables • St Lucia 125 J4
Anse Lavoutte • St Lucia 125 J2
Anse Royale • Seychelles 106 F1
Anse Royale Bay • Seychelles 106 F1
Anse Volbert Village • Seychelles 106 F1
Anshan • China 29 G2
Anshun • China 29 D5
Anson Bay • NT, Australia 34 F2
Ansongo • Mali 20 F5
Anta • Peru 127 B2
Antabamba • Peru 127 B2
Antagnod Ski • Italy ..... 70 [201]
Antalaha • Madagascar 24 I2
Antalya • Turkey 93 G3
Antalya [Adm] • Turkey 93 G3
Antalya Körfezi • Turkey 93 G4
Antananarivo • Madagascar 24 H3
Antarctic cruise area • Antarctica 59 A10
Antarctic Peninsula • Antarctica 46 (1) II2
Antelao • Italy 13 B11
Antequera • Spain 86 B3
Anthony I. Heritage C • BC, Canada ..... 62 [1]
Anti Atlas • Morocco 101 D3
Antibes Beach • France ..... 68 [117]
Antibes • France 85 H1
Antibes, Cap d' • France 85 H1
Anticosti, I. d' • QU, Canada 123 D2
Anticosti, I. d', Prov. Park • QU, Canada 123 D2
Antietam Nat. Battlefield • MD, United States 118 H3
Antietam Nat. Battlefield Park • MD, United States ..... 121 [271]
Antifer, Cap d' • France 5 D5
Antigua Heritage C • Guatemala ..... 62 [28]
Antigua • Fuerteventura, Canary Is. 87 E2
Antigua • Antigua & Barbuda ..... 125 F
Antigua & Barbuda • West Indies 37 I4
Antilla • Cuba 124 D8
Antioch • Turkey 92 A3
Antioch • Turkey 92 A3
Antioche, Pertuis d' • France 10 D7
Antiparos Monastery • Cyprus 93 J2
Antivari • Fed. Rep. of Yugoslavia 71 A14
Antofagasta • Chile 44 B3
Antofalla, Volcán • Argentina 44 C4
Antoing, Baie d' • Madagascar 24 H3
Antonina • Brazil 44 G4
Antonine Wall • United Kingdom 71 A2
Antrim • United Kingdom 7 F7
Antrim [Adm] • United Kingdom 75 A3
Antrim Mtns • United Kingdom 7 F6
Antrodoco • Italy 12 H6
Antsalova • Madagascar 24 G3
Antsirabe • Madagascar 24 H4
Antsiranana • Madagascar 24 H2
Antu • China 30 E3
Antwerp • Belgium 80 A10
Antwerpen • Belgium 80 A10
Antwerpen [Adm] • Belgium 80 A15
Anupgarh • India 105 C1
Anuradhapura Heritage C • Sri Lanka ..... 63 [134]
Anuradhapura • Sri Lanka 106 D15
Anxi • China 29 B2
Anyang • China 29 E3
Anyer • Java, Indonesia 110 D1
Anza-Borrego Desert • CA, United States 117 F6
Anzanigo • Spain 11 K2
Anzère • Switzerland 89 G6
Anzhero-Sudzhensk • Russian Fed. 26 O6
Anzhou, Ostrova • Russian Fed. 27 N1
Anzio • Italy 91 F3
Ao To Nong • Phuket, Thailand 109 K1
Aoba • Vanuatu 35 (2) B2
Aomori • Japan 30 I3
Aosta • Italy 91 E1
Aotea Harbour • New Zealand 112 K1
Aotou • China 107 H2
Aouk, Bahr • Central African Rep./Chad 21 C6
Aoukale • Central African Rep./Chad 23 C1
Aoulef • Algeria 20 D5
Aoukâr • Mauritania 20 D5
Aozou • Chad 21 C3
Ap Lei Chau • Hong Kong, China 107 H5
Apacha • Russian Fed. 27 Q6
Apalachee Bay • FL, United States 37 E2
Apalachicola • FL, United States 119 M2
Apalachicola [Riv] • FL, United States 119 M2
Apaporis • Colombia 43 D4
Aparecida do Norte • Brazil 127 C3
Apari • Philippines 31 G3
Apatity • Russian Fed. 17 E1
Apeldoorn • Netherlands 80 A8
Apere • Bolivia 44 C1
Apex Bay • BC, Canada ..... 116 [3]
Api • Nepal 28 D2
Apia • Western Samoa 35 (2) F1
Apiacás, Serra dos • Brazil 43 F6
Apio • Solomon Is. 35 (1) G2
Apo, Mt • Philippines 127 B4
Apolakkiá • Rhodes, Greece 93 F3
Apolda • Germany 9 G5
Apollo Bay • VI, Australia 111 G3
Apollo Beach • Greece 92 D7
Apollona • Rhodes, Greece 93 F2
Apollonia • Albania 15 A3
Apollonia • Libya 21 D1
Apopka • FL, United States 119 M5
Apostle Is. Nat. Lakeshore Park • WI, United States ..... 121 [157]
Apóstoli • Crete, Greece 93 E6

Apoteri • Guyana 43 F3
Appalachians • United States 41 J4
Appennines • Italy 12 G5
Appennino • Italy 12 E4
Appennino Calabro • Italy 12 K10
Appennino Campano • Italy 12 J8
Appennino Ligure • Italy 12 C4
Appennino Lucano • Italy 12 K8
Appennino Tosco-Emiliano • Italy 12 E4
Appenweier • Germany 5 K6
Appenzell • Switzerland 82 J5
Appleby • United Kingdom 7 J7
Appleton • WI, United States 41 I3
Appleton • WI, United States 124 C1
Appomattox Court House Nat. Hist. Park • VA, United States ..... 121 [254]
Aprica • Italy 91 E2
Aprilia • Italy 91 F3
Apt • France 85 H1
Aptera • Crete, Greece 93 E1
Apucarana • Brazil 44 F3
Apurímac • Peru 127 B2
Aqaba, Gulf of • Egypt/Saudi Arabia 101 F2
Aqabah, Al • Jordan 18 B4
Aqitag • China 26 P9
Aqtaü • Kazakhstan 28 E1
Aqtaü • Kazakhstan 17 I6
Aquidauana • Brazil 44 E3
Aquileia • Italy 91 E4
Aquitaine • France 10 F9
Ar Horqin Qi • China 27 J8
Ar Raqqah • Syria 18 C2
Ar Rawdâ' • Saudi Arabia 18 E5
Ar Ruways • United Arab Emirates 18 F5
Ara • India 105 C8
Arab, Bahr al • Sudan 23 D2
Arabba • Italy ..... 70 [227]
Arabba • Italy 90 B4
Arabian Oryx Sanctuary Heritage N • Oman ..... 61 [102]
Arabian Sea • Asia 18 H6
Arac • Turkey 15 O2
Aracaju • Brazil 44 I1
Aracati • Brazil 45 (1) D2
Araçatuba • Brazil 45 (1) C5
Aracena • Spain 86 B1
Aracena, Sierra de • Spain 11 E7
Araçuai • Brazil 45 (1) C5
Arad • Romania 14 I3
Arafali • Eritrea 21 G4
Arafura Sea • Australia/Indonesia 33 E7
Aragarças • Brazil 44 F2
Aragón [Adm] • Spain 11 K3
Aragón [Riv] • Spain 11 J2
Aragón • Sicily, Italy 12 H11
Araguacema • Brazil 45 (1) B3
Araguaia • Brazil 44 F1
Araguaina • Brazil 45 (1) B3
Araguari • Brazil 44 F2
Araguatins • Brazil 45 (1) B3
Arak • Iran 18 E3
Arak • Algeria 20 F3
Arakan Yoma • Myanmar 31 A2
Araks • Azerbaijan 18 E2
Aral Sea • Kazakhstan/Uzbekistan 26 J8
Aral'sk • Kazakhstan 26 J8
Aral'skoye More • Kazakhstan/Uzbekistan 26 I8
Aramac • QLD, Australia 111 F3
Arambol • Goa, India 105 B1
Arambol Beach • Goa, India 105 B1
Aran I. • Ireland 7 D7
Aran Is. • Ireland 79 E3
Aranda de Duero • Spain 11 H3
Aranjuez • Spain 11 H4
Araouane • Mali 20 E5
Arapahoe Basin Ski • CO, United States ..... 116 [92]
Arapiraca • Brazil 45 (1) D3
Arápis, Akra • Greece 15 F3
Arapongas • Brazil 44 F3
Arapuni Dam • New Zealand 112 K2
Araranguá • Brazil 44 G4
Araraquara • Brazil 44 G3
Ararat • Turkey 18 D2
Araruama, Lago de • Brazil 127 C4
Aras • Asia 18 E2
Arauca • Colombia 43 C3
Aravalli Range • India 105 C5
Arawale Game Reserve • Kenya 101 G4
Arawua Bay • New Zealand 112 L2
Araxá • Brazil 44 G2
Araxos, Akra • Greece 15 C5
Arba • Spain 11 D11
Arba Minch • Ethiopia 23 F2
Arbanasi • Bulgaria 97 D3
Arbaoua • Morocco 101 D1
Arbatax • Sardinia, Italy 90 C4
Arbil • Iraq 18 D2
Arboga • Sweden 95 D3
Arbon • Switzerland 9 E9
Arbroath • United Kingdom 74 B2
Arc • France 85 F1
Arc-et-Senans Heritage C • France ..... 64 [53]
Arcachon Beach • France ..... 68 [66]
Arcachon • France 85 G3
Arcachon, Bassin de • France 85 G3
Arches Nat. Park Park • UT, United States ..... 120 [87]
Archidona • Spain 11 G7
Arcidosso • Italy 12 F6
Arcos de Valdevez • Portugal 11 C3
Arcs, les Ski • France ..... 70 [29]
Arcs, les • France 85 F2
Arctic Bay • NU, Canada 36 J2
Arctic Red River • NT, Canada 38 E3
Arctic Red River [Riv] • NT, Canada 38 E3
Arctic Village • AK, United States 38 B3
Arda • Bulgaria 15 G2
Ardabil • Iran 18 E2
Ardakan • Iran 18 F3
Ardalstangen • Norway 94 C4
Ardee • Ireland 7 F8
Arden • Denmark 95 E5
Ardennes • Belgium 80 A19
Ardennes, Canal des • France 5 H5
Ardfert Beach • Ireland ..... 68 [45]
Ardfert • Ireland 79 F5
Ardila • Portugal 11 D6
Ardmore Beach • Ireland ..... 68 [39]
Ardmore • OK, United States 119 N1
Ardrossan • United Kingdom 6 H7
Ards • United Kingdom 75 A3
Are • Sweden 16 G5
Arecibo • Puerto Rico 125 E1
Arecibo, Observatorio de • Puerto Rico 125 E1
Arecibo, Río Grande de • Puerto Rico 125 E1

Arée, Monts d' • France ... 10 B5
Areia, Ponta de • Portugal ... 88 E8
Areiro, Pico de • Madeira ... 88 C2
Arena d'en Castell •
  Minorca, Spain ... 87 F2
Arenas, Punta de • Argentina ... 45 C6
Arend • Sweden ... 95 F8
Arendal • Norway ... 95 F1
Arenys de Mar • Spain ... 87 D4
Aréopoli • Greece ... 15 D7
Arequipa • Peru ... 127 B4
Ares • France ... 10 H3
Arès Beach • France ... 68 [66]
Arès • France ... 85 G3
Areuse, Gorges de l' •
  Switzerland ... 89 G1
Areyonga • NT, Australia ... 112 H3
Arezzo • Italy ... 91 E11
Arga • Spain ... 10 D11
Arganda • Spain ... 11 H4
Argássi • Greece ... 92 C3
Argássi • Greece ... 92 C3
Argelès-Gazost • France ... 85 J2
Argelès-sur-Mer Beach • France ... 68 [111]
Argen • Germany ... 82 J5
Argent, Côte d' • France ... 85 G
Argentan • France ... 10 G5
Argentera, Punta • Italy ... 91 E5
Argenteuil • France ... 10 G5
Argentia • NF, Canada ... 123 D4
Argentina • S. America ... 42 D8
Argentino, Lago • Argentina ... 45 B6
Argenton-sur-Creuse • France ... 84 D4
Arges • Romania ... 14 M5
Arghandab • Afghanistan ... 28 A2
Argonne • France ... 5 I5
Argopuro, Gunung •
  Java, Indonesia ... 110 D8
Argos • Greece ... 15 D6
Argostóli Beach • Greece ... 69 [150]
Arguineguín •
  Gran Canaria, Canary Is. ... 86 E4
Argun • Russian Fed. ... 27 J6
Argyle, Lake • WA, Australia ... 34 E3
Argyll & Bute • United Kingdom ... 75 A2
Arhángelos • Crete, Greece ... 93 E7
Arhángelos Beach •
  Rhodes, Greece ... 69 [187]
Arhángelos • Rhodes, Greece ... 93 F2
Århus • Denmark ... 95 F10
Århus [Adm] • Denmark ... 95 F10
Århus Bugt • Denmark ... 95 F10
Ari Atoll • Maldives ... 106 F1
Ariano Irpino • Italy ... 91 G2
Aribinda • Burkina Faso ... 20 E4
Arica • Chile ... 44 B2
Arica, Golfo de • Chile/Peru ... 127 B4
Aricha, El • Algeria ... 20 E2
Arid, Cape • WA, Australia ... 34 D6
Aride, I. • Seychelles ... 106 F4
Aridéa • Greece ... 14 J9
Ariège • France ... 10 G10
Aries • Romania ... 14 K3
Arild • Sweden ... 95 F11
Arima • Trinidad & Tobago ... 125 K3
Aripo Caves • Trinidad & Tobago ... 125 K1
Aripuaná • Brazil ... 43 E5
Arisa • Ethiopia ... 23 G1
Arish, El • Egypt ... 101 F2
Ariza • Spain ... 11 I3
Arizona • United States ... 118 J
Arjang • Sweden ... 94 B4
Arjeplog • Sweden ... 16 I3
Arjuna, Gunung •
  Java, Indonesia ... 110 D8
Arkadelphia • AR, United States ... 41 H5
Arkádi, Moní • Crete, Greece ... 93 E6
Arkalyk • Kazakhstan ... 26 K7
Arkansas • United States ... 41 H4
Arkansas City •
  KS, United States ... 41 G4
Arkansas Post Nat. Mem. Park •
  AR, United States ... 121 [194]
Arkansas [Riv] • United States ... 41 G4
Arkanu • Libya ... 21 D3
Arkatag • China ... 26 O10
Arkhangel'sk • Russian Fed. ... 17 G2
Arkí • Greece ... 92 D8
Arki • Greece ... 92 D8
Arklow Beach • Ireland ... 68 [36]
Arklow • Ireland ... 79 E4
Arkona, Kap • Germany ... 8 I2
Arkösund • Sweden ... 95 F4
Arkoúdi • Greece ... 92 C1
Arkoúdi • Greece ... 92 C1
Arkticheskogo Instituta, Ostrov •
  Russian Fed. ... 26 N2
Arla • Sweden ... 95 D3
Arlanda [Apt] • Sweden ... 95 D2
Arlanza • Spain ... 10 B11
Arles • France ... 10 J10
Arles Heritage C • France ... 64 [68]
Arlington • VA, United States ... 118 H3
Arlington • TX, United States ... 119 N1
Arlington House Park •
  VA, United States ... 121 [267]
Arlit • Niger ... 20 G5
Arlon • Belgium ... 80 A20
Arltunga Hist. Reserve •
  NT, Australia ... 112 H2
Arly, Parc nat. d' Park •
  Burkina Faso ... 103 [28]
Armação de Pera • Portugal ... 88 E6
Armadale • WA, Australia ... 34 C6
Armadale • United Kingdom ... 78 A1
Armageddon • Israel ... 98 A5
Armagh • United Kingdom ... 7 F7
Armagh [Adm] • United Kingdom ... 75 A3
Armagnac • France ... 84 B3
Armant • Egypt ... 21 F2
Armavir • Russian Fed. ... 17 G5
Arméni • Crete, Greece ... 93 E2
Armenia • Asia ... 18 D1
Armenia • Colombia ... 43 B3
Armentières • France ... 10 H3
Armidale • NS, Australia ... 34 J6
Armier Bay • Malta ... 93 H4
Armona, I. da • Portugal ... 88 E8
Armutcuk Dağ • Turkey ... 15 I3
Armutlu • Turkey ... 15 J3
Arnaud • QU, Canada ... 39 Q4
Arnaúti, Cape • Cyprus ... 93 J3
Arnel, Ponta de • Azores ... 88 B2
Arnes • Norway ... 94 B2
Arnhem • Netherlands ... 80 A8
Arnhem, Cape • NT, Australia ... 34 G1
Arnhem Land • NT, Australia ... 34 F2
Arno • Italy ... 91 E11
Arnøy • Norway ... 16 K1
Arnprior • OT, Canada ... 122 B6
Arnsberg • Germany ... 8 D5
Arnstadt • Germany ... 82 G1
Arnueró Beach • Spain ... 68 [70]
Aroab • Namibia ... 24 B5
Aroche, Pico de • Spain ... 11 E6
Arolsen • Germany ...
Arolsen Spa • Germany ... 83 [121]
Arona • Italy ... 91 E2
Arorae • Kiribati ... 33 I6

Arosa Ski • Switzerland ... 70 [114]
Arosa • Switzerland ... 89 G4
Arosa, Ria de • Spain ... 11 C2
Arpajon • France ... 85 E3
Arrábida, Serra da • Portugal ... 88 D2
Arraias • Brazil ... 45 (1) B4
Arran • United Kingdom ... 6 G6
Arras • France ... 10 H3
Arras, Burg • Germany ... 82 H3
Arrecife Beach •
  Lanzarote, Canary Is. ... 68 [94]
Arrecife •
  Lanzarote, Canary Is. ... 87 E3
Arrieta • Lanzarote, Canary Is. ... 87 E3
Arrochar • United Kingdom ... 74 B1
Arrosim Beach • Goa, India ... 105 B2
Arrow Lake • BC, Canada ... 38 H6
Arrow, Lough • Ireland ... 79 F2
Arrowhead, Lake •
  TX, United States ... 119 N1
Arrowtown • New Zealand ... 112 L2
Arroyo • Puerto Rico ... 125 E4
Arroyo de la Luz • Spain ... 11 E5
Arrufó • Argentina ... 44 D5
Ars • Denmark ... 95 F5
Arsenyev • Russian Fed. ... 30 G2
Arta • Greece ... 15 B4
Artà • Majorca, Spain ... 87 H2
Artà, Coves d' • Majorca, Spain ... 87 H2
Artem • Russian Fed. ... 30 G3
Artemovsk • Russian Fed. ... 26 P7
Artesia • NM, United States ... 40 F5
Arthur's Town • Bahamas ... 124 B2
Artigas • Uruguay ... 44 E5
Artillery Lake • NT, Canada ... 38 J4
Artois • France ... 10 G3
Artrutx, Cap d' •
  Minorca, Spain ... 87 F3
Artyk • Russian Fed. ... 27 O4
Aru, Kepulauan • Indonesia ... 32 (1) D4
Arua • Uganda ... 23 E3
Aruba • West Indies ... 37 G5
Arucas •
  Gran Canaria, Canary Is. ... 86 E4
Arunachal Pradesh • India ... 29 C1
Arundel • United Kingdom ... 74 E3
Arusha • Tanzania ... 102 H2
Arusha Nat. Park • Tanzania ... 102 H2
Arusha Nat. Park Park •
  Tanzania ... 103 [91]
Aruwimi • Dem. Rep. of Congo ... 23 D3
Arvalem Caves • Goa, India ... 105 B1
Arvayheer • Mongolia ... 29 C1
Arvi • Crete, Greece ... 93 E7
Arviat • NU, Canada ... 38 M4
Arvidsjaur • Sweden ... 16 J4
Arvika • Sweden ... 16 G2
Arviksand • Norway ... 16 K1
Arykanda • Turkey ... 93 G3
Arys • Kazakhstan ... 26 K9
Arzamas • Russian Fed. ... 17 G3
Arzew • Algeria ... 20 E1
Arzew, Gulf of • Algeria ... 11 K9
Arzgir • Russian Fed. ... 17 G5
Aš • Norway ... 94 B2
Aš • Czech Rep. ... 96 C1
As Sidr • Libya ... 21 C1
As Sidrah • Libya ... 21 C1
As Smara • Western Sahara ... 101 D5
Aså • Denmark ... 95 F6
Asa Wright Nature Centre •
  Trinidad & Tobago ... 125 K1
Asab • Namibia ... 24 B5
Asahan • Indonesia ... 110 B2
Asahikawa • Japan ... 30 L3
Asan-man • Rep. of Korea ... 30 D6
Asansol • India ... 28 E4
Asbury Park • NJ, United States ... 118 H1
Ascaín • France ... 85 J1
Ascension • Atlantic Ocean ... 19 C6
Aschaffenburg • Germany ... 82 G4
Aschau in Tirol Ski • Austria ... 70 [156]
Asco, Gorges de l' •
  Corsica, France ... 85 L2
Ascoli Piceno • Italy ... 91 E12
Ascona • Switzerland ... 89 G7
Ascot • United Kingdom ... 74 E1
Asdhu Sun I. • Maldives ... 106 E2
Ase • Belgium ... 95 F8
Asela • Ethiopia ... 23 F2
Asele • Sweden ... 16 I4
Asenovgrad • Bulgaria ... 14 L7
Aseral • Norway ... 95 F1
Aseri • Estonia ... 16 N7
Asfendioú Beach • Greece ... 69 [186]
Asgårdstrand • Norway ... 94 B4
Ash Shariqah •
  United Arab Emirates ... 18 G4
Ashante Heritage C • Ghana ... 63 [96]
Ashbourne • Ireland ... 79 E2
Ashburton • New Zealand ... 35 C6
Ashby Fort • St Kitts & Nevis ... 125 G2
Ashdod • Israel ... 98 A5
Ashdown Forest • United Kingdom ... 74 E3
Asher • Israel/Lebanon ... 98 A2
Asheville • NC, United States ... 41 J4
Ashford • United Kingdom ... 74 E4
Ashgabat • Turkmenistan ... 18 G2
Ashington • United Kingdom ... 7 K6
Ashizuri-Misaki • Japan ... 30 G8
Ashkharah, Al • Oman ... 18 G5
Ashland • OR, United States ... 40 B3
Ashland • ME, United States ... 118 G2
Ashmünien, El • Egypt ... 101 F3
Ashuanipi Lake • QU, Canada ... 39 R6
Asia, Kepulauan • Indonesia ... 32 (1) D2
Asiago Ski • Italy ... 70 [213]
Asikkala • Finland ... 95 E2
Asilah • Morocco ... 101 D1
Asinara, Golfo del' •
  Sardinia, Italy ... 90 C1
Asinara, I. • Sardinia, Italy ... 90 C1
Asinou Church • Cyprus ... 93 J3
Asir • Saudi Arabia ... 18 D6
Asker • Norway ... 94 B2
Askersund • Sweden ... 95 D4
Askham • United Kingdom ... 74 C2
Askim • Norway ... 94 B4
Asklipío Beach • Rhodes, Greece ... 69 [187]
Asklipío • Rhodes, Greece ... 93 F3
Askøy • Norway ... 94 C3
Askvoll • Norway ... 94 C3
Asmara • Eritrea ... 21 G4
Asnen • Sweden ... 95 F11
Asnes • Norway ... 101 D5
Asola • Italy ... 91 E7
Aspen • CO, United States ... 40 E4
Aspen Ski • CO, United States ... 116 [99]
Aspendos • Turkey ... 93 G4
Aspiring, Mt • New Zealand ... 112 L2
Asprókavos, Akra •
  Corfu, Greece ... 92 B1
Asprókavos, Akra •
  Corfu, Greece ... 92 B1
Apróvata Beach • Greece ... 69 [170]
Assab • Eritrea ... 21 H5
Assal, Lake • Ethiopia ... 21 H5

Assam • India ... 28 F3
Assamakka • Niger ... 20 G5
Assateague I. Nat. Seashore •
  MD, United States ... 118 H3
Assateague I. Nat. Seashore Park •
  MD, United States ... 121 [278]
Assen • Netherlands ... 80 A4
Assen • Denmark ... 95 F13
Assiniboine • MN, Canada ... 38 L7
Assiniboine, Mt • BC, Canada ... 38 I6
Assiniboine, Mt. Prov. Park •
  BC, Canada ... 122 C4
Assis • Brazil ... 44 F3
Assisi • Italy ... 91 E12
Assmannshausen • Germany ... 82 H4
Assomption • Seychelles ... 106 F3
Assos • Greece ... 92 C2
Assos • Sicily, Italy ... 15 C5
Astakós • Greece ... 15 C5
Astérix, Parc • France ... 85 E2
Asteroúsia • Crete, Greece ... 93 E7
Asti • Italy ... 91 E5
Astillero • Peru ... 127 B2
Astipálaia • Greece ... 15 E6
Astipálaia • Greece ... 92 D8
Astorga • Spain ... 11 E2
Astrakhan • Russian Fed. ... 117 E1
Astove • Seychelles ... 106 F3
Astrakhan • Russian Fed. ... 17 H5
Astura, Torre • Italy ... 91 F3
Asturias Heritage C • Spain ... 64 [82]
Asturias, Principado de • Spain ... 11 E1
Asuka [Base] • Antarctica ... 46 (1) H2
Asunción • Paraguay ... 44 E4
Asuwa • Uganda ... 23 E3
Asvem Beach • Goa, India ... 105 B1
Aswa • Uganda ... 23 E3
Aswân • Egypt ... 101 F5
Aswân Dam • Egypt ... 101 F5
Aswân High Dam • Egypt ... 101 F5
Asyût • Egypt ... 101 F3
Ata • Tonga ... 33 J8
Atacama • Chile ... 44 C3
Atafu • Tokelau ... 33 J6
Atalánti • Greece ... 15 D5
Atalaia Beach • Greece ... 69 [164]
Atalaya • Peru ... 43 C6
Atalaya de Femés •
  Lanzarote, Canary Is. ... 87 E3
Atambua • Indonesia ... 32 (1) B4
Atâr • Mauritania ... 20 C4
Atasu • Kazakhstan ... 26 L8
Ataturk [Apt] • Turkey ... 92 D3
Atatürk [Apt] • Turkey ... 92 D3
Atauri • Spain ... 11 I2
Atbarah • Sudan ... 21 G4
Atbara [Riv] • Sudan ... 21 G4
Atbasar • Kazakhstan ... 26 K7
Atchafalaya • LA, United States ... 118 K3
Atchafalaya Bay •
  LA, United States ... 118 K3
Atchinson • KS, United States ... 41 G4
Aterno • Italy ... 91 F2
Ath • Belgium ... 80 A14
Athabasca • AL, Canada ... 38 H6
Athabasca Lake • AL/SA, Canada ... 38 J5
Athboy • Ireland ... 79 E1
Athenry • Ireland ... 79 F4
Athens Heritage C • Greece ... 64 [183]
Athína • Greece ... 92 D4
Athína Heritage C • Greece ... 64 [183]
Athína • Greece ... 92 D4
Athlone • Ireland ... 7 E8
Athol I. • Bahamas ... 124 B3
Athos Heritage N • Greece ... 61 [61]
Athos Heritage C • Greece ... 64 [174]
Athos • Greece ... 92 D1
Athy • Ireland ... 79 E3
Ati • Chad ... 21 C5
Atibaia • Brazil ... 127 C3
Atico • Peru ... 127 B3
Atka • Russian Fed. ... 27 P4
Atka • AK, United States ... 36 (1) D2
Atlanta • GA, United States ... 41 J5
Atlanta • TX, United States ... 119 N2
Atlantic Beach •
  NC, United States ... 118 H5
Atlantic Beach •
  St Kitts & Nevis ... 125 G2
Atlantic City •
  NJ, United States ... 118 H3
Atlantic Islands cruise area •
  Atlantic Ocean ... 59 A5
Atlantic Ocean ... 2 K5
Atlántida • Uruguay ... 127 D2
Atlas Bogdo-Ula • Mongolia ... 29 B2
Atlas Mtns • Algeria/Morocco ... 19 D2
Atlas Saharien • Algeria ... 20 F2
Atlin • BC, Canada ... 38 E5
Atlin Lake • YT, Canada ... 38 E4
Atløy • Norway ... 94 C3
Atokos • Greece ... 92 C2
Atokos • Greece ... 92 C2
Atol das Rocas • Brazil ... 45 (1) E2
Atrak • Iran ... 18 G2
Atran • Sweden ... 95 F7
Atran [Riv] • Sweden ... 95 F7
Atrato • Colombia ... 43 B2
Atruk • Turkmenistan ... 18 G2
Atri • Italy ... 12 H6
Atrun, Al • Sudan ... 21 E4
Atsumi • Japan ... 30 J5
Attaf, El • Algeria ... 11 M8
Attapu • Laos ... 31 D4
Attáviros • Rhodes, Greece ... 93 F1
Attawapiskat • OT, Canada ... 39 O6
Attawapiskat [Riv] • OT, Canada ... 39 O6
Attersee • Austria ... 89 H4
Attila Line • Cyprus ... 93 J4
Attnash-Bear Peak Ski •
  NM, United States ... 116 [211]
Attre • Belgium ... 80 A14
Attu • AK, United States ... 36 (1) A2
Atvidaberg • Sweden ... 95 F4
Atyrau • Kazakhstan ... 17 I5
Au • Austria ... 89 H1
Aubagne • France ... 85 H3
Aube • France ... 10 J5
Aubigny Lake • NT, Canada ... 38 J3
Auburn • CA, United States ... 117 F3
Auburn • ME, United States ... 118 G2
Aubusson • France ... 85 G2
Aucanquilcha, Cerro • Chile ... 44 C3
Auch • France ... 85 G4
Auckland • New Zealand ... 35 E4
Auckland [Adm] • New Zealand ... 112 J2
Auckland I. • New Zealand ... 35 (4) H3
Aude • France ... 85 K2
Aude [Riv] • France ... 10 A5
Audierne • France ... 84 C3
Audierne, Baie d' • France ... 84 C3

Audincourt • France ... 9 B9
Audo • Ethiopia ... 23 G2
Aue • Germany ... 9 H6
Aue [Riv] • Germany ... 5 M2
Auer • Italy ... 90 B3
Auerbacher Schloß • Germany ... 82 H4
Auffach Ski • Austria ... 70 [147]
Augathella • QL, Australia ... 111 F5
Aughrim • Ireland ... 79 E4
Aughty, Slieve • Ireland ... 79 F4
Augier • St Lucia ... 125 J3
Augrabies Falls • South Africa ... 24 C5
Augsburg • Germany ... 82 J2
Augusta • WA, Australia ... 34 C6
Augusta • GA, United States ... 41 J5
Augusta • Sicily, Italy ... 90 D4
Augusta • ME, United States ... 118 G4
Augustenborg Beach • Denmark ... 68 [26]
Augustenborg • Denmark ... 95 F13
Augustin Codazzi • Colombia ... 43 C2
Augustów • Poland ... 13 M4
Augustus, Mt • WA, Australia ... 34 C4
Auki • Solomon Is. ... 35 (1) G2
Aukstaitija Nat. Park Park •
  Lithuania ... 72 [146]
Aulendorf • Germany ... 82 J1
Aulendorf Spa • Germany ... 83 [213]
Aulie-Ata • Kazakhstan ... 26 L9
Aulla • Italy ... 12 E4
Aulnay • France ... 85 G1
Aulne • France ... 84 C1
Aumale • France ... 5 E5
Auob • Africa ... 24 C5
Aurach Ski • Austria ... 70 [158]
Aurangabad • India ... 28 C5
Auray • France ... 84 C4
Aurdal • Norway ... 16 E6
Aurich • Germany ... 8 C3
Aurillac • France ... 10 H9
Aurina • Italy ... 90 B2
Aurina, Val • Italy ... 90 B2
Auris • France ... 85 F3
Auris-en-Oisans Ski • France ... 70 [57]
Aurlandsvangen • Norway ... 15 H4
Auron Ski • France ... 70 [71]
Auron • France ... 85 H2
Aurora • CO, United States ... 11 K5
Aurora • IL, United States ... 41 I3
Auroville • India ... 106 D7
Aurukun Mission • QL, Australia ... 34 H2
Aurunci, Monti • Italy ... 91 F4
Auschwitz • Poland ... 11 I1
Auschwitz Heritage C • Poland ... 64 [142]
Ausoni, Monti • Italy ... 91 F4
Aust Agder • Norway ... 16 E7
Austad • Norway ... 94 C6
Austin • NV, United States ... 117 F4
Austin • TX, United States ... 119 N3
Austin, Lake • WA, Australia ... 34 C5
Austnes • Norway ... 94 C1
Australasia cruise area •
  Oceania ... 59 A9
Australia • Oceania ... 34
Australia's Wonderland •
  NS, Australia ... 111 G2
Australian Alps •
  NS/VI, Australia ... 111 G4
Australian Capital Territory •
  QL, Australia ... 111 G2
Australian rainforest reserves Heritage N •
  Australia ... 61 [130]
Austria • Europe ... 4 M7
Austvågøy • Norway ... 16 H2
Autazes • Brazil ... 43 F4
Authie • France ... 10 G3
Autieul • France ... 85 E3
Autun • France ... 10 J7
Auvergne • France ... 10 I8
Auvernier • Switzerland ... 89 G1
Aux Sources, Mont •
  South Africa ... 24 D5
Auxerre • France ... 10 I6
Auxerre-le-Château • France ... 5 F4
Auyan Tepuy • Venezuela ... 43 E2
Auzangate, Nudo • Peru ... 127 B2
Avadh • India ... 105 C3
Avaldsnes • Norway ... 94 C5
Avalon Peninsula • NF, Canada ... 123 D4
Avarua • Cook Is. ... 33 L8
Avebury Heritage C •
  United Kingdom ... 64 [20]
Avebury • United Kingdom ... 74 F3
Aveiro • Portugal ... 11 C4
Aveiro [Adm] • Portugal ... 88 A1
Avellaneda • Argentina ... 127 D2
Avellino • Italy ... 91 G2
Averøya • Norway ... 16 D5
Aversa • Italy ... 91 G1
Aves • Venezuela ... 15 I2
Aves • West Indies ... 124 A3
Avesnes-sur-Helpe • France ... 5 G4
Avesta • Sweden ... 95 D1
Aveyron • France ... 85 G4
Aveyron, Gorges de l' • France ... 85 G4
Avezzano • Italy ... 91 F2
Avgó • Greece ... 92 C2
Aviano • Italy ... 90 B4
Aviés • Spain ... 11 I1
Avigliano • Italy ... 14 C9
Avignon • France ... 10 J10
Avignon Heritage C • France ... 64 [67]
Ávila • Spain ... 11 E3
Ávila Heritage C • Spain ... 64 [85]
Avilés • Spain ... 11 E1
Aviliótes Beach • Corfu, Greece ... 69 [149]
Avoca • Ireland ... 79 E4
Avoca, Vale of • Ireland ... 79 E4
Avola • Sicily, Italy ... 90 D4
Avon • United Kingdom ... 74 D2
Avon • United Kingdom ... 74 D2
Avon • United Kingdom ... 74 D2
Avon Downs • NT, Australia ... 34 G4
Avonmouth • United Kingdom ... 74 D3
Avoriaz Ski • France ... 70 [10]
Avranches • France ... 5 E6
Avre • France ... 5 E6
Avre • France ... 10 G6
Awa • Japan ... 30 J5
Awaji-shima • Japan ... 30 H6
Awakino Gorge • New Zealand ... 112 K1
Awara Mtns • Namibia ... 24 B4
Awasa • Ethiopia ... 85 H3
Awash • Ethiopia ... 21 G5
Awash Nat. Park Park • Ethiopia ... 103 [63]
Awash [Riv] • Ethiopia ... 23 G1
Awaso • Ghana ... 21 B2
Awbari • Libya ... 21 B2
Awbārī • Libya ... 21 B2
Awdal • Libya ... 21 B2
Awe, Loch • United Kingdom ... 6 G5
Awjilah • Libya ... 21 C2
Ax-les-Thermes • France ... 85 K1
Axarfjörður • Iceland ... 16 (1) E1
Axel Heiberg • Canada ... 36 K2
Axiós • Greece ... 92 C1
Axminster • United Kingdom ... 74 F3

Axós • Crete, Greece ... 93 E2
Ayabe • Japan ... 30 H7
Ayacucho • Peru ... 127 B1
Ayacucho • Argentina ... 127 D3
Ayaguz • Kazakhstan ... 26 N8
Ayakkum Hu • China ... 28 E1
Ayam Line • Russian Fed. ... 97 A6
Ayamonte • Spain ... 11 D7
Ayan • Russian Fed. ... 27 G5
Ayan • Russian Fed. ... 27 M5
Ayanka • Russian Fed. ... 27 S4
Ayas • Turkey ... 15 N3
Ayaviri • Peru ... 127 B2
Aybak • Afghanistan ... 28 A1
Aydin • Turkey ... 92 D9
Aydin • Turkey ... 92 D9
Aydin Dağlari • Turkey ... 15 I5
Aydingkol Hu • China ... 26 O9
Ayelinkent • Turkey ... 93 G2
Ayer Chawan • Singapore ... 108 E3
Ayer Hitam • Malaysia ... 108 D4
Ayer Merbau • Singapore ... 108 E3
Ayers Rock • NT, Australia ... 112 H3
Ayers Rock Resort •
  NT, Australia ... 112 H3
Ayía Nápia Beach • Cyprus ... 69 [195]
Ayía Nápia • Cyprus ... 93 J4
Ayíos Tychon Beach • Cyprus ... 69 [193]
Aykhal • Russian Fed. ... 27 H3
Ayn al Ghazal • Libya ... 21 D3
Ayn, Ras • Saudi Arabia ... 18 E4
Ayod • Sudan ... 23 E2
Ayodhya • India ... 105 C8
Ayorou • Niger ... 20 F6
Ayoun el Atroûs • Mauritania ... 20 D5
Ayr • QL, Australia ... 111 F1
Ayr • United Kingdom ... 6 H6
Aysha • Ethiopia ... 23 G1
Aytos • Bulgaria ... 97 D3
Ayutthaya Heritage C • Thailand ... 63 [174]
Ayutthaya • Thailand ... 109 H1
Ayvacik • Turkey ... 15 H4
Ayvalık • Turkey ... 15 H4
Az Zahran • Saudi Arabia ... 18 E4
Az Zawiyah • Libya ... 21 B1
Azahar, Costa del • Spain ... 11 K5
Azaila • Spain ... 11 K3
Azamgarh • India ... 105 C8
Azangaro • Peru ... 127 B4
Azaouâd • Mali ... 20 E5
Azaouak, Vallée de l' •
  Mali/Niger ... 20 F5
Azare • Nigeria ... 22 G2
Azay-le-Ferron [Château] •
  France ... 84 D4
Azay-le-Rideau [Château] •
  France ... 84 D2
Azbine • Niger ... 20 G5
Azday • Turkey ... 15 O2
Azemmour • Morocco ... 101 D1
Azerbaijan • Asia ... 18 E1
Azinhal • Portugal ... 88 E4
Azogues • Ecuador ... 43 B4
Azores • Atlantic Ocean ... 88 B
Azov, Sea of •
  Russian Fed./Ukraine ... 17 F5
Azpeitia • Spain ... 11 I1
Azrou • Morocco ... 101 D2
Aztec Ruins Nat. Mon. •
  NM, United States ... 118 J2
Aztec Ruins Nat. Mon. Park •
  NM, United States ... 120 [124]
Azúa • Spain ... 11 I1
Azuero, Peninsula de • Panama ... 37 E6
Azul • Galápagos Is. ... 43 (1) A2
Azul • Argentina ... 127 D3
Azul, Costa • Portugal ... 88 D1
Azulcocha, Cerro • Peru ... 127 B1
Azur, Côte d' • France ... 85 H
Azure Window • Malta ... 93 H1
Azzel Matti, Sebkha • Algeria ... 20 F3
Azzurra, Grotta • Italy ... 91 G3

Ba'qubah • Iraq ... 18 D3
Baa • Indonesia ... 32 (1) B5
Baába • New Caledonia ... 35 (2) A3
Baabe Beach • Germany ... 68 [13]
Baabe Spa • Germany ... 83 [280]
Baalbek Heritage C • Lebanon ... 64 [244]
Baarn • Netherlands ... 80 C2
Baba Burun • Çanakkale, Turkey ... 15 H4
Baba Burun • Zonguldak, Turkey ... 15 M2
Baba Dagi • Turkey ... 15 K7
Babadag • Romania ... 97 D2
Babaeski • Turkey ... 15 I2
Babanusah • Sudan ... 23 D1
Babaoyo • Ecuador ... 43 B4
Babar • Indonesia ... 32 (1) C4
Babayevo • Russian Fed. ... 97 E2
Babbacombe Bay • United Kingdom ... 74 F3
Babenhausen • Germany ... 82 J2
Babenro • South Africa ... 24 E5
Babian Jiang • China ... 29 C6
Babine Lake • BC, Canada ... 38 F6
Babiogórski Nat. Park Park •
  Poland ... 72 [96]
Babo • Indonesia ... 32 (1) D3
Babol • Iran ... 18 F2
Babonneau • St Lucia ... 125 J2
Babr • Poland ... 13 E6
Babruysk • Belarus ... 15 D4
Babuna • F.Y.R. of Macedonia ... 14 I8
Babuyan • Philippines ... 31 F4
Babuyan Is. • Philippines ... 31 G3
Babylon • Iraq ... 18 D3
Bac Lieu • Vietnam ... 108 B3
Bac Phan • Vietnam ... 31 D2
Bacabal • Brazil ... 45 (1) D2
Bacan • Indonesia ... 32 (1) C3
Bacău • Romania ... 14 N3
Baccarat • France ... 9 B8
Bacharach • Germany ... 82 H4
Back • NU, Canada ... 38 L3
Backa F.R. of Yugoslavia ... 14 G4
Bäckefors • Sweden ... 95 F2
Backnang • Germany ... 82 J2
Bacolod • Philippines ... 31 G4
Bad • Iran ... 18 E3
Bad Abbach Spa • Germany ... 83 [231]
Bad Aibling • Germany ... 82 J3
Bad Aibling Spa • Germany ... 83 [254]
Bad Alexandersbad Spa • Germany ... 83 [138]
Bad Aussee • Austria ... 89 H4
Bad Bayersoien • Germany ... 82 J6
Bad Bayersoien Spa • Germany ... 83 [203]
Bad Bederkesa Spa • Germany ... 83 [56]
Bad Bentheim • Germany ... 9 D6
Bad Bentheim Spa • Germany ... 83 [63]
Bad Bergzabern • Germany ... 82 G6
Bad Bergzabern Spa • Germany ... 83 [166]
Bad Berka Spa • Germany ... 83 [309]
Bad Berleburg • Germany ... 5 L3

Bad Berleburg Spa • Germany ... 83 [111]
Bad Berneck Spa • Germany ... 83 [226]
Bad Bertrich Spa • Germany ... 83 [157]
Bad Bevensen Spa • Germany ... 83 [58]
Bad Birnbach • Germany ... 82 J4
Bad Birnbach Spa • Germany ... 83 [263]
Bad Bocklet Spa • Germany ... 83 [220]
Bad Boll Spa • Germany ... 83 [193]
Bad Brambach Spa • Germany ... 83 [316]
Bad Bramstedt Spa • Germany ... 83 [33]
Bad Breisig • Germany ... 82 H1
Bad Breisig Spa • Germany ... 83 [150]
Bad Brückenau Spa • Germany ... 83 [219]
Bad Buchau • Germany ... 82 J1
Bad Buchau Spa • Germany ... 83 [140]
Bad Camberg Spa • Germany ... 83 [140]
Bad Colberg Spa • Germany ... 83 [305]
Bad Ditzenbach Spa • Germany ... 83 [194]
Bad Doberan • Germany ... 8 G2
Bad Doberan • Germany ... 13 A3
Bad Doberan Beach • Germany ... 68 [16]
Bad Doberan Spa • Germany ... 83 [271]
Bad Driburg Spa • Germany ... 83 [99]
Bad Düben Spa • Germany ... 83 [312]
Bad Dürkheim • Germany ... 82 G4
Bad Dürkheim Spa • Germany ... 83 [165]
Bad Dürrheim Spa • Germany ... 83 [200]
Bad Eilsen Spa • Germany ... 83 [68]
Bad Elster Spa • Germany ... 83 [315]
Bad Ems • Germany ... 82 H2
Bad Ems Spa • Germany ... 83 [155]
Bad Emstal Spa • Germany ... 83 [124]
Bad Endbach Spa • Germany ... 83 [128]
Bad Endorf • Germany ... 82 J4
Bad Endorf Spa • Germany ... 83 [255]
Bad Essen Spa • Germany ... 83 [67]
Bad Faulenberg Spa • Germany ... 83 [244]
Bad Feilnbach • Germany ... 82 J7
Bad Feilnbach Spa • Germany ... 83 [251]
Bad Frankenhausen Spa • Germany ... 83 [298]
Bad Fredeburg Spa • Germany ... 83 [110]
Bad Freienwalde • Germany ... 8 J4
Bad Freienwalde Spa • Germany ... 83 [288]
Bad Füssing Spa • Germany ... 83 [264]
Bad Gandersheim Spa • Germany ... 83 [74]
Bad Godesberg • Germany ... 82 H1
Bad Gögging Spa • Germany ... 83 [230]
Bad Goisern • Austria ... 89 H4
Bad Gottleuba Spa • Germany ... 83 [318]
Bad Griesbach Spa • Germany ... 83 [263]
Bad Grund • Germany ... 83 [75]
Bad Harzburg • Germany ... 8 F5
Bad Harzburg Spa • Germany ... 83 [78]
Bad Heilbrunn • Germany ... 82 J7
Bad Heilbrunn Spa • Germany ... 83 [251]
Bad Hermannsborn Spa • Germany ... 83 [99]
Bad Herrenalb Spa • Germany ... 83 [180]
Bad Hersfeld • Germany ... 9 E6
Bad Hersfeld Spa • Germany ... 83 [131]
Bad Hofgastein Ski • Austria ... 70 [169]
Bad Hofgastein • Austria ... 89 H8
Bad Homburg • Germany ... 83 [145]
Bad Homburg vor der Höhe •
  Germany ... 82 H2
Bad Honnef • Germany ... 82 H1
Bad Honnef Spa • Germany ... 83 [115]
Bad Hönningen • Germany ... 82 H1
Bad Hönningen Spa • Germany ... 83 [151]
Bad Imnau Spa • Germany ... 83 [64]
Bad Ischl • Austria ... 89 H4
Bad Karlshafen Spa • Germany ... 83 [119]
Bad Kissingen • Germany ... 9 F6
Bad Kissingen Spa • Germany ... 83 [220]
Bad Kleinkirchheim Ski •
  Austria ... 70 [189]
Bad Klosterlausnitz Spa •
  Germany ... 83 [311]
Bad Kohlgrub • Germany ... 82 J6
Bad Kohlgrub Spa • Germany ... 83 [147]
Bad König Spa • Germany ... 83 [147]
Bad Königshofen Spa • Germany ... 83 [222]
Bad Kösen Spa • Germany ... 83 [296]
Bad Kreuznach • Germany ... 82 H4
Bad Kreuznach Spa • Germany ... 83 [164]
Bad Krozingen • Germany ... 9 C9
Bad Krozingen Spa • Germany ... 83 [201]
Bad Laasphe Spa • Germany ... 83 [112]
Bad Laer Spa • Germany ... 83 [65]
Bad Langensalza • Germany ... 9 F5
Bad Langensalza Spa • Germany ... 83 [313]
Bad Lausick Spa • Germany ... 83 [313]
Bad Lauterberg • Germany ... 8 F5
Bad Lauterberg Spa • Germany ... 83 [87]
Bad Liebenstein Spa • Germany ... 83 [303]
Bad Liebenwerda Spa • Germany ... 83 [291]
Bad Liebenzell Spa • Germany ... 83 [177]
Bad Malente-Gremsmühlen Spa •
  Germany ... 83 [31]
Bad Marienberg Spa • Germany ... 83 [153]
Bad Meinberg Spa • Germany ... 83 [98]
Bad Mergentheim • Germany ... 9 E7
Bad Mergentheim Spa • Germany ... 83 [171]
Bad Münder • Germany ... 8 E4
Bad Münster am Stein Spa •
  Germany ... 83 [163]
Bad Münstereifel Spa • Germany ... 83 [116]
Bad Muskau Spa • Germany ... 83 [321]
Bad Nauheim • Germany ... 5 L4
Bad Nauheim Spa • Germany ... 83 [139]
Bad Nenndorf • Germany ... 9 D6
Bad Nenndorf Spa • Germany ... 83 [69]
Bad Neuenahr Spa • Germany ... 83 [99]
Bad Neuenahr-Ahrweiler •
  Germany ... 82 H1
Bad Neustadt Spa • Germany ... 83 [221]
Bad Neustadt an der Saale •
  Germany ... 9 F6
Bad Niederau Spa • Germany ... 83 [190]
Bad Oeynhausen Spa • Germany ... 83 [69]
Bad Oldesloe • Germany ... 16 F10
Bad Orb • Germany ... 5 M4
Bad Orb Spa • Germany ... 83 [137]
Bad Peterstal Spa • Germany ... 83 [182]
Bad Pyrmont • Germany ... 8 E5
Bad Pyrmont Spa • Germany ... 83 [71]
Bad Rappenau Spa • Germany ... 83 [173]
Bad Reichenhall • Germany ... 82 J3
Bad Reichenhall Spa • Germany ... 83 [261]
Bad Rippoldsau Spa • Germany ... 83 [188]
Bad Rothenfelde Spa • Germany ... 83 [66]
Bad Saarow Spa • Germany ... 83 [290]
Bad Sachsa Spa • Germany ... 83 [76]
Bad Säckingen Spa • Germany ... 83 [204]
Bad Salzdetfurth Spa • Germany ... 83 [73]
Bad Salzhausen Spa • Germany ... 83 [138]
Bad Salzschlirf Spa • Germany ... 83 [126]
Bad Salzuflen • Germany ... 8 E5
Bad Salzuflen Spa • Germany ... 83 [93]
Bad Salzungen • Germany ... 9 F6
Bad Salzungen Spa • Germany ... 83 [304]
Bad Sassendorf Spa • Germany ... 83 [104]
Bad Schandau Spa • Germany ... 83 [320]
Bad Schmiedeberg Spa • Germany ... 83 [292]
Bad Schönborn Spa • Germany ... 83 [172]
Bad Schussenried • Germany ... 82 J1
Bad Schussenried Spa • Germany ... 83 [216]

Bad Schwalbach

Bad Schwalbach • Germany 82 H4
Bad Schwartau Spa • Germany .... 83 [141]
Bad Schwartau • Germany 8 F3
Bad Schwarau • Germany .... 83 [30]
Bad Seebruch Spa • Germany .... 83 [92]
Bad Segeberg • Germany 8 F3
Bad Segeberg Spa • Germany .... 83 [34]
Bad Senkelteich Spa • Germany .... 83 [92]
Bad Sobernheim Spa • Germany .... 83 [162]
Bad Soden Spa • Germany .... 83 [144]
Bad Soden-Salmünster Spa • Germany .... 83 [136]
Bad Sooden Spa • Germany .... 83 [130]
Bad Steben Spa • Germany .... 83 [225]
Bad Suderode Spa • Germany .... 83 [295]
Bad Sulza Spa • Germany .... 83 [310]
Bad Sülze Spa • Germany .... 83 [272]
Bad Teinach Spa • Germany .... 83 [182]
Bad Tennstedt Spa • Germany .... 83 [299]
Bad Tölz • Germany 82 H7
Bad Tölz Spa • Germany .... 83 [252]
Bad Überkingen Spa • Germany .... 83 [194]
Bad Urach • Germany 82 G6
Bad Urach Spa • Germany .... 83 [192]
Bad Vilbel Spa • Germany .... 83 [146]
Bad Waldsee • Germany 82 J1
Bad Waldsee Spa • Germany .... 83 [216]
Bad Wiessee • Germany 82 J7
Bad Wiessee Spa • Germany .... 83 [253]
Bad Wildbad • Germany 82 G6
Bad Wildbad Spa • Germany .... 83 [183]
Bad Wildungen • Germany 5 M3
Bad Wildungen • Germany 9 E5
Bad Wildungen Spa • Germany .... 83 [125]
Bad Wilsnack Spa • Germany .... 83 [287]
Bad Wimpfen • Germany 82 G4
Bad Wimpfen Spa • Germany .... 83 [173]
Bad Windsheim • Germany 9 F7
Bad Windsheim Spa • Germany .... 83 [229]
Bad Wörishofen • Germany 82 J2
Bad Wörishofen Spa • Germany .... 83 [235]
Bad Wurzach • Germany 82 J1
Bad Wurzach Spa • Germany .... 83 [217]
Bad Zwesten Spa • Germany .... 83 [126]
Bad Zwischenahn • Germany 8 D3
Bad Zwischenahn Spa • Germany .... 83 [51]
Badain Jaran Shamo • Mongolia 29 C2
Badajoz • Spain 11 E6
Badalona • Spain 87 D4
Badami • India 106 D2
Badanah • Saudi Arabia 18 E3
Badda • Ethiopia 23 F2
Bade • Indonesia 32 (1) E4
Baden • Switzerland 9 D9
Baden • Austria 13 F9
Baden-Baden • Germany 82 G6
Baden-Baden Spa • Germany .... 83 [181]
Baden-Württemberg • Germany 9 E8
Badenweiler • Germany 82 G7
Badenweiler Spa • Germany .... 83 [202]
Badgastein Ski • Austria .... 70 [168]
Badgastein • Austria 89 H8
Badia, Val • Italy 90 B2
Badiyat ash Sham • Iraq/Jordan 18 C3
Badlands • United States 117 D2
Badlands Nat. Park Park • SD, United States .... 120 [153]
Badr Hunayn • Saudi Arabia 18 C5
Badu I. • QL, Australia 34 H2
Badulla • Sri Lanka 106 D15
Badung, Bukit • Bali, Indonesia 110 C4
Badung, Selat • Indonesia 110 C4
Badwater Basin • CA, United States 117 F4
Baena • Spain 86 B3
Bafang • Cameroon 22 G3
Bafatá • Guinea-Bissau 22 B2
Baffin Bay • Canada/Greenland 36 K2
Baffin Bay • TX, United States 119 N5
Baffin I. • NU, Canada 39 P2
Baffing • Guinea/Mali 22 B2
Bafia • Cameroon 22 G4
Bafoulabé • Mali 20 C6
Bafoussam • Cameroon 22 G3
Bafq • Iran 18 G3
Baga • Goa, India 105 B1
Baga Beach • Goa, India 105 B1
Bagamoyo • Tanzania 102 H2
Bagan Datuk • Malaysia 108 D1
Bagansiapiapi • Indonesia 110 B4
Bagata • Dem. Rep. of Congo 23 B4
Bagdarin • Russian Fed. 27 K5
Bagé • Brazil 44 F5
Bagenkop • Denmark 95 F14
Bagerhat Heritage C • Bangladesh .... 63 [133]
Baggs, Bill, Cape Florida State Recreation Area • FL, United States 119 M8
Baghdad • Iraq 18 D3
Baghelkhand Plateau • India 105 C8
Bagheria • Sicily, Italy 12 H10
Baghlan • Afghanistan 18 I2
Baghwan Mahaveer Wildlife Sanctuary • Goa, India 105 B2
Baginton [Apt] • United Kingdom 74 D2
Bagnères-de-Bigorre • France 11 L1
Bagnères-de-Luchon • France 11 L2
Bagno di Romagna • Italy 12 F5
Bagoe • Mali 22 C2
Bagua • Peru 43 B5
Baguio • Philippines 31 G3
Bagzane, Mts • Niger 20 G5
Bahama Is. • West Indies 37 F2
Bahama Sea • West Indies 124 D3
Bahamas • West Indies .... 124 B
Bahamas Nat. Trust Park • Bahamas 124 B4
Bahariya Oasis • Egypt 101 F3
Bahau • Malaysia 108 D4
Bahawalnagar • Pakistan 28 B3
Bahawalpur • Pakistan 28 B3
Bahia • Honduras 37 D4
Bahia • Brazil 44 H1
Bahía Blanca • Argentina 45 D3
Bahía Grande • Majorca, Spain 87 H3
Bahia Honda • Cuba 124 D1
Bahia Honda State Recreation Area • FL, United States 119 M8
Bahía Negra • Paraguay 44 E1
Bahías, Camarones Cabo dos • Argentina 45 C4
Bahla Heritage C • Oman .... 63 [105]
Bahr • Chad/Sudan 21 D5
Bahr al Abyad, Al • Sudan 21 F5
Bahr al Azraq, Al • Sudan 21 F5
Bahr al Ghazal • Sudan 23 D2
Bahr Dar • Ethiopia 21 F5
Bahr el Arab • Sudan 19 G4
Bahraich • India 105 C3
Bahrain • Asia 18 F4
Bai Bung, Mui • Vietnam 108 B3
Baia Mare • Romania 14 K2
Báia Sardinia • Sardinia, Italy 90 C2
Baião • Brazil 45 (1) B2
Baibokoum • Chad 21 C6
Baicheng • China 29 G1
Baie Comeau • QU, Canada 123 D1

Baie Lazare Village • Seychelles 106 F1
Baie Verte • NF, Canada 123 D3
Baiersbronn • Germany 82 G6
Baiersbronn Spa • Germany .... 83 [185]
Baiguan • China 107 J4
Baijiahohu • China 107 H3
Baikal, Lake • Russian Fed. 27 G6
Baikal, Lake Heritage N • Russian Fed. .... 61 [65]
Baikal-Amur Railway • Russian Fed. 97 A5
Baikonur Cosmodrome • Kazakhstan 96 A2
Baile Atha Cliath • Ireland 79 E2
Bailén • Spain 11 H6
Bailundo • Angola 23 B6
Baina Beach • Goa, India 105 B1
Bainbridge • FL, United States 119 M2
Baing • Indonesia 32 (1) B5
Baingoin • China 28 E2
Baio Grande • Spain 11 C1
Baird Peninsula • NU, Canada 39 P3
Bairiki • Kiribati 33 I5
Bairnsdale • VI, Australia 111 G3
Baise • France 10 F10
Baitenghu Resort • Zhuhai, China 107 H3
Baitou • D.P.R. of Korea 30 E4
Baixo Longa • Angola 24 B3
Baixo-Alentejo • Portugal 11 C6
Baiyun [Apt] • China 107 H1
Baja • Hungary 13 H11
Baja California • Mexico 40 D6
Baja California [Adm] • Mexico 40 C6
Baja California Sur • Mexico 40 D6
Baja Nuevo • West Indies 124 A1
Bajas, Rías • Spain 11 B2
Baka • Sudan 23 E3
Bakadzicite • Bulgaria 15 H1
Bakal • Russian Fed. 26 I7
Bakala • Central African Rep. 22 I3
Bakanas • Kazakhstan 26 M9
Bakaueni • Indonesia 110 D1
Bakchar • Russian Fed. 26 N6
Bake • Indonesia 32 C3
Baker • Senegal 22 B2
Baker • Pacific Ocean 33 J5
Baker • OR, United States 117 E4
Baker Lake • NU, Canada 38 L4
Baker Lake [Lake] • NU, Canada 38 L4
Bakersfield • CA, United States 117 F6
Bakhta • Russian Fed. 26 O5
Bakhtaran • Iran 18 E3
Bakhuhn, Kuh-e • Iran 18 G4
Baki • Azerbaijan 18 E1
Bakio Beach • Spain .... 68 [69]
Bakir • Turkey 15 I4
Bakken Park • Denmark .... 73 [17]
Bakony • Hungary 13 G10
Bakoye • Mali 22 B2
Baku • Azerbaijan 18 E1
Bakungan • Indonesia 110 B1
Bala • Turkey 15 O4
Bala Morghab • Afghanistan 26 J10
Balabac • Philippines 31 F5
Balabac I. • Philippines 31 F5
Balabac, Selat • Malaysia/Philippines 31 F5
Balaban • Turkey 15 O4
Balaghat • India 28 C4
Balagne • Corsica, France 85 L1
Balaguer • Spain 11 L3
Balakovo • Russian Fed. 17 H4
Balan Dagi • Turkey 15 J7
Balandra • Trinidad & Tobago 125 K2
Balashov • Russian Fed. 17 G4
Balassagyarmat • Hungary 13 I9
Balaton • Hungary 13 G11
Balatonfüred • Hungary 13 G11
Balawan • Indonesia 32 (1) B4
Balazote • Spain 11 I6
Balbi • Papua New Guinea 35 (1) J2
Balboa • Panama 58 B9
Balbriggan • Ireland 79 E2
Balcarce • Argentina 127 D4
Balchik Beach • Bulgaria .... 69 [212]
Balchik • Bulgaria 97 D4
Balclutha • New Zealand 112 L4
Balcones Escarpment • TX, United States 119 N3
Balderschwang • Germany 82 J5
Baldeyneysee • Germany 81 E2
Baldy Peak • AZ, United States 118 J4
Balé Gong Palace • Bali, Indonesia 110 C4
Bale Mtns Nat. Park Park • Ethiopia .... 103 [65]
Balearic Is. • Spain 11 N5
Balearic Is. • Spain 11 N5
Balease, Gunung • Indonesia 32 (1) B3
Baleia, Ponta de • Brazil 45 (1) D5
Baleine, Grande Rivière de la • QU, Canada 39 P5
Baleine, Rivière à la • QU, Canada 39 R5
Baler • Philippines 31 G3
Baleshwar • India 28 F4
Balestrand • Norway 94 C4
Baley • Russian Fed. 27 I6
Balhaf • Yemen 18 E7
Bali • Crete, Greece 93 E2
Bali • Kiribati 33 J4
Bali • Indonesia .... 110 C
Bali Aga • Bali, Indonesia 110 C2
Bali Handara • Bali, Indonesia 110 C2
Bali Sea • Indonesia 110 C2
Bali, Selat • Indonesia 110 C1
Balik Pulau Forest Reserve • Penang, Malaysia 108 C3
Balikesir • Turkey 92 D3
Balikesir • Turkey 15 K5
Balikpapan • Indonesia 32 F3
Balimbing • Indonesia 31 F5
Balimo • Papua New Guinea 35 (1) C2
Balingen • Germany 82 G6
Balkash Köli • Kazakhstan 26 M8
Balkhash • Kazakhstan 26 L8
Balkhash, Lake • Kazakhstan 26 M8
Ball's Pyramid • NS, Australia 34 K6
Balladonia • WA, Australia 34 E6
Ballaghaderreen • Ireland 79 F2
Ballangen • Norway 94 C4
Ballantrae • United Kingdom 7 H6
Ballarat • VI, Australia 111 G3
Ballás • Egypt 21 F3
Ballenita, Punta • Chile 44 B4
Balleny Is. • Antarctica 46 (1) V3
Ballestas, Is. • Peru 43 B6
Ballia • India 105 C8
Ballina • NS, Australia 111 F6
Ballina • Ireland 79 F4
Ballinasloe • Ireland 79 F4
Ballinrobe • Ireland 79 F4
Ballinskelligs Beach • Ireland .... 68 [41]
Ballinskelligs • Ireland 79 F7
Ballintober Abbey • Ireland 79 F1
Ballivor • Ireland 79 E1
Ballna • NS, Australia 111 G1
Ballybunion Beach • Ireland .... 68 [41]

Ballybunion • Ireland 79 F5
Ballycastle Beach • United Kingdom .... 75 [223]
Ballycastle • United Kingdom 78 A2
Ballycastle • Ireland 79 F2
Ballydehob • Ireland 79 F7
Ballyhaunis • Ireland 79 F1
Ballyheige Beach • Ireland .... 68 [41]
Ballyheige • Ireland 79 F5
Ballylynnan • Ireland 79 E3
Ballymena • United Kingdom 7 F7
Ballymena [Adm] • United Kingdom 75 A3
Ballymoney • United Kingdom 75 A3
Ballymore Eustace • Ireland 79 E3
Ballymote • Ireland 79 F2
Ballytore • Ireland 79 E3
Ballyvaughan Beach • Ireland .... 68 [42]
Ballyvaughan • Ireland 79 F4
Balmedie Beach • United Kingdom .... 75 [8]
Balmoral • United Kingdom 74 C1
Balochistan • Pakistan 18 H4
Balonne • QL, Australia 105 C5
Balotra • India 105 C5
Balranald • NS, Australia 34 H6
Bals • Romania 14 L5
Balsams, The Ski • NH, United States .... 116 [217]
Balsas • Brazil 45 (1) B3
Balsas • Mexico 123 E4
Bâlsta • Sweden 95 D2
Bâlti • Moldova 14 O2
Baltic Coast • Poland 96 B1
Baltic cruise area • Europe 59 A4
Baltic Republics • Europe 96 A1
Baltic Sea • Europe 16 J8
Baltim • Egypt 101 F1
Baltimore • Ireland 79 F8
Baltimore • MD, United States 118 H3
Baltimore Washington Int. Airport • MD, United States 118 H3
Baltinglass • Ireland 79 E3
Baltiysk • Russian Fed. 13 I3
Baltrum • Germany 8 C3
Baltum Spa • Germany .... 83 [39]
Balve • Germany 9 C5
Balya • Turkey 15 I4
Bam • Iran 18 G4
Bam Co • China 28 F2
BAM Railway • Russian Fed. 97 A5
Bama • Nigeria 22 H2
Bamaga • QL, Australia 34 H2
Bamako • Mali 22 C2
Bambari • Central African Rep. 23 C2
Bamberg • Germany 9 F7
Bamberg Heritage C • Germany .... 64 [46]
Bambili • Dem. Rep. of Congo 23 D3
Bambio • Central African Rep. 22 H4
Bambolim Beach • Goa, India 105 B1
Bambouto, Mts • Cameroon 22 G3
Bamburi • Brazil 127 C1
Bamburgh Beach • United Kingdom .... 75 [15]
Bamburi Beach • Kenya 101 G5
Bamenda • Cameroon 22 G3
Bamiangi • Afghanistan 18 I3
Bamingui-Bangoran, Parc nat. du Park • Central African Rep. .... 103 [45]
Bamovskoye • Russian Fed. 97 A6
Bampur • Iran 18 H4
Bampur [Riv] • Iran 18 G4
Ban Bang Po • Ko Samui, Thailand 109 J1
Ban Bophut • Ko Samui, Thailand 109 J1
Ban Chaweng • Ko Samui, Thailand 109 J1
Ban Chaweng Noi • Ko Samui, Thailand 109 J2
Ban Chiang Heritage C • Thailand .... 63 [172]
Ban Chiang • Thailand 109 H1
Ban Hong • Thailand 109 G3
Ban Houayxay • Laos 31 C2
Ban Hua Thanon • Ko Samui, Thailand 109 J2
Ban Klaeng • Thailand 109 H4
Ban Laem • Thailand 109 H3
Ban Lamai • Ko Samui, Thailand 109 J2
Ban Lipa Noi • Ko Samui, Thailand 109 J2
Ban Maenam • Ko Samui, Thailand 109 J1
Ban Me Thuot • Vietnam 108 B2
Ban Pae • Thailand 109 H4
Ban Phang Ka • Ko Samui, Thailand 109 J2
Ban Pong • Thailand 109 H1
Ban Sa Ket • Ko Samui, Thailand 109 J2
Ban Sa Kret • Ko Samui, Thailand 109 J2
Ban Tah • Thailand 109 H3
Ban Tai • Ko Samui, Thailand 109 J1
Ban Taling Ngam • Ko Samui, Thailand 109 J2
Ban Thale • Ko Samui, Thailand 109 J2
Ban Thong Krut • Ko Samui, Thailand 109 J2
Ban Thong Tanot • Ko Samui, Thailand 109 J2
Ban Thurian • Ko Samui, Thailand 109 J2
Ban Tong Yang • Ko Samui, Thailand 109 J2
Banaadir • Somalia 23 G3
Banaba • Kiribati 33 H5
Banados del Izozog • Bolivia 44 D2
Banalia • Dem. Rep. of Congo 23 D3
Banamba • Mali 22 C2
Banapur • India 28 E4
Banas • Egypt 101 F5
Banat • Romania 14 I4
Banaz • Turkey 15 K5
Banaz [Riv] • Turkey 15 K5
Banbury • United Kingdom 74 D4
Banc d'Arguin Nat. Park Heritage N • Mauritania .... 61 [70]
Banc d'Arguin Nat. Park Park • Mauritania .... 103 [13]
Banco Chinchorro • Mexico 37 D4
Bancroft • OT, Canada 122 B6
Banda • India 28 D3
Banda Aceh • Indonesia 110 B1
Banda, Kepulauan • Indonesia 32 (1) C3
Banda Sea • Indonesia 32 (1) C4
Bandama • Côte d'Ivoire 22 D3
Bandama • Gran Canaria, Canary Is. 86 E4
Bandar Seri Begawan • Brunei 31 E5
Bandar-e 'Abbas • Iran 18 G4
Bandar-e Anzali • Iran 18 F2
Bandar-e Khomeyni • Iran 18 E4
Bandar-e Langeh • Iran 18 G4
Bandar-e Maqam • Iran 18 F4
Bandar-e Torkeman • Iran 18 F2
Bandeira, Pico da • Brazil 127 C2
Bandelier Nat. Mon. • NM, United States 118 J2
Bandelier Nat. Mon. Park • NM, United States .... 120 [129]
Banderas, Bahía de • Mexico 37 (1) A1

Bandiagara Cliffs Heritage N • Mali .... 61 [69]
Bandipur Nat. Park • India 106 D6
Bandirma • Turkey 92 D3
Bandirma • Turkey 92 D3
Bandirma Körfezi • Turkey 15 J3
Bandol Beach • France .... 68 [116]
Bandon • France 85 H3
Bandon • Ireland 79 F8
Bandon • OR, United States 117 E3
Bandos • Maldives 106 E4
Bandundu • Dem. Rep. of Congo 23 B4
Bandundu [Adm] • Dem. Rep. of Congo 23 B4
Bandung • Java, Indonesia 110 D2
Bandungan • Java, Indonesia 110 D7
Baneasa [Apt] • Romania 97 C1
Banes • Cuba 124 D8
Banff • AL, Canada 122 C4
Banff Nat. Park • AL, Canada 122 C4
Bang Kaong Beach • Phuket, Thailand 109 K1
Bang Pa-In • Thailand 109 H1
Bang Saen • Thailand 109 H4
Bang Thao • Phuket, Thailand 109 K1
Bang Thao Beach • Phuket, Thailand 109 K1
Bangalore • India 106 D6
Banganapalle • India 106 D3
Bangang Co • China 28 C2
Bangaram I. • India 106 D9
Bangassou • Central African Rep. 23 C3
Bangeta • Papua New Guinea 35 (1) D2
Banggai • Indonesia 32 (1) B3
Banggi • Malaysia 31 F5
Banghazi • Libya 21 C1
Bangil • Java, Indonesia 110 D8
Bangka • Indonesia 32 D3
Bangkalan • Indonesia 110 D4
Bangkao Bay • Ko Samui, Thailand 109 J2
Bangkok • Thailand 109 H1
Bangkok, Bight of • Thailand 109 H3
Bangladesh • Asia 28 E4
Bangli • Bali, Indonesia 110 C4
Bangor • N. Ireland, UK 7 G7
Bangor • Wales, UK 7 H8
Bangor • Ireland 79 F1
Bangor • ME, United States 118 G4
Bangui • Central African Rep. 23 B3
Bangweulu, Lake • Zambia 24 D2
Bangyai • Phuket, Thailand 109 K2
Bani • Mali 22 C2
Bani Walid • Libya 21 B1
Banja • Syria 98 A2
Banja Luka • Bosnia-Herz. 14 E5
Banjar • Bali, Indonesia 110 C1
Banjar • Java, Indonesia 110 D6
Banjarmasin • Indonesia 32 E3
Banjul • Gambia 22 A2
Bank I. • BC, Canada 38 E6
Bankas • Mali 20 E6
Bankberg • South Africa 100 C4
Bankeryd • Sweden 95 F7
Banks I. • QL, Australia 34 H2
Banks I. • NT, Canada 38 G2
Banks Is. • Vanuatu 35 (1) B1
Banks Peninsula • New Zealand 35 D6
Banks Strait • TS, Australia 34 I8
Bann • United Kingdom 7 F7
Bannockburn • United Kingdom 74 B3
Bannu • Pakistan 28 B2
Banridge • United Kingdom 75 A3
Bansin Beach • Germany .... 69 [12]
Bansin Spa • Germany .... 83 [285]
Banská Bystrica • Slovak Rep. 13 I9
Banská Stiavnica • Slovak Rep. 13 H9
Banská Stiavnica Heritage C • Slovak Rep. .... 64 [149]
Banten • Java, Indonesia 110 D7
Bantham Beach • United Kingdom .... 75 [120]
Bantry • Ireland 79 F7
Bantry Bay • Ireland 79 F7
Bañuelo • Spain 11 G6
Banyak, Kepulauan • Indonesia 110 B3
Banyalbufar • Majorca, Spain 87 H1
Banyo • Cameroon 22 G3
Banyoles • Spain 11 N2
Banyuls • France 84 B4
Banyuls-sur-Mer Beach • France .... 68 [111]
Banyumas • Java, Indonesia 110 D8
Banyuwangi • Java, Indonesia 110 D8
Banyuwedang • Bali, Indonesia 110 C1
Bao Loc • Vietnam 108 B2
Bao'an • China 107 H3
Baoding • China 29 F3
Baoji • China 29 D4
Baoqing • China 27 L7
Baoshan • Yunnan, China 29 B5
Baoshan • Shanghai, China 107 J2
Baoting • China 29 C2
Baoulé • Côte d'Ivoire/Mali 22 C2
Bapaume • France 44 C3
Baquedano • Chile 44 C3
Bar • F.R. of Yugoslavia 14 G7
Bar • France 5 H5
Bar Am • Israel 98 A2
Bar Harbor • ME, United States 118 G4
Bar-le-Duc • France 10 K5
Barabinsk • Russian Fed. 26 M6
Barabinskaya Step • Russian Fed. 26 M6
Baracaldo • Spain 11 H1
Baracoa • Cuba 124 E8
Baracoa • Brazil 127 C1
Barahona • Dominican Rep. 37 G4
Baraki Barak • Afghanistan 18 I3
Baranja • Hungary 14 F4
Barano d'Ischia • Italy 91 N3
Baranov I. • AK, United States 38 D5
Baranovichi • Belarus 16 N10
Barat Daya, Kepulauan • Indonesia 110 A7
Baratang • India 28 G3
Barawe • Somalia 23 G3
Barbacena • Brazil 127 C1
Barbados • West Indies .... 125 H
Barbar • Sudan 21 F4
Bárbara • Colombia 43 C4
Barbaresco • Italy 91 E5
Barbaros • Turkey 15 I3
Barbary Coast • Africa 59 C5-6
Barbastro • Spain 11 L2
Barbate de Franco • Spain 86 B3

Barbate, Ensenada de • Spain 86 B3
Barbâte • Corfu, Greece 92 B1
Barbeau Peak • NU, Canada .... 36 [64]
Barbezieux • France 85 G1
Barbuda • Antigua & Barbuda 37 I4
Barca de Alva • Portugal 11 F3
Barcaldine • QL, Australia 111 F3
Barcarès, the Beach • France .... 68 [111]
Barcellona Pozzo di Gotto • Sicily, Italy 12 J10
Barcelona • Spain 11 L6
Barcelona • Venezuela 43 E2
Barcelona Heritage C • Spain .... 64 [71-72]
Barcelona Beach • Spain .... 68 [105]
Barcelona • Spain 87 D3
Barcelonette • France 85 H2
Barcelos • Brazil 43 E4
Barcoo • QL, Australia 111 E7
Barcs • Hungary 13 K8
Bardai • Chad 21 C3
Bardejov • Slovak Rep. 13 K8
Bardere • Somalia 23 G3
Bardeskan • Iran 26 I10
Bardo • Tunisia 12 E12
Bardolino • Italy 91 E7
Bardonecchia Ski • Italy .... 70 [196]
Bardonecchia • Italy 91 E5
Bareda • Somalia 23 I1
Barèges • France 85 J2
Bareilly • India 105 C3
Barentin • France 10 F4
Barents Sea • Arctic Ocean 4 S2
Barentsburg • Svalbard 46 N2
Barfleur • France 5 B5
Barfleur, Point de • France 5 B5
Barga • China 28 D2
Bargal • Somalia 23 I1
Bargarh • India 28 D4
Barguzinskiy Khrebet • Russian Fed. 27 H6
Bari • Italy 12 K7
Barinas • Venezuela 43 C2
Baringo, Lake • Kenya 101 G1
Baripada • India 28 E4
Barisal • Bangladesh 28 F4
Barisov • Belarus 17 D4
Barito • Indonesia 32 E3
Barka • Oman 18 G5
Barkat Nasser • Egypt 18 B5
Barkerville • BC, Canada 122 C1
Barkly Tableland • NT, Australia 34 G3
Barlee, Lake • WA, Australia 34 C5
Barletta • Italy 12 K7
Barlinek • Poland 13 E4
Barlovento de Jandia, Playa de • Fuerteventura, Canary Is. 87 E2
Barma • Indonesia 32 (1) B3
Barmer • India 105 C5
Barmera • SA, Australia 34 H6
Barmouth • United Kingdom 7 H9
Barmouth Beach • United Kingdom .... 75 [188]
Barnaul • Russian Fed. 26 N7
Barnes Hill • Antigua & Barbuda 125 F1
Barneville-Carteret • France 10 D4
Barneville-Carteret Beach • France .... 68 [58]
Barnsley • United Kingdom 7 K8
Barnstaple • United Kingdom 74 F2
Barnstaple Bay • United Kingdom 74 F2
Barolo • Italy 91 E5
Baronia • Sardinia, Italy 90 C2
Baros • Maldives 106 E2
Barossa Valley • SA, Australia 111 E7
Barqah al Bahriyah • Egypt/Libya 21 E1
Barqu, Jabal • Tunisia 12 D12
Barquisimeto • Venezuela 43 D2
Barra • Brazil 45 (1) C4
Barra de Navidad • Mexico 123 E3
Barra de Tijuca • Brazil 127 C3
Barra do Cuanza • Angola 23 A5
Barra Falsa, Ponta da • Mozambique 24 F4
Barra Mansa • Brazil 127 C3
Barra, Ponta da • Mozambique 24 F4
Barração do Barreto • Brazil 43 F5
Barranca • Peru 43 B4
Barrancabermeja • Colombia 43 C2
Barrancas • Venezuela 43 E2
Barranco del Velho • Portugal 88 E3
Barranqueras • Argentina 44 E4
Barranquilla • Colombia 43 C1
Barre • VT, United States 118 G3
Barre de l'Isle • St Lucia 125 J2
Barreiras • Brazil 45 (1) C4
Barreiro • Portugal 88 D2
Barreiros Beach • Brazil .... 68 [72]
Barren • Madagascar 24 G3
Barren Grounds • NU, Canada 122 A2
Barreta, I. da • Portugal 88 E7
Barretos • Brazil 44 G3
Barrie • OT, Canada 122 B5
Barrier Reef Reserve System Heritage N • Belize .... 60 [21]
Barrington, Fort • Antigua & Barbuda 125 F1
Barrington Tops • NS, Australia 34 J6
Barrow • Ireland 79 F4
Barrow • AK, United States 46 EE2
Barrow Creek • NT, Australia 112 H2
Barrow I. • WA, Australia 34 C4
Barrow, Point • AK, United States 36 B2
Barrow-in-Furness • United Kingdom 74 C1
Barry I. Pleasure Beach Park • United Kingdom .... 73 [33]
Barry I. Pleasure Beach • United Kingdom 74 F2
Barry's Amusement Park Park • United Kingdom .... 73 [21]
Barrys Bay • OT, Canada 122 B6
Barsac • France 84 B3
Barstow • CA, United States 117 F6
Bartin • Germany 8 E4
Bartin • Turkey 15 N2
Bartle Frere, Mt • QL, Australia 111 F1
Bartlet Town • Bahamas 124 B2
Bartoszyce • Poland 13 J3
Baru, Volcán • Panama 37 E6
Barúmini • Sardinia, Italy 90 C4
Barumun • Indonesia 110 B4
Barun Bagdo-Ula • Mongolia 29 B2
Barung • Indonesia 110 D8
Barwon • NS/QL, Australia 111 E8
Barycz • Poland 13 F6
Bas Médoc • France 84 B3
Bas-Rhin • France 10 M4
Basak • Cambodia 108 B1
Basankusu • Dem. Rep. of Congo 23 B3
Basauri • Spain 11 I1
Bascuñan, Cabo • Chile 44 B4
Basdorf • Germany 81 G2
Basel • Switzerland 9 C9
Basey • Philippines 31 H4
Bashi Haixia • Taiwan 29 G5
Bashkortostan • Russian Fed. 17 J3
Basilan • Philippines 31 G5
Basildon • United Kingdom 74 E2
Basilicata • Italy 91 N1
Basingstoke • United Kingdom 7 K10
Baskatong, Réservoir • QU, Canada 122 B3
Basle • Switzerland 82 G7
Basoko • Dem. Rep. of Congo 23 C3

Basque Coast • Spain 86 A1
Basque, Côte • France 85 J1
Basque Country • Spain 86 A1
Basque, Pays • France 85 J1
Basrah • Iraq 18 E3
Bass Lake • CA, United States 117 F3
Bass Strait • TS/VI, Australia 34 I7
Bassae Heritage C • Greece .... 64 [180]
Basse • Togo 22 E3
Bassas da India • Reunion 24 F3
Basse Normandie • France 84 A1
Basse Terre • Guadeloupe 37 I4
Basse-Casamance, Parc nat. de Park • Senegal .... 103 [9]
Bassein • Myanmar 31 A3
Bassenthwaite • United Kingdom 74 C1
Bassenthwaite Lake • United Kingdom 74 C1
Basseterre • St Kitts & Nevis 125 G1
Basseterre Bay • St Kitts & Nevis 125 G1
Bassila • Benin 22 E3
Basso, Plateau de • Chad 21 D4
Bassum • Germany 5 L2
Bâstad • Sweden 95 F11
Bastelica • Corsica, France 85 L3
Basti • India 105 C4
Bastia • Italy 12 G5
Bastia • Corsica, France 85 L2
Bastogne • Belgium 8 A19
Bastrop • LA, United States 118 K1
Bastrop • TX, United States 119 N3
Bat Heritage C • Oman .... 63 [106]
Bata • Equatorial Guinea 22 F4
Batabanó, Golfo de • Cuba 124 D1
Batagay • Russian Fed. 27 L3
Batagay-Alyta • Russian Fed. 27 L3
Batak • Bulgaria 14 L8
Bataklik Gölü • Turkey 15 O6
Batalha Heritage C • Portugal .... 64 [97]
Batan Is. • Philippines 31 G2
Batang • China 29 B5
Batangafo • Central African Rep. 23 B2
Batanghari • Indonesia 32 C3
Batangos • Philippines 31 G4
Batchelor • NT, Australia 34 F2
Batchelor, Mt • OR, United States 117 E3
Bâtdâmbâng • Cambodia 31 C4
Batéké, Plateaux • Congo 22 G5
Batemans Bay • NS, Australia 111 G2
Bath Heritage C • United Kingdom .... 64 [19]
Bath • United Kingdom 74 F3
Bath • Jamaica 124 C4
Bath • St Kitts & Nevis 125 G4
Batha • Chad 21 C5
Bathgate • United Kingdom 74 B4
Bathsheba • Barbados 125 H2
Bathurst • NU, Canada 38 J3
Bathurst • NS, Australia 111 G2
Bathurst • NB, Canada 123 D2
Bathurst, Cape • NT, Canada 38 F2
Bathurst I. • NT, Australia 34 F2
Bathurst Inlet • NU, Canada 46 J3
Batna • Algeria 20 G1
Bato-Bato • Philippines 31 F5
Baton Rouge • LA, United States 118 K4
Batouri • Cameroon 23 A3
Battenberg • Germany 9 D5
Batti Maly • India 28 F7
Batticaloa • Sri Lanka 106 D16
Battipaglia • Italy 91 G4
Battle • AL, Canada 38 I6
Battle • United Kingdom 74 E4
Battle Creek • MI, United States 41 I3
Battle Harbour • NF, Canada 39 T6
Battle Mountain • NV, United States 117 F2
Batu • Ethiopia 23 F2
Batu Berinchang, Gunung • Malaysia 108 D1
Batu Caves • Malaysia 108 D1
Batu Gajah • Malaysia 108 D1
Batu, Kepulauan • Indonesia 110 B4
Batu Pahat • Malaysia 32 C2
Batu Putih, Gunung • Malaysia 108 D1
Batuasa • Indonesia 32 (1) D3
Batukau, Gunung • Bali, Indonesia 110 C2
Batumi • Georgia 17 G6
Batur, Danau • Bali, Indonesia 110 C2
Batur, Gunung • Bali, Indonesia 110 C2
Batur Temple • Bali, Indonesia 110 C2
Baturaja • Indonesia 32 C3
Baturino • Russian Fed. 26 O6
Batusangkar • Indonesia 110 B4
Baubau • Indonesia 32 (1) B4
Baucau • East Indies 32 (1) C4
Bauchi • Nigeria 22 F2
Bauchi [Adm] • Nigeria 22 F2
Baudry • Switzerland 89 G1
Baudry [Château] • France 84 D2
Bauld, Cape • NF, Canada 123 D5
Baule-Escoublac, la • France 84 C4
Bauru • Brazil 44 G3
Bauska • Latvia 13 N1
Bautzen • Germany 9 J5
Bavaria • Germany 81 D4
Bavarian Alps • Germany 81 D4
Bavella, Col de • Corsica, France 85 L4
Båven • Sweden 95 D3
Baw Sang • Thailand 109 G1
Bawamataluo • Indonesia 110 B3
Bawe • Indonesia 32 (1) D3
Bawean • Indonesia 110 D4
Bawiti • Egypt 101 F3
Bawku • Ghana 22 D2
Baxoi • China 28 G2
Baxter State Park • ME, United States 118 G2
Bay City • MI, United States 118 F3
Bay City • NT, United States 118 F3
Bay City • TX, United States 119 N6
Bay Is. • Honduras 124 A1
Bay of Islands • New Zealand 35 E2
Bay of Plenty [Adm] • New Zealand 112 J2
Bay View • New Zealand 112 K4
Bayad, Al • Saudi Arabia 18 E5
Bayadh, El • Algeria 20 F2
Bayah Har Shan • China 28 H2
Bayamo • Cuba 124 D8
Bayamón • Puerto Rico 125 C1
Bayan • Mongolia 29 B2
Bayan Har Shan • China 28 H2
Bayan Lepas • Penang, Malaysia 108 C3
Bayan Lepas [Apt] • Penang, Malaysia 108 C3
Bayan Obo • China 29 D3
Bayan Ul • Mongolia 27 H7
Bayana • India 105 C4
Bayanga • Central African Rep. 23 B3
Bayda, Al • Libya 21 D1

Baydaratskaya Guba • Russian Fed. 26 K4
Bayerisch Gmain Spa • Germany .. 83 [261]
Bayerische Alpen • Germany.. 82 J7
Bayerischer Wald • Germany.. 9 I8
Bayern • Germany 9 G8
Bayeux • France 10 E4
Baykal, Ozero • Russian Fed.... 25 L4
Baykalskiy Khrebet • Russian Fed. 27 G6
Baykit • Russian Fed. 26 Q5
Baykonyr • Kazakhstan.. 26 K8
Bayona • Spain 11 C2
Bayonne • France 11 C2
Bayram-Ali • Turkmenistan.. 18 H2
Bayramiç • Turkey 15 H4
Bayreuth • Germany 9 G7
Bayrischer Wald, Nationalpark Park • Germany .... 72 [64]
Bayrischzell Ski • Germany .. 70 [4]
Bayrischzell • Germany.. 82 J7
Bayrischzell Spa • Germany .. 83 [259]
Bayrut • Lebanon 18 B3
Baytik Shan • China 26 O8
Baytown • TX, United States .. 119 N4
Bayy al Kabir • Libya 21 B1
Baza • Spain 86 B4
Bazardüzü • Azerbaijan .. 17 H6
Bazas • France 85 G3
Be'er Shiva • Israel 18 B3
Beachy Head • United Kingdom.. 74 E3
Beadnell Bay Beach • United Kingdom .... 75 [17]
Béalanga • Madagascar .. 24 H2
Béar, Cap • France 85 K2
Bear Cove • BC, Canada .. 122 C3
Bear Creek Ski • MI, United States .. 116 [127]
Bear I. • Ireland 79 F7
Bear Valley Ski • CA, United States .. 116 [60]
Beara Peninsula • Ireland.. 79 F7
Béarn • France 85 J2
Beas • India 28 E5
Beata, Cabo • Dominican Rep... 37 G4
Beatrice • NE, United States.. 41 G3
Beatty • NV, United States.. 117 F4
Beau Vallon, Baie • Seychelles.. 106 F1
Beaufort • Malaysia 32 F1
Beaufort • Luxembourg.. 80 A20
Beaufort • NC, United States.. 118 H5
Beaufort I. • Hong Kong, China.. 107 H6
Beaufort Sea • Arctic Ocean.. 36 C2
Beaufort West • South Africa.. 100 C3
Beaugency • France 84 D4
Beaujolais • France 84 B4
Beaulieu-sur-Mer • France.. 85 H2
Beaumaris Beach • United Kingdom .... 75 [216]
Beaumont • France 5 B5
Beaumont • New Zealand.. 112 L4
Beaumont • TX, United States.. 119 N4
Beaune • France 10 J6
Beauregard (Château) • France .. 84 D2
Beauséjour, Fort • NB, Canada.. 123 D7
Beauté, I. de • France 84 B4
Beauvais • France 85 E1
Beauval • SA, Canada.. 38 J5
Beauvoir-sur-Mer • France.. 10 C7
Beaver Creek Ski • CO, United States .. 116 [95]
Beaver Valley Ski • OT, Canada.. 116 [19]
Beawar • India 44 G3
Bebedouro • Brazil 44 G3
Bebra • Germany 9 E6
Becej • F.R. of Yugoslavia.. 14 H4
Béchar • Algeria 20 E2
Bechet • Romania 14 K6
Bechyne • Czech Rep... 96 C4
Beckley • WV, United States.. 41 J4
Beckum • Germany 8 D5
Bective Abbey • Ireland.. 79 E1
Bedarieux • France 10 I10
Bedarra I. • QL, Australia .. 111 F1
Bedburg • Germany 81 E3
Bedford • United Kingdom.. 7 L9
Bedford Level • United Kingdom.. 5 C2
Bedfordshire • United Kingdom.. 75 A5
Bedulu • Bali, Indonesia.. 110 C4
Beek [Apt] • Netherlands.. 80 A15
Beekse Bergen • Netherlands.. 80 A11
Beersheba • Israel 39 F5
Beesands Beach • United Kingdom 75 [115]
Beeston • United Kingdom.. 7 K9
Beeville • TX, United States.. 119 N5
Bega • NS, Australia 111 G4
Begejski Kanal • F.R. of Yugoslavia/Romania.. 14 H4
Beggars Point • Antigua & Barbuda.. 125 F1
Begna • Norway 95 C5
Begur Beach • Spain .... 68 [106]
Begur • Spain 87 D2
Behbahan • Iran 18 F2
Behshahr • Iran 18 F2
Bei Jiang • China 31 E2
Bei'an • China 27 K7
Beida He • China 29 B3
Beihai • China 29 D6
Beijing • China 9 H4
Beijing Heritage C • China.. 63 [146]
Beijing [Adm] • China.. 107 G3
Beila • Mauritania 20 B5
Beilstein • Germany 82 H3
Beira • Mozambique 24 E3
Beira Alta • Portugal 11 D4
Beira Baixa • Portugal 11 D4
Beira Litoral • Portugal 11 C4
Beirut • Lebanon 18 B3
Beit el Wali • Egypt 101 F5
Beitbridge • Zimbabwe.. 102 J4
Beius • Romania 14 J3
Beja • Portugal 11 D6
Béja • Tunisia 101 E1
Béja [Adm] • Portugal.. 88 A3
Bejaïa • Algeria 20 G1
Béjar • Spain 11 F4
Beji Temple • Bali, Indonesia.. 110 C2
Bekal • India 106 D6
Bekasi • Java, Indonesia.. 110 D1
Bekdash • Turkmenistan.. 18 F1
Békés • Hungary 13 K11
Bekily • Madagascar .. 24 H4
Bela • Pakistan 28 A3
Bela, Costa • Portugal.. 88 D2
Bela Crkva • F.R. of Yugoslavia.. 14 I5
Bela Pratapgarh • India.. 105 C8
Bela Vista • Mozambique.. 24 E5
Belaga • Malaysia 32 (1) B2
Belang • Indonesia 32 (1) B2
Belau • Europe 15 D4
Belawan • Indonesia.. 110 B2
Belaya • Russian Fed... 4 V6
Belaya • Russian Fed... 27 T3
Belayan • Indonesia.. 32 F2
Belchatów • Poland 13 I6
Belchen • Germany 82 G8
Belcher Is. • NU, Canada.. 39 P5
Belchite • Spain 10 E12
Beldibi Beach • Turkey .. 69 [201]

Beldibi • Turkey 93 G3
Beled Weyne • Somalia.. 23 H4
Belek • Turkey 93 G3
Belém • Brazil 45 (1) B2
Belém • Portugal 88 D1
Belen • NM, United States.. 118 J2
Belep, Is. • New Caledonia.. 35 (2) A2
Beleye • Ethiopia 23 F1
Belfast • United Kingdom.. 7 G7
Belford • United Kingdom.. 6 K6
Belfort • France 10 L6
Belfort • Lebanon 98 A2
Belfry, The • United Kingdom.. 74 D2
Belgaum • India 106 D2
Belgium • Europe 5 H4
Belgodere • Corsica, France.. 85 L1
Belgorod • Russian Fed... 17 F4
Belgrade • F.R. of Yugoslavia.. 14 H5
Belhaven Bay Beach • United Kingdom .... 75 [14]
Bélice • Sicily, Italy.. 90 D1
Beliche • Portugal 88 E5
Bélinga • Gabon 22 G4
Belitung • Indonesia.. 32 D3
Belize • C. America 37 D4
Belize City • Belize 37 D4
Beljanica • F.R. of Yugoslavia.. 14 I5
Bell • QU, Canada 39 P7
Bell Peninsula • NU, Canada.. 39 O4
Bell Ville • Argentina 44 C5
Bella Coola • BC, Canada.. 38 F6
Bellac • France 84 D4
Bellágio • Italy 91 E2
Bellamonte Ski • Italy.. 70 [219]
Bellamonte • Italy 90 B3
Bellanta • Italy 12 G4
Bellary • India 106 D15
Belle Glade • FL, United States.. 119 M6
Belle Isle • FL, United States.. 121 C2
Belle Isle, Strait of • NF, Canada 123 D5
Belleayre Ski • NY, United States .... 116 [180]
Bellegarde-sur-Valserine • France 85 F1
Bellplaine • Barbados.. 125 H1
Belleville • OT, Canada.. 122 B6
Bellevue • WA, United States.. 117 E1
Bellevue, Grotte de • France.. 85 G4
Bellewaerde Park Park • Belgium 73 [47]
Bellingham • WA, United States.. 117 E1
Bellinghausen [Base] • Antarctica 46 (1) JJ4
Bellingshausen Sea • Pacific Ocean 46 (1) GG4
Bellinzona • Switzerland.. 89 G7
Bello • Colombia 43 B2
Belluno • Italy 90 B4
Bellville • South Africa.. 100 C5
Bellwald • Switzerland.. 89 G6
Belm • Germany 8 D4
Belmonte • Brazil 44 I2
Belmopan • Belize 37 D4
Belo Horizonte • Brazil.. 127 C1
Belo-Tsiribihina • Madagascar.. 24 G3
Beloeil • Belgium 80 A14
Belogorsk • Russian Fed... 27 K6
Belomorsk • Russian Fed... 17 E2
Beloretsk • Russian Fed... 26 I7
Belot, Lac • NT, Canada.. 38 F3
Beloveshskaya Pushcha Heritage N • Belarus .... 61 [49]
Belovo • Russian Fed... 26 O7
Beloye More • Russian Fed... 17 F1
Beloye Ozero • Russian Fed... 17 F2
Belozersk • Russian Fed... 17 F3
Belp [Apt] • Switzerland.. 89 G2
Belukha, gora • Kazakhstan/Russian Fed... 26 O8
Belur • India 106 D6
Belvoir • Israel 98 A4
Belyando • QL, Australia.. 111 F3
Belyy, Ostrov • Russian Fed... 26 L3
Bemaraha, Plateau du • Madagascar 24 G3
Bembe • Angola 22 G6
Ben Gardane • Tunisia.. 101 E6
Ben Mehidi • Algeria.. 12 B12
Bena Dibele • Dem. Rep. of Congo.. 23 C4
Benabarre • Spain 10 F11
Benalla • VI, Australia.. 111 G3
Benalmádena Costa • Spain.. 86 B7
Benares • India 105 C8
Benaulim • Goa, India.. 105 B2
Benaulim Beach • Goa, India.. 105 B2
Benavente • Spain 11 F3
Benavente • Portugal.. 88 D2
Benbecula • United Kingdom.. 75 A1
Benbulbin • Ireland 79 F2
Bend • OR, United States.. 117 E3
Bendara, Bukit • Penang, Malaysia.. 108 C1
Bendel • Nigeria 22 F3
Bender • Moldova 14 O3
Bender Bayla • Somalia.. 23 I2
Bendigo • VI, Australia.. 111 G3
Bendinat, Castell de • Majorca, Spain.. 87 H3
Bendorf • Germany 82 H1
Bénéna • Mali 20 E6
Benesov • Severocesky, Czech Rep... 96 C2
Benesov • Stredocesky, Czech Rep... 96 C2
Benevento • Italy 91 G2
Bengal, Bay of • Indian Ocean.. 28 E5
Bengbu • China 29 F4
Benghazi • Libya 21 C1
Bengkalis • Indonesia.. 32 C2
Bengkulu • Indonesia.. 32 C3
Bengo, Baia do • Angola.. 22 G6
Bengtsfors • Sweden.. 95 E2
Benguela • Angola 23 A6
Benguerir • Morocco.. 101 D3
Bengut, Cap • Algeria.. 20 F1
Beni • Dem. Rep. of Congo.. 23 D3
Beni • Bolivia 44 C1
Beni Abbès • Algeria.. 20 E2
Beni Boufrah • Morocco.. 11 G9
Beni Hammâd Heritage C • Algeria .... 64 [221]
Beni Hasan • Egypt 101 F3
Beni Mellal • Morocco.. 20 D2
Beni Saf • Algeria 11 J9
Beni Suef • Egypt 101 F1
Benicarló • Spain 11 L4
Benicàssim Beach • Spain.. 68 [103]
Benidorm Beach • Spain.. 68 [101]
Benidorm • Spain 87 C2

Benin • Africa 22 E3
Benin, Bight of • Nigeria.. 22 E3
Benin City • Nigeria.. 22 F3
Benin Forcados • Nigeria.. 22 E3
Benisa Beach • Spain.. 68 [101]
Benisa • Spain 87 C2
Benito Juárez • Argentina.. 127 D3
Benitses • Corfu, Greece.. 92 B1
Benitses • Corfu, Greece.. 92 B1
Benjamin • Jordan 98 A6
Benjamin Constant • Brazil.. 43 D4
Benkovac • Croatia 14 C5
Benllech Beach • United Kingdom 75 [214]
Bennett, W.A.C., Dam • BC, Canada 122 C1
Bennington • VT, United States.. 118 G3
Benoa, Port • Bali, Indonesia.. 110 C4
Benom • Malaysia 108 D2
Benone Beach • United Kingdom 75 [219]
Benoni • South Africa.. 24 D5
Bénoué • Cameroon/Chad.. 22 G3
Bénoué, Parc nat. de la Park • Cameroon .... 103 [40]
Benrath, Schloß • Germany.. 81 E3
Bensafrim • Portugal.. 88 E5
Bensheim • Germany.. 82 H4
Benson • AZ, United States.. 118 J4
Bent's Old Fort Nat. Hist. Site Park • CO, United States.. 120 [98]
Benta Sebarang • Malaysia.. 108 D2
Benteng • Togian, Indonesia.. 32 (1) B3
Benteng • Selajar, Indonesia.. 32 (1) B4
Bentinck I. • QL, Australia.. 34 G3
Bentiu • Sudan 23 D2
Bento Gonçalves • Brazil.. 44 F4
Bentota • Sri Lanka 106 D15
Benue • Nigeria 22 G3
Benue [Adm] • Nigeria.. 22 G3
Benwee Head • Ireland.. 79 F1
Benxi • China 29 G2
Beo • Indonesia 32 (1) C2
Beograd • F.R. of Yugoslavia.. 14 H5
Berach • India 105 C6
Berat • Albania 15 A3
Beratus, Gunung • Indonesia.. 32 F3
Berber • Somalia 23 G1
Berbérati • Central African Rep... 23 B3
Berchtesgaden • Germany.. 82 J8
Berchtesgaden Spa • Germany.. 83 [262]
Berchtesgaden, Nationalpark Park • Germany .... 72 [65]
Berchtesgaden, Nationalpark • Germany 82 J8
Berck-sur-Mer Beach • France.. 68 [55]
Berdichev • Ukraine.. 17 D5
Berdyansk • Ukraine.. 17 F5
Berechid • Morocco.. 101 D1
Beregovo • Ukraine.. 13 L9
Berehove • Ukraine.. 14 I1
Berenice • Egypt 18 B5
Beresti • Romania 14 O3
Berettyóújfalu • Hungary.. 13 K10
Berezniki • Russian Fed... 17 G2
Berezovka • Russian Fed... 26 J5
Berezovo • Russian Fed... 26 J5
Berg • Germany 82 J3
Berga • Spain 87 D1
Berga • Sweden 95 F7
Bergama • Turkey 15 I4
Bergamo • Italy 91 E6
Bergara • Spain 11 I1
Bergeggi Beach • Italy.. 68 [121]
Bergen • Germany 8 E4
Bergen Heritage C • Norway.. 64 [1]
Bergen • Norway 94 C3
Bergen op Zoom • Netherlands.. 80 A10
Berger, David, Nat. Mem. Park • OH, United States.. 121 [189]
Bergerac • France 85 G2
Berggießhübel Spa • Germany.. 83 [319]
Bergisch Gladbach • Germany.. 81 F2
Bergisch Gladbach: Bensberg • Germany 81 E2
Bergischer Dom • Germany.. 81 E2
Bergkamen • Germany.. 81 E2
Bergkvara • Sweden.. 95 F12
Bergnaustadt • Germany.. 81 E4
Bergö • Sweden 95 D2
Bergün • Switzerland.. 89 D5
Berhampur • India 28 D5
Bering Land Bridge Nat. Preserve Park • AK, United States.. 120 [5]
Bering Sea • Pacific Ocean.. 46 HH4
Bering Strait • Russian Fed./United States.. 40 (2) G2
Beringa, Ostrov • Russian Fed... 27 S5
Beringen • Belgium.. 5 I3
Beringov Proliv • Russian Fed... 27 X3
Berja • Spain 11 I8
Berja Beach • Spain.. 68 [99]
Berkåk • Norway 95 F5
Berkakit • Russian Fed... 27 J5
Berkel • Netherlands.. 5 J2
Berkner I. • Antarctica.. 46 (1) JJ2
Berkshire • United Kingdom.. 75 A6
Berkshire Downs • United Kingdom 7 K10
Berkshire East Ski • MA, United States.. 116 [192]
Berlengas, Is. • Portugal.. 11 B5
Berlevåg • Norway.. 16 I1
Berlin Heritage C • Germany.. 64 [31]
Berlin • Germany 81 F2
Berlin • NH, United States.. 118 G3
Berlin [Adm] • Germany.. 81 F2
Berlin: Buch • Germany.. 81 F2
Berlin: Buchow • Germany.. 81 F2
Berlin: Dahlem • Germany.. 81 F3
Berlin: Köpenik • Germany.. 81 F2
Berlin: Kreuzberg • Germany.. 81 F2
Berlin: Lichtenberg • Germany.. 81 F2
Berlin: Lichtenrade • Germany.. 81 F2
Berlin: Marzahn • Germany.. 81 F2
Berlin: Mitte • Germany.. 81 F2
Berlin: Neukölln • Germany.. 81 F2
Berlin: Pankow • Germany.. 81 F2
Berlin: Prenzlauer Berg • Germany 81 F2
Berlin: Reinickendorf • Germany.. 81 F2
Berlin: Schöneberg • Germany.. 81 F2
Berlin: Spandau • Germany.. 81 E2
Berlin: Steglitz • Germany.. 81 F2
Berlin: Tegel • Germany.. 81 F2
Berlin: Tempelhof • Germany.. 81 F2
Berlin: Treptow • Germany.. 81 F4
Berlin: Wannsee • Germany.. 81 F2
Berlin: Wedding • Germany.. 81 F2
Berlin: Weissensee • Germany.. 81 F2
Berlin: Wilmersdorf • Germany.. 81 F2
Berlin: Zehlendorf • Germany.. 81 F2

Bermejo • Argentina 44 C5
Bermeo • Spain 10 C10
Bermeo Beach • Spain.. 68 [69]
Bermillo de Sayago • Spain.. 11 E3
Bermuda • Atlantic Ocean.. 36 K6
Bern Heritage C • Switzerland.. 64 [102]
Bern • Switzerland 89 G2
Bernalda • Italy .... 68 [145]
Bernau • Germany.. 91 E8
Bernam • Malaysia.. 108 D1
Bernau bei Berlin • Germany.. 81 F2
Bernau-Hof • Germany.. 82 G8
Bernay • France 10 F4
Bernburg • Germany.. 8 F5
Berne Heritage C • Switzerland.. 64 [102]
Berne • Switzerland.. 89 G2
Berner Alpen • Switzerland.. 89 G6
Berner Oberland • Switzerland.. 89 G2
Bernina, Passo del • Switzerland 89 G8
Bernina, Piz • Italy/Switzerland.. 89 G8
Bernkastel-Kues • Germany.. 81 E3
Berntorffs Isfjord • Greenland.. 39 W4
Beroroha • Madagascar.. 24 H4
Beroun • Germany 13 D8
Berounka • Czech Rep... 96 C1
Berovo • F.Y.R. of Macedonia.. 15 D2
Berri • S. Australia.. 10 H7
Berry Is. • Bahamas.. 124 B1
Bertioga • Brazil 127 C3
Bertoua • Cameroon.. 22 G4
Beruas • Malaysia 108 D1
Beruwala • Sri Lanka.. 106 D15
Berwick-upon-Tweed • United Kingdom 6 J6
Besakih Temple • Bali, Indonesia.. 110 C2
Besalampy • Madagascar.. 24 G3
Besançon • France 10 L6
Besar, Gunung • Indonesia.. 32 F3
Beshwar, Mt • Antarctica.. 46 (1) L2
Besikama • Indonesia.. 32 (1) B4
Besnyakh • Russian Fed... 27 J3
Besna Kobila • F.R. of Yugoslavia.. 14 J7
Besparmak Dagi • Turkey.. 15 I6
Bessarabia • Moldova.. 14 P2
Bestensee • Germany.. 81 F4
Bestobe • Kazakhstan.. 26 L7
Bet Guvrin • Israel 98 A7
Bet She'an • Israel 98 A4
Bet She'arim • Israel.. 98 A4
Betalbatim Beach • Goa, India.. 105 B2
Betancuria • Fuerteventura, Canary Is... 87 E2
Betanzos, Ría de • Spain.. 11 C1
Beth Horon • Jordan.. 98 A5
Beth-zur • Jordan.. 98 A7
Bethany • Jordan.. 98 A7
Bethany Beach • DE, United States.. 118 H3
Bethel • AK, United States.. 40 (2) E2
Bethel • AK, United States.. 46 FF3
Bethel • Jordan 98 A6
Bethesda • Antigua & Barbuda.. 125 [102]
Bethlehem • South Africa.. 24 D5
Bethlehem • Jordan.. 98 A7
Bethlehem • PA, United States.. 118 H3
Béthune • France 10 H3
Bethune, Mary McLeod, Council House Nat. Hist. Site Park • DC, United States.. 121 [289]
Betioky [Riv] • France.. 5 J8
Betis Nat. Park • India.. 105 C8
Béticos, Sistemas • Spain.. 11 G7
Betong • Malaysia.. 108 C3
Betsiboka • Madagascar.. 24 H3
Betsiamites • QU, Canada.. 39 M6
Bette • Libya 21 C3
Bettembourg • Luxembourg.. 70 [25]
Bettmeralp Ski • Switzerland.. 70 [99]
Bettmeralp • Switzerland.. 89 G6
Bettwiesen • Sweden.. 95 D3
Betty's Hope • Antigua & Barbuda.. 125 F4
Betul • Madhya Pradesh, India.. 28 C4
Betul • Goa, India.. 105 B2
Betul Beach • Goa, India.. 105 B2
Betwa • India 28 C4
Betzdorf • Germany.. 9 C6
Beuil-les-Launes Ski • France.. 70 [73]
Beuren Spa • Germany.. 83 [192]
Beuren, Kloster • Germany.. 82 H8
Beuvron • France 5 G5
Beverley • United Kingdom.. 7 L8
Beverungen • Germany.. 8 E5
Beverwijk • Netherlands.. 80 C1
Bexhill Beach • United Kingdom.. 75 [70]
Bexhill-on-Sea • United Kingdom 74 E4
Bexon • St Lucia 125 J1
Bey Daglari • Turkey.. 93 G3
Beykoz • Turkey 15 K2
Beyla • Guinea 22 C3
Beyneu • Kazakhstan.. 26 I8
Beypazari • Turkey.. 15 M3
Beyrouth • Lebanon.. 18 B3
Beysehir • Turkey 93 G2
Beysehir Gölü • Turkey.. 93 G3
Bezhetsk • Russian Fed... 17 E3
Béziers • France 10 I10
Bezwada • India 28 D5
Bhadravati • India 106 D6
Bhagalpur • India 105 C8
Bhaktapur • Nepal.. 105 C4
Bhamo • Myanmar.. 31 B2
Bharatpur • India 105 C2
Bharuch • India 28 B4
Bhatinda • India 28 B2
Bhatpara • India 28 E4
Bheemavaram • India.. 106 D4
Bheri • Nepal 105 C6
Bhilwara • India 105 C2
Bhima • India 106 D2
Bhiwani • India 28 C2
Bhopal • India 28 C4
Bhubaneswar • India.. 28 D4
Bhuj • India 28 B4
Bhumiphol Reservoir • Thailand.. 109 G3
Bhutan • Asia 28 E3
Bi'r al Hakim • Libya.. 21 D1
Bi'r al Wa'r • Libya.. 21 B1
Bi'r Allaq • Libya.. 21 B1
Bi'r Misrahah • Egypt.. 21 B1
Bia Nat. Park Park • Ghana.. 103 [26]
Biafra, Bight of • Africa.. 22 F4
Biak • Indonesia 32 (1) D3
Biala • Indonesia 32 (1) D3
Biala Podlaska • Poland.. 13 M5
Biala Slatina • Bulgaria.. 14 K6
Bialograd • Poland.. 13 E3
Bialowieski Nat. Park Park • Poland .... 72 [94]
Bialowieza Nat. Park Heritage N • Poland .... 61 [49]
Bialystok • Poland.. 13 M4

Biaora • India 105 C6
Biarritz • France 85 J1
Biasca • Switzerland.. 89 G7
Bibai • Japan 30 K3
Biberach • Germany.. 82 J1
Biberach-Jordanbad Spa • Germany .... 83 [215]
Bibione Beach • Italy.. 68 [145]
Bibione • Italy 91 E8
Bicaz • Romania 14 M3
Bicholim • Goa, India.. 105 B1
Bickerton I. • NT, Australia.. 34 G2
Bida • Nigeria 22 F3
Bidar • India 28 C5
Biddeford • ME, United States.. 118 G3
Bideford • United Kingdom.. 74 F2
Bideford Bay • United Kingdom.. 74 F2
Bidur • Malaysia 108 D1
Bidwell Mansion State Hist. Park • CA, United States.. 117 F1
Bié, Planalto do • Angola.. 23 B6
Biebrza • Poland 13 L4
Biebrzanski Nat. Park Park • Poland .... 72 [93]
Biedenkopf • Germany.. 9 D6
Biel • Switzerland.. 89 G2
Bielefeld • Germany.. 8 D4
Bieler See • Switzerland.. 89 G2
Biella • Italy 91 E5
Bielsk Podlaski • Poland.. 13 M5
Bielsko-Biala • Poland.. 13 I8
Bien Hoa • Vietnam.. 108 B1
Bienville, Lac • QU, Canada.. 39 Q5
Bierset [Apt] • Belgium.. 80 A15
Biertan Heritage C • Romania.. 64 [165]
Biervliet • Netherlands.. 80 A10
Biesbosch • Netherlands.. 80 C4
Biesenthal • Germany.. 81 F2
Bieszczady • Poland.. 13 L9
Bieszczadzki Nat. Park Park • Poland .... 72 [95]
Bifuka • Japan 30 L2
Big Bear Lake • CA, United States.. 117 F6
Big Bend Nat. Park Park • TX, United States.. 120 [138]
Big Boulder Ski • PA, United States.. 116 [166]
Big Cypress Nat. Preserve • FL, United States.. 119 M8
Big Cypress Nat. Preserve Park • FL, United States.. 121 [225]
Big Cypress Swamp • FL, United States.. 119 M8
Big Hole Nat. Battlefield Park • MT, United States.. 120 [69]
Big Mtn Ski • MT, United States.. 116 [73]
Big Pine Key • FL, United States.. 119 M8
Big Powderhorn Mtn Ski • MI, United States.. 116 [126]
Big Sioux • IA/SD, United States.. 38 L8
Big Sky Ski • MT, United States.. 116 [74]
Big Smoky Valley • NV, United States.. 117 F4
Big Spring • TX, United States.. 40 F5
Big Sur • CA, United States.. 117 F3
Big Thicket Nat. Preserve • TX, United States.. 119 N4
Big Thicket Nat. Preserve Park • TX, United States.. 121 [144]
Big Trout Lake • OT, Canada.. 39 M6
Big Vanilla at Davos Ski • NY, United States.. 116 [178]
Big White Ski • BC, Canada.. 116 [6]
Biga • Turkey 15 I3
Bigadiç • Turkey 15 J4
Bigbury Bay • United Kingdom.. 74 F5
Biggar • United Kingdom.. 74 B4
Bighorn • MT/WY, United States.. 38 J8
Bighorn Canyon Nat. Recreation Area Park • MT, United States.. 120 [70]
Bighorn Mtns • WY, United States.. 40 E3
Bigorre • France 85 J2
Biguglia, Etang de • Corsica, France.. 85 L2
Bihac • Bosnia-Herz... 14 C5
Bihar • India 28 E4
Bihar [Adm] • India.. 28 E4
Biharamulo • Tanzania.. 102 J2
Bihoro • Japan 30 M3
Bijapur • India 106 D2
Bijawar • India 105 C7
Bijelina • Bosnia-Herz... 14 G5
Bijouter • Seychelles.. 106 F4
Bikaner • India 105 C1
Bikin • Russian Fed... 29 I1
Bikin [Riv] • Russian Fed... 27 M7
Bikini • Marshall Is... 33 H4
Bikoro • Dem. Rep. of Congo.. 22 H5
Bila Tserkov • Ukraine.. 17 E5
Bilaspur • India 28 D4
Bilauktaung Range • Myanmar/Thailand.. 31 B4
Bilbao • Spain 10 C10
Bilecik • Turkey 15 K3
Bilesha Plain • Kenya.. 23 G3
Bilibino • Russian Fed... 27 S3
Bilin • Myanmar 109 G3
Bilin • China 30 B5
Billings • MT, United States.. 40 E2
Billund • Denmark.. 95 F9
Bilma • Niger 20 H5
Bilma, Grand Erg de • Niger.. 20 H5
Biloela • QL, Australia.. 111 F4
Bilogora • Croatia.. 13 L7
Biloku • Guyana 43 F3
Biloxi • MS, United States.. 118 K4
Bilthoven • Netherlands.. 80 C2
Bilthe • Chad 21 D5
Bimberi Peak • AC/NS, Australia.. 34 I7
Bimbo • Central African Rep... 23 B3
Bimini Is. • Bahamas.. 124 B1
Bin Ghunayah, Jabal • Libya.. 21 C2
Bina • India 105 C7
Bindura • Zimbabwe.. 102 J3
Binga • Zimbabwe.. 102 J1
Bingen • Germany.. 9 C6
Binghampton • NY, United States.. 118 H1
Bingöl • Turkey 17 G6
Binh Dinh • Vietnam.. 108 C1
Binic • France 84 B3
Binjai • Indonesia 110 B2
Bintan • Indonesia 32 C2
Bintulu • Malaysia.. 32 E2
Bintumani, Mt Park • Sierra Leone.. 103 [14]
Binz • Germany 8 G3
Binz Beach • Germany.. 68 [13]
Biograd na Moru • Croatia.. 14 D6
Biograd Gora Nat. Park Park • Fed. Rep. of Yugoslavia.. 72 [119]
Bioko • Equatorial Guinea.. 22 F4
Biokovo • Croatia.. 14 E6

Bir • India 28 C5
Bir Gandus • Western Sahara.. 20 B4
Bir Lehlú • Western Sahara.. 20 D3
Bir Mogrein • Mauritania.. 20 C3
Bir Shalatein • Egypt.. 21 G3
Bira Racing Circuit • Thailand.. 109 H4
Birak • Libya 21 B2
Birao • Central African Rep... 23 C1
Biratnagar • Nepal.. 28 E3
Birchington Beach • United Kingdom .... 75 [62]
Bird • MN, Canada.. 38 M5
Bird I. • Seychelles.. 106 F2
Bird I. • West Indies.. 124 A3
Bird, V.C. [Apt] • Antigua & Barbuda.. 125 F1
Birdsville • QL, Australia.. 34 G5
Bireuen • Indonesia.. 110 B1
Birganj • Nepal 28 D3
Birhet el Bibane • Tunisia.. 101 E6
Birao • Iran 18 G3
Bir, A. • Saudi Arabia.. 18 D6
Birka Heritage C • Sweden.. 64 [4]
Birkeland • Norway.. 95 F1
Birkenhead • United Kingdom.. 7 I8
Birkenwerder bei Berlin • Germany 81 F1
Bîrlad • Romania 14 O3
Bîrlad [Riv] • Romania.. 14 O3
Birling Gap Beach • United Kingdom .... 75 [73]
Birmingham • AL, United States.. 41 I5
Birmingham • United Kingdom.. 74 D2
Birni Nkonni • Niger.. 20 G6
Birnie • Kiribati 33 J6
Birnin Gwari • Nigeria.. 20 G6
Birnin Kebbi • Nigeria.. 22 E2
Birobidzhan • Russian Fed... 27 L7
Birr • Ireland 7 E8
Birsk • Russian Fed... 17 J3
Birsz • China 28 F2
Birun • Uzbekistan..
Biryusa • Russian Fed... 27 E5
Birzai • Lithuania 13 N1
Birzebbuga • Malta.. 93 H4
Bisanadi Game Reserve • Kenya.. 101 G2
Bisau • India 105 C2
Biscarosse • France.. 85 G3
Biscay, Bay of • France.. 4 J8
Biscayne Nat. Park • FL, United States.. 119 M8
Biscayne Nat. Park Park • FL, United States.. 121 [222]
Bisceglie • Italy 14 D8
Bischofsgrün Spa • Germany.. 83 [227]
Bischofshofen • Austria.. 9 I8
Bischofswerda • Germany.. 81 F3
Bischofswiesen Spa • Germany.. 83 [262]
Biserta • Tunisia 71 A18
Bisevo • Croatia.. 14 D7
Biševski Kanal • Croatia.. 14 D6
Bishkek • Kyrgyzstan.. 26 L8
Bishop • South Africa.. 24 D6
Bishop • CA, United States.. 117 F4
Bishop Auckland • United Kingdom 7 K7
Bishop's Stortford • United Kingdom 74 E1
Biskra • Algeria 20 G2
Bislig • Philippines.. 31 H5
Bismarck • ND, United States.. 40 F2
Bismarck Archipelago • Papua New Guinea.. 35 (1) D1
Bismarck Sea • Pacific Ocean.. 35 (1) D1
Bismo • Norway 94 C3
Bissau • Guinea-Bissau.. 22 A2
Bistcho Lake • AL, Canada.. 38 H5
Bistrita • Romania 14 L2
Bistrita [Riv] • Romania.. 14 M2
Bitam • Gabon 22 G4
Bitburg • Germany.. 82 H3
Bitche • France 5 K5
Bitea • Chad 21 D5
Bithia • Sardinia, Italy.. 90 C4
Bitkine • Chad 20 I6
Bitola • F.Y.R. of Macedonia.. 14 I8
Bitonto • Italy 12 K7
Bitra I. • India 106 D9
Bitterfeld • Germany.. 8 F5
Bitterfontein • South Africa.. 24 B6
Bitterroot Range • ID/MT, United States.. 117 E2
Bittersweet Ski • MI, United States.. 116 [142]
Bitti • Sardinia, Italy.. 12 D8
Bitumount • AL, Canada.. 38 I5
Biu • Nigeria 22 G2
Bivolari • Romania.. 14 O2
Biwako • Japan 30 I7
Biyadoo • Maldives.. 106 D7
Biysk • Russian Fed... 26 O7
Bizerte • Tunisia 101 E2
Bjarnahvölm • Sweden.. 95 F11
Bjelolasica • Croatia.. 14 B4
Bjelovar • Croatia.. 14 D4
Bjergsted Beach • Denmark.. 68 [24]
Bjerringbro • Denmark.. 95 F9
Bjeshkët e Nemuna • Albania/F.R. of Yugoslavia.. 14 G7
Bjerkelangen • Norway.. 94 B2
Bjørklinge • Sweden.. 95 D2
Bjørkö • Sweden.. 95 C2
Bjørkvik • Sweden.. 95 D3
Bjørna • Sweden.. 16 J5
Bjørnafjorden • Norway.. 94 C3
Bjørneborg • Finland.. 95 F11
Bjørnlunda • Sweden.. 95 D3
Bjørnön • Arctic Ocean.. 4 O2
Bla • Mali 20 E6
Blåbjerg Beach • Denmark.. 68 [32]
Black Canyon • AZ/NV, United States.. 118 J1
Black Canyon of the Gunnison Nat. Mon. Park • CO, United States.. 120 [91]
Black Country • United Kingdom.. 74 D2
Black Forest • Germany.. 82 G8
Black Head • United Kingdom.. 74 F4
Black Hills • SD, United States.. 40 F3
Black Lady Mtn • Vietnam.. 108 B1
Black Mountains • United Kingdom 74 D3
Black River • China/Vietnam.. 108 A1
Black River • Jamaica.. 124 C3
Black Rock • Barbados.. 125 H3
Black Rock Desert • NV, United States.. 117 F2
Black Sea • Europe.. 17 E6
Black Sea Coast • Turkey.. 92 A3
Black Sea Coast • Turkey.. 93 A3
Black Sea Coast • Bulgaria/Romania.. 97 D
Black sea cruise area • Asia/Europe.. 59 C
Black Sugarloaf, The • NS, Australia.. 34 J6
Blackall • QL, Australia.. 111 F3

Blackbeard's Grave • Bahamas 124 B3
Blackburn • United Kingdom 7 J8
Blackburn, Mt •
  AK, United States 38 C4
Blackcomb Ski • BC, Canada .. 116 [2]
Blackdown Hills •
  United Kingdom 74 F2
Blackmount • New Zealand 112 L3
Blackness Castle •
  United Kingdom 74 B4
Blackpool • United Kingdom 7 I8
Blackpool Pleasure Beach Park •
  United Kingdom .... 73 [22]
Blackpool Sands Beach •
  United Kingdom .... 75 [112]
Blacksburg • VA, United States ... 41 J4
Blacksod Bay • Ireland 79 F1
Blackstone River Valley Nat. Heritage
  Corridor Park •
  MA, United States .... 121 [341]
Blackwater • Neath, Ireland 79 E1
Blackwater • Cork, Ireland 79 F8
Blåfjellhatten • Norway 16 G4
Blagnac [Apt] • France 85 G4
Blagoevgrad • Bulgaria 14 K7
Blagoveshchensk • Russian Fed. ... 27 K6
Blaine • WA, United States 117 E1
Blair Athol • QL, Australia 111 F3
Blair Drummond Safari Park •
  United Kingdom 74 B3
Blairgowrie • United Kingdom 74 B2
Blaj • Romania 14 K3
Blambangan, Semenanjung •
  Java, Indonesia 110 D8
Blanc, Cap [Majorca, Spain 11 N5
Blanc, Cap • Tunisia 101 E2
Blanc, Mont • France/Italy 85 F2
Blanc Sablon • QU, Canada 123 D5
Blanca, Bahía • Argentina 45 D3
Blanca, Costa • Spain .... 87 C
Blanca Peak • CO, United States .. 40 E4
Blanche, Lake • SA, Australia 34 G5
Blanchisseuse •
  Trinidad & Tobago 125 K1
Blanco • Bolivia 44 D2
Blanco, Cape •
  OR, United States 117 E3
Blandford Forum •
  United Kingdom 74 F3
Blanes Beach • Spain .... 68 [106]
Blanes • Spain 87 D4
Blangkerejen • Indonesia 110 B1
Blangy-sur-Bresle • France 5 E5
Blankahoim • Sweden 95 F8
Blankenberge • Belgium 80 B2
Blankenburg Spa • Germany .. 83 [294]
Blankenfelde • Germany 81 F4
Blankenheim • Germany 82 H1
Blanquilla • Venezuela 43 E1
Blanquilla, I. • Venezuela 124 A6
Blansko • Czech Rep. 13 F8
Blantyre • Malawi 24 F3
Blantyre-Limbe • Malawi 24 F3
Blarney • Ireland 79 F8
Blåsjøen • Norway 94 C6
Blatna • Czech Rep. 96 C3
Blaubeuren • Germany 82 J1
Blåvands Huk Beach • Denmark .. 68 [32]
Blåvands Huk • Denmark 95 F9
Blavet • France 84 C4
Blaye • France 85 G1
Bledes, Is. • Ibiza, Spain 87 G1
Blefjell • Norway 94 B1
Bleking • Sweden 95 F12
Blenheim • New Zealand 35 D5
Blenheim Palace Heritage C •
  United Kingdom .... 64 [21]
Blenheim Palace •
  United Kingdom 74 D4
Blenhorst Spa • Germany ...... 83 [62]
Blessington • Ireland 79 E3
Bletchley • United Kingdom 7 L10
Blida • Algeria 11 N6
Blidö • Sweden 95 D2
Blies • Germany 5 K5
Blieskastel • Germany 82 G3
Blieskastel Spa • Germany .... 83 [169]
Bligh Sound • New Zealand 112 L1
Blind River • OT, Canada 39 O7
Blitar • Java, Indonesia 110 D7
Blitta • Togo 22 E3
Blizzard Beach •
  FL, United States 121 C1
Block I. • NY, United States 118 H2
Bloemfontein • South Africa 24 D5
Blois • France 84 D2
Blois [Château] • France 84 D2
Blommestein, W.J. van, Meer •
  Suriname 43 F3
Bloody Point • St Kitts & Nevis .. 125 G1
Bloomington • IL, United States .. 41 I3
Bloomington • IN, United States .. 41 I4
Bludenz • Austria 89 H5
Blue Basin Falls •
  Trinidad & Tobago 125 K1
Blue Grotto • Malta 93 H4
Blue Hole • Jamaica 124 C2
Blue Lagoon • Malta 93 H1
Blue Mtn Ski • OT, Canada .... 116 [20]
Blue Mtn Ski •
  PA, United States .... 116 [165]
Blue Mtn Peak • Jamaica 124 C4
Blue Mtns • NS, Australia 111 G2
Blue Mtns • OR, United States .. 117 E4
Blue Mtns • Jamaica 124 C4
Blue Nile • Sudan 21 F5
Blue Ridge • United States 117 D8
Blue Ridge Parkway Park •
  NC/VA, United States .... 121 [245]
Bluefields • Nicaragua 37 E5
Bluefields • Jamaica 124 C1
Bluefields Bay • Jamaica 124 C3
Bluenose Lake • NU, Canada 38 H3
Bluff • New Zealand 112 L4
Bluff Point • WA, Australia 34 B5
Blumberg • Germany 82 H5
Blumberg • Germany 81 F2
Blumenau • Brazil 44 G4
Blyth • United Kingdom 7 K6
Bø • Sierra Leone 22 B3
Bø • Norway 94 B3
Bo Hai • China 29 F3
Bo River • Sudan 23 D2
Bo Sai • Phuket, Thailand 109 K1
Boa Esperança, Reprêsa • Brazil .. 45 (1) C3
Boa Vista • Cape Verde 22 (1) B1
Boa Vista • Brazil 43 E1
Boac • Philippines 31 G4
Boaventura • Madeira 88 C1
Bobadilla • Spain 86 B2
Bobbejaanland Park • Belgium .. 73 [49]
Bóbbio • Italy 12 D4
Bobingen • Germany 82 J2
Böblingen • Germany 82 G6
Bobo Dioulasso • Burkina Faso ... 22 D2
Bôbr • Poland 13 E6
Bobrov • Russian Fed. 17 G4
Boby, Pic • Madagascar 24 H4
Boca de Valeria • Brazil 58 A3

Boca do Acre • Brazil 43 D5
Boca Grande • Venezuela 43 E2
Boca Raton • FL, United States .. 119 M6
Bocaranga •
  Central African Rep. 22 H3
Bocas del Amazonas • Brazil 43 F3
Bochnia • Poland 13 J8
Bocholt • Germany 8 B5
Bochum • Germany 81 E2
Bochum: Wattenscheid • Germany .. 81 E2
Bocognano • Corsica, France 85 L4
Boda • Central African Rep. 22 H4
Bodafors • Sweden 95 F7
Bodaybo • Russian Fed. 27 H5
Bode • Germany 8 G5
Bodegraven • Netherlands 80 C3
Bodelé • Chad 21 C4
Boden • Sweden 16 K4
Bodendorf Spa • Germany ... 83 [150]
Bodenmais Spa • Germany ... 83 [233]
Bodensee •
  Germany/Switzerland 82 J5
Bodenteich Spa • Germany .... 83 [59]
Bodhgaya • India 105 C8
Bodmin • United Kingdom 74 F4
Bodmin Moor • United Kingdom .. 74 F4
Bodø • Norway 16 G4
Bodrum Beach • Turkey .... 69 [207]
Bodrum • Turkey 92 D9
Bodrum • Turkey 92 D9
Bodufinolhu • Maldives 106 E4
Boduthithi Coral Isle • Maldives .. 106 C2
Bogalusa • LA, United States 118 K4
Bogarra • Spain 87 A2
Bogbonga • Dem. Rep. of Congo .. 22 H4
Bogcang Zangbo • China 28 E2
Bogda Feng • China 26 O9
Bogda Shan • China 26 O9
Bogen • Norway 16 I2
Bogenfels • Namibia 24 B5
Bogense • Denmark 95 F10
Boggeragh Mtns • Ireland 79 F8
Boggy Peak • Antigua & Barbuda .. 125 F3
Bogia • Papua New Guinea 35 (1) C1
Bogmalo Beach • Goa, India ... 105 B1
Bognor Regis • United Kingdom .. 74 E3
Bognor Regis Beach •
  United Kingdom .... 75 [77]
Bogolyubovo • Russian Fed. 97 E4
Bogor • Java, Indonesia 110 D1
Bogotá • Colombia 43 C3
Bogotol • Russian Fed. 26 O6
Bogey • Norway 16 H3
Boguchany • Russian Fed. 26 O6
Bogué • Mauritania 20 C5
Bogue Basin Ski •
  ID, United States .... 116 [71]
Bohan • Belgium 80 A19
Bohemia • Czech Rep. 96 C1
Bohemia, Garden of • Czech Rep. .. 96 C2
Bohemian Switzerland •
  Czech Rep. 96 C1
Böhmen • Czech Rep. 13 D8
Böhmerwald • Germany 9 H7
Boho • Philippines 31 G4
Bohol Sea • Philippines 31 G5
Boiaçu • Brazil 43 E4
Boina • Madagascar 24 H3
Bois d'Attilly, Parc zoologique du •
  France 85 E4
Bois, Lac des • NT, Canada 38 F3
Boise • ID, United States 117 E4
Boizenburg • Germany 8 F3
Bojador, Cabo • Morocco 20 C3
Bojano • Italy 12 I7
Bojnurd • Iran 18 G2
Bojonegoro • Java, Indonesia .. 110 D3
Bok Tower Gardens •
  FL, United States 119 M5
Boka Kotorska •
  F.R. of Yugoslavia 14 F7
Boké • Guinea 22 B2
Boknafjorden • Norway 94 C5
Boko • Congo 22 G5
Bokol Mayo • Ethiopia 23 G3
Bokoro • Chad 22 H2
Bokpyin • Myanmar 31 B4
Bol • Chad 21 B5
Bolama • Guinea-Bissau 20 B6
Bolans • Antigua & Barbuda 125 F3
Bolbec • France 10 F4
Bole • Ghana 22 D3
Bole • China 26 N9
Bolekhov • Ukraine 13 M9
Boleslawiec • Poland 13 E6
Bolgatanga • Ghana 22 D3
Bolgrad • Ukraine 14 P4
Bolia • Dem. Rep. of Congo 23 B4
Boliden • Sweden 16 K4
Bolifushi • Maldives 106 E4
Boliqueime • Portugal 88 E7
Bolívar, Cerro • Venezuela 43 C2
Bolívar, Pico • Venezuela 37 I6
Bolivia • S. America 44 C2
Bolivia, Altiplano de • Bolivia 44 C2
Bolkesjø • Norway 94 B1
Bollebygd • Sweden 95 H1
Bollnäs • Sweden 16 I6
Bollon • QL, Australia 111 F5
Bolmen • Sweden 95 F7
Bologna • Italy 12 I7
Bologne • France 84 C4
Bologoye • Russian Fed. 97 E1
Bolomba • Dem. Rep. of Congo ... 23 B3
Bolombo • Dem. Rep. of Congo ... 23 A3
Bolovens Plateau • Laos 108 A2
Bolsena • Italy 91 F1
Bolsena, Lago di • Italy 91 F1
Bolshaya Martá • Russian Fed. ... 26 P6
Bolshevik, Ostrov •
  Russian Fed. 97 A5
Bolshezemelskaya Tundra •
  Russian Fed. 26 I4
Bolshoy Anyuy • Russian Fed. 27 R3
Bolshoy Begichev, Ostrov •
  Russian Fed. 27 H2
Bolshoy Kamen • Russian Fed. .. 30 Q3
Bolshoy Lyakhovskiy, Ostrov •
  Russian Fed. 27 N2
Bolsón, Cerro del • Argentina 44 C4
Bolsón de Mapimí • Mexico 40 F6
Bolsward • Netherlands 80 A3
Boltenhagen • Germany 8 G2
Boltenhagen Beach • Germany .. 68 [17]
Boltenhagen Spa • Germany .. 83 [266]
Bolton • United Kingdom 7 J8
Bolton Valley Ski •
  VT, United States .... 116 [202]
Bolu • Turkey 15 M3
Bolu Daglari • Turkey 15 M3
Boluntay • China 28 F1
Bolvadin • Turkey 15 M5
Bolzano • Italy 91 B3
Bom Despacho • Brazil 127 C1
Bom Jesus da Lapa • Brazil 44 H1
Boma • Dem. Rep. of Congo 23 A5
Bomano, Cayo • Cuba 124 D3

Bomassa • Congo 22 H4
Bombay • India 28 B5
Bomberai, Jazirah • Indonesia .. 32 (1) D3
Bomboma • Dem. Rep. of Congo .. 22 H4
Bomi • China 28 F2
Bomi Hills • Liberia 22 B3
Bamiljorden • Norway 94 C5
Bomlo • Norway 94 C5
Bomu • Central African Rep./Dem. Rep. of
  Congo 23 C3
Bon, Cap • Tunisia 101 E2
Bona • Algeria 11 M6
Bonaire • West Indies 37 H5
Bonaparte Archipelago •
  WA, Australia 34 D3
Bonasse • Trinidad & Tobago .. 125 K3
Bonassola Beach • Italy .... 68 [123]
Bonavista • NF, Canada 123 D4
Bonavista Bay • NF, Canada ... 123 D4
Bondeno • Italy 12 F4
Bondla Wildlife Sanctuary •
  Goa, India 105 B1
Bondo • Dem. Rep. of Congo 23 C3
Bondoukou • Côte d'Ivoire 22 D3
Bondowoso • Java, Indonesia .. 110 D8
Bonerate, Kepulauan • Indonesia .. 110 A7
Bonete, Cerro • Argentina 44 C4
Bongabong • Philippines 31 G4
Bongandanga •
  Dem. Rep. of Congo 23 C3
Bongo, Massif des •
  Central African Rep. 23 C2
Bongolava • Madagascar 24 H3
Bongor • Chad 21 C5
Boni Game Reserve • Kenya 101 N5
Bonifacio • Corsica, France 85 L4
Bonifacio, Strait of •
  France/Italy 12 D7
Bonifica del Volturno • Italy 91 G1
Bonita, Playa • Cuba 124 D7
Bonita Springs •
  FL, United States 119 M7
Bonn • Germany 82 G1
Bonners Ferry •
  ID, United States 117 E2
Bonnerup Strand • Denmark 95 F10
Bonneval • France 84 D2
Bonneville • France 89 G5
Bonneville Salt Flats •
  UT, United States 117 F2
Bonny • Nigeria 22 F4
Bonorva • Sardinia, Italy 12 C8
Bontebok Nat. Park •
  South Africa 100 C6
Bontebok Nat. Park Park •
  South Africa .... 103 [118]
Bóolay I. • St Kitts & Nevis 125 G4
Booligar • NS, Australia 111 G1
Boon Point • Antigua & Barbuda .. 125 F1
Böön Tsagaan Nuur • Mongolia .. 29 B1
Boot • United Kingdom 74 C3
Boothbay Harbor •
  ME, United States 118 G4
Boothia, Gulf of • NU, Canada .. 38 M2
Boothia Peninsula • NU, Canada .. 38 M2
Booué • Gabon 22 G4
Bopfingen • Germany 82 J1
Bophut Beach •
  Ko Samui, Thailand 109 J1
Boppard • Germany 82 H2
Boppard Spa • Germany ...... 83 [156]
Boquerón • Puerto Rico 125 E2
Boquerón, Bahía de •
  Puerto Rico 125 E3
Bor • Russian Fed. 17 G3
Bor • Sudan 23 E2
Bor • Czech Rep. 96 C3
Bora Bora • French Polynesia 58 A1
Borah Peak • ID, United States .. 117 F4
Borås • Sweden 95 F7
Borborema, Planoalto da •
  Brazil 45 (1) D3
Borca di Cadore • Italy 90 B4
Borcham • Germany 8 D5
Bordeaux • France 85 G3
Borden • France 84 D1
Borden • Portugal 88 E5
Borden Peninsula • NU, Canada .. 39 O2
Borders • United Kingdom 74 B4
Bordertown • SA, Australia 34 H7
Bordeyri • Iceland 16 (1) C2
Bordighera Beach • Italy .... 68 [120]
Bordighera • Italy 91 E9
Bordj Bou Arreridj • Algeria 11 N7
Bordj el Kiffan • Algeria 11 O8
Bordj Fly St Marie • Algeria 20 E3
Bordj Menaïel • Algeria 11 O8
Bordj Messouda • Algeria 20 F2
Bordj Moktar • Algeria 20 F4
Bordj Omar Driss • Algeria 20 G3
Boreal Ski • CA, United States .. 116 [54]
Borensberg • Sweden 95 F6
Borgarfjördur • Iceland 16 (1) C2
Borgarnes • Iceland 16 (1) C2
Børgefjell • Norway 16 G4
Børgefjell Nat. Park Park •
  Norway .... 72 [10]
Borger • TX, United States 40 F4
Borgholm • Sweden 95 F8
Borglund stavkirke • Norway 94 B1
Borgo • Corsica, France 85 L4
Borislav • Ukraine 13 M8
Borisoglebsk • Russian Fed. 17 G4
Borj Bourguiba • Tunisia 101 E6
Borja • Peru 43 B4
Borken • Germany 8 B5
Borken • Germany 9 E5
Borkop Beach • Denmark ...... 68 [27]
Borkop • Denmark 95 F9
Borkou • Chad 21 C4
Borkum • Germany 8 B3
Borkum Spa • Germany .... 83 [36]
Borlänge • Sweden 16 H6
Borlu • Turkey 15 J5
Bornes-les-Mimosas Beach •
  France .... 68 [116]
Bormio Ski • Italy .... 70 [205]
Bormio • Italy 91 E3
Borna • Germany 9 H5
Borneo • East Indies 32 E3
Bornholm [Adm] • Denmark 94 A10
Bornholm [I.] • Denmark 95 F16
Bornholmsgattet •
  Denmark/Sweden 95 F1
Börnicke • Germany 81 F1
Bornova • Turkey 15 I5
Borobudur Heritage C •
  Java, Indonesia .... 63 [177]
Borobudur • Java, Indonesia ... 110 D8
Borodino • Russian Fed. 27 E5
Borohoro Shan • China 26 N9
Boromo • Burkina Faso 22 D3
Borovets • Bulgaria 96 B2
Borovichi • Russian Fed. 97 E1
Borrolola • NT, Australia 34 G3

Borrowdale • United Kingdom 74 C2
Borsa • Romania 14 L2
Borth Beach • United Kingdom .. 27 I6
Borya • Russian Fed. 27 I6
Bosa • Sardinia, Italy 90 C1
Bosanska Dubica • Croatia 12 K3
Bosanska Gradiska •
  Bosnia-Herz. 12 L3
Bosanski Petrovac •
  Bosnia-Herz. 12 K4
Bosaso • Somalia 23 H1
Boscastle • United Kingdom 74 F4
Boscobel • NY, United States ... 118 H1
Boscobel House • United Kingdom .. 74 D1
Boscobelle • Barbados 125 H1
Bosherston Beach •
  United Kingdom .... 75 [155]
Boshnyakovo, gora •
  Russian Fed. 27 N7
Boskoop • Netherlands 80 C3
Bosna • Bosnia-Herz. 14 F5
Bosna • Bulgaria 15 I1
Bosna-Herzegovina • Europe 14 F6
Bosnik • Indonesia 32 (1) D3
Boso • Japan 30 K7
Bosporus • Turkey 92 D3
Bosporus • Turkey 92 D3
Bosra Heritage C • Syria ...... 64 [242]
Bossangoa •
  Central African Rep. 23 B2
Bossentélé •
  Central African Rep. 23 A2
Bossier City •
  LA, United States 118 K1
Bosso • Niger 20 H6
Boston Hu • China 26 O9
Boston • United Kingdom 7 L7
Boston • MA, United States 118 G3
Boston African American Nat. Hist. Site
  Park •
  MA, United States .... 121 [344]
Boston Mills Ski •
  OH, United States .... 116 [148]
Boston Ski • MA, United States .. 41 H4
Boston Nat. Hist. Park Park •
  MA, United States .... 121 [345]
Boswachterij Wassenaar •
  Netherlands 80 C1
Bosworth Field • United Kingdom .. 74 D2
Botany Bay • NS, Australia 111 G2
Botevgrad • Bulgaria 15 E1
Bothnia, Gulf of •
  Finland/Sweden 16 J6
Botlek • Netherlands 80 C3
Botoșani • Romania 14 N2
Botrange • Belgium 5 J4
Botswana • Africa 24 C4
Botte Donato • Italy 12 K9
Bottrop • Germany 81 E1
Botucatu • Brazil 44 G3
Botwood • NF, Canada 123 D3
Bou Djébéha • Mali 20 E5
Bou Grara, Golfe de • Tunisia ... 101 E6
Bou Izakarn • Morocco 20 D3
Bou Maad, Djebel • Algeria 11 N8
Bou Saâda • Algeria 11 N8
Bouaké • Côte d'Ivoire 22 C3
Bouar • Central African Rep. 23 A2
Bouârfa • Morocco 20 E2
Bouba Ndjida, Parc nat. de Park •
  Cameroon .... 103 [41]
Bouca • Central African Rep. 22 H3
Bouchet, le [Château] • France .. 5 F6
Boudnib • Morocco 20 E2
Boudeuse • Seychelles 106 F2
Boufarik • Algeria 11 N8
Bougainville • Papua New Guinea .. 35 (1) F2
Bougouni • Mali 22 C2
Bouguenais • France 10 I7
Bouillon • Belgium 80 A19
Bouira • Algeria 11 O8
Boulder • CO, United States 40 E4
Boulder City •
  NV, United States 40 D4
Boulogne-Billancourt • France ... 5 F6
Boulogne-sur-Mer • France 10 G3
Boultoum • Niger 20 H6
Boumois [Château] • France 84 D1
Bouna • Côte d'Ivoire 22 D3
Bourail • New Caledonia 35 (2) B3
Bourbonnais • France 10 I7
Bourdeilles • France 85 G2
Bourem • Mali 20 E5
Bourg-en-Bresse • France 85 F1
Bourg-St-Maurice • France 85 F2
Bourges • Germany 82 H2
Bourges Heritage C • France ... 64 [56]
Bourget, le [Apt] • France 85 E2
Bourgneuf, Baie de • France 10 C6
Bourgogne • France 84 C4
Bourgueil • France 84 B1
Bourke • NS, Australia 34 I6
Bournemouth • United Kingdom .. 74 F3
Bournemouth Beach •
  United Kingdom .... 75 [84-85]
Bourscheid • Luxembourg 80 A20
Bourton-on-the-Water •
  United Kingdom 74 D4
Boussay [Château] • France 84 D4
Boussens • France 11 L1
Boutilimit • Mauritania 20 C5
Boutonne • France 85 F1
Bouvines • France 71 A7
Bova Marina • Italy 12 J11
Bovallstrand • Sweden 95 F2
Bovey Tracey • United Kingdom .. 74 F2
Boya • Peru 43 B4
Bowen • QL, Australia 111 F1
Bowie • TX, United States 119 N1
Bowie, Fort, Nat. Hist. Site •
  AZ, United States 118 J4
Bowie, Fort, Nat. Hist. Site Park •
  AZ, United States .... 120 [118]
Bowling Green •
  KY, United States 41 I4
Bowness-on-Windermere •
  United Kingdom 74 C4
Bowo • China 28 F2
Bowral • NS, Australia 111 G2
Bowron Lake Prov. Park •
  BC, Canada 122 C1
Boxholm • Sweden 95 F4
Boxmeer • Netherlands 5 I3
Boxtel • Netherlands 80 C6
Boyana Heritage C • Bulgaria ... 64 [167]
Boyle • Ireland 79 E1
Boyne • Ireland 79 E1
Boyne Highlands Ski •
  MI, United States .... 116 [129]
Boyne Mtn Ski •
  MI, United States .... 116 [128]
Boynton Beach •
  FL, United States 119 M6
Boz Burun • Turkey 15 J7
Boz Dag • Turkey 15 K6
Boz Daglari • Turkey 15 I5
Bozanski Novi • Croatia 12 K3

Bozburun • Turkey 15 J7
Bozburun Dagi • Turkey 15 M6
Bozcaada • Turkey 15 H4
Bozcaada [I.] • Turkey 92 D2
Bozdogan • Turkey 15 J6
Bozeman • MT, United States 40 D2
Bozen • Italy 90 B3
Bozene • Dem. Rep. of Congo 22 H4
Bozkir • Turkey 93 G2
Bozouls • France 10 H9
Bozoum • Central African Rep. ... 23 B2
Bozova • Turkey 93 G1
Bozovici • Romania 14 I5
Bozüyük • Turkey 15 L4
Bra • Italy 12 B4
Brabant • Belgium 80 A15
Brac • Croatia 14 D6
Bracciano • Italy 91 F1
Bracciano, Lago di • Italy 91 F1
Bräcke • Sweden 16 H5
Brackenheim • Germany 82 G6
Bracki kanal • Croatia 14 D6
Bracknell • United Kingdom 7 L10
Brad • Romania 14 J3
Bradano • Italy 12 K8
Bradenton • FL, United States . 119 M5
Bradford • United Kingdom 7 K8
Bradley [Apt] •
  CT, United States 118 H2
Braemar • United Kingdom 6 I4
Braga [Adm] • Portugal 88 A1
Braga [Adm] • Portugal 88 A1
Bragado • Argentina 127 D1
Bragança • Portugal 11 E3
Bragança [Adm] • Portugal 88 A1
Bragança [Adm] • Portugal 45 (1) B2
Bragança Paulista • Brazil 127 C3
Brahestad • Finland 16 M4
Brahmani • India 28 E4
Brahmaputra • Asia 28 E3
Braila • Romania 97 D2
Braithwaite • United Kingdom 74 C2
Braj • India 105 C2
Braja • Portugal 11 C3
Brake • Germany 8 D3
Brålanda • Sweden 95 F3
Bramadero, Bahía • Puerto Rico .. 125 E3
Bramming • Denmark 95 F9
Brampton • OT, Canada 122 B9
Brampton I. • QL, Australia 111 F3
Bramsche • Germany 8 C4
Branco • Brazil 43 E3
Brand • Austria 89 H5
Brandberg • Namibia 24 A4
Brandbu • Norway 94 B2
Brande • Denmark 95 F9
Brandenburg • Germany 8 H4
Brandenburg [Adm] • Germany .. 8 I4
Brandenburger Tor • Germany ... 81 F2
Brandon • MN, United States 38 L7
Brandon Mtn • Ireland 79 F5
Brands Hatch • United Kingdom .. 74 E1
Brandval • Norway 94 B2
Brandywine Ski •
  OH, United States .... 116 [148]
Brandywine Battlefield State Hist. Site •
  PA, United States 118 H1
Branesti • Romania 97 D1
Brânfeld, Parc zoologique de •
  France 84 C4
Brani • Singapore 108 E4
Braniewo • Poland 13 I3
Brantford • OT, Canada 122 B9
Brantôme • France 85 G2
Bras d'Or Lake • NS, Canada ... 123 D8
Brasil, Planalto do • Brazil 42 F6
Brasiléia • Brazil 43 D6
Brasília • Brazil 44 G2
Brasília Heritage C • Brazil .... 62 [57]
Braslav • Belarus 16 N9
Brasov • Romania 14 M4
Brass • Nigeria 22 F4
Brassac • France 5 H3
Brasschaat • Belgium 5 H3
Brastagi • Indonesia 110 B2
Brataj • Albania 15 A3
Bratan, Danau • Bali, Indonesia .. 110 C2
Bratislava • Slovak Rep. 13 G9
Bratsk • Russian Fed. 26 R6
Bratskoye Vdkhr. • Russian Fed. .. 27 F5
Brattleboro • VT, United States .. 118 G3
Brattvåg • Norway 94 C2
Braubach • Germany 82 H2
Braunau • Austria 13 C9
Braunfels • Germany 82 H2
Braunlage Spa • Germany ..... 83 [80]
Braunschweig • Germany 8 F4
Braunwald • Switzerland 89 G3
Brauweiler • Germany 81 E3
Brava • Cape Verde 22 (1) B2
Brava, Costa • Spain .... 87 D
Bravo del Norte, Rio •
  Mexico/United States 40 E5
Brawley • CA, United States 40 C5
Brawly • NL, Canada 39 P3
Bray • Ireland 79 E4
Bray Head • Ireland 79 E4
Brazil • S. America 42 E5
Brazilian Highlands • Brazil 127 A2
Brazo Casiquiare • Venezuela ... 43 D3
Brazos • TX, United States 119 N3
Brazzaville • Congo 22 H5
Brcko • Bosnia-Herz. 14 F5
Breadalbane • United Kingdom .. 74 B1
Breaksea Sound • New Zealand .. 112 L1
Bream Bay • New Zealand 35 E2
Brebes • Java, Indonesia 110 D2
Breckenridge Ski •
  CO, United States .... 116 [97]
Breckerfeld • Germany 81 E4
Breckland • United Kingdom 5 D2
Breclav • Czech Rep. 13 F9
Brecon • United Kingdom 7 I10
Brecon Beacons • United Kingdom .. 7 I10
Brecon Beacons Nat. Park Park •
  United Kingdom .... 72 [49]
Brecon Beacons Nat. Park •
  United Kingdom 75 A5
Breda • Netherlands 5 I3
Bredasdorp • South Africa 100 C6
Bredbo • Denmark 95 F13
Bredene-aan-Zee • Belgium 80 B1
Bredstedt • Germany 8 D2
Bree • Belgium 80 A11
Breede • South Africa 100 C6
Bregalnica •
  F.Y.R. of Macedonia 14 J3
Bregenz • Austria 89 H5
Brehal Beach • France .... 68 [58]
Bréhat, I. • France 84 C2
Breheimen • Norway 94 C2
Breidafjördur • Iceland 16 (1) B2
Breimsvatnet • Norway 94 C1
Breisach • Germany 82 G7
Breitachklamm • Germany 89 H5
Breitenfelde • Germany 71 A8
Breitscheid • Germany 81 E5
Brejeira, Serra da • Portugal 88 E2

Brekstad • Norway 16 E5
Bremangerlandet • Norway 94 C1
Bremen • Germany 8 D3
Bremen [Adm] • Germany 81 D1
Bremerhaven • Germany 8 D3
Bremerton • WA, United States .. 117 E1
Bremervörde • Germany 8 E3
Bremnes • Norway 94 C5
Brendon Hills • United Kingdom .. 74 F2
Brenham • TX, United States ... 119 N3
Brenner Pass • Austria/Italy 89 H7
Brenta • Italy 91 E3
Brenta [Riv] • Italy 12 F3
Brentwood • United Kingdom ... 7 M10
Brereton • Barbados 125 H4
Brescia • Italy 91 E6
Breskens • Netherlands 80 A10
Breslau • Poland 71 A9
Bressanone • Italy 90 B1
Bressay • United Kingdom 75 A7
Bresse-Hohneck, la Ski • France .. 70 [6]
Bressuire • France 84 D3
Brest • Belarus 13 M5
Brest • France 84 C1
Bretagne • France 10 B5
Brétignolles-sur-Mer Beach •
  France .... 68 [64]
Breton, Pertuis • France 10 D7
Breton Sound •
  LA, United States 118 K4
Bretonne Corniche • France 84 C1
Brett, Cape • New Zealand 35 E2
Bretten • Germany 9 D7
Bretton Woods Ski •
  NH, United States .... 116 [216]
Breueh • Indonesia 110 B1
Breuil-Cervinia Ski • Italy ...... 70 [199]
Breuil-Cervinia • Italy 91 E1
Breves • Brazil 43 G4
Bréville-sur-Mer Beach • France .. 68 [58]
Brewarrina • NS, Australia 34 I5
Brezno • Slovak Rep. 13 I9
Bria • Central African Rep. 23 C2
Brian Head Ski •
  UT, United States .... 116 [86]
Briançon Ski • France .... 70 [61]
Briançon • France 85 F4
Bribie • QL, Australia 111 F6
Brices Cross Roads Nat. Battlefield Site
  Park • MS, United States .. 121 [203]
Brides-les-Bains Ski • France .. 70 [38]
Bridge of Orchy •
  United Kingdom 74 B1
Bridgend • United Kingdom 7 I10
Bridgeport • CT, United States .. 118 H2
Bridgetown • WA, Australia 34 C6
Bridgetown • Barbados 125 H3
Bridgewater • NS, Canada 123 D7
Bridgnorth • United Kingdom 74 D1
Bridgwater • United Kingdom 74 F3
Bridlington • United Kingdom 7 L7
Bridlington Beach •
  United Kingdom .... 75 [34-35]
Bridport • United Kingdom 74 F3
Brie • France 85 E4
Brielle • Netherlands 80 C3
Brienzer See • Switzerland 89 G2
Brieselang • Germany 81 F1
Briey • France 5 I5
Brig • Switzerland 89 G6
Brigham City •
  ID, United States 40 D3
Brightlingsea Beach •
  United Kingdom .... 75 [55]
Brighton • United Kingdom 74 E3
Brighton Ski •
  UT, United States .... 116 [85]
Brignoles • France 85 H3
Brimstone Hill Fortress •
  St Kitts & Nevis 125 G1
Brindisi • Italy 12 L8
Brintz Apple Mtn Ski •
  MI, United States .... 116 [136]
Brisbane • QL, Australia 111 F6
Brissac [Château] • France 84 D1
Brissago • Switzerland 89 G7
Bristol • United Kingdom 74 F3
Bristol • RI, United States 118 H3
Bristol Bay • AK, United States .. 40 (2) B3
Bristol Channel •
  United Kingdom 74 F2
Bristol Mtn Ski •
  NY, United States .... 116 [175]
British Columbia • Canada 38 F5
British Indian Ocean Territory •
  Indian Ocean 3 R7
British Mtns •
  Canada/United States 38 C3
British Virgin Is. •
  West Indies 37 I4
Britstown • South Africa 24 C5
Brittany • France .... 84 C
Brittas Bay • Ireland 79 E4
Brive-la-Gaillarde • France 85 G2
Brixen • Italy 90 B1
Brixen im Thale Ski • Austria .. 70 [148]
Brixham • United Kingdom 74 F5
Brno • Czech Rep. 13 F8
Broad Haven Beach •
  United Kingdom .... 75 [162]
Broad Sound • QL, Australia 111 F3
Broadback • QU, Canada 39 P6
Broadford • United Kingdom 6 G4
Broads, The • United Kingdom 5 E2
Broadstairs • United Kingdom 74 E2
Broadstairs Beach •
  United Kingdom .... 75 [64]
Broadway • United Kingdom 74 D4
Broby • Sweden 95 F11
Brocken • Germany 8 F5
Brockhole Visitor Centre •
  United Kingdom 74 C4
Brockton • MA, United States .. 118 H4
Brockville • OT, Canada 122 B7
Brod • F.Y.R. of Macedonia 15 C2
Brodeur Peninsula • NU, Canada .. 39 N2
Brodick • United Kingdom 74 B2
Brodick Ski • MA, United States .. 116 [190]
Brodnica • Poland 13 I4
Broek in Waterland •
  Netherlands 80 C2
Broek op Langedijk •
  Netherlands 80 A7
Broich, Schloß • Germany 81 E1
Broken Arrow •
  OK, United States 41 G4
Brokopondo • Suriname 43 F3
Bromley Mtn Ski •
  VT, United States .... 116 [197]
Bromma [Apt] • Sweden 95 D2
Bromo, Gunung • Java, Indonesia .. 110 D8
Bromolla • Sweden 95 F11
Bromont Ski • QU, Canada .... 116 [38]
Brøndby Beach • Denmark .... 68 [20]
Brønderslev • Denmark 95 F6
Brønnøysund • Norway 16 F4
Bronte • Sicily, Italy 12 I11
Bronx • NY, United States 118 H2
Brook's Point • Philippines 31 F5

Brookhaven • MS, United States . 118 K2
Brookings • SD, United States . 41 G3
Brooklyn • NY, United States . 118 H2
Brooks • AL, Canada . 38 I6
Brooks Range •
AK, United States . 38 B3
Brookton • WA, Australia . 34 C6
Broome • WA, Australia . 34 D3
Brora • United Kingdom . 6 I3
Brouage • France . 85 G1
Brougham Castle •
United Kingdom . 74 C2
Broughton in Furness •
United Kingdom . 74 C2
Broughty Ferry • United Kingdom . 74 B2
Brovst Beach • Denmark . 68 [29]
Brovst • Denmark . 95 F5
Brown Pasture •
St Kitts & Nevis . 125 G4
Brown v. Board of Education Nat. Hist. Site
Park • KS, United States . 121 [171]
Brownsea I. • United Kingdom . 74 F3
Brownsville • TX, United States . 41 G6
Brownwood • TX, United States . 119 N3
Brú, Jökulsá á • Iceland . 16 (1) F2
Brú Na Bóinne Heritage C •
. 64 [12]
Brú Na Bóinne • Ireland . 79 E2
Bruay-en-Artois • France . 10 H3
Bruce, Mt • WA, Australia . 33 C8
Bruce Peninsula • OT, Canada . 38 F2
Bruce Rock • WA, Australia . 34 C6
Bruce Vale • Barbados . 125 H1
Bruche • France . 5 K6
Bruchhausen Spa • Germany . 83 [100]
Bruchsal • Germany . 82 G6
Bruck an der Mur • Austria . 13 E10
Bruckmühl • Germany . 82 J3
Bruges • Belgium . 80 B2
Brugge • Belgium . 80 B2
Brühl Heritage C • Germany . 64 [39]
Brühl • Germany . 82 G1
Brumado • Brazil . 44 H1
Brumunddal • Norway . 16 F6
Bruneck • Italy . 90 B2
Brunei • Asia . 31 E6
Brunico • Italy . 90 B2
Brunnen • Switzerland . 89 G3
Brunsbüttel • Germany . 8 E3
Brunswick • GA, United States . 41 J5
Brunswick • Germany . 71 A8
Brunswick • ME, United States . 118 G4
Brusa • Turkey . 71 A20
Bruson Ski • Switzerland . 70 [77]
Bruson • Switzerland . 89 G6
Brusque • Brazil . 44 G4
Brussel • Belgium . 80 A14
Brussels • Belgium . 80 A14
Bruxelles • Belgium . 80 A14
Bryansk • Russian Fed. . 17 E4
Bryce Canyon Nat. Park Park •
UT, United States . 120 [82]
Bryrup • Denmark . 95 F9
Brzeg • Poland . 13 G7
Bu Craa • Western Sahara . 20 C3
Bu'ayrat al Hasun • Libya . 21 C1
Bua • Sweden . 95 F6
Bua Yai • Thailand . 31 C3
Buala • Solomon Is. . 35 (1) F2
Buapinang • Indonesia . 32 (1) B3
Buatan • Indonesia . 32 C2
Buca • Turkey . 15 I5
Bucak • Turkey . 93 G1
Bucaramanga • Colombia . 43 C2
Buccoo Reef • Trinidad & Tobago . 125 K2
Buchanan • Liberia . 22 B3
Bucharest • Romania . 97 D1
Buchen • Germany . 9 E7
Buchholz in der Nordheide •
Germany . 8 E3
Buchloe • Germany . 82 J2
Buck Hill Ski •
MN, United States . 116 [113]
Buckeye • AZ, United States . 118 J3
Buckfastleigh • United Kingdom . 74 F5
Buckinghamshire •
United Kingdom . 75 A5
Buckland Abbey • United Kingdom . 74 F5
Buckland Tableland •
QL, Australia . 111 F3
Buckow Spa • Germany . 83 [289]
Bucksport • ME, United States . 118 G4
Buco Zau • Angola . 22 G5
Bucuresti • Romania . 97 D1
Bud • Norway . 71 A14
Budapest • Hungary . 13 I10
Budapest Heritage C • Hungary . 64 [153]
Budardalur • Iceland . 16 (1) C2
Budaun • India . 105 C3
Bude • United Kingdom . 74 F1
Bude Beach • United Kingdom . 75 [130-133]
Bude Bay • United Kingdom . 74 F1
Büdelsdorf • Germany . 8 E2
Budennovsk • Russian Fed. . 17 G6
Büdingen • Germany . 82 G2
Budleigh Salterton •
United Kingdom . 74 F5
Budzjak • Moldova . 14 P3
Buena Vista Ski •
MN, United States . 116 [108]
Buenaventura • Colombia . 43 B3
Buenos Aires • Argentina . 127 D1
Buenos Aires, Lago •
Argentina/Chile . 45 B5
Bueu Beach • Spain . 68 [74]
Buff Bay • Jamaica . 124 C2
Buffalo • SD, United States . 41 G3
Buffalo • NY, United States . 41 K3
Buffalo • TX, United States . 119 N4
Buffalo Lake • NT, Canada . 38 H4
Buffalo Narrows • SA, Canada . 38 J5
Buffalo Springs Game Reserve •
Kenya . 101 G2
Buffavento Castle • Cyprus . 93 J2
Buffels Bay • South Africa . 100 C7
Buftea • Romania . 97 D1
Buga • Colombia . 43 B3
Bugia • Algeria . 71 A17
Bugibba • Malta . 93 H2
Bugojno • Bosnia-Herz. . 12 I4
Buguruslan • Russian Fed. . 17 I4
Bühl • Germany . 9 D8
Buhusi • Romania . 14 N3
Bui Dam • Ghana . 21 A17
Bui Nat. Park Park • Ghana . 103 [23]
Builth Wells • United Kingdom . 7 I9
Buin • Papua New Guinea . 35 (1) F2
Buin • Chile . 44 B5
Buinsk • Russian Fed. . 17 H3
Buir Nur • Mongolia . 29 F1
Bujanovac • F.R. of Yugoslavia . 15 C1
Bujaraloz • Spain . 11 K3
Bujumbura • Burundi . 23 D4
Bük • Hungary . 14 D2
Buka • Papua New Guinea . 35 (1) F2
Bukama • Dem. Rep. of Congo . 23 D5
Bukavu • Dem. Rep. of Congo . 23 D4
Bukhara • Uzbekistan . 18 H2

Bukhara Heritage C • Uzbekistan . 63 [81]
Bukit Ferringhi •
Penang, Malaysia . 108 C1
Bukit Gemuruh Forest Reserve •
Penang, Malaysia . 108 C3
Bukit Genting Forest Reserve •
Penang, Malaysia . 108 C3
Bukit Juru Forest Reserve •
Penang, Malaysia . 108 E3
Bukit Kerajaan Forest Reserve •
Penang, Malaysia . 108 C4
Bukit Mertajam • Malaysia . 31 C5
Bukit Pulau • Penang, Malaysia . 108 C3
Bukit Relau Forest Reserve •
Penang, Malaysia . 108 C3
Bukit Tengah • Penang, Malaysia . 108 C4
Bukit Timah Nature Reserve •
Singapore . 108 E1
Bukittinggi • Indonesia . 110 B4
Bukk Nat. Park Park • Hungary . 72 [104]
Bukoba • Tanzania . 102 H1
Bukovina • Dem. Rep. of Congo . 24 D1
Bukovina • Ukraine . 14 M1
Bukum • Singapore . 108 E3
Bula • Indonesia . 32 (1) D3
Bulan • Philippines . 31 G4
Bulawayo • Zimbabwe . 102 J3
Buldan • Turkey . 15 J5
Bulgan • Mongolia . 29 B2
Bulgaria • Europe . 14 L7
Bull Point • Falkland Is. . 45 E6
Bulla Regia • Tunisia . 101 E1
Bullfinch • WA, Australia . 34 C6
Bulo Berde • Somalia . 23 H3
Bulolo • Papua New Guinea . 35 (1) D2
Bulukumba • Indonesia . 32 (1) B4
Bulungu • Dem. Rep. of Congo . 23 B4
Bumba • Dem. Rep. of Congo . 23 C3
Bumi Hills • Zimbabwe . 102 J1
Bunbury • WA, Australia . 34 C6
Bundaberg • QL, Australia . 111 F4
Bünde • Germany . 8 D4
Bundelkhand Riva • India . 105 C7
Bundoran • Ireland . 79 E2
Bungku • Indonesia . 32 (1) B3
Bungle Bungle • WA, Australia . 111 E2
Bungo • Angola . 22 H6
Bungo [Riv] • Angola/Zambia . 24 C2
Bungo-Suido • Japan . 30 G8
Bungu • Dem. Rep. of Congo . 23 E3
Bunmahon Beach • Ireland . 68 [39]
Bunratty Castle • Ireland . 79 F6
Buntenbock Spa • Germany . 83 [79]
Buntok • Indonesia . 32 (1) A3
Buorkhaya, Guba • Russian Fed. . 27 L2
Buqayq • Saudi Arabia . 18 G4
Bur Gabo • Somalia . 23 G4
Bur Hakkaba • Somalia . 23 G3
Bür Sa'id • Egypt . 101 F4
Bür Safâga • Egypt . 101 F4
Bur Sudan • Sudan . 21 G4
Bur'o • Somalia . 23 H2
Buran • Kazakhstan . 26 O8
Buraydah • Saudi Arabia . 18 D4
Burbach • Germany . 9 D6
Burdekin • QL, Australia . 111 F1
Burdur • Turkey . 93 G1
Burdur [Adm] • Turkey . 93 G1
Burdur Gölü • Turkey . 93 G1
Burdwan • India . 28 E4
Bure • United Kingdom . 5 E2
Bure • Ethiopia . 23 F1
Bureinskiy Khrebet •
Russian Fed. . 27 L6
Burela Beach • Spain . 68 [72]
Büren • Germany . 8 D5
Bürenhayrhan • Mongolia . 26 P8
Burg • Germany . 8 G2
Burg Spa • Germany . 83 [22]
Burg bei Magdeburg • Germany . 8 G4
Burgaski Zaliv • Bulgaria . 14 O7
Burgau • Germany . 82 J2
Burgau • Portugal . 88 E5
Burgdorf • Switzerland . 89 G2
Burgenland • Austria . 13 E10
Burghausen • Germany . 82 J4
Burgkirchen • Germany . 82 J4
Burglengenfeld • Germany . 9 H7
Burgos • Spain . 11 H2
Burgos Heritage C • Spain . 64 [78]
Burgsvik • Sweden . 16 J8
Burgundy • France . 84 A1
Burhaniye • Turkey . 15 I4
Burhanpur • India . 28 C4
Burhave Spa • Germany . 83 [52]
Burias • Philippines . 31 G4
Burica, Punta • Costa Rica . 43 A2
Burin Peninsula • NF, Canada . 123 D4
Burjal Hattabah • Tunisia . 21 K5
Burjasot • Spain . 11 K5
Burkina Faso • Africa . 20 E6
Burlington • IA, United States . 41 H3
Burlington • VT, United States . 118 G3
Burlington • NJ, United States . 118 H1
Burlington • OT, Canada . 122 B9
Burma • Asia . 31 B2
Burma Road • China/Myanmar . 29 B5
Burnah, Al • Tunisia . 21 A1
Burnazului, Câmpia • Romania . 14 M6
Burnham-on-Sea • United Kingdom . 74 F3
Burnham-on-Sea Beach •
United Kingdom . 75 [136]
Burnie • TS, Australia . 34 I8
Burnley • United Kingdom . 7 J8
Burns • OR, United States . 117 E4
Burns Lake • NT, Canada . 38 I3
Burqin • China . 26 O8
Burra • SA, Australia . 34 G6
Burreli • Albania . 15 B2
Burren, The • Ireland . 79 F4
Burriana • Spain . 11 L5
Bursa • Turkey . 92 D3
Burscheid • Germany . 81 E4
Bürstadt • Germany . 89 H5
Bürserberg • Austria . 89 H5
Burton-upon-Trent •
United Kingdom . 7 K9
Buru • Indonesia . 32 (1) C3
Burun Shibertuy, gora •
Russian Fed. . 27 G7
Burundi • Africa . 23 D4
Burutu • Nigeria . 22 F3
Buryn Urt • Mongolia . 27 F7
Bury • United Kingdom . 7 J8
Bury St Edmunds •
United Kingdom . 7 M9
Buryatia • Russian Fed. . 27 H6
Busch Gardens Tampa Bay •
FL, United States . 119 M5
Busch Gardens Tampa Bay Park •
FL, United States . 121 [DD]

Busch Gardens the Old Country Park •
VA, United States . 121 [GG]
Busch Gardens Williamsburg •
VA, United States . 118 H3
Bushehr • Iran . 18 F4
Busing • Singapore . 108 E3
Businga • Dem. Rep. of Congo . 23 C3
Buskerud • Norway . 16 E6
Busko-Zdrój • Poland . 13 J7
Bussana • Italy . 91 E9
Busselton • WA, Australia . 34 C6
Bussum • Netherlands . 80 C2
Busto Arsizio • Italy . 12 C3
Busuanga • Philippines . 31 F4
Büsum • Germany . 8 D2
Büsum Spa • Germany . 83 [8]
Buta • Dem. Rep. of Congo . 23 D3
Buta Ranquil • Argentina . 45 C3
Butanah, Al • Sudan . 18 B6
Butare • Rwanda . 23 D4
Butaritari • Kiribati . 33 I5
Bute • United Kingdom . 6 G6
Butembo • Dem. Rep. of Congo . 23 D3
Butha Qi • China . 29 G1
Butrotum Heritage C • Albania . 64 [163]
Butrotum • Albania . 92 B1
Buthrotum • Albania . 92 B1
Butiá • Brazil . 44 F5
Butjadingen Spa • Germany . 83 [52]
Butler, Lake •
FL, United States . 121 C1
Butrinti Heritage C • Albania . 64 [163]
Butt of Lewis • United Kingdom . 6 F3
Butte • MT, United States . 40 D2
Butterfly Valley •
Rhodes, Greece . 93 F2
Buttermere • United Kingdom . 74 C1
Buttermere [Lake] •
United Kingdom . 74 C1
Butternut Basin Ski •
MA, United States . 116 [188]
Butterworth • Penang, Malaysia . 108 C2
Buttevant • Ireland . 79 F6
Butuan • Philippines . 31 H5
Butung • Indonesia . 32 (1) B4
Butzbach • Germany . 82 H2
Buxar • India . 105 C8
Buxtehude • Germany . 8 E3
Buxton • United Kingdom . 7 K8
Buy • Russian Fed. . 17 G3
Buyan, Danau • Bali, Indonesia . 110 C2
Büyük Agri Dagi • Turkey . 18 D2
Büyük Kemiki Burnu • Turkey . 15 H3
Büyük Menderes • Turkey . 15 K5
Büyükanafarta • Turkey . 15 H3
Buyun • China . 30 B4
Buzachi, Poluostrov •
Kazakhstan . 17 I6
Buzau • Romania . 14 N4
Buzau [Riv] • Romania . 14 N4
Buzaymah, Al • Libya . 21 C1
Buzuluk • Russian Fed. . 17 I4
Búzios • Brazil . 127 C4
Bvumba Reserve • Zimbabwe . 102 J4
Bwindi Impenetrable Nat. Park Heritage N •
Uganda . 61 [87]
Bwindi Impenetrable Nat. Park Park •
Uganda . 103 [71]
Byala • Lovec, Bulgaria . 14 M6
Byala • Burgas, Bulgaria . 97 D4
Byam Martin, Cape • NU, Canada . 39 P2
Byam Martin I. • NU, Canada . 38 K1
Bydgoszcz • Poland . 13 G4
Bygdin • Norway . 94 C4
Bygland • Norway . 94 C6
Byglandsfjord • Norway . 95 F1
Bykle • Norway . 94 C4
Bykovo [Apt] • Russian Fed. . 97 E4
Bykovski • Russian Fed. . 27 K1
Bylot I. • NU, Canada . 39 P2
Byrd Field [Apt] •
VA, United States . 118 H3
Byrkjelo • Norway . 94 C2
Byron, Cape • NS, Australia . 111 F6
Byrranga, Gory • Russian Fed. . 26 P3
Bystrzyca Klodzka • Poland . 13 F7
Bytca • Slovak Rep. . 13 H8
Bytom • Poland . 13 H7
Bytów • Poland . 13 G3
Byxelkrok • Sweden . 95 F8
Bzura • Poland . 13 I5

Ca Mau • Vietnam . 108 B3
Caaguazú • Paraguay . 44 E4
Caballas • Peru . 127 B3
Caballo Cocha • Peru . 43 C4
Caballo Reservoir •
NM, United States . 118 J4
Cabana • Peru . 127 B1
Cabanatuan • Philippines . 31 G3
Caberfae Peaks Ski •
MI, United States . 116 [133]
Cabimas • Venezuela . 43 C1
Cabinda • Angola . 22 G6
Cabinda [Adm] • Angola . 22 G6
Cabinet Mtns •
MT, United States . 117 E2
Cable Beach • Bahamas . 124 C2
Cabo Bojador • Western Sahara . 20 C3
Cabo de Rama Fort • Goa, India . 105 D2
Cabo Negro • Morocco . 101 D2
Cabonga, Réservoir • QU, Canada . 39 P7
Caborca • Mexico . 40 D5
Cabora Bassa • Mozambique . 24 E3
Caboro Bassa, Lago • Mozambique . 24 E3
Cabot Strait • NF/NS, Canada . 123 D3
Cabra • Spain . 11 G7
Cabrera, I. de • Spain . 87 H4
Cabu • Spain . 11 J5
Cabrillo Nat. Mon. Park •
CA, United States . 120 [58]
Caçador • Brazil . 44 F4
Cacahuamilpa • Mexico . 123 E4
Cacak • F.R. of Yugoslavia . 14 H6
Caçapava do Sul • Brazil . 44 F5
Cáceres • Spain . 11 E5
Cáceres • Brazil . 44 E1
Cáceres Heritage C • Spain . 64 [80]
Cachimbo • Brazil . 43 G5
Cachimbo, Serra do • Brazil . 44 I1
Cachoeira •
Brazil . 45 (1) D3
Cachoeira do Sul • Brazil . 44 F5
Cachoeiro de Itapemirim •
Brazil . 127 C2
Cachopo • Portugal . 88 E3
Cacoctin Mtn Park •
MD, United States . 118 H3
Cacocum • Cuba . 124 D8
Caçolo • Angola . 24 B2
Caculé • Brazil . 44 H1
Cadaqués • Spain . 87 D2

Cadca • Slovak Rep. . 13 H8
Cadeirão, Serra do • Portugal . 88 E3
Cadenábbia • Italy . 91 E2
Cadillac • MI, United States . 41 I3
Cadiz • Philippines . 31 G4
Cádiz Beach • Spain . 68 [96]
Cádiz • Spain . 86 B5
Cádiz, Bahía de • Spain . 86 B5
Cádiz, Golfo de • Spain . 11 D3
Cadore • Italy . 90 B2
Cadouin • France . 85 G4
Caen • France . 10 E4
Caernarfon • United Kingdom . 7 H8
Caernarfon Bay • United Kingdom . 7 H8
Caernarfonshire & Merionethshire •
United Kingdom . 75 A4
Caerphilly • United Kingdom . 7 I10
Caesarea • Israel . 98 A3
Caesarea Philippi • Syria . 98 A2
Cafayate • Argentina . 44 C4
Cagayan • Philippines . 31 G3
Cagayan de Oro • Philippines . 31 H5
Cagayan Sulu • Philippines . 31 F5
Çagis • Turkey . 15 J4
Cágliari • Sardinia, Italy . 90 C4
Cágliari, Golfo di •
Sardinia, Italy . 90 C4
Cagnes-sur-Mer • France . 85 H4
Caguas • Puerto Rico . 125 E4
Cagyl • Turkmenistan . 18 G1
Caherciveen Beach • Ireland . 68 [41]
Caherciveen • Ireland . 79 F7
Caherdaniel Beach • Ireland . 68 [41]
Caherdaniel • Ireland . 79 F7
Cahir • United Kingdom . 117 F
Cahokia Mounds State Hist. Site Heritage C •
IL, United States . 62 [9]
Cahors • France . 85 G4
Cahul • Moldova . 14 P4
Caiapó, Serrra do • Brazil . 44 F2
Caibarién • Cuba . 124 D3
Caicara • Venezuela . 37 H6
Caimanera • Cuba . 124 D8
Caimito, Playa del • Cuba . 124 D2
Caine • Bolivia . 44 C2
Cairngorm Mtns • United Kingdom . 6 I4
Cairnryan • United Kingdom . 78 A4
Cairns • QL, Australia . 111 F1
Cairo • IL, United States . 41 I4
Cairo Heritage C • Egypt . 64 [237]
Cairo • Egypt . 101 F1
Calabozo • Angola . 24 B3
Cajabamba • Peru . 43 B5
Cajamarca • Peru . 127 B1
Cajapió • Brazil . 45 (1) C2
Cajun Country •
LA, United States . 118 K3
Çakirlar • Turkey . 93 G3
Cakovec • Croatia . 13 F11
Cala Antena • Majorca, Spain . 87 H4
Cala Bassa • Ibiza, Spain . 87 G1
Cala Blanca • Minorca, Spain . 87 F1
Cala Blanes • Minorca, Spain . 87 F1
Cala Blava • Majorca, Spain . 87 H3
Cala Bona • Majorca, Spain . 87 H2
Cala Conta • Ibiza, Spain . 87 G1
Cala d'Egos • Majorca, Spain . 87 H3
Cala d'Or • Majorca, Spain . 87 H4
Cala de Sant Vicenç •
Ibiza, Spain . 87 G2
Cala de Sant Vicenç •
Majorca, Spain . 87 H2
Cala de Santandría •
Minorca, Spain . 87 F1
Cala Lenya • Ibiza, Spain . 87 G2
Cala Llombarts • Majorca, Spain . 87 H4
Cala Llonga • Minorca, Spain . 87 F4
Cala Llonga • Ibiza, Spain . 87 G2
Cala Llonga • Majorca, Spain . 87 H4
Cala Major • Majorca, Spain . 87 H3
Cala Marçal • Majorca, Spain . 87 H4
Cala Millor • Majorca, Spain . 87 H2
Cala Mondragó • Majorca, Spain . 87 H4
Cala Morell • Minorca, Spain . 87 F1
Cala Pi • Majorca, Spain . 87 H3
Cala Ratjada • Majorca, Spain . 87 H2
Cala Sahona • Formentera, Spain . 87 G3
Cala Salada • Ibiza, Spain . 87 G1
Cala Santa Galdana •
Minorca, Spain . 87 F4
Cala Santanyí • Majorca, Spain . 87 H4
Cala Tarida • Ibiza, Spain . 87 G1
Cala Tirant • Minorca, Spain . 87 F2
Cala Torret • Minorca, Spain . 87 F4
Cala Vadella • Ibiza, Spain . 87 G1
Cala Vinyes • Majorca, Spain . 87 H3
Calabar • Nigeria . 22 F3
Calábria • Italy . 12 K9
Calábria, Parco Naz. della Park •
Italy . 72 [88]
Calaccuica • Corsica, France . 85 L1
Calafat • Portugal . 88 E3
Calafate • Argentina . 45 B6
Calafell Beach • Spain . 68 [104]
Calahonda • Spain . 11 I2
Calahorra • Spain . 87 C2
Calai • Angola . 24 B3
Calais Beach • France . 68 [55]
Calais • France . 10 G2
Calaiste, Sierra de •
Argentina . 44 C4
Calama • Chile . 44 C3
Calamian Group • Philippines . 31 F4
Calamocha • Spain . 11 J4
Calanche, les Heritage N •
Corsica, France . 61 [45]
Calangianus • Corsica, France . 85 L1
Calang • Indonesia . 110 B1
Calangute • Goa, India . 105 B1
Calangute Beach • Goa, India . 105 B1
Calanques, Côte des • France . 85 H5
Calapan • Philippines . 31 G4
Calarasi • Moldova . 14 P3
Calarasi • Romania . 97 D1
Calatayud • Spain . 11 J3
Calbayog • Philippines . 31 G4
Calbuco • Chile . 44 B5
Caldas da Rainha • Portugal . 11 B5
Caldas da Rainha Beach •
Portugal . 68 [79]

Caldbeck • United Kingdom . 74 C2
Caldeirão, Serra do • Portugal . 88 E3
Calder Hall • United Kingdom . 74 C3
Caldera • Chile . 44 B4
Caldera de Taburiente, Parque Nac. de Park •
La Palma, Canary Is. . 72 [76]
Caldera de Taburiente, Parque Nac. de •
La Palma, Canary Is. . 87 E5
Caldonazzo, Lago di • Italy . 90 B3
Caldwell • ID, United States . 117 E4
Caledon • South Africa . 100 C5
Caledon Ski • OT, Canada . 116 [22]
Caledon [Riv] • South Africa . 24 D6
Caledonian Canal •
United Kingdom . 6 H4
Calella Beach • Spain . 68 [105]
Calella • Spain . 87 D4
Calenzana • Corsica, France . 85 L1
Cales Coves • Minorca, Spain . 87 F4
Cales de Mallorca •
Majorca, Spain . 87 H4
Caleta Olivia • Argentina . 45 C5
Caleton Blanc • Cuba . 124 D8
Caletta, la • Sardinia, Italy . 90 C2
Calgary • AL, Canada . 122 C4
Calheta • Azores . 88 B2
Calheta • Madeira . 88 C1
Cali • Colombia . 43 B3
Calico Ghost Town •
CA, United States . 117 F6
Calicut • India . 106 D10
Calida, Costa • Spain . 87 C3
Caliente • NV, United States . 117 F4
California • United States . 117 F
California, Golfo de • Mexico . 40 D6
Callabonna, Lake •
SA, Australia . 34 G5
Callao • Peru . 127 B1
Callosa de Segura • Spain . 11 K6
Calma, Costa •
Fuerteventura, Canary Is. . 86 E5
Calonge Beach • Spain . 68 [106]
Calore • Italy . 91 G2
Caloundra • QL, Australia . 111 F6
Calpe Beach • Spain . 68 [101]
Calpe • Spain . 87 C2
Caltagirone • Sicily, Italy . 12 I11
Caltanissetta • Sicily, Italy . 90 D4
Calulo • Angola . 22 G6
Calvados, Côte du • France . 5 C5
Calvi • Corsica, France . 85 L1
Calvià Beach • Majorca, Spain . 68 [109]
Calvià • Majorca, Spain . 87 H1
Calvinia • South Africa . 100 C2
Calw • Germany . 82 G6
Cam • United Kingdom . 5 D2
Cam Ranh • Vietnam . 108 B2
Cam Ranh Bay • Vietnam . 108 B2
Camabatela • Angola . 23 B5
Camacã • Brazil . 44 I2
Camagüey • Cuba . 124 D7
Camagüey, Archipiélago de •
Cuba . 124 D2
Camaiore Beach • Italy . 68 [104]
Camamu • Brazil . 44 I1
Camaná • Peru . 127 B4
Camaquã • Brazil . 44 F5
Camará • Peru . 127 B2
Camargo • Spain . 11 H1
Camargue • France . 10 J10
Camariñas • Spain . 11 B1
Camarón, Cabo • Honduras . 37 D4
Camarones • Argentina . 45 C4
Camas • Spain . 11 F7
Cambados • Spain . 11 C2
Camber Beach • United Kingdom . 75 [68]
Cambo-les-Bains • France . 85 J1
Cambodia • Asia . 31 C4
Camborne • United Kingdom . 74 F4
Cambrai • France . 10 I3
Cambrian Mtns • United Kingdom . 7 I9
Cambridge • United Kingdom . 7 M9
Cambridge • New Zealand . 112 K1
Cambridge • MA, United States . 118 H2
Cambridge • MD, United States . 118 H3
Cambridge Bay • NU, Canada . 38 J3
Cambridgeshire • United Kingdom . 75 A5
Cambrils Beach • Spain . 68 [104]
Cambris de Mar • Spain . 87 D3
Camden • ME, United States . 118 G4
Camden • NJ, United States . 118 H1
Camden Park • SC, United States . 121 [241]
Camelback Ski •
PA, United States . 116 [167]
Camelford • United Kingdom . 74 F4
Camelot Theme Park Park •
United Kingdom . 73 [23]
Camenca • Moldova . 14 P1
Cameron Highlands • Malaysia . 108 C7
Cameron Hills • NT, Canada . 38 H4
Cameron Mtns • New Zealand . 112 L3
Cameroon • Africa . 22 G3
Cameroon, Mt • Cameroon . 22 F4
Cametá • Brazil . 43 G4
Caminha Beach • Portugal . 68 [75]
Camino de Santiago Heritage C •
Spain . 64 [80]
Çamliköyü • Turkey . 93 G2
Camocim • Brazil . 45 (1) C2
Camoowal • QL, Australia . 34 F3
Camopi • French Guiana . 43 G3
Camorta • India . 28 F7
Camp de Mar • Majorca, Spain . 87 H3
Campagna • Italy . 91 G4
Campal Beach • Goa, India . 105 B1
Campana, I. • Chile . 45 A5
Campanella, Punta • Italy . 91 G3
Campania • Italy . 12 J8
Campbell, Cape • New Zealand . 35 E5
Campbell Town • TS, Australia . 34 I8
Campbelltown • NB, Canada . 123 D2
Campbeltown • United Kingdom . 6 G6
Campeche • Mexico . 37 C4
Campeche [Adm] • Mexico . 37 C4
Campeche, Bahía de • Mexico . 37 C4
Campechuela • Cuba . 124 D7
Campello Beach • Spain . 68 [101]
Campello • Spain . 87 C2
Campi Dano • Sardinia, Italy . 12 C9
Campiglia Marittima • Italy . 12 E5
Campina Grande • Brazil . 45 (1) D3
Campinas • Brazil . 127 C3
Campitello di Fassa Ski • Italy . 70 [228]
Campo del Oro [Apt] •
Corsica, France . 85 L3
Campo Felice • Italy . 91 F2
Campo Grande • Brazil . 44 E2
Campo Maior • Brazil . 45 (1) C2
Campo Mourão • Brazil . 44 F3
Campo Tures • Italy . 90 B2
Campoalegre • Colombia . 43 B3
Campobasso • Italy . 91 G2
Campomarino Beach • Italy . 69 [138]
Campos • Brazil . 45 (1) C4
Campos • Majorca, Spain . 87 H4

Campos • Brazil . 127 C4
Campos do Jordão • Brazil . 127 C3
Campos, Lagoa de • Spain . 91 F2
Campsie Fells • United Kingdom . 74 B3
Camrose • AL, Canada . 38 J6
Camsell Portage • SA, Canada . 38 J5
Camyuva • Turkey . 93 G3
Can • Turkey . 15 I3
Can Pastilla • Majorca, Spain . 87 H3
Can Picafort • Majorca, Spain . 87 H3
Can Tho • Vietnam . 108 B3
Cana • United Kingdom . 75 A2
Cana of Galilee • Israel . 98 A4
Canaan Valley Ski •
WV, United States . 116 [155]
Canada • N. America . 36
Cañada de Gomez • Argentina . 44 D5
Canadaigua Lake •
NY, United States . 122 B10
Cañadas del Teide, Parque Nac. de las Park •
Tenerife, Canary Is. . 72 [78]
Cañadas del Teide, Parque Nac. de las •
Tenerife, Canary Is. . 86 E1
Canadian Rocky Mtns parks Heritage N •
AL/BC, Canada . 60 [4]
Canadian Shield • Canada . 38/39
Canaguinim Beach • Goa, India . 105 B2
Canaima, Parque Nac. Heritage N •
Venezuela . 60 [27]
Çanakkale • Turkey . 92 D2
Çanakkale • Turkey . 92 D2
Çanakkale Bogazi • Turkey . 92 D2
Çanakkale Bogazi • Turkey . 92 D2
Canal du Midi Heritage C •
France . 64 [64]
Canaria, Costa •
Gran Canaria, Canary Is. . 86 E4
Canarias • Atlantic Ocean . 86 E
Canaries • St Lucia . 125 J3
Canarreros, Archipiélago de los •
Cuba . 124 D2
Canary Is. • Atlantic Ocean . 86 E
Canaveral, Cape •
FL, United States . 41 J6
Canaveral Nat. Seashore •
FL, United States . 119 M6
Canaveral Nat. Seashore Park •
FL, United States . 121 [223]
Canazei Ski • Italy . 70 [228]
Canazei • Italy . 90 B3
Canberra • AC, Australia . 111 G2
Cancale Beach • France . 68 [59]
Cancale • France . 84 C2
Canche • France . 5 E4
Cancún • Mexico . 37 D3
Çandarli • Turkey . 15 H5
Çandarli Körfezi • Turkey . 15 H5
Candelaria •
Tenerife, Canary Is. . 86 E1
Candi Kuning Temple •
Bali, Indonesia . 110 C2
Candi Sukuh Temple •
Java, Indonesia . 110 D7
Candidasa Beach •
Bali, Indonesia . 110 C4
Candolim Beach • Goa, India . 105 B1
Cane River Creole Nat. Hist. Park & Nat.
Heritage Area Park •
LA, United States . 121 [196]
Canea Beach • Crete, Greece . 69 [188]
Canea • Crete, Greece . 93 E1
Canelones • Uruguay . 127 D2
Canet d'En Berenguer Beach •
Spain . 68 [102]
Canet en Roussillon Beach •
France . 68 [111]
Canet-Plage • France . 85 K2
Cañete • Spain . 11 J4
Canfranc • Spain . 11 K2
Cangamba • Angola . 24 B2
Cangas • Spain . 11 C2
Cangas Beach • Spain . 68 [74]
Canggu Beach • Bali, Indonesia . 110 C4
Cango Caves • South Africa . 100 C7
Cangzhou • China . 29 F3
Caniapiscau, Lac • QU, Canada . 39 R6
Caniçal • Madeira . 88 C2
Canicattì • Sicily, Italy . 12 H11
Caniço • Madeira . 88 C2
Canindé • Brazil . 45 (1) D2
Cankiri • Turkey . 15 O3
Canna • United Kingdom . 78 A1
Cannanore • India . 106 D6
Cannes Beach • France . 68 [117]
Cannes • France . 85 H4
Cannock • United Kingdom . 5 A2
Cannock Chase • United Kingdom . 74 D2
Cannon Ski • NH, United States . 116 [215]
Cannon [Apt] •
NV, United States . 117 F3
Cannon Beach •
OR, United States . 117 E1
Cannonsburg Ski •
MI, United States . 116 [141]
Canoas • Brazil . 44 F4
Canonica, la • Corsica, France . 85 L2
Canosa di Puglia • Italy . 14 D8
Canove Ski • Italy . 70 [213]
Cansaulim Beach • Goa, India . 105 B2
Canso, Strait of • NS, Canada . 123 D8
Cantabria • Spain . 11 G1
Cantábrica, Cordillera • Spain . 11 F2
Cantábrico, Mar • Spain . 11 E1
Cantanhede Beach • Portugal . 68 [78]
Cantera, I. de la • Spain . 87 C1
Canterbury Heritage C •
United Kingdom . 64 [25]
Canterbury • United Kingdom . 74 E4
Canterbury • New Zealand . 112 J3
Canterbury • NH, United States . 118 G3
Canterbury Bight • New Zealand . 35 J4
Canterbury Plains • New Zealand . 112 J3
Canton • OH, United States . 41 J3
Canton • China . 107 H1
Canton • MS, United States . 118 K2
Cañumá • Brazil . 43 F4
Canvey I. • United Kingdom . 74 E2
Canyon de Chelly Nat. Mon. •
AZ, United States . 118 J2
Canyon de Chelly Nat. Mon. Park •
AZ, United States . 120 [103]
Canyonlands Nat. Park Park •
UT, United States . 120 [86]
Canyons, The Ski •
UT, United States . 116 [82]
Caombo • Angola . 22 H6
Caorle • Italy . 90 B3
Cap aux Meules • QU, Canada . 123 D3
Cap d'Ail Beach • France . 68 [117]
Cap d'Ambre • Madagascar . 24 H2
Cap de la Madeleine •
QU, Canada . 122 B4
Cap Estate • St Lucia . 125 J3
Cap Esterel • France . 85 H4
Capanema • Brazil . 45 (1) B2
Caparaó, Serra do • Brazil . 127 C2
Caparica • Puerto Rico . 125 E2
Capbreton • France . 85 G3
Capdepera Beach •
Majorca, Spain . 68 [109]

Capdepera • Majorca, Spain ... 87 H2
Cape Breton Highlands Nat. Park •
  NS, Canada ... 123 D8
Cape Breton I. • NS, Canada ... 123 D8
Cape Canaveral •
  FL, United States ... 119 M6
Cape Coast • Ghana ... 22 D3
Cape Coral • FL, United States ... 119 M5
Cape Cross Reserve Park •
  Namibia ... 103 [115]
Cape Evans • Antarctica ... 59 A10
Cape Girardeau •
  MO, United States ... 41 I4
Cape Hatteras Nat. Seashore Park •
  NC, United States ... 121 [249]
Cape Krusenstern Nat. Mon. Park •
  AK, United States ... 120 [1]
Cape Lookout Nat. Seashore Park •
  NC, United States ... 121 [248]
Cape of Good Hope Nature Reserve Park •
  South Africa ... 103 [117]
Cape of Good Hope Nature Resrve •
  South Africa ... 100 C5
Cape Peninsula • South Africa ... 100 C5
Cape Sounio • Greece ... 92 D7
Cape Sounio • Greece ... 92 D7
Cape Town • South Africa ... 100 C5
Cape Verde • Atlantic Ocean ... 22 I1
Capella Telemin • Indonesia ... 32 (1) F3
Capelle, la • France ... 10 I4
Capernaum • Israel ... 98 A2
Capileira • Spain ... 86 B3
Capitán Arturo Prat [Base] •
  Antarctica ... 46 (1) JJ4
Capitol Reef Nat. Park Park •
  UT, United States ... 120 [83]
Capivara, Parque Nac. Serra da Heritage N •
  Brazil ... 60 [35]
Capivara, Parque Nac. Serra da Heritage C •
  Brazil ... 62 [58]
Capo Boi • Sardinia, Italy ... 90 C4
Capodichino [Apt] • Italy ... 91 G1
Capodimonte • Italy ... 91 F1
Cappadocia Heritage N • Turkey ... 61 [63]
Cappadocia Heritage C • Turkey ... 64 [193]
Cappenberg, Schloß • Germany ... 81 C2
Cápraia, I. di • Italy ... 91 E10
Caprera, I. • Sardinia, Italy ... 90 A1
Capri • Italy ... 91 G3
Capri, I. di • Italy ... 91 G3
Capriate San Gervasio • Italy ... 91 E6
Capricorn Channel •
  QL, Australia ... 111 F4
Capricorn Group • QL, Australia ... 111 F4
Caprivi Strip • Namibia ... 24 C3
Captain Cook •
  HI, United States ... 119 L8
Captiva I • FL, United States ... 119 M5
Càpua • Italy ... 91 G1
Capulin Volcano Nat. Mon. Park •
  NM, United States ... 120 [132]
Caputh • Germany ... 81 F3
Caqueta • Colombia ... 43 C4
Car Nicobar • India ... 28 F7
Caracal • Romania ... 14 I5
Caracara • Brazil ... 43 D3
Caracas • Venezuela ... 43 D1
Caracollo • Bolivia ... 44 C2
Caraguatatuba • Brazil ... 127 C3
Carais, Serra dos • Brazil ... 43 G5
Carajás • Brazil ... 43 G5
Caransebes • Romania ... 14 J4
Caranzalem Beach • Goa, India ... 105 B1
Caraquet • NB, Canada ... 123 D2
Caratasca, Laguna de • Honduras ... 37 C2
Caratinga • Brazil ... 43 D5
Caraúari • Brazil ... 43 C3
Caravaca de la Cruz • Spain ... 11 J6
Caravelas • Brazil ... 44 I2
Carázinho • Brazil ... 44 F4
Carballo • Spain ... 11 C1
Carballo Beach • Spain ... 68 [73]
Carbon, Cap • Algeria ... 11 K9
Carbonara, Capo •
  Sardinia, Italy ... 90 C4
Carbondale • IL, United States ... 41 I4
Carboneras Beach • Spain ... 68 [99]
Carboneras • Spain ... 86 B4
Carbonia • Sardinia, Italy ... 12 C9
Carbury • Ireland ... 79 E1
Carcans Beach • France ... 68 [66]
Carcans • France ... 85 G1
Carcassonne • France ... 10 H10
Carcassonne Heritage C • France ... 64 [69]
Carcavelos • Portugal ... 88 D1
Çardak • Çanakkale, Turkey ... 15 H3
Çardak • Denizli, Turkey ... 15 K6
Cardamom Hills • India ... 106 D10
Cardassar Beach •
  Majorca, Spain ... 86 [109]
Cárdenas • Cuba ... 124 D1
Cardiff • United Kingdom ... 74 F2
Cardigan • United Kingdom ... 7 H9
Cardigan Bay • United Kingdom ... 75 A5
Cardiganshire • United Kingdom ... 7 H9
Cardona • Uruguay ... 127 D2
Cardrona • New Zealand ... 112 L2
Carei • Romania ... 14 J2
Carentan • France ... 10 D4
Carey, Lake • WA, Australia ... 34 D5
Carezza, Lago di • Italy ... 90 B3
Cargados Carajos • Indian Ocean ... 19 J7
Cargèse Beach • Corsica, France ... 68 [118]
Cargèse • Corsica, France ... 85 L3
Carhaix-Plouguer • France ... 84 C1
Cariacica • Brazil ... 44 H3
Caribbean Beach •
  St Kitts & Nevis ... 125 G2
Caribbean Sea • America ... 37 G4
Caribbean/Florida cruise area •
  America ... 58 B
Cariboo Mtns • BC, Canada ... 38 G6
Caribou • MN, United States ... 38 L5
Caribou • ME, United States ... 118 G2
Caribou Mtns • AL, Canada ... 38 H5
Carié • Turkey ... 5 I5
Carignan • France ... 10 K7
Carinhanha • Brazil ... 44 H1
Carinthia • Austria ... 89 F3
Carinthia Ski •
  VT, United States ... 116 [195]
Caripito • Venezuela ... 43 E1
Carita • Java, Indonesia ... 110 D1
Carlet • Spain ... 11 K5
Carleton Place • OT, Canada ... 122 B6
Carlisle • PA, United States ... 118 H1
Carlisle Bay • Barbados ... 125 H3
Carlow • Ireland ... 79 E3
Carlow [Adm] • Ireland ... 79 D2
Carlsbad • NM, United States ... 40 F5
Carlsbad Caverns Nat. Park Heritage N •
  NM, United States ... 60 [13]
Carlsbad Caverns Nat. Park Park •
  NM, United States ... 120 [122]
Carmacks • YT, Canada ... 38 D4
Carmagnola • Italy ... 12 B4
Carmarthen • United Kingdom ... 7 H10
Carmarthen Bay • United Kingdom ... 7 H10
Carmarthenshire •
  United Kingdom ... 75 A5

Carmaux • France ... 10 H9
Carmel • CA, United States ... 117 F3
Carmel, Mount • Israel ... 98 A3
Carmelo • Uruguay ... 127 D2
Carmen • Mexico ... 40 D6
Carmensa • Argentina ... 44 C5
Carmona • Spain ... 86 B2
Carna • Ireland ... 79 F3
Carnac • France ... 84 C4
Carnamah • WA, Australia ... 34 C5
Carnarvon • WA, Australia ... 34 B4
Carnarvon • South Africa ... 100 C3
Carnarvon • India ... 106 C1
Carnegie, Lake • WA, Australia ... 34 D5
Carnot • Central African Rep. ... 23 B3
Carnoustie • United Kingdom ... 74 B2
Carnsore Point • Ireland ... 7 F9
Carolina • Brazil ... 45 (1) B3
Carolina • Puerto Rico ... 125 E2
Caroline • Kiribati ... 33 L7
Caroline, Fort Nat. Mem. •
  FL, United States ... 119 M3
Caroline, Fort, Nat. Mem. Park •
  FL, United States ... 121 [220]
Caroline Is. •
  Fed. States of Micronesia ... 33 F5
Carolinensiel Spa • Germany ... 83 [47]
Carondelet • Kiribati ... 33 J6
Caroni • Venezuela ... 37 I6
Caroni • Trinidad & Tobago ... 125 K3
Caroni Swamp •
  Trinidad & Tobago ... 125 K3
Carora • Venezuela ... 43 C1
Carpathians • Europe ... 4 O7
Carpatii Meridionali • Romania ... 14 K4
Carpatii Occidentali • Romania ... 13 L11
Carpentaria, Gulf of •
  NT/QL, Australia ... 34 G3
Carpi • Italy ... 12 E4
Carra, Lough • Ireland ... 79 F4
Carrapateira • Portugal ... 88 E5
Carrara • Italy ... 91 E10
Carraroe Beach • Ireland ... 68 [43]
Carraroe • Ireland ... 79 F3
Carrasco • Uruguay ... 127 D2
Carreño • Spain ... 11 F1
Carreta, Punta • Peru ... 127 B1
Carrick-on-Shannon • Ireland ... 7 D8
Carrick-on-Suir • Ireland ... 7 E9
Carrickfergus • United Kingdom ... 7 G7
Carrigadrohid Reservoir •
  Ireland ... 79 F8
Carroz, les Ski • France ... 70 [18]
Carroz-d'Arâches, les • France ... 85 F2
Carruantoohil • Ireland ... 79 F7
Carson City • NV, United States ... 117 F3
Cartagena • Colombia ... 43 B1
Cartagena Heritage C • Colombia ... 62 [42]
Cartagena Beach • Spain ... 68 [100]
Cartagena • Spain ... 87 C3
Cartago • Costa Rica ... 37 E6
Cartago • Colombia ... 43 B3
Cartaya Beach • Spain ... 68 [100]
Cartaya • Spain ... 86 B1
Carter, Jimmy, Nat. Hist. Site Park •
  GA, United States ... 121 [214]
Carter, Mt • QL, Australia ... 34 H2
Carthage • MO, United States ... 41 H4
Carthage Heritage C • Tunisia ... 64 [227]
Carthage • Tunisia ... 101 E2
Carthage [Apt] • Tunisia ... 101 E2
Caruaru • Brazil ... 45 (1) D3
Carúpano • Venezuela ... 43 D1
Carver, George Washington, Nat. Mon. Park •
  MO, United States ... 121 [174]
Carvoeiro • Portugal ... 88 E6
Carvoeiro, Cabo • Portugal ... 11 B5
Cas Concos • Majorca, Spain ... 87 H4
Casa de Campo, Parque de Atracciones Park •
  Spain ... 73 [78]
Casa Grande • AZ, United States ... 118 J3
Casa Grande Ruins Nat. Mon. •
  AZ, United States ... 118 J3
Casa Grande Ruins Nat. Mon. Park •
  AZ, United States ... 120 [113]
Casablanca • Morocco ... 101 D1
Casale Monferrato • Italy ... 91 B4
Casalmaggiore • Italy ... 12 E4
Casamari, Abbazia di • Italy ... 91 F4
Casares Beach • Spain ... 68 [97]
Casares • Spain ... 86 B6
Cascade Mtns Ski •
  WI, United States ... 116 [122]
Cascade Range •
  OR/WA, United States ... 117 E
Cascais Beach • Portugal ... 68 [80]
Cascais • Portugal ... 88 D1
Cascavel • Brazil ... 44 F4
Cascina • Italy ... 12 E5
Caserta Heritage C • Italy ... 64 [126]
Caserta • Italy ... 91 G1
Casey [Base] • Antarctica ... 46 (1) J3
Casey Bay • Antarctica ... 46 (1) J3
Caseyr, Râs • Somalia ... 23 I1
Cashel • Ireland ... 79 D2
Casilda • Argentina ... 127 D1
Casino • NS, Canada ... 111 F6
Cáslav • Czech Rep. ... 96 C2
Caspe • Spain ... 11 K3
Casper • WY, United States ... 40 E3
Caspian Sea • Asia ... 4 T8
Cassai • Angola ... 24 C2
Cassano allo Ionio • Italy ... 91 K3
Cassiar • BC, Canada ... 38 F5
Cassiar Mtns • BC, Canada ... 38 E5
Cassinga • Angola ... 24 B3
Cassino • Italy ... 91 G1
Castagneto Carducci Beach •
  Italy ... 68 [126]
Castagneto Carducci • Italy ... 91 E11
Castel del Monte Heritage C •
  Italy ... 64 [132]
Castel di Sangro • Italy ... 12 I7
Castel Gandolfo • Italy ... 91 F3
Castelfranco Vèneto • Italy ... 12 F3
Casteljaloux • France ... 85 G3
Castelló d'Empúries Beach •
  Spain ... 68 [106]
Castelló de la Plana • Spain ... 11 K4
Castellón • Spain ... 11 K4
Castelnaudary • France ... 11 M1
Castelnau • France ... 85 K2
Castelldefels Beach • Spain ... 87 D3
Castelli Romani • Italy ... 91 F3
Castello de Castelsardo Beach •
  Sardinia, Italy ... 68 [119]
Castelsardo • Sardinia, Italy ... 90 C1
Castelvetrano • Sicily, Italy ... 12 G1

Castiglioncello • Italy ... 91 E11
Castiglione del Lago • Italy ... 91 E11
Castiglione della Pescáia •
  Italy ... 91 E11
Castilla, Playa de • Spain ... 86 B1
Castilla-la Mancha • Spain ... 11 G5
Castilla-y-León • Spain ... 11 G3
Castillo de Jagua • Cuba ... 124 D2
Castillo de San Marcos Nat. Mon. •
  FL, United States ... 119 M4
Castillo de San Marcos Nat. Mon. Park •
  FL, United States ... 121 [221]
Castle Clinton Nat. Mon. Park •
  NY, United States ... 121 [325]
Castle Drogo • United Kingdom ... 74 F5
Castle Hill • NF, Canada ... 123 D4
Castle Matrix • Ireland ... 79 F6
Castle Peak • Hong Kong, China ... 107 H5
Castlebar • Ireland ... 79 F2
Castlebay • United Kingdom ... 74 B1
Castleconnell • Ireland ... 79 E3
Castledermot • Ireland ... 79 E3
Castledown House • Ireland ... 79 E1
Castlegregory Beach • Ireland ... 68 [41]
Castlegregory • Ireland ... 79 F5
Castleisland • Ireland ... 79 F6
Castlepoint • New Zealand ... 35 F5
Castlereagh • Ireland ... 79 F2
Castlereagh Bay • NT, Australia ... 34 G2
Castlerigg Stone Circle •
  United Kingdom ... 74 C2
Castletown • Jamaica ... 124 C2
Castletownbere • Ireland ... 79 F7
Castres • France ... 10 H10
Castries • St Lucia ... 125 J1
Castro • Brazil ... 44 F3
Castro • Chile ... 45 B4
Castro Marim Beach • Portugal ... 68 [82]
Castro Marim • Portugal ... 88 E4
Castrojeriz • Spain ... 11 G2
Castrop-Rauxel • Germany ... 81 E2
Castropol Beach • Spain ... 68 [71]
Castrovillari • Italy ... 12 K9
Caswell Bay Beach •
  United Kingdom ... 75 [140]
Caswell Sound • New Zealand ... 112 L1
Cat I. • Bahamas ... 124 B2
Cat Lake • OT, Canada ... 39 M6
Çatal Dag • Turkey ... 15 J4
Catalão • Brazil ... 44 G2
Catalca • Turkey ... 15 J2
Catalina • Chile ... 44 C4
Catalina, Punta • Chile ... 45 B6
Catalonia • Spain ... 11 M3
Catalunya • Spain ... 11 M3
Catamarca • Argentina ... 44 C4
Catanduanes • Philippines ... 31 G4
Catanduva • Brazil ... 44 G3
Catània • Sicily, Italy ... 90 D4
Catània, Golfo di •
  Sicily, Italy ... 90 D4
Catánia • Puerto Rico ... 125 E2
Catanzaro • Italy ... 12 K10
Catarata Ruancaná •
  Angola/Namibia ... 24 A3
Catarman • Philippines ... 31 G4
Catastrophe, Cape •
  SA, Australia ... 34 G6
Cataway Park • AL, Canada ... 122 C4
Catbalogan • Philippines ... 31 G4
Catena Costierra • Italy ... 12 K9
Catena dei Lagorai • Italy ... 90 B3
Catinàccio • Italy ... 90 B3
Catins, The • New Zealand ... 112 L4
Cato I. • CL, Australia ... 34 K4
Cato • Guinea-Bissau ... 22 A2
Catoctin Mtn Park Park •
  MD, United States ... 121 [282]
Catrilò • Argentina ... 44 D6
Catskill Mtns •
  NY, United States ... 118 H1
Cattòlica • Italy ... 91 E12
Catu • Brazil ... 44 I1
Cauca • Colombia ... 43 B2
Caucaisia • Colombia ... 43 B2
Caucasus • Asia/Europe ... 17 G6
Caucete • Argentina ... 37 A3
Caudry • France ... 5 G4
Caulnes • France ... 84 C2
Caulonia • Italy ... 12 K10
Cuanguia • Angola ... 24 B1
Cauquoican • Bolivia ... 44 C1
Cauquenes • Chile ... 44 B6
Caura • Venezuela ... 43 E2
Causanii • Moldova ... 14 O3
Causeway Bay • Hong Kong, China ... 107 H6
Cauterets • France ... 85 J2
Cauto • Cuba ... 124 D8
Cauvery • India ... 106 D6
Cauvery Delta • India ... 106 D11
Caux, Pays de • France ... 5 D5
Cava de' Tirreni • Italy ... 91 G4
Cavado • Portugal ... 11 C3
Cavaillon • France ... 85 H4
Cavalaire-sur-Mer • France ... 85 F3
Cavalese Ski • Italy ... 70 [216]
Cavalese • Italy ... 90 B3
Cavalleria, Cap de •
  Minorca, Spain ... 87 F2
Cavalli Is. • New Zealand ... 35 D2
Cavallo • I. • Corsica, France ... 85 L4
Cávally • Côte d'Ivoire/Liberia ... 22 C3
Cavan • Ireland ... 7 E8
Cavan [Adm] • Ireland ... 79 D1
Cavarzere • Italy ... 12 F3
Cavelossim Beach • Goa, India ... 105 B2
Caviana • Brazil ... 43 G3
Cavtat • Croatia ... 14 A4
Çavus Burun • Turkey ... 93 G3
Cawnpore • India ... 105 C7
Caxambu • Brazil ... 127 C3
Caxias • Brazil ... 45 (1) C2
Caxias do Sul • Brazil ... 44 F4
Caxito • Angola ... 23 A5
Çay • Turkey ... 15 M5
Cayambe, Volcán • Ecuador ... 43 B2
Cayenne • French Guiana ... 43 G3
Cayey • Puerto Rico ... 125 E2
Cayman Brac • Cayman Is. ... 124 D6
Cayman Is. • West Indies ... 37 E4
Cayo Guin • Cuba ... 124 D8
Cayon • St Kitts & Nevis ... 125 G1
Cayos del Este Sudeste •
  Colombia ... 43 A1
Cayuga Lake • NY, United States ... 122 B10
Cazombo • Angola ... 23 C6
Ceannannas Mór • Ireland ... 79 E1
Ceará • Brazil ... 45 (1) D2
Cebollera, Sierra • Spain ... 10 C11
Ceboruco • Spain ... 91 B1
Cebu [I.] • Philippines ... 31 G4
Cebu • Philippines ... 31 G4
Cebu [I.] • Philippines ... 90 B1

Cedar Breaks Nat. Mon. Park •
  UT, United States ... 120 [81]
Cedar City • UT, United States ... 40 D4
Cedar Falls • IA, United States ... 41 H3
Cedar Grove • Antigua & Barbuda ... 125 F1
Cedar Keys Nat. Wildlife Refuge •
  FL, United States ... 119 M3
Cedar Lake • MN, Canada ... 38 K6
Cedar Point Park •
  OH, United States ... 121 [T]
Cedar Rapids •
  IA, United States ... 41 H3
Cederberg • South Africa ... 100 C1
Cedros • Mexico ... 36 F7
Ceduna • SA, Australia ... 34 F6
Cefalù • Sicily, Italy ... 90 D2
Cegar Perah • Malaysia ... 108 D2
Ceglèd • Hungary ... 13 J10
Cegléd Heritage • Hungary ... 13 J6
Ceiba • Puerto Rico ... 125 E2
Cekik • Bali, Indonesia ... 110 C1
Celano • Italy ... 91 F2
Celaya • Mexico ... 36 E4
Celebes • Indonesia ... 32 (1) A3
Celebes Sea • Indonesia ... 32 (1) B2
Celerina Ski • Switzerland ... 70 [116]
Celerina • Switzerland ... 89 G4
Celje • Slovenia ... 13 E11
Celldömölk • Hungary ... 13 G10
Celle • Germany ... 8 F4
Celle Ligure Beach • Italy ... 68 [121]
Celtic Sea • Ireland/UK ... 7 E10
Celuk • Bali, Indonesia ... 110 C4
Cemaes Bay Beach •
  United Kingdom ... 75 [210]
Cenajo, Embalse de • Spain ... 11 J6
Cenderawasih, Teluk • Indonesia ... 35 (1) A1
Cento • Italy ... 12 E4
Central • Hong Kong, China ... 107 H5
Central African Rep. • Africa ... 23 C2
Central Australia Aboriginal Land •
  WA, Australia ... 112 H3
Central Highlands • Kenya ... 101 G3
Central I. Nat. Park Heritage N •
  Kenya ... 61 [88]
Central I. Nat. Park • Kenya ... 101 G1
Central Lowland •
  IL/MO, United States ... 41 H3
Central Makran Range • Pakistan ... 18 H4
Central Plains • Thailand ... 109 F2
Central Plateau • Russian Fed. ... 4 O8
Central Plateau • New Zealand ... 112 K4
Central Range •
  Papua New Guinea ... 35 (1) C2
Central Siberian Plateau •
  Russian Fed. ... 25 L3
Central Siberian Uplands •
  Russian Fed. ... 26 Q5
Centralia • WA, United States ... 117 E1
Centre • France ... 84 A1
Centreville • OT, Canada ... 122 B9
Cephalonia • Greece ... 92 C2
Cephalonia • Greece ... 92 C2
Cepu • Java, Indonesia ... 110 D3
Ceraino • Indonesia ... 32 (1) C3
Cerbère • France ... 85 L4
Cerbère Beach • France ... 68 [111]
Cèrbere • France ... 85 K2
Cerbicale, Is. •
  Corsica, France ... 85 L4
Ceres • Brazil ... 44 G2
Ceres • South Africa ... 100 C5
Ceres I. • Seychelles ... 106 F1
Cerf, I. au • Seychelles ... 106 F1
Cergnago • France ... 85 E1
Cerignola • Italy ... 12 J7
Cerigo • Greece ... 92 D7
Cerigo • Greece ... 92 D7
Çerkes • Turkey ... 15 N3
Çerkezköy • Turkey ... 15 I2
Cernavoda • Romania ... 13 K11
Cernei • Romania ... 13 K11
Cernika • Albania ... 14 H8
Cerna Skala •
  Bulgaria/F.Y.R. of Macedonia ... 15 D1
Cernavoda • Romania ... 15 E1
Cerni vrah • Bulgaria ... 15 E1
Cernòbbio • Italy ... 91 D5
Cerralvo • Mexico ... 40 E7
Cerritos • Mexico ... 36 E4
Cerro Azul • Brazil ... 44 G3
Cerro de las Mesas • Mexico ... 123 E4
Cerro de Pasco • Peru ... 43 B6
Cervantes • Spain ... 12 J7
Cervená Lhota • Czech Rep. ... 96 C4
Cervéteri • Italy ... 91 F1
Cervia Beach • Italy ... 68 [144]
Cérvia • Italy ... 91 E8
Cervialto, Monte • Italy ... 91 G4
Cervo • Spain ... 11 D4
Cervo Beach • Italy ... 68 [120]
Cervo • Spain ... 68 [72]
Cesana Ski • Italy ... 70 [192]
Cesena • Italy ... 12 G4
Cesenàtico Beach • Italy ... 68 [143]
Cesenàtico • Italy ... 91 E8
Cesis • Latvia ... 16 M8
Ceská Lipa • Czech Rep. ... 96 C4
Ceské Budejovice • Czech Rep. ... 96 C4
Ceské Svycarsko • Czech Rep. ... 96 C1
Ceské Zeme • Czech Rep. ... 13 D8
Ceskomoravská Vysocina •
  Czech Rep. ... 13 E8
Cesky Krumlov Heritage C •
  Czech Rep. ... 64 [146]
Cesky Krumlov • Czech Rep. ... 96 C4
Cesky Les • Czech Rep. ... 9 H7
Cesky Sternberk • Czech Rep. ... 96 C2
Çesme • Turkey ... 92 D5
Çesme • Turkey ... 92 D5
Cessnock • NS, Australia ... 111 F6
Cestos • Côte d'Ivoire/Liberia ... 22 C3
Cetarro • Italy ... 12 J9
Cetinje • F.R. of Yugoslavia ... 14 F7
Ceuta • Africa ... 101 D2
Ceva-i-Ra • Fiji ... 35 (2) C3
Cévennes, Parc nat. des Park •
  France ... 72 [70]
Cevizli • Turkey ... 93 G2
Ceyhan • Turkey ... 28 D7
Ch'onan • Rep. of Korea ... 30 E4
Ch'ongji • D.P.R. of Korea ... 30 E3
Ch'ongju • Rep. of Korea ... 30 E4
Ch'orwon • Rep. of Korea ... 30 D5
Ch'unch'on • Rep. of Korea ... 30 D5
Cha-Am • Thailand ... 109 H3
Chabala, Laguna de • Mexico ... 123 E1
Chachapoyas • Peru ... 43 B5
Chachoengsao • Thailand ... 109 H2
Chaco Austral • Argentina ... 44 D4

Chaco Boreal • Paraguay ... 44 D3
Chaco Central • Argentina ... 44 D3
Chaco Culture Nat. Hist. Park Heritage C •
  NM, United States ... 62 [7]
Chaco Culture Nat. Hist. Park •
  NM, United States ... 118 J2
Chaco Culture Nat. Hist. Park Park •
  NM, United States ... 120 [125]
Chad • Africa ... 21 C4
Chad, Lake • Africa ... 21 B5
Chadan • Russian Fed. ... 26 P7
Chadileuvú • Argentina ... 44 C6
Chadron • NE, United States ... 40 F3
Chafarinas, Is. • Spain ... 11 I9
Chagai Hills • Pakistan ... 18 I4
Chaghcharan • Afghanistan ... 18 I3
Chagda • Russian Fed. ... 27 T7
Chaguanas • Trinidad & Tobago ... 125 K3
Chaguaramas Bay •
  Trinidad & Tobago ... 125 K3
Chah Bahar • Iran ... 18 H4
Chahar Borjak • Afghanistan ... 18 H4
Chaillu, Massif du • Gabon ... 22 G5
Chainat • Thailand ... 31 C3
Chaitén • Chile ... 45 B4
Chake Chake • Tanzania ... 102 H2
Chakhansur • Afghanistan ... 18 H3
Chala • Peru ... 127 B3
Chalaki Desert • Kenya ... 101 G1
Chalaur Bay • NB/QU, Canada ... 123 D2
Chalky Hill • Barbados ... 125 H2
Chalky Inlet • New Zealand ... 112 L3
Challaborough Beach •
  United Kingdom ... 75 [121]
Challapata • Bolivia ... 44 C2
Challenger Deep •
  Fed. States of Micronesia ... 25 P8
Challengers • St Kitts & Nevis ... 125 G1
Chalon-sur-Saône • France ... 10 J7
Chalong • Phuket, Thailand ... 109 K2
Chalong Bay • Phuket, Thailand ... 109 K2
Chalons-sur-Marne • France ... 10 J5
Chalusset, Château de • France ... 85 G2
Cham • Germany ... 9 H7
Chám • Mauritania ... 20 C4
Chaman • Pakistan ... 28 A2
Chamba • India ... 28 D2
Chamba • Tanzania ... 102 H4
Chambal • India ... 105 C6
Chambers Pillar • NT, Australia ... 112 H4
Chambèry • France ... 85 F1
Chambeshi • Zambia ... 24 E2
Chambi, Jebel • Tunisia ... 101 E3
Chambly • France ... 5 J6
Chambly, Fort • QU, Canada ... 122 B7
Chambord Heritage C • France ... 64 [61]
Chambord [Château] • France ... 84 D2
Chamizal Nat. Mem. Park •
  TX, United States ... 120 [135]
Chamois • Italy ... 91 E1
Chamonix • France ... 85 F2
Chamonix-Mont Blanc Ski •
  France ... 70 [26]
Champ du Feu • France ... 10 M5
Champagne-Ardennes • France ... 84 A1
Champagnole • France ... 10 K7
Champagny-en-Vanoise Ski •
  France ... 70 [34]
Champaign • IL, United States ... 41 I3
Champaqui, Cerro • Argentina ... 44 D5
Champasak • Laos ... 108 A2
Champawat • India ... 105 C6
Champéry • Switzerland ... 89 G5
Champéry-Planachaux Ski •
  Switzerland ... 70 [76]
Champex • Switzerland ... 89 G6
Champigny-sur-Marne • France ... 85 E4
Champlain, Lake •
  NY/VT, United States ... 118 G3
Champmol Ski • Italy ... 70 [201]
Champoussin • Switzerland ... 89 G5
Chamrousse Ski • France ... 70 [52]
Chan Chan • Peru ... 43 B5
Chan Chan Heritage C • Peru ... 62 [47]
Chandalar • AK, United States ... 38 B3
Chandeleur Sound •
  LA, United States ... 118 K4
Chanderi • India ... 105 C7
Chandigarh • India ... 28 C2
Chandigarh [Adm] • India ... 105 A1
Chandler • QU, Canada ... 123 D2
Chandor • Goa, India ... 105 B2
Chandragiri • India ... 106 D7
Chandrapabha Wildlife Sanctuary •
  India ... 105 C8
Chang Jiang • China ... 29 G4
Chang, Ko • Thailand ... 31 C4
Chang Zhou • China ... 107 J1
Changan • China ... 98 B6
Changane • Mozambique ... 24 E4
Changbai • China ... 30 D4
Changbai Shan • China ... 30 D4
Changcheng • China ... 29 H2
Changchun • China ... 29 H2
Changde • China ... 29 G4
Changhua • Taiwan ... 29 G6
Changji [Apt] • Singapore ... 108 C3
Changjiang Kou • China ... 29 G4
Changjin-Up • D.P.R. of Korea ... 30 D4
Changping • China ... 107 H2
Changsha • China ... 29 E5
Changshu • China ... 107 J3
Changxing • China ... 107 J3
Changyon • D.P.R. of Korea ... 30 D5
Channel Country • QL, Australia ... 111 E7
Channel Is. • Europe ... 7 J12
Channel Is. • CA, United States ... 117 F5
Channel Is. Nat. Park •
  CA, United States ... 117 F5
Channel Is. Nat. Park Park •
  CA, United States ... 120 [56]
Channel Port-aux-Basques •
  NF, Canada ... 123 D3
Channel Tunnel • France/UK ... 74 E4
Chantada • Spain ... 11 D2
Chantada, Faro de • Spain ... 11 D2
Chantilly • France ... 31 C4
Chantilly, Forêt de • France ... 85 E2
Chao Phraya • Thailand ... 109 H1
Chaouèn • Morocco ... 101 D2
Chaozhou • China ... 29 F5
Chapada das Mangabeiras •
  Brazil ... 45 (1) B3
Chapada Diamantina • Brazil ... 44 H1
Chapala, Laguna de • Mexico ... 123 E1
Chapayevo • Kazakhstan ... 17 I5
Chapco • Argentina ... 44 D6
Chapeco • Brazil ... 44 F4
Chapleau • OT, Canada ... 39 O7
Chaplino, mys • Russian Fed. ... 27 V4
Chapora • Goa, India ... 105 B1
Chapora Fort • Goa, India ... 105 B1
Chapra • India ... 105 C8
Chara • Mauritania ... 20 C4
Chara • Russian Fed. ... 26 R6
Chard • United Kingdom ... 74 F3

Chardzhou • Turkmenistan ... 18 H2
Charentais • France ... 84 B3
Charente [Adm] • France ... 85 G1
Charente [Riv] • France ... 85 G1
Charente-Maritime • France ... 85 G1
Chari • Chad ... 21 C5
Charity • Guyana ... 43 F2
Charleroi • Belgium ... 80 A14
Charles, Cape • NF, Canada ... 39 T6
Charles, Cape •
  VA, United States ... 118 H3
Charles, Fort •
  St Kitts & Nevis ... 125 G4
Charles I. • NU, Canada ... 39 G4
Charles, Peak • WA, Australia ... 34 D6
Charles Sound • New Zealand ... 112 L1
Charleston • IL, United States ... 41 J4
Charleston • WV, United States ... 41 J4
Charleston • SC, United States ... 41 K5
Charlestown • Ireland ... 79 F2
Charlestown • St Kitts & Nevis ... 125 G4
Charleville • Australia ... 111 F5
Charleville • QL, Australia ... 111 F5
Charleville-Mézières • France ... 10 J4
Charlotte • NC, United States ... 41 J4
Charlotte Amalie •
  US Virgin Is. ... 58 B7
Charlotte, Fort • Bahamas ... 124 B3
Charlotte • St Lucia ... 125 J1
Charlotte Harbor •
  FL, United States ... 119 M5
Charlottenburg, Schloß •
  Germany ... 81 F1
Charlottesville •
  VA, United States ... 41 K4
Charlottesville Heritage C •
  VA, United States ... 62 [10]
Charlottetown • PE, Canada ... 123 D7
Charlotteville •
  Trinidad & Tobago ... 125 K2
Charlton • VI, Australia ... 111 G3
Charnwood Forest •
  United Kingdom ... 74 D2
Charters Towers • QL, Australia ... 111 F1
Chartres Heritage C • France ... 64 [60]
Chartres • France ... 85 E3
Chartwell • United Kingdom ... 74 E3
Chascomús • Argentina ... 127 D4
Chasong • D.P.R. of Korea ... 30 D4
Chassengue • Angola ... 23 B6
Chassin • St Lucia ... 125 J2
Château-Arnoux • France ... 10 L9
Château-d'Oex Ski • Switzerland ... 70 [85]
Château-d'Oex • Switzerland ... 89 G6
Château-du-Loir • France ... 10 F6
Château-Gontier • France ... 10 E6
Château-Salins • France ... 5 J6
Château-Thierry • France ... 84 A1
Châteaubriant • France ... 84 D1
Châteaudun • France ... 84 D2
Châteaulin • France ... 10 A5
Châteauneuf-du-Pape • France ... 85 H4
Châteauroux • France ... 84 A4
Châtel Ski • France ... 70 [9]
Châtel • France ... 85 F2
Châtelet • Belgium ... 5 H4
Châtellerault • France ... 84 A4
Chatham • United Kingdom ... 74 E2
Chatham • NB, Canada ... 123 D2
Chatham I. • New Zealand ... 35 (3) B1
Chatham Is. • New Zealand ... 33 J10
Chatham Is. • New Zealand ... 35 (3)
Châtillon-sur-Indre • France ... 84 D4
Chatkal-ský • Kyrgyzstan ... 26 L9
Chatra • India ... 105 C8
Châtre, la • France ... 10 H7
Chattahoochee River Nat. Recreation Area •
  GA, United States ... 121 [210]
Chattanooga • TN, United States ... 41 J4
Châtillon-sur-Seine • France ... 10 J6
Chau Doc • Vietnam ... 108 B1
Chaudi • Goa, India ... 105 B2
Chaudiere • QU, Canada ... 122 B4
Chauka • India ... 105 C3
Chaumont • France ... 10 K5
Chaumont [Château] • France ... 84 D2
Chaunskaya Guba • Russian Fed. ... 27 S3
Chaury • France ... 5 G5
Chauvigny • France ... 84 A4
Chavantina • Brazil ... 44 F1
Chaves • Portugal ... 11 D3
Chaves • Brazil ... 43 G4
Chavin Heritage C • Peru ... 62 [48]
Chavin de Huantar • Peru ... 127 B1
Chavuma • Zambia ... 24 C2
Chaweng Beach •
  Ko Samui, Thailand ... 109 J1
Chayamangkalaram, Wat •
  Penang, Malaysia ... 108 C2
Chbika • Tunisia ... 101 E3
Cheb • Czech Rep. ... 96 C1
Cheboksary • Russian Fed. ... 17 H3
Chech, Erg • Algeria ... 20 E4
Chechenia • Russian Fed. ... 17 H6
Chechuysk • Russian Fed. ... 27 G5
Cheddar • United Kingdom ... 74 F3
Cheddar Gorge • United Kingdom ... 74 F3
Cheduba • Myanmar ... 31 A3
Chedworth Roman Villa •
  United Kingdom ... 74 D4
Cheerala • India ... 106 D3
Chegga • Mauritania ... 20 D3
Chegutu • Zimbabwe ... 102 J2
Cheju • Rep. of Korea ... 30 D8
Cheju • Rep. of Korea ... 30 D8
Cheju [I.] • Rep. of Korea ... 30 D8
Cheju-Haehyop • Rep. of Korea ... 30 D8
Chek Lap Kok • Hong Kong, China ... 107 H5
Cheliff • Algeria ... 20 F1
Cheliff, Plaine du • Algeria ... 11 L8
Cheliff [Riv] • Algeria ... 20 F1
Chelkar • Kazakhstan ... 26 I8
Chelm • Poland ... 13 M4
Chelmno • Poland ... 13 H4
Chelmsford • United Kingdom ... 74 E2
Chelmza • Poland ... 13 H4
Chelsea • United Kingdom ... 74 E1
Cheltenham • United Kingdom ... 74 D4
Chelva • Spain ... 11 J5
Chelyabinsk • Russian Fed. ... 26 J6
Chelyuskin, mys • Russian Fed. ... 26 S2
Chemainis • Thailand ... 85 E2
Chemdal'sk • Russian Fed. ... 26 R6
Chémery [Château] • France ... 84 D2
Chemillé • France ... 10 E6
Chemnitz • Germany ... 9 H6
Chemult • OR, United States ... 117 E3
Chenab • Pakistan ... 28 B2
Chenachane • Algeria ... 20 E3
Chenachane [Riv] • Algeria ... 20 E3
Chengde • China ... 29 G2
Chengde Heritage C • China ... 63 [145]
Chengdu • China ... 29 E4
Chengshan Jiao • China ... 29 G3
Chenini • Tunisia ... 101 E6
Chenonceaux [Château] • France ... 84 D2
Chentijn Nuruu •
  Mongolia/Russian Fed. ... 27 H7
Chenxian • China ... 29 F5
Cheongmon Bay •
  Ko Samui, Thailand ... 109 J1

Chepca • Russian Fed. 17 I3
Chepes • Argentina 44 C5
Chepstow • United Kingdom 74 D3
Cher • France 10 G6
Cherangany Hills • Kenya 23 F3
Cherating • Malaysia 108 A4
Cherbaniani Reef • India 106 D5
Cherbourg • France 10 D4
Cherchell • Algeria 19 N8
Cheremkhovo • Russian Fed. 27 F6
Cherepovets • Russian Fed. 97 E2
Cheriton Terminal •
    United Kingdom 78 C4
Cheriyam I. • India 106 D9
Cherkassy • Ukraine 17 E5
Cherkessk • Russian Fed. 17 G6
Cherlak • Russian Fed. 26 L7
Cherigov • Ukraine 17 E4
Chernobyl • Ukraine 17 E4
Chernomorets • Bulgaria 97 D3
Chernovtsy • Ukraine 14 M1
Chernyakhovsk • Russian Fed. 13 K3
Chernysevskiy • Russian Fed. 27 N4
Cherrapunji • India 28 F3
Cherry Tree Hill • Barbados 125 H1
Cherskiy • Russian Fed. 27 R3
Cherskogo, Khrebet •
    Russian Fed. 27 N3
Chesapeake • VA, United States . . . 41 K4
Chesapeake Bay •
    VA, United States 41 J5
Chesapeake & Ohio Canal Nat. Hist. Park
    Park • MD, United States . . . . 121 [273]
Cheshire • United Kingdom 75 A4
Cheshkaya Guba • Russian Fed. . . . 17 H1
Chesil Beach • United Kingdom . . . 74 F6
Chesne, le • France 5 H5
Chessington World of Adventures Park •
    United Kingdom . . . . 73 [36]
Chessington World of Adventures •
    United Kingdom 74 E1
Chester • United Kingdom 7 J8
Chesterfield • United Kingdom 7 K8
Chesterfield Inlet • NU, Canada . . . 39 M4
Chestnut Mtn Ski •
    IL, United States . . . . 116 [117]
Chesuncook Lake •
    ME, United States 118 G2
Chettlatt I. • India 106 D5
Chetumal • Mexico 37 D4
Cheung Chau • Hong Kong, China . . 107 H5
Cheverny • France 84 B1
Cheverny [Château] • France 84 D2
Cheviot Hills • United Kingdom 7 J6
Cheviot, The • United Kingdom 7 J6
Chew Bahir • Ethiopia/Kenya 23 F3
Chewore safari area Heritage N •
    Zimbabwe . . . . 61 [96]
Cheyenne • WY, United States 40 F3
Cheyenne [Riv] • United States 38 K8
Cheyne Bay • WA, Australia 34 C6
Chi • Thailand 109 F2
Chia • Sardinia, Italy 90 C4
Chiang Dao • Thailand 109 G1
Chiang Kham • Thailand 109 G4
Chiang Khan • Thailand 109 G4
Chiang Khong • Thailand 109 G2
Chiang Mai • Thailand 109 G2
Chiang Rai • Thailand 109 G2
Chiang Saen • Thailand 109 G2
Chianje • Angola 24 A3
Chianti • Italy 91 E11
Chiapas • Mexico 37 C4
Chiaravalle • Italy 91 E6
Chiayi • Taiwan 29 E6
Chiba • Japan 30 K7
Chibougamou • QU, Canada 39 O6
Chicago • IL, United States 41 I3
Chicago Portage Nat. Hist. Site Park •
    IL, United States . . . . 121 [180]
Chichagof I. •
    AK, United States 38 D5
Chichaoua • Morocco 20 D2
Chichén Itzá • Mexico 37 D3
Chichén Itzá Heritage C •
    Mexico . . . . 62 [27]
Chichester • United Kingdom 7 K9
Chickamauga & Chattanooga Nat. Military
    Park Park •
    GA, United States . . . . 121 [208]
Chickasaw Nat. Recreation Area Park •
    OK, United States . . . . 121 [145]
Chickasawhay •
    MS, United States 118 K2
Chiclana de la Frontera Beach •
    Spain . . . . 68 [96]
Chiclana de la Frontera • Spain . . . 86 B5
Chiclayo • Peru 43 B5
Chico • CA, United States 117 F1
Chicoutimi • QU, Canada 123 D1
Chicualacuala • Mozambique 102 J4
Chidambaram • India 106 D11
Chidley, Cape • NU, Canada 39 S4
Chiemsee • Germany 82 J4
Chiengi • Zambia 23 D5
Chiesa • Italy 91 E2
Chieti • Italy 91 H4
Chiéuti Beach • Italy . . . . 69 [137]
Chifeng • China 29 F2
Chigu Co • China 28 F3
Chiloe • Mozambique 24 E4
Chihuahua • Mexico 40 E6
Chihuahua [Adm] • Mexico 40 E6
Chikurachki, Vulkan •
    Russian Fed. 27 Q6
Chilca • Peru 127 B1
Chilcott I. • CL, Australia 34 J3
Childers • QL, Australia 111 F6
Chile • S. America 42 C7
Chile-Chico • Chile 45 B5
Chiloé de • Argentina 44 C4
Chillán • Chile 44 B6
Chiloé, I. de • Chile 45 B4
Chilpancingo • Mexico 123 E4
Chiltern Hills • United Kingdom . . . 74 E1
Chilumba • Malawi 24 E2
Chilung • Taiwan 29 G5
Chilwa, Lake • Malawi 24 F3
Chimanimani • Zimbabwe 102 J4
Chimanimani Nat. Park •
    Zimbabwe 102 J4
Chimbay • Uzbekistan 26 I9
Chimborazo, Volcán • Ecuador 43 B5
Chimbote • Peru 43 B5
Chimkent • Kazakhstan 26 K9
Chimney Rock Nat. Hist. Site Park •
    NE, United States . . . . 120 [166]
Chin • Rep. of Korea 30 D7
Chin • Myanmar 31 A2
China • Asia 25 K6
China Folk Culture Villages •
    Shenzhen, China 107 H3
Chinandega • Nicaragua 37 E5
Chincha Alta • Peru 127 B1
Chinchilla • QL, Australia 111 F6
Chindwin • Myanmar 31 A2
Chinese & Japanese Garden •
    Singapore 108 E1
Chingola • Zambia 24 D2
Chinguetti • Mauritania 20 C4

Chinguetti Heritage C •
    Mauritania . . . . 63 [92]
Chinhae • Rep. of Korea 30 E7
Chinhoyi • Zimbabwe 102 J2
Chinju • Rep. of Korea 30 D7
Chinko • Africa 23 C2
Chinle • AZ, United States 118 J2
Chinon • France 84 B1
Chinon [Château] • France 84 D4
Chióggia • Italy 91 E8
Chios Heritage C • Greece . . . . . 64 [184]
Chios • Greece 92 D5
Chios • Greece 92 D5
Chipata • Zambia 24 E2
Chiperone • Mozambique 24 F3
Chipinda Pools • Zimbabwe 102 J4
Chipiona Beach • Spain . . . . 68 [96]
Chipiona • Spain 86 B5
Chipman • NB, Canada 123 D7
Chippenham • United Kingdom 74 F3
Chipunquira • Colombia 43 C2
Chiquitos, Llanos de • Bolivia 44 D2
Chiquitos missions Heritage C •
    Bolivia . . . . 62 [55]
Chirchik • Uzbekistan 26 K9
Chiredzi • Zimbabwe 102 J4
Chirfa • Niger 20 D7
Chiri • Rep. of Korea 30 D7
Chiricahua Nat. Mon. •
    AZ, United States 118 J4
Chiricahua Nat. Mon. Park •
    AZ, United States . . . . 120 [119]
Chirinda • Russian Fed. 26 R4
Chirip, Vulkan • Russian Fed. 27 O7
Chirpan • Bulgaria 97 D3
Chirripó • Costa Rica 37 E6
Chirundu • Zimbabwe 102 J1
Chisamba • Zambia 24 D2
Chisasibi • QU, Canada 39 P6
Chisinau • Moldova 14 M2
Chistopol • Russian Fed. 17 I3
Chita • Russian Fed. 27 H6
Chitina • AK, United States 38 C4
Chitradurga • India 106 D6
Chitrakut • India 105 C7
Chitral • Pakistan 28 B1
Chitré • Panama 37 E6
Chittagong • Bangladesh 28 F4
Chittaurgarh • India 105 C6
Chittoor • India 106 D7
Chitungwiza • Zimbabwe 102 J2
Chiumbe • Angola 24 C3
Chiume • Angola 24 C3
Chiunzi, Válico de • Italy 91 G4
Chiusa • Italy 90 B1
Chiusi • Italy 91 E11
Chivasso • Italy 91 E5
Chivhu • Zimbabwe 102 J4
Chivilcoy • Argentina 127 D1
Chiwan • Shenzhen, China 107 H5
Chizarira Nat. Park • Zimbabwe . . 102 J1
Chizha • Russian Fed. 17 F1
Chobe • Botswana/Namibia 24 C3
Chobe Nat. Park Park • Botswana 103 [110]
Choc Bay • St Lucia 125 J1
Chodov • Czech Rep. 13 B7
Chodziez • Poland 13 F5
Choele-Choel • Argentina 45 C3
Choiseul • Solomon Is. 35 (1) F2
Choiseul • St Lucia 125 J3
Chojnice • Poland 13 F4
Chojnów • Poland 13 E6
Chokai • Japan 30 K5
Chóke • Ethiopia 23 F1
Cholet • France 84 D3
Cholula • Mexico 123 E4
Chom Thong • Thailand 109 G3
Choma • Zambia 24 D3
Chomutov • Czech Rep. 96 C1
Chon Buri • Thailand 109 H4
Chone • Ecuador 43 A4
Chongkrum, Laem •
    Ko Samui, Thailand 109 J2
Chongming • China 107 J4
Chongming Dao • China 107 J2
Chongmyo Shrine Heritage C •
    Rep. of Korea . . . . 63 [160]
Chongqing • China 29 D5
Chongup • Rep. of Korea 30 D7
Chonju • Rep. of Korea 30 D7
Chonos, Archipiélago de los •
    Chile 45 A5
Chorao I. • Goa, India 105 B1
Chorzów • Poland 13 H7
Choshi • Japan 30 K7
Choszczno • Poland 13 E4
Chota Nagpur • India 105 A2
Chott Ech Chergui • Algeria 20 F2
Choum • Mauritania 20 C4
Choybalsan • Mongolia 27 H7
Choyr • Mongolia 29 D1
Chrisoskalitisas, Moni •
    Crete, Greece 93 E5
Christchurch • New Zealand 35 D6
Christchurch Beach •
    United Kingdom . . . . 75 [82-83]
Christian, Cape • NU, Canada 39 R2
Christian Sound •
    AK, United States 38 D5
Christian Valley •
    Antigua & Barbuda 125 F3
Christiana • Norway 71 A3
Christiana • Jamaica 124 C1
Christiansfeld • Denmark 95 F13
Christiansø • Denmark 95 F16
Christiansted • U.S. Virgin Is. 58 B7
Christie Bay • NT, Canada 38 I4
Christmas • Kiribati 33 L5
Christmas Creek • WA, Australia . . . 34 E3
Christmas I. • Indian Ocean 32 D5
Christiansbáb • Greenland 39 U3
Chrysoroyiatissa Monastery •
    Cyprus 93 J3
Chrzanów • Poland 13 I7
Chu • Kazakhstan 26 L9
Chu [Riv] • Kazakhstan 26 K9
Chu Xian • China 107 J1
Chu Yang Sin • Vietnam 108 B2
Chu Zhou • China 107 J1
Chuansha • China 107 J2
Chubukulakh, gora •
    Russian Fed. 27 P3
Chudjand • Tajikistan 18 I1
Chudovo • Russian Fed. 97 E1
Chudskoye Ozero •
    Estonia/Russia 16 N7
Chugoku-Sanchi • Japan 30 G7
Chukai • Malaysia 32 C4
Chukchi • Russian Fed. 97 A7
Chukchi Sea • Arctic Ocean 40 (2) D2
Chukotskiy Poluostrov •
    Russian Fed. 27 W3
Chukotskoye More • Russian Fed. . . 46 GG2
Chulman • Russian Fed. 27 J5
Chulucanas • Peru 43 A5
Chulym • Russian Fed. 26 N7
Chumikan • Russian Fed. 27 M6
Chumphon • Thailand 31 B4

Chun'an • China 107 J3
Chunar • India 105 C8
Chunski • Russian Fed. 26 Q6
Chuor Phnum Krâvanh •
    Cambodia/Thailand 31 C4
Chuquibamba • Peru 127 B4
Chuquicamata • Chile 44 C3
Chur Ski • Switzerland . . . . 70 [108]
Chur • Switzerland 89 G4
Churapcha • Russian Fed. 27 L4
Churchill • SA, Canada 38 K5
Churchill • MN, Canada 38 M5
Churchill • NF, Canada 39 S6
Churchill Falls • NF, Canada 122 A8
Churchill Falls (Falls) •
    NF, Canada 39 S6
Churchill Lake • SA, Canada 38 J5
Churchill Peak • BC, Canada 38 F5
Churu • India 105 C2
Churuguara • Venezuela 43 D1
Churún Merú • Venezuela 43 E2
Churwalden Ski • Switzerland . . . 70 [109]
Chusovoy • Russian Fed. 26 I6
Chute, la • France 13 M9
Chute-Montmorency, Parc de la •
    QU, Canada 123 D1
Chuuk •
    Fed. States of Micronesia 33 G5
Chuvashia • Russian Fed. 17 H3
Chuxiong • China 31 C2
Chynovska jeskyne • Czech Rep. . . . 96 C4
Chyulu Nat. Park • Kenya 101 G4
Ciamis • Java, Indonesia 110 D6
Ciampino [Apt] • Italy 91 F3
Cianjar • Java, Indonesia 110 D1
Cicarija • Croatia 14 B4
Ciceron • St Lucia 125 J4
Cide • Turkey 15 N2
Ciechanów • Poland 13 L5
Ciechanowiec • Poland 13 L5
Ciego de Avila • Cuba 124 D3
Ciénaga • Colombia 43 C1
Cienfuegos • Cuba 124 C2
Cieza • Spain 87 C1
Çifteler • Turkey 15 M4
Cihanbeyli Platosu • Turkey 15 N5
Cijara, Embalse de • Spain 11 G5
Cijulang • Java, Indonesia 110 D6
Cilacap • Java, Indonesia 110 D6
Ciledug • Java, Indonesia 110 D1
Cilento • Italy 91 G4
Cilo Dag • Turkey 18 D2
Cimahi • Java, Indonesia 110 D2
Cimini, Monti • Italy 91 F1
Cimone • Italy 12 E4
Cîmpina • Romania 14 M4
Cîmpulung • Romania 14 M4
Cina, Tanjung • Indonesia 32 C4
Çinarcik • Turkey 15 K3
Cinca • Spain 10 F11
Cincar • Bosnia-Herz. 14 E6
Cincinnati • OH, United States 41 J4
Cindrelu, Virful • Romania 14 K4
Çine • Turkey 15 J6
Ciney • Belgium 5 I6
Cinque Terre Heritage C • Italy . . 64 [119]
Cinque Terre • Italy 91 E10
Cinto, Monte • Corsica, France . . . 85 L1
Cintra, Golfo de •
    Western Sahara 20 B4
Ciotat, la • France 85 H3
Cipó • Brazil 127 F1
Circeo, Parco Naz. del Park •
    Italy . . . . 72 [87]
Circeo, Parco Naz. del • Italy 91 F4
Circle • AK, United States 38 C3
Circus Circus Park •
    NV, United States . . . . 120 [K]
Cirebon • Java, Indonesia 110 D2
Cirema, Gunung •
    Java, Indonesia 110 D2
Cirencester • United Kingdom 74 D4
Ciró Marina • Italy 91 H7
Cirque Mtn • NF, Canada 39 S5
Cisco • TX, United States 119 N1
Ciscoande • Romania 14 L4
Citlaltépetl • Mexico 37 B4
Città di Castello • Italy 91 E7
Cittadella • Italy 91 E7
City of Rocks Nat. Reserve •
    ID, United States 117 E4
City of Rocks Nat. Reserve Park •
    ID, United States . . . . 120 [63]
Ciucasu, Virful • Romania 14 M4
Ciudad Acuña • Mexico 37 A2
Ciudad Altamirano • Mexico 123 E3
Ciudad Bolívar • Venezuela 43 E2
Ciudad Camargo • Mexico 40 F6
Ciudad del Carmen • Mexico 37 C4
Ciudad Delicias • Mexico 40 E6
Ciudad Guayana • Venezuela 43 E2
Ciudad Juárez • Mexico 40 E5
Ciudad Lerdo • Mexico 40 F6
Ciudad Madero • Mexico 123 E2
Ciudad Mante • Mexico 123 E2
Ciudad Obregón • Mexico 40 E6
Ciudad Ojeda • Venezuela 43 C1
Ciudad Piar • Venezuela 37 I6
Ciudad Real • Spain 11 H6
Ciudad Rodrigo • Spain 11 E4
Ciudad Valles • Mexico 37 B3
Ciudad Valles • Mexico 123 E2
Ciudad Victoria • Mexico 123 E2
Ciudadela Beach •
    Minorca, Spain . . . . 68 [110]
Ciutadella • Minorca, Spain 87 F1
Cividale del Friuli • Italy 13 C11
Civita Castellana • Italy 91 F1
Civitanova Marche • Italy 91 E12
Civitavécchia • Italy 91 F1
Cixerri • Italy 15 K5
Cixi • China 107 J4
Cizre • Turkey 18 D2
Clackmannan • United Kingdom . . . 75 A2
Clacton-on-Sea • United Kingdom . . 7 N4
Clamecy • France 10 I6
Clanwilliam • South Africa 100 C1
Claonaig • United Kingdom 78 A2
Clara Barton Nat. Hist. Site Park •
    MD, United States . . . . 121 [274]
Clara Lara Fun Park Park •
    Ireland . . . . 73 [20]
Claraville • NF, Canada 123 D4
Clare • Ireland 79 B4
Clare Abbey • Ireland 79 F6
Clare Glens • Ireland 79 F6
Clare I. Beach • Ireland . . . . 68 [44]
Clare I. • Ireland 79 B4
Claregalway Abbey • Ireland 79 F4
Claremont • NH, United States . . . 118 G3
Claremont • Jamaica 124 C2
Claremorris • Ireland 79 C4
Clare Fork • ID, United States 117 E3
Clarence Town • Bahamas 124 B4
Clarence • NU, Australia 34 H7
Clark, George Rogers, Nat. Hist. Park Park •
    IN, United States . . . . 121 [182]
Clarksville • TN, United States 41 I4

Clatsop, Fort, Nat. Mem. •
    OR, United States 117 E1
Clatsop, Fort, Nat. Mem. Park •
    OR, United States . . . . 120 [33]
Clausholm • Denmark 95 F10
Clausthal-Zellerfeld Spa •
    Germany . . . . 83 [79]
Clavière Ski • Italy . . . . 70 [193]
Clavière • Italy 91 E5
Clay Belt • QT/QU, Canada 39 O6
Clayton • NM, United States 40 F4
Clear, Cape • Ireland 79 F7
Clear I. • Ireland 79 F7
Clear Water Bay •
    Hong Kong, China 107 H6
Clearwater • AL/SA, Canada 38 I5
Clearwater • FL, United States . . . 119 M5
Clearwater Mtns •
    ID, United States 38 H7
Cleator Moor • United Kingdom . . . 74 C1
Cleburne • TX, United States 119 N1
Cleethorpes • United Kingdom 7 L8
Clermont • France 85 E2
Clermont • QL, Australia 111 E5
Clermont • FL, United States 121 C1
Clermont-Ferrand • France 5 F7
Clervaux • Luxembourg 80 A20
Clevedon • United Kingdom 74 F3
Cleveland • OH, United States 41 J3
Cleveland • TX, United States 119 N4
Clew Bay • Ireland 79 F1
Clifden • Ireland 79 B4
Clifden • New Zealand 112 L3
Clifton • AZ, United States 118 J4
Clinton • BC, Canada 38 G6
Clinton-Colden Lake •
    NT, Canada 38 J4
Clodomira • Argentina 44 D4
Cloghane • Ireland 79 F5
Clogher Head • Ireland 79 E2
Clogherhead Beach • Ireland . . . 68 [34]
Clonakilty Beach • Ireland . . . . . 68 [40]
Clonakilty • Ireland 79 F8
Clonakilty Bay • Ireland 79 F8
Cloncurry • QL, Australia 34 H4
Clonea Beach • Ireland . . . . 68 [39]
Clonmel • Ireland 79 E1
Clonmellon • Ireland 79 E1
Clorinda • Argentina 44 E4
Cloud Peak • WY, United States . . . 40 E3
Clovelly • United Kingdom 74 F2
Clovis • NM, United States 40 F5
Cluane Lake • YT, Canada 38 D4
Cluj-Napoca • Romania 14 K3
Clun Forest • United Kingdom 74 D1
Clusaz, la Ski • France . . . . 70 [21]
Clusaz, la • France 85 F2
Clutha • New Zealand 112 L4
Clutha District • New Zealand 112 L4
Clyde • NU, Canada 46 V2
Clyde • United Kingdom 74 B3
Clyde, Firth of •
    United Kingdom 6 G6
Clydebank • United Kingdom 74 B3
Clydebank • United Kingdom 74 B3
Coahuila • Mexico 40 F6
Coal I. • New Zealand 112 L3
Coalville • United Kingdom 7 K8
Coamo • Puerto Rico 125 E4
Coari • Brazil 43 E4
Coast Mtns • BC, Canada 38 F6
Coast Ranges •
    CA/OR, United States 40 B3
Coastal Plain • United States . . . . 119 N
Coats I. • NU, Canada 39 O4
Coatzacoalcos • Mexico 37 C4
Cobán • Guatemala 37 D4
Çobanısa • Turkey 93 G3
Cobar • NS, Australia 34 I6
Cobblers Reef • Barbados 125 H4
Cóbh • Ireland 79 F8
Cobourg • FL, United States 90 E4
Cobourg • OT, Canada 39 P8
Cobourg Peninsula •
    NT, Australia 34 F2
Cóbue • Mozambique 23 E6
Coburg • Germany 9 F6
Cochabamba • Bolivia 44 C2
Cochem • Germany 82 H1
Coches, les Ski • France . . . . . . 70 [33]
Cochin • India 106 D10
Cochin China • Vietnam 108 B3
Cochino, Bahía de • Cuba 124 D2
Cochrane • OT, Canada 39 O7
Cockburn Town • Bahamas 124 B4
Cockermouth • United Kingdom . . . 74 C1
Cockpit Country, The • Jamaica . . . 124 C1
Coco • Pacific Ocean 42 A4
Coco, Cayo • Cuba 124 D3
Coco Channel • India 28 F6
Coco o Segovia •
    Honduras/Nicaragua 37 E5
Coco, Parque Nac. Isla del Heritage N •
    Costa Rica . . . . 60 [23]
Cocoa Beach • FL, United States . . 119 M6
Cocoa I. • Maldives 106 E4
Cod Bay, Cape •
    MA, United States 118 H2
Cod, Cape, Nat. Seashore Park •
    MA, United States . . . . 121 [342]
Coda Cavallo, Capo •
    Sardinia, Italy 12 D8
Codajás • Brazil 43 E4
Codigoro • Italy 12 G4
Codrington College • Barbados . . . 125 H4
Coesfeld • Germany 81 E3
Coëtivy • Seychelles 106 F4
Coeur d'Alene •
    ID, United States 117 E2
Coevorden • Netherlands 80 A8
Coffs Harbour • NS, Australia 34 J6
Cofrentes • Spain 11 K5
Cogalnic • Moldova 14 P3
Coglans, Monte • Austria/Italy 91 E14
Cognac • France 85 G1
Cogolin Beach • France . . . . 68 [116]
Cogolin • France 85 H4
Coiba • Panama 37 E6
Coihaique • Chile 45 B5
Coimar • Cuba 124 D2
Coimbatore • India 106 D10
Coimbra • Portugal 11 C4
Coimbra [Adm] • Portugal 88 A2
Coin • Spain 11 G8
Cointrin [Apt] •
    Switzerland/France 89 G5
Colac • VI, Australia 111 E3
Colac • New Zealand 112 L4
Çolakli Beach • Turkey . . . . 69 [199]
Colares • Portugal 88 A2
Colatina • Brazil 127 C2
Colbeck Castle • Jamaica 124 C4
Colca • Peru 127 B4
Colca, Cañon del • Peru 127 B4
Colchester • United Kingdom 74 E2
Coleraine • United Kingdom 7 F6

Coleraine [Adm] •
    United Kingdom 75 A3
Coles, Punta • Peru 127 B4
Colfosco Ski • Italy . . . . 70 [233]
Colfosco • Italy 90 B2
Coliciure • France 85 K2
Colima • Mexico 123 E3
Colima [Adm] • Mexico 37 (1) B2
Colintraive • United Kingdom 78 A2
Coll • United Kingdom 6 F5
College Station •
    TX, United States 119 N3
Collier Bay • WA, Australia 34 D3
Collingwood • New Zealand 35 D5
Collingwood • OT, Canada 122 B5
Collins • MS, United States 118 K2
Collinstown Beach • Ireland . . . . 68 [38]
Collinsville • QL, Australia 34 I4
Colliouire Beach • France . . . . . 68 [111]
Collioure • France 85 K2
Collonges-la-Rouge • France 85 G2
Collooney • Ireland 79 F2
Colmar • France 10 M5
Colmenar Viejo • Spain 11 H4
Colóane • Macau 107 H3
Colóane Village • Macau 107 H3
Cologne Heritage C • Germany . . 64 [38]
Cologne • Germany 81 E3
Coloma • CA, United States 117 F3
Colomb Beach • Goa, India 105 B2
Colombia • S. America 43 C3
Colombier • Switzerland 89 G1
Colombo • Sri Lanka 106 D15
Colombo, Cristofo [Apt] • Italy 91 E6
Colón • Panama 37 F6
Colón • Cuba 124 D2
Colón • Argentina 127 D1
Colón, Archipiélago de •
    Pacific Ocean 43 (1) A1
Colona • SA, Australia 34 H6
Colònia de Sant Jordi •
    Majorca, Spain 87 H4
Colonia del Sacramento Heritage C •
    Uruguay . . . . 62 [65]
Colonia del Sacramento •
    Uruguay 127 D2
Colonia Las Heras • Argentina 45 C5
Colonia Suiza • Uruguay 127 D2
Colonial Nat. Hist. Park •
    VA, United States 118 H3
Colonial Nat. Hist. Park Park •
    VA, United States . . . . 121 [257]
Colorado [Adm] • United States . . . 40 E4
Colorado • Argentina 45 C3
Colorado Desert •
    CA, United States 117 F6
Colorado Nat. Mon. Park •
    CO, United States . . . . 120 [90]
Colorado Plateau •
    United States 118 J1
Colorado [Riv] •
    Mexico/United States 40 D5
Colorado [Riv] •
    TX, United States 40 G5
Colorado Springs •
    CO, United States 40 F4
Colville • MO, United States 41 H4
Columbia • TN, United States 41 I4
Columbia • SC, United States 41 J5
Columbia • LA, United States 118 K1
Columbia Basin •
    WA, United States 117 E2
Columbia Gorge •
    OR/WA, United States 117 E1
Columbia Icefield • AL, Canada . . . 122 C4
Columbia Mtns • BC, Canada 38 G6
Columbia Plateau •
    United States 117 E4
Columbine, Cape • South Africa . . . 100 C1
Columbus • NE, United States 41 G3
Columbus • OH, United States 41 J4
Columbus • TX, United States 119 N3
Columbus Monument • Bahamas . . 124 B4
Columbus Park • Jamaica 124 C1
Colva • Goa, India 105 B2
Colva Beach • Goa, India 105 B2
Colville Channel • New Zealand . . . 35 E3
Colville Lake • NT, Canada 38 F3
Colwell Bay Beach •
    United Kingdom . . . . 75 [89]
Colwyn Bay • United Kingdom 7 I8
Comácchio • Italy 12 G4
Comácchio, Lido di • Italy 91 E8
Coman, Mt • Antarctica 46 (1) II2
Comarugo • Spain 87 D3
Combarelles, Groote des •
    France 85 G2
Combermere Bay • Myanmar 31 A3
Combloux Ski • France . . . . 70 [24]
Combrit Beach • France . . . . 68 [61]
Comerio • Puerto Rico 125 E4
Comillas Beach • Spain . . . . 68 [70]
Comino • Malta 93 H1
Comminotto • Malta 93 H1
Cómiso • Sicily, Italy 90 D4
Commercy • France 5 I6
Commingies • France 85 K1
Como • Italy 91 E2
Como, Lago di • Italy 91 E2
Comodoro Rivadavia • Argentina . . 45 C5
Comoé, Parc nat. de la Heritage N •
    Côte d'Ivoire . . . . 61 [74]
Comoé, Parc nat. de la Park •
    Côte d'Ivoire . . . . 103 [21]
Comorin, Cape • India 106 D14
Comoros, Archipel des • Comoros . . 24 G2
Compiègne • France 85 E2
Compiègne, Forêt de • France 85 E2
Comté • Moldova 14 P3
Comté Tolosan • France 84 B3
Comtés Rhodaniens • France 84 B4
Con Dao • Vietnam 108 B3
Conakry • Guinea 22 A2
Concarneau • France 88 E8
Conceição • Portugal 88 E8
Conceição do Araguaia • Brazil . . . 43 G5
Concepción • Chile 44 B6
Concepción • Argentina 44 C4
Concepción • Bolivia 44 D2
Concepción • Paraguay 44 D3
Concepción • Peru 127 B1
Concepción del Uruguay •
    Argentina 44 E5
Conception • Seychelles 106 F1
Conception I. • Bahamas 124 B4
Conception, Point •
    CA, United States 117 F5
Concord • NH, United States 118 G3
Concordia • Argentina 44 E5
Conde • Brazil 44 I1
Condobolin • NS, Australia 111 G1
Condor, Cordillera del •
    Ecuador/Peru 43 B4
Condrieu • France 84 B4
Condroz • Belgium 5 I4

Coneglianо • Italy 12 G3
Conero, Costa • Italy 91 E12
Coney Beach Park •
    United Kingdom . . . . 73 [32]
Confolens • France 85 G2
Cong • Ireland 79 F4
Congaree Swamp Nat. Mon. Park •
    SC, United States . . . . 121 [339]
Congo • Africa 22 H4
Congo Basin • Africa 100 A3
Congo, Democratic Republic of •
    Africa 23 C4
Congo [Riv] •
    Congo/Dem. Rep. of Congo . . . 23 D4
Congonhas Heritage C • Brazil . . 62 [63]
Congonhas • Brazil 127 C1
Conil de la Frontera Beach •
    Spain . . . . 68 [96]
Conil de la Frontera • Spain 86 B5
Conilera, I. • Spain 87 H4
Coniston • United Kingdom 74 C4
Coniston Water • United Kingdom . . 74 C4
Conn, Lough • Ireland 79 F2
Connah's Quay • United Kingdom . . 7 D8
Connaught • Ireland 7 D8
Connecticut [Adm] •
    United States 118 H2
Connecticut [Riv] •
    United States 118 G3
Connemara • Ireland 79 F3
Connemara Nat. Park Park •
    Ireland . . . . 72 [39]
Connemara Nat. Park • Ireland 79 F3
Conny-Land Park • Switzerland . . 73 [81]
Conroe • TX, United States 119 N4
Conselheiro Lafaiete • Brazil 127 C1
Consett • United Kingdom 7 K7
Consett Bay • Barbados 125 H4
Consett Point • Barbados 125 H4
Constance • Germany 82 G8
Constance, Lake • Germany 82 J5
Constanta • Romania 97 D2
Constantine • Spain 86 B2
Constantine • Algeria 20 G1
Constantinople • Turkey 71 A15
Constitución • Chile 44 B6
Constitution Gardens Park •
    DC, United States . . . . 121 [283]
Consuegra • Spain 11 H5
Consuelo Peak • QL, Australia 34 I4
Contamana • Peru 43 C5
Contamines-Montjoie, les Ski •
    France . . . . 70 [28]
Contamines-Montjoie, les •
    France 85 F2
Contreras, • Spain 11 J5
Contwoyto Lake • NT/NU, Canada . . 38 J3
Conway • Fiji 35 (2) C3
Conway • FL, United States 121 C2
Conway, Cape • QL, Australia 111 F1
Conway, Mt • NT, Australia 112 H2
Conway • United Kingdom 7 I8
Coober Pedy • SA, Australia 34 F5
Cook • SA, Australia 34 F6
Cook Is. • Pacific Ocean 33 K7
Cook, Mt • New Zealand 35 C6
Cook Strait • New Zealand 35 E5
Cookeville • TN, United States 41 I4
Cookhouse • South Africa 100 A3
Cookstown • United Kingdom 75 A3
Cooktown • QL, Australia 34 I3
Coolangatta • QL, Australia 111 F6
Coolgardie • WA, Australia 34 D6
Cooma • NS, Australia 111 G4
Coonabarabran • NS, Australia . . . 34 I6
Coonoor • India 106 D10
Cooper • AK, United States 38 C4
Cooper Creek • QL/SA, Australia . . 34 H5
Cooper I. • New Zealand 112 L3
Coorg • India 106 D6
Coos Bay • OR, United States 117 E3
Cootamundra • NS, Australia 111 G1
Copacabana • Bolivia 127 B4
Copacabana • Brazil 127 C4
Copán • Honduras 37 D5
Copán Heritage C • Honduras . . . 62 [30]
Copano Bay • TX, United States . . 119 N5
Copeland Forest •
    United Kingdom 74 C1
Copenhagen Beach • Denmark . . 68 [21]
Copenhagen • Denmark 95 F11
Copiapó • Chile 44 B4
Coporolo • Angola 24 A2
Copper Mtn Ski •
    CO, United States . . . . 116 [96]
Copperas Cove •
    TX, United States 119 N3
Coppermine • NU, Canada 38 H3
Coppermine [Riv] •
    NT/NU, Canada 38 H3
Coqen • China 28 F3
Coquimbo • Chile 44 B5
Corabia • Romania 14 L6
Coral Bay • Cyprus 93 J3
Coral Coast • Tunisia 101 C2
Coral Gables •
    FL, United States 119 M8
Coral Harbour • NU, Canada 39 O4
Coral Heights • Bahamas 124 B3
Coral Sea • Australia 33 G7
Coral Sea Is. Territory •
    Australia 34 I3
Coral Springs •
    FL, United States 119 M8
Coralarium, Sentosa • Singapore . . 108 E4
Coralito, Riviera del •
    Sardinia, Italy 90 C1
Corató • Italy 14 D8
Corbeil-Essonnes • France 85 E4
Corbett Nat. Park • India 105 C2
Corbier, le Ski • France . . . . . . 70 [47]
Corbières • France 85 K2
Corby • United Kingdom 7 L9
Corcaigh • Ireland 79 F8
Córcega • Puerto Rico 125 E1
Corcovado, Golfo de • Chile 45 B4
Corcovado, Volcán • Chile 45 B4
Cordele, GA, United States 41 J5
Cordévole • Italy 90 B2
Cordilheiras, Serra das •
    Brazil 45 (1) B3
Cordillera Central • Colombia 43 B3
Cordillera Central • Peru 43 B5
Cordillera Central • Bolivia 44 C2
Cordillera Central Heritage C •
    Philippines . . . . 63 [175]
Cordillera Central •
    Puerto Rico 125 E3
Cordillera Occidental •
    Colombia 43 B3
Cordillera Occidental •
    Bolivia/Chile 44 C2
Cordillera Oriental • Colombia 43 C2
Cordillera Oriental •
    Bolivia/Peru 44 C1
Cordillera Real • Ecuador 43 B4
Córdoba • Argentina 44 D5
Córdoba Heritage C • Spain . . . . 64 [93]

Córdoba

Córdoba • Spain.....86 B2
Córdoba • Mexico.....123 E4
Córdoba, Sierras de • Argentina.....44 D5
Cordova • AK, United States.....46 D3
Corfe Castle • United Kingdom.....74 F6
Corfu • Corfu, Greece.....69 [149]
Corfu • Corfu, Greece.....92 B1
Corfu • Corfu, Greece.....92 B1
Corfu [I.] • Greece.....92 B1
Corfu [I.] • Greece.....92 B1
Coria • Spain.....11 E5
Coria del Río • Spain.....11 E7
Coricudgy, Mt • NS, Australia.....34 J6
Corigliano Calabro • Italy.....12 K9
Corinaldo • Italy.....91 E12
Coringa Is. • CL, Australia.....34 J3
Corinth • Greece.....92 D4
Corinth • Greece.....92 D4
Corinth Canal • Greece.....15 D6
Corinto • Brazil.....44 H2
Corjuem Fort • Goa, India.....105 B1
Cork • Ireland.....79 F8
Cork [Adm] • Ireland.....79 F8
Çorlu • Turkey.....15 I2
Çorlu [Riv] • Turkey.....15 I10
Cornas • France.....84 B4
Cornélio • Brazil.....44 F3
Corner Brook • NF, Canada.....123 D3
Cornesti • Moldova.....14 P2
Corniche, La • France.....85 H2
Corno Grande • Italy.....91 F2
Cornouaille • France.....84 C3
Cornwall • United Kingdom.....74 F4
Cornwall • OT, Canada.....122 B7
Cornwall • Jamaica.....124 C1
Cornwall, Cape • United Kingdom.....74 F4
Cornwallis I. • NU, Canada.....38 L1
Coro • Venezuela.....43 D1
Coro Heritage C • Venezuela.....62 [41]
Corofin • Ireland.....79 F4
Coromandel • New Zealand.....35 E3
Coromandel Coast • India.....106 D7
Coromandel Peninsula • New Zealand.....35 E3
Coron • Philippines.....31 G4
Coronado Nat. Mem. • AZ, United States.....118 J4
Coronado Nat. Mem. Park • AZ, United States.....120 [116]
Coronation Gulf • NU, Canada.....38 I3
Coronation I. • Antarctica.....59 A1
Coronel • Chile.....44 B6
Coronel Fabriciano • Brazil.....127 C2
Coronel Oviedo • Paraguay.....44 E4
Coronel Pringles • Argentina.....45 D3
Coronel Suárez • Argentina.....127 D3
Coronet Peak • New Zealand.....112 L4
Coropuna, Nudo • Peru.....127 B4
Çorovodë • Albania.....15 B3
Corpus Christi • TX, United States.....119 N5
Corpus Christi Bay • TX, United States.....119 N5
Corralejo • Fuerteventura, Canary Is.....87 E2
Corralejo, Playas de • Fuerteventura, Canary Is.....87 E2
Corraun Peninsula • Ireland.....79 F1
Corrençon-en-Vercors Ski • France.....70 [54]
Correntina • Brazil.....44 H1
Corrib, Lough • Ireland.....79 F4
Corrientes • Argentina.....44 E4
Corrientes, Cabo • Mexico.....37 (1) A1
Corrientes, Cabo • Colombia.....43 B2
Corrientes, Cabo • Cuba.....124 D1
Corrigan • TX, United States.....119 N4
Corrigin • WA, Australia.....34 C6
Corse • France.....12 D6
Corse, Cap • Corsica, France.....85 L2
Corse-du-Sud • Corsica, France.....85 L3
Corsham Court • United Kingdom.....74 F3
Corsica • France.....85 L
Corsica, Canale di • France/Italy.....12 D6
Corsicana • TX, United States.....119 N1
Corte • Corsica, France.....85 L2
Cortés, Laguna de • Cuba.....124 D1
Cortina Ski • Italy.....70 [242]
Cortina d'Ampezzo • Italy.....90 B2
Cortona • Italy.....91 E11
Corubal • Guinea/Guinea-Bissau.....22 B2
Coruche • Portugal.....88 D2
Corumbá • Brazil.....44 E2
Corvara in Badia • Italy.....90 B2
Corvo • Azores.....88 B1
Cos Beach • Greece.....69 [186]
Cos • Greece.....92 D8
Cos • Greece.....92 D8
Cosenza • Italy.....12 K9
Cosmoledo, Atoll de • Seychelles.....106 F3
Cosne-sur-Loire • France.....10 H6
Costa, Cordillera de la • Venezuela.....43 E2
Costa d'en Blanes • Majorca, Spain.....87 H3
Costa da Caparica • Portugal.....88 D1
Costa Rica • C. America.....37 D5
Costa Teguise • Lanzarote, Canary Is.....87 E3
Costiera Amalfitana Heritage C • Italy.....64 [129]
Costières de Nîmes • France.....84 B4
Costinesti • Romania.....97 D2
Coswig • Germany.....13 C6
Cotabato • Philippines.....31 G5
Cotahuasi • Peru.....127 B4
Cotahuasi, Cañon del • Peru.....127 B4
Cote 2000 Ski • France.....70 [53]
Côte Chalonnaise • France.....84 B2
Côte d'Azur • France.....85 H
Côte d'Ivoire • Africa.....10 J6
Côte d'Or • France.....84 B2
Côte de Beaune • France.....84 B2
Côte de Nuits • France.....84 B2
Côte Rotie • France.....84 B4
Coteaux de Vendômois • France.....84 B4
Coteaux du Tricastin • France.....84 B4
Coteaux les Baux-de-Provence • France.....84 B4
Cotehele • United Kingdom.....74 F5
Cotentin • France.....10 D4
Côtes d'Armor • France.....84 B3
Côtes des Frontonnais • France.....84 B3
Côtes du Lubéron • France.....84 B4
Côtes des Marmandais • France.....84 B4
Côtes du Rhône • France.....84 B4
Côtes du Roussillon • France.....84 B4
Côtes du Ventoux • France.....84 B4
Côtes du Vivarais • France.....84 B4
Cotignaa Wildlife Sanctuary • Goa, India.....105 B2
Coto de Doñana, Parque Nac. Heritage N • Spain.....61 [47]
Coto de Doñana, Parque Nac. Park • Spain.....72 [75]

Coto de Doñana, Parque Nac. • Spain.....86 B1
Cotonou • Benin.....22 E3
Cotopaxi, Volcán • Ecuador.....43 B4
Cotswold Hills • United Kingdom.....74 D4
Cotswold Wildlife Park • United Kingdom.....74 D4
Cottbus • Germany.....8 J5
Cotton Ground • St Kitts & Nevis.....125 G4
Cotton Tower • Barbados.....125 H4
Coubre, Fôret de la • France.....85 G1
Coubre, Pointe de la • France.....85 G1
Coulee Dam Nat. Recreation Area • WA, United States.....117 E2
Coulee Dam Nat. Recreation Area Park • WA, United States.....120 [29]
Coulogne • QU, Canada.....122 B2
Coulommiers • France.....85 E4
Council Bluffs • IA, United States.....41 G3
Courances • France.....85 E4
Courchevel Ski • France.....70 [36]
Courchevel • France.....85 F4
Courmayeur Ski • Italy.....70 [198]
Courmayeur • Italy.....91 E1
Courseulles-sur-Mer Beach • France.....68 [57]
Courtenay • BC, Canada.....122 C3
Courtmacsherry • Ireland.....79 F8
Courtown Beach • Ireland.....68 [37]
Cousin • Seychelles.....106 F4
Cousine • Seychelles.....106 F4
Coutainville • France.....84 C2
Coutances • France.....10 D4
Couvin • Belgium.....5 H4
Covadonga, Parque Nac. de la Montaña de Park • Spain.....72 [73]
Coventry • United Kingdom.....74 D2
Coverack • United Kingdom.....74 F4
Covilhã • Portugal.....11 D4
Cowboy Country • NV, United States.....117 F2
Cowdenbeath • United Kingdom.....74 B4
Cowes • United Kingdom.....5 B4
Cowes Beach • United Kingdom.....75 [91-92]
Cowpens Nat. Battlefield Park • SC, United States.....121 [243]
Cowra • NS, Australia.....111 G2
Cox's Bazar • Bangladesh.....28 F4
Crab Hill • Antigua & Barbuda.....125 F3
Crabs Peninsula • Antigua & Barbuda.....125 F2
Cracow Heritage C • Poland.....64 [141]
Cradock • South Africa.....100 C4
Craig • CO, United States.....40 E3
Craigavon • United Kingdom.....75 A3
Craignure • United Kingdom.....78 A2
Crailsheim • Germany.....9 F7
Craiova • Romania.....14 K5
Cranborne Chase • United Kingdom.....74 F3
Cranbrook • WA, Australia.....34 C6
Cranbrook • BC, Canada.....122 C4
Crane Beach • Barbados.....125 H4
Cranfield Beach • United Kingdom.....75 [228]
Cranmore Ski • NH, United States.....116 [212]
Crans-Montana Ski • Switzerland.....70 [90]
Crans-Montana • Switzerland.....89 G6
Crasna • Romania.....14 J2
Crater Lake Nat. Park • OR, United States.....117 E3
Crater Lake Nat. Park Park • OR, United States.....120 [36]
Craters of the Moon Nat. Mon. Park • ID, United States.....120 [165]
Crateús • Brazil.....45 (1) D3
Crati • Italy.....12 L9
Crato • Brazil.....45 (1) D3
Craufordsburn Beach • United Kingdom.....68 [99]
Crawley • United Kingdom.....74 E3
Crécy • France.....71 A7
Crediton • United Kingdom.....74 F2
Cree Lake • SA, Canada.....38 J5
Creerlea Abbey • Ireland.....79 F2
Creil • France.....85 E6
Crema • Italy.....91 E6
Cremona • Italy.....91 E6
Crepy-en-Valois • France.....85 E6
Cres • Croatia.....14 B5
Cres [I.] • Croatia.....14 B5
Crescent City • NV, United States.....117 F1
Crescent I. • Hong Kong, China.....107 H4
Crespi d'Adda Heritage C • Italy.....64 [110]
Crested Butte Ski • CO, United States.....116 [100]
Creswell Bay • NU, Canada.....38 M2
Crete • Greece.....93 E
Crete, Sea of • Greece.....92 D11
Crete, Sea of • Greece.....35 (2) B1
Créteil • France.....85 E4
Creus, Cap de • Spain.....87 D2
Creuse • France.....84 D4
Creusot, le • France.....10 J7
Crevillente • Spain.....87 C1
Crewe • United Kingdom.....7 J8
Crianlarich • United Kingdom.....74 B1
Criccieth Beach • United Kingdom.....75 [190]
Crichton Castle • United Kingdom.....74 B4
Criciúma • Brazil.....44 G4
Crieff • United Kingdom.....74 B1
Crikvenica • Croatia.....12 I3
Crimea • Ukraine.....14 M7
Crimmitschau • Germany.....9 H6
Crinkley Bottom • United Kingdom.....74 F3
Crisan • Romania.....97 D2
Cristal, Sierra del • Cuba.....124 D8
Cristalândia • Brazil.....43 H6
Cristóbal • Panama.....43 C1
Cristóbal Colón • Colombia.....43 C1
Criuleni • Moldova.....14 P2
Crisul Negru • Romania.....13 L11
Crisul Repede • Romania.....13 L10
Crna • F.Y.R. of Macedonia.....15 C2
Crni Drim • Albania.....14 H8
Crni Vrh • Slovenia.....13 L11
Croagh Patrick • Ireland.....79 F1
Croatia • Europe.....14 B5
Crockett • TX, United States.....119 N4
Crocodile Farm • Singapore.....108 C1
Crocodile Paradise • Singapore.....108 C4
Croisic, le • France.....44 B5
Croix-Valmer, la Beach • France.....85 H4
Croker I. • NT, Australia.....34 F2
Cromer • United Kingdom.....7 N9

Cromer Beach • United Kingdom.....75 [43]
Cromwell • New Zealand.....112 L2
Crooked • BC, Canada.....122 C1
Crooked I. • Hong Kong, China.....107 H4
Crooked I. • Bahamas.....124 B4
Cross Cays • Bahamas.....124 B2
Cross River • Nigeria.....22 F3
Cross River Nat. Park Park • Nigeria.....103 [37]
Crosshaven • Ireland.....79 F8
Crossmolina • Ireland.....79 F2
Crotone • Italy.....12 L9
Crown Point • Trinidad & Tobago.....125 K2
Crown Prince Frederik • NU, Canada.....39 N2
Crowsnest Pass • AL, Canada.....38 I7
Croyde Bay Beach • United Kingdom.....75 [134]
Croydon • QL, Australia.....34 H3
Croydon • United Kingdom.....74 E1
Crozes-Hermitage • France.....84 B4
Crozet, Is. • Indian Ocean.....19 J10
Crozon, Presqu'île de • France.....84 C1
Crúcoli Beach • Italy.....69 [133]
Cruden Bay Beach • United Kingdom.....75 [7]
Cruces • Cuba.....124 D2
Cruese • France.....10 G7
Crummock Water • United Kingdom.....74 C1
Crump I. • Antigua & Barbuda.....125 F2
Cruz Alta • Brazil.....44 F4
Cruz, Cabo • Cuba.....124 D7
Cruz, Cayo • Cuba.....124 D3
Cruz del Eje • Argentina.....44 D5
Cruzeiro • Brazil.....127 C3
Cruzeiro do Oeste • Brazil.....44 F3
Cruzeiro do Sul • Brazil.....43 C5
Crystal Mtn Ski • WA, United States.....116 [45]
Crystal Mtn Ski • MI, United States.....116 [135]
Cserhát • Hungary.....14 L2
Csurgó • Hungary.....14 J3
Ctesiphon • Iraq.....98 B4
Cu Lao Hon • Vietnam.....108 B4
Cuamba • Mozambique.....24 F2
Cuangar • Angola.....24 B3
Cuango • Angola.....23 B5
Cuango [Riv] • Angola.....23 B6
Cuanza • Angola.....23 B6
Cuarto • Argentina.....45 D2
Cuba • Portugal.....11 D6
Cuba • West Indies.....124 D
Cubango • Angola/Namibia.....24 B3
Cubelles Beach • Spain.....68 [105]
Cubells • Ibiza, Spain.....87 G3
Cuchia • Spain.....86 B1
Cuchilla Grande • Uruguay.....45 F2
Cuchilla Grande • Uruguay.....127 D2
Cuchillas de Toa • Cuba.....124 D8
Cuckmere Haven Beach • United Kingdom.....75 [74]
Cuckold Point • Barbados.....125 H1
Cucq Beach • France.....68 [55]
Cucui • Brazil.....43 D3
Cúcuta • Colombia.....106 D7
Cuddalore • India.....106 D7
Cuddapah • India.....106 D6
Cue • WA, Australia.....34 C5
Cuéllar • Spain.....11 I4
Cuenca • Spain.....11 I4
Cuenca • Ecuador.....43 B4
Cuenca Heritage C • Spain.....64 [76]
Cuenca, Serranía de • Spain.....11 J4
Cuernavaca • Mexico.....123 E4
Cueto • Cuba.....124 D8
Cueva de Bellamar • Cuba.....124 D2
Cuevas de Almanzora Beach • Spain.....68 [99]
Cueva de Camuy • Puerto Rico.....125 E1
Cuevas del Indio • Cuba.....124 D1
Cui Heng • China.....107 H2
Cuiabá • Brazil.....44 E2
Cuilo • Angola.....23 B6
Cuima • Angola.....24 B2
Cuito • Angola.....24 B2
Cuitzeo • Mexico.....123 E1
Culara, l.da • Portugal.....88 E2
Culbone Church • United Kingdom.....74 F1
Culcairn • NS, Australia.....111 G1
Culdaff Beach • Ireland.....68 [46]
Culemborg • Netherlands.....80 C4
Culgoa • QL, Australia.....111 F5
Culiacán • Mexico.....40 E7
Culik • Bali, Indonesia.....110 C2
Culion • Philippines.....31 F4
Culion [I.] • Philippines.....31 F4
Cullen • Spain.....11 K5
Cullera • Spain.....68 [102]
Cullman • AL, United States.....41 I5
Culver, Point • WA, Australia.....34 D6
Cuma • Italy.....91 G3
Cumana • Venezuela.....43 E1
Cumbal, Volcán • Colombia.....43 B2
Cumberland • MD, United States.....41 K4
Cumberland, Cape • Vanuatu.....35 (2) B1
Cumberland Gap Nat. Hist. Park Park • KY, United States.....121 [234]
Cumberland I. Nat. Seashore Park • GA, United States.....121 [217]
Cumberland Peninsula • NU, Canada.....39 R3
Cumberland Sound • NU, Canada.....39 R3
Cumbernauld • United Kingdom.....74 B3
Cumbrae Slip • United Kingdom.....78 A3
Cumbre del Libertador General San Martin • Argentina.....44 C3
Cumbre, Paso de la • Argentina/Chile.....44 B5
Cumbria • United Kingdom.....74 C
Cumbrian Mtns • United Kingdom.....7 I7
Cumnock • United Kingdom.....74 F5
Cumra • Turkey.....15 N6
Cunene • Angola/Namibia.....24 C2
Cúneo • Italy.....91 E5
Cunit Beach • Spain.....68 [104]
Cunnamulla • QL, Australia.....111 F5
Cunningham • United Kingdom.....74 F5
Cunupia • Trinidad & Tobago.....125 K2
Cuokka rassa • Norway.....16 M2
Cupar • United Kingdom.....74 B2
Cupica, Golfo de • Colombia.....43 B2
Cupids • NF, Canada.....123 E1
Cupra Marittima • Italy.....91 F11
Cupra Marittima Beach • Italy.....69 [140]
Curaçao • West Indies.....37 H5
Curacautín • Chile.....44 B6
Curdimurka • SA, Australia.....34 G5
Curepipe • Mauritius.....24 [1]
Curepto • Venezuela.....43 E2
Curicó • Chile.....44 B5
Curieuse • Seychelles.....106 F4
Curitibanos • Brazil.....44 F4
Curitiba • Brazil.....44 G4

Curium • Cyprus.....93 J3
Curoca • Angola.....24 A3
Curracloe Beach • Ireland.....68 [37]
Curragh, The • Ireland.....79 E3
Currais Novos • Brazil.....45 (1) D3
Curral das Freiras • Madeira.....88 C1
Curral-Velho • Cape Verde.....22 (1) B1
Currane, Lough • Ireland.....79 F7
Currie • TS, Australia.....34 H7
Curtain Bluff • Antigua & Barbuda.....125 F3
Curtea de Arges • Romania.....14 L4
Curtis • New Zealand.....33 J9
Curtis Channel • QL, Australia.....111 F4
Curtis I. • QL, Australia.....111 F4
Curuguaty • Paraguay.....44 E3
Curupira, Sierra de • Brazil/Venezuela.....43 D3
Curuzú Cuatiá • Argentina.....44 E4
Curvelo • Brazil.....127 B2
Cusco • Peru.....127 B2
Cusco • Angola.....23 B5
Cutervo • Peru.....43 B5
Cutro • Italy.....12 L9
Cuttack • India.....28 E4
Cuxhaven • Germany.....8 D3
Cuya • Chile.....44 B3
Cuyahoga Valley Nat. Recreation Area Park • OH, United States.....121 [190]
Cuyuni • Guyana/Venezuela.....43 E2
Cuzco Heritage C • Peru.....62 [51]
Cuzco • Peru.....127 B2
Cwm-yr-Eglwys Beach • United Kingdom.....75 [168]
Cwmtydu Beach • United Kingdom.....75 [77]
Cyclades • Greece.....92 D8
Cyclades • Greece.....92 D8
Cypress Hills • AL/SA, Canada.....38 I7
Cyprus • Europe.....93 J
Cyrenaica • Libya.....21 D1
Cyrene • Libya.....21 D1
Cyrene Heritage C • Libya.....64 [235]
Czech Republic • Europe.....13 D8
Czechowice-Dziedzice • Poland.....13 G4
Czersk • Poland.....13 G4
Częstochowa • Poland.....13 I7

D'Arros • Seychelles.....106 F2
D'Entrecasteaux Is. • Papua New Guinea.....35 (1) E2
D'Urville I. • New Zealand.....35 D5
Da Hinggan Ling • China.....27 I8
Da Lat • Vietnam.....108 B2
Da Lat Plateau • Vietnam.....108 B2
Da Nang • Vietnam.....31 D3
Da Qaidam • China.....29 B3
Da Song • Vietnam.....108 A1
Da Xi • China.....31 F1
Da Yunhe • China.....27 H6
Daba Shan • China.....29 D4
Dabakala • Côte d'Ivoire.....22 D3
Dabas • Hungary.....13 I10
Dabeiba • Colombia.....43 B2
Dabie Shan • China.....29 F4
Dabola • Guinea.....22 B2
Dabolim [Apt] • Goa, India.....105 B1
Dabsan Hu • China.....28 F1
Dachau • Germany.....82 J3
Dachstein • Austria.....89 H4
Dadanawa • Guyana.....43 E2
Daday • Turkey.....15 O2
Dadès, Gorges du • Morocco.....101 D4
Dádejsö • Sweden.....95 F8
Dadra • India.....28 A3
Dadu • Pakistan.....28 A3
Dadu He • China.....29 C4
Daeni • Romania.....97 D2
Dafnoúdi, Akra • Greece.....92 C2
Dafnoúdi, Akra • Greece.....92 C2
Dafok, Am • Sudan.....23 C4
Dagali • Norway.....94 D3
Dagana • Senegal.....20 B5
Dagestan • Russian Fed.....17 H6
Dagg Sound • New Zealand.....112 L1
Dagomys • Russian Fed.....17 F6
Dagomys • Russian Fed.....96 A2
Dagupan • Philippines.....31 G3
Dahab • Egypt.....101 F4
Dahlak • Eritrea.....21 H4
Dahme • Germany.....83 [24]
Dahme Spa • Germany.....83 [24]
Dahna, Ad • Saudi Arabia.....21 F4
Dahongliutan • China.....28 C1
Dahra • Algeria.....11 L8
Dahra • Libya.....21 C2
Dahra • Senegal.....22 A1
Dahshur • Egypt.....101 F1
Dai Shan • China.....107 J4
Daiet el Kisria • Algeria.....11 N9
Dailekh • Nepal.....28 D3
Daimiel • Spain.....11 H5
Daimiel, Parque Nac. de las Tablas de Park • Spain.....72 [74]
Daio-Zaki • Japan.....30 I7
Daishan • China.....107 J4
Daito-Shoto • Japan.....29 I5
Dajarra • QL, Australia.....34 G4
Dajtit Nat. Park Park • Albania.....72 [125]
Dakar • Senegal.....22 A2
Dakhla • Western Sahara.....20 B3
Dakhla Oasis • Egypt.....101 F3
Dakoro • Niger.....20 G6
Dakovica • F.R. of Yugoslavia.....14 F4
Dakovo • Croatia.....14 B6
Dal • Norway.....94 B2
Dala • Angola.....24 C2
Dalaas • Austria.....89 H5
Dalaba • Guinea.....22 B2
Dalälven • Sweden.....16 I6
Dalaman • Turkey.....92 D9
Dalaman • Turkey.....92 D9
Dalaman [Riv] • Turkey.....15 J7
Dalandzadgad • Mongolia.....29 C2
Dalarnas • Sweden.....95 D4
Dalbandin • Pakistan.....28 H4
Dalbosjön • Sweden.....95 F11
Dalby • QL, Australia.....111 F6
Dalby • Sweden.....95 F8
Dale Beach • United Kingdom.....75 [158]
Dale • Sogn og Fjordane, Norway.....94 C3
Dale • Hordland, Norway.....94 C3
Dalem Temple • Bali, Indonesia.....110 C4
Dalen • Norway.....94 F4
Dalhart • TX, United States.....40 F4
Dalhousie Springs • SA, Australia.....34 G4
Dalhousie • India.....28 A2
Dali • China.....29 G3
Dalian • China.....29 G3
Dalkey • Ireland.....79 E2
Dalkey I. • Ireland.....79 E2

Dallas • TX, United States.....119 N1
Dallgow • Germany.....81 F1
Dallol Bosso • Niger.....20 F6
Dalmatia • Croatia.....14 C6
Dalmeny • United Kingdom.....74 B4
Dalnegorsk • Russian Fed.....27 M8
Dalnyaya, gora • Russian Fed.....27 U3
Daloa • Côte d'Ivoire.....22 C3
Dalou Shan • China.....29 D5
Dalqu • Sudan.....21 F3
Dalrymple, Mt • QL, Australia.....111 F3
Dalslands kanal • Sweden.....95 F2
Dalton • GA, United States.....41 J5
Dalton-in-Furness • United Kingdom.....74 C2
Daltongani • India.....105 C8
Daluis, Gorges de • France.....85 H2
Dalwallinu • WA, Australia.....34 F2
Daly • NT, Australia.....34 F3
Daly Waters • NT, Australia.....34 F3
Dalyan • Turkey.....92 D9
Dalyan • Turkey.....92 D9
Dam Qu • China.....28 F2
Daman • India.....28 B4
Daman [Adm] • India.....28 B4
Damanhûr • Egypt.....101 F1
Damar • Indonesia.....32 (1) C4
Damascus • Syria.....18 C3
Damascus Heritage C • Syria.....64 [241]
Damascus Heritage C • Syria.....64 [241]
Damar, Ad • Sudan.....21 F4
Damazin, Ad • Sudan.....22 H6
Damba • Angola.....23 B5
Dambulla Golden Rock Temple Heritage C • Sri Lanka.....61 [111]
Dambulla Golden Rock Temple Heritage C • Sri Lanka.....63 [137]
Dambulla Golden Rock Temple • Sri Lanka.....106 D15
Damietta • Egypt.....101 F1
Damietta Mouth • Egypt.....101 F1
Damme • Germany.....8 D4
Damoh • India.....105 C7
Damp Spa • Germany.....83 [13]
Damqoq Kanbab • China.....28 F2
Damüls • Austria.....89 H1
Dan • Israel.....98 A5
Danakil • Ethiopia.....21 H5
Dancheng • China.....107 J4
Dandawa • Zimbabwe.....102 J1
Dandeldhura • Nepal.....28 D3
Dandenong • VI, Australia.....111 G3
Dangan Liedao • Zhuhai, China.....107 H4
Dangast Spa • Germany.....83 [18]
Danger Point • South Africa.....100 C5
Dangoura, Mt • Central African Rep.....23 D2
Dangtu • China.....107 J1
Daníli • Russian Fed.....97 E2
Danilov • Russian Fed.....97 E2
Danish Riviera • Denmark.....95 F11
Danmarks Havn • Greenland.....36 O2
Dannemora • Sweden.....95 D2
Dannenberg • Germany.....8 G3
Dannevirke • New Zealand.....35 F6
Danshui • China.....107 H2
Danube Delta Heritage N • Romania.....61 [56]
Danube Delta • Romania.....97 D2
Danville • VA, United States.....41 K4
Danyang • China.....107 J1
Danzig • Poland.....13 H3
Dao Phu Quoc • Vietnam.....31 C4
Dao Timni • Niger.....20 H4
Dapaong • Togo.....22 E2
Daqing • China.....29 G1
Dar Boulzazi • Morocco.....101 D1
Dar es Salaam • Tanzania.....102 H4
Dar Rounga • Central African Rep./Sudan.....23 C2
Dar Sila • Chad.....23 C3
Dar'a • Syria.....18 C3
Darabani • Romania.....14 N1
Daracya Yarimadasi • Turkey.....15 J7
Daravica • F.R. of Yugoslavia.....14 H7
Darbhanga • India.....28 E3
Dardanelles • Turkey.....92 D2
Dardanelles • Turkey.....92 D2
Darfo Boario Terme • Italy.....91 E5
Darfur • Chad/Sudan.....100 A2
Darfur al Janubiyah • Sudan.....23 C1
Darganata • Uzbekistan.....18 H1
Dargaville • New Zealand.....35 D2
Darhan • Mongolia.....27 G7
Darién • Panama.....37 F6
Darién, Golfo del • Colombia/Panama.....43 B2
Darién, Parque Nac. del Heritage N • Panama.....60 [25]
Darién, Serranía del • Colombia/Panama.....43 B2
Darjeeling • India.....28 E3
Darkwood Beach • Antigua & Barbuda.....125 F3
Darling • NS, Australia.....34 H6
Darling Downs • QL, Australia.....111 F6
Darling, J.N. 'Ding', Nat. Wildlife Refuge • FL, United States.....119 M5
Darling Range • WA, Australia.....33 C9
Darlington • United Kingdom.....7 K7
Darlowo • Poland.....13 F3
Darmstadt • Germany.....82 H4
Darnah • Libya.....21 D1
Daroca • Spain.....11 J3
Darrah Wildlife Sanctuary • India.....105 C6
Darregueira • Argentina.....44 D6
Darss • Germany.....8 H2
Dart • United Kingdom.....74 F5
Dartmoor • United Kingdom.....74 F5
Dartmoor Nat. Park Park • United Kingdom.....72 [51]
Dartmoor Wildlife Centre • United Kingdom.....74 F5
Dartmouth • United Kingdom.....74 F5
Dartmouth • NS, Canada.....123 D7
Daru • Papua New Guinea.....35 (1) C2
Daruvar • Croatia.....14 E4
Darvaza • Turkmenistan.....18 G1
Darvel, Teluk • Malaysia.....31 F6
Darwen • United Kingdom.....74 F5
Darwin • NT, Australia.....34 F2
Darwin • Galapagos Is.....43 (1) A1
Daryacheh-ye Hamun-e Hirmand • Afghanistan/Iran.....28 H3
Dashen, Ras • Ethiopia.....21 H5
Dassel • Germany.....8 E4
Dassen I. • South Africa.....100 C5
Dassiá • Corfu, Greece.....92 B1
Dassiá • Corfu, Greece.....92 B1
Datça Beach • Turkey.....69 [206]
Datça • Turkey.....92 D9
Datça • Turkey.....92 D9
Date • Japan.....30 K3

Datia • India.....105 C7
Datong • China.....29 E2
Daugava • Latvia.....16 N8
Daugavpils • Latvia.....16 N9
Daun • Germany.....82 H1
Daun Spa • Germany.....83 [158]
Daunia, Monti della • Italy.....14 B8
Dauphin • MN, Canada.....38 L6
Dauphiné • France.....10 K8
Davangere • India.....106 D6
Davao • Philippines.....31 H5
Davao Gulf • Philippines.....31 H5
Davar Panah • Iran.....18 H4
Davenport • United States.....41 H3
David • Panama.....37 E6
Davis [Base] • Antarctica.....46 (1) N3
Davis Dam • AZ/NV, United States.....118 J1
Davis, Fort, Nat. Hist. Site Park • TX, United States.....120 [137]
Davis Strait • Canada/Greenland.....39 T3
Davos • Switzerland.....70 [113]
Davos • Switzerland.....89 G4
Dawa • China.....30 A4
Dawa • Ethiopia.....101 G2
Dawlish Beach • United Kingdom.....75 [101]
Dawlish Warren Beach • United Kingdom.....75 [100]
Dawson • YT, Canada.....38 D4
Dawson • QL, Australia.....111 F5
Dawson Creek • BC, Canada.....122 C1
Dawu • China.....29 C4
Dax • France.....85 G3
Daxue Shan • China.....29 C5
Daydream I. • QL, Australia.....111 F3
Daylesford • VI, Australia.....111 G3
Dayr • Sudan.....21 F5
Dayr az Zawr • Syria.....18 C2
Dayton • OH, United States.....41 J4
Dayton Aviation Nat. Hist. Park Park • OH, United States.....121 [185]
Daytona Beach • FL, United States.....119 M4
De Aar • South Africa.....24 C6
De Bay, Laguna • Philippines.....31 G4
De Efteling Park • Netherlands.....73 [45]
De Efteling • Netherlands.....80 A11
De Funiak Springs • FL, United States.....119 M2
De Gaulle, Charles [Apt] • France.....85 E2
De Grey • WA, Australia.....34 D4
De Haan • Belgium.....80 B2
De Haar • Netherlands.....80 C2
De Hoge Veluwe, Nat. Park Park • Netherlands.....72 [53]
De Hoge Veluwe, Nat. Park • Netherlands.....80 A7
De Hoop Nature Reserve • South Africa.....100 C6
De Jongs, Tanjung • Indonesia.....32 (1) E4
De Kalb • TX, United States.....119 N2
De Land • FL, United States.....119 M4
De Panne • Belgium.....80 B1
De Quincy Village • Seychelles.....106 F1
De Rust • South Africa.....100 C6
De Soto Nat. Mem. • FL, United States.....119 M5
De Soto Nat. Mem. Park • FL, United States.....121 [224]
De Timmoun, Sebkha • Algeria.....20 A3
De Zijpe • Netherlands.....80 A3
Dead Sea • Israel/Jordan.....98 A8
Deal • United Kingdom.....74 E4
Dean, Forest of • United Kingdom.....74 D3
Deán Funes • Argentina.....44 D5
Dease • BC, Canada.....38 F5
Dease Arm • NT/NU, Canada.....38 G3
Dease Lake • BC, Canada.....38 F5
Dease Strait • NT, Canada.....38 J3
Death Valley Nat. Park • CA, United States.....117 F4
Death Valley Nat. Park Park • CA, United States.....120 [55]
Deauville • France.....5 D5
Debica • Poland.....13 K7
Debin • Russian Fed.....27 P4
Deblin • Poland.....13 J6
Debno • Poland.....13 D5
Debo, Lac • Mali.....20 E5
Debre Berhan • Ethiopia.....23 E2
Debre Birhan • Ethiopia.....21 G5
Debre Markos • Ethiopia.....21 G5
Debrecen • Hungary.....13 K10
Debreuil • St Lucia.....125 J3
Decapolis • Asia.....98 A4
Decatur • IL, United States.....41 I4
Decatur • AL, United States.....41 I5
Decatur • TX, United States.....119 N1
Deception Bay • Papua New Guinea.....35 (1) C2
Decin • Czech Rep.....96 C2
Decize • France.....10 I7
Dedegöl Dag • Turkey.....93 G2
Dee • Scotland, UK.....6 J4
Dee • England/Wales, UK.....7 I9
Deeg • India.....105 C2
Deep Bay • China.....107 H3
Deep Bay • Antigua & Barbuda.....125 F1
Deep Cove • New Zealand.....112 L1
Deer I. • NB, Canada.....123 D6
Deer Lake • NF, Canada.....123 D3
Deer Lake [Lake] • NF, Canada.....123 D3
Deer Valley Ski • UT, United States.....116 [79]
Degeberga • Sweden.....95 F11
Degeh Bur • Ethiopia.....23 G2
Degerhamn • Sweden.....95 F12
Degerö • Germany.....9 H8
Deggendorf • Germany.....15 I5
Degirmendere • Turkey.....15 I5
Dehibat • Tunisia.....20 H2
Dehiwala • Sri Lanka.....106 D15
Dehra Dun • India.....28 C2
Dehui • China.....27 K8
Deià • Majorca, Spain.....87 H1
Deinze • Belgium.....5 G3
Deir el Beida • Morocco.....101 D1
Deir Mar Saba • Jordan.....98 A8
Déiva Marina Beach • Italy.....69 [123]
Dej • Romania.....14 K2
DeKalb • IL, United States.....41 I3
Dekese • Dem. Rep. of Congo.....23 B6
Dekoa • Central African Rep.....22 H3
Del Prat [Apt] • Spain.....87 D2
Del Rio • TX, United States.....40 F6
Delano • CA, United States.....117 F3
Delano Peak • UT, United States.....40 D4
Delareyville • South Africa.....100 C4
Delaware • United States.....118 H3
Delaware [St] • United States.....118 H3
Delaware, Fort, State Park • United States.....118 H3
Delaware & Lehigh Navigation Canal Nat. Heritage Corridor Park • PA, United States.....121 [313]
Delaware Water Gap Nat. Recreation Area Park • PA, United States.....121 [314]

Delegate • NS, Australia ... 111 G4
Delémont • Switzerland ... 9 C9
Delfi • Greece ... 15 D5
Delfi Heritage C • Greece ... 64 [178]
Delfland • Netherlands ... 80 C3
Delft • Netherlands ... 80 C3
Delfzijl • Netherlands ... 80 A4
Delgada, Punta • Argentina ... 45 D4
Delgado, Cabo • Mozambique ... 24 G2
Delhi Heritage C • India ... 63 [116-117]
Delhi • India ... 105 C2
Deli • Indonesia ... 110 D1
Delimara Point • Malta ... 93 H4
Delingha • China ... 28 G1
Delitzsch • Germany ... 8 H5
Delmenhorst • Germany ... 8 D3
Delnice • Croatia ... 14 B4
Deloraine • TS, Australia ... 34 I8
Delphi • Greece ... 15 D5
Delphi Heritage C • Greece ... 64 [178]
Delray Beach •
  FL, United States ... 119 M6
Delta Country •
  MS, United States ... 118 K2
Delta du Saloum, Parc nat. du Park •
  Senegal ... 103 [8]
Delta Junction •
  AK, United States ... 38 B4
Deltebre Beach • Spain ... 68 [104]
Delvin • Ireland ... 79 E1
Delvináki • Greece ... 15 B4
Demak • Java, Indonesia ... 110 D3
Demba • Dem. Rep. of Congo ... 23 C5
Dembi Dolo • Ethiopia ... 23 E2
Demidov • Russian Fed. ... 97 E3
Deming • NM, United States ... 119 N1
Demirci • Turkey ... 15 J4
Demirköy • Turkey ... 15 I2
Demirtas • Turkey ... 93 G4
Demmin • Germany ... 8 I3
Demone, Val • Sicily, Italy ... 90 D2
Dempo, Gunung • Indonesia ... 32 C3
Dêmqog • China ... 28 C2
Demta • Indonesia ... 32 (1) F3
Demyanskoye • Russian Fed. ... 26 K6
Den Chai • Thailand ... 109 G4
Den Haag • Netherlands ... 80 C1
Den Helder Beach • Netherlands ... 68 [48]
Den Helder • Netherlands ... 80 A3
Denain • France ... 10 I3
Denali Nat. Park & Preserve Park •
  AK, United States ... 120 [7]
Denau • Uzbekistan ... 18 I2
Denbighshire • United Kingdom ... 75 A4
Dendang • Indonesia ... 32 D3
Dender • Belgium ... 5 G4
Dendera • Egypt ... 101 F4
Denezkin Kamen • Russian Fed. ... 26 I5
Dengkou • China ... 28 F2
Dêngqên • China ... 28 F2
Denham • WA, Australia ... 34 B5
Denia Beach • Spain ... 68 [101]
Denia • Spain ... 87 C2
Deniliquin • NS, Australia ... 111 G1
Denis, I. • Seychelles ... 106 F2
Denison Dam •
  OK/TX, United States ... 119 N1
Denizli • Turkey ... 92 D9
Denizli • Turkey ... 92 D9
Denmark • WA, Australia ... 34 C6
Denmark • Europe ... 95 F
Denmark Strait •
  Greenland/Iceland ... 4 E3
Dennery • St Lucia ... 125 J2
Dennery I. • St Lucia ... 125 J4
Denpasar • Bali, Indonesia ... 110 C4
Denton • TX, United States ... 119 N1
Denver • CO, United States ... 40 F4
Deoli • India ... 105 C6
Deqing • China ... 107 J3
Der, Lac du • France ... 5 H6
Dera Ghazi Khan • Pakistan ... 28 B2
Dera Ismail Khan • Pakistan ... 28 B2
Derbent • Russian Fed. ... 17 H6
Derby • United Kingdom ... 7 K9
Derby • WA, Australia ... 34 D3
Derbyshire • United Kingdom ... 75 A4
Dereköy • Turkey ... 15 I2
Derg, Lough • Ireland ... 79 F4
Dernière Rivière • St Lucia ... 125 J2
Déroute, Passage de la • France ... 5 B5
Derrière Morne • St Lucia ... 125 J4
Derry City • United Kingdom ... 75 A3
Derrynasaggart Mtns • Ireland ... 79 F8
Derventa • Bosnia-Herz. ... 14 E5
Derwent • Derbyshire, UK ... 5 B1
Derwent • United Kingdom ... 74 C1
Derwent River • TS, Australia ... 34 I8
Derwent Water • United Kingdom ... 74 C2
Des Moines • IA, United States ... 41 H3
Desaguadero • Argentina ... 44 C5
Desaguadero • Peru ... 127 B4
Désappointement •
  French Polynesia ... 33 M7
Desaru • Malaysia ... 108 A4
Descartes • France ... 84 D4
Deschutes • OR, United States ... 117 E3
Dese • Ethiopia ... 21 G5
Deseado • Argentina ... 45 C5
Desengaño, Punta • Argentina ... 45 C5
Desenzano • Italy ... 91 E7
Deshnoke • India ... 105 C1
Deskáti • Greece ... 15 C4
Desna • Ukraine ... 17 E4
Desnœfs • Seychelles ... 106 F2
Desolacion, I. • Chile ... 45 B6
Desolation, Valley of •
  South Africa ... 100 C3
Despotikó • Greece ... 92 D7
Despotikó • Greece ... 92 D7
Desroches • Seychelles ... 106 F2
Desruisseaux • St Lucia ... 125 J4
Dessau • Germany ... 8 H5
Dessau Heritage C • Germany ... 64 [33]
Dessel Beach • Belgium ... 68 [52]
Destin • FL, United States ... 119 M2
Deta • Romania ... 14 I4
Dete • Zimbabwe ... 102 J1
Detmold • Germany ... 8 D5
Detroit • MI, United States ... 41 J3
Detva • Slovak Rep ... 13 I9
Deurne [Adm] • Belgium ... 80 A10
Deutsche Bucht • North Sea ... 8 C2
Deux Alpes, les Ski • France ... 70 [58]
Deux Alpes • France ... 85 F3
Deux Sèvres • France ... 84 D3
Deva • Romania ... 14 I4
Devil River Peak • New Zealand ... 35 D5
Devil's Bridge •
  Antigua & Barbuda ... 125 L2
Devil's I. • French Guiana ... 58 A3
Devils Head Ski •
  WI, United States ... 116 [123]
Devils Postpile Nat. Mon. •
  CA, United States ... 117 F4
Devils Postpile Nat. Mon. Park •
  CA, United States ... 120 [52]

Devils Tower Nat. Mon. Park •
  WY, United States ... 120 [72]
Devin • Bulgaria ... 14 L8
Devizes • United Kingdom ... 74 F3
Devoll • Albania ... 15 B3
Devon • United Kingdom ... 74 F2
Devonport I. • NU, Canada ... 39 N1
Devonport • TS, Australia ... 34 I8
Devonport • New Zealand ... 35 E3
Devrek • Turkey ... 15 M2
Devrez • Turkey ... 15 O3
Dewa • Ethiopia/Kenya ... 23 G3
Dey-Dey, Lake • SA, Australia ... 34 F5
Dezful • Iran ... 18 E3
Dezhnva, mys • Russian Fed. ... 25 U3
Dezhou • China ... 29 F3
Dháfni • Greece ... 15 C6
Dhahran • Saudi Arabia ... 18 E4
Dhaka • Bangladesh ... 28 E4
Dháli • Cyprus ... 93 J4
Dhamar • Yemen ... 18 D7
Dhamtari • India ... 28 D4
Dharwad • India ... 106 D2
Dhaulagiri • Nepal ... 28 D3
Dhefterá • Cyprus ... 93 J3
Dhekélia • Cyprus ... 98 J4
Dhíban • Jordan ... 93 J4
Dhiban • India ... 28 B4
Dhule • India ... 105 C6
Día • Greece ... 93 E3
Diable, I. du • French Guiana ... 43 G2
Diablo Range •
  CA, United States ... 117 F3
Diamante • Italy ... 12 J9
Diamante • Argentina ... 44 D5
Diamantina • QL, Australia ... 34 H4
Diamantina • Brazil ... 44 H2
Diamantina Lakes •
  QL, Australia ... 34 H4
Diamantino • Brazil ... 44 E1
Diamond Baths • St Lucia ... 125 J3
Diamond Head State Mon. •
  HI, United States ... 119 L6
Diamond Is. • CL, United States ... 111 F2
Diamond Jenness Peninsula •
  NT, Canada ... 38 H2
Diamond Peak Ski •
  NV, United States ... 116 [66]
Diani Beach • Kenya ... 101 G5
Diani Marina Beach • Italy ... 68 [120]
Diano Marina • Italy ... 91 E9
Dianópolis • Brazil ... 45 (1) B4
Diapaga • Burkina Faso ... 22 E2
Dibang • India ... 28 G3
Dibaya-Lubue •
  Dem. Rep. of Congo ... 23 B4
Dibella • Niger ... 20 H5
Dibrugarh • India ... 28 F3
Dickenson Bay •
  Antigua & Barbuda ... 125 F1
Dickinson • ND, United States ... 40 F2
Dicle • Turkey ... 18 D2
Didcot • United Kingdom ... 74 D4
Dideso • Ethiopia ... 23 F2
Didiéni • Mali ... 22 C2
Didim • Turkey ... 92 D8
Didima • Turkey ... 92 D8
Didyma • Turkey ... 92 D8
Didyma • Turkey ... 92 D8
Die • France ... 10 K9
Dieburg • Germany ... 9 D7
Diego Suarez • Madagascar ... 24 H2
Diekirch • Luxembourg ... 80 A20
Diéma • Mali ... 22 C2
Diemel • Germany ... 8 D5
Dien Bien Phu • Vietnam ... 31 C2
Dieng Plateau • Java, Indonesia ... 110 D6
Dienten am Hochkönig Ski •
  Austria ... 70 [166]
Diepholz • Germany ... 8 D4
Dieppe • France ... 10 G4
Dieppe Beach • France ... 68 [56]
Dieppe Bay Town •
  St Kitts & Nevis ... 125 G1
Dierhagen Beach • Germany ... 68 [14]
Dierhagen Spa • Germany ... 83 [274]
Dießen-Rieden • Germany ... 82 J2
Diest • Belgium ... 80 A15
Dieuze • France ... 5 J6
Diez • Germany ... 82 H2
Diffa • Niger ... 20 H6
Differdange • Luxembourg ... 5 I5
Digby • NS, Canada ... 123 D7
Digity Mud Volcano •
  Trinidad & Tobago ... 125 K3
Digne • France ... 85 H1
Digoin • France ... 10 I7
Digue, la • Seychelles ... 106 F4
Digul • Indonesia ... 32 (1) E4
Dihang • India ... 28 F3
Dijlah • Iraq ... 18 E3
Dijon • France ... 10 K6
Dik • Chad ... 23 B2
Dikili • Turkey ... 15 H4
Diksmuide • Belgium ... 80 B1
Dikson • Russian Fed. ... 26 N3
Diktêen Antron • Crete, Greece ... 93 E7
Diktinéon • Crete, Greece ... 93 E1
Dikwa • Nigeria ... 20 D1
Dili • East Indies ... 32 (1) B4
Dilila • Niger ... 22 E4
Dilling • Sudan ... 23 D1
Dillingen • Germany ... 71 A8
Dillon • MT, United States ... 40 D2
Dilly • Mali ... 20 D6
Dilolo • Dem. Rep. of Congo ... 23 C6
Dilos Heritage C • Greece ... 64 [186]
Dilos • Greece ... 92 D8
Dilos • Greece ... 92 D8
Dimashq • Syria ... 18 C3
Dimashq Heritage C • Syria ... 64 [241]
Dimbokro • Côte d'Ivoire ... 22 D3
Dimboola • VI, Australia ... 111 G2
Dimbovita • Romania ... 9 D7
Dimitrovgrad • Russian Fed. ... 17 H4
Dimitrovgrad • Bulgaria ... 97 D3
Dinagat • Philippines ... 31 H4
Dinajpur • Bangladesh ... 28 E3
Dinan • France ... 84 C2
Dinant • Belgium ... 80 A19
Dinar • Turkey ... 15 L5
Dinara • Bosnia-Herz./Croatia ... 14 D5
Dinard • France ... 84 C2
Dinaric Alps •
  Bosnia-Herz./Croatia ... 96 B2
Dinas Dinlle Beach •
  United Kingdom ... 75 [194]
Dinder Nat. Park Park • Sudan ... 103 [61]
Dindigul • India ... 106 D11
Dinga • Dem. Rep. of Congo ... 22 H6
Dinghai • China ... 107 J4
Dingle Bay • Ireland ... 79 F5
Dingle • Ireland ... 79 F7
Dingle Peninsula • Ireland ... 79 F5

Dingli Cliffs • Malta ... 93 H4
Dingolfing • Germany ... 9 H8
Dingwall • United Kingdom ... 6 H4
Dingxian • China ... 29 F3
Dinkelsbühl • Germany ... 9 F7
Dinosaur Nat. Mon. Park •
  CO, United States ... 120 [88]
Dinosaur Prov. Park Heritage N •
  AL, Canada ... 60 [6]
Dinosaurier Park Münchehagen Park •
  Germany ... 73 [56]
Dinotown • BC, Canada ... 122 C3
Dinslaken • Germany ... 81 E1
Dioila • Mali ... 22 C2
Dionisiades • Greece ... 93 E4
Dioura • Mali ... 20 D6
Diourbel • Senegal ... 22 A2
Dipolog • Philippines ... 31 G5
Dire Dawa • Ethiopia ... 23 G1
Dirfis, Oros • Greece ... 15 E5
Dirj • Libya ... 21 A1
Dirk Hartog I. • WA, Australia ... 34 B5
Dirkou • Niger ... 20 H5
Dirranbandi • QL, Australia ... 34 F5
Disappointment, Lake •
  WA, Australia ... 34 D4
Discovery Bay • Jamaica ... 124 C1
Discovery I. •
  United States ... 121 C1
Disentis • Switzerland ... 89 G3
Disko • Greenland ... 39 U3
Dismal Swamp •
  VA, United States ... 118 H5
Disney, Walt, World Int. Sports Complex •
  FL, United States ... 121 [Y]
Disney, Walt, World Resort Complex •
  FL, United States ... 121 C1
Disney-MGM Studios •
  FL, United States ... 121 C1
Disneyland • CA, United States ... 117 F6
Disneyland Park •
  CA, United States ... 120 [H]
Disneyland Paris Park • France ... 73 [73]
Disneyland Paris • France ... 85 E4
Dispur • India ... 28 E3
Distington • United Kingdom ... 74 C1
District of Columbia •
  United States ... 118 H3
Distrito Federal • Brazil ... 45 (1) B5
Ditiki Rodópi • Greece ... 15 F2
Diu • India ... 28 B4
Diu [Adm] • India ... 105 B1
Divar I. • Goa, India ... 105 B1
Dives • France ... 5 C5
Divinópolis • Brazil ... 127 C1
Divisoes, Serra das • Brazil ... 44 H2
Divisor, Serra de • Brazil/Peru ... 43 C5
Divjaka Nat. Park Park •
  Albania ... 72 [126]
Divo • Côte d'Ivoire ... 22 C3
Divriği Heritage C • Turkey ... 64 [194]
Diwaniyah, Ad • Iraq ... 18 D3
Dixon Entrance • BC, Canada ... 38 E6
Diyala • Iraq ... 18 E3
Diyarbakir • Turkey ... 18 D2
Dja • Cameroon/Congo ... 22 G4
Dja, Réserve du Heritage N •
  Cameroon ... 61 [80]
Dja, Réserve du Park • Cameroon ... 103 [164]
Djado • Niger ... 20 H4
Djado, Plateau de • Niger ... 20 H4
Djambala • Congo ... 22 G5
Djanet • Algeria ... 20 G4
Djaret • Algeria ... 20 F2
Djavat • F.Y.R. of Macedonia ... 15 C2
Djedi • Algeria ... 20 F2
Djelfa • Algeria ... 20 E1
Djemila • Algeria ... 20 G1
Djemila Heritage C • Algeria ... 64 [222]
Djenne • Mali ... 20 E6
Djenne Heritage C • Mali ... 63 [94]
Djerdap Nat. Park Park •
  Fed. Rep. of Yugoslavia ... 72 [116]
Djerem • Cameroon ... 22 G3
Djibo • Burkina Faso ... 22 D2
Djibouti • Djibouti ... 21 H5
Djibouti • Africa ... 21 H5
Djoua • Congo/Gabon ... 22 G4
Djoudj, Parc nat. des Oiseaux du Heritage N •
  Senegal ... 61 [71]
Djoudj, Parc nat. des Oiseaux du Park •
  Senegal ... 103 [6]
Djouf, El • Mali/Mauritania ... 20 D4
Djoum • Cameroon ... 22 G4
Djourab, Erg du • Chad ... 22 H1
Djupivogur • Iceland ... 16 (1) F2
Djurs Sommerland Park • Denmark ... 73 [15]
Djurs Sommerland • Denmark ... 95 F8
Djursdala • Sweden ... 95 F8
Djursland • Denmark ... 95 F10
Dmitriya Lapteva, Proliv •
  Russian Fed. ... 27 N2
Dmitrov • Russian Fed. ... 97 E4
Dnepr • Ukraine ... 17 E5
Dneprodzerzhinsk • Ukraine ... 17 F5
Dnepropetrovsk • Ukraine ... 17 F5
Dnestr • Moldova/Ukraine ... 17 D5
Dno • Russian Fed. ... 97 D2
Doaba • Chad ... 23 B2
Dobbiaco • Italy ... 90 B2
Dobel Spa • Germany ... 83 [180]
Dobele • Latvia ... 16 L8
Döbeln • Germany ... 9 I5
Doberai, Jazirah • Indonesia ... 32 (1) D3
Dobiacco Ski • Italy ... 70 [237]
Dobo • Indonesia ... 32 (1) D4
Doboj • Bosnia-Herz. ... 14 F5
Dobreta-Turnu Severin • Romania ... 14 J5
Dobrich • Bulgaria ... 97 D4
Dobrodzije • Romania ... 97 D2
Dobrudzansko Plato • Bulgaria ... 14 O6
Doce • Brazil ... 127 C2
Docker River • NT, Australia ... 112 H3
Doctor Phillips •
  FL, United States ... 121 [61]
Doda Betta • India ... 106 D10
Dodecanese • Greece ... 92 D8
Dodekánissa • Greece ... 15 I7
Dodge City • KS, United States ... 40 F4
Dodge Ridge Ski •
  CA, United States ... 116 [61]
Dodman Point • United Kingdom ... 74 C3
Dodoma • Tanzania ... 102 H2
Dodóni • Greece ... 15 B4
Dodori Game Reserve • Kenya ... 101 G4
Doe Mtn Ski • PA, United States ... 116 [164]
Doetinchem • Netherlands ... 5 J3
Dofa • Indonesia ... 32 (1) D3
Dog I. • FL, United States ... 119 M2
Dogai Coring • China ... 28 E2
Dogana • Turkey ... 93 G2
Doge • Japan ... 30 G6
Dogo • Japan ... 30 G6
Dogondoutchi • Niger ... 22 E2
Dogor • Hungary ... 13 H10
Dogubayazit • Turkey ... 92 A4
Dogubayazit • Turkey ... 92 A4
Dogwood Point •
  St Kitts & Nevis ... 125 G4

Doha • Qatar ... 18 F4
Dohad • India ... 18 J5
Doi Inthanon • Thailand ... 109 G3
Doi Inthanon Nat. Park •
  Thailand ... 109 G3
Doi Khun Tan Nat. Park •
  Thailand ... 109 G3
Doi Suthep Nat. Park • Thailand ... 109 G1
Dokhara, Dunes de • Algeria ... 20 G2
Dokkum • Netherlands ... 80 A3
Dokós • Greece ... 92 D7
Dokós • Greece ... 92 D7
Dol-de-Bretagne • France ... 84 C2
Dolak • Indonesia ... 32 (1) E4
Döle • France ... 10 K6
Dolent, Mt •
  France/Italy/Switzerland ... 89 G5
Dolgellau • United Kingdom ... 7 I9
Dolina • Ukraine ... 14 K1
Dollard • Germany/Netherlands ... 8 C3
Dollywood Park •
  TN, United States ... 121 [Y]
Dolny Kubin • Slovak Rep. ... 13 I8
Dolo • Ethiopia ... 23 G3
Dolomites • Italy ... 90 B
Dolomiti • Italy ... 90 B
Dolonnur • China ... 29 F2
Dolores • Uruguay ... 127 D2
Dolores • Argentina ... 127 D4
Dolphin, Cape • Falkland Is. ... 45 E6
Dolphin Coast • South Africa ... 100 D6
Dolus d'Oleron Beach • France ... 68 [65]
Dom Pedrito • Brazil ... 44 F5
Domažlice • Czech Rep. ... 96 C3
Dombås • Norway ... 94 C2
Dombóvár • Hungary ... 13 H11
Domburg • Belgium ... 5 G3
Domfront • France ... 5 C6
Dominica • West Indies ... 37 I4
Dominican Republic •
  West Indies ... 37 G4
Domme • France ... 85 G4
Dommel • Netherlands ... 5 I3
Domo • Ethiopia ... 23 H2
Domodedovo [Apt] • Russian Fed. ... 97 E4
Domodóssola • Italy ... 89 G4
Domokós • Greece ... 15 D4
Domuyo, Volcán • Argentina ... 44 B6
Don • United Kingdom ... 6 J4
Don • Russian Fed. ... 17 F4
Don Benito • Spain ... 11 F6
Don Muang [Apt] • Thailand ... 109 H2
Dona Paula Beach • Goa, India ... 105 B1
Donabate Beach • Ireland ... 68 [35]
Donabate • Ireland ... 79 E2
Donaghadee • Ireland ... 79 E2
Donaldsonville • Germany ... 8 G8
Donau • Austria/Germany ... 9 G8
Donaueschingen • Germany ... 82 G8
Donauwörth • Germany ... 9 F8
Doncaster • United Kingdom ... 7 K8
Dondo • Angola ... 23 A5
Dondo • Mozambique ... 24 E3
Dondra Head • Sri Lanka ... 25 J9
Dondra Head • Sri Lanka ... 106 D15
Donegal • Ireland ... 7 D7
Donegal [Adm] • Ireland ... 79 D1
Donegal Bay • Ireland ... 7 D7
Donegal Mtns • Ireland ... 7 D7
Donelson, Fort, Nat. Battlefield Park •
  TN, United States ... 121 [230]
Donets Basin •
  Russian Fed./Ukraine ... 96 A2
Donetsk • Ukraine ... 17 F5
Dong Bai • China ... 29 G1
Dong Hoi • Vietnam ... 31 D3
Dong Jiang • China ... 31 F2
Dong Ujmqin Qi • China ... 27 I7
Dongara • WA, Australia ... 34 B5
Dongchuan • China ... 31 D3
Dongfang • China ... 31 D3
Dongguan • China ... 30 C5
Dongka • Indonesia ... 32 (1) B4
Dongnan Qiuling • China ... 31 E2
Dongou • Congo ... 22 H4
Dongsha Qundao • China ... 31 F2
Dongting Hu • China ... 29 E5
Donga Nat. Park Ski •
  CA, United States ... 116 [51]
Donner Pass • CA, United States ... 117 F3
Donnybrook • WA, Australia ... 34 C6
Donoe • Ireland ... 79 E2
Donostia • Spain ... 11 J1
Donostia-San Sebastián Beach • Spain ... 68 [68]
Donoússa • Greece ... 92 D8
Donoússa • Greece ... 92 D8
Doolin • Ireland ... 79 F4
Doonass, Falls of • Ireland ... 79 F6
Doorn • Netherlands ... 5 I2
Dor • Israel ... 98 A3
Dora Baltea • Italy ... 91 E5
Dora Riparia • Italy ... 10 M8
Dorada, Costa • Spain ... 87 D3
Dorado • Puerto Rico ... 125 E2
Dorchester • United Kingdom ... 74 F3
Dordogne • France ... 85 G1
Dordogne [Adm] • France ... 85 G2
Dordogne, Gorges de la • France ... 85 G2
Dordrecht • Netherlands ... 80 C3
Döröö Nuur • Mongolia ... 28 D1
Doré Lake • SA, Canada ... 38 J6
Dores do Indaiá • Brazil ... 127 C1
Dorfen • Germany ... 82 J3
Dorfgastein • Austria ... 89 H4
Dorgali • Sardinia, Italy ... 12 D8
Dori • Burkina Faso ... 22 D2
Doring • South Africa ... 100 C2
Dormagen • Germany ... 81 E3
Dornoch • United Kingdom ... 6 H4
Dornoch Beach • United Kingdom ... 75 [2]
Dornoch Firth • United Kingdom ... 6 I4
Dornumersiel Spa • Germany ... 83 [44]
Dorog • Hungary ... 13 H10
Dorohoi • Romania ... 14 N2
Dorotea • Sweden ... 16 H4
Dorset • United Kingdom ... 74 F3
Dorsten • Germany ... 81 E1
Dortmund • Germany ... 81 E2
Dortmund, Florianturm • Germany ... 81 E2
Dortmund: Syburg • Germany ... 81 E2
Dortmund, Tierpark • Germany ... 81 E2
Dortmund-Ems-Kanal • Germany ... 8 C4
Dorum Spa • Germany ... 83 [53]
Dos Hermanas • Spain ... 11 F7
Dosatuy • Russian Fed. ... 27 K7
Dösemalti • Turkey ... 93 G1
Dospat • Bulgaria ... 15 F2
Dosso • Niger ... 20 F6
Dothan • AL, United States ... 119 M2
Douai • France ... 10 I3
Douala • Cameroon ... 22 F4
Douarnenez • France ... 84 C3
Double, Fôret de la • France ... 85 G1
Double I. • Hong Kong, China ... 107 H4

Doubs • France ... 10 L6
Doubtful Sound • New Zealand ... 112 L1
Douentza • Mali ... 20 E6
Douera • Algeria ... 11 N8
Dougga Heritage C • Tunisia ... 64 [225]
Dougga • Tunisia ... 101 E1
Douglas • Isle of Man ... 7 H7
Douglas • South Africa ... 24 C5
Douglas • GA, United States ... 41 J5
Douglas • AZ, United States ... 118 J4
Douglas, Mt • GL, Australia ... 111 F3
Douglass, Frederick, Nat. Hist. Site Park •
  DC, United States ... 121 [285]
Doukáto, Akra • Greece ... 92 C1
Doukáto, Akra • Greece ... 92 C1
Doullens • France ... 10 H3
Doumen • Zhuhai, China ... 107 H1
Dourada, Costa da • Portugal ... 88 A3
Dourados • Brazil ... 44 F3
Dourdan • France ... 85 E3
Douro • Portugal ... 11 D3
Douz • Tunisia ... 101 E5
Dove Cottage • United Kingdom ... 74 C2
Dover • United Kingdom ... 74 E4
Dover • DE, United States ... 118 H3
Dover, Strait of • France/UK ... 74 E4
Dover-Foxcroft •
  ME, United States ... 118 G2
Dovercourt Beach •
  United Kingdom ... 75 [54]
Dovrefjell • Norway ... 16 E5
Dovrefjell Nat. Park Park •
  Norway ... 72 [12]
Dovrefjell Nat. Park • Norway ... 94 C3
Down • United Kingdom ... 75 A3
Downpatrick • United Kingdom ... 7 G7
Downunderland • NS, Australia ... 111 G2
Dowth • Ireland ... 79 E2
Dráa • Algeria/Morocco ... 101 D5
Dráa, Cap • Morocco ... 101 D6
Dráa, Vallée du • Morocco ... 101 D6
Drac • France ... 85 F3
Drac, Coves del •
  Majorca, Spain ... 87 H2
Drachenfels • Germany ... 82 H1
Drachten • Netherlands ... 5 J1
Dragan • Sweden ... 16 H4
Dragasani • Romania ... 14 L5
Dragon's Mouths •
  Trinidad/Venezuela ... 125 K1
Dragonáda • Greece ... 93 E4
Dragonera, I. • Majorca, Spain ... 87 H1
Dragsholm Beach • Denmark ... 68 [24]
Draguignan • France ... 85 H1
Drake Passage • Antarctica ... 46 (1) HH4
Drakensberg • South Africa ... 24 D6
Dráma • Greece ... 92 D1
Drammen • Norway ... 94 B1
Drangajökull • Iceland ... 16 (1) B1
Drangedal • Norway ... 94 B3
Drápano, Akra • Crete, Greece ... 93 E2
Drau • Austria ... 13 D11
Drava • Croatia ... 14 E4
Drayton Manor Park Park •
  United Kingdom ... 73 [29]
Drayton Manor Park •
  United Kingdom ... 74 D2
Dreamworld • GL, Australia ... 111 F6
Dreihermspitze • Austria/Italy ... 90 B2
Drépano, Akra • Greece ... 15 E4
Dresden • Germany ... 9 I5
Dreux • France ... 10 G5
Drievliet, Familiepark Park •
  Netherlands ... 73 [44]
Drina • F.R. of Yugoslavia ... 14 G6
Drint, Gjiri i • Albania ... 14 G8
Driochead Atha • Ireland ... 79 E2
Drøbak • Norway ... 94 B2
Drochia • Moldova ... 14 O1
Drogheda • Ireland ... 79 E2
Drogobych • Ukraine ... 13 M8
Droichead Nua • Ireland ... 79 E2
Drôme • France ... 10 K9
Dronne • France ... 10 F8
Dronninglund Beach • Denmark ... 68 [29]
Drosia • Greece ... 92 D4
Drosia • Greece ... 92 D4
Drottningholm • Sweden ... 95 D4
Drottningholm Palace Heritage C •
  Sweden ... 64 [5]
Drovyanaya • Russian Fed. ... 26 H2
Drumcliff • Ireland ... 79 D1
Drumheller • AL, Canada ... 122 C4
Drummondville • QU, Canada ... 122 B4
Drusillas Park • United Kingdom ... 74 E3
Druzhba • Kazakhstan ... 26 C5
Druzba • Bulgaria ... 97 D4
Drvar • Bosnia-Herz. ... 14 D5
Drweca • Poland ... 13 I4
Dry Falls • WA, United States ... 117 E2
Dry Harbour Mtns • Jamaica ... 124 C1
Dry Tortugas Nat. Park •
  FL, United States ... 119 M7
Dry Tortugas Nat. Park Park •
  FL, United States ... 121 [228]
Drygalski Ice Tongue •
  Antarctica ... 46 (1) W2
Drysdale • WA, Australia ... 34 E2
Drysdale River Nat. Park •
  WA, Australia ... 34 E3
Dschang • Cameroon ... 22 G3
Dsungar Alatau •
  China/Kazakhstan ... 26 N8
Du'ayn, Ad • Sudan ... 23 D1
Duarte • Dominican Rep. ... 37 G4
Dubai • United Arab Emirates ... 18 G4
Dubawnt • NT, Canada ... 38 K4
Dubawnt Lake • NT/NU, Canada ... 38 K4
Dubbo • NS, Australia ... 34 I6
Dublin [Adm] • Ireland ... 79 E2
Dublin • Ireland ... 79 E2
Dublin Bay • Ireland ... 79 E2
Dubna • Russian Fed. ... 97 E4
Dubrovnik • Croatia ... 14 F6
Dubrovnik Heritage C • Croatia ... 64 [158]
Duc de Gloucester •
  French Polynesia ... 33 M8
Ducie • Pitcairn Is. ... 33 O8
Duddon • United Kingdom ... 74 C3
Duden • Turkey ... 93 G1
Düdenbasi • Turkey ... 93 G1
Düdensuyu • Turkey ... 93 G1
Dudhsagar Falls • Goa, India ... 105 B2
Dudhwa Nat. Park • India ... 105 C3
Dudinka • Russian Fed. ... 26 O4
Dudley • United Kingdom ... 74 D2
Düdüce • Turkey ... 15 M3
Dudweiler • Germany ... 82 F3
Duero • Spain ... 11 G3
Dugi Otok • Croatia ... 14 C5
Duino • Italy ... 91 E4

Duisburg: Homberg • Germany ... 81 E1
Duisburg: Rheinhausen • Germany ... 81 E1
Duitama • Colombia ... 43 C2
Duiveland • Netherlands ... 80 A10
Dujuma • Somalia ... 23 G3
Dukagjini • Albania ... 14 G7
Dukhan • Qatar ... 18 F4
Dukou • China ... 29 B5
Dulan • China ... 28 F2
Dulce • Argentina ... 44 D4
Duleek • Ireland ... 79 E2
Dulles [Apt] •
  VA, United States ... 118 H3
Dülmen • Germany ... 8 C5
Duluth • MN, United States ... 41 H2
Dumaguete • Philippines ... 31 G5
Dumai • Indonesia ... 110 B4
Dumas • TX, United States ... 40 F4
Dumbarton • United Kingdom ... 7 I6
Dumford, Punta • Western Sahara ... 20 B4
Dumfries • United Kingdom ... 7 I6
Dumfries & Galloway •
  United Kingdom ... 75 A3
Dümmersee • Germany ... 5 L2
Dumont d'Urville [Base] •
  Antarctica ... 46 (1) T3
Dumont d'Urville Sea •
  Antarctica ... 46 (1) S3
Dumpu • Papua New Guinea ... 35 (1) J2
Dümrek • Turkey ... 15 J5
Dumyât • Egypt ... 101 F2
Dún Aengus • Ireland ... 79 F3
Dún Dealgan • Ireland ... 7 F7
Dún Laoghaire • Ireland ... 79 E2
Duna • Hungary ... 13 H11
Duna-Tisza Köz • Hungary ... 14 G3
Dunafôldvár • Hungary ... 13 H11
Dunaj • Slovak Rep. ... 13 G9
Dunajská Sreda • Slovak Rep. ... 13 G9
Dunántúl • Hungary ... 13 G11
Dunărea • Romania ... 14 K6
Dunas Beach • Goa, India ... 105 B1
Dunaújváros • Hungary ... 13 H10
Dunav • Europe ... 14 L6
Dunblane • United Kingdom ... 74 B1
Dunboyne • Ireland ... 79 E2
Duncan • BC, Canada ... 122 C3
Duncan Passage • India ... 105 F5
Duncannon Beach • Ireland ... 68 [37]
Dundalk • Ireland ... 7 F7
Dundalk Bay • Ireland ... 7 F8
Dundas Peninsula • NT, Canada ... 38 I2
Dundee • United Kingdom ... 74 B2
Dunedin • New Zealand ... 35 C7
Dunfanaghy • Ireland ... 7 E6
Dunfermline • United Kingdom ... 74 B4
Dungannon • United Kingdom ... 75 A3
Dungarvan • Ireland ... 7 E9
Dungeness • United Kingdom ... 74 E4
Dunhua • China ... 29 A2
Dunhuang • China ... 29 A2
Dunk I. • QL, Australia ... 111 F1
Dunkeld • United Kingdom ... 74 B2
Dunkerque • France ... 10 H2
Dunkery Beacon • United Kingdom ... 7 I10
Dunkirk • France ... 80 A13
Dunlavin • Ireland ... 79 E3
Dunloe, Gap of • Ireland ... 79 F7
Dunmanus Bay • Ireland ... 79 F8
Dunmanway • Ireland ... 79 F8
Dunmarra • NT, Australia ... 34 F3
Dunmore • Ireland ... 79 F4
Dunmore East Beach • Ireland ... 68 [39]
Dunmore Town • Bahamas ... 124 D1
Dunn's River Falls • Jamaica ... 124 C2
Dunnet Head • United Kingdom ... 6 I3
Dunnville • OT, Canada ... 122 B9
Dunoon • United Kingdom ... 78 A3
Dunquin • Ireland ... 79 F5
Dunqulah • Sudan ... 21 F5
Dunshaughlin • Ireland ... 79 E1
Dunstan Mtns • New Zealand ... 112 L2
Dunster • United Kingdom ... 74 F2
Duntroon • New Zealand ... 35 C7
Duolun • China ... 29 F2
Dupnitsa • Bulgaria ... 15 E1
Duqm • Oman ... 18 G6
Duque de Caxias • Brazil ... 127 C4
Durack Range • WA, Australia ... 34 E3
Durance • France ... 85 G2
Durand • St Lucia ... 125 J1
Durango • Spain ... 11 I1
Durango • Mexico ... 40 F7
Durango • CO, United States ... 118 J2
Durango [Adm] • Mexico ... 40 F7
Durankulak • Bulgaria ... 97 C3
Durant • MS, United States ... 118 K2
Durant • OK, United States ... 119 N1
Durazno • Uruguay ... 127 D2
Durazzo • Albania ... 71 A19
Durban • South Africa ... 24 E5
Düren • Germany ... 82 G1
Durgapur • India ... 28 E4
Durham • United Kingdom ... 7 K7
Durham • NC, United States ... 41 K4
Durham Heritage C •
  United Kingdom ... 64 [16]
Durham [Adm] • United Kingdom ... 75 A3
Durmitor • F.R. of Yugoslavia ... 14 F6
Durmitor Nat. Park Heritage N •
  F.R. of Yugoslavia ... 61 [53]
Durmitor Nat. Park Park •
  Fed. Rep. of Yugoslavia ... 72 [118]
Durrës • Albania ... 14 G8
Durresit, Gjiri i • Albania ... 14 G8
Dursey I. • Ireland ... 79 F7
Dursunbey • Turkey ... 15 J4
Durusu Gölü • Turkey ... 15 J2
Duruz • Syria ... 21 G1
Dusa Mareb • Somalia ... 21 D1
Dushan • China ... 31 D1
Dushanbe • Tajikistan ... 18 I2
Dusky Sound • New Zealand ... 112 L3
Düsseldorf • Germany ... 81 E3
Düsseldorf: Kaiserswerth •
  Germany ... 81 E3
Dutch Harbor •
  AK, United States ... 36 (1) D4
Duvkh Tsirkov, gora •
  Russian Fed. ... 27 S3
Duvno • Bosnia-Herz. ... 14 E6
Duwayhin • United Arab Emirates ... 18 F5
Duwaym, Ad • Sudan ... 21 G6
Duyfken Point • QL, Australia ... 34 H2
Düzce • Turkey ... 15 M3
Dvinskaya Guba • Russian Fed. ... 16 P3
Dwingelderveld, Nat. Park Park •
  Netherlands ... 72 [52]
Dwingelderveld, Nat. Park •
  Netherlands ... 80 A4
Dyje • Czech Rep. ... 13 F9
Dylewska Góra • Poland ... 13 I4

Dymchurch

Dymchurch • United Kingdom 74 E4
Dymchurch **Beach** •
United Kingdom .... 75 [66]
Dyrehavsbakken **Park** • Denmark .. 73 [17]
Dzamin Üüd • Mongolia 29 E2
Dzanga-Sangha, Réserve du **Park** •
Central African Rep. .... 103 [46]
Dzaoudzi • Comoros 24 H2
Dzhagdy, Khrebet • Russian Fed. ... 27 L6
Dzhankoy • Ukraine 17 E5
Dzhardzhan • Russian Fed. 27 J3
Dzhebel • Bulgaria 15 G2
Dzhetygara • Kazakhstan 26 J7
Dzhezkazgan • Kazakhstan 26 K8
Dzhugdzhur, Khrebet •
Russian Fed. 27 M5
Dzhusaly • Kazakhstan 26 J8
Dzialdowo • Poland 13 J4
Dzialoszyce • Poland 13 J7
Dzierzoniów • Poland 13 F7
Dzukija Nat. Park **Park** •
Lithuania .... 72 [148]

Eagle Farm [**Apt**] •
QL, Australia 111 F6
Eagle Lake • ME, United States 118 G2
Eagle Pass • TX, United States 40 F6
Earn • United Kingdom 74 B1
Earn, Loch • United Kingdom 74 B1
Earnslaw, Mt • New Zealand 112 L2
East Alligator • NT, Australia 34 F2
East Ayrshire • United Kingdom ... 75 A3
East Cape • New Zealand 35 G3
East China Sea • Asia 29 H5
East Coast Park • Singapore 108 E4
East Falkland • Falkland Is. 45 E6
East Grinstead • United Kingdom ... 5 C3
East Kilbride • United Kingdom 74 B3
East Lake Tohopekaliga •
FL, United States 121 C2
East London • South Africa 24 D6
East of England •
United Kingdom 75 A5
East Prussia • Poland 13 J3
East Retford • United Kingdom 5 C1
East Riding of Yorkshire •
United Kingdom 75 A4
East Siberian Sea •
Arctic Ocean 46 II2
East Sussex • United Kingdom 74 E3
Eastbourne • United Kingdom 74 E3
Eastbourne **Beach** •
United Kingdom .... 75 [72]
Easter I. • Pacific Ocean 33 Q8
Eastern Cape • South Africa 24 D6
Eastern Desert • Egypt 101 F4
Eastern Mediterranean Coast •
Turkey 92 A3
Eastern Mediterranean Coast •
Turkey 92 A3
Eastern Valleys • Norway 94 A7
Eastleigh • United Kingdom 7 K11
Eastmain • QU, Canada 39 P6
Eastmain [Riv] • QU, Canada 39 P6
Eau Claire • WI, United States 41 H3
Ebbw Vale • United Kingdom 7 I10
Ebebiyin • Equatorial Guinea 22 G4
Ebeltoft **Beach** • Denmark .... 68 [28]
Ebeltoft • Denmark 95 F10
Eber Gölü • Turkey 15 M5
Eberbach • Germany 82 G4
Eberbach **Spa** • Germany .... 83 [170]
Eberbach, Kloster • Germany 82 H4
Ebersberg • Germany 82 J3
Eberswalde-Finow • Germany 8 I4
Ebey's Landing Nat. Hist. Reserve **Park** •
WA, United States .... 120 [25]
Eboli • Italy 91 G4
Ebolowa • Cameroon 22 G4
Ebre, Delta de l' • Spain 11 L4
Ebro • Spain 11 K3
Ebro, Embalse del • Spain 11 H2
Ebschloh • Germany 5 L3
Echdeina • Western Sahara 20 C3
Echo Bay • NT, Canada 38 H3
Echternach • Luxembourg 80 A20
Echuca • VI, Australia 111 G3
Ecija • Spain 10 D3
Eckenhagen **Spa** • Germany ..... 83 [133]
Eckental • Germany 9 G7
Eckernförde • Germany 8 E2
Eckernförde **Spa** • Germany ..... 83 [14]
Eckerö • Finland 95 E3
Eckwarden **Spa** • Germany ...... 83 [52]
Eclipse Sound • NU, Canada 39 P2
Ecouen • France 85 E1
Ecrins, Parc nat. des **Park** •
France .... 72 [67]
Ecrins, Parc nat. des • France 85 F4
Ecuador • S. America 43 B4
Ed • Sweden 95 F2
Edam • Netherlands 80 C2
Eday • United Kingdom 6 J2
Edchera • Western Sahara 20 C3
Eddystone Rocks •
United Kingdom 74 F5
Ede • Netherlands 22 E3
Ede • Netherlands 80 A7
Edea • Cameroon 22 G4
Edelsteinmine • Germany 82 H3
Edelweiss Valley **Ski** •
QU, Canada .... 116 [26]
Edemissen • Germany 8 F4
Eden • United Kingdom 74 C2
Eden • NS, Australia 111 G4
Eden Brown • St Kitts & Nevis 125 G4
Edendale • New Zealand 112 L4
Edenlandia **Park** • Italy .... 73 [86]
Eder • Germany 9 D5
Eder-Stausee • Germany 5 M3
Edessa • Greece 15 D3
Edewecht • Germany 8 D3
Edfu • Egypt 101 F5
Edgar Ranges • WA, Australia 34 D3
Edgeham • Algeria 21 E3
Edgell I. • NU, Canada 39 S4
Edinburgh **Heritage C** •
United Kingdom .... 64 [13]
Edinburgh • United Kingdom 74 B4
Edinik • Turkey 15 I3
Edirne • Turkey 15 H2
Edison Nat. Hist. Site **Park** •
NJ, United States .... 121 [334]
Edland • Norway 94 C6
Edmonton • AL, Canada 122 C6
Edmunston • NB, Canada 123 D1
Edremit • Turkey 92 D5
Edremit • Turkey 92 D5
Edremit Körfezi • Turkey 15 H4
Edsbro • Sweden 95 D2

Edson • AL, Canada 122 C2
Eduardo Castex • Argentina 44 D6
Edward, Lake •
Uganda/Dem. Rep. of Congo ... 23 D4
Edwards Creek • SA, Australia 34 G5
Edwards Plateau •
TX, United States 40 F5
Edzo • NT, Canada 38 H4
Eeklo • Netherlands 5 G3
Eelde [**Apt**] • Netherlands 80 A4
Eemshaven • Netherlands 80 A4
Efaté • Vanuatu 35 (2) B2
Eferding • Austria 9 I4
Efes • Turkey 92 D9
Efes • Turkey 92 D9
Effigy Mounds Nat. Mon. **Park** •
IA, United States .... 121 [168]
Eflani • Turkey 15 N2
Eforie Nord • Romania 97 D2
Eforie Sud • Romania 97 D2
Efxinoúpolis **Beach** • Greece .. 69 [165]
Ega • Spain 10 C11
Ega, Val d' • Italy 90 B3
Egadi, Is. • Italy 90 D1
Eger • Germany 9 H6
Eger • Hungary 13 J10
Egersund • Norway 16 D7
Egesko • Denmark 95 F14
Eggelfelden • Germany 82 J4
Eghezée • Belgium 5 H4
Egina • Greece 92 D7
Egina • Greece 92 D7
Egio • Greece 15 C5
Eglab Dersa • Algeria 20 E3
Eglab, El • Algeria 20 E3
Egmont, Cape • New Zealand 112 K3
Egmont, Mt • New Zealand 112 K3
Egmont Nat. Park • New Zealand . 112 K3
Egnazia • Italy 14 E9
Egremont • United Kingdom 74 C1
Egridir • Turkey 93 G2
Egridir Gölü • Turkey 15 L5
Egrigöz Dagi • Turkey 15 K4
Egvekinot • Russian Fed. 27 V3
Egypt • Africa 21 E3
Egypt • Africa 82 J1
Ehingen • Germany 82 D7
Ehlscheid **Spa** • Germany ... 83 [152]
Ehrenbreitstein • Germany 82 H2
Ehrwald **Ski** • Austria .... 70 [139]
Ehrwald • Austria 89 H2
Eibar • Spain 11 I1
Eichstätt • Germany 9 G8
Eichwalde • Germany 81 F4
Eidanger • Norway 94 B3
Eider • Germany 8 E2
Eidfjord • Norway 94 C4
Eidfjorden • Norway 94 C4
Eidsdal • Norway 94 B1
Eidsvoll • Norway 94 C2
Eidsvåg • Norway 94 B1
Eifel • Germany 82 G1
Eifelpark **Park** • Germany ... 73 [62]
Eifelpark • Germany 82 H3
Eigat • Egypt 21 G3
Eiger • Switzerland 89 G2
Eigg • United Kingdom 6 F5
Eight Degree Channel •
Indian Ocean 106 D13
Eikelandsosen • Norway 94 B1
Eiken • Norway 94 C2
Eikesdalsvatnet • Norway 18 B4
Eilat • Israel 92 C3
Eilethyia • Crete, Greece 93 E3
Einasleigh • QL, Australia 34 H3
Eindhoven • Netherlands 80 A11
Einsiedeln • Switzerland 89 G3
Einslow • AZ, United States 118 J1
Eirunepé • Brazil 43 D5
Eisenach • Germany 9 F6
Eisenberg • Germany 9 G6
Eisenerz • Austria 13 C10
Eisenhower Birthplace State Hist. Site •
TX, United States 119 N1
Eisenhower Nat. Hist. Site **Park** •
PA, United States .... 121 [304]
Eisenhüttenstadt • Germany 8 J4
Eisenstadt • Austria 13 F10
Eisenwurzen • Austria 14 B2
Eisleben • Germany 8 G5
Eisleben **Heritage C** • Germany . 64 [32]
Eitorf • Germany 5 K4
Eivissa • Ibiza, Spain 87 G2
Eivissa [I.] • Spain 11 E2
Eje, Sierra del • Spain .... 87 G
Ejea de los Caballeros • Spain ... 11 J2
Ekenäs • Finland 95 E4
Eketorpsborg • Sweden 95 F11
Ekibastuz • Kazakhstan 26 M7
Eklingji • India 105 C5
Ekoli • Dem. Rep. of Congo 23 C4
Ekoln • Sweden 95 D2
Ekonda • Russian Fed. 26 S3
Eksjö • Sweden 95 F8
Ekwan • OT, Canada 39 O6
El Abrigo •
Tenerife, Canary Is. 86 E1
El Arahal • Spain 11 F7
El Banco • Colombia 43 C2
El Baúl • Venezuela 43 D2
El Cabo de Gata • Spain 86 B8
El Callao • Venezuela 43 E2
El Campo • TX, United States 119 N5
El Cañuelo • Puerto Rico 125 E2
El Carmen de Bolívar • Colombia . 43 B2
El Cerro • Bolivia 44 D2
El Cerro de Aripo •
Trinidad & Tobago 125 K1
El Cuy • Argentina 45 C3
El Dorado • Venezuela 37 I6
El Dorado • AR, United States 41 H5
El Ejido **Beach** • Spain .... 68 [99]
El Ejido • Spain 86 B8
El Encanto • Colombia 43 C4
El Escorial • Spain 11 G4
El Escorial **Heritage C** • Spain .. 64 [87]
El Ferrol • Spain 11 C1
El Jem **Heritage C** • Tunisia ... 64 [230]
El Maestrazgo • Spain 11 K4
El Maitén • Argentina 45 B4
El Malpais Nat. Mon. •
NM, United States 118 J2
El Malpais Nat. Mon. **Park** •
NM, United States .... 120 [127]
El Masnou **Beach** • Spain .... 68 [105]
El Masnou • Spain 87 D4
El Medano •
Tenerife, Canary Is. 86 E1
El Molinar • Majorca, Spain 87 H1
El Morro • Cuba 124 D8
El Morro, Castillo •
Puerto Rico 125 E2
El Morro Nat. Mon. •
NM, United States 118 J2
El Morro Nat. Mon. **Park** •
NM, United States .... 120 [126]

El Nevado, Cerro • Argentina 44 C6
El Palo • Spain 86 B7
El Paso • TX, United States 118 J4
El Pico • Bolivia 44 D2
El Pilar • Formentera, Spain 87 G4
El Pital • Mexico 123 E2
El Port de la Selva **Beach** •
Spain .... 68 [106]
El Potosí • Mexico 37 A3
El Prat de Llobregat • Spain 11 N3
El Puerto de Santa María **Beach** •
Spain .... 68 [96]
El Puerto de Santa María •
Spain 86 B5
El Qâhira **Heritage C** • Egypt .. 64 [237]
El Rompido • Spain 86 B1
El Salto • Mexico 37 (1) A1
El Salvador • C. America 37 D5
El Sueco • Mexico 40 E6
El Tajín **Heritage C** • Mexico ... 62 [18]
El Tigre • Mexico 123 E2
El Tigre • Venezuela 43 E2
El Torro • Minorca, Spain 87 F2
El Turbio • Argentina 45 B6
El Vendrell **Beach** • Spain ..... 68 [104]
El Vendrell • Spain 87 D3
El Vizcaino whale sanctuary **Heritage N** •
Mexico .... 62 [18]
El Yunque • Puerto Rico 125 E2
Elafonísi • Crete, Greece 93 E5
Eland Sanctuary • Zimbabwe 102 J4
Elassóna • Greece 15 H3
Elat • Israel 18 B4
Eláti • Greece 15 H3
Eláziz • Turkey 18 C2
Elba, I. d' • Italy 91 E10
Elbasan • Albania 14 H8
Elbe • Germany 8 F3
Elbert, Mt • CO, United States ... 40 E4
Elbeuf • France 10 F4
Elblag • Poland 13 I3
Elbrus • Georgia/Russian Fed. ... 17 G6
Elbtal • Germany 18 E2
Elche **Beach** • Spain .... 68 [101]
Elche • Spain 87 C1
Elcho I. • NT, Australia 34 G2
Elda • Spain 87 C1
Eldab • Somalia 23 H2
Elde • Germany 8 G3
Eldikan • Russian Fed. 27 M4
Eldora Mtn **Ski** •
CO, United States .... 116 [89]
Eldoret • Kenya 101 G1
Elephant Butte Reservoir •
NM, United States 118 J4
Elephant Village •
Pattaya, Thailand 109 H4
Elephanta Caves **Heritage C** •
India .... 63 [125]
Elephantine I. • Egypt 101 F5
Eleuthera • Bahamas 124 B1
Elgin • United Kingdom 6 H3
Elgin • IL, United States 41 I3
Elginsky • Russian Fed. 27 N4
Elgon, Mt • Kenya/Uganda 101 G1
Elgoran • Ethiopia 23 G2
Elgyay • Russian Fed. 27 I4
Elía **Beach** • Crete, Greece .... 69 [190]
Elie **Beach** • United Kingdom .. 75 [11]
Elila • Dem. Rep. of Congo 23 D4
Elin Pelin • Bulgaria 14 K7
Eliot • NT, Australia 34 F3
Elista • Russian Fed. 17 G5
Elizabeth • SA, Australia 34 G6
Elizabeth City •
NC, United States 118 H5
Elizabeth Reef • Australia 33 H9
Elizabethtown •
KY, United States 41 I4
Elk • Poland 13 L4
Elk I. Nat. Park • AL, Canada 122 C4
Elkhovo • Bulgaria 97 D3
Elko • NV, United States 117 F2
Ellensburg • WA, United States .. 117 E1
Ellertrin, Plains of • Ireland 79 F4
Ellesmere I. • NU, Canada 36 I1
Ellice Is. • Tuvalu 33 I6
Elliot Lake • OT, Canada 36 L3
Elliott, Mt • QL, Australia 111 F1
Elliston • SA, Australia 34 F6
Ellmau **Ski** • Austria ...... 70 [153]
Ellmau • Austria 89 H3
Ellora Caves **Heritage C** • India . 63 [128]
Ellsworth Land • Antarctica .. 46 (1) FF2
Ellwangen • Germany 9 F8
Elmali • Turkey 93 G3
Elmdon [**Apt**] • United Kingdom . 74 D2
Elmira • NY, United States 118 H1
Elmshorn • Germany 8 F3
Elne • France 11 I2
Elorza • Venezuela 43 D2
Eloúnda **Beach** • Crete, Greece . 69 [191]
Eloúnda • Crete, Greece 93 E8
Elsdorf • Germany 82 H1
Else • Germany 5 L2
Elsen Nur • China 28 F1
Elstal • Germany 81 F1
Elsterwerda • Germany 8 I5
Eltanin Bay • Antarctica ... 46 (1) GG2
Eltham • New Zealand 112 K3
Eltville • Germany 82 H1
Eltz, Burg • Germany 82 H1
Elura • India 28 B5
Eluru • India 11 D6
Elvas • Portugal 11 D6
Elverum • Norway 94 C2
Elx **Beach** • Spain .... 68 [101]
Elx • Spain 87 C1
Ely • United Kingdom 7 M9
Ely • NV, United States 117 F4
Elzas • France 9 C8
Emal • Vanuatu 35 (2) B2
Emamshar • Iran 18 G2
Emân • Sweden 95 F8
Emanuel • Antigua & Barbuda ... 125 F3
Emae • Vanuatu 35 (2) B2
Emba • Kazakhstan 26 I8
Emba [Riv] • Kazakhstan 26 I8
Embarcación • Argentina 44 D3
Embarras Portage • AL, Canada .. 38 I5
Embay, Rhodes, Greece 93 F1
Embudhu • Maldives 106 E4
Embudhu Finolhu • Maldives 106 E4
Emden • Germany 8 C3
Emei Shan **Heritage N** • China .. 61 [117]
Emei Shan **Heritage C** • China .. 63 [156]
Emei Shan • China 107 G7
Emerald • QL, Australia 111 F3
Emeraude, Côte d' • France 15 K4
Emet • Turkey 15 K4
Emi Koussi • Chad 21 C4
Emilia-Romagna • Italy 91 E7
Emily Rock • Pacific Ocean 33 L9
Emine, Nos • Bulgaria 14 O7
Emirdag • Turkey 15 M4

Emlichheim • Germany 8 B4
Emmaboda • Sweden 95 F12
Emmaste • Estonia 16 L7
Emmeloord • Netherlands 80 A8
Emmen • Netherlands 80 A7
Emmendingen • Germany 9 C8
Emmerich • Germany 5 J3
Emmmen • QL, Australia 34 H4
Emory Peak • TX, United States .. 40 F6
Empalme • Mexico 40 D6
Empoli • Italy 12 E5
Emporda • Spain 87 D2
Emporia • KS, United States 41 G4
Empúries • Spain 87 D2
Ems • Germany 8 C4
Ems-Jade-Kanal • Germany 5 K1
Emsdetten • Germany 5 K2
Emsland • Germany 8 C4
En Colom, I. d' •
Minorca, Spain 87 F4
En Gedi • Israel 98 A8
Enaratoli • Indonesia 32 (1) E3
Enare träsk • Finland 16 N2
Encantada • Mexico 40 C5
Encarnación • Paraguay 44 E4
Enchi • Ghana 22 D3
Endako • SA, Australia 32 (1) B4
Ende • Indonesia 32 (1) B4
Endelave • Denmark 95 F10
Enderby Land • Antarctica .. 46 (1) K3
Endvale • France 85 A8
Enez • Turkey 15 H3
Enez Körfezi • Turkey 15 G3
Enfidaville • Tunisia 12 E12
Engelberg **Ski** • Switzerland . 70 [103]
Engelberg • Switzerland 89 G3
Engels • Russian Fed. 17 H4
Engelskirchen • Germany 81 E4
Engelsviken **Heritage C** • Sweden . 64 [3]
Engelskirchen • Germany 81 E4
Erlebnispark Tripsdrill **Park** •
Germany .... 73 [64]
England • United Kingdom 7
England, North West •
United Kingdom 75 A4
England, Southeast •
United Kingdom .... 74 E
Englee • NF, Canada 123 D4
English Channel • France/UK 10 D3
English Harbour •
Antigua & Barbuda 125 F4
English Harbour Town •
Antigua & Barbuda 125 F4
English Riviera •
United Kingdom 74 F5
Enh-Gayvan • Mongolia 26 Q8
Enid • OK, United States 41 G4
Eniwetok • Marshall Is. 33 H4
Enkhuizen • Netherlands 80 A7
Enköping • Sweden 95 D1
Enna • Sicily, Italy 90 D4
Ennadai Lake • NU, Canada 38 K4
Ennedi • Chad 21 D4
Ennepetal • Germany 81 E4
Ennepetal **Spa** • Germany .. 83 [107]
Ennerdale Water •
United Kingdom 74 C1
Ennri Miski • Chad 21 C4
Ennis • Ireland 79 F6
Enniscorthy • Ireland 7 F9
Enniskerry • Ireland 79 A4
Enniskillen • United Kingdom 7 E7
Ennistymon • Ireland 79 F4
Enns • Austria 13 D10
Eno • Finland 16 P5
Enontekiö • Finland 16 L2
Enschede • Netherlands 80 C5
Ensenada • Mexico 40 C5
Ensenada • Argentina 127 D2
Enshi • China 29 D4
Entebbe • Uganda 23 E3
Entenbühl • Czech Rep./Germany . 9 H7
Enterprise • NT, Canada 38 H4
Enterprise • MS, United States ... 118 K2
Entrance, The • NS, Australia ... 111 G4
Entre Ríos • Argentina 127 A3
Entre-Deux-Mers • France 84 B3
Entrecasteaux, Point d' •
WA, Australia 34 C6
Entrecasteaux, Récifs d' •
New Caledonia 35 (2) A2
Enugu • Nigeria 22 F3
Envigado • Colombia 43 C5
Envira • Brazil 43 D5
Enz • Germany 82 A2
Enzan • Japan 30 J7
Epanomí **Beach** • Greece ... 69 [168]
EPCOT Center •
FL, United States 121 C1
Epernay • France 10 I4
Ephesus • Turkey 92 D9
Ephesus • Turkey 92 D9
Ephraim, Mount • Jordan 98 A5
Epi • Vanuatu 35 (2) B2
Epidamnus • Albania 14 H8
Epidaurus **Heritage C** • Greece . 64 [182]
Epidauros • Greece 92 D7
Epidauros • Greece 92 D7
Epidavros **Heritage C** • Greece . 64 [182]
Epidavros • Greece 92 D7
Epinal • France 10 I5
Epirus • Greece 92 A1
Episkopi • Crete, Greece 93 E2
Episkopi Bay • Cyprus 93 J3
Epping • United Kingdom 74 E1
Epsom • United Kingdom 7 L10
Epsom Downs • United Kingdom . 34 D6
Epte • France 10 G4
Epupa Falls • Angola/Namibia ... 24 A3
Equateur • Dem. Rep. of Congo .. 23 C3
Equatorial Channel • Maldives .. 106 E3
Equatorial Guinea • Africa 101 D4
Er Rachidia • Morocco 20 D2
Eraclea Minoa • Sicily, Italy 90 D3
Eratini • Greece 5 M5
Erbach • Germany 82 J1
Erbalunga • Corsica, France 85 L2
Ercek • Turkey 18 E2
Erciyas Dagi • Turkey 15 O4
Erculano • Italy 91 G3
Erd • Hungary 13 H10
Erdao • China 30 D3
Erdek • Turkey 92 D3
Erdek Körfezi • Turkey 15 I3
Erdemli • Turkey 92 D3
Erdeven **Beach** • France .... 68 [76]
Erdeven • France 84 C4
Erdi Ma • Chad 21 D4
Erding • Germany 82 J3
Erdre • France 10 D6
Erebus, Mt • Antarctica ... 46 (1) W2

Erechim • Brazil 44 F4
Eregli • Turkey 15 M2
Ereke • Indonesia 32 (1) B3
Erenhot • China 29 E2
Eressós **Beach** • Greece ... 69 [176]
Eressós • Greece 92 D5
Eressós • Greece 92 D5
Erétria • Greece 15 E5
Erétria **Beach** • Greece .... 69 [163]
Erfoud • Morocco 101 D6
Erfurt • Germany 8 I6
Erfurt **Heritage C** • Germany ... 64 [62]
Ergene • Turkey 9 G6
Ergig, Bahr • Chad 22 H2
Erg Iguidi • Africa 21 E3
Ergun Zuoqi • China 27 J6
Erice **Beach** • Sicily, Italy ... 68 [131]
Erice • Sicily, Italy 90 D1
Ericeira • Portugal 11 C4
Ericht, Loch • United Kingdom ... 6 H5
Erie • PA, United States 41 K3
Erie Canal • NY, United States . 122 B10
Erie, Lake •
Canada/United States 39 O8
Erimanthos • Greece 23 H1
Erimantos • Greece 92 D7
Erimo-Misaki • Japan 30 L4
Eringsboda • Sweden 95 F9
Eritrea • Africa 21 G4
Eriyadu • Maldives 106 E2
Erken • Sweden 95 D2
Erkner • Germany 81 E3
Erkrath • Germany 81 E3
Erlach • India 105 C7
Erlangen • Germany 9 G7
Erlauf • NT, Australia 45 (1) B4
Erlebnispark Tripsdrill **Park** •
Germany .... 73 [64]
Erlong Shan • China 27 K8
Ermelo • South Africa 24 E5
Ermenek • Turkey 15 N7
Ermesinde • Portugal 11 C3
Ermióni • Greece 92 D7
Ermióni • Greece 92 D7
Ermones **Beach** • Corfu, Greece . 69 [149]
Ermones • Corfu, Greece 92 B1
Ermones • Corfu, Greece 92 B1
Ernabella • SA, Australia 112 H3
Erne • India 106 D10
Erne, Lough, Lower •
United Kingdom 7 E7
Erne, Lough, Upper •
United Kingdom 7 E7
Ernest Giles • Pacific Ocean ... 33 L9
Erode • India 106 D10
Erpeler Ley • Germany 82 H1
Erquy • France 84 C2
Errego • Mozambique 24 F3
Erritsø • Denmark 95 F9
Erromango • Vanuatu 35 (2) B2
Erstein • France 9 C8
Erve • Albania 15 A2
Erzberg • Germany 9 I6
Erzin • Russian Fed. 26 O7
Erzincan • Turkey 92 A4
Erzincan • Turkey 92 A4
Erzurum • Turkey 18 D2
Es Canutells • Minorca, Spain ... 87 F4
Es Canyar • Ibiza, Spain 87 G2
Es Delfins • Minorca, Spain 87 F1
Es Mercadal **Beach** •
Minorca, Spain .... 68 [110]
Es Mercadal • Minorca, Spain ... 87 F2
Es Migjorn Redones Gran Sant Cristóbal •
Minorca, Spain 87 F3
Es Pla • Majorca, Spain 87 H2
Es Pujols • Formentera, Spain ... 87 G4
Es Savina • Formentera, Spain ... 87 G4
Es Sclerne, Naveta d' •
Minorca, Spain 87 F1
Esashi • Japan 30 L2
Esbjerg • Denmark 95 F9
Esbo • Finland 95 E4
Escala, l' **Beach** • Spain ..... 68 [106]
Escala, l' • Spain 87 D2
Escambia • AL/FL, United States . 119 M1
Escambray, Sierra del • Cuba .. 124 D2
Escanaba • MI, United States 41 I3
Escaut • France 80 A14
Esch-sur-Alzette • Luxembourg .. 80 A20
Esch-sur-Sûre • Luxembourg 80 A20
Eschwege • Germany 9 F5
Eschweiler • Germany 82 G1
Escondido • CA, United States .. 117 F6
Escuintla • Guatemala 37 C5
Esens-Bensersiel **Spa** • Germany . 83 [45]
Esfahan • Iran 18 G2
Esfahan **Heritage C** • Iran .. 63 [108]
Eshtemoa • Jordan 98 A7
Esino • Italy 12 H5
Esk • United Kingdom 74 C3
Eskilstuna • Sweden 95 D3
Eskimo Lake • NT, Canada 38 E3
Eskisehir • Turkey 15 L4
Eslöv • Sweden 95 F11
Esme • Turkey 15 J5
Esmeraldas • Ecuador 43 B3
Esna • Egypt 101 F5
Espalmador, I. • Ibiza, Spain ... 87 G4
Español • Galapagos Is. ... 43 (1) B2
Esparadell, I. • Ibiza, Spain 87 G4
Espelkamp • Germany 5 L2
Esperance • WA, Australia 34 D6
Esperance Bay • WA, Australia .. 34 D6
Esperanza • Argentina 44 D5
Esperanza [Base] • Antarctica . 46 (1) JJ3
Espichel, Cabo • Portugal 11 C5
Espigäo Mestre • Brazil 44 G1
Espinal • Colombia 43 C3
Espinar • Peru 43 C7
Espinhaço de Cão, Serra de •
Portugal 88 E1
Espinho **Beach** • Portugal ... 68 [77]
Espinho • Brazil 44 H1
Espírito Santo • Brazil 44 H1
Espíritu Santo • Vanuatu ... 35 (2) B2
Espíritu Santo, Río •
Puerto Rico 125 E2
Esplanada • Brazil 44 H1
Espoo • Finland 95 E4
Esposende • Portugal 11 C3
Esposende **Beach** • Portugal .. 68 [76]
Espungabera • Mozambique 24 E4
Esquel • Argentina 45 B4
Essaouira • Morocco 101 D6
Essaouira **Beach** • Morocco . 69 [117]
Essen • Germany 81 E4
Essen: Werden • Germany 81 E4
Essendon, Mt • WA, Australia ... 34 D4
Essequibo • Guyana 43 F3

Essex • United Kingdom 74 E2
Essex • CT, United States 118 H2
Esslingen am Neckar • Germany . 82 G6
Esso • Russian Fed. 27 Q5
Essonne • France 85 E3
Est, Pointe de l' • QU, Canada .. 123 D2
Estados, I. de los • Argentina 45 D6
Estância • Brazil 44 I1
Estarreja • Portugal 11 C4
Estartit, l' • Spain 87 D2
Este • Italy 12 F3
Este, Playas del • Cuba 124 D2
Estelí • Nicaragua 37 D5
Estella • Spain 11 I2
Estellencs • Majorca, Spain 87 H1
Estepa • Spain 86 B2
Estepona **Beach** • Spain ...... 68 [97]
Estepona • Spain 86 B6
Esterel, l' • France 85 C7
Estevan • SA, Canada 38 K7
Estói • Portugal 88 D1
Estonia • Europe 16 M7
Estoril • Portugal 88 D1
Estoril, Costa do • Portugal 11 D4
Estrela, Serra da • Portugal 11 D5
Estremadura • Portugal 11 B5
Estremoz • Portugal 11 D6
Estrondo, Serra do • Brazil .. 45 (1) B4
Estuario do Tejo, Reserva Natural •
Portugal 88 D2
Esztergom • Hungary 13 H10
Et Tieta de Ouad Laou • Morocco . 88 E1
Étables-sur-Mer **Beach** • France . 68 [60]
Étables-sur-Mer • France 84 C2
Étain • France 5 I5
Étampes • France 85 E3
Étaples • France 10 G3
Étawah • India 105 C7
Etel **Beach** • France .... 68 [62]
Étel • France 84 C4
Eternity Range • Antarctica . 46 (1) II3
Ethiopia • Africa 19 H5
Etna, Monte • Sicily, Italy 90 D2
Etne • Norway 94 C5
Étoile • Seychelles 106 F2
Etolin I. • AK, United States 38 E5
Etosha Nat. Park **Park** • Namibia . 103 [114]
Etosha Pan • Namibia 24 B3
Etoumbi • Congo 23 C3
Etretat • France 84 D2
Étsaut • Germany 82 J6
Ettelbruck • Luxembourg 5 J5
Ettlingen • Germany 5 L6
Eu • France 5 E4
Euboea • Greece 92 D4
Euboea • Greece 92 D4
Eucla • WA, Australia 34 E6
Eucumbene, Lake • NS, Australia . 111 G4
Eugene • OR, United States 117 E3
Eugenia, Punta • Mexico 40 C6
Eugmo • Finland 16 L5
Eunice • LA, United States 118 K3
Eupen • Belgium 5 J4
Euphrates • Asia 18 D3
Eura • Finland 95 E1
Eurajoki • Finland 95 E1
Eure • France 10 G5
Eureka • CA, United States 117 F1
Eureka • NV, United States 117 F2
Euromast • Netherlands 80 C3
Europa Park **Park** • Germany .. 73 [67]
Europa Park • Germany 82 G7
Europa, Picos de • Spain 11 G1
Europa, Punta de • Gibraltar 86 B6
Europa, Punta de • Gibraltar 86 B6
Europoort • Netherlands 80 C3
Euskirchen • Germany 82 H1
Eutin • Germany 8 F2
Eutin **Spa** • Germany ...... 83 [32]
Evale • Angola 24 B3
Evanger • Norway 94 C3
Evans, Lac • QU, Canada 39 P6
Evans Strait • NU, Canada 39 O4
Evanston • WY, United States ... 40 D3
Evansville • IN, United States 41 I4
Eveciler • Turkey 15 H4
Evdir Hani • Turkey 93 G1
Evelyn, Mt • NT, Australia 34 F1
Evenes • Russian Fed. 27 O4
Everest, Mt • China/Nepal 28 E3
Everett • WA, United States 117 E1
Everglades • FL, United States .. 119 M8
Everglades Nat. Park **Heritage N** •
FL, United States .... 60 [17]
Everglades Nat. Park •
FL, United States 119 M8
Everglades Nat. Park **Park** •
FL, United States ...... 121 [226]
Evesham • United Kingdom 74 D4
Evesham, Vale of •
United Kingdom 74 D4
Evia • Greece 92 D4
Evia • Greece 92 D4
Évian-les-Bains • France 85 F4
Evinayong • Equatorial Guinea .. 22 G4
Evje • Norway 95 F1
Évora • Portugal 11 D6
Évora **Heritage C** • Portugal .. 64 [101]
Évora [Adm] • Portugal 88 A3
Évreux • France 10 G5
Evros • Greece 15 H2
Évry • France 85 E3
Ewa Beach • HI, United States .. 119 L5
Ewaso Ngiro • Kenya 101 G2
Ewo • Congo 22 G5
Exe • United Kingdom 74 F2
Exeter • United Kingdom 74 F2
Exmoor • United Kingdom 74 F2
Exmoor Nat. Park **Park** •
United Kingdom .... 72 [50]
Exmoor Nat. Park •
United Kingdom 74 F2
Exmouth • WA, Australia 34 B4
Exmouth • United Kingdom 74 F5
Exmouth Gulf • WA, Australia ... 33 C8
Exposition, Parc des • France 5 I3
Extremadura • Spain 11 F5
Exuma Cays • Bahamas 124 B1
Exuma Cays Land & Sea Park •
Bahamas 124 B1
Eyasi, Lake • Tanzania 102 H2
Eyl • Somalia 23 H2
Eymouthiers • France 85 G2
Eyre • WA, Australia 34 E6
Eyre Mtns • New Zealand 112 L2
Eyre, Lake • SA, Australia 34 G5
Eyre, Lake, North •
SA, United States 34 G5
Eyre, Lake, South •
SA, Australia 34 G5
Eyre Peninsula • SA, Australia .. 34 G6
Eze • France 85 H2
Ezeiza [**Apt**] • Argentina 127 D2
Ezequiel Ramos Mexia, Embalse •
Argentina 45 C3

Faan, Ko • Thailand ... 109 J1
Faber Lake • NT, Canada ... 38 F4
Fåborg Beach • Denmark ... 68 [25]
Fåborg • Denmark ... 95 F14
Fabriano • Italy ... 12 G5
Fachi • Niger ... 20 H5
Fada • Chad ... 21 D4
Fada-Ngourma • Burkina Faso ... 20 D5
Faddeya, Zaliv • Russian Fed. ... 26 S2
Faddeyevskiy, Ostrov •
   Russian Fed. ... 27 N1
Fadiffolu Atoll • Maldives ... 106 E1
Faenza • Italy ... 91 E7
Fafen • Ethiopia ... 23 G2
Fagaras • Romania ... 14 L4
Fagerhult • Sweden ... 95 F8
Fagernes • Norway ... 16 E6
Fagersta • Sweden ... 95 E1
Fagita • Indonesia ... 32 (1) D3
Faguibine, Lac • Mali ... 20 E5
Faguibine, Lac Park • Mali ... 103 [2]
Fahrland • Germany ... 81 F3
Fahrlander See • Germany ... 81 F3
Fahs, El • Tunisia ... 12 D12
Fai di Paganella • Italy ... 90 B3
Faial Beach • Azores ... 68 [83]
Faial • Azores ... 88 B1
Faial • Madeira ... 88 C2
Fair Isle • United Kingdom ... 6 K2
Fair Park Park •
   TX, United States ... 121 [M]
Fairbanks • AK, United States ... 38 B4
Fairbourne Beach •
   United Kingdom ... 75 [187]
Fairmont • MN, United States ... 41 H3
Fairmont • WV, United States ... 41 J4
Fairmount Hot Springs •
   BC, Canada ... 122 C4
Fairview Park •
   Hong Kong, China ... 107 H3
Fairweather, Mt •
   Canada/United States ... 38 D5
Fairyhouse • Ireland ... 79 E2
Faisalabad • Pakistan ... 28 B2
Faiyûm, El • Egypt ... 101 F1
Faizabad • India ... 105 C8
Fakfak • Indonesia ... 32 (1) D3
Fakse Bugt • Denmark ... 95 F14
Fakse Ladeplads • Denmark ... 95 F14
Falaise • France ... 10 E5
Falaise de Tiguidit • Niger ... 20 F6
Falam • Myanmar ... 31 A2
Falásarna • Crete, Greece ... 93 E1
Falcade Ski • Italy ... 70 [223]
Falcade • Italy ... 90 B4
Falcon, Cap • Algeria ... 11 K9
Falcon Reservoir •
   TX, United States ... 40 G6
Falconara • Italy ... 91 E12
Falconara Marittima • Italy ... 12 H5
Falcone, Capo del •
   Sardinia, Italy ... 90 C1
Falémé • Mali/Senegal ... 22 B2
Falfurrias • TX, United States ... 119 N5
Faliráki • Rhodes, Greece ... 93 F2
Faliráki [Beach] •
   Rhodes, Greece ... 93 F2
Falkenberg Beach • Sweden ... 68 [2]
Falkenberg • Sweden ... 95 F7
Falkensee • Germany ... 81 F1
Falkirk • United Kingdom ... 74 B3
Falkirk [Adm] • United Kingdom ... 74 B3
Falkland Is • Atlantic Ocean ... 45 J6
Falköping • Sweden ... 95 F3
Fall River • MA, United States ... 118 H2
Fallingbostel • Germany ... 8 E4
Fallingbostel Spa • Germany ... 83 [61]
Fallon • NV, United States ... 117 F4
Falls Creek • VI, Australia ... 111 G3
Falmouth • United Kingdom ... 74 F4
Falmouth • Jamaica ... 124 C1
Falmouth • Antigua & Barbuda ... 125 F4
Falmouth Harbour •
   Antigua & Barbuda ... 125 F4
False Bay • South Africa ... 100 C5
Falster • Denmark ... 95 F14
Falsterbo • Sweden ... 95 F15
Falticeni • Romania ... 14 N2
Falun • Sweden ... 16 H6
Famagusta • Cyprus ... 93 J4
Famagusta Bay • Cyprus ... 93 J2
Familien-Freizeitpark Tolk-Schau Park •
   Germany ... 73 [51]
Fan Si Pan • Vietnam ... 31 C2
Fana • Mali ... 20 C6
Fana • Norway ... 94 C3
Fanári Beach • Greece ... 69 [173]
Fanári • Greece ... 92 D2
Fanári • Greece ... 92 D2
Fanchang • China ... 107 J3
Fang • Thailand ... 107 H3
Fanling • Hong Kong, China ... 107 H3
Fanø Beach • Denmark ... 68 [32]
Fano • Italy ... 91 E12
Fanø • Denmark ... 95 F13
Fanø Bugt • Denmark ... 95 F13
Fantasylandia • Ibiza, Spain ... 87 G2
Far East cruise area • Asia ... 59 A8
Faraday [Base] • Antarctica ... 46 (1) I3
Faradje • Dem. Rep. of Congo ... 23 D3
Farafra Oasis • Egypt ... 101 D2
Farah • Afghanistan ... 18 H3
Farah [Riv] • Afghanistan ... 18 H3
Faranah • Guinea ... 22 B2
Farasan, Jaza'ir • Saudi Arabia ... 18 D6
Farbarin Reservoir •
   QL, Australia ... 111 F3
Fareham • United Kingdom ... 7 K11
Farewell, Cape • New Zealand ... 35 D5
Farewell Spit • New Zealand ... 35 D5
Fargo • ND, United States ... 41 G2
Faribault • MN, United States ... 41 H3
Faridabad • India ... 105 C2
Farilhões, Is • Portugal ... 11 B5
Farim • Guinea-Bissau ... 22 A2
Färjestaden • Sweden ... 95 F8
Farmakonissi • Greece ... 92 D8
Farmakonissi • Greece ... 92 D8
Farmington • NM, United States ... 118 J2
Färnebofjärden • Sweden ... 95 D1
Farnham • United Kingdom ... 74 E3
Färö • Sweden ... 16 J8
Faro • Portugal ... 88 E7
Faro • Portugal ... 88 E7
Faro [Adm] • Portugal ... 88 E7
Faro, Punta del • Italy ... 12 J10
Faroe Is • Atlantic Ocean ... 4 I4
Fårösund • Sweden ... 16 J8
Farquhar, Atoll de • Seychelles ... 106 F3
Farrukhabad • India ... 105 C3
Fársala • Greece ... 15 D4
Farsø Beach • Denmark ... 68 [44]
Farsø • Denmark ... 95 F5
Farsund • Norway ... 16 D7
Farukolhufushi • Maldives ... 106 E4

Fårup • Denmark ... 95 F9
Fårup Aquapark & Sommerland Park •
   Denmark ... 73 [14]
Fårup Sommerland • Denmark ... 95 F5
Farvel, Kap • Greenland ... 39 W5
Fasano • Italy ... 12 L8
Fashir, Al • Sudan ... 21 E5
Fasil Ghebbi Heritage C •
   Ethiopia ... 63 [85]
Fasillar • Turkey ... 93 G2
Fatehpur • Rajasthan, India ... 105 C2
Fatehpur • Uttar Pradesh, India ... 105 C7
Fatehpur Sikri Heritage C •
   India ... 63 [120]
Fatehpur Sikri • India ... 105 C3
Fátima • Portugal ... 11 C5
Fatrade Beach • Goa, India ... 105 B2
Fatu Hiva • French Polynesia ... 33 N7
Faucigny • France ... 85 F2
Faugères • France ... 84 B4
Faurei • Romania ... 9 D1
Fauske • Norway ... 16 H3
Faute-sur-Mer, la Beach •
   France ... 68 [64]
Favara • Sicily, Italy ... 12 H11
Faváritx, Cap de •
   Minorca, Spain ... 87 F2
Favignana, I • Italy ... 90 D1
Faw, Al • Iraq ... 41
Fawn • OT, Canada ... 39 N6
Faxälven • Sweden ... 16 H5
Faya-Largeau • Chad ... 21 C4
Faye, Pas de la • France ... 85 H2
Fayetteville •
   NC, United States ... 41 K5
Fazao-Malfakassa, Parc nat. de Park •
   Togo ... 103 [30]
Fazilka • India ... 18 J3
Fazzan • Libya ... 21 B2
Fderick • Mauritania ... 20 B2
Feale • Ireland ... 79 F6
Fear, Cape • NC, United States ... 41 K5
Fécamp • France ... 10 F4
Federación • Argentina ... 45 E2
Federal Hall Nat. Mem. Park •
   NY, United States ... 121 [326]
Fedje • Norway ... 94 C3
Fehmarn • Germany ... 8 G2
Fehmarnbelt • Germany ... 8 G2
Feia, Lago • Brazil ... 127 C4
Feijó • Brazil ... 43 C5
Feilding • New Zealand ... 35 E5
Feira de Santana • Brazil ... 44 I1
Felanitx Beach • Majorca, Spain ... 68 [109]
Felanitx • Majorca, Spain ... 87 H4
Feldafing • Germany ... 82 J3
Feldberg Ski • Germany ... 70 [1]
Feldberg • Germany ... 82 G8
Feldkirch • Austria ... 89 H5
Feliceto • Corsica, France ... 85 L1
Félicité • Seychelles ... 106 F4
Felidu Atoll • Maldives ... 106 E4
Felixstowe • United Kingdom ... 74 E2
Fell Foot Park • United Kingdom ... 74 C4
Feltre • Italy ... 90 B4
Femer Bælt • Denmark/Germany ... 95 F14
Femund • Norway ... 16 F5
Fen He • China ... 29 E3
Fendek, El • Morocco ... 11 F9
Fengcheng • China ... 30 C4
Fengjie • China ... 107 J4
Fengnie • China ... 29 D4
Fengshui Shan • China ... 27 J6
Fengxian • China ... 107 J4
Fenit Beach • Ireland ... 68 [41]
Fenit • Ireland ... 79 F5
Fenouillèdes • France ... 85 K2
Fens, The • United Kingdom ... 7 M9
Fensfjorden • Norway ... 94 C3
Fenyang • China ... 29 E3
Fer, Cap de • Algeria ... 20 G1
Ferdows • Iran ... 18 G3
Fère-Champenoise • France ... 5 H6
Féres • Greece ... 15 H3
Ferfer • Ethiopia ... 23 H2
Fergana • Uzbekistan ... 18 J1
Fergana Basin • Uzbekistan ... 96 A3
Ferguson Lake • NU, Canada ... 38 J4
Fergusson I • Papua New Guinea ... 35 (1) E2
Ferienzentrum Schloß Dankern Park •
   Germany ... 73 [53]
Ferkéssédougou • Côte d'Ivoire ... 22 C3
Ferlo • Senegal ... 20 C6
Ferlo [Riv] • Senegal ... 20 B5
Fermanagh • United Kingdom ... 79 D2
Fermo • Italy ... 12 H5
Fermoy • Ireland ... 79 F8
Fern Gully • Jamaica ... 124 C2
Fernandina • Galapagos Is. ... 43 (1) A2
Fernandina Beach •
   FL, United States ... 119 M3
Fernando de Noronha, Território do •
   Brazil ... 45 (1) F2
Fernando Póo •
   Equatorial Guinea ... 22 F4
Fernandópolis • Brazil ... 44 F3
Fernie Snow Valley Ski •
   BC, Canada ... 116 [10]
Fernmeldeturm • Germany ... 81 E3
Ferragudo • Portugal ... 88 E6
Ferrandina • Italy ... 12 K8
Ferrara Heritage C • Italy ... 64 [115]
Ferrara • Italy ... 91 E7
Ferraria, Ponta da • Azores ... 88 B1
Ferreira do Alentejo • Portugal ... 11 C6
Ferreras • Portugal ... 88 E6
Ferreries Beach •
   Minorca, Spain ... 68 [110]
Ferreries • Minorca, Spain ... 87 F1
Ferret, Cap • France ... 85 G3
Ferru, Monte • Sardinia, Italy ... 90 C1
Ferrutx, Es Cap de •
   Majorca, Spain ... 11 O5
Ferté-Bernard, la • France ... 84 D2
Ferté-Macé, la • France ... 84 C2
Fès Heritage C • Morocco ... 64 [214]
Fès • Morocco ... 101 D2
Fesdu Fun I • Maldives ... 106 E1
Feshi • Dem. Rep. of Congo ... 22 H6
Festós • Crete, Greece ... 93 E6
Fetesti • Romania ... 97 D2
Fethiye • Turkey ... 92 D9
Fethiye • Turkey ... 92 D9
Fethiye Körfezi • Turkey ... 15 J7
Fetlar • United Kingdom ... 6 L1
Fetsund • Norway ... 94 B2
Feuchtwangen • Germany ... 9 F7
Feuilles, Rivière aux •
   QU, Canada ... 39 Q5
Feurs • France ... 10 J8
Feyzabad • Afghanistan ... 18 J2
Fezzan • Libya ... 20 H3
Ffestiniog • United Kingdom ... 7 I8
Fiabilandia Park • Italy ... 73 [84]
Fianarantsoa • Madagascar ... 24 H4
Fiche • Ethiopia ... 23 F1
Fichtelgebirge • Germany ... 9 H6
Fichtenwalde • Germany ... 81 F3

Fidenza • Italy ... 91 E6
Fideris Ski • Switzerland ... 70 [112]
Fieberbrunn Ski • Austria ... 70 [155]
Fieberbrunn • Austria ... 89 H3
Fier • Albania ... 15 A3
Fiesch Ski • Switzerland ... 70 [101]
Fiesch • Switzerland ... 89 G6
Fiésole • Italy ... 91 E11
Fife • United Kingdom ... 74 B2
Fife Ness • United Kingdom ... 6 J5
Fifi, Al • Sudan ... 23 D1
Fig Tree • St Kitts & Nevis ... 125 G4
Fig Tree Drive •
   Antigua & Barbuda ... 125 F3
Figari • Corsica, France ... 85 L4
Figeac • France ... 85 G4
Figeholm • Sweden ... 95 F8
Figueira da Foz • Portugal ... 11 C4
Figueira da Foz Beach •
   Portugal ... 68 [78]
Figueres • Spain ... 87 D2
Figuig • Morocco ... 101 D4
Fihalhohi • Maldives ... 106 E4
Fiji • Pacific Ocean ... 35 (2) D2
Filadelfia • Brazil ... 13 L7
Filchner Ice Shelf • Antarctica ... 46 (1) B2
Filey Beach • United Kingdom ... 75 [32]
Filfla • Malta ... 93 H4
Filiasi • Romania ... 14 K5
Filiátes • Greece ... 15 C6
Filiatrá • Greece ... 15 C6
Filicudi, I • Italy ... 90 D2
Filingué • Niger ... 20 F6
Filípi • Greece ... 92 D1
Filípi • Greece ... 92 D1
Filipiáda • Greece ... 15 B4
Filipstad • Sweden ... 16 H7
Fillefjell • Norway ... 94 C4
Filosorma • Corsica, France ... 85 L1
Filzmoos Ski • Austria ... 70 [180]
Filzmoos • Austria ... 89 H4
Fimaina • Greece ... 15 H6
Fimi • Dem. Rep. of Congo ... 23 B4
Finale Ligure • Italy ... 12 C4
Finale Ligure Beach • Italy ... 68 [121]
Findel [Apt] • Luxembourg ... 80 A20
Finestrat Beach • Spain ... 68 [101]
Finestrat • Spain ... 87 C2
Finger Lakes •
   NY, United States ... 122 B10
Fingly • BC, Canada ... 38 F5
Finhaut • Switzerland ... 89 G5
Finike • Turkey ... 93 G3
Finike Körfezi • Turkey ... 93 G3
Finikoúndas Beach • Greece ... 69 [158]
Finistère • France ... 84 C1
Finisterre, Cabo • Spain ... 11 B2
Finland • Europe ... 16
Finland, Gulf of • Europe ... 16 N7
Finnemarka • Norway ... 94 B1
Finnigan, Mt • QL, Australia ... 34 I3
Finnish Archipelago • Finland ... 94 A9
Finnish Lakeland • Finland ... 94 A9
Finnis, Cape • SA, Australia ... 34 F6
Finnmark • Norway ... 16 O2
Finnsnes • Norway ... 95 F7
Finschhafen • Papua New Guinea ... 35 (1) D2
Finse • Norway ... 94 C4
Finspång • Sweden ... 95 D3
Finsteraarhorn • Switzerland ... 89 G6
Finsterwalde • Germany ... 8 I5
Fionnphort • United Kingdom ... 6 F5
Fiordland • New Zealand ... 112 L1
Fiordland Nat. Park •
   New Zealand ... 112 L1
Firat • Turkey ... 18 C2
Fire I. Nat. Seashore Park •
   NY, United States ... 121 [333]
Firefly • Jamaica ... 124 C2
Firenze Heritage C • Italy ... 64 [118]
Firenze • Italy ... 91 E11
Firmat • Argentina ... 127 D1
Firminy • France ... 10 J8
Firozabad • India ... 105 C3
Firozpur • India ... 28 B2
Fischen • Germany ... 82 J6
Fischen Spa • Germany ... 83 [241]
Fish River Canyon • Namibia ... 24 B4
Fishbourne • United Kingdom ... 78 C8
Fisher Strait • NU, Canada ... 39 O4
Fishguard • United Kingdom ... 7 H10
Fishnish • United Kingdom ... 78 A2
Fiskárdo • Greece ... 92 C2
Fiskárdo • Greece ... 92 C2
Fiskö • Portugal ... 88 E2
Fiskarhalvön • Russian Fed. ... 17 E1
Fiskebäckskil • Sweden ... 95 F2
Fitou • France ... 84 B4
Fitri, Lac • Chad ... 22 H2
Fitzcarrald • Peru ... 127 B2
Fitzroy • WA, Australia ... 34 D3
Fitzroy • QL, Australia ... 111 F4
Fitzroy Crossing •
   WA, Australia ... 34 E3
Fitzroy I • QL, Australia ... 111 F3
Fiumicino • Italy ... 91 F3
Fiumorbo • Corsica, France ... 85 L4
Five Islands Harbour •
   Antigua & Barbuda ... 125 F1
Five Islands Village •
   Antigua & Barbuda ... 125 F1
Fjällbacka • Sweden ... 95 F2
Fjärdsbräcka • Sweden ... 95 F6
Fjerritslev Beach • Denmark ... 68 [29]
Fjerritslev • Denmark ... 95 F5
Fjöllum, Jökulsá á • Iceland ... 16 (1) F2
Flå • Norway ... 94 B1
Flachau Ski • Austria ... 70 [173]
Flachau • Austria ... 89 H4
Flachauwinkel Ski • Austria ... 70 [171]
Flagstaff • AZ, United States ... 118 J1
Flagstaff Lake •
   ME, United States ... 118 G2
Flaine Ski • France ... 70 [19]
Flaine • France ... 85 F2
Flåm • Norway ... 94 C4
Flambards Victorian Village •
   United Kingdom ... 74 F4
Flamborough Beach •
   United Kingdom ... 75 [33]
Fläming • Germany ... 13 B5
Flanders • Belgium/France ... 80 A13
Flannan Isles • United Kingdom ... 75 A1
Flåsjön • Sweden ... 16 H4
Flat I • South China Sea ... 31 F4
Flateby • Norway ... 94 B2
Flathead Lake •
   MT, United States ... 117 E2
Flattery, Cape •
   WA, United States ... 117 E1

Flåvatn • Norway ... 94 B3
Flaxaflói • Iceland ... 16 (1) B2
Flèche, la • France ... 84 D1
Fleetwood • United Kingdom ... 7 I8
Flekkefjord • Norway ... 16 D7
Flen • Sweden ... 95 D3
Flensburg • Germany ... 8 E2
Flers • France ... 5 C6
Flesberg • Norway ... 94 B1
Flesland [Apt] • Norway ... 94 C3
Fleury-d'Aude Beach • France ... 68 [112]
Fleuve Maroni •
   French Guiana/Suriname ... 43 G3
Flevoland • Netherlands ... 80 A7
Flevoland [Adm] • Netherlands ... 80 A7
Flims Ski • Switzerland ... 70 [106]
Flims • Switzerland ... 89 G3
Flin Flon • MN, Canada ... 38 K6
Flinders • QL, Australia ... 34 H3
Flinders I • TS, Australia ... 34 I8
Flinders Passage •
   QL, Australia ... 111 F1
Flinders Ranges • SA, Australia ... 34 G6
Flinders Reefs • CL, Australia ... 111 F1
Flint • United Kingdom ... 7 I8
Flint • Kiribati ... 33 L7
Flint • MI, United States ... 41 J3
Flintshire • United Kingdom ... 75 A4
Flisa • Norway ... 16 F6
Flix • Spain ... 10 F12
Flöha • Germany ... 9 I6
Florence • AL, United States ... 41 I5
Florence • SC, United States ... 41 K5
Florence Heritage C • Italy ... 64 [118]
Florence • Italy ... 91 E11
Florence • OR, United States ... 117 E3
Florencia • Colombia ... 43 B3
Florenville • Belgium ... 80 A19
Flores • Indonesia ... 32 (1) B4
Flores • Guatemala ... 37 C4
Flores • Azores ... 88 B1
Flores • Argentina ... 127 D3
Flores, I. de • Uruguay ... 127 D2
Flores, Laut • Indonesia ... 25 N10
Flores Sea • Indonesia ... 32 (1) B4
Floreşti • Moldova ... 14 N2
Floresville • TX, United States ... 119 N5
Floriano • Brazil ... 45 (1) C3
Florianópolis • Brazil ... 44 G4
Florida • United States ... 119 M
Florida • Cuba ... 124 D7
Florida • Uruguay ... 127 D3
Florida Caverns State Park •
   FL, United States ... 119 M2
Florida Citrus Bowl •
   FL, United States ... 121 C2
Florida Citrus Tower •
   FL, United States ... 121 C1
Florida City •
   FL, United States ... 119 M8
Florida Keys •
   FL, United States ... 119 M8
Florida, Straits of •
   FL, United States ... 41 J7
Florida's Cypress Gardens •
   FL, United States ... 119 M5
Florida's Silver Springs •
   FL, United States ... 119 M3
Florida's Silver Springs Park •
   FL, United States ... 121 [AA]
Floridablanca • Colombia ... 43 C2
Flórina • Greece ... 15 C3
Florissant Fossil Beds Nat. Mon. Park •
   CO, United States ... 120 [93]
Florø • Norway ... 94 C1
Flotte-en-Rie, la Beach •
   France ... 68 [65]
Flower Forest • Barbados ... 125 H1
Flowers Cove • NF, Canada ... 39 T6
Flumendosa • Sardinia, Italy ... 90 C4
Flumserberg Ski • Switzerland ... 70 [105]
Flumserberg • Switzerland ... 89 G3
Flushing • Netherlands ... 80 A10
Fluviá • Spain ... 10 H11
Fly • Papua New Guinea ... 35 (1) C2
Flying Fish Cove • Indian Ocean ... 32 D5
Flying Tigers Warbird Air Museum •
   FL, United States ... 121 C2
Foça • Bosnia-Herz. ... 14 F6
Foça • Turkey ... 92 D5
Foça • Turkey ... 92 D5
Focsani • Romania ... 14 O4
Fódele • Greece ... 93 E5
Foggia • Italy ... 12 J7
Foggo • Nigeria ... 20 H6
Fogo • Cape Verde ... 22 (1) B2
Fogo • NF, Canada ... 123 D4
Fogo [I.] • NF, Canada ... 123 D4
Fohnsdorf • Austria ... 13 D10
Föhr • Germany ... 8 D2
Föhr Spa • Germany ... 83 [4]
Foia • Portugal ... 88 E2
Foix • France ... 85 K1
Foix [Region] • France ... 85 K1
Folda • Norway ... 16 G4
Foldereid • Norway ... 16 G4
Folégandros • Greece ... 92 D7
Folégandros • Greece ... 92 D7
Folelli • Corsica, France ... 85 L2
Foley I • NU, Canada ... 39 O3
Folgaria Ski • Italy ... 70 [211]
Folgárida Ski • Italy ... 70 [206]
Folgefonn • Norway ... 94 C4
Folgôet, le • France ... 84 C1
Foligno • Italy ... 91 E12
Folkestone • United Kingdom ... 74 E4
Folkestone Underwater Park •
   Barbados ... 125 H3
Follónica • Italy ... 91 E11
Folmava • Comoros ... 24 G2
Fomento • Cuba ... 124 D2
Fond Assau • St Lucia ... 125 J2
Fond d'Or Bay • St Lucia ... 125 J2
Fond du Lac • SA, Canada ... 38 J5
Fond du Lac • WI, United States ... 41 I3
Fond St Jacques • St Lucia ... 125 J2
Fondi • Italy ... 91 F4
Fonsagrada • Spain ... 11 D2
Fonseca, Golfo de •
   El Salvador/Nicaragua ... 37 D5
Font • Switzerland ... 89 F5
Font-Romeu • France ... 85 K2
Fontainebleau Heritage C •
   France ... 64 [57]
Fontainebleau • France ... 5 H6
Fontainebleau, Forêt de •
   France ... 85 E4
Fontana Rossa • Sicily, Italy ... 90 D4
Fontas • BC, Canada ... 38 G5
Fonte alla Róccia • Italy ... 90 B3
Fonte Boa • Brazil ... 43 D4
Fontenay Heritage C • France ... 64 [54]
Fontenay-le-Comte • France ... 84 D3
Fontevraud • France ... 84 D2
Fontur • Iceland ... 16 (1) F1
Fonualei • Tonga ... 35 (2) F2
Fóppolo • Italy ... 91 E12

Föra • Sweden ... 95 F8
Fora, I. de • Madeira ... 88 C2
Forbach • France ... 10 L4
Forbes • NS, Australia ... 111 G2
Forchheim • Germany ... 9 G7
Ford's Theatre Nat. Hist. Site Park •
   DC, United States ... 121 [284]
Førde •
   Sogn og Fjordane, Norway ... 94 C1
Fordefjorden • Norway ... 94 C1
Fore Abbey • Ireland ... 79 E1
Forel, Mt • Greenland ... 39 X3
Forest Finland • Finland ... 94 A6
Forestville • QU, Canada ... 123 D1
Forez, Mts du • France ... 10 I8
Forfar • United Kingdom ... 74 B2
Forggensee • Germany ... 82 J6
Forillon Nat. Park • QU, Canada ... 123 E1
Forío • Italy ... 91 G3
Forlì • Italy ... 91 E7
Formby Beach • United Kingdom ... 75 [217]
Formentera Beach • Spain ... 68 [107]
Formentera • Spain ... 87 G4
Formentor • Majorca, Spain ... 87 H2
Formentor, Cap de •
   Majorca, Spain ... 87 H2
Formia • Italy ... 91 F4
Formiga • Brazil ... 127 C1
Formigas • Azores ... 88 B2
Formosa • Argentina ... 44 E4
Formosa • Brazil ... 44 G2
Formosa Strait • China ... 29 F6
Fornebu [Apt] • Norway ... 94 B2
Fornells • Minorca, Spain ... 87 F2
Forrest • WA, Australia ... 34 E6
Forrest City •
   AR, United States ... 41 H4
Fors • Sweden ... 95 D3
Forsayth • QL, Australia ... 34 H3
Forssa • Finland ... 95 B5
Forst • Germany ... 8 J5
Fort Albany • OT, Canada ... 39 O6
Fort Apache Indian Reservation •
   AZ, United States ... 118 J3
Fort Archambault • Chad ... 21 C6
Fort Augustus • United Kingdom ... 6 H4
Fort Beaufort • South Africa ... 100 C4
Fort Bragg • CA, United States ... 117 F1
Fort Chipewyan • AL, Canada ... 38 I5
Fort Collins •
   CO, United States ... 40 E3
Fort-de-France • Martinique ... 37 I5
Fort Dodge • IA, United States ... 41 H3
Fort Erie • OT, Canada ... 122 B9
Fort Frances •
   OT, Canada ... 40 E3
Fort George • QU, Canada ... 39 P6
Fort Good Hope • NT, Canada ... 46 BB3
Fort Hope • OT, Canada ... 39 N6
Fort Kent • ME, United States ... 118 G2
Fort Lauderdale •
   FL, United States ... 119 M8
Fort Macleod • AL, Canada ... 122 C4
Fort McMurray • AL, Canada ... 38 I5
Fort McPherson • NT, Canada ... 38 E3
Fort Médoc • France ... 85 G1
Fort Mirbel • Algeria ... 20 F2
Fort Myers • FL, United States ... 119 M5
Fort Nelson • BC, Canada ... 38 G5
Fort Nelson [Riv] • BC, Canada ... 38 G5
Fort Norman • NT, Canada ... 38 F4
Fort Peck Lake •
   MT, United States ... 40 E2
Fort Pierce • FL, United States ... 119 M6
Fort Providence • NT, Canada ... 38 H4
Fort Resolution • NT, Canada ... 38 I4
Fort St James • BC, Canada ... 122 C1
Fort St John • BC, Canada ... 122 C1
Fort Severn • OT, Canada ... 39 N5
Fort Shevchenko • Kazakhstan ... 17 I6
Fort Simpson • NT, Canada ... 38 G4
Fort Smith • NT, Canada ... 38 I4
Fort Smith • AR, United States ... 41 H4
Fort Stockton •
   TX, United States ... 40 F5
Fort Union Trading Post Nat. Hist. Site Park •
   ND, United States ... 120 [147]
Fort Vermilion • AL, Canada ... 38 H5
Fort Walton Beach •
   FL, United States ... 119 M2
Fort Wayne • IN, United States ... 41 I3
Fort Wilderness •
   FL, United States ... 121 C1
Fort William • United Kingdom ... 6 G5
Fort Worth • TX, United States ... 119 N1
Fort Yukon • AK, United States ... 38 B3
Forte dei Marmi Beach • Italy ... 68 [124]
Forte dei Marmi • Italy ... 91 E10
Fortescue • WA, Australia ... 34 C4
Forth • United Kingdom ... 74 B4
Forth, Firth of •
   United Kingdom ... 74 B4
Fortín Coronel Eugenio Garay •
   Paraguay ... 44 D3
Fortress Mtn Ski • AL, Canada ... 116 [14]
Fortune • NF, Canada ... 123 D3
Fortune Bay • NF, Canada ... 123 D3
Fortuneswell • United Kingdom ... 74 F6
Fosforescente, Bahía •
   Puerto Rico ... 125 E3
Foshan • China ... 107 H1
Fosnavåg • Norway ... 94 C1
Fossano • Italy ... 12 B4
Fossnova, Abbazia di • Italy ... 91 F4
Fougères • France ... 10 D5
Foúla • United Kingdom ... 6 J1
Foulness I • United Kingdom ... 74 E3
Foulwind, Cape • New Zealand ... 35 C5
Foumban • Cameroon ... 22 G4
Fountain • St Kitts & Nevis ... 125 G4
Fountains Abbey Heritage C •
   United Kingdom ... 64 [17]
Fouras Beach • France ... 68 [65]
Fourfourás • Crete, Greece ... 93 E6
Fourmies • France ... 5 H4
Foúrnoi Beach • Greece ... 69 [169]
Foúrnoi • Greece ... 92 D8
Foúrni • Greece ... 92 D8
Fouta • Senegal ... 20 B5
Fouta Djallon • Guinea ... 22 B2
Foux-d'Allos, la Ski • France ... 70 [70]
Foveaux Strait • New Zealand ... 112 L4
Fowey • United Kingdom ... 74 F4
Fowlers Bay • SA, Australia ... 34 E6
Fox • MN, Canada ... 38 M5
Fox Is • AK, United States ... 36 (1) D2
Foxe Basin • NU, Canada ... 39 P3

Foxe Channel • NU, Canada ... 39 O4
Foxe Peninsula • NU, Canada ... 39 P4
Foxen • Sweden ... 94 B4
Foxford • Ireland ... 79 F2
Foyle, Lough • Ireland/UK ... 7 E6
Foynes • Ireland ... 79 F6
Foz • Spain ... 11 D2
Foz Beach • Spain ... 68 [72]
Foz do Cunene • Namibia ... 24 A4
Foz do Iguaçu • Brazil ... 44 F4
Frabosa • Italy ... 91 E5
Fraga • Spain ... 11 L3
France • Europe ... 10
Francés, Punta • Cuba ... 124 D1
Franceville • Gabon ... 22 G5
Franche Comté • France ... 10 K6
Francis Case, Lake •
   SD, United States ... 40 G3
Francisco Beltrão • Brazil ... 44 F4
Franciscus Bay • Namibia ... 24 A5
Francistown • Botswana ... 24 D4
Franconia • NH, United States ... 118 G3
Franeker • Netherlands ... 8 A3
Frangokástelo • Crete, Greece ... 9 D5
Frankenberg • Germany ... 9 I6
Frankenberg • Germany ... 9 I6
Frankenstein, Burg • Germany ... 82 H4
Frankenwald • Germany ... 9 G6
Frankfort • KY, United States ... 41 J4
Frankfurt am Main • Germany ... 82 H4
Frankfurt an der Oder • Germany ... 8 J4
Fränkisch Alb • Germany ... 9 G7
Fränkische Saale • Germany ... 9 E6
Franklin Bay • NT, Canada ... 38 F3
Franklin, Benjamin, Nat. Mem. Park •
   PA, United States ... 121 [308]
Franklin Mtns • NT, Canada ... 38 G4
Franklin Strait • NU, Canada ... 38 L2
Frantiskovy Lazne • Czech Rep. ... 96 C1
Frantsa-Iosifa, Zemlya •
   Russian Fed. ... 96 A2
Franz Josef Land • Arctic Ocean ... 26 G1
Franz Joseph Strauss [Apt] •
   Germany ... 82 J3
Frasassi, Grotta di • Italy ... 91 E12
Frascati • Italy ... 91 F3
Fraser • BC, Canada ... 122 C3
Fraser I. Heritage N •
   QL, Australia ... 61 [135]
Fraser I • QL, Australia ... 111 F6
Fraser Range • WA, Australia ... 34 D6
Fraser's Hill • Malaysia ... 108 D2
Fraserburgh Beach •
   United Kingdom ... 75 [5]
Fraserburgh • South Africa ... 100 C2
Frauenfeld • Switzerland ... 9 D9
Fray Bentos • Uruguay ... 127 D2
Frederica, Fort. Nat. Mon. Park •
   GA, United States ... 121 [216]
Fredericia Beach • Denmark ... 68 [29]
Fredericia • Denmark ... 95 F9
Fredericksburg •
   VA, United States ... 118 H3
Fredericksburg •
   TX, United States ... 119 N3
Fredericksburg & Spotsylvania County
   Battlefields Mem. •
   VA, United States ... 118 H3
Fredericksburg & Spotsylvania County
   Battlefields Mem. Park •
   VA, United States ... 121 [263]
Fredericton • NB, Canada ... 123 D7
Frederiksberg • Denmark ... 95 F10
Frederikshåb • Greenland ... 39 V4
Frederikshavn Beach • Denmark ... 68 [29]
Frederikshavn • Denmark ... 95 F6
Frederiksted • US Virgin Is. ... 58 B7
Frederiksværk Beach • Denmark ... 68 [22]
Frederiksværk • Denmark ... 95 F10
Fredrikstad • Norway ... 16 F7
Free State • South Africa ... 24 D5
Freels, Cape • NF, Canada ... 123 D4
Freeport • TX, United States ... 119 N6
Freeport • Bahamas ... 124 D5
Freetown • Sierra Leone ... 22 B3
Freetown • Antigua & Barbuda ... 125 F4
Frégate • Seychelles ... 106 F2
Fréhel, Cap • France ... 84 C2
Freiberg • Germany ... 9 I6
Freiberger Mulde • Germany ... 9 I6
Freiburg im Breisgau • Germany ... 82 G8
Freiburg im Breisgau Spa •
   Germany ... 83 [195]
Freilassing • Germany ... 82 J8
Freising • Germany ... 82 J8
Freistadt • Austria ... 13 D9
Freital • Germany ... 9 I6
Freizeit- und Miniaturpark Allgäu Park •
   Germany ... 73 [66]
Freizeit- und Miniaturpark Allgäu •
   Germany ... 82 J5
Freizeit-Land Park • Germany ... 73 [65]
Freizeitpark Lochmuhle •
   Germany ... 82 H2
Freizeitpark Schloß Beck •
   Germany ... 81 E1
Fréjus • Var, France ... 10 L5
Fréjus Beach • France ... 68 [116]
Fréjus • Hautes-Alpes, France ... 85 H4
Fréjus, Tunnel du •
   France/Italy ... 85 H4
Fremantle • WA, Australia ... 34 C6
Fremont • NE, United States ... 41 G3
Fremont • CA, United States ... 117 F3
Fremont Mtns •
   OR, United States ... 117 E3
French Guiana • S. America ... 43 G3
French Guiana • S. America ... 43 G3
French Pass • New Zealand ... 35 D5
French Polynesia •
   Pacific Ocean ... 33 M8
Frenchman • SA, Canada ... 38 J7
Freshwater Beach •
   United Kingdom ... 75 [153]
Fresnillo • Mexico ... 37 (1) B1
Fresno • CA, United States ... 117 F3
Freu, Cap de • Majorca, Spain ... 11 O5
Freudenberg • Germany ... 9 G6
Freudenstadt • Germany ... 9 E8
Freudenstadt Spa • Germany ... 83 [186]
Fri • Greece ... 15 I8
Fria • Guinea ... 22 B2
Frías • Argentina ... 44 D4
Fribourg • Switzerland ... 89 G2
Fridtjof Nansen, Mt •
   Antarctica ... 46 (1) Y1
Friedberg • Hessen, Germany ... 9 D6
Friedberg • Bavaria, Germany ... 82 J6
Friedenweiler Spa • Germany ... 83 [210]
Friedersdorf • Germany ... 81 G3
Friedland • Germany ... 83 [302]
Friedrichroda Spa • Germany ... 83 [9]
Friedrichshafen • Germany ... 82 J5
Friedrichshafen Spa • Germany ... 83 [9]
Friendship Hill Nat. Hist. Site Park •
   PA, United States ... 121 [300]

Friesland • Germany/Neths. ... 5 K1
Friesland [Adm] • Netherlands ... 80 A3
Friesoythe • Germany ... 8 C3
Frigate Bay • St Kitts & Nevis ... 125 G2
Frigate Bay Beach •
  St Kitts & Nevis ... 125 G2
Frio, Cabo • Brazil ... 127 C4
Frisian Is. • Germany/Neths. ... 8 B3
Frisian Is., East • Germany ... 8 C3
Frisian Is., North • Germany ... 8 D2
Frisian Is., West • Netherlands ... 8 A3
Fristad • Sweden ... 95 F7
Fritzlar • Germany ... 9 E5
Friuli-Venezia Giulia • Italy ... 91 E4
Frobisher Bay • NU, Canada ... 39 R4
Frobisher Bay [Bay] •
  NU, Canada ... 39 R4
Frobisher Lake • SA, Canada ... 38 J5
Frolovo • Russian Fed. ... 17 G5
Frome • United Kingdom ... 74 F3
Frome, Lake • SA, Australia ... 34 G6
Fronsac • France ... 84 B3
Frontenac Prov. Park •
  QU, Canada ... 122 B4
Frontignan-la Peyrade Beach •
  France ... 68 [113]
Frosinone • Italy ... 91 F4
Frøya • Norway ... 16 E5
Frozen Strait • NU, Canada ... 39 O3
Frunzivka • Ukraine ... 15 E12
Fruska Gora •
  F.R. of Yugoslavia ... 14 G4
Fruska Gora Nat. Park Park •
  Fed. Rep. of Yugoslavia ... 72 [115]
Frutal • Brazil ... 44 G3
Frýdek Místek • Czech Rep. ... 13 H8
Frýdlant • Czech Rep. ... 96 C2
Fu Yang • China ... 107 J3
Fuah Mulah Atoll • Maldives ... 106 E3
Fuchskauten • Germany ... 5 L4
Fuchun Jiang • China ... 107 J3
Fucino, Piana del • Italy ... 91 F2
Fuding • China ... 29 G5
Fuengirola Beach • Spain ... 68 [97]
Fuengirola • Spain ... 86 B6
Fuente Alto • Chile ... 44 B5
Fuentesaúco • Spain ... 11 F3
Fuerteventura • Canary Is. ... 87 E2
Fügen • Austria ... 89 H3
Fuggerschloß • Germany ... 82 J2
Fuhai • China ... 26 O8
Fuji-san • Japan ... 30 J7
Fujian • China ... 107 G8
Fujin • China ... 29 I1
Fukagawa • Japan ... 30 K3
Fukuchiyama • Japan ... 30 H7
Fukue • Japan ... 30 E8
Fukue [I.] • Japan ... 30 E8
Fukueichiao • Taiwan ... 29 G5
Fukui • Japan ... 30 I6
Fukuoka • Japan ... 30 K6
Fukuyama • Japan ... 30 H7
Fulda • Germany ... 9 E6
Fulda [Riv] • Germany ... 9 E5
Fuling • China ... 29 D5
Full Moon • Maldives ... 106 E4
Fulpmes • Austria ... 89 H6
Fulton • MO, United States ... 41 H4
Fulton • AR, United States ... 119 N2
Fumay • France ... 5 H4
Fuminimaggiore •
  Sardinia, Italy ... 12 C9
Fun Acres Park • United Kingdom ... 73 [37]
Fun I. • Maldives ... 106 E4
Funabashi • Japan ... 30 J7
Funafuti • Kiribati ... 33 I6
Funafuti [I.] • Kiribati ... 33 I6
Funchal • Madeira ... 88 C2
Funchal Beach • Madeira ... 68 [90]
Funchal • Portugal ... 11 D4
Fundy, Bay of • NB/NS, Canada ... 123 D7
Fundy Nat. Park • NB, Canada ... 123 D7
Fünen • Denmark ... 95 F14
Fünfkirchen • Hungary ... 71 A14
Fungus Rock • Malta ... 93 H1
Fur • Denmark ... 95 F5
Furana • Maldives ... 106 E4
Furancungo • Mozambique ... 24 E2
Furano • Japan ... 30 L3
Furat, Al • Iraq/Syria ... 18 D3
Furkapass • Switzerland ... 89 G3
Furnas • Azores ... 88 B1
Furnas Dam • Brazil ... 127 C1
Furnas, Represa de • Brazil ... 127 C1
Furneaux Group • TS, Australia ... 34 C3
Furness Abbey • United Kingdom ... 74 C3
Furness Fells • United Kingdom ... 74 C3
Fürstenfeld • Austria ... 14 D2
Fürstenfeldbruck • Germany ... 82 J3
Fürstenwalde • Germany ... 8 J4
Fürth • Germany ... 9 G7
Fürth im Wald • Germany ... 9 H8
Furtwangen • Germany ... 82 G8
Furukawa • Japan ... 30 J6
Furuviksparken Park • Sweden ... 73 [8]
Fury & Hecla Strait •
  NU, Canada ... 39 O3
Fusa • Norway ... 94 C4
Fushë-Lura • Albania ... 15 B2
Fushun • China ... 29 H2
Fusong • China ... 30 D3
Füssen • Germany ... 82 J6
Füssen Spa • Germany ... 83 [244]
Futuna • Vanuatu ... 35 (2) C2
Futuna • Wallis & Futuna ... 35 (2) J6
Futuroscope Park • France ... 73 [74]
Futuroscope • France ... 84 D4
Fuxian • China ... 30 A5
Fuxin • China ... 29 H2
Fuyang • China ... 29 F4
Fuyu • China ... 27 J8
Fuyun • China ... 26 O8
Fuzhou • Fujian, China ... 29 F5
Fuzhou • Jiangxi, China ... 29 F5
Fyn [Adm] • Denmark ... 95 F14
Fyn [I.] • Denmark ... 95 F14
Fyne, Loch • United Kingdom ... 75 F13
Fynshav • Denmark ... 95 F13
Fyresdal • Norway ... 94 C6
Fyresvatn • Norway ... 94 C6

Gaafaru Atoll • Maldives ... 106 E2
Gabbs • NV, United States ... 117 F4
Gabela • Angola ... 23 A6
Gabès • Tunisia ... 101 E4
Gabès, Golfe de • Tunisia ... 101 E4
Gabicce Mare Beach • Italy ... 68 [142]
Gabicce Mare • Italy ... 91 E12
Gabon • Africa ... 22 G5
Gaborone • Botswana ... 24 D4
Gabriel Strait • NU, Canada ... 39 R4
Gabrovo • Bulgaria ... 97 D3
Gad • Jordan ... 98 A6

Gadag • India ... 106 D2
Gadara • Jordan ... 98 A4
Gäddede • Sweden ... 16 H4
Gadsden • AL, United States ... 41 I5
Gadsden, Fort, State Hist. Site •
  FL, United States ... 119 M2
Gaesti • Romania ... 97 D1
Gaeta • Italy ... 91 F4
Gaeta, Golfo di • Italy ... 12 H7
Gaferut •
  Fed. States of Micronesia ... 33 F5
Gafsa • Tunisia ... 101 E3
Gagarin • Russian Fed. ... 97 E3
Gagenau Spa • Germany ... 83 [181]
Gagnoa • Côte d'Ivoire ... 22 C3
Gagnon • QU, Canada ... 39 R6
Gai Xian • China ... 30 B4
Gaillac • France ... 85 G4
Gaillimh • Ireland ... 79 F4
Gaillster Alpen • Austria ... 89 H8
Gainer Wildlife Sanctuary •
  India ... 105 C1
Gainesville • FL, United States ... 119 M3
Gainesville • TX, United States ... 119 N1
Gainsborough • United Kingdom ... 7 L8
Gairdner, Lake • SA, Australia ... 34 G6
Gairloch • United Kingdom ... 6 G4
Gal Oya Nat. Park • Sri Lanka ... 106 D16
Gala Gölü • Turkey ... 15 H3
Galán, Cerro • Argentina ... 44 C4
Galana • Kenya ... 101 G4
Galanta • Slovak Rep. ... 13 G9
Galápagos Is. • Pacific Ocean ... 43 (1) A1
Galápagos, Parque Nac. Heritage N •
  Pacific Ocean ... 60 [30]
Galashiels • United Kingdom ... 74 B4
Galata • Cyprus ... 93 J3
Galata • Bulgaria ... 97 D4
Galati • Romania ... 97 C2
Galatina • Italy ... 12 M8
Galdhøpiggen • Norway ... 94 C2
Galé, Costa da • Portugal ... 88 A3
Galeão • Brazil ... 127 C4
Galeota Point •
  Trinidad & Tobago ... 125 K4
Galera Point •
  Trinidad & Tobago ... 125 K2
Galgibaga Beach • Goa, India ... 105 B2
Galhak, El • Sudan ... 21 F5
Galicia • Spain ... 11 C2
Galicia • Poland ... 13 L8
Galicica Nat. Park Park •
  F.Y.R. of Macedonia ... 72 [123]
Galilee • Israel ... 98 A2
Galilee, Sea of • Israel ... 98 A4
Galilei, Galileo [Apt] • Italy ... 91 E11
Galina Point • Jamaica ... 124 C2
Galite, Canal de la • Tunisia ... 12 C11
Galite, La • Tunisia ... 101 E1
Galka'yo • Somalia ... 23 H2
Gallarus Oratory • Ireland ... 79 F5
Galle Heritage C • Sri Lanka ... 63 [139]
Galle • Sri Lanka ... 106 D15
Gallipoli • Italy ... 12 M8
Gallipoli • Turkey ... 92 D2
Gallipoli • Turkey ... 92 D2
Gallipoli Peninsula • Turkey ... 92 D2
Gallipoli Peninsula • Turkey ... 92 D2
Gällivare • Sweden ... 16 K3
Gällö • Sweden ... 16 H5
Galloway, Mull of •
  United Kingdom ... 7 H7
Gallup • NM, United States ... 118 J2
Gallur • Spain ... 11 J3
Galtür • Austria ... 89 H5
Galty Mtns • Ireland ... 79 F6
Galu Beach • Kenya ... 101 G5
Galveston • TX, United States ... 119 N6
Galveston Bay •
  TX, United States ... 119 N6
Galveston I. •
  TX, United States ... 119 N6
Gálvez • Argentina ... 44 D5
Galway • Ireland ... 79 F4
Galway [Adm] • Ireland ... 79 F4
Galway Bay • Ireland ... 79 F4
Galway City Beach • Ireland ... 68 [43]
Gamarra • Colombia ... 43 C2
Gamasa • Egypt ... 101 F2
Gambia [Riv] • Gambia/Senegal ... 20 B6
Gambia, The • Africa ... 20 B6
Gambie • Senegal ... 22 B2
Gambier • Bahamas ... 124 B3
Gambona • Congo ... 22 E1
Gamkonora, Gunung • Indonesia ... 32 (1) C2
Gamla Uppsala • Sweden ... 95 D2
Gamleby • Sweden ... 95 F4
Gammarth • Tunisia ... 101 E2
Gammelstad Heritage C • Sweden ... 63 [72]
Gammertingen • Germany ... 82 J1
Gamph, Slieve • Ireland ... 79 F2
Gamud • Ethiopia ... 23 F3
Gamvik • Norway ... 16 O1
Gan • Maldives ... 106 E3
Gan Jiang • China ... 29 F5
Ganado • AZ, United States ... 40 E4
Gand • Belgium ... 80 A14
Gandadiwata, Bulu • Indonesia ... 32 (1) A3
Gandajika • Dem. Rep. of Congo ... 23 C5
Gandak • India ... 105 C8
Gander • NF, Canada ... 123 D4
Ganderkesee • Germany ... 5 L1
Gandhi Dam • India ... 105 C6
Gandhi, Indira [Apt] • India ... 105 C2
Gandhi, Indira, Nahar • India ... 105 C1
Gandhi, Indira, Wildlife Sanctuary •
  India ... 106 D10
Gandhi Sagar • India ... 105 C6
Gandhinagar • India ... 28 B4
Gandía • Spain ... 11 K6
Gandía Beach • Spain ... 68 [102]
Gandria • Switzerland ... 89 G7
Gandu • Brazil ... 44 I1
Ganetti • Sudan ... 21 F4
Ganga • India ... 28 D3
Gangaikondacholapuram • India ... 106 D11
Gangaw • Myanmar ... 28 F4
Gangca • China ... 28 B2
Gangdhar • India ... 105 C6
Ganges • India ... 28 D3
Ganges Plain • India ... 105 C7
Gangtok • India ... 28 B3
Gani • Indonesia ... 32 (1) C3
Gannett Peak •
  WY, United States ... 40 E3
Gansbaai • South Africa ... 100 C5
Gansu • China ... 28 C2
Ganta • Liberia ... 20 C7
Ganteng • China ... 107 J3
Ganzano di Roma • Italy ... 91 F3
Ganzhou • China ... 28 D5
Gao • Mali ... 20 E5
Gaochun • China ... 107 J1
Gaolan • Zhuhai, China ... 107 H3
Gaolan Dao • Zhuhai, China ... 107 H3
Gaotingzhen • China ... 107 J4

Gaoual • Guinea ... 22 B2
Gaoula • Burkina Faso ... 22 D2
Gaoyou Hu • China ... 29 F4
Gap • France ... 85 F3
Gara, Lough • Ireland ... 79 F2
Gara Muleta • Ethiopia ... 23 G2
Gara'ad • Somalia ... 23 H2
Garachico •
  Tenerife, Canary Is. ... 86 E1
Garajonay, Parque Nac. de Heritage N •
  Gomera, Canary Is. ... 61 [48]
Garajonay, Parque Nac. de •
  Gomera, Canary Is. ... 72 [77]
Garajonay, Parque Nac. de Park •
  Gomera, Canary Is. ... 87 E5
Garama • Libya ... 21 B2
Garamba, Parc nat. de Heritage N •
  Dem. Rep. of Congo ... 61 [82]
Garamba, Parc nat. de Park •
  Dem. Rep. of Congo ... 103 [54]
Garango • Burkina Faso ... 45 (1) D3
Garba • Central African Rep. ... 23 C2
Garbsen • Germany ... 8 E4
Garching bei München • Germany ... 82 J3
Garda, Lago di • Italy ... 91 E7
Gardaland Park • Italy ... 73 [83]
Gardaland • Italy ... 91 E7
Gardelegen • Germany ... 8 G4
Garden City • KS, United States ... 40 F4
Garden Route • South Africa ... 100 C7
Gardermoen [Apt] • Norway ... 94 B2
Gardez • Afghanistan ... 18 I3
Gardiki • Corfu, Greece ... 92 B1
Gardiki • Corfu, Greece ... 92 B1
Gardone Riviera • Italy ... 91 E7
Gärdsjö • Sweden ... 95 F3
Gärdslösa • Sweden ... 95 F4
Garfield, James A., Nat. Hist. Site Park •
  OH, United States ... 121 [188]
Gargaliani • Greece ... 15 C6
Gargano • Italy ... 12 J7
Gargellen • Austria ... 89 H5
Garibaldi Prov. Park •
  BC, Canada ... 122 C3
Garicin Grad •
  F.R. of Yugoslavia ... 14 I7
Garigliano • Italy ... 91 F4
Garissa • Kenya ... 101 G4
Gariwerd • VI, Australia ... 111 F1
Garmisch-Partenkirchen Ski •
  Germany ... 70 [3]
Garmisch-Partenkirchen •
  Germany ... 82 J6
Garmisch-Partenkirchen Spa •
  Germany ... 83 [246]
Garonne • France ... 10 E9
Garonne, Canal latéral à la •
  France ... 10 F9
Garoua • Cameroon ... 22 G3
Garowe • Somalia ... 23 H2
Garphyttan Nat. Park Park •
  Sweden ... 72 [25]
Garrison • Barbados ... 125 H3
Garry Lake • NU, Canada ... 38 K3
Garsa, Chott el • Tunisia ... 101 E3
Garsen • Kenya ... 23 F4
Gärtringen • Germany ... 9 D8
Garut • Java, Indonesia ... 110 D6
Garvie Mtns • New Zealand ... 112 L2
Garwa • India ... 105 C8
Garwolin • Poland ... 13 K6
Gary • IN, United States ... 41 I3
Garyarsa • China ... 28 C4
Garze • China ... 29 C4
Garzón • Colombia ... 43 B3
Gasan-Kuli • Turkmenistan ... 18 F2
Gaschurn Ski • Austria ... 70 [125]
Gaschurn • Austria ... 89 H5
Gascogne • France ... 10 F10
Gascony • France ... 84 A2
Gascoyne • WA, Australia ... 34 C5
Gasfinolhu • Maldives ... 106 E2
Gashaka Game Reserve Park •
  Nigeria ... 103 [35]
Gashua • Nigeria ... 22 G2
Gaspé • QU, Canada ... 123 D2
Gaspé, Cap • QU, Canada ... 123 D2
Gaspésie, Péninsule de •
  QU, Canada ... 123 D2
Gassol • Nigeria ... 22 G3
Gastonia • NC, United States ... 41 J4
Gastoúni • Greece ... 15 C6
Gastoúri • Corfu, Greece ... 92 B1
Gastoúri • Corfu, Greece ... 92 B1
Gastre • Argentina ... 45 C4
Gata, Cabo de • Spain ... 86 B8
Gata, Cape • Cyprus ... 93 J3
Gata, Sierra de • Spain ... 11 E4
Gatchina • Russian Fed. ... 97 E1
Gates of the Arctic Nat. Park & Preserve
  Park • AK, United States ... 120 [3]
Gateshead • United Kingdom ... 7 K7
Gateway Nat. Recreation Area Park •
  NJ/NY, United States ... 121 [327]
Gatineau • QU, Canada ... 122 B2
Gatineau Park • QU, Canada ... 122 B2
Gatorland • FL, United States ... 121 C2
Gatwick [Apt] • United Kingdom ... 74 E3
Gauja • Latvia ... 16 M8
Gauja Nat. Park Park • Latvia ... 72 [144]
Gauley River Nat. Recreation Area Park •
  WV, United States ... 121 [269]
Gaume, Fonte de • France ... 85 G2
Gaupne • Norway ... 94 C4
Gaustá • Norway ... 94 B1
Gaustablikk • Norway ... 94 B1
Gauteng • South Africa ... 24 D5
Gavarnie • France ... 85 F2
Gavdopoúla • Greece ... 93 E5
Gávdos • Greece ... 92 D10
Gávdos • Greece ... 92 D10
Gävle • Sweden ... 16 I6
Gävleborg • Sweden ... 16 I6
Gávrio • Greece ... 92 D7
Gávrio • Greece ... 92 D7
Gawler • SA, Australia ... 34 G6
Gawler Ranges • SA, Australia ... 34 G6
Gaya • Niger ... 22 E2
Gaya • India ... 105 C8
Gayndah • QL, Australia ... 111 F6
Gaya • Russian Fed. ... 97 E2
Gaza • Palestine ... 98 B3
Gázi Beach • Crete, Greece ... 69 [190]
Gazi Beach • Kenya ... 101 G5
Gaziantep • Turkey ... 18 C2
Gazipasa • Turkey ... 93 G4
Gdańsk • Poland ... 13 H3
Gdańsk, Gulf of • Poland ... 13 I3
Gdynia • Poland ... 13 H3
Gê'gyai • China ... 28 D2
Gebiz • Turkey ... 93 G2
Gebze • Turkey ... 15 H4
Gedi • Kenya ... 23 G4
Gedi Nat. Mon. • Kenya ... 101 G5
Gediz • Turkey ... 15 K4
Gediz [Riv] • Turkey ... 92 D6
Gediz [Riv] • Turkey ... 92 D6
Gedser • Denmark ... 95 F14

Gedung • Malaysia ... 108 C4
Geel • Belgium ... 5 H3
Geelen • Netherlands ... 80 A16
Geelong • VI, Australia ... 111 G3
Geesthacht • Germany ... 8 F3
Géfira • Greece ... 15 D3
Gefle • Sweden ... 16 H6
Geidam • Nigeria ... 22 G2
Geilo • Norway ... 94 C4
Geiranger • Norway ... 94 C2
Geirangerfjorden • Norway ... 94 C2
Geishügelhof • Germany ... 82 H1
Geislingen an der Steige •
  Germany ... 9 E8
Geita • Tanzania ... 102 H1
Geithus • Norway ... 94 B1
Gejiu • China ... 29 C6
Gela • Sicily, Italy ... 90 D4
Gela, Golfo di • Sicily, Italy ... 90 D4
Geladi • Ethiopia ... 23 H2
Gelgendeng • Chad ... 23 B1
Gelibolu • Turkey ... 92 D2
Gelibolu • Turkey ... 92 D2
Gelibolu Yarimadasi • Turkey ... 92 D2
Gelibolu Yarimadasi • Turkey ... 92 D2
Gelinsor • Somalia ... 23 H2
Gelnhausen • Germany ... 82 G2
Gelsenkirchen • Germany ... 81 E2
Gelsenkirchen: Buer • Germany ... 81 E2
Gelting Spa • Germany ... 83 [117]
Gelugur • Penang, Malaysia ... 108 C4
Gemas • Malaysia ... 108 D4
Gembloux • Belgium ... 71 A7
Gemena • Dem. Rep. of Congo ... 23 B3
Gemlik • Turkey ... 92 D3
Gemlik Körfezi • Turkey ... 15 J3
Gemünd Spa • Germany ... 83 [117]
Gemünden • Germany ... 9 E6
Genádio Beach • Rhodes, Greece ... 69 [187]
Genádio • Rhodes, Greece ... 93 F3
Genale • Ethiopia ... 23 G2
Gencek • Turkey ... 93 G2
General Acha • Argentina ... 45 D3
General Alvear • Argentina ... 44 C5
General Belgrano Station [Base] •
  Antarctica ... 46 (1) B2
General Bernardo O'Higgins [Base] •
  Antarctica ... 46 (1) JJ3
General Carrera, Lago • Chile ... 45 B5
General Lavalle • Argentina ... 127 D4
General Manuel Belgrano, Cerro •
  Argentina ... 44 C4
General Pico • Argentina ... 44 D4
General Pinedo • Argentina ... 44 D3
General Roca • Argentina ... 45 C3
General Santos • Philippines ... 14 P6
General Toševo • Bulgaria ... 97 C3
General Villegas • Argentina ... 45 D3
Geneva • Switzerland ... 89 G5
Geneva, Lake •
  Switzerland/France ... 89 G5
Genève • Switzerland ... 89 G5
Gengenbach • Germany ... 82 G6
Genil • Spain ... 86 B2
Genk • Belgium ... 80 A15
Gennargentu, Monte dei •
  Sardinia, Italy ... 90 C2
Genoa • Italy ... 91 E6
Génova • Italy ... 91 E6
Génova, Golfo di • France/Italy ... 91 E10
Genovesa • Galapagos Is. ... 43 (1) B1
Gent • Belgium ... 80 A14
Gent naar Oostende, Kanaal van •
  Belgium ... 80 B2
Genteng • Indonesia ... 110 D5
Genteng [I.] • Indonesia ... 110 D6
Genteng • Indonesia ... 8 H4
Genting Highlands • Malaysia ... 32 (1) F3
Genyem • Indonesia ... 32 (1) F3
Geographe Bay • WA, Australia ... 34 C6
Geok-Tepe • Turkmenistan ... 18 G2
Georg von Neumayer [Base] •
  Antarctica ... 46 (1) JJ1
Georga, Zemlya • Russian Fed. ... 96 A2
George • George ... 39 S5
George • South Africa ... 100 C7
George, Fort • OT, Canada ... 122 B9
George, Fort •
  Trinidad & Tobago ... 125 K1
George, Lake • NS, Australia ... 111 G2
George Sound • New Zealand ... 112 L1
George Town • TS, Australia ... 34 I8
George Town • Cayman Is. ... 37 E4
George Town • Penang, Malaysia ... 108 C2
George V Sound • Antarctica ... 46 (1) I11
Georgetown • Ascension ... 19 C6
Georgetown • QL, Australia ... 34 H3
Georgetown • Guyana ... 43 F2
Georgetown • TX, United States ... 119 N3
Georgia • Asia ... 17 G6
Georgia • United States ... 41 J5
Georgia, Strait of • BC, Canada ... 38 G7
Georgian Bay • OT, Canada ... 39 O7
Georgian Bay Is. Nat. Park •
  OT, Canada ... 122 B5
Georgina • NT/QL, Australia ... 111 E3
Georgioúpoli • Crete, Greece ... 93 E2
Georgsmarienhütte • Germany ... 8 D4
Gera • Germany ... 9 H6
Gera [Riv] • Germany ... 9 G5
Gérardmer • France ... 10 L5
Geráki • Greece ... 92 D7
Gerakiní Beach • Greece ... 69 [169]
Gerakiní • Greece ... 92 D1
Gávdopoúla • Greece ... 92 D1
Geral do Goiás, Serra • Brazil ... 45 (1) B4
Geral do Paraná, Serra • Brazil ... 44 G2
Geral, Serra • Brazil ... 44 F4
Geraldine • New Zealand ... 35 C7
Geraldton • WA, Australia ... 34 B5
Geraniou Beach • Crete, Greece ... 69 [188]
Gerasa • Jordan ... 98 A4
Gerbichi, gora • Russian Fed. ... 26 S3
Gerede • Turkey ... 15 N3
Gerede [Riv] • Turkey ... 15 N3
Gerês, Serra do • Portugal ... 11 D3
Gergei • Afghanistan ... 18 H2
Geretsried • Germany ... 82 J3
Gérgeri • Crete, Greece ... 93 E7
Gerizim, Mount • Jordan ... 98 A6
Gerlachovsky Stit • Slovak Rep. ... 13 J8
Gerlos Ski • Austria ... 70 [145]
Gerlos • Austria ... 89 H7
Gerlovo • Bulgaria ... 14 N6
Germany • Europe ... 8/9
Germersheim • Germany ... 83 [101]
Germi • Iran ... 17 I5
Gernona del Friuli • Italy ... 12 H2
Gerolstein • Germany ... 82 H4
Gerolzhofen • Germany ... 9 F7
Gêrzê • China ... 28 D3
Gerze • Turkey ... 15 N1
Gersau • Switzerland ... 89 G3

Gertak Sanggul •
  Penang, Malaysia ... 108 C3
Gertak Sanggul, Tanjong •
  Penang, Malaysia ... 108 C3
Gerze • China ... 28 D2
Gesundaberget • Sweden ... 16 H6
Geta • Finland ... 95 E3
Getafe • Spain ... 11 H4
Gete • Belgium ... 5 I4
Gets, les Ski • France ... 70 [13]
Gets, les • France ... 85 F2
Gettysburg Nat. Military Park •
  PA, United States ... 118 H1
Gettysburg National Military Park Park •
  PA, United States ... 121 [305]
Getxo Beach • Spain ... 68 [69]
Geureudong, Gunung • Indonesia ... 110 B1
Gevelsberg • Germany ... 81 E2
Gevgelija • Macedonia ... 14 H4
Gevik Dagi • Turkey ... 15 N7
Geyikli • Turkey ... 15 H4
Geyve • Turkey ... 15 L3
Gezer • Israel ... 98 A5
Ghajnsielem Heritage C • Malta ... 64 [196]
Ghajntuja • Malta ... 93 H1
Ghadamis • Libya ... 21 A1
Ghadames Heritage C • Libya ... 64 [232]
Ghaghara • India ... 105 C8
Ghajn Tuffieha Bay • Malta ... 93 H3
Ghajnsielem • Malta ... 93 H1
Ghana • Africa ... 22 D3
Ghar Dalam • Malta ... 93 H1
Gharb • Malta ... 93 H1
Gharbi • Tunisia ... 101 E4
Gharbiyah, Al Istiwa'iyah al •
  Sudan ... 23 D2
Ghard Abu Muharik • Egypt ... 21 E2
Ghardaia • Algeria ... 20 F2
Gharib • Egypt ... 21 F2
Gharyan • Libya ... 21 B1
Ghat • Libya ... 21 A2
Ghats, Eastern • India ... 106 D3
Ghats, Western • India ... 106 D6
Ghazal, Bahr al • Sudan ... 23 E2
Ghazal, Bahr el • Chad ... 21 C5
Ghazaouet • Algeria ... 11 J9
Ghaziabad • India ... 105 C2
Ghazipur • India ... 105 C8
Ghazni • Afghanistan ... 18 I3
Ghent • Belgium ... 80 A14
Gherla • Romania ... 14 K2
Ghisonaccia • Corsica, France ... 85 L4
Ghisoni • Corsica, France ... 85 L4
Ghoumrassen • Tunisia ... 101 E6
Ghuzayyil, Sabkhat • Libya ... 21 C2
Giali • Greece ... 92 D8
Giali • Greece ... 92 D8
Gianades Beach • Corfu, Greece ... 69 [149]
Gianades • Corfu, Greece ... 92 B1
Gianades • Corfu, Greece ... 92 B1
Gianisáda • Greece ... 93 G3
Giannutri, I. di • Italy ... 90 A2
Giant's Castle Game Reserve Park •
  South Africa ... 103 [129]
Giant's Causeway •
  United Kingdom ... 7 F6
Giant's Causeway Heritage N •
  United Kingdom ... 61 [41]
Giants Ridge Ski •
  MN, United States ... 116 [109]
Gianyar • Bali, Indonesia ... 110 C4
Giao • Vietnam ... 31 D4
Giardini-Naxos • Sicily, Italy ... 90 D2
Giáros • Greece ... 92 D7
Giáros • Greece ... 92 D7
Giarre • Sicily, Italy ... 12 J11
Gibara • Cuba ... 124 D8
Gibb River • WA, Australia ... 34 D3
Gibbs Beach • Barbados ... 125 H1
Gibeon • Namibia ... 24 B5
Gibibon • Jordan ... 98 A5
Gibostad • Norway ... 16 I2
Gibraltar • Europe ... 86 B6
Gibraltar, Strait of •
  Morocco/Spain ... 11 F9
Gibson Desert • WA, Australia ... 34 D4
Gičan • France ... 10 H6
Gießen • Germany ... 85 H3
Giethoorn • Netherlands ... 80 B2
Gifford • NU, Canada ... 39 O2
Gifhorn • Germany ... 8 F4
Gifu • Japan ... 30 I7
Giglio • Italy ... 12 E6
Giglio • Italy ... 12 E6
Giglio • United Kingdom ... 78 A2
Gijón • Spain ... 11 F1
Gila • AZ/NM, United States ... 118 J3
Gila Bend • AZ, United States ... 118 J3
Gila Cliff Dwellings Nat. Mon. •
  NM, United States ... 118 J4
Gila Cliff Dwellings Nat. Mon. Park •
  NM, United States ... 120 [120]
Gilbert • AZ, United States ... 34 H3
Gilbert Is. • Kiribati ... 33 I6
Gilbo'a, Mount • Israel/Jordan ... 98 A4
Gilbués • Brazil ... 45 (1) B3
Giles Meteorological Station •
  WA, Australia ... 34 E5
Gilgit • Jammu & Kashmir ... 28 B1
Gilgit [Riv] • Jammu & Kashmir ... 28 B1
Gilimanuk • Bali, Indonesia ... 110 C1
Gili, Lough • Ireland ... 79 F2
Gillam • MN, Canada ... 38 M5
Gilleleje • Denmark ... 95 F10
Gillette • WY, United States ... 40 E3
Gillingham • United Kingdom ... 74 F3
Gimbi • Ethiopia ... 23 F2
Gimie, Mt • St Lucia ... 125 J3
Gin Gin • QL, Australia ... 111 F6
Gin Gin • QL, Australia ... 111 F6
Gíngoog • Philippines ... 31 G5
Gingin • WA, Australia ... 34 C6
Gioia del Colle • Italy ... 12 K8
Gioia, Golfo di • Italy ... 12 K10
Gioúra • Greece ... 92 D4
Gioúra • Greece ... 92 D4

Giulianova • Italy ... 91 E12
Giumalau, Vârful • Romania ... 14 M2
Giurgeni • Romania ... 97 D2
Giurgiu • Romania ... 97 D2
Give • Denmark ... 95 F9
Givet • France ... 5 H4
Giza Pyramids • Egypt ... 101 F1
Gizeh • Egypt ... 101 F1
Gizhinskaya Guba • Russian Fed. ... 27 R4
Gizo • Solomon Is. ... 35 (1) F2
Gizycko • Poland ... 13 K3
Gjegnni • Norway ... 94 B3
Gjirokastër • Albania ... 15 B3
Gjoa Haven • NU, Canada ... 38 L3
Gjerstad • Norway ... 94 B3
Gjøl • Norway ... 94 B3
Gjøvik • Norway ... 94 B3
Gjuhëzës, Kep i • Albania ... 15 A3
Glace Bay • NS, Canada ... 123 D8
Glacier Bay • AK, United States ... 58 A2
Glacier Bay Nat. Park & Preserve Heritage N •
  AK, United States ... 60 [1]
Glacier Bay Nat. Park •
  AK, United States ... 120 [13]
Glacier Nat. Park •
  MT, United States ... 117 E2
Glacier Nat. Park Park •
  MT, United States ... 120 [67]
Glacier Nat. Park • BC, Canada ... 122 C4
Glacier Peak •
  WA, United States ... 38 G7
Gladbach • Germany ... 81 E1
Gladbeck • Germany ... 9 D6
Gladstone Spa • Germany ... 83 [127]
Gladstone • QL, Australia ... 111 F4
Gláma • Iceland ... 16 F6
Glamis Castle • United Kingdom ... 74 B2
Glan • Germany ... 9 C7
Glane • Sweden ... 95 F4
Glanvilles • Antigua & Barbuda ... 125 F4
Glarner Alpen • Switzerland ... 89 G3
Glasgow • MT, United States ... 40 E2
Glasgow • United Kingdom ... 74 B3
Glashütte • Germany ... 9 I6
Glaskär • Sweden ... 95 F8
Glass Country • Sweden ... 95 F8
Glass Window Bridge • Bahamas ... 124 B5
Glasshouse Mtns Nat. Park •
  QL, Australia ... 111 F6
Glastonbury • United Kingdom ... 74 F3
Glastonbury Tor •
  United Kingdom ... 13 B7
Glauchau • Germany ... 13 B7
Glazov • Russian Fed. ... 17 I3
Glen • NH, United States ... 118 G3
Glen Canyon Dam •
  AZ, United States ... 118 J1
Glen Canyon Nat. Recreation Area •
  AZ/UT, United States ... 118 J1
Glen Canyon Nat. Recreation Area Park •
  AZ/UT, United States ... 120 [101]
Glen Eden Ski • OT, Canada ... 116 [23]
Glen Helen • NT, Australia ... 112 H1
Glen Innes • NS, Australia ... 34 J5
Glen Shee • United Kingdom ... 74 B2
Glenbeigh Beach • Ireland ... 68 [41]
Glenbeigh • Ireland ... 79 F7
Glencoe • Ireland ... 79 E4
Glendalough • Ireland ... 79 E4
Glendive • MT, United States ... 40 F2
Gleneagles • United Kingdom ... 74 B1
Glengarriff • Ireland ... 79 E4
Glenmalure • Ireland ... 79 E4
Glenorchy • New Zealand ... 112 L2
Glenridding • United Kingdom ... 74 C2
Glenrothes • United Kingdom ... 74 B1
Glens Falls • NY, United States ... 118 G3
Glenveagh Nat. Park Park •
  Ireland ... 72 [38]
Glenwood Springs •
  CO, United States ... 40 E4
Gletsch • Switzerland ... 89 G3
Glifáda • Corfu, Greece ... 92 D7
Glifáda • Greece ... 92 D7
Glifáda • Corfu, Greece ... 92 B1
Glifáda • Greece ... 92 D7
Glinde • Germany ... 8 F3
Glindow • Germany ... 8 I3
Glittertind • Norway ... 94 C2
Gliwice • Poland ... 13 H7
Globe • AZ, United States ... 118 J3
Glódós • Greece ... 92 D7
Glomfjord • Norway ... 16 G3
Glommersträsk • Sweden ... 16 J4
Glorenza • Italy ... 91 E3
Gloria Dei Church Nat. Hist. Site Park •
  PA, United States ... 121 [310]
Glorieuses • Réunion ... 24 H2
Gloucester • United Kingdom ... 74 F3
Gloucester • MA, United States ... 118 G3
Gloucester, Cape •
  Papua New Guinea ... 35 (1) D2
Gloucestershire •
  United Kingdom ... 74 D4
Głogów • Poland ... 13 I6
Glubokoye • Belarus ... 16 N9
Glucholazy • Poland ... 13 G7
Glücksburg Spa • Germany ... 83 [10]
Glückstadt • Germany ... 8 E3
Glurns • Italy ... 91 E3
Glyngøre • Denmark ... 95 F5
Gmünd • Germany ... 9 H9
Gmünd • Austria ... 89 H8
Gmünd • Austria ... 89 H4
Gmunden • Austria ... 89 H4
Gnarp • Sweden ... 16 I5
Gnesen • Poland ... 71 A9
Gnesta • Sweden ... 95 F3
Gniezno • Poland ... 13 G5
Gnjilane • Yugoslavia ... 14 H4
Gnowangerup • WA, Australia ... 34 C6
Goa Heritage C • India ... 63 [126]
Goa • India ... 105 B
Goa Lawah Cave •
  Bali, Indonesia ... 110 C4
Goba • Ethiopia ... 23 G2
Gobabis • Namibia ... 24 B4
Gobernador Gregores • Argentina ... 45 B5
Gobi • China/Mongolia ... 28 D2
Gobo • Japan ... 30 H8
Gochas • Namibia ... 24 B4
Göd • Hungary ... 13 I10
Godavari, Mouths of the • India ... 106 D4
Godbout • QU, Canada ... 123 D1
Gode • Ethiopia ... 23 G2
Godelbukta Breidvika •
  Antarctica ... 46 (1) H2
Godech • Bulgaria ... 93 G3
Godhab • Greenland ... 39 U3
Godhra • India ... 28 B4
Godinne • Belgium ... 80 A15
Godoy Cruz • Argentina ... 44 C5
Gods Lake • MN, Canada ... 38 M5
Goéland, Lac-au- • QU, Canada ... 39 P6
Goeree Beach • Netherlands ... 68 [49]
Goeree • Netherlands ... 80 A10

Goes • Netherlands 5 G3
Gogrial • Sudan 23 D2
Göhren Spa • Germany ... 83 [280]
Goianésia • Brazil 44 G2
Goiânia • Brazil 44 G3
Goiás • Brazil 44 F2
Goiás [Adm] • Brazil 44 G1
Goiatuba • Brazil 44 G2
Goifulhia Fehendhu Atoll •
Maldives 106 E1
Going Ski • Austria .... 70 [153]
Göinge • Sweden 95 F11
Góis • Portugal 11 C4
Gök Tepe • Turkey 15 K7
Gokarn • India 106 D5
Gokayama Heritage C • Japan .. 63 [168]
Gökçe • Turkey 15 G3
Gökçeada • Turkey 92 D2
Gökçeada • Turkey 92 D2
Gökdere • Turkey 15 N7
Gokova Körfezi • Turkey 15 I7
Göksu • Turkey 15 K3
Göktepe • Turkey 15 J6
Gokwe • Zimbabwe 102 J1
Gol • Norway 94 C4
Gola Forest Reserve Park •
Sierra Leone .... 103 [16]
Golan Heights • Syria 98 A2
Golancz • Poland 13 G5
Golaninha • Brazil 45 (1) D3
Gölcük • Turkey 15 K3
Gold Beach • OR, United States .. 117 E3
Gold Coast • China ....
Gold Coast • QL, Australia .. 111 F6
Goldap • Poland 13 L3
Goldau • Switzerland 89 G3
Golden Bay • New Zealand ... 35 D5
Golden Bay • Malta 93 H3
Golden Coast • Sweden 95 F6
Golden Gate • CA, United States .. 40 B4
Golden Gate Nat. Recreation Area Park •
CA, United States .... 120 [45]
Golden Horseshoe • OT, Canada .. 122 B9
Golden Ring • Russian Fed. .. 97 E4
Golden Rock [Apt] •
St Kitts & Nevis 125 G1
Golden Sands • Bulgaria 97 D4
Golden Spike Nat. Hist. Site Park •
UT, United States .... 120 [78]
Golden Triangle • India 105 C2
Golden Triangle •
Laos/Myanmar/Thailand ... 108 A1
Golden Valley • United Kingdom .. 74 D3
Golden Winde • BC, Canada .. 40 A1
Goldsboro • NC, United States .. 41 K4
Goldsworthy • WA, Australia .. 34 C4
Goldthwaite • TX, United States .. 119 N3
Goléa, El • Algeria 20 F2
Goleniów • Poland 13 D4
Golfe-Juan • France 85 H4
Golfito • Costa Rica 37 E6
Golfo Aranci Beach •
Sardinia, Italy .... 68 [119]
Golfo Aranci • Sardinia, Italy .. 90 C2
Golfo de Chiriquí • Panama .. 37 E6
Golija • F.R. of Yugoslavia 14 H6
Golm • Germany 81 F3
Gölmarmara • Turkey 15 I5
Golmud • China 28 F1
Golmud He • China 28 F1
Golo • Corsica, France 85 L2
Goma • Dem. Rep. of Congo .. 23 D4
Gombe • Nigeria 22 G2
Gombe Nat. Park • Tanzania .. 102 H1
Gombe Nat. Park Park • Tanzania .. 103 [93]
Gomera • Canary Is. 87 E5
Gómez Palacio • Mexico 36 C3
Gomi • Ethiopia/Sudan 21 F6
Gomo • China 28 E2
Gonabad • Iran 18 G3
Gonaïves • Haiti 37 G4
Gonarezhou Nat. Park • Zimbabwe .. 102 J4
Gonâve, I. de • Haiti 124 A2
Gonbad-e Cabus • Iran 18 G2
Gonder • Ethiopia ....
Gonder monuments Heritage C •
Ethiopia .... 63 [85]
Gondia • India 28 C4
Gondomar • Portugal 11 C3
Gönen • Turkey 92 D3
Gönen • Turkey 92 D3
Gönen [Riv] • Turkey 15 I3
Gongbai • Zhuhai, China 107 H1
Gongbo'gyamda • China 28 F3
Gongga Shan • China 29 C5
Gonghe • China 29 C3
Gongola [Adm] • Nigeria 22 G3
Gongola [Riv] • Nigeria 22 G2
Gongshan • China 31 B1
Good Hope, Cape of •
South Africa 100 C5
Goodenough • Papua New Guinea .. 35 (1) A2
Goodhouse • South Africa 24 B5
Gooding • ID, United States .. 117 E4
Goodrich • United Kingdom ... 74 D3
Goodwood • United Kingdom .. 74 E3
Goole • United Kingdom 7 L8
Goomalling • WA, Australia ... 34 C6
Goondiwindi • QL, Australia .. 111 F6
Goonhilly Downs •
United Kingdom 74 F4
Goor • Netherlands 5 J2
Goose Bay • NF, Canada 39 S6
Goose Lake •
CA/OR, United States 117 E3
Gooty • India 106 D2
Göppingen • Germany 9 E8
Gora • New Zealand 112 L4
Gora Stoy • Ukraine 13 M9
Gorakhpur • India 105 C4
Gorczanski Nat. Park Park •
Poland .... 72 [96]
Gorda, Punta •
CA, United States 117 F1
Gordes • Turkey 15 J5
Gordion • Turkey 15 N4
Gordonvale • QL, Australia 34 I3
Goré • Chad 22 H3
Gore • Ethiopia 23 E3
Gore Bay • NH, United States .. 116 [183]
Gorée Ski •
NY, United States .... 116 [183]
Gorée, I. de Heritage C •
Senegal .... 63 [95]
Göreme Nat. Park Heritage N •
Turkey .... 61 [63]
Göreme Nat. Park Heritage C •
Turkey .... 64 [193]
Görenez Dagi • Turkey 15 J5
Gorgan • Iran 18 G2
Gorgona • Colombia 43 B3
Gorgona, I. di • Italy 91 E10
Gorham • NH, United States .. 118 G3
Gorinchem • Netherlands 80 C4
Gorizia • Italy 91 E4
Gorjanci • Croatia/Slovenia .. 14 C4
Gorkovskoye Vdkhr. •
Russian Fed. 17 G2
Gørlev Beach • Denmark ..... 68 [24]

Gørlev • Denmark 95 F10
Gorlice • Poland 13 K8
Görlitz • Germany 9 J5
Gorna Orjahovica • Bulgaria .. 97 D3
Gorno-Altaysk • Russian Fed. .. 26 O7
Gornozavodsk • Russian Fed. .. 29 K1
Gorochan • Ethiopia 23 F2
Gorodets • Russian Fed. 17 G3
Gorodok • Ukraine 13 M8
Goroka • Papua New Guinea .. 35 (1) D2
Gorong, Kepulauan • Indonesia .. 32 (1) D3
Gorongosa, Parque Nac. da Park •
Mozambique .... 103 [135]
Gorongoza, Serra da •
Mozambique 24 E3
Gorontalo • Indonesia 32 (1) B2
Górowo Ilaweckie • Poland ... 13 J3
Gorriti, I. de • Uruguay 127 D2
Gorski Kotar • Croatia/Slovenia .. 14 B4
Gort • Ireland 79 F4
Gortipohl Ski • Austria ...... 70 [126]
Görtis • Crete, Greece 93 E7
Gortyna • Crete, Greece 93 E7
Goru, Virful • Romania 14 N4
Gorumna I. • Ireland 79 F3
Gory Stolowe Nat. Park Park •
Poland .... 72 [98]
Górzów Wielkopolski • Poland .. 13 E5
Gosau Ski • Austria .... 70 [177]
Gosau • Austria 89 H4
Gosford • NS, Australia 111 G2
Goshen • Canada 124 C2
Goslar • Germany 8 F5
Goslar Heritage C • Germany .. 64 [35]
Gospic • Croatia 14 C5
Gosport • United Kingdom 7 K11
Gossau • Switzerland ....
Gossi • Mali 20 E5
Gossilies [Apt] • Belgium 80 A14
Gostivar • F.Y.R. of Macedonia .. 15 B2
Gostyn • Poland 13 G6
Gostynin • Poland 13 I5
Göta älv • Sweden 95 F2
Göta kanal • Sweden 95 F6
Göteborg • Sweden 95 F6
Göteborg och Bohus • Sweden .. 95 F2
Götel Mtns • Cameroon/Nigeria .. 22 G3
Götene • Sweden 95 F3
Gotha • Germany 8 F6
Goto-Retto • Japan 30 E8
Gotowasi • Indonesia 32 (1) C2
Gotse Delchev • Bulgaria 14 K8
Gotska Sandön • Sweden 16 J7
Gotsu • Japan 30 G7
Göttingen • Germany 8 E5
Gouda • Netherlands 80 C3
Goudiri • Senegal 20 C6
Goudoumaria • Niger 22 G2
Gough I. • Atlantic Ocean 19 C9
Gough I. Wildlife Reserve Heritage N •
Atlantic Ocean .... 61 [101]
Gouin, Réservoir • QU, Canada .. 39 Q7
Goulburn • NS, Australia 111 G2
Goulburn [Riv] • VI, Australia .. 111 G3
Goulimine • Morocco 101 D5
Gouménissa • Greece 14 J9
Gouna • Cameroon 23 A2
Goundam • Mali 20 E5
Gourdon • France 10 G9
Gouré • Niger 20 H6
Gouritsmond • South Africa .. 100 C6
Gourma Rharous • Mali 20 E5
Gourmay-en-Bray • France 85 E1
Gournià • Crete, Greece 93 E8
Gourock • United Kingdom 78 A3
Gourock Range • NS, Australia .. 111 G2
Gourrama • Morocco 20 E2
Goúves Beach • Crete, Greece .. 69 [190]
Goúves • Crete, Greece 93 E3
Gouviá • Corfu, Greece 92 B1
Gouviá • Corfu, Greece 92 B1
Gov'Altyan Nuruu • Mongolia .. 29 C2
Gove Peninsula • NT, Australia .. 34 G2
Govena, mys • Russian Fed. .. 27 S5
Governador Valadares • Brazil .. 127 C2
Governor Ballabh Pant Sagar •
India 105 C8
Goya • Argentina 44 E4
Göynük • Turkey 15 L3
Göynük Beach • Turkey ..... 69 [202]
Göynük • Turkey 93 G3
Goz Beïda • Chad 23 C1
Gozha Co • China 28 D1
Gozo • Malta 93 H1
Graaff-Reinet • South Africa .. 100 C4
Graal-Müritz • Germany 8 H2
Graal-Müritz Beach • Germany .. 68 [15]
Graal-Müritz Spa • Germany .. 83 [273]
Grabo • Côte d'Ivoire 22 D3
Grächen • Switzerland 89 G6
Gracias a Dios, Cabo •
Nicaragua 37 E4
Graciosa Beach • Azores .... 68 [365]
Graciosa • Canary Is. 87 E3
Graciosa • Azores 88 B2
Gradaus, Serra dos • Brazil .. 43 G5
Grado Beach • Italy .... 68 [147]
Grado • Spain 11 E1
Grado • Italy 91 E4
Græsted-Gilleleje Beach •
Denmark .... 68 [22]
Grafton • NS, Australia 34 J5
Grafton • ND, United States .. 41 G2
Graham • TX, United States .. 119 N1
Graham I. • BC, Canada 38 E6
Graham Land • Antarctica .. 46 (1) II3
Graham Moore, Cape • NU, Canada .. 39 P2
Grahamstown • South Africa .. 100 C8
Grain Coast •
Liberia/Sierra Leone 22 B3
Grainau • Germany 82 J6
Grajaú • Brazil 45 (1) B3
Grajewo • Poland 13 L4
Gram • Denmark 95 F13
Gramat, Causse de • France .. 85 G4
Grampian Mtns • United Kingdom .. 6 H5
Grampians • TV, Australia 111 E7
Gramvoúsa • Crete, Greece ... 93 E1
Gramvoúsa, Akria •
Crete, Greece 93 E1
Gran • Hungary 71 A14
Gran • Norway 94 B2
Gran Canaria • Canary Is. 86 E4
Gran Chaco • Argentina/Paraguay .. 44 D3
Gran Paradiso • Italy 91 E5
Gran Paradiso, Parco Naz. del Park •
Italy .... 72 [85]
Gran Paradiso, Parco Naz. del •
Italy 91 E5
Gran Piedra • Cuba 124 D8
Gran Pilastro • Austria/Italy .. 90 B1
Gran San Bernardo •
Italy/Switzerland 12 B3
Gran Sasso d'Italia • Italy 91 F2
Gran Tarajal •
Fuerteventura, Canary Is. .. 87 E2

Granada • Nicaragua 37 D5
Granada Heritage C • Spain .. 64 [94]
Granada • Spain 86 B3
Granby • QU, Canada 122 B8
Grand Anse • St Lucia 125 J2
Grand Bahama I. • Bahamas .. 124 B2
Grand Ballon • France 9 C9
Grand Bank • NF, Canada 123 D3
Grand Bassam • Côte d'Ivoire .. 22 D3
Grand Brière • France 84 C4
Grand Canal • Ireland 7 E8
Grand Canal • China 29 F4
Grand Canyon •
AZ, United States 118 J1
Grand Canyon Nat. Park Heritage N •
AZ, United States .... 60 [12]
Grand Canyon Nat. Park •
AZ, United States 118 J1
Grand Canyon Nat. Park Park •
AZ, United States .... 120 [100]
Grand Canyon of Pennsylvania •
PA, United States 118 H1
Grand Causses • France 10 I9
Grand Cayman • Cayman Is. .. 124 C6
Grand Cess • Liberia 22 C4
Grand Coulee •
WA, United States 40 C2
Grand Coulee Dam •
WA, United States 117 E2
Grand Erg Occidental • Algeria .. 20 F2
Grand Erg Oriental •
Algeria/Tunisia 20 G2
Grand Falls • NB, Canada ... 123 D1
Grand Falls • NF, Canada ... 123 D1
Grand Forks • ND, United States .. 41 G2
Grand Harbour • Malta 93 H4
Grand Island •
NE, United States 41 G3
Grand Isle • VT, United States .. 118 F1
Grand Junction •
CO, United States 40 E4
Grand Junction •
CO, United States .... 116 A
Grand Lake •
Canada/United States 118 G2
Grand Lake • LA, United States .. 118 K3
Grand Lake • NF, Canada 123 D3
Grand Lake • NB, Canada 123 D6
Grand Manan I. • NB, Canada .. 123 D6
Grand Morin, Vallée du • France .. 85 E4
Grand Portage Nat. Mon. Park •
MN, United States .... 121 [156]
Grand Prairie •
TX, United States 119 N1
Grand Pré • NS, Canada 123 D5
Grand Pressigny, le [Château] •
France 84 D4
Grand Rapids • MN, Canada .. 38 L6
Grand Rapids •
MN, United States 41 H2
Grand Rapids •
MI, United States 41 I3
Grand Ravine • St Lucia 125 J2
Grand Récif de Cook •
New Caledonia 35 (2) A2
Grand St-Bernard, Col du •
Italy/Switzerland 89 G6
Grand Teton • WY, United States .. 40 E3
Grand Teton Nat. Park Park •
WY, United States .... 120 [76]
Grand-Bornand, le Ski • France .. 70 [20]
Grand-Village-Plage, le Beach •
France .... 68 [65]
Grandcamp-Maisy • France ... 10 D4
Grande • Brazil 44 G2
Grande, Bahía • Argentina ... 45 C6
Grande, Ilha de I. • Brazil ... 127 C3
Grande Casse • France 10 I3
Grande Cul de Sac Bay •
St Lucia 125 J1
Grande I. • Brazil 127 C3
Grande Lande, Ecomusée de la •
France 85 G3
Grande Morin • France 5 G6
Grande Ronde • AL, Canada .. 122 C2
Grande, Rio •
Mexico/United States 40 F6
Grande, Rio • Bolivia 44 D2
Grande, Rio • Jamaica 124 C4
Grande Rivière •
Dennery, St Lucia 125 J2
Grande Rivière •
Gros Islet, St Lucia 125 J2
Grande, Serra • Brazil 45 (1) C3
Gredos, Sierra de • Spain 11 F4
Greece • Europe 17
Greek Peak Ski •
NY, United States .... 116 [176]
Greeley • CO, United States .. 40 F3
Greem Bell, Ostrov •
Russian Fed. 96 A3
Green Bay • WI, United States .. 41 I3
Green Bay [Bay] •
WI, United States 39 N7
Green I. • QL, Australia 111 F1
Green I. • Antigua & Barbuda .. 125 F4
Green Meadows Petting Farm •
FL, United States 121 C2
Green Mtns • VT, United States .. 118 G3
Green [Riv] •
UT/WY, United States 40 E3
Green River • WY, United States .. 40 E3
Green Springs Hist. District Park •
VA, United States .... 121 [260]
Green Turtle Cay • Bahamas .. 124 B1
Green Valley •
AZ, United States 118 J3
Greenbelt Park Park •
MD, United States .... 121 [280]
Greendale • United Kingdom .. 74 D3
Greenland • N. America 36 M2
Greenland Sea • Arctic Ocean .. 46 P2
Greenock • United Kingdom ... 74 B3
Greensboro • NC, United States .. 41 K4
Greenville • Liberia 22 C3
Greenville • SC, United States .. 117 F3
Greenville • NC, United States .. 118 H5
Greenville • MS, United States .. 118 K2
Greenville • TX, United States .. 119 N2
Greenwich • United Kingdom .. 7 M10
Greenwood • MS, United States .. 118 K2
Greenwood Great House • Jamaica .. 124 C3
Gregório • Brazil ....
Gregory [Riv] • WA, Australia .. 34 G3
Gregory Lake • WA, Australia .. 34 E3
Grenå Beach • Denmark .... 68 [28]
Grenada • West Indies 37 I5
Grenadines, The • St Vincent .. 37 I5
Gresik • Java, Indonesia 110 D4

Great Barrier Reef Heritage N •
QL, Australia .... 61 [131]
Great Barrier Reef •
QL, Australia .... 111 F
Great Barrier Reef Marine Park •
QL, Australia 111 F4
Great Basin • NV, United States .. 117 F2
Great Basin Nat. Park •
NV, United States 117 F4
Great Basin Nat. Park Park •
NV, United States .... 120 [62]
Great Bear • NT, Canada 38 G4
Great Bear Lake • NT/NU, Canada .. 38 G3
Great Bend • KS, United States .. 40 F4
Great Bernera • United Kingdom .. 75 A1
Great Bird I. •
Antigua & Barbuda 125 F2
Great Blasket I. • Ireland 79 F7
Great Coxwell Barn •
United Kingdom 74 D4
Great Dividing Range •
Australia 34 I4
Great Exhibition Bay •
New Zealand 35 D2
Great Exuma • Bahamas 124 B3
Great Falls • MT, United States .. 40 E2
Great Fish • South Africa 100 C8
Great Gable • United Kingdom .. 74 C1
Great George Resort Action Park •
NJ, United States 118 H1
Great Gorge Resort Action Park Park •
NJ, United States .... 121 [LL]
Great Harbour Cay • Bahamas .. 124 B1
Great Harbour Deep • NF, Canada .. 123 D5
Great Inagua • Bahamas 124 B4
Great Kappel I. • QL, Australia .. 111 F4
Great Karoo • South Africa .. 100 C3
Great Keppel I. • QL, Australia .. 111 F4
Great Lakes •
Canada/United States 117 D4
Great Malvern • United Kingdom .. 74 D3
Great Nicobar • India 28 F7
Great Oasis, The • Egypt 101 F3
Great Palm I. • QL, Australia .. 111 F1
Great Pedro Bluff • Jamaica .. 124 C3
Great Plains •
Canada/United States 40 E2
Great [Riv] • Jamaica 124 C1
Great Ruaha • Tanzania 102 H4
Great Salt Lake •
UT, United States 40 D3
Great Salt Lake Desert •
UT, United States 40 D3
Great Salt Pond •
St Kitts & Nevis 125 G4
Great Sand Dunes Nat. Mon. Park •
CO, United States .... 120 [97]
Great Sandy Desert •
WA, Australia 34 D4
Great Sandy Desert •
OR, United States 117 E4
Great Slave Lake • NT, Canada .. 38 H4
Great Smoky Mtns Nat. Park Heritage N •
NC/TN, United States ..... 60 [16]
Great Smoky Mtns Nat. Park Park •
NC/TN, United States ... 121 [232]
Great Torrington •
United Kingdom 74 F2
Great Valley •
TN/VA United States 41 J4
Great Victoria Desert •
SA/WA, Australia 34 E5
Great Victoria Desert Nature Reserve •
SA/WA, Australia 34 E5
Great Wall Heritage C • China .. 63 [144]
Great White Heron Nat. Wildlife Refuge •
FL, United States 119 M7
Great Yarmouth • United Kingdom .. 7 N9
Great Yarmouth Beach •
United Kingdom .... 75 [45-46]
Great Zimbabwe Nat. Mon. Heritage C •
Zimbabwe .... 63 [100]
Great Zimbabwe Nat. Mon. •
Zimbabwe 102 J4
Greater Antilles • West Indies .. 37 G4
Greater St Lucia Wetland Park Park •
South Africa .... 103 [127]
Greater Sunda Is. • Indonesia .. 32 E4
Greatstone-on-Sea Beach •
United Kingdom .... 75 [67]
Grebbestad • Sweden 95 F2
Gréboun, Mt • Niger 20 G4
Greco, Cape • Cyprus 93 J4
Gredos, Sierra de • Spain 11 F4
Green, I. • QL, Australia 111 F1
Grein • Austria ....
Greene • NY, United States .. 116 [176]
Greenfield • MA, United States .. 118 G3
Grünstadt • Germany 81 F2
Grüsch • Switzerland 89 G4
Gruyères • Switzerland 89 G4
Gryazovets • Russian Fed. 17 F3
Gryfice • Poland 13 E4
Gryfino • Poland 13 D4
Gryon Ski • Switzerland ..... 70 [83]
Gryon • Switzerland 89 G4
Gryt • Sweden 95 F4
Grytviken • South Georgia .. 46 (1) D4
Gstaad • Switzerland 89 G6
Gstaad-Saanenland Ski •
Switzerland .... 70 [86]
Guacanayabo, Golfo de • Cuba .. 124 D7
Guadalajara • Spain 11 G3
Guadalajara Heritage C • Mexico .. 62 [19]
Guadalcanal • Solomon Is. .. 35 (1) G2
Guadaleste • Spain 87 C2
Guadalimar • Spain 11 K4
Guadalope • Spain 11 K4
Guadalquivir • Spain 11 F5
Guadalupe • Mexico 37 A2
Guadalupe • Mexico ....
Guadalupe Heritage C • Spain .. 64 [89]
Guadalupe • TX, United States .. 119 N5
Guadalupe Peak • TX, United States .. 40 F5
Guadalupe Mtns Nat. Park Park •
TX, United States .... 120 [105]
Guadarrama, Sierra de • Spain .. 11 G4
Guadeloupe • West Indies 37 I4
Guadiana • Portugal/Spain 11 D7
Guadix, Bahía de • Cuba 124 C3
Guadix • Spain 86 B4
Guaíba • Brazil 45 E5
Guaira • Brazil 44 F3
Guajaba, Cayo • Cuba 124 D3

Gressámoen Nat. Park Park •
Norway .... 72 [11]
Gressoney-la-Trinité Ski •
Italy .... 70 [202]
Gressoney-St Jean Ski • Italy .. 70 [202]
Greve Beach • Denmark ..... 68 [19]
Greven • Germany 8 C4
Grevená • Greece 15 C3
Grevenbroich • Germany 81 E3
Grevesmühlen • Germany 8 G3
Grey Is. • NF, Canada 123 D5
Grey Range • QL, Australia 34 H5
Greymouth • New Zealand 35 C6
Greystones • Ireland 79 E4
Greytown • New Zealand 35 E5
Gribës • Albania 15 A3
Gribingu •
Central African Rep./Chad .. 22 H3
Grieben Spa • Germany ..... 83 [278]
Griesheim • Germany 82 H4
Griffin • GA, United States 118 K5
Grimari • Central African Rep. .. 23 B2
Grimaud Beach • France ... 68 [116]
Grimentz • Switzerland 89 G6
Grimmen • Germany 8 I2
Grimsby • United Kingdom 7 L8
Grimselpass • Switzerland ... 89 G3
Grimsey • Iceland 16 (1) E1
Grímsstadir • Iceland 16 (1) E1
Grimstad • Norway 95 F1
Grindavík • Iceland 16 (1) B3
Grindelwald Ski • Switzerland .. 70 [97]
Grindelwald • Switzerland 89 G2
Grindsted • Denmark 95 F9
Gríntavec • Slovenia 13 D11
Gripsholm • Sweden 95 G3
Gris-Nez, Cap • France 10 G3
Grise Fjord • NU, Canada 36 I2
Grisons • Switzerland 89 G4
Grisslehamn • Sweden 95 D2
Grizedale Forest •
United Kingdom 74 C1
Grmec • Bosnia-Herz. 14 D5
Grodno • Belarus 13 M4
Grodzisk Mazowiecki • Poland .. 13 J5
Groix, I. de • France 84 C3
Grójec • Poland 13 J6
Grömitz Spa • Germany ..... 83 [25]
Gröna Lunds Tivoli Park •
Sweden .... 73 [7]
Gronau • Germany 82 J2
Grönenbach • Germany 82 J2
Grönenbach Spa • Germany .. 83 [237]
Grong • Norway 16 G4
Groningen • Netherlands 80 A4
Groningen [Adm] • Netherlands .. 80 A4
Groot • South Africa 100 C7
Groot-Karasberge • Namibia .. 24 B5
Groote Eylandt • NT, Australia .. 34 G2
Grootfontein • Namibia 24 B3
Gros Islet • St Lucia 125 J2
Gros Morne • St Lucia 125 J3
Gros Morne Nat. Park Heritage N •
NF, Canada .... 60 [7]
Gros Morne Nat. Park •
NF, Canada ....
Gros Piton • St Lucia 125 J3
Gros Piton Point • St Lucia .. 125 J3
Groß-Gerau • Germany 82 H4
Großarl Ski • Austria .... 70 [170]
Großbeeren • Germany 81 F4
Großenbrode • Spa • Germany .. 83 [23]
Großer Arber • Germany 82 J4
Großer Feldberg • Germany ... 82 H2
Großer Inselsberg • Germany .. 9 F6
Großer Müggelsee • Germany .. 81 F4
Großer Plöner See • Germany .. 81 F3
Großer Seddiner See • Germany .. 81 F3
Großenthiming Stausee • Germany.. 81 E4
Grosseto • Italy 91 E11
Grosseto-Prugna Beach •
Corsica, France .... 68 [118]
Grosseto-Prugna •
Corsica, France 85 L3
Großglockner • Austria 89 H8
Großostheim • Germany 9 E7
Großräschen • Germany 81 F4
Großrotte • Austria 89 H7
Großvenediger • Austria 13 B10
Großwardein • Romania 71 A14
Groton • United Kingdom 7 N9
Grottaglie • Italy 12 L8
Grottammare • Italy 12 G5
Groux • Morocco 101 D1
Groznyy • Russian Fed. 17 H6
Grudovo • Bulgaria 97 D3
Grudziądz • Poland 13 H4
Gruissan Beach • France .. 68 [112]
Grumeti • Tanzania 23 E4
Grünau • Namibia 24 B5
Grünberg • Germany 82 G2
Grundy Lake Prov. Park •
OT, Canada 122 B1
Grunewald • Germany 81 F3
Gruyères • Switzerland 89 G4

Guajará Mirim • Brazil 43 D6
Guajataca • Puerto Rico 125 E1
Guajira, Península de •
Colombia 43 C1
Guakolak, Tanjung •
Java, Indonesia 110 D1
Gualdo Tadino • Italy 71 A13
Gualeguay • Argentina 127 D1
Gualeguaychú • Argentina ... 127 D1
Guam • Pacific Ocean 33 F4
Guamá Indian Village • Cuba .. 124 D2
Guampi, Sierra de • Venezuela .. 37 H6
Guanajay • Cuba 124 D1
Guanajuato Heritage C • Mexico .. 62 [15]
Guanajuato • Mexico 123 E1
Guanajuato • Mexico 37 (1) D1
Guanare • Venezuela 43 D2
Guane • Cuba 124 D1
Guangde • China 107 J3
Guangdong • China 107 G7
Guangmao Shan • China 31 C1
Guangming Ding • China 107 J3
Guangxi Zhuangzu Zizhiqu •
China 29 D6
Guangyuan • China 107 H1
Guangzhou East • China 107 H2
Guanica • Puerto Rico 125 E3
Guanimar, Playa • Cuba 124 D1
Guantánamo • Cuba 124 D8
Guantánamo Bay • Cuba 124 D8
Guapay • Bolivia 44 D2
Guapi • Colombia 43 B3
Guaporé • Bolivia/Brazil 43 E6
Guaqui • Bolivia 44 C2
Guarabira • Brazil 45 (1) D3
Guaraparí • Brazil 127 C2
Guarapuava • Brazil 44 F4
Guaratuba • Brazil ....
Guarda • Portugal 11 D4
Guarda [Adm] • Portugal 88 A1
Guardalaberca, Playa • Cuba .. 124 D8
Guardamar del Segura Beach •
Spain .... 68 [101]
Guardamar del Segura • Spain .. 87 C3
Guárdia Sanframondi • Italy .. 91 G2
Guarujá • Brazil 127 C3
Guarulhos • Brazil 127 C3
Guarulhos [Apt] • Brazil 127 C3
Guasave • Mexico 40 E6
Guatemala • C. America 37 C4
Guatemala City • Guatemala .. 37 C5
Guatuaro Point •
Trinidad & Tobago 125 K4
Guaviare • Colombia 43 D3
Guaxupé • Brazil 127 C1
Guayaguayare •
Trinidad & Tobago 125 K4
Guayama • Puerto Rico 125 E3
Guayaneco, Archipiélago • Chile .. 45 A5
Guayanilla, Bahía de •
Puerto Rico 125 E3
Guayaquil • Ecuador 43 B4
Guayaquil, Golfo de • Ecuador .. 43 A4
Guaymas • Mexico 40 D6
Gubakha • Russian Fed. 26 I6
Guban • Somalia 23 H1
Gubbat Sawqirah • Oman 18 I6
Gúbbio • Italy 91 E12
Guben • Germany 8 J5
Gubin • Poland 8 J5
Güdar, Sierra de • Spain 11 K4
Gudbrandsdalen • Norway 16 E6
Gudhjem • Denmark 95 F16
Güdül • Turkey 15 N3
Gudur • India 106 D7
Gudvangen • Norway 94 C4
Guebwiller • France 9 C9
Guédi, Mt • Chad 23 B1
Guelma • Algeria 101 E6
Guelmim • Morocco 20 D3
Guelph • OT, Canada 122 B9
Guelta Zemmur • Western Sahara .. 20 C3
Guéné • Benin 22 F3
Guéra, Massif de • Chad 21 C5
Guérande • France 84 C4
Guéret • France 85 G2
Guernica • Spain 11 I1
Guernsey • Channel Is. 7 J12
Guerrero • Mexico 37 (1) B2
Guerrero Negro • Mexico 40 D6
Guge • Ethiopia 23 F2
Guglionesi • Italy 12 H6
Guiana Highlands • S. America .. 43 E3
Guiana I. • Antigua & Barbuda .. 125 F2
Guide • China 29 C3
Guider • Cameroon 23 A2
Guiglo • Côte d'Ivoire 22 C3
Guignes • France 85 E4
Guildford • United Kingdom ... 7 L11
Guilford Courthouse Nat. Military Park Park •
NC, United States .... 121 [246]
Guilin • China 29 D5
Guimar • Tenerife, Canary Is. .. 86 E1
Guimarães • Portugal 11 C3
Guincho • Portugal 88 D1
Guinea • Africa 22 B2
Guinea, Gulf of • Africa 22 F4
Guinea-Bissau • Africa 20 B6
Guinea Basin • Atlantic Ocean .. 19 D8
Guineguinte • France 84 C2
Guiria • Venezuela 43 E1
Guitiriz • Spain 11 D1
Guiuan • Philippines 31 H4
Guixi • China 29 E5
Guiyang • China 29 D5
Guizhou • China 107 G7
Gujarat • India 28 B4
Gujranwala • Pakistan 28 B2
Gujrat • Pakistan 28 B2
Gulbarga • India 106 D2
Gulbene • Latvia 16 N8
Gulen • Norway 94 C3
Gulf Is. Nat. Seashore •
MS, United States 118 K4
Gulf Is. Nat. Seashore Park •
FL/MS, United States ... 121 [218]
Gulf, The • Asia 18 G4
Gulfport • MS, United States .. 118 K4
Gulfstream Park •
FL, United States 119 M8
Gulhi • Maldives 106 E4
Gulian • China 27 J6
Gulistan • Uzbekistan 26 K9
Gulkana • AK, United States .. 38 B3
Gullane Bents Beach •
United Kingdom .... 75 [13]
Gullivers Kingdom Park •
United Kingdom .... 73 [26]
Güllüpinar • Sweden 92 D9
Güllük • Turkey 92 D9
Güllük Körfezi • Turkey 15 I6
Gülnar • Turkey 15 H4
Gülpinar • Turkey 15 H4
Gulu • Uganda 23 E3
Gumbiri, Jabal • Sudan 23 E3
Gummersbach • Germany 81 E4

Gummi

Gummi • Nigeria ... 20 G6
Gümüssu • Turkey ... 15 K5
Gun Hill Tower • Barbados ... 125 H3
Guna • Ethiopia ... 21 G5
Guna • India ... 105 C6
Gündogmus • Turkey ... 93 G4
Gungu • Dem. Rep. of Congo ... 23 B5
Gunnar • SA, Canada ... 38 J5
Gunnbjørns Fjeld • Greenland ... 46 S2
Gunnedah • NS, Australia ... 34 A6
Gunnislake • United Kingdom ... 74 F5
Gunstock Ski •
  NH, United States ... 116 [209]
Guntakal • India ... 106 D2
Guntur • India ... 106 D3
Gunung Kawi • Bali, Indonesia ... 110 C2
Gunungsitoli • Indonesia ... 110 B3
Günz • Germany ... 9 F8
Günzburg • Germany ... 82 J2
Gunzenhausen • Germany ... 9 F7
Gur, Lough • Ireland ... 79 F6
Guradu • Maldives ... 106 E4
Güre • Turkey ... 15 K5
Gurgel • Sudan ... 21 D5
Gurha • India ... 105 C5
Gurktaler Alpen • Austria ... 14 A3
Gurnard Beach • United Kingdom ... 75 [90]
Gürskey • Norway ... 94 C1
Gurupá • Brazil ... 43 G4
Gurupi • Brazil ... 45 (1) B4
Gurupi [Riv] • Brazil ... 45 (1) B2
Gurupi, Serra do • Brazil ... 45 (1) B2
Guruvayur • India ... 106 D10
Guruve • Zimbabwe ... 102 J2
Gusau • Nigeria ... 22 F2
Gusev • Russian Fed. ... 13 L3
Gush Halav • Israel ... 98 A2
Gushan • China ... 28 B5
Gusinaya, Guba • Russian Fed. ... 27 P2
Gusinoozersk • Russian Fed. ... 27 C6
Guspini • Sardinia, Italy ... 12 C9
Güstrow • Germany ... 8 H3
Gusum • Sweden ... 95 F4
Gutach • Germany ... 82 G8
Güterfelde • Germany ... 81 F3
Gütersloh • Germany ... 8 D5
Guthega • NS, Australia ... 111 G4
Guttenberg, Burg • Germany ... 82 G4
Guwahati • India ... 28 F3
Guyana • S. America ... 43 F2
Guyang • China ... 29 E2
Guyenne • France ... 10 F9
Guymon • OK, United States ... 40 F4
Güzelsu • Turkey ... 93 G4
Güzelyurt • Cyprus ... 15 N8
Güzelyurt Körfezi • Cyprus ... 15 N8
Gvardeysk • Russian Fed. ... 13 K3
Gvarv • Norway ... 94 B3
Gwadar • Pakistan ... 18 H4
Gwalior • India ... 105 C7
Gwanda • Zimbabwe ... 102 J3
Gwda • Poland ... 13 F4
Gweebarra Bay • Ireland ... 7 D7
Gwei • Zimbabwe ... 102 J3
Gweru • Zimbabwe ... 102 J2
Gyaca • China ... 28 F3
Gyandzha • Azerbaijan ... 18 E1
Gyangze • China ... 28 E3
Gyaring Co • China ... 28 E2
Gyaring Hu • China ... 28 G2
Gyda • Russian Fed. ... 26 M3
Gydan Peninsula • Russian Fed. ... 96 A3
Gydanskiy Poluostrov •
  Russian Fed. ... 26 M3
Gympie • QL, Australia ... 111 F6
Gyoma • Hungary ... 13 J11
Gyöngyös • Hungary ... 13 I10
Györ • Hungary ... 13 H9
Gypsumville • MN, Canada ... 38 L6
Gyula • Hungary ... 13 K11
Gyumri • Armenia ... 18 D1

Ha Giang • Vietnam ... 31 C2
Ha Long Bay Heritage N •
  Vietnam ... 61 [121]
Ha Long Bay • Vietnam ... 108 A1
Ha Tien • Vietnam ... 108 B3
Ha Tinh • Vietnam ... 31 D3
Ha'apai Group • Tonga ... 35 (2) F2
Ha'il • Saudi Arabia ... 18 D4
Ha-ad Chao Samran • Thailand ... 109 H3
Haag • Germany ... 82 J4
Haan • Germany ... 81 E3
Haapsalu • Estonia ... 16 L7
Haardt • Germany ... 9 C7
Haarlem • Netherlands ... 80 C1
Haarlemmermeer Polder •
  Netherlands ... 80 C1
Haast • New Zealand ... 35 B6
Haast Bluff • NT, Australia ... 112 H1
Haast Pass • New Zealand ... 35 B7
Haasts Bluff Aboriginal Land •
  NT, Australia ... 112 H1
Habarane • Sri Lanka ... 106 D15
Habaswein • Kenya ... 23 F3
Haboro • Japan ... 30 K2
Hachijo • Japan ... 30 M4
Hachinohe • Japan ... 30 K4
Hacilar • Turkey ... 93 G1
Hackås • Sweden ... 16 H5
Hackleton's Cliff • Barbados ... 125 H4
Hadamar • Germany ... 81 E2
Hadaribah, Ra's al • Sudan ... 18 C5
Hadd, Al • Oman ... 18 G5
Hadd, Ra's al • Oman ... 18 G5
Hadded • Somalia ... 23 H1
Haddington • United Kingdom ... 74 B4
Haddummati Atoll • Maldives ... 106 E13
Hadejia • Nigeria ... 22 F2
Hadejia [Riv] • Nigeria ... 22 F2
Hadejia-Nguru Wetlands Park •
  Nigeria ... 103 [33]
Hadeland • Norway ... 94 B2
Haderslev Beach • Denmark ... 68 [26]
Haderslev • Denmark ... 95 F13
Hadijah • Saudi Arabia ... 18 C4
Hadim • Turkey ... 15 N7
Hadithah, Al • Iraq ... 18 D3
Hadjout • Algeria ... 20 G4
Hadley Bay • NU, Canada ... 38 J2
Hadrian • United Kingdom ... 18 E6
Hadrian's Wall • United Kingdom ... 7 J6
Hadrian's Villa • Italy ... 91 F1
Hadrian's Wall Heritage C •
  United Kingdom ... 64 [15]
Hadsund Beach • Denmark ... 68 [29]
Hadsund • Denmark ... 95 F6
Hae, Ko • Thailand ... 109 K2
Haeinsa Temple Heritage C •
  Rep. of Korea ... 63 [159]
Haeju • D.P.R. of Korea ... 30 C6
Hafar al Batin • Saudi Arabia ... 18 E4
Hafibah, Ra's • Saudi Arabia ... 18 C5
Hafirat al 'Ayda • Saudi Arabia ... 18 C4

Hafnarfjördur • Iceland ... 16 (1) B2
Hafun, Rås • Somalia ... 23 I1
Hagadera • Kenya ... 23 G3
Hagby • Sweden ... 95 F12
Hagen • Germany ... 81 E2
Hagen-Hohen-Limburg • Germany ... 81 E2
Hagenow • Germany ... 8 G3
Hagerman Fossil Beds Nat. Mon. •
  ID, United States ... 117 E4
Hagerman Fossil Beds Nat. Mon. Park •
  ID, United States ... 120 [64]
Haghpat Heritage C • Armenia ... 63 [79]
Hagi • Japan ... 30 F7
Hagondange • France ... 10 L4
Hague, Cap de la • France ... 10 D4
Hague, The • Netherlands ... 80 C1
Haguenau • France ... 10 M5
Hagunia • Western Sahara ... 20 C3
Hahnenklee Spa • Germany ... 83 [77]
Hai Phong • Vietnam ... 31 D2
Hai'an • China ... 107 J2
Haiku • China ... 31 E2
Hailar • China ... 27 I7
Hailong • China ... 29 H2
Hailun • China ... 29 H1
Hailuoto • Finland ... 16 M4
Haimen • China ... 107 J2
Hainan • China ... 31 E3
Hainaut • Belgium ... 80 A14
Haines • AK, United States ... 46 CC4
Haines Junction • YT, Canada ... 38 D4
Hainichen • Germany ... 9 I6
Haining • China ... 107 J4
Haiti • West Indies ... 37 G4
Haïtien, Cap • Haiti ... 37 G4
Haixin Shui • China ... 29 C3
Haiyan • China ... 107 J4
Haizhou Wan • China ... 29 F3
Hajarah, Al • Iraq ... 18 D4
Hajdúböszörmény • Hungary ... 13 K10
Hajdúdorog • Hungary ... 13 K10
Hajdúhadhás • Hungary ... 13 K10
Hajdúnánás • Hungary ... 13 K10
Hajik • F.R. of Yugoslavia ... 14 H7
Hajnówka • Poland ... 13 M5
Hakken • Japan ... 30 H7
Hakodate • Japan ... 30 K4
Haku • Japan ... 30 I6
Hal Saflieni Hypogeum Heritage C •
  Malta ... 64 [197]
Hal Saflieni Hypogeum • Malta ... 93 H4
Hala Sultan Tekke • Cyprus ... 93 J4
Hala'ib • Egypt ... 21 E5
Hala'ib • Syria ... 18 C2
Halab Heritage C • Syria ... 64 [239]
Hålaveden • Sweden ... 95 F3
Halban • Mongolia ... 26 Q8
Halberstadt • Germany ... 8 G5
Halcon, Mt • Philippines ... 31 G4
Hald • Denmark ... 95 F9
Halden • Norway ... 94 B4
Haldensleben • Germany ... 8 G4
Hale, Mt • WA, Australia ... 34 C5
Haleakala Crater •
  HI, United States ... 119 L3
Haleakala Nat. Park •
  HI, United States ... 119 L3
Haleakala Nat. Park Park •
  HI, United States ... 120 [18]
Halebid • India ... 106 D6
Haleiwa • HI, United States ... 119 L1
Half Moon Bay •
  Antigua & Barbuda ... 125 G1
Half Moon I. • Antarctica ... 59 A10
Half Way Tree •
  St Kitts & Nevis ... 125 G1
Halfa, Wadi • Egypt ... 21 F3
Halfmoon Bay • New Zealand ... 35 B8
Haliburton Highlands •
  OT, Canada ... 122 B6
Halifax • NS, Canada ... 123 D7
Halifax Bay • QL, Australia ... 111 F1
Halifax, Mt • QL, Australia ... 111 F1
Halikarnassos • Turkey ... 92 D9
Halikarnassos • Turkey ... 92 D9
Halil • Iran ... 18 G4
Halim Perdana Kusuma [Apt] •
  Java, Indonesia ... 110 D1
Hálki • Greece ... 93 F1
Hálki [I.] • Greece ... 93 F1
Halkida Beach • Greece ... 69 [163]
Halkida • Greece ... 92 D4
Halkida • Greece ... 92 D4
Halkidi • Greece ... 92 D1
Halkidiki • Greece ... 92 D1
Hall Beach • NU, Canada ... 39 O3
Hall in Tirol • Austria ... 89 H2
Hall Peninsula • NU, Canada ... 39 R4
Halla • Rep. of Korea ... 30 D8
Halland • Sweden ... 95 F7
Hallandsås • Sweden ... 95 F11
Halle • Belgium ... 5 H4
Halle • Germany ... 8 G5
Halleberg • Sweden ... 95 D3
Halleforsnäs • Sweden ... 95 D3
Hallein • Austria ... 89 H4
Hallet, Cape • Antarctica ... 59 A10
Halley Bay • Antarctica ... 46 (1) J1
Hallingdalselva • Norway ... 16 E6
Hallingskarvet • Norway ... 94 C4
Halls Creek • WA, Australia ... 34 E3
Hallsberg • Sweden ... 95 D2
Hallstadt-Dachstein-Salzkammergut
  Heritage C • Austria ... 64 [106]
Hallstahammar • Sweden ... 95 D1
Hallstavik • Sweden ... 95 D1
Halmahera • Indonesia ... 32 (1) I2
Halmeu • Romania ... 14 K2
Halmstad Beach • Sweden ... 68 [3]
Halmstad • Sweden ... 95 F11
Halsa • Slovenia ... 14 C3
Hals Beach • Denmark ... 68 [29]
Hals • Denmark ... 95 F6
Halsskov • Denmark ... 95 F14
Halstad • Austria ... 89 H4
Halti • Finland ... 16 K2
Halver • Germany ... 81 E2
Hamad, Al • Saudi Arabia ... 21 H1
Hamada de Tinrhert • Algeria ... 20 G3
Hamada el Haricha • Mali ... 20 E4
Hamada al Hamrah, Al • Libya ... 21 B1
Hamadan • Iran ... 18 E2
Hamah • Syria ... 18 C2
Hamamatsu • Japan ... 30 I7
Hamar • Norway ... 16 F6
Hamat Gader • Israel ... 98 A4
Hamatah • Egypt ... 21 G3
Hamatonbetsu • Japan ... 30 L2
Hambantota • Sri Lanka ... 106 D15
Hamber Prov. Park • BC, Canada ... 122 C4
Hamburg • Germany ... 8 F3
Hamburg [Adm] • Germany ... 81 D1
Hamburgisches Wattenmeer, Nationalpark
  Park • Germany ... 72 [56]
Hamd, Wadi al • Saudi Arabia ... 21 G2

Häme • Finland ... 95 E2
Hämeenlinna • Finland ... 95 E4
Hameln • Germany ... 8 E4
Hamero Hadad • Ethiopia ... 23 G2
Hamersley Range • WA, Australia ... 34 C4
Hamgyong-Sanmaek •
  D.P.R. of Korea ... 30 E4
Hamhung • D.P.R. of Korea ... 30 D5
Hami • China ... 26 P9
Hamilton • VI, Australia ... 34 H7
Hamilton • OH, United States ... 41 J4
Hamilton • Bermuda ... 58 A2
Hamilton • United Kingdom ... 74 B3
Hamilton • New Zealand ... 112 K1
Hamilton • OT, Canada ... 122 B9
Hamilton Grange Nat. Mem. Park •
  NY, United States ... 121 [329]
Hamilton I. • QL, Australia ... 111 F1
Hamina • Finland ... 16 N6
Hamm • Germany ... 8 C5
Hamm Spa • Germany ... 83 [106]
Hamman Lif • Tunisia ... 101 E2
Hammamet • Tunisia ... 101 E2
Hammamet, Golfe de • Tunisia ... 101 E2
Hammarsjön • Sweden ... 95 F11
Hammel • Denmark ... 95 F9
Hammelburg • Germany ... 9 E6
Hammerdal • Sweden ... 16 H5
Hammerfest • Norway ... 16 L1
Hammershus • Denmark ... 95 F16
Hammond • LA, United States ... 118 K4
Hamoyet, Jabal • Eritrea/Sudan ... 18 C6
Hampden • New Zealand ... 35 C7
Hampi Heritage C • India ... 63 [128]
Hampi • India ... 106 D2
Hampshire • United Kingdom ... 75 A6
Hampstead • United Kingdom ... 74 E1
Hampton • VA, United States ... 118 H3
Hampton Court • United Kingdom ... 74 E1
Hampton Nat. Hist. Site Park •
  MD, United States ... 121 [281]
Hamra Nat. Park Park • Sweden ... 72 [24]
Hamun-e Jaz Murian • Iran ... 18 G4
Han • Rep. of Korea ... 30 D6
Han Shui • China ... 29 E4
Han-sur-Lesse • Belgium ... 80 A19
Hana • HI, United States ... 119 L4
Hanamaki • Japan ... 30 K5
Hanang • Tanzania ... 102 H2
Hanau • Germany ... 82 G4
Hancesti • Moldova ... 14 P3
Handan • China ... 29 E3
Handen • Sweden ... 95 D4
Handlová • Slovak Rep. ... 13 H9
Hanford • CA, United States ... 117 F3
Hangklip, Cape • South Africa ... 100 C5
Hangö • Finland ... 95 E4
Hangzhou • China ... 107 J3
Hangzhou Wan • China ... 107 J4
Haniá Beach • Crete, Greece ... 69 [188]
Haniá • Crete, Greece ... 93 E3
Haniá [Adm] • Crete, Greece ... 93 E1
Haninge • Sweden ... 16 J7
Hanión, Kólpos • Crete, Greece ... 93 E1
Haniótis Beach • Greece ... 69 [169]
Haniótis • Greece ... 92 D1
Haniótis • Greece ... 92 D1
Hanita • Israel ... 98 A1
Hankey • South Africa ... 100 C8
Hanko • Finland ... 95 E4
Hanmer Springs • New Zealand ... 35 D6
Hann, Mt • WA, Australia ... 34 E3
Hanna • AL, Canada ... 38 I6
Hannover • Germany ... 8 E4
Hannut • Belgium ... 80 A16
Hanöbukten • Sweden ... 95 F12
Hanoi • Vietnam ... 31 D2
Hanover • NH, United States ... 118 H1
Hansapark Park • Germany ... 73 [52]
Hanshan • China ... 107 J1
Hansi • India ... 105 C2
Hantsholm • Denmark ... 95 F6
Hanumangarh • India ... 105 C2
Hanzhong • China ... 29 D4
Hao • French Polynesia ... 33 M7
Haora • India ... 28 E4
Haouaria, El • Tunisia ... 101 E2
Haparanda • Sweden ... 16 M4
Hapsu • D.P.R. of Korea ... 30 E4
Har Sai Shan • China ... 29 B3
Harad • Saudi Arabia ... 18 E5
Hárakas • Crete, Greece ... 15 G9
Haraki • Rhodes, Greece ... 93 F4
Haramachi • Japan ... 30 K6
Haraz • Chad ... 22 H2
Harazah • Sudan ... 21 F4
Harazé Mangueigne • Chad ... 23 C2
Harbin • China ... 29 H1
Harbo • Sweden ... 95 D1
Harboør • Denmark ... 95 F9
Harbour Breton • NF, Canada ... 123 D3
Harbour Grace • NF, Canada ... 123 D4
Harbour, Lake • NU, Canada ... 39 R4
Harbour Park, Littlehampton Park •
  ... 73 [38]
Hardangerfjorden • Norway ... 94 C3
Hardangerjøkulen • Norway ... 94 C4
Hardangervidda • Norway ... 94 C4
Hardangervidda Nat. Park Park •
  Norway ... 72 [15]
Hardangervidda Nat. Park •
  Norway ... 94 C4
Hardenberg • Netherlands ... 5 J2
Harderwijk • Netherlands ... 80 A7
Harderwijk, Zeedierenpark •
  Netherlands ... 80 A7
Hardheim • Germany ... 82 G5
Harding • South Africa ... 24 E6
Hardknott Pass • United Kingdom ... 74 C3
Hare Indian • NT, Canada ... 38 F3
Haredaland • Norway ... 94 C1
Haren • Germany ... 8 C4
Harer • Ethiopia ... 23 G2
Harestua • Norway ... 94 B2
Hargeysa • Somalia ... 23 G2
Hargeysa Nat. Park Park •
  Somalia ... 103 [67]
Harghita, Muntii • Romania ... 14 N2
Haría Beach •
  Lanzarote, Canary Is. ... 68 [94]
Haridwar • India ... 105 C3
Haringvliet • Netherlands ... 80 C3
Haringvliet Dam • Netherlands ... 80 C3
Harirud • Afghanistan ... 18 I3
Harjavalta • Finland ... 95 E1
Harlingen • Netherlands ... 80 A3
Harlow • United Kingdom ... 74 E1
Harmal • Goa, India ... 105 B1
Harmancik • Turkey ... 15 K4
Harmil • Eritrea ... 21 H4
Harney Basin •
  OR, United States ... 117 E4
Harney Lake • OR, United States ... 117 E4
Harney Peak • SD, United States ... 40 F3
Harnösand • Sweden ... 16 I5
Harpalpur • India ... 105 C7
Harper • Liberia ... 22 C4

Harpers Ferry Nat. Hist. Park Park •
  WV, United States ... 121 [270]
Harrachov • Czech Rep. ... 96 C2
Harrah, Al • Saudi Arabia ... 21 G1
Harrat al 'Uwayrid •
  Saudi Arabia ... 21 G2
Harricana • QU, Canada ... 39 P6
Harrington Harbour • QU, Canada ... 39 T6
Harris • United Kingdom ... 6 F4
Harrisburgh • PA, United States ... 118 H1
Harrismith • South Africa ... 24 D5
Harrison Point • Barbados ... 125 H1
Harrison's Cave • Barbados ... 125 H3
Harrisonburg •
  VA, United States ... 41 K4
Harrogate • United Kingdom ... 7 K8
Harsho • Somalia ... 23 H1
Harstad • Norway ... 16 I2
Harsum • Germany ... 8 E4
Hart, Lake • FL, United States ... 121 C2
Hartgeipen • Norway ... 94 C4
Hartford • CT, United States ... 118 H2
Hartland Covered Bridge •
  NB, Canada ... 123 D6
Hartland Point • United Kingdom ... 74 F1
Hartlepool • United Kingdom ... 7 K7
Hartola • Finland ... 95 E2
Haruj al Aswad, Al • Libya ... 21 C2
Harun, Bukit • Indonesia ... 31 F6
Harun, Bukit • Indonesia ... 32 F2
Harvey • WA, Australia ... 34 C6
Harwich • United Kingdom ... 74 E2
Haryana • India ... 105 C2
Harz • Germany ... 8 G5
Hasa, Al • Saudi Arabia ... 18 E4
Hasakah, Al • Syria ... 18 D2
Hasbaya • Lebanon ... 98 A2
Hase • Germany ... 8 C4
Hasi Ausert • Western Sahara ... 20 C4
Haslemere • United Kingdom ... 7 L10
Haslev • Denmark ... 95 F14
Hassan • India ... 106 D6
Hasselt • Belgium ... 80 A15
Hassi Bel Guebbour • Algeria ... 20 G2
Hassi Messaoud • Algeria ... 20 G2
Hassi Seouenout • Algeria ... 20 G2
Hässleholm • Sweden ... 95 F11
Hastings • FL, United States ... 118 E4
Hastings • New Zealand ... 112 K4
Hasvik • Norway ... 16 L1
Hat Yai • Thailand ... 31 C5
Hatfield • United Kingdom ... 74 E1
Hatgal • Mongolia ... 27 F6
Hathras • India ... 105 C3
Hatillo • Puerto Rico ... 125 E1
Hatra Heritage C • Iraq ... 64 [250]
Hatteras, Cape •
  NC, United States ... 118 H5
Hatteras, Cape, Nat. Seashore •
  NC, United States ... 118 H5
Hattiesburg • MS, United States ... 118 K2
Hattingen • Germany ... 81 E2
Hattula • Finland ... 95 E2
Hattusha Heritage C • Turkey ... 64 [192]
Hatvan • Hungary ... 13 I10
Haugesund • Norway ... 94 C5
Hauhungaroa Range • New Zealand ... 112 K4
Haukeligrend • Norway ... 16 E7
Haukipudas • Finland ... 16 M4
Haukivesi • Finland ... 16 O5
Hauraki Gulf • New Zealand ... 35 E3
Hauroko, Lake • New Zealand ... 112 J3
Haus in Ennstal Ski • Austria ... 70 [182]
Hausa • Western Sahara ... 20 C3
Haut Atlas • Morocco ... 101 D4
Haut Médoc • France ... 84 B3
Haut Zaïre • Dem. Rep. of Congo ... 23 D3
Haute Corse • Corsica, France ... 85 L2
Haute Normandie • France ... 84 A1
Haute Savoie • France ... 85 F2
Haute-Touche, Parc de la •
  France ... 84 D4
Hautefort • France ... 85 G2
Hautes Fagnes • Belgium ... 5 I4
Hautes Pyrénées • France ... 85 J2
Hautmont • France ... 5 G4
Hauts Plateaux • Algeria ... 20 F2
Hauula • HI, United States ... 119 L1
Hauzenberg • Germany ... 9 J8
Havana Heritage C • Cuba ... 62 [34]
Havana • Cuba ... 124 D1
Havant • United Kingdom ... 7 L11
Havasu, Lake •
  AZ/NV, United States ... 118 J1
Havel • Germany ... 8 I3
Havelkanal • Germany ... 81 F1
Havelland • Germany ... 81 D2
Havelock North • New Zealand ... 112 K4
Havelte • Netherlands ... 80 A6
Haverthwaite • United Kingdom ... 74 C3
Havirov • Czech Rep. ... 13 H8
Havlickuv Brod • Czech Rep. ... 96 C2
Havnsø • Denmark ... 95 F10
Havøysund • Norway ... 16 M1
Havre • MT, United States ... 40 E2
Havre, le • France ... 10 F4
Havre-Aubert • QU, Canada ... 123 D2
Havre-St Pierre • QU, Canada ... 123 D2
Havsa • Turkey ... 15 H2
Haw Par Dragon World •
  Singapore ... 108 E3
Hawaii • Pacific Ocean ... 119 L
Hawaii [I.] • HI, United States ... 119 L8
Hawaii Volcanoes Nat. Park Heritage N •
  HI, United States ... 60 [8]
Hawaii Volcanoes Nat. Park •
  HI, United States ... 119 L8
Hawaii Volcanoes Nat. Park Park •
  HI, United States ... 120 [22]
Hawaiian Is. cruise area •
  Pacific Ocean ... 58 A1
Hawalli • Kuwait ... 18 E4
Hawd • Ethiopia/Somalia ... 23 H2
Hawea • New Zealand ... 112 L2
Hawea, Lake • New Zealand ... 112 L2
Hawera • New Zealand ... 112 K3
Haweswater Reservoir •
  United Kingdom ... 74 C2
Hawi • HI, United States ... 119 L8
Hawick • United Kingdom ... 6 J6
Hawke Bay • New Zealand ... 35 F4
Hawke's Bay [Adm] • New Zealand ... 112 K4
Hawkes, Mt • Antarctica ... 46 (1) JJ1
Hawkshead • United Kingdom ... 74 C4
Hawkshead Beach •
  Antigua & Barbuda ... 125 F1
Hawng Tuk • Myanmar ... 31 B2
Hawrami • NT, Australia ... 112 H4
Hawthorne • FL, United States ... 117 M8
Hawthorne, Mt • Antarctica ... 46 (1) FF3
Hay • AL, Canada ... 38 H5
Hay • NS, Australia ... 111 G1
Hay River • NT, Canada ... 38 H4
Hay River • TX, United States ... 119 N2
Hay-on-Wye • United Kingdom ... 74 D3
Hayes • MN, United States ... 38 M5
Hayes, Mt • AK, United States ... 46 EE3
Hayling I. Beach •
  United Kingdom ... 75 [79]

Hayman I. • QL, Australia ... 111 F1
Haymana • Turkey ... 15 N4
Haynesville • LA, United States ... 118 K1
Hayrabolu • Turkey ... 15 H2
Haystack Ski •
  VT, United States ... 116 [195]
Hayya • Sudan ... 21 G4
Hazebrouck • France ... 10 H3
Hazleton • PA, United States ... 118 H1
Hazor • Israel ... 98 A2
He Xian • China ... 107 J1
Heacham Beach • United Kingdom ... 75 [39]
Head of Bight • SA, Australia ... 34 H6
Head-Smashed-In Buffalo Jump Heritage C •
  AL, Canada ... 62 [2]
Healdsburg • CA, United States ... 117 F3
Heard I. • Indian Ocean ... 19 (1) B2
Heard Island N •
  Indian Ocean ... 61 [138]
Hearne • TX, United States ... 119 N3
Hearst San Simeon State Hist. Mon. •
  CA, United States ... 117 F3
Heart of England •
  United Kingdom ... 74 D
Heathrow [Apt] • United Kingdom ... 74 E1
Heavenly Ski •
  NV, United States ... 116 [68]
Hebbronville •
  TX, United States ... 119 N5
Hebei • China ... 107 G3
Hebi • China ... 29 E3
Hebrides, Inner •
  United Kingdom ... 6 F5
Hebrides, Outer •
  United Kingdom ... 6 E4
Hebrides, Sea of •
  United Kingdom ... 6 E4
Hebron • NF, Canada ... 39 S5
Hebron • Jordan ... 98 A7
Hecate Strait • BC, Canada ... 38 E6
Hechingen • Germany ... 82 G7
Hechuan • China ... 29 D4
Hed • Sweden ... 95 D1
Heddal stavkirke • Norway ... 94 B3
Heddalsvatnet • Norway ... 94 B3
Hedehusum • Sweden ... 95 F11
Hedemora • Sweden ... 16 F5
Hedesundafjärden • Sweden ... 95 D1
Hedmark • Norway ... 16 F5
Hedon • United Kingdom ... 74 E1
Heemstede • Netherlands ... 80 C1
Heerde • Netherlands ... 80 A3
Heerenlogement Cave •
  South Africa ... 100 C1
Heerenveen • Netherlands ... 80 A3
Heerlen • Netherlands ... 80 A16
Hefa • Israel ... 98 A3
Hefei • China ... 29 F4
Hegang • China ... 29 I1
Hegura • Japan ... 30 I6
Hei Ling Chau •
  Hong Kong, China. ... 107 H5
Heide • Germany ... 8 E2
Heide-Park Park • Germany ... 73 [54]
Heidelberg • Germany ... 82 G4
Heidenheim an der Brenz •
  Germany ... 9 F8
Heilbron • Germany ... 82 G6
Heilbronn • Germany ... 82 G6
Heiligenberg, Schloß • Germany ... 82 J5
Heiligenblut • Austria ... 89 H8
Heiligendamm Spa • Germany ... 83 [269]
Heiligenhafen • Germany ... 8 G2
Heiligenhafen Spa • Germany ... 83 [21]
Heiligenhaus • Germany ... 81 E1
Heiligenstadt • Germany ... 8 F5
Heilong Jiang • China ... 27 K7
Heilongjiang • China ... 107 G4
Heimaey • Iceland ... 16 (1) C3
Heimdal • Norway ... 16 F5
Heinola Beach • Finland ... 69 [11]
Heinola • Finland ... 95 E2
Heishan Xia • China ... 29 D3
Hekla • Iceland ... 16 (1) D2
Hel • Poland ... 13 H3
Helagsfjället • Sweden ... 16 G5
Helen Reef • Palau ... 32 (1) D2
Helen's Bay Beach •
  United Kingdom ... 75 [226]
Helena • MT, United States ... 40 D2
Helengeli • Maldives ... 106 E2
Helensburgh • United Kingdom ... 74 B3
Helgasjön • Sweden ... 95 F7
Helgeland • Norway ... 16 G4
Helgoland • Germany ... 8 D2
Helgolander Bucht • Germany ... 8 D2
Heliopolis • Egypt ... 101 F2
Hellendorn, Avonturenpark •
  Netherlands ... 80 A8
Hellesylt • Norway ... 94 C2
Hellevoetsluis • Netherlands ... 80 C3
Hellin • Spain ... 11 J6
Hellinikon [Apt] • Greece ... 92 D4
Hellinikon [Apt] • Greece ... 92 D4
Hells Canyon Nat. Recreation Area •
  ID/OR, United States ... 117 E4
Hells Gate Nat. Park • Kenya ... 101 G3
Hellshire Hills • Jamaica ... 124 C4
Helme • Germany ... 8 G5
Helmond • Afghanistan ... 18 I4
Helmond • Netherlands ... 80 A11
Helmsdorf • Germany ... 8 G4
Helong • China ... 30 E3
Helsingborg • Sweden ... 95 F11
Helsinge Beach • Denmark ... 68 [22]
Helsingfors Heritage C •
  Finland ... 64 [8]
Helsingfors • Finland ... 95 E4
Helsingør Beach • Denmark ... 68 [22]
Helsinki Heritage C • Finland ... 64 [8]
Helsinki • Finland ... 95 E4
Helston • United Kingdom ... 74 F4
Helvellyn • United Kingdom ... 74 C2
Helwân • Egypt ... 101 F2
Hemel Hempstead •
  United Kingdom ... 7 L10
Hemer • Germany ... 81 E2
Hemmoor • Germany ... 8 E3
Hempstead • TX, United States ... 119 N4
Hemsedal • Norway ... 94 C4
Henan • China ... 107 G7
Henares • Spain ... 11 I4
Henbury • NT, Australia ... 112 H4
Henbury meteorite craters •
  NT, Australia ... 112 H4
Hendaye • France ... 85 J1
Henderson • NV, United States ... 117 F4
Henderson • TX, United States ... 119 N4
Henderson I. Heritage N •
  Pacific Ocean ... 60 [142]
Heng Shan • Shanxi, China ... 107 G3
Heng Shan • Hunan, China ... 107 G7
Hengduan Shan • China ... 31 B1
Hengelo • Netherlands ... 80 A8

Hengqin • China ... 107 H3
Hengshui • China ... 29 F3
Hengyang • China ... 29 E5
Hénin-Beaumont • France ... 5 F3
Hennebont • France ... 84 C4
Hennigsdorf • Germany ... 81 F1
Henrietta Maria, Cape •
  OT, Canada ... 39 O5
Henry, Cape • VA, United States ... 118 H5
Henzada • Myanmar ... 31 B3
Heping • China ... 29 F6
Heptapegon • Israel ... 98 A4
Héradsvötn • Iceland ... 16 (1) D2
Herakleion • Crete, Greece ... 93 E3
Herald Cays • CL, Australia ... 111 F1
Herat • Afghanistan ... 18 H3
Herborn • Germany ... 82 G2
Herbstein Spa • Germany ... 83 [135]
Herculaneum Heritage C • Italy ... 64 [128]
Herculaneum • Italy ... 91 G3
Herdecke • Germany ... 81 E2
Heredia • Costa Rica ... 37 E5
Hereford • TX, United States ... 40 F5
Hereford • United Kingdom ... 74 D3
Hereford & Worcester •
  United Kingdom ... 74 D1
Hereke • Turkey ... 15 K3
Herentals • Belgium ... 80 A11
Herford • Germany ... 8 D4
Hergiswil • Switzerland ... 89 G3
Hergla • Tunisia ... 101 E2
Heringsdorf • Germany ... 8 J3
Heringsdorf Spa • Germany ... 83 [285]
Herisau • Switzerland ... 9 E9
Heritage Quay •
  Antigua & Barbuda ... 125 F1
Herm • Channel Is. ... 75 A8
Hermannsburg • NT, Australia ... 112 H2
Hermannsburg Aboriginal Land •
  NT, Australia ... 112 H2
Hermanus • Venezuela ... 43 E1
Hermansverk • Norway ... 94 C4
Hermanus • South Africa ... 100 C5
Hermitage • France ... 84 B4
Hermitage, The • Bahamas ... 124 B2
Hermon, Mount • Lebanon/Syria ... 98 A2
Hermosillo • Mexico ... 40 D6
Hermsdorf • Germany ... 9 G6
Hernád • Slovak Rep. ... 13 K9
Hernani • Spain ... 11 J1
Herne • Germany ... 81 E2
Herne Bay • United Kingdom ... 74 E2
Herne: Wanne-Eickel • Germany ... 81 E2
Herning • Denmark ... 95 F9
Herodium • Jordan ... 98 A8
Heroine's monument •
  Phuket, Thailand ... 109 K1
Herolds Bay • South Africa ... 100 C7
Heron I. • QL, Australia ... 111 F4
Herouval, le Bois • France ... 5 F4
Herräng • Sweden ... 95 D2
Herrenchiemsee, Schloß •
  Germany ... 82 J4
Herra de Pisuerga • Spain ... 11 G2
Herrljunga • Sweden ... 95 F3
Herrnsheim • Germany ... 82 H4
Herrsching • Germany ... 82 H4
Hershey • PA, United States ... 118 H1
Herstal • Belgium ... 5 I4
Herten • Germany ... 81 E2
Hertford • United Kingdom ... 74 E1
Hertfordshire • United Kingdom ... 74 E1
Hervey Bay • QL, Australia ... 111 F4
Herzberg • Germany ... 8 F5
Herzogenaurach • Germany ... 9 F7
Herzogenrath • Germany ... 5 I4
Hesdin • France ... 5 F4
Heshbon • Jordan ... 98 A7
Hesse • Germany ... 81 D3
Hessen • Germany ... 9 D6
Hessisch Lichtenau • Germany ... 8 F5
Hettstedt • Germany ... 8 G5
Hever Castle • United Kingdom ... 74 E1
Heves • Hungary ... 13 J10
Hevananorra [Apt] • St Lucia ... 125 J4
Hexham • United Kingdom ... 74 C2
Hexrivierberge • South Africa ... 100 C5
Heysham • United Kingdom ... 78 A5
Heyuan • China ... 107 G7
Heywood • VI, Australia ... 34 H7
Heywoods Beach • Barbados ... 125 H1
Heze • China ... 29 F3
Hialeah • FL, United States ... 119 M8
Hibbing • MN, United States ... 118 K1
Hicacos, Peninsula de • Cuba ... 124 C2
Hida-Sanmyaku • Japan ... 30 J6
Hidaka-Sammyaku • Japan ... 37 B3
Hidalgo • Mexico ... 40 E6
Hidalgo del Parral • Mexico ... 40 E6
Hidalgo, Miguel [Apt] • Mexico ... 40 E6
Hidcote Manor • United Kingdom ... 74 D4
Hidden Valley Ski •
  PA, United States ... 116 [159]
Hiddensee • Germany ... 8 I2
Hiddensee Spa • Germany ... 83 [278]
Hiddensee • Germany ... 83 [95]
Hienghene • New Caledonia ... 35 (1) F4
Hierakonpolis • Egypt ... 101 F5
Hierapolis • Turkey ... 92 D6
Hierapolis • Turkey ... 92 D6
Hierapolis-Pamukkale Heritage N •
  Turkey ... 61 [62]
Hierapolis-Pamukkale Heritage C •
  Turkey ... 64 [189]
Hierro • Canary Is. ... 87 E5
High Island Reservoir •
  Hong Kong, China ... 107 H6
High Point • NC, United States ... 41 K4
High Rock • Bahamas ... 124 B2
High Street • United Kingdom ... 74 C2
High Willhays • United Kingdom ... 74 F1
High Wycombe • United Kingdom ... 7 L10
Highland • Jamaica ... 124 C4
Highland • United Kingdom ... 75 A1
Highland Park •
  Ko Samui, Thailand. ... 109 J1
Highlands Forest Reserve •
  Penang, Malaysia. ... 108 C2
Highlands Hammock State Recreation Area •
  FL, United States ... 119 M5
Highlands, North West •
  ... 6 G4
Highveld • Zimbabwe ... 102 J4
Higüero, Punta • Puerto Rico ... 125 E1
Higüey • Dominican Rep. ... 37 H4
Hiiiumaa • Estonia ... 16 L7
Hiitola • Russian Fed. ... 16 L6
Hijar • Spain ... 11 J3
Hijaz, Al • Saudi Arabia ... 18 C5
Hikkaduwa • Sri Lanka ... 106 D15
Hikurangi [Mtn] • New Zealand ... 35 G3
Hila • Indonesia ... 32 (1) C4
Hildburghausen • Germany ... 9 F6

Hilden • Germany 81 E3
Hildesheim • Germany 8 E4
Hildesheim Heritage C • Germany .. 64 [36]
Hilisimaetano • Indonesia 110 B3
Hill End • NS, Australia 111 G2
Hill Head Beach •
  United Kingdom .... 75 [80]
Hillaby, Mt • Barbados 125 H1
Hillah, Al • Iraq 18 D3
Hillah, Al • Saudi Arabia 18 E5
Hillegom • Netherlands 80 C1
Hillerød • Denmark 95 F10
Hillsboro • TX, United States 119 N1
Hilo • HI, United States 119 L8
Hilpoltstein • Germany 9 G7
Hilvarenbeek • Netherlands 80 A11
Hilversum • Netherlands 80 C2
Himachal Pradesh • India 28 C2
Himalaya • Asia 28 E3
Himarë • Albania 15 A3
Himeji • Japan 30 H7
Himeji Heritage C • Japan .... 63 [165]
Himmafushi • Maldives 106 E2
Himmerland • Denmark 95 F5
Himos • Finland 95 E2
Hin Khom, Laem •
  Ko Samui, Thailand 109 J2
Hinakiyah, Al • Saudi Arabia 18 D5
Hinca Renancó • Argentina 44 D5
Hinchinbrook I. • QL, Australia ... 111 F1
Hindelang • Germany 82 J6
Hindelang Spa • Germany .... 83 [243]
Hindsholm • Denmark 95 F10
Hindu Kush • Asia 28 B1
Hindupur • India 106 D6
Hindustan • India 28 C3
Hinganghat • India 28 C4
Hinggan Ling • China 25 M5
Hinlad Falls •
  Ko Samui, Thailand 109 J1
Hinnøya • Norway 16 H2
Hinojosa del Duque • Spain 11 F6
Hins • Syria 18 C3
Hinterglemm • Austria 89 H3
Hintertux Ski • Austria .... 70 [141]
Hintertux • Austria 89 H7
Hinterzarten Spa • Germany ..... 83 [209]
Hios Heritage C • Greece .... 64 [184]
Hios • Greece 92 D5
Hios • Greece 92 D5
Hios [I.] • Greece 92 D5
Hios [I.] • Greece 92 D5
Hippos • Israel 98 A4
Hirado • Japan 30 E8
Hirara • Japan 29 H6
Hirebhasgar Reservoir • India ... 106 D6
Hirfanli Baraji Gölü • Turkey 15 O4
Hirhafok • Algeria 20 G4
Hiroo • Japan 30 L3
Hirosaki • Japan 30 K4
Hiroshima • Japan 30 F7
Hiroshima Heritage C • Japan ... 63 [163]
Hirschegg Ski • Austria .... 70 [128]
Hirschegg • Austria 89 H1
Hirson • France J4
Hirsova • Romania 97 D2
Hirtshals Beach • Denmark .... 68 [29]
Hirtshals • Denmark 95 F6
Hisar • India 105 C2
Hispaniola • West Indies 37 G3
Histria • Romania 97 D2
Hitachi • Japan 30 F8
Hitoyoshi • Japan 30 F8
Hitra • Norway 16 E5
Hjallerup • Denmark 95 F6
Hjälmaren • Sweden 95 D3
Hjelm Bugt • Denmark 95 F15
Hjelmeland • Norway 94 C5
Hjo • Sweden 95 F3
Hjørring Beach • Denmark .... 68 [29]
Hjørring • Denmark 95 F6
Hlane Game Sanctuary Park •
  Swaziland .... 103 [131]
Hlohovec • Slovak Rep. 13 G9
Hluboká • Czech Rep. 96 C4
Hluhluwe/Umfolozi Game Reserve Park •
  South Africa .... 103 [128]
Ho • Ghana 22 E3
Ho Chi Minh City • Vietnam 108 B1
Hoa Da • Vietnam 108 B2
Hoanib • Namibia 24 A3
Hobart • TS, Australia 34 I8
Hobbs • NM, United States 40 F5
Hobq Shamo • China 29 D3
Hobro • Denmark 95 F9
Hobya Obbia • Somalia 23 H2
Hoch Harz, Nationalpark Park •
  Germany .... 72 [63]
Hochbrig • Switzerland 89 G3
Höchenschwand Spa • Germany ... 83 [207]
Hochfeiler • Austria/Italy 90 B1
Hochgolling • Austria 9 H3
Hochgurgl Ski • Austria .... 70 [136]
Hochgurgl • Austria 89 H6
Höchneukirch • Germany 81 E3
Hochschwab • Austria 13 E10
Höchseiden • Austria 89 H6
Höchstadt an der Aisch •
  Germany 9 F7
Hockenheim • Germany 5 L5
Hockenheim • Germany 82 G4
Hodeida • Yemen 18 D7
Hodh • Mauritania 20 D5
Hódmezővásárhely • Hungary 13 J11
Hodna, Chott el • Algeria 20 F1
Hodonín • Czech Rep. 13 G9
Hoek van Holland • Netherlands ... 80 C3
Hoekse Waard • Netherlands 80 C3
Höfn • Iceland .... 16 I (1) F2
Hofors • Sweden 16 I6
Höfsjökull • Iceland .... 16 I (1) D2
Höfu • Japan 30 E7
Höganäs • Sweden 95 F11
Hogarth, Mt • NT, Australia 34 G4
Högby • Sweden 95 F8
Hoggar • Algeria 100 A1
Hogland • Russian Fed. 16 N6
Högsby • Sweden 82 J8
Hogsfjorden • Norway 94 C5
Hagsforden • Norway 95 C4
Hoh Xil Nur • China 28 F1
Hoh Zil Shan • China 28 E1
Hohe Acht • Germany 82 H1
Hohe Tauern, Nationalpark Park •
  Austria .... 72 [82]
Hohe Tauern, Nationalpark Park •
  Austria 89 H6
Hohe Wilde • Austria/Italy 90 B1
Hohenau • Germany .... 83 [81]
Hohenbrunn • Germany 81 F1
Hohenheck Spa • Germany .... 83 [175]
Hohenschwangau • Germany 82 J6
Hohentwiel • Germany 82 G8
Hohenzollern, Schloß • Germany ... 82 G6

Hohhot • China 29 E2
Hohneck • France 10 L5
Hohneck, Burg • Germany 82 H4
Hohokam Pima Nat. Mon. Park •
  AZ, United States .... 120 [112]
Hohwacht Spa • Germany .... 83 [19]
Hoima • Uganda 23 E3
Hok-Kai • Japan 30 M2
Hokensås • Sweden 95 F3
Hokitika • New Zealand 35 C6
Hokkaido • Japan 30 M3
Hokksund • Norway 94 B1
Hol • Norway 94 C4
Holasovice • Czech Rep. 96 C4
Holbæk Beach • Denmark .... 68 [24]
Holbæk • Denmark 95 F10
Holbrook • AZ, United States 40 D5
Holburgen • Sweden 16 J8
Hølen • Norway 94 B4
Holetown • Barbados 125 H3
Holguín • Cuba 124 D8
Holiday Mtn Ski •
  NY, United States .... 116 [179]
Holiday Park Park • Germany ..... 73 [63]
Holiday Valley Ski •
  NY, United States .... 116 [172]
Höljes • Sweden 16 G6
Hollabrunn • Austria 13 F9
Hollandse IJssel • Netherlands 80 C4
Hollant Beach • Goa, India 105 B2
Holleia • Norway 94 B1
Hollókö Heritage C • Hungary .... 64 [152]
Hollywood • CA, United States ... 117 F6
Hollywood • FL, United States ... 119 M8
Holman I. • NT, Canada 38 H2
Holmes Hill • St Kitts & Nevis .. 125 C4
Holmes Reefs • C, Australia 33 F7
Holmestrand • Norway 94 B3
Holmsland Beach • Denmark .... 68 [31]
Holmsland Klit • Denmark 95 F9
Holmsund • Sweden 16 K5
Holö • Sweden 95 D4
Holomóndas • Greece 15 E3
Holsnøy • Norway 94 C3
Holstebro • Denmark 95 F9
Holsteinsborg • Greenland 39 U3
Holsworthy • United Kingdom 74 F2
Holtyn-Daba • Mongolia 27 G7
Holy I. • England, UK 6 K6
Holy I. • Wales, UK 7 H8
Holy I. Beach • United Kingdom 75 [205-208]
Holy Land • Asia .... 98 A
Holyhead • United Kingdom 7 H8
Holywood Park Park • Germany .... 73 [58]
Holzgau • Austria 89 H2
Holzkirchen • Germany 82 J3
Holzminden • Germany 8 E5
Holzwickede • Germany 81 E2
Homa Bay • Kenya 101 G3
Homalin • Myanmar 31 B2
Homberg • Germany 9 E5
Hombori • Mali 20 E4
Homburg • Germany 9 C7
Home Bay • NU, Canada 39 R3
Home Hill • QL, Australia 111 F1
Homer • Belarus 17 E4
Homer • AK, United States 46 EE4
Homestead • FL, United States ... 119 M8
Homestead Nat. Mon. of America Park •
  NE, United States .... 121 [167]
Homewood Ski •
  CA, United States .... 116 [56]
Homoljske Planina •
  F.R. of Yugoslavia 14 I5
Homossassa Springs State Wildlife Park •
  FL, United States 119 M5
Homr, El • Algeria 20 F3
Hon Chong • Vietnam 108 B3
Hon Khoai • Vietnam 108 B3
Hon Lon • Vietnam 108 B2
Hon Quan • Vietnam 108 B2
Hon Tre • Vietnam 108 B2
Honakaa • HI, United States 119 L8
Honavar • India 106 D5
Honaz Dagi • Turkey 15 K6
Honda • Colombia 43 C2
Hondo • Japan 30 E8
Hondo • Belize/Mexico 37 D4
Honduras • C. America 37 D5
Honduras, Golfo de • C. America ... 37 D4
Hønefoss • Norway 94 B1
Honey Lake Resort •
  Shenzhen, China 107 H3
Honfleur • France 10 F4
Hong Kong Central •
  Hong Kong, China 107 H5
Hong Kong I. • Hong Kong, China .. 107 H5
Hong Kong Special Administrative Region •
  China 107 H2
Hong, Song • Vietnam 108 A1
Hongch'on • Rep. of Korea 30 D6
Hongor • Mongolia 29 E1
Hongqiao [Apt] • China 107 J2
Hongsong • Rep. of Korea 30 D6
Honguedo, Détroit d' •
  QU, Canada 123 D2
Hongwon • D.P.R. of Korea 30 D5
Honiara • Solomon Is. 35 (1) F2
Honister Pass • United Kingdom ... 74 C1
Honiton • United Kingdom 74 F2
Honjo • Japan 30 K5
Honkajoki • Finland 95 F9
Hanne Strand • Denmark 95 F9
Honningsvåg • Norway 16 M1
Honolulu • HI, United States 119 L6
Honrubia • Spain 11 I5
Hons • Syria 18 C3
Honshu • Japan 30 J5
Hood, Fort • TX, United States ... 119 N3
Hood, Mt • OR, United States 117 E3
Hoofddorp • Netherlands 80 C1
Hoogeveen • Netherlands 80 A8
Hoogezand • Netherlands 80 A4
Hoogvliet • Netherlands 80 C3
Hook I. • QL, Australia 111 F1
Hook of Holland • Netherlands 80 C3
Hoonah • AK, United States 38 D5
Hooper, Cape • NU, Canada 39 R3
Höör • Sweden 95 F11
Hoorn • Netherlands 80 A7
Hoover Dam •
  AZ/NV, United States 118 J1
Hoover, Herbert, Nat. Hist. Site Park •
  IA, United States .... 121 [169]
Hope • AR, United States 41 H5
Hope • BC, Canada 122 C3
Hope Bay • Antarctica 59 A10
Hope Bay • Jamaica 124 C2
Hope Town • Bahamas 124 B2
Hopes Advance, Cap • QU, Canada .. 39 R4
Hopetoun • WA, Australia 34 D6
Hopetoun • VI, Australia 34 H7
Hopewell Culture Nat. Hist. Park Park •
  OH, United States .... 121 [186]
Hopewell Furnace Nat. Hist. Site Park •
  PA, United States .... 121 [306]

Hopfen am See Spa • Germany ... 83 [244]
Hopfenberg Spa • Germany .... 83 [89]
Hopfgarten im Brixental Ski •
  Austria .... 70 [149]
Hopi Indian Reservation •
  AZ, United States 118 J1
Hopkins, Lake • WA, Australia ... 112 H3
Hóra • Greece 15 C6
Horain • Turkey 93 G3
Horb • Germany 9 D8
Horbat Ashdod Yam • Israel 98 A5
Hörby • Sweden 95 F11
Hordaland • Norway 94 C4
Horefto • Greece 92 D4
Horefto • Greece 92 D4
Horezu Heritage C • Romania .... 64 [164]
Horlivka • Ukraine 17 F5
Hormiguéros • Puerto Rico 125 E3
Hormoz, Küh-e • Iran 18 F4
Hormoz • Iran 18 G4
Hormuz, Strait of • Iran/Oman 18 G4
Horn • Iceland .... 16 I (1) B1
Horn, Cape • Chile 45 C7
Horn, Is. de • Wallis & Futuna . 35 (2) E1
Horn Plateau • NT, Canada 38 H4
Hornavan • Sweden 16 J3
Hornberg, Burg • Germany 82 G4
Horncastle • United Kingdom 5 C1
Hornefors • Sweden 16 J5
Hornindalsvatn • Norway 94 C1
Horngrindie • Germany 82 G8
Hornos, Cabo de • Chile 45 C7
Horovice • Czech Rep. 96 C1
Horqin Youyi Qiangqi • China 29 G1
Horqin Zuoyi Zhongqi • China 27 J8
Horse Is. • NF, Canada 123 D3
Horsens Beach • Denmark .... 68 [27]
Horsens • Denmark 95 F9
Horseshoe Bend Nat. Military Park Park •
  AL, United States .... 121 [205]
Horsham • VI, Australia 34 H7
Horsham • United Kingdom 74 E3
Horst, Schloß • Germany 81 E2
Horta • Azores 88 B1
Hortas do Tabual • Portugal 88 E5
Hórto • Greece 92 D4
Hortobágyi Nat. Park Park •
  Hungary .... 72 [105]
Horton • NT, Canada 38 F3
Horumersil Spa • Germany .... 83 [48]
Horyuji Heritage C • Japan .... 63 [166]
Hosaina • Ethiopia 23 F2
Hösbach • Germany 9 E6
Hoséré Vokré • Cameroon 22 G3
Hoskins • Papua New Guinea 35 (1) E2
Hosokawa • Japan 106 D2
Hospet • India 106 D2
Hospitalet de Llobregat, l' •
  Spain 11 N3
Hossegor • France 85 G3
Hossmo • Sweden 95 F8
Hoste, I. • Chile 45 C7
Hot • Thailand 109 G3
Hot Springs • SD, United States .. 40 F3
Hot Springs Nat. Park Park •
  AR, United States .... 121 [193]
Hotan • China 26 M10
Hotazel • South Africa 24 C5
Hoting • Sweden 16 J4
Hottah Lake • NT, Canada 38 H3
Hottentots Holland Nature Reserve •
  South Africa 100 C5
Hotton • Belgium 80 A15
Houdan • France 85 E3
Houlton • ME, United States 118 G2
Houma • LA, United States 118 K4
Houma • China 29 E3
Houmt-Souk • Tunisia 101 E4
Houmt-Souq • Tunisia 101 E4
Houndé • Burkina Faso 22 D2
Hourtin Beach • France .... 68 [66]
Houston • TX, United States 119 N4
Houston • BC, Canada 122 C1
Houtribdijk • Netherlands 80 A7
Hov • Denmark 95 F10
Hovdevtta • Norway 94 C6
Hove • United Kingdom 7 L11
Hovenweep Nat. Mon. Park •
  CO, United States .... 120 [94]
Hovgården Heritage C • Sweden .. 64 [4]
Howa • Chad/Sudan 21 D4
Howe, Cape • NS/VI, Australia ... 111 G4
Howland • Pacific Ocean 33 J5
Howletts Park • United Kingdom ... 74 E3
Howth • Ireland 79 E2
Hoxie • AR, United States 41 H4
Hoy • United Kingdom 6 I3
Hayanger • Norway 94 C3
Hoyerswerda • Germany 8 J5
Hpunhpu • Myanmar 31 B1
Hradec Králové • Czech Rep. 96 C2
Hrissi • Greece 93 E8
Hrissoúpoli • Greece 15 F3
Hristianí • Greece 92 D11
Hristianí • Greece 92 D11
Hrodna • Belarus 13 M4
Hron • Slovak Rep. 13 H9
Hrubieszów • Poland 13 M7
Hruby Nisky Jeseník •
  Czech Rep. 13 G7
Hsinchu • Taiwan 29 G6
Hsophang • Myanmar 31 B2
Hu Men • China 107 H2
Hua Hin • Thailand 109 H3
Hua Shan • China 107 G3
Huacho • Peru 43 B5
Huacrachuco • Peru 43 B5
Huaira • China 29 F4
Huairen • China 29 E3
Huajuápan de León • Mexico 123 E4
Hualalai Indian Reservation •
  AZ, United States 118 J1
Hualien • Taiwan 29 G6
Huambo • Angola 23 B6
Hualcabamba • Peru 43 B6
Huancaní • Peru 127 B1
Huancavelica • Peru 127 B1
Huancayo • Peru 127 B1
Huang Hai • Asia 29 G3
Huang He • China 29 E3
Huang Shan Heritage N • China .. 61 [114]
Huang Shan Heritage C • China .. 63 [154]
Huang Shan • China 107 J3
Huang Shui • China 29 C3
Huanggang Liang • China 27 J8
Huanggang Heritage N • China ... 61 [116]
Huangmao Jian • China 31 F1
Huangshan • China 107 H1
Huangshan • China 107 H3
Huangtian [Apt] • China 107 H3
Huanren • China 30 C4
Huanta • Peru 127 B1
Huánuco • Peru 43 B6
Huaráz • Peru 127 B1
Huarás • Peru 43 B5
Huascarán • Peru 43 B5

Huascarán, Parque Nac. Heritage N •
  Peru .... 60 [32]
Huatabampo • Mexico 40 E6
Hubbell Trading Post Nat. Hist. Site •
  AZ, United States 118 J2
Hubbell Trading Post Nat. Hist. Site Park •
  AZ, United States .... 120 [104]
Hubei • China 107 G3
Hubli • India 106 D2
Hubsugul Nur • Mongolia 27 F6
Hückeswagen • Germany 81 E4
Hucknall • United Kingdom 7 K8
Hudaydah, Al • Yemen 18 D7
Huddersfield • United Kingdom 7 K8
Huddinge • Sweden 95 D4
Huddvheli • Maldives 106 E2
Hudhuveli • Maldives 106 E2
Hudiksvall • Sweden 16 I6
Hudson • United States 41 L3
Hudson Bay • SA, Canada 38 K6
Hudson Bay [Bay] • Canada 39 N5
Hudson Strait • NU/QU, Canada 39 Q4
Hue • Vietnam 31 D3
Hue Heritage C • Vietnam .... 63 [169]
Huedin • Romania 14 K3
Huelgoat • France 84 C1
Huelva • Spain 86 B1
Huercal-Overa • Spain 86 B4
Huertas, Cabo de las • Spain 11 K6
Huesca • Spain 11 K2
Huéscar • Spain 86 B4
Huevos I. • Trinidad & Tobago ... 125 K1
Huexotla • Mexico 123 E4
Huftarøy • Norway 94 C3
Húǐfǎh, Al • Saudi Arabia 18 E5
Hügel, Villa • Germany 81 E1
Hughenden • QL, Australia 34 H4
Hugo • OK, United States 119 N2
Hui • Brazil 43 C4
Hui Cheng • China 107 J3
Huiarau Range • New Zealand 112 K2
Huich'on • D.P.R. of Korea 29 H2
Huila • Colombia 43 B3
Huila • China 31 F2
Huiñamarca, Lago de •
  Bolivia/Peru 127 B4
Huisne • France 10 F5
Huiten Nur • China 28 F1
Huittinen • Finland 95 E2
Huiyang • China 107 H2
Huizen • Netherlands 80 C2
Huizhou • China 107 H2
Hula Falls • New Zealand 112 K2
Hukou • China 29 E3
Hukuntsi • Botswana 24 C4
Hula Valley • Israel 98 A2
Hulayfa' • Saudi Arabia 18 D4
Hulin • China 29 J1
Hull • QU, Canada 122 B7
Hüllhorst Spa • Germany .... 83 [85]
Hulst • Netherlands 80 A13
Hultsfred • Sweden 95 F8
Hulun Nur • China 27 I7
Hulwan • Egypt 101 G4
Humacao • Puerto Rico 125 E3
Humaita • Brazil 43 E5
Humber • United Kingdom 7 L8
Humboldt • New Caledonia 35 (2) B3
Humboldt • NV, United States 117 F2
Hume, Lake • NS, Australia 111 G3
Humenné • Slovak Rep. 13 K9
Humera • Brazil 107 H2
Humphreys Peak •
  AZ, United States 118 J1
Humppila • Finland 95 E2
Hun • Libya 21 C2
Hun • China 30 C4
Húnaflói • Iceland .... 16 I (1) C2
Hunan • China 107 G2
Hunchun • China 30 F3
Hundested Beach • Denmark .... 68 [22]
Hundested • Denmark 95 F10
Hundoara • Romania 14 J4
Hünfeld • Germany 9 E6
Hungarian Plain • Hungary 96 B2
Hungary • Europe 13 I10
Hüngnam • D.P.R. of Korea 30 D5
Hunjiang • China 30 D4
Hunneberg • Sweden 95 F3
Hunnebostrand • Sweden 95 F3
Hunsrück • Germany 82 H3
Hunstanton • United Kingdom 7 M9
Hunstanton Beach •
  United Kingdom .... 75 [40]
Hunte • Germany 8 D4
Hunter • New Caledonia 35 (2) C3
Hunter • NS, Australia 111 G2
Hunter Mtn Ski •
  NY, United States .... 116 [181]
Hunter Mtns • New Zealand 112 L3
Hunter Valley • NS, Australia ... 111 E4
Huntingdon • NY, United States .. 118 H2
Huntingdon • WV, United States ... 41 J4
Huntly • New Zealand 112 K1
Huntsville • AL, United States ... 41 I5
Huntsville • TX, United States .. 119 N4
Huntsville • OT, Canada 122 B5
Hünxe • Germany 81 E1
Huon • Papua New Guinea 35 (1) D2
Huon Gulf • Papua New Guinea .. 35 (1) D2
Huonville • TS, Australia 34 I8
Hura • Maldives 106 E2
Hurdalsjøen • Norway 94 B2
Hurdiyo • Somalia 23 I1
Hurghada • Egypt 101 F4
Huron • SD, United States 41 G3
Huron, Lake •
  Canada/United States 39 O7
Hürth • Germany 5 J4
Hurunui • New Zealand 35 D6
Húsavík • Iceland .... 16 I (1) E1
Hushan • China 107 J4
Husi • Romania 14 F3
Huskvarna • Sweden 95 F7
Hust • Ukraine 13 K4
Husum • Germany 8 E2
Husum • Sweden 16 J5
Hutag • Mongolia 27 F7
Hutchinson • KS, United States ... 41 G4
Hutchinson • South Africa 100 C3
Huvhoyfun, gora • Russian Fed. ... 27 R5
Huwaimi, Al • Yemen 18 E7
Huxley, Mt • New Zealand 35 C5
Huy • Belgium 80 A15
Hüzhou • China 107 J3
Hvannadalshnúkur • Iceland ... 16 I (1) E2
Hvar • Croatia 12 K5
Hvar [I.] • Croatia 12 K5
Hvaler • Norway 94 B4
Hvannadalshnúkur • Iceland ... 16 I (1) E2
Hvar • Croatia 12 K5
Hvar [I.] • Croatia 14 D6
Hvarski kanal • Croatia 14 D6
Hvidbjerg • Denmark 95 F5
Hvítá • Iceland .... 16 I (1) D2
Hvitsten • Norway 94 B4

Hvittingfoss • Norway 94 B3
Hwang-Hae • Asia 29 G3
Hwange • Zimbabwe 102 J1
Hwange Nat. Park Zimbabwe 102 J3
Hwange Nat. Park Park •
  Zimbabwe .... 103 [109]
Hyak Ski • WA, United States ... 116 [44]
Hyannis • MA, United States 118 H2
Hyargas Nur • Mongolia 27 E6
Hyde Park • NY, United States .. 118 H2
Hyderabad • Pakistan 28 A3
Hyderabad • India 106 D3
Hyderabad • India 106 D3
Hydra • Greece 92 D7
Hydra • Greece 92 D7
Hyères Beach • France .... 68 [116]
Hyères • France 85 H3
Hyères, Is. d' • France 85 H3
Hyères-Plage • France 85 H3
Hyesan • D.P.R. of Korea 30 E4
Hyland Post • BC, Canada 38 F5
Hylestad • Norway 94 C6
Hyltebruk • Sweden 95 F7
Hyndman Peak •
  ID, United States 38 I8
Hythe • United Kingdom 74 E4
Hyuga • Japan 30 F8
Hyvinkää • Finland 95 E4

I-n-Abanrherit • Niger 20 G5
I-n-Afaleleh • Algeria 20 G4
I-n-Amenas • Algeria 20 G3
I-n-Azaoua • Niger 20 G4
I-n-Ezzane • Algeria 20 H4
I-n-Gall • Niger 20 G5
I-n-Guezzàm • Algeria 20 G5
I-n-Saleh • Algeria 20 F3
I-n-Tabezas • Mali 20 F5
I-n-Tallak • Mali 20 F5
I-n-Techerème • Mali 20 G5
I-n-Tessoum • Niger 20 G5
Ialisos Beach • Rhodes, Greece . 69 [187]
Ialisos • Rhodes, Greece 93 F2
Ialomita • Romania 14 O5
Iao Valley State Mon. •
  HI, United States 119 L3
Iar-Chonnacht • Ireland 79 F4
Iasi • Romania 14 O2
Ibadan • Nigeria 22 E3
Ibague • Colombia 43 C3
Ibarra • Ecuador 43 B3
Ibarreta • Argentina 44 E4
Ibbenbüren • Germany 8 C4
Ibérico, Sistema • Spain 11 I3
Ibi • Nigeria 22 F3
Ibi • Spain 11 K6
Ibi • Nigeria 21 A6
Ibicaraí • Brazil 44 I1
Ibiza • Ibiza, Spain 87 G2
Ibiza [I.] • Spain .... 87 G
Ibra • Oman 18 G5
Ica • Peru 127 B1
Icacos Point •
  Trinidad & Tobago 125 K3
Icama • Brazil 43 D3
Ice Age Nat. Scientific Reserve Park •
  WI, United States .... 121 [158]
Iceland • Atlantic Ocean ...... 16 I (1) D2
Ichinskaya Sopka, Vulkan •
  Russian Fed. 27 Q5
Ichkeul Nat. Park Heritage N •
  Tunisia .... 61 [67]
Ichkeul Nat. Park • Tunisia 101 E2
Içmeler Beach • Turkey .... 69 [205]
Icod de los Vinos Beach •
  Tenerife, Canary Is. .... 68 [91]
Icod de los Vinos •
  Tenerife, Canary Is. 86 E1
Idah • Nigeria 22 F3
Idaho • United States 40 C3
Idaho City • ID, United States .. 117 E4
Idaho Falls • ID, United States .. 40 D3
Idan • Somalia 23 H2
Idar-Oberstein • Germany 82 H3
Ideles • Algeria 20 G4
Idéon Antron • Crete, Greece ... 93 E6
Idfu • Egypt 101 F4
Idhan Awbari • Libya 21 B2
Idhan Murzuq • Libya 21 B3
Idi Oros • Crete, Greece 93 E6
Idra • Greece 92 D7
Idra [I.] • Greece 92 D7
Idstein • Germany 9 D6
Ieper • Belgium 80 A13
Ierápetra Beach • Crete, Greece . 69 [191]
Ierápetra • Crete, Greece 93 E6
Ierissós • Beach • Greece ...... 69 [169]
Ierissós Beach • Greece .... 69 [169]
Ifach, Peñon de • Spain 87 C2
Ifakara • Tanzania 102 H4
Ife • Nigeria 22 E3
Iferouâne • Niger 20 G5
Ifetesene • Algeria 20 F3
Igarapé Miri • Brazil 45 (1) B2
Igarka • Russian Fed. 26 O4
Iglesias • Sardinia, Italy 90 A14
Igloolik • NU, Canada 39 O3
Igls • Austria 89 H6
Ignalina Nat. Park Park •
  Lithuania .... 72 [146]
Igneada Burun • Turkey 15 I2
Igneada • Turkey 15 I2
Igombe • Tanzania 23 E4
Igoumenitsa • Greece 92 D3
Igoumenítsa Beach • Greece ..... 69 [152]
Igrim • Russian Fed. 26 J5
Iguaçu • Brazil 44 F4
Iguaçu, Parque Nac. do Heritage N •
  Brazil .... 60 [36]
Iguaçu, Parque Nacional do •
  Brazil 44 F4
Iguala • Mexico 123 E4
Igualada • Spain 87 D3
Iguatu • Brazil 45 (1) D3
Iguazu, Parque Nac. de Heritage N •
  Argentina .... 60 [37]
Iguéla • Gabon 22 F5
Iguéla, Réserve d' Park • Gabon . 103 [49]
Iguidi, Erg •
  Algeria/Mauritania 20 E2
Ih-Obo-Ula • Mongolia 26 Q9
Iharana • Madagascar 24 H2
Ihavandiffulu Atoll • Maldives .. 106 E2
Ihosy • Madagascar 24 H4
Ihu • Maldives 106 E2
Iida • Japan 30 I7
Iijoki • Japan 30 J6
IJ-Meer • Netherlands 80 C2
IJmuiden • Netherlands 80 C1
IJssel • Netherlands 80 A8
IJsselmeer • Netherlands 80 A7

Ijui • Brazil 44 F4
IJzendijke • Netherlands 80 A10
IJzer • Belgium 5 F4
Ikaalinen • Finland 95 E2
Ikali • Dem. Rep. of Congo 23 C4
Ikaría • Greece 92 D8
Ikaría • Greece 92 D8
Ikast • Denmark 95 F9
Ikeda • Japan 30 L3
Ikegami • Japan 30 I7
Ikeja • Nigeria 22 E3
Ikela • Dem. Rep. of Congo 23 C4
Ikopa • Madagascar 24 H3
Ilagan • Philippines 31 G3
Ilawa • Poland 13 I4
Ilbenge • Russian Fed. 27 K4
Ile de France • France 10 H4
Ilebo • Dem. Rep. of Congo 23 C4
Ilek • Kazakhstan/Russian Fed. ... 17 I6
Ilerh • Algeria 20 F4
Ilesha • Nigeria 22 E3
Ilfracombe • United Kingdom 74 F2
Ilgaz • Turkey 15 O2
Ilgaz Daglari • Turkey 15 O2
Ilgin • Turkey 15 M5
Ilha do Bananal • Brazil 45 (1) B4
Ilhabela • Brazil 127 C3
Ilhavo • Portugal 11 C4
Ilhavo Beach • Portugal .... 68 [77]
Ilhéus • Brazil 44 I1
Iligan • Philippines 31 G5
Ilir • Russian Fed. 27 F6
Iljia • Romania 14 N2
Ilagui • Chile 44 B5
Iller • Germany 82 J1
Illertissen • Germany 82 J1
Illetes • Majorca, Spain 87 H3
Illimani, Nevado del • Bolivia ... 44 C2
Illinois • United States 41 I4
Illinois & Michigan Canal Nat. Heritage
  Corridor Park •
  IL, United States .... 121 [179]
Illizi • Algeria 20 G3
Ilm • Germany 9 G6
Ilman, Ozero • Russian Fed. 97 E1
Ilmenau • Thüringen, Germany 9 F6
Ilmenau • Sachsen, Germany 9 F6
Ilo • Peru 127 B4
Iloilo • Philippines 31 G4
Ilomantsi • Finland 16 P5
Ilorin • Nigeria 22 E3
Iluíissat • Greenland 46 U3
Ilwaki • Indonesia 32 (1) C4
Imabari • Japan 30 G7
Imandra, Ozero • Russian Fed. 17 E1
Imari • Japan 30 E8
Imata • Peru 127 B4
Imatra • Finland 16 O6
Imbtuba • Brazil 44 G4
Imeni Gastello • Russian Fed. 27 O4
Imi • Ethiopia 23 G2
Imilili • Western Sahara 20 B4
Imjin • D.P.R. of Korea 30 D5
Immenstadt • Germany 82 J6
Imo • Nigeria 22 F3
Imogiri • Java, Indonesia 110 D7
Imola • Italy 91 E7
Imotski • Croatia 14 E6
Imperatorskaya Gavan •
  Russian Fed. 27 M7
Imperatriz • Brazil 45 (1) B3
Imperia • Italy 91 E9
Impfondo • Congo 22 H4
Imphal • India 28 F4
Imst • Austria 89 H6
Imzouren • Morocco 11 H9
Ina • Japan 30 I7
Inambari • Peru 127 B2
Inanga • Japan 30 L3
Inangahua Junction •
  New Zealand 35 C5
Inanwatan • Indonesia 32 (1) D3
Iñapari • Peru 43 D6
Inari • Finland 16 N2
Inarijarvi • Finland 16 N2
Inca • Majorca, Spain 87 H1
Inca de Oro • Chile 44 C4
Incaguasi • Chile 44 B4
Ince Burun • Turkey 15 I3
Incekum • Turkey 93 G4
Inch'on • Rep. of Korea 30 D6
Inch'on Ferry • Turkey 93 G1
Indalsälven • Sweden 16 I5
Indawgyi • Myanmar 28 G3
Independence •
  MO, United States 41 H4
Independence Nat. Hist. Park Park •
  PA, United States .... 121 [311]
Independência • Brazil 45 (1) C3
Independencia, I. • Peru 127 B1
India • Asia 28 C3
Indian Ocean 3 S8
Indian Town Point •
  Antigua & Barbuda 125 F2
Indiana • United States 41 I4
Indiana Dunes Nat. Lakeshore Park •
  IN, United States .... 121 [181]
Indianapolis •
  IN, United States 41 I4
Indianhead Mtn Ski •
  MI, United States .... 116 [127]
Indianola • MS, United States ... 118 K2
Indiga • Russian Fed. 17 I1
Indigirka • Russian Fed. 27 O3
Indonesia • Asia 25 N10
Indore • India 28 C4
Indragiri • Indonesia 32 C3
Indramayu • Java, Indonesia 110 D2
Indravati • India 28 D5
Indre • France 84 D4
Indre [Adm] • France 84 D4
Indre Arna • Norway 94 C3
Indre-et-Loire • France 84 D2
Indus • Pakistan 28 A3
Inebolu • Turkey 15 O2
Inecik • Turkey 15 I3
Inegöl • Turkey 15 K3
Ingape • Morocco 20 C2
Inezgane [Apt] • Morocco 101 D5
Infanta, Cape • South Africa 100 C6
Infantado • Portugal 88 D2
Ingelstad • Sweden 95 F8
Ingeniero Jacobaci • Argentina ... 45 C4
Ingenio •
  Gran Canaria, Canary Is. 86 E4
Ingenio Santa Ana • Argentina 44 D3
Ingenios, Valley of the Heritage C •
  Cuba .... 62 [35]
Ingham • QL, Australia 111 F1
Inglewood • QL, Australia 111 E3
Inglewood • New Zealand 112 K3
Ingolstadt • Germany 9 G8
Ingulets • Russian Fed. 17 H6
Inhambane • Mozambique 24 F4
Inhambane, Baia de • Mozambique . 24 F4
Inhisar • Turkey 15 L3
Inhumas • Brazil 44 G2
Inírida • Colombia 43 D3

Inishark • Ireland 79 F3
Inishbofin • Ireland 79 F3
Inishcrone **Beach** • Ireland ..... 68 [45]
Inishcrone • Ireland 79 F2
Inisheer • Ireland 79 F3
Inishkea North • Ireland 79 F1
Inishkea South • Ireland 79 F1
Inishmaan • Ireland 79 F3
Inishmore • Ireland 79 F3
Inishmurray • Ireland 79 F2
Inishowen Peninsula • Ireland .. 79 D1
Inishturk • Ireland 79 F1
Injune • QL, Australia 111 F5
Inkisi • Dem. Rep. of Congo .. 23 B5
Inland Kaikoura Range •
New Zealand 35 D5
Inland Sea • Japan 30 G7
Inland Sea • Malta 93 H1
Inn • Austria/Germany 9 I8
Innamincka • SA, Australia .. 34 H5
Innbygda • Norway 16 G6
Inner Hope **Beach** •
United Kingdom .... 75 [117]
Inner Mongolia • China 29 E2
Inner Sound • United Kingdom .. 6 G4
Innfield • Ireland 79 E1
Innichen **Ski** • Italy ..... 70 [239]
Innichen • Italy 90 B2
Innisfail • QL, Australia 111 F1
Innsbruck • Austria 89 H6
Innvikfjorden • Norway 16 G2
Inongo • Dem. Rep. of Congo .. 23 B4
Inönü • Turkey 15 L4
Inoússes • Greece 92 D5
Inoússes • Greece 92 D5
Inowrocław • Poland 13 H5
Inscription, Cape •
WA, Australia 34 B5
Insuyu • Turkey 93 G1
Inta • Russian Fed. 26 J4
Intepe • Turkey 15 H4
Interlaken **Ski** • Switzerland .. 70 [93]
Interlaken • Switzerland 89 G2
International Drive •
FL, United States 121 C2
International Peace Garden **Park** •
ND, United States .... 120 [146]
Intracoastal Waterway •
United States 118 K4
Inukjuak • QU, Canada 39 P5
Inuvik • NT, Canada 38 E3
Inverboynde **Beach** •
United Kingdom .... 75 [4]
Invercargill • New Zealand .. 112 L4
Invergordon • United Kingdom .. 59 D1
Inverness • United Kingdom .. 6 H4
Inverness • NS, Canada 123 D7
Investigator Group •
SA, Australia 34 F6
Investigator Strait •
SA, Australia 34 G7
Inya • Russian Fed. 27 N5
Inya [Riv] • Russian Fed. 27 N5
Inza • Dem. Rep. of Congo .. 22 H5
Ioánina • Greece 15 B4
Ion Corvin • Romania 97 D2
Iona • United Kingdom 75 A2
Ionian Is. • Greece .... 92 B/C
Ionian Is. • Greece .... 92 B/C
Ionian Sea • Europe 4 N9
Iónion Pélagos • Greece 15 B6
Íos **Beach** • Greece .... 69 [185]
Íos • Greece 92 D8
Íos • Greece 92 D8
Íos [I.] • Greece 92 D8
Íos [I.] • Greece 92 D8
Iowa • United States 41 H3
Iowa City • IA, United States .. 41 H3
Ipameri • Brazil 44 G2
Ipanema • Brazil 127 C4
Ipatinga • Brazil 127 C2
Ipek • Fed. Rep. of Yugoslavia .. 71 A14
Ipiales • Colombia 43 B3
Ipiaú • Brazil 44 I1
Ipirós • Greece 92 A1
Ipirós • Greece 92 A1
Ipixuna • Brazil 43 C5
Ipoh • Malaysia 108 D1
Ipoly • Slovak Rep. 14 G1
Iporá • Brazil 44 F2
Ipsala • Turkey 14 N9
Ipsos • Corfu, Greece 92 B1
Ipsos • Corfu, Greece 92 B1
Ipswich • United Kingdom .. 7 N9
Ipswich • QL, Australia 111 F6
Ipswich • Jamaica 124 C1
Iqaluit • NU, Canada 39 R4
Iquitos • Chile 44 B3
Iquitos • Peru 43 C4
Iracoubo • French Guiana 43 G2
Iráklia • Greece 92 D8
Iráklia • Greece 92 D8
Iráklio • Crete, Greece 93 E3
Iráklio [Adm] • Crete, Greece .. 93 E7
Iran • Asia 18 F3
Iranshahr • Iran 18 H4
Irapuato • Mexico 123 E1
Iraq • Asia 18 D3
Irati • Brazil 44 F4
Irazú, Volcán • Costa Rica 37 E5
Irbid • Jordan 18 C3
Irbid • Russian Fed. 26 J6
Irebu • Dem. Rep. of Congo .. 23 B4
Irecê • Brazil 45 (1) C4
Ireland • Europe 4 I6
Irelands Eye • Ireland 79 E2
Irgiz • Kazakhstan 26 J8
Irgiz [Riv] • Kazakhstan 26 J8
Iri • Rep. of Korea 30 D7
Irian • I • Indonesia 32 (1) E4
Irian Jaya • Indonesia 32 (1) E3
Iringa • Tanzania 102 H4
Irinya, gora • Russian Fed. .. 26 R6
Iriri • Brazil 43 F5
Irish Sea • Ireland/UK 7 H8
Iritula • Brazil 45 (1) B2
Irkutsk • Russian Fed. 27 F6
Iroise • France 84 C1
Ironbridge • United Kingdom .. 74 D1
Ironbridge Gorge **Heritage C** •
United Kingdom .... 64 [18]
Ironwood • MI, United States .. 41 I2
Irouléguy • France 84 B3
Irqah, Al • Yemen 18 F7
Irrawaddy • Myanmar 31 B3
Irrsdorf • Austria 89 H4
Irtysh • Asia 26 L6
Irun • Spain 11 I1
Irurzun • Spain 11 J2
Irvine • United Kingdom 6 H6
Isa, Ra's • Yemen 21 H5
Isaba • Philippines 31 G5
Isabela • Galapagos Is. 43 (1) A2
Isabela • Puerto Rico 125 E1
Isabela de Sagua • Cuba 124 D2
Isabelia, Cordillera •
Nicaragua 37 D5

Isafjördur • Iceland 16 (1) B1
Isalo, Massif de l' •
Madagascar 24 H4
Isalo, Parc nat. de l' **Park** •
Madagascar .... 103 [139]
Isangi • Dem. Rep. of Congo .. 23 C3
Isar • Germany 9 H8
Isarco • Italy 90 B1
Isarkanal • Germany 82 J3
Ischgl **Ski** • Austria ..... 70 [134]
Ischgl • Austria 89 H6
Ischia • Italy 91 G3
Ischia, I. d' • Italy 91 G3
Ise • Japan 30 I7
Ise-Wan • Japan 30 I7
Isefjord • Denmark 95 F10
Isel • Austria 90 B2
Iseo, Lago d' • Italy 91 E2
Isère • France 85 E3
Isère [Adm] • France 85 F3
Iserlohn • Germany 81 E2
Iset • Russian Fed. 26 K6
Iseyin • Nigeria 22 E3
Isfahan • Iran 18 F3
Isfahan **Heritage C** • Iran ..... 63 [108]
Isfendiyar Daglari • Turkey .. 15 O2
Isfjorden • Norway 94 C2
Isha Baydabo • Somalia 23 G3
Isherton • Guyana 43 F3
Ishikari-Wan • Japan 30 K3
Ishim • Russian Fed. 26 K6
Ishim [Riv] •
Kazakhstan/Russian Fed. .. 26 K7
Ishimskaya Step • Russian Fed. .. 26 K6
Ishinomaki • Japan 30 K5
Ishodnaya, gora • Russian Fed. .. 27 W4
Ishøj **Beach** • Denmark ..... 68 [20]
Isigny-sur-Mer • France 5 B5
Isikli • Russian Fed. 26 L7
Isiolo • Kenya 101 G2
Isiro • Dem. Rep. of Congo .. 23 D3
Iskandariya, El • Egypt 102 H1
Iskenderun • Turkey 18 C2
Iskur • Bulgaria 14 L6
Isle Royale Nat. Park **Park** •
MI, United States .... 121 [159]
Islote de Hilario •
Lanzarote, Canary Is. 87 E3
Ismá'iliya • Egypt 101 F2
Isna • Egypt 101 F4
Isny • Germany 82 J5
Isny **Spa** • Germany ..... 83 [218]
Isoka • Zambia 24 E2
Isola 2000 • France 85 H2
Isonzo • Italy 91 E4
Isparta • Turkey 93 I1
Isparta [Adm] • Turkey 93 G2
Isparta [Riv] • Turkey 93 G1
Íspica • Sicily, Italy 12 I12
Íspico, Cava d' • Sicily, Italy .. 90 D4
Israel • Asia 18 B3
Issachar • Israel 98 A4
Issoire • France 10 I8
Issoudun • France 10 H7
Issum • Germany 81 E1
Issyk-Kul • Kyrgyzstan 26 M9
Issyk-Kul [Lake] • Kyrgyzstan .. 26 M9
Ist • Croatia 14 B5
Istanbul **Heritage C** • Turkey .. 64 [190]
Istanbul • Turkey 92 D3
Istanbul • Turkey 92 D3
Istanbul-Bakirköy • Turkey .. 15 J3
Istanbul-Kadiköy • Turkey .. 15 J3
Istiéa • Greece 15 E5
Isto, Mt • AK, United States .. 40 (1) G2
Istra • Croatia 14 A4
Istra • Croatia 96 B2
Itabaianinha • Brazil 44 I1
Itabapoana • Brazil 127 C2
Itaberaba • Brazil 44 I1
Itaberaí • Brazil 44 G2
Itabira • Brazil 127 C2
Itabuna • Brazil 44 I1
Itacoatiara • Brazil 43 F4
Itaguí • Colombia 43 B2
Itaipu, Represa de •
Brazil/Paraguay 44 F3
Itaitube • Brazil 43 F4
Itajaí • Brazil 44 G4
Itajubá • Brazil 127 B1
Italian Lake District • Italy .. 90 A1
Italy • Europe 12
Itambacuri • Brazil 44 H1
Itambé, Pico de • Brazil 44 H1
Itanagar • India 28 F3
Itanós • Crete, Greece 93 E8
Itaperuna • Brazil 127 C2
Itapetinga • Brazil 44 H2
Itapetininga • Brazil 44 G3
Itapicuru • Brazil 45 (1) C2
Itapicuru-Mirim • Brazil 45 (1) C2
Itápolos • Brazil 44 G3
Itaqui • Brazil 44 E4
Itarsi • India 28 C4
Itatiaia • Brazil 127 C1
Itaúna • Brazil 127 C1
Itbay • Egypt 21 H2
Itchan Kala **Heritage C** •
Uzbekistan .... 63 [80]
Itéa **Beach** • Greece ..... 69 [154]
Ithaca • NY, United States .. 41 K3
Itháki • Greece 92 C2
Itháki • Greece 92 C2
Itháki [I.] • Greece 92 C2
Itháki [I.] • Greece 92 C2
Iti • Greece 15 D5
Iti Oros Nat. Park **Park** •
Greece .... 72 [138]
Ito • Japan 30 J7
Iton • France 5 B5
Itremo, Massif de l' •
Madagascar 24 H4
Itsukushima Shrine **Heritage C** •
Japan .... 63 [164]
Itter • Austria 89 H3
Ituiutaba • Brazil 44 G2
Itumbiara • Brazil 44 G2
Iturup, Ostrov • Russian Fed. .. 27 O8
Itzehoe • Germany 8 E3
Iúna • Brazil 127 C2
Ivai • Brazil 44 F4
Ivajlovgrad • Bulgaria 15 H2
Ivalo • Finland 16 N2
Ivalojoki • Finland 16 N2
Ivangorod • Russian Fed. 16 O1
Ivangrad • F.R. of Yugoslavia .. 14 G7

Ivanhoe • NS, Australia 111 G1
Ivanic-Frankovsk • Ukraine .. 17 C5
Ivanovo **Heritage C** • Bulgaria .. 64 [169]
Ivanovo • Bulgaria 97 D3
Ivanovo • Russian Fed. 97 E4
Ivdel • Russian Fed. 26 J5
Iveragh Peninsula • Ireland .. 79 F7
Ivigut • Greenland 39 V4
Ivindo • Congo/Gabon 22 G4
Ivory Coast • Africa 22 C4
Ivösjön • Sweden 95 F11
Ivrea • Italy 91 E5
Ivujivik • QU, Canada 39 P4
Iwaki • Japan 30 K6
Iwaki [Mtn] • Japan 30 K4
Iwakuni • Japan 30 G7
Iwanai • Japan 30 K3
Iwate • Japan 30 K5
Iwate [Mtn] • Japan 30 K5
Iwo Jima • Japan 25 P7
Iwon • D.P.R. of Korea. 30 E4
Ixiá • Rhodes, Greece 93 F2
Ixiá [Bay] • Rhodes, Greece .. 93 F2
Ixiamas • Bolivia 44 C1
Ixtapa • Mexico 123 E3
Ixtapan del Oro • Mexico 123 E4
Izabel, Lago de • Guatemala .. 37 D4
Izhevsk • Russian Fed. 17 I3
Izmail • Ukraine 14 P4
Izmir • Turkey 92 D5
Izmir • Turkey 92 D5
Izmir Körfezi • Turkey 15 H5
Izmit • Turkey 15 K3
Izmit • Turkey 92 D3
Iznik • Turkey 92 D3
Iznik • Turkey 92 D3
Iznik Gölü • Turkey 92 D3
Iznik Gölü • Turkey 15 K3
Iznajar, Embalse de • Spain .. 11 G7
Iznik • Turkey 92 D3
Iznik • Turkey 92 D3
Iztochni Rodópi • Bulgaria .. 14 M8
Izu • Japan 30 J7
Izu-Shoto • Japan 30 J8
Izúcar de Matamoros • Mexico .. 123 E4
Izuhara • Japan 30 E7
Izumo • Japan 30 H7
Izvestsiy Tsik, Ostrova •
Russian Fed. 26 N2
Izyum • Ukraine 17 F5

J.A.D. Jensens Nunatakker •
Greenland 39 V4
Ja'el • Somalia 23 I1
Jabal al Qarantal • Jordan. 98 A6
Jabal, Bahr al • Sudan 23 E2
Jabalpur • India 28 C4
Jabbabah, Wadi • Egypt. 21 F3
Jablanica • Bosnia-Herz. 14 E6
Jablonec nad Nisou • Czech Rep. .. 13 E7
Jablonne v Podjestedi •
Czech Rep. 96 C1
Jabonovskij • Ukraine 14 L1
Jabridge Wilderness Area •
NV, United States 117 F2
Jabuticabal • Brazil 44 G3
Jaca • Spain 11 K2
Jacarezinho • Brazil 44 G4
Jáchal • Argentina 44 C4
Jáchymov • Czech Rep. 96 C1
Jack Frost **Ski** •
PA, United States .... 116 [168]
Jackson • WY, United States. 40 D3
Jackson • TN, United States .. 41 I4
Jackson • MS, United States. .. 118 K2
Jackson Head • New Zealand .. 35 B7
Jackson Hole, Teton **Ski** •
WY, United States .... 116 [76]
Jackson, Mt • Antarctica 46 (1) II2
Jackson Prairie •
MS, United States 118 K2
Jacksonville •
IL, United States 41 H4
Jacksonville •
NC, United States 41 K5
Jacksonville •
FL, United States 118 H5
Jacksonville •
FL, United States 119 M3
Jacksonville •
TX, United States 119 N2
Jacob's Well • Jordan ..... 98 [22]
Jacobabad • Pakistan 28 A3
Jacobina • Brazil 45 (1) C4
Jacques-Cartier, Détroit de •
QU, Canada 123 D2
Jacques-Cartier, Mt •
QU, Canada 123 D2
Jacques-Cartier Prov. Park •
QU, Canada 123 D1
Jacuí, Rio • Brazil 44 F5
Jaddi, Ras • Pakistan 28 A4
Jadebusen • Germany 5 L1
Jadida, El • Morocco 101 D1
Jadu • Libya 21 B1
Jægerspris **Beach** • Denmark .. 68 [22]
Jaén • Spain 86 B3
Jaeren • Norway 16 C7
Jaffa • Israel 98 A5
Jaffa, Cape • SA, Australia .. 34 G7
Jaffar, Cirque de • Morocco .. 101 D4
Jaffna • Sri Lanka 106 D11
Jagaraga Temple •
Bali, Indonesia 110 C2
Jagdalpur • India 28 D5
Jagodina • F.R. of Yugoslavia .. 14 I6
Jagst • Germany 9 G7
Jaguaquara • Brazil 44 I1
Jaguari • Brazil 44 F5
Jagüey Grande • Cuba 124 D2
Jahrom • Iran 18 F4
Jailolo • Indonesia 32 (1) C2
Jaipur • India 105 C6
Jaisalmer • India 105 C6
Jajce • Bosnia-Herz. 12 L4
Jakarta • Java, Indonesia .. 110 D1
Jakobshavn • Greenland 46 U3
Jakobstad • Finland 16 L5
Jakupica • F.Y.R. of Macedonia .. 15 C2
Jalalabad • Afghanistan 28 B2
Jalapa • Mexico 123 E2
Jälasjärvi • Finland 16 L5
Jalgaon • India 28 C4
Jalisco • Mexico 37 (1) B1
Jalon • Spain 11 C12
Jalor • India 105 C5
Jamaare • Nigeria 22 G3
Jamaica • West Indies .... 124 C
Jamalpur • Bangladesh 28 E4
Jamame • Somalia 23 G3
Jamantau, gora • Russian Fed. .. 32 C3
Jambi • Indonesia 32 C3
Jameos del Agua •
Lanzarote, Canary Is. 87 E3
James • ND/SD, United States .. 40 F3
James Bay • NU, Canada 39 O6

James, Fort • Antigua & Barbuda .. 125 F1
James, Fort • Trinidad & Tobago .. 125 K2
James Ross Strait • NU, Canada .. 38 L2
Jamestown • SA, Australia 34 G6
Jamestown • ND, United States .. 41 G2
Jamestown • NY, United States .. 41 K3
Jamestown Nat. Hist. Site •
VA, United States 118 H3
Jamestown Nat. Hist. Site **Park** •
VA, United States .... 121 [256]
Jammerbugten • Denmark 95 F5
Jammu • Jammu & Kashmir 28 B2
Jammu & Kashmir • India 28 B4
Jammu & Kashmir • Asia 28 C2
Jamnagar • India 28 B4
Jämsä • Finland 95 E2
Jämsänkoski • Finland 95 E2
Jamshedpur • India 28 E4
Jämtland • Sweden 16 G5
Jan Mayen • Greenland Sea 4 I2
Janaucu • Brazil 43 H3
Jandía •
Fuerteventura, Canary Is. .. 87 E2
Jandía Playa •
Fuerteventura, Canary Is. .. 87 E2
Jesús **Heritage C** • Paraguay .. 62 [56]
Jandia, Punta de •
Fuerteventura, Canary Is. .. 87 E2
Jane Peak • New Zealand .. 112 L2
Janesville • WI, United States .. 41 I3
Jánoshalma • Hungary 13 I11
Jánosháza • Hungary 12 L1
Jánské Lázne • Czech Rep. .. 96 C2
Januária • Brazil 44 H2
Japan • Asia 30
Japan, Sea of • Asia 30 G4
Japan Trench • Pacific Ocean .. 30 M6
Japim • Brazil 43 C5
Japurá • Brazil 43 D4
Jaramillo • Argentina 45 C5
Jarandilla • Spain 11 F6
Jardim • Brazil 44 E3
Jardín d'Acclimation **Park** •
France .... 73 [71]
Jardin de la France • France. .. 84 B7
Jardines de la Reina, Archipiélago de •
Cuba 124 D7
Jare • Norway 94 B2
Jari • Brazil 43 G3
Järlåsa • Sweden 95 D1
Jarmah • Libya 21 B2
Järna • Sweden 95 D1
Jarny • France 5 I9
Jarocin • Poland 13 G6
Jaromer • Czech Rep. 96 C2
Jaroslaw • Poland 13 L8
Järvenpää • Finland 95 E4
Jarvis • Pacific Ocean 33 K5
Jask • Iran 18 G4
Jaslo • Poland 13 K8
Jason Islands • Falkland Is. 45 D6
Jasper • TX, United States .. 119 N4
Jasper • AL, Canada 122 C2
Jasper Nat. Park • AL, Canada .. 122 C2
Jassy • Romania 71 A15
Jastrzebie Zdrój • Poland 13 H8
Jászárokszállás • Hungary .. 13 I10
Jászberény • Hungary 13 I10
Jataí • Brazil 44 F2
Jatibarang • Java, Indonesia .. 110 D2
Jatibonico • Cuba 124 D3
Jatijajar Caves •
Java, Indonesia 110 D6
Jatiwangi • Java, Indonesia .. 110 D2
Jaú • Brazil 44 G3
Jauja • Peru 127 B1
Jaunpur • India 105 C8
Java • Indonesia .... 110 D
Java Sea • Indonesia 32 D3
Java Trench • Indonesia 32 C4
Jávea **Beach** • Spain ..... 68 [101]
Jávea • Spain 11 J2
Javier • Spain 11 J2
Javor Osa • Bosnia-Herz. 14 F5
Javorov • Ukraine 13 M8
Jawa • Indonesia 32 D4
Jawa Barat • Java, Indonesia .. 110 D1
Jawa Tengah • Java, Indonesia .. 110 D3
Jawa Timur • Java, Indonesia .. 110 D8
Jawf, Al • Saudi Arabia 18 C4
Jawi • Penang, Malaysia .. 108 C4
Jawor • Poland 13 I7
Jaworzno • Poland 13 I7
Jay Peak **Ski** •
VT, United States .... 116 [205]
Jaya Ancol Dreamland •
Java, Indonesia 110 D1
Jaya, Puncak • Indonesia .. 32 (1) E3
Jayapura • Indonesia 32 (1) F3
Jayawijaya, Pegunungen •
Indonesia 32 (1) E3

Jerada • Morocco 101 D2
Jerantut • Malaysia 108 D2
Jerba • Tunisia 101 E6
Jerez de la Frontera • Spain .. 86 A6
Jericho • Jordan 18 C3
Jericho • QL, Australia 111 F3
Jerid, Chott el • Tunisia 101 E5
Jersey • Channel Is. 7 J12
Jersey City • NJ, United States .. 118 H1
Jerusalem **Heritage C** •
Israel/Jordan .... 64 [247]
Jerusalem • Israel/Jordan .. 98 A5
Jervis Bay • AC, Australia .. 111 G2
Jesenica • Slovenia 13 I13
Jesi • Italy 91 E12
Jésolo • Italy 12 G3
Jesperhus Blomsterpark •
Denmark 95 F5
Jesperhus Blomsterpark **Park** •
Denmark .... 73 [13]
Jessheim • Norway 94 B2
Jestr, Wabe • Ethiopia 23 G2
Jesup • GA, United States .. 41 J5
Jesup, Fort • LA, United States .. 118 K1
Jever • Germany 8 C3
Jevnaker • Norway 94 C3
Jewel Cave Nat. Mon. **Mon.** •
SD, United States .... 120 [150]
Jeypore • India 28 D5
Jezercës • Albania 15 A1
Jezioro Lebsko • Poland 13 G3
Jezioro Mamry • Poland 13 K3
Jezioro Sniardwy • Poland 13 L4
Jezreel, Valley of • Israel 98 A4
Jhajjar • India 105 C2
Jhalarapatan • India 105 C6
Jhalawar • India 105 C6
Jhang Sadar • Pakistan 28 B2
Jhansi • India 105 C7
Jhelum • Pakistan 28 B2
Jhelum [Riv] • Pakistan 28 B2
Jhunjhunun • India 105 C2
Ji'an • Jilin, China 30 D4
Ji'an • Jiangxi, China 31 F1
Jiading • China 107 J2
Jialing Jiang • China 29 D4
Jiamusi • China 29 I1
Jiangdu • China 107 H1
Jiangmen • China 107 I4
Jiangsu • China 107 G4
Jiangxi • China 107 G8
Jiangyin • China 107 J2
Jianyang • China 29 F5
Jiaozuo • China 29 E3
Jiashan • China 107 J4
Jiaxing • China 107 J4
Jiayuguan • China 29 C3
Jibacoa • Cuba 124 D2
Jicín • Czech Rep. 96 C2
Jida • Zhuhai, China 107 H1
Jiddah • Saudi Arabia 18 C5
Jiddat al Harasis • Oman 18 G6
Jihlava • Czech Rep. 96 C4
Jijiga • Ethiopia 23 G2
Jilib • Somalia 23 G3
Jilin • China 29 H2
Jilin [Adm] • China 107 G4
Jima • Ethiopia 23 F2
Jimbaran Beach •
Bali, Indonesia 110 C4
Jimbe • Angola 23 C6
Jimbolia • Romania 14 H4
Jiménez de la Frontera • Spain .. 11 F8
Jimmy Peak **Ski** •
MA, United States .... 116 [191]
Jin I. • Hong Kong, China 107 H6
Jinan • China 29 F3
Jindrichuv Hradec • Czech Rep. .. 96 C4
Jing Xian • China 107 J3
Jingde • China 107 J3
Jingdezhen • China 29 F5
Jinggang Shan • China 31 E1
Jinghe • China 26 N9
Jingjiang • China 107 J2
Jingjiang • China 30 D3
Jinhua • China 29 F5
Jining • Nei Monggol, China .. 29 E2
Jining • Shandong, China .. 29 F3
Jinja • Uganda 23 E3
Jinmen • Taiwan 31 F2
Jinsha • China 107 J2
Jinsha Jiang • China 31 C2
Jinshan • China 107 J4
Jintan • China 107 J1
Jinzhou • China 29 G2
Jiparaná • Brazil 43 E5
Jipijapa • Ecuador 43 A4
Jiuhua Shan • China 107 G8
Jiujiang • China 29 F5
Jiuquan • China 29 B3
Jiuzhaigou Valley **Heritage N** •
China .... 61 [115]
Jixi • Zhuhai, China 107 H1
Jiwani, Ras • Pakistan 18 H4
Jixi • Heilongjiang, China 29 I1
Jixi • Anhui, China 107 J3
Jizan • Saudi Arabia 18 D6
Jizo-Zaki • Japan 30 G7
Jizzakh • Uzbekistan 26 K9
João Pessoa • Brazil 45 (1) D3
João Pinheiro • Brazil 44 G2
Jochberg **Ski** • Austria ..... 70 [159]
Jochgrimm • Italy 90 B3
Jódar • Spain 11 H7
Jodhpur • India 105 C5
Joensuu • Finland 16 O5
Joetsu • Japan 30 J6
Jog Falls • India 106 D6
Jogeva • Estonia 16 N7
Johannesburg • South Africa .. 24 D5
John Day • OR, United States .. 38 H4
John Day Fossil Beds Nat. Mon. •
OR, United States 117 F3
John Day Fossil Beds Nat. Mon. **Park** •
OR, United States .... 120 [35]
John o'Groats • United Kingdom .. 6 I3
Johns Lake • FL, United States .. 121 C1
Johnson, Andrew, Nat. Hist. Site **Park** •
TN, United States .... 121 [233]
Johnson, Lyndon B., Mem. Grove **Park** •
DC, United States .... 121 [288]
Johnson, Lyndon B., Nat. Hist. Park •
TX, United States 119 N3
Johnson, Lyndon B., Nat. Hist. Park **Park** •
TX, United States .... 120 [140]
Johnson Space Center •
TX, United States 119 N6
Johnsons Point •
Antigua & Barbuda 125 F3
Johnsons Point Beach •
Antigua & Barbuda 125 F3
Johnstown • PA, United States .. 41 K3

Johnstown Flood Nat. Mem. **Park** •
PA, United States .... 121 [302]
Johor • Malaysia 31 C6
Johor Baharu • Malaysia 108 E1
Johor Strait •
Malaysia/Singapore 108 E2
Joigny • France 10 I6
Joinvile • Brazil 44 G4
Joinville • France 10 K5
Jokkmokk • Sweden 16 J3
Jokulsargljufur Nat. Park **Park** •
Iceland .... 72 [1]
Joliet • IL, United States 41 I3
Joliette • QU, Canada 122 B3
Jolly Harbour •
Antigua & Barbuda 125 F3
Jolo • Philippines 31 G5
Jolo Group • Philippines 31 G5
Jølstravatnet • Norway 94 C1
Jombang • Java, Indonesia .. 110 D7
Jomfruland • Norway 94 B3
Jomsom • Nepal 105 C4
Jonava • Lithuania 13 N2
Jonesboro • AR, United States .. 41 H4
Jonesville • LA, United States .. 118 K1
Jonglei • Sudan 23 E2
Jonglei Canal • Sudan 23 E2
Jönköping • Sweden 95 F7
Jönköping [Adm] • Sweden .. 95 F7
Jonquera, la • Spain 87 D2
Jonquière • QC, Canada .. 123 D1
Joplin • MO, United States .. 41 H4
Joppa • Israel 98 A5
Jordan • Asia 18 B3
Jordan [Riv] • Israel/Jordan .. 98 A6
Jorhat • India 16 K4
Jörn • Sweden 16 K3
Jørpeland • Norway 94 C5
Jos • Nigeria 22 F3
Jos Plateau • Nigeria 22 F3
José de San Martin • Argentina .. 45 B4
José Miguel, Cuevas de • Cuba .. 124 D1
Joseph Bonaparte Gulf •
WA, Australia 34 E2
Joseph, Lac • NF, Canada .. 39 R6
Joshua Tree Nat. Park •
CA, United States 117 F6
Joshua Tree Nat. Park **Park** •
CA, United States .... 120 [59]
Josselin • France 84 C4
Jostedalen • Norway 94 C2
Jostedalsbreen • Norway 94 C2
Jotunheimen • Norway 94 C3
Jotunheimen Nat. Park **Park** •
Norway .... 72 [14]
Jotunheimen Nat. Park • Norway .. 94 C2
Joubertina • South Africa 100 C7
Joue du Loup, la **Ski** • France .. 70 [63]
Joumâa • Tunisia 101 E6
Joutsa • Finland 95 E2
Joutseno • Finland 16 O6
Jovellanos • Cuba 124 D2
Jowhar Giohar • Somalia 23 H3
Joya de Cerén **Heritage C** •
El Salvador .... 62 [31]
Joyce's Country • Ireland 79 F3
Juan de Fuca, Strait of •
Canada/United States 122 C3
Juan de Nova • Réunion. 24 G3
Juan Fernandez, Archipiélago •
Pacific Ocean 42 B8
Juan Francisco, Playa • Cuba .. 124 D2
Juan les Pins • France 85 H4
Juarez, Benito [Apt] • Mexico .. 123 E4
Juàzeiro • Brazil 45 (1) C3
Juàzeiro do Norte • Brazil .. 45 (1) D3
Juba • Sudan 23 E3
Juba • Sudan 23 E3
Jubaland • Somalia 23 G3
Jubba, Webi • Somalia 23 G3
Juby, Cap • Morocco 20 C3
Júcar • Spain 11 J5
Júcaro • Cuba 124 D3
Jüchen • Germany 81 E3
Judaberg • Norway 94 C5
Judaea • Israel/Jordan 98 A4
Judaea, Wilderness of •
Israel/Jordan 98 A4
Judah • Jordan 98 A4
Judenburg • Austria 13 I10
Juegang • China 107 J2
Juelsminde **Beach** • Denmark .. 68 [22]
Juelsminde • Denmark 95 F10
Jui • Romania 14 K5
Juist • Germany 8 B3
Juist **Spa** • Germany ..... 83 [37]
Juiz de Fora • Brazil 127 C1
Jukleegga • Norway 94 C3
Juli • Peru 127 B4
Julia Creek • QL, Australia .. 34 H4
Juliaca • Peru 127 B4
Julian Alps • Slovenia 96 B2
Juliana Kanaal • Netherlands .. 5 I3
Juliana Top • Suriname 43 F3
Julianehåb • Greenland 39 V4
Jülich • Germany 9 B6
Julijske Alpe • Slovenia 12 H2
Julita • Sweden 95 D3
Jullundur • India 28 C2
Juma, Pampas de **Heritage C** •
Peru .... 62 [52]
Jumba • Kenya 101 G5
Jumilla • Spain 87 C1
Junagadh • India 28 B4
Junaynah, Al • Sudan 21 D3
Junction • TX, United States .. 40 G5
Junction City •
KS, United States 41 G4
June Mtn **Ski** •
CA, United States .... 116 [62]
Juneau • AK, United States .. 38 E5
Junee • NS, Australia 111 G1
Jungfrau • Switzerland 89 G2
Junggar Basin • China 107 G1
Junggar Pendi • China 26 O8
Jungutbatu • Indonesia 110 C4
Junin • Argentina 127 D1
Junsele • Sweden 16 I5
Jupiá, Represa de • Brazil .. 44 F3
Jupiter • Romania 97 D2
Jura • United Kingdom 6 G5
Jura, Sound of • United Kingdom .. 6 G6
Jurado • Colombia 43 B3
Jurançon • France 84 B3
Jurbarkas • Lithuania 16 L9
Jurilovca • Romania 97 D2
Jurmala • Latvia 16 L8
Jurong • China 107 J1
Jurong Bird Park • Singapore .. 108 E1
Jurong New Town • Singapore .. 108 E1
Juru • Penang, Malaysia .. 108 C4
Jurua • Brazil 43 C5
Juruá • Brazil 43 F6
Juruena • Brazil 43 F6
Juruena [Riv] • Brazil 43 F6
Juruti • Brazil 43 F4
Justo Daract • Argentina 44 C5
Juticalpa • Honduras 37 D5
Jütai [Riv] • Brazil 43 C5
Jütai [Riv] • Brazil 43 D4
Jüterbog • Germany 8 I5

Jutland • Denmark 95 F9
Juuka • Finland 16 O5
Juva • Finland 16 N6
Juventud, I. de la • Cuba 124 D1
Jyderup • Denmark 95 F10
Jylland • Denmark 95 F9
Jyväskylä • Finland 95 E2

K2 • China/Kashmir 28 C1
Ka • Nigeria 22 E2
Ka, Laem • Phuket, Thailand . . 109 K2
Kaabong • Uganda 23 E3
Kaakhka • Turkmenistan 18 G2
Kaala • HI, United States 119 L5
Kaamanen • Finland 16 N2
Kaarst • Germany 81 E3
Kaarta • Mali 22 C2
Kaatsheuvel • Netherlands . . . 80 A11
Kabaena • Indonesia 32 (1) B4
Kabala • Sierra Leone 22 B3
Kabale • Uganda 102 H1
Kabalega Falls • Uganda 23 E3
Kabalo • Dem. Rep. of Congo . . 23 D5
Kabanjahe • Indonesia 110 B2
Kabardino-Balkaria •
   Russian Fed. 17 G6
Kabba • Nigeria 22 F3
Kåbdalis • Sweden 16 K3
Kabin Buri • Thailand 109 H2
Kabinda • Dem. Rep. of Congo . . 23 C5
Kableshkovo • Bulgaria 15 I1
Kablow-Ziegelei • Germany . . 81 F4
Kabo • Central African Rep. . . . 22 H3
Kabompo • Zambia 24 C2
Kabongo • Dem. Rep. of Congo . . 23 D5
Kabul • Afghanistan 18 I3
Kabunda • Dem. Rep. of Congo . . 24 D2
Kabwe • Zambia 24 D2
Kacanik • F.R. of Yugoslavia . . 15 C1
Kachin • Myanmar 31 B1
Kachug • Russian Fed. 27 G6
Kacina • Czech Rep. 96 C2
Kackar Dagi • Turkey 18 D1
Kadamatt I. • India 106 D9
Kadan • Czech Rep. 96 C1
Kadan Kyun • Myanmar 31 B4
Kadei •
   Cameroon/Central African Rep. . . 22 G4
Kadinhani • Turkey 15 N5
Kadoma • Zimbabwe 102 J2
Kaduna • Nigeria 22 F2
Kaduna Plateau • Nigeria 22 F2
Kaduna [Riv] • Nigeria 22 F2
Kaduqli • Sudan 21 E5
Kaduy • Russian Fed. 97 E2
Kadzherom • Russian Fed. . . . 17 J2
Kaédi • Mauritania 20 C5
Kaena Point • HI, United States . . 119 L5
Kaesong • D.P.R. of Korea . . . 30 D6
Kaew Noi, Ko • Thailand 109 K1
Kaew Yai, Ko • Thailand 109 K1
Kafakumba • Dem. Rep. of Congo . . 24 C1
Kaffrine • Senegal 20 B6
Kafiréa, Stenó • Greece 15 F4
Kafiréas, Akra • Greece 15 F5
Kafue • Zambia 24 D3
Kafue Dam • Zambia 24 D3
Kafue Flats • Zambia 24 D3
Kafue Nat. Park Park • Zambia . . 103 [105]
Kaga • Japan 30 I6
Kaga Bandoro •
   Central African Rep. 23 B2
Kagan • Uzbekistan 18 H2
Kagera • Africa 23 E4
Kagera • Rwanda/Tanzania . . 102 H1
Kagoshima • Japan 30 F9
Kahaluu • HI, United States . . 119 L6
Kahama • Tanzania 102 H1
Kahana Valley State Park •
   HI, United States 119 L5
Kahemba • Dem. Rep. of Congo . . 23 B5
Kahla • Germany 9 G6
Kahler Asten • Germany 9 D5
Kahoolawe • HI, United States . . 119 L7
Kahovka • Ukraine 17 E5
Kahuku Point •
   HI, United States 119 L1
Kahului • HI, United States . . . 119 L3
Kahuzi-Biega, Parc nat. du Heritage N •
   Dem. Rep. of Congo . . . . . . 61 [85]
Kahuzi-Biega, Parc nat. du Park •
   Dem. Rep. of Congo . . . . . 103 [58]
Kai Besar • Indonesia 35 (1) A2
Kai, Kepulauan • Indonesia . . 32 (1) D4
Kai Tak [Apt] •
   Hong Kong, China 107 H6
Kaiama • Nigeria 22 E3
Kaiapoi • New Zealand 35 D6
Kaieteur Falls • Guyana 43 F2
Kaifeng • China 29 E4
Kaikohe • New Zealand 35 D2
Kaikoura • New Zealand 35 D6
Kailu • China 27 J8
Kailua • HI, United States 119 L8
Kailua Kona • HI, United States . . 119 L8
Kaimana • Indonesia 32 (1) D3
Kaimanawa Mtns • New Zealand . . 112 K4
Kaianatu • Papua New Guinea . . 35 (1) D2
Kainji Reservoir • Nigeria 22 E2
Kainuu • Finland 94 M3
Kairouan Heritage C • Tunisia . . 64 [231]
Kairouan • Tunisia 101 E4
Kaiserslautern • Germany 82 G4
Kaiserstuhl • Germany 82 G7
Kaitaia • New Zealand 35 D2
Kaiwi Channel •
   HI, United States 119 L3
Kaiyuan • China 31 C2
Kajaani • Finland 16 N4
Kajapuy • Indonesia 32 C4
Kajabbi • QL, Australia 34 H3
Kajang • Malaysia 108 D4
Kajmakcalan •
   Greece/F.Y.R. of Macedonia . . 15 C2
Kaka • Ethiopia 23 F2
Kakadu Nat. Park •
   NT, Australia 34 F2
Kakadu Nat. Park Heritage N •
   NT, Australia . . . . 61 [128]
Kakadu Nat. Park Heritage C •
   Australia . . . . 63 [180]
Kakamega • Kenya 101 G1
Kakamega Forest Game Reserve •
   Kenya 101 G1
Kakar Range • Pakistan 28 A2
Kakata • Liberia 22 B3
Kakinada • India 106 D4
Kakopetriá • Cyprus 93 J2
Kaktovik • AK, United States . . 38 G3
Kakum Nature Park Park • Ghana . . 103 [27]
Kala • Phuket, Thailand 109 K1
Kalá Nerá Beach • Greece . . 69 [165]
Kalaa Kasbah • Tunisia 101 E3

Kalaallit Nunaat • Greenland . . 39 V3
Kalabahi • Indonesia 32 (1) B4
Kalabsha • Egypt 101 F5
Kalacha Beach • Goa, India . . 105 B1
Kaladan • India/Myanmar 28 F4
Kaladar • OT, Canada 122 B6
Kalahari Desert • Botswana . . 24 C4
Kalahari Gemsbok Nat. Park Park •
   South Africa . . . . 103 [113]
Kalai Mor • Turkmenistan 26 J10
Kalajoki • Finland 16 L4
Kalajoki Beach • Finland . . . . 69 [9]
Kalakan • Russian Fed. 27 I5
Kalalau Lookout •
   HI, United States 119 L2
Kalamáki • Zante, Greece 15 E6
Kalamáki • Zante, Greece 92 C3
Kalamáki • Zante, Greece 92 C3
Kalamáta • Greece 15 D6
Kalamáta Beach • Greece . . 69 [158]
Kalamazoo • MI, United States . . 41 I3
Kalambo Falls • Tanzania . . . 102 H3
Kalámi • Crete, Greece 93 E1
Kálamos • Greece 92 C1
Kálamos • Greece 92 C1
Kalamunda • WA, Australia . . 34 C6
Kalándra Beach • Greece . . 69 [169]
Kalándra • Greece 92 D1
Kalándra • Greece 92 D1
Kalao • Indonesia 32 (1) B4
Kalapana • HI, United States . . 119 L8
Kalasin • Indonesia 32 E2
Kalat • Pakistan 28 A3
Kálathos Beach • Rhodes, Greece . . 69 [187]
Kálathos • Rhodes, Greece . . 93 F4
Kalaupapa Nat. Hist. Park •
   HI, United States 119 L3
Kalaupapa Nat. Hist. Park Park •
   HI, United States . . . . 120 [17]
Kalavárda • Rhodes, Greece . . 93 F1
Kale • Denizli, Turkey 15 J6
Kale • Alanya, Turkey 93 G3
Kale • Antalya, Turkey 93 G4
Kalecik • Turkey 15 O3
Kalemie • Dem. Rep. of Congo . . 23 D5
Kalevala • Russian Fed. 16 P4
Kalgoorlie • WA, Australia . . . 34 D6
Kali Liménes • Crete, Greece . . 93 E6
Kaliákra, Nos • Bulgaria 14 P6
Kalima • Dem. Rep. of Congo . . 23 D4
Kalimantan • Indonesia 32 E3
Kálimnos • Greece 15 I7
Kálimnos [I.] • Greece 92 D8
Kálimnos [I.] • Greece 92 D8
Kaliningrad • Russian Fed. . . . 13 J3
Kálix • Sweden 105 C7
Kalispell • MT, United States . . 117 E2
Kaliste • Czech Rep. 96 C4
Kalisz • Koszalinskie, Poland . . 13 E4
Kalisz • Kaliskie, Poland 13 E4
Kalithéa Beach • Greece . . . 69 [169]
Kalithiés Beach •
   Rhodes, Greece . . . . 69 [187]
Kalithiés • Rhodes, Greece . . 93 F2
Kalitva • Tanzania 102 H1
Kaliurang • Java, Indonesia . . 110 D7
Kalives Beach • Crete, Greece . . 69 [188]
Kalives • Crete, Greece 93 E1
Kálix • Sweden 16 L4
Kalix älv • Sweden 16 L3
Kalkan • Turkey 92 D9
Kalkan • Turkey 92 D9
Kalkim • Turkey 15 I4
Kalkrand • Namibia 24 B4
Kalkudah • Sri Lanka 106 D16
Kállandsö • Sweden 95 F3
Kallavesi • Finland 16 N5
Kallithéa • Jordan 98 A3
Kalloní Beach • Greece . . . . 69 [176]
Kalloní • Greece 92 D5
Kalloní • Greece 92 D5
Kallsjön • Sweden 16 G5
Kalmar • Sweden 95 F8
Kalmar [Adm] • Sweden 95 F8
Kalmarsund • Sweden 95 F8
Kalmykia • Russian Fed. 17 G5
Kaló Horió Beach •
   Crete, Greece . . . . 69 [191]
Kaló Horió • Crete, Greece . . 93 E8
Kalocsa • Hungary 13 H11
Kalofer • Bulgaria 14 L7
Kaloko-Honokohau Nat. Hist. Park •
   HI, United States 119 L8
Kaloko-Honokohau Nat. Hist. Park Park •
   HI, United States . . . . 120 [20]
Kalólimnos • Greece 92 D8
Kalólimnos • Greece 92 D8
Kalomo • Zambia 102 J1
Kalopanayiotis • Cyprus 93 J3
Kalpáki • Greece 15 B4
Kalpeni I. • India 106 D9
Kalsubai • India 25 I8
Kaluga • Russian Fed. 17 F4
Kalumburu Mission •
   WA, Australia 34 E2
Kalundborg Beach • Denmark . . 68 [24]
Kalundborg • Denmark 95 F10
Kalvåg • Norway 94 C1
Kalvarija • Lithuania 13 M3
Kalyazin • Russian Fed. 97 E4
Kam Shan Country Park •
   Hong Kong, China 107 H5
Kama • Russian Fed. 26 H6
Kamai • Chad 20 I4
Kamaishi • Japan 30 K5
Kaman • Turkey 15 O4
Kamanjab • Namibia 24 A3
Kamaran • Yemen 18 D6
Kamarang • Guyana 43 F2
Kamáres • Greece 92 D7
Kamáres • Greece 92 D7
Kambalda • WA, Australia . . . 34 D6
Kambalnaya Sopka, Vulkan •
   Russian Fed. 27 Q6
Kambanós, Akra • Greece . . . 15 F6
Kamchatka Peninsula •
   Russian Fed. 97 A7
Kamchatka, Poluostrov •
   Russian Fed. 27 Q5
Kamchatka [Riv] • Russian Fed. . . 27 Q6
Kamchatka volcanoes Heritage N •
   Russian Fed. . . . . 61 [66]
Kamchatskiy Zaliv •
   Russian Fed. 27 R5
Kamchiya • Bulgaria 97 D4
Kamchiya [Riv] • Bulgaria 14 O6
Kamen • Germany 81 E2
Kamen • Czech Rep. 96 C4
Kamen-na-Obi • Russian Fed. . . 26 N7
Kaména Voúrla Beach • Greece . . 69 [164]
Kaména Voúrla • Greece 92 D4
Kaména Voúrla • Greece 92 D4
Kamenka • Ukraine 17 E5
Kamenka • Russian Fed. 17 G4
Kamensk-Uralskiy • Russian Fed. . . 26 J6

Kamenz • Germany 9 J5
Kamet • India 28 C2
Kamien Pomorski • Poland . . . 13 D4
Kamina • Dem. Rep. of Congo . . 23 C5
Kamiros • Rhodes, Greece . . . 93 F1
Kámiros Skala • Rhodes, Greece . . 93 F1
Kamloops • BC, Canada 122 C3
Kammam • India 106 D3
Kamnarok Game Reserve • Kenya . . 101 G1
Kamp-Lintfort • Germany 81 E1
Kampala • Uganda 23 E3
Kampar • Malaysia 31 C6
Kampar • Indonesia 32 C2
Kampen • Netherlands 80 A7
Kampen Spa • Germany . . . . . 83 [2]
Kampenwand • Germany 82 J8
Kampinoski Nat. Park Park •
   Poland . . . . 72 [91]
Kâmpóng Saôm • Cambodia . . 31 C4
Kamrau, Teluk • Indonesia . . 35 (1) A1
Kamuela • HI, United States . . 119 L8
Kamui-Misaki • Japan 30 K3
Kamuku Wildlife Reserve Park •
   Nigeria . . . . 103 [32]
Kamvoúnia Ori • Greece 15 C4
Kamyshin • Russian Fed. 17 H4
Kanaauspcov • QU, Canada . . 39 P6
Kanariktok • NF, Canada 39 S6
Kanáli • Corfu, Greece 92 B1
Kanáli • Corfu, Greece 92 B1
Kananga • Dem. Rep. of Congo . . 30 I6
Kanazawa • Japan 30 I6
Kanchanaburi • Thailand . . . 109 H1
Kandanghaur • Java, Indonesia . . 110 D7
Kándanos • Crete, Greece . . . 93 E1
Kandavu • Fiji 35 (2) D2
Kandel • Germany 82 G8
Kandersteg • Switzerland 89 G6
Kandi • Benin 22 E2
Kandira • Turkey 15 L2
Kandla • India 28 B4
Kandooma • Maldives 106 E4
Kandrian • Papua New Guinea . . 35 (1) D2
Kandy Heritage C • Sri Lanka . . 63 [138]
Kandy • Sri Lanka 106 D15
Kanem • Chad 21 B5
Kaneohe • HI, United States . . 119 L6
Kaneohe Bay • HI, United States . . 119 L6
Kang • Botswana 24 C4
Kang Kra Chan • Thailand . . . 109 H3
Kangaba • Mali 20 D6
Kangar • Malaysia 32 C1
Kangaroo I. • SA, Australia . . . 34 G7
Kangasniemi • Finland 16 N6
Kangean, Kepulauan • Indonesia . . 32 F4
Kangerlussuaq • Greenland . . . 46 I3
Kangguq • D.P.R. of Korea . . . 30 D4
Kangiqsualujjuaq • QU, Canada . . 39 R5
Kangirsuk • QU, Canada 39 Q5
Kangmar • China 28 E3
Kangnung • Rep. of Korea . . . 30 E6
Kango • Gabon 22 G4
Kangribogê Feng • China 28 D2
Kanifinolhu • Maldives 106 E2
Kanin Nos • Russian Fed. 17 G1
Kanin Nos, mys • Russian Fed. . . 17 G1
Kanin, Poluostrov •
   Russian Fed. 17 I1
Kanjiza • F.R. of Yugoslavia . . 13 J11
Kankaanpää • Finland 95 E1
Kankan • Guinea 22 C2
Kankesanturai • Sri Lanka . . 106 D11
Kankroli • India 105 C4
Kankunskiy • Russian Fed. . . . 27 K5
Kannauj • India 105 C3
Kannonyakumari • India 106 D14
Kano • Nigeria 22 F2
Kano [Adm] • Nigeria 22 F2
Kanona • Zambia 24 D2
Kanoya • Japan 30 F9
Kanpur • India 105 C3
Kansas • United States 40 G4
Kansas City •
   KS/MO, United States 41 H4
Kansk • Russian Fed. 26 O6
Kansong • Rep. of Korea 30 E5
Kansyat • Indonesia 32 (1) E3
Kantara Castle • Cyprus 93 J2
Kantchari • Burkina Faso 20 F6
Kante • Togo 22 E3
Kanturk Castle • Ireland 79 F6
Kanuku Mtns • Guyana 43 F2
Kanya • Botswana 24 D4
Kanyemba • Zimbabwe 102 J2
Kanyu • Botswana 24 C4
Kaohsiung • Taiwan 29 G6
Kaolack • Senegal 22 A2
Kaole • Tanzania 102 H4
Kapanga • Dem. Rep. of Congo . . 23 C5
Kapchagay • Kazakhstan 26 M9
Kapellskär • Sweden 95 D2
Kapenguria • Kenya 101 G1
Kapfenberg • Austria 13 E10
Kapidagi Yarim Adasi • Turkey . . 15 I3
Kapit • Malaysia 32 E2
Kapka, Massif du • Chad/Sudan . . 21 D5
Kapos • Hungary 13 H11
Kappeln • Germany 8 E2
Kaprun Ski • Austria . . . . . . 70 [163]
Kaprun • Austria 89 H4
Kapuas • D.P.R. of Korea 30 E4
Kapuas • Indonesia 32 E2
Kapuskasing • OT, Canada . . . 39 O7
Kapuvár • Hungary 13 F10
Kara • Togo 22 E3
Kara Bogaz Gol • Turkmenistan . . 26 H9
Kara Burun • Turkey 15 J7
Kara Dong • China 26 N10
Kara Gölü • Turkey 15 O6
Kara Kum • Turkmenistan 18 G2
Kara Sea • Arctic Ocean 26 I4
Kara Strait • Russian Fed. 26 I4
Karaburun • Istanbul, Turkey . . 15 H5
Karaburun • Izmir, Turkey . . . 15 I5
Karabutak • Kazakhstan 26 J8
Karacabey • Turkey 15 J3
Karachay-Cherkessia •
   Russian Fed. 17 G6
Karachayevsk •
   Russian Fed. 27 R5
Karachi • Pakistan 28 A3
Karadeniz Bogazi • Turkey . . . 92 D7
Karadeniz Bogazi • Turkey . . . 15 I3
Karaginskiy, Ostrov •
   Russian Fed. 27 R5
Karagos, gora • Russian Fed. . . 26 O7

Karaikal • India 106 D11
Karain • Turkey 93 G1
Karak • Kazakhstan 26 J9
Karakalpakstan • Uzbekistan . . 26 I9
Karakax He • China 28 C1
Karakelong • Indonesia 32 (1) C2
Karakol • Kyrgyzstan 26 M9
Karakoram • Asia 28 C1
Karakorum • Mongolia 98 B3
Karakul, Ozero • China 18 J2
Karakumskiy Kanal •
   Turkmenistan 18 H2
Karam • Russian Fed. 15 O6
Karaman • Turkey 15 O6
Karamanli • Turkey 93 G1
Karamay • China 26 N9
Karamea • New Zealand 35 D5
Karamea Bight • New Zealand . . 35 C5
Karamiran He • China 28 E1
Karamiran Shankou • China . . 26 O10
Karamürsel • Turkey 15 K3
Karangsari Cave • Indonesia . . 110 D1
Karapsburg • Namibia 24 B5
Karasjok • Norway 16 M2
Karasu • Turkey 15 L2
Karasu [Riv] • Turkey 18 D1
Karasuk • Russian Fed. 26 M7
Karatas • Turkey 15 J5
Karatau • Kazakhstan 26 L9
Karatsu • Japan 30 E8
Karaul • India 105 C6
Karauli • India 105 C6
Karavastase, Gjiri i • Albania . . 14 G9
Karavostási • Cyprus 93 J1
Kárdamena Beach • Greece . . 69 [186]
Kardámena • Greece 92 D8
Kardámena • Greece 92 D8
Kardámila Beach • Greece . . 69 [177]
Kárditsa • Greece 15 C4
Kárdla • Estonia 16 L7
Kardoedouw • South Africa . . 100 C3
Kareha, Jbel • Morocco 11 F9
Karelia • Russian Fed. 16 P3
Karelia, Northern • Finland . . . 94 A6
Karelska Naset • Russian Fed. . . 17 O2
Karen • India 28 F6
Karen • Myanmar 31 B3
Karesuando • Sweden 16 L2
Kargi • China 17 F2
Kargopol • Russian Fed. 17 F2
Karhula • Finland 16 N6
Kari • Nigeria 20 H6
Kariai • Greece 15 F3
Kariani Beach • Greece . . . . 69 [171]
Karianous Nat. Park • Kenya . . 101 G3
Kariba • Zimbabwe 102 J1
Kariba Dam • Zambia/Zimbabwe . . 102 J1
Kariba, Lake • Zambia/Zimbabwe . . 102 J1
Karibib • Namibia 24 B4
Karidia Atoll • Maldives 106 E1
Kariega • South Africa 100 C3
Karigasniemi • Finland 17 D1
Karikari, Cape • New Zealand . . 35 D2
Karimata, Kepulauan • Indonesia . . 32 D3
Karimnagar • India 28 C5
Karimunjawa, Kepulauan •
   Indonesia 110 D3
Karin • Somalia 23 H1
Karisimbi • Rwanda 23 D4
Káristos • Greece 92 D4
Káristos • Greece 92 D4
Karjaa • Finland 95 E4
Karjala • Russian Fed. 17 P2
Karkar • Papua New Guinea . . 102 H3
Karkinitskiy Zaliv • Ukraine . . 14 P4
Karkonoski Nat. Park Park •
   Poland . . . . 72 [98]
Karlcby • Finland 16 L5
Karlik Shan • China 29 A2
Karlobag • Croatia 12 J4
Karlovac • Croatia 14 C4
Karlovo • Bulgaria 14 L7
Karlovy Vary • Czech Rep. . . . 96 C1
Karlsbad • Czech Rep. 96 C1
Karlsborg • Sweden 95 F3
Karlshamn • Sweden 95 F12
Karlskoga • Sweden 16 H7
Karlskrona • Sweden 95 F11
Karlslunde • Denmark 95 F10
Karlsruhe • Germany 82 G7
Karlstad • Sweden 16 G7
Karlstadt • Germany 82 H5
Karlstein-Nonn Spa • Germany . . 83 [261]
Karlstejn • Czech Rep. 96 C2
Karmah • Sudan 21 F4
Karmoy • Norway 94 C5
Karnak • Egypt 101 F4
Karnal • India 105 C2
Karnataka • India 106 D2
Karnataka Plateau • India . . . 106 D2
Karnische Skiregion Ski •
   Austria . . . . 70 [190]
Karnobat • Bulgaria 97 D3
Kärnten • Austria 13 C11
Karo Batak Villages • Indonesia . . 110 B2
Karoi • Zimbabwe 102 J2
Karon • Phuket, Thailand . . . 109 K2
Karon Beach • Phuket, Thailand . . 109 K2
Karonga • Malawi 24 E2
Karnataka • Sri Lanka 106 D15
Karoo, Great • South Africa . . 100 C3
Karoo, Little • South Africa . . 100 C3
Karoo Nat. Park Park •
   South Africa . . . . 103 [119]
Karora • Sudan 21 G4
Karpackie, Pogórze • Poland . . 13 J2
Karpas Peninsula • Cyprus . . . 93 J2
Kárpathos • Greece 92 D11
Kárpathos • Greece 92 D11
Kárpathos [I.] • Greece 92 D11
Kárpathos [I.] • Greece 92 D11
Karpathou, Stenó • Greece . . 92 D11
Karratha • WA, Australia 34 C4
Kars • Turkey 15 J3
Kars [Riv] • Turkey 15 I2
Karsakpay • Kazakhstan 26 K8
Karsiyaka • Turkey 15 I5
Karskiye Vorota, Proliv •
   Russian Fed. 26 I3
Karskoye More • Russian Fed. . . 15 K3
Karskaya • Kazakhstan 15 K3
Kartal • Turkey 15 H3
Karumba • QL, Australia 34 H3
Karun • Iran 18 F4
Karungi • Sweden 16 L3

Karungu • Kenya 23 E4
Karup • Denmark 95 F9
Karur • India 106 D11
Karviná • Czech Rep. 13 H8
Karwandelgebirge • Austria . . . 9 G9
Karwar • India 106 D11
Karymskoye • Russian Fed. . . 27 H6
Kas Beach • Turkey . . . . 69 [204]
Kas • Turkey 93 G3
Kasaba • Zambia 23 E6
Kasai • Dem. Rep. of Congo . . 23 C4
Kasai [Riv] •
   Dem. Rep. of Congo 23 C5
Kasama • Zambia 24 E2
Kasaragod • India 106 D6
Kasba Lake • NT/NU, Canada . . 38 K4
Kasba Tatla • Morocco 20 D2
Kasempa • Zambia 24 D2
Kasenga • Dem. Rep. of Congo . . 23 D6
Kasese • Uganda 23 E3
Kashan • Iran 18 F3
Kashgar • China 18 K2
Kashi • China 26 M10
Kashin • Russian Fed. 97 E4
Kashiwazaki • Japan 30 J6
Kashmar • Iran 18 G2
Kasimov • Russian Fed. 17 G3
Kaskinen • Finland 95 E1
Kaskö • Finland 95 E1
Kasongo • Dem. Rep. of Congo . . 23 D4
Kasongo-Lunda •
   Dem. Rep. of Congo 23 B5
Kaspiyskiy • Russian Fed. . . . 17 H5
Kassala • Sudan 21 G4
Kassándra • Greece 92 D1
Kassándra • Greece 92 D1
Kassándra, Akra • Greece . . . 15 E4
Kassándras, Kólpos • Greece . . 15 E3
Kassándria Beach • Greece . . 69 [166]
Kassel • Germany 9 E5
Kassel-Wilhelmshöhe Spa •
   Germany . . . . 83 [123]
Kasselburg • Germany 82 H1
Kasserine • Tunisia 101 E3
Kassiópi Beach • Corfu, Greece . . 69 [149]
Kassiópi • Corfu, Greece 92 B1
Kassiópi • Corfu, Greece 92 B1
Kássos • Greece 92 D11
Kássos • Greece 92 D11
Kastamonu • Turkey 15 O2
Kastaniés • Greece 15 H2
Kastelholm • Finland 95 E3
Kastéli • Crete, Greece 93 E7
Kastelruth • Italy 90 B1
Kasterlee Beach • Belgium . . . 68 [52]
Kasterlee • Belgium 80 A11
Kastoriá • Greece 15 C3
Kastoriás, Limni • Greece . . . 15 C3
Kastós • Greece 92 C1
Kastós • Greece 92 C1
Kástro Beach • Greece . . . . . 69 [157]
Kástro • Greece 92 D4
Kástro • Greece 92 D4
Kastrup [Apt] • Denmark 95 F11
Kasumiga-ura • Japan 30 K6
Kasungu • Malawi 24 E2
Kasungu Nat. Park Park • Malawi . . 103 [97]
Kasur • Pakistan 18 J3
Kata • Phuket, Thailand 109 K2
Kata Noi Beach •
   Phuket, Thailand 109 K2
Kata Noi Beach •
   Phuket, Thailand 109 K2
Kataba • Zambia 24 D3
Katahdin, Mt •
   ME, United States 118 G2
Katanga • Dem. Rep. of Congo . . 23 C5
Katanning • WA, Australia . . . 34 C6
Katikati • New Zealand 112 K2
Katiola • Côte d'Ivoire 22 D3
Katiti Aboriginal Land •
   NT, Australia 112 H3
Katmai Nat. Park & Preserve Park •
   AK, United States . . . . 120 [10]
Káto Ahaía • Greece 15 C5
Káto Korakiana Beach •
   Corfu, Greece . . . . 69 [149]
Káto Stavrós Beach • Greece . . 69 [170]
Káto Zákros • Crete, Greece . . 93 E8
Katong • Singapore 108 E2
Katoomba • NS, Australia . . . 111 G2
Katowice • Poland 13 H7
Katrine, Loch • United Kingdom . . 74 B1
Katrineholm • Sweden 95 D3
Katsina • Nigeria 22 F2
Katsuura • Japan 30 K7
Kattakurgan • Uzbekistan 18 I2
Kattegat • Denmark/Sweden . . 95 F6
Katu • Phuket, Thailand 109 K2
Katun • Russian Fed. 26 O7
Katwijk • Netherlands 80 C1
Katwijkse Duinen • Netherlands . . 80 C1
Katz, Burg • Germany 82 H2
Kau • Indonesia 32 (1) C2
Kau Paulamada, Gunung •
   Indonesia 32 (1) C3
Kau Sai Chau • Hong Kong, China . . 107 H6
Kauai • HI, United States 119 L2
Kauai Channel •
   HI, United States 119 L2
Kaub • Germany 82 H4
Kaufbeuren • Germany 82 J2
Kaufungen • Germany 9 E5
Kauhajoki • Finland 16 L5
Kauhava • Finland 16 L5
Kauhaveld • Botswana/Namibia . . 24 C3
Kauiainen • Finland 95 E4
Kaula • HI, United States . . . 119 L1
Kaunakakai • HI, United States . . 119 L3
Kaunas • Lithuania 13 M3
Kaunos • Turkey 92 D9
Kauvaki • Finland 95 E3
Kavadarci • F.Y.R. of Macedonia . . 14 J8
Kavajë • Albania 14 H8
Kavak • Turkey 15 H3
Kaval • India 25 I4
Kavála Beach • Greece . . . . 69 [171]
Kavála • Greece 92 D1

Kavála • Greece 92 D1
Kaválas, Kólpos • Greece 15 F3
Kavalerovo • Russian Fed. . . . 30 H2
Kavali • India 106 D3
Kavaratti • India 106 D9
Kavaratti I. • India 106 D9
Kavarna Beach • Bulgaria . . 69 [212]
Kavendou, Mt • Guinea 22 B2
Kavieng • Papua New Guinea . . 35 (1) E1
Kavir, Dasht-e • Iran 18 G3
Kávos • Corfu, Greece 92 B1
Kávos • Corfu, Greece 92 B1
Kavoúri • Greece 92 D7
Kavoúri • Greece 92 D7
Kavoúsi • Crete, Greece 93 E8
Kawa • Sudan 21 F4
Kawaikini • HI, United States . . 119 L2
Kawambwa • Zambia 24 D1
Kawasaki • Japan 30 J7
Kaweka Range • New Zealand . . 112 K4
Kawerau • New Zealand 112 K2
Kawhia • New Zealand 112 K1
Kawhia Harbour • New Zealand . . 112 K1
Kaxgar He • China 26 M10
Kaya • Burkina Faso 20 E6
Kayah • Myanmar 31 B3
Kayak • Russian Fed. 26 R3
Kayali Dagi • Turkey 15 H4
Kayan • Indonesia 32 F2
Kayes • Mali 22 B2
Kayseri • Turkey 18 C2
Kazachye • Russian Fed. 27 M2
Kazakhstan • Asia 26 K8
Kazan • Russian Fed. 17 H3
Kazan • NU, Canada 38 L4
Kazan Retto • Japan 25 P7
Kazandzik • Turkmenistan . . . 18 G2
Kazanluk Heritage C • Bulgaria . . 64 [172]
Kazanluk • Bulgaria 97 D3
Kazerun • Iran 18 F4
Kazincbarcika • Hungary 13 J9
Kaziranga Nat. Park Heritage N •
   India . . . . 61 [108]
Kazuma Pan Nat. Park • Zimbabwe . . 102 J1
Ké • Chad 20 I5
Kéa • Greece 92 D7
Kéa • Greece 92 D7
Kearney • NE, United States . . 40 G3
Kebili • Tunisia 101 E5
Kebnekaise • Sweden 16 J3
Kebumen • Java, Indonesia . . 110 D6
Kecel • Hungary 13 I11
Kechika • BC, Canada 38 F5
Kecskemét • Hungary 13 I11
Kedah • Malaysia 31 C5
Kedainiai • Lithuania 13 N2
Kédia d'Idjil • Mauritania 20 C4
Kediri • Java, Indonesia 110 D7
Kédougou • Senegal 22 B2
Kedzierzyn-Kozle • Poland . . . 13 G7
Keekorok Lodge • Kenya . . . 101 G3
Keel • Ireland 79 F1
Keele Peak • YT, Canada 38 F4
Keene • NH, United States . . 118 G3
Keetmanshoop • Namibia . . . 24 B5
Kef Lakhdar Chergui • Algeria . . 11 O9
Kefalonía • Greece 92 C2
Kefalonía • Greece 92 C2
Kefalonía Nat. Park • Greece . . 92 C2
Kefalonía Nat. Park • Greece . . 92 C2
Keflavik • Iceland 16 (1) B2
Kehl • Germany 9 C8
Kehlheim • Germany 9 G8
Kehlstein • Germany 82 J8
Keighley • United Kingdom . . . 7 K8
Keilah • Jordan 98 A7
Keitele • Finland 16 M5
Keith • SA, Australia 34 H7
Keith Arm • NT, Canada 38 G3
Keitum Spa • Germany . . . . . . 83 [2]
Kejimkujik Nat. Park •
   NS, Canada 123 D7
Kek Lok Si Temple •
   Penang, Malaysia 108 C1
Kekaha • HI, United States . . 119 L2
Kékes • Hungary 13 I10
Kekova • Turkey 93 G3
Kel Tepe • Izmit, Turkey 15 L3
Kel Tepe • Zonguldak, Turkey . . 15 N2
Kelafo • Ethiopia 23 G2
Kelang • Malaysia 108 D3
Kelang [I.] • Malaysia 108 D3
Kelantan • Malaysia 31 C5
Keld Chapel • United Kingdom . . 74 C2
Kelem • Ethiopia 23 F2
Kelibia • Tunisia 101 E2
Kellberg Spa • Germany . . . 83 [265]
Kelle • Congo 22 G4
Kellenhusen Spa • Germany . . 83 [24]
Kellerwand • Austria/Italy 89 H8
Kellet, Cape • NT, Canada . . . 38 F2
Kellie's Castle • Malaysia . . . 108 C2
Kellogg • Russian Fed. 27 C4
Kellogg • MT, United States . . 117 E2
Kells • Ireland 79 E1
Kélo • Chad 22 I3
Kelowna • BC, Canada 122 C4
Kelsey • MN, Canada 38 L5
Kelsey Bay • BC, Canada 38 F6
Kelti, Jbel • Morocco 11 F9
Keluang • Malaysia 31 C6
Kem • Russian Fed. 17 E2
Kemalpasa • Turkey 15 J6
Kemaman • Malaysia 108 A4
Kemer • Turkey 15 J6
Kemer • Mugla, Turkey . . . . 69 [203]
Kemer • Antalya, Turkey 93 G3
Kemer Barji • Turkey 15 J6
Kemerovo • Russian Fed. 26 O6
Kemijärvi • Finland 16 N3
Kemijärvi [Lake] • Finland . . . 16 N3
Kemijoki • Finland 16 N3
Kemiö • Finland 95 E3
Kempen • Belgium 5 I3
Kempen • Germany 81 E1
Kempendyay • Russian Fed. . . 27 J4
Kempens Kanaal • Belgium . . . 5 I3
Kempsey • NS, Australia 34 J6
Kempt, Lac • OT, Canada . . . 39 O7
Kempten • Germany 82 J6
Kenai Peninsula •
   AK, United States 46 E3
Kenai Peninsula •
   AK, United States . . . . 120 [11]
Kenai Fjords Nat. Park Park •
   AK, United States . . . . 120 [11]
Kendal • United Kingdom 74 C4
Kendari • Indonesia 32 (1) B3
Kendawangan • Indonesia . . . 32 E3
Kenema • Sierra Leone 22 B3
Keng Tung • Myanmar 31 B2
Kenge • Dem. Rep. of Congo . . 23 B4
Kengur Shan • China 26 M10
Kenhardt • South Africa 24 C5

Kenitra • Morocco 101 D1
Kenkoure • Guinea 22 B2
Kenmare • Ireland 79 F7
Kenmare [Riv] • Ireland 79 F7
Kennacraig • United Kingdom 78 A2
Kennebec • ME, United States 118 G2
Kennebunkport • ME, United States 118 G3
Kennedy, John F. [Apt] • NY, United States 118 H2
Kennedy, John F., Nat. Hist. Site Park • MA, United States 121 [347]
Kennedy, John F., Space Center • FL, United States 119 M6
Kennemerduinen, Nat. Park de • Netherlands 80 C1
Kennesaw Mtn Nat. Battlefield Park Park • GA, United States 121 [209]
Kennet • United Kingdom 5 B3
Kennewick • WA, United States 117 C2
Keno Hill • YT, Canada 38 D4
Kenogami • OT, Canada 39 N6
Kenora • OT, Canada 38 M7
Kenosha • WI, United States 41 I3
Kensington • United Kingdom 74 E1
Kensington Oval • Barbados 125 H3
Kent • United Kingdom 74 E4
Kent Peninsula • NU, Canada 38 J3
Kentau • Kazakhstan 26 K9
Kentucky • United States 41 I4
Kentucky Kingdom Park • KY, United States 121 [W]
Kentwood • LA, United States 118 K4
Kenya • Africa 101 G
Kenya, Mt • Kenya 101 G3
Kenya, Mt, Nat. Park Heritage N • Kenya 61 [89]
Kenyatta, Jomo [Apt] • Kenya 101 G3
Keoladeo Nat. Park Heritage N • India 61 [106]
Keoladeo Nat. Park • India 105 C2
Kepi • Indonesia 32 (1) E4
Kepice • Poland 13 F3
Kepler Mtns • New Zealand 112 L1
Kepno • Poland 13 G6
Kepsut • Turkey 15 J4
Kerala • India 106 D10
Kéran, Parc nat. de la Park • Togo 103 [29]
Kerang • VI, Australia 111 G1
Kerava • Finland 95 E4
Keraz • Algeria 20 E3
Kerch • Ukraine 17 F5
Kerema • Papua New Guinea 35 (1) D2
Kerempe Burun • Turkey 15 O1
Keren • Eritrea 21 G4
Kerguelen Is. • Indian Ocean 19 (1) J1
Keri • Greece 92 C3
Keri • Greece 92 C3
Kerinci, Gunung • Indonesia 32 C3
Kerio Valley Game Reserve • Kenya 101 G1
Keriya • China 28 D1
Keriya He • China 28 D1
Kerken • Germany 81 E1
Kerki • Turkmenistan 18 I2
Kérkira Beach • Corfu, Greece 69 [149]
Kérkira • Corfu, Greece 92 B1
Kérkira • Corfu, Greece 92 B1
Kérkira • Corfu, Greece 92 B1
Kérkira [I.] • Greece 92 B1
Kérkira [I.] • Greece 92 B1
Kerkouane Heritage C • Tunisia 64 [228]
Kerkouane • Tunisia 101 D2
Kermadec Is. • New Zealand 33 J9
Kerman • Iran 18 G3
Kerme • Turkey 15 J6
Kerni • Finland 16 M4
Kéros • Greece 92 D8
Kéros • Greece 92 D8
Kérouane • Guinea 22 C3
Kerpen • Germany 9 B6
Kerry • Ireland 79 F5
Kerry Head • Ireland 79 F5
Kerry, Ring of • Ireland 79 F7
Kerteminde • Denmark 95 F14
Kertosono • Java, Indonesia 110 D7
Kesan • Turkey 15 H3
Kesen'numa • Japan 30 K5
Keski-Suomi • Finland 16 M5
Keski-Suomi • Finland 94 A9
Keskin • Turkey 15 O4
Kessingland Beach • United Kingdom 75 [49]
Kestel Beach • Turkey 69 [196]
Keswick • United Kingdom 74 C2
Keszthely • Hungary 13 G11
Ket • Russian Fed. 26 O6
Ketapang • Borneo, Indonesia 32 E3
Ketapang • Java, Indonesia 110 D8
Ketchikan • AK, United States 38 E5
Ketou • Benin 22 E3
Ketrzyn • Poland 13 K3
Kettering • United Kingdom 7 L9
Ketzin • Germany 81 F3
Keukenhof • Netherlands 80 C1
Keurusselka • Finland 95 E2
Keuruu • Finland 95 E2
Keweenaw Nat. Hist. Park Park • MI, United States 121 [160]
Key • St Kitts & Nevis 125 G1
Key Biscayne • FL, United States 119 M8
Key Deer Nat. Wildlife Refuge • FL, United States 119 M8
Key Largo • FL, United States 119 M8
Key, Lough • Ireland 79 F2
Key West • FL, United States 119 M7
Keystone Ski • CO, United States 116 [93]
Kezhma • Russian Fed. 26 R6
Kezmarok • Slovak Rep. 13 J8
Khabarovsk • Russian Fed. 27 M7
Khaburah, Al • Oman 18 G5
Khadra • Algeria 11 L8
Khairpur • Pakistan 28 A3
Khajuraho Heritage C • India 63 [121]
Khajuraho • India 105 C7
Khakassia • Russian Fed. 26 O7
Khalesavey • Russian Fed. 26 M5
Khalij Sirt • Libya 21 C1
Khaluf • Oman 18 G5
Khambhat, Gulf of • India 28 B4
Khami Ruins Nat. Mon. Heritage C • Zimbabwe 63 [101]
Khami Ruins Nat. Mon. • Zimbabwe 102 J3
Khamir • Yemen 18 D6
Khamis Ash Shallal al • Sudan 21 F4
Khamra • Russian Fed. 27 H4
Khan al Ahmar • Jordan 98 A6
Khandwa • India 28 C4
Khanka, Ozero • Russian Fed. 27 L8
Khanpur • Pakistan 28 B3
Khanty-Mansiysk • Russian Fed. 26 K5
Khao Chamao • Thailand 109 H4
Khao Kheaw • Thailand 109 H2

Khao Kheaw Zoo • Thailand 109 H4
Khao Laem • Thailand 109 H2
Khao Mokochu • Thailand 31 B3
Khao Saming • Thailand 31 C4
Khao Yai • Thailand 109 H2
Kharabali • Russian Fed. 17 H5
Kharagpur • India 28 E4
Kharevaddo Beach • Goa, India 105 B1
Khârga, El • Egypt 101 F3
Kharkov • Ukraine 17 F4
Kharmanli • Bulgaria 14 M8
Kharovsk • Russian Fed. 17 F3
Khartoum • Sudan 21 F4
Khasan • Russian Fed. 30 F3
Khash • Afghanistan 18 H3
Khaskovo • Bulgaria 97 D3
Khatangha • Russian Fed. 26 R3
Khatt Atoui • Mauritania 20 B4
Khemis Miliana • Algeria 11 N8
Khemisset • Morocco 20 D2
Khenchela • Algeria 20 G1
Khenifra • Morocco 101 D1
Kherson • Ukraine 17 E5
Kheta • Russian Fed. 27 E2
Kheta [Riv] • Russian Fed. 26 R3
Khilok • Russian Fed. 27 H6
Khilok [Riv] • Russian Fed. 27 H6
Khimki • Russian Fed. 97 E4
Khionótripa • Greece 15 F2
Khiva • Uzbekistan 18 H1
Khizi Pogost Heritage C • Russian Fed. 63 [77]
Khizi Pogost • Russian Fed. 96 A2
Khmel'nitskiy • Ukraine 17 D5
Kho Khot Kra • Myanmar 31 B4
Khodzheyli • Uzbekistan 18 G1
Khok Pip • Thailand 109 H2
Kholm • Afghanistan 28 A1
Kholm • Russian Fed. 97 E3
Kholmsk • Russian Fed. 27 N7
Khon Kaen • Thailand 31 C3
Khonuu • Russian Fed. 27 N3
Khoper • Russian Fed. 17 G4
Khor • Russian Fed. 27 M7
Khorasan • Iran 18 G3
Khorat • Thailand 109 F2
Khorog • Tajikistan 18 J2
Khorramabad • Iran 18 E3
Khorranshahr • Iran 18 E3
Khotan • China 98 B2
Khouribga • Morocco 101 D1
Khram, Ko • Thailand 109 H4
Khrysokhou Bay • Cyprus 93 J1
Khufayfiyah, Al • Saudi Arabia 18 D5
Khulna • Bangladesh 28 E4
Khun Yuam • Thailand 109 G1
Khuriya Muriya, Jaza'ir • Oman 18 G6
Khurtum, Al • Sudan 21 F4
Khurtum Bahri, Al • Sudan 21 F4
Khwae Noi • Thailand 109 H1
Khyber Pass • Pakistan 28 B2
Kiamba • Philippines 31 G5
Kiang Nat. Park Park • Gambia 103 [12]
Kiangaroan, WA • QL, Australia 34 J5
Kiantajärvi • Finland 16 O4
Kiáton • Greece 15 D6
Kiboko • Kenya 23 F4
Kibombo • Dem. Rep. of Congo 23 D4
Kibondo • Tanzania 102 H1
Kicevo • F.Y.R. of Macedonia 15 B2
Kicking Horse Pass • AL/BC, Canada 122 C4
Kidal • Mali 20 F5
Kidderminster • United Kingdom 74 D1
Kidira • Senegal 22 B2
Kidnappers, Cape • New Zealand 112 K4
Kiedrich • Germany 82 H4
Kiel • Germany 8 F2
Kielce • Poland 13 J7
Kieler Bucht • Germany 8 F2
Kierspe • Germany 81 E4
Kieta • Papua New Guniea 35 (1) F2
Kiev • Ukraine 17 E4
Kiev Heritage C • Ukraine 64 [204]
Kiffa • Mauritania 20 C5
Kifisós • Greece 15 D5
Kigoma • Tanzania 102 H1
Kihei • HI, United States 119 L3
Kihnu • Estonia 16 L7
Kii-Suido • Japan 30 H8
Kiikoinen • Finland 95 E1
Kikai • Japan 29 H5
Kikambala • Kenya 101 G5
Kikinda • F.R. of Yugoslavia 15 F6
Kikládes • Greece 15 G6
Kikonai • Japan 30 K4
Kikori • Papua New Guinea 35 (1) C2
Kikori [Riv] • Papua New Guinea 35 (1) C2
Kikwit • Dem. Rep. of Congo 23 B5
Kil-Sanchi • Japan 30 H7
Kilauea Caldera • HI, United States 119 L8
Kilchoan • United Kingdom 78 A2
Kilchu • D.P.R. of Korea 30 E4
Kilcock • Ireland 79 E1
Kilconnell Friary • Ireland 79 F4
Kilcrea Abbey • Ireland 79 F8
Kilcreggan • United Kingdom 78 A3
Kilcullen • Ireland 79 E3
Kildare • Ireland 79 E3
Kildare [Adm] • Ireland 79 E3
Kilfenora • Ireland 79 E4
Kilgore • TX, United States 119 N2
Kilifi • Kenya 101 G5
Kilimanjaro, Mt • Tanzania 102 H2
Kilimanjaro Nat. Park Heritage N • Tanzania 61 [92]
Kilimanjaro Nat. Park • Tanzania 102 H2
Kilimanjaro Nat. Park Park • Tanzania 103 [90]
Kilindoni • Tanzania 102 H4
Kiliya • Ukraine 14 O4
Kiliya • Ukraine 14 O4
Kilkee • Ireland 79 F4
Kilkeel • Ireland 79 E9
Kilkenny • Ireland 79 E7
Kilkenny [Adm] • Ireland 79 E3
Kilkieran • Ireland 79 F3
Kilkis • Greece 15 D3
Killala Beach • Ireland 68 [44]
Killala • Ireland 79 F2
Killala Bay • Ireland 79 F2
Killaloe • Ireland 79 F6
Killarney • Ireland 79 F6
Killarney, Lake • Bahamas 124 B3
Killarney Nat. Park Park • Ireland 72 [40]
Killarney Nat. Park • Ireland 79 F7
Killary Harbour • Ireland 79 F3
Killerton House • United Kingdom 74 F2
Killiecrankie, Pass of • United Kingdom 74 B1
Killimer • Germany 82 J3
Killiney Beach • Ireland 68 [35]
Killiney • Ireland 79 E4

Killington Ski • VT, United States 116 [199]
Killington • VT, United States 118 G3
Killorglin • Ireland 79 F7
Killybegs Beach • Ireland 68 [46]
Kilmacduagh • Ireland 79 F4
Kilmallock • Ireland 79 F6
Kilmichael Point • Ireland 79 E5
Kilombero • Tanzania 102 H4
Kiloja • Tanzania 102 H4
Kilpisjärvi • Finland 16 K2
Kilronan Beach • Ireland 68 [43]
Kilronan • Ireland 79 F3
Kilrush Beach • Ireland 68 [42]
Kilrush • Ireland 79 F6
Kilttan I. • India 106 D9
Kilwa • Dem. Rep. of Congo 24 D1
Kilwa Kisiwani Heritage C • Tanzania 63 [99]
Kilwa Kisiwani • Tanzania 102 H4
Kilwa Kivinje • Tanzania 102 H4
Kilwa Masoko • Tanzania 102 H4
Kilyos • Turkey 92 D3
Kilyos • Turkey 92 D3
Kimbe • Papua New Guinea 35 (1) E2
Kimbe Bay • Papua New Guinea 35 (1) E2
Kimberley • South Africa 24 C5
Kimberley Ski • BC, Canada 116 [9]
Kimberley Plateau • WA, Australia 34 E3
Kimch'aek • D.P.R. of Korea 30 E4
Kimch'on • Rep. of Korea 30 D6
Kimi • Greece 92 D4
Kimi • Greece 92 D4
Kimito • Finland 16 L6
Kimito [I.] • Finland 16 L6
Kimolos • Greece 92 D7
Kimolos • Greece 92 D7
Kimry • Russian Fed. 97 E4
Kinabalu, Gunung • Malaysia 32 F1
Kinabatangan • Malaysia 32 F1
Kinaros • Greece 92 D8
Kinaros • Greece 92 D8
Kinbasket Lake • BC, Canada 122 C4
Kincardine • OT, Canada 39 O8
Kincardine • United Kingdom 74 B4
Kind • Sweden 95 F4
Kinda • Sweden 95 F4
Kinder • LA, United States 118 K3
Kinder Scout • United Kingdom 5 B1
Kinderdijk • Netherlands 80 C3
Kinderdijk-Elshout Heritage C • Netherlands 64 [28]
Kindersley • SA, Canada 38 J6
Kindia • Guinea 22 B2
Kindu • Dem. Rep. of Congo 23 D4
Kineshma • Russian Fed. 17 G3
King Country, The • New Zealand 112 K1
King George, Fort • Trinidad & Tobago 125 K2
King George I. • Antarctica 59 A10
King I. • TS, Australia 34 H7
King Jr., Martin Luther, Nat. Historic Site Park • GA, United States 121 [211]
King Leopold • WA, Australia 34 E3
King Ridge Ski • NH, United States 116 [207]
King Sound • WA, Australia 34 D3
King William I. • NU, Canada 38 L3
King William's Town • South Africa 24 D6
King's Bay Waterfall • Trinidad & Tobago 125 K2
King's Lynn • United Kingdom 7 M9
Kingaroy • QL, Australia 111 F6
Kingisepp • Russian Fed. 97 E3
Kingman • Pacific Ocean 33 K5
Kingman • AZ, United States 118 J1
Kingoonya • SA, Australia 34 G6
Kings Canyon • NT, Australia 34 F5
Kings Canyon Nat. Park • CA, United States 117 F4
Kings Canyon Nat. Park Park • CA, United States 120 [53]
Kings Landing • NB, Canada 123 D6
Kings Mtn Nat. Military Park Park • SC, United States 121 [242]
Kings, Valley of the • Egypt 101 F4
Kingsbarns Beach • United Kingdom 75 [10]
Kingsbridge • United Kingdom 74 F2
Kingscote • SA, Australia 34 G7
Kingsford Smith [Apt] • NS, Australia 111 G2
Kingston • New Zealand 112 L2
Kingston • NY, United States 118 H1
Kingston • OT, Canada 122 B6
Kingston • Jamaica 124 C4
Kingston South East • SA, Australia 34 G7
Kingston upon Hull • United Kingdom 7 L8
Kingston upon Hull [Adm] • United Kingdom 75 A4
Kingston-upon-Thames • United Kingdom 74 E1
Kingstown • St Vincent 37 I5
Kingsville • TX, United States 119 N5
Kingussie • United Kingdom 74 A3
Kinik • Turkey 15 I4
Kinna • Sweden 95 F3
Kinnairds Head • United Kingdom 6 K4
Kinnegad • Ireland 79 E2
Kinnekulle • Sweden 95 F3
Kinoosao • MN, Canada 38 K5
Kinross • United Kingdom 74 B2
Kinsale • Ireland 79 F7
Kinsarvik • Norway 94 C4
Kinshasa • Dem. Rep. of Congo 23 B4
Kinston • NC, United States 118 H5
Kintap • Indonesia 32 F3
Kintyre • United Kingdom 6 G6
Kintyre, Mull of • United Kingdom 7 G6
Kinvarra Beach • Ireland 68 [43]
Kinvarra • Ireland 79 F4
Kinyeti • Sudan 23 E3
Kínzig • Germany 9 D8
Kióni • Greece 92 C2
Kióni • Greece 92 C2
Kiparissia Beach • Greece 69 [158]
Kiparissiakós Kolpos • Greece 15 C6
Kipembawe • Tanzania 102 H3
Kipengere Range • Tanzania 102 H3
Kipili • Tanzania 102 H3
Kipushi • Dem. Rep. of Congo 24 D2
Kirakira • Solomon Is. 35 (1) G3
Kirazli • Turkey 15 H3
Kirbyville • TX, United States 119 N4
Kirchberg in Tirol Ski • Austria 70 [156]
Kirchdorf • Austria 89 H3
Kirchenlamitz • Germany 82 H2
Kirchheim, Pass of • United Kingdom 74 B1
Kirchheim • Germany 82 J3
Kirchheim bei München • Germany 82 J3
Kirchheim unter Teck • Germany 9 E8
Kirchheim-Bolanden • Germany 82 H4

Kireç • Turkey 15 J4
Kirenç • Turkey 93 G2
Kirensk • Russian Fed. 27 G5
Kirgiz Steppe • Kazakhstan 26 I8
Kirgöz Hani • Turkey 93 G1
Kiri • Dem. Rep. of Congo 22 H5
Kiribati • Pacific Ocean 33 J6
Kirikkale • Turkey 15 O4
Kirinyaga • Kenya 23 F3
Kirishi • Russian Fed. 97 E1
Kiritimati • Kiribati 33 L5
Kirkagaç • Turkey 15 I4
Kirkby Lonsdale • United Kingdom 7 J7
Kirkcaldy • United Kingdom 74 B4
Kirkenær • Norway 94 B2
Kirkenes • Norway 16 P2
Kirkintilloch • United Kingdom 74 B3
Kirkjubæjarklaustur • Iceland 16 (1) D3
Kirkkonummi • Finland 95 E4
Kirkland Lake • OT, Canada 39 O7
Kirklareli • Turkey 15 I2
Kirkpatrick, Mt • Antarctica 46 (1) V1
Kirkstone Pass • United Kingdom 74 C2
Kirkuk • Iraq 18 D2
Kirkwall • United Kingdom 6 J3
Kirkwood • South Africa 100 C8
Kirkwood Ski • CA, United States 116 [59]
Kirn • Germany 5 K5
Kirov • Russian Fed. 17 E4
Kirovograd • Ukraine 17 E5
Kirovsk • Russian Fed. 17 E1
Kirovskiy • Russian Fed. 27 K6
Kirriemuir • United Kingdom 74 B2
Kirs • Russian Fed. 17 I3
Kiruna • Sweden 16 K3
Kisa • Sweden 95 F4
Kisakata • Japan 30 L3
Kisangani • Dem. Rep. of Congo 23 D3
Kisangarh • India 105 G5
Kishiwada • Japan 30 H7
Kisii • Kenya 101 G3
Kisite Nat. Park • Kenya 101 G5
Kiskörei Víztároló • Hungary 13 I10
Kiskörös • Hungary 13 I11
Kisköre Víztározó • Hungary 13 I11
Kiskunfélegyháza • Hungary 13 I11
Kiskunhalas • Hungary 13 I11
Kiskunmajsa • Hungary 13 I11
Kiskunság • Hungary 13 I11
Kiskunság Nat. Park Park • Hungary 72 [106]
Kislovodsk • Russian Fed. 17 G6
Kismayo • Somalia 23 G4
Kismayo Nat. Park Park • Somalia 103 [68]
Kismayu • Somalia 23 G4
Kiso • Japan 30 I7
Kissámou Kástéli • Crete, Greece 93 E1
Kissámou, Kólpos • Crete, Greece 93 E1
Kissidougou • Guinea 22 B3
Kissimmee • FL, United States 121 C2
Kisújszállás • Hungary 13 J10
Kisumu • Kenya 101 G3
Kita • Mali 22 C2
Kitakyushu • Japan 30 F8
Kitale • Kenya 101 G1
Kitami • Japan 30 L3
Kitami-Sanchi • Japan 30 L3
Kitay, Ozero • Ukraine 14 O4
Kitchener-Waterloo • OT, Canada 16 P5
Kitee • Finland 16 P5
Kitessa • Central African Rep. 23 B2
Kitgum • Uganda 23 E3
Kithira • Greece 92 D10
Kithira • Greece 92 D10
Kithira [I.] • Greece 92 D7
Kithira [I.] • Greece 92 D7
Kithnos • Greece 92 D7
Kithnos • Greece 92 D7
Kithnou, Stenó • Greece 15 F6
Kiti • Cyprus 93 J4
Kiti, Cape • Cyprus 93 J4
Kitimat • BC, Canada 38 F5
Kitimat Ranges • BC, Canada 38 F6
Kitridge Point • Barbados 125 H4
Kitros • Greece 15 D3
Kittilä • Finland 16 M3
Kittul • Kenya 23 F4
Kitunda • Tanzania 102 H3
Kitwe-Nkana • Zambia 24 D2
Kiu Tsui Chau • Hong Kong, China 107 H6
Kiunga • Papua New Guinea 35 (1) C2
Kiunga Marine Game Reserve • Kenya 101 G4
Kiuruvesi • Finland 16 N5
Kivijärvi • Finland 16 M5
Kivik • Sweden 95 F11
Kivioli • Estonia 16 N7
Kivu • Dem. Rep. of Congo 23 D4
Kivu, Lac • Rwanda/Dem. Rep. of Congo 23 D4
Kiwai • Papua New Guinea 35 (1) C2
Kizikkaya • Turkey 93 G1
Kizil Adalar • Turkey 18 J1
Kizil Adalar • Turkey 92 D3
Kizil Dag • Turkey 15 N7
Kizil Irmak • Turkey 15 O3
Kizilcahaman • Turkey 15 N3
Kizilhisar • Turkey 15 K6
Kizilkadag • Turkey 93 G1
Kizimen Sopka, Vulkan • Russian Fed. 27 R5
Kizyl-Arvat • Turkmenistan 18 G2
Kjellerup • Denmark 95 F9
Kjøllefjord [Apt] • Norway 95 F9
Kladanj • Bosnia-Herz. 14 F5
Kladno • Czech Rep. 96 C3
Kladruby • Czech Rep. 96 C3
Klaeng • Thailand 109 H4
Klagenfurt • Austria 13 D11
Klaipéda • Lithuania 13 K2
Klamath • CA/OR, United States 117 F1
Klamath Falls • OR, United States 117 F1
Klamath Mtns • CA, United States 117 F1
Kla • Russian Fed. 16 I2
Kola Peninsula • Russian Fed. 16 I2
Kolaka • Indonesia 32 (1) B3
Kolar • India 106 D7
Kolar Gold Fields • India 106 D7
Kolari • Finland 16 M3
Kolárovo • Slovak Rep. 13 G10
Kolayat • India 105 C1
Kolbäck • Sweden 95 D1

Kleinburg • OT, Canada 122 B9
Kleinmachnow • Germany 81 F3
Kleinwalsertal Ski • Austria 70 [128]
Klenci pod Cerchovem • Czech Rep. 96 C3
Klerksdorp • South Africa 24 D5
Kleve • Germany 8 B5
Klibreck, Ben • United Kingdom 6 H3
Klin • Russian Fed. 97 E4
Klincy • Russian Fed. 17 E4
Klingenburg • Germany 82 G4
Klingenthal • Germany 13 B7
Klinovec • Czech Rep. 96 C1
Klitehamn • Sweden 16 J8
Klió Beach • Greece 69 [176]
Klippan • Sweden 95 F11
Klitmøller • Denmark 95 D1
Klobuck • Poland 13 H7
Klodzko • Poland 13 F6
Klöfta • Norway 94 B2
Klondike • YT, Canada 38 D4
Klondike Gold Rush Nat. Hist. Park • AK, United States 120 [15]
Klosterneuburg • Austria 13 F3
Klosters Ski • Switzerland 70 [112]
Klosters • Switzerland 89 G4
Kloten • Switzerland 9 D9
Kluane Nat. Park Heritage N • YT, Canada 60 [1]
Kluczbork • Poland 13 H7
Klungkung • Bali, Indonesia 110 C4
Klyuchevskaya Sopka, Vulkan • Russian Fed. 27 R5
Knäred • Sweden 95 F11
Knarvik • Norway 94 C3
Knebworth House • United Kingdom 74 E1
Knechtsteden • Germany 81 E3
Knife River Indian Villages Nat. Hist. Site Park • ND, United States 120 [149]
Knightshayes Court • United Kingdom 74 F2
Knin • Croatia 12 K4
Knislinge • Sweden 95 F11
Knittelfeld • Austria 13 D10
Knivsjkellodden • Norway 16 M1
Knivsta • Sweden 95 D2
Knock • Ireland 79 F2
Knock [Apt] • Ireland 79 F2
Knockmealdown Mtns • Ireland 7 E9
Knoebels Grove • PA, United States 118 H1
Knokke-Heist • Belgium 80 B2
Knóssós • Crete, Greece 93 E1
Knott's Berry Farm Park • CA, United States 120 [G]
Knott's Camp Snoopy Park • MN, United States 121 [R]
Knowth • Ireland 79 E2
Knox, Cape • BC, Canada 38 E6
Knoxville • TN, United States 41 J4
Knutby • Sweden 95 D2
Knuthenborg Park • Denmark 95 F14
Knysna • South Africa 100 C7
Knysna Nat. Lake Area • South Africa 100 C7
Ko • Japan 30 J4
Kobayashi • Japan 30 F9
Kobe • Japan 30 H7
København Beach • Denmark 68 [21]
København • Denmark 95 F11
Kobern-Gondorf • Germany 82 H1
Kobetdag • Turkmenistan 18 G2
Koblenz • Germany 82 H2
Kobrin • Belarus 13 N5
Kobuk Valley Nat. Park Park • AK, United States 120 [4]
Koca • Balikesir, Turkey 15 I3
Koca • Zonguldak, Turkey 15 N2
Kocabas • Turkey 93 G1
Kocaeli • Turkey 15 I3
Kochechum • Russian Fed. 26 Q4
Kochel • Germany 82 J7
Kochelsee • Germany 82 J7
Kocher • Germany 9 E7
Kochi • Japan 30 G8
Koçhisar Ovasi • Turkey 93 H2
Kochubey • Russian Fed. 17 H6
Kodagu • India 106 D9
Kodaikanal • India 106 D10
Kodiak I. • AK, United States 40 (2) F2
Kodikkarai Bird Sanctuary • India 106 D11
Kodok • Sudan 21 F5
Kodungallur • India 106 D10
Kodyma • Ukraine 14 O1
Kodyma [Riv] • Ukraine 14 O1
Kodzha Balkan • Bulgaria 14 N7
Koës • Namibia 24 B5
Köflach • Austria 13 E10
Kofu • Japan 30 J7
Kogalniceanu, Mihail [Apt] • Romania 97 D2
Køge • Denmark 95 F14
Køge Bugt • Denmark 95 F15
Kohat • Pakistan 28 B2
Kohima • India 28 F3
Kohtla-Järve • Estonia 16 N7
Kohu Dagi • Turkey 15 K7
Koje • D.P.R. of Korea 30 E7
Kojo • D.P.R. of Korea 30 D5
Kojonup • WA, Australia 34 C6
Kokand • Uzbekistan 32 (1) D3
Kokatea • Indonesia 32 (1) D3
Kokchetav • Kazakhstan 26 K7
Kokemäenjoki • Finland 95 E2
Kokemäki • Finland 95 E1
Kokini Hani • Crete, Greece 93 E3
Kokkina • Cyprus 15 (1) B1
Kokkola • Finland 16 L5
Kokkoni Beach • Greece 69 [155]
Koko • Nigeria 22 E2
Koko Head Natural Park • HI, United States 119 L6
Koko Nor • China 29 C3
Kokoda • Papua New Guinea 34 I1
Kokonau • Indonesia 32 (1) D3
Kokorin • Czech Rep. 96 C1
Kokside-Bad • Belgium 80 B1
Kokstad • CA/OR, United States 39 R5
Kol'skiy Poluostrov • Russian Fed. 17 F1
Kola • Russian Fed. 16 I2
Kola • Russian Fed. 16 I2
Kola Peninsula • Russian Fed. 16 I2

Kolbermoor • Germany 82 J3
Kolda • Senegal 22 A2
Kolding Beach • Denmark 68 [27]
Kolding • Denmark 95 F9
Koléa • Algeria 11 N8
Kolente • Guinea/Sierra Leone 22 B3
Kolguyev, Ostrov • Russian Fed. 17 I1
Kolhapur • India 106 D1
Kolimbia • Rhodes, Greece 93 F2
Kolimbia [Beach] • Rhodes, Greece 93 F2
Kolimvári • Crete, Greece 93 E1
Kolin • Czech Rep. 96 C2
Kollfuschg • Italy 90 B2
Kolmården • Sweden 95 D3
Kolmårdens Djurpark • Sweden 95 D3
Köln Beach • Germany 64 [38]
Köln • Germany 81 E3
Kolo • Poland 13 H5
Kolobrzeg • Poland 13 E3
Kolokani • Mali 22 C2
Kololo • Ethiopia 21 H6
Kolomna • Russian Fed. 97 E4
Kolomyya • Ukraine 13 L2
Kolonodale • Indonesia 32 (1) B3
Kolpashevo • Russian Fed. 26 N6
Kolpino • Russian Fed. 97 E1
Kölpinsee Spa • Germany 83 [284]
Kolsva • Sweden 95 D1
Kolumadulu Atoll • Maldives 106 E3
Kolwezi • Dem. Rep. of Congo 23 D6
Kolyma • Russian Fed. 27 O4
Kolyma Lowlands • Russian Fed. 97 A7
Kolymskaya Nizmennost • Russian Fed. 27 P3
Kolymskoye Nagorye • Russian Fed. 27 Q4
Kom • Bulgaria 14 K6
Kom • Africa 22 G4
Kom Ombo • Egypt 101 F5
Kóma tou Yialoú • Cyprus 93 J2
Komadugu Gana • Nigeria 20 H6
Komandorskiye Ostrova • Russian Fed. 27 S5
Komárno • Slovak Rep. 14 F2
Komárom • Hungary 14 F2
Komi • Russian Fed. 17 J2
Komi virgin forests Heritage N • Russian Fed. 61 [64]
Komló • Hungary 13 H11
Kommunizm, Qullai • Tajikistan 18 J2
Komodo • Indonesia 32 (1) A4
Komodo Nat. Park Heritage N • Indonesia 61 [126]
Komoé • Burkina Faso/Côte d'Ivoire 22 D3
Komoran • Indonesia 32 (1) E4
Komotini • Greece 92 D2
Komotini • Greece 92 D2
Kompong Cham • Cambodia 108 B1
Kompong Chhnang • Cambodia 108 B1
Komsa • Russian Fed. 26 O5
Komsomol'sk-na-Amure • Russian Fed. 27 M6
Komsomolets, Ostrov • Russian Fed. 96 A4
Komsomolskiy • Russian Fed. 27 T3
Kömür Burnu • Turkey 15 H5
Kona • Mali 20 E6
Konakovo • Russian Fed. 97 E4
Konar • Afghanistan 28 B1
Konarak • India 28 E5
Konarak Heritage C • India 63 [131]
Kondagaon • India 28 D5
Kondinin • WA, Australia 34 C6
Kondoa • Tanzania 102 H2
Kondopoga • Russian Fed. 17 E2
Koné • New Caledonia 35 (2) B3
Kong Christian IX Land • Greenland 39 W3
Kong Frederik VI Kyst • Greenland 39 W4
Kongolo • Dem. Rep. of Congo 23 D5
Kongsberg • Norway 94 B2
Kongsvinger • Norway 94 B2
Königs Wusterhausen • Germany 81 F3
Königsberg • Russian Fed. 71 A4
Königsbrunn • Germany 82 H5
Königssee • Germany 83 [198]
Königslein Ski • Austria 70 [146]
Königssee • Germany 82 J8
Königssee Spa • Germany 83 [262]
Königstein • Germany 82 H2
Königstein Spa • Germany 83 [143]
Königswinter • Germany 81 H1
Konin • Poland 13 H5
Konispol • Albania 15 B4
Konjic • Bosnia-Herz. 14 E6
Konkan • India 105 A3
Konopiste • Czech Rep. 96 C2
Konosha • Russian Fed. 17 F2
Konskie • Poland 13 J6
Konstanz • Germany 82 G8
Konstanz • Germany 82 G8
Kontagora • Nigeria 22 G3
Kontcha • Cameroon 22 G3
Kontich • Belgium 5 H3
Kontiomäki • Finland 16 O4
Kontókali • Corfu, Greece 92 B1
Kontókali • Corfu, Greece 92 B1
Kontum Plateau • Vietnam 108 A2
Konya • Turkey 15 N6
Konya Ovasi • Turkey 15 N6
Konz • Germany 5 J5
Konz • Germany 82 H3
Koolau Range • HI, United States 119 L5
Koorda • WA, Australia 34 C6
Kootenay • Canada/United States 122 C4
Kootenay Nat. Park • BC, Canada 122 C4
Kopaonik • F.R. of Yugoslavia 14 H6
Kópavogur • Iceland 16 (1) C2
Koper • Slovenia 12 H3
Kopervik • Norway 94 C5
Kopeysk • Russian Fed. 26 J6
Köping • Sweden 95 D1
Kopliku • Albania 15 A1
Koppang • Norway 16 F6
Kopparberg • Sweden 95 D1
Koprivnica • Croatia 12 K2
Köprülü • Turkey 93 G2
Kora Nat. Park • Kenya 101 G4
Korahe • Ethiopia 23 G2
Korak Plateau • Thailand 109 F2
Korba • Tunisia 12 E12
Korba • India 28 D4
Korbach • Germany 9 D5
Korçë • Albania 15 B3
Korçula • Croatia 12 L6
Korcula [I.] • Croatia 14 D6
Korculanski kanal • Croatia 14 D6
Korea, Democratic People's Republic of • Asia 30 D6

Korea, Republic of • Asia 30 D5
Korea Strait •
Japan/Rep. of Korea 30 E8
Korea War Veterans Memeorial Park •
DC, United States .... 121 [286]
Köreglu Daglari • Turkey 15 M3
Korf • Russian Fed. 46 II3
Korhogo • Côte d'Ivoire 22 C3
Korinós Beach • Greece .... 69 [167]
Korinthiakós Kólpos • Greece 15 D5
Kórinthos • Greece 92 D4
Kórinthos • Greece 92 D4
Koriolei • Somalia 23 G3
Korithi • Greece 92 C3
Korithi • Greece 92 C3
Koritnik •
Albania/F.R. of Yugoslavia 14 H7
Koriyama • Japan 30 K6
Korkuteli • Turkey 93 C1
Korla • China 28 D5
Kormakiti Burun • Cyprus 15 (1) B1
Kormakiti, Cape • Cyprus 93 J1
Körmend • Hungary 13 F10
Kormy, gora • Russian Fed. 26 S5
Kornati • Croatia 14 C6
Kornati Nat. Park Park •
Croatia .... 72 [111]
Kornelimünster • Germany 82 G1
Kornsjø • Norway 94 B4
Koro Sea • Fiji .... 35 (D) D2
Koro Toro • Chad 20 I5
Koroba • Papua New Guinea 35 (1) C2
Köroglu Tepe • Turkey 15 M3
Korogwe • Tanzania 102 H2
Korónia, Limni • Greece 15 E3
Koronída Beach • Greece .... 69 [183]
Koronowo • Poland 13 G4
Koror • Palau 33 E5
Körös • Hungary 13 J11
Korosten • Ukraine 17 D4
Korpilahti • Finland 95 E2
Korpo • Finland 95 E3
Korppoo • Finland 95 E3
Korsakov • Russian Fed. 27 N7
Korschenbroich • Germany 81 E3
Korsnäs • Finland 16 K5
Korsør Beach • Denmark .... 68 [24]
Korsør • Denmark 95 F14
Kortrijk • Belgium 80 A13
Koru Dagi • Turkey 15 H3
Korucu • Turkey 15 I4
Korup, Parc nat. du Park •
Cameroon .... 103 [38]
Koryakskiy Nagorye •
Russian Fed. 27 T4
Koryakskaya, Vulkan •
Russian Fed. 27 Q6
Koryazhma • Russian Fed. 17 H2
Kos Beach • Greece .... 69 [186]
Kos • Greece 92 D8
Kos • Greece 92 D8
Kos [I.] • Greece 92 D8
Kos [I.] • Greece 92 D8
Koscian • Poland 13 F5
Koscierzyna • Poland 13 G3
Kosciusko • MS, United States 118 K2
Kosciusko, Mt • NS, Australia 111 G4
Kosciuszko, Thaddeus, Nat. Mem. Park •
PA, United States .... 121 [312]
Koserow Beach • Germany .... 83 [284]
Koshiki-Retto • Japan 30 E9
Kosice • Slovak Rep. 13 K9
Koski • Finland 95 E4
Koskinoú Beach • Rhodes, Greece. 69 [187]
Koskinoú • Rhodes, Greece 93 F2
Koson • Russian Fed. 17 H2
Kosong • D.P.R. of Korea 30 E5
Kosovo • F.R. of Yugoslavia 14 I7
Kosovska Mitrovica •
F.R. of Yugoslavia 14 H7
Kosrae •
Fed. States of Micronesia 33 H5
Kossou, Barrage de •
Côte d'Ivoire 22 C3
Kosta • Sweden 95 F8
Koster • Sweden 95 F2
Kostomuksha • Russian Fed. 16 P4
Kostroma • Russian Fed. 97 E2
Kostromskoe Vdkhr. •
Russian Fed. 97 E2
Kostrzyn • Gorzowskie, Poland. 13 D5
Kostrzyn • Poznanskie, Poland . 13 G5
Koszalin • Poland 13 F3
Kőszeg • Hungary 13 F10
Kota • India 105 C6
Kota Baharu • Malaysia 32 C1
Kota Kinabalu • Malaysia 32 F1
Kotabaru • Indonesia 32 F3
Kotabumi • Indonesia 32 D3
Kotadabok • Indonesia 32 D3
Kotare Gorge • New Zealand 112 K3
Kotel • Bulgaria 14 N7
Kotelnich • Russian Fed. 17 H3
Kotelnyy, Ostrov • Russian Fed. . 27 M1
Köthen • Germany 8 G5
Kotka • Finland 16 N6
Kotlas • Russian Fed. 17 H2
Kotlin, Ostrov • Russian Fed. 97 E1
Kotlina Sandomierska • Poland . 13 K9
Kotopasa, Gunung • Indonesia. 32 (1) B3
Kotor Heritage N •
F.R. of Yugoslavia .... 61 [54]
Kotor Heritage C •
F.R. of Yugoslavia .... 64 [159]
Kotovo • Russian Fed. 17 G4
Kotovsk • Ukraine 14 O2
Kotsifoú, Farági •
Crete, Greece 93 E6
Kottayam • India 106 D10
Kotte • Sri Lanka 106 D15
Kotto • Central African Rep. 23 C2
Kotuy • Russian Fed. 26 R3
Kotzebue • AK, United States 46 FF3
Kötzting Spa • Germany .... 83 [232]
Kouba Modounga • Chad 22 H1
Kouchibouguac Nat. Park •
NB, Canada 123 D7
Koudougou • Burkina Faso 22 D2
Koufonísi • Aegean Sea, Greece . 92 D8
Koufonísi • Aegean Sea, Greece . 92 D8
Koufonísi •
Mediterranean Sea, Greece . 93 E8
Kougaberge • South Africa 100 C7
Koukdjuak, Great Plain of the •
NU, Canada 39 G3
Koulamoutou • Gabon 23 G5
Koulikoro • Mali 20 D6
Koumbi-Saleh • Mauritania 20 D5
Koumpentoum • Senegal 20 C6
Kounoupidiana Beach •
Crete, Greece .... 69 [188]
Koupéla • Burkina Faso 22 D2
Kourim • Czech Rep. 96 C2
Kourou • French Guiana 43 G2
Kouroussa • Guinea 20 D6
Kourtaliótiko Farági •
Crete, Greece 93 E6

Koutiala • Mali 22 C2
Koutsounari • Crete, Greece 93 E8
Kouvola • Finland 16 N6
Kovalam • India 106 D14
Kovdor • Russian Fed. 16 P3
Kovdozero • Russian Fed. 16 P3
Kovel • Ukraine 17 C4
Kovriga, gora • Russian Fed. 26 P5
Kovrov • Russian Fed. 17 G3
Kowloon • Hong Kong, China.... 107 H6
Kowloon City • Hong Kong, China. 107 H6
Kowon • D.P.R. of Korea 30 D5
Koycegiz • Turkey 15 J7
Koytezek • Tajikistan 26 L10
Kozagaci • Turkey 93 G3
Kozáni • Greece 15 C3
Kozara • Bosnia-Herz. 14 D4
Kozhim • Russian Fed. 17 J1
Kozienice • Poland 13 K6
Kozlu • Turkey 15 M2
Kozu • Japan 30 J7
Kozuf • F.Y.R. of Macedonia 14 J8
Kpalimé • Togo 22 E3
Kra, Isthmus of • Thailand 109 F3
Kraaifontein • South Africa 100 C5
Krabbfjärden • Sweden 95 D4
Kråchéh • Cambodia 31 D4
Kragerø • Norway 94 B3
Kragujevac • F.R. of Yugoslavia . 14 H5
Krajiste •
Bulgaria/F.R. of Yugoslavia . 14 J7
Krakatau • Java, Indonesia 110 D1
Krakatau Nature Reserve Heritage N •
Indonesia .... 61 [125]
Krakow • Poland 13 I8
Kraków Heritage C • Poland .. 64 [141]
Kraljevo • F.R. of Yugoslavia 14 H6
Kralupy nad Vltavou •
Czech Rep. 13 D7
Kramsach • Austria 89 H3
Kramsfors • Sweden 16 I5
Kranebitten [Apt] • Austria 89 H2
Kranidi • Greece 15 E6
Kranj • Slovenia 13 D11
Krapina • Croatia 12 J2
Krapkowice • Poland 13 G7
Krasavino • Russian Fed. 17 H2
Kraskino • Russian Fed. 30 F3
Krasnik • Poland 13 L7
Krasnodar • Russian Fed. 17 F5
Krasnogorsk • Russian Fed. 27 N7
Krasnokamensk • Russian Fed. . 27 I7
Krasnokamsk • Russian Fed. 17 J3
Krasnoselkup • Russian Fed. 26 N4
Krasnoufimsk • Russian Fed. 26 I6
Krasnoural'sk • Russian Fed. 26 J6
Krasnovishersk • Russian Fed. . 26 I5
Krasnoyarsk • Russian Fed. 26 P6
Krasnozatonsky • Russian Fed. . 17 I2
Krasnystaw • Poland 13 M7
Krasnyy Chikoy • Russian Fed. . 27 G6
Kratochvíle • Czech Rep. 96 C4
Kratovo • F.Y.R. of Macedonia . 14 J7
Krazh Khara-Tas • Russian Fed. . 26 S3
Krefeld • Germany 81 E1
Kremasti • Rhodes, Greece 93 F2
Kremastón, Tehnití Límni •
Greece 15 C5
Kremenchug • Ukraine 17 E5
Kremenchugskoye Vdkhr. •
Ukraine 17 E5
Kremna • Turkey 93 G1
Krems • Austria 14 C1
Kresta, Zaliv • Russian Fed. 27 V3
Kretinga • Lithuania 13 K2
Kreuzlingen • Switzerland 9 D6
Kreuztal • Germany 9 D6
Kribi • Cameroon 22 F4
Krichev • Belarus 17 E4
Krichim • Bulgaria 15 F1
Krim • Ukraine 17 E5
Krimpenerwaard • Netherlands .. 80 C4
Krimskie Gory • Ukraine 17 E6
Kriopigi Beach • Greece .... 69 [169]
Kriopigi • Greece 92 D1
Kriopigi • Greece 92 D1
Krios, Akra • Crete, Greece 93 E5
Krishna • India 106 D3
Krishna, Mouths of the • India .. 106 D3
Krishnagiri • India 106 D7
Kristdala • Sweden 95 F8
Kristianopel • Sweden 95 F12
Kristiansand • Norway 95 F1
Kristiansand Dyrepark Park •
Norway .... 73 [1]
Kristiansand Dyrepark • Norway .. 95 F11
Kristianstad • Sweden 95 F11
Kristiansund • Norway 16 D5
Kristiinankaupunki • Finland 95 E1
Kristinestad • Finland 95 E1
Kritinía • Rhodes, Greece 93 F1
Kritsá Beach • Crete, Greece . 69 [191]
Kritsá • Crete, Greece 93 E7
Krivoklát • Czech Rep. 96 C1
Krivolátska Vrchovina •
Czech Rep. 96 C1
Krivoy Rog • Ukraine 17 E5
Krk • Croatia 14 B4
Krk [I.] • Croatia 14 B4
Krka Nat. Park Park • Croatia .. 72 [112]
Krkonose Nat. Park Park •
Czech Rep. .... 72 [99]
Krkonose Nat. Park • Czech Rep.. 96 C2
Krnov • Czech Rep. 13 G7
Krøderen • Norway 94 B1
Krøderen [Lake] • Norway 94 B1
Krokek • Sweden 95 D3
Krokom • Sweden 16 H5
Kromeríz • Czech Rep. 13 G8
Kronach • Germany 9 G6
Kronoberg • Sweden 95 F7
Kronoki • Russian Fed. 27 R6
Kronotskaya Sopka, Vulkan •
Russian Fed. 27 R5
Kronotskiy Zaliv • Russian Fed.. 27 R6
Kronshagen • Germany 8 F2
Kronstadt • Russian Fed. 97 E1
Kroonstad • South Africa 24 D5
Kropotkin • Russian Fed. 17 G5
Kropotkin • Russian Fed. 27 I5
Kroppefjäll • Sweden 95 F2
Krosno • Poland 13 K8
Krotoszyn • Poland 13 G6
Kroussónas • Crete, Greece 93 E7
Krueng • Java, Indonesia 110 D6
Krsko • Slovenia 14 C4
Kruger Nat. Park • South Africa . 24 E4
Kruger Nat. Park Park •
South Africa .... 103 [124]
Krugersdorp • South Africa 24 D5
Krujë • Albania 14 G8
Krumbach • Germany 82 J2
Krumbad • Germany 82 J2
Krumbad Spa • Germany .... 83 [234]

Krumovgrad • Bulgaria 14 M8
Krung Thep • Thailand 109 H1
Krüpelsee • Germany 81 F4
Krusevac • F.R. of Yugoslavia 14 I6
Krusne Hory • Czech Rep. 96 C1
Krynica • Poland 13 J8
Krynica, gora • Russian Fed. 26 P5
Kryzyz • Poland 13 F5
Ksar el Boukhari • Algeria 11 N9
Ksar el Kebir • Morocco 101 D1
Ksar es Srhir • Morocco 11 F9
Ksar Hadada • Tunisia 101 E6
Ksar Hellal • Tunisia 101 E4
Ksar Dulec Soltane • Tunisia 101 E6
Ksour, Mts des • Algeria 101 D2
Ktikados Beach • Greece .... 69 [179]
Ku-Ring-Gai Chase Nat. Park •
NS, Australia 111 G2
Kuala Belait • Brunei 32 E2
Kuala Dungun • Malaysia 32 C2
Kuala Kelawang • Malaysia 108 D2
Kuala Kerai • Malaysia 32 C1
Kuala Kubu Baharu • Malaysia . 108 D2
Kuala Lipis • Malaysia 108 D2
Kuala Lumpur • Malaysia 108 D4
Kuala Selangor • Malaysia 108 D3
Kuala Terengganu • Malaysia 32 C1
Kuandang • Indonesia 32 (1) B2
Kuandian • China 30 C4
Kuantan • Malaysia 32 C2
Kuba • Azerbaijan 17 H6
Kuban • Russian Fed. 17 G5
Kubenskoye, Ozero •
Russian Fed. 97 E2
Kubokawa • Japan 30 G8
Küçük Menderes • Turkey 15 A3
Kucurgan • Ukraine 14 O2
Kudahithi • Maldives 106 E2
Kudat • Malaysia 32 F1
Kuda • Java, Indonesia 110 D3
Kudymkar • Russian Fed. 17 I3
Kuenga • Russian Fed. 97 A5
Kufrah Oasis • Libya 21 D3
Kufstein • Austria 89 H3
Kugaaruk • NU, Canada 38 H3
Kugluktuk • NU, Canada 38 H3
Kühlungsborn • Germany 8 G2
Kühlungsborn Beach • Germany.. 68 [16]
Kühlungsborn Spa • Germany. 83 [268]
Kuhmo • Finland 16 O4
Kuhmoinen • Finland 16 N5
Kuito • Angola 23 B6
Kujani Game Reserve Park •
Ghana .... 103 [24]
Kujawy • Poland 13 H5
Kuji • Japan 30 K4
Kuji • Japan 30 F8
Kul • Iran 18 F4
Kul • F.R. of Yugoslavia 14 G4
Kula • Bulgaria 14 J6
Kula • Turkey 15 J5
Kular • Russian Fed. 27 M2
Kulata • Bulgaria 14 K8
Kuldiga • Latvia 95 E7
Kulgera • NT, Australia 112 H4
Kulmbach • Germany 9 G6
Kulob • Tajikistan 18 I2
Kulsary • Kazakhstan 26 H8
Kulu • Turkey 15 O4
Kulu • Turkey 15 O4
Kulunda • Russian Fed. 26 M7
Kum-Dag • Turkmenistan 18 F2
Kuma • Russian Fed. 4 T7
Kumagaya • Japan 30 J6
Kumai • Indonesia 32 E3
Kumamoto • Japan 30 E8
Kumano • Japan 30 H8
Kumanovo • F.Y.R. of Macedonia. 14 I7
Kumasi • Ghana 22 D3
Kumaun • India 105 C3
Kumba • Cameroon 22 F4
Kumbakonam • India 106 D11
Kumbe • Indonesia 32 (1) H4
Kumbhalgarh • India 105 C5
Kumbh • Saudi Arabia 21 I3
Kume • Japan 29 H5
Kumhwa • Rep. of Korea 30 D7
Kumköy • Turkey 15 K2
Kumkuduk • China 26 P9
Kumla • Orebro, Sweden 16 H7
Kumla • Västmanland, Sweden. . 95 D1
Kumluca • Turkey 93 G3
Kumo alv • Finland 95 E2
Kumul • China 29 A2
Kunashir, Ostrov • Russian Fed.. 30 D7
Kunashiri-To • Russian Fed. 27 O8
Kunashirskiy Proliv •
Russian Fed. 27 O8
Kundapura • India 106 D6
Kundelungu, Mtns •
Dem. Rep. of Congo 23 D6
Kundelungu, Parc nat. de Park •
Dem. Rep. of Congo .... 103 [60]
Kundiawa • Papua New Guinea .. 35 (1) C2
Kunduchi • Tanzania 102 H4
Künes He • China 28 D5
Kung Bay • Phuket, Thailand 109 K1
Kungagraven • Sweden 95 F11
Kungälv • Sweden 95 F6
Kungey-Alatau • Kazakhstan 26 M9
Kungsbacka • Sweden 95 F6
Kungshamn • Sweden 95 F2
Kungsör • Sweden 95 D3
Kungu • Dem. Rep. of Congo 23 B3
Kungur • Russian Fed. 17 J3
Kunhing • Myanmar 31 B2
Kunlun Shan • China 28 F1
Kunlun Shankou • China 28 F1
Kunming • China 29 C5
Kunsan • Rep. of Korea 30 D7
Kunshan • China 107 J2
Kununurra • WA, Australia 34 E3
Künzelsau • Germany 9 E7
Kuopio • Finland 16 N5
Kuopio Beach • Finland .... 69 [10]
Kuopio [Adm] • Finland 16 N5
Kuopio [Adm] • Finland 94 A6
Kupa • Croatia 14 C4
Kupang • Indonesia 32 (1) E5
Kupiano • Papua New Guinea 35 (1) D3
Kupino • Russian Fed. 26 M7
Kupiskis • Lithuania 13 D2
Kupreanof Is. •
AK, United States 38 E5
Kuqa • China 26 N9
Kura • Azerbaijan 18 E1
Kuramathi • Maldives 106 E2
Kuranda • QL, Australia 111 F1
Kuraymah • Sudan 21 F4
Kurayoshi • Japan 30 F7
Kurdistan • Asia 18 D2
Kurdufan al Janubiyah • Sudan . 23 D1
Kurdzhali • Bulgaria 14 M8
Küre • Turkey 15 O2

Kure • Japan 30 G7
Kuressaare • Estonia 16 L7
Kurgan • Russian Fed. 26 K6
Kuri Bay • WA, Australia 34 D3
Kurikka • Finland 16 L5
Kuril Is. • Russian Fed. 27 P7
Kuril'sk • Russian Fed. 27 O7
Kurilskoye Ostrova •
Russian Fed. 25 P5
Kurland • Latvia 16 K8
Kurmuk • Sudan 23 E1
Kurnool • India 106 D3
Kurobe • Japan 30 I6
Kuroishi • Japan 30 K4
Kurort Krakow am See Spa •
Germany .... 83 [286]
Kurort Oberwiesenthal Spa •
Germany .... 83 [317]
Kurort Schmalkalden • Germany.. 9 F6
Kurpfalzpark • Germany 82 G4
Kursenai • Lithuania 13 L1
Kursk • Russian Fed. 17 F4
Kurski Zaliv •
Lithuania/Russian Fed. 13 J2
Kürten • Germany 81 E4
Kuru • Finland 95 E2
Kurucasile • Turkey 15 N2
Kurukshetra • India 105 C2
Kuruman • South Africa 24 C5
Kurumbu • Maldives 106 E4
Kurume • Japan 30 F8
Kurunegala • Sri Lanka 106 D15
Kurutag • China 26 O9
Kus Gölü • Turkey 92 D3
Kus Gölü • Turkey 92 D3
Kusadasi • Turkey 92 D8
Kusadasi • Turkey 92 D8
Kusadasi Körfezi • Turkey 15 H6
Kusamba • Bali, Indonesia 110 C4
Kushikino • Japan 30 F9
Kushimoto • Japan 30 H8
Kushinagar • India 105 C4
Kushiro • Japan 30 M3
Kushka • Turkmenistan 18 H2
Kushmurun • Kazakhstan 26 J7
Kusong • D.P.R. of Korea 30 C5
Kussharo-Ko • Japan 30 M3
Kussnacht • Switzerland 89 G3
Kustanay • Russian Fed. 26 J7
Kusti • Sudan 21 F5
Kusva • Russian Fed. 26 I6
Kut, Al • Iraq 18 E3
Kut, Ko • Thailand 31 C4
Kuta • Bali, Indonesia 110 C4
Kuta Beach • Bali, Indonesia 110 C4
Kutahia • Turkey 15 K4
Kutaisi • Georgia 17 G6
Kutaisi Heritage C • Georgia .. 64 [212]
Kutch, Gulf of • India 28 A4
Kutch, Rann of • India 28 A4
Kutná Hora • Czech Rep. 14 D4
Kutná Hora Heritage C •
Czech Rep. .... 64 [144]
Kutná Hora • Czech Rep. 13 I5
Kutno • Poland 13 I5
Kuttanad • India 106 D10
Kuty • Ukraine 14 M1
Kuujjuaq • QU, Canada 39 R5
Kuujjuarapik • QU, Canada 39 P5
Kuusamo • Finland 16 O4
Kuwait • Asia 18 E4
Kuwait City • Kuwait 18 E4
Kuygan • Kazakhstan 26 L8
Kuytun • China 26 O9
Kuznetsk • Russian Fed. 17 H4
Kuznetskiy Alatau •
Russian Fed. 26 O7
Kuzomen • Russian Fed. 17 F1
Kvænangen • Norway 16 K2
Kvaløy • Norway 16 J2
Kvaløya • Norway 37 F6
Kvarner • Croatia 14 B5
Kvarnerić • Croatia 14 B5
Kvicksund • Sweden 95 D3
Kvikkjokk • Sweden 16 I3
Kviteseid • Norway 94 C6
Kwa • Dem. Rep. of Congo 23 B4
Kwaiharo Plateau • Ghana 22 D3
Kwajalein • Marshall Is. 33 H5
Kwakoegron • Suriname 43 F2
Kwale • Kenya 101 G5
Kwando • Africa 24 C3
Kwangju • Rep. of Korea 30 D7
Kwanmo • D.P.R. of Korea 30 E4
Kwara • Nigeria 22 F3
Kwazulu Natal • South Africa 24 E5
Kwekwe • Zimbabwe 102 J2
Kwidzyn • Poland 13 H4
Kwikila • Papua New Guinea 34 I1
Kwilu • Dem. Rep. of Congo 23 B4
Kwoka, Gunung • Indonesia.. 32 (1) D3
Kyabé • Chad 21 C6
Kyaikkami • Myanmar 31 B3
Kyancutta • SA, Australia 34 G6
Kyaukpyu • Myanmar 28 C2
Kyelang • India 105 C3
Kyiv • Ukraine 17 D4
Kyklo Monastery • Cyprus 93 J3
Kyle, Lake • Zimbabwe 102 J3
Kyle of Lochalsh •
United Kingdom 6 G4
Kyleakin • United Kingdom 78 A1
Kylerhea • United Kingdom 78 A1
Kyll • Germany 82 H3
Kyllburg Spa • Germany .... 83 [159]
Kymi • Finland 16 N6
Kymi alv • Finland 94 A9
Kymijoki • Finland 16 N6
Kymmene alv • Finland 16 N6
Kyneton • VA, Australia 34 I3
Kyoga, Lake • Uganda 23 E3
Kyoga-Misaki • Japan 30 H7
Kyongju-man • Rep. of Korea 30 E7
Kyongju • Rep. of Korea 30 E7
Kyoto Heritage C •
Rep. of Korea .... 63 [161]
Kyongsong • D.P.R. of Korea 30 E4
Kyoto • Japan 30 H7
Kyoto Heritage C • Japan .... 63 [167]
Kyperoúda • Cyprus 93 J3
Kyra • Russian Fed. 91 F2
Kyrenia • Cyprus 93 J1
Kyrenia Mtns • Cyprus 93 J1
Kyrgyzstan • Asia 26 L9
Kythira • Greece 15 E7
Kyulik • Sweden 95 F11
Kythréa • Cyprus 93 J1
Kyushu • Japan 30 F8
Kyushu-Sanchi • Japan 30 F8
Kyustendil • Bulgaria 14 J7
Kyusyur • Russian Fed. 27 K2
Kyyiv • Ukraine 17 E4

Kyyiv Heritage C • Ukraine .... 64 [204]
Kyzyl • Russian Fed. 26 P7
Kyzyl-Kum •
Kazakhstan/Uzbekistan 26 J9
Kyzylart • China 26 M10
Kyzylkum • Uzbekistan 18 H1
Kzilca Dagi • Turkey 15 K7
Kzyl-Orda • Kazakhstan 26 K9
Kzyltu • Kazakhstan 26 L7

L'Abbaye • St Lucia 125 J1
L'Ancresse Beach •
United Kingdom .... 75 [232]
L'Anse au Loup • NF, Canada .. 123 D5
L'Anse aux Meadows • NF, Canada. 123 D5
L'Anse aux Meadows Hist. Park Heritage C •
NF, Canada .... 62 [5]
L'Aquila • Italy 91 F2
L'Erèe Beach • United Kingdom . 75 [229]
L'Europa • Reunion 24 G4
L'gov • Russian Fed. 17 F4
L'Île Rousse • Corsica, France 85 L1
La Almunia de Doña Godina •
Spain 11 J3
La Ametlla de Mar • Spain 11 L4
La Amistad, Parque Int. Heritage N •
Costa Rica/Panama .... 60 [24]
La Antilla • Spain 86 B1
La Banda • Argentina 44 D4
La Bañeza • Spain 11 F2
La Borne • St Lucia 125 J2
La Brea • Trinidad & Tobago .. 125 K3
La Cadena • Puerto Rico 125 E1
La Canal • Ibiza, Spain 87 G3
La Ceiba • Honduras 37 D4
La Chaux-de-Fonds • Switzerland. 89 G1
La Chorrera • Panama 43 B2
La Chorrera • Colombia 43 B3
La Croix Maingot • St Lucia .. 125 J1
La Crosse • WI, United States 41 H3
La Dorada • Colombia 43 C2
La Esmeralda • Venezuela 43 D3
La Española • West Indies 37 G3
La Esperanza • Cuba 124 D1
La Estrada • Spain 11 C2
La Fé • Cuba 124 D1
La Fortaleza Heritage C •
Puerto Rico .... 62 [39]
La Fortaleza • Puerto Rico 125 E2
La Goulette • Tunisia 101 E2
La Gran Sabana • Venezuela 43 E2
La Grande • OR, United States .. 117 E4
La Grande Rivière • QU, Canada. 39 P6
La Grita • Venezuela 43 C2
La Guaira • Venezuela 37 H5
La Guardia • Portugal 11 C3
La Habana Heritage C • Cuba .. 62 [34]
La Habana • Cuba 124 D1
La Isleta •
Lanzarote, Canary Is. 87 E3
La Laguna •
Tenerife, Canary Is. 86 E1
La Línea • Spain 86 B6
La Maddalena Beach •
Sardinia, Italy .... 68 [119]
La Mancha • Spain 11 H5
La Manche • France/UK 10 D3
La Manga del Mar Menor • Spain . 87 C3
La Mármora, Punta •
Sardinia, Italy 90 C4
La Marsa • Tunisia 101 E2
La Montaña • Peru 43 C5
La Neuveville • Switzerland 89 G2
La Oliva •
Fuerteventura, Canary Is. 87 E2
La Orotava •
Tenerife, Canary Is. 86 E1
La Oroya • Peru 127 B1
La Palma • Panama 37 F6
La Palma • Canary Is. 87 E5
La Panchita • Cuba 124 D2
La Paragua • Venezuela 43 E2
La Paz, Istmo de •
Fuerteventura, Canary Is. 87 E2
La Paz • Mexico 40 D7
La Paz • Bolivia 44 C2
La Paz • Mendoza, Argentina.... 44 C5
La Paz • Entre Ríos, Argentina .. 44 E5
La Pedrera • Colombia 43 D4
La Peraleja • Spain 11 I4
La Pérouse Strait •
Russian Fed. 27 N7
La Plata • Argentina 127 D2
La Plata, Río de •
Argentina/Uruguay 127 D2
La Playa de Mogán •
Gran Canaria, Canary Is. 86 E6
La Pointe Beach • St Lucia 125 J3
La Puntilla • Ecuador 43 A3
La Purisima Mission State Hist. Park •
CA, United States 117 F5
La Quiaca • Argentina 44 C3
La Rapita • Majorca, Spain 87 H4
La Ressource • St Lucia 125 J3
La Rioja • Spain 11 I2
La Rioja • Argentina 44 C4
La Robla • Spain 11 F2
La Roche-en-Ardenne • Belgium. 80 A19
La Rochelle Beach • France .... 68 [53]
La Rochelle • France 84 D3
La Ronge • SA, Canada 38 J5
La Sabana • Colombia 43 D3
La Serena • Spain 11 F6
La Serena • Chile 44 B4
La Solana • Spain 11 H6
La Spézia • Italy 91 F1
La Tagua • Colombia 43 C4
La Tzoumas Ski • Switzerland . 70 [79]
La Unión • Chile 45 B4
La Unión • Spain 87 C3
La Vache Bay •
Trinidad & Tobago 125 K1
La Veguita •
Lanzarote, Canary Is. 87 E3
La Vela • Venezuela 43 D1
La Verna, Abbazia • Italy 91 E11
La Victoria • Venezuela 43 D1
La Viña • Peru 43 B5
La Yeguada • Panama 28 D2
La-Punt-Chaumes-ch. Ski •
Switzerland .... 70 [115]
Laarne • Belgium 80 A14
Laax • Switzerland .... 70 [107]
Laax • Switzerland 89 G3
Laben Beach • France .... 68 [67]
Labenne • Niger 22 F2
Laboe Spa • Germany .... 83 [17]
Laborie • St Lucia 125 J3
Laborie Bay • St Lucia 125 J3

Labota • Indonesia 32 (1) B3
Labouheyre • France 85 G3
Laboulaye • Argentina 44 D5
Labrador • NF/QU, Canada 39 R6
Labrador City • NF, Canada 39 R6
Labrador, Coast of • NF, Canada. 39 S5
Labrador Mtn Ski •
NY, United States .... 116 [177]
Labrador Sea • Atlantic Ocean .. 36 M4
Lábrea • Brazil 43 E5
Labuan • Indonesia 32 (1) C3
Labuha • Indonesia 32 (1) C3
Labuhan • Java, Indonesia 110 D1
Labuhanbajo • Indonesia 32 (1) A4
Labuhanbalai • Indonesia 110 B2
Labuk, Teluk • Malaysia 31 F5
Lábuta • Myanmar 31 A3
Labytnangi • Russian Fed. 26 K4
Lac • Albania 15 A2
Lac la Biche • AL, Canada 38 I6
Lac La Martre • NT, Canada 38 H4
Lac Mégantic • QU, Canada .. 122 B4
Lacanau • France 85 G1
Laccadive Is. • India 25 H8
Lacepede Bay • SA, Australia 34 G7
Lachay, Punta • Peru 43 B6
Lachi • Cyprus 93 J3
Lachlan • NS, Australia 111 G1
Lachute • QU, Canada 122 B3
Lacken Reservoir • Ireland 79 E4
Lackenhof • Austria 95 F3
Ladakh • Jammu & Kashmir 28 C2
Ladhiqiyah, Al • Syria 18 C2
Ladiko • Rhodes, Greece 93 F2
Ladispoli • Italy 91 F1
Ladoga, Lake • Russian Fed. 17 E2
Ladozhskoye, Ozero •
Russian Fed. 17 E2
Lady Ann Strait • NU, Canada .. 39 P1
Lady Elliot I. • QL, Australia 111 H4
Ladysmith • South Africa 24 E5
Lae • Papua New Guinea 35 (1) D2
Laem Chabang • Thailand 109 H4
Laem So Pagoda •
Ko Samui, Thailand 109 J2
Lærdalsøyri • Norway 94 C4
Læsø Beach • Denmark .... 68 [29]
Læsø • Denmark 95 F6
Læsø Rende • Denmark 95 F6
Lafayette • LA, United States .. 118 K3
Lafia • Nigeria 22 F3
Lafiagi • Nigeria 22 F3
Lafite, Château • France 85 G1
Lafitte, Jean, Nat. Hist. Park •
LA, United States 118 K4
Lafitte, Jean, Nat. Hist. Park Park •
LA, United States .... 121 [198]
Lågan • Sweden 95 F7
Laganás • Greece 92 C3
Laganás • Greece 92 C3
Lågen • Norway 16 F6
Laghouat • Algeria 20 F2
Laghy Beach • Ireland .... 68 [46]
Lago de Moreno • Mexico 123 E1
Lagoa Beach • Portugal .... 68 [82]
Lagoa • Azores 88 B7
Lagoa • Azores 88 B1
Lagoa • Portugal 88 E6
Lagoa Vermelha • Brazil 44 F4
Lagonissi • Greece 92 D7
Lagonissi • Greece 92 D7
Lagos • Nigeria 22 E3
Lagos Beach • Portugal .... 68 [82]
Lagos • Portugal 88 E6
Lagos • Greece 92 D2
Lágos • Greece 92 D2
Lagos [Adm] • Nigeria 22 E3
Lagos, Baía de • Portugal 88 E6
Lagosa • Tanzania 102 H1
Lagrán • Spain 11 I2
LaGuardia [Apt] •
NY, United States 118 H2
Laguna • Brazil 44 G4
Laguna • NM, United States .. 118 J2
Lagunillas • Bolivia 44 C3
Lahad Datu • Malaysia 32 F1
Lahaina • HI, United States 119 L3
Lahat • Indonesia 32 C3
Lahemaa Nat. Park Park •
Estonia .... 72 [143]
Lahewa • Indonesia 110 B3
Lahn • Germany 82 G2
Lahnstein • Germany 82 H2
Lahnstein Spa • Germany. 83 [155]
Laholm Beach • Sweden .... 68 [4]
Laholm • Sweden 95 F11
Laholmsbukten • Sweden 95 F11
Lahore • Pakistan 28 B2
Lahore Heritage C • Pakistan .. 63 [115]
Lahr • Germany 82 G6
Lahti • Finland 95 E4
Lai • Chad 23 B2
Lai Chau • Vietnam 31 C2
Lai'an • China 107 J1
Laiagam • Papua New Guinea .. 35 (1) C2
Laie • HI, United States 119 L1
Laiguéglia Beach • Italy .... 68 [121]
Laiguéglia • Italy 91 E9
Laikipia Game Reserve • Kenya . 101 G1
Laingsburg • South Africa 100 C6
Lainio älv • Sweden 16 K2
Laitila • Finland 95 E3
Laiwui • Indonesia 32 (1) C3
Laja • Chile 44 B6
Lajes • Brazil 44 F4
Lajes do Pico • Azores 88 B1
Lajosmizse • Hungary 13 I10
Lake Bogoria Game Reserve •
Kenya 101 G1
Lake Buena Vista •
FL, United States 121 C2
Lake Charles •
LA, United States 118 K3
Lake City • FL, United States .. 119 M3
Lake Clark Nat. Park & Preserve Park •
AK, United States .... 120 [8]
Lake District • United Kingdom . 74 C
Lake District Nat. Park Park •
United Kingdom .... 72 [43]
Lake District Nat. Park •
United Kingdom .... 74 C
Lake Grace • WA, Australia 34 C6
Lake Havasu City •
AZ, United States 118 J1
Lake King • WA, Australia 34 C6
Lake Louise Ski • AL, Canada . 116 [12]
Lake Louise • AL, Canada 122 C4
Lake Mackay Aboriginal Land •
NT, Australia .... 34 [11]
Lake Malawi Nat. Park Heritage N •
Malawi .... 61 [94]
Lake Malawi Nat. Park Park •
Malawi .... 103 [98]

162 INDEX

Lake Mead Nat. Recreation Area

Lake Mead Nat. Recreation Area **Park** •
  NV, United States .... 120 [61]
Lake Meredith Nat. Recreation Area **Park** •
  TX, United States .... 120 [133]
Lake Monroe • FL, United States .. 119 M4
Lake Murray • Papua New Guinea 35 (1) C2
Lake Nakuru Nat. Park • Kenya .. 101 G3
Lake Nakuru Nat. Park **Park** •
  Kenya .... 103 [81]
Lake Placid • NY, United States 41 L3
Lake Placid • NY, United States .... 116 C
Lake River • OT, Canada 39 O6
Lake Tekapo • New Zealand 35 C7
Lake Wales • FL, United States ... 119 M5
Lakefield Nat. Park •
  QL, Australia 34 H3
Lakeland • FL, United States 119 M5
Lakemba • Fiji 35 (2) E2
Lakes Beach • Barbados 125 H1
Lakes Entrance • VI, Australia ... 111 G3
Lakeview • OR, United States 117 E3
Lákmos • Greece 15 C4
Lakonikós Kólpos • Greece 15 D5
Laköpetra **Beach** • Greece ..... 69 [156]
Laksamana Forest Reserve •
  Penang, Malaysia 108 C1
Laksefjorden • Norway 16 N1
Lakselv • Norway 16 M1
Lakshadweep • India 106 D9
Lakshadweep Sea • India 106 D10
Lalapasa • Turkey 15 H2
Lalibela • Ethiopia 21 G5
Lalibela **Heritage C** • Ethiopia .. 63 [86]
Lalitpur • India 105 C7
Lalzit, Gjiri i • Albania 14 G8
Lam Po Reservoir • Thailand 109 F2
Lam Tseun Country Park •
  Hong Kong, China 107 H3
Lamai Beach •
  Ko Samui, Thailand 109 J2
Lamar • CO, United States 40 F4
Lambaréné • Gabon 22 G5
Lambari • Brazil 127 C3
Lambasa • Fiji 35 (2) D2
Lambay I. • Ireland 79 E2
Lambert's Bay • South Africa 100 C1
Lambton, Cape • NT, Canada 38 G2
Lamego • Portugal 11 D3
Lamèque, I. • NB, Canada 123 D2
Lamesa • TX, United States 40 F5
Lamezia Terme • Italy 12 K10
Lamía • Greece 15 D5
Lamington Nat. Park •
  QL, Australia 111 F6
Lamma I. • Hong Kong, China ... 107 H5
Lammermuir Hills •
  United Kingdom 74 B4
Lammhult • Sweden 95 F7
Lamon Bay • Philippines 31 G4
Lamongan • Java, Indonesia 110 D4
Lampang • Thailand 109 G4
Lampasas • TX, United States .. 119 N3
Lampedusa • Italy 12 G13
Lampertheim • Germany 9 D7
Lamphun • Thailand 109 G3
Lamu • Kenya 101 G4
Lamu I. • Kenya 101 G4
Lan Hsu • Taiwan 29 G6
Lan, Ko • Thailand 109 H4
Lanai • HI, United States 119 L3
Lanai City • HI, United States ... 119 L3
Lanao, Lake • Philippines 31 G5
Lanark • United Kingdom 74 B3
Lancang Jiang • China 29 B5
Lancashire • United Kingdom 7 J8
Lancaster • United Kingdom 7 J7
Lancaster • PA, United States ... 118 H1
Lancaster Sound • NU, Canada .. 39 O2
Lancelin • WA, Australia 34 C6
Lancha He • China 29 F2
Lanciano • Italy 12 I6
Lancut • Poland 13 L1
Land of the Midnight Sun cruise area •
  Norway 59 A4
Land van Altena • Netherlands ... 80 C4
Landau an der Isar • Germany ... 13 E9
Landau in der Pfalz • Germany 9 D7
Landeck • Austria 89 H6
Lander • NT, Australia 34 F4
Landes, les • France 85 G3
Landete • Spain 11 J5
Lands End • United Kingdom 74 F4
Landsberg am Lech • Germany ... 82 J2
Landshut • Germany 9 H8
Landskrona • Sweden 95 F11
Landsort • Sweden 95 D4
Landvetter [Apt] • Sweden 95 F6
Lanerbach • Austria 89 H7
Lang Son • Vietnam 31 D2
Langada • Greece 92 D5
Langada • Greece 92 D5
Langano & Shala-Abiyata Lakes Nat. Park
  Park • Ethiopia .... 103 [64]
Langara • Indonesia 32 (1) B3
Langcang Jiang • China 28 G2
Langdale Fell • United Kingdom .. 74 C2
Langeais [Château] • France 84 D2
Langeberg • South Africa 100 C6
Langeland • Denmark 95 F14
Längelmävesi • Finland 95 E2
Langen • Germany 8 D3
Langenfeld • Germany 81 E3
Langenhagen • Germany 9 E6
Langenselbold • Germany 8 C3
Langeoog • Germany 9 E8
Langeoog **Spa** • Germany ... 83 [40]
Langer See • Germany 81 F4
Langesund • Norway 94 B3
Langevåg •
  More og Romsdal, Norway 94 C3
Langevåg • Rogaland, Norway ... 94 C5
Langfjorden • Norway 94 C2
Langjökull • Iceland 16 (1) C2
Langkawi • Malaysia 32 B1
Langnau • Switzerland 89 G2
Langogne • France 10 I9
Langon • France 85 G2
Langreo • Spain 11 F1
Langres • France 10 K6
Langsa • Indonesia 110 B1
Langsele • Sweden 94 B1
Langue de Barbarie, Parc nat. de la **Park** •
  Senegal .... 103 [7]
Languedoc • France 10 I10
Languedoc-Roussillon • France .. 84 A2
Langwedel • Germany 8 E4
Langxi • China 107 J1
Langzhong • China 29 D4
Lanhydrock House •
  United Kingdom 74 F4
Lanín, Volcán • Argentina 45 B3
Lankarihohlu • Maldives 106 E2
Lannemezan • France 85 J2
Lannion • France 84 C1
Lansing • MI, United States 41 J3

Lanta, Ko • Thailand 109 F4
Lantau I. • Hong Kong, China ... 107 H5
Lantau Peak • Hong Kong, China 107 H5
Lante, Villa • Italy 91 F1
Lanzarote • Canary Is. 87 E3
Lanzhou • China 29 C3
Lao • Thailand 109 G2
Lao Cai • Vietnam 31 C2
Lao Ling • China 30 D4
Laoag • Philippines 31 G3
Laocheng • China 29 F3
Laois • Ireland 79 D2
Laon • France 10 I4
Laos • Asia 31 C2
Laou • Morocco 11 F9
Lapa • Brazil 44 G4
Lápithos • Cyprus 93 J1
Lappeenranta • Finland 16 O6
Lappersdorf • Germany 9 H7
Lappi • Finland 16 N3
Lappijärvi • Finland 16 L5
Lapland area **Heritage N** •
  Sweden .... 61 [39]
Lapland area **Heritage C** •
  Sweden .... 63 [71]
Laprida • Argentina 127 D3
Lapseki • Turkey 15 H3
Laptev Sea • Arctic Ocean 46 C2
Laptevykh, More • Arctic Ocean .. 46 C2
Lapua • Finland 16 L5
Łapy • Poland 13 L4
Laquiat al Arba'in • Sudan 21 E3
Lar • Iran 18 F4
Lara, Plaj • Turkey 93 G3
Larache • Morocco 101 D1
Laramie • WY, United States 40 E3
Laramie, Fort, Nat. Hist. Site **Park** •
  WY, United States .... 120 [73]
Laramie Mtns •
  WY, United States 89 G1
Larantuka • Indonesia 32 (1) B4
Larat • Indonesia 32 (1) D4
Larba • Algeria 11 O8
Lárdos **Beach** • Rhodes, Greece 69 [187]
Lárdos • Rhodes, Greece 93 F4
Lárdos, Akra • Rhodes, Greece .. 93 F4
Laredo • Spain 11 H1
Laredo • TX, United States 40 G6
Laredo **Beach** • Spain .... 68 [70]
Laren • Netherlands 80 C2
Larestan • Iran 18 G4
Largo, Cayo • Cuba 124 D2
Largs • United Kingdom 74 B3
Larino • Italy 11 E8
Lárissa • Greece 15 C5
Lárissa • Greece 28 A3
Larkana • Pakistan 28 A3
Larnaca **Beach** • Cyprus .... 69 [194]
Larnaca • Cyprus 93 J4
Larnaca Bay • Cyprus 93 J4
Larne • United Kingdom 7 G7
Larne [Adm] • United Kingdom ... 75 A3
Larned, Fort, Nat. Hist. Site **Park** •
  KS, United States .... 120 [170]
Larochette • Luxembourg 80 A20
Larrau • France 85 J1
Larrimah • NT, Australia 34 F3
Larsen Ice Shelf • Antarctica .. 46 (1) I3
Larsen, Mt • Antarctica 46 (1) V2
Larvik • Norway 94 B3
Las Aves, Is. • Venezuela 124 A5
Las Casitas • Mexico 40 E7
Las Cruces • NM, United States . 118 J4
Las Cuevas Bay •
  Trinidad & Tobago 125 K1
Las Flores • Argentina 127 D3
Las Galletas •
  Tenerife, Canary Is. 86 E1
Las Heras • Argentina 44 C5
Las Leñas • Argentina 45 C3
Las Marismas • Spain 86 B1
Las Médulas **Heritage C** • Spain 64 [79]
Las Navas de Tolosa • Spain 71 A16
Las Palmas de Gran Canaria **Beach** •
  Gran Canaria, Canary Is. ..... 68 [92]
Las Palmas de Gran Canaria •
  Gran Canaria, Canary Is. 86 E4
Las Piedras • Uruguay 44 E5
Las Piedras, Río de • Peru 44 C3
Las Pipinas • Argentina 127 D4
Las Plumas • Argentina 45 C4
Las Qoray • Somalia 23 H1
Lascano • NM, United States 40 E4
Las Vegas • NV, United States .. 117 F4
Las'anod • Somalia 23 H2
Lascaux, Grotte de • France 85 G2
Lash-e Joveyn • Afghanistan 18 H3
Lashio • Myanmar 31 B2
Lashkar Gah • Afghanistan 18 H3
Lask • Poland 13 I6
Lassen Volcanic Nat. Park •
  CA, United States 117 F1
Lassen Volcanic Nat. Park **Park** •
  CA, United States .... 120 [41]
Lassithi • Crete, Greece 93 E7
Lassithi [Adm] • Crete, Greece .. 93 E8
Last Mountain Lake • SA, Canada .. 38 J6
Lastovo • Croatia 14 D7
Latakia • Syria 18 C2
Late • Tonga 35 (2) F2
Latémar • Italy 90 B3
Latina • Italy 11 C2
Lató • Crete, Greece 93 E8
Latoritza • Ukraine 13 L9
Latrobe Valley • VI, Australia .. 111 G3
Lattari, Monti • Italy 91 G3
Latur • India 28 C5
Lau Group • Fiji 35 (2) E2
Lauchammer • Germany 8 I5
Lauderburg • Germany 9 F7
Laufen • Germany 9 G7
Laufen • Germany 9 G7
Laughlin • NV, United States ... 117 F6
Laukaa • Finland 95 E2
Launceston • TS, Australia 34 I8
Launceston • United Kingdom 74 F4
Laupheim • Germany 82 J1
Laurel • MS, United States 118 K2
Laurentian • QU, Canada 122 B3
Laurentides, Plateau •
  QU, Canada 39 R6
Laurentides Prov. Reserve •
  QU, Canada 123 D1
Lauru • Indonesia 32 F3
Laut • Indonesia 32 (1) C4
Laut • East Indies 32 (1) C4
Lauter • Germany 9 C7
Lauter • Germany 82 G2
Lauterbrunnen **Ski** • Switzerland 70 [94]
Lauterbrunnen • Switzerland 89 G2
Lauttawar, Danau • Indonesia .. 110 B1

Lava Beds Nat. Mon. •
  CA, United States 117 F1
Lava Beds Nat. Mon. **Park** •
  CA, United States .... 120 [39]
Lavagna • Italy 91 E6
Laval • France 84 D1
Lavandou, le **Beach** • France .. 68 [116]
Lavandou, le • France 85 H3
Lavapié, Punta • Chile 44 B6
Lavarone **Ski** • Italy .... 70 [212]
Lavayai, Ko • Thailand 109 K1
Laverton • WA, Australia 34 D5
Lavik • Norway 94 C3
Lavon Lake • TX, United States . 119 N1
Lávra • Brazil 127 C1
Lávrio • Greece 92 D7
Lávrio • Greece 92 D7
Lavumisa • Swaziland 24 E5
Lawang • Java, Indonesia 110 D8
Lawit, Gunung • Indonesia 32 E2
Lawra • Burkina Faso 20 E6
Lawrah • Afghanistan 28 A2
Lawrence • KS, United States ... 41 G4
Lawson • Papua New Guinea .. 35 (1) D2
Lawton • OK, United States 40 G5
Lawu, Gunung • Java, Indonesia 110 D7
Layar • Saudi Arabia 21 G2
Laxá • Sweden 95 F3
Laycock Abbey • United Kingdom . 74 E4
Layla • Saudi Arabia 18 E5
Lázaro Cárdenas • Mexico 123 E3
Lazdijai • Lithuania 13 M3
Lazio • Italy 91 F1
Le Bourget [Apt] • France 85 E2
Le Brassus • Switzerland 89 G1
Le Châble **Ski** • Switzerland .. 70 [77]
Le Havre • France 10 F4
Le Kef • Tunisia 101 E1
Le Locle • Switzerland 89 G1
Le Mans • France 84 D2
Le Phang Bay • Phuket, Thailand 109 K1
Le Relais **Ski** • QU, Canada 116 [36]
Le Roeulx • Belgium 80 A14
Le Vaud • Switzerland 89 G1
Lea • United Kingdom 5 C3
Leamington • United Kingdom 79 F8
Learmonth • WA, Australia 34 B4
Leba • Poland 13 G3
Lebanon • Asia 18 B3
Lebanon • NH, United States ... 118 G3
Leblon • Brazil 127 C4
Lebombo Mtns • South Africa 24 E4
Lebork • Poland 13 G3
Lebrija • Spain 11 E8
Lebu • Chile 45 B3
Lecce • Italy 12 M8
Lecco • Italy 91 E2
Lech **Ski** • Austria .... 70 [129]
Lech • Austria 89 H5
Lech [Riv] • Austria/Germany ... 82 J6
Lechtaler Alpen • Austria 89 H2
Leczna • Poland 13 L6
Leczyca • Poland 13 I5
Ledbury • United Kingdom 74 D3
Ledesma • Spain 86 A2
Lednice-Valtice **Heritage C** •
  Czech Rep. .... 64 [148]
Lédo, Cabo • Angola 24 A1
Ledyanaya, gora • Russian Fed. .. 27 T4
Lee • United Kingdom 79 F8
Lee, Robert E., Mem. **Park** •
  VA, United States .... 121 [268]
Leeds • United Kingdom 7 K8
Leeds Castle • United Kingdom .. 74 E4
Leegebruch • Germany 81 F2
Leer • Germany 8 C3
Leerdam • Netherlands 80 C4
Leeuwarden • Netherlands 80 A3
Leeuwin, Cape • WA, Australia .. 34 C6
Lefka Ori Nat. Park •
  Crete, Greece 93 E5
Lefkáda • Greece 92 C1
Lefkáda • Greece 92 C1
Lefkáda [I.] • Greece 92 C1
Lefkáda [I.] • Greece 92 C1
Lefkara • Cyprus 93 J3
Lefkimi **Beach** • Corfu, Greece 69 [149]
Lefkimi • Corfu, Greece 92 B1
Lefkimi • Corfu, Greece 92 B1
Lefkoniko • Cyprus 93 J1
Leganés • Spain 11 H4
Legazpi • Philippines 31 G4
Legendes, Côte des • France 84 C1
Leghorn • Italy 91 E11
Legian Beach • Bali, Indonesia . 110 C4
Legionowo • Poland 13 J5
Legnano • Lombardia, Italy 12 C3
Legnano • Véneto, Italy 91 E7
Legnica • Poland 13 F6
Legoland **Park** • Denmark .... 73 [16]
Legoland **Park** • United Kingdom 73 [34]
Legoland • Denmark 95 F9
Legundi • Indonesia 110 D1
Lehi • Jammu & Kashmir 28 B1
Lehená • Greece 15 C6
Lehinch **Beach** • Ireland .... 68 [42]
Lehinch • Ireland 8 E4
Leicester • United Kingdom 74 D2
Leichlingen • Germany 81 E3
Leiden • Netherlands 80 C1
Leie • Belgium 5 G4
Leigh Creek • SA, Australia 34 G6
Leignitz • Poland 71 A9
Leikanger • Norway 94 C4
Leine • Germany 9 F5
Leinefelde • Germany 9 F5
Leinster • Ireland 7 E8
Leipheim • Germany 82 J1
Leipnitzsee • Germany 9 H5
Leipzig • Germany 9 G5
Leiria • Portugal 11 C5
Leiria [Adm] • Portugal 88 A2
Leirvik • Norway 94 C5
Leisure I. • Maldives 106 E2
Leith • United Kingdom 74 B4
Leitha • Austria 13 F10
Leitrim • Ireland 79 D1
Leiva • Colombia 43 C3
Leixlip • Ireland 79 D2
Lejre **Beach** • Denmark ..... 68 [23]
Leka • Norway 94 A5
Lékáni • Greece 15 D4
Lekitobi • Indonesia 32 (1) B3
Lékitob • Indonesia .... 32 [176]
Lekness • Norway 16 H2
Leksozero • Russian Fed. 16 P5
Leksula • Indonesia 32 (1) C3
Lelång • Sweden 94 B4
Lelystad • Netherlands 80 C2
Léman, Lac • Switzerland 89 G5

Lemba Harau Reserve • Indonesia 110 B4
Lemesós • Cyprus 93 J3
Lemgo • Germany 8 D4
Lemieux Is. • NU, Canada 39 S4
Lemland • Finland 95 E3
Lemmenjoki Nat. Park **Park** •
  Finland .... 72 [29]
Lemmer • Netherlands 80 B3
Lemnos • Greece 92 D2
Lemnos • Greece 92 D2
Lemsid • Western Sahara 20 C3
Lemvig **Beach** • Denmark .... 68 [31]
Lemwig • Denmark 95 F9
Lena • Russian Fed. 27 J3
Lena Delta • Russian Fed. 97 A6
Lena, Mt • Crete, Greece 93 E7
Lengerich • Germany 8 D4
Lenggries • Germany 82 J7
Lengua de Vaca, Punta • Chile .. 44 B5
Leninabad • Crete, Greece 93 J1
Lenina, pik • Kyrgyzstan 18 J2
Lénina, pik • Kyrgyzstan 18 J2
Leningradskaya [Base] •
  Antarctica 46 (1) U3
Leningradsky • Russian Fed. .. 46 HH3
Leninsk-Kuznetsky •
  Russian Fed. 26 O7
Lenk **Ski** • Switzerland .... 70 [89]
Lenk • Switzerland 89 G6
Lenkoran • Azerbaijan 18 E2
Lenne • Germany 9 C5
Lennox, Fort • QU, Canada 122 B8
Leno-Angarskoye Plato •
  Russian Fed. 27 F6
Lens • France 10 H3
Lensk • Russian Fed. 27 I4
Lent • Hungary 14 D3
Lentini • Sicily, Italy 12 J11
Lenwa • Finland 16 O4
Lenzerheide • Switzerland 89 G4
Lenzerheide-Valbella **Ski** •
  Switzerland .... 70 [110]
Lenzkirch **Spa** • Germany .. 83 [209]
Léo • Burkina Faso 22 D2
Leoben • Austria 13 E10
Leogang **Ski** • Austria .... 70 [162]
Leok • Indonesia 32 (1) B2
Leominster • United Kingdom 74 D1
Leominster • MA, United States 118 G3
León • Spain 11 F2
León • Nicaragua 37 D5
León • Mexico 123 E1
León, Montes de • Spain 11 E2
León, Pays de • France 84 C1
Leonardville • Namibia 24 B4
Leonberg • Germany 9 E8
Leone, Monte •
  Italy/Switzerland 89 G6
Leonora • WA, Australia 34 D5
Leontes • Lebanon 98 A2
Leopardstown • Ireland 79 E2
Leópolis • Brazil 127 C2
Léova • Moldova 14 F3
Lepanto • Greece 71 A20
Lepe **Beach** • Spain .... 68 [95]
Lepe • Spain 86 B1
Lepe Country Park **Beach** •
  United Kingdom .... 75 [81]
Lephepe • Botswana 24 C4
Lepini, Monti • Italy 91 F4
Leptis Magna • Libya 21 B1
Leptis Magna **Heritage C** • Libya 64 [234]
Lercara Fridi • Sicily, Italy .. 12 H11
Léré • Chad 22 G3
Lérici • Italy 91 E10
Lérida • Spain 11 L3
Lérida • Colombia 43 C4
Lérins, Is. de • France 85 H4
Lerma • Spain 11 B1
Lermoos **Ski** • Austria .... 70 [138]
Léros • Greece 92 D8
Léros • Greece 92 D8
Lerum • Sweden 95 F6
Lerwick • United Kingdom 6 K1
Les Amirantes • Seychelles 106 F2
Les Bioux • Switzerland 89 G1
Les Cayes • Haiti 15 D5
Les Collons **Ski** • Switzerland 70 [82]
Les Crosets **Ski** • Switzerland 70 [76]
Les Diablerets **Ski** •
  Switzerland .... 70 [84]
Les Diablerets • Switzerland ... 89 A16
Les Mosses • Switzerland 89 A16
Lesbos • Greece 92 D5
Lesbos • Greece 92 D5
Lesh • China 29 C5
Leshan Giant Buddha **Heritage N** •
  China .... 61 [117]
Leshan Giant Buddha **Heritage C** •
  China .... 63 [156]
Lésina, Lago di • Italy 12 J7
Lesjaskog • Norway 94 C2
Lesjaskogsvatnet • Norway 94 C2
Lesjöfors • Sweden 16 H7
Leskovac • F.R. of Yugoslavia .. 14 I7
Leskovik • Albania 15 B3
Lesnevem • France 84 C1
Lesnoy • Russian Fed. 17 I3
Lesosibirsk • Russian Fed. 26 P6
Lesotho • Africa 24 D5
Lesozavodsk • Russian Fed. 27 L7
Lesser Antilles • West Indies .. 37 I5
Lesser Sunda Is. • Indonesia . 32 (1) B4
Leszno • Poland 13 F6
Lethbridge • AL/Canada 38 I7
Lethem • Guyana 43 F3
Leticia • Colombia 43 D4
Letmathe • Germany 81 E2
Letoon • Turkey 92 D9
Letoon • Turkey 92 D9
Letterie • Portugal 31 B3
Letterfrack • Ireland 79 F3
Letterkenny • United Kingdom 7 E7
Lettermore • Ireland 79 F3
Leu • Romania 14 L5
Leucate **Beach** • France .... 68 [112]
Leucate • France 85 K2
Leucate, Étang de • France 85 K2
Leukerbad • Switzerland 89 G6
Leuna • Germany 9 H5
Leuser, Gunung • Indonesia 110 B1
Leutkirch • Germany 82 J5
Leutze Spa • Germany .... 83 [157]
Leuven • Belgium 80 A15
Levanger • Norway 16 H6
Levant • Asia 59 C8
Levant, I. du • France 85 H3
Lim • F.R. of Yugoslavia 14 G6

Lévanto, I. de • Italy 90 D1
Leven, Loch • United Kingdom ... 74 B2
Levens Hall • United Kingdom ... 74 C4
Lévêque, Cape • WA, Australia .. 34 D3
Leverkusen • Germany 81 E3
Levern **Spa** • Germany ..... 83 [87]
Lévice • Slovak Rep. 13 H9
Lévico Terme • Italy 90 B3
Levin • New Zealand 35 E5
Lévis • QU, Canada 122 B4
Levítha • Greece 92 D8
Levítha • Greece 92 D8
Levkas • Greece 92 C1
Levkási • Greece 92 C1
Levkosia • Cyprus 93 J2
Levoca • Slovak Rep. 13 J8
Levski • Bulgaria 97 D3
Lewes • United Kingdom 74 E3
Lewes • DE, United States 118 H3
Lewis • United Kingdom 6 F3
Lewis Hills • NF, Canada 123 D3
Lewis Pass • New Zealand 35 D6
Lewis Range •
  Canada/United States 38 I7
Lewiston • ID, United States .. 117 E2
Lewiston • ME, United States .. 118 G4
Lewistown • MT, United States .. 40 E2
Lewisville • TX, United States 119 N1
Lexington • KY, United States .. 41 J4
Leyre • France 10 E9
Leysdown-on-Sea **Beach** •
  United Kingdom .... 75 [61]
Leysin • Switzerland 89 G5
Leyte • Philippines 31 H4
Lezha • Albania 15 A2
Lhasa • China 28 E3
Lhasa **Heritage C** • China .. 63 [142]
Lhaze • China 28 E3
Lhazhong • China 28 E2
Lho-Nga **Beach** • Indonesia . 110 B3
Lhohifushi • Maldives 106 E2
Lhokseumawe • Indonesia 110 B1
Lhozhag • China 28 F3
Liákoura • Greece 15 D5
Liamuga, Mt • St Kitts & Nevis 125 G1
Liangspran, Gunung • Indonesia . 32 E2
Lianhuashan • China 107 H2
Lianxian • China 29 E5
Lianyungang • China 29 F4
Liao He • China 29 G2
Liaodong • China 29 G2
Liaodong Wan • China 29 G2
Liaoning • China 107 G4
Liaoyang • China 29 G2
Liard • Canada 38 G4
Liard River • BC, Canada 38 F5
Libby • MT, United States 40 C2
Libechov • Czech Rep. 96 C2
Libenge • Dem. Rep. of Congo .. 23 B3
Liberal • KS, United States 40 F4
Liberec • Czech Rep. 96 C2
Liberia • Africa 22 B3
Liberia • Costa Rica 37 D5
Liberta • Antigua & Barbuda .. 125 [157]
Liberty • TX, United States ... 119 N4
Libiyah, As Sahra al • Africa .. 21 D2
Lobobo, Tanjung • Indonesia . 32 (1) C3
Liber • Kenya 101 G4
Libourne • France 84 B3
Libourne • France 85 G1
Libreville • Gabon 22 F4
Libya • Africa 21 C2
Libyan Desert • Egypt 21 E2
Licantén • Chile 45 B2
Licata • Sicily, Italy 12 H11
Lichfield • United Kingdom 74 D2
Lichinga • Mozambique 24 F2
Lichnice • Czech Rep. 96 C2
Lichtenfels • Germany 9 G6
Licosa, Punta • Italy 91 G3
Lida • Belarus 16 M10
Lidice • Czech Rep. 96 C2
Lidingö • Sweden 95 D4
Lidköping • Sweden 95 F3
Lido de Camaiore • Italy 91 E10
Lido de Jésolo • Italy 91 E8
Lido di Ostia • Italy 12 G7
Lidoríki • Greece 15 D5
Lidzbark Warminski • Poland 13 J3
Liebenback, Burg • Germany 82 H2
Liebenstein, Burg • Germany 82 H2
Liebig, Mt • NT, Australia 112 H1
Liechtenstein • Europe 89 H5
Liège • Belgium 80 A16
Liège [Adm] • Belgium 80 A16
Lieksa • Finland 16 P5
Lienz • Austria 89 H8
Liepaja • Latvia 13 J1
Lier • Belgium 80 A11
Lierbyen • Norway 94 B1
Liesjärvi Nat. Park **Park** •
  Finland .... 73 [12]
Liesjärvi Nat. Park **Park** •
  Finland .... 72 [34]
Linnhe, Loch • United Kingdom ... 6 G5
Linping • China 107 J4
Lins • Brazil 44 G3
Linstead • Jamaica 124 C4
Lintorf • Germany 81 E1
Linxi • China 29 F2
Linyi • China 29 F3
Linz • Austria 13 D9
Linz • Germany 82 H1
Lion, Golfe du •
  Mediterranean Sea 10 J11
Lion Rock Country Park •
  Hong Kong, China 107 H6
Lioppa • Indonesia 32 (1) C4
Liouesso • Congo 22 H4
Lipa • Philippines 31 G4
Lípari • Italy 90 D2
Lípari, Is. • Italy 90 D2
Lipcani • Moldova 14 N1
Lipenská Prehradní Nádrz •
  Czech Rep. 96 C4
Liperi • Finland 16 O5
Lipetsk • Russian Fed. 17 F4
Lipez, Cordillera de • Bolivia .. 44 C3
Lipnice nad Sázavou •
  Czech Rep. 96 C4
Lipno • Poland 13 I5
Lipova • Romania 14 I3
Lippe • Germany 9 D5
Lippstadt • Germany 8 D5
Lipsí • Greece 92 D8
Lipsí • Greece 92 D8
Liptovský Mikuláš • Slovak Rep. 13 I8
Lira • Uganda 23 E3
Liranga • Congo 22 H5
Líri • Italy 12 H7
Lisala • Dem. Rep. of Congo ... 23 C3
Lisalmi • Finland 16 N5
Lisboa **Heritage C** • Portugal 64 [100]
Lisboa • Portugal 88 D2
Lisboa [Adm] • Portugal 88 A2
Lisboa, Costa de • Portugal 88 A3
Lisbon **Heritage C** • Portugal 64 [100]
Lisbon • Portugal 88 D2
Lisburn • United Kingdom 7 F7

Lisburn [Adm] • United Kingdom **75** A3
Lisdoonvarna • Ireland **79** F4
Liseberg **Park** • Sweden **73** [5]
Lishui • Zhejiang, China **31** F1
Lishui • Jiangsu, China **107** J1
Lisichansk • Ukraine **17** F5
Lisieux • France **10** F4
Liskeard • United Kingdom **74** F5
Liski • Romania **14** N3
Lismore • United Kingdom **75** A2
Lismore • NS, Australia **111** F6
Lissadell House • Ireland **79** F2
Lisse • Netherlands **80** C1
List **Spa** • Germany **83** [2]
Lista • Norway **16** D7
Lister, Mt • Antarctica **46** (1) V2
Listowel • Ireland **79** F5
Lit-et-Mixe **Beach** • France **68** [67]
Lit-et-Mixe, Fôret de • France **85** G3
Litani • Lebanon **98** A2
Liternum • Italy **91** G1
Lith, Al • Saudi Arabia **18** D5
Lithgow • NS, Australia **111** G2
Líthino, Akra • Crete, Greece **93** E6
Lithuania • Europe **16** M9
Litle Abaco • Bahamas **124** B1
Litohóro **Beach** • Greece **69** [167]
Litomerice • Czech Rep. **96** C2
Little • TX, United States **119** N3
Little Andaman • India **28** F6
Little Bighorn Battlefield Nat. Mon. **Park** • MT, United States **120** [71]
Little Cayman • Cayman Is. **124** D6
Little Current • OT, Canada **39** O7
Little Exuma • Bahamas **124** B4
Little Hura • Maldives **106** E2
Little Inagua • Bahamas **124** B4
Little Karoo • South Africa **100** C6
Little Missouri • United States **38** K7
Little Nicobar • India **28** F7
Little River Canyon Nat. Preserve **Park** • AL, United States **121** [206]
Little Rock • AR, United States **41** H5
Little Skellig • Ireland **79** F7
Little Tobago • Trinidad & Tobago **125** K2
Littlehampton • United Kingdom **74** E3
Littlehampton **Beach** • United Kingdom **75** [76]
Litvínov • Czech Rep. **96** C1
Liuhe • China **30** C3
Liullaillaco, Volcán • Argentina/Chile **44** C3
Liuzhou • China **29** D6
Livadiá • Greece **15** D5
Livanátes **Beach** • Greece **69** [164]
Liverpool • United Kingdom **7** J8
Liverpool • NS, Canada **123** D7
Liverpool Bay • United Kingdom **7** I8
Liverpool Bay • NT, Canada **38** E3
Livigno **Ski** • Italy **70** [204]
Livigno • Italy **91** E2
Livingston • MT, United States **40** D2
Livingston • United Kingdom **74** B4
Livingston • TX, United States **119** N4
Livingston, Lake • TX, United States **119** N4
Livingstone • Zambia **24** D3
Livingstone, Chutes de • Dem. Rep. of Congo **23** A5
Livingstone Falls • Dem. Rep. of Congo **23** A5
Livingstone Mtns • Tanzania **23** E5
Livingstone Mtns • New Zealand **112** L2
Livingstonia • Malawi **23** E6
Livland • Estonia/Latvia **16** N8
Livno • Bosnia-Herz. **14** D6
Livorno • Italy **91** E11
Liwale • Tanzania **102** H4
Liwonde Nat. Park **Park** • Malawi **103** [99]
Lixoúri • Greece **92** C2
Lixoúri • Greece **92** C2
Liyang • China **107** J1
Liyuan • China **107** J2
Lizard Point • United Kingdom **74** F4
Ljubinje • Bosnia-Herz. **14** F7
Ljubisnja • Bosnia-Herz./F.R. of Yugoslavia **14** F6
Ljubljana • Slovenia **13** D11
Ljugarn • Sweden **16** J8
Ljungan • Sweden **16** I5
Ljungby • Sweden **95** F7
Ljungsbro • Sweden **95** F4
Ljusdal • Sweden **16** I6
Ljusnan • Sweden **16** I6
Ljusterö • Sweden **95** D2
Ljusterö [I.] • Sweden **95** D2
Llançá **Beach** • Spain **68** [106]
Llançá • Spain **87** D2
Llandanwg **Beach** • United Kingdom **75** [189]
Llanddona **Beach** • United Kingdom **75** [215]
Llandrindod Wells • United Kingdom **7** I9
Llandudno **Beach** • United Kingdom **75** [197]
Llaneilian **Beach** • United Kingdom **75** [211]
Llanelli • United Kingdom **7** H10
Llanes • Spain **11** G1
Llanes **Beach** • Spain **68** [71]
Llanfachraeth **Beach** • United Kingdom **75** [209]
Llanfaelog **Beach** • United Kingdom **75** [203]
Llanfairfechan **Beach** • United Kingdom **75** [195]
Llangennith **Beach** • United Kingdom **75** [143]
Llangollen • United Kingdom **7** I9
Llangorwen **Beach** • United Kingdom **75** [184]
Llangrannog **Beach** • United Kingdom **75** [175-176]
Llano • TX, United States **119** N3
Llano Estacado • NM/TX, United States **40** F5
Llano [Riv] • TX, United States **119** N3
Llanos • Colombia/Venezuela **43** D2
Llanos de Concepcion • Fuerteventura, Canary Is. **87** E2
Llanrhystud **Beach** • United Kingdom **75** [182]
Llantwit Major • United Kingdom **74** F2
Llerena • Spain **11** F6
Llevant, Costa de • Spain **87** D2
Llevant, Serra de • Majorca, Spain **87** H4
Lliria • Spain **11** K5
Llívia • Spain **87** D1
Llobregat • Spain **87** D1
Llogara Nat. Park **Park** • Albania **72** [127]
Lloret de Mar **Beach** • Spain **68** [106]
Lloret de Mar • Spain **87** D4
Lloyd George, Mt • BC, Canada **38** F5
Lloydminster • SA, Canada **38** J6
Lluc Alcari • Majorca, Spain **87** H1
Lluc, Monestir de • Majorca, Spain **87** H1
Llucmajor • Majorca, Spain **87** H3
Lo Wu • Hong Kong, China **107** H3
Loa • Chile **44** C3
Loano • Italy **12** C4
Löbau • Germany **9** J5
Lobaye • Central African Rep. **23** B2
Lobéria • Argentina **127** D3
Lobito • Angola **23** A6
Lobo • Indonesia **32** (1) D3
Lobos • Canary Is. **87** E2
Lobos • Argentina **127** D1
Lobos, I. de • Uruguay **127** D2
Locarno • Switzerland **89** G7
Lochaline • United Kingdom **78** A2
Lochboisdale • United Kingdom **6** E4
Loches [Château] • France **84** D4
Lochgilphead • United Kingdom **6** G5
Lochinver • United Kingdom **6** G3
Lochmaddy • United Kingdom **6** E4
Lochnagar • United Kingdom **6** I5
Lochranza • United Kingdom **78** A2
Lochy, Loch • United Kingdom **6** H5
Lockhart • TX, United States **119** N3
Locmariaquer • France **84** C4
Locminé • France **10** C6
Locri • Italy **12** K10
Locronan • France **84** C3
Lod • Israel **98** A5
Lodève • France **10** I10
Lodeynoye Pole • Russian Fed. **17** E2
Lodi • Italy **91** E6
Lødingen • Norway **16** H2
Lodja • Dem. Rep. of Congo **23** C4
Lodore Falls • United Kingdom **74** C2
Lodwar • Kenya **101** G1
Lódz • Poland **13** I6
Loei • Thailand **109** G4
Loerie • South Africa **100** C8
Loffa • Liberia **22** B3
Lofoten • Norway **16** G2
Loftahammar • Sweden **95** F4
Lofthus • Norway **94** C4
Logan • UT, United States **40** D3
Logan [Apt] • MA, United States **118** G3
Logan, Mt • YT, Canada **38** C4
Logansport • LA, United States **118** K1
Loge • Angola **23** A5
Logone • Chad **21** C5
Logroño • Spain **11** I2
Løgstør **Beach** • Denmark **68** [29]
Løgstør • Denmark **95** F5
Logudoro • Sardinia, Italy **12** C8
Løgumkloster • Denmark **95** F13
Lögurinn • Iceland **16** (1) F2
Lohja • Finland **95** E4
Lohmar • Germany **82** G1
Löhne • Germany **8** D4
Lohne • Germany **8** D4
Lohr • Germany **9** E6
Lohria • Crete, Greece **93** E6
Loi-kaw • Myanmar **31** B3
Loibl • Slovenia **13** D11
Loimaa • Finland **95** E4
Loir • France **84** D2
Loir-et-Cher • France **84** D2
Loire • France **10** G6
Loíza Aldea • Puerto Rico **125** E2
Loíza, Río Grande de • Puerto Rico **125** E4
Loja • Ecuador **43** B4
Loja • Spain **86** B3
Lokan tekojärri • Finland **16** N3
Løken • Norway **94** B2
Lokeren • Belgium **5** G3
Loket • Czech Rep. **96** C1
Lokitaung • Kenya **23** F3
Løkken • Denmark **95** F5
Løkken-Vrå **Beach** • Denmark **68** [29]
Lokoja • Nigeria **22** F3
Lokomo • Cameroon **23** B3
Loks Land • NU, Canada **39** S4
Lokwe Kangole • Kenya **101** G1
Lolland • Denmark **95** F14
Lolo Pass • MT, United States **117** E2
Lom • Bulgaria **14** K6
Lom • Norway **94** C2
Lom Sak • Thailand **109** G4
Loma Mtns • Guinea/Sierra Leone **22** B3
Lomami • Dem. Rep. of Congo **23** C5
Lombarda, Serra • Brazil **43** G3
Lombardia • Italy **91** E6
Lombardsijde-Bad • Belgium **80** B1
Lombardy • Italy **90** A1
Lombok • Indonesia **32** F4
Lomé • Togo **22** E3
Lomela • Dem. Rep. of Congo **23** C4
Lomié • Cameroon **22** G4
Lommel • Belgium **5** I3
Lomond, Loch • United Kingdom **74** B3
Lomonosov • Russian Fed. **17** D3
Lomza • Poland **13** L4
Lon, Ko • Thailand **109** K2
Londe-les-Maures, la **Beach** • France **68** [116]
Londerzeel **Beach** • Belgium **68** [54]
Londerzeel • Belgium **80** A14
London • OT, Canada **39** O8
London **Heritage C** • United Kingdom **64** [22-24]
London • United Kingdom **74** E1
London City [Apt] • United Kingdom **74** E1
Londonderry • United Kingdom **7** E7
Londonderry, Cape • WA, Australia **34** E2
Long Akah • Malaysia **31** E6
Long Bay • Jamaica **124** C4
Long Bay • Antigua & Barbuda **125** F2
Long Bay • Barbados **125** H4
Long Bay [Bay] • Jamaica **124** C3
Long Beach • CA, United States **117** F6
Long Branch • NJ, United States **118** H1
Long Cay • Bahamas **124** B4
Long Hai • Vietnam **108** B4
Long I. • Papua New Guinea **35** (1) D2
Long I. • QL, Australia **111** F1
Long I. • New Zealand **112** L3
Long I. • NY, United States **118** H2
Long I. • Bahamas **124** B4
Long I. • Antigua & Barbuda **125** F2
Long Island Sound • CT/NY, United States **41** L3
Long Kloof • South Africa **100** C7
Long Mynd, The • United Kingdom **74** D1
Long Point • New Zealand **112** L3
Long Point • OT, Canada **122** B9
Long Range Mtns • NF, Canada **123** D3
Long Xuyen • Vietnam **108** B3
Longa, Proliv • Russian Fed. **27** U3
Longarone • Italy **90** B4
Longboat Key • FL, United States **119** M5
Longchamp • France **85** E3
Longeville-sur-Mer **Beach** • France **68** [64]
Longfellow Nat. Hist. Site **Park** • MA, United States **121** [348]
Longford • Ireland **7** E8
Longford [Adm] • Ireland **79** D1
Longgang • China **107** H2
Longlac • OT, Canada **39** N7
Longleat House & Safari Park • United Kingdom **74** F3
Longmalinau • Indonesia **32** F2
Longmont • CO, United States **40** F3
Longnan • China **31** E2
Longonot Nat. Park • Kenya **101** G3
Longpujungan • Indonesia **32** F2
Longreach • QL, Australia **34** H4
Longs Peak • CO, United States **40** E3
Longue, I. • Seychelles **106** F1
Longuyon • France **10** K4
Longview • WA, United States **117** E1
Longview • TX, United States **119** N2
Longwood Gardens • PA, United States **118** H3
Longwy • France **5** I5
Longxi • China **29** C3
Longxi Shan • China **31** F1
Longyearbyen • Svalbard **46** N2
Löningen • Germany **8** C4
Lons-le-Saunier • France **10** K7
Looe • United Kingdom **74** F5
Looe Key Nat. Marine Sanctuary • FL, United States **119** M8
Lookout, Cape • NC, United States **118** H5
Lookout, Cape, Nat. Seashore • NC, United States **118** H5
Lookout Pass • MT, United States **40** C2
Loolmalassin • Tanzania **23** F4
Loon **Ski** • NH, United States **116** [214]
Loop Head • Ireland **79** F5
Loosdrechtse Plassen • Netherlands **80** C2
Lop Buri • Thailand **31** C4
Lop Nur • China **26** P9
Lopatina, gora • Russian Fed. **27** N6
Lopatka, mys • Russian Fed. **25** Q4
Lopé, Réserve de **Park** • Gabon **103** [47]
Lopez, Cap • Gabon **22** F5
Lopez, Cap, Baie du • Gabon **22** F5
Lopikerwaard • Netherlands **80** C4
Loppem • Belgium **80** B2
Lora del Rio • Spain **11** F7
Lorain • OH, United States **41** J3
Lorca • Spain **11** J7
Lorch • Germany **82** H4
Lord Howe I. • NS, Australia **34** K6
Lord Howe I. **Heritage N** • NS, Australia **61** [137]
Lordsburg • NM, United States **118** J4
Loreley • Germany **82** H4
Lorengau • Papua New Guinea **35** (1) D1
Loreto • Bolivia **44** D2
Loreto **Heritage C** • Argentina **62** [64]
Loreto • Italy **91** E12
Loreto • Mexico **123** E1
Lorian Swamp • Kenya **101** G2
Lorient • France **84** C3
Lörinci • Hungary **13** I10
Lorn, Firth of • United Kingdom **6** G5
Lörrach • Germany **82** G7
Lorraine • France **10** K4
Lorsach • Germany **82** J3
Lorsch **Heritage C** • Germany **64** [44]
Lorsch • Germany **82** H4
Los Alamos • NM, United States **118** J2
Los Alcázares **Beach** • Spain **68** [100]
Los Alcázares • Spain **87** C3
Los Angeles • Chile **45** B3
Los Angeles • CA, United States **117** F6
Los Arenales del Sol • Spain **87** C1
Los Blancos • Argentina **44** D3
Los Cristianos • Tenerife, Canary Is. **86** E1
Los Gigantes • Tenerife, Canary Is. **86** E1
Los Glaciares, Parque Nac. **Heritage N** • Argentina **60** [38]
Los, Is. de • Guinea **22** B3
Los Katios, Parque Nac. **Heritage N** • Colombia **60** [28]
Los Mochis • Mexico **40** E6
Los Monegros • Spain **11** K3
Los Monos • Mexico **123** E3
Los Padres, Laguna de • Argentina **127** D4
Los Palacios • Cuba **124** D1
Los Palacios y Villafranca • Spain **11** F7
Los Pinos, Costa de • Majorca, Spain **87** H2
Los Pocillos • Lanzarote, Canary Is. **87** E3
Los Rodeos [Apt] • Tenerife, Canary Is. **86** E1
Los Teques • Venezuela **43** D2
Los Vilos • Chile **44** B5
Losai Game Reserve • Kenya **101** G2
Losinj • Croatia **14** B5
Lost Trail Pass • MT, United States **117** E2
Lostwithiel • United Kingdom **74** F4
Lot • France **10** G9
Lot • Sudan **21** E6
Lot [Adm] • France **85** G4
Lota • Chile **44** B6
Lothian • United Kingdom **74** B4
Lotkipi Plain • Kenya **101** G1
Loto • Dem. Rep. of Congo **23** C4
Lotuka, Jabal • Sudan **23** E3
Lotus Mtn • China **107** H2
Louangphrabang • Laos **31** C3
Louangphrabang **Heritage C** • Laos **63** [170]
Loubomo • Congo **22** G5
Loudéac • France **84** C2
Loudima • Congo **22** G5
Loudun • France **84** D3
Loué • France **10** E6
Louga • Senegal **22** A1
Loughborough • United Kingdom **74** D2
Loughrea **Beach** • Ireland **68** [43]
Loughrea • Ireland **79** F4
Loughwood Meeting House • United Kingdom **74** F3
Louisa, Lake • FL, United States **121** C1
Louisa, Lake, State Park • FL, United States **121** C1
Louisbourg, Fortress of • NS, Canada **123** D8
Louisburgh **Beach** • Ireland **68** [44]
Louisburgh • Ireland **79** F1
Louisiade Archipelago • Papua New Guinea **35** (1) E2
Louisiana • United States **118** K1
Louisville • KY, United States **41** I4
Louisville • MS, United States **118** K2
Loulan • China **98** B3
Loulan Yiji • China **26** O9
Loulé **Beach** • Portugal **68** [82]
Loulé • Portugal **88** E7
Louny • Czech Rep. **96** C1
Loup • France **85** H2
Loup, Gorges du • France **85** H2
Lourdes • France **85** J2
Lourinha **Beach** • Portugal **68** [80]
Louth • United Kingdom **7** M8
Louth • Ireland **79** D1
Loutrá • Greece **92** D7
Loutrá • Greece **92** D7
Loutrá Edipsoú • Greece **92** D4
Loutrá Edipsoú • Greece **92** D4
Loutráki **Beach** • Greece **69** [155]
Louvière, la • Belgium **5** H4
Louviers • France **10** G4
Lövanger • Sweden **16** K4
Lovat • Russian Fed. **97** E3
Lovcan • F.R. of Yugoslavia **14** F7
Lovcen Nat. Park **Park** • Fed. Rep. of Yugoslavia **72** [120]
Lovech • Bulgaria **14** L6
Loveland **Ski** • CO, United States **116** [91]
Lovelock • NV, United States **117** F2
Lover's Leap • Jamaica **124** C3
Lovina Beach • Bali, Indonesia **110** C2
Lovoi • Dem. Rep. of Congo **23** D5
Lovosice • Czech Rep. **96** C1
Lövstad • Sweden **95** F4
Low, Cape • NU, Canada **39** N4
Low Newton **Beach** • United Kingdom **75** [18]
Lowa • Dem. Rep. of Congo **23** D4
Lowell • MA, United States **118** G3
Lowell Nat. Hist. Park **Park** • MA, United States **121** [351]
Lower Austria • Austria **89** F4
Lower Egypt • Egypt **101** F1
Lower Hutt • New Zealand **35** E5
Lower Post • YT, Canada **38** F4
Lower Saxony • Germany **81** D2
Lower Zambezi Nat. Park **Park** • Zambia **103** [106]
Lowestoft • United Kingdom **7** N9
Lowestoft **Beach** • United Kingdom **75** [47-48]
Loweswater • United Kingdom **74** C1
Lowicz • Poland **13** I5
Loxstedt • Germany **5** L1
Loxstedt • Germany **8** D3
Loxton • South Africa **100** C3
Loyalty Is. • New Caledonia **35** (2) B3
Loyangalani • Kenya **101** G1
Loyauté, Is. • New Caledonia **35** (2) B3
Lozenets • Bulgaria **97** D4
Lozère, Mt • France **10** I9
Loznica • F.R. of Yugoslavia **14** G5
Lu Shan **Heritage C** • China **63** [155]
Lu'an • China **29** F4
Lua • Dem. Rep. of Congo **22** H4
Luacano • Angola **24** C2
Luachimo • Angola **23** C5
Luachimo [Riv] • Angola **23** C5
Luahasibuka • Indonesia **110** B4
Lualaba • Dem. Rep. of Congo **23** D5
Luama • Dem. Rep. of Congo **23** D4
Luana Point • Jamaica **124** C3
Luanda • Angola **23** A5
Luando • Angola **23** B6
Luang Po Ban Laem • Thailand **109** H3
Luang Prabang **Heritage C** • Laos **63** [170]
Luang Prabang Range • Laos/Thailand **109** G4
Luanginga • Angola/Zambia **24** C2
Luangwa • Zambia **102** J2
Luangwa [Riv] • Zambia **24** E2
Luanshya • Zambia **24** D2
Luao • Angola **23** C6
Luapula • Dem. Rep. of Congo/Zambia **23** D6
Luarca • Spain **11** E1
Luba • Equatorial Guinea **22** F4
Luban • Poland **13** E6
Lubang • Philippines **31** G4
Lubango • Angola **24** A2
Lubao • Dem. Rep. of Congo **23** D5
Lubartow • Poland **13** L6
Lübbecke • Germany **8** D4
Lübben • Germany **8** I5
Lübbenau • Germany **8** I5
Lubbock • TX, United States **40** F5
Lübeck • Germany **8** F3
Lübeck **Heritage C** • Germany **64** [30]
Lübecker Bucht • Germany **8** G2
Lubenec • Czech Rep. **9** I6
Lubilash • Dem. Rep. of Congo **23** C5
Lubin • Poland **13** F6
Lublin • Poland **13** L6
Lubliniec • Poland **13** H7
Lubmin **Spa** • Germany **83** [282]
Lubnàn, Jabal • Lebanon **18** C3
Lubny • Ukraine **17** E4
Lubon • Poland **13** F5
Lubsko • Poland **13** D6
Lubudi • Dem. Rep. of Congo **23** C6
Lubuklinggau • Indonesia **32** C3
Lubumbashi • Dem. Rep. of Congo **23** D6
Luc • France **85** F3
Luc, le • France **85** H3
Lucala • Angola **22** H6
Lucala [Riv] • Angola **22** H6
Lucan • Ireland **79** E2
Lucapa • Angola **23** C5
Lucaya • Bahamas **124** B2
Lucaya Estates • Bahamas **124** B2
Lucca • Italy **91** E11
Luce Bay • United Kingdom **7** H7
Lucea • Jamaica **124** C1
Lucena • Spain **11** G7
Lucena del Cid • Spain **11** K4
Lucenec • Slovak Rep **13** I9
Lucera • Italy **14** C8
Lucerne • Switzerland **89** G3
Lucerne, Lake of • Switzerland **89** G3
Lucheringo • Mozambique **23** F6
Lucira • Angola **24** A2
Luckau • Germany **8** I5
Luckenwalde • Germany **8** I4
Lucknow • India **105** C3
Luçon • France **84** D3
Lucrecia, Cabo • Cuba **124** D8
Lucusse • Angola **23** C6
Lüda • China **29** G3
Lude, le • France **84** D1
Lüdenscheid • Germany **81** E4
Lüderitz • Namibia **24** B5
Lüderitz Bay • Namibia **24** B5
Ludhiana • India **28** C2
Ludlow • United Kingdom **74** D1
Ludogorije • Bulgaria **14** O6
Ludogorsko Plato • Bulgaria **14** O6
Ludus • Romania **14** L3
Ludvika • Sweden **16** H6
Ludwigsburg • Germany **82** G6
Ludwigsfelde • Germany **81** F3
Ludwigshafen • Germany **82** G4
Ludwigslust • Germany **8** G3
Luebo • Dem. Rep. of Congo **23** C5
Luena • Angola **24** C2
Luena [Riv] • Zambia **24** C2
Luenha • Mozambique/Zimbabwe **24** E3
Lufira • Dem. Rep. of Congo **23** D6
Lufkin • TX, United States **119** N4
Luga • Russian Fed. **17** D3
Lugano • Switzerland **89** G7
Lugano, Lago di • Italy/Switzerland **89** G7
Lugansk • Ukraine **17** F5
Luganville • Vanuatu **35** (2) B2
Lugenda • Mozambique/Tanzania **24** F2
Lugnaquillia • Ireland **79** E4
Lugo • Spain **11** D1
Lugo • Italy **12** F4
Lugoj • Romania **14** I4
Luhayyah, Al • Yemen **18** D6
Luhe • China **107** J1
Luhit • India **28** G3
Luhur Batukau Temple • Bali, Indonesia **110** C2
Lui • Angola **22** H6
Luiana • Angola **24** C3
Luiana [Riv] • Africa **24** C3
Luilaka • Dem. Rep. of Congo **23** C4
Luimneach • Ireland **79** F6
Luing • United Kingdom **75** A2
Luján • Argentina **127** D1
Lukenie • Dem. Rep. of Congo **23** C4
Lukolela • Dem. Rep. of Congo **22** H5
Lukovit • Bulgaria **14** L6
Luków • Poland **13** L6
Lukuga • Dem. Rep. of Congo **23** D5
Lukulu • Zambia **24** C2
Lule älv • Sweden **16** K4
Lulea • Sweden **16** L4
Luleå **Heritage C** • Sweden **63** [72]
Lüleburgaz • Turkey **15** I2
Lulimba • Dem. Rep. of Congo **23** D4
Lulonga • Dem. Rep. of Congo **23** B3
Lulua • Dem. Rep. of Congo **23** C5
Lumajang • Java, Indonesia **110** D8
Lumajangdong Co • China **28** D2
Lumbala • Angola **24** C2
Lumberton • NC, United States **41** K5
Lumbini **Heritage C** • Nepal **63** [140]
Lumi • Papua New Guinea **35** (1) C1
Lumjiag, Laem • Phuket, Thailand **109** K2
Lumsden • New Zealand **112** L4
Lumut • Malaysia **108** D1
Lumut • Malaysia **108** D3
Lunar Crater • NV, United States **117** F4
Lund • Sweden **95** F11
Lunda • Angola **23** B5
Lundazi • Zambia **24** E2
Lunde • Norway **94** B3
Lunds Tivoli **Park** • Norway **73** [3]
Lundu • Malaysia **32** D2
Lundy • United Kingdom **74** F1
Lüneburg • Germany **8** F3
Lüneburg **Spa** • Germany **83** [57]
Lüneburger Heide • Germany **8** F3
Lünen • Germany **5** K3
Lünen • Germany **81** E2
Lunenburg **Heritage C** • NS, Canada **62** [4]
Lunenburg • NS, Canada **123** D7
Luneur **Park** • Italy **73** [85]
Lunéville • France **10** L5
Lung Kwu Chau • Hong Kong, China **107** H5
Luni • India **105** C5
Luo He • China **29** D3
Luohe • China **29** E4
Luoyang • China **29** E4
Lupeni • Romania **14** K4
Lupilichi • Mozambique **24** F2
Luputa • Dem. Rep. of Congo **23** C5
Luq • Somalia **23** G3
Luqa [Apt] • Malta **93** H4
Luque • Paraguay **44** E4
Luquillo • Puerto Rico **125** E2
Luquillo, Sierra de • Puerto Rico **125** E2
Lura Nat. Park **Park** • Albania **72** [125]
Lure • France **9** B9
Luremo • Angola **23** B5
Lurgan • United Kingdom **7** F7
Lúrio • Mozambique **24** F2
Lusaka • Zambia **24** D3
Lusambo • Dem. Rep. of Congo **23** C4
Luserna **Ski** • Italy **70** [212]
Lushnjë • Albania **14** G9
Lushoto • Tanzania **102** H2
Lushui • China **29** B5
Lüshun • China **29** G3
Lussac-les-Châteaux • France **84** D4
Lut, Dasht-e • Iran **18** G3
Lutembo • Angola **24** C2
Lutolim • Goa, India **105** B2
Luton • United Kingdom **74** E1
Lutselk'e • NT, Canada **38** I4
Lutsk • Ukraine **17** D4
Lützen • Germany **9** H5
Lützow-Holmbukta • Antarctica **46** (1) I3
Luvua • Dem. Rep. of Congo **23** D5
Luwaymi, Al • Saudi Arabia **18** D4
Luwego • Tanzania **24** F1
Luwuk • Indonesia **32** (1) B3
Luxembourg • Europe **80** A20
Luxembourg [Adm] • Belgium **80** A19
Luxembourg-Ville **Heritage C** • Luxembourg **64** [29]
Luxembourg-Ville • Luxembourg **80** A20
Luxeuil-les-Bains • France **10** L6
Luxi • China **29** B6
Luxor • Egypt **101** F4
Luxus • Morocco **101** D1
Luy • France **10** E10
Luz • France **85** J2
Luz, Costa de la • Spain **86** B5
Luza • Russian Fed. **17** H2
Luzern • Switzerland **89** G3
Luzhou • China **29** D5
Luziânia • Brazil **44** G2
Luznice • Czech Rep. **96** C4
Luzon • Philippines **31** G3
Luzon Strait • Philippines **31** G2
Lviv • Ukraine **17** C5
Lvov • Ukraine **17** C5
Lyakhovskiy Ostrova • Russian Fed. **97** A5
Lyall, Mt • New Zealand **112** L1
Lycksele • Sweden **16** J4
Lydd • United Kingdom **5** D4
Lydd [Apt] • United Kingdom **74** E4
Lydford Cay • Bahamas **124** B3
Lydië • Turkey **15** I5
Lydstep **Beach** • United Kingdom **75** [150]
Lyme Bay • United Kingdom **74** F6
Lyme Regis • United Kingdom **74** F3
Lymington • United Kingdom **7** K11
Lymira • Turkey **93** G3
Lyna Alie • Poland **13** J3
Lynchburg • VA, United States **41** K4
Lynd • QL, Australia **34** H3
Lynn Lake • MN, Canada **38** K5
Lynnay, gora • Russian Fed. **27** R4
Lynton • United Kingdom **74** F2
Lynx Lake • NT, Canada **38** J4
Lyon • France **85** F1
Lyons • WA, Australia **34** C4
Lys • France **5** F4
Lysebotn • Norway **94** C6
Lysefjorden • Norway **94** C5
Lysekil • Sweden **95** F2
Lysva • Russian Fed. **26** I6
Lytham St Anne's • United Kingdom **7** I8
Lyubertsy • Russian Fed. **97** E4
Lyubimets • Bulgaria **15** H2

M

M'Sila • Algeria **20** F1
M'Zab Valley **Heritage C** • Algeria **64** [224]
Ma On Shan Country Park • Hong Kong, China **107** H6
Ma, Oued el • Mauritania **20** D4
Ma Wan • Hong Kong, China **107** H5
Ma'an • Jordan **18** B3
Ma'anshan • China **107** J1
Ma'aza Plateau • Egypt **101** F4
Ma'tan as Sarra • Libya **21** D3
Maafushi • Maldives **106** E4
Maam Turk Mtns • Ireland **79** F3
Maarianhamina • Finland **95** E3
Maarssen • Netherlands **80** C2
Maas • Netherlands **80** A12
Maas en Waal, Land van • Netherlands **80** C4
Maaseik • Belgium **5** I3
Maassluis • Netherlands **80** C3
Maastricht • Netherlands **80** A15
Maasvlakte • Netherlands **80** C3
Mablethorpe **Beach** • United Kingdom **75** [36]
Mabote • Mozambique **24** E4
Macaé • Brazil **127** C4
Maçanet • Spain **87** D2
Macapá • Brazil **43** G3
Macará • Ecuador **43** B4
Macas • Ecuador **43** B4
Macau • Brazil **45** (1) D2
Macau • Asia **107** H1
Macaúbas • Brazil **44** H1
Macauley • New Zealand **33** J9
Macclesfield • United Kingdom **7** J8
Macclesfield Bank • South China Sea **107** G8
Macdhui, Ben • United Kingdom **6** I4
Macdonald, Lake • NT/WA, Australia **112** H1
Macdonnell Ranges • NT, Australia **112** H2
Macedo de Cavaleiros • Portugal **11** E3
Macedonia • Greece **92** A1
Macedonia • Greece **92** A1
Macedonia, F.Y.R. of • Europe **14** I8
Maceió • Brazil **45** (1) D3
Macenta • Guinea **22** C3
Macerata • Italy **12** H5
Macfarlane, Lake • SA, Australia **34** G6
Macgillicuddy's Reeks • Ireland **79** F7
Machaerus • Jordan **98** A8
Machakos • Kenya **101** G3
Machala • Ecuador **43** B4
Machareti • Bolivia **44** D3
Macheng • China **29** F4
Mácher • Lanzarote, Canary Is. **87** E3
Machico • Madeira **88** C2
Machilipatnam • India **106** D3
Machiques • Venezuela **43** C2
Machu Picchu • Peru **127** B2
Machu Picchu, Santuario histórico **Heritage N** • Peru **60** [33]
Machu Picchu, Santuario histórico **Heritage C** • Peru **62** [50]
Macia • Mozambique **24** E4
Macina Gourma • Mali **22** D1
Macinaggio • Corsica, France **85** L2
Macizo Galaico • Spain **11** D2
Mackay • QL, Australia **111** F3
Mackay, Lake • NT/WA, Australia **112** H1
Mackenzie • NT, Canada **38** E3
Mackenzie Bay • YT, Canada **38** D3
Mackenzie Bay • Kerguelen Is. **46** (1) L3
Mackenzie Delta • NT, Canada **122** A1
Mackenzie Mtns • NT/YT, Canada **38** F4
Mackerricher State Park • CA, United States **117** F1
Mackinac, Strait of • MI, United States **39** O7
Mackinnon Road • Kenya **101** G5
Maclear • South Africa **24** D6
MacLeod, Lake • WA, Australia **34** B4
Macmillan • YT, Canada **38** E4
Macomer • Sardinia, Italy **90** C1
Macon • GA, United States **41** J5
Mâcon • France **85** F1
Macondo • Angola **24** C2
Mâconnais • France **84** B2
Macquarie I. • Pacific Ocean **3** X10
Macquarie I. **Heritage N** • Southern Ocean **61** [139]
Macroom • Ireland **79** F8
Macugnaga • Italy **91** E1
Macujer • Colombia **43** C3
Macusani • Peru **127** B2
Madaba • Jordan **98** A8
Madagascar • Indian Ocean **24** H3
Madama • Niger **20** H4
Madan • Bulgaria **14** M8
Madang • Papua New Guinea **35** (1) D2
Madaoua • Niger **20** G6
Madara **Heritage C** • Bulgaria **64** [170]
Madara • Bulgaria **97** D3
Maddalena, I. • Sardinia, Italy **90** C2
Madeira • Brazil **43** E5
Madeira • Atlantic Ocean **88** C
Mädelegabel • Austria/Germany **82** J6
Madeleine, Is. de la • QU, Canada **123** D2
Madera • CA, United States **40** B4
Madera • Mexico **40** E6
Madésimo • Italy **91** E2
Madhar, Ra's • Saudi Arabia **21** G2
Madhya Pradesh • India **28** C4
Madikeri • India **106** D6
Madinah, Al • Saudi Arabia **18** C5

Madiran • France 84 B3
Madison • WI, United States 41 I3
Madison • IN, United States 41 I4
Madiun • Java, Indonesia 110 D7
Madoi • China 28 G1
Madone d'Utelle • France 85 H2
Madonie • Sicily, Italy 90 D2
Madonna di Campiglio Ski •
  Italy ....70 [209]
Madonna di Campiglio • Italy 91 E3
Madra Dagi • Turkey 15 I4
Madrakah, Ra's al • Oman 18 G6
Madras • India 106 D7
Madre de Dios • Peru 127 B2
Madre de Dios [Riv] •
  Bolivia/Peru 44 C1
Madre Occidental, Sierra •
  Mexico 40 E6
Madre Oriental, Sierra • Mexico ...40 F7
Madre, Sierra • Mexico 37 C4
Madrid • Spain 11 H4
Madrid, Comunidad de • Spain ..11 H4
Madridejos • Spain 11 H5
Madura • Indonesia 110 D4
Madura, Selat • Java, Indonesia ..110 D8
Madurai • India 106 D11
Madurodam • Netherlands 80 C3
Madyan • Saudi Arabia 21 G2
Mae Hong Son • Thailand 109 G1
Mae La Noi • Thailand 109 G3
Mae Ping Nat. Park • Thailand ...109 G3
Mae Rim • Thailand 109 G3
Mae Sai • Thailand 109 G1
Mae Sariang • Thailand 109 G3
Mae Suai • Thailand 109 G3
Mae Taeng • Thailand 109 G1
Maebashi • Japan 30 J6
Mael • Norway 94 B1
Maenam Beach •
  Ko Samui, Thailand 109 J1
Maestra, Sierra • Cuba 124 D8
Maevatanana • Madagascar 24 H3
Maéwo • Vanuatu 35 (2) B1
Mafeteng • Lesotho 24 D5
Mafia I. • Tanzania 102 H4
Mafikeng • South Africa 24 C5
Mafra • Brazil 44 G4
Mafra • Portugal 88 D1
Magadan • Russian Fed. 27 P5
Magadi • Kenya 101 G3
Magadino • Switzerland 89 G7
Magalluf • Majorca, Spain 87 H3
Magangué • Colombia 43 C2
Magaria • Niger 22 F2
Magarida • Papua New Guinea 34 I2
Magda Plateau • NU, Canada 39 O2
Magdagachi • Russian Fed. 27 K6
Magdalena • Mexico 40 D5
Magdalena • Colombia 43 C2
Magdalena • Bolivia 44 D1
Magdalena • Argentina 127 D2
Magdalena, I. • Mexico 123 E3
Magdeburg • Germany 8 G4
Magdelaine Cays • CL, Australia ..34 J3
Magelang • Java, Indonesia 110 D7
Magellan, Strait of • Chile 45 B6
Magerøya • Norway 16 N1
Maggiore, Lago • Italy 91 E2
Maghâgha • Egypt 101 F3
Magherafelt • United Kingdom 75 A3
Maghnia • Algeria 20 E2
Magic Hill Farm • OT, Canada ...122 B5
Magic Kingdom •
  FL, United States 121 C1
Magic Valley • NS, Canada 123 D7
Magical World of Fantasy Island Park •
  United Kingdom ....73 [28]
Maglaj • Bosnia-Herz. 12 M4
Maglic • F.R. of Yugoslavia 14 F6
Maglie • Italy 12 M9
Maglie • Italy 12 M9
Magnetic I. • QL, Australia 111 F1
Magnitogorsk • Russian Fed. 26 I7
Magnor • Norway 94 B2
Magny-en-Vexin • France 85 E1
Mago • Russian Fed. 27 N6
Mago Nat. Park Park • Ethiopia ..103 [66]
Magoebaskloof • South Africa 24 D4
Magoulades Beach •
  Corfu, Greece ....69 [149]
Magouládes • Corfu, Greece 92 B1
Magouládes • Corfu, Greece 92 B1
Maguarinho, Cabo • Brazil ...45 (1) B2
Magwe • Myanmar 31 B2
Maha Sarakham • Thailand 31 C3
Mahabad • Iran 18 E2
Mahabalipuram Heritage C •
  India ....63 [130]
Mahabalipuram • India 106 D7
Mahafaly, Plateau • Madagascar ..24 G4
Mahajan • India 105 C2
Mahajanga • Madagascar 24 H3
Mahakam • Indonesia 32 F3
Mahalapye • Botswana 24 D3
Mahanadi • India 28 D4
Maharashtra • India 28 B4
Mahaweli Ganga • Sri Lanka 106 D15
Mahbubnagar • India 106 D3
Mahdia • Guyana 43 F2
Mahdia • Tunisia 101 E4
Mahe • India 106 D10
Mahé • Seychelles 106 F1
Mahenge • Tanzania 102 H4
Mahesana • India 28 B4
Mahi • India 28 B4
Mahia Peninsula • New Zealand ..35 F4
Mahilov • Belarus 17 E4
Mahín • Germany 81 F4
Mahón Beach • Minorca, Spain ..68 [110]
Mahón • Minorca, Spain 87 F4
Mähren • Czech Rep. 13 F8
Mahrès • Tunisia 101 E4
Mai Khao Beach •
  Phuket, Thailand 109 K1
Mai Ndombe, Lac •
  Dem. Rep. of Congo 23 B4
Mai Po Marsh • Hong Kong, China ..107 H3
Mai-Ndombe, Lac •
  Dem. Rep. of Congo 22 H5
Maicao • Colombia 43 C1
Maidan Castle • United Kingdom ..74 F3
Maiden I. • Antigua & Barbuda ..125 F2
Maidstone • United Kingdom 74 E4
Maiduguri • Nigeria 105 C7
Maihar • India 105 C7
Maiko, Parc nat. de la Park •
  Dem. Rep. of Congo ....103 [57]
Maikona • Kenya 23 F3
Maili • HI, United States 119 L5
Main • Germany 9 E7
Main Barrier Range •
  NS, Australia 34 H6
Main-Donau-Kanal • Germany 9 E6
Mainalon • Greece 15 D6
Mainau • Germany 82 J5
Mainburg • Germany 9 G8

Maine • France 10 D5
Maine • United States 118 G2
Maine, Gulf of •
  Canada/United States 39 R8
Maine-et-Loire • France 84 D1
Mainistir, Pongo • Peru 127 B2
Mainland • Orkney, UK 6 I2
Mainland • Shetland, UK 6 K1
Mainz • Germany 82 H4
Maio • Cape Verde 22 (1) B1
Maipo, Volcá • Argentina 44 C5
Maipú • Argentina 127 D4
Maira • Italy 10 M9
Maisí, Cabo • Cuba 124 D8
Maitland • NS, Australia 111 G2
Maíz, Is. del • Nicaragua 43 A1
Maizhokunggar • China 28 F3
Majunro • Japan 30 H7
Majalengka • Java, Indonesia 110 D2
Majene • Indonesia 32 (1) A3
Majertén • Somalia 23 H2
Majete Game Reserve Park •
  Malawi ....103 [100]
Majevica • Bosnia-Herz. 14 F5
Maji • Ethiopia 23 F2
Major, Puig • Majorca, Spain 87 H1
Major's Bay • St Kitts & Nevis ...125 G4
Majorca • Spain ....87 H
Majorda • Goa, India 105 B2
Majorda Beach • Goa, India 105 B2
Majuro • Marshall Is. 33 I5
Makaha • HI, United States 119 L5
Makakan • Indonesia 32 F3
Makakilo City •
  HI, United States 119 L5
Makale • Indonesia 32 (1) A3
Makallé • Argentina 44 E4
Makalondi • Niger 20 F6
Makambako • Tanzania 102 H3
Makanza • Dem. Rep. of Congo ..22 H3
Makari Mts • Tanzania 102 H1
Makarikari • Botswana 24 C3
Makarov • Russian Fed. 27 N7
Makarska • Croatia 14 E6
Makassar, Selat • Indonesia 25 M10
Makassar Strait • Indonesia 32 F3
Makat • Kazakhstan 17 I5
Makó • Hungary 13 J11
Makokou • Gabon 22 G4
Makongolosi • Tanzania 102 H3
Makorako, Mt • New Zealand 112 K4
Makoua • Congo 22 H4
Makran • Iran/Pakistan 18 H4
Makrigialós Beach • Greece .....69 [167]
Makrigialós • Crete, Greece 93 E8
Makthar • Tunisia 101 E1
Makunudhoo • Maldives 106 E2
Makunudu Atoll • Maldives 106 E1
Makurazaki • Japan 30 F9
Makurdi • Nigeria 22 F5
Malá • Sweden 16 J4
Mala Kapela • Croatia 14 C5
Mala, Punta • Panama 37 E6
Malabang • Philippines 31 G5
Malabar Coast • India 106 D10
Malabo • Equatorial Guinea 22 F4
Malacca • Malaysia 108 A4
Malacca, Strait of •
  Indonesia/Malaysia 32 B2
Malacky • Slovak Rep. 13 G9
Málaga • Colombia 43 C2
Málaga Beach • Spain ....68 [97]
Málaga • Spain 86 B7
Malagarasi • Tanzania 102 H1
Malahide • Ireland 78 E2
Malambandy • Madagascar 24 H4
Malaita • Solomon Is. 35 (1) G2
Malakal • Sudan 23 E2
Malakula • Vanuatu 35 (2) B2
Malan, D.F. [Apt] •
  South Africa 100 C5
Malang • Java, Indonesia 110 D8
Malanje • Angola 23 B5
Malanville • Benin 20 F6
Malaren • Sweden 95 D3
Malatya • Turkey 18 C2
Malawi • Africa 24 E2
Malawi, Lake • Africa 24 E2
Malay Peninsula • Malaysia 31 C5
Malaya Vishera • Russian Fed. 97 E1
Malaybalay • Philippines 31 G5
Malaysia • Asia 31 C6
Malbork • Poland 13 I3
Malbork Heritage C • Poland ...64 [136]
Malbun • Liechtenstein 89 H5
Malcésine • Italy 91 E3
Malchin • Germany 8 H3
Malchow • Germany 8 H3
Malden • Germany 8 H3
Malden • Kiribati 33 L6
Maldives • Indian Ocean 106 D10
Maldon • United Kingdom 7 M10
Maldonado • Uruguay 127 D2
Malé • Maldives 106 E4
Malé Atoll • Maldives 106 E2
Maléas, Akra • Greece 92 D7
Maléas, Akra • Greece 92 D7
Malegaon • India 28 B4
Máleme Beach • Crete, Greece ..69 [188]
Máleme • Crete, Greece 93 E1
Málerás • Sweden 95 F9
Malgomaj • Sweden 16 H4
Malgrat de Mar • Spain 87 D4
Malha Wells • Sudan 21 E4
Malhalla el Kubra, El • Egypt 101 F1
Malheur Lake •
  OR, United States 117 E4
Mali • Africa 20 E4
Mali i Krabit • Albania 14 G7
Mália Beach • Crete, Greece ....69 [190]
Mália • Crete, Greece 93 E7
Mália [Hist.] • Crete, Greece 93 E7
Malibu • CA, United States 117 F6
Malik, Wadi al • Sudan 21 E4
Malin, Mtns •
  Dem. Rep. of Congo 23 D5
Malin Head • Ireland 6 E6
Malindi • Kenya 101 G3
Malindi Marine Game Reserve •
  Kenya 101 G5
Malindi Marine Nat. Park •
  Kenya 101 G5

Malindidzimu • Zimbabwe 102 J3
Malino, Bukit • Indonesia 32 (1) B3
Malion, Kólpos • Crete, Greece ...93 E3
Maljen • F.R. of Yugoslavia 14 G5
Malkara • Turkey 15 H3
Malko Turnovo • Bulgaria 15 I2
Malkorbe Beach • Spain ....68 [68]
Mallacoota • VI, Australia 111 G4
Mallaig • United Kingdom 6 G4
Mallawi • Egypt 18 A4
Mallorca • Spain ....87 H
Mallow • Ireland 79 F8
Malmberget • Sweden 16 K3
Malmédy • Belgium 5 J4
Malmesbury • United Kingdom 74 D4
Malmesbury • South Africa 100 C5
Malmköping • Sweden 95 D3
Malmö • Sweden 95 F11
Malo • Vanuatu 35 (2) B2
Malolotja Nature Reserve Park •
  Swaziland ....103 [132]
Malónas • Rhodes, Greece 93 F2
Malonga • Dem. Rep. of Congo ..24 C2
Malosmadulu Atoll North •
  Maldives 106 E1
Malosmadulu Atoll South •
  Maldives 106 E1
Maløy • Norway 94 C1
Malpelo • Colombia 43 A3
Malpensa [Apt] • Italy 91 E6
Malpica Beach • Spain ....68 [73]
Malprabha • India 28 C5
Malsch • Germany 82 G6
Malta • MT, United States 40 E2
Malta • Europe ....93 H
Malta Channel • Italy/Malta 12 I12
Maltepe • Turkey 15 K3
Maluku, Kepulauan • Indonesia ..32 (1) C2
Malunda • Indonesia 32 (1) A3
Malung • Sweden 16 G6
Malut • Sudan 23 E1
Maluu • Solomon Is. 35 (1) G2
Malvasia • Greece 71 A20
Malveira da Serra • Portugal 88 D1
Malvern Hills • United Kingdom ..74 D3
Malvinas, Is. • Atlantic Ocean 44 E6
Malwan • India 106 D1
Maly Karmakuly • Russian Fed. ..26 H3
Malyy Lyakhovskiy, Ostrov •
  Russian Fed. 27 N2
Mama • Russian Fed. 27 H5
Mamaia-Bai • Romania 97 H2
Mamaia-Sat • Romania 97 D2
Mambéré • Africa 23 A2
Mambrui • Kenya 101 G3
Mammoth Cave Nat. Park Heritage N •
  KY, United States ....60 [15]
Mammoth Cave Nat. Park Park •
  KY, United States ....121 [235]
Mammoth Lakes •
  CA, United States 117 F4
Mammoth Mtn Ski •
  CA, United States ....116 [63]
Mamonovo • Russian Fed. 13 J3
Mamoré • Bolivia 44 C1
Mamou • Guinea 22 B2
Mamoutzou • Mayotte 23 H6
Mamuju • Indonesia 32 (1) A3
Mamuno • Botswana 24 C4
Mamunta-Mayoso Wildlife Sanctuary Park •
  Sierra Leone ....103 [15]
Man • Côte d'Ivoire 22 C3
Man, Isle of • Europe 7 H7
Man of War Bay •
  Trinidad & Tobago 125 K2
Mana Pools Nat. Park Heritage N •
  Zimbabwe ....61 [96]
Mana Pools Nat. Park • Zimbabwe ..102 J2
Mana Pools Nat. Park Park •
  Zimbabwe ....103 [107]
Manacapuru • Brazil 43 E4
Manacor Beach • Majorca, Spain ..68 [109]
Manacor • Majorca, Spain 87 H2
Manado • Indonesia 32 (1) B2
Managua • Nicaragua 37 D5
Manakara • Madagascar 24 H4
Manamah, Al • Bahrain 18 F4
Manambolo • Madagascar 24 H3
Manapouri • New Zealand 112 L3
Manapouri, Lake • New Zealand ..112 L3
Manar • Yemen 21 H5
Manas • China 19 J2
Manas Wildlife Sanctuary Heritage N •
  India ....60 [34]
Manassas Nat. Battlefield Park Park •
  VA, United States ....121 [265]
Manasseh • Israel/Jordan 98 A4
Manati • Puerto Rico 125 E2
Manati, Rio Grande de •
  Puerto Rico 125 E2
Manaus • Brazil 43 E4
Manavgat Beach • Turkey ....69 [198]
Manavgat • Turkey 93 G4
Manche, la • France/UK 10 D3
Manchester • United Kingdom 7 J8
Manchestkaya Vpadina •
  Russian Fed. 17 G5
Manchuria • China 107 G4
Mand • Iran 18 F4
Manda • Tanzania 102 H3
Manda I. • Kenya 101 G4
Manda, Jabal • Sudan 23 C2
Mandab, Bab al • Africa/Asia 21 H5
Mandaguari • Brazil 44 F3
Mandal • Norway 94 C3
Mandala, Puncak • Indonesia ..32 (1) F3
Mandalay • Myanmar 31 B2
Mandalgovi • Mongolia 29 D1
Mandalselva • Norway 95 F1
Mandan • ND, United States 40 F2
Mandara, Mts • Cameroon 21 B5
Mandas • Sardinia, Italy 12 D9
Mandawa • India 105 C2
Mandera • Kenya 101 G2
Mandera [Region] • Kenya 101 G2
Manderscheid • Germany 82 H7
Manderscheid Spa • Germany ...83 [160]
Mandeville • Jamaica 124 C3
Mandingues, Mts • Mali 22 B2
Mandla • India 28 C4
Mandore • India 105 C5
Mandoudi • Greece 15 E5
Mandrem Beach • Goa, India 105 B1
Mandritsara • Madagascar 24 H3
Mandsaur • India 105 C6
Mandurah • WA, Australia 34 C6
Manduria • Italy 12 L8
Mandvi • India 28 A4
Mandzavinata Beach • Greece ..69 [150]
Mandzavinata • Greece 92 C2
Mandzavinata • Greece 92 C2
Manendragarh • India 28 D4
Manfalût • Egypt 18 A4
Manfredonia • Italy 12 J7

Manfredonia, Golfo di • Italy 12 K7
Manga • Niger 20 H6
Manga • Brazil 45 (1) C4
Mangalia • Romania 97 D2
Mangalore • India 106 D6
Mángana Beach • Greece ....69 [172]
Mangaratiba • Brazil 127 C3
Mangareva • French Polynesia 33 N8
Manger • Norway 94 C3
Mangfall • Germany 82 J3
Manggar • Indonesia 32 D3
Mangin Yoma • Myanmar 31 B2
Mangnai • China 28 F1
Mangoky • Madagascar 24 G4
Mangole • Indonesia 32 (1) C3
Mangueira, Lago • Brazil 44 F5
Manguéni, Plateau de • Niger 20 H4
Mangui • China 27 J6
Manhattan • NY, United States ...118 H2
Manhuaçu • Brazil 127 C2
Mani • Colombia 43 C3
Mania • Madagascar 24 H3
Manica • Mozambique 102 J2
Manicaland • Zimbabwe 102 J2
Manicouagan • QU, Canada 39 R6
Manicouagan, Réservoir •
  QU, Canada 39 R6
Manihiki • Cook Is. 33 K7
Manila • Philippines 31 G4
Manila Heritage C • Philippines ..63 [176]
Manila Bay • Philippines 31 G4
Manila Beach • Spain ....68 [97]
Manilva • Spain 86 B6
Maningrida Settlement •
  NT, Australia 34 F2
Maninjau, Danau • Indonesia 110 B4
Manipur • India 28 F4
Manises • Spain 11 K5
Manitoba • Canada 38 L5
Manitou, Lake • MN, Canada 38 L6
Manitoulin • OT, Canada 39 O7
Maniwaki • QU, Canada 122 B2
Manizales • Colombia 43 B3
Manja • Madagascar 24 G4
Manjimup • WA, Australia 34 C6
Manjra • India 28 C5
Mankarbo • Sweden 95 D1
Mankato • MN, United States 41 H3
Mankono • Côte d'Ivoire 22 C3
Manley, Norman [Apt] • Jamaica ..124 C4
Manlleu • Spain 11 N3
Manly • Russian Fed. 27 S4
Manmad • India 28 B4
Mann Ranges • NT/SA, Australia ..112 H3
Manna • Indonesia 32 C3
Mannar • Sri Lanka 106 D11
Mannar, Gulf of •
  India/Sri Lanka 106 D15
Mannheim • Germany 82 G4
Manning • AL, Canada 38 H5
Mannu, Capo • Sardinia, Italy 12 C8
Mannu, Rio • Sardinia, Italy 12 C8
Manoa • Bolivia 44 C1
Manokwari • Indonesia 32 (1) D3
Manolada • Madagascar 24 G4
Manòn Beach • Spain ....68 [73]
Manono • Dem. Rep. of Congo 23 D4
Manorbier Beach •
  United Kingdom ....75 [152]
Manosque • France 85 H1
Manovo-Gounda St Floris, Parc nat. de
  Heritage N • Central African Rep.61 [79]
Manovo-St Floris, Parc nat. Park •
  Central African Rep. ....103 [44]
Manp'ojin • D.P.R. of Korea 30 D4
Manra • Kiribati 33 J6
Manresa • Spain 87 D3
Mans, le • France 84 D2
Mansa Konko • Gambia 22 A2
Mansel I. • NU, Canada 39 P4
Mansfield • United Kingdom 7 K8
Mansfield • OH, United States 41 J3
Mansfield • LA, United States 118 K1
Mansion • St Kitts & Nevis 125 G4
Mansura • LA, United States 118 K3
Mansūra, El • Egypt 101 F2
Manta • Ecuador 43 A4
Manta, Bahía de • Ecuador 43 A4
Mantaro • Peru 127 B1
Mantes-la-Jolie • France 85 E1
Mantiqueira, Serra de • Brazil ...127 C3
Mantova • Italy 91 E7
Mänttälä • Finland 95 E4
Mänttä • Finland 95 E2
Mantua • Italy 91 E7
Manturovo • Russian Fed. 17 G3
Manú • Peru 127 B2
Manu Bay • New Zealand 112 K1
Manú, Parque Nac. Heritage N •
  Peru ....60 [34]
Manú, Parque Nac. • Peru 127 B2
Manua • American Samoa 35 (2) G1
Manukau • New Zealand 35 E3
Manuhoa, Mt • New Zealand 112 K2
Manyara Nat. Park • Tanzania ...102 H2
Manyas-Kuscenneti Nat. Park Heritage N •
  Turkey ....72 [142]
Manyas-Kuscenneti Nat. Park •
  Turkey 92 D3
Manyas-Kuscenneti Nat. Park •
  Turkey 92 D3
Manyoni • Tanzania 102 H1
Manzanar Nat. Hist. Site Park •
  CA, United States ....120 [54]
Manzanares • Spain 11 H5
Manzanilla Point •
  Trinidad & Tobago 125 K4
Manzanillo • Mexico 123 D4
Manzanillo • Cuba 124 D7
Manzhouli • China 27 I7
Mao • Chad 21 B5
Maó Beach • Minorca, Spain ....68 [110]
Maó • Minorca, Spain 87 F4
Mao Shan • China 107 J1
Maoke, Pegunungan • Indonesia ..32 (1) F3
Maomao Shan • China 29 E6
Maoming • China 29 E6
Maotou Shan • China 29 D6
Mapi • Indonesia 32 (1) E4
Mapi [Riv] • Indonesia 32 (1) E4
Mapia, Kepulauan • Indonesia ..32 (1) D2
Maple Creek • SA, Canada 38 J7
Mapou • Thailand 109 K2
Mapuera • Brazil 43 E4
Mapusa • Goa, India 105 B1
Maputo • Mozambique 24 E3
Maputo, Baia de • Mozambique ..24 E3
Maputo Elephant Reserve Park •
  Mozambique ....103 [134]
Maqaman Nabi Músá • Jordan 98 A8
Maquan He • China 28 D3
Maquinchao • Argentina 44 C5
Mar Chiquita, Lago • Argentina ..127 D4

Mar Chiquita, Laguna •
  Argentina 44 D3
Mar del Plata • Argentina 127 D4
Mar del Tuyú • Argentina 127 D4
Mar, Serra de • Brazil 127 C3
Mara • Kenya/Tanzania 23 E4
Marabá • Brazil 43 H5
Maracã • Brazil 43 G3
Maracaibo • Venezuela 43 C1
Maracaibo, Lago de • Venezuela ..43 C2
Maracaju • Brazil 44 E3
Maracaju, Serra de • Brazil 44 E3
Maracás • Brazil 43 H1
Maracas Bay • Trinidad & Tobago ..125 K1
Maracay • Venezuela 43 D1
Maradi • Niger 20 G6
Marahoué, Parc nat. de la Park •
  Côte d'Ivoire ....103 [20]
Marahuaca • Venezuela 43 D3
Marajó, Baía de • Brazil 45 (1) B2
Marajó, I. de • Brazil 43 G4
Maralal Game Reserve • Kenya ..101 G1
Maralinga • SA, Australia 34 F6
Maramba • Zambia 24 D3
Marand • Iran 18 E2
Maranhão • Brazil 45 (1) D3
Marano, Laguna di • Italy 12 H3
Marañón • Peru 43 B4
Marão, Serra do • Portugal 11 D3
Maratea Beach • Italy ....69 [129]
Maratea • Italy 90 A2
Marateca • Portugal 88 D2
Marathiá, Akra • Greece 92 C3
Marathiás, Akra • Greece 92 C3
Marathon • OT, Canada 39 N7
Marathon • OT, Canada 41 I2
Marathon • Greece 92 D4
Marathon • FL, United States 119 M8
Márathopolis • Crete, Greece 93 E2
Marawar • Sudan 21 F4
Marbella Beach • Spain ....68 [97]
Marbella • Spain 86 B6
Marble Bar • WA, Australia 34 C4
Marble Canyon •
  AZ, United States 118 J1
Marburg • Germany 82 G2
Marcali • Hungary 12 L2
Marco I. • FL, United States 119 M7
Marconi, G [Apt] • Italy 91 E7
Marcos Juárez • Argentina 44 D5
Marcus • Pacific Ocean 33 G3
Marcy • NY, United States 41 L3
Mardan • Pakistan 28 B2
Mardin • Turkey 92 A4
Maré • New Caledonia 35 (2) B3
Maree, Loch • United Kingdom 6 G4
Mareeba • QL, Australia 111 F1
Mareg • Somalia 23 H3
Maremma • Italy 91 E11
Marennes • France 85 G1
Maret • Tunisia 101 E6
Marettimo, I. • Italy 90 D1
Marfa Point • Malta 93 H1
Margai Caka • China 28 E1
Margam • United Kingdom 74 E2
Marganets • Ukraine 92 A4
Margaret • WA, Australia 34 C6
Margarita • Venezuela 43 E1
Margaret • Greece 15 B4
Margate Beach • United Kingdom ..75 [63]
Margate • United Kingdom 74 E2
Margaux • France 85 G1
Margeride, Mts de la • France 10 I8
Marguerite Bay • Antarctica ...46 (1) HH3
Mari-El • Russian Fed. 17 H3
Maria •
  Tubuai Is., French Polynesia ...33 L8
Maria •
  Gambier Is., French Polynesia ..33 N8
Maria Alm Ski • Austria ....70 [165]
Maria Elena • Chile 44 C3
Maria Is. • St Lucia 125 J4
Maria Laach • Germany 82 H1
Mariana • Brazil 127 C2
Marianao • Cuba 37 E3
Marianas Trench • Pacific Ocean ..25 C8
Mariankenni • Kenya 101 G2
Marianna • FL, United States 119 M2
Marianne • Seychelles 106 F4
Mariannelund • Sweden 95 F8
Mariánské Lázne • Czech Rep. ...96 C1
Mariapfarr Ski • Austria ....70 [186]
Marias, Is. • Mexico 123 E7
Marias, Is. • Mexico 37 (1) A1
Mariato, Punta • Panama 37 E6
Maribo • Denmark 95 F4
Maribor • Slovenia 13 E11
Marie Byrd Land • Antarctica ..46 (1) BB2
Marie I. • LA, United States 118 K3
Marie Louise • Seychelles 106 F2
Marie-Galante • Guadeloupe 37 I4
Marienbad • Czech Rep. 96 C1
Marienheide • Germany 81 E4
Mariental • Namibia 24 B4
Mariestad • Sweden 95 D2
Marietta • GA, United States 41 J5
Marignane [Apt] • France 85 H3
Marigot Bay • St Lucia 125 J1
Marigot Harbour • St Lucia 125 J1
Marijampolé • Lithuania 16 M3
Marília • Brazil 44 F3
Marilléva Ski • Italy ....70 [207]
Marimba • Angola 24 B1
Marín Beach • Spain ....68 [74]
Marín, Luis Muñoz [Apt] •
  Puerto Rico 125 E2
Marina Bay • Singapore 108 E4
Marina del Rey •
  CA, United States 117 F6
Marina di Massa • Italy 91 E10
Marina di Pietrasanta • Italy 91 E10
Marina di Pisa • Italy 12 G5
Marinduque • Philippines 31 G4
Marine World Africa USA Park •
  CA, United States ....120 [A]

Marineland of Florida •
  FL, United States 119 M4
Marinella, Golfo di •
  Sardinia, Italy 90 C2
Maringá • Dem. Rep. of Congo ...23 C3
Maringá • Brazil 44 F3
Marinha Grande • Portugal 11 C5
Marino • Italy 12 G7
Marion Reef • CL, Australia 111 F2
Maripa • Venezuela 43 D2
Maripa • CA, United States 117 F3
Marisa • Indonesia 32 (1) B2
Mariscal Estigarribia •
  Paraguay 44 D3
Marismas, Las • Spain 86 B1
Maritime Museum • Singapore ...108 E4
Maritsa • Europe 14 M7
Mariupol • Ukraine 17 F5
Marj, Al • Libya 21 D1
Marka • Somalia 23 G3
Markaryd • Sweden 95 F11
Marken • Netherlands 80 C2
Markermeer • Netherlands 80 C2
Market Harborough •
  United Kingdom 7 L9
Markha • Russian Fed. 27 J4
Markham, Mt • Antarctica 46 (1) V1
Marki • Poland 13 K5
Märkisch Wilmersdorf • Germany ..81 F3
Markópoulo Beach • Greece .....69 [162]
Markounda •
  Central African Rep. 22 H3
Markovo • Russian Fed. 27 T4
Markschellenberg Spa • Germany ..83 [262]
Marktheidenfeld • Germany 9 E7
Marktoberdorf • Germany 82 J6
Marktredwitz • Germany 9 H6
Marl • Germany 5 K3
Marl • Germany 81 E2
Marlboro • VT, United States 118 G3
Marlborough • QL, Australia 111 F4
Marlborough • New Zealand 112 J4
Marle • France 5 G5
Marlin • TX, United States 119 N3
Marlin Coast • QL, Australia 111 F1
Marloes Beach • United Kingdom ..75 [159]
Marlow • United Kingdom 74 E1
Marmande • France 85 G3
Marmara • Turkey 15 I3
Marmara Adasi • Turkey 92 D3
Marmara Adasi • Turkey 92 D3
Marmara Ereglisi • Turkey 15 I5
Marmara Gölü • Turkey 15 I3
Marmara, Sea of • Turkey 92 D3
Marmara, Sea of • Turkey 92 D3
Marmári • Greece 92 D4
Marmári • Greece 92 D4
Marmaris Beach • Turkey ....69 [205]
Marmaris • Turkey 92 D9
Marmaro • Greece 92 C5
Mármaro • Greece 92 C5
Mármaro • Greece 92 C5
Marmolada, Gruppo delle • Italy ..91 E3
Marmolejo • Spain 86 B4
Marmot Basin Ski • AL, Canada ..116 [11]
Marne • France 10 I4
Marne au Rhin, Canal de la •
  France 10 J5
Maro • Chad 21 C6
Maro [Riv] • Chad 20 I5
Maroa • Venezuela 43 D3
Maroantsetra • Madagascar 24 H3
Maromokotro • Madagascar 24 H3
Marondera • Zimbabwe 102 J2
Marónia • Greece 92 D2
Maroochydore • QL, Australia 111 F6
Maroua • Cameroon 22 G2
Márpissa Beach • Greece ....69 [182]
Marquesas • French Polynesia ...33 N6
Marquette • MI, United States 41 I2
Marquette, Father, Nat. Mem. & Museum
  Park • MI, United States ....121 [162]
Marquis • St Lucia 125 J2
Marquis, Cape • St Lucia 125 J2
Marrah, Jabal • Sudan 21 D5
Marrakech Heritage C • Morocco ..64 [217]
Marrakech • Morocco 101 D3
Marree • SA, Australia 34 G5
Marromeu • Mozambique 24 F3
Marromeu, Reserve de Park •
  Mozambique ....103 [136]
Marsá al Burayquah • Libya 21 C1
Marsa Alam • Egypt 101 F5
Marsa, El • France 11 L8
Marsabit • Kenya 101 G2
Marsabit Game Reserve • Kenya ..101 G2
Marsabit Nat. Park • Kenya 23 F3
Marsabit Nat. Park Park • Kenya ..103 [75]
Marsala Beach • Sicily, Italy .....68 [131]
Marsala • Sicily, Italy 90 D1
Marsalforn • Malta 93 H1
Marsalforn Bay • Malta 93 H1
Marsaskala • Malta 93 H4
Marsaxlokk • Malta 93 H4
Marsaxlokk Bay • Malta 93 H4
Marsberg • Germany 8 D5
Marsh Harbour • Bahamas 124 E4
Marsh I. • LA, United States 118 K3
Marshall • MN, United States 41 H3
Marshall • TX, United States 119 N2
Marshfield • WI, United States 41 H3
Marssum • Netherlands 80 A3
Marstal • Denmark 95 F4
Marston Moor • United Kingdom ..71 A7
Marstrand • Sweden 95 F6
Martaban, Gulf of • Myanmar 31 B3
Martha Brae • Jamaica 124 C1
Martha's Vineyard •
  MA, United States 118 H2
Marthaville • LA, United States ...118 K1
Martigné • France 10 F6
Martigny • Switzerland 89 H7
Martigues • France 10 K10
Martil Beach • France ....68 [115]
Martil • Morocco 101 D2
Martim Longo • Portugal 88 D4
Martin • Slovak Rep. 13 H8
Martin, Lac •
  Atlantic Ocean 19 B8
Martin, Is. • Brazil 45 (1) A2
Martin's Haven Beach •
  United Kingdom ....75 [160]
Martinique • West Indies 37 I4
Martins Bay • New Zealand 112 L2
Marton • New Zealand 35 E5
Martorell • Spain 87 D3
Martos • Spain 11 H7
Martre, Lac la • NT, Canada 38 H4

Martti • Finland ... 16 O3
Marungu, Mtns •
  Dem. Rep. of Congo ... 23 D5
Marv-Dasht • Iran ... 18 F4
Marvão • Portugal ... 11 D5
Marwar • India ... 105 C5
Mary • Turkmenistan ... 18 H2
Mary Jane Ski •
  CO, United States ... 116 [90]
Maryborough • QL, Australia ... 111 F6
Maryborough • VI, Australia ... 111 G3
Maryport • United Kingdom ... 74 C1
Marysville • CA, United States ... 40 B4
Maryville • MO, United States ... 41 H3
Maryville • TN, United States ... 41 J4
Masada • Israel ... 98 A8
Masai • Malaysia ... 108 E2
Masai Mara Game Reserve • Kenya 101 [53]
Masai Mara Nat. Reserve Park •
  Kenya ... 103 [82]
Masai Steppe • Tanzania ... 102 H2
Masaka • Uganda ... 23 E4
Masalembo, Kepulauan •
  Indonesia ... 110 D4
Masan • Rep. of Korea ... 30 E7
Másari • Rhodes, Greece ... 93 F2
Masasi • Tanzania ... 102 H4
Masbate • Philippines ... 31 G4
Masbate [I.] • Philippines ... 31 G4
Mascara • Algeria ... 20 F1
Maseru • Lesotho ... 24 D5
Mashabih • Saudi Arabia ... 21 G2
Mashhad • Iran ... 18 G2
Mashonaland • Zimbabwe ... 102 J2
Masindi • Uganda ... 23 E3
Masirah, Jazirat • Oman ... 18 G5
Masirah, Khalij • Oman ... 18 G5
Mask, Lough • Ireland ... 79 F4
Maskad, Al • Somalia ... 23 H1
Mason City • IA, United States ... 41 H3
Mason's Limestone Valley •
  New Zealand ... 112 K1
Maspalomas •
  Gran Canaria, Canary Is. ... 86 E4
Massa • Italy ... 12 E4
Massa Lubrense • Italy ... 91 G3
Massa Marittima • Italy ... 91 E11
Massachusetts • United States ... 115 L3
Massafra • Italy ... 12 L8
Massaguet • Chad ... 23 B1
Massangena • Mozambique ... 24 E4
Massanutten Ski •
  VA, United States ... 116 [157]
Massawa • Eritrea ... 21 G4
Masséna • Chad ... 20 I6
Masserberg Spa • Germany ... 83 [307]
Masset • BC, Canada ... 38 E6
Massif Central • France ... 10 H8
Massinga • Mozambique ... 24 F4
Massy • France ... 85 E3
Masterton • New Zealand ... 35 E5
Mastigouche Prov. Park •
  QU, Canada ... 122 B3
Masuda • Japan ... 30 F7
Masuguru • Tanzania ... 102 H4
Masurai, Gunung • Indonesia ... 32 C3
Masuria • Poland ... 96 Bi
Masuriska Sjöarna • Poland ... 13 K4
Masvingo • Zimbabwe ... 102 J4
Mat Lang, Ko • Thailand ... 109 J1
Mata-Utu • Wallis & Futuna ... 35 (2) E1
Matabeleland • Zimbabwe ... 102 J3
Matadi • Dem. Rep. of Congo ... 23 A5
Matagalpa • Nicaragua ... 37 D5
Matagami • QU, Canada ... 39 P7
Matagorda • TX, United States ... 119 N6
Matagorda Bay •
  TX, United States ... 119 N5
Matagorda I. •
  TX, United States ... 119 N5
Matagorda Peninsula •
  TX, United States ... 119 N6
Matakana I. • New Zealand ... 112 K2
Matala • Angola ... 24 B2
Matala • Crete, Greece ... 93 E6
Matale • Sri Lanka ... 106 D15
Matam • Senegal ... 20 C5
Matamata • New Zealand ... 112 K2
Matamoros • Mexico ... 37 B2
Matane • QU, Canada ... 123 D1
Matanzas • Cuba ... 124 D2
Matanzas, Fort. Nat. Mon. •
  FL, United States ... 119 M4
Matanzas, Fort. Nat. Mon. Park •
  FL, United States ... 121 [222]
Matapédia • QU, Canada ... 123 D2
Matara • Eritrea ... 23 G2
Matara • Sri Lanka ... 106 D15
Mataram • Indonesia ... 32 F4
Matarani • Peru ... 127 B4
Mataranka • NT, Australia ... 34 F2
Mataró • Spain ... 87 D4
Mataura • New Zealand ... 112 L4
Mataura [Riv] • New Zealand ... 112 L4
Matehuala • Mexico ... 123 E1
Matélica • Italy ... 91 E12
Matelot • Trinidad & Tobago ... 125 K2
Matera • Italy ... 12 K8
Matera Heritage C • Italy ... 64 [130]
Matese, Monti del • Italy ... 91 G1
Mátészalka • Hungary ... 13 L10
Mateur • Tunisia ... 101 E2
Mathura • India ... 105 C2
Mati • Albania ... 14 H8
Mati • Philippines ... 31 H5
Matlock • United Kingdom ... 7 K8
Matmata • Tunisia ... 101 E6
Mato Grosso • Brazil ... 44 E2
Mato Grosso [Adm] • Brazil ... 44 E1
Mato Grosso do Sul • Brazil ... 44 E2
Mato Grosso, Planalto do •
  Brazil ... 42 E6
Matobo Nat. Park • Zimbabwe ... 102 J3
Matochkin Shar • Russian Fed. ... 26 I3
Matosinhos • Portugal ... 11 C3
Matra • Hungary ... 13 I10
Matrah • Oman ... 18 G5
Matre • Norway ... 94 C3
Matrei • Austria ... 89 H7
Matrûh • Egypt ... 101 F1
Matsu Liehtao • Taiwan ... 29 G5
Matsudona Nat. Park • Zimbabwe ... 102 J1
Matsue • Japan ... 30 G7
Matsumoto • Japan ... 30 I6
Matsusyama • Japan ... 30 G8
Mattagami • OT, Canada ... 39 O7
Mattancheri • India ... 106 D10
Mattawa • OT, Canada ... 122 B1
Matterdale • United Kingdom ... 74 C2
Matterhorn • Italy/Switzerland ... 89 H6
Matthew Town • Bahamas ... 124 B4
Matthews Ridge • Guyana ... 127 B1
Matucana • Peru ... 127 B1
Matuku • Fiji ... 35 (2) D2
Matura Bay • Trinidad & Tobago ... 125 K2

Maturin • Venezuela ... 43 E2
Mau • India ... 105 C8
Mau Escarpment • Kenya ... 23 F4
Mau Kyun • Myanmar ... 31 B4
Maubeuge • France ... 10 I3
Maubuisson • France ... 85 G1
Mauganj • India ... 105 C8
Mauguio Carnon Beach • France ... 68 [113]
Maui • HI, United States ... 119 L3
Maulbronn Heritage C • Germany ... 64 [42]
Mauléon • France ... 85 J1
Maullin • Chile ... 45 B4
Maumere • Indonesia ... 32 (1) B4
Maun • Botswana ... 24 C3
Mauna Kea • HI, United States ... 119 L8
Mauna Loa • HI, United States ... 119 L8
Maunoir, Lac • NT, Canada ... 38 F3
Maurepas, Lake •
  LA, United States ... 118 K4
Maures, Massif des • France ... 85 H3
Maurice, Lake • SA, Australia ... 34 F5
Mauricie, la, Nat. Park •
  QU, Canada ... 122 B4
Maurienne • France ... 85 F4
Mauritania • Africa ... 20 C5
Maus, Burg • Germany ... 82 H2
Mäuseturm • Germany ... 82 H4
Mauterndorf Ski • Austria ... 70 [186]
Mavinga • Angola ... 24 C3
Mavrovo Nat. Park Park •
  F.Y.R. of Macedonia ... 72 [122]
Mavrovoúni • Greece ... 14 K8
Mawan • Shenzhen, China ... 107 H3
Mawkmai • Myanmar ... 109 G1
Mawlaik • Myanmar ... 28 F4
Mawsil, Al • Iraq ... 18 D2
Mawson [Base] • Antarctica ... 46 (1) L3
Maxglan [Apt] • Austria ... 89 H4
Máximo Gómez • Cuba ... 124 D3
May, Cape • NJ, United States ... 118 H3
May Day Mtns • Jamaica ... 124 C3
May Pen • Jamaica ... 124 C4
Maya • Russian Fed. ... 27 M5
Maya • Indonesia ... 32 D3
Mayaguana • Bahamas ... 124 B4
Mayagüez • Puerto Rico ... 125 E3
Mayagüez, Bahía de •
  Puerto Rico ... 125 E3
Mayapán • Mexico ... 37 D3
Mayari • Cuba ... 124 D8
Mayaro Bay • Trinidad & Tobago ... 125 K4
Maychew • Ethiopia ... 23 G2
Mayen • Germany ... 82 H1
Mayenne • France ... 10 E6
Mayenne [Riv] • France ... 10 E6
Mayens-de-l'Ours Ski •
  Switzerland ... 70 [81]
Mayens-de-Riddes Ski •
  Switzerland ... 70 [79]
Maykain • Kazakhstan ... 26 M7
Maykop • Russian Fed. ... 17 G6
Maynas • Peru ... 43 B4
Maynooth • Ireland ... 79 F6
Mayo • Ireland ... 79 F2
Mayo, Plains of • Ireland ... 79 F2
Mayon, Mt • Philippines ... 25 N8
Mayor I. • New Zealand ... 112 K2
Mayrhofen Ski • Austria ... 70 [143]
Mayrhofen • Austria ... 89 H7
Mayshoß • Germany ... 82 H1
Mazabuka • Zambia ... 24 D3
Mazagão • Brazil ... 43 G4
Mazagón • Spain ... 86 Bi
Mazamet • France ... 10 H10
Mazar • China ... 26 M10
Mazar-e Sharif • Afghanistan ... 18 I2
Mazara del Vallo •
  Sicily, Italy ... 12 G11
Mazara, Val di • Sicily, Italy ... 90 D1
Mazarrón Beach • Spain ... 68 [100]
Mazarrón • Spain ... 87 C3
Mazarrón, Golfo de • Spain ... 11 J7
Mazartag • China ... 26 N10
Mazatenango • Guatemala ... 37 C5
Mazatlán • Mexico ... 37 (1) A1
Mazeikiai • Lithuania ... 13 L1
Mazong Shan • China ... 29 B2
Mazowe • Zimbabwe ... 102 J2
Mazowe [Riv] •
  Mozambique/Zimbabwe ... 102 J2
Mazurski Nat. Park Park •
  Poland ... 72 [92]
Mazzarò • Sicily, Italy ... 90 D2
Mbabane • Swaziland ... 24 E5
Mbaiki • Central African Rep. ... 23 B3
Mbala • Zambia ... 23 E5
Mbalabala • Zimbabwe ... 24 D4
Mbale • Uganda ... 23 E3
Mbalmayo • Cameroon ... 22 G4
Mbamba Bay • Tanzania ... 102 H3
Mbandaka • Dem. Rep. of Congo ... 23 B3
Mbanga • Cameroon ... 22 F4
Mbanza Congo • Angola ... 23 A5
Mbanza-Ngungu •
  Dem. Rep. of Congo ... 23 A5
Mbé • Cameroon ... 23 A2
Mbéré •
  Cameroon/Central African Rep. ... 22 H3
Mbeya • Tanzania ... 102 H3
Mbinda • Congo ... 22 G5
Mbomou • Central African
  Rep./Dem. Rep. of Congo ... 23 D2
Mbour • Senegal ... 20 A2
Mbout • Mauritania ... 20 C5
Mbua • Fiji ... 35 (2) D2
Mbuji-Mayi • Dem. Rep. of Congo ... 23 C5
Mbulu • Tanzania ... 102 H2
Mbwemburu • Tanzania ... 24 F2
McAlester • OK, United States ... 41 G5
McAllen • TX, United States ... 40 G6
McCall • ID, United States ... 117 E4
McCarran [Apt] •
  NV, United States ... 117 F4
McClintock Channel • NU, Canada ... 38 K2
McClintock, Mt • Antarctica ... 46 (1) V1
McClure Strait • NT, Canada ... 36 E2
McComb • MS, United States ... 118 K2
McCook • NE, United States ... 40 F3
McDonald I. • Indian Ocean ... 3 R10
McDonald I. Heritage N •
  Indian Ocean ... 61 [138]
McHenry, Fort, Nat. Mon. & Hist. Shrine
  Park • MD, United States ... 121 [279]
Mchinga • Tanzania ... 102 H4
McIlwraith Range •
  QL, Australia ... 34 H2
McKerrow, Lake • New Zealand ... 112 L2
McKinley, Mt •
  AK, United States ... 40 (2) F2
McKinney • TX, United States ... 119 N1
McLean's Town • Bahamas ... 124 B2
McLoughlin House Nat. Hist. Site Park •
  OR, United States ... 120 [34]
McMinnville • OR, United States ... 117 E3
McMurdo [Base] • Antarctica ... 46 (1) V2
Mdennah • Algeria/Mali ... 20 D4

Mdina • Malta ... 93 H4
Mdiq • Morocco ... 101 D1
Me'arot Hever • Israel ... 98 A8
Mead, Lake •
  AZ/NV, United States ... 118 J1
Mead, Lake, Nat. Recreation Area •
  AZ/NV, United States ... 118 J1
Meadow Lake • SA, Canada ... 38 J6
Mealhada • Portugal ... 11 C4
Mealy Mtns • NF, Canada ... 39 T6
Meander • AL, Canada ... 38 H5
Meath • Ireland ... 79 E1
Meaux • France ... 85 E2
Mebridege • Angola ... 23 A5
Mecca • Saudi Arabia ... 18 D5
Mechelen • Belgium ... 80 A14
Mecheria • Algeria ... 20 E2
Mecidiye • Turkey ... 15 H3
Mecitözü • Turkey ... 82 H1
Mecklenburg-Vorpommern •
  Germany ... 8 G2
Mecklenburger Bucht • Germany ... 8 G2
Mecklenburgische Seenplatte •
  Germany ... 8 H3
Mecsek • Hungary ... 13 H11
Mecula • Mozambique ... 24 F2
Meda • Indonesia ... 110 B2
Medan • Indonesia ... 32 (1) A4
Medellín • Colombia ... 43 B2
Medenine • Tunisia ... 101 E6
Mederdra • Mauritania ... 20 B5
Medewi Beach • Bali, Indonesia ... 110 C1
Medford • OR, United States ... 117 E4
Medgidia • Romania ... 97 D2
Media Luna • Cuba ... 124 D7
Medias • Romania ... 14 L3
Medicine Hat • AL, Canada ... 38 I6
Medina • Saudi Arabia ... 18 C5
Medina de Ríoseco • Spain ... 11 F3
Medina del Campo • Spain ... 11 G3
Medina-Sidonia • Spain ... 11 F8
Medinaceli • Spain ... 11 H4
Mediterranean cruise area •
  Africa/Europe ... 59 C
Mediterranean Sea • Europe ... 4 N11
Medjerda, Mts de la •
  Algeria/Tunisia ... 12 C12
Mednogorsk • Russian Fed. ... 26 I7
Mednyy, Ostrov • Russian Fed. ... 27 S6
Médoc • France ... 85 G1
Médon • France ... 10 L5
Medouneu • Gabon ... 22 G4
Medvedítsa • Russian Fed. ... 17 G3
Medvednica • Croatia ... 14 C4
Medvezh'yegorsk • Russian Fed. ... 17 E2
Medvezhi, Ostrovo •
  Russian Fed. ... 27 R2
Meekatharra • WA, Australia ... 34 C5
Meelpaeg lake • NF, Canada ... 123 D3
Meerane • Germany ... 9 H6
Meerbusch • Germany ... 81 B14
Meersburg • Germany ... 82 J5
Meerufenfushi • Maldives ... 106 E2
Mega • Ethiopia ... 23 F3
Mega • Indonesia ... 32 (1) D3
Megalgan Khorion • Greece ... 15 I7
Megalópolis • Greece ... 15 D6
Meganíssi • Greece ... 92 C1
Meganíssi • Greece ... 92 C1
Meganom, mys • Ukraine ... 15 E6
Mégara • Greece ... 15 E6
Megève Ski • France ... 70 [23]
Megève • France ... 85 F2
Meghalaya • India ... 28 F3
Megísti • Greece ... 93 G3
Meharry, Mt • WA, Australia ... 34 C4
Mehdiya-Plage • Morocco ... 101 D1
Mehran • Iran ... 18 E4
Mei Yuan • China ... 107 J1
Meiganga • Cameroon ... 22 G3
Meiktila • Myanmar ... 31 B2
Meinershagen • Germany ... 81 E4
Meiningen • Germany ... 9 F5
Meiringen • Switzerland ... 89 G2
Meiringspoort • South Africa ... 100 C7
Meisenheim • Germany ... 82 H4
Meixian • China ... 29 F6
Mejez el Bab • Tunisia ... 101 E2
Mékambo • Gabon ... 22 G4
Mejillones • Chile ... 44 C6
Mekele • Ethiopia ... 21 G5
Mekherrhane, Sebkha • Algeria ... 20 F3
Meknassy • Tunisia ... 101 E3
Meknès Heritage C • Morocco ... 64 [216]
Meknès • Morocco ... 101 D1
Mekong • Asia ... 31 D3
Mekong, Mouths of the • Vietnam ... 108 B3
Mekongga, Gunung • Indonesia ... 32 (1) B3
Mékrou • Africa ... 22 E2
Melaka • Malaysia ... 32 C2
Melamo, Cabo • Mozambique ... 24 G2
Melanesia • Pacific Ocean ... 33 H6
Melaque • Mexico ... 123 E2
Melaselkä • Russian Fed. ... 16 P5
Melawi • Indonesia ... 32 E3
Melbourne • VI, Australia ... 111 G3
Melbourne • FL, United States ... 119 M6
Melbu • Norway ... 16 H2
Melchsee-Frutt • Switzerland ... 89 G3
Meldorf • Germany ... 82 B1
Melele • Mozambique ... 24 F3
Melendugno • Italy ... 12 M8
Melendugno Beach • Italy ... 69 [135]
Melfi • Italy ... 12 J8
Melfi • Chad ... 23 B1
Meli Park Park • Belgium ... 73 [46]
Melilla • Africa ... 20 F1
Melidoni • Crete, Greece ... 93 E2
Melilla • Africa ... 101 D2
Melincué • Argentina ... 127 D1
Melipilla • Chile ... 44 B5
Melíssani • Greece ... 92 C2
Melíssani • Greece ... 92 C2
Melíta [Apt] • Tunisia ... 101 E4
Melitopol' • Ukraine ... 17 F5
Melíti • Greece ... 92 D1
Melívia • Greece ... 92 D1
Melk • Austria ... 14 C1
Melle Spa • Germany ... 83 [66]
Mellègue • Algeria/Tunisia ... 101 E1
Mellerud • Sweden ... 95 F3
Mellieha • Malta ... 93 H1
Mellieha Bay • Malta ... 93 H1
Melmerby Abbey • France ... 79 E2
Melník • Czech Rep. ... 96 C2
Melo • Uruguay ... 44 F5
Melsungen • Germany ... 9 E5
Melton Mowbray • United Kingdom ... 7 L9
Melun • France ... 85 E4
Melville • SA, United States ... 38 K6
Melville Bay • NT, Australia ... 34 G2
Melville, Cape • QL, Australia ... 34 H2
Melville Hills • NT/NU, Canada ... 38 G3

Melville I. • NT, Australia ... 34 F2
Melville I. • NT/NU, Canada ... 36 F2
Melville, Lake • NF, Canada ... 39 T6
Melville Peninsula • NU, Canada ... 24 G2
Memba, Baía de • Mozambique ... 24 G2
Memberamo • Indonesia ... 32 (1) E3
Memboro • Indonesia ... 32 (1) A4
Memmert • Germany ... 8 B3
Memmingen • Germany ... 82 J2
Memphis • TN, United States ... 41 I4
Memphis Heritage C • Egypt ... 64 [238]
Memphis • Egypt ... 101 F1
Menabe • Madagascar ... 24 G4
Menaggio • Italy ... 91 E2
Ménaka • Mali ... 20 F5
Menay • Angola ... 23 A5
Menangalaku • Indonesia ... 32 (1) A4
Menara [Apt] • Morocco ... 101 D3
Mendaya • Bali, Indonesia ... 110 C1
Mende • France ... 10 I9
Mendebo • Ethiopia ... 23 F2
Menden • Germany ... 8 C5
Menemen • Turkey ... 92 D5
Mendenka Beach • Spain ... 68 [69]
Mendi • Papua New Guinea ... 35 (1) C2
Mendip Hills • United Kingdom ... 74 F3
Mendocino • CA, United States ... 117 E5
Mendocino, Cape •
  CA, United States ... 40 B3
Mendoza • Argentina ... 44 C5
Menemen • Turkey ... 15 I5
Menen • Belgium ... 80 A15
Menfi • Sicily, Italy ... 12 G11
Mengen • Germany ... 82 J1
Menggala • Indonesia ... 32 D3
Mengkalihat, Tanjung •
  Indonesia ... 32 (1) A2
Menikio • Greece ... 15 E2
Menindee • NS, Australia ... 34 H6
Meningie • SA, Australia ... 34 G7
Menjangan • Bali, Indonesia ... 110 C1
Menjapa, Gunung • Indonesia ... 32 (1) A1
Menongue • Angola ... 24 B2
Menor, Mar • Spain ... 87 C3
Menorca • Spain ... 11 M5
Mensk • Belarus ... 17 D4
Mentakab • Malaysia ... 108 D4
Mentawai, Kepulauan • Indonesia ... 32 B3
Mentawai, Selat • Indonesia ... 32 B3
Mentigi • Indonesia ... 110 C4
Menton • France ... 85 H2
Menuires, les Ski • France ... 70 [41]
Menuires, les • France ... 85 F4
Menzel Bourguiba • Tunisia ... 12 D11
Menzies • WA, Australia ... 34 D5
Menzies, Mt • Antarctica ... 46 (1) L2
Meppel • Netherlands ... 80 A8
Meppen • Germany ... 8 C4
Meran • Italy ... 90 B1
Merano • Italy ... 90 B1
Merapi, Gunung • Indonesia ... 110 B4
Merauke • Indonesia ... 32 (1) F4
Merbabu, Gunung •
  Java, Indonesia ... 110 D7
Mercantour, Parc nat. du Park •
  France ... 72 [68]
Mercantour, Parc nat. du •
  France ... 85 H2
Mercato • Italy ... 91 G4
Merced • CA, United States ... 40 B4
Mercedario, Cerro • Argentina ... 44 C5
Mercedes • San Luis, Argentina ... 44 C5
Mercedes •
  Corrientes, Argentina ... 44 E4
Mercedes • Uruguay ... 127 D2
Mercers Creek Bay •
  Antigua & Barbuda ... 125 F2
Mercier Dam • SA, Canada ... 122 B2
Mercury I. • New Zealand ... 35 E3
Mercy, Cape • NU, Canada ... 39 S4
Méré Lava • Vanuatu ... 35 (2) B1
Meredoua • Algeria ... 20 F3
Merefa • Ukraine ... 17 F5
Mergenev • Kazakhstan ... 17 I5
Mergui • Myanmar ... 31 B4
Mergui Archipelago • Myanmar ... 31 B4
Méribel Ski • France ... 70 [39]
Méribel • France ... 85 F4
Mérida • Spain ... 11 E6
Mérida • Mexico ... 37 D3
Mérida • Venezuela ... 43 C2
Mérida Heritage C • Spain ... 64 [91]
Mérida, Cordillera de •
  Venezuela ... 43 C2
Meridian • MS, United States ... 118 K2
Mérig • Vanuatu ... 35 (2) B1
Mérignac • France ... 10 E9
Mérignac [Apt] • France ... 85 G3
Merikarvia • Finland ... 95 E1
Merimbula • NS, Australia ... 111 G4
Mering • Germany ... 82 J2
Merlette • France ... 85 F4
Merlimau • Singapore ... 108 E3
Meron • Israel ... 98 A2
Merowe • Sudan ... 21 F4
Meroe [Adm] • Sudan ... 21 F4
Merrick • United Kingdom ... 7 H6
Merrimack •
  MA/NH, United States ... 118 G3
Merritt I. Nat. Wildlife Refuge •
  FL, United States ... 119 M6
Merryville • LA, United States ... 118 K3
Mersa Fatma • Eritrea ... 18 D7
Mersch • Luxembourg ... 80 A20
Merseburg • Germany ... 9 H5
Mersin • Turkey ... 84 B4
Mersing • Malaysia ... 32 C2
Merta Road • India ... 84 A2
Mertert • Luxembourg ... 5 J5
Merthyr Tydfil • United Kingdom ... 7 J9
Merti • Kenya ... 23 F3
Mértola • Portugal ... 11 D7
Meru • Kenya ... 101 G2
Meru, Mt • Tanzania ... 102 H2
Meru Nat. Park • Kenya ... 103 [78]
Merville-Franceville-Plage Beach •
  France ... 68 [57]
Meryemana • Turkey ... 92 D3
Meryemana • Turkey ... 92 D3
Merzig • Germany ... 9 B7
Mesa • AZ, United States ... 117 G6
Mesa Verde Nat. Park •
  CO, United States ... 118 J2
Mesa Verde Nat. Park Park •
  CO, United States ... 120 [96]

Mesagne • Italy ... 12 L8
Meschede • Germany ... 5 L3
Meschers-sur-Gironde Beach •
  France ... 68 [65]
Meset • Turkey ... 15 I2
Meski • Morocco ... 101 D3
Meská • Crete, Greece ... 93 E1
Meso Gerakari Beach • Greece ... 69 [151]
Mesopotamia • Iraq/Syria ... 18 D3
Mesopotamia • Trinidad & Tobago ... 125 K2
Mesquer-Quimiac Beach • France ... 68 [63]
Messalo • Mozambique ... 23 F6
Messanges Beach • France ... 68 [67]
Messanges • France ... 85 G3
Messaôria Plain • Cyprus ... 93 J3
Messarás, Ormos • Crete, Greece ... 93 E6
Messel • Germany ... 82 G4
Messel Pit Heritage N • Germany ... 61 [42]
Messina • South Africa ... 24 E4
Messina • Sicily, Italy ... 90 D2
Messina, Stretto di • Italy ... 90 D2
Messíni • Greece ... 15 C6
Messíni Beach • Greece ... 69 [158]
Messiniakós Kólpos • Greece ... 15 D7
Messolóngi • Greece ... 15 C5
Messongi • Corfu, Greece ... 92 B1
Messongi • Corfu, Greece ... 92 B1
Messótopos Beach • Greece ... 69 [176]
Mesta • Bulgaria ... 15 E2
Mestá • Greece ... 92 D5
Mestá • Greece ... 92 D5
Mesuji • Indonesia ... 32 D3
Meta • Colombia ... 43 C2
Meta • Italy ... 91 G3
Meta Incognita Peninsula •
  NU, Canada ... 39 R4
Metabief Ski • France ... 70 [7]
Metamórfossi Beach • Greece ... 69 [169]
Metán • Argentina ... 44 D4
Metaponto • Italy ... 12 K8
Metéora Heritage N • Greece ... 61 [59]
Metéora Heritage C • Greece ... 64 [177]
Methana • Greece ... 15 E6
Methana [Peninsula] • Greece ... 92 D1
Methana [Peninsula] • Greece ... 92 D1
Methil • United Kingdom ... 74 B2
Methóni Beach • Greece ... 69 [158]
Methven • New Zealand ... 35 C6
Metkovic • Croatia ... 12 L5
Metlika • Slovenia ... 12 J3
Metmárfalg • Western Sahara ... 2 C1
Metóhi Beach • Greece ... 69 [156]
Metohija • F.R. of Yugoslavia ... 14 H7
Mettlach • Germany ... 82 G3
Mettmann • Germany ... 81 E3
Metz • France ... 10 L4
Meulaboh • Indonesia ... 110 B1
Meurthe • France ... 10 L5
Meurudu • Indonesia ... 110 B1
Meuse • Belgium/France ... 10 K5
Meuse Valley • Belgium ... 80 A15
Meuselwitz • Germany ... 9 H5
Mevagissey • United Kingdom ... 74 F4
Mexiana • Brazil ... 43 H4
Mexicali • Mexico ... 40 C5
Mexican Riviera cruise area •
  Mexico/United States ... 58 A3
Mexicana, Altiplanicie • Mexico ... 40 F6
Mexico • N. America ... 36 G8
Mexico City Heritage C • Mexico ... 62 [21]
Mexico City • Mexico ... 123 E4
Mexico, Gulf of • N. America ... 37 C2
Meymaneh • Afghanistan ... 18 I2
Mezen • Russian Fed. ... 17 G1
Mezen [Riv] • Russian Fed. ... 17 G2
Mezenskaya Guba • Russian Fed. ... 17 G1
Mezhdurechensk • Russian Fed. ... 26 N7
Mezőberény • Hungary ... 13 J10
Mezőkövesc • Hungary ... 13 J10
Mfanganu I. • Uganda ... 101 G3
Mgarr • Malta ... 93 H1
Mhamid • Morocco ... 101 D6
Mi • Japan ... 30 F7
Miami • FL, United States ... 119 M8
Miami Beach • FL, United States ... 119 M8
Miami Seaquarium •
  FL, United States ... 121 [FF]
Miami Seaquarium Park •
  FL, United States ... 121 [FF]
Mianyang • China ... 29 C4
Miarinarivo • Madagascar ... 24 H3
Miass • Russian Fed. ... 26 J6
Miastko • Poland ... 13 F3
Michalovce • Slovak Rep. ... 13 K9
Michelstadt • Germany ... 82 G4
Michendorf • Germany ... 81 F3
Michigan • United States ... 41 I2
Michigan, Lake • United States ... 41 I3
Michipicoten • OT, Canada ... 39 N7
Michoacán • Mexico ... 37 (I) D2
Michurin • Bulgaria ... 97 D4
Michurinsk • Russian Fed. ... 17 G4
Micoud • St Lucia ... 125 J4
Micra [Apt] • Greece ... 92 D1
Micra [Apt] • Greece ... 92 D1
Micronesia • Pacific Ocean ... 33 F5
Micronesia, Federated States of •
  Pacific Ocean ... 33 F5
Middelburg • South Africa ... 24 E5
Middelburg • Netherlands ... 80 A10
Middelfart Beach • Denmark ... 68 [73]
Middelfart • Denmark ... 95 F9
Middelharnis • Netherlands ... 80 B1
Middelkirke-Bad • Belgium ... 80 B1
Middle Andaman • India ... 106 F2
Middle Island •
  St Kitts & Nevis ... 125 G1
Middlesbrough • United Kingdom ... 7 K7
Middlesex • Jamaica ... 124 C2
Middleton • NS, Canada ... 123 D7
Middleton Reef • Australia ... 33 H8
Middlt • Morocco ... 20 E2
Midelt • Morocco ... 101 E3
Midi • France ... 84 B4
Midi, Canal du • France ... 10 G10
Midi-Pyrénées • France ... 84 A2
Midland • TX, United States ... 40 F5
Midland • OT, Canada ... 122 B1
Midleton • Ireland ... 79 F8
Midnight Sun Coast • Sweden ... 16 L4
Midongy Atsimo • Madagascar ... 24 H4
Midor • F.R. of Yugoslavia ... 14 J6
Miedzyrzecz • Poland ... 13 E5
Miercurea Cuic • Romania ... 14 M3
Mières • Spain ... 11 F1
Miesbach • Germany ... 82 J7
Migiorn, Platja de •
  Formentera, Spain ... 87 G4
Mihailçgik • Turkey ... 92 D6
Mijares • Spain ... 11 K4
Mijas Beach • Spain ... 68 [65]
Mijas • Spain ... 86 B6
Mijas Costa • Spain ... 86 B6
Mijdrecht • Netherlands ... 80 C2
Mikhaylovka • Russian Fed. ... 17 G4
Mikínes • Greece ... 15 D6

Mikkeli • Finland ... 16 N6
Mikkeli [Adm] • Finland ... 16 N6
Mikkeli [Adm] • Finland ... 16 N6
Mikonos Beach • Greece ... 69 [181]
Mikonos • Greece ... 92 D8
Mikonos • Greece ... 92 D8
Mikonou, Stenó • Greece ... 15 G6
Mikra Mándina Beach • Greece ... 69 [158]
Mikrá Préspa, Limni • Greece ... 15 C3
Mikumi • Tanzania ... 102 H4
Mikumi Nat. Park • Tanzania ... 102 H4
Mikun • Russian Fed. ... 17 I2
Mikuni • Japan ... 30 J6
Mikuni-Sanmyaku • Japan ... 30 J6
Milan Heritage C • Italy ... 64 [109]
Milan • Italy ... 91 E6
Milange • Mozambique ... 24 F3
Milano Heritage C • Italy ... 64 [109]
Milano • Italy ... 91 E6
Milano Maritima • Italy ... 91 E8
Milas • Turkey ... 92 D9
Milas • Turkey ... 92 D9
Milatos • Crete, Greece ... 93 E3
Milazzo • Sicily, Italy ... 90 D2
Miles • QL, Australia ... 111 F6
Miles City • MT, United States ... 40 E2
Milet • Turkey ... 92 D8
Milet • Turkey ... 92 D8
Milevsko • Czech Rep. ... 96 C4
Milford Beach • New Zealand ... 68 [46]
Milford Haven • United Kingdom ... 7 G10
Milford Haven Beach •
  United Kingdom ... 75 [157]
Milford Sound • New Zealand ... 112 L2
Milford Sound (Fiord) •
  New Zealand ... 112 L1
Milford Track • New Zealand ... 112 L2
Milh, Ra's al • Libya ... 21 D3
Miliana • Algeria ... 11 N8
Miliès • Greece ... 15 E4
Milikapiti • NT, Australia ... 34 F2
Milk • Canada/United States ... 38 I7
Milk River Spa • Jamaica ... 124 C3
Milky Way • Russian Fed. ... 27 O6
Mill I. • NU, Canada ... 39 S4
Millau • France ... 10 I9
Millerovo • Russian Fed. ... 17 G5
Millevaches, Plateau de •
  France ... 85 G2
Millicent • SA, Australia ... 34 H7
Millinocket • ME, United States ... 118 G2
Millom • United Kingdom ... 74 C3
Millstatt • Austria ... 89 H3
Millstatter See • Austria ... 89 H8
Millstreet • Ireland ... 79 F6
Milltown Malbay • Ireland ... 79 F6
Milltown-Malbay Beach • Ireland ... 68 [42]
Milnthorpe • United Kingdom ... 74 C3
Milos Beach • Greece ... 69 [184]
Milos • Greece ... 92 D7
Milos • Greece ... 92 D7
Milparinka • NS, Australia ... 34 H5
Miltenberg • Germany ... 82 G4
Milton • New Zealand ... 35 B8
Milton • FL, United States ... 119 M1
Milton Keynes • United Kingdom ... 7 L9
Milwaukee • WI, United States ... 41 I3
Milyas • Turkey ... 93 G3
Mimaland • Malaysia ... 108 D4
Mimizan • France ... 85 G3
Mimizan, Fôret de • France ... 85 G3
Min • China ... 31 F1
Min Shan • China ... 29 C4
Mina • Algeria ... 11 L9
Mina Sa'ud • Kuwait ... 18 E4
Minami-Tori-Shima •
  Pacific Ocean ... 33 G3
Minas • Uruguay ... 127 D2
Minas Gerais • Brazil ... 44 G2
Minbu • Myanmar ... 31 A2
Minch, Little • United Kingdom ... 6 F4
Minch, North • United Kingdom ... 6 G3
Minchinmávida, Volcán • Chile ... 45 B4
Mincio • Italy ... 91 E7
Mindanao • Philippines ... 31 H5
Mindel • Germany ... 9 F8
Mindelheim • Germany ... 82 J2
Mindelo • Cape Verde ... 22 (1) B1
Minden • Germany ... 8 D4
Minden Spa • Germany ... 83 [90]
Minden • LA, United States ... 118 K1
Mindoro • Philippines ... 31 G4
Mindoro Strait • Philippines ... 31 G4
Minehead • United Kingdom ... 74 F2
Mineiros • Brazil ... 44 F2
Mineola • TX, United States ... 119 N2
Mineral Wells •
  TX, United States ... 119 N1
Minerva Reefs • Pacific Ocean ... 33 J8
Minervois • France ... 84 B3
Minfeng • China ... 28 D1
Ming Village • Singapore ... 108 E3
Mingan • QU, Canada ... 123 D2
Mingan Archipelago • QU, Canada ... 123 D2
Mingenew • WA, Australia ... 34 C5
Minglanilla • Spain ... 11 J5
Minho • Portugal ... 11 C3
Minho, Rio • Jamaica ... 124 C4
Minicoy I. • India ... 106 D13
Minilya • WA, Australia ... 34 B4
Minna • Nigeria ... 22 F3
Minneapolis • MN, United States ... 41 H3
Minnehaha, Lake •
  FL, United States ... 121 C1
Minnesota • United States ... 41 H2
Miño • Spain ... 11 D2
Miño Beach • Spain ... 68 [73]
Minorca • Spain ... 87 F
Minot • ND, United States ... 40 F2
Minquiers, Îles • Channel Is. ... 75 A8
Minsk • Belarus ... 17 D4
Minsk Mazowiecki • Poland ... 13 K5
Minto, Lac • QU, Canada ... 39 P5
Minto, Mt • Antarctica ... 46 (1) V2
Minusinsk • Russian Fed. ... 26 P7
Minute Man Nat. Hist. Park Park •
  MA, United States ... 121 [352]
Minya, El • Egypt ... 101 F3
Mira • Italy ... 12 G3
Mira Beach • Portugal ... 68 [78]
Mira • Portugal ... 11 C4
Mirabad • Afghanistan ... 18 I3
Mirabel [Apt] • QU, Canada ... 122 B3
Miraflores • Peru ... 127 B3
Miraflores • Boyaca, Colombia ... 43 C2
Miraflores • Guaviare, Colombia ... 43 C3
Miraj • India ... 106 D11
Miramar • Argentina ... 127 D4
Miramar Beach • Goa, India ... 105 D11
Mirambeau • France ... 10 E8
Mirambélou, Kólpos •
  Crete, Greece ... 93 E8
Miranda de Ebro • Spain ... 11 H2
Mirándela • Portugal ... 11 D3
Mirándola • Italy ... 91 E7

Mirapolis **Park** • France ....73 [68]
Mirapolis • France 85 E1
Mirbat • Oman 18 F6
Mirepoix • France 11 M1
Mires • Crete, Greece 15 F8
Miri • Malaysia 32 E2
Miria • Niger 20 G6
Mirim, lagoa • Brazil/Uruguay 44 F5
Mirina **Beach** • Greece ....69 [175]
Mirina • Greece 92 D2
Mirina • Greece 92 D2
Mirny [Base] • Antarctica 46 (1) O3
Mirnyy • Russian Fed. 27 H4
Mirpur Khas • Pakistan 28 A3
Mirs Bay • China 107 H4
Mirtoan Sea • Greece 92 D7
Mirtoan Sea • Greece 92 D7
Mirtóo Pélagos • Greece 92 D7
Mirtos • Crete, Greece 93 E7
Mirzapur • India 105 C8
Misano Adriático • Italy 91 E12
Miscou I. • NB, Canada 123 D2
Miseno, Capo • Italy 91 G3
Mish, Slieve • Ireland 79 F5
Mishan • China 27 L7
Misima • Papua New Guinea 35 (1) E3
Miskito, Cayos • Nicaragua 124 A4
Miskitos, Costa de • Nicaragua 37 E5
Miskolc • Hungary 13 J9
Misoöl • Indonesia 32 (1) D3
Misratah • Libya 105 C3
Misrikh • India 105 C8
Mission Beach • QL, Australia 111 F1
Mississauga • OT, Canada 122 B9
Mississippi [Adm] •
    United States 41 I5
Mississippi [Riv] •
    United States 41 H5
Mississippi River Delta •
    LA, United States 118 K4
Missoula • MT, United States 117 E2
Missouri [Adm] • United States 40 F2
Missouri [Riv] • United States 39 O6
Mistassini • QU, Canada 39 O6
Mistassini, Lac • QU, Canada 39 O6
Mistassini [Riv] • QU, Canada 39 Q7
Mistegná **Beach** • Greece ....69 [176]
Misterhult • Sweden 95 F8
Mistrás • Greece 15 D6
Mistrás **Heritage C** • Greece ....64 [181]
Misty Fjords •
    AK, United States 58 A2
Mitchell • SD, United States 41 G3
Mitchell • QL, Australia 111 F5
Mitchell, Mt •
    NC, United States 41 J4
Mitchell [Riv] • QL, Australia 34 H3
Mitchell River Mission •
    QL, Australia 34 H3
Mitchelstown • Ireland 79 F6
Mithimna **Beach** • Greece ....69 [176]
Mithimna • Greece 92 D5
Mithimna • Greece 92 D5
Mitikas **Beach** • Greece ....69 [153]
Mitikas • Epirus, Greece 92 C1
Mitikas • Ditiki Elláda, Greece 92 C1
Mitikas • Epirus, Greece 92 C1
Mitikas • Ditiki Elláda, Greece 92 C1
Mitilíni **Beach** • Greece ....69 [176]
Mitilíni • Greece 92 D5
Mitilíni • Greece 92 D5
Mitla • Mexico 123 E4
Mito • Japan 30 K6
Mittelberg **Ski** • Austria ....70 [128]
Mittelfranken • Germany 9 G7
Mittelland • Switzerland 89 G2
Mittellandkanal • Germany 8 D4
Mittenwald • Germany 82 J7
Mittenwalde • Germany 81 F4
Mittersill **Ski** • Austria ....70 [160]
Mittweida • Germany 9 H6
Mitú • Colombia 43 C3
Mitumba, Mtns •
    Dem. Rep. of Congo 23 D5
Mitwaba • Dem. Rep. of Congo 23 D5
Mitzic • Gabon 22 G4
Miyake • Japan 30 J7
Miyake • Japan 30 K5
Miyako • Japan 30 F9
Miyanoura • Japan 30 F9
Miyazaki • Japan 30 G7
Miyoshi • Japan 30 G7
Mizdah • Libya 21 B1
Mizen Head • Wicklow, Ireland 79 E4
Mizen Head • Cork, Ireland 79 E4
Mizil • Romania 14 N5
Mizoram • India 28 F4
Mizuho [Base] • Antarctica 46 (1) J2
Mjölby • Sweden 95 F4
Mjøndalen • Norway 94 B1
Mjörn • Sweden 95 F3
Mjøsa • Norway 16 F6
Mkhaya Nature Reserve **Park** •
    Swaziland ....103 [133]
Mkushi • Zambia 24 D2
Mkuzi Game Reserve **Park** •
    South Africa ....103 [126]
Mladá Boleslav • Czech Rep. 96 C2
Mlawa • Poland 13 J4
Mlibizi • Zimbabwe 102 J1
Mljet • Croatia 14 E7
Mljet Nat. Park **Park** • Croatia ....72 [113]
Mmabatho • South Africa 24 D5
Mnajdra • Malta 93 H4
Mnarani • Kenya 101 G5
Mnichovo Hradiste • Czech Rep. 96 C2
Mo i Rana • Norway 16 H3
Moa • Sierra Leone 22 B3
Moa • QL, Australia 34 H2
Moa • Cuba 124 D8
Moab • UT, United States 40 D4
Moab • Jordan 98 A8
Moala • Fiji 35 (2) D2
Moanda • Dem. Rep. of Congo 23 A5
Moba • Dem. Rep. of Congo 23 D5
Mobaye • Central African Rep. 23 C3
Mobayi-Mbongo •
    Dem. Rep. of Congo 23 C3
Mobile • AL, United States 119 M1
Mobile Bay • AL, United States 119 M1
Mober Beach • Goa, India 105 B2
Mobridge • SD, United States 40 F2
Moçambique • Mozambique 24 F3
Moçambique, Canal de •
    Madagascar/Mozambique 24 G3
Moçambique, Ilha da **Heritage N** •
    Mozambique ....61 [97]
Mochudi • Botswana 24 D4
Mocimboa da Praia • Mozambique 23 G6
Mocka • Yemen 18 E7
Möckeln • Sweden 95 F11
Môco, Serra • Angola 23 B6
Mocoa • Colombia 43 B3
Mocuba • Mozambique 24 F3

Modane • France 85 F4
Modave • Belgium 80 A15
Modena **Heritage C** • Italy ....64 [117]
Modena • Italy 91 E7
Moder • France 9 C8
Módica • Sicily, Italy 12 I12
Mödling • Austria 13 F9
Moe • VI, Australia 111 G3
Moelfre **Beach** • United Kingdom ....75 [212-213]
Moelv • Norway 16 F6
Moena • Italy 90 B3
Moena di Fassa **Ski** • Italy ....70 [218]
Moengo • Suriname 43 G2
Moers • Germany 80 A12
Moers • Germany 81 E1
Mogadishu • Somalia 23 H3
Mogadouro • Portugal 11 E3
Mogami, Serra do • Portugal 11 E3
Mogami • Japan 30 K5
Mogán **Beach** •
    Gran Canaria, Canary Is. ....68 [92]
Mogán •
    Gran Canaria, Canary Is. 86 E4
Mogao Caves **Heritage C** • China ....63 [143]
Mogho • Ethiopia 23 G3
Mogoca • Russian Fed. 27 I6
Moguer **Beach** • Spain ....68 [95]
Moguer • Spain 86 B1
Mohács • Hungary 13 H12
Mohammadia • Algeria 11 L9
Mohammed V [Apt] • Morocco 101 D1
Mohammédia • Morocco 101 D1
Mohrraq, El • Egypt 101 F5
Mohave, Lake •
    AZ/NV, United States 118 J1
Mohawk Mtn **Ski** •
    CT, United States ....116 [186]
Mohéli • Comoros 24 G2
Mohenjodaro • Pakistan 28 A3
Mohenjodaro **Heritage C** •
    Pakistan ....63 [111]
Moher, Cliffs of • Ireland 79 F4
Möhne • Germany 8 D5
Moi • Myanmar/Thailand 109 G3
Moi [Apt] • Kenya 101 G5
Moinesti • Romania 14 N3
Mointy • Kazakhstan 26 L8
Moisie • QU, Canada 39 R6
Moissac • France 85 G4
Moïta • Corsica, France 85 L2
Mõja • Sweden 95 D4
Mojácar **Beach** • Spain ....68 [99]
Mojácar • Spain 86 B4
Mojave Desert •
    CA, United States 117 F6
Mojave Nat. Preserve •
    CA, United States 117 F6
Mojave Nat. Preserve **Park** •
    CA, United States ....120 [60]
Mojokerto • Java, Indonesia 110 D8
Mojos, Llanos de • Bolivia 44 C1
Mokapu Peninsula •
    HI, United States 119 L6
Mokau • New Zealand 112 K3
Mokau [Riv] • New Zealand 112 K1
Moknine • Tunisia 101 E4
Mokp'o • Rep. of Korea 30 D7
Mokuleia Baech •
    HI, United States 119 L1
Mol • Belgium 5 I3
Mola di Bari • Italy 12 L7
Mólai • Greece 15 D7
Molara, I. • Sardinia, Italy 90 C2
Molat • Croatia 14 J5
Molatón **Beach** • Spain 11 J5
Mold • United Kingdom 7 I8
Moldau • Czech Rep. 13 D8
Moldova • Romania 14 N2
Moldova • Europe 15 D5
Moldova Noua • Romania 14 I5
Moldova [Riv] • Romania 14 M2
Moldoveanu, Vîrful • Romania 14 L4
Mole Nat. Park **Park** • Ghana ....103 [22]
Molepolole • Botswana 24 D4
Molfetta • Italy 12 K7
Moliets-en-Maa **Beach** • France ....68 [67]
Molina de Aragón • Spain 11 J4
Molina de Segura • Spain 11 J6
Molise • Italy 12 F3
Mollafeneri • Turkey 15 K3
Mölle • Sweden 95 F11
Mollendo • Peru 127 B4
Mölln • Germany 8 F3
Mölln **Spa** • Germany ....83 [35]
Mollösund • Sweden 95 F2
Mölndal • Sweden 95 F6
Molodechno • Belarus 16 N9
Molodezhnaya [Base] •
    Antarctica 46 (1) J3
Molokai • HI, United States 119 L3
Molong • NS, Australia 111 G2
Molopo • Botswana/South Africa 24 C5
Moloundou • Cameroon 22 H4
Molucca • Indonesia 32 (1) C3
Molucca Sea • Indonesia 32 (1) C2
Molygino • Russian Fed. 27 D5
Molyneux • St Kitts & Nevis 125 G1
Moma • Mozambique 24 F3
Moma • Russian Fed. 27 O3
Mombasa • Kenya 101 G5
Mombasa Marine Game Reserve •
    Kenya 101 G5
Mombasa Marine Nat. Park •
    Kenya 101 G5
Mombetsu • Japan 30 L2
Mompós • Colombia 43 C2
Mompós **Heritage C** • Colombia ....62 [43]
Momski Khrebet • Russian Fed. 27 O3
Møn • Denmark 95 F15
Mon Repos • St Lucia 125 J4
Mona, Isla • Puerto Rico 124 D1
Monaco • Europe 85 H2
Monadhliath Mtns •
    United Kingdom 6 H4
Monadnock • NH, United States 118 G3
Monaghan • Ireland 7 F7
Monaghan [Adm] • Ireland 79 D1
Monasterevin • Ireland 79 D3
Monastir • Tunisia 101 E4
Monastir • Japan 30 L3
Moncalieri • Italy 12 B4
Monção • Portugal 11 C2
Moncarapacho • Portugal 88 E8
Moncayo • Spain 11 H4
Monchegorsk • Russian Fed. 17 E1
Mönchengladbach • Germany 81 E3
Monchique • Portugal 88 E2
Monchique, Serra de • Portugal 88 E2
Monchy • St Lucia 125 J3
Monclova • Mexico 37 A2
Moncófar **Beach** • Spain ....68 [103]
Moncton • NB, Canada 123 D7

Mondego • Portugal 11 D4
Mondi • Italy 90 D1
Mondo • Chad 22 H2
Mondorf-les-Bains • Luxembourg 80 A20
Mondorf • Italy 91 E5
Mondragone • Italy 91 G1
Mondsee • Austria 89 H4
Mondsee [Lake] • Austria 89 H4
Mondy • Russian Fed. 27 F6
Monéglia **Beach** • Italy ....68 [122]
Monéglia • Italy 91 E6
Monemvassia • Greece 92 D7
Monemvassia • Greece 92 D7
Monesterio • Spain 11 D2
Monforte de Lemos • Spain 11 D2
Mong Hpayak • Myanmar 109 G1
Mong Kok • Hong Kong, China 107 H5
Monga • Dem. Rep. of Congo 23 C3
Mongalla • Sudan 28 E3
Monghyr • India 28 E3
Mongie, la • France 85 J2
Mongo • Chad 21 C5
Mongo • Russian Fed. 27 H6
Mongol Altayn Nuruu •
    China/Mongolia 26 O8
Mongolia • Asia 25 L5
Mongonu • Nigeria 22 G2
Mongororo • Chad 23 C1
Mongouge • St Lucia 125 J3
Mongstad • Norway 94 C3
Mony • Zambia 24 C3
Monheim • Germany 81 E3
Monjes • West Indies 43 C1
Monkey Hill • St Kitts & Nevis 125 G1
Monmouth • United Kingdom 74 D3
Monmouthshire • United Kingdom 74 D3
Monnickendam • Netherlands 80 C2
Monnow • Lake • CA, United States 117 F4
Monocacy Nat. Battlefield **Park** •
    MD, United States ....121 [272]
Monólithos • Rhodes, Greece 93 F3
Monopoli • Italy 12 L8
Monor • Hungary 13 I10
Monos I. • Trinidad & Tobago 125 K1
Monovar • Spain 11 K6
Monowai, Lake • New Zealand 112 L3
Monpazier • France 85 G4
Monreal del Campo • Spain 11 J4
Monreale • Sicily, Italy 90 D1
Monroe • LA, United States 118 K1
Monrovia • Liberia 22 B3
Mons • Belgium 80 A14
Møns Klint • Denmark 95 F15
Monschau • Germany 82 G1
Monselice • Italy 12 F3
Monselice • Italy 82 H4
Mont Blanc • France/Italy 85 F2
Mont Blanc **Ski** • QU, Canada ....116 [32]
Mont Blanc, Tunnel du •
    France/Italy 85 F2
Mont Cenis, Col du • France 85 F4
Mont d'Or, le **Ski** • France ....70 [7]
Mont de Marsan • France 85 G3
Mont Gabriel **Ski** • QU, Canada ....116 [27]
Mont Joli • QU, Canada 123 D1
Mont Laurier • QU, Canada 122 B3
Mont Louis • France 11 N2
Mont Mégantic Prov. Park •
    QU, Canada 122 B8
Mont Olympia **Ski** • QU, Canada ....116 [28]
Mont Orford **Ski** • QU, Canada ....116 [41]
Mont Orford Prov. Park •
    QU, Canada 122 B8
Mont St Bruno Prov. Park •
    QU, Canada 122 B8
Mont St Michel **Heritage N** •
    France ....61 [43]
Mont St Michel **Heritage C** •
    France ....64 [48]
Mont St Michel, Baie du •
    France 5 B6
Mont St Michel, le • France 84 C2
Mont Ste Anne **Ski** • QU, Canada ....116 [35]
Mont Ste Anne Prov. Park •
    QU, Canada 123 D1
Mont Ste Saveur **Ski** •
    QU, Canada ....116 [29]
Mont Sutton **Ski** • QU, Canada ....116 [39]
Mont Tremblant Prov. Park •
    QU, Canada 122 B3
Mont Video **Ski** • QU, Canada ....116 [25]
Mont-roig del Camp **Beach** •
    Spain ....68 [104]
Montabaur • Germany 82 H2
Montacute House •
    United Kingdom 74 F3
Montagnana • Italy 91 E7
Montagnes Noires • France 84 C2
Montagu • South Africa 100 C6
Montalbán • Spain 11 K4
Montalegre • Portugal 11 D3
Montana • Bulgaria 14 K6
Montana • United States 40 E2
Montaña Blanca •
    Lanzarote, Canary Is. 87 E3
Montaña Clara • Canary Is. 87 E3
Montanhàs • Portugal 88 A1
Montargis • France 10 H6
Montauban • France 85 G4
Montauk • NY, United States 118 H2
Montbéliard • France 10 L6
Montblanc • Spain 11 L3
Montchavin **Ski** • France ....70 [33]
Montchanin • France 85 F2
Monte Albán **Heritage C** • Mexico ....62 [24]
Monte Albán • Mexico 123 E4
Monte Alegre • Brazil 45 (1) C4
Monte Azul • Brazil 45 (1) C4
Monte Carlo • Monaco 85 H2
Monte Caseros • Argentina 44 E5
Monte Fogo, Serra de • Portugal 88 E7
Monte Gordo • Portugal 88 E8
Monte Lindo • Paraguay 44 E4
Monte Oliveto Maggiore, Abbazia di •
    Italy 91 E11
Monte Quemado • Argentina 44 D4
Monte Sant' Angelo • Italy 12 J7
Monte Santu, Capo di •
    Sardinia, Italy 12 D8
Montealegre del Castillo •
    Spain 11 J6
Montebelluno • Italy 91 E7
Montecassino, Abbazia di •
    Italy 91 F4
Montecatini • Italy 91 E11
Montechoro • Portugal 88 E6
Montecorvino • Italy 91 G4
Montecristo • Italy 12 E6
Montefalco • Italy 91 E12
Montego Bay • Jamaica 124 C1
Montélier • France 85 F3
Montélimar • France 85 F3
Montella • Italy 91 G2
Montemor-o-Novo • Portugal 11 C6

Montenegro • F.R. of Yugoslavia 14 G7
Montenegro • Brazil 44 F4
Montepulciano • Italy 91 E11
Montereau-Faut-Yonne • France 85 E4
Monterey • CA, United States 117 F3
Monterey Bay •
    CA, United States 117 F3
Montería • Colombia 43 B2
Monteriggioni • Italy 91 E11
Montero • Bolivia 44 D2
Monterotondo • Italy 12 G6
Monterrey • Mexico 37 A2
Montes Claros • Brazil 44 H2
Montesárchio • Italy 91 G2
Montevarchi • Italy 12 F5
Montevideo • Uruguay 127 D2
Montezuma Castle Nat. Mon. •
    AZ, United States 118 J1
Montezuma Castle Nat. Mon. **Park** •
    AZ, United States ....120 [109]
Montfort • Israel 98 A1
Montgenèvre **Ski** • France ....70 [62]
Montgenèvre • France 85 F4
Montgomery • AL, United States 41 I5
Montgomery • United Kingdom 74 D1
Monthey • Switzerland 89 G5
Monticello • Corsica, France 85 L1
Montignac • France 85 G2
Montigny-lès-Metz • France 10 L4
Montijo • Spain 11 E6
Montijo • Portugal 88 D2
Montilla • Spain 86 B2
Montivilliers • France 5 D5
Montlouis • France 84 B1
Montluçon • France 10 H7
Montmagny • QU, Canada 118 D1
Montmédy • France 5 I5
Montmélian • France 85 F1
Montmorillon • France 85 F1
Mont-Oriol • QL, Australia 111 F4
Montoro • Spain 11 G6
Montpelier • VT, United States 118 G3
Montpellier • France 10 I10
Montpoupon [Château] • France 84 D2
Montréal • QU, Canada 122 B7
Montreuil • France 5 E4
Montreux • Switzerland 89 G5
Montrose • United Kingdom 6 J5
Montrose • CO, United States 40 E4
Monts Chic-Chocs prov. parks •
    QU, Canada 123 D2
Montsen • Spain 11 L2
Montserrat • West Indies 37 I4
Montserrat Hills •
    Trinidad & Tobago 125 K3
Montserrat, Monestir de • Spain 87 D3
Monywa • Myanmar 31 B2
Monza • Italy 91 E6
Monzón • Spain 11 L3
Moone • Ireland 79 E3
Moonie • QL, Australia 111 F6
Moonstone **Ski** • OT, Canada ....116 [17]
Moor Abbey • Ireland 79 F6
Moora • WA, Australia 34 C6
Moorba Lobenstein **Spa** •
    Germany ....83 [308]
Moore, Lake • WA, Australia 34 C5
Moorea • French Polynesia 58 A1
Moores Creek Nat. Battlefield **Park** •
    NC, United States ....121 [247]
Moorfoot Hills • United Kingdom 74 B4
Moorhead • MN, United States 41 G2
Moosburg • Germany 82 J3
Moose • OT, Canada 39 O6
Moose Jaw • SA, Canada 38 J6
Moosehead • NB, United States 118 G2
Moosehead Lake •
    ME, United States 118 G2
Moosonee • OT, Canada 39 O6
Mopti • Mali 20 E6
Moquegua • Peru 127 B4
Mór • Hungary 13 H10
Mora • Portugal 11 C6
Mora • Spain 11 I5
Mora • Sweden 16 H6
Mora • Cameroon 22 G2
Mòra d'Ebre • Spain 11 L3
Moradabad • India 105 C3
Morag • Poland 13 I4
Moraira • Spain 87 C2
Moraítika • Corfu, Greece 92 B1
Moraítika • Corfu, Greece 92 B1
Morane • French Polynesia 33 N8
Morant Bay • Jamaica 124 C4
Morant Point • Jamaica 124 C4
Morar, Loch • United Kingdom 6 G5
Moratalla • Spain 11 J6
Moratuwa • Sri Lanka 106 D15
Morava • Czech Rep. 13 G9
Moravia • Czech Rep. 96 B1
Morawa • WA, Australia 34 C5
Morawhanna • Guyana 43 F2
Moray • United Kingdom 74 A1
Moray Firth • United Kingdom 6 I4
Morbach • Germany 82 H3
Morbihan • France 84 C4
Morbihan, Golfe du • France 84 C4
Mörbylånga • Sweden 95 F12
Morcenx • France 85 G3
Morcote • Switzerland 89 G7
Mordovia • Russian Fed. 17 G4
Möre • Sweden 95 F12
More, Glen • United Kingdom 6 H4
More og Romsdal • Norway 16 D5
Morecambe • United Kingdom 7 J7
Morecambe Bay • United Kingdom 7 J7
Moree • NS, Australia 111 F6
Morehead • Papua New Guinea 35 (1) D2
Moreiz, gora • Russian Fed. 27 M3
Mörel-Breiten **Ski** • Switzerland ....70 [100]
Morelia **Heritage C** • Mexico ....62 [20]
Morelia • Mexico 123 E4
Morella • Spain 11 K4
Moremi Wildlife Reserve **Park** •
    Botswana ....103 [111]
Morena, Sierra • Spain 11 G6
Moreni • Romania 14 M5
Moresby I. • BC, Canada 38 E6
Moreton Bay • QL, Australia 34 J5
Moreton I. • QL, Australia 111 F6
Moreton-in-Marsh •
    United Kingdom 74 D4
Moreuil • France 5 F5
Mörfelden • Germany 5 L5
Morgan • UT, United States ....116 B
Morgan City • LA, United States 118 K4
Morgan Lewis Beach • Barbados 125 H1
Morgan Lewis Mill • Barbados 125 H1
Morgan, Mt • QL, Australia 34 J4
Morgan, Carleton Prov. Park •
    NB, Canada 123 D2
Morgaüb • Afghanistan 18 I2
Morgins **Ski** • Switzerland ....70 [75]
Morgins • Switzerland 89 G5
Morhange • France 9 B8
Mori • China 26 P9
Mori • Japan 30 K3

Morib • Malaysia 108 D3
Morillon les Essert **Ski** •
    France ....70 [15]
Morioka • Japan 30 K5
Morjärv • Sweden 16 L3
Morjim Beach • Goa, India 105 B1
Morko • Sweden 95 D4
Morlaix • France 84 C1
Mörlunda • Sweden 95 F8
Mormagao • Goa, India 105 B1
Morne Fortune • St Lucia 125 J1
Morne Seychellois • Seychelles 106 F1
Morne Seychellois Nat. Park •
    Seychelles 106 F1
Morne Trois Pitons Nat. Park **Heritage N** •
    Dominica ....60 [26]
Mornington I. • QL, Australia 34 H3
Morobe • Papua New Guinea 35 (1) D2
Morocco • Africa 102 H4
Morogoro • Tanzania 24 G4
Morombe • Madagascar 24 G4
Mörön • Mongolia 27 F7
Morón • Cuba 124 D3
Morón de la Frontera • Spain 11 F7
Morón • France 28 F2
Moroni • Comoros 24 G2
Morotai • Indonesia 32 (1) C2
Moroto • Uganda 23 F3
Morotu • Japan 30 H8
Morpeth • United Kingdom 7 K6
Mórphou • Cyprus 93 J1
Mórphou Bay • Cyprus 93 J1
Morrinhos • Brazil 44 G2
Morrinsville • New Zealand 112 K2
Morris Jessup, Kap • Greenland 36 N1
Morristown Nat. Hist. Park **Park** •
    NJ, United States ....121 [335]
Morro Bay State Park •
    CA, United States 117 F5
Morro de Chapéu • Brazil 44 H1
Mörrum • Sweden 95 F12
Mors Beach • Denmark ....68 [30]
Mors • Denmark 95 F5
Morshansk • Russian Fed. 17 G4
Mort, Costa de la • Spain 87 D2
Mortagne • France 10 L5
Mortain • France 5 C6
Moruga • Trinidad & Tobago 125 K3
Morvan • France 85 C7
Morven • QL, Australia 111 F5
Morwell • VI, Australia 111 G3
Morzine **Ski** • France ....70 [12]
Morzine • France 85 F2
Mosbach • Germany 82 G4
Moscow **Heritage C** •
    Russian Fed. ....64 [207-208]
Moscow • Russian Fed. 97 E4
Moscow • ID, United States 117 E2
Mosel • Germany 82 H3
Mosel Valley • Germany 82 H3
Moselle • France 5 I5
Moses Lake • WA, United States 40 C2
Mosgiel • New Zealand 35 C7
Moshi • Tanzania 102 H2
Mosi-oa-Tunya **Heritage N** •
    Zambia/Zimbabwe ....61 [95]
Mosjøen • Norway 16 G4
Moskenesøya • Norway 16 G3
Moskva **Heritage C** •
    Russian Fed. ....64 [207-208]
Moskva • Russian Fed. 97 E4
Moskva [Riv] • Russian Fed. 97 E4
Moskviy, Kanal im •
    Russian Fed. 97 E4
Moslavačka Gora • Croatia 14 D4
Mosonmagyaróvár • Hungary 13 G10
Mosquito Bluff •
    St Kitts & Nevis 125 G4
Mosquitos, Costa de • Nicaragua 58 B9
Mosquitos, Golfo de •
    Costa Rica/Panama 37 E6
Moss • Norway 94 B4
Moss Park • FL, United States 121 C2
Moss Town • Bahamas 124 B3
Mossaka • Congo 23 B4
Mossel Bay • South Africa 100 C6
Mossendjo • Congo 22 G5
Mossman • QL, Australia 34 I3
Mossoró • Brazil 45 (1) D3
Most • Czech Rep. 96 C1
Mosta • Malta 93 H4
Mostaganem • Algeria 20 F1
Mostar • Bosnia-Herz. 14 E6
Mostul • Iraq 18 D2
Mosty • Russian Fed. 94 C6
Morghab • Afghanistan 18 I2
Mota Lava • Vanuatu 35 (2) B1
Motala • Congo 22 H4
Motaga • Guatemala 22 D1
Motala • Sweden 95 F4
Motherwell • United Kingdom 74 B3
Motihari • India 105 C8
Motilla del Palancar • Spain 11 J5
Motiti I. • New Zealand 112 K2
Motril • Spain 86 B7
Motru • Romania 14 J5
Motu One • French Polynesia 33 L7
Motueka • New Zealand 35 D5
Motuhora I. • New Zealand 112 K2
Mouchard • France 10 K7
Mouche, Anse a la • Seychelles 106 F1
Moudjéria • Mauritania 20 C5
Moúdros • Greece 92 D2
Moúdros • Greece 92 D2
Mouila • Gabon 22 G5
Moukalaba, Réserve de la **Park** •
    Gabon ....103 [51]
Moul • Niger 20 H5
Moulay Bousselham • Morocco 101 D1
Moulay Idriss • Morocco 101 D1
Moule à Chique, Cape • St Lucia 125 J4
Moulin [Château] • France 84 D2
Moulins • France 10 I7
Moulins • France 31 B3
Moulmein • Myanmar 31 B3
Moulouya • Morocco 101 D2
Moúnda, Akra • Greece 92 C2
Moúnda, Akra • Greece 92 C2
Mounaba • Chad 21 C6
Mount Abu • India 105 C5
Mount Aspiring Nat. Park •
    New Zealand 112 L2
Mount Bachelor **Ski** •
    OR, United States ....116 [49]
Mount Baker **Ski** •
    WA, United States ....116 [42]
Mount Barker • WA, Australia 34 C6
Mount Brighton **Ski** •
    MI, United States ....116 [138]
Mount Buffalo • VI, Australia 111 G3
Mount Carleton Prov. Park •
    NB, Canada 123 D2
Mount Darwin • Zimbabwe 102 J2
Mount Desert I. •
    ME, United States 118 G4
Mount Douglas • QL, Australia 34 I4
Mount Elgon Nat. Park • Kenya 101 G5

Mount Elgon Nat. Park **Park** •
    Kenya ....103 [76]
Mount Gambier • SA, Australia 34 H7
Mount Hagen • Papua New Guinea 35 (1) C2
Mount Holly **Ski** •
    MI, United States ....116 [139]
Mount Hood Meadows **Ski** •
    OR, United States ....116 [47]
Mount Isa • QL, Australia 34 G4
Mount Kato **Ski** •
    MN, United States ....116 [115]
Mount Kenya Nat. Park • Kenya 101 G3
Mount Kenya Nat. Park **Park** •
    Kenya ....103 [79]
Mount Lavinia • Sri Lanka 106 D15
Mount Magnet • WA, Australia 34 C5
Mount Mansfield **Ski** •
    VT, United States ....116 [203]
Mount Maunganui • New Zealand 112 K2
Mount Pleasant •
    MI, United States 41 J3
Mount Rainier Nat. Park •
    WA, United States 117 E1
Mount Rainier Nat. Park **Park** •
    WA, United States ....120 [31]
Mount Revelstoke Nat. Park •
    BC, Canada 122 C4
Mount Robson Prov. Park •
    AL, United States 122 C2
Mount Rose **Ski** •
    NV, United States ....116 [67]
Mount Rushmore Nat. Mem. **Park** •
    SD, United States ....120 [151]
Mount Snow **Ski** •
    VT, United States ....116 [195]
Mount St Helens Nat. Volcanic Mon. •
    WA, United States 117 E1
Mount St Louis **Ski** • OT, Canada ....116 [16]
Mount Sunapee **Ski** •
    NH, United States ....116 [208]
Mount Tom **Ski** •
    MA, United States ....116 [189]
Mount Vernon • WA, Australia 34 C4
Mount Vernon •
    WA, United States 40 B2
Mount Vernon •
    IL, United States 41 I4
Mount Washington **Ski** •
    BC, Canada ....116 [1]
Mount Wise • United Kingdom 74 F4
Mountain High **Ski** •
    CA, United States ....116 [64]
Mountain Zebra Nat. Park •
    South Africa 100 C4
Mountain Zebra Nat. Park **Park** •
    South Africa ....103 [120]
Mountshannon • Ireland 79 F4
Moura • Portugal 11 D6
Moura • Spain 11 D6
Mourão • Portugal 11 D6
Mourdi, Dépression du • Chad 21 D4
Mourdiah • Mali 20 D6
Mourési **Beach** • Greece ....69 [165]
Mourne Mtns • United Kingdom 7 G7
Mouscron • Belgium 5 G4
Moussoro • Chad 22 H2
Moutiers • France 85 F2
Mouton, Château • France 85 G1
Moutong • Indonesia 32 (1) B2
Mouydir • Algeria 20 F3
Moxey Town • Bahamas 124 B1
Moy • Ireland 79 F2
Moyale • Kenya 101 G2
Moyle • United Kingdom 75 A3
Moyne Abbey • Ireland 79 F2
Moyobamba • Peru 127 B1
Moyto • Chad 20 I6
Mozambique • Africa 24 F3
Mozambique, Canal de •
    Madagascar/Mozambique 24 G3
Mozambique Channel •
    Madagascar/Mozambique 24 G3
Mozyr • Belarus 17 D4
Mpanda • Tanzania 102 H1
Mpika • Zambia 24 E2
Mpouya • Congo 23 B4
Mpulungu • Zambia 24 D5
Mpumalanga • South Africa 24 D5
Mpunga Marine Nat. Park • Kenya 101 G5
Mragowo • Poland 13 K4
Mràyer, El • Mauritania 20 D4
Mreiti, El • Mauritania 20 D4
Mrewa • Zimbabwe 102 J2
Mreyyé, El • Mali/Mauritania 20 D5
Msasani • Tanzania 102 H1
Msta • Russian Fed. 97 E1
Mtarazi Falls Nat. Park •
    Zimbabwe 102 J2
Mtelo • Kenya 23 F3
Mtsensk • Russian Fed. 17 F4
Mtskheta **Heritage C** • Georgia ....63 [78]
Mtwara • Tanzania 102 H1
Muang Khammouan • Laos 31 C3
Muang Khong • Laos 31 D4
Muang Mai • Phuket, Thailand 109 K1
Muang Pakxan • Laos 31 C2
Muang Sing • Laos 31 C2
Muang Xaignabouri • Laos 31 C2
Muar • Malaysia 32 C2
Murasiberut • Indonesia 32 B3
Muaratebe • Indonesia 32 E3
Muaro Takus • Indonesia 32 B3
Mubarak, Al • Saudi Arabia 18 E4
Mubi • Nigeria 20 H6
Muchinga Mtns • Zambia 24 E2
Muck • United Kingdom 79 F7
Muckross Abbey • Ireland 79 F7
Muconda • Angola 23 B6
Mudan Jiang • China 29 H2
Mudanjiang • China 29 H2
Mudanya • Turkey 92 D3
Muddus Nat. Park **Park** • Sweden ....72 [18]
Mudgee • NS, Australia 111 G2
Mudug • Somalia 23 H2
Mudumalai Wildlife Sanctuary •
    India 106 D10
Mudurnu • Turkey 15 L3
Muela • Mozambique 24 F2
Muela de San Juan • Spain 11 J4
Muertos, I. Caja de •
    Puerto Rico 125 E3
Muezenti • Chad 20 I5
Mufulira • Zambia 24 D2
Muge •
    Dem. Rep. of Congo 23 D9
Mugía • Turkey 92 D9
Mugla • Turkey 92 D5
Mugla • Turkey 92 D9
Mugodzhary • Kazakhstan 26 I8
Muhammad 'Qawl • Sudan 21 C3
Muhammad, Râs • Egypt 101 F4
Mühlberg • Germany 71 A8
Mühldorf am Inn • Germany 82 J4
Mühlenbeck • Germany 81 F2

Mühlhausen • Germany 9 F5
Mühltal **Ski** • Austria.... 70 [147]
Muhos • Finland.... 16 N4
Muhu • Estonia.... 16 L7
Mui Wo • Hong Kong, China.. 107 H5
Muiden • Netherlands.... 80 C2
Muiderslot • Netherlands.... 80 C2
Muir, John, Nat. Hist. Site **Park** • CA, United States.... 120 [48]
Muir Woods Nat. Mon. **Park** • CA, United States.... 120 [43]
Muirfield • United Kingdom.... 74 B4
Muite • Mozambique.... 24 F2
Muizenberg • South Africa.... 100 C5
Mujeres, I. • Mexico.... 123 E6
Muji • China.... 28 C1
Muka Head • Penang, Malaysia.. 108 C1
Mukacevo • Ukraine.... 14 J1
Mukacevo • Ukraine.... 13 L9
Mukah • Malaysia.... 32 E2
Mukalla, Al • Yemen.... 18 E7
Mukawwar • Sudan.... 21 G3
Mukdahan • Thailand.... 31 C3
Mukha, Al • Yemen.... 18 D7
Mukinbudin • WA, Australia.... 34 C6
Mula • Spain.... 11 J6
Mulaku Atoll • Maldives.... 106 E3
Mulan • China.... 27 K7
Mulanje Mtns • Malawi.... 24 F3
Mulde • Germany.... 8 H5
Mulgrave I. • Australia.... 32 (1) F4
Mulhacén • Spain.... 86 B3
Mülheim an der Ruhr • Germany.. 81 E1
Mulhouse • France.... 10 M6
Mull • United Kingdom.... 6 G5
Mullaghareirk Mtns • Ireland.. 79 F6
Mullaghmore **Beach** • Ireland.. 68 [45]
Mullaittivu • Sri Lanka.... 106 D11
Mullet Peninsula • Ireland.... 79 F1
Mullewa • WA, Australia.... 34 C5
Müllheim • Germany.... 9 C9
Mullingar • Ireland.... 7 E8
Mullsjö • Sweden.... 95 F3
Mulobezi • Zambia.... 102 J1
Mulranny **Beach** • Ireland.. 68 [44]
Multan • Pakistan.... 28 B2
Multan • Pakistan.... 28 B2
Mumbué • Angola.... 24 B2
Mummelsee • Germany.... 82 G6
Mun • Thailand.... 109 F2
Mun, Ko • Thailand.... 109 K2
Muna • Russian Fed.... 27 P4
Muna • Indonesia.... 32 (1) B3
Munabao • India.... 18 J4
Münchberg • Germany.... 9 G6
München • Germany.... 82 J3
Muncie • IN, United States.... 41 I3
Munda • Solomon Is.... 35 (1) F2
Mundaring • WA, Australia.... 34 C6
Munden • Germany.... 8 E5
Mundesley **Beach** • United Kingdom.... 75 [44]
Mundiwindi • WA, Australia.... 34 D4
Mundo Nôvo • Brazil.... 44 H1
Munellës • Albania.... 15 B2
Mungbere • Dem. Rep. of Congo.. 23 D3
Müngstener Brücke • Germany.. 81 E4
Munhango • Angola.... 23 B6
Munich • Germany.... 82 J3
Munapa • Spain.... 11 K3
Munifah • Saudi Arabia.... 18 E4
Munkedal • Sweden.... 95 F2
Munku Sardyk, gora • Mongolia/Russian Fed.... 27 F6
Munnar • India.... 106 D10
Munster • Ireland.... 7 C9
Münster • Germany.... 8 C5
Münsterland • Germany.... 8 C5
Muntenia • Romania.... 97 D1
Muntii Apuseni • Romania.... 14 J3
Muntok • Indonesia.... 32 D3
Munyati • Zimbabwe.... 102 J1
Münzenberg • Germany.... 82 G2
Muojärvi • Finland.... 16 O3
Muong Sen • Vietnam.... 31 C3
Muonio • Finland.... 16 L3
Muonio älv • Sweden.... 16 L2
Muonionjoki • Finland.... 16 L2
Muqdisho • Somalia.... 23 H3
Mur • Austria.... 13 D10
Mur, la • France.... 10 K9
Mura • Croatia.... 13 F11
Murad, Gunong • Malaysia.. 32 F2
Muranga • Kenya.... 101 G3
Murashi • Russian Fed.... 17 H3
Murat • Turkey.... 18 D2
Murat Dagi • Turkey.... 15 K5
Murati • Turkey.... 15 I2
Muratpasa **Beach** • Turkey.. 69 [200]
Murau • Austria.... 14 B2
Murchison Falls • Uganda.... 23 E3
Murchison • WA, Australia.... 34 C5
Murchison, Mt • New Zealand.. 35 C6
Murcia • Spain.... 87 C3
Murcia [Adm] • Spain.... 11 J7
Müreffe • Turkey.... 15 I3
Mures • Romania.... 14 K4
Muret • France.... 10 L10
Murg • Germany.... 9 D8
Murgab • Turkmenistan.... 18 H2
Murgab • Tajikistan.... 18 J2
Murgon • QL, Australia.... 111 F6
Müritz • Germany.... 8 H3
Müritz, Nationalpark **Park** • Germany.... 72 [60]
Murlaé • Brazil.... 127 C2
Murmansk • Russian Fed.... 17 E1
Murmashi • Russian Fed.... 17 E1
Murnau • Germany.... 82 J7
Murnau **Spa** • Germany.. 83 [250]
Muro **Beach** • Majorca, Spain.. 68 [100]
Muro • Majorca, Spain.... 87 F2
Murom • Russian Fed.... 17 G3
Muroran • Japan.... 30 K3
Muros • Spain.... 11 B2
Muros **Beach** • Spain.. 68 [73]
Muroto y Nova, Ria de • Spain.. 11 B2
Muroto-Zaki • Japan.... 30 G7
Murray • Australia.... 33 H6
Murray **Beach** • Australia.... 34 F8
Murray, Lake • Papua New Guinea 32 (1) F4
Murraysburg • South Africa.... 100 C3
Mürren **Ski** • Switzerland.. 70 [96]
Mürren • Switzerland.... 88 G2
Murrisk **Beach** • Ireland.. 68 [44]
Murrisk • Ireland.... 79 F1
Murrumbidgee • NS, Australia.. 111 G1
Murten • Switzerland.... 89 G2
Murtensee • Switzerland.... 89 G2
Murter • Croatia.... 93 G2
Murtosa **Beach** • Portugal.. 68 [77]
Murupara • New Zealand.... 112 K2
Muruoa • French Polynesia.. 33 N8

Murwara • India.... 105 C7
Murwillumbah • NS, Australia.. 111 F6
Murzuq • Libya.... 21 B2
Mürzzuschlag • Austria.... 13 E10
Mus • Turkey.... 18 D2
Mus-Haya • Russian Fed.... 27 N4
Musala • Lithuania.... 13 N1
Musala • Bulgaria.... 110 B4
Musala • Indonesia.... 110 C5
Musan • D.P.R. of Korea.... 30 E3
Muscadet • France.... 84 B1
Muscat • Oman.... 18 G5
Muscatine • IA, United States.. 41 H3
Musgrave • QL, Australia.... 34 H2
Musgrave Ranges • SA, Australia.. 112 H3
Mushie • Dem. Rep. of Congo.. 23 B4
Muskegon • MI, United States.. 41 I3
Muskö • Sweden.... 95 D4
Muskö [I.] • Sweden.... 95 D4
Musoma • Tanzania.... 102 H1
Musselshell • MT, United States.. 38 J7
Mussende • Angola.... 23 B6
Mustafa Kemalpasa • Turkey.. 15 J3
Müstair **Heritage C** • Switzerland.... 64 [104]
Müstair • Switzerland.... 89 G4
Mustvee • Estonia.... 16 N7
Musu-dan • D.P.R. of Korea.... 30 E4
Mut • Turkey.... 15 O7
Mut • Egypt.... 101 F3
Mutaf, Ra's al • Iran.... 18 F4
Mutare • Zimbabwe.... 102 J4
Muting • Indonesia.... 32 (1) F4
Mutirikwi, Lake • Zimbabwe.. 102 J4
Mutis, Gunung • Indonesia.. 32 (1) B4
Mutoko • Zimbabwe.... 24 E3
Mutoray • Russian Fed.... 26 R5
Mutsamudu • Comoros.... 24 G2
Mutshatsha • Dem. Rep. of Congo 24 C1
Mutsu • Japan.... 30 K4
Mutsu-Wan • Japan.... 30 K4
Mutters • Austria.... 89 H6
Muwayh, Al • Saudi Arabia.. 21 H3
Muyinga • Burundi.... 23 E4
Muynak • Uzbekistan.... 26 I9
Muyun Kum • Kazakhstan.... 26 L9
Muzaffarnagar • India.... 105 C3
Muzaffarpur • India.... 105 C8
Muzhi • Russian Fed.... 26 J4
Muztag • China.... 26 N10
Muztag • China.... 26 R5
Muztagh • China.... 102 J4
Mvuma • Zimbabwe.... 102 J4
Mwabvi Game Reserve **Park** • Malawi.... 103 [102]
Mwanza • Tanzania.... 102 H1
Mwaya • Tanzania.... 102 H3
Mwea Game Reserve • Kenya.. 101 G4
Mweelrea • Ireland.... 79 F3
Mweka • Dem. Rep. of Congo.. 23 C4
Mwene-Ditu • Dem. Rep. of Congo.. 23 C5
Mwense • Zambia.... 23 D6
Mweru, Lake • Dem. Rep. of Congo/Zambia.. 23 D5
Mwinilunga • Zambia.... 24 C2
Mwnt **Beach** • United Kingdom.. 75 [171]
My Tho • Vietnam.... 108 B3
Myakit • Russian Fed.... 27 P4
Myakka River State Park • FL, United States.... 119 M5
Myako-Retto • Japan.... 29 H6
Myanaung • Myanmar.... 31 B3
Myanmar • Asia.... 31 B2
Mycene • Greece.... 15 D6
Myingyan • Myanmar.... 31 B4
Myinmoletkat Taung • Myanmar 31 B4
Myitkyina • Myanmar.... 31 B1
Mymensingh • Bangladesh.... 28 E4
Myra • Turkey.... 93 G3
Myrdal • Norway.... 94 C4
Myrdalsjökull • Iceland.. 16 (1) D3
Myre • Norway.... 16 H2
Myrtle Beach • SC, United States.... 41 K5
Mys Shmidta • Russian Fed.... 27 V3
Mysen • Norway.... 94 B4
Mysil • Turkey.... 15 I4
Myslenice • Poland.... 13 I8
Mysore • India.... 106 D6
Mystic • CT, United States.. 118 H2
Myszków • Poland.... 13 I7
Myszyniec • Poland.... 13 K4
Mytishchi • Russian Fed.... 97 E4
Myvatn • Iceland.. 16 (1) E2
Mze • Czech Rep.... 96 C1

N'Djamena • Chad.... 21 B5
Na Cailíghe, Sliabh • Ireland.... 79 E1
Na Pali Coast State Park • HI, United States.... 119 L2
Na Phra Lan, Laem • Ko Samui, Thailand.. 109 J1
Naab • Germany.... 9 H7
Naalehu • HI, United States.. 119 L8
Naantali • Finland.... 95 E3
Naarden • Netherlands.... 80 C2
Naas • Ireland.... 79 E3
Nabadid • Somalia.... 21 H6
Naberezhnyye Chelny • Russian Fed.... 17 I3
Nabeul • Tunisia.... 101 E2
Nabi Shu'ayb • Yemen.... 25 F8
Nabi Shu'ayb, Jabal an • Yemen.. 21 H4
Nabire • Indonesia.. 32 (1) E3
Nablus • Jordan.... 98 A6
Nacala • Mozambique.... 24 F2
Nachingwea • Tanzania.... 102 H4
Nachod • Czech Rep.... 13 F7
Nadiad • India.... 28 F6
Nacka • Sweden.... 95 D4
Nacogdoches • TX, United States.. 119 N4
Nädendal • Finland.... 95 E3
Nadiad • India.... 28 B4
Nador • Morocco.... 101 D2
Nadur • Malta.... 93 H1
Nadvoitsy • Russian Fed.... 17 F2
Nadym • Russian Fed.... 26 L4
Nadym [Riv] • Russian Fed.... 26 L5
Næstved **Beach** • Denmark.. 68 [18]
Næstved • Denmark.... 95 F14
Náfpaktos **Beach** • Greece.. 69 [153]
Náfplio • Greece.... 15 C5
Náfplio **Beach** • Greece.. 69 [161]
Nafud, An • Saudi Arabia.... 18 D4
Nafusah, Jabal • Libya.... 21 B1
Nag's Head • St Kitts & Nevis.. 125 G4
Naga • Philippines.... 31 G4
Naga Hills • India.... 105 A2
Nagaland • India.... 28 F3
Nagaland • India.... 28 C5
Nandi • Fiji.. 35 (2) D2
Nagaoka • Japan.... 30 J6

Nagappattinam • India.... 106 D11
Nagar Haveli • India.... 28 B4
Nagarhole Nat. Park • India.. 106 D6
Nagarjuna Sagar • India.... 106 D3
Nagarjunakona • India.... 106 D3
Nagasaki • Japan.... 30 E8
Nagato • Japan.... 30 F7
Nagaur • India.... 28 B3
Nagda • India.... 105 C5
Nagercoil • India.... 106 D14
Nagina • India.... 105 C3
Nago • Japan.... 29 H5
Nagold • Germany.... 82 G6
Nagornyy • Russian Fed.... 27 J5
Nagoya • Japan.... 30 I7
Nagpur • India.... 28 C4
Nagqu • China.... 28 F2
Nagruawahia • New Zealand.. 112 K1
Nags Head • NC, United States.. 118 H5
Nagy-Milic • Slovak Rep.... 14 I1
Nagyatád • Hungary.... 13 G11
Nagykálló • Hungary.... 13 K10
Nagykanizsa • Hungary.... 13 G11
Nagykáta • Hungary.... 13 I10
Nagykörös • Hungary.... 13 I10
Naha • Japan.... 29 H5
Nahariyya • Israel.... 98 A1
Nahe • Germany.... 9 C7
Nahr Ouassei • Algeria.... 11 N9
Nai Harn Beach • Phuket, Thailand.... 109 K2
Nai Yang • Phuket, Thailand.. 109 I3
Nai Yang Beach • Phuket, Thailand.... 109 K1
Nailsworth • United Kingdom.. 74 D3
Naiman • India.... 105 C3
Naimisharanya • India.... 105 C3
Nain • NF, Canada.... 39 S5
Naintal • India.... 105 C3
Nairobi **Beach** • United Kingdom.. 75 [3]
Nairobi • Kenya.... 101 G3
Nairobi Nat. Park • Kenya.... 101 G4
Nairobi Nat. Park **Park** • Kenya.. 103 [83]
Najaf, An • Iraq.... 18 D3
Najd • Saudi Arabia.... 21 H2
Najin • D.P.R. of Korea.... 30 F3
Najrán • Saudi Arabia.... 18 D6
Naka Noi, Ko • Thailand.... 109 K1
Naka Yai, Ko • Thailand.... 109 K1
Naka-No • Japan.... 30 G6
Nakaina Mtns • Papua New Guinea 35 (1) E1
Nakajo • Japan.... 30 J5
Nakamura • Japan.... 30 G8
Nakasongola • Uganda.... 23 E3
Nakatchafushi • Maldives.. 106 E2
Nakatsu • Japan.... 30 F8
Nakatsugawa • Japan.... 30 I7
Nakhichen • Iran.... 18 E2
Nakhodka • Russian Fed.... 27 L8
Nakhon Nayok • Thailand.... 109 H2
Nakhon Pathom • Thailand.. 109 H1
Nakhon Phanom • Thailand.. 31 C3
Nakhon Ratchasima • Thailand.. 31 C3
Nakhon Sawan • Thailand.... 31 C3
Nakhon Si Thammarat • Thailand.. 31 C5
Nakina • OT, Canada.... 39 N6
Nakiska **Ski** • AL, Canada.. 116 [15]
Nakło • Poland.... 13 G4
Nakonde • Zambia.... 24 E1
Naksskov **Beach** • Denmark.. 68 [18]
Naksskov • Denmark.... 95 F14
Naktong • Rep. of Korea.... 30 E7
Nakuru • Kenya.... 101 G3
Nal • Pakistan.... 18 I4
Nalayha • Mongolia.... 27 G6
Nalchik • Russian Fed.... 17 G6
Nalgonda • India.... 106 D3
Nallamalla Range • India.... 106 D3
Nallıhan • Turkey.... 15 M3
Nalón • Spain.... 11 F1
Nalut • Libya.... 21 B1
Nam Cat Tien Nat. Park • Vietnam.... 108 B2
Nam Co • China.... 28 C2
Nam Dinh • Vietnam.... 31 D2
Nam Tok Surin Nat. Park • Thailand.... 109 G1
Nam Wu Wu • Phuket, Thailand.. 109 K1
Namakwaland • South Africa.. 24 B6
Namangan • Uzbekistan.... 18 I2
Namatanai • Papua New Guinea.. 35 (1) E1
Namatjira Mem. • NT, Australia.. 112 H2
Namber • Indonesia.. 32 (1) D3
Nambour • QL, Australia.... 111 F6
Namdalen • Norway.... 16 G4
Nämdö • Sweden.... 95 D4
Nametil • Mozambique.... 24 F2
Namib Desert • Namibia.... 24 A3
Namib-Naukluft Nat. Park **Park** • Namibia.... 103 [116]
Namibe • Angola.... 24 A3
Namibia • Africa.... 24 B4
Namja Namse La Shankou • China/Nepal.... 28 D2
Namkham • Myanmar.... 31 B2
Namlea • Indonesia.. 32 (1) C3
Namous • Algeria.... 20 E2
Nampo • D.P.R. of Korea.... 30 C5
Nampa • ID, United States.... 117 E4
Nampula • Mozambique.... 24 F2
Namrud • Syria.... 98 A2
Namsen • Norway.... 16 F4
Namsos • Norway.... 16 F4
Namuang Falls • Ko Samui, Thailand.... 109 J2
Namuli, Serra • Mozambique.. 24 F3
Namur • Belgium.... 80 A15
Namur [Adm] • Belgium.... 80 A15
Namur, Rep. of Korea.... 30 D7
Namyslow • Poland.... 13 H6
Nan • Thailand.... 109 G2
Nan Hai • China.... 29 F6
Nan Hulsan Hu • China.... 28 G1
Nan Jing • China.... 107 J1
Nan Ling • China.... 29 E5
Nan [Riv] • Thailand.... 109 G2
Nanaimo • BC, Canada.... 122 C3
Nanam • D.P.R. of Korea.... 30 E4
Nanango • QL, Australia.... 111 F6
Nanao • Japan.... 30 I6
Nanchang • China.... 29 F5
Nanchong • China.... 29 D4
Nancowry • India.... 28 F7
Nancy • France.... 10 L5
Nancy **Heritage C** • France.. 64 [51]
Nancy Sound • New Zealand.. 112 L1
Nanda • India.... 28 A3
Nanded • India.... 28 C5
Nandi • Fiji.. 35 (2) D2
Nandikanima Pass • India.. 106 D3

Nandyal • India.... 106 D3
Nanfen • China.... 30 B4
Nanga Parbat • Jammu & Kashmir.. 28 B1
Nangapinoh • Indonesia.... 32 E3
Nangatayap • Indonesia.... 32 E3
Nangis • France.... 85 E4
Nangnim • D.P.R. of Korea.... 30 D4
Nangnim-Sanmaek • D.P.R. of Korea.... 30 D4
Nanhui • China.... 107 J4
Nanning • China.... 29 D6
Nankoku • Japan.... 30 G8
Nanling • China.... 107 J3
Nannup • WA, Australia.... 34 C6
Nanpan Jiang • China.... 29 C6
Nanping • China.... 29 F5
Nanqiao • China.... 107 J4
Nansei-Shoto • Japan.... 31 H1
Nansha • China.... 107 H2
Nansha Qundao • South China Sea.. 31 E5
Nanshan • Shenzhen, China.. 107 H3
Nantais, Lac • QU, Canada.... 39 O4
Nantes • France.... 84 D1
Nanton Point • Antigua & Barbuda.. 125 F4
Nantong • China.... 107 J2
Nantucket • MA, United States.. 58 A2
Nantucket I. • MA, United States.... 118 H2
Nanumea • Tuvalu.... 33 I6
Nanuque • Brazil.... 44 H2
Nanus Fort • Goa, India.... 105 B1
Nanwei Dao • South China Sea.. 31 E5
Nanyandang Shan • China.... 29 G5
Nanyang • China.... 29 E4
Nanyo • Japan.... 30 K5
Nanyuki • Kenya.... 101 G1
Nao, Cabo de la • Spain.... 87 C2
Naococane, Lac • QU, Canada.. 39 O6
Náoussa • Greece.... 15 D3
Napa Valley • CA, United States.. 117 F3
Napata • Sudan.... 21 F4
Naphtali • Israel/Lebanon.... 98 A2
Napier • New Zealand.... 112 K4
Naples **Heritage C** • Italy.. 64 [127]
Naples • Italy.... 91 G3
Naples • FL, United States.. 119 M7
Napo • Peru.... 43 C4
Napoléon, Route • France.... 85 H1
Nápoli **Heritage C** • Italy.. 64 [127]
Nápoli • Italy.... 91 G3
Nápoli, Golfo di • Italy.... 91 G3
Napoule-Plage, la • France.. 95 H4
Nar'yan Mar • Russian Fed.... 17 I1
Nara • Japan.... 30 I2
Nara • Mali.... 22 C1
Nara • Pakistan.... 28 A3
Nara • India.... 105 C3
Naracoorte **Heritage N** • SA, Australia.... 61 [133]
Narberth • United Kingdom.. 74 D3
Narbonne **Beach** • France.. 68 [112]
Narca, Punta da • Angola.... 22 G6
Narcondam • India.... 28 F6
Nardò • Italy.... 12 M8
Nares Strait • Canada/Greenland.. 39 V1
Narew • Poland.... 13 K4
Narin Gol • China.... 28 G2
Narithiwat • Thailand.... 109 F4
Nariva Swamp • Trinidad & Tobago.. 125 K4
Narmada • India.... 28 C4
Narnaul • India.... 105 C2
Narni • Italy.... 12 G6
Naro • Sicily, Italy.... 90 D3
Narodnaya, gora • Russian Fed.. 17 J1
Narrabri • NS, Australia.... 111 G1
Narrandera • NS, Australia.. 111 G1
Narrogin • WA, Australia.... 34 C6
Narromine • NS, Australia.... 34 I6
Narrows, The • St Kitts & Nevis.. 125 G4
Narsarsuaq • Greenland.... 39 V4
Narsimhapur • India.... 28 C4
Narva • Estonia.... 16 N7
Narva • Norway.... 94 C4
Narym • Russian Fed.... 26 N6
Naryn • Kazakhstan.... 26 M9
Naryn [Riv] • Kazakhstan/Uzbekistan.. 26 M9
Naryn • Kyrgyzstan.... 26 M9
Näsåker • Sweden.... 16 I5
Nasalot Game Reserve • Kenya 101 G1
Naseby • United Kingdom.. 71 A7
Nashoba Valley **Ski** • MA, United States.... 116 [194]
Nashua • NH, United States.. 118 G3
Nashville • TN, United States.. 41 I4
Nasice • Croatia.... 12 M3
Näsijärvi • Finland.... 95 E2
Nasir • India.... 28 B4
Nasir • Sudan.... 23 E2
Nasiriyah, An • Iraq.... 18 E3
Nass • BC, Canada.... 38 F5
Nassau • Cook Is.... 33 K7
Nassau • Bahamas.... 124 B3
Nasser, Lake • Egypt.... 101 F5
Nässjö • Sweden.... 95 F7
Nata [Riv] • Botswana/Zimbabwe.. 24 D3
Natal • Brazil.... 45 (1) D3
Natal • Indonesia.... 110 B4
Natal • QU, Canada.... 123 O2
Natashquan [Riv] • QU, Canada.. 39 S6
Natchez • MS, United States.. 119 O4
Natchez Nat. Hist. Park **Park** • MS, United States.... 121 [199]
Natchez Trace Parkway • United States.... 118 K2
Natchez Trace Parkway **Park** • United States.... 121 [201]
Natchitoches • LA, United States.... 118 K1
Nathdwara • India.... 105 C5
Nathon • Ko Samui, Thailand.. 109 J1
National Agricultural Centre • United Kingdom.... 74 D3
National Birds of Prey Centre • United Kingdom.... 74 D3
National Capital parks **Park** • DC, United States.... 121 [290]
National Exhibition Centre • United Kingdom.... 74 D3
National Mall **Park** • DC, United States.... 121 [291]
National Park • New Zealand.. 112 K3
National Stadium • Singapore.. 108 E4
National Theatre • Myanmar.... 31 B4
Natividade • Brazil.... 43 H6
Natori • Japan.... 30 K5
Natron, Lake • Tanzania.... 102 H2
Nattawasaga Bay • OT, Canada.. 123 B5
Natuna Besar • Indonesia.... 32 D2
Natuna Is. • Indonesia.... 31 D6
Natuna, Kepulauan • Indonesia 110 A2

Natural Bridges Nat. Mon. **Park** • UT, United States.... 120 [85]
Naturaliste, Cape • WA, Australia.... 34 C6
Nature's Valley • South Africa.. 100 C7
Nauders • Austria.... 89 H6
Nauen • Germany.... 81 F1
Naujoji-Akmene • Lithuania.. 13 L1
Naukluft Mtns • Namibia.... 24 B4
Naul • Ireland.... 79 E2
Naumburg • Germany.... 9 G5
Naumburg **Spa** • Germany.. 83 [223]
Nauplia • Greece.... 71 A20
Nauru • Pacific Ocean.... 33 H6
Nauta • Peru.... 43 C4
Navahermosa • Spain.... 11 G5
Navajo Indian Reservation • AZ/NM, United States.... 118 J2
Navajo Nat. Mon. • AZ, United States.... 118 J1
Navajo Nat. Mon. **Park** • AZ, United States.... 120 [102]
Navajo Reservoir • CO/NM, United States.... 118 J2
Navalmoral de la Mata • Spain.. 11 F5
Navan • Ireland.... 79 E1
Navarin, mys • Russian Fed.. 27 U4
Navarino • Greece.... 71 A20
Navarino, I. • Chile.... 45 C7
Navarra • Spain.... 11 J2
Navasota • TX, United States.. 119 N4
Navian, Pointe • New Caledonia.. 35 (2) A3
Navoi • Uzbekistan.... 18 I1
Navrongo • Ghana.... 22 D2
Nawabshah • Pakistan.... 28 A3
Nawalgarh • India.... 105 C2
Nawiliwili • HI, United States.. 119 L2
Náxos **Beach** • Greece.. 69 [183]
Náxos • Greece.... 92 D8
Náxos • Greece.... 92 D8
Náxos [I.] • Greece.... 92 D8
Náxos [I.] • Greece.... 92 D8
Nayarit • Mexico.... 37 (1) A1
Nayoro • Japan.... 30 L2
Nazaré • Portugal.... 11 B5
Nazaré • Brazil.... 44 I1
Nazaré **Beach** • Portugal.. 68 [79]
Nazareth • Israel.... 98 A4
Nazarovo • Russian Fed.... 26 Q6
Nazca **Heritage C** • Peru.. 62 [52]
Nazca • Peru.... 127 B1
Nazca Lines • Peru.... 127 B1
Naze • Japan.... 29 H5
Nazili • Turkey.... 15 I5
Nazimovo • Russian Fed.... 26 P6
Naznan • Russian Fed.... 17 G6
Nazret • Ethiopia.... 23 F2
Nazwa • Oman.... 18 G5
Nchelenge • Zambia.... 23 D5
Ndalatando • Angola.... 23 B5
Ndali • Benin.... 22 E3
Ndélé • Central African Rep.... 23 C2
Ndendé, Réserve de **Park** • Gabon 103 [52]
Ndere I. Nat. Park • Kenya.... 101 G3
Ndola • Zambia.... 24 D2
Ndrhamcha, Sebkha du • Mauritania.... 20 B5
Nduindui • Solomon Is.. 35 (1) F2
Ndumo Game Reserve **Park** • South Africa.... 103 [125]
Né • Norway.... 16 F5
Néa Artáki • Greece.... 15 E5
Néa Fókea **Beach** • Greece.. 69 [169]
Néa Kalikrátia • Greece.... 92 D4
Néa Kidonia **Beach** • Crete, Greece.... 69 [188]
Néa Mihaniona **Beach** • Greece.. 69 [168]
Néa Moni • Greece.... 92 D4
Néa Moni • Greece.... 92 D4
Nea Póri **Beach** • Greece.. 69 [167]
Néa Róda **Beach** • Greece.. 69 [169]
Néa Skióni **Beach** • Greece.. 69 [169]
Néa Stira • Greece.... 92 D4
Néa Stira • Greece.... 92 D4
Néa Zihni • Greece.... 15 E2
Neagh, Lough • United Kingdom.. 7 F7
Neale, Lake • NT, Australia.... 112 H3
Neander tal • Germany.... 81 E3
Néapoli • Macedonia, Greece.. 15 C3
Néapoli • Pelopónnisos, Greece.. 15 E7
Néapoli • Crete, Greece.... 93 F7
Neapolitan Riviera • Italy.... 91 G4
Neath • United Kingdom.... 7 I10
Nebbio • Corsica, France.... 85 L2
Nebbou • Burkina Faso.... 20 E6
Nebel **Spa** • Germany.. 83 [8]
Nebit-Dag • Turkmenistan.... 18 F2
Neblina • Brazil/Venezuela.... 43 D3
Nebo • QU, Canada.... 41 I3
Nebo, Mount • Jordan.... 98 A8
Nebraska • United States.... 38 H4
Nebrodi • Sicily, Italy.... 12 I11
Necessity, Fort, Nat. Battlefield **Park** • PA, United States.... 121 [301]
Nechako • BC, Canada.... 122 C1
Neches • TX, United States.. 119 N4
Neckar • Germany.... 8 D8
Neckargemünd • Germany.... 5 I5
Neckarsulm • Germany.... 9 E7
Necochea • Argentina.... 127 D3
Neder-Rijn • Netherlands.... 5 I3
Nedong • China.... 28 E3
Nedstrand • Norway.... 94 C5
Needham's Point • Barbados.. 125 H3
Needles • CA, United States.. 117 F6
Needles, The • United Kingdom.. 5 B4
Nefedova • Russian Fed.... 26 L6
Neftegorsk • Russian Fed.... 17 I3
Nefta • Tunisia.... 101 E3
Neftekamsk • Russian Fed.... 17 I3
Nefteyugansk • Russian Fed.... 26 L5
Nefza • Tunisia.... 12 D12
Negage • Angola.... 23 B5
Negara • Bali, Indonesia.... 110 C1
Negele • Ethiopia.... 23 F2
Negeri Sembilan • Malaysia.. 31 C6
Negev • Israel.... 21 F1
Negombo • Sri Lanka.... 106 D15
Negra • Peru.... 43 A5
Negra, Punta • Peru.... 43 A5
Negra, Cape • Myanmar.... 31 C2
Negreira • Spain.... 11 C2
Negril • Jamaica.... 124 C2
Negro • Brazil.... 43 E4
Negro • Uruguay.... 45 C4
Negro • Argentina.... 45 D4
Negroponte • Greece.... 15 [?]
Negros • Philippines.... 31 G4
Negru Voda • Romania.... 14 I4
Negru • Peru.... 43 A5
Nehe • China.... 29 F2
Neheim-Hüsten • Germany.. 8 C5
Nei Mongol Zizhiqu • China.. 29 E2
Neiderau **Ski** • Austria.. 70 [147]

Neidpath Castle • United Kingdom.. 74 B4
Neijiang • China.... 29 D5
Neiva • Colombia.... 43 F2
Nekemt • Ethiopia.... 23 F2
Nekheb • Egypt.... 101 F5
Nekso • Denmark.... 95 F16
Nelidovo • Russian Fed.... 97 E3
Nellore • India.... 106 D7
Nelma • Russian Fed.... 27 M7
Nelson • New Zealand.... 35 D5
Nelson • BC, Canada.... 38 H7
Nelson • MN, Canada.... 38 L5
Nelson, Cape • VI, Australia.. 34 H7
Nelson Museum • St Kitts & Nevis.... 125 G4
Nelson's Dockyard • Antigua & Barbuda.... 125 F4
Nelspoort • South Africa.... 100 C3
Nelspruit • South Africa.... 24 E5
Néma • Mauritania.... 20 D5
Neman • Russian Fed.... 13 K2
Neman [Riv] • Belarus.. 13 M10
Nembrala • Indonesia.. 32 (1) B5
Neméa • Greece.... 15 D6
Neméa [Adm] • Greece.... 15 D6
Nëmërçkë • Albania.... 15 B3
Nemi, Lagi di • Italy.... 91 F3
Nemrut Dag **Heritage C** • Turkey.. 64 [195]
Nemunas • Lithuania.... 13 L2
Nemuro • Japan.... 30 M3
Nen Jiang • China.... 27 K6
Nenagh • Ireland.... 79 F6
Nenana • AK, United States.. 38 B4
Nendaz **Ski** • Switzerland.. 70 [80]
Nene • United Kingdom.... 7 M9
Nenjiang • China.... 27 K7
Néo Itilo **Beach** • Greece.. 69 [159]
Neohóri **Beach** • Greece.. 69 [177]
Néos Marmarás **Beach** • Greece.. 69 [169]
Néos Marmarás • Greece.... 92 D1
Néos Marmarás • Greece.... 92 D1
Nepal • Asia.... 28 D3
Nepalganj • Nepal.... 28 D3
Nephi • UT, United States.... 40 D4
Nephin Beg Range • Ireland.. 79 F1
Neport **Beach** • CA, United States.... 40 C5
Neptun-Olimp • Romania.... 97 D2
Nera • Italy.... 91 F1
Nerántza **Beach** • Greece.. 69 [155]
Neratovice • Czech Rep.... 13 D7
Neretva • Bosnia-Herz.... 12 L5
Neringa • Lithuania.... 13 J2
Nerja **Beach** • Spain.. 68 [97]
Nerja • Spain.... 86 B7
Nerpio • Spain.... 11 E7
Nerva • Spain.... 86 A5
Nesbyen • Norway.... 94 C4
Nesebur **Heritage C** • Bulgaria.. 64 [171]
Nesebur **Beach** • Bulgaria.. 69 [211]
Nesebur • Bulgaria.... 97 D3
Nesselwang • Germany.... 82 J6
Neßmersiel **Spa** • Germany.. 83 [44]
Nesterov • Russian Fed.... 13 L3
Nesterov • Ukraine.... 13 N8
Nesterov • Norway.... 95 F2
Nesttun • Norway.... 94 C3
Nesvizh • Belarus.. 16 N10
Netanya • Israel.... 98 A3
Netherlands • Europe.... 5 I4
Netherlands Antilles • West Indies.... 37 H5
Neto • Italy.... 12 K9
Nette • Germany.... 82 H1
Nettling Lake • NU, Canada.. 39 Q3
Nettuno • Italy.... 91 F3
Nettuno, Grotta di • Sardinia, Italy.... 90 C1
Neu-Anspach • Germany.... 82 H2
Neu-Ulm • Germany.... 82 J1
Neubrandenburg • Germany.. 8 I3
Neuburg • Germany.... 9 G8
Neuchâtel • Switzerland.... 89 G1
Neuchâtel, Lac de • Switzerland.. 89 G1
Neuendorf **Spa** • Germany.. 83 [278]
Neuenhagen bei Berlin • Germany.. 81 F2
Neufchâteau • France.... 10 K5
Neufchâteau • Belgium.... 80 A19
Neufchâtel-en-Bray • France.. 10 G4
Neuharlingersiel **Spa** • Germany.. 83 [46]
Neuhaus **Spa** • Germany.. 83 [55]
Neuhof • Germany.... 9 E6
Neukirchen • Germany.... 81 E1
Neukirchen **Spa** • Germany.. 83 [132]
Neuleiningen • Germany.... 82 G4
Neumagen-Dhron • Germany.. 82 H3
Neumarkt in der Oberpfalz • Germany.... 9 G7
Neumarkt-St Veit • Germany.. 82 J4
Neumarkter Sattel • Austria.. 14 B2
Neumünster • Germany.... 8 E2
Neunkirchen • Germany.... 82 G3
Neunkirchen • Austria.... 13 F10
Neuquén • Argentina.... 45 C3
Neuruppin • Germany.... 8 H3
Neuschwanstein • Germany.. 82 J6
Neusiedler See • Austria.... 13 F10
Neusiedler See • Austria.... 81 E3
Neustadt **Spa** • Germany.. 83 [26]
Neustadt an der Aisch • Germany.. 9 F7
Neustadt an der Weinstraße • Germany.... 82 G4
Neustadt bei Coburg • Germany.. 9 G6
Neustadt in Holstein • Germany.. 8 F2
Neustift • Austria.... 89 H6
Neustift im Stubaital **Ski** • Austria.... 70 [140]
Neustrelitz • Germany.... 8 I3
Neuwied • Germany.... 82 H1
Nevada • United States.... 117 F4
Nevada City • CA, United States.. 117 F3
Nevada, Sierra • United States.. 38 F4
Nevada, Sierra • Colombia.... 43 F1
Nevada, Sierra • Spain.... 86 B3
Nevada, Sierra Nat. Park • CA, United States.... 117 F3
Nevado • Colombia.... 43 C3
Neve, Serra da • Angola.... 24 A2
Nevel • Russian Fed.... 17 D3

Nevers • France 10 I7
Nevesinje • Bosnia-Herz. 14 F6
Neviges • Germany 81 E2
Néville-sur-Mer Beach • France ....68 [58]
Nevinnomyssk • Russian Fed. 17 G6
Nevis • St Kitts & Nevis 125 G4
Nevis, Ben • United Kingdom 6 H5
Nevis, Ben • St Kitts & Nevis 125 G4
Nevyansk • Russian Fed. 26 J6
New Amsterdam • Suriname 43 F2
New Bedford • MA, United States 118 H4
New Bern • NC, United States 118 H5
New Braunfels •
  TX, United States 119 N3
New Brighton • New Zealand 35 D6
New Britain • Papua New Guinea 35 (1) E2
New Brunswick • Canada 123 D2
New Caledonia • Pacific Ocean 35 (2) B3
New Castle • DE, United States 118 H3
New Delhi • India 105 C2
New Forest • United Kingdom 5 B4
New Georgia • Solomon Is. 35 (1) F2
New Georgia Sound • Solomon Is. 35 (1) F2
New Glasgow • NS, Canada 123 D7
New Guinea • Oceania 35 (1) G2
New Hampshire • United States 118 G3
New Hanover • Papua New Guinea 35 (1) E1
New Haven • CT, United States 118 H2
New Hazleton • BC, Canada 122 C1
New Hebrides • Vanuatu 35 (2) B2
New Iberia • LA, United States 118 H4
New Ireland • Papua New Guinea 35 (1) E1
New Jersey • United States 118 H1
New London • CT, United States 118 H2
New Mexico • United States 8 F5
New Norfolk • TAS, Australia 34 I8
New Orleans • LA, United States 118 H4
New Orleans Jazz Nat. Hist. Park •
  LA, United States ....121 [197]
New Paltz • NY, United States 118 H1
New Plymouth • New Zealand 112 K3
New Providence • Bahamas 124 B3
New Quay Beach •
  United Kingdom ....75 [178-180]
New Ross • Ireland 7 F9
New Siberian Is. • Russian Fed. 27 N1
New South Wales • NS, Australia 34 I6
New Territories •
  Hong Kong, China 107 H5
New Ulm • MN, United States 41 H3
New Valley, The • Egypt 101 F3
New Westminster • BC, Canada 38 G7
New York • NY, United States 118 H2
New York [Adm] • United States 41 K3
New Zealand • Oceania 35
Newark • NJ, United States 118 H1
Newark-on-Trent •
  United Kingdom 7 L8
Newborough Beach •
  United Kingdom ....75 [201]
Newbury • United Kingdom 7 K10
Newcastle • United Kingdom 7 G7
Newcastle • South Africa 24 E5
Newcastle • WY, United States 40 F3
Newcastle • NS, Australia 111 G4
Newcastle • NB, Canada 123 D2
Newcastle • Jamaica 124 C4
Newcastle • St Kitts & Nevis 125 G4
Newcastle Creek • NT, Australia 34 F3
Newcastle under Lyme •
  United Kingdom 7 J8
Newcastle upon Tyne •
  United Kingdom 7 K7
Newcastle West • Ireland 79 F6
Newfield • Antigua & Barbuda 125 F4
Newfoundland • NF, Canada 123 D3
Newfoundland & Labrador •
  Canada 39 T6
Newgale Beach • United Kingdom ....75 [164]
Newgrange • Ireland 79 E2
Newhaven • United Kingdom 74 E3
Newman • WA, Australia 34 C4
Newmarket • United Kingdom 7 M9
Newmarket • Ireland 79 F6
Newmarket • OT, Canada 39 N6
Newmarket on Fergus • Ireland 79 F6
Newnham • Isle of Wight, UK 7 K11
Newport • Wales, UK 74 D3
Newport • Ireland 79 F1
Newport • OR, United States 117 E3
Newport • VT, United States 118 G1
Newport Beach •
  CA, United States 40 C5
Newport News •
  VA, United States 118 H5
Newport Sands Beach •
  United Kingdom ....75 [169]
Newquay • United Kingdom 74 F4
Newry • United Kingdom 7 F7
Newton • KS, United States 41 G4
Newton Abbot • United Kingdom 74 F5
Newton Ground •
  St Kitts & Nevis 125 G1
Newtontoppen • Svalbard 46 N2
Newtown • United Kingdom 7 I9
Newtownabbey • United Kingdom 7 G7
Newtownards • United Kingdom 7 G7
Neya • Russian Fed. 17 G3
Neyshabur • Iran 18 E2
Neyveli • India 106 D11
Nez Perce Nat. Hist. Park •
  ID, United States 117 C2
Nez Perce Nat. Hist. Park •
  ID, United States ....120 [66]
Nga, Laem • Phuket, Thailand 109 K2
Ngabé • Congo 22 H5
Ngami, Lake • Botswana 24 C4
Ngamiland • Botswana 24 C3
Ngangerabeli Plain • Kenya 23 G4
Ngangla Ringco • China 28 D2
Nganglong Kangri • China 28 D2
Nganze Co • China 28 E2
Ngaoundéré • Cameroon 22 G3
Ngaruroro • New Zealand 112 K4
Ngauruhoe, Mt • New Zealand 112 K4
Ngo • Congo 22 H5
Ngoan Muc Pass • Vietnam 108 B2
Ngoc Linh • Vietnam 25 L8
Ngoko • Cameroon/Congo 23 B3
Ngola Shankou • China 29 B3
Ngoma • Zambia 24 D3
Ngoring Hu • China 29 B3
Ngorongoro Conservation Area Heritage N •
  Tanzania ....61 [91]
Ngorongoro Conservation Area •
  Tanzania 102 H2
Ngorongoro Conservation Area Park •
  Tanzania ....103 [89]
Ngorongoro Crater • Tanzania 102 H2
Ngounie • Gabon 22 G3
Ngounie • Niger 20 H6
Nguigmi • Niger 20 H6
Ngum, Ko • Thailand 109 K1
Nguni • Kenya 23 F4
Ngurah Rai [Apt] •
  Bali, Indonesia 110 C4
Nguru • Nigeria 22 H2
Nha Trang • Vietnam 108 B2
Nhulunbuy • NT, Australia 34 G2

Nia-Nia • Dem. Rep. of Congo 23 D3
Niafounké • Mali 20 E5
Niagara Falls •
  NY, United States 122 B9
Niagara Falls • OT, Canada 122 B9
Niagara Falls [Waterfall] •
  Canada/United States 122 B9
Niah • Malaysia 32 E2
Niamey • Niger 20 F6
Niangara • Dem. Rep. of Congo 23 D3
Niangay, Lac • Mali 20 E5
Niangoloko • Burkina Faso 22 D2
Nianzishan • China 29 B3
Nibe • Denmark 95 F5
Nicaragua • C. America 37 D5
Nicaragua, Lago de • Nicaragua 37 D5
Nice • France 85 H2
Nice-Côte d'Azur [Apt] • France 85 H2
Nichicun, Lac • QU, Canada 39 G6
Nicholls Town • Bahamas 124 B1
Nicholson • WA, Australia 34 E3
Nicobar Is. • India 28 F7
Nicosia • Cyprus 93 J2
Nidda • Germany 5 M4
Nidda • Germany 9 E6
Nidda [Riv] • Germany 9 E6
Nideggen • Germany 82 G1
Niedersächsisches Wattenmeer,
  Nationalpark Park • Germany ....72 [55]
Nidri • Greece 92 C1
Nidri • Greece 92 C1
Nidzica • Poland 13 J4
Nieblum Spa • Germany ....83 [4]
Niebüll • Germany 8 D2
Niecka Sieradzka • Poland 13 H6
Nied • France 5 J5
Niederau • Austria 89 H3
Niederbayern • Germany 9 H8
Niederdorf Ski • Italy ....70 [238]
Niederlausitz • Germany 81 D2
Niederösterreich • Austria 13 E10
Niederrachsen • Germany 8 E4
Nienburg • Germany 8 E4
Nienhagen Spa • Germany ....83 [270]
Niers • Germany 5 J3
Niesky • Germany 81 D2
Nieuw Amsterdam • Suriname 43 F2
Nieuwpoort • Belgium 80 B1
Nieuwpoort-aan-Zee • Belgium 80 B1
Nieves, Pico de las •
  Gran Canaria, Canary Is. 86 E4
Niger • Africa 20 G5
Niger [Adm] • Africa 22 F3
Niger Delta • Nigeria 22 F3
Niger [Riv] • Africa 22 D1
Nigrán Beach • Spain ....68 [74]
Nigrita • Greece 14 K9
Niigata • Japan 30 J7
Niigata • Japan 30 J6
Niihama • Japan 30 G8
Niihau • HI, United States 119 L2
Niimi • Japan 30 G7
Nijar Beach • Spain ....68 [99]
Nijar • Spain 86 B4
Nijmegen • Netherlands 80 A11
Nika • Maldives 106 E1
Nikel' • Russian Fed. 17 E1
Nikitas Beach • Greece ....69 [169]
Nikitas • Greece 92 D1
Nikitas • Greece 92 D1
Nikolayev • Ukraine 22 E5
Nikolayevsk-na-Amure •
  Russian Fed. 27 N6
Nikolsk • Russian Fed. 17 H3
Nikopol • Ukraine 17 E5
Nikópoli • Greece 15 B4
Niksic • F.R. of Yugoslavia 14 F7
Nil, Bahr el • Africa 21 F6
Nilanda Atoll North • Maldives 106 E1
Nilanda Atoll South • Maldives 106 E3
Nilaveli • Sri Lanka 106 D11
Nile • Africa 21 F2
Nile Delta • Egypt 101 F1
Nile [Riv] • India 106 D10
Nilgiri Hills • India 106 C10
Nilometer • Egypt 101 F5
Nilüfer • Turkey 15 J3
Nimba, Mts • Africa 22 C3
Nimba, Réserve du Monts Heritage N •
  Côte d'Ivoire/Guinea ....61 [73]
Nimba, Mts • Côte d'Ivoire/Guinea 22 C3
Nîmes • France 10 J10
Nin • Croatia 12 J4
Nine Degree Channel •
  Indian Ocean 106 D9
Ninety Mile Beach • New Zealand 35 D2
Ninety Mile Beach •
  VI, United States 111 G3
Ninety Six Nat. Hist. Site Park •
  SC, United States ....121 [240]
Nineveh • Iraq 18 D2
Ning Zhen Shan • China 107 J11
Ningbo • China 107 J4
Ningde • China 29 F5
Ningguo • China 107 J3
Ninghai • China 107 J4
Ningjing Shan • China 28 E2
Ningjing Shan • China 29 E3
Ningwu • China 29 E3
Ningxia Huizu Zizhiqu • China 29 D3
Ninh Hoa • Vietnam 108 B2
Ninigo Group • Papua New Guinea 35 (1) C1
Niobrara • NE/WY, United States 38 K8
Niokolo Koba, Parc nat. de Park •
  Senegal ....103 [10]
Niokolo Koba, Parc du Heritage N •
  Senegal ....61 [72]
Niolo • Corsica, France 85 L1
Nioro du Sahel • Mali 20 D5
Nioro du Sahel • Mali 84 D3
Niort • France 10 F8
Nipigon, Lake • OT, Canada 39 N7
Nipissing, Lake • OT, Canada 122 D7
Niquelândia • Brazil 44 G1
Niquero • Cuba 124 D7
Nirmal • India 28 C5
Nis • F.R. of Yugoslavia 14 H7
Nisab • Yemen 18 E7
Nisava • F.R. of Yugoslavia 14 H7
Nisbet Plantation Inn •
  St Kitts & Nevis 125 G4
Niscemi • Sicily, Italy 12 I11
Nishi-No • Japan 30 G6
Nishino'omote • Japan 30 G8
Nisiporeni • Moldova 14 P2
Nisko • Poland 13 L7
Nissáki • Corfu, Greece 92 B5
Nissan • Sweden 94 C5
Nissedal • Norway 94 C6
Nisser • Norway 92 D8
Nissiros • Greece 92 D8
Nissum Bredning • Denmark 95 F5
Nissum Fjord • Denmark 95 F5
Niterói • Brazil 127 C4
Nith • United Kingdom 7 I6
Nithavris • Crete, Greece 15 K5
Nitra • Slovak Rep. 13 H9
Nitra [Riv] • Slovak Rep. 13 H9
Nitray [Château] • France 84 D2
Nittedal • Norway 94 B2
Niuafo'ou • Tonga 35 (2) E2
Niuatoputapu • Tonga 35 (2) E2

Niue • Pacific Ocean 35 (2) G2
Niut, Gunung • Indonesia 32 D2
Nivala • Finland 16 M5
Nivelles • Belgium 80 A14
Nivernais • France 10 I6
Niya • China 28 D1
Nizamabad • India 28 C5
Nizhneangarsk • Russian Fed. 27 G5
Nizhnekamsk • Russian Fed. 17 I3
Nizhneudinsk • Russian Fed. 26 F6
Nizhnevartovsk • Russian Fed. 26 M5
Nizhneyansk • Russian Fed. 27 M2
Nizhniy Novgorod • Russian Fed. 17 G3
Nizhniy Tagil • Russian Fed. 26 I6
Nizhnyaya Pesha • Russian Fed. 17 H1
Nizhnyaya Tunguska •
  Russian Fed. 26 P5
Nizina • Slovak Rep. 14 L2
Nizina Podlaska • Poland 13 L4
Nizke Tatry • Slovak Rep 13 I9
Nízke Tatry Nat. Park Park •
  Slovak Rep. ....72 [101]
Njandoma • Russian Fed. 17 G2
Njavve • Sweden 16 J3
Njombe • Tanzania 102 H3
Njudung • Sweden 95 F8
Njunes • Norway 16 J2
Nkayi • Congo 23 A4
Nkongsamba • Cameroon 22 F4
Nkululu • Tanzania 23 E5
No Name City • Germany 82 J3
Noatak Nat. Preserve Park •
  AK, United States ....120 [2]
Nobeoka • Japan 30 F8
Noce • Italy 90 B3
Nockberge, Nationalpark Park •
  Austria ....72 [83]
Noën • Mongolia 29 C2
Nogales • AZ, United States 118 J3
Nogent-le-Rotrou • France 84 D2
Noginsk • Siberia, Russian Fed. 26 P5
Noginsk • Moscow, Russian Fed. 97 E4
Nogliki • Russian Fed. 27 N6
Nogoa • QL, Australia 111 F3
Nogoyá • Argentina 44 E5
Nogueira, Serra da • Portugal 11 E3
Nohfelden • Germany 5 K5
Noia • Spain 11 C2
Noirmoutier, I. de • France 10 C7
Noirmoutier-en-l'Ile Beach •
  France ....68 [64]
Noja Beach • Spain ....68 [70]
Nok Kundi • Pakistan 18 H4
Nokaneng • Botswana 24 C3
Nokhra • India 105 C1
Nokia • Finland 95 E2
Nola • Central African Rep. 23 B3
Nola • Italy 91 G1
Nola • Italy 91 G1
Nolinsk • Russian Fed. 17 H3
Noman Haven Beach •
  United Kingdom ....75 [163]
Nomad • Papua New Guinea 35 (1) C2
Nome • AK, United States 40 (2) E2
Nomuka Group • Tonga 35 (2) F3
Non, Val di • Italy 90 B3
Nonacho Lake • NT, Canada 38 J4
Nong Khai • Thailand 31 C3
Nong Nooch Garden • Thailand 109 H4
Nonnweiler Spa • Germany ....83 [168]
Nonsuch Bay • Antigua & Barbuda 125 F4
Nonthaburi • Thailand 109 H1
Noord-Beveland • Netherlands 80 A10
Noord-Brabant • Netherlands 80 A11
Noord-Holland • Netherlands 80 A7
Noordoostpolder • Netherlands 80 A7
Noordwijk Beach • Netherlands ....68 [49]
Noordwijk • Netherlands 80 C1
Noordzee Kanaal • Netherlands 80 C2
Noormarkku • Finland 95 E1
Noosa Heads • QL, Australia 111 F6
Nora • Sardinia, Italy 90 B7
Nora • QU, Canada 39 P7
Nordborg • Sweden 95 D1
Nord, I. du • Seychelles 106 F2
Nord-Ostsee-Kanal • Germany 81 A1
Nord-Pas de Calais • France 10 H4
Nord-Trøndelag • Norway 94 B3
Nordaustlandet • Svalbard 46 V2
Nordborg Beach • Denmark ....68 [26]
Nordborg • Denmark 95 F9
Nordby • Denmark 95 F9
Norddeich Spa • Germany ....83 [3]
Norddorf Spa • Germany ....83 [43]
Norden • Germany 8 C4
Norden Spa • Germany ....83 [43]
Nordenham • Germany 8 E3
Nordenskjöld [Base] •
  Antarctica 46 (1) D2
Norderney • Germany 8 C3
Norderney Spa • Germany ....83 [38]
Norderstedt • Germany 81 E1
Nordeste Beach • Azores ....68 [87]
Nordeste • Azores 86 G8
Nordfjord • Norway 94 C1
Nordfjordeid • Norway 94 C1
Nordfriesische Inseln • Germany 8 D2
Nordfriesland • Germany 81 A1
Nordfrisiska Öarna •
  Denmark/Germany 16 E9
Nordhausen • Germany 81 C2
Nordhorn • Germany 8 C4
Nordic Mtn Ski •
  WI, United States ....116 [121]
Nordjylland • Denmark 95 F5
Nordkapp • Norway 16 N1
Nordkapp • Norway 16 N1
Nordkinn-Halvøya • Norway 16 N1
Nordkjosbotn • Norway 16 J2
Nordland • Norway 16 G3
Nördlingen • Germany 9 F8
Nordrhein-Westfalen • Germany 8 C5
Nordstrand • Germany 8 D2
Nordstrand Spa • Germany ....83 [6]
Nore • Norway 94 B1
Nore og Uvdal • Norway 94 B1
Norefjell • Norway 94 B1
Noresund • Norway 94 B1
Norfolk • United Kingdom 7 M9
Norfolk • Australia 33 H8
Norfolk • NE, United States 41 G3
Norfolk • VA, United States 118 H5
Norfolk I. • Pacific Ocean 33 H8
Norg • Netherlands 80 A8
Norge • Europe 16 G3
Norheimsund • Norway 94 A1
Norias • Greece 92 D8
Norilsk • Russian Fed. 26 O4
Noril'sk • Russian Fed. 26 O4
Norman • OK, United States 41 G4
Norman Wells • NT, Canada 38 F3
Normanby • Papua New Guinea 35 (1) E2
Normandie • France 10 E5
Normandie, Collines de • France 10 E5
Normanton • QL, Australia 34 H3
Norra Kvarken • Finland/Sweden 16 K5
Norra Storfjället • Sweden 16 H4
Norrbotten • Sweden 16 K3
Nørre Djurs Beach • Denmark ....68 [28]
Nørre Nebel • Denmark 95 F9
Nørre Snede • Denmark 95 F9
Nørre Vorupør • Denmark 95 F5
Nørresundby • Denmark 95 F5
Norrhult • Sweden 95 F8
Norrköping • Sweden 94 B5

Norrland Riviera • Sweden 94 A5
Norrtälje • Sweden 34 D6
Norseman • WA, Australia 34 D6
Norsjö • Norway 94 B3
Norsjö • Sweden 16 J4
Norsk • Russian Fed. 27 L6
Norsoup • Vanuatu 35 (2) B2
Norte, Cabo • Brazil 43 G3
Norte, Punta • Argentina 45 D4
North Andaman • India 28 F6
North Arm • NT, Canada 38 I4
North Ayrshire • United Kingdom 74 B3
North Belcher Is. • NU, Canada 39 P5
North Bay • OT, Canada 122 B1
North Berwick • United Kingdom 74 B4
North Cape • Norway 16 M1
North Cape • New Zealand 35 D2
North Cape • NS, Canada 123 D3
North Cape cruise area • Norway 39 M6
North Carolina • United States 41 K4
North Cascades Nat. Park •
  WA, United States 117 E1
North Cascades Nat. Park Park •
  WA, United States ....120 [26]
North Channel • United Kingdom 7 G7
North Channel • OT, Canada 39 O7
North Conway •
  United States 118 G3
North Dakota • United States 40 F2
North Downs • United Kingdom 74 E3
North East Lincolnshire •
  United Kingdom 75 A4
North Foreland • United Kingdom 7 N10
North Frisian Is. •
  St Kitts & Nevis 125 G2
North Geomagnetic Pole •
  Greenland 46 V2
North I. • New Zealand 35 E4
North Kitui Game Reserve •
  Kenya 101 G4
North Land • Russian Fed. 97 A5
North Lincolnshire •
  United Kingdom 75 A4
North Luangwa Nat. Park Park •
  Zambia ....103 [103]
North Magnetic Pole • Canada 46 Z2
North Negril Point • Jamaica 124 C1
North Ossetia • Russian Fed. 26 S3
North Platte •
  NE, United States 40 F3
North Point • Seychelles 106 F2
North Point • Barbados 125 H1
North Rona • United Kingdom 6 G2
North Ronaldsay •
  United Kingdom 75 A7
North Saskatchewan • AL, Canada 38 I6
North Sea • Europe 4 K6
North Sentinel • India 28 F6
North Siberian Lowlands •
  Russian Fed. 97 A5
North Stradbroke I. •
  QL, Australia 111 F6
North Sydney • NS, Canada 123 D8
North Uist • United Kingdom 6 G4
North West • South Africa 24 D5
North West Cape • WA, Australia 34 B4
North York Moors Nat. Park Park •
  United Kingdom ....72 [45]
North York Moors Nat. Park •
  United Kingdom 75 A3
Northam • WA, Australia 34 C6
Northampton • United Kingdom 7 L9
Northampton • WA, Australia 34 B5
Northamptonshire •
  United Kingdom 75 A5
Northeast Aegean Is. • Greece 92 D5
Northeast Aegean Is. • Greece 92 D5
Northeast Passage cruise area •
  N. America 58 A2
Northeim • Germany 8 F5
Northern Cape • South Africa 24 C6
Northern Capitals cruise area •
  Europe 59 A4
Northern Hills • Thailand 109 F1
Northern Indian Lake •
  MN, Canada 38 L5
Northern Ireland •
  United Kingdom 7 F7
Northern Mariana Is. •
  Pacific Ocean 33 F4
Northern Province •
  South Africa 24 D4
Northern Range •
  Trinidad & Tobago 125 K1
Northern Territory • Australia 34 F3
Northfield • MN, United States 41 H3
Northland • New Zealand 112 J2
Northstar-at-Tahoe Ski •
  United States ....116 [52]
Northumberland • United Kingdom 75 A3
Northumberland Is. •
  QL, Australia 111 F4
Northumberland Nat. Park Park •
  United Kingdom ....72 [42]
Northumberland Nat. Park •
  United Kingdom 75 A3
Northumbria • United Kingdom 75 A3
Northway • AK, United States 38 C4
Northwest Territories • Canada 38 F4
Norton Sound •
  AK, United States 40 (2) E2
Norway • Europe 16 G3
Norwegian Fjords cruise area •
  Norway 59 A4
Norwegian Sea • Europe 4 K3
Norwich • United Kingdom 7 N9
Norwich • OT, United States 118 H2
Noshiro • Japan 30 J4
Nosratabad • Iran 18 G4
Nossa Senhora das Candeias •
  Brazil 44 I1
Nossebro • Sweden 95 F3
Nossob • Africa 24 B4
Nostalgia Town • QL, Australia 111 F6
Nostra Señora de Guadelupe •
  Portugal 88 E5
Nosy Bé • Madagascar 24 H2
Nosy Ste Marie • Madagascar 24 H3
Notec • Poland 13 F5
Noto • Sicily, Italy 12 I12
Noto • Japan 30 I6
Noto [Adm] • Japan 30 I6
Noto, Golfo di • Sicily, Italy 90 D4
Noto, Val di • Sicily, Italy 12 I12
Notoden • Norway 94 B3
Notre-Dame Bay • NF, Canada 123 D3
Notre-Dame-des-Landes • France ....70 [22]
Notre-Dame-de-Bellecombe Ski •
  France ....70 [22]
Nottaway • QU, Canada 39 P6
Nottekanal • Germany 82 F5
Nottingham • United Kingdom 7 K9
Nottingham I. • NU, Canada 39 P4
Nottinghamshire •
  United Kingdom 75 A4

Nouadhibou • Mauritania 20 B4
Nouadhibou, Dakhet • Mauritania 20 B4
Nouadhibou, Ras • Mauritania 20 B4
Nouakchott • Mauritania 20 B5
Nouamrhar • Mauritania 20 B5
Nouméa • New Caledonia 35 (2) B3
Nouna • Burkina Faso 22 D2
Nouvelle Caledonie •
  Pacific Ocean 35 (2) A3
Nouvelle France, Cap de •
  QU, Canada 39 Q4
Nouvelles Hébrides • Vanuatu 35 (2) B2
Nouzha, El [Apt] • Egypt 101 F1
Nova Friburgo • Brazil 127 C4
Nova Gaia • Angola 23 B6
Nova Iguaçu • Brazil 127 C3
Nova Lamego • Guinea-Bissau 22 B2
Nova Levante • Italy 90 B3
Nova Lima • Brazil 127 C1
Nova Lisboa • Angola 24 B2
Nova Mambone • Mozambique 24 E4
Nova Scotia • Canada 123 D7
Nova Zagora • Bulgaria 97 D3
Novara • Italy 91 E6
Novaya Sibir, Ostrov •
  Russian Fed. 27 O1
Novaya Zemlya • Russian Fed. 26 H3
Nové Zámky • Slovak Rep. 13 H10
Novelda • Spain 87 C1
Novgorod Heritage C •
  Russian Fed. ....64 [206]
Novgorod • Russian Fed. 97 E1
Novi Ligure • Italy 12 C4
Novi Pazar • Russian Fed. 14 H6
Novi Pazar • Bulgaria 97 D3
Novi Sad • F.R. of Yugoslavia 14 G4
Novo Gradiska • Croatia 12 B3
Nôvo Hamburgo • Brazil 44 F4
Nôvo Mesto • Slovenia 13 G9
Novo Mesto • Slovenia 14 C4
Novo Orjahovo • Bulgaria 97 D4
Novocherkassk • Russian Fed. 17 G5
Novodvinsk • Russian Fed. 17 G2
Novojoa • Mexico 40 E6
Novokhalinsk • Russian Fed. 29 I1
Novokuybyshev • Russian Fed. 17 H4
Novokuznetsk • Russian Fed. 26 O7
Novolazarevskaya [Base] •
  Antarctica 46 (1) G2
Novomoskovsk • Russian Fed. 17 F4
Novomoskovsk • Ukraine 17 F5
Novorossiysk • Russian Fed. 17 F5
Novorybnoye • Russian Fed. 26 S3
Novosaya • Russian Fed. 17 I1
Novoshakhtinsk • Russian Fed. 17 F5
Novosibirskoye Ostrova •
  Russian Fed. 27 N1
Novosibirsk • Russian Fed. 26 N7
Novotroitsk • Russian Fed. 17 I4
Novouzensk • Russian Fed. 26 P6
Novovoronezh • Ukraine 13 N1
Novoyeniseysk • Russian Fed. 26 P6
Novoyerudinsky • Russian Fed. 26 P6
Novozybkov • Russian Fed. 17 G2
Novvy Port • Russian Fed. 26 L4
Novyy Uzen • Kazakhstan 26 S8
Novyy Vasyugan • Russian Fed. 26 M6
Nowa Ruda • Poland 13 F6
Nowa Sól • Poland 13 E6
Nowgong • India 105 C2
Nowgaard • Poland 13 E4
Nowra • NS, Australia 111 G2
Nowy Dwór Mazowiecki • Poland 13 J5
Nowy Sacz • Poland 13 J8
Nowy Targ • Poland 13 I8
Noyon • France 10 H4
Nsukka • Nigeria 22 F3
Ntem •
  Cameroon/Equatorial Guinea 22 G4
Nu Jiang • China 28 F2
Nub's Nob Ski •
  MI, United States ....116 [130]
Nubah, Jibal an • Sudan 21 F5
Nubian Desert • Sudan 21 F3
Nubiyah, As Sahra an • Sudan 21 F3
Nudow • Germany 82 F5
Nueces • TX, United States 119 N5
Nuellin Lake • NU, Canada 38 L4
Nueva Gerona • Cuba 124 C1
Nueva Palmira • Uruguay 127 C5
Nueva San Salvador •
  El Salvador 37 D5
Nueve (9) de Julio • Argentina 127 D3
Nuevitas • Cuba 124 D3
Nuevo Casas Grandes • Mexico 40 E5
Nuevo, Golfo • Argentina 45 D4
Nuevo Laredo • Mexico 37 B2
Nuevo Leon • Mexico 37 A2
Nuevo Mundo, Cerro • Bolivia 44 C3
Nuevo Rocafuerte • Ecuador 43 B4
Nuevo Rosita • Mexico 37 A2
Nugal • Somalia 23 H2
Nugget Point • New Zealand 35 B8
Nugssuaq • Greenland 39 U2
Nuhud, An • Sudan 21 E5
Nui Ba Den • Vietnam 108 B2
Nui Sam • Vietnam 108 B3
Nui'u'Erhu Shan • China 29 F2
Nukhaylak • Sudan 21 E4
Nuku Hiva • French Polynesia 33 M6
Nuku'alofa • Tonga 35 (2) E3
Nukunonu • Tokelau 33 J6
Nukus • Uzbekistan 18 G1
Nullagine • WA, Australia 34 C6
Nullarbor • SA, Australia 34 F6
Nullarbor Plain •
  SA/WA, Australia 34 E6
Numan • Nigeria 22 G3
Numancia • Philippines 31 H4
Numazu • Japan 30 J7
Nümbrecht Spa • Germany ....83 [114]
Numedal • Norway 94 B1
Numedalslågen • Norway 94 B1
Numfoor • Indonesia 35 (1) A1
Nummela • Finland 95 E4
Nunavut • Canada 38 L3
Nuneaton • United Kingdom 7 K9
Nungan • WA, Australia 34 C6
Nungnain Sum • China 27 I7
Nungo • Mozambique 24 F2
Nunivak I. • AK, United States 40 (2) C3
Nuoro • Sardinia, Italy 90 C2
Nuqui • Colombia 43 B2
Nura • Kazakhstan 26 I7
Nuraghe Santu Antine •
  Sardinia, Italy 12 B8
Nure • Italy 82 H1
Nurek • Tajikistan 26 I8
Nuri • Sudan 21 F4
Nuristan • Afghanistan 18 I3
Nürnberg • Germany 9 G8
Nurra, la • Sardinia, Italy 90 C1
Nusa Barung • Indonesia 110 C4
Nusa Dua • Bali, Indonesia 110 C4
Nusa Dua Beach •
  Bali, Indonesia 110 C4
Nusa Penida • Indonesia 110 C4
Nusa Tenggara • Indonesia 25 N10
Nusa Tenggara Barat • Indonesia 110 A4
Nusa Tenggara Timur • Indonesia 110 A4
Nutak • NF, Canada 39 S5
Nuthe • Germany 81 D2

Nuuk • Greenland 39 U4
Nuwara Eliya • Sri Lanka 106 D15
Nuweiba • Egypt 101 F2
Nuweveldberge • South Africa 100 C2
Nyainqentanglha Feng • China 28 E2
Nyainqentanglha Shan • China 28 F2
Nyaka • Zimbabwe 102 J1
Nyala • Sudan 21 E5
Nyali • Kenya 101 G5
Nyalam • China 28 D2
Nyamandhlovu • Kenya 101 G3
Nyamanett • Sudan 23 D2
Nyampanda • Zimbabwe 102 J2
Nyanga • Congo/Gabon 22 G5
Nyanga Nat. Park • Zimbabwe 102 J2
Nyangani • Zimbabwe 102 J2
Nyanza-Lac • Burundi 23 D4
Nyborg • Denmark 95 F14
Nybro • Sweden 95 F8
Nyda • Russian Fed. 26 L4
Nydala • Sweden 95 F7
Nyeri • Kenya 101 G3
Nyika Nat. Park • Malawi ....103 [96]
Nyíregyháza • Hungary 13 K10
Nyírség • Hungary 14 L2
Nyiru • Kenya 23 F3
Nykarleby • Finland 16 L5
Nykøbing • Sjælland, Denmark 95 F14
Nykøbing • Falster, Denmark 95 F10
Nykøbing • Mors, Denmark 95 F5
Nykøbing Rørvig Beach • Denmark ....68 [24]
Nyköping • Sweden 95 B3
Nynäshamn • Sweden 95 B3
Nyngan • NS, Australia 34 I6
Nyon • Switzerland 89 G5
Nyong • Cameroon 22 G4
Nyrud • Norway 16 O2
Nysa • Poland 13 G6
Nysa • Russian Fed. 27 N6
Nyslott • Finland 16 O6
Nystad • Finland 95 E3
Nysted • Denmark 95 F14
Nyudo-Zaki • Japan 30 J5
Nyurba • Russian Fed. 27 I4
Nyuya • Russian Fed. 27 H4
Nzega • Tanzania 102 H1
Nzérékoré • Côte d'Ivoire 22 C3
Nzeto • Angola 23 A5
Nzi • Côte d'Ivoire 22 D3
Nzilo, Barrage de •
  Dem. Rep. of Congo 24 D2

O • Sea of Japan, Japan 30 J4
O • Izu-Shoto, Japan 30 J7
O Grove Beach • Spain ....68 [74]
O'Neill, Eugene, Nat. Hist. Site Park •
  CA, United States ....120 [49]
Oahe, Lake • SD, United States 40 F2
Oahu • HI, United States 119 L5
Oak Harbor • WA, United States 40 B2
Oak Ridge • TN, United States 41 J4
Oakland • CA, United States 117 E3
Oakley • KS, United States 40 F4
Oakura • New Zealand 112 K3
Oakwood Adventure Park •
  United Kingdom ....73 [31]
Oamaru • New Zealand 35 C7
Oaro • New Zealand 35 D6
Oasis de Nazaret •
  Lanzarote, Canary Is. 87 E3
Oaxaca Heritage C • Mexico ....62 [24]
Oaxaca • Mexico 123 E4
Oaxaca • Mexico 26 K4
Ob Estuary • Russian Fed. 96 A3
Obala • Cameroon 22 G4
Obama • Japan 30 H5
Oban • United Kingdom 6 H5
Oban • New Zealand 35 B8
Oban Hills • Nigeria 22 F3
Obando • Colombia 43 D3
Ober Engadin • Switzerland 89 G8
Ober Gatlinburg Ski •
  TN, United States ....116 [150]
Oberá • Argentina 44 E4
Oberammergau • Germany 82 J6
Oberasbach • Germany 9 F7
Oberau • Germany 9 H3
Oberaula Spa • Germany ....83 [262]
Oberau • Austria 89 H3
Oberaudorf • Germany 82 J8
Oberbayern • Germany 9 G8
Obereggen Ski • Italy ....70 [214]
Oberegg • Italy 90 B3
Oberfranken • Germany 9 G6
Obergurgl Ski • Austria ....70 [185]
Obergurgl • Austria 89 H6
Oberharz Spa • Germany ....83 [79]
Oberhausen • Germany 81 E1
Oberhausen: Sterkrade • Germany 81 E1
Oberhof • Germany 9 F6
Oberjoch • Germany 82 G6
Oberkirch • Germany 82 G6
Oberlausitz • Germany 81 D2
Oberlech Ski • Austria ....70 [129]
Oberndorf • Germany 9 D8
Oberndorf • Austria 89 H4
Oberösterreich • Austria 13 D10
Oberpfalz • Germany 9 H7
Oberpfälzerwald • Germany 89 G3
Oberstaufen • Germany 82 G3
Oberstaufen Spa • Germany ....83 [240]
Oberstdorf Ski • Germany ....70 [2]
Oberstdorf • Germany 82 J5
Oberstdorf Spa • Germany ....83 [242]
Obertauern Ski • Austria ....70 [185]
Obertauern • Austria 89 H8
Obertauern • Austria 89 H4
Obervellach • Germany 82 H4
Oberwald • Switzerland 89 G8
Obi • Indonesia 32 (1) C3
Óbidos • Brazil 43 F4
Obihiro • Japan 30 L3
Obninsk • Russian Fed. 97 E4
Obo • Central African Rep. 23 C3
Obock • Djibouti 23 G1
Oborníki • Poland 13 F5
Obozerskiy • Russian Fed. 17 G2
Obskaya Guba • Russian Fed. 26 L4
Obzor • Bulgaria 97 D3
Oc, d' • France 84 B4
Ocala • FL, United States 119 M3
Ocaña • Spain 11 D3
Ocaña • Colombia 43 C2
Ocean City • MD, United States 118 H3
Ocean City • NJ, United States 118 H3
Ocean Falls • BC, Canada 38 F6
Ocean Hole • Bahamas 124 C2
Ocean I. • Kiribati 33 I6
Ocean Park • Hong Kong, China 107 H6
Ocean World Water Park •
  Thailand 109 H4
Oceanside • CA, United States 40 C5

Pahang [Riv] • Malaysia ... 32 C2
Paharpur Heritage C • Bangladesh ... 63 [132]
Pahiatua • New Zealand ... 35 E5
Pähnes • Crete, Greece ... 93 E5
Pai • Thailand ... 109 G1
Paia • Vanuatu ... 35 (2) B2
Paide • Estonia ... 16 M7
Paignton • United Kingdom ... 74 F5
Päijanne • Finland ... 95 E2
Paimpol • France ... 84 C2
Paine, Cerro • Chile ... 45 B6
Paine, Mt • Antarctica ... 46 (1) AA1
Painted Desert • AZ, United States ... 118 J1
País-Vasco • Spain ... 11 I1
Paisley • United Kingdom ... 74 B3
Paita • Peru ... 43 A5
Pajala • Sweden ... 16 L3
Pájara Beach • Fuerteventura, Canary Is. ... 68 [93]
Pájara • Fuerteventura, Canary Is. ... 87 E2
Pajarito Mtn Ski • NM, United States ... 116 [103]
Pajaten • Peru ... 43 B5
Pakch'on • D.P.R. of Korea ... 30 C4
Pakhachi • Russian Fed. ... 46 II3
Paki • Nigeria ... 20 G6
Pakistan • Asia ... 18 I4
Paklenica Nat. Park Park • Croatia ... 72 [110]
Pakokku • Myanmar ... 31 B2
Pakrac • Croatia ... 12 L3
Paks • Hungary ... 13 H11
Pakse • Laos ... 108 A2
Pakwach • Uganda ... 23 E3
Pala • Chad ... 23 A2
Palafrugell Beach • Spain ... 68 [106]
Palafrugell • Spain ... 87 D2
Palagruza • Croatia ... 14 D7
Palamau Nat. Park • India ... 105 C8
Palamós Beach • Spain ... 68 [106]
Palamós • Spain ... 87 D2
Palana • Russian Fed. ... 27 Q5
Palanga • Lithuania ... 13 J2
Palangkaraya • Indonesia ... 32 E3
Palani • India ... 106 D10
Palanpur • India ... 105 C5
Palapye • Botswana ... 24 D4
Palatka • FL, United States ... 119 M3
Palau • Pacific Ocean ... 33 E5
Palau • Sardinia, Italy ... 90 D2
Palauli • Western Samoa ... 35 (2) F1
Palawan • Philippines ... 31 F4
Paldiski • Estonia ... 16 M7
Palea Paphos • Cyprus ... 93 J3
Palékastro Beach • Crete, Greece ... 69 [191]
Palékastro • Crete, Greece ... 93 E8
Palembang • Indonesia ... 32 C3
Palencia • Spain ... 11 G3
Paléndria • Cyprus ... 93 J3
Palenque • Mexico ... 37 C4
Palenque Heritage C • Mexico ... 62 [25]
Paleo Faliro Beach • Greece ... 92 D7
Paleo Faliro • Greece ... 92 D7
Paleohóra Beach • Crete, Greece ... 69 [188]
Paleohóra • Crete, Greece ... 93 E5
Paleokastritsa • Corfu, Greece ... 92 B1
Paleokastritsa • Corfu, Greece ... 92 B1
Palermo • Sicily, Italy ... 90 D1
Páleros • Greece ... 92 C1
Páleros • Greece ... 92 C1
Palestine • TX, United States ... 119 N4
Palestrina • Italy ... 91 F4
Palghat • India ... 106 D10
Pali • India ... 105 C5
Palioúri Beach • Greece ... 92 D1
Palioúri • Greece ... 92 D1
Palisades • NJ/NY, United States ... 118 H1
Palisadoes • Jamaica ... 124 C4
Pak Bay • Sri Lanka ... 106 D11
Palk Strait • India/Sri Lanka ... 106 D11
Palkane • Finland ... 95 E2
Pallas-Ounastunturi Nat. Park Park • Finland ... 72 [28]
Pallasovka • Russian Fed. ... 17 H4
Palliser, Cape • New Zealand ... 35 E5
Palliser, Is. • French Polynesia ... 33 M7
Palm Beach • FL, United States ... 119 M6
Palm Springs • CA, United States ... 117 F6
Palm Valley • NT, Australia ... 112 H4
Palma • Mozambique ... 24 G2
Palma, Badia de • Majorca, Spain ... 87 H3
Palma de Mallorca Beach • Majorca, Spain ... 68 [109]
Palma de Mallorca • Majorca, Spain ... 87 H1
Palma del Rio • Spain ... 86 B2
Palma Nova • Majorca, Spain ... 87 H3
Palma, Playa de • Majorca, Spain ... 87 H3
Palma Soriano • Cuba ... 124 D8
Palma Sur • Costa Rica ... 43 A2
Palmanova • Italy ... 91 E4
Palmares • Brazil ... 45 (1) D3
Palmária, I. Heritage C • Italy ... 64 [119]
Palmarito • Venezuela ... 43 C2
Palmas, Cape • Liberia ... 22 C4
Pálmas, Golfo di • Sardinia, Italy ... 90 C3
Palmeira das Missões • Brazil ... 44 F4
Pálmela • Portugal ... 88 D2
Palmer Station [Base] • Antarctica ... 46 (1) II3
Palmerston • Cook Is. ... 33 K7
Palmerston • New Zealand ... 35 C7
Palmerston North • New Zealand ... 35 E5
Pálmi • Italy ... 12 J10
Palmira • Colombia ... 43 B3
Palmyra • Syria ... 18 J4
Palmyra Atoll • Pacific Ocean ... 33 K5
Palo Alto Battlefield Nat. Hist. Site Park • TX, United States ... 121 [142]
Paloh • Indonesia ... 32 D2
Palolem Beach • Goa, India ... 69 [189]
Palomani, Nevado • Bolivia/Peru ... 127 B2
Palopo • Indonesia ... 32 (1) B3
Palos, Cabo de • Spain ... 87 C3
Palpa • Peru ... 127 B1
Palpala • Argentina ... 44 C3
Palu • Indonesia ... 32 (1) A3
Palyavaam • Russian Fed. ... 27 T2
Pama • Burkina Faso ... 22 E2
Pamekasan • Indonesia ... 110 D4
Pameungpeuk • Java, Indonesia ... 110 D6
Pamiers • France ... 11 G10
Pamir • Tajikistan ... 18 J2
Pâmiut • Greenland ... 39 V4
Pamlico Sound • NC, United States ... 118 H5
Pampa • TX, United States ... 40 F4
Pampa Húmida • Argentina ... 127 D3
Pampas • Argentina ... 127 B3
Pampas • Peru ... 127 B1

Pamplona • Spain ... 11 J2
Pamplona • Colombia ... 43 C2
Pamporovo • Bulgaria ... 96 B2
Pampus • Netherlands ... 80 C2
Pamukkale • Turkey ... 92 D6
Pamukkale • Turkey ... 92 D6
Pamukova • Turkey ... 15 L3
Panagiá Beach • Greece ... 69 [171]
Panagyurishte • Bulgaria ... 15 F1
Panaitan • Indonesia ... 110 D1
Panaji • Goa, India ... 105 B1
Panajá Kerá • Crete, Greece ... 93 E8
Panaiánes, Canal des • Madagascar ... 24 H4
Panama • C. America ... 37 E6
Panama Canal • Panama ... 37 F6
Panama City • Panama ... 37 F6
Panama City Heritage C • Panama ... 62 [33]
Panama City • FL, United States ... 119 M2
Panamá, Golfo de • Panama ... 43 B2
Panamá, Istmo de • Panama ... 43 B2
Panao • Peru ... 43 B6
Panarea • Italy ... 12 J10
Panarea, I. • Italy ... 90 D2
Panaro • Italy ... 91 E7
Panay • Philippines ... 31 G4
Pancevo • F.R. of Yugoslavia ... 14 H5
Pancicav vrh • F.R. of Yugoslavia ... 14 H6
Pandan • Philippines ... 31 G4
Pandava Caves • Goa, India ... 105 B2
Pandean • Indonesia ... 110 C1
Pandeleimónas Beach • Greece ... 69 [167]
Pandharpur • India ... 28 C5
Pandheon • Greece ... 15 D4
Pando • Uruguay ... 44 E5
Pandrup Beach • Denmark ... 68 [29]
Panevezys • Lithuania ... 13 N2
Panfilov • Kazakhstan ... 26 M9
Pangani • Tanzania ... 23 F4
Pangandaran • Java, Indonesia ... 110 D6
Panggó • Greece ... 15 F3
Panggoe • Solomon Is. ... 35 (1) F2
Pangkalanbrandan • Indonesia ... 110 B1
Pangkalaseang, Tanjung • Indonesia ... 32 (1) B3
Pangkalpinang • Indonesia ... 32 D3
Pangkor • Malaysia ... 108 D1
Pangnirtung • NU, Canada ... 39 R3
Pangrango, Gunung • Indonesia ... 110 D1
Pangutaran Group • Philippines ... 32 (1) B1
Panhala • India ... 106 D1
Panié • New Caledonia ... 35 (2) A3
Panipat • India ... 105 C2
Panja • Afghanistan/Tajikistan ... 28 A1
Panjang • Indonesia ... 110 D1
Panmunjom • D.P.R. of Korea ... 30 D6
Panna • India ... 105 C7
Pannonhalma Heritage C • Hungary ... 64 [154]
Panorama • Brazil ... 44 F3
Panorama Ski • BC, Canada ... 116 [8]
Panoramapark Sauerland Park • Germany ... 73 [60]
Pánormos • Crete, Greece ... 93 E2
Panshan • China ... 30 B4
Pantai Aceh Forest Reserve • Penang, Malaysia ... 108 C1
Pantai Suluban • Bali, Indonesia ... 110 C4
Pantanal • Brazil ... 44 E2
Pantar • Indonesia ... 32 (1) B4
Pante Makassar • Indonesia ... 32 (1) B4
Pantelleria • Italy ... 12 G12
Pantoja • Peru ... 43 B4
Pánuco • Mexico ... 37 B3
Pánuco • Mexico ... 123 E2
Panug, Ko • Thailand ... 109 K1
Panyu • China ... 107 H1
Panzi • Dem. Rep. of Congo ... 22 H6
Paola • Italy ... 12 K9
Paola • Malta ... 93 H4
Paoli Peaks Ski • IN, United States ... 116 [145]
Pápa • Hungary ... 13 G10
Papago Indian Reservation • AZ, United States ... 118 J3
Papatowai • New Zealand ... 112 L4
Papeete • French Polynesia ... 33 M7
Papendorp • South Africa ... 100 C1
Papey • Iceland ... 16 (1) F2
Paphos Heritage C • Cyprus ... 64 [199]
Paphos Beach • Cyprus ... 69 [192]
Paphos • Cyprus ... 93 J3
Papija • Bulgaria ... 15 I1
Papineau-Labelle Prov. Reserve • QU, Canada ... 122 B3
Papua, Gulf of • Papua New Guinea ... 35 (1) C2
Papua New Guinea • Oceania ... 35 (1) C1
Papuk • Croatia ... 14 E4
Papun • Myanmar ... 109 G3
Papunya • NT, Australia ... 112 H1
Pará • Brazil ... 43 G4
Paraburdoo • WA, Australia ... 34 C4
Paracatu • Brazil ... 44 G2
Paracel Is. • South China Sea ... 107 G7
Paradise Bay • Antarctica ... 59 A10
Paradise Bay • Malta ... 93 H1
Paradise I. • Bahamas ... 124 B3
Paradise Sea-Side Resort • BC, Canada ... 122 C3
Paradísi [Apt] • Rhodes, Greece ... 93 F2
Paragould • AR, United States ... 41 H4
Paragua • Venezuela ... 43 E2
Paraguay • Bolivia ... 44 E1
Paraguarí • Paraguay ... 44 E4
Paraguay • S. America ... 44 E3
Paraguay [Riv] • S. America ... 44 E3
Paraíba • Brazil ... 45 (1) D3
Paraíba do Sul • Brazil ... 127 E4
Parainen • Finland ... 95 E3
Parakou • Benin ... 22 E3
Parálimni Beach • Cyprus ... 69 [195]
Parálimni • Cyprus ... 93 J4
Parálio Astros Beach • Greece ... 69 [160]
Paramaribo • Suriname ... 43 E2
Paramo Frontino • Colombia ... 43 B2
Paramount Canada's Wonderland • ON, Canada ... 122 B9
Paramount's Great America • CA, United States ... 117 F3
Paramount's Great America Park • CA, United States ... 120 [B]
Paramount's Kings Dominion • VA, United States ... 118 H3
Paramount's Kings Dominion Park • VA, United States ... 121 [HH]
Paramount's Kings I. Park • OH, United States ... 121 [V]
Paramushir, Ostrov • Russian Fed. ... 27 I5
Paraná • Argentina ... 44 D5
Paraná [Adm] • Brazil ... 44 F3
Paraná [Riv] • S. America ... 44 E4
Paraná [Riv] • Brazil ... 45 (1) D4
Paranaguá • Brazil ... 44 F3
Paranaíba • Brazil ... 44 G2
Paranapanema • Brazil ... 44 F3

Paranavaí • Brazil ... 44 F3
Parangtritis • Java, Indonesia ... 110 D7
Parati • Brazil ... 127 C3
Parbati • India ... 28 C5
Parbhani • India ... 28 C5
Parc Astérix Park • France ... 73 [70]
Parc Astérix • France ... 85 E2
Parc des Princes, Paris • France ... 85 E3
Parc Floral Park • France ... 73 [72]
Parchim • Germany ... 8 G3
Pardo • Brazil ... 45 (1) C5
Pardubice • Czech Rep. ... 96 C2
Parecis, Chapada dos • Brazil ... 43 E6
Paren • Russian Fed. ... 27 R4
Parepare • Indonesia ... 32 (1) A3
Pares • Antigua & Barbuda ... 125 F2
Párga • Greece ... 15 B4
Pargas • Finland ... 95 E3
Pargo, Ponta do • Madeira ... 88 C1
Parguera • Puerto Rico ... 125 I10
Parham • Antigua & Barbuda ... 125 F2
Parham Harbour • Antigua & Barbuda ... 125 F2
Paria, Gulf of • Trinidad & Tobago ... 125 K3
Pariaguán • Venezuela ... 43 E2
Pariaman • Indonesia ... 110 B4
Parika • Guyana ... 43 F2
Parima, Serra • Brazil/Venezuela ... 43 E3
Pariñas, Punta • Peru ... 43 A4
Parintins • Brazil ... 43 E4
Paris Heritage N • France ... 61 [44]
Paris Heritage C • France ... 64 [58]
Paris • France ... 85 E3
Paris, TX, United States ... 119 N2
Parish Closes • France ... 84 C1
Park City • UT, United States ... 116 B
Park City Ski • UT, United States ... 116 [80]
Park West Ski • UT, United States ... 116 [81]
Parkano • Finland ... 95 E2
Parken Zoo i Eskilstuna Park • Swedens ... 73 [6]
Parker • AZ, United States ... 118 J3
Parker Dam • AZ/NV, United States ... 118 J3
Parkes • NS, Australia ... 111 G2
Parma • Italy ... 91 E7
Parnaíba • Brazil ... 45 (1) C2
Parnaíba [Riv] • Brazil ... 45 (1) C3
Parnassós • Greece ... 15 D5
Parnassós Nat. Park Park • Greece ... 72 [139]
Parnassus • New Zealand ... 35 D6
Párnitha Nat. Park Park • Greece ... 72 [140]
Párnitha, Oros • Greece ... 15 E5
Párnonas, Oros • Greece ... 15 D6
Párnu • Estonia ... 16 M7
Páros • Greece ... 92 D8
Páros • Greece ... 92 D8
Páros [I.] • Greece ... 92 D8
Páros [I.] • Greece ... 92 D8
Parpaillon • France ... 12 A4
Parpan Ski • Switzerland ... 70 [111]
Parramatta • NS, Australia ... 111 G2
Parrett • United Kingdom ... 74 F3
Parry Is. • NT/NU, Canada ... 38 L2
Parry Peninsula • NT, Canada ... 38 L2
Parry Sound • ON, Canada ... 122 B5
Parsons • KS, United States ... 41 G4
Partenen Ski • Austria ... 70 [124]
Partenen • Austria ... 89 H5
Parthenay • France ... 84 D3
Partinico • Sicily, Italy ... 12 H10
Partnachklamm • Germany ... 82 J6
Partry Mtns • Ireland ... 79 F4
Paru • Brazil ... 43 G4
Pas de la Casa • Andorra ... 85 K1
Pasadena • CA, United States ... 117 F6
Pasadena • TX, United States ... 119 M1
Pascagoula • MS, United States ... 119 M1
Pascani • Romania ... 14 N2
Pasco • WA, United States ... 117 E2
Pascol, Mt • Brazil ... 44 H2
Pascua, I. de • Pacific Ocean ... 33 Q8
Pasewalk • Germany ... 8 I3
Pasir Panjang • Penang, Malaysia ... 108 C3
Pasir Ras New Town • Singapore ... 108 [7]
Pasirputih • Java, Indonesia ... 110 D8
Páskallavik • Sweden ... 95 E4
Pasni • Pakistan ... 18 H4
Paso de Indios • Argentina ... 45 C4
Paso de los Libres • Argentina ... 44 E4
Paso de los Toros • Uruguay ... 127 D2
Paso Real • Costa Rica ... 37 E6
Passage to the Indian cruise area • Indian Ocean ... 59 A5/8
Pássaro, Capo • Sicily, Italy ... 90 D4
Passau • Germany ... 9 I8
Passendale [Battlefield] • Belgium ... 80 A13
Passer • Italy ... 90 B1
Passo Fundo • Brazil ... 44 F4
Passo Rolle Ski • Italy ... 70 [220]
Passo Tonale Ski • Italy ... 70 [208]
Passos • Brazil ... 127 C1
Pasto • Colombia ... 43 B3
Pastos Bons • Brazil ... 45 (1) C3
Pasuruan • Java, Indonesia ... 110 D8
Pasvikelva • Norway ... 16 O2
Pat Sin Leng Country Park • Hong Kong, China ... 107 H4
Patagonia • Argentina ... 45 B5
Patagonia, Cordillera • Argentina/Chile ... 45 B5
Patan • Nepal ... 28 E3
Patani • Indonesia ... 32 (1) C2
Patara • Turkey ... 92 D9
Patara • Turkey ... 92 D9
Pate I. • Kenya ... 101 G4
Pate Manda • Kenya ... 112 K3
Paternó • Sicily, Italy ... 12 J10
Paterson • South Africa ... 100 C8
Paterson Range • WA, Australia ... 34 C4
Patia • Colombia ... 43 B3
Patillas, Puerto • Puerto Rico ... 125 E4
Pativilca • Peru ... 43 B6
Pátmos • Greece ... 92 D4
Pátmos • Greece ... 92 D4
Pátmos [I.] • Greece ... 92 D4
Patnem Beach • Goa, India ... 105 B2
Pato Branco • Brazil ... 44 F4
Patomskoye Nagorye • Russian Fed. ... 27 I5
Patong • Phuket, Thailand ... 109 K2
Patong Bay • Phuket, Thailand ... 109 K2
Patong Beach • Phuket, Thailand ... 109 K2
Patos • Brazil ... 45 (1) D3
Patos de Minas • Brazil ... 44 G2
Patos, Lagoa dos • Brazil ... 44 F5
Patquía • Argentina ... 44 C4
Pátra • Greece ... 15 C5
Patras • Greece ... 15 C5

Patrocinio • Brazil ... 44 G2
Pats Peak Ski • NH, United States ... 116 [206]
Pattadakal Heritage C • India ... 63 [127]
Pattadakal • India ... 106 D2
Pattaya • Thailand ... 109 H4
Patterdale • United Kingdom ... 74 C2
Patti • Sicily, Italy ... 12 I10
Patuca • Honduras ... 37 E4
Pátzcuaro • Mexico ... 123 E3
Pau • France ... 85 J2
Pauillac • France ... 85 G1
Pauini [Riv] • Brazil ... 43 D5
Pau de Serra • Madeira ... 88 C1
Paul Sauer Bridge • South Africa ... 100 C7
Pauli I. • Antarctica ... 59 A10
Paulo Alfonso • Brazil ... 45 (1) D3
Pavia • Italy ... 91 E6
Pavia, Certosa di • Italy ... 91 E6
Pavlodar • Kazakhstan ... 26 M7
Pavlovsk • Russian Fed. ... 97 E1
Pawai • Singapore ... 108 E3
Pawna • Greece ... 15 B4
Paximada • Greece ... 93 E4
Paximádia • Greece ... 93 E6
Payakumbuh • Indonesia ... 110 B4
Payangan • Bali, Indonesia ... 110 C2
Payerne • Switzerland ... 89 G1
Paynesville • VT, Australia ... 111 G3
Pays de la Loire • France ... 84 A1
Paysandú • Uruguay ... 44 E5
Payyer, gora • Russian Fed. ... 26 J4
Pazarbasi Burun • Turkey ... 15 L2
Pazardzik • Bulgaria ... 14 L7
Pazaryeri • Turkey ... 15 K4
Pazin • Croatia ... 14 A4
Pea Ridge Nat. Military Park Park • AR, United States ... 121 [191]
Peace [Riv] • AL/BC, Canada ... 38 G5
Peace River • AL, Canada ... 122 C2
Peak District Nat. Park Park • United Kingdom ... 72 [46]
Peak District Nat. Park • United Kingdom ... 75 A4
Pearl • MS, United States ... 118 K2
Pearl City • HI, United States ... 119 L5
Pearl Harbor • HI, United States ... 119 L5
Pearl Land • Zhuhai, China ... 107 H2
Pearson, Lester B. [Apt] • OT, Canada ... 122 B9
Pearston • South Africa ... 100 C4
Peary Land • Greenland ... 36 O1
Peatland World • Ireland ... 79 E1
Peauges, Safari de • France ... 85 F3
Pebane • Mozambique ... 24 F3
Pebas • Peru ... 43 C4
Pec • F.R. of Yugoslavia ... 14 H7
Peche-Merle, Grotte du • France ... 85 G4
Pechenga • Russian Fed. ... 17 E1
Pechora • Russian Fed. ... 17 J1
Pechora [Riv] • Russian Fed. ... 17 I1
Pechorskaya Guba • Russian Fed. ... 26 H4
Pechorskoye More • Russian Fed. ... 17 I1
Pecos • TX, United States ... 40 F5
Pecos Nat. Hist. Park • NM, United States ... 118 J1
Pecos Nat. Hist. Park Park • NM, United States ... 120 [130]
Pecos [Riv] • NM/TX, United States ... 40 F5
Pécs • Hungary ... 13 H11
Pedde Beach • Goa, India ... 105 B2
Pedra Azul • Brazil ... 44 H2
Pedráces Ski • Italy ... 70 [233]
Pedráces • Italy ... 90 B2
Pedraisches • Italy ... 90 B2
Pedreiras • Brazil ... 45 (1) C2
Pedro Afonso • Brazil ... 45 (1) B3
Pedro Juan Caballero • Paraguay ... 44 E3
Pedro Luro • Argentina ... 45 D3
Pedro Osorio • Brazil ... 44 F5
Peebles • United Kingdom ... 74 B4
Peek'n Peak Ski • NY, United States ... 116 [171]
Peel • YT, Canada ... 38 D3
Peel Sound • NU, Canada ... 38 L2
Peel's Grave, John • United Kingdom ... 74 C2
Peene • Germany ... 8 I3
Peera Peera Poolanna Lake • SA, Australia ... 34 G5
Pefka • Rhodes, Greece ... 93 F4
Péfki Beach • Crete, Greece ... 69 [191]
Péfki • Crete, Greece ... 93 E8
Pefkohóri Beach • Greece ... 69 [166]
Pefkohóri • Greece ... 92 D1
Pefkohóri • Greece ... 92 D1
Péfkos • Crete, Greece ... 93 E8
Péfkos • Rhodes, Greece ... 93 F2
Peg Barisan • Indonesia ... 25 L10
Pegasus Bay • New Zealand ... 35 D6
Peggys Cove • NS, Canada ... 123 D7
Pegnitz • Germany ... 9 G7
Pegnitz [Riv] • Germany ... 9 G7
Pegu • Myanmar ... 31 B2
Pegu Yoma • Myanmar ... 31 B2
Péguère, Monte • Martinique ... 72 L8
Pehlivanköy • Turkey ... 15 H2
Pehuajó • Argentina ... 127 D3
Peillon • France ... 85 H2
Peine • Germany ... 8 F4
Peipsi jarv • Estonia/Russian Fed. ... 16 N7
Peipus, Lake • Estonia/Russian Fed. ... 17 D3
Peisey-Nancroix-Vallandry Ski • France ... 70 [30]
Peißenberg • Germany ... 82 J6
Peixe • Brazil ... 45 (1) B3
Peixoto, Reprêsa de • Brazil ... 44 G3
Pekalongan • Java, Indonesia ... 110 D2
Pekan • Malaysia ... 32 C2
Pekanbaru • Indonesia ... 110 B4
Peking • China ... 29 F3
Peking Heritage C • China ... 63 [146]
Pekin • Portugal ... 88 E4
Pekulney, Khrebet • Russian Fed. ... 27 U3
Péla • Greece ... 15 D3
Pelabuhan Kelang • Malaysia ... 108 D3
Pelabuhanratu • Java, Indonesia ... 110 D1
Pelagonija • F.Y.R. of Macedonia ... 14 I8
Pélagos • Greece ... 92 D4
Pélagos • Greece ... 92 D5
Pelat, Mont • France ... 85 H2
Pelawanbesar • Indonesia ... 32 F2
Peleaga, Virful • Romania ... 14 J4
Peleduy • Russian Fed. ... 27 H5
Peleé, Montagne • Martinique ... 72 L8
Pélekas Beach • Corfu, Greece ... 69 [149]
Pelican I. • Antigua & Barbuda ... 125 F2
Pelican Cay Nat. Park • Bahamas ... 124 B1
Pelican • Antigua & Barbuda ... 125 F2
Pelinaíon • Greece ... 15 E5
Pelister Nat. Park Park • F.Y.R. of Macedonia ... 72 [124]

Peljesac • Croatia ... 14 E7
Pelkosenniemi • Finland ... 16 N3
Pella • Jordan ... 98 A4
Pello • Finland ... 16 M3
Pellworm • Germany ... 8 D2
Pellworm Spa • Germany ... 83 [5]
Pelly • YT, Canada ... 38 E4
Pelly Mtns • YT, Canada ... 38 E4
Pelopónnisos • Greece ... 15 D6
Pelotas • Brazil ... 44 F5
Pelusium • Egypt ... 101 F2
Pemalang • Java, Indonesia ... 110 D2
Pematangsiantar • Indonesia ... 110 B2
Pemba • Mozambique ... 24 G2
Pemba I. • Tanzania ... 102 H2
Pemberton • WA, Australia ... 34 C6
Pembina • Canada/United States ... 38 H7
Pembrey Beach • United Kingdom ... 75 [144]
Pembroke Beach • United Kingdom ... 75 [232]
Pembroke • OT, Canada ... 122 B2
Pembroke • United Kingdom ... 75 A5
Pembrokeshire Coast Nat. Park • United Kingdom ... 75 A5
Pembrokeshire Nat. Park Park • United Kingdom ... 72 [48]
Pembuang • Indonesia ... 32 E3
Peña, Sierra de la • Spain ... 11 K2
Peña Nevada • Mexico ... 40 F7
Penang • Malaysia ... 108 C
Penang Botanic Gardens • Penang, Malaysia ... 108 C1
Penang Hill • Penang, Malaysia ... 108 C1
Penang I. Bridge • Penang, Malaysia ... 108 C4
Penara Bukit Forest Reserve • Penang, Malaysia ... 108 C3
Penarroya-Pueblonuevo • Spain ... 11 F6
Peñas, Cabo de • Spain ... 11 F1
Penbryn Beach • United Kingdom ... 75 [174]
Pend Oreille • Canada/United States ... 38 H7
Pend Oreille Lake • ID, United States ... 117 E2
Pendennis Castle • United Kingdom ... 74 F4
Pendik • Turkey ... 15 K3
Pendjari, Parc nat. de la Park • Benin ... 103 [31]
Pendleton • OR, United States ... 117 E4
Penebel • Bali, Indonesia ... 110 C2
Peneda, Serra da • Portugal ... 88 A1
Peneda-Gerês, Parque Nac. da Park • Portugal ... 72 [80]
Penedo • Brazil ... 45 (1) D4
Penelokan • Bali, Indonesia ... 110 C2
Penetanguishene • OT, Canada ... 122 B5
Peng Chau • Hong Kong, China ... 107 H5
Pengambengan • Bali, Indonesia ... 110 C1
Penganga • India ... 28 C5
Pengastulan • Bali, Indonesia ... 110 C1
Penghu • Taiwan ... 107 G8
Penghu Liehtao • Taiwan ... 31 F2
Penóbtico, Sistema • Spain ... 11 G8
Peniche • Portugal ... 11 B5
Peniche Beach • Portugal ... 68 [79]
Penicuik • United Kingdom ... 6 I6
Peninsula [Apt] • CA, United States ... 117 F3
Peñíscola • Spain ... 11 K3
Peñíscola Beach • Spain ... 68 [103]
Penjat, I. des • Formentera, Spain ... 87 G4
Penmaenmawr Beach • United Kingdom ... 75 [196]
Penmarc'h, Pointe de • France ... 84 C3
Penn's Cave • PA, United States ... 118 H1
Penne • India ... 106 D3
Penne • France ... 12 L8
Pennekamp, John, Coral Reef State Park • FL, United States ... 119 M8
Pennines • United Kingdom ... 7 J7
Pennsylvania • United States ... 41 K3
Pennsylvania Avenue Nat. Hist. Site Park • DC, United States ... 121 [292]
Penny Highland • NU, Canada ... 39 R3
Penobscot • ME, United States ... 118 G2
Penobscot Bay • ME, United States ... 118 G4
Penola • SA, Australia ... 34 H7
Penong • SA, Australia ... 34 F6
Penrhyn • Cook Is. ... 33 L6
Penrith • NS, Australia ... 111 G2
Penrith • United Kingdom ... 74 C2
Pensacola • FL, United States ... 119 M1
Pensarn Beach • United Kingdom ... 75 [198]
Penshurst Place • United Kingdom ... 74 E3
Pensiangan • Malaysia ... 32 F2
Pentecôte • Vanuatu ... 35 (2) B2
Penticton • BC, Canada ... 122 C4
Pentland Firth • United Kingdom ... 6 I3
Pentland Hills • United Kingdom ... 74 B4
Penukonda • India ... 106 D6
Penza • Russian Fed. ... 17 G4
Penzance • United Kingdom ... 74 F4
Penzberg • Germany ... 82 J7
Penzhinskaya Guba • Russian Fed. ... 27 R4
Peoria • IL, United States ... 41 I3
Pequeno I. • Goa, India ... 105 B1
Perabumulih • Indonesia ... 32 C3
Peraea • Jordan ... 98 A6
Perai • Penang, Malaysia ... 108 C2
Perak [Adm] • Malaysia ... 31 C5
Perak [Riv] • Malaysia ... 108 D1
Perama • Corfu, Greece ... 92 B1
Perama • Corfu, Greece ... 92 B1
Perama • Crete, Greece ... 93 E2
Percé • QU, Canada ... 123 D2
Perche, Collines du • France ... 5 D6
Perdido, Monte Heritage N • France/Spain ... 61 [46]
Perdido, Monte Heritage C • France/Spain ... 64 [70]
Perdido, Mt • France/Spain ... 11 L2
Perê Beach • Greece ... 69 [168]
Pereira • Colombia ... 43 B3
Pereiro • Portugal ... 88 E4
Perenjori • WA, Australia ... 34 C5
Pereslavl-Zalesskiy • Russian Fed. ... 17 E3
Pereyaslav • Ukraine ... 71 A10
Perfect North Slopes Ski • IN, United States ... 116 [146]
Pergamino • Argentina ... 127 D1
Pergamon • Turkey ... 92 D5
Pergamon • Turkey ... 92 D5
Pérgamo • Turkey ... 93 G1
Péribonca • QU, Canada ... 39 Q7
Perico • Argentina ... 44 C3
Périgord Blanc • France ... 85 G2
Périgord Noir • France ... 85 G3
Périgord Vert • France ... 85 G2
Périgueux • France ... 85 G2
Perija, Sierra de • Colombia/Venezuela ... 43 C2
Perim • Djibouti ... 21 H5
Perinet, Réserve de Park • Madagascar ... 103 [137]
Perisher Blue • NS, Australia ... 111 G4
Peristási Beach • Greece ... 69 [167]

Peristéra • Greece ... 92 D4
Peristéra • Greece ... 92 D4
Periyar Wildlife Sanctuary • India ... 106 D10
Perkam, Tanjung • Indonesia ... 32 (1) E3
Perks Pleasure Park Park • Ireland ... 73 [19]
Perl • Germany ... 82 G3
Perlak, Kuala • Malaysia ... 108 D1
Perleberg • Brandenburg, Germany ... 8 G3
Perleberg • Niedersachsen, Germany ... 8 G4
Perlis • Malaysia ... 31 C5
Pernambuco • Brazil ... 45 (1) D3
Pernem • Goa, India ... 105 B1
Pernik • Bulgaria ... 14 K7
Perniö • Finland ... 95 E4
Pernis • Netherlands ... 80 C3
Péronne • France ... 5 F5
Peroulades Beach • Corfu, Greece ... 69 [149]
Perpignan • France ... 85 K2
Perranporth • United Kingdom ... 74 F4
Perros-Guirec • France ... 84 C1
Perry's Victory & Int. Peace Mem. Park • OH, United States ... 121 [187]
Persek • Bulgaria ... 15 F2
Persepolis Heritage C • Iran ... 63 [109]
Perseverancia • Bolivia ... 44 D1
Perstorp • Sweden ... 95 F11
Perth • WA, Australia ... 34 C6
Perth • United Kingdom ... 74 B2
Perth • OT, Canada ... 122 B6
Perthshire & Kinross • United Kingdom ... 74 B1
Pertusato, Capo • Corsica, France ... 85 L4
Peru • S. America ... 42 C5
Peru, Altiplano del • Peru ... 127 B2
Peru-Chile Trench • Pacific Ocean ... 44 B3
Perúgia • Italy ... 91 E12
Perumal Par I. • India ... 106 D9
Pervomay • Bulgaria ... 15 G1
Pésaro • Italy ... 91 E12
Pescadores • Taiwan ... 107 G8
Pescara • Italy ... 12 I6
Pescara [Riv] • Italy ... 12 H6
Peschanyy, Ostrov • Russian Fed. ... 27 I2
Pesek • Singapore ... 108 E3
Peshawar • Pakistan ... 18 B2
Peshtera • Bulgaria ... 15 F2
Pesmes • France ... 10 E9
Pessac • France ... 85 J2
Pessac-Léognan • France ... 84 B3
Pessáda • Greece ... 92 C2
Pessáda • Greece ... 92 C2
Pest • Hungary ... 71 A14
Pestovo • Russian Fed. ... 97 E1
Petäjävesi Heritage C • Finland ... 63 [74]
Petäjävesi • Finland ... 95 E2
Petalión, Kólpos • Greece ... 15 F5
Petalúdes • Rhodes, Greece ... 93 F2
Petaluma • CA, United States ... 117 F3
Petare • Venezuela ... 43 D1
Petauke • Zambia ... 24 E2
Petchaburi • Thailand ... 109 H3
Peterborough • United Kingdom ... 7 I9
Peterborough • SA, Australia ... 34 G6
Peterborough • OT, Canada ... 122 B5
Peterhead • United Kingdom ... 6 K4
Peterlee • United Kingdom ... 7 K7
Petermann Aboriginal Land • NT, Australia ... 112 H3
Petermann Ranges • NT/WA, Australia ... 112 H3
Petersburg • AK, United States ... 38 E5
Petersburg • VA, United States ... 118 H3
Petersfield Nat. Battlefield Park • VA, United States ... 121 [255]
Petersmanns Bjerg • Greenland ... 36 O2
Petiot • BC, Canada ... 38 G5
Petit Mécatina, Rivière du • NF/QU, Canada ... 39 S6
Petit Piton • St Lucia ... 125 J3
Petit St Bernard, Col de • France/Italy ... 85 F2
Petit-Loango, Réserve de Park • Gabon ... 103 [50]
Petites Pyrénées • France ... 11 M1
Petitsikapau Lake • NF, Canada ... 39 R6
Petkeljärvi Nat. Park Park • Finland ... 72 [33]
Petra Heritage C • Jordan ... 64 [249]
Petra Velikogo, Zaliv • Russian Fed. ... 30 F4
Petralona • Greece ... 92 D1
Petralona • Greece ... 92 D1
Petre, Point • OT, Canada ... 122 B6
Petrel [Base] • Antarctica ... 46 (1) JJ3
Petreto-Bicchisano • Corsica, France ... 85 L3
Petrich • Bulgaria ... 14 K8
Pétre, Récifs • New Caledonia ... 35 (2) A2
Petrified Forest Nat. Park • AZ, United States ... 118 J2
Petrified Forest Nat. Park Park • AZ, United States ... 120 [110]
Petrila • Romania ... 14 K4
Petroglyph Nat. Mon. Park • NM, United States ... 120 [128]
Petrolina • Brazil ... 45 (1) C3
Petropavl • Kazakhstan ... 26 K7
Petropavlovsk-Kamchatskiy • Russian Fed. ... 27 Q6
Petrópolis • Brazil ... 127 C4
Petrosani • Romania ... 14 K4
Petrovsk-Zabaykalskiy • Russian Fed. ... 27 G6
Petrozavodsk • Russian Fed. ... 17 E2
Petsamo • Russian Fed. ... 17 E1
Peuetsagoe, Gunung • Indonesia ... 110 B1
Pevek • Russian Fed. ... 27 T3
Pevensey Bay Beach • United Kingdom ... 75 [71]
Péyia Beach • Cyprus ... 69 [192]
Peyia Basilica • Cyprus ... 93 J3
Pezinok • Slovak Rep. ... 13 G9
Pfalz • Germany ... 82 G4
Pfälzer Wald • Germany ... 82 G4
Pfarrkirchen • Germany ... 9 H8
Pfeiffer Big Sur State Park • CA, United States ... 117 F3
Pforzheim • Germany ... 82 J4
Pfronten • Germany ... 82 J6
Pfullendorf • Germany ... 82 J5
Pfullingen • Germany ... 9 E8
PGA National • FL, United States ... 119 M6
Pha Tai Caves • Thailand ... 109 G4
Phaestos • Crete, Greece ... 93 E6
Phai Rong Wua, Wat • Thailand ... 109 H1
Phalodi • India ... 105 C5
Phalut • India ... 105 G8
Phan Rang • Vietnam ... 108 B2
Phan Thiet • Vietnam ... 108 B2
Phanat Nikhom • Thailand ... 109 H4
Phangan, Ko • Thailand ... 31 C5

Phangnga • Thailand....31 B5
Phanom Dong Rak • Cambodia/Thailand....31 C4
Phanom Rung • Thailand....109 F2
Phantasialand Park • Germany....73 [61]
Phantasialand • Germany....82 G1
Phara • Phuket, Thailand....109 K1
Phaselis • Turkey....93 G3
Phayao • Thailand....109 G2
Phi Phi, Ko • Thailand....109 K2
Philadelphia Heritage C • PA, United States....62 [11]
Philadelphia • Jordan....98 A6
Philadelphia • PA, United States....118 H1
Philae Heritage C • Egypt....63 [83]
Philae • Egypt....101 F5
Philippeville • Belgium....5 H4
Philippi • Greece....92 D1
Philippi • Greece....92 D1
Philippine Trench • Philippines....31 G4
Philippines • Asia....31 G4
Philippopolis • Bulgaria....71 A15
Philipsburg • St Maarten....58 B7
Philistia • Israel....98 A7
Phillip I. • VI, Australia....111 G3
Phillippsburg • Germany....5 L5
Phimai • Thailand....109 F2
Phitsanulok • Thailand....109 G4
Phlu, Khao • Ko Samui, Thailand....109 J2
Phnom Penh • Cambodia....108 B1
Phoenicia • Israel/Lebanon....98 A1
Phoenix • AZ, United States....118 J3
Phoenix Is. • Kiribati....33 K6
Phoenix Park • Ireland....79 E2
Phoi, Ko • Thailand....109 H4
Phong Bia • Laos....31 C2
Phra Buddha Sothorp • Thailand....109 H2
Phra Pathom Chedi • Thailand....109 H1
Phra Phutthabat • Thailand....109 H1
Phra Srirattana Mahathat, Wat • Thailand....109 H3
Phra Thong, Ko • Thailand....109 F4
Phra Thong, Wat • Phuket, Thailand....109 K1
Phrae • Thailand....109 G4
Phu Hin Rongkla Nat. Park • Thailand....109 G4
Phu Luang Nat. Park • Thailand....109 G4
Phu Rua Nat. Park • Thailand....109 G4
Phuket • Thailand....109 K
Phumi Mlu Prey • Cambodia....31 D4
Piacenza • Italy....91 E6
Piana • Corsica, France....85 L1
Piancavallo • Italy....90 B4
Pianosa • Tyrrhenian Sea, Italy....90 B5
Pianosa • Adriatic Sea, Italy....12 J6
Piarco [Apt] • Trinidad & Tobago....125 K3
Piaseczno • Poland....13 K5
Piatra Neamt • Romania....14 N3
Piau-Engaly • France....85 H3
Piauí • Brazil....45 (1) C3
Piave • Italy....91 E3
Piaye • St Lucia....125 J3
Piazza Armerina • Sicily, Italy....90 D4
Pibor • Sudan....23 E2
Pibor Post • Sudan....23 E2
Pic Touside • Chad....21 C3
Picardie • France....10 H4
Picardy • France....84 A1
Piceno • Italy....12 H6
Picentini, Monti • Italy....91 G4
Pichilemu • Chile....44 B5
Pickens, Fort • FL, United States....119 M1
Pickle Lake • OT, Canada....39 M6
Pico • Azores....88 B1
Pico Ski • VT, United States....116 [200]
Pico dei Tre Signori • Austria/Italy....90 B2
Pico Truncado • Argentina....45 C5
Picos • Brazil....45 (1) D3
Picton • New Zealand....35 E5
Picton • OT, Canada....38 B6
Pictured Rocks Nat. Lakeshore Park • MI, United States....121 [161]
Pidurutalagala • Sri Lanka....106 D15
Piedade, Ponta da • Portugal....88 E6
Piedmont • Italy....90 A1
Piedmonte Matese • Italy....43 C6
Piedras • Peru....43 C5
Piedras Negras • Mexico....37 A2
Piedras, Punta • Argentina....127 D4
Piekary Slaskie • Poland....13 H7
Pieksämäki • Finland....16 N5
Pielavesi • Finland....16 N5
Pielavesi [Lake] • Finland....94 A6
Pielinen • Finland....16 P5
Pieljekaise Nat. Park Park • Sweden....72 [20]
Piemonte • Italy....91 E5
Pieniński Nat. Park Park • Poland....72 [96]
Pienza Heritage C • Italy....64 [123]
Pienza • Italy....91 E11
Pierce Reservoirs • Singapore....108 E1
Pieria • Greece....15 D3
Pierre • SD, United States....40 F3
Pierrefonds • France....85 E2
Pierreville • Trinidad & Tobago....125 K4
Piešťany • Slovak Rep....13 G9
Pietarsaari • Finland....16 L5
Pietermaritzburg • South Africa....24 E5
Pietersburg • South Africa....24 D4
Pietra Ligure • Italy....91 E9
Pietrasanta • Italy....12 E5
Pietrosu, Vîrful • Romania....14 M2
Pieve di Cadore • Italy....90 B4
Pigeon I. Nat. Park • St Lucia....125 J2
Piggotts • Antigua & Barbuda....125 J7
Pigi Beach • Crete, Greece....69 [189]
Pigi • Crete, Greece....93 E2
Pigs, Bay of • Cuba....124 D2
Pihlajavesi • Finland....16 O6
Piilanhale Heiau Temple • HI, United States....119 L4
Pikes Peak • CO, United States....116 A
Piketberg • South Africa....100 C1
Pila • Italy....13 H4
Pila • Italy....91 E1
Pilanesberg Nat. Park Park • South Africa....103 [123]
Pilar • Paraguay....44 D3
Pilar de la Horadada Beach • Spain....68 [101]
Pilar de la Horadada • Spain....87 C3
Pilaya • Bolivia....44 D3
Pilbara • WA, Australia....111 E1
Pilcomayo • S. America....44 D3
Pilibhit • India....105 C3
Pilica • Poland....13 J7
Pilio • Greece....92 D4
Pilio • Greece....92 D4
Pilón • Cuba....124 D7
Pilónas • Rhodes, Greece....93 F4

Pílos • Greece....15 C7
Pilsen • Czech Rep....96 C1
Pinamar • Argentina....127 D4
Pinang • Malaysia....108 C
Pinar • Spain....11 F8
Pinar, Cap d'es • Majorca, Spain....87 H2
Pinar del Rio • Cuba....124 D1
Pinarello • Corsica, France....85 L4
Pinarhisar • Turkey....15 I2
Pinatubo, Mt • Philippines....31 G3
Pinckney, Charles, Nat. Hist. Site Park • SC, United States....121 [238]
Pinçon, Mt • France....5 C6
Pinde Nat. Park Park • Greece....72 [135]
Pindos Oros • Greece....15 C4
Pine Bluff • AR, United States....41 H5
Pine Castle • FL, United States....121 C2
Pine Creek • NT, Australia....34 F2
Pine Hills • FL, United States....121 C2
Pine I. • FL, United States....119 M5
Pine I. Bay • Antarctica....46 (1) EE2
Pine Keys • FL, United States....119 M7
Pine Knob Ski • MI, United States....116 [140]
Pine Pass • BC, Canada....38 G5
Pineda de Mar • Spain....87 D4
Pineda, la • Spain....87 D3
Pinega • Russian Fed....17 G2
Pinega [Riv] • Russian Fed....17 H2
Pinehouse Lake • SA, Canada....38 J5
Pinelands Nat. Reserve Park • NJ, United States....121 [336]
Pinerolo • Italy....91 E5
Pineta • Sardinia, Italy....90 C4
Ping • Thailand....109 G3
Ping Chau • Hong Kong, China....107 H4
Pingding Shan • China....29 H1
Pinghu • China....107 J4
Pingliang • China....29 D3
Pingtung • Taiwan....29 G6
Pingvallavatn • Iceland....16 (1) C2
Pingvellir • Iceland....16 (1) C2
Pingwu • China....29 C4
Pingxiang • Guangxi, China....29 D6
Pingxiang • Jiangxi, China....29 E5
Pingyao Heritage C • China....63 [148]
Pinhel • Portugal....11 D4
Pini • Indonesia....110 B4
Piniós • Greece....15 C6
Pinnacles Nat. Mon. Park • CA, United States....120 [50]
Pinnacles, The • WA, Australia....111 E5
Pinneberg • Germany....8 E3
Pinnes, Akra • Greece....15 F3
Pinney's Beach • St Kitts & Nevis....125 G4
Pino • Corsica, France....85 L2
Pinolosaen • Indonesia....32 (1) B2
Pinos, I. de • Cuba....124 D1
Pins, Anse aux • Seychelles....106 F1
Pins, I. des • New Caledonia....35 (2) B3
Pinsk • Belarus....17 D4
Pinta • Galapagos Is....43 (1) A1
Pinto • Argentina....44 D4
Pintu Gedong • Malaysia....108 D3
Piombino • Italy....91 E11
Pioneer Territory • NV, United States....117 F4
Pioner, Ostrov • Russian Fed....96 A4
Pionerskiy • Russian Fed....13 J3
Pionki • Poland....13 K6
Piopio • New Zealand....112 K1
Piotrków Trybunalski • Poland....13 I6
Pipa Dingzi • China....29 H2
Pipalyatjara • SA, Australia....112 H3
Pipamuaran, Réservoir • QU, Canada....123 D1
Pipe Spring Nat. Mon. • AZ, United States....118 J1
Pipe Spring Nat. Mon. Park • AZ, United States....120 [99]
Pipestone Nat. Mon. Park • MN, United States....121 [154]
Pipiriki • New Zealand....112 K3
Pipri Dam • India....105 C8
Piquiri • Brazil....44 F3
Piracicaba • Brazil....44 G3
Piraeus • Greece....92 D4
Piraeus • Greece....92 D4
Piran • Slovenia....12 H3
Pirapora • Brazil....44 H4
Pireás • Greece....92 D4
Pireás • Greece....92 D4
Pirgos • Pelopónnisos, Greece....15 C6
Pirgos • Crete, Greece....15 D3
Pirgos • Crete, Greece....93 E7
Piriac-sur-Mer Beach • France....68 [63]
Piran • Corsica, France....84 C4
Piriápolis • Uruguay....127 D2
Pirin Nat. Park Heritage N • Bulgaria....61 [58]
Pirin Nat. Park Park • Bulgaria....72 [132]
Pirineos • Spain....11 L2
Piripiri • Brazil....45 (1) D2
Pirmasens • Germany....82 G5
Pirna • Germany....9 J6
Pirongia, Mt • New Zealand....112 K1
Pirot • F.R. of Yugoslavia....14 J6
Piru • Indonesia....32 (1) C3
Pisa Heritage C • Italy....64 [120]
Pisa • Italy....91 E11
Pisa Range • New Zealand....112 L2
Pisac • Peru....127 B2
Piscataway Park Park • MD, United States....121 [276]
Pisco • Peru....127 B1
Písek • Czech Rep....96 C4
Pissouri Beach • Cyprus....69 [193]
Pissouri • Cyprus....93 J3
Pisticci • Italy....12 K8
Pistillfjörður • Iceland....16 (1) F1
Pistóia • Italy....91 E11
Pisz • Poland....13 K4
Pit • CA, United States....117 H1
Pitalito • Colombia....43 B3
Pitcairn • Pitcairn Is....33 08
Pitcairn Is. • Pacific Ocean....33 08
Pitch Lake • Trinidad & Tobago....125 K3
Pite älv • Sweden....16 K4
Piteå • Sweden....16 L4
Pitești • Romania....14 L5
Pitjantjatjara Aboriginal Land • SA, Australia....112 H3
Pitkyaranta • Russian Fed....17 E2
Pitlochry • United Kingdom....74 B1
Pitsidia Beach • Crete, Greece....69 [190]
Pitt I. • New Zealand....35 (3) A2
Pitt I. • BC, Canada....38 E6
Pittsburgh • PA, United States....118 K3
Pittsfield • MA, United States....118 D3
Piura • Peru....43 A5
Pjórsá • Iceland....16 (1) D2
Placentia Bay • NF, Canada....123 D4
Placetas • Cuba....124 D2
Plackovica • F.Y.R. of Macedonia....15 D2
Plage de la Corniche • Tunisia....101 E2

Plage des Nations • Morocco....101 D1
Plagne, la Ski • France....70 [33]
Plagne, la • France....85 F2
Plagne Montalbert Ski • France....70 [33]
Pláka Beach • Crete, Greece....69 [188]
Pláka, Akra • Greece....15 C2
Plakías • Crete, Greece....93 E6
Plana Cays • Bahamas....124 B4
Planachaux • Switzerland....89 G5
Planícies • Portugal....11 G3
Plano • TX, United States....119 N1
Plános Beach • Greece....69 [151]
Plános • Greece....92 C3
Plános • Greece....92 C3
Plasencia • Spain....11 E4
Plastun • Russian Fed....30 I2
Plasy • Czech Rep....96 C1
Platamónas Beach • Greece....69 [167]
Plataneás • Crete, Greece....93 E2
Plátani • Sicily, Italy....90 D3
Plataniás Beach • Crete, Greece....69 [188]
Plataniás • Crete, Greece....93 E1
Plátanos • Crete, Greece....93 E1
Plate, I. • Seychelles....106 F2
Plate, River • Argentina/Uruguay....127 D2
Platí • Greece....15 D3
Platja d'Aro • Spain....87 D2
Platja d'En Bossa • Ibiza, Spain....87 G3
Platja de Muro • Majorca, Spain....87 H2
Platja dels Dols • Majorca, Spain....87 H4
Platja Talamanca • Ibiza, Spain....87 G2
Platre • Colombia....43 C2
Platte • CO/NE, United States....40 G3
Plattsburgh • NY, United States....118 G3
Plau • Germany....8 H3
Plauen • Germany....9 H6
Plauer See • Germany....8 H3
Playa Azul • Mexico....123 E3
Playa Blanca • Lanzarote, Canary Is....87 E3
Playa de Fajardo • Puerto Rico....125 E2
Playa de Guayanés • Puerto Rico....125 E4
Playa de Guyanilla • Puerto Rico....125 E3
Playa de las Americas • Tenerife, Canary Is....86 E1
Playa del Inglés • Gran Canaria, Canary Is....86 E4
Playa Girón • Cuba....124 D2
Playa Larga • Cuba....124 D2
Playa Paraíso • Tenerife, Canary Is....86 E1
Pleasure I. • FL, United States....121 C2
Pleasurewood Hills Park • United Kingdom....73 [30]
Plechy • Czech Rep....96 C4
Pleiku • Vietnam....31 D4
Pleiney, le Ski • France....70 [51]
Plenty • New Zealand....35 F3
Plenty, Bay of • New Zealand....35 F3
Plérin Beach • France....68 [60]
Plérin • France....84 C2
Plesetsk • Russian Fed....17 G2
Plessis-Bourré, le [Château] • France....84 D1
Pleszew • Poland....13 G6
Plettenberg • Germany....82 F3
Plettenberg Bay • South Africa....100 C7
Pleven • Bulgaria....14 L6
Plimiri • Rhodes, Greece....93 F3
Pliska • Bulgaria....14 N6
Plitvice • Croatia....12 J4
Plitvice Lakes Nat. Park Heritage N • Croatia....61 [52]
Plitvice Lakes Nat. Park Park • Croatia....72 [109]
Pljesevica • Bosnia-Herz./Croatia....14 G6
Pljevlja • F.R. of Yugoslavia....14 G6
Ploca, Rt • Croatia....12 L5
Ploce • Croatia....12 L5
Ploce • Bosnia-Herz....12 L5
Plock • Poland....13 I5
Plöckenstein • Austria/Czech Rep....9 I8
Ploërmel • France....84 C4
Plogmagen Spa • Germany....83 [278]
Ploiesti • Romania....97 D1
Plomári Beach • Greece....69 [176]
Plomb du Cantal • France....10 H8
Plön • Germany....8 H3
Plonge, Lac la • SA, Canada....38 J5
Plonsk • Poland....13 J5
Plötzin • Germany....84 C1
Plougrenan • France....84 C1
Plouha • France....84 C1
Ploumanac'h • France....84 C1
Plovdiv • Bulgaria....14 L7
Plover Cove Country Park • Hong Kong, China....107 H4
Plover Cove Reservoir • Hong Kong, China....107 H4
Plumtree • Zimbabwe....102 J3
Plunge • Lithuania....13 K2
Plymouth • Montserrat....58 B7
Plymouth • United Kingdom....74 F5
Plymouth • Trinidad & Tobago....125 K2
Plzen • Czech Rep....96 C1
Po • Italy....91 E7
Po Basin • Italy....90 A1
Po, Colline di • Italy....91 E5
Po, Foci del • Italy....91 E8
Po Lin Monastery • Hong Kong, China....107 H5
Po Toi • Hong Kong, China....107 H6
Poarta Orientala • Romania....14 J5
Pobeda, gora • Russian Fed....25 P3
Pobedy, pik • Kyrgyzstan....26 N9
Pobla de Segur, la • Spain....11 M2
Poblet Heritage C • Spain....64 [73]
Poblet, Reial Monestir de • Spain....87 D3
Pobrezeje • Bulgaria....8 G2
Pocano Mtns • PA, United States....118 H1
Pocatello • ID, United States....40 J3
Pochentong [Apt] • Cambodia....108 B1
Poço das Antas, Reserva biológica • Brazil....127 E4
Poções • Brazil....44 H1
Poços de Caldas • Brazil....127 C3
Podebrady • Czech Rep....96 C2
Podgorica • F.R. of Yugoslavia....14 G7
Podkammennaya Tunguska • Russian Fed....96 E4
Podolsk • Russian Fed....17 F4
Podor • Senegal....20 J5
Podravina • Croatia....14 E4
Poduri • F.R. of Yugoslavia....14 E1
Podunajska • Slovak Rep....14 E1
Poe, Edgar Allen, Nat. Hist. Site Park • PA, United States....121 [309]
Poel • Germany....8 G2
Pogradec • Albania....15 B3
Pohjois-Karjala • Finland....16 O5
Pohjois-Karjala • Finland....94 A6
Pohnpei • Fed. States of Micronesia....33 G5

Pohnpei • Fed. States of Micronesia....33 G5
Pohorje • Slovenia....13 E11
Point au Fer I. • LA, United States....118 K4
Point, Fort, Nat. Hist. Site Park • CA, United States....120 [44]
Point Fortin • Trinidad & Tobago....125 K3
Point Lake • NT, Canada....38 I3
Point Lisas • Trinidad & Tobago....125 K3
Point Pleasant • NJ, United States....118 H1
Point Reyes Nat. Seashore Park • CA, United States....120 [42]
Pointe à Pierre • Trinidad & Tobago....125 K3
Pointe à Pitre • Guadeloupe....37 I4
Pointe au Sel • Seychelles....106 F1
Pointe du Cap • St Lucia....125 J2
Pointe Noire • Congo....22 G5
Pointe Seraphine • St Lucia....125 J1
Poissy • France....5 F6
Poitevin, Marais • France....84 D3
Poitiers • France....84 D4
Poitou • France....84 D3
Poitou-Charentes • France....84 A1
Poivre • Seychelles....106 F2
Poix-de-Picardie • France....10 G4
Pojezierze Chelminskie • Poland....13 I4
Pojezierze Dobrzynskie • Poland....13 I5
Pojezierze Mazurskie • Poland....13 J4
Pojezierze Pomorskie • Poland....13 H4
Pojezierze Wielkopolsko-Kujawskie • Poland....13 F5
Pok Pu Lam Country Park • Hong Kong, China....107 H5
Pokaran • India....105 C1
Pokhara • Nepal....28 D3
Poko • Dem. Rep. of Congo....23 D2
Pol-e Khomri • Afghanistan....26 K10
Pola de Laviana • Spain....11 F1
Pola de Lena • Spain....11 F1
Pola de Siero • Spain....11 F1
Poland • Europe....13
Polatli • Turkey....15 N4
Polem Beach • Goa, India....105 B2
Polesine • Italy....91 E7
Polesie • Russian Fed....13 N6
Polessk • Russian Fed....13 K3
Poli • Cameroon....22 G3
Polican • Albania....15 B3
Policastro, Golfo di • Italy....12 J9
Police • Poland....13 D4
Police, Pointe • Seychelles....106 F3
Policoro • Italy....12 K8
Policoro Beach • Italy....69 [134]
Poliegos • Greece....92 D7
Poliegos • Greece....92 D7
Poligus • Russian Fed....96 D4
Polihnitos • Greece....15 H4
Polihnitos Beach • Greece....69 [169]
Polihrono Beach • Greece....69 [169]
Polikastro • Greece....15 D2
Polillo • Philippines....31 G4
Polirinia • Crete, Greece....93 E1
Pólis • Cyprus....93 J3
Polis-Khrysokhoú Beach • Cyprus....69 [192]
Polistena • Italy....12 K10
Polk, Fort • LA, United States....118 K3
Polkowice • Poland....13 F6
Pollachi • India....106 D10
Pollença • Majorca, Spain....87 H2
Póllica • Italy....12 J8
Póllica Beach • Italy....69 [128]
Polo, Marco [Apt] • Italy....91 E8
Polonia [Apt] • Indonesia....110 B2
Polonnaruwa Heritage C • Sri Lanka....63 [136]
Polonnaruwa • Sri Lanka....106 D15
Polotsk • Belarus....17 D3
Polousny Kryazh • Russian Fed....27 N3
Polson • MT, United States....117 E2
Poltava • Ukraine....17 E5
Polyarnyy • Russian Fed....17 E1
Polynesia • Pacific Ocean....33 K6
Polzeath Beach • United Kingdom....75 [129]
Pomarkku • Finland....95 E1
Pomerania • Poland....96 B1
Pomerol • France....84 B3
Pomio • Papua New Guinea....35 (1) D2
Pommersche Bucht • Germany/Poland....8 J2
Pomongwe Cave • Zimbabwe....102 J3
Pomorie • Bulgaria....97 D3
Pomorska, Zatoka • Germany/Poland....8 J2
Pomorskiy Proliv • Russian Fed....17 I1
Pompadour, Château de • France....85 G2
Pompano Beach • FL, United States....119 M8
Pompei • Italy....12 J8
Pompei and Heritage C • Italy....64 [128]
Ponape • Fed. States of Micronesia....33 G5
Ponca City • OK, United States....41 G4
Ponce • Puerto Rico....125 E3
Pond Inlet • NU, Canada....39 P2
Ponda • Goa, India....105 B1
Pondicherry • India....106 D7
Ponferrada • Spain....11 E2
Pong Qu • China/Nepal....28 E3
Pongola • Mozambique/South Africa....24 E5
Ponmudi • India....106 D10
Ponoy • Russian Fed....17 G1
Pons • Spain....10 G12
Pont-à-Mousson • France....5 J6
Pont-Audemer • France....10 F4
Pont-Aven • France....84 C3
Pont-l'Abbé • France....84 C3
Ponta Delgada Beach • Azores....68 [87]
Ponta Delgada • Azores....88 B1
Ponta do Sol • Madeira....88 C1
Ponta Grossa • Brazil....44 F4
Ponta Porã • Brazil....44 E3
Pontal • Portugal....88 E6
Pontarlier • France....89 G1
Pontchartrain, Lake • LA, United States....118 K4
Ponte di Legno • Italy....91 E4
Ponte Leccia • Corsica, France....85 L2
Ponte Nova • Brazil....127 C2
Pontecagnano • Italy....91 G4
Ponte María • Italy....91 C2
Pont Menier • QU, Canada....123 D2
Pont Morant • France....84 C4
Pontevedra, Ria de • Spain....11 C2
Pontianak • Indonesia....32 D3
Pontivy • France....84 B6
Pontorson • France....84 C1
Pontrémoli • Italy....91 E6
Pontresina Ski • Switzerland....70 [102]
Pontresina • Switzerland....89 G8
Pontypool • United Kingdom....7 I10
Pony Express Territory • NV, United States....117 F2
Ponypark Park • Netherlands....73 [39]
Ponypark • Netherlands....80 A8
Ponza • Italy....12 G8

Ponziane, Is. • Italy....12 G8
Pool Plateau • Antarctica....46 (1) A1
Poole • United Kingdom....74 F3
Poole Beach • United Kingdom....75 [86]
Poona • India....28 B5
Poopó • Bolivia....44 C2
Poopó, Lago de • Bolivia....44 C2
Popayán • Colombia....43 B3
Popeye Village • Malta....93 H1
Popigay • Russian Fed....27 N2
Poplar Bluff • MO, United States....41 H4
Popocatépetl Heritage C • Mexico....62 [22]
Popocatépetl • Mexico....123 E4
Pópoli • Italy....91 F2
Popondetta • Papua New Guinea....35 (1) D2
Popovo • Bulgaria....97 D3
Poprad • Slovak Rep....13 J8
Porbandar • India....28 B4
Porcupine • Canada/United States....38 C3
Porcupine Plain • YT, Canada....38 D3
Pordenone • Italy....90 B4
Porec • Croatia....12 H3
Porec Heritage C • Croatia....64 [155]
Poretta [Apt] • Corsica, France....85 L2
Pori • Finland....95 E1
Porirua • New Zealand....35 E5
Pórisvatn • Iceland....16 (1) D2
Porkkala • Finland....95 E4
Porlamar • Venezuela....43 E1
Porlock • United Kingdom....74 F2
Pornic Beach • France....68 [63]
Pornichet • France....84 C4
Poronaysk • Russian Fed....27 N7
Póros • Greece....15 E6
Póros • Cephalonia, Greece....92 C2
Póros • Cephalonia, Greece....92 C2
Póros [I.] • Greece....92 D7
Póros [I.] • Greece....92 D7
Porpoise Bay • Antarctica....46 (1) R3
Porpoise Bay • New Zealand....112 L4
Porquerolles, I. de • France....85 H3
Porsangen • Norway....16 M1
Porsanger-Halvøya • Norway....16 M1
Porsgrunn • Norway....94 B3
Pórshöfn • Iceland....16 (1) F1
Porsuk • Turkey....15 M4
Porsuk Baraji • Turkey....15 L4
Port Alberni • BC, Canada....122 C3
Port Alfred • South Africa....24 D6
Port Alice • BC, Canada....38 F6
Port Angeles • WA, United States....117 E1
Port Antonio • Jamaica....124 C2
Port Aransas • TX, United States....119 N5
Port Arthur • TS, Australia....34 I8
Port Arthur • TX, United States....119 N4
Port Askaig • United Kingdom....6 F6
Port Augusta • SA, Australia....34 G6
Port aux Français • Kerguelen Is....19 (1) B1
Port Aventura Park • Spain....73 [76]
Port Aventura • Spain....87 D3
Port Barcarès • France....85 K2
Port Beaufort • South Africa....100 C6
Port Blair • India....28 F6
Port Burwell • NU, Canada....39 S4
Port Campbell Nat. Park • VI, Australia....111 G3
Port Canaveral • FL, United States....119 M6
Port Cartier • QU, Canada....39 R6
Port Chalmers • New Zealand....35 C7
Port Charlotte • FL, United States....119 M5
Port Chicago Naval Magazine Nat. Mem. Park • CA, United States....120 [47]
Port Cros, Ile de • France....85 H3
Port Cros, Parc nat. de Park • France....72 [60]
Port Cros, Parc nat. de • France....85 H3
Port d'Addaia • Minorca, Spain....87 F2
Port de Alcúdia • Majorca, Spain....87 H2
Port de Andratx • Majorca, Spain....87 H3
Port de Bouc • France....10 K10
Port de Pollença • Majorca, Spain....87 H2
Port de St Miquel • Ibiza, Spain....87 G2
Port de Sóller • Majorca, Spain....87 H1
Port Dickson • Malaysia....108 D4
Port el Kantaoui • Tunisia....101 E2
Port Elizabeth • South Africa....100 C8
Port Ellen • United Kingdom....6 H7
Port Erin • Isle of Man....7 H7
Port Eynon Beach • United Kingdom....75 [142]
Port Fitzroy • New Zealand....35 E3
Port Gentil • Gabon....22 F5
Port Gibson • MS, United States....118 K2
Port Grimaud • France....85 H4
Port Harcourt • Nigeria....22 E4
Port Hardy • BC, Canada....38 F6
Port Hawkesbury • NS, Canada....123 D7
Port Hedland • WA, Australia....34 C4
Port Hope • OT, Canada....122 B5
Port Hope Simpson • NF, Canada....39 T6
Port Huron • MI, United States....41 J3
Port I. • Hong Kong, China....107 H4
Port Jackson • NS, Australia....111 G2
Port Kelang • Malaysia....108 D3
Port Kembla • NS, Australia....111 G2
Port la Nouvelle • France....11 I2
Port Lairge • Ireland....79 E3
Port Lavaca • TX, United States....119 N5
Port Leucate • France....85 K2
Port Lincoln • SA, Australia....34 G6
Port Lockroy • Antarctica....59 A10
Port Louis • Mauritius....24 (1) B2
Port Lympne Wildlife Park • United Kingdom....74 E3
Port Macquarie • NS, Australia....34 I6
Port Maria • Jamaica....124 C2
Port Menier • QU, Canada....123 D2
Port Morant • Jamaica....124 C4
Port Moresby • Papua New Guinea....35 (1) D2
Port O'Connor • TX, United States....119 N5
Port of Spain • Trinidad & Tobago....125 K3
Port Pirie • SA, Australia....34 G6

Port Saunders • NF, Canada....123 D5
Port Shelter • Hong Kong, China....107 H6
Port Shepstone • South Africa....100 B2
Port Soif Bay Beach • United Kingdom....75 [231]
Port Stanley • Falkland Is....59 A10
Port Stephens • NS, Australia....111 E8
Port Sudan • Sudan....23 E5
Port Talbot • United Kingdom....7 I10
Port Vendres • France....10 I11
Port Vendres Beach • France....68 [111]
Port Vila • Vanuatu....35 (2) B2
Port Wakefield • SA, Australia....34 G6
Port-la-Nouvelle Beach • France....68 [112]
Porta, la • Corsica, France....85 L2
Porta Westfalica Spa • Germany....83 [91]
Portadown • United Kingdom....6 F8
Portage la Prairie • MN, Canada....38 L6
Portalegre • Portugal....11 D5
Portalegre [Adm] • Portugal....88 A2
Portalegre • NM, United States....40 F5
Portals Nova • Majorca, Spain....87 H3
Portals Vells • Majorca, Spain....87 H3
Portarlington • Ireland....79 E3
Portbou Beach • Spain....68 [106]
Portbou • Spain....87 D2
Porté Puymorens • France....85 K1
Porté • Brazil....43 G4
Porte, le Beach • France....68 [55]
Portela • Madeira....88 C2
Portela de Sacavém [Apt] • Portugal....88 D2
Portelet Bay Beach • United Kingdom....75 [233]
Porterville • South Africa....24 B6
Porterville • CA, United States....117 F3
Portes du Soleil • France....89 G5
Portes, Punta de ses • Ibiza, Spain....87 G3
Porthcawl • United Kingdom....74 F2
Porthcawl Beach • United Kingdom....75 [139]
Porthmadog • United Kingdom....7 H9
Porticcio • Corsica, France....85 L3
Portici • Italy....91 G3
Portile de Fier • Corsica, France....85 L3
Portillo • Corsica, France....85 L3
Portimão Beach • Portugal....68 [82]
Portimão • Portugal....88 E6
Portinão da Arrábida • Portugal....88 D2
Portinatx • Ibiza, Spain....87 G2
Portiragnes Beach • France....68 [113]
Portland • VI, Australia....34 H7
Portland • OR, United States....117 E3
Portland • ME, United States....118 G4
Portland Bight • Jamaica....124 C4
Portland Bill • United Kingdom....74 F6
Portland, Isle of • United Kingdom....74 F6
Portland Point • Jamaica....124 C4
Portlaoise • Ireland....7 E8
Portmarnock • Ireland....79 E2
Portmore • Jamaica....124 C4
Portnoo Beach • Ireland....68 [46]
Porto • Portugal....11 C3
Porto Heritage C • Portugal....64 [95]
Porto • Corsica, France....85 L2
Porto Acre • Brazil....43 D5
Porto • Corsica, France....85 L1
Porto [Adm] • Portugal....88 A1
Pôrto Alegre • Brazil....44 F5
Porto Amboim • Angola....23 A6
Pôrto Azzurro • Italy....91 E11
Porto Cervo • Sardinia, Italy....90 C4
Porto Colom • Majorca, Spain....87 H4
Porto Conte • Sardinia, Italy....90 C1
Porto Cristo • Majorca, Spain....87 H2
Porto da Cruz • Madeira....88 C2
Porto de Moz • Brazil....43 G4
Porto Empédocle • Sicily, Italy....90 D4
Porto Franco • Brazil....45 (1) B3
Porto Garibaldi • Italy....91 E8
Porto, Golfe de Heritage N • Corsica, France....61 [45]
Porto, Golfe de • Corsica, France....85 L1
Pôrto Moniz Beach • Madeira....68 [90]
Porto Moniz • Madeira....88 C1
Porto Novo • Cape Verde....22 (1) A1
Porto Petro • Majorca, Spain....87 H4
Pôrto Potenza Picena • Italy....91 E12
Porto Rafael • Sardinia, Italy....90 C2
Pôrto Ráfti • Greece....92 D7
Pôrto Ráfti • Greece....92 D7
Porto Recanati • Italy....91 E12
Porto Rotondo • Sardinia, Italy....90 C2
Porto San Giórgio • Italy....12 H5
Porto Santana • Brazil....43 G4
Porto Santo • Madeira....88 [89]
Porto Santo Stefano • Italy....12 F6
Porto Seguro • Brazil....44 I2
Porto Tolle • Italy....12 G4
Porto Tórres • Sardinia, Italy....90 C1
Porto Vélez • Brazil....43 C5
Porto Vecchio • Corsica, France....85 L4
Porto Velho • Brazil....43 E5
Portobelo Heritage C • Panama....62 [32]
Portoferraio • Italy....91 E10
Portofino Beach • Italy....68 [122]
Portofino • Italy....91 E6
Portogruaro • Italy....12 G3
Portohéli Beach • Greece....69 [161]
Portohéli • Greece....92 D7
Portomaggiore • Italy....91 E8
Portonovo • Benin....22 E3
Portopalo • Italy....91 E8
Portoscuso • Sardinia, Italy....90 C3
Portovénere Heritage C • Italy....64 [119]
Portovénere • Italy....91 E10
Portoviejo • Ecuador....43 A4
Portreath • United Kingdom....74 F4
Portrush Beach • United Kingdom....75 [221-222]
Portsmouth • United Kingdom....7 K11
Portsmouth • OH, United States....41 J4
Portsmouth • Dominica....58 B11
Portsmouth • NH, United States....118 G3
Portsmouth • VA, United States....118 H5
Portstewart Beach • United Kingdom....75 [220]
Porttipahdan tekojarvi • Finland....16 N2
Portugal • Europe....11
Portugalete • Spain....11 H1
Portumna • Ireland....79 F4
Porvenir • Bolivia....45 B6
Porvenir • Chile....45 B6
Porvoo • Finland....95 E4
Posada • Sardinia, Italy....90 C2
Posadas • Argentina....44 E4
Posavina • Bosnia-Herz./Croatia....14 F5
Poschiavo • Switzerland....89 G8
Poseidon, Temple of • Greece....92 D7
Poseidon, Temple of • Greece....92 D7
Posio • Finland....16 O3
Positano • Italy....91 G3
Poso • Indonesia....32 (1) B2
Poso, Danau • Indonesia....32 (1) B3
Posse • Brazil....45 (1) B4
Postavy • Belarus....16 N9

Postojna • Slovenia ... 14 B4
Potamiés • Crete, Greece ... 93 E7
Potenza • Italy ... 12 J8
Potenza [Riv] • Italy ... 12 H5
Potenteri, Lake • New Zealand ... 112 L3
Poti • Georgia ... 17 G6
Potiskum • Nigeria ... 22 G2
Potnarvin • Vanuatu ... 35 (2) B2
Poto • Peru ... 127 B2
Potomac • MD/VI, United States ... 118 H3
Potosí • Bolivia ... 127 B2
Potosí Heritage C • Bolivia ... 62 [53]
Potsdam Heritage C • Germany ... 64 [31]
Potsdam • Germany ... 81 F3
Potsdam Neues Palais • Germany ... 81 F3
Potters Village •
   Antigua & Barbuda ... 125 F1
Pottsville • PA, United States ... 41 K3
Pottuvil • Sri Lanka ... 106 D16
Potworks Dam •
   Antigua & Barbuda ... 125 F4
Poughkeepsie •
   NY, United States ... 118 H2
Pouilly-Fumé • France ... 84 B2
Pouso Alegre • Brazil ... 127 C3
Pouthisat • Cambodia ... 31 C4
Považská Bystrica • Slovak Rep. ... 13 H8
Poverty Bay • New Zealand ... 35 F4
Poverty Point Nat. Mon. •
   LA, United States ... 118 K1
Poverty Point Nat. Mon. Park •
   LA, United States ... 121 [195]
Póvoa de Varzim • Portugal ... 11 C3
Povoação • Azores ... 88 B1
Powder • MT/WY, United States ... 38 J7
Powder Mtn Ski •
   UT, United States ... 116 [77]
Powell • WY, United States ... 40 E3
Powell, Lake •
   AZ/UT, United States ... 118 J1
Powell River • BC, Canada ... 38 G7
Powerscourt House • Ireland ... 79 E4
Powys • United Kingdom ... 75 A5
Poyang Hu • China ... 29 F5
Pöytyä • Finland ... 95 E3
Poza Rica • Mexico ... 123 E2
Pozarevac • F.R. of Yugoslavia ... 14 I5
Poznan • Poland ... 13 F5
Pozoblanco • Spain ... 11 G6
Pozos, Punta • Argentina ... 45 C5
Pozuelos • Venezuela ... 43 E2
Pozza di Fassa Ski • Italy ... 70 [221]
Pozza di Fassa • Italy ... 90 B3
Pozzallo • Sicily, Italy ... 90 D4
Pozzuoli • Italy ... 91 G3
Pra • Ghana ... 23 E8
Pra-Loup Ski • France ... 70 [69]
Pra-Loup • France ... 85 H2
Prachatice • Czech Rep. ... 96 C3
Prachin Buri • Thailand ... 109 H2
Praded • Czech Rep. ... 13 G7
Prades • France ... 85 K2
Præstø • Denmark ... 95 F14
Prague Heritage C • Czech Rep. ... 64 [143]
Prague • Czech Rep. ... 96 C2
Praha Heritage C • Czech Rep. ... 64 [143]
Praha • Czech Rep. ... 96 C2
Praia • Cape Verde ... 22 (1) B2
Praia da Falésia • Portugal ... 88 E7
Praia da Luz • Portugal ... 88 E7
Praia da Oura • Portugal ... 88 E6
Praia da Rocha • Portugal ... 88 E7
Praia das Macas • Portugal ... 88 D1
Praia da Balaia • Portugal ... 88 E7
Praia de Castelo • Portugal ... 88 E6
Praia de Galé • Portugal ... 88 E6
Praia de Vale do Lobo •
   Portugal ... 88 E7
Praia Grande • Portugal ... 88 D1
Praia Parede • Portugal ... 88 D1
Praia Verde • Portugal ... 88 E7
Prainha • Brazil ... 43 G4
Prainha • Madeira ... 88 C2
Prambanan Heritage C •
   Java, Indonesia ... 63 [178]
Prambanan • Java, Indonesia ... 63 [178]
Pranauron Ski • Italy ... 70 [231]
Pranita • India ... 28 C5
Prapat • Indonesia ...
Prapoutel Ski • France ... 70 [51]
Praslin • Seychelles ... 106 F4
Praslin Bay • St Lucia ... 125 J4
Prasonisi, Akra •
   Rhodes, Greece ... 93 F3
Prat Matavu • France ... 85 K1
Prata • Brazil ... 44 G2
Prata, Costa de • Portugal ... 88 A2
Pratas Is. • China ... 107 G8
Prato • Italy ... 91 E11
Prats-de-Mollo • France ... 85 K2
Pravdinsk • Russian Fed. ... 13 K3
Pravia • Spain ... 11 E1
Prawl Point • United Kingdom ... 74 F5
Praz du Lys, le Ski • France ... 70 [14]
Prazeres • Madeira ... 88 C1
Predazzo Ski • Italy ... 70 [217]
Predazzo • Italy ... 90 B3
Preetz • Germany ... 8 F2
Pregolya • Russian Fed. ... 13 J3
Prekmurje • Slovenia ... 14 D3
Premnitz • Germany ... 8 H4
Premuda • Croatia ... 14 B5
Prenj • Bosnia-Herz. ... 14 E6
Prenn Falls • Vietnam ... 108 B2
Prenzlau • Germany ... 8 I3
Preobrazhenka • Russian Fed. ... 27 G5
Preparis North Channel •
   Myanmar ... 31 A3
Prerov • Czech Rep. ... 13 G8
Prerov nad Labem • Czech Rep. ... 96 C2
Prerow Beach • Germany ... 68 [14]
Prerow Spa • Germany ... 83 [276]
Prescott • AZ, United States ... 118 J1
Preservation Inlet •
   New Zealand ... 112 L3
Presidencia Roque Sáenz Peña •
   Argentina ... 44 D4
Presidente Epitácio • Brazil ... 44 F3
Presidente Frei [Base] •
   Antarctica ... 46 (1) JJ4
Presidente Prudente • Brazil ... 44 F3
Presidio • TX, United States ... 40 F6
Preslav • Bulgaria ... 97 D3
Presov • Slovak Rep. ... 13 K8
Préspa Nat. Park Park • Greece ... 72 [133]
Presque Isle •
   ME, United States ... 118 G2
Pressburg • Slovak Rep. ... 71 A14
Prestice • Czech Rep. ... 9 I7
Preston • United Kingdom ... 7 J8
Prestwick [Apt] •
   United Kingdom ... 6 H6
Pretoria • South Africa ... 24 D5
Pretorius, Willem Game Reserve Park •
   South Africa ... 103 [122]
Preußisch-Oldendorf Spa •
   Germany ... 83 [86]
Prevel, Fort • QU, Canada ... 123 D2
Préveza • Greece ... 92 C1
Préveza • Greece ... 92 C1

Priboj • F.R. of Yugoslavia ... 14 G6
Pribram • Czech Rep. ... 96 C3
Pribyslav • Czech Rep. ... 96 C4
Price • UT, United States ... 40 D4
Prickley Pear I. •
   Antigua & Barbuda ... 125 F1
Pridz Bay • Antarctica ... 46 (1) M3
Priego • Spain ... 11 I4
Priego de Córdoba • Spain ... 11 G7
Prien • Germany ... 82 J4
Prien Spa • Germany ... 83 [256]
Priene • Turkey ... 93 D9
Priene • Turkey ... 92 D9
Prieros • Germany ... 81 F4
Prieska • South Africa ... 24 C5
Prievidza • Slovak Rep. ... 13 H9
Prignitz • Germany ... 81 D1
Prijedor • Bosnia-Herz. ... 12 K4
Prilep • F.Y.R. of Macedonia ... 14 I8
Priluki • Ukraine ... 17 E4
Primavera [Base] • Antarctica ... 46 (1) II3
Primeira Cruz • Brazil ... 45 (1) C2
Primorsk • Russian Fed. ... 16 O6
Primorsko Beach • Bulgaria ... 69 [211]
Primorsko • Bulgaria ... 97 D3
Primorsko-Akhtarsk •
   Russian Fed. ... 17 F5
Primosten • Croatia ... 12 J5
Prince Albert • SA, Canada ... 38 J6
Prince Albert • South Africa ... 100 C7
Prince Albert Peninsula •
   NT, Canada ... 38 H2
Prince Albert Road •
   South Africa ... 100 C2
Prince Albert Sound •
   NT, Canada ... 38 H2
Prince Alfreds Pass •
   South Africa ... 100 C7
Prince Charles I. • NU, Canada ... 39 P3
Prince Charles Mtns •
   Antarctica ... 46 (1) L2
Prince de Galles, Cap de •
   QU, Canada ... 39 Q4
Prince Edward I. • Canada ... 123 D7
Prince Edward I. Nat. Park •
   PE, Canada ... 123 D7
Prince Edward Is. •
   Indian Ocean ... 19 H10
Prince George • BC, Canada ... 122 C1
Prince of Wales, Cape •
   AK, United States ... 36 A3
Prince of Wales I. •
   QL, Australia ... 34 H2
Prince of Wales I. •
   AK, United States ... 38 E5
Prince of Wales I. • NU, Canada ... 38 L2
Prince of Wales Strait •
   NT, Canada ... 38 H2
Prince Regent Inlet •
   NU, Canada ... 39 N2
Prince Rupert • BC, Canada ... 38 F6
Prince Rupert Bay • Dominica ... 58 B11
Princes Is. • Turkey ... 92 D3
Princes Is. • Turkey ... 92 D3
Princes Town •
   Trinidad & Tobago ... 125 K3
Princess Charlotte Bay •
   QL, Australia ... 34 H2
Princess Royal I. • BC, Canada ... 38 F6
Princeton • NJ, United States ... 118 H1
Principe • Sao Tomé e Principe ... 22 F4
Prinos [Base] • Kavála, Greece ... 69 [171]
Prinos Beach • Kavála, Greece ... 69 [189]
Prinos • Crete, Greece ... 93 E2
Prinzapolka • Nicaragua ... 43 A1
Pripyat • Belarus ... 17 D4
Priskaspiyskaya Nizmennost •
   Kazakhstan ... 17 I5
Pristina • F.R. of Yugoslavia ... 14 I7
Pritzwalk • Germany ... 8 H3
Privas • France ... 10 J9
Priverno • Italy ... 91 F4
Prizren • F.R. of Yugoslavia ... 14 H8
Probolinggo • Java, Indonesia ... 110 D8
Prócida, I. di • Italy ... 91 G3
Procópio • Brazil ... 44 F3
Pródhromos • Cyprus ... 93 J3
Profitis Ilias • Greece ... 15 D7
Profondeville • Belgium ... 80 A15
Progonati • Albania ... 92 A1
Progress [Base] • Antarctica ... 46 (1) N3
Prokop'yevsk • Russian Fed. ... 26 O7
Prokupje • F.R. of Yugoslavia ... 14 I6
Prome • Myanmar ... 31 B3
Promthep, Laem •
   Phuket, Thailand ... 109 K2
Propriá • Brazil ... 45 (1) D4
Propriano • Corsica, France ... 85 L3
Proserpine • QL, Australia ... 111 F1
Prosna • Poland ... 13 G5
Prosperidad • Philippines ... 31 H5
Prostejov • Czech Rep. ... 13 G8
Provadiya • Bulgaria ... 97 D3
Provence • France ... 85 H1
Provence-Alpes-Côte d'Azur •
   France ... 84 A2
Providence • Seychelles ... 106 F2
Providence • RI, United States ... 118 H2
Providence, Bancs • Seychelles ... 106 F2
Providencia • Colombia ... 37 E5
Providenia • Russian Fed. ... 46 GG3
Provins • France ... 85 E4
Provo • UT, United States ... 40 D3
Provost • AL, Canada ... 38 I6
Prozor • Bosnia-Herz. ... 12 L5
Prudnik • Poland ... 13 G7
Prüm • Germany ... 82 G1
Pruszcz Gdanski • Poland ... 13 H3
Pruszków • Poland ... 13 J5
Prut • Ukraine ... 14 L1
Pruzhany • Belarus ... 13 N5
Przasnysz • Poland ... 13 J4
Przemysl • Poland ... 13 L8
Psará • Greece ... 92 D5
Psará • Greece ... 92 D5
Psérimos • Greece ... 92 D8
Psérimos • Greece ... 92 D8
Psiloritis • Crete, Greece ... 93 E6
Psínthos • Rhodes, Greece ... 93 F2
Pskov • Russian Fed. ... 17 D3
Ptolemais • Libya ... 21 D1
Ptolemais • Israel ... 98 A1
Pu'er • China ... 29 C6
Pu'uhonua o Honaunau Nat. Hist. Park •
   HI, United States ... 119 L8
Pu'uhonua o Honaunau Nat. Hist. Park Park •
   HI, United States ... 120 [71]
Pucallpa • Peru ... 43 C5
Puck • Poland ... 13 H3
Pudasjärvi • Finland ... 16 N4
Pudent, Estany •
   Formentera, Spain ... 87 G4
Pudoz • Russian Fed. ... 17 F2
Pudukkottai • India ... 106 D11
Puebla Heritage C • Mexico ... 62 [23]
Puebla • Mexico ... 123 E4
Puebla • CO, United States ... 40 E4
Pueblo de Taos Heritage C •
   NM, United States ... 62 [8]
Puelches • Argentina ... 45 C3
Puente Genil • Spain ... 11 G7

Puenteáreas • Spain ... 11 C2
Puerto Acosta • Bolivia ... 44 C2
Puerto Aisén • Chile ... 45 B5
Puerto Alegre • Bolivia ... 44 D1
Puerto Angel • Mexico ... 123 E4
Puerto Armuelles • Panama ... 37 E6
Puerto Asis • Colombia ... 43 B3
Puerto Ayacucho • Venezuela ... 43 D2
Puerto Ayora • Galapagos Is. ... 43 (1) A2
Puerto Banús • Spain ... 88 B6
Puerto Baquerizo Morena •
   Galapagos Is. ... 43 (1) B2
Puerto Berrio • Guatemala ... 37 D4
Puerto Berrio • Colombia ... 43 C2
Puerto Cabello • Venezuela ... 37 H5
Puerto Cabezas • Nicaragua ... 37 E5
Puerto Caldera • Costa Rica ... 58 B9
Puerto Carreño • Colombia ... 43 D2
Puerto Carreño • Colombia ... 43 D2
Puerto Cumarebo • Venezuela ... 43 D1
Puerto de la Cruz •
   Tenerife, Canary Is. ... 86 E1
Puerto de la Peña •
   Fuerteventura, Canary Is. ... 87 E2
Puerto de Lajas • Mexico ... 40 E6
Puerto de Mazarrón • Spain ... 87 C3
Puerto de Santiago •
   Tenerife, Canary Is. ... 86 E1
Puerto del Carmen •
   Lanzarote, Canary Is. ... 87 E3
Puerto del Rosario •
   Fuerteventura, Canary Is. ... 87 E2
Puerto del Santiago Beach •
   Tenerife, Canary Is. ... 68 [91]
Puerto Deseado • Argentina ... 45 C5
Puerto Escondido • Mexico ... 123 E4
Puerto Francisco de Orellana •
   Ecuador ... 43 B4
Puerto Heath • Bolivia ... 43 D6
Puerto Huasco • Chile ... 44 B4
Puerto Huitoto • Colombia ... 43 C3
Puerto Inca • Peru ... 127 B3
Puerto la Concordia • Colombia ... 43 C3
Puerto la Cruz • Venezuela ... 43 E1
Puerto Leguizamo • Colombia ... 43 C4
Puerto Limón • Costa Rica ... 37 E6
Puerto Limón • Colombia ... 43 B3
Puerto Lopez • Colombia ... 43 C3
Puerto Madryn • Argentina ... 58 A3
Puerto Maldonado • Peru ... 127 B2
Puerto Montt • Chile ... 45 B4
Puerto Nariño • Venezuela ... 43 D3
Puerto Natales • Chile ... 45 B6
Puerto Ordaz • Venezuela ... 43 E2
Puerto Padre • Cuba ... 124 D8
Puerto Paez • Venezuela ... 43 D2
Puerto Plata • Dominican Rep. ... 37 G4
Puerto Portals • Majorca, Spain ... 87 H3
Puerto Prado • Peru ... 127 B3
Puerto Princesa • Philippines ... 31 F5
Puerto Providencia • Peru ... 127 B2
Puerto Real • Spain ... 11 E8
Puerto Rico • Colombia ... 43 B3
Puerto Rico • Bolivia ... 43 D6
Puerto Rico •
   Gran Canaria, Canary Is. ... 86 E4
Puerto Rico • West Indies ... 125 E
Puerto Rico Trench •
   West Indies ... 37 H4
Puerto San José • Guatemala ... 37 C5
Puerto Santa Cruz • Argentina ... 45 C6
Puerto Siles • Bolivia ... 44 C1
Puerto Suárez • Bolivia ... 44 E2
Puerto Vallarta • Mexico ... 123 E1
Puerto Varas • Chile ... 45 B4
Puesti • Romania ... 14 O3
Puglia • Italy ... 12 K8
Puigcerdà • Spain ... 87 D1
Puigmal • France/Spain ... 11 N2
Puk'chong • D.P.R. of Korea ... 30 E4
Puka • Albania ... 15 A1
Pukapuka • French Polynesia ... 33 N7
Puksoozero • Russian Fed. ... 17 G2
Puksubaek • D.P.R. of Korea ... 30 D4
Pula • Croatia ... 12 H4
Pulaski, Fort, Nat. Mon. Park •
   GA, United States ... 121 [215]
Pulau Pinang [Adm] • Malaysia ... 31 C5
Pulau Tikus • Penang, Malaysia ... 108 C2
Pulawy • Poland ... 13 K6
Pulguksa Temple Heritage C •
   Rep. of Korea ... 63 [162]
Pulheim • Germany ... 81 E3
Pulicat Lake • India ... 106 D7
Pulkkila • Finland ... 16 M4
Pulkovo [Apt] • Russian Fed. ... 95 B4
Pullman • WA, United States ... 117 E2
Pulog, Mt • Philippines ... 31 G3
Pultusk • Poland ... 13 K5
Puma Yumco • China ... 28 D2
Pump Bay • St Kitts & Nevis ... 125 G1
Puná • Ecuador ... 43 A4
Punchestown • Ireland ... 79 E3
Pune • India ... 28 B5
Punggol • Singapore ... 108 E2
Púngoe • Mozambique ... 24 D4
Punia • Dem. Rep. of Congo ... 23 D4
Punjab [Adm] • India/Pakistan ... 28 B2
Punjab [Adm] • Pakistan ... 28 B2
Punjab [Adm] • India ... 28 C2
Puno • Peru ... 127 B4
Punta Almina • Spain ... 11 F9
Punta Alta • Argentina ... 45 D3
Punta Arenas • Chile ... 45 B6
Punta Cana • Dominican Rep. ... 37 H4
Punta, Cerro de • Puerto Rico ... 125 C3
Punta del Este • Uruguay ... 45 E3
Punta Gorda • Belize ... 37 D4
Punta Prieta • Mexico ... 40 B4
Punta Prima • Minorca, Spain ... 87 F4
Punta Räisi [Apt] •
   Sicily, Italy ... 90 D1
Punta Umbria Beach • Spain ... 68 [95]
Punta Umbria • Spain ... 86 B1
Puntarenas • Costa Rica ... 37 E6
Punto Fijo • Venezuela ... 43 D1
Puolanka • Finland ... 16 N4
Pupapuka • Cook Is. ... 33 K7
Puquio • Peru ... 127 B1
Pur • Russian Fed. ... 26 M4
Purace, Volcán • Colombia ... 43 B3
Purbeck, Isle of •
   United Kingdom ... 74 F6
Purépero • Indonesia ... 110 D6
Purcell Mtns • AL/BC, Canada ... 38 I7
Purcell Forest Park •
   New Zealand ... 112 K2
Purgatory Ski •
   CO, United States ... 116 [102]
Purmerend • Netherlands ... 80 C2
Purnia • India ... 28 E4
Purulya • India ... 28 E4
Purus • Brazil ... 43 D5
Purwakarta • Java, Indonesia ... 110 D1
Purwodadi • Java, Indonesia ... 110 D6
Purwokerto • Java, Indonesia ... 110 D6
Pusan • Rep. of Korea ... 30 E7
Pushkin • Russian Fed. ... 17 E3
Puspökladany • Hungary ... 13 K10
Pusteria, Val • Italy ... 90 B2

Pustertal • Austria/Italy ... 90 B2
Pusula Dagi • Turkey ... 15 N6
Puszcza Notecka • Poland ... 13 F5
Putao • Myanmar ... 31 B1
Putaruru • New Zealand ... 112 K2
Puteran • Indonesia ... 110 D4
Putian • China ... 29 F5
Putila • Ukraine ... 14 M2
Putorana, Plato • Russian Fed. ... 26 P4
Puttalam • Sri Lanka ... 106 D5
Puttaparthy • India ... 106 D1
Putten • Netherlands ... 80 C3
Puttgarden • Germany ... 8 G2
Putumayo • S. America ... 43 C4
Putuo Shan • China ... 29 G4
Putussibau • Indonesia ... 32 E2
Puukohola Heiau Nat. Hist. Site •
   HI, United States ... 119 L8
Puukohola Heiau Nat. Hist. Site Park •
   HI, United States ... 120 [19]
Puulavesi • Finland ... 16 N6
Puuwai • HI, United States ... 119 L2
Puy, le • France ... 10 I8
Puy-l'Evêque • France ... 85 G4
Puysegur Point • New Zealand ... 112 L3
Pweto • Dem. Rep. of Congo ... 23 D5
Pwllheli • United Kingdom ... 7 H9
Pwllheli Beach • United Kingdom ... 75 [191]
Pyalma • Russian Fed. ... 17 F2
Pyanskiy Zaliv • Russian Fed. ... 26 N3
Pyaozero • Russian Fed. ... 16 P3
Pyapon • Myanmar ... 28 G5
Pyasina • Russian Fed. ... 26 P3
Pyhä-Häkki Nat. Park Park •
   Finland ... 72 [35]
Pyhäjärvi • Finland ... 95 E3
Pyhäjoki • Finland ... 16 L4
Pyhäntä • Finland ... 16 N3
Pyhätunturi Nat. Park Park •
   Finland ... 72 [31]
Pyhrnpaß • Austria ... 14 B2
Pyräjoki • Finland ... 16 M4
Pyramid Canyon •
   AZ/NV, United States ... 118 J1
Pyramid Lake •
   NV, United States ... 117 F1
Pyrénées Occidentales, Parc nat. des Park •
   France ... 72 [71]
Pyrénées-Occidentales, Parc Nat. des •
   France ... 85 J2
Pyrénées-Orientales • France ... 85 K
Pyrénées-Orientales [Adm] •
   France ... 85 K2
Pyrzice • Poland ... 13 D4
Pyu • Myanmar ... 31 B3

Qaanaaq • Greenland ... 36 K2
Qadarif, Al • Sudan ... 21 G5
Qadimah, Al • Saudi Arabia ... 21 G3
Qadub • Yemen ... 18 F7
Qâhira, El • Egypt ... 101 F1
Qaidam Basin • China ... 107 G2
Qaidam He • China ... 28 C1
Qaidam Pendi • China ... 28 C1
Qaiouan Heritage C • Tunisia ... 64 [231]
Qairouan • Tunisia ... 101 E4
Qal'at al Jundi • Egypt ... 101 F2
Qal'at Bishah • Saudi Arabia ... 18 D6
Qal'eh-ye Now • Afghanistan ... 18 H3
Qala • Malta ... 93 H1
Qalat • Afghanistan ... 18 I3
Qalibah, Al • Saudi Arabia ... 18 C5
Qamdo • China ... 29 B4
Qamiac • France ... 84 C4
Qang Ngai • Vietnam ... 31 D3
Qang Tri • Vietnam ... 31 D3
Qaqortoq • Greenland ... 39 V4
Qar Wager • Somalia ... 20 H2
Qarabuli, Al • Libya ... 21 C2
Qarat as Sab'ah • Libya ... 21 C2
Qardo • Somalia ... 20 H3
Qarqan • China ... 28 C1
Qarqan He • China ... 28 C1
Qarshi • Uzbekistan ... 18 I2
Qasigiannguit • Greenland ... 39 U3
Qasr Amra Heritage C • Jordan ... 64 [248]
Qasr, El • Egypt ... 21 E2
Qasr Farâfra • Egypt ... 21 E2
Qasr Hamam • Saudi Arabia ... 18 E5
Qasr Ibrîm • Egypt ... 101 F5
Qasserine • Tunisia ... 101 E4
Qatar • Asia ... 18 E4
Qatif, Al • Saudi Arabia ... 18 E4
Qâttâra • Egypt ... 21 E2
Qattâra Depression • Egypt ... 101 F1
Qattâra, Munkhaffad al • Egypt ... 21 E2
Qawra • Malta ... 93 H2
Qayihah, Al • Saudi Arabia ... 18 D5
Qazrin • Syria ... 98 A1
Qazvin • Iran ... 18 E2
Qena • Egypt ... 101 F4
Qeqertarssuaq • Greenland ... 39 U3
Qerqenah Is. • Tunisia ... 101 E4
Qeshm • Iran ... 18 G4
Qezel Owzan • Iran ... 18 E2
Qian Gorlos • China ... 29 G1
Qianshan • Zhuhai, China ... 107 H2
Qiao Dao • Zhuhai, China ... 107 H2
Qiaowan • China ... 28 C1
Qidong • China ... 107 J2
Qijiaojing • China ... 28 C1
Qikiqtaluk • NU, Canada ... 122 A3
Qilian Shan • China ... 28 C1
Qin Ling • China ... 29 D4
Qingdao • China ... 29 F3
Qinghai • China ... 107 G2
Qinghai Hu • China ... 29 C3
Qingshan • China ... 107 J2
Qingyang • China ... 29 D3
Qingyuan • China ... 29 F5
Qing Jiang • China ... 107 G4
Qinhuangdao • China ... 29 F3
Qinzhou • China ... 29 D5
Qiong Hai • China ... 29 G1
Qiqihar • China ... 29 G1
Qira • China ... 28 B1
Qishn • Yemen ... 18 F6
Qitai • China ... 26 O9
Qixiashan • China ... 107 J2
Qog Feng • China/Kashmir ... 28 C1
Qoineng-Ve Damavand • Iran ... 18 F3
Qom • Iran ... 18 F3
Qomolangma Feng • China/Nepal ... 28 D2
Qomsheh • Iran ... 18 F3
Qorveh • Iran ... 18 E2
Qu'Appelle • MN/SA, Canada ... 38 K6
Qu'Appelle • China ... 29 C3
Quadane • Mauritania ... 22 D2
Quakenbrück • Germany ... 8 G4
Quanjiao • China ... 108 B3
Quanzhou • Guangxi, China ... 29 E5
Quanzhou • Fujian, China ... 29 F6
Quaqtaq • QU, Canada ... 39 R4
Quarry Bay • Hong Kong, China ... 107 H6

Quarteira • Portugal ... 88 E7
Quartu Sant' Elena •
   Sardinia, Italy ... 12 D9
Quatre Bornes • Seychelles ... 106 F3
Quchan • Iran ... 18 G2
Queanbeyan • NS, Australia ... 111 G2
Québec Heritage C • QU, Canada ... 62 [3]
Québec • QU, Canada ... 122 B4
Québec [Adm] • Canada ... 39 P6
Qued el Kehir • Algeria ... 12 C12
Quedlinburg • Germany ... 8 G5
Quedlinburg Heritage C •
   Germany ... 64 [34]
Queen Alexandra Range •
   Antarctica ... 46 (1) U1
Queen, Cape • NU, Canada ... 39 P4
Queen Charlotte Is. •
   BC, Canada ... 38 E6
Queen Charlotte Sound •
   BC, Canada ... 38 E6
Queen Charlotte Strait •
   BC, Canada ... 38 F6
Queen Elizabeth Is. •
   NU, Canada ... 38 K2
Queen Elizabeth Nat. Park Park •
   Uganda ... 103 [70]
Queen Maud Gulf • NU, Canada ... 38 K3
Queen Maud Land • Antarctica ... 46 (1) G2
Queen Maud Mtns • Antarctica ... 46 (1) CC1
Queen of Spains Valley •
   Jamaica ... 124 C1
Queens • NY, United States ... 118 H2
Queensland • Australia ... 34 H4
Queensland wet tropics Heritage N •
   QL, Australia ... 61 [129]
Queenstown • South Africa ... 24 D6
Queenstown • TS, Australia ... 34 I8
Queenstown • New Zealand ... 112 L2
Queenstown New Town • Singapore 108 E2
Quela • Angola ... 22 H6
Quelimane • Mozambique ... 24 D4
Quelpart Rep. of Korea ... 30 D7
Queluz • Portugal ... 88 D1
Quemoy • Taiwan ... 31 F2
Quenza • Corsica, France ... 85 L4
Queopán • Argentina ... 127 D3
Quepem • Goa, India ... 105 B1
Quepos • Costa Rica ... 37 E6
Querétaro Heritage C • Mexico ... 62 [16]
Querétaro • Mexico ... 123 E3
Quesa • Spain ... 11 H7
Quesada • Spain ... 11 H7
Queretaro Beach • Goa, India ... 105 B1
Queseda • Spain ... 11 H7
Quesnel • BC, Canada ... 122 C1
Quesnel Lake • BC, Canada ... 38 G6
Quetta • Pakistan ... 28 A2
Quevedo • Ecuador ... 43 B4
Queyras • France ... 85 F4
Quezaltenango • Guatemala ... 62 [29]
Quezon • Palawan, Philippines ... 31 F5
Quezon City •
   Luzon, Philippines ... 31 G3
Qufu Heritage C • China ... 63 [152]
Qui Nhon • Vietnam ... 31 D4
Quibdó • Colombia ... 43 B2
Quickborn • Germany ... 8 E3
Quiberon • France ... 84 C4
Quilán, Cabo • Chile ... 45 B5
Quilengues • Angola ... 23 G6
Quillacollo • Bolivia ... 44 C2
Quillan • France ... 85 K2
Quillota • Chile ... 44 E5
Quilmes • Argentina ... 44 E5
Quilon • India ... 106 D10
Quilpie • QL, Australia ... 34 H5
Quilpué • Chile ... 44 E5
Quimbele • Angola ... 23 B5
Quime • Bolivia ... 84 C4
Quimiac • France ... 84 C4
Quimili • Argentina ... 44 D4
Quimper • France ... 84 C3
Quimperlé • France ... 84 C3
Quincy • IL, United States ... 41 H4
Quincy • France ... 84 C4
Quincy • CA, United States ... 117 F1
Quindfrabah, Al • Saudi Arabia ... 18 D6
Quoin I. • QL, Australia ... 111 F4
Qurdud • Sudan ... 23 E1
Qurghoteppa • Tajikistan ... 18 I2
Quseir • Egypt ... 101 F4
Quthing • Lesotho ... 24 D6
Quxian • China ... 29 F5
Qüxü • China ... 28 F3

Radøy • Norway ... 94 C3
Radstadt Ski • Austria ... 70 [176]
Radviliskis • Lithuania ... 13 M2
Radzyn Podlaski • Poland ... 13 L6
Rae • NT, Canada ... 38 H4
Raetea • New Zealand ... 35 D2
Raetihi • New Zealand ... 112 K3
Raevavae • French Polynesia ... 33 M8
Raf-Raf • Tunisia ... 101 E2
Rafaela • Argentina ... 44 D5
Rafaï • Central African Rep. ... 23 C2
Rafina • Greece ... 92 D4
Rafina • Greece ... 92 D4
Rafsanjan • Iran ... 18 G3
Ragged I. • Bahamas ... 124 B4
Ragged I. Range • Bahamas ... 124 B3
Ragged, Mt • WA, Australia ... 34 D6
Ragged Point • Barbados ... 125 H4
Raging Waters Park •
   CA, United States ... 120 [F]
Raglan • New Zealand ... 112 K1
Raglan Castle • United Kingdom ... 74 D3
Raglan Harbour • New Zealand ... 112 K1
Ragley Hall • United Kingdom ... 74 D2
Ragusa • Croatia ... 71 A14
Ragusa • Sicily, Italy ... 90 D4
Raha • Indonesia ... 32 (1) B3
Rahad, Ar • Sudan ... 21 F5
Râhes Beach • Greece ... 69 [164]
Rahimyar Khan • Pakistan ... 28 B3
Rahole Game Reserve • Kenya ... 101 G2
Raichur • India ... 106 D2
Raiatea • French Polynesia ... 33 L7
Rainbow Bridge Nat. Mon. •
   UT, United States ... 118 J1
Rainbow Bridge Nat. Mon. Park •
   UT, United States ... 120 [84]
Rainbow Springs • New Zealand ... 112 K2
Rainier, Mt • WA, United States ... 117 E1
Rainy Lake •
   Canada/United States ... 38 M7
Rajpalpuoto • Finland ... 16 K5
Raipur • India ... 28 D4
Rasio • Finland ... 95 E3
Raja • Indonesia ... 110 D8
Raja Noi, Ko • Thailand ... 109 K2
Raja Yai, Ko • Thailand ... 109 K2
Rajahmundry • India ... 106 D4
Rajang • Malaysia ... 32 E2
Rajapalaiyam • India ... 106 D10
Rajasthan • India ... 28 B3
Rajasthan Canal • India ... 28 B3
Rajbag Beach • Goa, India ... 105 B2
Rajkot • India ... 28 B4
Rajshahi • Bangladesh ... 28 E4
Raka Zangbo • China ... 28 D2
Rakhine • Myanmar ... 31 A2
Rakhiv • Ukraine ... 14 L1
Rakhmanovskiye Klyuchi •
   Russian Fed. ... 26 O8
Rakit • Indonesia ... 110 D2
Rakistra • Russian Fed. ... 94 L8
Rakkestad • Norway ... 94 B4
Rakoniewice • Poland ... 13 F5
Rakops • Botswana ... 24 C4
Rakovnik • Czech Rep. ... 9 I6
Råkvåg • Norway ... 94 B2
Rakvere • Estonia ... 16 N7
Raleigh • NC, United States ... 41 K4
Raleigh, Fort, Nat. Hist. Site •
   NC, United States ... 118 H5
Raleigh, Fort, Nat. Hist. Site Park •
   NC, United States ... 121 [250]
Ralik Chain • Marshall Is. ... 33 H5
Rama • Nicaragua ... 43 A1
Ramadi, Ar • Iraq ... 18 D3
Ramatuelle Beach • France ... 68 [116]
Ramatuelle • France ... 85 H4
Rambervillers • France ... 9 B8
Ramberget, Fort de • France ... 85 E3
Rambouillet, Fort de • France ... 85 E3
Rambut Siwi Temple •
   Bali, Indonesia ... 110 C1
Rameswaram • India ... 106 D11
Ramgarh • India ... 28 E4
Ramiers Hist. Park Heritage C •
   Haiti ... 62 [37]
Ramisi • Kenya ... 101 G5
Ramla • Israel ... 98 A5
Ramla Bay • Malta ... 93 H1
Ramlat Dahm • Saudi Arabia ... 21 A4
Ramlu • Ethiopia ... 18 D7
Ramnagar • India ... 105 C8
Ramnäs • Sweden ... 95 C3
Rampur • India ... 105 C1
Ramree • Myanmar ... 31 A3
Ramsau • Germany ... 82 J8
Ramsau am Dachstein Ski •
   Austria ... 70 [183]
Ramsele • Sweden ... 16 I5
Ramsgate • United Kingdom ... 74 E2
Ramsgate Beach • United Kingdom ... 75 [65]
Ramsjö • Sweden ... 16 H5
Rana • Laos ... 31 C2
Rana • Norway ... 16 H3
Ranai • Indonesia ... 110 D8
Ranakpur • India ... 105 C5
Ranai • Norway ... 16 H3
Ranau • Malaysia ... 32 F1
Rancagua • Chile ... 45 B2
Rance • France ... 84 C2
Ranchi • India ... 28 D4
Rancho Luna, Playa • Cuba ... 124 D2
Randaberg • Norway ... 94 C5
Randers • Denmark ... 95 F10
Random I. • NF, Canada ... 123 D4
Randringhausen Spa • Germany ... 83 [85]
Ranfurly • New Zealand ... 35 D6
Rangae • New Zealand ... 112 K2
Rangitaiki • New Zealand ... 112 K2
Rangitikei • New Zealand ... 112 K4
Rangkasbitung • Java, Indonesia ... 110 D1
Rangoon • Myanmar ... 31 B3
Rangpur • Bangladesh ... 28 E3
Rangsdorf • Germany ... 81 F4
Rangsdorfer See • Germany ... 81 F4
Ranikhet • India ... 105 C3
Rannalhi • Maldives ... 106 F4
Rannoch, Loch • United Kingdom ... 74 B1
Ranomafana, Parc nat. de Park •
   Madagascar ... 103 [138]
Ranong • Thailand ... 31 B5
Ransdfjorden • Norway ... 94 B2
Ranski • Finland ... 32 (1) J3
Rantaunprapat • Indonesia ... 32 D3
Rantauprapat • Indonesia ... 110 B4
Ranthambor Nat. Park • India ... 105 C6
Rantum Spa • Germany ... 83 [2]
Ranua • Finland ... 16 N3
Ranyah, Wadi • Saudi Arabia ... 21 H3
Rapa • French Polynesia ... 33 M8
Rapa Nui • Pacific Ocean ... 33 M9
Rapa Nui, Parque Nac. Heritage C •
   Pacific Ocean ... 62 [66]
Rapallo • Italy ... 91 E6
Raper, Cape • NU, Canada ... 39 R3

Rapid City • SD, United States 40 F3
Rapla • Estonia 16 N7
Raposeira • Portugal 88 E5
Rapperswil • Switzerland 89 G3
Rapulo • Bolivia 44 C1
Raroia • French Polynesia 33 M7
Rarotonga • Cook Is. 33 L8
Ras Beddouza • Morocco 20 D2
Râs el Bar • Egypt 101 F2
Râs el Mâ • Mali 20 E5
Râs el Ma Niafounke • Mali 22 D1
Râs Ghârib • Egypt 101 F4
Râs Jumbo • Somalia 23 G4
Râs Sidi Ali el Mekki • Tunisia 12 E11
Rasa, Punta • Argentina 45 D4
Rasa, Punta • Argentina 127 D4
Rascani • Moldova 14 O2
Rasdhu Atoll • Maldives 106 E1
Raseiniai • Lithuania 13 M2
Rashid • Egypt 101 F1
Rasht • Iran 18 E2
Raso, Cabo • Portugal 88 D1
Rason Lake • WA, Australia 34 D5
Rastatt • Germany 82 G6
Rastede • Germany 9 G7
Rat I. • St Lucia 125 J1
Rat Is. • AK, United States 36 (1) B2
Ratak Chain • Marshall Is. 33 I5
Ratangarh • India 18 J4
Ratchaburi • Thailand 109 H1
Ráth Luirc • Ireland 79 F6
Rathangan • Ireland 79 E3
Rathcoole • Ireland 79 E2
Rathdrum • Ireland 79 E4
Rathnew • Germany 8 H4
Rathkeale • Ireland 79 F6
Rathlin I. • United Kingdom 7 F6
Rathmullen Beach • Ireland .... 68 [46]
Rathvilly • Ireland 79 E3
Ratiborice • Czech Rep. 96 C2
Ratingen • Germany 81 E3
Ratlam • India 28 C4
Ratnagir • India 106 D1
Ratno • Ukraine 13 N6
Raton • NM, United States 40 F4
Ratta • Russian Fed. 26 N5
Rattenberg • Austria 89 H3
Rattlesnake Nat. Recreation Area •
    MT, United States 117 E2
Ratz, Mt • BC, Canada 38 E5
Ratzeburg • Germany 8 F3
Rauch • Argentina 127 D3
Rauland • Norway 94 C6
Rauma Heritage C • Finland .... 63 [73]
Rauma • Norway 94 B2
Rauma • Finland 95 E1
Raung, Gunung • Java, Indonesia 28 D4
Raurkela • India 28 D4
Ravello • Italy 91 G4
Ravenglass • United Kingdom 74 C3
Ravenglass & Eskdale Railway •
    United Kingdom 74 C3
Ravenglass Estuary •
    United Kingdom 74 C3
Ravenna Heritage C • Italy .... 64 [116]
Ravenna • Italy 91 E8
Ravensburg • Germany 82 J5
Ravenshoe • QL, Australia 111 F1
Ravensthorpe • WA, Australia 34 D6
Ravi • Pakistan 28 D2
Ravnina • Turkmenistan 18 H2
Rawa Mazowiecka • Poland 13 J6
Rawai • Phuket, Thailand 109 K2
Rawai Beach • Phuket, Thailand 109 J5
Rawaki • Kiribati 33 J6
Rawalpindi • Pakistan 28 B2
Rawicz • Poland 13 F6
Rawlinna • WA, Australia 34 E6
Rawlins • WY, United States 40 E3
Rawlinson Ranges •
    NT/WA, Australia 34 E5
Rawson • Argentina 45 C4
Raxaul • India 105 C4
Raya, Bukit • Indonesia 32 E3
Rayburn, Sam, Reservoir •
    TX, United States 119 N4
Raychikhinsk • Russian Fed. 27 K7
Rayong • Thailand 109 H4
Rayy • Iran 98 B4
Raz, Pointe de • France 84 C3
Razelm, Lacul • Romania 97 D2
Razgrad • Bulgaria 97 D3
Razlog • Bulgaria 14 K8
Ré, Île de • France 84 D3
Reach Falls • Jamaica 124 C4
Reading • PA, United States 118 H1
Realico • Argentina 44 D5
Reboly • Russian Fed. 16 P5
Rebord Manambien • Madagascar 23 J4
Rebun • Japan 30 K2
Recherche, Archipelago of the •
    WA, Australia 34 D6
Recife • Brazil 45 (1) E3
Recife, Cape • South Africa 100 C8
Recklinghausen • Germany 81 E2
Recknitz • Germany 8 H2
Reconquista • Argentina 44 E4
Recreo • Argentina 44 C4
Red • China/Vietnam 29 C6
Red Basin • China 107 G7
Red Bluff • CA, United States 117 F1
Red Centre, The • NT, Australia .... 112 H
Red Cliff • St Kitts & Nevis 125 G4
Red Deer • AL, Canada 2 D4
Red Deer [Riv] • AL, Canada 38 D4
Red Hill Patrick Henry Nat. Mem. Park •
    VA, United States .... 121 [253]
Red Lodge Mtn Ski •
    MT, United States .... 116 [75]
Red Mtn Ski • BC, Canada .... 116 [7]
Red River • United States 40 G5
Red River Ski •
    NM, United States .... 116 [104]
Red River of the North •
    United States 41 G2
Red Sea • Africa/Asia 21 G3
Red Sea cruise area •
    Africa/Asia 59 A5/7
Redcar • United Kingdom 7 K7
Redding • CA, United States 117 F1
Redditch • United Kingdom 7 J9
Redeyef • Tunisia 84 C4
Redon • France 84 C4
Redondo • Portugal 11 D6
Redondo, Monte •
    Corsica, France 85 L2
Redruth • United Kingdom 74 F4
Réduit Beach • St Lucia 125 J2
Redwood Nat. Park Heritage N •
    CA, United States .... 60 [10]
Redwood Nat. Park •
    CA, United States 117 F1
Redwood Nat. Park Park •
    CA, United States .... 120 [38]
Ree, Lough • Ireland 7 D8
Reethi Rah • Maldives 106 E2
Refugio • TX, United States 119 N5
Regen • Germany 9 H6
Regen [Riv] • Germany 9 H7

Regensburg • Germany 9 H7
Regenstauf • Germany 9 H6
Reggane • Algeria 20 F3
Regge • Netherlands 5 J2
Réggio di Calabria • Italy 90 D2
Réggio nell' Emilia • Italy 91 E7
Regina • SA, Canada 14 L3
Regina • SA, Canada 38 K6
Regina • French Guiana 43 G3
Regnitz • Germany 9 G7
Reguengos de Monsaraz •
    Portugal 11 D6
Rehoboth • Namibia 24 B4
Rehoboth Beach •
    DE, United States 118 H3
Rei, Costa • Sardinia, Italy 90 C4
Reichenbach • Germany 9 H6
Reichenstein, Burg • Germany 82 H4
Reichstag • Germany 81 F2
Reigate • United Kingdom 74 E3
Reims • France 10 J4
Reims Heritage C • France .... 64 [50]
Reina Adelaida, Archipiélago •
    Chile 45 A6
Reina Sofía [Apt] •
    Tenerife, Canary Is. 86 E1
Reindeer • SA, Canada 38 K5
Reindeer Lake • MN/SA, Canada 38 K5
Reiner's Beach • Goa, India 105 B2
Reinga, Cape • New Zealand 35 D2
Reinhardstein, Château de •
    Belgium 80 A16
Reis Magos Fort • Goa, India 105 B1
Reisa Nat. Park Park • Norway .... 72 [6]
Reisselva • Norway 16 K2
Reischach Ski • Italy .... 70 [235]
Reischach • Italy 90 B2
Reit im Winkl Ski • Germany .... 70 [5]
Reit im Winkl • Germany 82 J8
Rejmyre • Sweden 95 D3
Rekarne • Sweden 95 D3
Reliance • NT, Canada 11 D1
Relizane • Algeria 20 F1
Remada • Tunisia 101 E6
Remagen • Germany 82 H1
Remarkables, The • New Zealand 112 L2
Rembang • Java, Indonesia 110 D3
Rembau • Malaysia 108 D4
Remich • Luxembourg 80 A20
Rémire • Seychelles 106 F2
Remiremont • France 10 L5
Remoulins Heritage C • France .... 64 [65]
Remscheid • Germany 81 E4
Rémuzat • France 10 K9
Rendsburg • Germany 8 E2
Renfrew • ON, Canada 39 P7
Rengat • Indonesia 32 C3
Rengdorf Spa • Germany .... 83 [152]
Reni • Ukraine 14 P4
Renmark • SA, Australia 34 H6
Rennell • Solomon Is. 33 H7
Rennes • France 84 C4
Rennesøy • Norway 94 C5
Reno • Italy 12 F4
Reno • NV, United States 117 F1
Renqiu • China 29 F3
Reo • Indonesia 32 (1) B4
Réole, la • France 85 G3
Reposaari • Finland 95 E1
Repulse Bay • NU, Canada 39 M1
Repulse Bay • Hong Kong, China 107 H6
Repulse Bay • QL, Australia 111 F3
Repvåg • Norway 16 M1
Requena • Spain 11 J5
Requena • Peru 43 C5
Réquista • France 10 H9
Rerik Spa • Germany .... 83 [267]
Résheni • Albania 14 G8
Resistencia • Argentina 44 E4
Resita • Romania 14 I4
Resolute • NU, Canada 38 M2
Resolution I. • NU, Canada 39 S4
Resolution I. • New Zealand 112 L3
Restonica, Gorges de la •
    Corsica, France 85 L2
Retezat Nat. Park Park •
    Romania .... 72 [129]
Rethel • France 10 K4
Réthimno Beach • Crete, Greece .... 69 [189]
Réthimno • Crete, Greece 93 E2
Réthimno [Adm] • Crete, Greece 93 E6
Rettenberg • Germany 82 J6
Retz • Austria 96 C4
Reuben • Jordan 98 A8
Reuilly • France 84 B1
Réunion, la • Seychelles 106 F4
Reus • Spain 87 D3
Reuss • Switzerland 89 G3
Reutlingen • Germany 82 G6
Reval • Estonia 71 A4
Revelstoke • BC, Canada 122 C4
Revillagigedo, Is. • Mexico 36 F8
Revin • France 10 J4
Rewa • India 105 C7
Rewari • India 105 C2
Rex, Mt • Antarctica 46 (1) HH2
Rexburg • ID, United States 40 D3
Rey • Iran 18 F2
Rey • Panama 43 B2
Reyes, Point •
    CA, United States 117 F3
Reykjahlid • Iceland 16 (1) E2
Reykjanes • Iceland 16 (1) B3
Reykjavik • Iceland 16 (1) B2
Reynolds Range • NT, Australia 112 H2
Reynosa • Mexico 37 B2
Rezé • France 10 D6
Rezekne • Latvia 16 N8
Rezovo • Bulgaria 97 E4
Rezvaya • Bulgaria/Turkey 15 I2
Rheda-Wiedenbrück • Germany 8 D5
Rhein • Germany/Switzerland 9 C6
Rhein-Main [Apt] • Germany 82 H1
Rheinbach • Germany 82 H1
Rheinberg • Germany 81 D2
Rheine • Germany 8 C4
Rheineck, Burg • Germany 82 H1
Rheinfelden • Germany 82 G8
Rheinfels, Burg • Germany 82 H4
Rheingau • Germany 82 H4
Rheinhessen • Germany 82 H4
Rheinisches Schiefergebirge •
    Germany 5 K4
Rheinland-Pfalz • Germany 8 H3
Rheinsberg • Germany 8 H3
Rheinturm • Germany 81 D3
Rhenen • Netherlands 80 A11
Rhens • Germany 82 H1
Rhêmes • Morocco 81 E1
Rheydt, Schloß • Germany 81 D3
Rhin • France 10 M5
Rhine • Europe 9 C6
Rhine Gorge • Germany 82 H2
Rhineland-Palatinate • Germany 82 H3
Rhir, Cap • Morocco 101 D5
Rhode I. • United States 118 H2
Rhodes Heritage C • Greece .... 64 [187]

Rhodes Beach • Greece .... 69 [187]
Rhodes • Rhodes, Greece 93 F2
Rhodes' Grave • Zimbabwe 102 J3
Rhodes [I.] • Greece .... 93 F
Rhodopi • Bulgaria/Greece 14 L8
Rhön • Germany 81 D3
Rhondda • United Kingdom 7 I10
Rhone • France/Switzerland 10 J9
Rhône au Rhin, Canal du •
    France 9 C8
Rhône-Alpes • France 84 A2
Rhosneigr Beach •
    United Kingdom .... 75 [204]
Rhossili Beach • United Kingdom .... 75 [143]
Rhubodach • United Kingdom 78 A2
Rhyl • United Kingdom 7 I8
Rhyl Beach • United Kingdom .... 75 [199]
Riaño • Spain 11 F2
Riau • Indonesia 110 B4
Riau, Kepulauan • Indonesia 32 C2
Riaza • Spain 10 B12
Rib Mtn Ski • WI, United States .... 116 [120]
Ribadeo • Spain 11 D1
Ribadeo Beach • Spain .... 68 [72]
Ribamontán al Mar Beach • Spain .... 68 [70]
Ribatejo • Portugal 11 C5
Ribble • United Kingdom 7 J8
Ribe [Adm] • Denmark 95 F9
Ribe • Denmark 95 F10
Ribeira • Spain 11 C2
Ribeira Grande Beach • Azores .... 68 [87]
Ribeira Grande • Azores 88 B1
Ribeirão Prêto • Brazil 44 G3
Ribnica • Slovenia 14 B4
Ribnitz-Damgarten • Germany 11 F3
Ricabayo, Embalse de • Spain 11 F3
Ricardi Beach • Italy .... 69 [130]
Ricard, Circuit Paul • France 85 H3
Riccione • Italy 91 E12
Rich • Morocco 20 E2
Richard Collinson Inlet •
    NT, Canada 38 I2
Richard Toll • Senegal 20 B5
Richard's Bay • South Africa 24 E5
Richardson Mtns • NT/YT, Canada 38 D3
Richardson Mtns • New Zealand 112 L2
Richat, Guelb er • Mauritania 20 C4
Richborough Castle •
    United Kingdom 74 E2
Richelieu • France 10 F7
Richelieu • QU, Canada 122 B8
Richfield • UT, United States 40 D4
Richland • WA, United States 117 E2
Richmond • SA, Canada 35 D5
Richmond • KY, United States 41 J4
Richmond • South Africa 100 C3
Richmond • WA, United States 118 H3
Richmond, Mt • New Zealand 35 D5
Richmond Nat. Battlefield Park Park •
    VA, United States .... 121 [259]
Ridderkerk • Netherlands 80 A8
Ried • Austria 13 C9
Riederalp Ski • Switzerland .... 70 [98]
Riederalp • Switzerland 89 G6
Riedlingen • Germany 82 J1
Rienz • Italy 90 B1
Riesa • Germany 9 I5
Riesco, I. • Chile 45 B6
Rietavas • Lithuania 13 L1
Rieti • Italy 91 F2
Rietini, Monti • Italy 91 F4
Riezlern Ski • Austria .... 70 [128]
Riezlern • Austria 89 I1
Rif • Morocco 101 D2
Rifstangi • Iceland 16 (1) I1
Rift Valley • Africa 100 A3
Riga • Latvia 16 M8
Riga Heritage C • Latvia .... 64 [202]
Riga, Gulf of • Estonia/Latvia 16 M8
Rigestan • Afghanistan 18 I7
Rihiveli Beach • Maldives 106 E4
Rihveli • Maldives 95 E4
Rijeka • Croatia 14 B4
Rijnsburg • Netherlands 80 C1
Rijswijk • Netherlands 80 C3
Rika • Ukraine 14 K1
Rila • Bulgaria 14 K8
Rila Heritage C • Bulgaria .... 64 [173]
Rima • Nigeria .... 22 [108]
Rimau • Malaysia 108 C3
Rimavská Sobota • Slovak Rep. 13 J9
Rímini • Italy 91 E12
Rîmnicu Sarat • Romania 14 O4
Rîmnicu Vîlcea • Romania 14 L4
Rimouski • QU, Canada 123 D1
Rimouski Prov. Reserve •
    QU, Canada 123 D1
Rincón, Bahía de • Puerto Rico 125 E4
Rincón del Bonete, Lago Artificial de •
    Uruguay 127 D2
Ringe • Denmark 95 F14
Ringerike • Norway 94 B6
Ringkøbing Beach • Denmark .... 68 [31]
Ringkøbing • Denmark 95 F9
Ringkøbing [Adm] • Denmark 95 F9
Ringkøbing Fjord • Denmark 95 F9
Ringlades • Corfu, Greece 15 A4
Ringsjön • Sweden 95 F7
Ringsted Beach • Denmark .... 68 [24]
Ringsted • Denmark 95 F14
Ringvassøy • Norway 16 J1
Rinia • Greece 92 D8
Rinns • Greece 92 D8
Rinjani, Gunung • Indonesia 32 F4
Rinteln • Germany 8 E5
Río Abiseo, Parque Nac. Heritage N •
    Peru .... 60 [31]
Río Branco • Brazil 43 D6
Rio Bueno • Jamaica 124 C1
Río Caribe • Venezuela 43 E1
Río Claro • Trinidad & Tobago 125 K4
Río Colorado • Argentina 44 D5
Río Cuarto • Argentina 44 D5
Rio das Ostras • Brazil 127 C4
Río de Janeiro • Brazil 127 C4
Río de Janeiro [Adm] • Brazil 127 C4
Río de la Plata • Puerto Rico 125 E2
Río de Oro, Bahía de •
    Western Sahara 20 B4
Río Gallegos • Argentina 45 B6
Rio Grande • Brazil 44 E6
Río Grande • Argentina 45 C6
Río Grande do Sul • Brazil 45 (1) D3
Rio Grande do Sul • Brazil 44 F4
Río Largo • Italy 91 E11
Rio Negro • Brazil 44 F2
Rio Pardo • Argentina 16 G8
Río Platano, Reserva de la Biósfera Heritage
    N • Honduras .... 60 [22]
Rio Rancho • NM, United States 118 J2
Río Verde • Brazil 44 F3
Río Verde • Mexico 123 E2
Riobamba • Ecuador 43 B4

Riohacha • Colombia 43 C1
Riom • France 10 I8
Rionero in Vulture • Italy 12 J8
Ripoll • Spain 11 N2
Ripon • United Kingdom 7 K7
Riposto • Sicily, Italy 12 J11
Riscone Ski • Italy .... 70 [235]
Riscone • Italy 90 B2
Rishiri • Japan 30 K2
Rishø • France 5 D6
Risinge • Croatia 14 B4
Risnjak Nat. Park Park •
    Croatia .... 72 [108]
Risør • Norway 95 F1
Risoul Ski • France .... 70 [66]
Risoul • France 85 F4
Ritchie's Archipelago • India 28 F6
Riva del Garda • Italy 91 E3
Rivadavia • Argentina 44 C5
River Cess • Liberia 22 C3
River Kwai Bridge • Thailand 109 H1
Rivera • Argentina 44 D6
Rivera • Uruguay 44 E5
Riverina • NS, Australia 111 G1
Rivers • Nigeria 22 F3
Riversdale • South Africa 100 C6
Riverside • CA, United States 117 F6
Riverside [Apt] •
    United Kingdom 74 B2
Riversleigh Heritage N •
    QL, Australia .... 61 [133]
Riverton • WY, United States 40 E3
Riverton • New Zealand 112 L4
Rivesaltes [Apt] • France 85 K2
Rivera à France/Italy 91 E10
Riviera di Levante • Italy 91 E10
Rive di Ponente • Italy 91 E9
Rivière du Loup • QU, Canada 123 D1
Rivoli • Italy 12 B3
Rixensart • Belgium 80 A14
Riyadh • Saudi Arabia 18 E5
Rizhao • China 29 F3
Rizokárpasso • Cyprus 93 J2
Rjukan • Norway 94 B1
Roa • Spain 11 G5
Roa • Norway 94 B2
Road Bay • Anguilla 58 B7
Roanne • France 10 J7
Roanoke • VA, United States 41 K4
Roanoke • NC, United States 118 H5
Roatán • Honduras 37 D4
Roh Roy's Grave •
    United Kingdom 74 B1
Robben I. • South Africa 100 C5
Robe • Ireland 79 F4
Robe, Mt • NS, Australia 34 H6
Röbel • Germany 8 H3
Roberts, Mt • QL, Australia 111 F6
Robertsfors • Sweden 16 K4
Robertsganj • India 105 C8
Robertson • South Africa 100 C6
Robertstown • Ireland 79 E3
Roberval • QU, Canada 123 D1
Robin Hood's Bay Beach •
    United Kingdom .... 75 [30]
Robinson Range • WA, Australia 34 C5
Robson, Mt • AL, Canada 122 C2
Roca, Cabo da • Portugal 88 D1
Rocamadour, Château de • France 85 G4
Rocas, Atol das • Brazil 127 A1
Rocca di Papa • Italy 91 F3
Rocha • Uruguay 44 E5
Rochdale • United Kingdom 7 J8
Roche-Guyon, la • France 85 E1
Roche-Racan [Château] • France 84 D2
Roche-sur-Yon, la • France 84 D2
Rochefort • Belgium 80 A19
Rochefort • France 85 G1
Rochefoucauld, la • France 85 G2
Rochegda • Russian Fed. 17 E2
Rochehaut • Belgium 80 A19
Rochelle, la Beach • France .... 68 [65]
Rochelle, la • France 84 D3
Rocher River • NT, Canada 38 I4
Rochester • MN, United States 41 H3
Rochester • NY, United States 41 K3
Rochester • United Kingdom 74 E2
Rochester • NH, United States 118 G3
Rochford [Adm] • United Kingdom 74 B2
Rock Creek Park Park •
    DC, United States .... 121 [293]
Rock Hill • SC, United States 41 J5
Rock Sound • Bahamas 124 B1
Rock Springs •
    WY, United States 40 E3
Rockall • Atlantic Ocean 4 H5
Rockefeller Jr., John D., Mem. Parkway
    Park •
    WY, United States .... 120 [75]
Rockefeller Plateau •
    Antarctica 46 (1) BB1
Rockford • IL, United States 41 I3
Rockhampton • WA, Australia 34 C6
Rockland • ME, United States 118 G4
Rockley Beach • Barbados 125 H3
Rockport • TX, United States 119 N5
Rocky Mtn Nat. Park Park •
    CO, United States .... 120 [89]
Rocky Mtns •
    Canada/United States 36 F5
Rocky Point • Jamaica 124 C4
Rocque-Gageac, la • France 85 G4
Rocreai • France 5 H5
Rod Hill, Fort • BC, Canada 122 B3
Róda • Corfu, Greece 92 B1
Róda • Corfu, Greece 92 B1
Rodach Spa • Germany .... 83 [223]
Rødby • Denmark 16 F9
Rødby Beach • Denmark .... 68 [18]
Rødbyhavn • Denmark 95 F14
Rødberg • Norway 94 B1
Rødenes • Norway 94 B2
Rödental • Germany 9 H8
Rode • France 10 H9
Rodgau • Germany 5 L5
Rodez • France 10 I9
Rodi Gargánico • Italy 12 J7
Rodiá Beach • Crete, Greece .... 69 [190]
Rodiá • Crete, Greece 93 E3
Rosière, la Ski • France .... 70 [37]
Rosière, la • France 85 F3
Roding • United Kingdom 5 H7
Rodnei, Muntii • Romania 14 L3
Rodney Bay • St Lucia 125 J2
Rodolivos • Greece 93 E1
Rodonit, Kep i • Albania 14 G8
Rodopi • Greece 93 E1
Rodopi Planina •
    Bulgaria/Greece 14 L8
Rodópoi, Hersónisos •
    Crete, Greece 93 E1
Ródos Heritage C • Greece .... 64 [187]
Ródos Beach • Rhodes, Greece .... 69 [187]
Ródos • Rhodes, Greece 93 F2
Ródos [I.] • Greece 93 F2
Rodrigues • Indian Ocean 19 K8
Roebourne • WA, Australia 34 B4
Roermond • Netherlands 80 A12
Roes Welcome Sound • NU, Canada 39 N4
Roeselare • Belgium 5 G4

Rogaguado, Laguna • Bolivia 44 C1
Rogaland • Norway 16 F7
Rogliano • Corsica, France 85 L2
Rohtak • India 105 C2
Rohtas Heritage C • Pakistan .... 63 [114]
Rohtas • India 105 C8
Rojo, Cabo • Puerto Rico 125 E3
Rokan • Indonesia 110 B4
Rokitnokárren • Belarus 13 N5
Rokycany • Czech Rep. 96 C1
Rola Co • China 28 E1
Rolandsbogen • Germany 82 H1
Røldal • Norway 94 C6
Rolla • MO, United States 41 H4
Rollag • Norway 94 B1
Rolle, Passo di • Italy 90 B3
Rolvsøya • Norway 94 A3
Roma Heritage C • Italy .... 64 [125]
Roma • QL, Australia 111 F5
Roma • NY, United States 14 N3
Roman • Romania 14 N3
Romang • Indonesia 32 (1) C4
Romania • Europe 14 M4
Romans-sur-Isère • France 10 J8
Romanshorn • Switzerland 89 H1
Romantische Straße • Germany 82 J2
Rombo Pass • Austria/Italy 90 B1
Rome • CA, United States 41 J5
Rome Heritage C • Italy .... 64 [125]
Rome • NY, United States 122 B10
Romeleåsen • Sweden 95 F11
Romerike • Norway 94 B2
Romilly-sur-Seine • France 10 I5
Romkamhang Nat. Park •
    Thailand 109 G4
Romney • United Kingdom 74 A7
Romney, Hythe & Dymchurch Light Railway •
    United Kingdom 74 B2
Romney Manor • St Kitts & Nevis 125 G1
Rømø • Denmark 95 F13
Romorantin-Lanthenay • France 84 D2
Romsdalfjorden • Norway 94 C2
Romsey • United Kingdom 74 B1
Ronda • Spain 86 B6
Ronda, Serranía de • Spain 86 B6
Rondane • Norway 16 E6
Rondane Nat. Park Park • Norway .... 72 [13]
Rønde • Denmark 95 F10
Rondón • Brazil 43 E3
Rondônia • Brazil 43 E6
Rondonópolis • Brazil 44 F2
Ronge, Lac la • SA, Canada 38 K5
Ronne • Belgium 95 F16
Ronne Bay • Antarctica 46 (1) HH2
Ronne Ice Shelf • Antarctica 46 (1) JJ2
Ronneby • Sweden 95 F12
Ronse • Belgium 5 G4
Roosendaal • Netherlands 80 A10
Roosevelt • Brazil 43 E6
Roosevelt Campobello Int. Park Park •
    NB, Canada .... 121 [356]
Roosevelt Campobello Int. Park •
    NB, Canada 123 D6
Roosevelt, Eleanor, Nat. Hist. Site Park •
    NY, United States .... 121 [321]
Roosevelt, Franklin D., Lake •
    WA, United States 117 E2
Roosevelt, Home of F.D., Nat. Hist. Site Park •
    NY, United States .... 121 [323]
Roosevelt, Mt • BC, Canada 38 F5
Roosevelt, Theodore, Birthplace Nat. Hist.
    Site Park • NY, United States .... 121 [332]
Roosevelt, Theodore, Dam •
    AZ, United States 118 J3
Roosevelt, Theodore, Inaugural Nat. Hist.
    Site Park • NY, United States .... 121 [316]
Roosevelt, Theodore, Island Park •
    DC, United States .... 121 [295]
Roosevelt, Theodore, Lake •
    ND, United States 118 J3
Roosevelt, Theodore, Nat. Park Park •
    ND, United States .... 120 [148]
Roper • NT, Australia 34 F2
Roques • Venezuela 43 D1
Roquetas de Mar Beach • Spain .... 68 [99]
Roquetas de Mar • Spain 86 B8
Roraima [Adm] • Brazil 43 E3
Roraima [Mtn] • S. America 43 E2
Røros • Norway 16 F5
Røros Heritage C • Norway .... 63 [69]
Rørvig • Denmark 95 F14
Rørvik • Norway 16 F4
Rosa, Lake • Bahamas 124 B4
Rosa, Monte • Italy/Switzerland 89 G6
Rosário • Brazil 45 (1) C2
Rosario • Argentina 127 D1
Rosario • Uruguay 127 D2
Rosario de Arriba • Mexico 40 C5
Rosario de Lerma • Argentina 44 C3
Rosário do Sul • Brazil 44 F5
Rosario, Sierra del • Cuba 124 D1
Rosarno • Italy 12 K10
Roscoff Beach • France .... 68 [61]
Roscoff • France 84 C4
Roscommon • Ireland 79 F4
Roscommon [Adm] • Ireland 79 F2
Roscrea • Ireland 7 E9
Rose Hall • Jamaica 124 C1
Rosebery • TS, Australia 34 I9
Roseburg • OR, United States 40 B3
Rosenberg • TX, United States 119 N6
Rosendal • Norway 94 C5
Rosenheim • Germany 82 J3
Rosenholm • Denmark 95 F10
Roses Beach • Spain .... 68 [106]
Roses • Spain 87 D2
Roses, Golf de • Spain 11 O2
Roses, Valley of • Bulgaria 97 D3
Rosetherm • SA, Canada 14 L3
Rosetown • SA, Canada 38 J6
Rosetta • Egypt 101 F1
Rosetta Mouth • Egypt 101 F1
Rosetto degli Abruzzi • Italy 12 I6
Rosière, la Ski • France .... 70 [37]
Rosière, la • France 85 F3
Rosignano Marittimo • Italy 91 E11
Rosiori de Vede • Romania 97 D1
Roskilde Beach • Denmark .... 64 [10]
Roskilde • Denmark 95 F10
Roskilde [Adm] • Denmark 95 F10
Roslagen • Sweden 95 D2
Roslavl • Russian Fed. 17 E4
Ross • TS, Australia 34 I8
Ross, Mt • Kerguelen Is. 46 (1) L5
Ross, Mt • NT, Australia 112 H2
Ross Sea • Antarctica 46 (1) Y2
Ross-on-Wye • United Kingdom 74 D3
Rossan Point • Ireland 7 D7
Rossano • Italy 12 K9
Rosses Point Beach • Ireland .... 68 [45]
Rosses Point • Ireland 79 F2
Rossignol, Lake • NS, Canada 123 E5
Rosslare Beach • Ireland .... 68 [37]
Rosslare Harbour • Ireland 7 F9
Rosslau • Germany 8 H5
Rossnowlagh Beach • Ireland .... 68 [46]
Rosso • Mauritania 20 B5
Rossosh • Russian Fed. 17 F4
Rossvatnet • Norway 16 G3
Rostock • Germany 8 H2
Rostock • Poland 13 M7
Rostov • Russian Fed. 98 E4
Rostov-na-Donu • Russian Fed. 17 F5
Rostrenen • France 84 C1
Roswell • NM, United States 40 F5
Rot • Germany 82 J1
Rota • Northern Mariana Is. 33 F4
Rota Beach • Spain .... 68 [96]
Rota • Spain 86 A7
Rote • Indonesia 110 A7
Rotenburg an der Fulda •
    Germany 9 F6
Rotenburg • Germany 9 G5
Roth • Germany 82 J1
Rothaargebirge • Germany 9 D5
Rothenburg ob der Tauber •
    Germany 9 F7
Rothenuffeln Spa • Germany .... 83 [88]
Rothera [Base] • Antarctica 46 (1) II3
Rotherham • United Kingdom 7 K8
Rothesay • United Kingdom 78 A2
Rotoehu, Lake • New Zealand 112 K2
Rotoiti, Lake • New Zealand 112 K2
Rotoma, Lake • New Zealand 112 K2
Rotorua • New Zealand 112 K2
Rotorua, Lake • New Zealand 112 K2
Rott • Germany 9 I8
Rottach-Egern • Germany 82 J7
Rottach-Egern Spa • Germany .... 83 [258]
Rottal • Germany 82 J6
Rottenbuch • Germany 82 J6
Rottenburg am Neckar • Germany 82 G6
Rotterdam • Netherlands 80 C3
Rottne • Sweden 95 F8
Rottumerplaat • Netherlands 82 G8
Rottweil • Germany 82 G8
Rotuma • Fiji 35 (2) D1
Roubaix • France 10 I3
Roudnice nad Labem • Czech Rep. 96 C1
Rouen • France 10 G4
Rouergue • France 85 G4
Rouge-Matawan Prov. Reserve •
    NS, Australia 122 B3
Rougemont • Switzerland 89 G6
Rougsø Beach • Denmark .... 68 [28]
Round Mountain, The •
    NS, Australia 34 J6
Roundstone • Ireland 79 F3
Rousay • United Kingdom 6 I2
Roussillon • France 85 K2
Rouyn • QU, Canada 39 P7
Rovaniemi • Finland 16 M3
Rovereto • Italy 91 E3
Roviés • Greece 92 D4
Roviés • Greece 92 D4
Rovigo • Italy 91 E7
Rovinj • Italy 17 D4
Rovno • Ukraine 17 D4
Rovuma • Mozambique 23 G6
Rowena • I • NU, Canada 33 P3
Rowley Shoals • QL, Australia 33 C7
Roxas • Palawan, Philippines 31 I4
Roxas • Panay, Philippines 31 G4
Roxborough • Trinidad & Tobago 125 L2
Roxburgh • New Zealand 112 L4
Roxburgh, Lake • New Zealand 112 L2
Roxen • Sweden 95 F4
Roy, Cap • Senegal 20 B6
Roy Hill • WA, Australia 34 C4
Roya • France 85 H2
Royal & Ancient, The •
    United Kingdom 74 B2
Royal • France 7 E8
Royal Chitwan Nat. Park Heritage N •
    Nepal .... 61 [104]
Royal Dockyard • Bermuda 58 A2
Royal Leamington Spa •
    United Kingdom 74 D2
Royal St George's •
    United Kingdom 74 E4
Royal Tunbridge Wells •
    United Kingdom 74 E3
Royan • France 85 G1
Royaumont, Abbaye de • France 85 E1
Roye • France 5 F5
Røyrvik • Norway 16 G4
Røysheim • Norway 94 C3
Rožnav • Poland 13 K5
Rozmberk • Czech Rep. 96 C4
Roznava • Slovak Rep. 13 J9
Rtishchevo • Russian Fed. 17 G4
Ruaha Nat. Park • Tanzania 102 H3
Ruaha Nat. Park Park • Tanzania .... 103 [94]
Ruahine Range • New Zealand 112 K4
Ruapehu, Mt • New Zealand 112 K4
Ruapuke I. • New Zealand 35 B8
Rub 'al Khali, Ar •
    Saudi Arabia 18 E6
Rubiku • Albania 15 A2
Rubio • Venezuela 43 C2
Rubondo I. Nat. Park • Tanzania 102 H1
Rubondo I. Nat. Park Park •
    Tanzania .... 103 [87]
Rubtsovsk • Russian Fed. 26 N7
Ruby Mtns • NV, United States 117 F2
Rudall River Nat. Park •
    WA, Australia 34 D4
Rudbar • Afghanistan 18 I3
Rudbjerg Beach • Denmark .... 68 [18]
Rüdersdorf • Germany 8 I4
Rüdesheim • Germany 82 H4
Rudkøbing Beach • Denmark .... 68 [25]
Rudkøbing • Denmark 95 F14
Rudná • F.R. of Yugoslavia 14 H5
Rudnik • Bulgaria 15 I1
Rudny • Kazakhstan 26 J7
Rudolstadt • Germany 9 G6
Rudong • China 107 J2
Rudozem • Bulgaria 15 F2
Rue • France 5 E5
Rueil Malmaison • France 85 E1
Rufiji • Tanzania 102 H2
Rufino • Argentina 44 D5
Rufisque • Senegal 22 A2
Rufunsa • Zambia 24 D3

Rugao

Rugao • China 107 J2
Rugby • United Kingdom 74 F4
Rügen • Germany 8 I2
Rügen Spa • Germany .... 83 [279-281]
Ruhnu • Estonia 16 L8
Ruhpolding • Germany 82 J8
Ruhr • Germany 9 D5
Ruhrgebiet • Germany .... 81 E
Ruien •
  Bulgaria/F.Y.R. of Macedonia 15 D1
Ruijin • China 31 F1
Ruivo, Pico • Madeira 88 C1
Ruki • Dem. Rep. of Congo 23 B4
Rukwa, Lake • Tanzania 102 H3
Rum • United Kingdom 6 F4
Rum Cay • Bahamas 124 B4
Rum Jungle • NT, Australia 34 F2
Ruma • F.R. of Yugoslavia 14 G4
Ruma Nat. Park • Kenya 101 G3
Rumbek • Sudan 23 D2
Rumburk • Czech Rep. 96 C2
Rumia • Poland 13 H3
Runanga • New Zealand 35 C6
Runaway Bay • Jamaica 124 C1
Runaway Bay • Antigua & Barbuda 125 F1
Runaway, Cape • New Zealand 35 F3
Runde • Zimbabwe 102 J4
Rundu • Namibia 24 B3
Rung, Ko • Thailand 109 K2
Rungwa • Tanzania 102 H3
Rungwa [Riv] • Tanzania 23 E5
Runhällen • Sweden 95 D1
Runkel • Germany 82 H2
Runmarö • Sweden 95 D4
Runnymede • United Kingdom 74 E1
Runö • Estonia 16 L8
Runswick Bay Beach •
  United Kingdom .... 75 [27]
Ruo Shui • China 29 C2
Ruokolahti • Finland 16 O6
Ruoqiang • China 26 I10
Ruovesi • Finland 95 E2
Rupat • Indonesia 110 B4
Rupert • QU, Canada 39 P6
Ruppiner Kanal • Germany 81 F1
Rur • Germany 80 B2
Rurutu • French Polynesia 33 L8
Rusalka • Bulgaria 97 D4
Rusape • Zimbabwe 102 J2
Rusayris, Ar • Sudan 21 F5
Rusayris, Khazzan ar • Sudan 21 F5
Rusayris, Lake • Sudan 23 E1
Ruse • Bulgaria 97 D1
Rusenski Lom Nat. Park Park •
  Bulgaria .... 72 [130]
Rusenski Lom Nat. Park •
  Romania 97 D1
Rush • Ireland 79 E2
Rusk • TX, United States 119 N4
Rußbach Ski • Austria .... 70 [178]
Russborough House • Ireland 79 E3
Russel I. • NU, Canada 38 L2
Russell • New Zealand 35 E2
Russell Cave Nat. Mon. Park •
  AL, United States .... 121 [207]
Rüsselsheim • Germany 9 D6
Russian Black Sea Coast •
  Russian Fed. 96 A2
Russian Federation •
  Europe/Asia 25 I3
Russkaya [Base] • Antarctica 46 (1) BB2
Rustavi • Georgia 97 H6
Ruston • LA, United States 118 K1
Rutanzige, Lac •
  Uganda/Dem. Rep. of Congo 23 D4
Rutbah, Ar • Iraq 18 C3
Ruteng • Indonesia 32 (1) B4
Rutenga • Zimbabwe 102 J4
Rutland • India 28 F6
Rutland • VT, United States 118 G3
Rutog • China 28 C2
Ruvu • Tanzania 102 H2
Ruvuma • Mozambique/Tanzania 102 H4
Ruwenzori Mtns Nat. Park Heritage N •
  Uganda .... 61 [86]
Ruwenzori Nat. Park Park •
  Uganda .... 103 [0]
Ruya • Mozambique/Zimbabwe 24 E3
Ruzomberok • Slovak Rep. 13 I8
Ruzyne [Apt] • Czech Rep. 96 C2
Rwanda • Africa 23 E4
Ry Beach • Denmark .... 68 [28]
Ry • Denmark 95 F9
Ryazan • Russian Fed. 17 F4
Rybachiy, Poluostrov •
  Russian Fed. 16 O2
Rybinsk • Russian Fed. 97 E2
Rybinskoye Vdkhr. •
  Russian Fed. 97 E2
Rybnik • Poland 13 H7
Rydaholm • Sweden 95 F7
Rydal Mt • United Kingdom 74 C2
Ryde • United Kingdom 78 C8
Rye • United Kingdom 74 E4
Ryfylke • Norway 94 C6
Rygge • Norway 94 B4
Ryotsu • Japan 30 J5
Rypin • Poland 13 I4
Ryukyu Is. • Japan 29 H5
Ryukyu-Shoto • Japan 29 H5
Rzepin • Poland 13 D5
Rzeszów • Poland 13 L8
Rzhev • Russian Fed. 97 E3

S'Albufeira • Minorca, Spain 87 F2
S'Albufeira • Majorca, Spain 87 H2
S'Algar • Minorca, Spain 87 F4
S'Arenal • Majorca, Spain 87 H3
S'Argamassa • Ibiza, Spain 87 G2
S'Horta • Majorca, Spain 87 H2
S'Illot • Majorca, Spain 87 H2
s-Gravenhage • Netherlands 80 C1
s-Hertogenbosch • Netherlands 80 A11
Sa Calobra • Majorca, Spain 87 H1
Sa Conillera • Ibiza, Spain 87 G1
Sa Keo • Thailand 109 H2
Sa Talaiassa de Sant Josep •
  Ibiza, Spain 87 G1
Sa'dah • Yemen 18 D6
Sa'idabad • Iran 18 G4
Saalach • Austria/Germany 82 J8
Saalbach • Austria 89 H3
Saalbach Hinterglemm Ski •
  Austria .... 70 [161]
Saale • Germany 8 G5
Saalfeld • Germany 9 G6
Saalfelden • Austria 89 H4
Saane • Switzerland 10 M7
Saanen • Switzerland 89 G6
Saanenmöser • Switzerland 89 G6
Saar • Germany 82 G3
Saarbrücken • Germany 82 G3
Saaremaa • Estonia 16 L7
Saarijärvi • Finland 16 M5

Saaristomeri Nat. Park Park •
  Finland .... 72 [37]
Saaristomeri Nat. Park •
  Finland 95 E3
Saarland • Germany 82 G3
Saarlouis • Germany 82 G3
Saas Fee Ski • Switzerland .... 70 [92]
Saas Fee • Switzerland 89 G6
Saba • West Indies 37 I4
Sabac • F.R. of Yugoslavia 14 G5
Sabadell • Spain 87 D3
Sabah • Malaysia 32 F2
Sabaki • Kenya 101 G5
Saban, Archipiélago de • Cuba 124 D2
Sabang • Sulawesi, Indonesia 32 (1) A2
Sabang • Indonesia 110 B1
Sabanözü • Turkey 15 O3
Sabará • Brazil 127 C1
Sabarei • Kenya 23 F3
Sabàudia • Italy 91 F4
Sabàudia, Lago di • Italy 91 F4
Sabha • Libya 21 B2
Sabi • Mozambique/Zimbabwe 102 J4
Sabina • Italy 91 F1
Sabinal, Cayo • Cuba 124 D3
Sabiñánigo • Spain 11 K2
Sabine • LA/TX, United States 119 N2
Sabine Lake •
  LA/TX, United States 118 K3
Sabkhat Tawurgha • Libya 21 B1
Sable, Cape • FL, United States 119 M8
Sable, Cape • NS, Canada 123 D7
Sable I. • NS, Canada 123 D8
Sablé-sur-Sarthe • France 84 D1
Sables d'Olonne, Les • France 10 D7
Sablukah, Ash Shallal as •
  Sudan 21 F4
Sabrata • Libya 21 B1
Sabratha Heritage C • Libya .... 64 [233]
Sabya • Saudi Arabia 18 D6
Sabzevar • Iran 18 G2
Saché [Château] • France 84 D2
Sachigo • OT, Canada 39 M6
Sachs Harbour • NT, Canada 38 G2
Sachsen • Germany 9 I5
Sachsen-Anhalt • Germany 8 G4
Sächsische Schweiz • Germany 9 J5
Sächsische Schweiz, Nationalpark Park •
  Germany .... 72 [62]
Sacramento • Brazil 44 G2
Sacramento • CA, United States 117 F3
Sacramento, Pampa del • Peru 43 B5
Sacramento [Riv] •
  CA, United States 117 F1
Sacramento Valley •
  CA, United States 40 B3
Sacred Falls State Park •
  HI, United States 119 L5
Sada Temple • Bali, Indonesia 110 C4
Sádaba • Spain 11 J2
Sadani • Tanzania 102 H2
Sadao • Thailand 109 F4
Sadiklar • Turkey 93 G4
Sadiya • India 28 G3
Sadlers • St Kitts & Nevis 125 G1
Sado • Portugal 88 D2
Sado • Japan 30 J5
Sado • Portugal 88 D2
Sadr, As • United Arab Emirates 18 F5
Saduak • Thailand 109 H1
Sæby Beach • Denmark .... 68 [29]
Sæby • Denmark 95 F6
Safad • Israel 98 A2
Safari und Abenteuerpark Park •
  Austria .... 73 [82]
Säffle • Sweden 16 G7
Saffron Walden • United Kingdom 7 M9
Safi • Morocco 101 D3
Safid • Iran 18 E2
Safonovo • Russian Fed. 17 E3
Safranbolu • Turkey 15 N2
Safranbolu Heritage C • Turkey .... 64 [191]
Sag Harbor • NY, United States 118 H2
Saga • Japan 30 F8
Saga • Myanmar 30 B2
Sagalassos • Turkey 93 G1
Sagamihara • Japan 30 J7
Sagamore Hill Nat. Hist. Site Park •
  NY, United States .... 121 [324]
Sagar • India 105 C7
Sagarmatha • China/Nepal 28 E3
Sagarmatha Nat. Park Heritage N •
  Nepal .... 61 [103]
Saggat • Sweden 16 I3
Saginaw • MI, United States 41 J3
Saginaw Bay • MI, United States 39 O8
Sagiz • Kazakhstan 26 H8
Saglouc • QU, Canada 36 J3
Sagone • Corsica, France 85 L3
Sagone, Golfe de •
  Corsica, France 85 L3
Sagres • Portugal 88 E5
Sagres, Ponta de • Portugal 88 E5
Sagua de Tánamo • Cuba 124 D8
Sagua Grande • Cuba 124 D2
Saguaro Nat. Park •
  AZ, United States 118 J3
Saguaro Nat. Park Park •
  AZ, United States .... 120 [117]
Saguenay • QU, Canada 39 Q7
Saguenay Prov. Park •
  QU, Canada 123 D1
Saguia el-Hamra •
  Western Sahara 20 C3
Sagunto • Spain 11 K5
Sagunto Beach • Spain .... 68 [102]
Sahagún • Spain 11 F2
Saharanpur • India 28 C2
Sahel • Tunisia 101 E4
Sahiwal • Pakistan 28 B2
Sahlabad • Iran 18 G3
Sahr-i-Bahlol Heritage C •
  Pakistan .... 63 [112]
Sahra Bayyudah • Sudan 21 F4
Sahra Murzuq • Libya 21 B3
Sahra Rabyanah • Libya 21 C3
Sahuayo • Mexico 123 E1
Sahyadri • India 28 B5
Sai Gon [Riv] • Vietnam 108 B1
Sai Kung • Hong Kong, China 107 H6
Sai Kung Country Park •
  Hong Kong, China 107 H6
Sai, Laem • Ko Samui, Thailand 109 J1
Saïda • Algeria 20 F2
Saïdia • Morocco 101 D2
Saidor • Papua New Guinea 35 (1) D2
Saigon • Vietnam 108 B1
Saiki • Japan 30 F8
Saimaa Kanal •
  Finland/Russian Fed. 16 O6
Saimaa • Finland 16 N6
Saimaa Kanava •
  Finland/Russian Fed. 16 O6
St Agnes • United Kingdom 74 F4
St Alban's Head •
  United Kingdom 74 F6
St Albans • United Kingdom 74 E1
St Albans • VT, United States 118 G1
St André, Cap • Madagascar 24 G3

St Andreasberg Spa • Germany .... 83 [80]
St Andrews • United Kingdom 74 B2
St Andrews Beach •
  United Kingdom .... 75 [9]
St Andrews • NB, Canada 123 D6
St Ann's Bay • Jamaica 124 C2
Ste-Anne-de-Beaupré • QU, Canada 123 D1
St Annes • Channel Is. 7 J12
St Anthony • NF, Canada 123 D5
St Anton am Arlberg Ski •
  Austria .... 70 [132]
St Anton am Arlberg • Austria 89 H6
St Arnaud • VI, Australia 111 G3
St Augustin • Germany 9 C6
St Augustin-Saguenay •
  QU, Canada 39 T6
St Augustine •
  FL, United States 119 M4
St Augustine, Baie de •
  Madagascar 24 G4
St Austell • United Kingdom 74 F4
St Austell Beach •
  United Kingdom .... 75 [122]
St Avold • France 5 J5
St Barbe • NF, Canada 123 D5
St Barthélemy • West Indies 37 I4
St Bee's Head • United Kingdom 74 C1
St Berg Spa • Germany .... 83 [176]
St Blais, Cape • South Africa 100 C6
St Blaise • Switzerland 89 G1
St Blasien • Germany 82 G8
St Blasien Spa • Germany .... 83 [206]
St Boniface • MN, Canada 38 L7
St Brevin • France 84 C4
St Brevin-les-Pins Beach •
  France .... 68 [63]
St Brides Haven Beach •
  United Kingdom .... 75 [161]
St Brieuc • France 84 C2
St Brieuc, Baie de • France 10 C5
St Calais • France 84 D2
St Cast • France 84 C2
St Catharines • OT, Canada 122 B9
St Cast • France 84 C2
St Catherine's Point •
  United Kingdom 5 B4
St Catherine, Monastery of •
  Egypt 101 F4
St Chamond • France 10 J8
St Charles • MO, United States 41 H4
St Chinian • France 84 B4
St Christina in Gröden • Italy 90 B1
St Christoph am Arlberg Ski •
  Austria .... 70 [133]
St Christoph am Arlberg •
  Austria 89 H5
St Christopher •
  St Kitts & Nevis 125 G1
St Christophe, Rocque • France 85 G2
St Cirq-Lapopie • France 85 G3
St Cloud • MN, United States 41 H2
St Croix • WI, United States 39 M7
St Croix I. Int. Hist. Site Park •
  ME, United States .... 121 [355]
St Croix I. Int. Hist. Site •
  Canada/United States 123 D6
St Cyprien Beach • France .... 68 [111]
St Cyr-sur-Mer Beach • France .... 68 [116]
St Cyr-sur-Mer • France 85 H3
St David's Beach •
  United Kingdom .... 75 [165-166]
St Denis • Réunion 24 (1) B2
St Denis • France 85 E1
St Dié • France 10 L5
St Dizier • France 10 J5
St Dogmaels Beach •
  United Kingdom .... 75 [170]
St Elias Mts, MT, Canada 38 C4
St Elias Mtns •
  Canada/United States 38 D4
St Elie • French Guiana 43 G3
St Emilion • France 85 G1
St Estephe • France 84 B3
St Etienne • France 10 J8
St Étienne-de-Tinée Ski •
  France .... 70 [71]
St Etienne-du-Rouvray • France 5 E5
St Eustatius • West Indies 37 I4
St Florent • Corsica, France 85 L2
St Florent, Golfe de •
  Corsica, France 85 L2
St Florentin • France 10 I6
St Flour • France 10 I8
St Francis Bay • South Africa 100 C8
St Francis, Cape • South Africa 100 C8
St Francis •
  LA, United States 118 K4
St François • Seychelles 106 F4
St François • QU, Canada 122 B4
St François-Longchamp Ski •
  France .... 70 [45]
St Gallen • Switzerland 9 E9
St Gallen Heritage C •
  Switzerland .... 64 [103]
St Gallenkirch Ski • Austria .... 70 [127]
St Gaudens • France 85 J2
St Gaudens Nat. Hist. Site •
  NH, United States 118 G3
St Gaudens Nat. Hist. Site Park •
  NH, United States .... 121 [353]
St George • UT, United States 40 D4
St George • QL, Australia 111 F5
St George, Cape •
  Papua New Guinea 35 (1) E1
St George I. •
  FL, United States 119 M2
St George, Monastery of •
  Jordan 98 A6
St George's • Grenada 37 I5
St George's Bermuda 58 A2
St George's Bay • NF, Canada 123 D3
St George's Channel •
  Ireland/UK 7 F10
St George's Church • Barbados 125 H3
St Georges-de-Didonne Beach •
  France .... 68 [65]
St Georges-de-la-Rivière Beach •
  France .... 68 [58]
St Germain, Forêt de • France 85 E1
St Germain-en-Laye • France 85 E1
St Gervais Ski • France .... 70 [25]
St Gervais-les-Bains • France 85 F2
St Gilgen • Austria 89 H4
St Gilles-de-Croix-de-Vie Beach •
  France .... 68 [64]
St Girons • France 85 K1
St Goar • Germany 82 H2
St Helena • Atlantic Ocean 19 D7
St Helena Bay • South Africa 100 C1
St Helens • United Kingdom 74 C3
St Helens • TS, Australia 34 I8
St Helens Beach •
  United Kingdom .... 75 [95]
St Helens, Mt •
  WA, United States 117 E1
St Helier • Channel Is. 7 J12

St Hilaire-de-Riez Beach •
  France .... 68 [64]
St Hilarion Castle • Cyprus 93 J1
St Hubert • Belgium 9 H8
St Hyacinthe • QU, Canada 122 B4
St Idesbald • Belgium 80 B1
St Ingbert • Germany 5 K5
St Ives • United Kingdom 74 F4
St Ives Beach • United Kingdom 75 [124-125]
St Ives Bay • United Kingdom 74 F4
St Jacut • France 84 C2
St Jakob am Arlberg Ski •
  Austria .... 70 [132]
St James, Cape • BC, Canada 38 E6
St James, The Way of Heritage C •
  Spain .... 64 [80]
St Jean • QU, Canada 122 B8
St Jean d'Arves Ski • France .... 70 [48]
St Jean, Lac • QU, Canada 123 D1
St Jean-Cap-Ferrat • France 85 H2
St Jean-d'Angély • France 85 G1
St Jean-d'Aulps Ski • France .... 70 [11]
St Jean-de-Luz • France 85 J1
St Jean-de-Monts Beach • France .... 68 [64]
St Jean-Pied-de-Port • France 85 J1
St Jérôme • QU, Canada 39 P7
St Johann im Pongau Ski •
  Austria .... 70 [167]
St Johann im Pongau • Austria 89 H4
St Johann in Tirol Ski •
  Austria .... 70 [154]
St Johann in Tirol • Austria 89 H3
St John • NB, Canada 123 D7
St John [Riv] •
  Canada/United States 123 D6
St John's • NF, Canada 123 D4
St John's • Antigua & Barbuda 125 F1
St John's Church • Barbados 125 H4
St John's Harbour •
  Antigua & Barbuda 125 F1
St Johns • AZ, United States 118 J2
St Johnsbury •
  VT, United States 118 G3
St Johnstone Village •
  Antigua & Barbuda 125 F1
St Joseph • Réunion 24 (1) B2
St Joseph • MO, United States 41 H4
St Joseph • Seychelles 106 E4
St Joseph • Seychelles 106 F2
St Joseph, Lake • OT, Canada 39 M6
St Julian's • Malta 93 H4
St Julien • France 84 B3
St Julien-en-Born Beach •
  France .... 68 [67]
St Just • United Kingdom 74 F4
St Kassian Ski • Italy .... 70 [233]
St Kassian • Italy 90 B2
St Kilda • United Kingdom 6 D4
St Kilda • New Zealand 35 C7
St Kilda Heritage N •
  United Kingdom .... 61 [40]
St Kitts • St Kitts & Nevis 125 G1
St Kitts & Nevis • West Indies .... 125 G
St Lary Soulan • France 85 J2
St Laurent • QU, Canada 39 R7
St Laurent • French Guiana 43 G2
St Lawrence • QU, Canada 39 R7
St Lawrence • QL, Australia 111 F3
St Lawrence • Barbados 125 H3
St Lawrence, Gulf of •
  QU, Canada 123 D2
St Lawrence I. • Bering Sea 40 (2) D2
St Lawrence Is. Nat. Park •
  OT, Canada 122 B6
St Lazaire • France 10 I11
St Léonard-de-Noblat • France 85 G2
St Leonard • Russian Fed. 15 H2
St Leonard in Passeier • Italy 90 B1
St Lizier • France 85 K1
St Lô • France 10 D4
St Louis • France 9 C9
St Louis • Senegal 22 A1
St Louis • MO, United States 41 H4
St Lucia • West Indies .... 125 J
St Lucia, Cape • South Africa 24 F5
St Maarten • West Indies 37 I4
St Malo • France 84 C2
St Malo, Golfe de • France 84 C2
St Margarethen im Lungau Ski •
  Austria .... 70 [187]
St Mårgen • Germany 82 G8
St Marie, Cap • Madagascar 24 H5
St Marie-de-Belleville Ski •
  France .... 70 [40]
St Martinville •
  LA, United States 118 K3
St Mary Peak • SA, Australia 34 H4
St Mary's, Cape • NF, Canada 123 D5
St Marys • TS, Australia 34 I8
St Marys City •
  MO, United States 118 H3
St Mathieu, Point de • France 84 C1
St Maur-des-Fossés • France 5 F6
St Maurice • QU, Canada 124 D1
St Maurice Prov. Reserve •
  QU, Canada 122 B4
St Mawes • United Kingdom 74 F4
St Maximin la Ste Baume •
  France 85 H3
St Merryn Beach •
  United Kingdom .... 75 [126-128]
St Michael im Lungau Ski •
  Austria .... 70 [188]
St Michael's Mount •
  United Kingdom 74 F4
St Michel • Finland 16 N6
St Michel-Chef-Chef Beach •
  France .... 68 [63]
St Mihiel • France 5 H6
St Moritz Ski • Switzerland .... 70 [118]
St Moritz • Switzerland 89 G8
St Nazaire • France 84 C4
St Nicholas' Abbey • Barbados 125 G1
St Nicolas-de-Port • France 5 J6
St Nicolas-de-Véroce Ski •
  France .... 70 [27]
St Niklaas Beach • Belgium .... 68 [51]
St Niklaas • Belgium 80 B1
St Omer • France 10 H3
St Paul • Réunion 24 (1) B2
St Paul • AL, Canada 38 I6
St Paul • MN, United States 41 H3
St Paul • France 85 H2
St Paul I. • NS, Canada 123 D3
St Paul, Monastery of • Egypt 101 F4
St Paul's Bay • Malta 93 H4
St Paul's Church Nat. Hist. Site Park •
  NY, United States .... 121 [330]
St Pé, Parc zoologique • France 85 G3
St Peter • Germany 82 G8
St Peter Ording • Germany .... 83 [7]
St Peter Ording Spa • Germany .... 83 [7]
St Peter Port • Channel Is. 7 J8
St Peterburg • Russian Fed. 97 E1
St Petersburg Heritage C •
  Russian Fed. .... 64 [205]
St Petersburg • Russian Fed. 97 E1

St Petersburg •
  FL, United States 119 M5
St Philips • Antigua & Barbuda 125 F4
St Phillip • St Lucia 125 F3
St Pierre • Réunion 24 (1) B2
St Pierre • Seychelles 106 F3
St Pierre •
  St Pierre et Miquelon 123 D3
St Pierre, Lac • QU, Canada 122 B4
St Pierre and Miquelon •
  N. America 123 D3
St Pierre, Lac • QU, Canada 122 B4
St Pölten • Austria 13 E9
St Quay-Portrieux Beach •
  France .... 68 [60]
St Quay-Portrieux • France 84 C2
St Quentin • France 10 I4
St Raphaël • France 85 H4
St Sauveur-des-Monts •
  QU, Canada 122 B3
St Savin • France 84 D4
St Savin-sur-Gartempe Heritage C •
  France .... 64 [62]
St Sebastien, Cap • Réunion 123 D1
St Siméon • QU, Canada 123 D1
St Stephen • NB, Canada 123 D6
St Théodorit • France 84 C1
St Thomas Bay • Malta 93 H4
St Tropez Beach • France .... 68 [116]
St Tropez • France 85 H4
St Truiden • Belgium 5 I4
St Ulrich Ski • Italy .... 70 [230]
St Ulrich • Italy 90 B1
St Valéry-en-Caux • France 5 D5
St Veit an der Glan • Austria 13 D11
St Vigil in Enneberg • Italy 90 B2
St Vincent, Gulf •
  SA, Australia 34 G6
St Vincent •
  FL, United States 119 M2
St Vincent & the Grenadines •
  West Indies 37 I5
St Vith • Belgium 80 A16
St Wendel • Germany 9 H4
St Wolfgang • Austria 89 H4
Ste Agathe-des-Monts •
  QU, Canada 122 B3
Ste Anne • Seychelles 106 F1
Ste Anne Marine Nat. Park •
  Seychelles 106 F1
Ste Anne-des-Monts • QU, Canada 123 D2
Ste Croix • Switzerland 89 G1
Ste Engrâce • France 85 J1
Ste Foy • QU, Canada 122 B4
Ste Foy-la-Grande • France 85 G1
Ste Maries-de-la-Mer Beach •
  France .... 68 [111]
Ste Maxime Beach • France .... 68 [116]
Ste Maxime • France 85 H4
Ste Menehould • France 5 H5
Saintes • France 85 G1
Stes Maries-de-la-Mer • France 10 J10
Saintonge • France 10 E8
Saipan • Northern Mariana Is. 33 G4
Sairecabur, Cerro • Bolivia 44 C2
Sais [Apt] • Morocco 101 D2
Saiwa Swamp Nat. Park • Kenya 101 G3
Sajak • Kazakhstan 26 M8
Sajama • Bolivia 44 C2
Sajama, Nevado de • Bolivia 44 C2
Sajó • Hungary 13 J9
Sajószentpéter • Hungary 13 J9
Sakai • Japan 30 H7
Sakakah • Saudi Arabia 18 C4
Sakakawea, Lake •
  ND, United States 40 I11
Sakar • Bulgaria 15 H2
Sakaraha • Madagascar 24 G4
Sakarya • Turkey 15 L3
Sakata • Japan 30 J5
Sakaman Temple •
  Bali, Indonesia 110 C4
Sakha • Russian Fed. 27 N6
Sakhalin, Ostrov • Russian Fed. 27 N6
Sakhalinskiye Zaliv •
  Russian Fed. 27 N6
Sakhira • Tunisia 101 E4
Sakishima-Shoto • Japan 31 G2
Sakjiang • Singapore 108 E4
Sakjiang • Singapore 108 E3
Sakködeng • Denmark 95 F14
Sal • Cape Verde 22 (1) B1
Sal • Slovak Rep. 13 G9
Sala • Chad 21 D6
Sala • Sweden 95 D1
Sala Consilina • Italy 12 J8
Sala y Gómez • Pacific Ocean 33 Q8
Salabangka, Kepulauan •
  Indonesia 32 (1) B3
Salacgriva • Latvia 16 M8
Saladillo • Argentina 127 D3
Salado • Argentina 44 C5
Salado • Argentina 44 D5
Salado • Cuba 124 D1
Salado • Argentina 127 D3
Salagle • Somalia 23 G3
Sálakos • Rhodes, Greece 93 F1
Salal • Chad 21 D6
Salalah • Oman 18 F6
Salamanca • Spain 11 F4
Salamanca • Mexico 123 C5
Salamat, Bahr • Chad 21 C5
Salamina [I.] • Greece 92 D4
Salamina [I.] • Greece 92 D4
Salamis • Cyprus 93 J2
Salamiyah, As • Saudi Arabia 18 E5
Salas • Spain 11 H2
Salas de los Infantes • Spain 11 H2
Salatiga • Java, Indonesia 110 D8
Salavat • Russian Fed. 4 V6
Salawati • Indonesia 32 (1) D3
Salbris • France 10 H6
Salcantay, Nevado de • Peru 127 B2
Salcombe • United Kingdom 74 F5
Salcombe Beach • United Kingdom 75 [116]
Salda Gölü • Turkey 93 G1
Saldae • Portugal 88 E5
Saldanha • South Africa 100 C1
Saldanha Bay • South Africa 100 C1
Saldus • Latvia 16 L8
Salé • Morocco 101 D1
Salé [Apt] • Morocco 101 D1
Salekhard • Russian Fed. 26 K4
Salem • India 106 D11
Salem • OR, United States 117 E1
Salem • MA, United States 118 G2
Salem Maritime Nat. Hist. Site Park •
  MA, United States .... 121 [350]
Salema • Portugal 88 E5
Salemo • Italy 91 G4
Salerno, Golfo di • Italy 91 G4
Salgótarján • Hungary 13 I9
Salgueiro • Brazil 45 (1) D3
Salhus • Norway 94 B1
Sali • Egypt 101 G4
Salina • KS, United States 41 G4
Salina Bay • Malta 93 H2
Salina Cruz • Mexico 123 E4

Salina, I. • Italy 90 D2
Salinas • Ecuador 43 A4
Salinas • Puerto Rico 125 E4
Salinas, Bahia • Puerto Rico 125 E3
Salinas Cliff Dwellings Nat. Mon. •
  NM, United States 118 J4
Salinas Grandes • Argentina 44 D4
Salinas Pueblo Missions Nat. Mon. Park •
  NM, United States .... 120 [123]
Salines, Cap de ses •
  Majorca, Spain 11 O5
Salisbury • United Kingdom 88 E3
Salisbury • MD, United States 118 H3
Salisbury I. • NU, Canada 39 P4
Salisbury Plain •
  United Kingdom 74 F3
Salla • Finland 16 O3
Sallingsund Beach • Denmark .... 68 [30]
Sallins • Ireland 79 E3
Salmon • ID, United States 39 F4
Sálpyana • Nepal 105 C4
Salmon • ID, United States 117 E4
Salmon Arm • BC, Canada 38 G6
Salmon Falls •
  ID, United States 117 E4
Salmon River Mtns •
  ID, United States 117 E4
Salmonsdam Nature Reserve •
  South Africa 100 C6
Saló • Italy 91 E7
Salo • Finland 95 E4
Salobreña • Spain 86 B7
Salon-de-Provence • France 10 K10
Salonga, Parc nat. de la Heritage N •
  Dem. Rep. of Congo .... 61 [81]
Salonga, Parc nat. de la Park •
  Dem. Rep. of Congo .... 103 [53]
Salonika Heritage C • Greece .... 64 [175]
Salonika • Greece 92 D1
Salonika • Greece 92 D1
Salonta • Romania 14 I3
Salor • Spain 11 E5
Salou Beach • Spain .... 68 [104]
Salou • Spain 87 D3
Salsk • Russian Fed. 17 G5
Salso • Sicily, Italy 90 D4
Salsomaggiore • Italy 91 E6
Salt • AZ, United States 118 J3
Salt Cay • Bahamas 124 B3
Salt Lake City •
  UT, United States 40 D3
Salt Pond Estate •
  St Kitts & Nevis 125 G4
Salta • Argentina 44 C3
Saltash • United Kingdom 74 F5
Saltburn-by-the-Sea •
  United Kingdom 7 L7
Salten • Norway 16 H3
Saltfjellet-Svartisen Nat. Park Park •
  Norway .... 72 [9]
Saltholm • Denmark 95 F11
Saltibus • St Lucia 125 J3
Saltillo • Mexico 37 A2
Salto • Uruguay 44 E5
Salto • Italy 91 F2
Salto Angostura • Colombia 43 C3
Salto Sete • CA, United States 117 F3
Saltram • United Kingdom 74 F5
Saltsjöbaden • Sweden 95 D4
Salut, Is. du • French Guiana 58 A3
Saluzzo • Italy 10 M9
Salvador de Bahia • Brazil 44 I1
Salvador de Bahia Heritage C •
  Brazil .... 62 [61]
Salween • Myanmar 3 I4
Salzach • Austria/Germany 9 I49
Salzburg Heritage C • Austria .... 64 [105]
Salzburg • Austria 89 H4
Salzburg [Adm] • Austria 89 H4
Salzburger Alpen •
  Austria/Germany 82 J8
Salzelmen Spa • Germany .... 83 [293]
Salzgitter • Germany 8 F4
Salzgitter Bad Spa • Germany .... 83 [76]
Salzmmendorf Spa • Germany .... 83 [72]
Salzkammergut • Austria 89 H4
Salzwedel • Germany 8 G4
Sam • India 105 C1
Sam Lord's Castle • Barbados 125 H4
Sam Ngao • Thailand 109 G3
Samae San • Thailand 109 H4
Samae San, Ko • Thailand 109 H4
Samaipata • Bolivia 44 C2
Samana Cay • Bahamas 124 B4
Samani • Japan 30 L3
Samar • Philippines 31 H4
Samara [Riv] • Russian Fed. 26 H7
Samaria • Jordan 98 A5
Samaria [Region] •
  Israel/Jordan 98 A5
Samariás, Farági •
  Crete, Greece 93 E5
Samarinda • Indonesia 32 F3
Samarkand • Uzbekistan 18 I2
Samarra • Iraq 18 D3
Samate • Indonesia 32 (1) D3
Samawah, As • Iraq 18 D3
Samba-Caju • Angola 22 H6
Sambalpur • India 28 D4
Sambas • Indonesia 32 D2
Sambhal • India 105 C3
Sambir • Ukraine 15 I5
Samborombón, Bahía • Argentina 127 D3
Sambre • Belgium 80 A14
Samburg • Russian Fed. 26 M4
Samburu Game Reserve • Kenya 101 G2
Samburu Nat. Reserve Park •
  Kenya .... 103 [77]
Samch'ongp'o • Rep. of Korea 30 D7
Samdong-ni • D.P.R. of Korea 30 D5
Same • Tanzania 102 H2
Samedan • Switzerland .... 70 [117]
Samedan • Switzerland 89 G8
Samet, Ko • Thailand 109 H4
Samfya-Mwamfuli • Zambia 23 D6
Sámi • Greece 92 C2
Sámi • Greece 92 C2
Samnaun Ski • Switzerland .... 70 [120]
Samnaun • Switzerland 89 G4
Samoa • Pacific Ocean 35 (2) F1
Samoa Is. • Pacific Ocean 35 (2) F1
Samoëns Ski • France .... 70 [16]
Samoëns • France 85 F2
Samokov • Bulgaria 14 K7
Samos • Portugal 11 H2
Sámos Heritage C • Greece .... 64 [185]
Sámos Beach • Greece .... 69 [178]
Sámos • Greece 92 D2
Sámos • Greece 92 D2
Sámos [I.] • Greece 92 D2
Sámos [I.] • Greece 92 D2
Samosir • Indonesia 110 B2
Samothrace • Greece 92 D2

Samothrace • Greece.................92 D2
Samothráki • Greece...............15 G3
Samothráki [I.] • Greece...........92 D2
Samothráki [I.] • Greece...........92 D2
Sampang • Java, Indonesia.......110 D8
Sampit • Indonesia................32 E3
Sampwe • Dem. Rep. of Congo....24 D1
Samrong, Laem •
  Ko Samui, Thailand.............109 J1
Samsø • Denmark.................95 F10
Samsø Bælt • Denmark............95 F10
Samuel, Mt • NT, Australia........34 F3
Samut Prakan • Thailand..........109 H2
Samut Sakhon • Thailand.........109 H1
Samut Songkhram • Thailand.....109 H3
San • Poland.......................13 L7
San Agustín •
  Gran Canaria, Canary Is..........86 E4
San Agustín, Parque Arqueológico Heritage
  C • Colombia..................62 [45]
San Ambrosio • Pacific Ocean.....42 C7
San Andrés • Colombia............37 E5
San Andrés del Rabanedo • Spain...11 F2
San Angelo • TX, United States....40 F5
San Antonio • Chile...............44 B5
San Antonio • TX, United States...119 N5
San Antonio Bay •
  TX, United States..............119 N5
San Antonio, Cabo • Cuba.........124 D1
San Antonio, Cabo • Argentina.....127 D4
San Antonio de los Cobres •
  Argentina......................44 C3
San Antonio Missions Nat. Hist. Park •
  TX, United States..............119 N5
San Antonio Missions Nat. Hist. Park Park •
  TX, United States...........120 [141]
San Antonio Oeste • Argentina.....45 D4
San Augustin, Cap • Philippines....31 H5
San Augustine •
  TX, United States..............119 N4
San Bartolomé de Tirajana Beach •
  Gran Canaria, Canary Is.......68 [92]
San Bartolomé de Tirajana •
  Gran Canaria, Canary Is.........86 E4
San Benedetto del Tronto •
  Italy..........................91 E12
San Bernardino • Switzerland......89 G7
San Bernardino •
  CA, United States.............117 F6
San Bernardino, Passo del •
  Switzerland....................89 G7
San Bernardo • Chile.............44 B5
San Blas • Mexico...............123 E1
San Blas Bay • Malta.............93 H1
San Blas, Cape •
  FL, United States.............119 M2
San Borja • Bolivia...............44 C1
San Cándido Ski • Italy.......70 [239]
San Cándido • Italy...............90 B2
San Carlos • Philippines..........31 G4
San Carlos • Nicaragua...........37 E5
San Carlos • Venezuela...........43 D2
San Carlos • Chile...............44 B6
San Carlos • Uruguay.............44 F5
San Carlos de Bariloche •
  Argentina......................45 B4
San Carlos de Bolívar •
  Argentina.....................127 D3
San Carlos del Zulia •
  Venezuela......................43 C2
San Carlos Indian Reservation •
  AZ, United States.............118 J4
San Cassiano Ski • Italy......70 [233]
San Cassiano • Italy..............90 B2
San Cataldo • Sicily, Italy.......12 H11
San Clemente • Spain..............11 I5
San Clemente del Tuyú •
  Argentina.....................127 D4
San Clemente I. •
  CA, United States.............117 F6
San Cristóbal • Solomon Is.....35 (1) G3
San Cristóbal • Galapagos Is...43 (1) A2
San Cristóbal • Venezuela.........43 C2
San Cristóbal • Argentina.........44 D5
San Diego • CA, United States....117 F6
San Diego, Cabo • Argentina......45 C6
San Donà di Piave • Italy.........12 G3
San Esteban de Gormaz • Spain....11 H3
San Felice Circéo • Italy..........91 F4
San Felipe • Venezuela............43 D1
San Felipe • Colombia.............43 D3
San Felipe • Chile...............44 B5
San Felix • Pacific Ocean.........42 C7
San Fernando • Philippines........31 G3
San Fernando • Mexico............40 G7
San Fernando • Chile..............44 B5
San Fernando Beach • Spain.....68 [96]
San Fernando • Spain.............86 B5
San Fernando •
  Trinidad & Tobago.............125 K3
San Fernando de Apure •
  Venezuela......................43 D2
San Fernando de Atabapo •
  Venezuela......................43 D3
San Floriano • Italy..............90 B3
San Francique •
  Trinidad & Tobago.............125 K3
San Francisco • Argentina.........44 D5
San Francisco •
  CA, United States.............117 F3
San Francisco Maritime Nat. Hist. Park Park •
  CA, United States...........120 [46]
San Francisco, Sierra de la Heritage C •
  Mexico........................62 [13]
San Galgano • Italy..............91 E11
San Gallán, I. • Peru............127 B1
San Germán • Puerto Rico.......125 E3
San Gil • Colombia...............43 C2
San Gimignano Heritage C •
  Italy.........................64 [121]
San Gimignano • Italy...........91 E11
San Gottardo, Passo del •
  Switzerland....................89 G3
San Ignacio • Paraguay...........44 E4
San Ignacio Mini Heritage C •
  Argentina.....................62 [64]
San Isidro • Argentina...........44 D5
San Javier • Chile...............44 B6
San Javier Beach • Spain......68 [100]
San Javier • Spain...............87 C3
San Joaquín • Bolivia............44 C1
San Joaquín • CA, United States...117 F3
San Joaquín Valley •
  CA, United States..............40 B4
San Jorge • Argentina............44 D5
San Jorge, Golfo de • Argentina...45 C5
San Jose • Philippines...........31 G4
San José • Costa Rica............37 E6
San José • Mexico...............40 D7
San José • Bolivia...............44 C2
San José • Bolivia...............44 D2
San José • CA, United States....117 F3
San José de Jáchal • Argentina....44 C5
San José de Mayo • Uruguay......127 D2
San José de Ocune • Colombia.....43 D3
San José del Guaviare •
  Colombia.......................43 C3
San Juan • Costa Rica/Nicaragua...37 E6
San Juan • Argentina.............44 C5
San Juan Heritage C •
  Puerto Rico...................62 [39]

San Juan • CO/UT, United States...118 J2
San Juan • Puerto Rico...........125 E2
San Juan • Trinidad & Tobago....125 K3
San Juan • Peru.................127 B3
San Juan Bautista •
  CA, United States.............117 F3
San Juan, Cabo •
  Equatorial Guinea...............22 F4
San Juan de los Morros •
  Venezuela......................43 D2
San Juan del Norte • Nicaragua....43 A1
San Juan I. Nat. Hist. Park •
  WA, United States.............117 E1
San Juan I. Nat. Hist. Park Park •
  WA, United States............120 [23]
San Juan, Pico • Cuba...........124 D2
San Juan y Martínez • Cuba......124 D1
San Julián • Argentina...........45 C6
San Just, Sierra de • Spain.......11 K4
San Lázaro • Paraguay...........44 E3
San Lázaro, Cabo • Mexico.......40 D7
San Leo • Italy.................91 E12
San Leonardo Ski • Italy......70 [233]
San Leonardo in Passiria •
  Italy..........................90 B1
San Lorenzo Heritage C • Panama...62 [32]
San Lorenzo, I. • Peru..........127 B1
San Lucas, Cabo • Mexico.........40 E7
San Luis • Argentina.............44 C5
San Luis • Cuba.................124 D8
San Luis Obispo •
  CA, United States.............117 F5
San Luis Potosí • Mexico........123 E1
San Luis Potosí [Adm] • Mexico...37 (1) B1
San Luis Río Colorado • Mexico....40 D5
San Mamete • Italy..............91 E2
San Marcos • Colombia...........43 B2
San Marcos • TX, United States...119 N3
San Marino •Europe.............91 E12
San Martín • Argentina...........44 C5
San Martín • Bolivia.............44 C2
San Martín [Base] • Antarctica...46 (1) II3
San Martín, Lago •
  Argentina/Chile.................45 B5
San Martino de Lota •
  Corsica, France.................85 L2
San Martino di Castrozza Ski •
  Italy.........................70 [220]
San Martino di Castrozza •
  Italy..........................90 B3
San Mateo • CA, United States....117 F3
San Matías, Golfo • Argentina.....45 C5
San Michele, Grotta di • Italy.....91 G2
San Miguel • El Salvador.........37 D5
San Miguel • Bolivia.............44 D2
San Miguel • CA, United States...117 F3
San Miguel de Allende • Mexico...123 E1
San Miguel de Tucumán •
  Argentina......................44 C4
San Miguel I. •
  CA, United States.............117 F5
San Millán Heritage C • Spain...64 [77]
San Miniato • Italy...............12 E5
San Nicolás de los Arroyos •
  Argentina.....................127 D1
San Nicolás de Tolentino •
  Gran Canaria, Canary Is.........86 E4
San Nicolas I. •
  CA, United States.............117 F5
San Pablo • Philippines..........31 G4
San Pawl il-Baħar • Malta........93 H2
San Pedro • Jujuy, Argentina......44 D3
San Pedro •
  Buenos Aires, Argentina......127 D1
San Pedro Alcántara • Spain......86 B6
San Pedro de Lloc • Peru.........43 B5
San Pedro de Macorís •
  Dominican Rep..................37 H4
San Pedro del Pinatar Beach •
  Spain........................68 [100]
San Pedro del Pinatar • Spain.....87 C3
San Pedro Sula • Honduras........37 C4
San Philippe, Cayos de • Cuba....124 D1
San Pietro, I. di •
  Sardinia, Italy.................90 C3
San Quintín • Mexico............40 C5
San Rafael • Argentina..........44 C5
San Ramón de la Nueva Orán •
  Argentina......................44 D3
San Remo • Italy................91 E9
San Rocque • Spain..............86 B6
San Saba • TX, United States....119 N3
San Salvador • El Salvador........37 D5
San Salvador • Galapagos Is....43 (1) A2
San Salvador de Jujuy •
  Argentina......................44 C4
San Salvador I. • Bahamas.......124 B4
San Sebastián • Spain............11 J1
San Sebastián •
  Gomera, Canary Is..............87 E5
San Sebastián • Puerto Rico.....125 E1
San Severo • Italy...............12 J7
San Sicário Ski • Italy........70 [192]
San Tin • Hong Kong, China.....107 H3
San Valentin • Chile.............45 B5
San Vicente de Cañete • Peru.....127 B1
San Vicente de la Barquera •
  Spain.........................11 G1
San Vicente de la Barquera Beach •
  Spain.........................68 [70]
San Vicente del Raspeig • Spain...11 K6
San Vigilio di Marebbe Ski •
  Italy........................70 [234]
San Vigilio in Marebbe • Italy....90 B2
San Vicente del Caguán •
  Colombia.......................43 C3
San Vincenzo • Italy............91 E11
San Vito, Capo • Sicily, Italy....12 G10
San Vito lo Capo •
  Sicily, Italy...................90 D1
San'a • Yemen..................18 D6
San'a Heritage C • Yemen......63 [103]
Sanae [Base] • Antarctica.....46 (1) II2
Sanaga • Cameroon..............23 G4
Sanana • Indonesia............32 (1) C3
Sanana [I.] • Indonesia.......32 (1) C3
Sanandaj • Iran..................18 E2
Sanary-sur-Mer • France.........85 H3
Sancai • Ethiopia................21 G5
Sancti-Spíritus • Cuba..........124 D3
Sancy, Puy de • France...........10 H8
Sandane • Mali..................20 C6
Sandøy • United Kingdom.........6 J2
Sand • Hedmark, Norway.........94 D5
Sand • Rogaland, Norway........94 C2
Sand Cay • Seychelles..........106 F2
Sand Hills • NE, United States....40 F3
Sand in Taufers • Italy..........90 B2
Sand Key • FL, United States....119 NM5
Sandakan • Malaysia.............32 F1
Sandane • Norway...............94 C1
Sandanski • Bulgaria............14 K8
Sandane • Mali..................20 C6
Sanday • United Kingdom.........6 J2
Sandefjord • Norway.............94 D4
Sandhamn • Sweden.............95 D4
Sandhornøya • Norway..........16 G3
Sandıklı • Turkey................15 L5

Sandlings • United Kingdom........5 E2
Sandnes • Norway...............94 C5
Sandnessjøen • Norway..........16 G3
Sandoa • Dem. Rep. of Congo....23 C5
Sandomierz • Poland.............13 K7
Sandoná • Colombia..............43 B3
Sandover • NT, Australia........112 H2
Sandøya • United Kingdom........7 K11
Sandown Beach • United Kingdom...75 [97]
Sandown Park • United Kingdom....74 E1
Sandras Dagi • Turkey...........15 J6
Sandringham • United Kingdom......7 M9
Sandsend Beach • United Kingdom...75 [28]
Sandur • India.................106 D2
Sandvig-Allinge • Denmark.......95 F16
Sandviken • Sweden..............16 I6
Sandwich • United Kingdom.......71 A7
Sandy Bay • Jamaica............124 C1
Sandy Bay • St Kitts & Nevis....125 G1
Sandy Cape • QL, Australia.....111 F4
Sandy Hook • NJ, United States...118 H1
Sandy Lake • OT, Canada.........38 M6
Sandy Point Town •
  St Kitts & Nevis..............125 G1
Sandycove • Ireland..............79 E2
Sandzak • F.R. of Yugoslavia.....14 G6
Sânfjället Nat. Park Park •
  Sweden........................72 [23]
Sanford • ME, United States.....118 G3
Sanford • FL, United States.....119 M6
Sanford, Mt • AK, United States...38 B4
Sanganer • India...............105 C6
Sangar • Russian Fed............27 K4
Sangareddy • India.............106 D3
Sangatte Terminal • France.......78 C4
Sangay, Parque Nac. Heritage N •
  Ecuador.......................60 [29]
Sangay, Volcán • Ecuador........43 B4
Sangerhausen • Germany..........8 G5
Sanggau • Indonesia.............32 E2
Sangha • Africa.................22 H4
Sanghe • Indonesia...........32 (1) C2
Sanghe, Kepulauan • Indonesia...32 (1) C2
Sangiran Heritage C •
  Java, Indonesia..............63 [179]
Sangju • Rep. of Korea...........30 D6
Sangli • India.................106 D2
Sango • Zimbabwe..............102 J4
Sangre Grande •
  Trinidad & Tobago.............125 K4
Sangro • Italy..................12 I7
Sangster, Sir Donald [Apt] •
  Jamaica.......................124 C1
Sanguem • Goa, India..........105 B2
Sangüesa • Spain................10 D11
Sanguinaires, Is. •
  Corsica, France.................85 L3
Sani • Greece...................92 D1
Sani • Greece...................92 D1
Sanibel I. • FL, United States...119 M5
Sanjo • Japan...................30 J6
Sankaisia • India..............105 C3
Sankt-Peterburg Heritage C •
  Russian Fed..................64 [205]
Sankuru • Dem. Rep. of Congo....23 C4
Sanli Urfa • Turkey.............18 C2
Sanlúcar de Barrameda • Spain....86 B5
Sanluri • Sardinia, Italy........12 C9
Sanming • China.................29 E4
Sannar • Sudan..................21 F5
Sannikova, Proliv •
  Russian Fed....................27 N2
Sanok • Poland..................13 L8
Sans-Souci Heritage C • Haiti...62 [37]
Sansepolcro • Italy.............12 G5
Sanski Most • Bosnia-Herz.......14 D5
Sanssouci, Schloß • Germany.....81 F3
Sant' Agata di Militello •
  Sicily, Italy..................12 I10
Sant Agustí • Majorca, Spain.....87 H3
Sant' Andria Priu, Necropoli di •
  Sardinia, Italy................90 C2
Sant' Angelo dei Lombardi •
  Italy..........................91 G2
Sant' Angelo in Formis • Italy....91 G1
Sant Antoni de Portmany •
  Ibiza, Spain...................87 G1
Sant Carles de la Ràpita Beach •
  Spain........................68 [104]
Sant Carles de Peralta •
  Ibiza, Spain...................87 G2
Sant Celoni • Spain.............11 N3
Sant Climent • Minorca, Spain....87 F4
Sant Feliu de Guíxols Beach •
  Spain........................68 [106]
Sant Feliu de Guíxols • Spain.....11 N3
Sant Fransesc de Formentera •
  Formentera, Spain..............87 G4
Sant Jaume Mediterrani •
  Minorca, Spain.................87 F4
Sant Joan de Labritja Beach •
  Ibiza, Spain..................68 [108]
Sant Joan de Labritja •
  Ibiza, Spain...................87 G2
Sant Jordi, Golf de • Spain.......11 L4
Sant Josep Beach • Ibiza, Spain..68 [108]
Sant Josep • Ibiza, Spain........87 G1
Sant Llorenç des Cardassar Beach •
  Majorca, Spain...............68 [109]
Sant Llorenç des Cardassar •
  Majorca, Spain.................87 H2
Santes Creus, Monestir de •
  Spain.........................87 D3
Sant Lluís Beach •
  Minorca, Spain...............68 [110]
Sant Lluís • Minorca, Spain.......87 F4
Sant Miquel de Balansat •
  Ibiza, Spain...................87 G2
Sant Pere de Rodes • Spain......87 D2
Sant Pere Pescador • Spain......87 D2
Sant Rafael de Forca •
  Ibiza, Spain...................87 G1
Sant Salvador, Santuari de •
  Majorca, Spain...............87 H2
Sant Telm • Majorca, Spain.......87 H1
Sant Tomàs • Minorca, Spain......87 F4
Santa Ana • El Salvador..........37 D5
Santa Ana • Mexico..............40 C2
Santa Ana Heritage C •
  Argentina.....................62 [64]
Santa Ana • CA, United States...117 F6
Santa Barbara •
  CA, United States.............117 F5
Santa Barbara I. •
  CA, United States.............117 F6
Santa Catalina I. •
  CA, United States.............117 F6
Santa Catarina • Brazil..........44 G4
Santa Catarina [Adm] • Brazil....44 F4
Santa Caterina di Pittinuri •
  Sardinia, Italy................90 C2
Santa Clara • CA, United States...117 F6
Santa Clara • Cuba.............124 D2
Santa Clara, Barragem de •
  Portugal.......................88 E2
Santa Clara Park •
  NM, United States.............118 J2
Santa Clara-a-Velha • Portugal...88 E2
Santa Comba • Spain.............11 C1
Santa Cristina Ski • Italy.....70 [231]
Santa Cristina Valgardena •
  Italy..........................90 B1

Santa Croce, Lago di • Italy......90 B4
Santa Cruz • Philippines.........31 G4
Santa Cruz • Galapagos Is....43 (1) A2
Santa Cruz • Brazil.............43 H4
Santa Cruz • Bolivia............44 D2
Santa Cruz • Argentina..........45 B6
Santa Cruz Beach • Madeira....68 [90]
Santa Cruz • CA, United States...117 F3
Santa Cruz Beach Boardwalk Park •
  CA, United States............120 [C]
Santa Cruz da Graciosa • Azores..88 B1
Santa Cruz das Flores • Azores....88 B1
Santa Cruz de La Palma •
  La Palma, Canary Is............87 E5
Santa Cruz de Tenerife •
  Tenerife, Canary Is............86 E1
Santa Cruz del Sur • Cuba.......124 D7
Santa Cruz do Sul • Brazil.......44 F4
Santa Cruz I. •
  CA, United States.............117 F5
Santa Cruz Is. • Solomon Is......33 H7
Santa Elena • Ecuador...........43 A4
Santa Elena • Costa Rica........37 D5
Santa Eufémia, Faro di • Italy....91 F4
Santa Eufémia, Golfo di • Italy...12 J10
Santa Eugénia • Spain...........11 C2
Santa Eulalia del Río Beach •
  Ibiza, Spain.................68 [108]
Santa Eulalia del Río •
  Ibiza, Spain...................87 G2
Santa Fe • Argentina............44 D5
Santa Fe Ski •
  NM, United States...........116 [106]
Santa Fe • NM, United States....118 J2
Santa Fé • Cuba................124 D1
Santa Helena • Brazil..........45 (1) C2
Santa Inês • Brazil...........45 (1) C2
Santa Inês, I. • Chile...........45 B6
Santa Isabel • Solomon Is......35 (1) F2
Santa Isabel • Argentina.........44 C6
Santa Lucía • Argentina.........44 C5
Santa Lucía, Playa • Cuba.......124 D3
Santa Luzia • Cape Verde.......22 (1) B1
Santa Margalida Beach •
  Majorca, Spain...............68 [109]
Santa Margalida •
  Majorca, Spain.................87 H2
Santa Margarita, I. • Mexico....123 E3
Santa Margherita di Pula •
  Sardinia, Italy................90 C4
Santa Margherita Ligure • Italy...91 E6
Santa Maria • Vanuatu.......35 (2) B1
Santa Maria • CA, United States...40 B5
Santa Maria • Galapagos Is...43 (1) A2
Santa Maria • Chile.............44 B6
Santa Maria • Brazil............44 F4
Santa Maria • Azores............88 B2
Santa Maria • Azores............88 B2
Santa Maria • Mexico...........123 E2
Santa Maria, Cabo • Uruguay....44 F5
Santa Maria, Cabo de • Portugal...88 E2
Santa Maria Cápua Vetere •
  Italy..........................91 G1
Santa Maria di Leuca, Capo •
  Italy.........................12 M9
Santa Maria Mayor Heritage C •
  Argentina.....................62 [64]
Santa Marinella • Italy..........91 F1
Santa Marta • Colombia..........43 C1
Santa Marta, Cabo de • Angola...24 A2
Santa Marta, Ria de • Spain......11 D1
Santa Monica Mtns Nat. Recreation Area
  Park • CA, United States.....120 [57]
Santa Pola Beach • Spain......68 [101]
Santa Pola • Spain..............87 C1
Santa Ponça • Majorca, Spain....87 H1
Santa Rosa • Argentina..........44 D6
Santa Rosa • Brazil.............44 F4
Santa Rosa • CA, United States...117 F3
Santa Rosa I. •
  CA, United States.............117 F5
Santa Rosa •
  FL, United States............119 M1
Santa Rosalía • Mexico..........40 D6
Santa Severina • Italy..........71 A19
Santa Teresa • NT, Australia....112 H4
Santa Teresa Aboriginal Land •
  NT, Australia.................112 H2
Santa Teresa di Gallura Beach •
  Sardinia, Italy..............68 [119]
Santa Teresa di Gallura •
  Sardinia, Italy................90 C2
Santa Vitória do Palmar •
  Brazil.........................44 F5
Santa's Village • OT, Canada.....122 B5
Santan • Indonesia...............32 F3
Santana • Madeira...............88 C2
Santana da Serra • Portugal......88 E2
Santana do Livramento • Brazil...44 F5
Santander • Spain...............11 H1
Santander • Colombia............43 B3
Santander Beach • Spain......68 [64]
Santander, Bahía de • Spain......11 H1
Santanyí Beach • Majorca, Spain..68 [109]
Santanyí • Majorca, Spain........87 H4
Santarém • Portugal.............11 C5
Santarém • Brazil...............43 G4
Santarém [Adm] • Portugal......88 A2
Santiago • Panama...............37 E6
Santiago • Dominican Rep........37 G4
Santiago • Brazil...............44 F4
Santiago • Mexico..............123 E1
Santiago de Compostela •
  Spain.........................11 C2
Santiago de Compostela Heritage C •
  Spain........................64 [83]
Santiago de Cuba Heritage C •
  Cuba.........................62 [36]
Santiago de Cuba • Cuba........124 D8
Santiago de la Ribera • Spain.....87 C3
Santiago del Estero • Argentina...44 C4
Santiago do Cacém • Portugal....11 C6
Santiago Ixcuintla • Mexico....37 (1) A1
Santiago Tuxtla • Mexico.......123 E4
Santíssima Trinità di Saccargia •
  Sardinia, Italy................90 C1
Santo André • Brazil..........45 (1) B6
Santo André • Brazil...........127 C3
Santo Ângelo • Brazil..........44 F4
Santo Antão • Cape Verde.....22 (1) A1
Santo Antônio de Jesus • Brazil...44 I1
Santo Antônio de Pádua • Brazil..127 C2
Santo Antônio do Içá • Brazil.....43 D4
Santo da Serra • Madeira........88 C2
Santo Domingo • Dominican Rep...37 H4
Santo Domingo Heritage C •
  Dominican Rep................62 [38]
Santo Domingo • Cuba..........124 D2
Santo Domingo de los Colorados •
  Ecuador........................43 B4
Santo Estêvão • Portugal.........88 E2
Santoña Beach • Spain........68 [70]
Santorini • Greece..............92 D8
Santos • Brazil.................127 C3
Santos Dumont • Brazil.........127 C1

Santpoort • Netherlands.........80 C1
Santurce-Antiguo • Spain........11 H1
Sanur • Bali, Indonesia........110 C4
Sanur • Bali, Indonesia........110 C4
Sanxenxo Beach • Spain.......68 [74]
Sanya • China..................31 D3
Sanzao • Zhuhai, China........107 H3
Sanzao Dao • Zhuhai, China....107 H3
São Bartolomeu de Messines •
  Portugal.......................88 E2
São Borja • Brazil..............44 E4
São Brás de Alportel • Portugal...88 E7
São Caetano do Sul • Brazil......44 G3
São Carlos • Brazil.............44 G3
São Félix do Xingu • Brazil......43 G5
São Francisco • Brazil..........44 G4
São Francisco do Sul • Brazil....44 G4
São Francisco [Riv] • Brazil...45 (1) D4
São Gabriel • Brazil...........44 F5
São Gabriel da Cachoeira •
  Brazil.........................43 D4
São Gonçalo • Brazil...........44 H3
São Gotardo • Brazil...........127 C1
São João da Barra • Brazil.....127 C4
São João da Madeira • Portugal...11 C4
São João del Rei • Brazil.......127 C1
São Joaquim • Brazil............44 G4
São Jorge Beach • Azores.....68 [84]
São Jorge • Azores..............88 B2
São Jorge • Madeira.............88 C2
São Jorge I. • Goa, India......105 B2
São José do Rio Pardo • Brazil...44 G3
São José do Rio Prêto • Brazil...44 G3
São José dos Campos • Brazil...127 C3
São Leopoldo • Brazil...........44 F5
São Lourenço do Sul • Brazil.....44 F5
São Luís Heritage C • Brazil...62 [59]
São Luís Gonzaga • Brazil.......44 F4
São Manuel • Brazil.............43 F5
São Marcos, Baía de • Brazil...45 (1) C2
São Marcos da Serra • Portugal...88 E2
São Mateus • Brazil..........45 (1) C5
São Miguel Heritage C • Brazil...62 [64]
São Miguel • Azores..........22 (1) B1
São Nicolau • Cape Verde.....22 (1) B1
São Paulo • Brazil.............127 A1
São Paulo [Adm] • Brazil........44 G3
São Paulo de Olivença • Brazil...43 D4
São Pedro • Brazil.............127 A1
São Raimundo Nonato • Brazil...45 (1) D3
São Roque, Cabo de • Brazil...45 (1) D3
São Sebastião do Paraíso •
  Brazil.........................44 G3
São Sebastião, I. de • Brazil....127 C3
São Teotónio • Portugal.........88 E1
São Tiago • Cape Verde......22 (1) B1
São Tomé • Sao Tomé e Príncipe...22 F4
São Tomé, Cabo de • Brazil.....127 C4
São Tomé e Príncipe • Africa.....22 F4
São Tomé [I.] •
  Sao Tomé e Príncipe...........22 F4
São Vicente • Cape Verde.....22 (1) A1
São Vicente • Brazil............44 G3
São Vicente • Madeira...........88 C1
São Vicente, Cabo de • Portugal...88 E5
Saolat, Buku • Indonesia.....32 (1) C2
Saon Beach • Phuket, Thailand....109 K1
Saône • France..................10 K6
Saonek • Indonesia...........32 (1) D3
Saoura • Algeria................20 E3
Sapai Bay • Phuket, Thailand....109 K1
Sapanca • Turkey................15 L3
Sapele • Nigeria................22 F3
Sápes • Greece.................15 G2
Saphane Dagi • Turkey..........15 L5
Sapi & Chewore Safari Areas •
  Zimbabwe......................102 J2
Sapi safari area Heritage N •
  Zimbabwe.....................61 [96]
Sapiendza • Greece..............15 C7
Sapo Nat. Park Park • Liberia...103 [18]
Saposoa • Peru..................43 B5
Sappada • Italy.................90 B2
Sapporo • Japan.................30 L2
Sapri • Italy....................12 J8
Sapudi • Indonesia.............110 D4
Saqqara • Egypt.................101 F2
Saquarema • Brazil.............127 C4
Sar Planina • Europe............14 H7
Sarahuri • Thailand............109 H2
Saragossa • Spain...............71 A12
Sarai • Russian Fed..............98 B1
Sarajevo • Bosnia-Herz..........14 F6
Saramati • India/Myanmar........28 F3
Saran, Gunung • Indonesia......32 E3
Saranci • Bulgaria...............15 E1
Sarandë • Albania...............15 A4
Sarandí del Yi • Uruguay.......127 D2
Sarangani • Philippines.........31 H5
Sarantey • Somalia..............23 G3
Saransk • Russian Fed...........17 I3
Sarapul • Russian Fed...........17 I3
Sarasin Bridge •
  Phuket, Thailand..............109 K1
Sarasota • FL, United States...119 M5
Saratoga Nat. Hist. Park Park •
  NY, United States...........121 [319]
Saratov • Russian Fed...........17 H4
Saravan • Laos..................31 D3
Sarawak • Malaysia.............15 I2
Saray • Turkey..................15 J5
Sarayköy • Turkey...............15 J6
Sárbogárd • Hungary...........13 H11
Sardarshahar • India...........105 C2
Sardegna • Italy................90 C
Sardes • Turkey.................92 D6
Sardindida Plain • Kenya.......101 G2
Sardinia • Italy.................90 C
Sarek Nat. Park Park • Sweden...72 [19]
Sarektjåkkå • Sweden...........16 I3
Sargasso Sea • Atlantic Ocean....E2
Sarh • Chad.....................21 G4
Sarhro, Jebel • Morocco........20 D2
Sari • Iran.....................18 F2
Sari d'Orcino • Corsica, France...85 L3
Sária • Greece..................92 D11
Sárieri • Turkey................15 J2
Sariñena • Spain................11 K3
Sarir Kalanshiyu • Libya........21 D2
Sarir Tibasti • Libya...........21 C3
Sariska Nat. Park • India......105 C2
Sariwon • D.P.R. of Korea.......30 C5
Sariyer • Turkey................15 J2
Sark • Channel Is................7 J12
Sarkad • Hungary..............13 K11
Sarkand • Kazakhstan...........26 M8
Sarkikaraagaç • Turkey.........15 M5
Şarlat-la-Canéda • France.......85 G2
Sarmi • Indonesia............32 (1) E3
Sarmiento • Argentina...........45 B6
Särna • Sweden..................16 G6

Sarnath • India................105 C8
Sarnen • Switzerland............89 G3
Sarnia • OT, Canada.............39 O8
Sarny • Ukraine.................17 D4
Saroma-Ko • Japan..............30 L2
Saronic Gulf • Greece...........92 D7
Saronic Gulf • Greece...........92 D7
Saronikós Kólpos • Greece.......92 D7
Saronikós Kólpos • Greece.......92 D7
Saronno • Italy.................12 D3
Saros Körfezi • Turkey..........15 H3
Sárospatak • Hungary..........13 K9
Sarot • St Lucia...............125 J1
Sarovar • Russian Fed...........17 G3
Sarpsborg • Norway.............94 B4
Sarralbe • France................5 J5
Sarre • France.................10 M5
Sarrebourg • France............10 L5
Sarreguemines • France.........10 M4
Sarria • Spain..................11 D2
Sarrión • Spain.................11 K4
Sarstedt • Germany..............8 E4
Sartène • Corsica, France.......85 L3
Sarthe [Adm] • France..........84 D2
Sarthe • France................10 F5
Särti Beach • Greece.........69 [169]
Sárti • Greece..................92 D1
Sárti • Greece..................92 D1
Sárvár • Hungary..............13 F10
Särviz • Hungary................14 F3
Sarych, mys • Ukraine...........17 E6
Sarykamysh • Turkmenistan.......26 I9
Sarysu • Kazakhstan............26 K8
Sarzana • Italy................91 E10
Sasaram • India................105 C3
Sasbachwalden Spa • Germany...83 [184]
Sasebo • Japan.................30 E8
Sasenkov • Russian Fed.........38 J5
Saskatchewan [Riv] •
  MN/SA, Canada...............38 K6
Saskatoon • SA, Canada.........38 J6
Saskylakh • Russian Fed........27 H2
Sasovo • Russian Fed...........17 G4
Sassandra • Côte d'Ivoire.......22 C3
Sassandra [Riv] • Côte d'Ivoire...22 C2
Sassari • Sardinia, Italy........90 C1
Sassenberg • Germany............8 I2
Sasso Marconi • Italy..........12 F4
Sassuolo • Italy...............12 E4
Sata-Misaki • Japan............30 F9
Satan, Pointe de • Vanuatu...35 (2) B2
Satara • India..................28 B5
Sater • Sweden.................16 H6
Satipo • Peru...................43 C6
Satna • India...................28 D4
Satna • India..................105 C7
Satolas [Apt] • France..........85 F1
Sátoraljaújhely • Hungary......13 K9
Satpayev • Kazakhstan..........26 K8
Satsunan-Shoto • Japan.........31 H1
Satthip • Thailand.............109 H4
Satu Mare • Romania............14 J2
Saturn • Romania...............97 D2
Saualpe • Austria..............13 J4
Sauce • Argentina...............44 E5
Sauda • Norway.................94 C5
Saudárkrókur • Iceland......16 (1) D2
Saudi Arabia • Asia.............18 E5
Sauer • Germany.................9 B7
Sauerland • Germany............9 C5
Saugus Iron Works Nat. Hist. Site Park •
  MA, United States..........121 [349]
Saül • French Guiana...........43 G3
Sauland • Norway...............94 B1
Saulgau • Germany..............82 J1
Saulgau Spa • Germany.......83 [214]
Sault Ste Marie • OT, Canada....39 O7
Saum, Laem • Phuket, Thailand...109 K1
Saumlaki • Indonesia.........32 (1) D4
Saumur • France................84 D1
Saumur [Château] • France......84 D1
Saundersfoot Beach •
  United Kingdom............75 [146-147]
Saurimo • Angola...............23 C5
Sausalito • CA, United States...117 F3
Sauternes • France.............84 C3
Sauvage, Côte • France.........84 C4
Sauve, la • France..............85 J1
Sauveterre • France............85 J1
Sâuze d'Oulx Ski • Italy.....70 [195]
Sâuze d'Oulx • Italy............14 E4
Sava • Europe..................14 E4
Savai'i • Western Samoa.....35 (2) F1
Savalou • Benin................22 E3
Savanna-la-Mar • Jamaica......124 C1
Savannah • GA, United States....41 J5
Savannah [Riv] •
  GA/SC, United States..........41 J5
Savannakhét • Laos.............31 C3
Savant Lake • OT, Canada.......39 M6
Savanur • India................106 D2
Savârsin • Romania.............13 L11
Savastepe • Turkey.............15 I4
Save • Benin...................22 E3
Save • Mozambique.............24 E4
Save • Sweden..................95 F6
Saverdun • France.............11 M1
Saverne • France...............10 M5
Savinjske Alpe •
  Austria/Slovenia...............14 B3
Savinski • Russian Fed..........17 G2
Savognin • Switzerland.........89 G4
Savoie • France................85 F2
Savona • Italy.................91 E6
Savonlinna • Finland...........16 O6
Savoy • France.................84 A2
Savoie • Sweden................95 F7
Sawai Madhopur • India.........105 C6
Sawakin • Sudan................21 G4
Sawakin, Jaza'ir • Sudan........21 G4
Sawankhalok • Thailand........109 G4
Sawantwadi • India............106 D1
Sawda, Jabal as • Libya.........21 B2
Sawkanah • Libya...............21 B2
Sawqirah • Oman................18 G6
Sawtooth Nat. Recreation Area •
  ID, United States............117 E4
Sawu • Indonesia..............32 (1) B4
Sawu Sea • Indonesia.......32 (1) B4
Saxony • Germany...............81 D2
Say • Niger....................20 F6
Saya • Russian Fed..............25 K4
Sayda • Lebanon................18 B3
Saydā • Yemen..................18 F6
Saynshand • Mongolia...........29 C3
Sázava • Czech Rep.............96 C2
Sázava [Riv] • Czech Rep........96 C2
Sbaa • Algeria.................20 E3
Sbeïtla • Tunisia..............101 E3
Scafell Pike • United Kingdom....74 C1
Scalby • United Kingdom.........75 J3
Scandinavia • Europe............16
Scandola, Réserve Naturelle Heritage N •
  Corsica, France..............61 [45]

Scandola, Réserve Naturelle

Scandola, Réserve Naturelle •
  Corsica, France 85 L1
Scanzano Iónico Beach • Italy 69 [134]
Scanzano Iónico • Italy 90 A2
Scapa Flow • United Kingdom 6 I3
Scarba • United Kingdom 75 A2
Scarborough • United Kingdom ... 7 L7
Scarborough Beach •
  United Kingdom .... 75 [31]
Scarborough • St Kitts & Nevis .. 125 G4
Scarborough • Trinidad & Tobago 125 K2
Scariff I. • Ireland 79 F7
Scarp • United Kingdom 6 F3
Schaalsee • Germany 8 F3
Schaffhausen • Switzerland 9 D9
Schäftlarn • Germany 82 J3
Schalksmühle • Germany 81 E4
Scharbeutz • Germany 8 F2
Scharbeutz-Haffkrug Spa •
  Germany .... 83 [27]
Schärding • Austria 9 I8
Scharhörn • Germany 8 D3
Scharmützelsee • Germany 8 J4
Schauinsland • Germany 82 G8
Scheffau Ski • Austria .... 70 [152]
Schefferville • QU, Canada 39 R5
Scheidegg • Switzerland 89 G2
Scheidegg • Germany 82 J3
Scheidegg Spa • Germany ..... 83 [239]
Schelde • Belgium 80 A14
Schenectady • NY, United States .. 41 L3
Schermbeck • Germany 81 E1
Scherpenheuvel-Zichem Beach •
  Belgium .... 68 [54]
Scherpenheuvel-Zichem • Belgium 80 A15
Scheveningen • Netherlands 80 C3
Schiedam • Netherlands 80 C3
Schieder Spa • Germany .... 83 [98]
Schieland • Netherlands 80 C3
Schiermonnikoog • Netherlands .. 80 A4
Schiltach • Germany 82 G8
Schiltigheim • France 5 K6
Schiphol [Apt] • Netherlands 80 C2
Schladming Ski • Austria .... 70 [184]
Schladming • Austria 89 H4
Schlangenbad Spa • Germany .. 83 [141]
Scharigna • Switzerland 89 B6
Schleiden • Germany 9 B6
Schlema Spa • Germany .... 83 [314]
Schleswig • Germany 8 E2
Schleswig-Holstein • Germany ... 8 E2
Schleswig-Holsteinisches Wattenmeer,
  Nationalpark Park •
  Germany .... 72 [57]
Schliersee • Germany 82 J7
Schluchsee • Germany 82 G8
Schluchsee Spa • Germany ... 83 [208]
Schlüchtern • Germany 9 H6
Schmallenberg • Germany 9 D5
Schneeberg • Germany 9 H6
Schneverdingen • Germany 5 M1
Schoberpaß • Austria 14 B2
Schokland Heritage C •
  Netherlands .... 64 [26]
Schokland • Netherlands 80 A7
Schömberg Spa • Germany .... 83 [178]
Schönau Spa • Germany 86 B1
Schönau am Königssee • Germany 82 J8
Schönberg Spa • Germany .... 83 [18]
Schönburg • Germany 82 H4
Schönebeck • Germany 8 G4
Schönefeld [Apt] • Germany 81 E4
Schöneiche bei Berlin • Germany 81 F4
Schongau • Germany 82 J6
Schönhagen Spa • Germany ... 83 [12]
Schöningen • Germany 8 F4
Schönwald Spa • Germany .... 83 [197]
Schönwalde • Germany 81 F1
Schönwalde • Germany 8 F2
Schoonhoven • Netherlands 80 C4
Schopfheim • Germany 82 G8
Schortens • Germany 8 C3
Schotten • Germany 82 G2
Schouwen • Netherlands 80 A10
Schouwen-Duiveland Beach •
  Netherlands .... 68 [50]
Schramberg • Germany 9 D8
Schreiber • OT, Canada 39 G7
Schröken • Austria 89 H5
Schruns • Austria 89 H5
Schulenberg Spa • Germany ... 83 [79]
Schull • Ireland 79 F7
Schultz Lake • NU, Canada 38 L3
Schulzendorf • Germany 81 F4
Schuss Mtn Ski •
  MI, United States .... 116 [132]
Schwabach • Germany 9 G7
Schwäbisch • Germany 9 G8
Schwäbisch Gmünd • Germany .. 9 E8
Schwäbisch Hall • Germany 9 E8
Schwäbisch Hall Spa • Germany 83 [174]
Schwäbisch Alb • Germany 9 E8
Schwäbisch-Bayerisches Alpenvorland •
  Germany .... 82 J
Schwäbmünchen • Germany ... 82 J2
Schwalefeld Spa • Germany ... 83 [120]
Schwalmstadt • Germany 5 M4
Schwandorf • Germany 9 H7
Schwangau • Germany 82 J6
Schwangau Spa • Germany ... 83 [245]
Schwante • Germany 81 F1
Schwarzach • Germany 9 H7
Schwarze Elster • Germany 8 H5
Schwarzenberg • Austria 89 H1
Schwarzwald • Germany 82 G8
Schwarzwaldbahn • Germany ... 82 G8
Schwaz • Austria 9 G9
Schwedt an der Oder • Germany . 8 J3
Schweinfurt • Germany 9 F6
Schweitzer Mtn Ski •
  ID, United States .... 116 [69]
Schwerin • Germany 81 E4
Schwerin • Germany 8 G3
Schweriner See • Germany 8 G3
Schwerte • Germany 5 K3
Schwerte • Germany 81 E2
Schwetzingen • Germany 82 G4
Schwielochsee • Germany 8 J4
Schwielowsee • Germany 81 F3
Schwyz • Switzerland 89 C7
Sciacca • Sicily, Italy 12 H11
Scicli • Sicily, Italy 12 I12
Scilly, Isles of •
  United Kingdom 7 F12
Scone Palace • United Kingdom . 74 B2
Sconser • United Kingdom 78 A1
Scoresbysund • Greenland 36 O2
Scorpion I. • St Lucia 125 J4
Scotland • United Kingdom 6
Scotlandville •
  LA, United States 118 K4
Scott [Base] • Antarctica 46 (1) V2
Scott, Cape • NT, Australia 34 E2
Scott, Cape • BC, Canada 38 F6
Scott, Fort, Nat. Hist. Site Park •
  KS, United States .... 121 [172]
Scott I. • Antarctica 46 (1) X3
Scottish Lowlands •
  United Kingdom .... 74 B

Scotts Bluff Nat. Mon. Park •
  NE, United States .... 120 [165]
Scottsbluff • NE, United States .. 40 F3
Scottsdale • TS, Australia 34 I8
Scottsdale • AZ, United States .. 118 J3
Scrabster • United Kingdom 78 B3
Scranton • PA, United States .. 118 H1
Scunthorpe • United Kingdom ... 7 L8
Scuol • Switzerland 89 G4
Scutari • Turkey 92 D3
Scutari • Turkey 92 D3
Scutari, Lake •
  Albania/F.R. of Yugoslavia ... 14 G7
Scythopolis • Israel 98 A4
Se Mesquida de Baix •
  Majorca, Spain 87 H2
Sea Is. • GA, United States 41 I5
Sea Life Park •
  HI, United States 119 L6
Sea View Farm •
  Antigua & Barbuda 125 F1
Sea World • QL, Australia 111 F6
Sea World of California •
  CA, United States 117 F6
Sea World of California Park •
  CA, United States .... 120 [J]
Sea World of Florida •
  FL, United States 121 C2
Sea World of Ohio Park •
  OH, United States .... 121 [U]
Sea World of Texas •
  TX, United States 119 N5
Sea World of Texas Park •
  TX, United States .... 121 [O]
Seaford • United States 74 E3
Seaford Town • Jamaica 124 C1
Seagrove Bay Beach •
  United Kingdom .... 75 [94]
Seahouses North Beach •
  United Kingdom .... 75 [16]
Seal, Cape • South Africa 100 C7
Seal River • MN, Canada 38 L5
Seapoint Beach • Ireland ..... 68 [35]
Seapoint • Ireland 79 E2
Seascale • United Kingdom 74 C3
Seaside • OR, United States ... 117 E1
Seaside • FL, United States .. 119 M2
Seaton • United Kingdom 74 F3
Seaton Carew Beach •
  United Kingdom .... 75 [26]
Seatons • Antigua & Barbuda .. 125 F2
Seattle • WA, United States ... 117 E1
Seaward Kaikoura Range •
  New Zealand 35 D6
Seaworld • Shenzhen, China ... 107 H3
Seba • Indonesia 32 (1) B5
Sebarok • Singapore 108 E3
Sebastiansweiler Spa • Germany 83 [191]
Sebes • Romania 14 K4
Sebesi • Indonesia 110 D1
Sebis • Romania 14 J3
Sebkha de Tindouf • Algeria .. 20 D2
Sebou • Morocco 101 D2
Sebu • Morocco 101 E5
Sebuca, El • Egypt 101 F5
Sebuku • Indonesia 110 D1
Sècheis • Italy 91 E7
Sechura, Bahía de • Peru 43 A5
Sechura, Desierto de • Peru .. 43 A5
Secretary I. • New Zealand ... 112 L1
Secunderabad • India 106 D3
Sécure • Bolivia 44 C2
Sedalia • MO, United States .. 41 H4
Sedan • France 10 J4
Sedano • Spain 10 B11
Seddenga • Sudan 21 F3
Seddülbahir • Turkey 15 H3
Sedona • AZ, United States .. 118 J1
Sedrun • Switzerland 89 G3
Sée • France 5 B6
Seefeld • Austria 89 H2
Seeheim • Namibia 24 B5
Seelig, Mt • Antarctica 46 (1) EE1
Seeon • Germany 82 J4
Sées • France 10 F5
Seesen • Germany 8 F5
Sefrou • Morocco 101 D2
Segesta • Sicily, Italy 90 D1
Segezha • Russian Fed 17 E2
Ségou • Mali 22 C2
Segovia • Spain 11 G4
Segovia Heritage C • Spain .. 64 [86]
Segre, el • Spain 11 L3
Séguédine • Niger 20 H4
Séguéla • Côte d'Ivoire 22 C3
Segura • TX, United States .. 119 N3
Segura • Spain 11 J6
Sehlabathebe Nat. Park Park •
  Lesotho .... 103 [130]
Seignosse Beach • France .... 68 [67]
Seiland • Norway 16 L1
Seille • France 5 J6
Seinäjoki • Finland 16 L5
Seine • France 10 G4
Seine, Baie de la • France ... 10 E4
Seine, Val de • France 85 E4
Seine-et-Marne • France 85 E4
Seixal • Madeira 88 C1
Seixal • Portugal 88 D2
Sejerø Bugt • Denmark 95 F10
Sejlflod Beach • Denmark .... 68 [29]
Sekincau, Gunung • Indonesia . 32 C3
Sekinchan • Malaysia 108 D3
Sekondi-Takoradi • Ghana 22 D4
Selajar • Indonesia 32 (1) B4
Selangor • Malaysia 31 C6
Selaön • Sweden 95 D3
Selaru • Indonesia 32 (1) D4
Selatan, Selat •
  Penang, Malaysia 108 C4
Selatan, Tanjung • Indonesia .. 32 E3
Selb • Germany 9 H6
Selb • Germany 13 B7
Selby • United Kingdom 7 K8
Selçuk • Turkey 15 I6
Sele • Italy 91 G4
Sele, Piana del • Italy 91 G4
Selebi-Phikwe • Botswana ... 24 D4
Selecka Planina •
  F.Y.R. of Macedonia 15 C2
Selendi • Turkey 15 J5
Selendi [Riv] • Turkey 15 J5
Selenga • Mongolia/Russian Fed. 27 G7
Selenge • Dem. Rep. of Congo .. 23 B4
Selennyakh • Russian Fed 27 N3
Selenter See • Germany 8 F2
Sélestat • France 10 E1
Seletar Reservoir • Singapore .. 108 E1
Seleucia • Iraq 16 (1) C3
Selfoss • Iceland 16 (1) C2
Selga • Turkey 90 C2
Selibabi • Mauritania 20 C5
Seliger, Ozero • Russian Fed. . 97 E3
Selimiye • Mugla, Turkey 92 C3
Selimye • Marmara, Turkey ... 93 G4
Selinunte • Sicily, Italy 90 D1
Selje • Norway 94 C1
Seljord • Norway 94 B3
Seljord stavkirke • Norway ... 94 B3

Seljordsvatnet • Norway 94 B3
Selkirk • United Kingdom 6 J6
Selkirk • MN, Canada 38 L6
Selkirk Mtns • BC, Canada ... 38 H7
Sella Nevea • Italy 91 E4
Sella, Passo di • Italy 90 B3
Sellafield • United Kingdom ... 74 C3
Selle • France 5 F5
Sellin Spa • Germany .... 83 [280]
Selma • AL, United States ... 41 I5
Selsey Bill • United Kingdom ... 5 C4
Sélune • France 5 C6
Selva di Cadore Ski • Italy ... 70 [226]
Selva di Cadore • Italy 90 B4
Selva di Val Gardena • Italy ... 90 B3
Selva Gardena Ski • Italy .... 70 [232]
Selvagens, Is. • Madeira 20 B2
Selva • Brazil 42 D5
Selworthy • United Kingdom .. 74 F2
Selwyn Lake • NT/SA, Canada .. 38 K5
Selwyn Mtns • NT/YT, Canada .. 38 E4
Selwyn Range • QL, Australia .. 34 G4
Semakau • Singapore 108 E3
Semani • Albania 15 A3
Semarang • Java, Indonesia .. 110 D3
Sembé • Congo 22 G4
Semeru, Gunung •
  Java, Indonesia 110 D8
Semey • Kazakhstan 26 N7
Semitau • Indonesia 110 D1
Semmering • Austria 13 E10
Semnan • Iran 18 F2
Semnon • France 10 D6
Semois • Belgium/France 80 A19
Semporna • Malaysia 32 F2
Semuda • Indonesia 110 D8
Sena Madureira • Brazil 43 D5
Senaja • Malaysia 32 F1
Senang • Singapore 108 E3
Senanga • Zambia 24 C2
Sénart, Forêt de • France 85 E4
Sendai • Kyushu, Japan 30 D4
Sendai • Honshu, Japan 30 K5
Sendai-Wan • Japan 30 K5
Seneca • WA, United States .. 82 J1
Seneca Lake • NY, United States 122 B10
Senegal • Africa 20 B6
Senegal [Riv] •
  Mauritania/Senegal 20 C5
Senftenberg • Germany 8 J5
Senftenberg • Germany 32 F2
Sengwa • Zimbabwe 24 D3
Senhor do Bonfim • Brazil 45 (1) C4
Senica • Slovak Rep 13 D8
Senigàllia Beach • Italy ..... 69 [141]
Senigàllia • Italy 91 E12
Senj • Croatia 14 B5
Senja • Norway 16 I2
Senkaku-Shoto • Japan 29 G5
Senlin • China 30 F3
Senlis • France 85 E2
Sennen Cove Beach •
  United Kingdom .... 75 [123]
Senneterre • QU, Canada 39 P7
Sens • France 10 H5
Senta • F.R. of Yugoslavia ... 14 H4
Sentosa • Singapore 108 E4
Senyavin •
  Fed. States of Micronesia ... 25 N9
Seoni • India 28 C4
Seoul • Rep. of Korea 30 D6
Seoul Heritage C •
  Rep. of Korea .... 63 [158]
Sepetiba, Baía de • Brazil ... 127 C3
Sepik • Papua New Guinea .. 35 (1) C1
Sept Laux, les Ski • France ... 70 [51]
Sept-Îles • QU, Canada 123 D2
Septemvri • Bulgaria 15 F1
Sepúlveda • Spain 11 H3
Sequoia Nat. Park •
  CA, United States 117 F4
Sequoia Nat. Park Park •
  CA, United States .... 120 [53]
Seráqta Han • Turkey 93 G4
Seraing • Belgium 5 I4
Seram • Indonesia 35 (1) A1
Seram, Laut • Indonesia 110 D1
Serang • Java, Indonesia ... 110 D1
Serangan • Bali, Indonesia .. 110 C4
Serangoon New Town • Singapore 108 E2
Seraya • Singapore 108 E3
Serbia • F.R. of Yugoslavia .. 14 H6
Serdo • Ethiopia 23 G3
Sered' • Slovak Rep 13 G9
Seredka • Turkey 15 J4
Serefiköçhisar • Turkey 15 J4
Serein • France 10 I6
Seremban • Malaysia 108 D4
Serengeti Nat. Park Heritage N •
  Tanzania .... 61 [90]
Serengeti Nat. Park • Tanzania 102 H2
Serengeti Plain • Tanzania ... 102 H1
Serengeti Playa Park •
  Tanzania .... 103 [88]
Serengeti Safaripark Park •
  Germany .... 73 [55]
Séres • Greece 92 D1
Séres • Greece 92 D1
Serfaus Ski • Austria .... 70 [135]
Serfaus • Austria 89 H6
Sergeya Kirova, Ostrova •
  Russian Fed 26 P2
Sergipe • Brazil 46 I3
Sergipe • Brazil 44 I1
Sergiyev Posad Heritage C •
  Russian Fed .... 64 [209]
Sergiyev Posad • Russian Fed. 97 F4
Serian • Malaysia 32 E3
Sérifos • Greece 92 D7
Sérifos • Greece 92 D7
Serifou, Stenó • Greece 15 F6
Serik • Turkey 93 G4
Sermata, Kepulauan • Indonesia 32 (1) C4
Serón • Spain 11 I7
Serov • Russian Fed 26 J6
Serowe • Botswana 24 D4
Serpa • Portugal 11 D7
Serpent's Mouth •
  Trinidad & Tobago 125 K3
Serpukhov • Russian Fed 97 E4
Serra • Malaysia 28 B3
Serra do Bonfim • Brazil 45 (1) C4
Serra do Caiapó • Brazil 44 F2
Serra do Navio • Brazil 43 G3
Serra Orrios, Villaggio nuragico di •
  Sardinia, Italy 90 C2
Serrant [Château] • France ... 84 D1
Serrat, Cap • Tunisia 21 I8
Serre • France 5 G5
Serre-Chevalier Ski • France .. 70 [60]
Serre-Chevalier • France 85 H5
Serres • France 10 K9
Serrinha • Brazil 44 I2
Serrinha • Brazil 44 I2

Serui • Indonesia 32 (1) E3
Servion • Switzerland 89 G1
Ses Animas, Mirador de •
  Majorca, Spain 87 H1
Ses Figueretes • Ibiza, Spain .. 87 G2
Ses Salines Beach •
  Majorca, Spain .... 68 [109]
Ses Salines • Majorca, Spain .. 87 H4
Sesayap • Indonesia 32 F2
Seseh Beach • Bali, Indonesia 110 C4
Sesheke • Zambia 24 C3
Sesimbra • Portugal 88 D2
Sesimbra Beach • Portugal ... 88 D2
Sesri • Sudan 21 F3
Sessa Aurunca • Italy 91 I1
Sestao • Spain 11 I1
Sesto Ski • Italy .... 70 [240]
Sesto • Italy 90 B2
Sesto Fiorentino • Italy 12 F5
Sestri Levante • Italy 91 E6
Sestriere Ski • Italy .... 70 [194]
Sestriere • Italy 91 E5
Set, Laem • Ko Samui, Thailand . 109 J2
Seta • Japan 30 J3
Sète • France 10 I10
Sète Beach • France .... 68 [113]
Sete Cidades, Caldeiras das •
  Azores 88 B1
Sete Lagoas • Brazil 127 C1
Sete Quedas, Saltos das •
  Brazil/Paraguay 44 F3
Setesdal • Norway 94 C6
Sétif • Algeria 20 G1
Seto • Japan 30 I7
Settat • Morocco 101 D1
Setúbal • Portugal 88 D1
Setúbal [Adm] • Portugal 88 A3
Setúbal, Baía de • Portugal .. 11 B6
Seu d'Urgell, la • Spain 87 F1
Seul, Lac • OT, Canada 38 M6
Seul • Azerbaijan 18 E1
Sévaré • Mali 20 E6
Sevastopol • Ukraine 97 E6
Sevelen • Germany 81 E1
Seven Springs Ski •
  PA, United States .... 116 [160]
Sévérac-le-Château • France .. 10 I9
Severn • OT, Canada 39 N5
Severn • United Kingdom 74 D1
Severn Gorge • United Kingdom . 74 D1
Sévérnaya • AK, United States 68 [34]
Severnaya Dvina • Russian Fed. 17 G2
Severnaya Zemlya • Russian Fed. 26 M6
Severnoye • Russian Fed 26 J4
Severny • Russian Fed 26 I4
Severny Ural • Russian Fed... 26 I5
Severny • Russian Fed 17 G3
Severo Donets • Ukraine 4 R7
Severo-Sibirskaya Nizmennost' •
  Russian Fed 26 R3
Severobaikalsk • Russian Fed. . 97 R3
Severodvinsk • Russian Fed... 17 F1
Severomorsk • Russian Fed... 17 E1
Severoural'sk • Russian Fed... 26 J5
Sevilla • Colombia 43 B3
Sevilla Heritage C • Spain ... 64 [92]
Sevilla • Spain 11 E7
Seville Heritage C • Spain ... 64 [92]
Seville • Spain 86 B1
Seville Nueva • Jamaica 124 C2
Sevlievo • Bulgaria 97 D3
Sèvre • France 10 E7
Sèvre Nantaise • France 84 D3
Sewa • Sierra Leone 22 B3
Sewall-Belmont House Nat. Hist. Site Park •
  DC, United States .... 121 [294]
Seward Peninsula •
  AK, United States 36 A3
Sexten Ski • Italy .... 70 [240]
Sexten • Italy 90 B2
Seyakha • Russian Fed 26 L3
Seychelles • Indian Ocean ... 100 A
Seydişehir • Turkey 93 G2
Seydisfjördur • Iceland 16 (1) F2
Seyitgazi • Turkey 15 L4
Seyla' • Somalia 23 G1
Seymchan • Russian Fed ... 27 P4
Seymour • VI, Australia 111 G3
Seyne-sur-Mer, la • France .. 10 K10
Sézanne • France 10 I5
Sfakiá • Crete, Greece 15 C7
Sfaktiría • Greece 15 C7
Sfax • Tunisia 101 E4
Sfîntu Gheorghe •
  Covasna, Romania 14 M4
Sfîntu Gheorghe •
  Tulcea, Romania 97 D2
Sha Tin • Hong Kong, China .. 107 H6
Shaanxi • China 107 G3
Shaba • Dem. Rep. of Congo .. 23 C5
Shaba Game Reserve • Kenya 101 G2
Shabelle, Webi • Somalia 23 G3
Shablá • Bulgaria 97 D4
Shache • China 26 M10
Shackleton Ice Shelf •
  Antarctica 46 (1) O3
Shadrinsk • Russian Fed 26 K6
Shaftesbury • United Kingdom . 74 F3
Shah Alam • Malaysia 108 D4
Shahdol • India 105 C8
Shahganj • India 105 C8
Shahjahanpur • India 105 C3
Shahpura • India 105 C6
Shahrud • Iran 18 F2
Shakhrisabz • Uzbekistan ... 18 I2
Shakhtyorsk • Russian Fed... 27 Q6
Shaki • Nigeria 22 E3
Shala, Lake • Ethiopia 23 G3
Shaldon Beach • United Kingdom 75 [103]
Shaldor Mtn • NT, Canada... 38 I2
Shallal, Ash • Egypt 21 F3
Shaluli Shan • China 29 B4
Sham, Jabal ash • Oman ... 18 G6
Shama, El • Somalia 23 G3
Shamiyah • Iraq/Syria 18 D3
Shammar, Jabal • Saudi Arabia 18 C4
Shamo, Lake • Ethiopia 23 G3
Shamva • Zimbabwe 102 J2
Shan • Myanmar 31 B2
Shanagarry Beach • Ireland .. 68 [40]
Shandi • Sudan 21 F4
Shandong • China 107 G4
Shandong Bandao • China... 107 G4
Shandong Peninsula • China .. 107 H4
Shangani • Zimbabwe 102 J1
Shanghai • China 107 J4
Shanghai [Adm] • China 107 J4
Shangqiu • China 31 F1
Shangqiu • China 29 F4
Shangqiu • China 29 F4
Shangri-La • Minorca, Spain .. 87 F4
Shangzhi • China 30 E2
Shanhaiguan • China 107 H3
Shankar Cave • China 107 J1
Shanklin Beach • United Kingdom 75 [98]
Shannon [Apt] • Ireland 7 D9
Shannon [Apt] • Ireland 79 F6

Shannon, Mouth of the • Ireland .. 79 F5
Shantarskiye Ostrova •
  Russian Fed 27 M5
Shantou • China 29 F6
Shanty Creek Ski •
  MI, United States .... 116 [132]
Shanxi • China 107 G3
Shanzu Becah • Kenya 101 G5
Shaoguan • China 29 E6
Shaowu • China 31 F1
Shaoxing • China 107 J4
Shaoyang • China 29 E5
Shap • United Kingdom 74 C2
Shap Abbey • United Kingdom 74 C2
Shap Fells • United Kingdom .. 74 C2
Shapinsay • United Kingdom .. 75 A7
Shaqra • Yemen 18 E4
Shaqra, Ash • Saudi Arabia .. 18 E4
Sharafah • Sudan 23 D1
Shari • Japan 30 M3
Shark Bay • WA, Australia ... 34 B5
Shark Bay Heritage N •
  WA, Australia .... 61 [127]
Sharkiyah, Al Istiwa'iyah al •
  Sudan 23 E2
Sharm el Sheikh • Egypt 101 F4
Sharon • Israel 98 A3
Sharp I. • Hong Kong, China .. 107 H6
Sharqiyah, Ash • Oman 18 G5
Shary • Saudi Arabia 17 H3
Sharya • Russian Fed 17 H3
Shashe • Botswana/Zimbabwe 24 D4
Shashe • Botswana/Zimbabwe 102 J3
Shashi • China 29 E4
Shasta, Mt • CA, United States 117 F1
Shati, Wadi ash • Libya 21 B2
Shatoujiao • Shenzhen, China 107 H4
Shatt al Arab • Iraq 18 E3
Shau Tau Kok • Hong Kong, China 107 H4
Shawnee Mtn Ski •
  PA, United States .... 116 [169]
Shawnigan • QU, Canada 122 B4
Shayb el Banat • Egypt 21 F2
Shaykh 'Uthman • Yemen ... 18 E7
Shchel'yayur • Russian Fed... 17 I1
Shchuchinsk • Kazakhstan ... 26 L7
Shchuchyn • Belarus 13 N4
She Xian • China 31 F1
Shebele, Wabe • Ethiopia ... 23 G2
Sheberghan • Afghanistan ... 26 K10
Sheenjek • AK, United States .. 38 C3
Sheep's Head • Ireland 79 F7
Sheerness • United Kingdom .. 74 E2
Sheerness Beach •
  United Kingdom .... 75 [59-60]
Sheet Harbour • NS, Canada .. 123 D7
Sheffield • United Kingdom ... 7 K8
Shek Kwu Chau •
  Hong Kong, China 107 H5
Shek O • Hong Kong, China .. 107 H6
Shekhawati • India 105 C2
Sheki • Azerbaijan 17 H6
Shekou • Shenzhen, China .. 107 H3
Sheksna • Russian Fed 97 E2
Shelagskiy, mys • Russian Fed. 27 T2
Shelburne • NS, Canada 123 D7
Shelby • MT, United States .. 40 D2
Shelikhova, Zaliv •
  Russian Fed 27 Q5
Shelley Beach • Kenya 101 G5
Shellharbour • NS, Australia .. 111 G2
Shelling Hill Beach • Ireland .. 68 [34]
Shelter Point • New Zealand .. 35 B8
Shenandoah Nat. Park Park •
  VA, United States .... 121 [262]
Shengsi Liedao • China 107 J4
Shengxian • China 107 J4
Shenkursk • Russian Fed.... 17 G2
Shenmu • China 29 E3
Shenton, Mt • WA, Australia .. 34 D5
Shenyang • China 107 H3
Shenzhen • China 107 H3
Shenzhen Special Economic Zone •
  China 107 H3
Shepparton • VI, Australia ... 111 G3
Sheppey, Isle of •
  United Kingdom 74 E2
Sherard, Cape • NU, Canada .. 39 P2
Sherborne • United Kingdom .. 74 F3
Sherbro I. • Sierra Leone 22 B3
Sherbrooke • QU, Canada 122 B8
Sherbrooke Village • NS, Canada 123 D7
Sherda • Chad 20 I4
Sherding Shan • China 29 F3
Shere Hill • Nigeria 22 F3
Sheremetyevo [Apt] •
  Russian Fed 97 E4
Shergui • Tunisia 101 E4
Sheridan • WY, United States .. 40 E3
Sheringham • United Kingdom . 5 E2
Sheringham Beach •
  United Kingdom .... 75 [42]
Sherkin I. • Ireland 79 F8
Sherman • TX, United States 119 N1
Sherwood Forest •
  United Kingdom 5 B1
Shetland Is. • United Kingdom .. 6 K1
Sheung Shui • Hong Kong, China 107 H3
Sheung Wan • Hong Kong, China 107 H5
Sheyenne • ND, United States .. 118 F1
Shibam • Yemen 18 E6
Shibam Heritage C • Yemen .. 63 [104]
Shibetsu • Japan 30 L2
Shibetsu • Japan 30 M3
Shibukawa • Japan 30 J6
Shibushi-Wan • Japan 30 D4
Shiel, Loch • United Kingdom .. 6 G5
Shihezi • China 28 C2
Shihr, Ash • Yemen 18 F7
Shijiazhuang • China 29 E3
Shikarpur • Pakistan 28 A3
Shikoku • Japan 30 G8
Shikoku-Sanchi • Japan 30 G8
Shikotan, Ostrov • Russian Fed. 27 O8
Shikotan-To • Russian Fed.... 27 O8
Shikotsu-Ko • Japan 30 K3
Shilega • Russian Fed 17 G2
Shilka • Russian Fed 27 J6
Shilka [Riv] • Russian Fed.... 27 I6
Shillá • India 28 C2
Shillong • India 28 D3
Shiloh • Jordan 98 A6
Shiloh Nat. Military Park Park •
  TN, United States .... 121 [229]
Shilong • China 107 H2
Shimabara • Japan 30 D4
Shimada • India 106 D6
Shimizu • Japan 30 I7
Shimoda • Japan 30 J7
Shimoga • India 106 D6
Shimoni • Kenya 101 G5
Shimonoseki • Japan 30 F8
Shin, Loch • United Kingdom .. 6 H3
Shindand • Afghanistan 18 H3

Shing Mun Country Park •
  Hong Kong, China 107 H5
Shingu • Japan 30 H8
Shingu • Japan 30 K5
Shinóussa • Greece 92 D8
Shinóussa • Greece 92 D8
Shintuya • Peru 127 B2
Shinyanga • Tanzania 102 H1
Shio-no-Misaki • Japan 30 H8
Shipka Pass • Bulgaria 97 D3
Shipki La • China/India 28 C2
Shiprock • NM, United States . 40 E4
Shiqi • China 107 H1
Shiquan He • China 28 B2
Shiquanhe • China 28 C2
Shirakami-Sanchi Heritage N •
  Japan .... 61 [120]
Shirakawa • Japan 30 I6
Shirakawa-Go Heritage C • Japan 63 [168]
Shirane • Gumma/Tochigi, Japan 30 J6
Shirane • Yamanashi, Japan .. 30 J7
Shiraz • Iran 18 F4
Shiren • China 30 D4
Shiretoko-Misaki • Japan 30 M2
Shiriya-Zaki • Japan 30 K4
Shirley Heights •
  Antigua & Barbuda 125 F4
Shishaldin Volcano •
  AK, United States 46 FF4
Shitou Shan • China 27 K6
Shiucheng • China 31 C1
Shiveluch Sopka, Vulkan •
  Russian Fed 27 R5
Shivpuri • India 105 C6
Shivpuri Nat. Park • India ... 105 C6
Shiwa Ngandu • Zambia 24 E2
Shiyan Lake Hot Springs Resort •
  China 107 H2
Shiza • Greece 15 C7
Shizuoka • Japan 30 J7
Shköder • Albania 14 G7
Shoalhaven • NS, Australia .. 111 G2
Shobara • Japan 30 G7
Shoeburyness East Beach •
  United Kingdom .... 75 [56]
Shoreham-by-Sea •
  United Kingdom 7 L11
Shortland • Solomon Is. 35 (1) F2
Shoshone Falls •
  ID, United States 117 E4
Shoshone Mtns •
  NV, United States 117 F4
Shreveport • LA, United States 118 K1
Shrewsbury • United Kingdom . 74 D1
Shri Mahalsa Temple •
  Goa, India 105 B1
Shri Mallikarjun Temple •
  Goa, India 105 B2
Shri Mangesh Temple •
  Goa, India 105 B1
Shropshire • United Kingdom . 74 D1
Shropshire Hills •
  United Kingdom 74 D1
Shuangyashan • China 29 I1
Shuguri Falls • Tanzania 24 F1
Shule • China 18 K2
Shule He • China 29 B2
Shumen • Bulgaria 97 D3
Shumerlya • Russian Fed.... 17 H3
Shumshu, Ostrov • Russian Fed. 27 O6
Shunayn, Sabkhat • Libya.... 21 D2
Shunde • China 107 H1
Shurayk, Ash • Sudan 18 B6
Shurab • Iran 18 G3
Shute Harbour • QL, Australia 111 F3
Shuwak • Sudan 21 G5
Shuya • Russian Fed 17 G3
Shwebo • Myanmar 31 B2
Si Racha • Thailand 109 H4
Si Satchanalai • Thailand.... 109 H4
Si Satchanalai Nat. Park Park •
  Thailand 109 G4
Sia • Indonesia 32 (1) D4
Siak Kecil Reserve • Indonesia 110 B4
Sialkot • Pakistan 28 B2
Sian Ka'an, Reserva de la Biósfera Heritage
  N • Mexico .... 60 [19]
Siána • Rhodes, Greece 93 F3
Siargao • Philippines 31 H5
Siauliai • Lithuania 13 M2
Sibay • Russian Fed 26 I7
Sibenik • Croatia 14 C6
Siberia • Russian Fed 25 K3
Siberimanua • Indonesia ... 32 B3
Siberut, Pulau • Indonesia .. 32 B3
Sibga • Indonesia 110 B1
Sibi • Pakistan 28 A3
Sibigo • Indonesia 110 B1
Sibiloi Nat. Park Heritage N •
  Kenya .... 61 [88]
Sibiloi Nat. Park • Kenya 101 G1
Sibiloi Nat. Park • Kenya.... 103 [74]
Sibiryakovo, Ostrov •
  Russian Fed 26 M3
Sibiti • Congo 22 G5
Sibiu • Romania 14 K4
Sibolga • Indonesia 110 B4
Siboney, Playa • Cuba 124 E3
Sibsey • Russia 32 E2
Sibu • Malaysia 32 E2
Sibut • Central African Rep. .. 23 B2
Sibuyan • Philippines 31 G4
Sibuyan Sea • Philippines ... 31 G4
Sichang, Ko • Thailand 109 H4
Sichuan • China 107 F4
Sichuan Pendi • China 107 G2
Sicié, Cap • France 85 H3
Sicilia • Italy .... 9 D
Sicilia, Canale di •
  Mediterranean Sea 12 F11
Sicily • Italy .... 90 D
Sicuani • Peru 127 B2
Sidari • Corfu, Greece 92 B1
Sidari • Corfu, Greece 92 B1
Side • Turkey 93 G4
Sideby • Finland 95 E1
Sidensjö • Sweden 16 I4
Sideros, Akra • Crete, Greece 93 E4
Siderno • Italy 12 K10
Sidi Aïssa • Algeria 11 09
Sidi Ali • Algeria 11 L8
Sidi Barrâni • Egypt 21 E1
Sidi Bel Abbès • Algeria ... 20 E1
Sidi Bou Saïd • Tunisia 101 E2
Sidi Daoud • Tunisia 101 E2
Sidi Ifni • Morocco 101 C2
Sidi Kacem • Morocco 101 D1
Sidi Moussa • Morocco 101 D1
Sidlaw Hills • United Kingdom 74 B2
Sidmouth • United Kingdom .. 74 E3
Sidorovsk • Russian Fed..... 27 B3
Sidra, Gulf of • Libya 21 C2
Siebengebirge • Germany ... 82 G1
Siedlce • Poland 13 L5
Sieg • Germany 9 C6
Siegburg • Germany 82 G1
Siegen • Germany 82 G2
Siegerwald • Germany 9 F7
Siemiatycze • Poland 13 L5
Siemréab • Cambodia 31 C4

Siena Heritage C • Italy ...... 64 [122]
Siena • Italy 91 E11
Sienne • France 5 B6
Sieradz • Poland 13 H6
Sierksdorf Spa • Germany ...... 83 [26]
Sierpc • Poland 13 I5
Sierra Blanca Peak • NM, United States 40 E5
Sierra Colorado • Argentina 45 C4
Sierra Leone • Africa 22 B3
Sierra Madre del Sur • Mexico 123 E4
Sierra Madre Occidental • Mexico 40 E6
Sierra Madre Oriental • Mexico 40 F7
Sierra Nevada • Colombia 43 C1
Sierra Nevada • Spain 86 B3
Sierra-at-Tahoe Ski • CA, United States ...... 116 [58]
Sierre • Switzerland 89 G6
Siesta Key • FL, United States 119 M5
Sifnos • Greece 92 D7
Sifnos • Greece 92 D7
Sig • Algeria 20 E1
Sigdal • Norway 94 B1
Sigean, Réserve africaine de • France 85 K2
Sighetu Marmatiei • Romania 14 K2
Sighisoara • Romania 14 L3
Sigiriya Heritage C • Sri Lanka ...... 63 [135]
Sigiriya • Sri Lanka 106 D15
Sigli • Indonesia 28 G7
Sigmaringen • Germany 82 J1
Signy I. [Base] • Antarctica 46 (1) A3
Sigri • Greece 92 D5
Sigri • Greece 92 D5
Sigtuna • Sweden 95 D2
Siguanea • Cuba 124 D1
Siguenza • Spain 71 A1
Siguiri • Guinea 22 C2
Sihuas • Peru 43 B5
Siilinjärvi • Finland 16 N5
Siippy • Finland 95 E1
Siirt • Turkey 18 D2
Sijunjung • Indonesia 110 B4
Sikakap • Indonesia 32 C3
Sikanni Chief • BC, Canada 38 G5
Sikar • India 105 C2
Sikasso • Mali 22 C2
Sikeston • MO, United States 41 I4
Sikhote-Alin • Russian Fed. 29 J1
Sikía • Pelopónnisos, Greece 15 D7
Sikía • Halkidikí, Greece 15 E3
Sikinos • Greece 92 D8
Sikinos • Greece 92 D8
Sikkim • India 28 E3
Siktyakh • Russian Fed. 27 K3
Sila, As • United Arab Emirates 18 F5
Silalè • Lithuania 13 L2
Silba • Croatia 14 B5
Silchar • India 28 F4
Sile • Turkey 15 K2
Sileiro, Cabo • Spain 11 C2
Silencio, Costa del • Tenerife, Canary Is. 86 E1
Silesia • Poland 13 G7
Silet • Algeria 20 F4
Silhouette • Seychelles 106 F2
Siliana • Tunisia 12 D12
Siliguri • India 28 E3
Siling Co • China 28 A2
Silistra • Bulgaria 97 D1
Silivri • Turkey 15 J2
Siljan • Sweden 16 H6
Siljan • Norway 94 B3
Silk Road • Asia 98 B4
Silkeborg • Denmark 95 F9
Sillamäe • Estonia 16 N7
Sillé-le-Guillaume [Château] • France 84 D1
Sillí • Somalia 23 G1
Sillyon • Turkey 93 G2
Siloana Plains • Zambia 24 C3
Siloso, Fort • Singapore 108 E3
Sils • Switzerland 89 G8
Sils-Maria Ski • Switzerland ...... 70 [119]
Siltou • Chad 21 C4
Siluatan, Gunung • Indonesia 110 B2
Silutè • Lithuania 13 K2
Silvaplana • Switzerland 89 G8
Silvaplana-Surlej Ski • Switzerland ...... 70 [120]
Silver City • NM, United States 116 (1)
Silver Lake Resort • Shenzhen, China 107 H3
Silver Mtn Ski • ID, United States ...... 116 [70]
Silver Star Ski • BC, Canada ...... 116 [5]
Silverwood • ID, United States 117 E2
Silves • Portugal 88 E6
Silvretta • Austria ...... 70 [134]
Silvretta • Austria 89 H5
Sim, Cap • Morocco 20 D2
Simanggang • Malaysia 32 E2
Simareh • Iran 18 E3
Simav • Turkey 15 J4
Simav Gölü • Turkey 15 J4
Simav [Riv] • Turkey 15 J4
Simbach • Germany 82 K4
Simbirsk • Russian Fed. 17 H4
Simbruini, Monti • Italy 91 F4
Simcoe, Lake • OT, Canada 122 B5
Simei New Town • Singapore 108 E2
Simeon • Israel 21 G5
Simeto • Sicily, Italy 90 D4
Simeulué • Indonesia 110 B1
Simferopol • Ukraine 17 E5
Simi • Greece 15 I7
Simi [I.] • Greece 92 D9
Simi [I.] • Greece 92 D9
Simien Nat. Park Heritage N • Ethiopia ...... 61 [78]
Simien Nat. Park Park • Ethiopia ...... 103 [62]
Simla • India 28 C2
Simlångsdalen • Sweden 95 F7
Simleu Silvaniei • Romania 14 J2
Simmer • Germany 82 H3
Simmerath • Germany 5 J4
Simon's Town • South Africa 100 C5
Simonstorp • Sweden 95 D3
Simplonpass • Switzerland 89 G6
Simpson Desert • Australia 34 G5
Simpson Desert Nat. Park • QL, Australia 34 G5
Simpson Gap Nat. Park • NT, Australia 112 H2
Simpson Hill • WA, Australia 34 K5
Simpson Peninsula • NU, Canada 39 N3
Simrishamn • Sweden 95 F11
Simsee • Germany 82 J4
Sin Cow • South China Sea 31 E5
Sinabang • Indonesia 110 B3
Sinai • Egypt 101 F2
Sinai, Mt • Egypt 101 F4
Sinaia • Romania 96 B2
Sinaloa • Mexico 40 E7

Sincelejo • Colombia 43 B2
Sindal • Denmark 95 F6
Sindangbarang • Java, Indonesia 110 D5
Sindelfingen • Germany 9 E8
Sindh • Pakistan 28 A3
Sindirgi • Turkey 15 J4
Sinekli • Turkey 15 J2
Sines • Portugal 11 C7
Sines Beach • Portugal ...... 68 [81]
Sines, Cabo de • Portugal 11 C7
Singa • Majorca, Spain 87 H2
Singako • Chad 23 B2
Singapore • Asia 32 C2
Singapore • Asia ...... 108 E
Singapore City • Singapore 108 E4
Singapore Crocodilarium • Singapore 108 E4
Singapore Science Centre • Singapore 108 E1
Singapore, Straits of • Asia 108 E4
Singapore Zoological Gardens • Singapore 108 E1
Singaraja • Bali, Indonesia 110 C2
Singen • Germany 9 D9
Singh Beach • Phuket, Thailand 109 K2
Singida • Tanzania 102 H1
Singkaling Hkamti • Myanmar 28 G3
Singkarak, Danau • Indonesia 110 B4
Singkawang • Indonesia 32 D2
Singkep • Indonesia 32 C3
Singkil • Indonesia 110 B3
Singleton • NS, Australia 111 G2
Singleton, Mt • WA, Australia 34 C5
Singö • Sweden 95 D2
Singö [I.] • Sweden 95 D2
Sinharaja Forest Reserve Heritage N • Sri Lanka ...... 61 [112]
Sinharaja Forest Reserve • Sri Lanka 106 D15
Sinis • Sardinia, Italy 90 C3
Siniscola • Sardinia, Italy 12 D8
Sinj • Croatia 14 D6
Sinjah • Sudan 21 F5
Sinjajevina • F.R. of Yugoslavia 14 G6
Sinnicolau Mare • Romania 14 H3
Sinoe, Lacul • Romania 97 D2
Sinop • Turkey 17 F6
Sin'p'o • D.P.R. of Korea 30 C5
Sinquerim Beach • Goa, India 105 B1
Sinsheim • Germany 9 D7
Sintana • Romania 14 I3
Sintang • Indonesia 32 E2
Sintra Heritage C • Portugal ...... 64 [99]
Sintra Beach • Portugal ...... 68 [80]
Sintra • Portugal 88 D1
Sintra, Serra de • Portugal 88 D1
Sinuiju • D.P.R. of Korea 30 C4
Sinzig • Germany 82 H1
Siófok • Hungary 13 H11
Sion • Switzerland 89 G6
Sioux City • IA, United States 41 G3
Sioux City Park • Gran Canaria, Canary Is. ...... 73 [79]
Sioux City • Gran Canaria, Canary Is. 86 E4
Sioux Falls • SD, United States 41 G3
Sioux Lookout • OT, Canada 39 M6
Sipalay • Philippines 31 G5
Sipan • Croatia 14 E7
Siparia • Trinidad & Tobago 125 K3
Sipcenski prohod • Bulgaria 97 D3
Siping • China 29 G2
Sipiwesk • MN, Canada 39 L5
Siple • China 105 C2
Siple, Mt • Antarctica 46 (1) G2
Siple Station [Base] • Antarctica 46 (1) G2
Siponto • Italy 71 A19
Siquijor • Philippines 31 G5
Sir Edward Pellew Group • NT, Australia 34 G3
Sir Sam's Ski • OT, Canada ...... 116 [16]
Sira • Norway 16 D7
Siracusa • Sicily, Italy 90 D4
Siraf • Iran 98 B4
Sirba • Burkina Faso/Niger 20 E6
Sire, Ko • Thailand 109 K2
Siret • Romania 14 N3
Siridao Beach • Goa, India 105 B1
Sirik • Iran 18 G4
Sirik, Tanjong • Malaysia 32 E2
Sirikit Reservoir • Thailand 109 G4
Sirino • Italy 12 J8
Sirmione • Italy 91 E7
Sirna • Greece 92 D8
Sirna • Greece 92 D8
Sirohi • India 105 C5
Sirolo Beach • Italy ...... 69 [141]
Sirolo • Italy 91 E12
Siros • Greece 92 D7
Siros • Greece 92 D7
Sirsa • India 18 K4
Sirsa • India 105 C2
Sisak • Croatia 14 D4
Sisimiut • Greenland 39 U3
Sisophon • Cambodia 31 C4
Sissano • Papua New Guinea 35 (1) C1
Sisteron • France 85 H1
Sistiana • Italy 91 E4
Sistranda • Norway 16 E5
Sitapur • India 105 C3
Sitges Beach • Spain ...... 68 [105]
Sitges • Spain 87 D3
Sithonia • Greece 92 D1
Sithonía • Greece 92 D1
Sitia Beach • Crete, Greece ...... 69 [191]
Sitía • Crete, Greece 93 E8
Sitka • AK, United States 38 D5
Sitka Nat. Hist. Park Park • AK, United States ...... 120 [14]
Sittard • Netherlands 80 A16
Situbondo • Java, Indonesia 110 D8
Sivas • Turkey 18 C2
Sivasli • Turkey 15 K5
Sivrice Beach • Turkey ...... 69 [210]
Sivrihisar • Turkey 15 M4
Sivry-sur-Meuse • France 5 I5
Siwa • Egypt 21 E2
Siwalik Range • India/Nepal 28 C3
Six Flags AstroWorld • TX, United States 119 N4
Six Flags AstroWorld Park • TX, United States ...... 121 [P]
Six Flags Fiesta • TX, United States 119 N3
Six Flags Fiesta Park • TX, United States ...... 121 [N]
Six Flags Great Adventure • NJ, United States 118 H1
Six Flags Great Adventure Park • NJ, United States ...... 121 [KK]
Six Flags Great America Park • IL, United States ...... 121 [S]
Six Flags Magic Mtn • CA, United States 117 F6
Six Flags Magic Mtn Park • CA, United States ...... 120 [D]

Six Flags over Georgia Park • GA, United States ...... 121 [Z]
Six Flags over Mid-America Park • MO, United States ...... 121 [Q]
Six Flags over Texas • TX, United States 119 N1
Six Flags over Texas Park • TX, United States ...... 121 [L]
Six Flags WaterWorld • TX, United States 119 N4
Six Flags WaterWorld Park • TX, United States ...... 121 [P]
Six Flags Wild Safari Animal Park • NJ, United States 118 H1
Six Men's Bay • Barbados 125 H1
Sixt Ski • France ...... 70 [17]
Sizergh Castle • United Kingdom 74 C4
Sizewell Beach • United Kingdom ...... 75 [51]
Sjælland • Denmark 95 F10
Sjenica • F.R. of Yugoslavia 14 H6
Sjöbo • Sweden 95 F11
Skadarsko jezero • F.R. of Yugoslavia 14 G7
Skadarsko jezero Nat. Park Park • Fed. Rep. of Yugoslavia ...... 72 [121]
Skadovsk • Ukraine 17 E5
Skælskør Beach • Denmark ...... 68 [24]
Skælskør • Denmark 95 F14
Skærbæk Beach • Denmark ...... 68 [24]
Skærbæk • Denmark 95 F9
Skaftafell Nat. Park Park • Iceland ...... 72 [2]
Skálfthamar • Sweden 95 D2
Skagen Beach • Denmark ...... 68 [29]
Skagen • Denmark 95 F6
Skagern • Sweden 95 F3
Skaggerak • Europe 95 F5
Skagway • AK, United States 58 A2
Skála Beach • Greece ...... 69 [150]
Skála • Greece 92 C2
Skála • Greece 92 C2
Skáldervíken • Sweden 95 F11
Skalistyy Golets • Russian Fed. 27 I5
Skalitys Golec • Russian Fed. 46 B4
Skanderborg • Denmark 95 F9
Skándzoura • Greece 92 D4
Skándzoura • Greece 92 D4
Skåne • Sweden 95 F11
Skaneateles Lake • NY, United States 122 B10
Skanés [Apt] • Tunisia 101 E4
Skanevik • Norway 94 C5
Skänninge • Sweden 95 F4
Skanör • Sweden 95 F15
Skara • Sweden 95 F3
Skaraborg • Sweden 95 F3
Skaralid • Sweden 95 F11
Skardu • Jammu & Kashmir 28 C1
Skarnes • Norway 94 B2
Skarzysko-Kamienna • Poland 13 J6
Skawina • Poland 13 I8
Skeena • BC, Canada 38 F6
Skeena Mtns • BC, Canada 38 F5
Skegness • United Kingdom 7 M8
Skegness Beach • United Kingdom ...... 75 [37]
Skei • Norway 94 C2
Skeleton Coast • Namibia 24 A3
Skellefteå • Sweden 16 K4
Skellefteälven • Sweden 16 J4
Skellig Michael Heritage C • Ireland ...... 64 [11]
Skellig Michael • Ireland 79 F7
Skëndërbout • Albania 15 A2
Skerries • Ireland 79 E2
Skhirat-Plage • Morocco 101 D1
Skhíza • Greece 92 B2
Ski • Norway 94 B2
Ski Acres Ski • WA, United States ...... 116 [44]
Ski Apache Ski • NM, United States ...... 116 [107]
Ski Beech Mtn Ski • NC, United States ...... 116 [151]
Ski Dagmar Ski • OT, Canada ...... 116 [24]
Ski le Chantecler Ski • QU, Canada ...... 116 [30]
Ski Liberty Ski • PA, United States ...... 116 [161]
Ski Morin Heights Ski • QU, Canada ...... 116 [31]
Ski Roundtop Ski • PA, United States ...... 116 [163]
Ski Snow Valley Ski • OT, Canada ...... 116 [18]
Ski Sundown Ski • CT, United States ...... 116 [187]
Ski Windham Ski • NY, United States ...... 116 [154]
Skiathos Beach • Greece ...... 69 [165]
Skíathos • Greece 92 D4
Skíathos • Greece 92 D4
Skibbereen Beach • Ireland ...... 68 [40]
Skibbereen • Ireland 79 F8
Skibotn • Norway 16 K2
Skidda • Algeria 20 G1
Skien • Norway 94 B3
Skierniewice • Poland 13 J6
Skiftet Kihti • Finland 95 E3
Skilingaryd • Sweden 95 F7
Skinári, Akra • Greece 92 C3
Skinári, Akra • Greece 92 C3
Skinnskatteberg • Sweden 95 D1
Skipton • United Kingdom 7 J8
Skíros • Greece 15 F5
Skíros • Greece 92 D4
Skíti Beach • Greece ...... 69 [166]
Skive • Denmark 95 F8
Skjærhalden • Norway 94 B4
Skjálfandafljót • Iceland 16 (1) H4
Skjálfandi • Iceland 16 (1) E1
Skjeberg • Norway 94 B4
Skjern • Denmark 95 F9
Skjolden • Norway 94 C1
Sklad • Russian Fed. 27 J2
Sklavopoúla • Crete, Greece 93 E5
Skocjan Caves Heritage N • Slovenia ...... 61 [51]
Skole • Ukraine 14 K1
Skópelos Beach • Magnissía, Greece ...... 69 [165]
Skópelos • Lesbos, Greece ...... 69 [176]
Skópelos • Greece 92 D4
Skópelos • Greece 92 D4
Skopje • F.Y.R. of Macedonia 14 I8
Skorba • Malta 93 H3
Skørping • Denmark 95 F7
Skotfoss • Norway 94 B3
Skotina Beach • Greece ...... 69 [167]
Skotselv • Norway 94 B1
Skotterud • Norway 94 B2
Skoura • Morocco 20 D2
Skövde • Sweden 95 F3
Skovorodino • Russian Fed. 27 J6
Skowhegan • ME, United States 118 G4
Skrimfjella • Norway 94 B3
Skrinkle Beach • United Kingdom ...... 75 [151]

Skudeneshavn • Norway 94 C5
Skuleskogen Nat. Park Park • Sweden ...... 72 [21]
Sky Harbor [Apt] • AZ, United States 118 J3
Sky Lake • FL, United States 121 C2
Skye • United Kingdom 6 F4
Slagelse Beach • Denmark ...... 68 [24]
Slagelse • Denmark 95 F14
Slamet, Gunung • Java, Indonesia 110 D6
Slane • Ireland 79 E1
Slaney • Ireland 7 F9
Slano • Croatia 14 E7
Slantsy • Russian Fed. 16 O7
Slany • Czech Rep. 13 D7
Slask • Poland 13 G7
Slatina • Romania 14 L5
Slave Coast • Africa 22 E3
Slave Lake • AL, Canada 39 I5
Slave Lake, Lesser • AL, Canada 122 C2
Slavgorod • Russian Fed. 26 M7
Slavjanka • Bulgaria/Greece 15 B1
Slavonice • Czech Rep. 13 E8
Slavonski Brod • Croatia 14 F4
Slavsko • Ukraine 14 J1
Slavskovsky Les • Czech Rep. 96 C1
Slavyansk • Ukraine 17 F4
Slawno • Poland 13 F3
Sleat, Sound of • United Kingdom 6 G4
Sleeper Is. • NU, Canada 39 P5
Sleeping Bear Dunes Nat. Lakeshore Park • MI, United States ...... 121 [163]
Slemmestad • Norway 94 B2
Slidell • LA, United States 118 K4
Slidre • Norway 94 C1
Sliedrecht • Netherlands 80 C4
Sliema • Malta 93 H4
Slieve Aughty Mtns • Ireland 79 F4
Slieve Mish Mtns • Ireland 79 F8
Slievefelim Mtns • Ireland 7 D9
Sligo • Ireland 79 F2
Sligo [Adm] • Ireland 79 F2
Sligo Bay • Ireland 79 F2
Slimbridge • United Kingdom 7 J10
Sliven • Bulgaria 97 D3
Slobodskoy • Russian Fed. 17 J2
Slobozia • Ialomita, Romania 97 D1
Slobozia • Pitesti, Romania 97 D1
Slough • United Kingdom 7 L10
Slovak karst Heritage N • Slovak Rep. ...... 61 [50]
Slovak Republic • Europe 13 H9
Slovenia • Europe 12 I2
Slovensko • Slovak Rep. 13 J9
Slowinski Nat. Park Park • Poland ...... 72 [90]
Slunchev Bryag • Bulgaria 97 D3
Slunj • Croatia 14 C4
Slupsk • Poland 13 F3
Slutsk • Belarus 17 D4
Slyne Head • Ireland 79 F3
Smålandsfarvandet • Denmark 95 F14
Smålandsstenar • Sweden 95 F7
Smallwood Reservoir • NF, Canada 39 S6
Smederevo • F.R. of Yugoslavia 14 I5
Smedjebacken • Sweden 16 H6
Smeralda, Costa • Sardinia, Italy 90 C2
Smirdaki, Grotta di • Italy 91 G4
Smir-Restinga • Morocco 101 D2
Smith Arm • NT, Canada 38 I3
Smith, Cape • NU, Canada 39 P4
Smith, Fort, Nat. Hist. Site Park • AR, United States ...... 121 [192]
Smith I. • MD, United States 118 H3
Smiths Falls • OT, Canada 39 P7
Smithton • TS, Australia 34 I8
Smögen • Sweden 95 F2
Smoky • AL, Canada 38 H6
Smøla • Norway 16 D5
Smolensk • Russian Fed. 17 E4
Smólikas • Greece 15 B3
Smolyan • Bulgaria 14 L8
Smorgon • Belarus 16 N9
Smuggler's Notch Ski • VT, United States ...... 116 [204]
Smyadovo • Bulgaria 97 D3
Smyrna • Turkey 92 D5
Smyrna • Turkey 92 D5
Smyrna • DE, United States 118 H3
Snake • YT, Canada 38 E4
Snake • AK, United States 40 C3
Snake River Plain • United States 117 E4
Snake Temple, Penang • Penang, Malaysia 108 C3
Snasavatnet • Norway 16 G4
Sneek • Netherlands 80 A3
Sneem • Ireland 79 F7
Snettisham Beach • United Kingdom ...... 75 [38]
Snezka • Czech Rep./Poland 96 C2
Snezka • Slovak Rep. 13 L9
Snehetta • Norway 94 C2
Snoqualmie • WA, United States ...... 116 [44]
Snow Lake • MN, Canada 38 K6
Snow Summit Ski • CA, United States ...... 116 [65]
Snow Trails Ski • OH, United States ...... 116 [147]
Snowbasin Ski • UT, United States ...... 116 [78]
Snowbird Ski • UT, United States ...... 116 [83]
Snowdon • United Kingdom 7 H8
Snowdonia • United Kingdom 7 H8
Snowdonia Nat. Park Park • United Kingdom ...... 72 [47]
Snowmass Ski • CO, United States ...... 116 [98]
Snowshill Manor • United Kingdom 74 D4
Snowshoe Ski • WV, United States ...... 116 [154]
Snowy Mtns • NS/VI, Australia 111 G4
Snowy [Riv] • NS/VI, Australia 111 G4
Snug Corner • Bahamas 124 B4
Snuol • Cambodia 108 B1
Snyder • TX, United States 40 F5
So, Laem • Ko Samui, Thailand 109 J2
Soar • United Kingdom 5 B2
Soave • Italy 91 E7
Soba • Nigeria 20 G6
Sobaek-Sanmaek • Rep. of Korea 30 D7
Sobat • Ethiopia/Sudan 23 E2
Sobotka • Czech Rep. 96 C2
Sobradinho, Reprêsa • Brazil 45 (1) D2
Sobral • Brazil 45 (1) D2
Soc Trang • Vietnam 108 B3
Sochaczew • Poland 13 J5
Sochi • Russian Fed. 17 F6
Society Is. • French Polynesia 33 L7

Socompa, Paso • Argentina/Chile 44 C3
Socorro • Colombia 43 C2
Socorro • NM, United States 118 J4
Socorro, I. • Mexico 123 E7
Socotra • Yemen 18 F7
Sodankylä • Finland 16 N3
Söderåsen • Sweden 95 F11
Söderfors • Sweden 16 I6
Söderhamn • Sweden 16 I6
Söderköping • Sweden 95 F4
Södermanland • Sweden 95 D3
Södertälje • Sweden 95 D4
Södra Kvarken • Finland/Sweden 16 J6
Soekarno-Hatta [Apt] • Java, Indonesia 110 D1
Soest • Germany 8 D5
Soest • Germany 71 A8
Soest • Netherlands 80 C2
Sofala • NS, Australia 111 G2
Sœurs, Ies • Seychelles 106 F4
Sofala, Baía de • Mozambique 24 E4
Sofia • Bulgaria 14 K7
Sofía • Madagascar 24 E4
Sofiya • Bulgaria 14 K7
Sofiysk • Russian Fed. 27 L6
Sofporog • Russian Fed. 17 E1
Sofrino • Russian Fed. 97 E4
Sogamoso • Colombia 43 C2
Soganli • Turkey 15 N2
Sogel • Germany 71 A8
Sogeri • Papua New Guinea 35 (1) D2
Sogn og Fjordane • Norway 94 C1
Sogndal • Norway 94 C4
Sognefjorden • Norway 94 C1
Sogod • Philippines 31 G4
Söğüt Gölü • Turkey 15 K6
Söğüt • Egypt 101 F4
Sohano • Papua New Guinea 35 (1) E2
Sohna • India 105 C2
Sohuksan • Rep. of Korea 30 C7
Soignies • Belgium 5 H4
Soissons • France 85 E2
Sojoson-man • D.P.R. of Korea 30 C5
Soka Beach • Bali, Indonesia 110 C3
Sokal • Ukraine 13 L5
Söke • Turkey 92 D9
Söke • Turkey 92 D9
Sokele • Dem. Rep. of Congo 23 C5
Sokkuram Grotto Heritage C • Rep. of Korea ...... 63 [162]
Soko • Russian Fed. 94 B1
Soko Is. • Hong Kong, China 107 H5
Sokodé • Togo 22 E3
Sokol • Russian Fed. 97 E2
Sokólka • Poland 13 M4
Sokolo • Mali 22 C2
Sokolov • Czech Rep. 96 C1
Sokolów Podlaski • Poland 13 L5
Sokosti • Finland 17 D1
Sokoto • Nigeria 22 F2
Sokoto [Adm] • Nigeria 22 F2
Sokoto [Riv] • Nigeria 22 F2
Sol, Costa del • Spain 86 B3
Sol, Costa do • Portugal 88 D1
Sol y Nieve • Spain 86 B3
Sola • Vanuatu 35 (2) B1
Sola • Venezuela 43 E1
Sola [Apt] • Norway 94 C5
Solapur • India 28 C5
Solda • Italy 91 E3
Sölden Ski • Austria ...... 70 [137]
Soldeu • Spain 87 F3
Soledad • Brazil 44 F4
Solenara • Corsica, France 85 L4
Solignac • France 85 G2
Solihull • United Kingdom 7 K9
Solikamsk • Russian Fed. 26 I6
Solimões • Brazil 44 C2
Solingen • Germany 81 E4
Solitude Ski • UT, United States ...... 116 [82]
Sollevita • Spain 11 M3
Sóller • Austria 89 H3
Söll • Austria 89 H3
Sollefteå • Sweden 16 I5
Sollentuna • Sweden 95 D4
Sóller • Majorca, Spain 87 G3
Solna • Sweden 95 D4
Solo • Java, Indonesia 110 D7
Solo [Riv] • Java, Indonesia 110 B4
Solok • Indonesia 110 B4
Solola • Guatemala 37 C5
Soloru • Ukraine 14 L1
Solomon Is. • Pacific Ocean 33 H6
Solomon Sea • Papua New Guinea/Solomon Is. 35 (1) E2
Solor, Kepulauan • Indonesia 32 (1) B4
Solovetskiye Ostrova Heritage C • Russian Fed. ...... 63 [76]
Soloyovsk • Russian Fed. 27 I7
Solsvik • Norway 94 C3
Solta • Croatia 14 D6
Soltau • Germany 8 E4
Soltau Spa • Germany ...... 83 [60]
Solund • Norway 94 C3
Solvang • CA, United States 117 F5
Solvesborg • Sweden 95 F11
Solway Firth • United Kingdom 7 I7
Som, Ko • Thailand 109 J1
Soma • Turkey 15 I4
Soma • Japan 30 H8
Somali Peninsula • Somalia 100 A2
Somalia • Africa 23 G1
Sombor • F.R. of Yugoslavia 14 G4
Sombrerete • Mexico 37 (1) B1
Somerset • Australia 34 H2
Somerset • KY, United States 41 J4
Somerset I. • NU, Canada 39 N2
Somerset East • South Africa 100 C4
Somerset West • South Africa 100 C5
Somerton • United Kingdom 74 C4
Somes • Romania 14 J2
Somme • France 10 H4
Sommen • Sweden 95 F4
Sömmerda • Germany 9 G5
Son • Norway 94 B4
Son Moll • Minorca, Spain 87 F3
Son Bou, Platja de • Minorca, Spain 87 F3
Son Parc • Minorca, Spain 87 F2
Son Sant Joan [Apt] • Majorca, Spain 87 H1

Son Servera Beach • Majorca, Spain ...... 68 [109]
Sonagiri • India 105 C7
Sonch'on D.P.R. of Korea 30 C5
Sønderborg Beach • Denmark ...... 68 [26]
Sønderborg • Denmark 95 F13
Sønderjylland • Denmark 95 F13
Sondershausen • Germany 9 F5
Søndervig • Denmark 95 F9
Søndre Strømfjord • Greenland 39 V3
Sondrio • Italy 91 E2
Songea • China 107 G3
Songea • Tanzania 102 H4
Songhua Hu • China 29 H2
Songhua Jiang • China 29 G1
Songjiang • China 107 J4
Songkhla • Thailand 31 C5
Songnim • D.P.R. of Korea 30 C5
Songo • Mozambique 24 E3
Songo Mnara Heritage C • Tanzania ...... 63 [99]
Songo Mnara • Tanzania 102 H4
Sonid Youqi • China 29 E2
Sonipat • India 105 C2
Sonneberg • Germany 9 G6
Sonoma • CA, United States 117 F3
Sonora • Mexico 40 D5
Sonora • CA, United States 117 F3
Sonoran Desert • AZ, United States 118 J3
Sonsbeck • Germany 81 E1
Sonsorol Is. • Palau 32 (1) D2
Sonthofen • Germany 82 J6
Sooneck, Burg • Germany 81 H4
Soontornpoi Mon • Thailand 109 H4
Soorts-Hossegor Beach • France ...... 68 [67]
Sopelana Beach • Spain ...... 68 [60]
Sopi, Tanjung • Indonesia 32 (1) C2
Sopocani Monastery Heritage C • F.R. of Yugoslavia ...... 64 [160]
Sopot • Poland 13 H3
Sopot • Bulgaria 15 F1
Sopron • Hungary 13 F10
Sopur • Jammu & Kashmir 28 B2
Sør-Trøndelag • Norway 16 F5
Sora • Italy 91 F4
Sorak • Rep. of Korea 30 E5
Sorbas • Spain 11 I7
Sorel • QU, Canada 39 Q7
Sörenberg Ski • Switzerland ...... 70 [102]
Sörenberg • Switzerland 89 G2
Sorfjorden • Norway 94 C4
Soria • Spain 11 I3
Sørø Beach • Denmark ...... 68 [24]
Sorø • Denmark 95 F14
Soroca • Moldova 14 P1
Sorocaba • Brazil 44 G3
Sorong • Indonesia 32 (1) D3
Soroni • Rhodes, Greece 93 F2
Soroti • Uganda 23 E3
Søröya • Norway 16 L1
Sørøya • Norway 16 L1
Sørreisa • Norway 16 J2
Sorrento • Italy 91 G3
Sorsele • Sweden 16 I4
Sorsogon • Philippines 31 G4
Sortland • Norway 16 H2
Søsan • Rep. of Korea 30 D6
Sösdala • Sweden 95 F11
Sosnogorsk • Russian Fed. 17 I2
Sosnovka • Ukraine 13 N7
Sosnowiec • Poland 13 I7
Sosva • Khanty-Mansi, Russian Fed. 26 J5
Sosva • Yekaterinburg, Russian Fed. 26 J6
Sotavento de Jandia, Playa de • Fuerteventura, Canary Is. 87 E2
Sotavento, Is. de • West Indies 43 D1
Sotkamo • Finland 16 O4
Sotra • Norway 94 C3
Sottern • Sweden 95 D3
Sotteville-les-Rouen • France 5 E5
Souahel, Boukhalef [Apt] • Morocco 101 D1
Souanké • Congo 22 G4
Soúda • Crete, Greece 93 E1
Soúda, Órmos • Crete, Greece 93 E2
Soufli • Greece 92 D2
Soufli • Greece 92 D2
Soufrière • St Lucia 125 J3
Soufrière Bay • St Lucia 125 J3
Soúgia • Crete, Greece 93 E5
Souillac • France 85 G2
Souilly • France 5 I5
Souk Ahras • Algeria 20 G1
Souk el Arba du Rharb • Morocco 101 D1
Soul • Rep. of Korea 30 D6
Soulac-sur-Mer Beach • France ...... 68 [66]
Soulac-sur-Mer • France 85 G1
Soúnio, Akra • Greece 92 D7
Soúnion • Greece 92 D7
Soúnion Nat. Park Park • Greece ...... 72 [141]
Soûr Heritage C • Lebanon ...... 64 [246]
Sour el Ghozlane • Algeria 20 F1
Soure • Brazil 43 H4
Souris • Canada/United States 38 K7
Souris • PE, Canada 123 D7
Sous • Morocco 20 D2
Sous le Vent, Is. • French Polynesia 33 L7
Sousa • Brazil 45 (1) D3
Sousse Heritage C • Tunisia ...... 64 [229]
Sousse • Tunisia 101 E2
Souterraine, la • France 84 D4
South Africa • Africa 24 C6
South America cruise area • S. America 58 A3
South Andaman • India 28 F6
South Australia • Australia 34 F5
South Ayrshire • United Kingdom 75 A3
South Beach • Bahamas 124 B3
South Bend • IN, United States 41 I3
South Carolina • United States 41 J5
South China Sea • Asia 31 E3
South Dakota • United States 40 F3
South Downs • United Kingdom 74 E3
South East Cape • TS, Australia 34 I8
South East Point • VI, Australia 111 G4
St Kitts & Nevis 125 G2
South Friar's Bay • St Kitts & Nevis 125 G2
South Geomagnetic Pole • Antarctica 46 (1) Q2
South Georgia • Atlantic Ocean 42 G10
South I. • New Zealand 35 B6
South I. • Kenya 101 A1
South Kitui Game Reserve • Kenya 101 G4
South Lanarkshire • United Kingdom 74 B3
South Luangwa Nat. Park Park • Zambia ...... 103 [104]
South Magnetic Pole • Antarctica 46 (1) T3

South Moll I. • QL, Australia 111 F1
South Nahanni • NT, Canada 38 F4
South Negril Point • Jamaica 124 C1
South Orkney Is • Antarctica 46 (1) A3
South Pacific cruise area •
  Pacific Ocean 58 A1
South Pacific cruise area •
  Pacific Ocean 59 A9
South Pass • WY, United States 40 E3
South Point • Barbados 125 H4
South Pole • Antarctica 59 A10
South Ronaldsay •
  United Kingdom 6 J3
South Sandwich Is. • Antarctica 46 (1) C4
South Saskatchewan • SA, Canada 38 J6
South Shields • United Kingdom 7 K7
South Shields Beach •
  United Kingdom ...... 75 [23]
South Turkana Game Reserve •
  Kenya 101 G1
South Uist • United Kingdom 6 E4
Southampton • United Kingdom 7 K11
Southampton, Cape • NU, Canada 39 O4
Southampton I. • NU, Canada 38 L5
Southend • SA, Canada 38 K5
Southend-on-Sea •
  United Kingdom 74 E2
Southend-on-Sea Beach •
  United Kingdom ...... 75 [57-58]
Southern [Adm] • United Kingdom 75 A6
Southern Alps • New Zealand 35 C6
Southern Cross • WA, Australia 34 C6
Southern Indian Lake •
  MN, Canada 38 L5
Southern Uplands •
  United Kingdom 6 I6
Southerndown Beach •
  United Kingdom ...... 75 [138]
Southland • New Zealand ...... 112 L
Southport • QL, Australia 111 F6
Southwest Cape • New Zealand 35 A8
Southwold • United Kingdom 5 E2
Southwold Beach •
  United Kingdom ...... 75 [50]
Soutpansberg • South Africa 24 D4
Sovetsk • Russian Fed. 13 K2
Sovetsky • Russian Fed. 26 J5
Soya-Misaki • Japan 30 K2
Soyo • Angola 23 A5
Sozopol Beach • Bulgaria ...... 69 [211]
Sozopol • Bulgaria 97 D3
Spa • Belgium 80 A16
Spa-Francorchamps • Belgium 80 A16
Spaandem • Netherlands 80 C1
Spain • Europe 11
Spalato • Croatia 71 A14
Spalding • United Kingdom 7 L9
Spánda, Akra • Crete, Greece 93 E1
Spanish Town • Jamaica 124 C4
Spanish Wells • Bahamas 124 B1
Spargi • Sardinia, Italy 12 J9
Sparks • NV, United States 117 F1
Sparreholm • Sweden 95 D3
Sparta • Greece 15 D6
Spartel, Cap • Morocco 101 D1
Spárti • Greece 15 D6
Spartias Beach • Corfu, Greece ...... 69 [149]
Spartivento, Capo •
  Calàbria, Italy 12 K11
Spartivento, Capo •
  Sardinia, Italy 90 C4
Spassk-Dalniy • Russian Fed. 27 L8
Speichersee • Germany 82 J3
Speightstown • Barbados 125 H1
Spello • Italy 91 E12
Spence Bay • NU, Canada 36 H3
Spencer, Cape • SA, Australia 34 G7
Spencer Gulf • SA, Australia 34 G6
Spenser Mtns • New Zealand 35 D6
Sperillen • Norway 94 B1
Sperlonga • Italy 91 E14
Sperone, Capo • Sardinia 12 C10
Sperrin Mtns • United Kingdom 7 F7
Spessart • Germany 9 E7
Spetsai • Greece 92 D7
Spétsai • Greece 92 D7
Spétses • Greece 92 D7
Spétses • Greece 92 D7
Spétses [I.] • Greece 15 E6
Spey • United Kingdom 6 I4
Speyer Heritage C • Germany ...... 64 [43]
Speyer • Germany 82 E4
Speyside • Trinidad & Tobago 125 K2
Sphinx • Egypt 101 F1
Spice Is. • Indonesia ...... 110 A
Spiddal Beach • Ireland ...... 68 [43]
Spiddal • Ireland 79 F4
Spiekeroog • Germany 8 C3
Spiekeroog Spa • Germany ...... 83 [41]
Spiez • Switzerland 89 G2
Spijkenisse • Netherlands 80 C3
Spili • Crete, Greece 93 E6
Spílion Kamarón • Crete, Greece 93 E6
Spinalonga, Herson •
  Crete, Greece 93 E8
Spingdale • NF, Canada 123 D3
Spirit Mtn Ski •
  MN, United States ...... 116 [110]
Spisská-Nová Ves • Slovak Rep. 13 J9
Spisské Pohradie Heritage C •
  Slovak Rep. ...... 64 [151]
Spithead • United Kingdom 5 B4
Spitsbergen • Arctic Ocean 4 M1
Spitsbergen I. • Arctic Ocean 46 N2
Spittal • Austria 89 H8
Spitzingsee • Germany 82 J7
Spjelkavik • Norway 94 B1
Splendid China •
  Shenzhen, China 107 H3
Splendid China •
  FL, United States 121 C1
Split • Croatia 14 C6
Split Heritage C • Croatia ...... 64 [157]
Split Lake • MN, Canada 38 L5
Splügen • Switzerland 89 G3
Spodsbjerg • Denmark 95 F14
Spokane • WA, United States 117 E2
Spoleto • Italy 91 F11
Spongeorama • FL, United States 119 M5
Spontin • Belgium 80 A15
Sporades, N • Greece 92 D4
Sporades, N • Greece 92 D4
Sportgastein • Austria 89 H8
Spottorno • Italy 91 E6
Søttrup Beach • Denmark ...... 68 [30]
Spratly Is. • South China Sea 31 E5
Spree • Germany 8 I4
Spreepark Berlin • Germany 81 F4
Spremberg • Germany 82 J3
Sprengisandur • Iceland 16 (1) D2
Spring Hill • FL, United States 119 M5
Springbok • South Africa 24 B5
Springdale • AR, United States 41 H4
Springe • Germany 8 E4
Springfield • New Zealand 35 C6
Springfield Mtn • United States 41 13
Springfield • IL, United States 41 I4
Springfield • OH, United States 41 J4
Springfield • OR, United States 117 E3

Springfield • MA, United States 118 H2
Springfield Armory Nat. Hist. Site Park •
  MA, United States ...... 121 [340]
Springhill • NS, Canada 123 D7
Springs • South Africa 24 D5
Springvale Beach •
  United Kingdom ...... 75 [93]
Sprockhövel • Germany 81 E2
Spruce Knob • WV, United States 41 K4
Spui • Netherlands 80 C3
Spurn Head • United Kingdom 7 M8
Squamish • BC, Canada 38 G7
Squaw Creek Ski •
  CA, United States ...... 116 [57]
Squaw Valley Ski •
  CA, United States ...... 116 [57]
Squillace • Italy 12 K10
Squillace, Golfo di • Italy 12 K10
Sravanabelgola • India 106 D6
Sravasti • India 105 C4
Srbija • F.R. of Yugoslavia 97 D1
Srbarna Nature Reserve Heritage N •
  Bulgaria ...... 61 [57]
Srebarna • Bulgaria 14 G5
Srebrenica • Bosnia-Herz. 14 G5
Sredinny Khrebet • Russian Fed. 27 Q5
Sredna Gora • Bulgaria 15 F1
Sravasti • India 14 H6
Srednesibirskoye Ploskogorye •
  Russian Fed. 26 Q4
Sredni Verecki • Ukraine 14 K1
Sredniy Ural • Russian Fed. 26 I6
Srednrusskaya Vozvyshennost •
  Russian Fed. 17 E4
Srednyaya Olëkma • Russian Fed. 27 J5
Srem • Poland 13 G5
Sremska Mitrovica •
  F.R. of Yugoslavia 14 G5
Sretensk • Russian Fed. 27 I6
Srikakulam • India 28 D5
Srikalahasti • India 106 D7
Srinagar • Jammu & Kashmir 28 B2
Srirangam • India 106 D11
Srirangapatnam • India 106 D6
Srisailam • India 106 C3
Sroda Wielkopolska • Poland 13 G5
Staaten River Nat. Park •
  QL, Australia 34 H3
Stabbursdalen Nat. Park Park •
  Norway ...... 72 [4]
Stade • Germany 8 E3
Stade de France, Paris • France 85 E1
Stadskanaal • Netherlands 5 J7
Stadtallendorf • Germany 8 E6
Stadthagen • Germany 8 E4
Staffelsee • Germany 82 J7
Staffelstein • Germany 9 F6
Staffelstein Spa • Germany ...... 83 [224]
Stafford • United Kingdom 7 L9
Stagnone, I. della • Italy 90 D1
Stahnsdorf • Germany 81 F3
Staigue Fort • Ireland 79 F7
Stalham • Norway 94 C4
Stalin, NP • BC, Canada 38 G5
Stalingrad • Russian Fed. 4 T7
Stalowa Wola • Poland 13 L7
Stamford • United Kingdom 7 L9
Stamford • CT, United States 118 H2
Stamford Bridge •
  United Kingdom 71 A7
Stamnes • Norway 94 C3
Stampalia • Greece 92 D8
Stampalia • Greece 92 D8
Stamsund • Norway 16 G2
Standley Chasm • NT, Australia 112 H2
Stanford • TS, Australia 34 I8
Stanley • Falkland Is. 45 E6
Stanley • Hong Kong, China 107 H6
Stanley Falls •
  Dem. Rep. of Congo 23 D3
Stanley, Mt • Uganda 23 E3
Stanorove Nagorye •
  Russian Fed. 27 H5
Stanovoy Khrebet • Russian Fed. 27 J6
Stansted [Apt] • United Kingdom 74 E1
Stanthorpe • QL, Australia 34 J5
Stanwix, Fort. Nat. Mon. Park •
  NY, United States ...... 121 [318]
Star Buck • Kiribati 33 L6
Stara Zagora • Bulgaria 97 D3
Staraplanina • Bulgaria 14 K7
Staraya Russa • Russian Fed. 97 E1
Stargard Szczecinski • Poland 13 E4
Stari Ras Heritage C •
  F.R. of Yugoslavia ...... 64 [160]
Starkenburg • Germany 82 H3
Starkville • MS, United States 118 K2
Starnberg • Germany 82 J3
Starnberger See • Germany 82 J3
Starogard Gdanski • Poland 13 H4
Start Bay • United Kingdom 74 F5
Start Point • United Kingdom 74 F5
Starry Oskol • Russian Fed. 17 F4
Staszów • Poland 13 K7
State College •
  PA, United States 118 H1
Staten I. • NJ, United States 118 H1
Statesboro • GA, United States 41 J5
Stathelle • Norway 94 B3
Statue of Liberty Heritage C •
  NJ, United States ...... 62 [12]
Statue of Liberty •
  NJ, United States 118 H2
Statue of Liberty Nat. Mon. Park •
  NY, United States ...... 121 [331]
Stavanger • Norway 94 C5
Stavern • Norway 94 B3
Staverton [Apt] •
  United Kingdom 74 D4
Stavoren • Netherlands 80 A3
Stavropol • Russian Fed. 17 G5
Stavropolskaya Vozvyshennost •
  Russian Fed. 17 G5
Stavrós • Thessaly, Greece 15 D4
Stavrós • Halkidikí, Greece 92 D1
Stavrós • Halkidikí, Greece 92 D1
Stavrós, Akra • Crete, Greece 93 E3
Stavrovouni Monastery • Cyprus 93 J4
Steamboat Ski •
  CO, United States ...... 116 [88]
Steamboat Springs •
  CO, United States 40 E3
Steamboat Springs •
  CO, United States ...... 116 A
Steamtown Nat. Hist. Site Park •
  PA, United States ...... 121 [315]
Stebnik • Ukraine 13 M8
Stechelberg Ski • Switzerland ...... 70 [96]
Steenwijk • Netherlands 5 J7
Stefansson I. • NU, Canada 38 J2
Steg • Denmark 95 F14
Steiermark • Austria 13 D10
Steigen • Norway 16 F2
Steinach an der Straße • Germany 82 G2
Steinbeck Spa • Germany ...... 83 [84]
Steinfurt • Germany 8 C4
Steinau an der Straße • Germany 82 G2
Steinbeck Spa • Germany ...... 83 [84]
Steinfurt • Germany 8 C4
Steingaden • Germany 82 J6

Steinhuder Meer • Germany 5 M2
Steinkjer • Norway 16 F4
Steinsel • Luxembourg 80 A20
Stella Maris • Bahamas 124 B4
Stellenbosch • South Africa 100 C5
Stèlvio • Italy 91 E3
Stelvio, Parco Naz. dello Park •
  Italy ...... 72 [84]
Stelvio, Parco Naz. dello •
  Italy 91 E2
Stenay • France 10 K4
Stenbrohult • Sweden 95 F11
Stendal • Germany 8 F2
Stenge • Rhodes, Greece 93 F2
Stenhouse Bay • SA, Australia 34 G7
Stenó Andíkithiron • Greece 15 E8
Stenó Elafónissou • Greece 15 D7
Stenungsund • Sweden 95 F2
Stephenville • NF, Canada 123 D3
Stephens, Mt • Antarctica 46 (1) A1
Stephenville •
  TX, United States 119 N1
Sterling • CO, United States 40 F3
Stern Ski • Italy ...... 70 [233]
Stern Ski • Italy 90 B2
Sternbeck • Czech Rep. 13 G8
Stérnes Beach • Crete, Greece ...... 69 [188]
Sterrenberg, Burg • Germany 82 H2
Sterzing • Italy 90 B1
Stessor Peak • Antarctica 46 (1) II3
Stettin • Poland 13 D4
Stettiner Haff • Germany/Poland 8 J8
Stevenage • United Kingdom 7 L10
Stevens Pass Ski •
  WA, United States ...... 116 [43]
Stewart I. • New Zealand 35 A8
Steyr • Austria 13 D9
Steyr [Riv] • Austria 9 J9
Steytlerville • South Africa 100 C7
Stikine • BC, Canada 38 E5
Stilfs • Italy 91 E3
Stilida • Greece 15 D5
Still Bay • South Africa 100 C6
Stip • F.Y.R. of Macedonia 14 J8
Stirling • United Kingdom 74 B3
Stirling [Adm] • United Kingdom 74 B1
Stjørnøya • Norway 16 L1
Stjørdal • Norway 16 F5
Stobi • F.Y.R. of Macedonia 15 C2
Stockerau • Austria 13 F9
Stockholm Heritage C • Sweden ...... 64 [6]
Stockholm Beach • Sweden ...... 69 [8]
Stockholm • Sweden 95 D4
Stockholm [Adm] • Sweden 95 D4
Stockport • United Kingdom 7 J8
Stockton • CA, United States 117 F3
Stockton-on-Tees •
  United Kingdom 7 K7
Stoeng Trêng • Cambodia 31 D4
Stogovo • F.Y.R. of Macedonia 14 H8
Stoke-on-Trent • United Kingdom 7 J8
Stoke-sub-Hamdon Priory •
  United Kingdom 74 F3
Stokksund • Norway 16 F4
Stolberg • Germany 9 B6
Stolbovoy, Ostrov •
  Russian Fed. 27 M2
Stolzenfels, Schloß • Germany 82 H1
Stone, Mountain. Nat. Hist. Site Park •
  MD, United States ...... 121 [277]
Stoneham Ski • QU, Canada ...... 116 [37]
Stonehaven • United Kingdom 6 J5
Stonehenge Heritage C •
  United Kingdom ...... 64 [20]
Stonehenge • United Kingdom 74 F3
Stones River Nat. Battlefield & Cemetery
  Park •
  TN, United States ...... 121 [231]
Stonington I. • Antarctica 59 A10
Stora Lule • Norway/Sweden 94 B4
Stora Lulevatten • Sweden 16 J3
Stora Sjöfället Nat. Park Park •
  Sweden ...... 72 [19]
Storavan • Sweden 16 J4
Stord • Norway 94 C5
Stordal • Norway 94 C3
Store • Norway 94 C3
Store Bælt • Denmark 95 F13
Store Heddinge • Denmark 95 F15
Store Mosse Nat. Park • Sweden 95 F7
Støren • Norway 16 F5
Størfjorden • Norway 94 C2
Storis Passage • NU, Canada 38 K3
Storkerson Bay • NT, Canada 38 F2
Storlien • Sweden 16 G4
Storm Lake • IA, United States 41 G3
Stornoway • United Kingdom 6 E4
Storsjøen • Norway 94 B2
Storstrøm • Denmark 95 F14
Storuman • Sweden 16 I4
Storuman [Lake] • Sweden 16 I4
Stöttingfjället • Sweden 16 I4
Stour • United Kingdom 5 D2
Stour • United Kingdom 5 E3
Stour • United Kingdom 74 F3
Stourbridge • United Kingdom 7 J9
Stourhead • United Kingdom 74 F3
Stourport • United Kingdom 74 D1
Stow-on-the-Wold •
  United Kingdom 74 D4
Stowe Ski • VT, United States ...... 116 [203]
Stowe • VT, United States 118 G3
Strå • Italy 91 E7
Strabane • United Kingdom 75 A3
Stradbally • Ireland 79 E3
Strakonice • Czech Rep. 13 E8
Straldzha • Bulgaria 15 H1
Stralsund • Germany 8 I2
Stranda • Norway 94 C2
Strande Spa • Germany ...... 83 [15]
Strangford Lough •
  United Kingdom 7 G7
Strängnäs • Sweden 95 D3
Strängsjö • Sweden 95 D3
Stranraer • United Kingdom 7 H7
Strasbourg • France 10 M5
Strasburg Heritage C • France ...... 64 [52]
Strasburg • PA, United States 118 H1
Strasbourg • France 71 A8
Stratford • New Zealand 112 K3
Stratford-upon-Avon •
  United Kingdom 74 D4
Strath Earn • United Kingdom 74 B1
Strathmore • United Kingdom 74 B2
Strathcona Prov. Park •
  BC, Canada 122 C3
Strathgordon • TS, Australia 34 I8
Strathmore • United Kingdom 74 B2
Stratton Mtn •
  VT, United States ...... 116 [196]
Stratton Mtn •
  VT, United States 118 G3
Straubing • Germany 9 H8

Straumsjøen • Norway 16 H2
Strausberg • Germany 8 I4
Streaky Bay • SA, Australia 34 F6
Streaky Bay [Gulf] •
  SA, Australia 34 F6
Strehaia • Romania 14 K5
Strelka • Russian Fed. 26 P6
Stresa • Italy 91 E2
Strete Gate Beach •
  United Kingdom ...... 75 [113]
Strezhevoy • Russian Fed. 26 M5
Strib • Denmark 95 F9
Strickland • Papua New Guinea 32 (1) H4
Strigno • Italy 90 B3
Strimónas • Greece 15 E3
Strimonikós Kolpos • Greece 15 E3
Strjama • Bulgaria 15 F1
Strómboli, I. • Italy 90 D4
Strømfjord, Nordre • Greenland 39 U3
Strømfjord, Søndre • Greenland 39 U3
Stromness • United Kingdom 6 I3
Strömsnäsbruk • Sweden 95 F11
Strömstad • Sweden 95 F2
Strömsund • Sweden 16 I5
Stronsay • United Kingdom 6 J3
Stroud • United Kingdom 74 D3
Struer Beach • Denmark ...... 68 [31]
Struer • Denmark 95 F9
Struga • F.Y.R. of Macedonia 15 B2
Struisbaai • South Africa 100 C6
Struma • Bulgaria 14 K8
Strumica • F.Y.R. of Macedonia 14 J8
Stry • Ukraine 13 M8
Stryn • Norway 94 C2
Strynsvatn • Norway 94 C2
Strzelin • Poland 13 G7
Stuart Mem. • NT, Australia 112 H2
Stuart Mtns • New Zealand 112 L1
Stubbekøbing • Denmark 95 F14
Stubbenkammer • Germany 8 I2
Stuben • Austria 89 H5
Stubice • Poland 13 D5
Studen • Switzerland 89 G2
Studholme Heritage C •
  F.R. of Yugoslavia ...... 64 [161]
Studley Royal Park Heritage C •
  United Kingdom ...... 64 [17]
Sturgeon Falls • OT, Canada 122 B1
Sturt Creek • WA, Australia 34 E3
Sturt Desert • QL/SA, Australia 34 H5
Sturt Nat. Park • NS, Australia 34 H5
Sturup [Apt] • Sweden 95 F11
Stuttgart • BR, United States 41 H5
Stuttgart • Germany 82 E4
Stuttgart Spa • Germany ...... 83 [176]
Stützerbach Spa • Germany ...... 83 [306]
Stykkishólmur • Iceland 16 (1) D2
Styr • Ukraine 17 D4
Styria • Austria 89 F4
Su Nuraxi • Sardinia, Italy 90 C4
Su Nuraxi di Barúmini Heritage C •
  Sardinia, Italy ...... 64 [135]
Suavango • Solomon Is. 35 (1) F2
Subang • Java, Indonesia 110 D2
Subang [Apt] • Malaysia 108 D4
Subbético • Spain 11 I6
Submeseta •
  Castilla y León, Spain 11 F2
Submeseta •
  Castilla-La Mancha, Spain 11 H5
Subotica • F.R. of Yugoslavia 14 G3
Suceava • Romania 14 N2
Sucia, Bahía • Puerto Rico 125 E3
Suck • Ireland 79 F4
Suckling • Papua New Guinea 35 (1) D2
Sucre • Bolivia 44 C2
Sucre Heritage C • Bolivia ...... 62 [54]
Sud, Costa del •
  Sardinia, Italy 90 C3
Sudan • Africa 19 H4
Sudan [Region] • Africa 22 F2
Sudan • Sardinia, Italy 90 C3
Sudd, As • Sudan 23 E2
Sude • Germany 8 G3
Sudeten • Poland/Czech Rep. 13 F7
Sudety • Poland/Czech Rep. 13 E7
Sudirman, Pegunungan •
  Indonesia 32 (1) E3
Sudong • Singapore 108 E3
Sue • Sudan 23 D2
Suea Beach • Spain 11 K5
Sueca Beach • Spain ...... 68 [102]
Suez • Egypt 101 F2
Suez Canal • Egypt 101 F2
Suez, Gulf of • Egypt 101 F4
Suffolk • United Kingdom 7 N9
Sugar Bowl Ski •
  CA, United States ...... 116 [53]
Sugar Loaf Ski •
  ME, United States ...... 116 [134]
Sugar Mtn Ski •
  NC, United States ...... 116 [152]
Sugarbush Ski •
  VT, United States ...... 116 [201]
Sugarloaf USA Ski •
  ME, United States ...... 116 [219]
Sugla Gölü • Turkey 93 G2
Sugoy • Russian Fed. 27 Q4
Suhar • Oman 18 G5
Suheli I. • India 106 D9
Suhl • Germany 8 F6
Suide • China 29 D3
Suihua • China 29 H1
Suippe • France 5 H5
Suippes • France 5 H5
Suir • Ireland 7 E9
Suizhong • China 29 G2
Sukabumi • Java, Indonesia 110 D1
Sukadana • Indonesia 32 D3
Sukaraja • Indonesia 32 D3
Sukhona • Russian Fed. 13 M10
Sukhothai Heritage N • Thailand ...... 61 [122]
Sukhothai Heritage C • Thailand ...... 63 [173]
Sukhothai • Thailand 109 G4
Sukhumi • Georgia 17 G6
Suki • Sudan 21 F5
Sukkur • Pakistan 28 B4
Sukon • Indonesia 32 (1) B3
Suksès • Namibia 24 B4
Sukumo • Japan 30 G8
Sula • Norway 94 C2
Sula, Kepulauan • Indonesia 110 A3
Sulaiman Range • Pakistan 28 B3
Sulawesi • Indonesia 32 (1) A3
Sulayyil, As • Saudi Arabia 18 E5
Sulb • Egypt 21 F3
Suldalsvatn • Norway 94 C6
Sulden • Italy 91 E3
Sulechów • Poland 13 E5
Suleskar • Norway 94 C6
Sulima • Sierra Leone 22 B3
Sulina • Romania 97 D2
Sulingen • Germany 5 L2
Sulitjelma • Norway 16 H3
Sulkava • Finland 95 B1
Susquehanna • PA, United States 118 H1
Sullana • Peru 43 A4
Sulmona • Italy 91 F2
Sulphur • AR/TX, United States 119 N2

Sulphur Springs •
  TX, United States 119 N2
Sultan Daglari • Turkey 15 M5
Sultan Daglari • Turkey 15 05
Sultanhani • Turkey 105 C8
Sultanpur • India 105 C4
Sulu Archipelago • Philippines 31 G5
Sulu Sea • Philippines 31 F5
Sülüklü • Turkey 15 N5
Sulz am Neckar • Germany 82 G6
Sulzbach-Rosenberg • Germany 9 G7
Sulzberger Bay • Antarctica 46 (1) AA2
Sumadija • F.R. of Yugoslavia 14 H5
Sumalata • Indonesia 32 (1) B2
Sumatera • Indonesia 32 A3
Sumatera Barat • Indonesia 110 B4
Sumatera Utara • Indonesia 110 B4
Sumatra • Indonesia 32 A3
Sumava • Czech Rep. 96 C3
Sumayh, As • Sudan 23 D2
Sumba • Indonesia 32 (1) A4
Sumbawa • Indonesia 32 (1) A4
Sumbawa Besar • Indonesia 32 (1) A4
Sumbawanga • Tanzania 102 N3
Sumbe • Angola 23 A6
Sumbing, Gunung •
  Java, Indonesia 110 D7
Sumbu • Zambia 23 E5
Sumburg Head • United Kingdom 6 K2
Sumenep • Indonesia 110 D4
Sumgait • Azerbaijan 18 E1
Summerside • PE, Canada 123 D7
Summit Lake • BC, Canada 38 G5
Sumperk • Czech Rep. 13 F8
Sumter • SC, United States 41 J5
Sumter, Fort, Nat. Mon. Park •
  SC, United States ...... 121 [237]
Sumy • Ukraine 17 E4
Sun Kosi • Nepal 28 E3
Sun Peaks Ski • BC, Canada ...... 116 [4]
Sun Valley Ski •
  ID, United States ...... 116 [72]
Sun Valley • ID, United States 117 E4
Sun Yat-sen's residence • China 107 H2
Sunak, gora • Kazakhstan 26 J5
Sunan • D.P.R. of Korea 30 C5
Sunapee • NH, United States 118 G3
Sunbury • VI, Australia 34 H7
Sunbury House and Museum •
  Barbados 125 H4
Sunch'on • Rep. of Korea 30 D7
Sunchales • Argentina 44 D5
Sunda, Selat • Java, Indonesia 110 D1
Sunda Strait • Indonesia 32 C4
Sundan • Bangladesh/India 28 E4
Sundarbans Heritage N •
  Bangladesh ...... 61 [110]
Sundarbans Nat. Park Heritage N •
  India ...... 61 [109]
Sunday River Ski •
  ME, United States ...... 116 [218]
Sunde • Norway 94 C5
Sunderland • United Kingdom 7 K7
Sunderland Sound • New Zealand 112 L1
Sundern • Germany 5 K3
Sundern • Germany 9 D5
Sündiken Daglari • Turkey 15 L4
Sundridge • United Kingdom 74 E1
Sundsli • Norway 94 C6
Sundsvall • Sweden 16 I5
Sundybyberg • Sweden 95 D4
Sungai Petani • Malaysia 31 C5
Sungaigurung • Indonesia 110 C2
Sungaipenuh • Indonesia 110 C2
Sunndalsøra • Norway 94 C2
Sunne • Sweden 16 G7
Sunnerbo • Sweden 95 F7
Sunnersta • Sweden 95 D2
Sunny Beach • Bulgaria 97 D3
Sunrise Park Ski •
  AZ, United States ...... 116 [81]
Sunset Beach •
  HI, United States 119 L1
Sunset Crater Nat. Mon. •
  AZ, United States 118 J1
Sunset Crater Nat. Mon. Park •
  AZ, United States ...... 120 [106]
Sunshine Coast • QL, Australia 111 F6
Sunshine Village Ski •
  AL, Canada ...... 116 [13]
Suntar • Russian Fed. 27 I4
Suntar Khayata, Khrebet •
  Russian Fed. 27 M4
Sunyani • Ghana 22 D3
Suolahti • Finland 95 E2
Suomenlinna • Finland 95 E4
Suomussalmi • Finland 16 O4
Suonenjoki • Finland 16 N5
Suoyarvi • Russian Fed. 17 E2
Sup'ung-Chosuji • China 30 C4
Super-Sauze • France 85 F2
Super-St-Bernard • Switzerland 89 G6
Super-Sterbegérène • France 85 K1
Superdévoluy Ski • France ...... 70 [64]
Superior • WI, United States 41 H2
Superior, Lake •
  Canada/United States 41 I2
Suphan Buri • Thailand 109 H1
Supiori • Indonesia 32 (1) E3
Sur • Oman 18 G5
Sur • Lebanon 98 A1
Surabaya • Java, Indonesia 110 D8
Surahammar • Sweden 95 D1
Surak • Iran 18 G4
Surakarta • Java, Indonesia 110 D7
Surat • India 28 B4
Surat • QL, Australia 111 F5
Surat Thani • Thailand 31 B5
Suratgarh • India 105 C2
Surduc • Romania 13 M10
Súre • Luxembourg 80 A20
Surfers Paradise •
  QL, Australia 111 F6
Surgidero de Bataband • Cuba 124 D2
Surgutikha • Russian Fed. 26 O5
Surhob • Asia 18 J2
Surigao • Philippines 31 H5
Surin Beach • Phuket, Thailand 109 K1
Surin, Ko • Thailand 109 F3
Surinam Quarters • Jamaica 124 C3
Suriname • S. America 103 H4
Surrey • United Kingdom 74 E3
Surrey • United Kingdom 74 E1
Surt • Libya 20 C2
Surtsey • Iceland 16 (1) C3
Surud Ad • Somalia 100 D3
Suruga-Wan • Japan 30 J5
Susa • Italy 12 B3
Susak • Croatia 14 D7
Susaki • Japan 30 G8
Susanville • CA, United States 117 F1
Susice • Czech Rep. 13 E8
Suso Heritage C • Spain ...... 64 [77]
Suso • Indonesia 32 (1) B3

Sutherland • South Africa 100 C2
Sutjeska Nat. Park Park •
  Bosnia-Herz. ...... 72 [114]
Sutlej • India/Pakistan 28 B2
Suursaari • Russian Fed. 16 N6
Suva • Fiji 35 (2) J2
Suva Planina •
  F.R. of Yugoslavia 14 J6
Suvadiva Atoll • Maldives 106 E3
Suwa • Japan 30 J6
Suwalki • Poland 13 L3
Suwannee • FL/GA, United States 119 M3
Suweis, El • Egypt 101 F2
Suzdal Heritage C •
  Russian Fed. ...... 64 [210]
Suzdal • Russian Fed. 97 E4
Suzhou Heritage C • China ...... 63 [153]
Suzhou • China 107 J2
Suzu • Japan 29 J3
Suzu • Japan 30 I6
Suzu-Misaki • Japan 30 I6
Suzun • Turkey 93 G1
Suzuz Han • Turkey 93 G1
Svalbard • Arctic Ocean 46 N2
Svaljava • Ukraine 13 M9
Svaneke • Denmark 95 F16
Svaneti area Heritage C •
  Georgia ...... 64 [211]
Svarstad • Norway 94 B3
Svartenhuk Halvø • Greenland 39 U2
Svärtinge • Sweden 95 D3
Svartisen • Norway 16 H3
Svatoy Nos, mys • Russian Fed. 27 N2
Svedala • Sweden 16 E5
Svedala • Sweden 16 H5
Sveg • Sweden 16 H5
Svelvik • Norway 94 B2
Svendborg Beach • Denmark ...... 68 [25]
Svendborg • Denmark 95 F14
Svene • Norway 94 B1
Svenljunga • Sweden 95 F7
Sverdrup Is. • NU, Canada 36 H2
Sveshtari Heritage C • Bulgaria ...... 64 [168]
Svetac • Croatia 14 C6
Svetlaya • Russian Fed. 27 M7
Svetlograd • Russian Fed. 17 G5
Svetly • Russian Fed. 13 J3
Svetly • Russian Fed. 27 I5
Sivaihnókar • Iceland 16 (1) E2
Sviatoy Nos, mys • Russian Fed. 27 M4
Svihov • Czech Rep. 96 C3
Svilaja • Croatia 14 N8
Svilengrad • Bulgaria 14 N8
Svinecea Mare, Vîrful • Romania 14 J5
Svir • Russian Fed. 17 E2
Svishtov • Bulgaria 97 D1
Svitava • Czech Rep. 13 F8
Svitavy • Czech Rep. 13 F8
Svobodnyy • Russian Fed. 27 K6
Svolvær • Norway 16 H2
Svrljig • F.R. of Yugoslavia 14 J6
Swain Ski • NY, United States ...... 116 [174]
Swain Reefs • QL, Australia 111 F4
Swakopmund • Namibia 24 A4
Swan • Honduras 37 E4
Swan Hill • VI, Australia 111 G1
Swanage • United Kingdom 5 C3
Swanage Beach • United Kingdom ...... 75 [87]
Swanage • United Kingdom 7 I10
Swartberg Pass • South Africa 100 B7
Swaziland • Africa 24 E5
Sweden • Europe 14
Swedish Lakeland • Sweden 95 F3
Sweetwater • WY, United States 38 J4
Sweetwater • TX, United States 40 F5
Swellendam • South Africa 100 C6
Swetes • Antigua & Barbuda 125 F3
Swidnica • Poland 13 F7
Swidnik • Poland 13 L6
Swidwin • Poland 13 E4
Swiebodzin • Poland 13 E5
Swiecie • Poland 13 H4
Swietokrzyskie, Góry • Poland 13 K7
Swift Current • SA, Canada 38 J6
Swilly, Lough • Ireland 7 E6
Swinburne, Cape • NU, Canada 38 L2
Swindon • United Kingdom 7 K10
Swinemünde • Poland 13 D4
Swiss Nat. Park Park •
  Switzerland ...... 72 [81]
Swiss Valley Ski •
  MI, United States ...... 116 [144]
Switzerland • Europe 4 L7
Swords • Ireland 79 E2
Sybaris • Italy 12 K9
Sydals Beach • Denmark ...... 68 [25]
Sydfangeland Beach • Denmark ...... 68 [25]
Sydney • NS, Australia 111 G2
Sydney • NS, Canada 123 D8
Sydney Mines • NS, Canada 123 D8
Sydthy Beach • Denmark ...... 68 [30]
Sykkylven • Norway 94 C2
Syktyvkar • Russian Fed. 17 I2
Sylhet • Bangladesh 28 F4
Sylling • Norway 94 B2
Sylt • Germany 8 D2
Sylt Spa • Germany ...... 83 [2]
Sylt-Ost Spa • Germany ...... 83 [2]
Sylvan Ski • MI, United States ...... 116 [131]
Sylvensteinsee • Germany 82 J7
Symond's Yat • United Kingdom 74 D3
Syowa [Base] • Antarctica 46 (1) J3
Syr Darya • Kazakhstan 26 K9
Syracuse • NY, United States 41 K3
Syracuse • Sicily, Italy 90 D4
Syria • Asia 18 C3
Syrian Desert • Asia 18 C3
Syutkya • Bulgaria 14 K8
Syvde • Norway 94 C1
Syzran • Russian Fed. 17 H4
Szamotuly • Poland 13 F5
Szarvas • Hungary 13 J11
Szczecin • Poland 13 D4
Szczecinek • Poland 13 F4
Szczytno • Poland 13 J4
Szeged • Hungary 13 J11
Székesfehérvár • Hungary 13 H10
Szekszárd • Hungary 13 H11
Szentendre • Hungary 13 J10
Szentes • Hungary 13 J11
Szeskie Wzgórza • Poland 13 L3
Szigetvár • Hungary 13 G11
Szolnok • Hungary 13 J10
Szombathely • Hungary 13 G10
Szprotawa • Poland 13 E6
Szubin • Poland 13 G4

T'aech'on • D.P.R. of Korea 30 C4
Ta'if, At • Saudi Arabia 18 D5
Ta'izz • Yemen 18 D7
Taba • Egypt 101 F3
Tabar Is. • Papua New Guinea 35 (1) E1
Tabarca • Tunisia 101 E1
Tabarz Spa • Germany ...... 83 [301]
Tabasco • Mexico 37 C4

Tabasco y Campeche, Llanos de • Mexico 37 C4
Tabelbala • Algeria 20 E3
Taberg • Sweden 95 F7
Tabernacle • St Kitts & Nevis 125 G1
Tabla • Niger 20 F6
Tablas • Philippines 31 G4
Table Bay • South Africa 100 C5
Table Cape • New Zealand 35 G4
Table Mtn • South Africa 100 C5
Tabor • Czech Rep. 96 C4
Tabor, Mount • Israel 98 A4
Tabora • Tanzania 102 H1
Tabou • Côte d'Ivoire 22 C4
Tabriz • Iran 18 E2
Tabuaeran • Kiribati 33 L5
Tabuk • Saudi Arabia 18 C4
Tabwemasana • Vanuatu 35 (2) B2
Täby • Sweden 95 D2
Tacheng • China 26 N8
Tachilek • Myanmar 109 G2
Tachov • Czech Rep. 13 B8
Tacloban • Philippines 31 G4
Tacna • Peru 127 B4
Tacoma • WA, United States 117 E1
Tacoronte Beach • Tenerife, Canary Is. ...... 68 [91]
Tacoronte • Tenerife, Canary Is. 86 E1
Tacuarembó • Uruguay 44 E5
Tademaït, Plateau du • Algeria 20 F3
Tadjourah • Djibouti 21 H5
Tadmur • Syria 18 C3
Tadmur Heritage C • Syria ...... 64 [240]
Tadrart Acacus Heritage C • Libya ...... 63 [90]
Taebaek-Sanmaek • D.P.R. of Korea/Rep. of Korea 30 E6
Taegu • Rep. of Korea 30 E7
Taehan-Haehyop • Rep. of Korea 29 H4
Taehuksan • Rep. of Korea 30 C7
Taejon • Rep. of Korea 30 D6
Tafahi • Tonga 35 (2) F2
Tafassaset • Algeria 20 G4
Tafers • Switzerland 89 G2
Taff • United Kingdom 10 B2
Tafi Viejo • Argentina 44 C4
Tafilalt • Morocco 101 D6
Tafiré • Côte d'Ivoire 22 C3
Tafraoute • Morocco 101 D5
Taft, William Howard, Nat. Hist. Site Park • OH, United States ...... 121 [184]
Taftan, Kuh-e • Iran 18 H4
Taga Dzong • Bhutan 28 E3
Taganrog • Russian Fed. 17 F5
Tagant • Mauritania 20 C5
Tagbilaran • Philippines 31 G5
Tàggia • Italy 91 E9
Tagliacozzo • Italy 91 F2
Tagliamento • Italy 12 G2
Tagomago, I. de • Ibiza, Spain 87 G2
Tagounit • Morocco 20 D3
Taguersimet • Western Sahara 20 B4
Taguish Lake • YT, Canada 38 D4
Tagus • Portugal/Spain 89 H4
Tahan, Gunung • Malaysia 32 C2
Tahat • Algeria 20 G4
Tahiti • French Polynesia 33 M7
Tahoe, Lake • CA/NV, United States 117 F3
Tahoua • Niger 20 G6
Tahuna • Indonesia 32 (1) C2
Tai • Côte d'Ivoire 22 C3
Tai Hu • China 29 G5
Tai Lam Country Park • Hong Kong, China 107 H5
Tai Mo Shan • Hong Kong, China 107 H5
Tai Mo Shan Country Park • Hong Kong, China 107 H5
Tai O • Hong Kong, China 107 H5
Taï, Parc nat. de Heritage N • Côte d'Ivoire ...... 61 [75]
Taï, Parc nat. de Park • Côte d'Ivoire ...... 103 [19]
Tai Po • Hong Kong, China 107 H6
Tai Shan Heritage N • China ...... 61 [113]
Tai Shan Heritage C • China ...... 63 [151]
Tai Shan • China 29 F4
Tai Tam Country Park • Hong Kong, China 107 H6
Taibai Shan • China 29 D4
Taibilla, Sierra de • Spain 11 I6
Taicang • China 107 J2
Taichung • Taiwan 29 G6
Taigetos, Oros • Greece 15 D6
Taihape • New Zealand 112 K4
Taimba • Russian Fed. 26 Q5
Tainan • Taiwan 29 G6
Taipa • Macau 107 H1
Taipa Village • Macau 107 H1
Taipei • Taiwan 29 G6
Taiping • Malaysia 32 C2
Taiping • China 107 J3
Taiping Ling • China 29 G1
Taisetsu • Japan 30 L3
Taitao, Península de • Chile 45 B5
Taitung • Taiwan 29 G6
Taivalkoski • Finland 16 O4
Taiwan • Asia 29 G6
Taixing • China 107 J1
Taiyuan • China 29 E3
Taizhou • China 107 J1
Taizʻ • China 30 C4
Taj Mahal Heritage C • India ...... 63 [119]
Tajikistan • Asia 26 L10
Tajima • Japan 30 J6
Tajo • Spain 11 D5
Tajrish • Iran 18 F2
Tajumulco, Volcán • Guatemala 37 C4
Tajura • Libya 21 B1
Tak • Thailand 31 B3
Takahe, Mt • Antarctica 46 (1) DD2
Takamatsu • Japan 30 H7
Takaoka • Japan 30 I6
Takapuna • New Zealand 35 E3
Takasaki • Japan 30 J6
Take • Japan 30 F6
Take Lake • BC, Canada 38 F5
Takeo • Cambodia 108 B1
Takern • Sweden 95 F3
Takht-i-Bakhi Heritage C • Pakistan ...... 63 [112]
Takijuq Lake • NU, Canada 38 I3
Takingeun • Indonesia 110 B1
Takitimu Mtns • New Zealand 112 L1
Takli Makan Shamo • China 26 N10
Taklimakan Desert • China 107 G1
Takum • Nigeria 22 G3
Takutea • Cook Is. 33 L7
Talacre Beach • United Kingdom ...... 75 [200]
Talaion • Crete, Greece 93 E2
Talak • Niger 20 G5
Talamanca, Cordillera de Heritage N • Costa Rica ...... 60 [24]
Talara • Peru 43 A4
Talata Mafara • Nigeria 20 G6
Talaud, Kepulauan • Indonesia 35 H6
Talaud, Kepulauan • Indonesia 32 (1) C2
Talavera de la Reina • Spain 11 G5
Talbot, Mt • WA, Australia 34 E5

Talca • Chile 44 B6
Talcahuano • Chile 44 B6
Talcy [Château] • France 84 D2
Taldy-Kurgan • Kazakhstan 26 M9
Talence • France 10 E9
Talgar • Kazakhstan 26 M9
Taliabu • Indonesia 32 (1) B3
Taling Ngam Beach • Ko Samui, Thailand 109 J2
Talisajan • Indonesia 32 F2
Talisman Ski • OT, Canada ...... 116 [21]
Talitsa • Russian Fed. 17 N6
Tallahassee • FL, United States 119 M2
Tallinn • Estonia 16 M7
Tallinn Heritage C • Estonia ...... 64 [201]
Talmest • Morocco 20 D2
Talmont-St Hilaire Beach • France ...... 68 [64]
Talo • Ethiopia 23 F1
Taloqan • Afghanistan 28 A1
Taloyoak • NU, Canada 38 M3
Talpona Beach • Goa, India 105 B2
Taltal • Chile 44 B4
Tam • France 10 G10
Tamale • Ghana 22 D3
Taman Negara Nat. Park • Malaysia 108 A4
Taman Nuga Temple • Bali, Indonesia 110 C4
Tamanrasset • Algeria 20 G4
Tamanrasset [Riv] • Algeria 20 F4
Tamar • United Kingdom 74 F5
Tamarinda • Minorca, Spain 87 F3
Tamarugal, Pampa del • Chile 44 C2
Tamasag-Bulak • Mongolia 29 F1
Tamatave • Madagascar 24 H3
Tamaulipas • Mexico 37 B3
Tamazunchale • Mexico 123 E2
Tambacounda • Senegal 22 B2
Tambelan, Kepulauan • Indonesia 110 A2
Tambo • QL, Australia 111 F3
Tambo • Peru 127 B4
Tambo Colorado • Peru 127 B3
Tambora, Gunung • Indonesia 32 (1) A4
Tambre • Spain 11 C2
Tambunan • Malaysia 31 F5
Tambura • Sudan 23 D2
Tamchaket • Mauritania 20 C5
Tamdi Surla Temple • Goa, India 105 B1
Tame • Colombia 43 C2
Támega • Portugal 11 C3
Tamegroute • Morocco 101 D6
Tamel Aike • Argentina 45 B5
Tamenghest • Algeria 20 G4
Tamerza • Tunisia 101 E2
Tamgak, Mts • Niger 20 G5
Tamgue, Massif du • Guinea 22 B2
Tamiahua, Laguna de • Mexico 123 E2
Tamil Nadu • India 106 D7
Tamlingan, Danau • Bali, Indonesia 110 C2
Tammerfors • Finland 95 E2
Tammisaari • Finland 95 D3
Tämnaren • Sweden 95 D1
Tampa • FL, United States 119 M5
Tampa Bay • FL, United States 119 M5
Tampere • Finland 95 E2
Tampereen Sarkanniemi Oy Park • Finland ...... 73 [11]
Tampico • Mexico 123 E2
Tampin • Malaysia 108 D4
Tampines • Singapore 108 C2
Tamsweg • Austria 13 C10
Tamu • Myanmar 28 F3
Tamuda • Morocco 101 D2
Tamuin • Mexico 37 B3
Tamworth • NS, Australia 34 J6
Tamworth • United Kingdom 74 D2
Tan An • Vietnam 108 B3
Tan Son Nhat [Apt] • Vietnam 108 B1
Tan-Tan • Morocco 101 D5
Tana • Norway 16 O1
Tana • Kenya 16 O1
Tana, Lake • Ethiopia 21 G5
Tana [Riv] • Norway 16 N1
Tana River Primate Game Reserve • Kenya 101 G4
Tanabe • Japan 30 H8
Tanacross • AK, United States 38 C4
Tanafjorden • Norway 16 O1
Tanagro • Italy 12 J8
Tanah Lot Temple • Bali, Indonesia 110 C4
Tanah Rata • Malaysia 108 D1
Tanahbala • Indonesia 110 B4
Tanahgrogot • Indonesia 32 F3
Tanahmasa • Indonesia 110 B4
Tanami Desert • NT, Australia 34 F3
Tanami Desert Wildlife Sanctuary • NT, Australia 112 H1
Tanana • AK, United States 38 A4
Tanana [Riv] • AK, United States 38 A4
Tanargue, le • France 10 J9
Tânaro • Italy 91 E5
Tanch'on • D.P.R. of Korea 30 E4
Tandil • Argentina 127 D3
Tando Adam • Pakistan 28 A3
Tanega • Japan 30 F9
Tanezrouft • Mali/Algeria 20 E4
Tanezrouft-n-Ahenet • Algeria 20 F4
Tang Kem Bay • Phuket, Thailand 109 K2
Tanga • Kenya 23 F5
Tanga • Tanzania 102 H2
Tanga Is. • Papua New Guinea 35 (1) E1
Tangalla • Sri Lanka 106 D15
Tanganyika, Lake • Dem. Rep. of Congo/Tanzania 102 H3
Tanger • Morocco 101 D1
Tangermünde • Germany 8 G4
Tanggu • China 29 F3
Tanggula Shan • China 28 F2
Tangier • Morocco 101 D1
Tangier I. • VA, United States 118 H3
Tangkuban Perahu, Gunung • Java, Indonesia 110 D2
Tangra Yumco • China 28 E2
Tangshan • China 29 F3
Tania, la Ski • France ...... 70 [35]
Tanimbar Is. • Indonesia 25 O10
Tanimbar, Kepulauan • Indonesia 32 (1) B4
Tanjung Bunga • Penang, Malaysia 108 C1
Tanjung Malim • Malaysia 108 D1
Tanjung Tokong • Penang, Malaysia 108 C2
Tanjungbalai • Indonesia 110 B2
Tanjungpandan • Indonesia 32 D3
Tanjungpinang • Indonesia 32 C2
Tanjungredep • Indonesia 32 F2
Tanjungselor • Indonesia 32 F2
Tankwa-Karoo Nat. Park • South Africa 100 C5
Tanna • Vanuatu 35 (2) B2
Tannenberg • Poland 71 A9
Tannis Bugt • Denmark 95 F6
Tannu Ola • Russian Fed. 26 P7
Tanout • Niger 20 G6

Tantã • Egypt 101 F1
Tantallon Castle • United Kingdom 74 B4
Tanum Heritage C • Sweden ...... 64 [2]
Tanum • Sweden 95 F2
Tanzania • Africa ...... 102 H
Talabu • Indonesia 109 F3
Tao, Ko • Thailand 31 G4
Tao'er He • China 29 G1
Taormina Beach • Sicily, Italy ...... 69 [132]
Taormina • Sicily, Italy 90 D2
Taos Ski • NM, United States ...... 116 [105]
Taoudenni • Mali 20 E4
Taounate • Morocco 101 D2
Taourirt • Morocco 101 D2
Taouz • Morocco 20 E2
Tap Mun Chau • Hong Kong, China 107 H4
Tapa • Estonia 16 N7
Tapachula • Mexico 37 C5
Tapah • Malaysia 108 D1
Tapajós • Brazil 43 F4
Tapaktuan • Indonesia 110 B1
Tapanui • New Zealand 112 L4
Tapauá • Brazil 43 E5
Taphan Hin • Thailand 31 C3
Taphao Noi, Ko • Thailand 109 K2
Taphao Yai, Ko • Thailand 109 K2
Tapia de Casariego Beach • Spain ...... 68 [71]
Tapini • Papua New Guinea 35 (1) D2
Tapolca • Hungary 13 G11
Tappi-Zaki • Japan 30 K4
Tapti • India 28 B4
Tapul Group • Philippines 32 (1) B1
Tapuaé • Brazil 44 F4
Taquile, I. • Peru 127 B4
Tara • F.R. of Yugoslavia 14 G6
Tara • Russian Fed. 26 L6
Tara • Ireland 79 E1
Tara Nat. Park Park • Fed. Rep. of Yugoslavia ...... 72 [117]
Tara [Riv] • F.R. of Yugoslavia 14 G6
Taraba • Nigeria 22 G3
Tarabuco • Bolivia 44 D2
Tarabulus • Libya 21 B1
Taraclia • Moldova 14 P4
Taradale • New Zealand 112 K4
Tarakan • Indonesia 31 F5
Tarakan • Indonesia 32 F2
Tarakan [I.] • Indonesia 32 F2
Tarakan [Adm] • New Zealand 112 K3
Taranaki Bight, North • New Zealand 112 K3
Taranaki Bight, South • New Zealand 112 K3
Taranaki, Mt • New Zealand 112 K3
Tarangire Nat. Park • Tanzania 102 H2
Tarangire Nat. Park Park • Tanzania ...... 103 [92]
Taransay • United Kingdom 75 A1
Tarantaise • France 71 A13
Táranto • Italy 12 L8
Táranto, Golfo di • Italy 12 L8
Tarapoto • Peru 43 B5
Taraqua • Brazil 43 D3
Tararua Range • New Zealand 35 E5
Tarascon-sur-Ariège • France 85 K1
Tarasp-Vulpera • Switzerland 89 G4
Tarat • Algeria 20 G3
Tarata • Peru 127 B4
Tarauacá • Brazil 43 C5
Taravilla • Spain 11 I4
Taravo • Corsica, France 85 L3
Tarawa • Kiribati 33 I5
Tarawera, Lake • New Zealand 112 K2
Tarazona • Spain 11 J3
Tarazona de la Mancha • Spain 11 J5
Tarbagatay • Kazakhstan 26 N8
Tarbert • United Kingdom 6 E4
Tarbes • France 85 J2
Tarcoola • SA, Australia 34 F6
Tardienta • Spain 11 K3
Tardoki Yani, gora • Russian Fed. 27 M7
Taree • NS, Australia 34 J6
Tarentais • France 85 F2
Tarfa • Morocco 101 D5
Tarhankut, mys • Ukraine 17 E5
Tarifa • Spain 86 B6
Tarifa o Marroqui, Punta de • Spain 86 B6
Tarija • Bolivia 44 D3
Tariku • Indonesia 32 (1) E3
Tariku-Taritatu • Indonesia 32 (1) A3
Tarim • Yemen 18 E6
Tarim Basin • China 107 G1
Tarim He • China 26 N10
Tarim Pendi • China 26 N10
Tarin Kowt • Afghanistan 18 I3
Taritatu • Indonesia 32 (1) E3
Tarko-Sale • Russian Fed. 26 M5
Tarm • Denmark 95 F9
Tarma • Peru 43 B6
Tarma • Peru 127 B1
Tarn • France 10 H9
Tarn Hows • United Kingdom 74 C4
Tårnaby • Sweden 16 H4
Tarnobrzeg • Poland 13 J7
Tarnów • Poland 13 J8
Tårnsjö • Sweden 95 D1
Taro • Italy 12 E4
Taroom • QL, Australia 111 F5
Taroudant • Morocco 101 D5
Tarpon Springs • FL, United States 119 M5
Tarquínia • Italy 91 F1
Tarragona Beach • Spain ...... 68 [104]
Tarragona • Spain 87 D3
Tàrrega • Spain 11 K4
Tarrytown • NY, United States 118 H2
Tarso Emisou • Chad 21 C3
Tarsus • Turkey 18 B2
Tart • China 28 F1
Tartagal • Argentina 44 D3
Tartu • Estonia 16 N7
Tarutao, Ko • Thailand 32 B1
Tarutung • Indonesia 110 B4
Tarxien Temples • Malta 93 H4
Tasagil • Turkey 93 B2
Tasawaih • Libya 21 B2
Tash Kurgan • China 98 B2
Tash-Kumyr • Kyrgyzstan 18 J1
Tashauz • Turkmenistan 18 G1
Tashk, Daryachech-ye • Iran 18 F3
Tashkent • Uzbekistan 26 K9
Tashkepri • Turkmenistan 18 H2
Tashtagol • Russian Fed. 26 O7
Tasikmalaya • Java, Indonesia 110 D6
Tasinge • Denmark 8 F2
Tåsinge • Denmark 95 E3
Taskan • Russian Fed. 27 P4
Tasker • Niger 20 H5
Tasman • New Zealand 112 J3
Tasman Bay • New Zealand 35 D5
Tasman Sea • Australia/New Zealand 33 H9
Tasmania • TS, Australia 34 I8

Tasmanian wilderness Heritage N • TS, Australia ...... 61 [136]
Tasmanian wilderness Heritage C • Australia ...... 63 [183]
Tassa Takorat • Niger 20 G5
Tassara • Niger 20 G5
Tassili n'Ajjer Heritage N • Algeria ...... 61 [68]
Tassili n'Ajjer Heritage C • Algeria ...... 63 [91]
Tassili-Oua-n-Ahaggar • Algeria 20 G4
Tata • Hungary 13 H10
Tata • Morocco 20 D3
Tata Mailau • East Indies 32 (1) C4
Tataba • Indonesia 32 (1) B3
Tatabánya • Hungary 13 H10
Tataouine • Tunisia 101 E6
Tatarbunary • Ukraine 14 C4
Tatarsk • Russian Fed. 26 M6
Tatarskiy Proliv • Russian Fed. 17 I3
Tatarstan • Russian Fed. 17 I3
Tateyama • Japan 30 J7
Tathlina Lake • NT, Canada 38 H4
Tathlith • Saudi Arabia 18 D6
Tatilya Turizm Park • Turkey ...... 73 [87]
Tatilya Turizm • Turkey 92 D3
Tatnam, Cape • MN, Canada 39 M5
Tatry • Poland/Slovak Rep. 13 J8
Tatra • Poland ...... 72 [96]
Tatshenshini-Alsek Prov. Wilderness Park Heritage N • BC, Canada ...... 60 [1]
Tatuí • Brazil 127 C3
Taubaté • Brazil 127 C3
Tauberbischofsheim • Germany 9 E7
Tauchik • Kazakhstan 26 H9
Tauern, Hohe • Austria 89 H7
Tauern, Niedere • Austria 89 H8
Taufkirchen • Germany 82 J3
Taufstein • Germany 9 E6
Taumarunui • New Zealand 112 K3
Taungdwingyi • Myanmar 28 G4
Taunggyi • Myanmar 31 A3
Taungup • Myanmar 28 G5
Taunton • United Kingdom 74 E4
Taunus • Germany 82 H2
Taunus-Wunderland • Germany 82 H4
Taupiti Ski • Austria ...... 70 [181]
Taupo • New Zealand 112 K4
Taupo, Lake • New Zealand 112 K4
Taurage • Lithuania 13 L2
Tauranga • New Zealand 112 K3
Tauroa Point • New Zealand 35 D2
Tausuk • Russian Fed. 27 O5
Tauyskaya Guba • Russian Fed. 27 O5
Tavas • Turkey 15 K6
Tavas Ovasi • Turkey 15 K6
Tavda • Russian Fed. 26 J6
Tavda [Riv] • Russian Fed. 26 J6
Tavernes de la Valldigna Beach • Spain ...... 68 [102]
Tavestehus • Finland 95 E2
Taveuni • Fiji 35 (2) E2
Taviano • Italy 12 M9
Tavignano • Corsica, France 85 L2
Tavira Beach • Portugal ...... 68 [82]
Tavira • Portugal 88 E8
Tavira, I. de • Portugal 88 E8
Tavistock • United Kingdom 74 F5
Tavolara, I. • Sardinia, Italy 90 C2
Tavoy • Myanmar 31 B4
Tavropoú, Tehniti Limni • Greece 15 C4
Tavsanli • Turkey 15 K4
Taw • United Kingdom 74 F2
Tawakoni, Lake • TX, United States 119 K4
Tawangmangu • Java, Indonesia 110 D7
Tawau • Malaysia 32 F2
Tawitawi • Philippines 31 F5
Tawkar • Sudan 21 G4
Taxco • Mexico 123 E4
Taxila Heritage C • Pakistan ...... 63 [113]
Taxila • Pakistan 98 B5
Taxkorgan • China 98 B2
Tay • United Kingdom 74 B1
Tay, Firth of • United Kingdom 74 B1
Tay, Loch • United Kingdom 74 B1
Tay Ninh • Vietnam 108 B1
Tayga • Russian Fed. 26 O6
Taygonos, mys • Russian Fed. 27 R4
Taygonos, Poluostrov • Russian Fed. 27 R4
Tayinloan • United Kingdom 78 A2
Taylor • TX, United States 119 N3
Tayma • Saudi Arabia 18 C4
Taymyr Peninsula • Russian Fed. 26 R3
Taymyr, Poluostrov • Russian Fed. 26 S2
Taymyra • Russian Fed. 26 Q3
Taymyr(r) • Russian Fed. 27 J2
Tayshet • Russian Fed. 26 P6
Taytay • Philippines 31 F4
Taz • Russian Fed. 26 N4
Taz • Russian Fed. 101 D2
Tazovsky • Russian Fed. 4 Z3
Tbilisi • Georgia 17 G6
Tchad, Lac • Africa 21 B5
Tchin Tabardem • Niger 20 G5
Tchogha Zanbil Heritage C • Iran ...... 63 [107]
Tczew • Poland 13 H3
Te Ana-Au Caves • New Zealand 112 L1
Te Anau • New Zealand 112 L1
Te Anau, Lake • New Zealand 112 L1
Te Araroa • New Zealand 35 G3
Te Awamutu • New Zealand 112 K2
Te Kaha • New Zealand 35 D2
Te Kao • New Zealand 35 D2
Te Kuiti • New Zealand 112 K1
Te Puke • New Zealand 112 K1
Te Urewera Nat. Park • New Zealand 112 K2
Te Waewae Bay • New Zealand 112 L1
Te Wahipounamu-SW New Zealand Heritage N • New Zealand ...... 61 [141]
Teano • Italy 91 G1
Tebay • United Kingdom 74 C4
Tébessa • Algeria 101 E3
Tebingtinggi • Indonesia 110 B2
Téboursouk, Mts de • Tunisia 12 C12
Techirghiol • Romania 97 D2
Tecka • Argentina 45 B4
Tecomán • Mexico 123 E3
Tecuci • Romania 14 O4
Tedzhen • Russian Fed. 27 F4
Tedzhen [Riv] • Iran/Turkmenistan 18 H2
Tees • United Kingdom 7 J7
Tees Bay • United Kingdom 7 K7
Tefe • Brazil 43 E4
Tefenni • Turkey 93 B2

Tegal • Java, Indonesia 110 D2
Tegea • Greece 15 D6
Tegeh Koripan Temple • Bali, Indonesia 110 C2
Tegel • Germany 81 F1
Tegeler See • Germany 81 F1
Tegernsee • Germany 82 J7
Tegernsee Spa • Germany ...... 83 [258]
Teguas • Lanzarote, Canary Is. ...... 68 [94]
Tegucigalpa • Honduras 37 D5
Teguid • Niger 20 G5
Teguise Beach • Lanzarote, Canary Is. ...... 68 [94]
Teguise • Lanzarote, Canary Is. 87 E3
Tehek Lake • NU, Canada 38 M4
Tehi-n-Isser • Algeria 20 G3
Tehoru • Indonesia 32 (1) C3
Tehran • Iran 18 E2
Tehuantepec • Mexico 37 B4
Tehuantepec, Golfo de • Mexico 37 B4
Tehuantepec, Istmo de • Mexico 37 C4
Teiche, la • France 85 G3
Teide, Pico de • Tenerife, Canary Is. 86 E1
Teifi, Afon- • United Kingdom 7 H9
Teignmouth • United Kingdom 74 F5
Teignmouth Beach • United Kingdom ...... 75 [102]
Teisendorf • Germany 82 J4
Teixeira • Portugal 74 B1
Tejakula • Bali, Indonesia 110 C2
Tejo • Portugal 11 C5
Tejupan, Punta • Mexico 123 D4
Teke Burun • Turkey 15 H5
Tekeli • Kazakhstan 26 N10
Tekeze • Africa 21 G5
Tekiliktag • China 26 N10
Tekirdağ • Turkey 15 I3
Tekirova • Turkey 93 C2
Tekkeli Lake • NT, Canada 39 I4
Tekong, Pulau • Singapore 108 C2
Tel 'Arad • Israel 98 A7
Tel Ashqelon • Israel 98 A5
Tel Aviv • Israel 98 A5
Tel Bet Shemesh • Israel 98 A5
Tel Dan • Israel 98 A2
Tel Lakhish • Israel 98 A7
Tel Meggido • Israel 98 A4
Tela • Honduras 37 D4
Teladgama Plateau • India 106 D3
Telavi • Georgia 17 H6
Telc Heritage C • Czech Rep. ...... 64 [147]
Telc • Czech Rep. 96 C4
Telciu • Romania 14 L2
Tele • Gran Canaria, Canary Is. 86 E4
Telegraph Creek • BC, Canada 38 E5
Telemark • Norway 16 E7
Telemark Sommarland Park • Norway ...... 73 [2]
Telemark Sommerland • Norway 94 B3
Telen • Indonesia 32 F2
Telén • Argentina 44 C6
Telenesti • Moldova 14 P2
Telese • Italy 12 I7
Telford • United Kingdom 74 H6
Teli • Russian Fed. 26 P7
Tell Atlas • Algeria 4 K10
Tell Deir 'Alla • Jordan 98 A6
Tell el Amarna • Egypt 101 F3
Telluride Ski • CO, United States ...... 116 [101]
Telmessos • Turkey 92 D9
Telmessos • Turkey 92 D9
Telposiz, gora • Russian Fed. 17 J3
Telsen • Argentina 45 C4
Telsiai • Lithuania 13 L2
Teltow • Germany 81 F3
Teltowkanal • Germany 81 F3
Teluk Anson • Malaysia 108 D1
Teluk Bahang • Penang, Malaysia 108 C1
Teluk Bahang Forest Reserve • Penang, Malaysia 108 C1
Teluk Duyung • Penang, Malaysia 108 C1
Teluk Intan • Malaysia 108 D1
Teluk Kumbar • Penang, Malaysia 108 C1
Telukbetung • Indonesia 110 D1
Telukbutun • Indonesia 32 C2
Telukdalem • Indonesia 110 B3
Temanggung • Java, Indonesia 110 D7
Temara Plage • Morocco 101 D1
Témara • Morocco 101 D2
Tembeling • Malaysia 108 C4
Tembeling [Riv] • Malaysia 32 C3
Tembilahan • Indonesia 110 B3
Tembo • Angola 24 D5
Tembo, Mt • Gabon 22 G4
Teme Valley • United Kingdom 74 H6
Temerloh • Malaysia 108 D4
Temesvár • Romania 14 I4
Teminabuan • Indonesia 32 (1) D3
Temirtau • Kazakhstan 26 L7
Témiskaming • QU, Canada 122 B1
Temmler • United Kingdom 74 D1
Temora • NS, Australia 111 G1
Tempelhof [Apt] • Germany 81 F4
Tempio Pausania • Sardinia, Italy 12 D8
Templar Park • Malaysia 108 D4
Temple • TX, United States 119 N3
Templemore • Ireland 7 E9
Templetown Beach • Ireland ...... 68 [34]
Templin • Germany 8 H4
Templiner See • Germany 81 F3
Temuco • Chile 45 B3
Temuka • New Zealand 35 C7
Ten Degree Channel • India 28 F6
Ten Thousand Is. • FL, United States 119 M8
Tenali • India 106 D3
Ténaro, Akra • Greece 15 D7
Tenasserim • Myanmar 31 B4
Tenby Beach • United Kingdom 75 [148-149]
Tenby • United Kingdom 74 E2
Tendaho • Ethiopia 23 G1
Tende • France 10 M9
Tendrara • Morocco 101 D2
Ténéré • Niger 20 H5
Ténéré du Tafassasset • Niger 20 H4
Ténéré, Erg du • Niger 20 H4
Ténéré, Réserve du Heritage N • Niger ...... 61 [77]
Ténéré, Réserve du Park • Niger ...... 103 [5]
Tenerife • Canary Is. 86 E1
Ténès • Algeria 11 M8
Ténès, Cap • Algeria 11 M8
Tengchong • Indonesia 32 (1) A4
Tengkuala • Indonesia 32 (1) A4
Tengrela • Côte d'Ivoire 22 C2
Tenente • Dem. Rep. of Congo 24 D5
Tenke • Dem. Rep. of Congo 24 D5
Tenkeli • Russian Fed. 27 N3
Tenkodogo • Burkina Faso 20 F6
Tennant Creek • NT, Australia 34 F3
Tennessee • United States 119 L3
Tennessee [Riv] • United States 119 L3
Tenojoki • Finland 94 A3
Tenom • Malaysia 31 F5
Tenosique • Mexico 123 F4
Tentefield • NS, Australia 34 J5
Teófilo Otoni • Brazil 44 H2
Teos • Turkey 92 D5

Teos • Turkey 92 D5
Teotepec, Cerro • Mexico 37 A4
Teotihuacán Heritage C • Mexico ...... 62 [17]
Teotihuacán • Mexico 123 E2
Tepa • Indonesia 32 (1) C4
Tepic • Mexico 123 E1
Teplá • Czech Rep. 96 C1
Teplice • Czech Rep. 96 C1
Teposcolula • Mexico 123 E4
Tequila • Mexico 123 E1
Ter • Spain 87 D2
Ter Heijde • Netherlands 80 C3
Téra • Niger 20 F6
Teramo • Italy 91 F2
Terceira • Azores 88 B2
Tercero, Rio • Argentina 45 D2
Terengganu • Malaysia 31 C6
Teresina • Brazil 43 G3
Teresinha • Brazil 43 G3
Teresópolis • Brazil 127 C4
Teressa • India 28 F7
Terezin • Czech Rep. 96 C2
Tergnier • France 10 I4
Terhazza • Mali 20 D4
Termas de Río Hondo • Argentina 44 D4
Terme • Italy 12 E5
Termessos • Turkey 93 G1
Termez • Uzbekistan 18 I2
Términi Imerese • Sicily, Italy 12 H11
Términi Imerese, Golfo di • Sicily, Italy 90 D2
Terminille • Italy 12 G6
Termit, Massif de • Niger 20 H5
Térmoli • Italy 12 I7
Térmoli Beach • Italy ...... 69 [138]
Ternate • Indonesia 32 (1) C2
Ternezen • Netherlands 80 A10
Terney • Russian Fed. 27 M7
Terni • Italy 91 F1
Ternopil • Ukraine 17 D5
Terpeniya, mys • Russian Fed. 27 N7
Terpeniya, Zaliv • Russian Fed. 27 N7
Terra Firma • South Africa 24 C5
Terra Nova Nat. Park • NF, Canada 123 D4
Terracina • Italy 91 F4
Terralba • Sardinia, Italy. 12 C9
Terrassa • Spain 87 D3
Terre Adelie • Antarctica 46 (1) S3
Terre Haute • IN, United States 41 I4
Terre-Neuve, Bancs de • NF, Canada 39 T7
Terreiro da Luta • Madeira 88 C2
Terrell • TX, United States 119 N1
Tersakan Gölü • Turkey 15 N5
Terschelling Beach • Netherlands ...... 68 [47]
Terschelling • Netherlands 80 A3
Tersef • Chad 22 H2
Teruel • Spain 11 J4
Teruel Heritage C • Spain ...... 64 [75]
Tervola • Finland 16 M3
Teseney • Eritrea 21 G4
Tésero Ski • Italy ...... 70 [215]
Tésero • Italy 90 B3
Teshio • Japan 30 K2
Teshio [Mtn] • Japan 30 L2
Teshio [Riv] • Japan 30 L2
Teskraia • Tunisia 101 E1
Teslin • YT, Canada 38 E4
Teslin [Riv] • YT, Canada 38 E4
Tesovo-Netyl'skiy • Russian Fed. 97 E1
Tessalit • Mali 20 F4
Tessaoua • Niger 20 G6
Test • United Kingdom 5 B3
Testa, Capo • Sardinia, Italy 90 C2
Testa del Gargano • Italy 14 D8
Teste-de-Buch, la Beach • France ...... 68 [66]
Teste-de-Buch, la • France 85 G3
Testigos • Venezuela 43 E1
Têt • France 85 K2
Tetas, Punta • Chile 44 B3
Tete • Mozambique 24 B3
Teterow • Germany 8 H3
Teteven • Bulgaria 14 L7
Tétouan Heritage C • Morocco ...... 64 [213]
Tétouan • Morocco 101 D2
Tetovo • F.Y.R. of Macedonia 14 H7
Tettnang • Germany 82 H3
Teulada Beach • Spain ...... 68 [101]
Teulada • Spain 87 C2
Teulada, Capo • Sardinia 12 C10
Teutoburger Wald • Germany 8 D5
Teverya • Italy 12 G6
Tewkesbury • United Kingdom 74 D4
Texarkana • AR/TX, United States 119 N2
Texas • United States 40 G5
Texas City • TX, United States 119 N6
Texas Safari Wildlife Park • TX, United States 119 N3
Texel • Netherlands 80 A3
Texoma, Lake • OK/TX, United States 119 N1
Teya • Russian Fed. 26 P5
Teykovo • Russian Fed. 97 F4
Tha Chin • Thailand 109 H1
Thabana Ntlenyana • South Africa 24 D5
Thabazimbi • South Africa 24 D4
Thai Binh • Vietnam. 31 C3
Thailand • Asia 31 C3
Thailand, Gulf of • Thailand 109 F4
Thailand, Peninsular • Thailand 109 F4
Thalang • Phuket, Thailand 109 K1
Thale • Germany 8 G5
Thalith, Ash Shallal ath • Sudan 21 F4
Thames • United Kingdom 7 K10
Thames • New Zealand 35 E3
Thames Estuary • United Kingdom 7 L10
Thana • India 28 B5
Thanet, Isle of • United Kingdom 74 E2
Thanh Hoa • Vietnam 31 D3
Thani, Ash Shallal ath • Sudan 21 F4
Thanjavur Heritage C • India ...... 63 [129]
Thanjavur • India 106 D11

Thann • France 9 C9
Thannhausen • Germany 82 J2
Thar Desert • India/Pakistan 105 C1
Thar Ua • Phuket, Thailand 109 K1
Thargomindah • QL, Australia 34 H5
Thárros • Sardinia, Italy 90 C3
Thasi Gang Dzong • Bhutan 28 F3
Thassos Beach • Greece .... 69 [171]
Thássos • Greece 92 D1
Thássos • Greece 92 D1
Thássos • Greece 92 D1
Thássos [I.] • Greece 92 D1
Thássos [I.] • Greece 92 D1
Thaton • Myanmar 31 B3
Thatta Heritage C • Pakistan ..... 63 [110]
Thayetmyo • Myanmar 31 B3
The Dalles • OR, United States 117 E3
The Pas • MN, Canada 38 K6
The Potteries • Barbados 125 H1
Thebes Heritage C • Egypt ...... 63 [82]
Thebes • Egypt 101 F4
Thelle • France 85 E1
Thelon • NT/NU, Canada 38 K4
Theodore • QL, Australia 111 F4
Theódori, Agii • Crete, Greece ... 93 E1
Theológos • Thássos, Greece 15 F3
Theológos Beach •
    Rhodes, Greece .... 69 [187]
Theológos • Rhodes, Greece 93 F2
Thérain • France 5 F5
Thérèse, I. • Seychelles 106 F1
Thérma • Greece 15 G3
Thermaïkós Kólpos • Greece 15 D3
Thermí • Greece 92 D5
Thermí • Greece 92 D7
Thermia • Greece 92 D7
Thermisía Beach • Greece ...... 69 [161]
Thermisía • Greece 92 D7
Thermisía • Greece 92 D7
Thessalía • Greece 15 D4
Thessaloníki Heritage C •
    Greece .... 64 [175]
Thessaloníki • Greece 92 D1
Thessaloníki • Greece 92 D1
Thessaly • Greece 92 A1
Thessaly • Greece 92 A1
Thetford • United Kingdom 7 M9
Thetford Mines • QU, Canada 123 D6
Thethi Nat. Park Park • Albania .. 72 [125]
Thibodaux • LA, United States ... 118 K4
Thief River Falls •
    MN, United States 41 G2
Thierbach Ski • Austria .... 70 [147]
Thies • Senegal 22 A2
Thießow Spa • Germany .... 83 [281]
Thika • Kenya 101 G3
Thillot, le • France 9 B9
Thimphu • Bhutan 28 E3
Thinalio Beach • Corfu, Greece .. 69 [149]
Thio • New Caledonia 35 (2) B3
Thionville • France 10 L4
Thíra • Greece 92 D8
Thíra • Greece 92 D8
Thíra [I.] • Greece 92 D8
Thíra [I.] • Greece 92 D8
Thirlmere • United Kingdom 74 C2
Thiruvarur • India 106 D11
Thisted Beach • Denmark .... 68 [30]
Thisted • Denmark 95 F5
Thitu • South China Sea 31 E4
Thíva • Greece 15 E5
Thiviers • France 85 G2
Thoen • Thailand 31 B3
Thoiry, Parc zoologique de •
    France 85 E3
Tholen • Netherlands 80 A10
Thomas, Fort • St Kitts & Nevis .. 125 G1
Thompson • MN, Canada 38 L5
Thompson • BC, Canada 122 C3
Thompson Sound • New Zealand . 112 L1
Thomson • QL, Australia 34 H4
Thon Buri • Thailand 109 H1
Thon Buri floating market •
    Thailand 109 H1
Thong Krok, Laem •
    Ko Samui, Thailand 109 J2
Thonon-les-Bains • France 85 F2
Thorn • Poland 71 A9
Thoronet, Abbaye du • France ... 85 H3
Thorpe Park Park •
    United Kingdom .... 73 [35]
Thorpe Park • United Kingdom ... 74 E1
Thorpeness Beach •
    United Kingdom .... 75 [52]
Thorshavn • Faroe Is. 4 I4
Thouars • France 84 D3
Thrace • Greece/Turkey 14 N8
Thráki • Greece 15 H2
Thrakikó Pélagos • Greece 15 G3
Thredbo • NS, Australia 111 G4
Three Kings Is. • New Zealand ... 35 D2
Three Pagodas Pass •
    Myanmar/Thailand 31 B3
Three Points, Cape • Ghana 22 D4
Threlkeld • United Kingdom 74 C2
Thuburbo Majus • Tunisia 101 E2
Thuile, la Ski • Italy .... 70 [197]
Thuile, la • Italy 91 E1
Thuin • Belgium 5 K4
Thule • Greenland 36 K2
Thule, Mt • NU, Canada 39 P2
Thulhagiri • Maldives 106 E2
Thulusdhu • Maldives 106 E2
Thun • Switzerland 89 G2
Thunder Bay • OT, Canada 39 N7
Thuner See • Switzerland 89 G2
Thung Salaeng Nat. Park •
    Thailand 109 G4
Thung Song • Thailand 31 B5
Thung Yai-Huai Kha Khaeng Wildlife
    Sanctuaries Heritage N •
    Thailand .... 61 [123]
Thur • Switzerland 89 D9
Thüringen • Germany 9 F5
Thüringer Wald • Germany 9 F6
Thuringia • Germany 81 D3
Thurlestone Beach •
    United Kingdom .... 75 [119]
Thurn, Pass Ski • Austria .... 70 [159-160]
Thursday Island • QL, Australia ... 34 H2
Thurso • United Kingdom 6 I3
Thuy Duong • TX, Australia 108 B4
Thy • Denmark 95 F5
Thyborøn • Denmark 95 F5
Thyborøn-Harboør Beach •
    Denmark .... 68 [31]
Thyon 2000 • Switzerland 89 G6
Ti Tree • NT, Australia 112 H2
Ti-n-Alkoum • Algeria 20 G4
Ti-n-Tarabiné • Algeria 20 G4
Ti-n-Toumma • Niger 20 D5
Ti-n-Zaoâtene • Algeria 20 F4
Tianbaoshan • China 30 E3
Tianjin • China 29 F3
Tianjin [Adm] • China 107 G4
Tianjun • China 29 B3
Tianmu Shan • China 107 J3

Tianshui • China 29 D4
Tiaret • Algeria 20 F1
Tías Beach •
    Lanzarote, Canary Is. .... 68 [94]
Tías • Lanzarote, Canary Is. 87 E3
Tib, Ras el • Tunisia 101 E2
Tibati • Cameroon 22 G3
Tiber • Italy 91 F1
Tiberias • Israel 98 A4
Tiberias, Lake • Israel 98 A4
Tibério, Villa di • Italy 91 F4
Tibesti • Chad 21 C3
Tibet • Italy 28 E2
Tibet, Lake • FL, United States ... 121 C1
Tibet, Plateau of • China 107 G1
Tibidabo, Parque de Atracciones Park •
    Spain .... 73 [75]
Tibro • Sweden 95 F3
Tiburón • Mexico 40 D6
Tichit • Mauritania 20 D5
Tichitt Heritage C • Mauritania .. 63 [92]
Tichka, Tizi n • Morocco 20 D2
Tichla • Western Sahara 11 K4
Ticino • Switzerland 89 G7
Ticino [Riv] •
    Italy/Switzerland 91 E6
Ticul • Mexico 37 D3
Tidaholm • Sweden 95 F3
Tidjikja • Mauritania 20 C5
Tidra, I. • Mauritania 20 B5
Tiefenbronn • Germany 82 G6
Tiel • Netherlands 80 C4
Tielerwaard • Netherlands 80 C4
Tielongtan • China 28 C1
Tielt • Belgium 80 B2
Tien Shan • Asia 26 N9
Tiène • Côte d'Ivoire 22 C3
Tienen • Belgium 80 A15
Tieroko, Tarso • Chad 20 I4
Tierp • Sweden 95 E2
Tierpark Friedrichsfelde •
    Germany 81 F2
Tierra Amarilla • Chile 44 B4
Tierra del Fuego, I. Grande de •
    Argentina/Chile 45 C6
Tierradentro, Parque Arqueológico Nac.
    Heritage C • Colombia ...... 62 [44]
Tieté • Brazil 44 F3
Tiflet • Morocco 101 D1
Tifton • GA, United States 119 M3
Tiga • New Caledonia 35 (2) B3
Tigani, Hersónisos •
    Crete, Greece 93 E1
Tighina • Moldova 14 D3
Tigil • Russian Fed. 27 Q5
Tignes Ski • France .... 70 [31]
Tignes • France 85 F2
Tigre • Ecuador 43 B4
Tigris • Asia 18 D3
Tihamat • Saudi Arabia 18 D5
Tijuana • Mexico 40 C5
Tikal • Guatemala 37 D4
Tikal, Parque Nacional Heritage N •
    Guatemala .... 60 [20]
Tikhoretsk • Russian Fed. 17 G5
Tikhvin • Russian Fed. 97 E1
Tikitere • New Zealand 112 K2
Tiksi • Russian Fed. 27 K2
Tikus • Malaysia 10 K6
Til-Châtel • France 85 E2
Tiladummati-Miladummadulu Atoll •
    Maldives 106 E1
Tilburg • Netherlands 80 A11
Tilbury • United Kingdom 74 E1
Tileagd • Romania 14 J2
Tilemsi, Vallée du • Mali 20 F5
Tílichiki • Russian Fed. 27 S4
Tilisos • Crete, Greece 93 E7
Tillabéry • Niger 20 F6
Tillanchong • India 28 E2
Tímbedra • Mauritania 20 D5
Timber Ridge Ski •
    MI, United States .... 116 [143]
Timberline Ski •
    OR, United States .... 116 [48]
Timbuktu • Mali 20 I1
Timbuktu Heritage C • Mali .... 63 [93]
Timgad Heritage C • Algeria ... 64 [223]
Timimoun • Algeria 20 F2
Timișoara • Romania 14 I4
Timiris, Cap • Mauritania 20 B5
Timmendorf-Niendorf Spa •
    Germany .... 83 [28]
Timmernabben • Sweden 95 F8
Timmins • OT, Canada 39 O7
Timor • East Indies 32 (1) B4
Timor, Laut •
    Australia/Indonesia 25 N11
Timor Sea • Australia/Indonesia . 34 E2
Timote • Argentina 44 D6
Timpanogos Cave Nat. Mon. Park •
    UT, United States .... 120 [79]
Timpson • TX, United States 119 N4
Timrå • Sweden 16 I5
Timucuan Ecological & Hist. Preserve •
    FL, United States 119 M3
Timucuan Ecological & Hist. Preserve Park •
    FL, United States .... 121 [219]
Tin Can Bay • QL, Australia 111 F6
Tin Shui Wai • Hong Kong, China 107 H5
Tinaca, Kaap • Philippines 31 H5
Tinahely • Ireland 79 E4
Tinaztepe • Turkey 14 B7
Tíndari • Sicily, Italy 90 D2
Tíneo • Spain 20 D3
Tinerhir • Morocco 101 D4
Tinetto, I. del Heritage C •
    Italy .... 64 [119]
Tinghert, Hamadat • Libya 21 B2
Tinglev • Denmark 95 F13
Tingo María • Peru 43 B5
Tingsryd • Sweden 95 F12
Tinjil • Indonesia 110 D1
Tinker Field •
    United States 121 C2
Tinnoset • Norway 95 F2
Tinos, I. del Heritage C • Italy .. 64 [119]
Tinogasta • Argentina 44 C4
Tínos • Greece 92 D8

Tínos • Greece 92 D8
Tínos [I.] • Greece 92 D8
Tínos [I.] • Greece 92 D8
Tinou, Stenó • Greece 15 G6
Tintagel • United Kingdom 74 F4
Tintern Abbey • United Kingdom . 74 D3
Tipasa Heritage C • Algeria .... 64 [219]
Tipitapa • Nicaragua 37 D5
Tipperary • Ireland 7 D9
Tipperary • Ireland 7 E9
Tipperary • Ireland 79 E6
Tiracambu, Serra do • Brazil ... 45 (1) B2
Tiracol Fort • Goa, India 105 B1
Tiradentes • Brazil 127 C1
Tirana • Albania 14 G8
Tirana • Albania 14 G8
Tirano • Italy 91 E2
Tiraspol • Moldova 14 D3
Tire • Turkey 92 D6
Tire • Turkey 92 D6
Tiree • United Kingdom 6 F5
Tîrgoviste • Romania 97 D1
Tîrgu Jiu • Romania 14 K4
Tîrgu Mures • Romania 14 L3
Tîrgu Neamt • Romania 14 N2
Tírintha • Greece 15 D6
Tírnava Mare • Romania 14 M3
Tírnava Mica • Romania 14 L3
Tírnaveni • Romania 14 L3
Tírnavos • Greece 15 D5
Tírnovo • Bulgaria 71 A15
Tirol • Austria 89 H3
Tirrénia Beach • Italy .... 68 [125]
Tirrénia • Italy 91 F11
Tirso • Sardinia, Italy 90 C2
Tirstrup [Apt] • Denmark 95 F5
Tirtha Empul Temple •
    Bali, Indonesia 110 C2
Tiruchirappalli • India 106 D11
Tirukalikundram • India 106 D7
Tirumala • India 106 D7
Tirunelveli • India 106 D10
Tirupati • India 106 D10
Tiruppur • India 106 D10
Tiruvannamalai • India 106 D7
Tíryns • Greece 15 D6
Tisa • Europe 14 K1
Tisnaren • Sweden 95 D3
Tissemsilt • Algeria 11 M9
Tisvildeleje • Denmark 95 F6
Tísza • Hungary 13 J11
Tiszaföldvár • Hungary 13 J10
Tiszakecske • Hungary 13 J11
Tiszaújváros • Hungary 13 J11
Tit-Ary • Russian Fed. 27 K2
Titicaca, Lago • Bolivia/Peru ... 127 B4
Titisee • Germany 82 G8
Titisee Spa • Germany .... 83 [209]
Titlagarh • India 28 D4
Titov Veles •
    F.Y.R. of Macedonia 14 I8
Titov vrh • F.Y.R. of Macedonia . 14 H8
Titovo Užice •
    F.R. of Yugoslavia 14 G6
Tittmoning • Germany 82 J4
Titu • Romania 97 D1
Titus Mtn Ski •
    NY, United States .... 116 [185]
Titusville • FL, United States ... 119 M6
Titz • Germany 81 E3
Tivaouane • Mauritania 20 B6
Tiveden • Sweden 95 F3
Tiveden Nat. Park • Sweden ... 72 [26]
Tiveden Nat. Park • Sweden ... 95 F3
Tiverton • United Kingdom 74 F2
Tívoli Park • Denmark .... 73 [18]
Tívoli • Italy 91 F2
Tiwai I. Wildlife Sanctuary Park •
    Sierra Leone .... 103 [17]
Tiwi Beach • Kenya 101 G5
Tiya Heritage C • Ethiopia .... 63 [88]
Tizi Ouzou • Algeria 20 F1
Tiznit • Morocco 101 D3
Tjällmo • Sweden 95 F4
Tjeggelvas • Sweden 16 I3
Tjeukemeer • Netherlands 5 I2
Tjolöholm • Sweden 95 F6
Tjøme • Norway 94 B4
Tjørn • Sweden 95 F2
Tjust • Sweden 95 F8
Tlaxcala • Mexico 37 B4
Tlaxcala [Adm] • Mexico 37 B4
Tlaxco • Mexico 123 E4
Tlimsen • Algeria 20 (1) E4
Tnahmerah • Indonesia 32 (1) H4
Toamasina • Madagascar 24 H3
Toapoon, Ko • Thailand 109 J1
Toay • Argentina 44 D6
Toba, Danau • Indonesia 32 B2
Toba, Lake • Indonesia 110 B2
Toba Range • Pakistan 28 A2
Tobago • Trinidad & Tobago 125 K2
Tobelo • Indonesia 32 (1) C2
Tobercurry • Ireland 79 D3
Tobermory • United Kingdom 6 F5
Tobi • Palau 32 (1) D2
Toblach Ski • Italy .... 70 [237]
Toblach • Italy 90 B2
Toboali • Indonesia 32 D3
Tobol • Kazakhstan 26 J7
Tobol [Riv] •
    Kazakhstan/Russian Fed. ... 26 K6
Tobolsk • Russian Fed. 26 K6
Tobruk • Libya 21 D1
Tobseda • Russian Fed. 17 I1
Tocantins [Adm] • Brazil 45 (1) B4
Tocantins [Riv] • Brazil 45 (1) B4
Toco • Trinidad & Tobago 125 K2
Tocopilla • Chile 44 B3
Tod Mtn Ski • BC, Canada .... 116 [4]
Todd • NT, Australia 112 H4
Todi • Italy 91 E12
Todo-qa-Saki • Japan 30 L5
Todos os Santos, Baía de •
    Brazil 44 I1
Todra, Gorges du • Morocco 101 D4
Todtmoos Spa • Germany ..... 83 [205]
Todtnau • Germany 82 G8
Tödy • Switzerland 12 C2
Toekomstig Reservoir • Suriname . 43 J3
Toetoes Bay • New Zealand 112 L4
Töfsingdalen Nat. Park Park •
    Sweden .... 72 [22]
Tofte • Norway 94 B4
Toftlund • Denmark 95 F5
Tofua • Tonga 35 (2) E2
Toggenburg • Switzerland 89 D9
Togian, Kepulauan • Indonesia . 32 (1) B2
Togo • Africa 22 E4
Togwotee Pass •
    WY, United States 38 I8
Toi-Misaki • Japan 30 F9
Toijala • Finland 95 E2
Toivakka • Finland 95 E2
Tok • Japan 30 F6
Tokelau • Pacific Ocean 33 J6
Tokkevatn • Norway 94 B3

Tokmak • Kyrgyzstan 26 M9
Tokoroa • New Zealand 112 K2
Tokur • Russian Fed. 27 L6
Tokushima • Japan 30 H7
Tokyo • Japan 30 J7
Tokyo-Wan • Japan 30 J7
Tol'yatti • Russian Fed. 17 H4
Tolaga Bay • New Zealand 35 G4
Tolanáro • Madagascar 24 H5
Toleant • Mexico 123 E2
Toledo • Spain 11 G5
Toledo • OH, United States 11 J3
Toledo • Brazil 44 F3
Toledo Heritage C • Spain .... 64 [88]
Toledo Bend Reservoir •
    LA/TX, United States 118 K1
Toledo, Montes de • Spain 11 G5
Tolfa • Italy 91 F1
Tolfa, Monti della • Italy 91 F1
Toliara • Madagascar 24 G4
Tolimo • Colombia 43 B3
Tolitoli • Indonesia 32 (1) B2
Tollarp • Sweden 95 F11
Tolmezzo • Italy 13 H2
Tolmin • Slovenia 14 A3
Tolo • Dem. Rep. of Congo 22 H5
Tolo Beach • Greece .... 69 [161]
Tolo Harbour • Hong Kong, China 107 H6
Tolosa • Spain 11 I1
Tolstoy, mys • Russian Fed. 27 Q5
Toluca • Mexico 123 E4
Toluca, Nevado de • Mexico ... 123 E4
Tom Price • WA, Australia 34 C4
Tomakomai • Japan 30 K3
Tomar • Portugal 11 C5
Tomar Heritage C • Portugal .. 64 [96]
Tomaszow Lubelski • Poland .. 13 M7
Tomaszów Mazowiecki • Poland 13 J6
Tombôco • Angola 22 G6
Tombouctou • Mali 20 E5
Tombstone • AZ, United States . 118 J4
Tomé • Chile 44 B6
Tomé-Açu • Brazil 45 (1) B2
Tomelilla • Sweden 95 F11
Tomelloso • Spain 11 H5
Tomkinson Ranges •
    SA/WA, Australia 112 H3
Tommot • Russian Fed. 27 K5
Tomo • Colombia 43 C3
Tomorit • Albania 14 H8
Tomorri Nat. Park Park •
    Albania .... 72 [128]
Tompe • Indonesia 32 (1) A3
Tompo • Russian Fed. 27 M4
Tomsk • Russian Fed. 26 O6
Tonalá • Mexico 37 C4
Tonale, Passo del • Italy 91 E3
Tonbridge • United Kingdom 74 E3
Tondano • Indonesia 32 (1) B2
Tønder • Denmark 8 D2
Tender • Denmark 95 F13
Tonesai Falls •
    Phuket, Thailand 109 K1
Toney • Antarctica 46 (1) DD2
Tong Pha Phum • Thailand 31 B4
Tonga • Pacific Ocean 35 (2) E2
Tonga Trench • Tonga 35 (2) F2
Tongariro Nat. Park Heritage N •
    New Zealand .... 61 [140]
Tongariro Nat. Park •
    New Zealand 112 K4
Tongatapu • Tonga 59 A9
Tongatapu Group • Tonga ... 35 (2) E3
Tongchuan • China 29 D3
Tongeren • Belgium 5 I4
Tonghe • China 29 H1
Tonghua • China 29 H2
Tongjoson-man • D.P.R. of Korea 30 D5
Tongking • Vietnam 108 A1
Tongliao • China 29 F2
Tongling • China 29 F4
Tongoa • Vanuatu 35 (2) B2
Tongtian Hei • China 28 G2
Tongue • United Kingdom 6 H3
Tongue • MT/WY, United States . 38 J7
Tônisvorst • Germany 81 E1
Tonk • India 105 C6
Tonkin, Gulf of • China/Vietnam . 31 D2
Tonle Sap • Cambodia 31 C4
Tönning • Germany 8 D2
Tonopah • NV, United States ... 117 F4
Tønsberg • Norway 94 B4
Tonto Nat. Mon. •
    AZ, United States 118 J3
Tonto Nat. Mon. Park •
    AZ, United States .... 120 [111]
Tooele • ID, United States 40 D3
Toowoomba • QL, Australia 111 F6
Top End, The • NT, Australia ... 111 E2
Topçam Plaji • Turkey 93 G3
Topeka • KS, United States 41 G4
Topki • Russian Fed. 26 O6
Topko, gora • Russian Fed. 27 M5
Toplita • Romania 14 M3
Töplitz • Germany 81 F3
Topol'cany • Slovak Rep. 13 H9
Topolnica • Bulgaria 15 F1
Topolovgrad • Bulgaria 97 D3
Tor Bay • United Kingdom 74 F2
Tor Bay Beach • United Kingdom 75 [106-111]
Torbali • Turkey 15 I5
Torbat-e Heydarieh • Iran 18 G2
Torbat-e Jam • Iran 18 G2
Torblous • Lebanon 18 C3
Torcross Beach • United Kingdom 75 [114]
Tordesillas • Spain 11 G3
Töreboda • Sweden 95 F3
Toreghali • Spain 92 C3
Toreno • Spain 92 C3
Torgau • Germany 81 D3
Torgelow • Germany 81 C4
Torgon Ski • Switzerland ..... 70 [74]
Torhamn • Sweden 95 F12
Torhout • Belgium 80 B2
Tori • India 105 C8
Torino Heritage C • Italy ..... 64 [108]
Torino • Italy 91 E5
Torkovichi • Russian Fed. 97 E1
Tormes • Spain 11 F3
Tornado Ski • Sweden 16 K3
Torne älv • Sweden 16 K3
Torne-träsk • Sweden 16 J2
Torneå • Finland 16 J4
Tornesch • Germany 8 E3
Torngat Mtns • NF/QU, Canada . 39 S5
Tornio • Finland 16 M4
Tornionjoki • Finland 16 M3
Toro, Cerro del •
    Argentina/Chile 44 C4
Toro Muerto • Peru 127 B4
Törökszentmiklós • Hungary .. 13 J10
Toronto • OT, Canada 122 B9
Toropets • Russian Fed. 97 E1
Trápani • Sicily, Italy 90 D1
Toraalgon VI, Australia 111 G3
Tororo • Uganda 101 G1
Toros Daglari • Turkey 15 N7
Torquay • United Kingdom 74 F5
Torquay Beach •
    United Kingdom .... 75 [104-105]

Torralba • Portugal 88 E6
Torre Annunziata Heritage C •
    Italy .... 64 [128]
Torre Annunziata • Italy 91 G3
Torre de Areas • Portugal 88 E8
Torre de Carredo • Spain 11 G1
Torre de la Higuera • Spain 86 B1
Torre de Moncorvo • Portugal .. 11 E3
Torre del Greco • Italy 91 G3
Torre del Mar • Spain 86 B7
Torre-Pacheco • Spain 11 K7
Torreblanca Beach • Spain .... 68 [103]
Torredembarra Beach • Spain .. 68 [104]
Torredembarra • Spain 86 B3
Torrejoncillo • Spain 86 B3
Torrelles Beach • France ...... 68 [111]
Torrelavega • Spain 11 G1
Torremolinos Beach • Spain ... 68 [97]
Torremolinos • Spain 86 B7
Torrens Creek • QL, Australia .. 111 F3
Torrens, Lake • SA, Australia .. 34 G6
Torreón • Mexico 40 F6
Torres • Vanuatu 35 (2) B1
Torres Strait • Australia 34 H1
Torres Vedras Beach • Portugal 68 [80]
Tolo Beach • Greece .... 69 [161]
Torrevieja Beach • Spain 87 C3
Torrevieja • Spain 87 C3
Torridge • United Kingdom 74 F2
Torrox • Spain 86 B7
Torsby • Sweden 95 D3
Torshälla • Sweden 95 D3
Torsö • Sweden 95 F3
Tortola • British Virgin Is. 58 B7
Tortona • Italy 91 E6
Tortosa • Spain 11 L4
Tortosa, Cabo de • Spain 11 L4
Tortuga • Venezuela 43 D1
Toruguart • China 26 M9
Torul • Turkey 13 H4
Toruń Heritage C • Poland .... 64 [137]
Torup • Sweden 95 F7
Torver • United Kingdom 74 C4
Tory I. • Ireland 79 D1
Torzhok • Russian Fed. 97 E3
Toscana • Italy 91 E11
Toshka Depression • Egypt 101 F5
Toson Hu • China 28 G1
Töss • Switzerland 9 D9
Tossa de Mar Beach • Spain .. 68 [106]
Tossa de Mar • Spain 87 D4
Tossens Spa • Germany ..... 83 [52]
Tostado • Argentina 44 D4
Tosted • Germany 8 E3
Tosterön • Sweden 95 D3
Tostón •
    Fuerteventura, Canary Is. ... 87 E2
Totak • Norway 94 C6
Totana • Spain 11 J7
Totes • France 5 E5
Totland Bay Beach •
    United Kingdom .... 75 [173]
Totma • Russian Fed. 17 G2
Totnes • United Kingdom 74 F5
Totness • Suriname 43 F2
Totora • Bolivia 44 C2
Totoya • Fiji 35 (2) E2
Tottori • Japan 30 H7
Touba • Côte d'Ivoire 22 C3
Toubkal, Jebel • Morocco 101 D5
Tougan • Burkina Faso 22 D2
Touggourt • Algeria 20 F2
Tougué • Guinea 22 B3
Touïl • Algeria 20 F2
Toul • France 10 K5
Toulon • France 85 H3
Toulouse • France 85 G4
Toummo • Niger 21 B3
Toungoo • Myanmar 31 B3
Touquet-Paris-Plage, le •
    France 5 E4
Touraine • France 84 D4
Tourcoing • France 10 H3
Tourlan, Cabo • Spain 11 B1
Tourine • Mauritania 20 C4
Tourmalet, Col du • France 85 J2
Tournai • Belgium 80 A14
Touro Orongo Nat. Hist. Site Park •
    RI, United States .... 121 [338]
Touroparc • France 85 F1
Toury • France 10 G5
Toussoro • Central African Rep. . 23 C2
Toussuire, la Ski • France .... 70 [46]
Toussuire, la • France 85 F2
Touws • South Africa 100 C6
Touws River • South Africa 100 C6
Tovdal • Norway 94 C6
Townshend, Cape • QL, Australia 111 F4
Townshend I. • QL, Australia ... 111 F4
Townsville • QL, Australia 111 F1
Towton • United Kingdom 71 A7
Towuti, Danau • Indonesia .. 32 (1) J3
Toya • Japan 30 J6
Toyama • Japan 30 I6
Toyama-Wan • Japan 30 J6
Toyapadah • Indonesia 110 C4
Toyo'oka • Japan 30 H7
Toyohashi • Japan 30 J7
Tozeur • Tunisia 101 E3
Traben-Trarbach • Germany ... 82 H3
Traben-Trarbach Spa • Germany 83 [161]
Trablous • Lebanon 18 C3
Trabzon • Turkey 18 D1
Trafalgar, Cabo • Spain 86 B5
Tragaki Beach • Greece ...... 69 [151]
Tragaki • Greece 92 C3
Tragaki • Greece 92 C3
Traighli • Ireland 79 E6
Trail • BC, Canada 122 C4
Trakai Nat. Park Park •
    Lithuania .... 72 [147]
Tralee • Ireland 79 F5
Tralee Bay • Ireland 79 F5
Tramore • Ireland 7 E9
Tramuntana, Serra de •
    Majorca, Spain 87 H1
Tranås • Sweden 95 F4
Traneberg • Denmark 95 F4
Tranemo • Sweden 95 F7
Trang • Thailand 31 B5
Trangan • Indonesia 32 (1) D4
Trani • Italy 12 K7
Trans-Siberian Railway •
    Russian Fed. 96 A3
Transylvania • Romania 14 L3
Transylvanian Alps • Romania .. 13 J10
Tranum Strand • Denmark 95 F5
Trápani • Sicily, Italy 90 D1
Traralgon VI, Australia 111 G3
Trasimeno, Lago • Italy 91 E11
Trasvase, Canal de • Spain 11 I5
Traunland • Germany 82 G6

Traun • Austria 13 C9
Traun [Riv] • Austria 13 D9
Traunreut • Germany 82 J4
Traunsee • Austria 89 H4
Traunstein • Germany 82 J4
Travemünde • Germany 8 F3
Travemünde Spa • Germany .. 83 [29]
Travers, Mt • New Zealand 35 D5
Traverse City •
    MI, United States 41 I3
Travnik • Bosnia-Herz. 14 E5
Travo • Corsica, France 85 L4
Trbovlje • Slovenia 13 E11
Treasure Beach • Jamaica ... 124 C3
Treasure Cay • Bahamas 124 B1
Trebaluger • Minorca, Spain ... 87 F4
Trebinje • Bosnia-Herz. 81 F3
Trebeurden Beach • France ... 68 [60]
Trébeurden • France 84 C1
Trebic • Czech Rep. 96 C4
Trebisov • Slovak Rep. 13 K9
Trebizond • Turkey 98 B1
Trebon • Czech Rep. 96 C4
Trébrez Beach • France ...... 68 [60]
Trédrez • France 84 C1
Treetops Ski •
    United States .... 116 [131]
Trégastel Beach • France ..... 68 [60]
Trégastel • France 84 C1
Tregosse Is. • CL, Australia 111 F2
Tréguier • France 84 C2
Treinta y Tres • Uruguay 44 F5
Treis-Karden • Germany 82 H1
Trelew • Argentina 45 C4
Trelleborg • Sweden 95 F15
Tremblante, la Beach • France . 68 [65]
Tremblant, la • France 85 G1
Tremblant Ski • QU, Canada .. 116 [33]
Tremezzo • Italy 91 E2
Tremitti, Is. • Italy 81 F1
Tremmen • Germany 81 F1
Tremp • Spain 11 L2
Trencin • Slovak Rep. 13 H9
Trenque Lauquen • Argentina .. 44 D6
Trent • United Kingdom 75 A4
Trentino-Südtirol • Italy 91 E1
Trento • Italy 91 E1
Trenton • NJ, United States ... 118 H1
Trenton • OT, Canada 122 B6
Trepassey • NF, Canada 123 D4
Tres • Italy 10 G3
Tres Arboles • Uruguay 44 F5
Três Corações • Brazil 127 C1
Tres Esquinas • Colombia 43 B3
Três Lagoas • Brazil 44 G2
Três Marias, Repr êsa • Brazil . 44 G2
Tres Picos • Argentina 45 C4
Tres Puntas, Cabo • Argentina . 45 C5
Tres Zapotes • Mexico 123 E4
Tresaith Beach • United Kingdom 75 [173]
Tresta • F.Y.R. of Macedonia ... 15 C2
Treskavica • Bosnia-Herz. 14 F6
Treuchtlingen • Germany 82 H5
Treuer Range • NT, Australia .. 112 H1
Treviglio • Italy 91 E6
Trevinca, Peña • Spain 11 E2
Treviño • Spain 11 I2
Treviso • Italy 91 E8
Trevose Head • United Kingdom 74 F4
Trianda • Rhodes, Greece 93 F2
Triberg • Germany 82 G8
Triberg Spa • Germany ..... 83 [197]
Tricase • Italy 12 M9
Trichur • India 106 D10
Trier Heritage C • Germany ... 64 [40]
Trier • Germany 82 H3
Trieste Beach • Italy .... 69 [148]
Trieste • Italy 91 E8
Trieste, Golfo di •
    Italy/Slovenia 91 E8
Trieux • France 10 B5
Triglav • Slovenia 14 A3
Triglav Nat. Park Park •
    Slovenia .... 72 [107]
Trigno • Italy 14 B8
Trihonida, Limni • Greece 15 C5
Trikala • Greece 15 C5
Trikora, Puncak • Indonesia . 32 (1) E3
Trim • Ireland 79 E1
Trincomalee • Sri Lanka 106 D15
Trindade, I. da •
    Atlantic Ocean 19 B7
Trinec • Czech Rep. 13 H8
Trinidad • Bolivia 44 D1
Trinidad Heritage C • Cuba .. 62 [35]
Trinidad • Uruguay 44 F5
Trinidad & Tobago • West Indies 125 K
Trinidad, I. da • Brazil 127 A2
Trinitapoli • Italy 12 K7
Trinity • TX, United States 119 N4
Trinity Bay • NF, Canada 123 D4
Trinity Hills •
    Trinidad & Tobago 125 K4
Triomoto • Japan 30 F9
Tripoli • Greece 15 D6
Tripoli • Lebanon 18 C3
Tripoli • Libya 21 B1
Tripolitania • Libya 21 B2
Tripura • India 28 F4
Tristan da Cunha •
    Atlantic Ocean 19 C9
Trivandrum • India 106 D14
Trnava • Slovak Rep. 13 G9
Trobriand • Papua New Guinea . 35 (1) E2
Troglav • Croatia 14 D6
Trogir Heritage C • Croatia .. 64 [156]
Troglav • Bosnia-Herz. 14 D5
Tróia • Portugal 88 D2
Trois Fourches, Cap de •
    Morocco 101 D2
Trois-Rivières • QU, Canada ... 122 B4
Troisdorf • Germany 5 K4
Troitsk •
    Chelyabinsk, Russian Fed. .. 26 J7
Troitsk •
    Krasnoyarsk, Russian Fed. . 26 P6
Troitsko-Pechorsk •
    Russian Fed. 17 J2
Trollhättan • Sweden 95 F2
Trollhaugen Ski •
    WI, United States .... 116 [119]
Troms • Norway 16 J2
Tromsø • Norway 16 J2
Trondheim • Norway 16 F5
Trondheimsfjorden • Norway .. 16 F5
Trondøya • Norway 94 B1
Troódos • Cyprus 93 J3
Troódos Mtns • Cyprus 93 J3
Troódos region Heritage C •
    Cyprus .... 64 [200]

Troon **Beach** • United Kingdom . . . . 75 [1]
Tropea • Italy 12 J10
Tropical, Costa • Spain 86 B7
Trosa • Sweden 95 D4
Trossachs, The • United Kingdom . 74 B1
Trostberg • Germany 82 J4
Trotus • Romania 14 N3
Troussay [Château] • France 84 D2
Trout Lake • NT, Canada 38 G4
Trout Lake • OT, Canada 38 M6
Troutbeck • United Kingdom 74 C4
Troutbeck • Zimbabwe 102 J2
Trouville-sur-Mer • France 10 F4
Trowbridge • United Kingdom 74 F3
Trowulan • Java, Indonesia 110 D8
Troy • AL, United States 41 I5
Troy • Turkey 92 D2
Troy • Turkey 92 D2
Troyan • Bulgaria 14 L7
Troyes • France 10 J5
Trujillo • Spain 11 F5
Trujillo • Peru 43 B5
Trujillo • Venezuela 43 C2
Truman, Harry S., Nat. Hist. Site **Park** •
   MO, United States . . . . 121 [173]
Trundholm **Beach** • Denmark . . . . 68 [24]
Trung Phan • Vietnam 31 D3
Truro • United Kingdom 7 H5
Truro • NS, Canada 123 D7
Truth or Consequences •
   NM, United States 118 J4
Trutnov • Czech Rep. 96 C2
Truva • Greece 92 D2
Truva • Greece 92 D2
Tryavna • Bulgaria 97 D3
Trysilelva • Norway 16 G6
Trzcianka • Poland 13 F4
Tsabong • Botswana 24 C5
Tsambika • Rhodes, Greece 93 F2
Tsangaráda **Beach** • Greece . . . . 69 [165]
Tsarkoye Selo • Russian Fed. 97 E1
Tsau • Botswana 24 C4
Tsavo • Kenya 23 F4
Tsavo East Nat. Park • Kenya 101 G4
Tsavo Nat. Park • Kenya . . . . . . 103 [85]
Tsavo West Nat. Park • Kenya 101 G4
Tseung Kwan O •
   Hong Kong, China 107 H6
Tshane • Botswana 24 C4
Tshikapa • Dem. Rep. of Congo . . . 23 C5
Tshuapa • Dem. Rep. of Congo . . . 23 C4
Tshwaane • Botswana 24 C4
Tsiafajavona • Madagascar 24 H3
Tsim Sha Tsui •
   Hong Kong, China 107 H6
Tsimlyanskoye Vdkhr. •
   Russian Fed. 17 G5
Tsing Yi • Hong Kong, China 107 H5
Tsingy Bemaraha, Réserve de **Heritage N** •
   Madagascar . . . . 61 [98]
Tsiroanomandidy • Madagascar . . . 24 H3
Tsitsikamma Mtns • South Africa . 100 C7
Tsitsikamma Nat. Park •
   South Africa 100 C7
Tsodilo Hills • Botswana 24 C3
Tsetsserleg • Mongolia 29 C1
Tsu • Japan 30 J7
Tsuchiura • Japan 30 I7
Tsuen Wan • Hong Kong, China . . 107 H5
Tsugaru-Kaikyo • Japan 30 K4
Tsumeb • Namibia 24 B3
Tsurugi • Japan 30 J5
Tsuruoka • Japan 30 J5
Tsushima • Japan 30 E7
Tsushima-Kaikyo • Japan 30 E8
Tsuyama • Japan 30 G7
Tua • Portugal 11 D3
Tual • Indonesia 32 (1) D4
Tuam • Ireland 79 F4
Tuamotu • French Polynesia 33 M7
Tuapse • Russian Fed. 17 E6
Tuas • Singapore 108 L1
Tuatapere • New Zealand 112 L3
Tuba City • AZ, United States 118 J1
Tubai Is. • French Polynesia 33 L8
Tuban • Java, Indonesia 110 D3
Tubarão • Brazil 44 D4
Tubayq, Jabal at • Saudi Arabia . . 21 G2
Tubbataha Reef Marine Park **Heritage N** •
   Philippines . . . . 61 [124]
Tübingen • Germany 82 G6
Tubize • Belgium 5 H4
Tubruq • Libya 21 D1
Tubuai • French Polynesia 33 M8
Tuchola • Poland 13 G4
Tucson • AZ, United States 118 J3
Tucumcari • NM, United States . . . 40 F4
Tucupita • Venezuela 43 E2
Tucurui, Reprêsa de • Brazil . . . 45 (1) B2
Tudela • Spain 11 J2
Tuen Mun • Hong Kong, China . . . 107 H5
Tufi • Papua New Guinea 35 (1) D2
Tugela • South Africa 100 B2
Tuguegarara • Philippines 31 G3
Tugur • Russian Fed. 27 M6
Tuineje •
   Fuerteventura, Canary Is. 87 E2
Tuk Tuk • Indonesia 110 B2
Tukangbesi, Kepulauan •
   Indonesia 32 (1) B4
Tuktoyaktuk • NT, Canada 38 E3
Tukums • Latvia 16 L8
Tula • Mexico 123 E2
Tulamben • Bali, Indonesia 17 F4
Tulancingo • Mexico 123 E2
Tulayat al Ghassul • Jordan 98 A6
Tulbagh • South Africa 100 B2
Tulcan • Colombia 43 B3
Tulcea • Romania 97 D2
Tuli, Fort • Zimbabwe 102 J3
Tulla • Ireland 79 F6
Tullamarine [Apt] •
   VI, Australia 111 G3
Tullamore • Ireland 7 E8
Tulle • France 85 G2
Tullow • Ireland 79 E3
Tully • QL, Australia 111 F1
Tuloma • Russian Fed. 16 Q2
Tulovo • Bulgaria 97 D3
Tulsa • OK, United States 41 G4
Tulsk • Ireland 79 F2
Tuluá • Colombia 43 B3
Tulum • Mexico 37 D3
Tulum **Beach** • Mexico 26 R7
Tulungagung • Java, Indonesia . . 110 D7
Tumacacori Nat. Mon. •
   AZ, United States 118 J3
Tumacacori Nat. Mon. **Park** •
   AZ, United States . . . . 120 [115]
Tumaco • Colombia 43 B3
Tumbes • Peru 43 A4
Tumen • China 30 E3
Tumen [Riv] •
   China/D.P.R. of Korea 30 F3
Tumkur • India 106 D6

Tummel • United Kingdom 74 B1
Tumucumaque, Serra • Brazil 43 G3
Tun • Sweden 95 F3
Tun Chung • Hong Kong, China . . 107 H5
Tunapuna • Trinidad & Tobago . . 125 K3
Tunas de Zaza • Cuba 124 D2
Tunduma • Tanzania 102 H3
Tunduru • Tanzania 102 H4
Tundzha • Bulgaria 14 N7
Tunel •
   Hong Kong, China 107 H6
Tung Ling Chau •
   Hong Kong, China 107 H6
Tungabhadra • India 106 D2
Tungelsta • Sweden 95 D4
Tunis **Heritage C** • Tunisia . . . . 64 [226]
Tunis • Tunisia 101 E2
Tunis, Golfe de • Tunisia 101 E2
Tunisia • Africa . . . . 101 E
Tunja • Colombia 43 C2
Tunnsjøen • Norway 16 G4
Tunxi • China 107 J3
Tuostakh • Russian Fed. 27 M3
Tupã • Brazil 44 F3
Tupanciretã • Brazil 44 F4
Tupelo Nat. Battlefield **Park** •
   MS, United States . . . . 121 [202]
Tupiza • Bolivia 44 C3
Tupungato, Cerro • Argentina 44 C5
Tuquan • China 27 J7
Túquerres • Colombia 43 B3
Túr, El • Egypt 101 F4
Tura • Russian Fed. 26 R5
Turabah • Saudi Arabia 18 D4
Turabah • Saudi Arabia 18 D4
Turan • Russian Fed. 26 P7
Turana, Khrebet • Russian Fed. . . 27 L6
Turangi • New Zealand 112 K4
Turayf, At • Saudi Arabia 18 C3
Turbah, At • Yemen 21 F5
Turballe, la **Beach** • France . . . 68 [63]
Turballe, la • France 84 C4
Turbat • Pakistan 18 H4
Turbo • Colombia 43 B2
Turda • Romania 14 K3
Turek • Poland 13 H5
Turenne • France 85 G2
Turfan • China 98 B3
Turgay • Kazakhstan 26 J8
Turgay Basin • Kazakhstan 96 A3
Turgayskoye Plato • Kazakhstan . . 26 J7
Turgovishte • Bulgaria 97 D3
Turgut • Turkey 15 M5
Turgutlu • Turkey 15 I5
Turia • Spain 11 K5
Turiaçu, Baía de • Brazil 45 (1) C2
Turimiquire • Venezuela 43 E2
Turin **Heritage C** • Italy . . . . . . 64 [108]
Turin • Italy 91 E5
Turinsk • Russian Fed. 26 J6
Turkana • Africa 23 F3
Turkana, Lake • Kenya 101 G1
Turkestan • Kazakhstan 26 K9
Turkey • Asia/Europe 4 R8
Turkey Creek • WA, Australia 34 E3
Turkmenbashi • Turkmenistan 18 F1
Turkmenistan • Asia 26 I10
Turks & Caicos Is. •
   West Indies 37 G3
Turku • Finland 95 E3
Turku Archipelago • Finland 95 E3
Turkwel • Kenya 101 G1
Turnagain, Cape • New Zealand . . 35 F5
Turneffe • Belize 37 D4
Turner's Hall Woods • Barbados . . 125 I1
Turnhout • Belgium 80 A11
Turnov • Czech Rep. 96 C2
Turnu Magurele • Romania 14 L6
Turoa • New Zealand 112 K4
Turpan • China 26 Q9
Turpan Depression • China 26 P9
Turquino, Pico • Cuba 124 D8
Turquoise Coast • Turkey . . . . 93 G
Turtkul • Uzbekistan 18 H1
Turtle I. • Bali, Indonesia 110 C4
Turtle I. • CL, Australia 111 F2
Turukhansk • Russian Fed. 26 O4
Turun Ja Pori • Finland 95 E3
Turuntu • Turkey 92 D9
Turunç • Turkey 92 D9
Tuscaloosa • AL, United States . . . 41 I5
Tuscania • Italy 91 F1
Tuscany • Italy 90 A1
TusenFryd **Park** • Norway . . . . . . 73 [4]
TusenFryd • Norway . . . . 73 [4]
Tuskegee Institute Nat. Hist. Site **Park** •
   AL, United States . . . . 121 [204]
Tuticorin • India 106 D11
Tutóia • Brazil 45 (1) C2
Tuttlingen • Germany 82 G8
Tutuala • East Indiea 32 (1) C4
Tutuila • American Samoa 35 (2) F1
Tutupaca, Volcán • Peru 44 C3
Tuul • Mongolia 27 G7
Tuva • Russian Fed. 26 G7
Tuvalu • Pacific Ocean 33 I6
Tuvana-i-Ra • Fiji 35 (2) E3
Tuvana-i-Tholo • Fiji 35 (2) D3
Tuwayq, Jabal • Saudi Arabia 18 E5
Tuxpán • Mexico 37 (1) A1
Tuxpan • Mexico 123 E2
Tuxtla Gutiérrez • Mexico 37 C4
Tuy • France 11 C2
Tuy Hoa • Vietnam 31 D5
Tuz Gölü • Turkey 15 O5
Tuz, Lake • Turkey 92 A3
Tuz, Lake • Turkey 92 A3
Tuzigoot Nat. Mon. •
   AZ, United States 118 J1
Tuzigoot Nat. Mon. **Park** •
   AZ, United States . . . . 120 [108]
Tuzla • Bosnia-Herz. 14 F5
Tuzlata • Bulgaria 97 D4
Tvedestrand • Norway 95 F1
Tverrfjell • Norway 94 E4
Tver' • Russian Fed. 97 E1
Tverfjellet • Norway 94 C2
Tvertsa • Russian Fed. 97 E3
Tvøroyri • Faroe Is. 15 G1
Tweed • United Kingdom 74 C4
Tweedsmuir Prov. Park •
   BC, Canada 122 C1
Twelve Apostles, The •
   VI, Australia 111 G3
Twelve Bens • Ireland 79 F3
Twente [Apt] • Netherlands 80 A8
Twilight Cove • WA, Australia 34 E6
Twin Falls • ID, United States . . . 117 E4
Twin Peaks • UT, United States . . 116 B
Twistringen • Germany 8 D4
Two Thumb Range • New Zealand . 35 C6
Twycross • United Kingdom 74 D2
Txiki Park **Park** • Spain . . . . 73 [77]
Tychy • Poland 13 H7
Tygda • Russian Fed. 27 K6
Tyin • Norway 94 C4
Tyler • TX, United States 119 N2

Tylösand • Sweden 95 F11
Tylskog • Sweden 95 F4
Tym • Russian Fed. 26 N6
Tymovskoye • Russian Fed. 46 A4
Tynda • Russian Fed. 27 J5
Tyndrum • United Kingdom 74 B1
Tyne • United Kingdom 7 K7
Tynemouth • United Kingdom 7 K6
Tynemouth **Beach** •
   United Kingdom . . . . 75 [21-22]
Tynset • Norway 16 F5
Typhoon Lagoon •
   FL, United States 121 C1
Tyre • Lebanon 98 A1
Tyrella **Beach** • United Kingdom 75 [227]
Tyrifjorden • Norway 94 B1
Tyrrhenian Sea •
   Mediterranean Sea 12 G9
Tyrresnøy • Norway 94 C5
Tyssedal • Norway 94 C4
Tystberga • Sweden 95 D3
Tyukalinsk • Russian Fed. 26 L6
Tyulenovo • Bulgaria 97 D4
Tyumen • Russian Fed. 26 K6
Tywi, Afon • United Kingdom 7 I10
Tywyn • United Kingdom 7 H9
Tywyn **Beach** • United Kingdom 75 [186]
Tzermiádo • Crete, Greece 93 E7

Uaroo • WA, Australia 34 C4
Uaupés • Brazil 43 D4
Ubá • Brazil 127 C2
Ubaitaba • Brazil 44 I1
Ubangi • Dem. Rep. of Congo 23 B3
Ubatuba • Brazil 127 C3
Ubayyid, Al • Sudan 21 F5
Ube • Japan 30 F8
Ubeda • Spain 11 H6
Ubekendt Ejland • Greenland 39 U2
Uberaba • Brazil 44 G2
Uberlândia • Brazil 44 G2
Uberlingen • Germany 82 J5
Überlingen **Spa** • Germany . . . . 83 [212]
Ubin • Singapore 108 E2
Ubiña, Peña • Spain 11 F1
Ubon Rat Reservoir • Thailand . . 109 F2
Ubon Ratchathani • Thailand 31 C3
Ubstadt-Weiher • Germany 9 D7
Ubsu-Nur • Mongolia 26 P8
Ubud • Bali, Indonesia 110 C4
Ubundu • Dem. Rep. of Congo . . . 23 D4
Ucayali • Peru 43 C5
Uchami • Russian Fed. 26 Q5
Uchiura-Wan • Japan 30 K3
Uchte • Germany 8 D4
Ückeritz **Spa** • Germany . . . . . 83 [284]
Uckermark • Germany 8 I3
Uçpinar • Turkey 93 G2
Udachnyy • Russian Fed. 26 T4
Udaipur • India 105 C5
Udayapur • India 105 C7
Uddevalla • Sweden 95 F2
Uddjaure • Sweden 16 I4
Udgir • India 28 C5
Udhagamandalam • India. 106 D10
Udine • Italy 91 E4
Udmurtia • Russian Fed. 17 I3
Udon Thani • Thailand 31 C3
Udskaya Guba • Russian Fed. 27 M5
Udupi • India 106 D6
Ueberisi • Indonesia 32 (1) B3
Uecker • Germany 8 J3
Ueckermünde • Germany 8 J3
Ueda • Japan 30 J6
Uele • Dem. Rep. of Congo 23 C3
Uelen • Russian Fed. 27 X3
Uelzen • Germany 8 F4
Uetze • Germany 8 F4
Ufa • Russian Fed. 17 J4
Ufa [Riv] • Russian Fed. 26 I6
Ugab • Namibia 24 A4
Uganda • Africa 23 E3
Ugine • France 85 J2
Uglekamensk • Russian Fed. 30 G3
Uglian Pasman • Croatia 14 C5
Uglich • Russian Fed. 97 E4
Uherské Hradiste • Czech Rep. . . . 13 G8
Uhlava • Czech Rep. 96 C3
Uig • United Kingdom 6 F4
Uige • Angola 23 B5
Uitenhage • South Africa 100 C8
Uithoorn • Netherlands 80 C2
Uithuizen • Netherlands 80 A4
Ujfehértó • Hungary 13 K10
Uji-Gunto • Japan 30 E9
Ujjain • India 28 C4
Ujung • Bali, Indonesia 110 C4
Ujung Kulon Nat. Park **Heritage N** •
   Indonesia . . . . 61 [125]
Ujung Pandang • Indonesia . . . 32 (1) A4
Ukhta • Russian Fed. 17 I2
Ukiah • CA, United States 40 B4
Ukmerge • Lithuania 13 N2
Ukraine • Europe 15 E4
Uku • Russian Fed. 27 I4
Ulá, Al • Saudi Arabia 18 C4
Ulaanbaatar • Mongolia 27 G2
Ulaangom • Mongolia 26 P8
Ulan Bator • Mongolia 27 G2
Ulan Ude • Russian Fed. 27 G6
Ulan Tajga • Mongolia 27 G6
Ulan Uul Hu • China 28 F2
Ulanhad • China 29 F2
Ular • Singapore 108 E3
Ulàssai • Sardinia, Italy 90 C4
Ulchin • Rep. of Korea 30 E6
Ulcinj • F.R. of Yugoslavia 15 A2
Ule älv • Finland 16 M4
Uleåborg • Finland 16 M4
Ulefoss • Norway 94 B3
Ulfborg • Denmark 95 F9
Ulfborg-Vemb **Beach** • Denmark . 68 [31]
Ulgiy • Mongolia 26 P8
Ulhasnagar • India 28 B5
Uliastay • Mongolia 26 Q8
Ulja • Marshall Is. 33 I5
Ullapool • United Kingdom 6 G4
Ullared • Sweden 95 F7
Ulldecona • Spain 11 L4
Ullswater • United Kingdom 74 C2
Ullung do • Rep. of Korea 30 H6
Ulm • Germany 82 J1
Ulmen • Germany 82 H1
Ulricehamn • Sweden 95 F7
Ulsan • Rep. of Korea 30 E7
Ulsteinvik • Norway 94 C1
Ulster • Ireland/UK 7 E5
Ulu • Russian Fed. 92 D6
Ulu • Russian Fed. 27 L4
Ulu Watu Temple •
   Bali, Indonesia 110 C4
Uluabat Gölü • Turkey 92 D3
Uluabat Gölü • Turkey 92 D3
Ulubey • Turkey 15 K5
Uludag • Turkey 92 D3

Uludag • Turkey 92 D3
Uluguru Mtns • Tanzania 23 F5
Ulundi • South Africa 100 B1
Uluru • NT, Australia 112 H3
Uluru-Kata Tjuta Nat. Park **Heritage N** •
   NT, Australia . . . . 61 [132]
Uluru-Kata Tjuta Nat. Park **Heritage C** •
   Australia . . . . 63 [181]
Uluru-Kata Tjuta Nat. Park •
   NT, Australia 112 H3
Ulus Dag • Turkey 15 J4
Ulverston • United Kingdom 74 C4
Ulverstone • TS, Australia 34 I8
Ulvik • Norway 94 C4
Ulya • Russian Fed. 27 N5
Ulytau • Kazakhstan 26 K8
Uman • Ukraine 17 E5
Umánarssuaq • Greenland 39 W5
Umba • Russian Fed. 17 E1
Umbrbey • Turkey 15 H3
Umbria • Italy 12 G6
Ume älv • Sweden 16 J4
Umeå • Sweden 16 K5
Umm ar Rasan • Libya 21 D1
Umm as Samim • Oman 18 G5
Umm Durman • Sudan 21 F4
Umm Lajj • Saudi Arabia 18 C4
Umm Qasr • Iraq 26 K8
Umnak I. • AK, United States 36 (1) C2
Umtata • South Africa 24 D6
Umuarama • Brazil 44 F3
Umurbaba Dagi • Turkey 15 J5
Umurbey • Turkey 15 H3
Una • Bosnia-Herz. 14 D5
Unalaska • AK, United States . . . 36 (1) C2
Unayzah • Saudi Arabia 18 D4
Uncompahgre Peak •
   CO, United States . . . . 116 A
Undandita • NT, Australia 112 H1
Undre • Norway 94 C4
Undredal • Norway 94 C4
Undu Point • Fiji 35 (2) D2
Ungava, Baie d' • QU, Canada . . . 39 R5
Ungava Peninsula • QU, Canada . . 39 Q4
Ungava, Péninsule d' •
   QU, Canada 39 Q4
Unggi • D.P.R. of Korea 30 F3
Ungheni • Moldova 14 O2
Ungwana Bay • Kenya 101 G4
União da Vitória • Brazil 44 F4
Unicov • Czech Rep. 13 G8
Unije • Croatia 14 B5
Unimak • AK, United States 36 (1) C2
Union, Fort, Nat. Mon. **Park** •
   NM, United States . . . . 120 [131]
Uniondale • South Africa 100 C7
United Arab Emirates • Asia 18 F5
United Kingdom • Europe 6/7
United States • N. America 36
Unity • SA, Canada 38 J6
Universal Studios Florida •
   FL, United States 121 C2
Universal Studios Hollywood **Park** •
   CA, United States . . . . 120 [E]
Universales, Montes • Spain 11 J4
Unna • Russian Fed. 5 K3
Unna • Germany 81 E2
Unst • United Kingdom 6 L1
Unstrut • Germany 9 F5
Unter Engadin • Switzerland 89 G4
Unteres Odertal, Nationalpark **Park** •
   Germany/Poland . . . . 72 [61]
Unterfranken • Germany 9 E7
Unterinntal • Austria 89 H3
Unterwasser • Switzerland 89 G3
Unzha • Russian Fed. 17 G3
Uozu • Japan 30 J6
Upala • Costa Rica 43 E2
Upemba, Parc nat. de l' **Park** •
   Dem. Rep. of Congo . . . . 103 [59]
Upernavik • Greenland 39 T2
Upin • Indonesia 32 (1) C3
Upington • South Africa 24 C5
Uplands [Apt] • OT, Canada 122 B7
Upolu • Western Samoa 35 (2) F1
Upper Austria • Austria 89 F3
Upper Canada Village •
   OT, Canada 122 B7
Upper Egypt • Egypt 101 F4
Upper Hutt • New Zealand 35 E5
Upper Klamath Lake •
   OR, United States 117 E3
Uppsala • Sweden 95 D2
Uppsala [Adm] • Sweden 95 D2
Upshi • Jammu & Kashmir 28 C2
Uqsat as Sugur • Saudi Arabia . . . 21 H2
Ur • Iraq 18 E3
Urakawa • Japan 30 L3
Ural • Kazakhstan/Russian Fed. . . 17 I4
Ural • Kazakhstan/Russian Fed. . . 26 H8
Urals • Russian Fed. 26 I6
Uranium City • SA, Canada 38 J5
Urawa • Japan 30 J7
Urbano Santos • Brazil 45 (1) C2
Urbino • Italy 91 E12
Uren • Russian Fed. 17 H3
Urengoy • Russian Fed. 26 M4
Urenui • New Zealand 112 K4
Uréparapara • Vanuatu 35 (2) B1
Urgal • Russian Fed. 27 L6
Urgench • Uzbekistan 18 H1
Urjhro Kekkonen Nat. Park **Park** •
   Finland . . . . 72 [30]
Urla • Turkey 15 H5
Urlings • Antigua & Barbuda 125 F3
Urnes **Heritage C** • Norway . . . 63 [68]
Urnes stavkirke • Norway 94 C5
Urosevac • F.R. of Yugoslavia 14 I7
Urshult • Sweden 95 F12
Ursus • Poland 13 J5
Uruapan • Mexico 123 E3
Urubamba • Peru 127 B2
Urubamba • Peru 127 B2
Uruçui • Brazil 45 (1) C3
Urucurituba • Brazil 43 F4
Uruguaiana • Brazil 44 E4
Uruguay • S. America 44 E5
Uruguay [Riv] • S. America 44 E4
Urumqi • China 26 Q9
Urup, Ostrov • Russian Fed. 27 P7
Urupinsk • Russian Fed. 17 G4
Urzhum • Russian Fed. 17 H3
Urziceni • Romania 97 D1
Ullung do • Rep. of Korea 82 H3
US East Coast cruise area •
   N. America 58 A2
US Virgin Is. • West Indies 37 I4
Usa • Russian Fed. 64 W3
Usa • Russian Fed. 17 J1
Usak • Turkey 92 D6
Usak • Turkey 92 D6
Usambara Mtns • Tanzania 102 H2
Usborne, Mt • Falkland Is. 44 D8
Use • Crete, Greece 93 E8
Vail • SC, United States . . . . 116 [94]
Vainguinim Beach • Goa, India . . 105 B1
Vaishali • India 105 C8

Ushakovskoye • Russian Fed. 27 V2
Ushkaniy, Ostrov • Russian Fed. . . 97 A5
Ushuaia • Argentina 45 C6
Usinsk • Russian Fed. 17 J1
Usk • United Kingdom 10 B2
Uskedal • Norway 94 C5
Uskemen • Kazakhstan 26 N7
Usküdar • Turkey 92 D3
Usküdar • Turkey 92 D3
Usküp • Turkey 15 I2
Uslar • Germany 8 E5
Usogorsk • Russian Fed. 17 H2
Usolye-Sibirskoye •
   Russian Fed. 27 F6
USS Arizona Mem. •
   HI, United States 119 L5
USS Arizona Mem. **Park** •
   HI, United States . . . . 120 [16]
Ussé [Château] • France 84 D2
Ussel • France 10 H8
Usseln **Spa** • Germany . . . . . . 83 [120]
Ust-Barguzin • Russian Fed. 27 G6
Ust-Corna • Ukraine 14 K1
Ust-Ilimsk • Russian Fed. 26 R6
Ust-Kamchatsk • Russian Fed. . . . 27 R5
Ust-Kara • Russian Fed. 26 J4
Ust-Khayruzovo • Russian Fed. . . 46 JJ4
Ust-Kut • Russian Fed. 27 G5
Ust-Kuyga • Russian Fed. 27 M3
Ust-Lyzha • Russian Fed. 17 J1
Ust-Maya • Russian Fed. 27 L4
Ust-Muya • Russian Fed. 27 I5
Ust-Nem • Russian Fed. 17 I2
Ust-Nera • Russian Fed. 27 N4
Ust-Nyukzha • Russian Fed. 27 J5
Ust-Olenëk • Russian Fed. 27 I2
Ust-Omchug • Russian Fed. 27 O4
Ust-Ordynskiy • Russian Fed. 27 F6
Ust-Pit • Russian Fed. 26 P6
Ust-Tsilma • Russian Fed. 17 I1
Ustaoset • Norway 94 C4
Ustek • Czech Rep. 96 C2
Usti nad Labem • Czech Rep. 96 C1
Usti nad Orlici • Czech Rep. 13 F8
Ustica, I. di • Italy 90 D7
Ustka • Poland 13 F3
Ustyurt Plato • Kazakhstan 96 A2
Ustyurt, Plato •
   Kazakhstan/Uzbekistan 26 I9
Usu • China 26 N9
Usuki • Japan 30 F8
Usumacinta • Guatemala/Mexico . 37 C4
Utah • United States 40 D4
Utara, Selat • Penang, Malaysia . 108 C2
Utena • Lithuania 16 M9
Utersum **Spa** • Germany . . . . . . 83 [4]
Utete • Tanzania 102 H4
Utica • NY, United States 41 K3
Utica • Tunisia 101 E2
Utiel • Spain 11 J4
Utlängen • Sweden 95 F12
Utne • Norway 94 C4
Utö • Sweden 95 D4
Utö [I.] • Sweden 95 D4
Utopia Aboriginal Land •
   NT, Australia 112 H2
Utorda Beach • Goa, India 105 B2
Utrecht • Netherlands 80 C4
Utrecht [Adm] • Netherlands 80 C4
Utrera • Spain 11 F7
Utsjoki • Finland 16 N2
Utsunomiya • Japan 30 J6
Uttar Pradesh • India 105 C7
Uttaradit • Thailand 109 G4
Uttoxeter • United Kingdom 74 D2
Utuado • Puerto Rico 125 E1
Utvær • Norway 94 C3
Uummaa • Finland 16 M4
Uusikaupunki • Finland 95 E3
Uva • Russian Fed. 17 I3
Uvalde • TX, United States 40 G6
Uvdal • Norway 94 C4
Uvéa • Wallis & Futuna 35 (2) E1
Uvinza • Tanzania 102 H1
Uvira • Dem. Rep. of Congo 23 D4
Uwajima • Japan 30 G8
Uwaynat Sudan •
   Egypt/Libya/Sudan 21 B2
Uwaynat Wannin • Libya 21 B2
Uxmal • Mexico 37 D3
Uxmal **Heritage C** • Mexico . . . 62 [26]
Uyar • Russian Fed. 26 P6
Uyedinennya, Ostrov •
   Russian Fed. 26 N2
Uygur Zizhiqu • China 29 A2
Uyuni, Salar de • Bolivia 44 C2
Uz • Slovak Rep. 13 L9
Uzbekistan • Asia 26 J9
Uzerche • France 85 G1
Uzhur • Russian Fed. 26 O6
Uzum • Turkey 92 D5
Uzum • Turkey 92 D5
Üzümlü • Turkey 93 G2
Uzungna Range • Tanzania 23 F5
Uzunköprü • Turkey 15 H2

Vaadhu Diving Paradise •
   Maldives 106 C4
Vaal • South Africa 24 C5
Vaala • Finland 16 N4
Vaaldam • South Africa 24 D5
Vaasa • Finland 16 K5
Vaasa [Adm] • Finland 94 A9
Vabbinfaru • Maldives 106 E2
Vác • Hungary 13 I10
Vacaria • Brazil 44 F4
Vaches, l. aux • Seychelles 106 F2
Vadehavet • Denmark 8 D1
Vadheim • Norway 94 C5
Vadodara • India 28 B4
Vadsø • Norway 16 O1
Vadstena • Sweden 95 F4
Vadvetjåkka Nat. Park **Park** •
   Sweden . . . . 72 [16]
Værlose **Beach** • Denmark . . . . 68 [20]
Værøy • Norway 16 G3
Vågåmo • Norway 94 B1
Vaganski vrh • Croatia 14 C5
Vagator Beach • Goa, India 105 B1
Vågåvatn • Norway 94 C2
Vagnhärad • Sweden 95 D3
Vágos **Beach** • Portugal . . . . . . 68 [77]
Vágsfjorden • Norway 16 I2
Vágsli • Norway 94 C1
Vah • Slovak Rep. 96 D3

Vaksdal • Norway 94 C3
Val André, le • France 84 C2
Val Camónica **Heritage C** • Italy . 64 [111]
Val Camónica • Italy 91 E3
Val Cenis **Ski** • France . . . . 70 [43]
Val d'Illiez **Ski** • Switzerland . . . 70 [76]
Val d'Isère **Ski** • France . . . . . . 70 [32]
Val d'Oise • France 85 E9
Val d'Or • QU, Canada 39 P7
Val St Come **Ski** • QU, Canada . 116 [34]
Val Thorens **Ski** • France . . . . . 70 [42]
Val Thorens • France 85 F4
Valahmia • Romania 14 K5
Valais • Switzerland 89 G6
Valandovo • F.Y.R. of Macedonia . 14 J8
Valasské Mezirici • Czech Rep. . . 13 G8
Valbella • Switzerland 89 G4
Valberg **Ski** • France . . . . 70 [72]
Valcabrère • France 85 J2
Valcheta • Argentina 45 C4
Valdagno • Italy 12 F3
Valdáora **Ski** • Italy . . . . 70 [236]
Valdáora • Italy 90 B2
Valday • Russian Fed. 4 O5
Valday • Russian Fed. 97 E1
Valdayskaya Vozvyshennost •
   Russian Fed. 97 E3
Valdecañas, Embalse de • Spain . 11 F5
Valdeganga • Spain 11 J5
Valdemarsslot • Denmark 95 F14
Valdemarsvik • Sweden 95 F3
Valdepeñas • Spain 11 H6
Valderrama • Spain 86 B6
Valdés **Beach** • Spain . . . . 68 [71]
Valdés, Peninsula • Argentina . . . 45 C4
Valdez • AK, United States 46 DD3
Valdivia • Chile 45 B3
Valdosta • GA, United States . . . 119 M3
Valdovino **Beach** • Spain . . . . . 68 [73]
Vale de Parra • Portugal 88 E7
Vale Navío • Portugal 88 E7
Vale of Trent • United Kingdom . . 74 D2
Valea lui Mihai • Romania 14 J2
Valença • Brazil 44 I1
Valençay • France 84 B1
Valençay [Château] • France 84 D4
Valence • France 85 F3
Valencia • Spain 11 J5
Valencia • Venezuela 43 D2
Valencia **Heritage C** • Spain . . 64 [74]
Valencia **Beach** • Spain . . . . . . 68 [102]
Valencia • Trinidad & Tobago . . . 125 K4
Valencia, Costa de • Spain 86 A2
Valencia de Don Juan • Spain . . . 11 F2
Valencia, Golfo de • Spain 11 L5
Valenciana, Comunidad de •
   Spain 11 K5
Valenciennes • France 10 I3
Valentia I. • Ireland 79 F7
Valentin • Russian Fed. 30 H3
Valentine, NE, United States 40 F3
Valera • Venezuela 43 C2
Valga • Estonia 16 N8
Valinco, Golfe de •
   Corsica, France 85 L3
Valjevo • F.R. of Yugoslavia 14 G5
Valkeakoski • Finland 95 E2
Valkenburg • Netherlands 80 A16
Valkenswaard • Netherlands 5 I3
Valladolid • Spain 11 G3
Valldal • Norway 94 C2
Valdemossa • Majorca, Spain . . . 87 I
Valls • Spain 87 D3
Valmeinier **Ski** • France . . . . . . 70 [49]
Valmiera • Latvia 16 M8
Vámos • Crete, Greece 93 E2
Van • Turkey 18 D2
Van Buren, Martin, Nat. Hist. Site **Park** •
   NY, United States . . . . 121 [320]
Van Diemen Gulf • NT, Australia . . 34 F2
Van Göla • Turkey 18 D2
Van Horn • TX, United States 40 F5
Van, Lake • Turkey 92 A4
Van, Lake • Turkey 92 A4
Van Rees, Pegunungan •
   Indonesia 32 (1) E3
Vanavara • Russian Fed. 26 R5
Vancouver • BC, Canada 122 C3
Vancouver I. Nat. Hist. Site **Park** •
   WA, United States . . . . 120 [32]
Vancouver I. • BC, Canada 122 C3
Vanda • Finland 95 E4
Vandellós l'Hospitalet de l'Infant **Beach** •
   Spain . . . . 68 [104]
Vanderbilt Mansion Nat. Hist. Site **Park** •
   NY, United States . . . . 121 [322]
Vanderhoof • BC, Canada 122 C1

Vänern • Sweden....16 G7
Vänersborg • Sweden....95 F2
Vang • Norway....94 C4
Vangsnes • Norway....16 J1
Vanimo • Papua New Guinea....35 (1) F2
Vanna • Norway....16 J1
Vännäs • Sweden....16 J5
Vannes Beach • France....68 [62]
Vannes • France....84 C4
Vannsjø • Norway....94 B4
Vanoise, Massif de la • France....12 A3
Vanoise, Parc nat. de la • Park • France....72 [66]
Vanoise, Parc nat. de la • France....85 F4
Vansbro • Sweden....16 H6
Vansittart Is. • NU, Canada....39 O3
Vantaa • Finland....95 E9
Vanua Lava • Vanuatu....35 (2) B1
Vanua Levu • Fiji....35 (2) D2
Vanuatu • Pacific Ocean....35 (2) B2
Vao, Ko • Thailand....109 K2
Var • France....85 H2
Var [Adm] • France....85 H3
Vara • Sweden....95 F3
Vara, Pico da • Azores....88 B1
Varadero • Cuba....124 D2
Varanasi • India....105 C8
Varanger-Halvaya • Norway....16 O1
Varangerfjorden • Norway....16 P1
Varano, Lago di • Italy....12 J7
Varano, Lago di • Italy....14 C8
Varazdin • Croatia....14 D3
Varberg Beach • Sweden....68 [1]
Varberg • Sweden....95 F6
Varca • Goa, India....105 B2
Varca Beach • Goa, India....105 C2
Vardar • F.Y.R. of Macedonia....95 F9
Varde • Denmark....95 E11
Varde • Norway....94 D4
Varel • Germany....5 L1
Varel • Germany....8 D3
Varese • Italy....12 C3
Vårgårda • Sweden....95 F3
Varginha • Brazil....127 C11
Varkala • India....106 D14
Varkaus • Finland....16 N5
Varkiza • Greece....92 D7
Varkiza • Greece....95 D4
Värmdölandet • Sweden....95 D4
Värmland • Sweden....16 G6
Värmlandsnäs • Sweden....95 F3
Varna Beach • Bulgaria....69 [236]
Varna • Bulgaria....97 A4
Värnamo • Sweden....95 F7
Varnenski Zaliv • Bulgaria....14 P6
Városha • Cyprus....93 J4
Várpalota • Hungary....13 H10
Vars Ski • France....70 [67]
Vars • France....85 F4
Varzea Grande • Brazil....44 E2
Vasa • Finland....16 K5
Vasco, Costa • Spain....86 A1
Vascao • Portugal....88 E4
Vasco da Gama • Goa, India....105 B1
Vashka • Russian Fed....17 H2
Vasilikí • Crete, Greece....93 E8
Vaslui • Romania....14 O3
Vassdalsegga • Norway....94 C6
Vassilikí • Greece....15 E3
Vassilikí • Greece....92 C1
Vassilikí • Greece....92 C1
Vassilikós • Greece....92 C3
Vassilikós • Greece....92 C3
Vasterås • Sweden....95 D1
Västerbotten • Sweden....16 K4
Västerdalälven • Sweden....16 G6
Västerhaninge • Sweden....95 D4
Västerlen • Sweden....95 F11
Västermo • Sweden....95 D3
Västernorrland • Sweden....16 J5
Västervik Beach • Sweden....69 [7]
Västervik • Sweden....95 F6
Västmanland • Sweden....95 D1
Vasto • Italy....12 I6
Vasto Beach • Italy....69 [139]
Vathi • Crete, Greece....93 E1
Vathipetro • Crete, Greece....93 E7
Vathy • Greece....92 C2
Vathy • Greece....92 C2
Vatican City Heritage C • Italy....64 [124]
Vatican City • Italy....91 F1
Vatili • Cyprus....93 J4
Vatnajökull • Iceland....16 (1) D2
Vatne • Norway....94 C2
Vatoa • Fiji....35 (2) E2
Vatra Dornei • Romania....14 M2
Vättern • Sweden....95 F3
Vattholma • Sweden....95 D2
Vaucouleurs • France....5 I6
Vaughans • St Kitts & Nevis....125 G4
Vaujany Ski • France....70 [56]
Vava'u Group • Tonga....35 (2) F2
Väversunda • Sweden....95 F3
Vavuniya • Sri Lanka....106 I11
Vaxholm • Sweden....95 D4
Växjö • Sweden....95 F7
Vaygach, Ostrov • Russian Fed....26 I3
Vaygach, Ostrov • Russian Fed....96 A3
Vazon Bay Beach • United Kingdom....75 [230]
Vechelde • Germany....8 F4
Vechta • Germany....8 D4
Vechte • Germany....8 C4
Veckholm • Sweden....95 D1
Vecsés • Hungary....13 I10
Vedbæk • Denmark....95 F11
Veddige • Sweden....95 F6
Vedra, I. es • Ibiza, Spain....87 G3
Veendam • Netherlands....5 I2
Veenendaal • Netherlands....5 I2
Veere Beach • Netherlands....68 [50]
Veere • Netherlands....80 A10
Vega • Norway....16 F4
Vega Baja • Puerto Rico....125 E2
Vegår • Norway....94 B1
Veggli • Norway....15 C3
Veinge • Sweden....95 F11
Vejbystrand • Sweden....95 F11
Vejen • Denmark....95 E11
Vejer de la Frontera • Spain....11 F8
Vejle Beach • Denmark....68 [27]
Vejle • Denmark....95 F11
Vejle [Adm] • Denmark....95 E11
Vel Vaddo Beach • Goa, India....105 B2
Velassaru • Maldives....106 E4
Velay, Mts du • France....10 I8
Velbazdski •
  Bulgaria/F.Y.R. of Macedonia....15 D1
Velbert • Germany....81 E2
Velddrif • South Africa....100 C1
Veldenz, Schloß • Germany....82 H3
Veldhoven • Netherlands....5 I3
Velebit • Croatia....14 C5

Velenje • Slovenia....13 E11
Veleta, Pico de • Spain....86 B3
Velez, Pico de • Spain....14 F6
Vélez-Málaga • Spain....86 B7
Vélez-Rubio • Spain....86 B4
Veligandu Huraa • Maldives....106 E4
Velika Kapela • Croatia....14 B4
Velikaya • Pskov, Russian Fed....16 O8
Velikaya •
  Magadan, Russian Fed....27 T4
Veliki Drvenik • Croatia....14 D6
Velikiy Ustyug • Russian Fed....17 H2
Velikiye-Luki • Russian Fed....97 E3
Veliko Turnovo • Bulgaria....97 A3
Velikovisochnoye • Russian Fed....17 I1
Velingara • Senegal....22 B2
Velingrad • Bulgaria....15 F1
Velino [Mtn] • Italy....12 H6
Velino [Riv] • Italy....91 F2
Velletri • Italy....91 F3
Vellinge Beach • Sweden....68 [5]
Vellinge • Sweden....95 F15
Vellore • India....106 D7
Velmerstot • Germany....5 L3
Velsao Beach • Goa, India....105 B2
Velsk • Russian Fed....17 G2
Velten • Germany....81 F1
Veluwezoom, Nat. Park Park •
  Netherlands....72 [54]
Veluwezoom, Nat. Park •
  Netherlands....80 A8
Ven • Sweden....95 F11
Venaco • Corsica, France....85 L2
Venado Tuerto • Argentina....44 D5
Venca • France....85 J3
Venda • South Africa....24 E4
Vendays-Montalivet Beach •
  France....68 [66]
Vendays-Montalivet • France....85 G1
Vendée • France....84 D3
Vendôme • France....84 D2
Vendres Beach • France....68 [113]
Véneta, Laguna • Italy....91 E8
Venetian Riviera • Italy....91 E8
Veneto • Italy....91 E7
Venezia Heritage C • Italy....64 [114]
Venézia • Italy....91 E8
Venézia, Golfo di •
  Croatia/Italy....91 E8
Venézia-Lido • Italy....12 G3
Venezuela • S. America....43 D2
Venezuela, Golfo de • Venezuela....43 C1
Venice Heritage C • Italy....64 [114]
Venice • Italy....91 E8
Vennesla • Norway....95 F1
Vénnisieux • France....10 J8
Vensyssel • Denmark....95 F5
Venta • Latvia/Lithuania....95 F4
Ventadour, Château de • France....85 G2
Ventimiglia • Italy....91 I9
Ventry Beach • Ireland....68 [41]
Ventry • Ireland....79 F5
Ventspils • Latvia....16 K8
Ventura • CA, United States....117 F5
Venus Bay • VI, Australia....111 G3
Venus-Aurora • Romania....91 E4
Venzone • Italy....91 E4
Vera • Argentina....44 D4
Vera Beach • Spain....68 [99]
Vera • Spain....86 B4
Veracruz • Mexico....123 E4
Veracruz [Adm] • Mexico....37 B3
Veraval • France....28 B4
Verbánia • Italy....91 E2
Verbier Ski • Switzerland....70 [78]
Verbier • Switzerland....89 G6
Vercelli • Italy....91 E6
Vercors • France....85 F3
Verdala Palace • Malta....93 H4
Verdalsøra • Norway....94 C5
Verde • Paraguay....44 E3
Verde, Costa • Spain....11 E1
Verde, Costa • Portugal....88 A1
Verde, Costa • Sardinia, Italy....90 C3
Verden • Germany....8 E4
Verdon • France....85 H1
Verdon, Basses Gorges du •
  France....85 H1
Verdon, Grand Canyon du •
  France....85 H1
Verdun-sur-Mer, le • France....85 H1
Verdun • France....10 K4
Vereeniging • South Africa....24 D5
Vérendrye, la, Prov. Reserve •
  QU, Canada....122 B2
Verga, Cap • Guinea....22 B2
Vergina Heritage C • Greece....64 [176]
Véria • Greece....15 D3
Verín • Spain....11 D1
Veringenstadt • Germany....82 I2
Verkhneimbatsk • Russian Fed....27 C4
Verkhnetulomskiy • Russian Fed....16 P2
Verkhnetulomskoye Vdkhr. •
  Russian Fed....16 P2
Verkhni Kuyto, Ozero •
  Russian Fed....16 P4
Verkhoyansk • Russian Fed....27 L3
Verkhoyanskiy Khrebet •
  Russian Fed....27 K3
Verla Heritage C • Finland....63 [75]
Vermeille, Côte • France....85 G3
Vermilion • SD, United States....41 G3
Vermont • United States....53 K3
Vernal • UT, United States....40 E3
Verneuil-sur-Avre • France....10 F5
Verno • Greece....15 C3
Vernon • BC, Canada....38 H6
Vernon • TX, United States....40 G5
Vernon • France....68 [74]
Vernon, Mt • VA, United States....118 H3
Vernon Valley Ski •
  NJ, United States....116 [170]
Verona • Italy....91 E7
Versailles Heritage C • France....64 [59]
Versailles • France....85 E3
Versciaco Ski • Italy....70 [241]
Vert, Cap • Senegal....22 A2
Vertientes • Cuba....124 D7
Vertiskos • Greece....15 D3
Vervins • France....5 G5
Vesheinskaya • Russian Fed....17 G5
Vesijärvi • Finland....95 E4
Vesoul • France....10 L6
Vest Agder • Norway....95 F1
Vest Sjælland • Denmark....95 F10
Vesterålen • Norway....16 H2
Vestern Havn • Denmark....95 F11
Vesterøy • Norway....16 H2
Vestfjorden • Norway....16 H2
Vestfold • Norway....95 E1
Vestmannaeyjar • Iceland....16 (1) C3
Vestnes • Norway....94 C4
Vestvågøy • Norway....16 G2

Vesubie • France....85 H2
Vesuvio • Italy....91 G3
Vesuvius • Italy....91 G3
Veszprém • Hungary....13 G10
Vetlanda • Sweden....95 F8
Vetralla • Italy....91 F1
Vette, le • Italy....90 B4
Veules-les-Roses Beach • France....68 [56]
Veurne • Belgium....80 B1
Vevey • Switzerland....89 G5
Vexin • France....85 E1
Veysonnaz Ski • Switzerland....70 [82]
Vézelay Heritage C • France....64 [55]
Vezen • Bulgaria....15 F1
Vézère • France....85 G2
Vézère, Gorges de la • France....85 G2
Vézère Valley Heritage C •
  France....64 [63]
Vezzani • Corsica, France....85 L2
Viana do Bollo • Spain....11 D2
Vianden • Luxembourg....80 A20
Viangchan • Laos....31 C3
Viareggio Beach • Italy....68 [124]
Viaréggio • Italy....91 E10
Vias Beach • France....68 [113]
Vibo Valentia • Italy....12 K10
Viborg • Russian Fed....17 D2
Viborg • Denmark....95 F9
Viborg [Adm] • Denmark....95 F9
Vic • Spain....87 D2
Vicarstown • Ireland....79 E3
Viccessors • France....85 K1
Vicecomodoro Marambio [Base] •
  Antarctica....46 (1) JJ3
Vicedo Beach • Spain....68 [72]
Vicenza Heritage C • Italy....64 [112]
Vicenza • Italy....91 E7
Vichuga • Russian Fed....17 F3
Vichy • France....10 I7
Vicksburg • MS, United States....118 K2
Vicksburg Nat. Military Park Park •
  MS, United States....121 [200]
Vico • Corsica, France....85 L1
Vico Equense • Italy....91 G3
Vico, Lago di • Italy....91 F1
Victor Harbour • SA, Australia....34 G7
Victoria • NT, Australia....34 F3
Victoria • VI, Australia....34 H7
Victoria • Papua New Guinea....35 (1) D2
Victoria • Chile....45 B3
Victoria • Malta....93 H1
Victoria • Seychelles....106 F1
Victoria • TX, United States....119 N5
Victoria de Las Tunas • Cuba....124 D7
Victoria Falls Heritage N •
  Zambia/Zimbabwe....61 [95]
Victoria Falls • Zambia/Zimbabwe....102 J1
Victoria Falls [Waterfall] •
  Zambia/Zimbabwe....102 J1
Victoria Harbour •
  Hong Kong, China....107 H5
Victoria • NT/NU, Canada....38 J2
Victoria, Lake • Africa....23 E4
Victoria, Lake • NF, Canada....123 D3
Victoria Land • Antarctica....46 (1) V2
Victoria Lines • Malta....93 H4
Victoria, Mt • Myanmar....28 F4
Victoria, Mt • Myanmar....31 A2
Victoria Nile • Uganda....23 E3
Victoria Peak •
  Hong Kong, China....107 H5
Victoria River Downs •
  NT, Australia....34 F3
Victoria Strait • NU, Canada....38 K3
Victoria West • South Africa....100 C3
Victory • Papua New Guinea....35 (1) D2
Vicuña Mackenna • Argentina....44 D5
Videira • Brazil....44 F4
Videle • Romania....97 D1
Vidin • Bulgaria....14 J6
Vidisha • India....28 C4
Vidöstern • Sweden....16 K4
Viechtach • Germany....9 H7
Viedma • Argentina....45 D4
Viejo • Spain....11 L2
Viella, Túnel de • Spain....85 K1
Viella • Spain....11 L2
Vienenburg • Germany....8 F4
Vienna Heritage C • Austria....64 [107]
Vienne • France....85 F1
Vienne [Adm] • France....84 D3
Vienne [Riv] • France....10 F6
Vientiane • Laos....31 C3
Vieques • Puerto Rico....125 E4
Vierschacht Ski • Italy....70 [241]
Viersen • Germany....81 E3
Vierwald Stätter See •
  Switzerland....89 G3
Vierzon • France....85 E2
Vieste • Italy....12 K7
Viet Tri • Vietnam....31 D2
Vietnam • Asia....31 D3
Vietnam Veterans Mem. Park •
  DC, United States....121 [297]
Vieux Fort Bay • St Lucia....125 J4
Vieux-Boucau-les-Bains • France....85 G3
Vigan • Philippines....31 G3
Vigévano • Italy....91 E6
Vigia • Brazil....45 (1) B2
Vigie [Apt] • St Lucia....125 J1
Vigie Beach • St Lucia....125 J1
Vigo • Spain....11 C2
Vigo Beach • Spain....68 [74]
Vigo di Fassa Ski • Italy....70 [222]
Vigo di Fassa • Italy....91 E7
Vigo, Ria de • Spain....11 C2
Vigso Bugt • Denmark....95 F9
Vihorlat • Slovak Rep....14 J1
Vihula • Finland....95 E2
Vijayadurg • India....106 D1
Vijayanagar • India....106 D2
Vijayapura • India....106 D3
Vijayawada • India....106 D3
Vijfhenerlanden • Netherlands....80 C4
Vijose • Albania....15 A3
Vik • Iceland....16 (1) D3
Vikbolandet • Sweden....95 F4
Vikedal • Norway....94 C5
Viken • Sweden....95 F11
Vikersund • Norway....94 B1
Viking Landet Park • Norway....73 [4]
Viking Landet • Norway....94 B2
Vikna • Norway....16 F4
Vikos-Aóos Nat. Park Park •
  Greece....72 [136]
Viksøyri • Norway....94 C4
Vila de Conde • Portugal....11 C3

Vila do Bispo Beach • Portugal....68 [82]
Vila do Bispo • Portugal....88 E5
Vila do Porto • Azores....88 B2
Vila Franca de Xira • Portugal....88 D2
Vila Franca do Campo Beach •
  Azores....68 [87]
Vila Franca do Campo • Azores....88 B1
Vila Nogueira de Azeitão •
  Portugal....88 D2
Vila Nova de Gaia • Portugal....11 C3
Vila Nova do Sales • Angola....23 A6
Vila Praia da Vitória Beach •
  Azores....68 [86]
Vila Real • Portugal....11 D3
Vila Real [Adm] • Portugal....88 A1
Vila Real de Santo António Beach •
  Portugal....68 [82]
Vila Real de Santo António •
  Portugal....88 E8
Vila Velha • Brazil....127 C2
Vilafranca del Penédes • Spain....87 D3
Vilagarcía Beach • Spain....68 [74]
Vilaine • France....84 C4
Vilamoura • Portugal....88 E7
Vilanova i la Geltrú Beach •
  Spain....68 [105]
Vilanova i la Geltrú • Spain....87 D3
Vilcabamba • Peru....127 C2
Vilconta • Peru....127 B2
Vilcheka, Zemlya • Russian Fed....96 A3
Vileyka • Belarus....16 N9
Vilhelmina • Sweden....16 J4
Vilhena • Brazil....43 E6
Vilija • Lithuania....13 N3
Viljandi • Estonia....16 N7
Vilkaviskis • Lithuania....13 M3
Vilkitskogo, Proliv •
  Russian Fed....26 R2
Villa Angela • Argentina....44 D4
Villa Carlos • Minorca, Spain....87 F4
Villa Constitución • Argentina....127 D1
Villa de María • Argentina....44 D4
Villa Dolores • Argentina....44 C5
Villa General Roca • Argentina....44 C5
Villa Gesell • Argentina....127 D4
Villa Hayes • Paraguay....44 E3
Villa Huidobro • Argentina....44 D5
Villa, la Ski • Italy....70 [233]
Villa, la • Italy....90 B2
Villa María • Argentina....44 D5
Villa Nova • Barbados....125 H4
Villa Nueva • Argentina....44 D5
Villa Romana del Casale Heritage C •
  Sicily, Italy....64 [133]
Villa San Martín • Argentina....44 D4
Villablasss Ski • Italy....70 [238]
Villalbino • Spain....11 E2
Villacañas • Spain....11 H5
Villach • Austria....89 H8
Villafranca del Bierzo • Spain....11 E2
Villafranca di Verona • Italy....91 E6
Villaguay • Argentina....44 E5
Villahermosa • Mexico....37 C4
Villajoyosa Beach • Spain....68 [101]
Villajoyosa • Spain....87 C2
Villalba • Spain....11 D1
Villalon de Campos • Spain....11 F2
Villamil • Galapagos Is....43 (1) A2
Villandry [Château] • France....84 D2
Villanueva de Córdoba • Spain....11 G6
Villanueva de la Serena • Spain....11 F6
Villanueva del Rio y Minas •
  Spain....11 F7
Villaputzu • Sardinia, Italy....12 D9
Villar del Rey • Spain....11 E5
Villarcayo • Spain....11 K5
Villard-de-Lans Ski • France....70 [53]
Villard-de-Lans • France....85 F3
Villard-Reculas Ski • France....70 [57]
Villarica • Chile....45 B3
Villarreal de los Infantes •
  Spain....11 K5
Villarrica • Paraguay....44 E4
Villars-sur-Ollon Ski •
  Switzerland....70 [83]
Villars-sur-Ollon • Switzerland....89 G6
Villasimius • Sardinia, Italy....90 C4
Villavicencio • Colombia....43 C3
Villaviciosa • Spain....11 F1
Villaviciosa Beach • Spain....68 [71]
Villefranche-de-Rouergue •
  France....85 G4
Villefranche-sur-Mer • France....85 H2
Villefranche-sur-Sâone • France....85 F1
Villena • Spain....87 C1
Villeneuve • Switzerland....89 G5
Villeneuve-les-Maguelone Beach •
  France....68 [113]
Villeneuve-Loubet • France....85 H4
Villeneuve-sur-Lot • France....85 G4
Villerupt • France....5 I5
Villesavin [Château] • France....84 D2
Villeurbanne • France....10 J8
Villingen Spa • Germany....83 [199]
Villingen-Schwenningen •
  Germany....9 D8
Villingili Beach • Maldives....106 E4
Villiarai • Maldives....106 E4
Vilmanstrand • Finland....16 O6
Vilm • Germany....8 I2
Vilnius • Lithuania....16 M9
Vilnius Heritage C • Lithuania....64 [203]
Vilppula • Finland....95 E2
Vils • Germany....9 H8
Vilsbiburg • Germany....9 H7
Vilseck • Germany....9 H7
Vilshofen • Germany....5 N9
Vilvoorde • Belgium....5 H4
Vilyuy • Russian Fed....27 I4
Vilyuysk • Russian Fed....27 J4
Vimmerby • Sweden....95 E9
Vimperk • Czech Rep....96 C3
Vina del Mar • Chile....44 B5
Vinaros Beach • Spain....68 [103]
Vinarós • Spain....86 A4
Vincennes • IN, United States....41 I4
Vincennes Beach • France....68 [31]
Vindelälven • Sweden....16 J4
Vinderup Beach • Denmark....68 [31]
Vinderup • Denmark....95 F9
Vindhya Range • India....28 C4
Vindö • Sweden....95 D4
Vingåker • Sweden....95 D3
Vingrom • France....95 F7
Vinh • Vietnam....31 D3
Vinh Long • Vietnam....108 B3
Vinh Long • Vietnam....108 B3
Vinica • Croatia....14 F4
Vinkovci • Croatia....14 F4
Vinniki • Ukraine....13 O5
Vinnitsa • Ukraine....14 O1
Vinogradov • Ukraine....13 M9
Vinslöv • Sweden....95 F11
Vinson Massif • Antarctica....46 (1) GG2
Vipiteno • Italy....90 B1
Vir • Croatia....14 C5
Virac • Philippines....31 G4
Vire • France....10 E5
Vire [Riv] • France....10 D5
Viré • Angola....24 A3
Virful Curcubata • Romania....13 L1
Virgenes, Cabo • Argentina....45 C6
Virgin • United States....118 J1
Virgin Gorda •
  British Virgin Is....58 B7
Virgin Is., UK • West Indies....37 I4
Virgin Is., US • West Indies....37 I4
Virginia • MN, United States....41 H2
Virginia • United States....41 K4
Virginia Beach •
  VA, United States....118 H5
Virginia City •
  NV, United States....117 F3
Virihaure • Sweden....16 I3
Virochey • Cambodia....31 D4
Virovitica • Croatia....14 E4
Virrat • Finland....95 E2
Virsbo • Sweden....95 D1
Virton • Belgium....80 A19
Virunga • Dem. Rep. of Congo....23 D4
Virunga Heritage C • Heritage N •
  Dem. Rep. of Congo....61 [84]
Virunga, Parc nat. des Park •
  Dem. Rep. of Congo....103 [56]
Vis • Croatia....14 D6
Visayan Sea • Philippines....31 G4
Visby • Sweden....16 J8
Visby Heritage C • Sweden....64 [7]
Viscount Melville Sound •
  NU, Canada....38 J2
Viseu • Portugal....11 D3
Viseu [Adm] • Portugal....88 A1
Viseu de Sus • Romania....14 L2
Vishakhapatnam • India....28 D5
Vishniy Volochek • Russian Fed....97 E3
Visiko • Bosnia-Herz....14 E5
Vislanda • Sweden....95 F7
Viso, Monte • Italy....91 E5
Visoko • Bosnia-Herz....14 E5
Visselhövede • Germany....8 E4
Vistonias, Ormos • Greece....15 G3
Vistonida, Limni • Greece....15 G2
Vitebsk • Belarus....17 E3
Viterbo • Italy....91 F1
Viti Levu • Fiji....35 (2) D2
Vitiaz Strait •
  Papua New Guinea....35 (1) D2
Vitigudino • Spain....11 E4
Vitim • Russian Fed....27 H5
Vitim [Riv] • Russian Fed....27 I5
Vitón • Svalbard....46 L2
Vitória • Brazil....127 C2
Vitória da Conquista • Brazil....44 H1
Vitoria Gasteiz • Spain....11 I2
Vitorog • Bosnia-Herz....14 D5
Vitosa Nat. Park Park •
  Bulgaria....72 [131]
Vitré [Château] • France....84 D1
Vitry-le-François • France....10 J5
Vittangi • Sweden....16 K3
Vittel • France....10 A8
Vittoria • Sicily, Italy....12 I12
Vittorio Véneto • Italy....90 B4
Vittoriosa • Malta....93 H4
Vittsjö • Sweden....95 F11
Vitznau • Switzerland....89 G3
Viveiro • Spain....11 D1
Viveiro Beach • Spain....68 [72]
Viver • Spain....11 K5
Vivian • LA, United States....118 K1
Vivonne • France....84 D3
Vizianagaram • India....28 D5
Vizinga • Russian Fed....17 I2
Vlaanderen • Belgium....5 F3
Vlaardingen • Netherlands....80 C3
Vladikavkaz • Russian Fed....17 G7
Vladimir Heritage C •
  Russian Fed....64 [210]
Vladimir • Russian Fed....97 E4
Vladimir-Volynski • Ukraine....13 N7
Vladivostok • Russian Fed....27 L8
Vlasic • Bosnia-Herz....14 E5
Vlasic • Bosnia-Herz....14 E5
Vlasovo • Russian Fed....27 M2
Vlieland • Netherlands....80 A3
Vlihada, Paralia •
  Crete, Greece....93 E4
Vliho • Greece....92 C1
Vlikos • Ukraine....14 Q4
Vlissingen • Netherlands....80 A10
Vlitasaari • Finland....16 M5
Vlkolinec Heritage C •
  Slovak Rep....64 [150]
Vlorë • Albania....15 A3
Vlotho Spa • Germany....83 [92]
Vltava • Czech Rep....96 C4
Vluyn • Germany....81 E1
Vnukovo [Apt] • Russian Fed....97 E4
Vöcklabruck • Austria....13 E9
Vodice • Croatia....12 J5
Voerde • Germany....81 E1
Voergård • Denmark....95 F6
Vogel Peak • Nigeria....22 G3
Vogelsberg • Germany....82 G2
Voghera • Italy....91 D6
Voh • Kenya....101 G4
Voi • Kenya....101 G4
Voiron • France....85 F3
Voitsberg • Austria....13 F10
Vojens • Denmark....95 E11
Vojvodina • F.R. of Yugoslavia....14 G4
Voknavolok • Russian Fed....96 B3
Volary • Czech Rep....96 C3
Volcano • HI, United States....119 L8
Volcans, Parc des Park • Rwanda....103 [72]
Volda • Norway....94 C1
Volendam • Netherlands....80 A7
Volga • Russian Fed....17 H5
Volga, Cities of the •
  Russian Fed....96 A2
Volga Delta • Russian Fed....17 H6
Volga Plateau • Russian Fed....96 A2
Volga, Ozero • Russian Fed....97 E3
Volgodonsk • Russian Fed....17 G5
Volgograd • Russian Fed....17 G5
Volgogradskoye Vdkhr. •
  Russian Fed....17 H4
Volissós • Greece....15 F4
Völkermarkt • Austria....13 E11
Völklingen Heritage C • Germany....64 [141]
Völklingen • Germany....82 G3
Volkovsk • Belarus....13 N4
Volkov [Riv] • Russian Fed....97 E3
Volochanka • Russian Fed....27 S4
Vologda • Russian Fed....97 E2

Vólos Beach • Greece....69 [165]
Vólos • Greece....92 D4
Vólos • Greece....92 D4
Volovets • Ukraine....14 K1
Volta area Heritage C • Ghana....63 [97]
Volta Blanche •
  Burkina Faso/Ghana....22 D2
Volta Noire • Ghana....22 E3
Volta Rouge •
  Burkina Faso/Ghana....22 D2
Volta Redonda • Brazil....127 C3
Volterra • Italy....91 E11
Volturno • Italy....91 G1
Volubilis Heritage C • Morocco....64 [215]
Volubilis • Morocco....101 D1
Volvi, Limni • Greece....15 E3
Volzhskiy • Russian Fed....17 F3
Voma • Fiji....35 (2) D2
Vóni • Crete, Greece....93 E7
Vónitsa • Greece....92 C1
Vónitsa • Greece....92 C1
Voorburg • Netherlands....80 C3
Voorne Beach • Netherlands....68 [49]
Voorne • Netherlands....80 C1
Voorschoten • Netherlands....80 C1
Vorarlberg • Austria....89 H1
Vordingborg Beach • Denmark....68 [18]
Vordingborg • Denmark....95 F14
Vorë • Albania....15 A2
Vóries Sporádes • Greece....92 D4
Voringsfossen • Norway....94 C4
Vórios Evoïkós Kólpos • Greece....15 E5
Vorkuta • Russian Fed....26 J4
Vorma • Norway....94 B2
Vormsi • Estonia....16 L7
Vorogovo • Russian Fed....27 C4
Voronezh • Russian Fed....17 F4
Vorpommersche Boddenlandschaft,
  Nationalpark Park • Germany....72 [58]
Vóru • Estonia....16 N8
Vosges • France....10 L5
Vosnesensk • Ukraine....17 E5
Vosnesensk • Russian Fed....94 C4
Vostochno Sibirskoye More •
  Arctic Ocean....46 II2
Vostochnyy Sayan • Russian Fed....26 Q7
Vostok • Kiribati....35 (1) P2
Vostok [Base] • Antarctica....46 (1) P2
Votkinsk • Russian Fed....17 I3
Vøtterøy • Norway....94 B4
Voukoliés • Crete, Greece....93 E1
Voúla • Greece....92 D7
Voúla • Greece....92 D7
Vouliagméni • Greece....92 D7
Vouliagméni • Greece....92 D7
Voúrinos • Greece....15 C3
Vouvray • France....84 D2
Vouvray • France....84 D2
Voúxa, Akra • Crete, Greece....93 E1
Vouziers • France....10 J4
Voyage to the Glaciers cruise area •
  N. America....58 A2
Voyageurs Nat. Park Park •
  MN, United States....121 [155]
Voyvozh • Russian Fed....17 J2
Vrå • Denmark....95 F6
Vrådal • Norway....94 B1
Vrahási Beach • Crete, Greece....69 [191]
Vrahási • Crete, Greece....93 E7
Vraháti Beach • Greece....69 [155]
Vrakhiónas • Greece....15 B6
Vran • Bosnia-Herz....14 E6
Vrangelya, Ostrov •
  Russian Fed....27 V2
Vrana • Bosnia-Herz....14 E6
Vrana • F.R. of Yugoslavia....14 I7
Vrassná Beach • Greece....69 [170]
Vratsa • Bulgaria....14 K6
Vrbas • Bosnia-Herz....14 E5
Vrchlabí • Czech Rep....13 F7
Vredenburg • South Africa....100 C1
Vredendal • South Africa....100 C2
Vrindabam • India....105 C2
Vrine • Albania....92 B1
Vrissa Beach • Greece....69 [176]
Vrontisiou, Moni •
  Crete, Greece....93 E6
Vrsac • F.R. of Yugoslavia....14 I4
Vryburg • South Africa....100 B1
Vryheid • South Africa....24 E5
Vsetin • Czech Rep....13 G8
Vukovar • F.R. of Yugoslavia....14 G4
Vuktyl • Russian Fed....17 J2
Vulcano • Italy....90 D2
Vulkaneifel • Germany....82 G3
Vulture • Italy....12 J8
Vung Tao • Vietnam....108 B3
Vuokatti • Finland....94 A6
Vuollerim • Sweden....16 K3
Vuotso • Finland....17 D1
Vyartsilya • Russian Fed....17 I3
Vyatka • Russian Fed....17 I3
Vyatka [Riv] • Russian Fed....17 I3
Vyatko-Chepetsk • Russian Fed....29 I1
Vyazemskiy • Russian Fed....27 L8
Vyazma • Russian Fed....97 E3
Vyazniki • Russian Fed....17 F3
Vychegda • Russian Fed....17 I2
Vym • Russian Fed....17 I2
Vym [Riv] • Russian Fed....17 I2
Vynohradiv • Ukraine....96 C2
Vysehrad • Czech Rep....96 C2
Vyškov • Czech Rep....13 G8
Vyskovski • Ukraine....14 K1
Vysoké Tatry Nat. Park Park •
  Slovak Rep....72 [100]
Vysokovsk • Russian Fed....13 M5
Vyssi Brod • Czech Rep....96 C4
Vytegra • Russian Fed....17 E2
Vyvenka • Russian Fed....27 S4

W, Parc nat. du Heritage N •
  Niger....61 [76]
W, Parc nat. du Park • Niger....103 [3]
Wa • Ghana....22 D2
Waal • Netherlands....80 A11
Waalwijk • Netherlands....80 A4
Wabasca • AL, Canada....38 I5
Wabrezno • Poland....13 H4
Wachadima Plain • Kenya....101 G2
Wachau • Austria....89 F4
Wächtendonk • Germany....81 E1
Wächtersbach • Germany....82 G2
Waco • TX, United States....119 N3
Wad Madani • Sudan....21 F5
Waddan • Libya....21 C2
Waddan, Jabal • Libya....21 C2
Waddeneilanden • Netherlands....80 A3
Waddenzee • Netherlands....80 A3

Waddi Beach • Goa, India **105** B2
Waddington, Mt • BC, Canada **122** C3
Wadebridge • United Kingdom **74** F4
Wadi • India **106** D2
Wadi ar Ru'ays • Libya **21** C2
Wageningen • Netherlands **5** I3
Wager Bay • NU, Canada **39** N3
Wagga Wagga • NS, Australia **111** G1
Wagin • WA, Australia **34** C6
Waging • Germany **82** J4
Waginger See • Germany **82** J4
Wagrain Ski • Austria .... **70** [174]
Wagrain • Austria **89** H4
Wagrowiec • Poland **13** G5
Wah • Pakistan **18** J3
Waha • Libya **21** C2
Wahai • Indonesia **32** (1) C3
Wahat al Kufrah • Libya **21** D3
Wāhāt, El • Egypt **21** F2
Wadi Jalu • Libya **21** C2
Wahat Salimah • Sudan **21** E3
Wahiawa • HI, United States **119** L5
Waialua • HI, United States **119** L5
Waianae Range •
HI, United States **119** L5
Waiau • New Zealand **112** L3
Waigama • Indonesia **32** (1) C3
Waigeo • Indonesia **32** (1) D3
Waihi • New Zealand **35** F3
Waihi Beach • New Zealand **112** K2
Waikaremoana, Lake •
New Zealand **112** K4
Waikato [Adm] • New Zealand ... **112** J2
Waikato [Riv] • New Zealand **112** K2
Waikawa • New Zealand **112** L4
Waikiki • HI, United States **119** L6
Waikokopu • New Zealand **35** F4
Wailua Falls •
HI, United States **119** L4
Wailuku • HI, United States **119** L3
Wailuku River State Park •
HI, United States **119** L8
Waimanalo Beach •
HI, United States **119** L6
Waimangu Volcanic Valley •
New Zealand **112** K2
Waimate • New Zealand **35** C7
Waimea •
Kauai, HI, United States **119** L2
Waimea •
Hawaii, HI, United States **119** L8
Waimea Bay • HI, United States .. **119** L1
Waimea Canyon State Park •
HI, United States **119** L2
Waingapa • India **28** C4
Waingapu • Indonesia **32** (1) B4
Waingaro • New Zealand **112** K1
Wainiha • HI, United States **119** K1
Wainwright • AL, Canada **38** I6
Waiouru • New Zealand **112** K4
Waipahu • HI, United States **119** L5
Waipawa • New Zealand **112** K4
Waipio Valley •
HI, United States **119** L8
Waipukurau • New Zealand **112** K4
Wairakei Thermal Valley •
New Zealand **112** K2
Wairoa • New Zealand **112** K4
Waitaki • New Zealand **35** C6
Waitara • New Zealand **112** K3
Waitemata • New Zealand **112** J2
Waitomo Caves • New Zealand ... **112** K1
Waiuku • New Zealand **35** E3
Wajh, Al • Saudi Arabia **18** C4
Wajima • Japan **30** I6
Wajir • Kenya **101** G2
Wak, El • Kenya **23** G3
Wakasa-Wan • Japan **30** H7
Wakatipu, Lake • New Zealand ... **35** A7
Wakayama • Japan **30** H7
Wake • Marshall Is. **33** H4
Wakefield • United Kingdom **7** K8
Wakhan • Afghanistan **18** J2
Wakkanai • Japan **30** K2
Walachia • Romania **14** L5
Walbrzych • Poland **13** F7
Walchensee • Germany **82** J7
Walcz • Poland **13** F4
Waldbronn Spa • Germany .. **83** [179]
Waldkirch • Germany **82** G8
Waldkirch Spa • Germany ... **83** [196]
Waldkraiburg • Germany **82** J4
Waldshut • Germany **82** G8
Walensee • Switzerland **89** G3
Wales • United Kingdom **7**
Wales I. • NU, Canada **39** N3
Wales, northwest Heritage C •
Kae .... **64** [14]
Walibi Park • Belgium .... **73** [50]
Walibi • Belgium **80** A15
Walibi Flevo Park • Netherlands . **73** [41]
Walibi Flevo • Netherlands **80** A7
Walker Lake • NV, United States . **117** F4
Walker, Maggie L., Nat. Hist. Site Park •
VA, United States .... **121** [258]
Walkers Beach • Barbados **125** H1
Walkerston • QL, Australia **111** F3
Walla Walla • WA, United States . **117** E2
Wallasey • United Kingdom **7** I8
Walldürn • Germany **9** F7
Wallenhorst • Germany **5** K2
Wallis & Futuna • Pacific Ocean . **35** (2) E1
Wallis, Is. de •
Wallis & Futuna **35** (2) E1
Wallonie • Belgium **5** H4
Wallowa Mtns •
OR, United States **117** E4
Walnut Canyon Nat. Mon. •
AZ, United States **118** J1
Walnut Canyon Nat. Mon. Park •
AZ, United States .... **120** [107]
Walsall • United Kingdom **74** D2
Walsertal, Grosser • Austria **89** H5
Walsertal, Kleiner • Austria **89** H1
Walsrode • Germany **8** E4
Walsershausen • Germany **9** F5
Walton Heath • United Kingdom . **74** E3
Waltrop • Germany **81** E2
Walvis Bay • Angola **19** F8
Walvis Bay • Namibia **24** A4
Wamba • Nigeria **22** F3
Wamba • Kenya **23** G3
Wamba • Dem. Rep. of Congo **23** D3
Wamba [Riv] •
Dem. Rep. of Congo **23** B5
Wamena • Indonesia **35** (1) B1
Wami • Tanzania **23** H3
Wan • Indonesia **32** (1) E4
Wan Chai • Hong Kong, China ... **107** H6
Wan Hsa-la • Myanmar **109** G1
Wan • China **107** J1
Wanaka • New Zealand **112** L2
Wanaka, Lake • New Zealand **112** L2
Wanapiri • Indonesia **32** (1) E3
Wandlitz • Germany **81** F2
Wandlitzer See • Germany **81** F2

Wang • Thailand **109** G3
Wang Phetburi Mtn • Thailand ... **109** H3
Wang Takhrai • Thailand **109** H2
Wang Takhrai Gardens • Thailand **109** H2
Wanganui • New Zealand **112** K3
Wanganui [Riv] • New Zealand ... **112** K3
Wangaratta • VI, Australia **111** G3
Wangen • Germany **82** J5
Wangerooge • Germany **8** C3
Wangerooge Spa • Germany .. **83** [42]
Wangpanyang • China **107** J4
Wangqing • China **30** E3
Wanneperveen • Netherlands **80** A8
Wanshan Qundao • Zhuhai, China **107** H4
Wanxian • China **29** D4
Wanzai • Zhuhai, China **107** H1
Warangal • India **28** C5
Waratah Bay • VI, Australia **111** G3
Warburg • Germany **8** E5
Warburton • SA, Australia **34** G5
Warburton Mission •
WA, Australia **34** E5
Wardija Point • Malta **93** H1
Wareham • United Kingdom **74** F6
Waremme • Belgium **5** I4
Waren • Germany **8** H3
Waren • Indonesia **32** (1) E3
Warendorf • Germany **5** K3
Warendorf • Germany **8** C5
Warkworth • New Zealand **35** E3
Warkworth Beach •
United Kingdom .... **75** [19]
Warmbad • South Africa **24** D4
Warminster • United Kingdom ... **74** F3
Warnemünde • Germany **8** H2
Warnemünde Beach • Germany . **68** [15]
Warnemünde Spa • Germany . **83** [270]
Warner Brothers Movie World Park •
Germany .... **73** [57]
Warner Brothers Movie World •
QL, Australia **111** F6
Warner Mtns • United States **38** G8
Warner Valley •
OR, United States **117** E3
Warnow • Germany **8** H3
Waroona • WA, Australia **34** C6
Warrego • NS/QL, Australia **34** I5
Warren • OH, United States **41** J3
Warri • Nigeria **22** F3
Warrington • United Kingdom **7** J8
Warrior Reefs • Australia **35** (1) C2
Warrnambool • VI, Australia **34** H7
Warsaw • Poland **13** J5
Warsaw Heritage C • Poland .. **64** [138]
Warstein • Germany **5** L3
Warszawa • Poland **13** J5
Warszawa Heritage C • Poland . **64** [138]
Warta • Poland **13** H6
Wartberge • South Africa **24** C6
Warth • Austria **89** H5
Waru • Indonesia **32** (1) D3
Warwick • United Kingdom **74** D2
Warwick • QL, Australia **111** F6
Warwickshire • United Kingdom . **74** D2
Wasalandia Park • Finland ... **73** [10]
Wasatch Range •
UT, United States **40** D4
Wash, The • United Kingdom **7** M9
Washago • OT, Canada **122** B5
Washington • United Kingdom **7** K7
Washington [Adm] •
United States **117** E1
Washington, Booker T., Nat. Mon. Park •
VA, United States .... **121** [252]
Washington Crossing State Hist. Site •
PA, United States **118** H1
Washington DC • United States .. **118** H3
Washington, Fort, Park Park •
MD, United States .... **121** [275]
Washington, George, Birthplace Nat. Mon. •
VA, United States .... **121** [261]
Washington, George, Mem. Parkway Park •
VA, United States .... **121** [266]
Washington Mon. Park •
DC, United States .... **121** [298]
Washington, Mt •
NH, United States **118** G3
Washington Nat. Airport •
VA, United States **118** H3
Wasiłków • Poland **13** M4
Wasior • Indonesia **32** (1) D3
Waskaganish • QU, Canada **39** P6
Waspám • Nicaragua **37** E5
Wassenaar • Netherlands **80** C1
Wasserburg • Germany **82** J4
Wasserkuppe • Germany **9** E6
Wast Water • United Kingdom ... **74** C3
Wat Phra That Doi Suthep •
Thailand **109** G1
Watampone • Indonesia **32** (1) B3
Watarrka Nat. Park •
NT, Australia **112** H3
Water Cay • Bahamas **124** B2
Water Mania • FL, United States . **121** C1
Water of Philorth Beach •
United Kingdom .... **75** [6]
Waterbury • CT, United States ... **118** H2
Waterfoot Beach •
United Kingdom .... **75** [224]
Waterford • Ireland **79** D2
Waterford [Adm] • Ireland **79** D2
Waterland • Netherlands **80** C2
Waterloo • Belgium **5** H4
Waterloo • IA, United States **41** H3
Waterloo [Battlefield] •
Belgium **80** A14
Watermouth Castle •
United Kingdom **74** F2
Waterport • NY, United States ... **122** B9
Waterton Lakes Nat. Park •
AL, Canada **38** H6
Waterton-Glacier Int. Peace Park Heritage
N • Canada/United States ... **60** [5]
Waterton-Glacier Int. Peace Park •
Canada/United States **122** C1
Watertown • SD, United States ... **41** G3
Watertown • NY, United States ... **41** K3
Waterville • Ireland **79** F7
Waterville • ME, United States ... **41** J6
Waterville Valley Ski •
NH, United States .... **116** [213]
Waterways • AL, Canada **38** I5
Watford • United Kingdom **74** E1
Watheroo • WA, Australia **34** C6
Watrous • SA, Canada **38** J6
Watsa • Dem. Rep. of Congo **22** H5
Watsi Kengo •
Dem. Rep. of Congo **22** H5
Watson • SA, Canada **38** F4
Watumu Marine Game Reserve •
Kenya **101** G5
Watumu Marine Nat. Park • Kenya **101** G5

Watzmann • Germany **82** J8
Wau • Papua New Guinea ... **35** (1) D2
Waukara, Gunung • Indonesia ... **32** (1) A3
Waukegan • IL, United States **41** I3
Waurika • OK, United States **119** N1
Wausau • WI, United States **41** I3
Wavre • Belgium **5** H4
Waw • Sudan **23** D2
Waw al Kabir • Libya **21** B2
Waw an Namus • Libya **21** B2
Wawa • SA, Canada **39** O7
Waxahachie • TX, United States . **119** N1
Wayabula • Indonesia **32** (1) C2
Waycross • GA, United States **119** M3
Waza, Parc nat. de Park •
Cameroon .... **103** [42]
Wé • New Caledonia **35** (2) B3
We • Indonesia **110** B1
Weald, The • United Kingdom **74** E3
Wear • United Kingdom **7** J7
Weatherford • TX, United States . **119** N1
Weda • Indonesia **32** (1) C2
Weddel Sea • Antarctica **46** (1) A2
Wedel • Germany **8** E3
Weeki Wachee Spring •
FL, United States **119** M5
Weener • Germany **8** C3
Weert • Netherlands **5** I3
Weesp • Netherlands **80** C2
Weggis • Switzerland **89** G3
Wei Ho • China **29** D4
Wei He • China **29** F3
Weichsel • Poland **13** H4
Weida • Germany **9** H7
Weifang • China **29** F3
Weilburg • Germany **82** H2
Weiler-Simmerberg • Germany ... **82** J5
Weiler-Simmerberg Spa • Germany **83** [238]
Weilheim • Germany **82** J5
Weimar • Germany **9** G6
Weimar Heritage C • Germany . **64** [33]
Weingarten • Germany **82** J5
Weinheim • Germany **9** D7
Weinsberg • Germany **9** E7
Weipa • QL, Australia **34** I2
Weir Farm Nat. Hist. Site Park •
CT, United States .... **121** [337]
Weiskirchen Spa • Germany .. **83** [167]
Weiße Elster • Germany **9** H5
Weißenburg • France **82** G6
Weißenburg in Bayern • Germany **9** F7
Weißenfels • Germany **9** G5
Weißenhaus Spa • Germany .. **83** [20]
Weißensee Spa • Germany ... **83** [244]
Weißwasser • Germany **8** J5
Wejherowo • Poland **13** H3
Welbourn Hill • SA, Australia **34** F5
Welch Village Ski •
MN, United States .... **116** [114]
Welchman Hall Gully • Barbados **125** H3
Welden • Germany **82** J2
Weldiya • Ethiopia **23** F1
Welel • Ethiopia **23** E2
Weleri • Java, Indonesia **110** D3
Welkom • South Africa **24** D5
Welland • OT, Canada **7** L9
Welland Canal • OT, Canada **122** B9
Wellesley Is. • QL, Australia **33** E7
Wellingborough • United Kingdom **7** L9
Wellington • NS, Australia **34** I6
Wellington • New Zealand **35** E5
Wellington [Adm] • New Zealand **112** J4
Wellington, I. • Chile **45** A5
Wells • United Kingdom **74** F3
Wells • NV, United States **117** F2
Wells Gray Prov. Park •
BC, Canada **122** C4
Wells-next-the-Sea •
United Kingdom **5** D2
Wells-next-the-Sea Beach •
United Kingdom .... **75** [41]
Wellsford • New Zealand **35** E3
Wels • Austria **13** C9
Welschap [Apt] • Netherlands ... **80** A11
Welschnofen • Italy **90** B3
Welshpool • United Kingdom **74** D1
Welwyn Garden City •
United Kingdom **5** C3
Wembley Stadium •
United Kingdom **74** E1
Wembury Old Mill •
United Kingdom **74** F5
Wemyss Bay • United Kingdom .. **78** A3
Wenatchee • WA, United States . **117** E1
Wenchi • Ghana **22** D3
Wendelstein • Germany **82** J7
Wendover • UT, United States ... **117** F2
Wenduine • Belgium **80** B2
Wengen Ski • Switzerland .... **70** [95]
Wengen • Switzerland **89** G2
Wenlock • QL, Australia **34** H2
Wenlock Edge • United Kingdom **74** D1
Wenningstedt Spa • Germany . **83** [2]
Wenquan • China **28** F2
Wenshan • China **29** C6
Wenshan • China **31** C2
Wentworth • NS, Australia **34** H6
Wenzhou • China **29** G5
Werda • Botswana **24** C5
Werder • Germany **81** F3
Wermelskirchen • Germany **81** E4
Werneuchen • Germany **81** F2
Wernergerode • Germany **8** F5
Werra • Germany **9** E5
Werris Creek • NS, Australia **34** J6
Wertach • Germany **82** J5
Wertheim • Germany **9** E7
Wesel • Germany **81** E1
Weser • Germany **8** E4
Wesergebirge • Germany **8** E5
Wesleyville • NF, Canada **123** D4
Wessel, Cape • NT, Australia **34** G2
Wessel Is. • NT, Australia **34** G2
West Africa cruise area •
Africa **59** A5
West Angle Bay Beach •
United Kingdom .... **75** [156]
West Bali Nat. Park •
Bali, Indonesia **110** C1
West Bank • Jordan **98** A6
West Bend • WI, United States ... **41** I3
West Bengal • India **28** E4
West Bromwich • United Kingdom **74** D2
West Cape • New Zealand **33** H10
West Cape • New Zealand **112** L3
West Coast • New Zealand **112** J3
West Coast Nat. Park •
South Africa **100** C1
West Country • United Kingdom .. **74** F
West End • Bahamas **124** B2
West Falkland • Falkland Is. **45** D6
West Lake • China **107** J3
West Midland Safari Park •
United Kingdom **74** D1
West Nicholson • Zimbabwe **102** J3

West Palm Beach •
FL, United States **119** M6
West Point • Falkland Is. **59** A10
West Point • NY, United States .. **118** H1
West Siberian Plain •
Russian Fed. **26** M5
West Sussex • United Kingdom .. **74** E3
West Virginia • United States **41** J4
West Vlaanderen • Netherlands . **80** A13
West Wittering Beach •
United Kingdom .... **75** [78]
West Wyalong • NS, Australia ... **111** G1
Westbury • St Kitts & Nevis **125** G4
Westeinder Plassen •
Netherlands **80** C1
Westendorf Ski • Austria ..... **70** [150]
Westendorf • Austria **89** H3
Westerland • Germany **8** D2
Westerland Spa • Germany ... **83** [2]
Western Australia • Australia **34** D5
Western, Bukit •
Penang, Malaysia **108** C1
Western Cape • South Africa ... **100** C6
Western Desert • Egypt **21** E3
Western Isles • United Kingdom . **75** A1
Western Lakeland • Finland **95** E2
Western Sahara • Africa **20** C4
Western Samoa • Pacific Ocean . **35** (2) F1
Westernkotten Spa • Germany . **83** [103]
Westerschelde • Netherlands **5** G3
Westerschouwen • Netherlands .. **5** G3
Westerwald • Germany **82** G2
Westkapelle • Netherlands **5** G3
Westland • Netherlands **80** C3
Westland Nat. Park •
New Zealand **112** L3
Westliche Karwendelspitze •
Austria/Germany **82** J7
Westmeath • Ireland **79** D1
Westminster • United Kingdom .. **74** E1
Weston • Malaysia **32** F1
Weston-super-Mare •
United Kingdom **74** F3
Weston-super-Mare Beach •
United Kingdom .... **75** [137]
Westport • New Zealand **35** C5
Westport • Ireland **79** F1
Westport House • Ireland **79** F1
Westray • United Kingdom **6** I2
Westward Ho! • United Kingdom **74** F2
Westwego • LA, United States ... **118** K4
Wet'n'Wild • QL, Australia **111** F6
Wet'n'Wild • FL, United States . **119** F10
Wetar • Indonesia **32** (1) C4
Wetaskiwin • AL, Canada **38** I6
Wethersfield •
CT, United States **118** H2
Wetter • Germany **5** L4
Wetter • Germany **81** E2
Wetteren • Belgium **5** G3
Wetzlar • Germany **82** G2
Wewak • Papua New Guinea . **35** (1) C1
Wexford • Ireland **7** F9
Wexford [Adm] • Ireland **79** D2
Weyburn • SA, Canada **38** K7
Weymouth • United Kingdom **74** F6
Weymouth Beach • United Kingdom **75** [99]
Whakapapa • New Zealand **112** K4
Whakatane • New Zealand **112** K2
Whalsay • United Kingdom **75** A7
Whampoa • China **107** H1
Whanganui Nat. Park •
NS, Australia **112** K3
Whangarei • New Zealand **35** E2
Wheeler Peak •
NM, United States **40** E4
Wheeler Peak •
NV, United States **117** F4
Wheeling • WV, United States ... **41** J3
Whiddy I. • Ireland **79** F7
Whipsnade Zoo • United Kingdom **74** E1
Whiskeytown-Shasta-Trinity Nat.
Recreation Area Park •
CA, United States .... **120** [40]
Whistler Ski • BC, Canada ... **116** [207]
Whistler • BC, Canada **122** C3
Whitburn Beach • United Kingdom **75** [24-25]
Whitby • United Kingdom **7** L7
Whitby Beach • United Kingdom **75** [29]
Whitby • OT, Canada **122** B9
White Bay • NF, Canada **123** D4
White Horse Hills •
United Kingdom **5** B3
White House Bay •
St Kitts & Nevis **125** G4
White House, The Park •
DC, United States .... **121** [299]
White I. • NU, Canada **39** O3
White I. • New Zealand **112** K2
White, Lake • NT/WA, Australia . **34** E4
White Lake • LA, United States .. **118** K3
White Mtn Peak •
CA, United States **40** C4
White Mtns • AK, United States . **38** B3
White Mtns • NH, United States . **118** G3
White Nile • Sudan **23** E2
White Pass Village Ski •
WA, United States .... **116** [46]
White River • SD, United States . **38** K8
White River Junction •
VT, United States **118** G3
White Sands Nat. Mon. •
NM, United States **118** J4
White Sands Nat. Mon. Park •
NM, United States .... **120** [121]
White Sea • Russian Fed. **17** F1
Whitecap Mtns Ski •
WI, United States .... **116** [118]
Whiteface Mtn Ski •
NY, United States .... **116** [184]
Whitefish Bay •
MI, United States **39** N7
Whitehaven • United Kingdom ... **74** C1
Whitehorse • YT, Canada **38** D4
Whitehouse • Jamaica **124** C3
Whiteman Range •
Papua New Guinea **35** (1) D2
Whitemark • TS, Australia **34** I8
Whitesand Bay • United Kingdom **74** F5
Whitetail Ski •
PA, United States .... **116** [162]
Whitman Mission Nat. Hist. Site •
WA, United States **117** E2
Whitman Mission Nat. Hist. Site Park •
WA, United States .... **120** [30]
Whitmore Village •
HI, United States **119** L5
Whitney, Mt • CA, United States **117** F4
Whitsunday Group •
QL, Australia **111** E4
Whitsunday I. • QL, Australia ... **111** F4
Whoidala Lake • NT, Canada **38** K4
Whyalla • SA, Australia **34** G6
Wiang Ko Sai Nat. Park •
Thailand **109** G4
Wichita • KS, United States **41** G4

Wichita Falls •
TX, United States **119** N1
Wick • United Kingdom **6** I3
Wickenburg • AZ, United States . **118** J3
Wicklow • Ireland **79** E4
Wicklow [Adm] • Ireland **79** E4
Wicklow Head • Ireland **79** E4
Wicklow Mtns • Ireland **79** E4
Wicklow Mtns Nat. Park Park •
Ireland .... **72** [41]
Widgiemooltha • WA, Australia .. **34** D6
Widyan, Al • Iraq/Saudi Arabia .. **18** D3
Wied • Germany **82** H2
Wieda Spa • Germany .... **83** [81]
Wiefelstede • Germany **8** D3
Wiehl • Germany **81** E3
Wien Heritage C • Austria .... **64** [107]
Wien [Adm] • Austria **89** F4
Wiener Becken • Austria **14** D1
Wiener Neustadt • Austria **13** F10
Wieprz • Poland **13** L6
Wieringermeer • Netherlands ... **80** A3
Wies Heritage C • Germany ... **64** [47]
Wiesbaden • Germany **82** H4
Wiesbaden Spa • Germany ... **83** [142]
Wiese • Germany **10** M6
Wieskirche • Germany **82** J5
Wiesloch • Germany **5** L5
Wiesmoor • Germany **5** K1
Wieża • Poland **13** H3
Wigan • United Kingdom **7** J8
Wiggins • MS, United States **118** K4
Wight, Isle of • United Kingdom . **7** K11
Wigierski Nat. Park Park •
Poland .... **72** [92]
Wigtown • United Kingdom **7** H7
Wigtown Bay • United Kingdom .. **7** H7
Wil • Switzerland **89** G3
Wilcannia • NS, Australia **34** H6
Wild Coast • South Africa **100** D2
Wild Mtn Ski •
MN, United States .... **116** [111]
Wildau • Germany **81** F4
Wildbad Spa • Germany ..... **83** [257]
Wildbad Kreuth • Germany **82** J7
Wildcat Ski • NH, United States . **116** [210]
Wildemann Spa • Germany ... **83** [79]
Wildenbruch • Germany **81** F3
Wilderness Nat. Lake Area •
South Africa **100** C7
Wilderswil bei Interlaken Ski •
Switzerland .... **70** [93]
Wildeshausen • Germany **8** D4
Wildhaus • Switzerland **89** G3
Wildlife Reserve • Barbados **125** H1
Wildschönau Ski • Austria .... **70** [147]
Wildspitze • Austria **89** H6
Wildwood • NJ, United States ... **118** H3
Wilhelmshaven • Germany **8** D3
Wilhelmshaven Spa • Germany . **83** [49]
Wilkes Barre •
PA, United States **118** H1
Wilkes Land • Antarctica **46** (1) R2
Willamette • OR, United States . **117** E3
Willamette Pass Ski •
OR, United States .... **116** [50]
Willamette Pass •
OR, United States **117** E3
Willandra Lakes Heritage N •
NS, Australia .... **61** [134]
Willandra Lakes Heritage C •
Australia .... **63** [182]
Willandra Lakes • NS, Australia . **117** E1
Willapa Bay • WA, United States **117** E1
Willebroek • Belgium **5** H3
Willemstad • Curaçao **37** H5
Willeroo • NT, Australia **34** F3
William, Prince, Forest Park Park •
VA, United States .... **121** [264]
Williams • AZ, United States ... **122** C3
Williams, Roger, Nat. Mem. Park •
RI, United States .... **121** [339]
Williamsburg •
VA, United States **118** H3
Williamsport •
PA, United States **41** K3
Williamsport •
PA, United States **118** H1
Willich • Germany **81** E3
Willikies • Antigua & Barbuda .. **125** F2
Willingen Spa • Germany ... **83** [120]
Willis Group • CL, Australia **34** J3
Williston • ND, United States **40** F2
Williston • South Africa **100** C2
Williston Lake • BC, Canada **122** C1
Willmar • MN, United States **41** G2
Willoughby Bay •
Antigua & Barbuda **125** F4
Willowmore • South Africa **100** C7
Wills, Lake • WA, Australia **34** E4
Wilmington • NC, United States . **41** K5
Wilmington • DE, United States . **118** H3
Wilmot Mtn Ski •
WI, United States .... **116** [125]
Wilnsdorf • Germany **81** E3
Wilok • Poland **13** K8
Wilpattu Nat. Park • Sri Lanka .. **106** D15
Wilson • NC, United States **41** K4
Wilson Bluff • Antarctica **46** (1) U2
Wilson, Cape • NU, Canada **39** O3
Wilson's Creek Nat. Battlefield Park •
MO, United States .... **121** [175]
Wilsons Promontory •
VI, Australia **111** G3
Wiltshire • United Kingdom **74** F3
Wiltz • Luxembourg **80** A20
Wiluna • WA, Australia **34** D5
Wimbledon • United Kingdom ... **74** E1
Wincanton • United Kingdom **74** F3
Winchelsea Beach •
United Kingdom .... **75** [69]
Wind Cave Nat. Park Park •
SD, United States .... **120** [152]
Wind River Range •
WY, United States **38** J8
Windermere [Lake] •
United Kingdom **74** C4
Windhoek • Namibia **24** B4
Windmill, Pointe • Vanuatu ... **35** (2) K2
Windmere • United Kingdom **74** C3
Window Rock • AZ, United States **118** J2
Windows of the World •
Shenzhen, China **107** H3
Windrush • United Kingdom **5** B3
Windsor • OT, Canada **39** O8
Windsor • United Kingdom **74** E1
Windsor • NS, Canada **123** C9
Windward Beach •
St Kitts & Nevis **125** G4
Windward Is. • West Indies **37** I5
Windward Passage • Cuba/Haiti . **37** G4

Winisk • OT, Canada **39** N5
Winisk Lake • OT, Canada **39** N6
Winisk • OT, Canada **39** N5
Winneba • Ghana **22** D3
Winnebago, Lake •
WI, United States **39** N8
Winnemucca • NV, United States **117** F2
Winnfield • LA, United States ... **118** K1
Winningen • Germany **82** H1
Winnipeg • MN, Canada **38** L6
Winnipeg, Lake • MN, Canada ... **38** L6
Winnipeg [Riv] • MN/OT, Canada **38** L6
Winnipegosis, Lake •
MN, Canada **38** K6
Winnipesaukee, Lake •
NH, United States **118** G3
Winschoten • Netherlands **5** K1
Winsen • Germany **8** E4
Winsen • Germany **8** F3
Winslow • Kiribati **33** J6
Winston • OR, United States **117** E3
Winston-Salem •
NC, United States **41** J4
Winter Gardens •
FL, United States **121** C1
Winter Harbour • NT/NU, Canada **38** I2
Winter Haven •
FL, United States **119** M5
Winter Park Ski •
CO, United States .... **116** [90]
Winter Park • FL, United States . **119** D5
Winterberg • Germany **9** D5
Winterberg Spa • Germany ... **83** [109]
Winterberg • South Africa **100** C4
Winterevergreen Ski •
VA, United States .... **116** [156]
Winterlace Ski •
WV, United States .... **116** [153]
Winterswijk • Netherlands **80** A8
Winterthur • Switzerland **9** D9
Winton • QL, Australia **34** H4
Winton • New Zealand **112** L4
Winton Heights • Bahamas **124** B3
Wipperfürth • Germany **81** E4
Wirliyajarrayi Aboriginal Land •
NT, Australia **112** H1
Wisbech • United Kingdom **7** M9
Wiscasset • ME, United States . **118** G4
Wisconsin • United States **41** H2
Wisconsin [Riv] • United States . **39** M8
Wisła • Poland **13** H8
Wisła [Riv] • Poland **13** I8
Wislany, Zalev •
Poland/Russian Fed. **13** I3
Wisłoka • Poland **13** K8
Wismar • Germany **8** G3
Wisnar Ski • MD, United States . **116** [158]
Witbank • South Africa **24** D5
Witjira Nat. Park •
SA, Australia **112** H4
Witney • United Kingdom **7** K10
Wittdün Spa • Germany ...... **83** [3]
Witten • Germany **81** E2
Wittenberg • Germany **8** H5
Wittenberg Heritage C • Germany **64** [32]
Wittenberge • Germany **8** G3
Wittingen • Germany **8** F4
Wittlich • Germany **82** H3
Wittmund • Germany **8** D3
Wittstock • Germany **8** H4
Witwatersrand • South Africa **24** D5
Witzenhausen Spa • Germany . **83** [129]
Wloclawek • Poland **13** I5
Wlodawa • Poland **13** M6
Wodonga • VI, Australia **111** G3
Wodzisław Slaski • Poland **13** H8
Woerden • Netherlands **80** C4
Wokam • Indonesia **32** (1) D4
Woking • United Kingdom **74** E1
Wolds, The • United Kingdom **5** C1
Wolf (Galápagos Is. **43** (1) A1
Wolf Mtn Ski •
UT, United States .... **116** [81]
Wolf Point • MT, United States .. **40** E2
Wolf Trap Farm Park Park •
VA, United States .... **121** [266]
Wolf, Volcán • Galápagos Is. .. **43** (1) A2
Wolfen • Germany **82** J5
Wolfen • Germany **8** H5
Wolfenbüttel • Germany **8** F4
Wolfhagen • Germany **9** E5
Wolfratshausen • Germany **82** J3
Wolfsberg • Austria **13** D11
Wolfsburg • Germany **8** F4
Wolgast • Germany **8** I3
Wolin • Poland **13** D4
Woliński Nat. Park Park •
Poland .... **72** [89]
Wolkenstein Ski • Italy ...... **90** [232]
Wolkenstein in Gröden • Italy ... **90** B1
Wollaston, Isla • Chile **45** C7
Wollaston Lake • SA, Canada ... **38** K5
Wollaston Peninsula •
NU, Canada **38** H3
Wolomin • Poland **13** K5
Wolstenholm, Cape • QU, Canada **39** P4
Woltersdorf • Germany **81** F4
Wolvega • Netherlands **5** I2
Wolverhampton • United Kingdom **74** D2
Women's Rights Nat. Hist. Park Park •
NY, United States .... **121** [317]
Wondsorejo • Indonesia **110** C3
Wonju • Rep. of Korea **30** E6
Wonosobo • Java, Indonesia ... **110** D7
Wonsan • D.P.R. of Korea **30** D5
Wonthaggi • VI, Australia **111** G3
Wood Buffalo Nat. Park Heritage N •
AL/NT, Canada .... **60** [3]
Woodbridge • United Kingdom **5** E2
Woodbury Bay • Dominica **125** E4
Woodford • OK, United States ... **40** G4
Woodley Hole • United Kingdom **74** F3
Woolacombe Beach •
United Kingdom .... **75** [135]
Woollongong • NS, Australia ... **111** G2
Woolroffe, Mt • SA, Australia .. **112** H3
Wooramel • WA, Australia **34** B5
Worcester • MA, United States . **41** L3
Worcester • United Kingdom **74** D1
Worcester • South Africa **100** C5
Wordsworth House •
United Kingdom **74** C1
Worgl • Austria **9** H9
Workington • United Kingdom ... **74** C1
Worksop • United Kingdom **7** K8
World's View • Zimbabwe **102** J3

Wormerveer • Netherlands **80** C2
Worms • Germany **82** H4
Wörth • Germany **5** L5
Wörther See • Austria **13** D11
Worthing • United Kingdom **74** E3
Worthing Town **Beach** •
United Kingdom .... **75** [75]
Worthsee • Germany **82** J3
Wosi • Indonesia **32** (1) C3
Wowoni • Indonesia **32** (1) B3
Woy Woy • NS, Australia **34** J6
Wrangel I. • Russian Fed. **27** V2
Wrangell • AK, United States **38** E5
Wrangell, Mt •
AK, United States **40** (2) G2
Wrangell Mtns •
AK, United States **38** C4
Wrangell-St Elias Nat. Park & Preserve
Heritage N •
AK, United States .... **60** [1]
Wrangell-St Elias Nat. Park & Preserve **Park** •
AK, United States .... **120** [12]
Wrath, Cape • United Kingdom **6** G3
Wrekin, The • United Kingdom **74** D1
Wremen **Spa** • Germany .... **83** [53]
Wrexham • United Kingdom **7** J8
Wrexham [Adm] • United Kingdom **75** A4
Wright Brothers Nat. Mem. •
NC, United States **118** H5
Wright Brothers Nat. Mem. **Park** •
NC, United States .... **121** [251]
Wrigley • NT, Canada **38** G4
Wrka • Poland **13** J5
Wrocław • Poland **13** F6
Wronki • Poland **13** F5
Wrzesnia • Poland **13** G5
Wschowa • Poland **13** F6
Wu Jiang • China **29** D5
Wu Xia • China **29** E5
Wudangshan **Heritage C** • China .... **63** [150]
Wudaoliang • China **28** F1
Wudu • China **29** C4
Wuhan • China **29** E4
Wuhu • China **107** J1
Wujiang • China **107** J2
Wukari • Nigeria **22** F3
Wulferdingsen **Spa** • Germany .... **83** [94]
Wuliang Shan • China **29** C6
Wulingyuan **Heritage N** • China .... **61** [118]
Wur • Indonesia **32** (1) C4
Wum • Cameroon **22** G3
Wümme • Germany **5** M1
Wun Rog • Sudan **23** D2
Wünnenberg **Spa** • Germany .... **83** [102]
Wunsiedel • Germany **9** H6
Wunstorf • Germany **8** E4
Wupatki Nat. Mon. •
AZ, United States **118** J1
Wupatki Nat. Mon. **Park** •
AZ, United States .... **120** [105]
Wupper • Germany **81** E4
Wuppertal • Germany **81** E4
Würm • Germany **82** J2
Wurno • Nigeria **22** F2
Wursten **Spa** • Germany .... **83** [53]
Würzburg • Germany **9** E7
Würzburg **Heritage C** • Germany .... **64** [45]
Wurzen • Germany **8** H5
Wushaoling • China **29** C3
Wusheng Guan • China **29** E4
Wusong • China **59** A8
Wustermark • Germany **81** F1
Wustrow **Spa** • Germany .... **83** [275]
Wutach • Germany **9** E9
Wutai Shan • China **29** E3
Wutong Shan • China **107** H4
Wuwei • China **29** C3
Wuxi • China **107** J2
Wuyi Shan • China **29** F5
Wuyiling • China **27** K7
Wuyuan • China **29** D2
Wuyuanzhen • China **107** J4
Wuzhi Shan • China **31** D3
Wyandra • QL, Australia **111** F5
Wye • United Kingdom **74** E3
Wye Valley • United Kingdom **74** D3
Wyk **Spa** • Germany .... **83** [4]
Wyndham • WA, Australia **34** E3
Wyndham • New Zealand **112** L4
Wynyard • TS, Australia **34** I8
Wynyard • SA, Canada **38** K6
Wyoming • United States **40** E3
Wyre Forest • United Kingdom **74** D1
Wysoczna Ciechanowska • Poland **13** J4
Wyszków • Poland **13** K5
Wyzyna Krakowsko-Czestochowsk •
Poland **13** I7
Wyzyna Lubelska • Poland **13** L6
Wyzyna Lubelska • Poland **13** M6

Xaghra • Malta **93** H1
Xai-Xai • Mozambique **24** E4
Xainza • China **28** E2
Xalapa • Mexico **123** E2
Xangongo • Angola **24** B3
Xanten • Germany **80** A12
Xanten • Germany **81** E1
Xánthi • Greece **92** D1
Xánthi • Greece **92** D1
Xanthos • Turkey **92** D9
Xanthos • Turkey **92** D9
Xanthos-Letoon **Heritage C** •
Turkey .... **64** [188]
Xanxerê • Brazil **44** F4
Xapuri • Brazil **43** D6
Xàtiva • Spain **11** K5
Xeraco **Beach** • Spain .... **68** [102]
Xewkija • Malta **93** H1
Xi Hu • China **107** J3
Xi'an • China **29** D4
Xi'an area **Heritage C** • China .... **63** [149]
Xiaguan • China **29** C5
Xiamen • China **29** F6
Xiang Jiang • China **29** E5
Xiangfan • China **29** E4
Xiangshan • China **107** J4
Xiangtan • China **29** E5
Xiangzhou • Zhuhai, China **107** H1
Xianqunmiao • China **107** J3
Xianquan He • China **107** C2
Xianxia Ling • China **29** F5
Xiao Hinggan Ling • China **27** K7
Xiaobole Shan • China **27** J6
Xiaolan • China **107** H1
Xiaomeisha Beach Resort •
Shenzhen, China **107** H4
Xiaoshan • China **107** J4
Xiapu • China **31** F1
Xichang • China **29** C5
Xigaze • China **28** E2
Xijir Ulan Hu • China **28** E1
Xili Lake Resort •
Shenzhen, China **107** H3
Xilókastro • Greece **15** D5

Xilókastro **Beach** • Greece .... **69** [155]
Ximiao • China **29** C2
Xingtai • China **29** E3
Xingu • Brazil **43** G5
Xingxingxia • China **101** G4
Xingyi • China **31** C2
Xining • China **29** C3
Xinjiang Uygur Zizhiqu • China **26** N10
Xinxian • China **29** E3
Xinxiang • China **29** E3
Xinyang • China **29** E4
Xinzo de Limia • Spain **11** D2
Xiongyuecheng • China **30** B4
Xiró • Greece **15** E5
Xisha Qundao • South China Sea **31** E3
Xisha Qundao • South China Sea **107** G7
Xitianmu Shan • China **107** J3
Xiuyan • China **30** B4
Xixabangma Feng • China **28** E3
Xizang Zizhiqu • China **28** E2
Xkendi • Malta **93** H1
Xlendi Bay • Malta **93** H1
Xochimilco **Heritage C** • Mexico .... **62** [21]
Xuan Loc • Vietnam **108** B2
Xuanhua • China **29** E3
Xuanwei • China **29** C5
Xuanzhou • China **107** J3
Xuefeng Shan • China **29** D5
Xupu • China **31** E1
Xuwen • China **29** E6
Xuzhou • China **29** F4
Xylóskalo • Crete, Greece **93** E5

Ya Men • China **107** H3
Ya'an • China **29** C4
Yabelo • Ethiopia **23** F3
Yablonovyy Khrebet •
Russian Fed. **27** H6
Yabu, Laem • Phuket, Thailand **109** K1
Yabulu • QL, Australia **111** F1
Yacuma • Bolivia **44** C1
Yadé, Massif du •
Cameroon/Central African Rep. **22** H3
Yaeyama-Retto • Japan **29** G6
Yafo • Israel **98** A5
Yafran • Libya **21** B1
Yagoua • Cameroon **22** H2
Yagradagzê Shan • China **29** B3
Yai, Khao • Ko Samui, Thailand **109** J1
Yai, Laem • Ko Samui, Thailand **109** J1
Yaiza **Beach** •
Lanzarote, Canary Is. .... **68** [94]
Yaiza • Lanzarote, Canary Is. **87** E3
Yakawa • WA, United States **117** E1
Yako • Burkina Faso **22** D2
Yaku • Japan **30** F9
Yakumo • Japan **30** K3
Yakushima **Heritage N** • Japan .... **61** [119]
Yakutat • AK, United States **38** D5
Yakutat Bay • AK, United States **38** C5
Yakutsk • Russian Fed. **27** K4
Yala • Thailand **31** B5
Yala Nat. Park • Sri Lanka **106** D16
Yalgoo • WA, Australia **34** C5
Yalinga • Central African Rep. **23** C2
Yaloké • Central African Rep. **22** H3
Yalong Jiang • China **29** C4
Yalongxue Shan • China **29** C4
Yalova • Turkey **92** D3
Yalpug, Ozero • Ukraine **14** P4
Yalta • Ukraine **17** E6
Yalu • China/D.P.R. of Korea **30** D4
Yalutorovsk • Russian Fed. **26** K6
Yamagata • Japan **30** K5
Yamaguchi • Japan **30** F7
Yamal Peninsula • Russian Fed. **96** A3
Yamal, Poluostrov •
Russian Fed. **26** K3
Yamarovka • Russian Fed. **27** H6
Yamaska Prov. Park • QU, Canada **122** B8
Yambio • Sudan **23** C3
Yambol • Bulgaria **97** D3
Yamdena • Indonesia **32** (1) D4
Yamma Yamma, Lake •
Australia **34** H5
Yamoussoukro • Côte d'Ivoire **22** C3
Yamsk • Russian Fed. **27** P4
Yamuna • India **105** C7
Yanagino Yumco • China **28** F3
Yan'an • China **29** D3
Yana • Russian Fed. **27** M2
Yanam • India **106** C4
Yanbu • Saudi Arabia **18** C5
Yancheng • China **26** N9
Yancheng • China **29** G4
Yanchep • QL, Australia **34** A4
Yandongo • Dem. Rep. of Congo **23** C3
Yangiyul • Uzbekistan **18** I1
Yangjiang • China **29** E6
Yangon • Myanmar **31** B3
Yangtze • China **29** F4
Yangtze Gorges • China **107** G1
Yangzhou • China **107** J1
Yanji • China **29** H2
Yankari Nat. Park **Park** •
Nigeria .... **103** [34]
Yankee Harbour • Antarctica **59** A10
Yankton • SD, United States **41** G3
Yano-Indigirskaya Nizmennost •
Russian Fed. **27** N2
Yanqi • China **26** O9
Yanskiy Zaliv • Russian Fed. **27** M2
Yaransk • Russian Fed. **17** H3
Yardimci Burun • Turkey **93** G3
Yare • United Kingdom **5** E2
Yari • Colombia **43** C3
Yariga • Japan **30** I6
Yarim • Yemen **18** D7
Yarkand • China **28** K2
Yarkant • China **98** B2
Yarkant He • China **26** M10
Yarlung Zangbo Jiang • China **28** E3
Yarmouth • United Kingdom **78** C8
Yarmouth • NS, Canada **123** D7
Yaroslavl' • Russian Fed. **97** E2
Yarra • United Kingdom **43** B2
Yarrumal • Colombia **43** B2
Yasawa Group • Fiji **35** (2) D2
Yashi • Nigeria **22** F2

Yass • NS, Australia **111** G2
Yatagan • Turkey **15** J6
Yateritas • Cuba **124** D8
Yatsushiro • Japan **30** F8
Yatta Plateau • Kenya **101** G4
Yau Ma Tei • Hong Kong, China **107** H6
Yauca • Peru **127** B3
Yáuco • Puerto Rico **125** E3
Yauyos • Peru **127** B1
Yavari • Brazil/Peru **43** C4
Yaverland **Beach** •
United Kingdom .... **75** [96]
Yavero • Peru **127** B2
Yawatahama • Japan **30** G8
Yaxchilán • Mexico **37** C4
Yazd • Iran **18** F3
Yazoo • MS, United States **118** K2
Yazoo City • MS, United States **118** K2
Ydre • Sweden **95** F8
Ye • Myanmar **31** B3
Ye-u • Myanmar **28** F4
Yebbi Bou • Chad **20** I4
Yecheng • China **28** C1
Yecla • Spain **87** C1
Yedi Burun • Turkey **15** J7
Yefremov • Russian Fed. **17** F4
Yéhe • Eritrea **21** G5
Yeji • Ghana **22** D3
Yekaterinburg • Russian Fed. **26** J6
Yelapa • Mexico **123** E1
Yelets • Russian Fed. **17** F4
Yelizavety, mys • Russian Fed. **27** N6
Yelizovo • Russian Fed. **27** Q6
Yell • United Kingdom **6** K1
Yellice Dagi • Turkey **15** K4
Yellow Mountains • China **107** J3
Yellow Sea • Asia **29** G3
Yellowhead Pass • AL/BC, Canada **122** C2
Yellowknife • NT, Canada **38** I4
Yellowstone •
MT/WY, United States **40** E2
Yellowstone Nat. Park **Heritage N** •
WY, United States .... **60** [14]
Yellowstone Nat. Park **Park** •
WY, United States .... **120** [74]
Yelwa • Nigeria **22** E2
Yemen • Asia **18** E7
Yenashimsky Polkan, gora •
Russian Fed. **26** P6
Yendi • Ghana **22** D3
Yengo • Congo **23** B3
Yenice • Turkey **15** I4
Yenifoça • Turkey **15** H5
Yenisey • Russian Fed. **26** O4
Yeniseysk • Russian Fed. **27** D5
Yeniseyskiy Kryazh •
Russian Fed. **26** P5
Yeniseyskiy Zaliv •
Russian Fed. **26** N3
Yeo Lake • WA, Australia **34** D5
Yeovil • United Kingdom **74** F3
Yeppoon • QL, Australia **111** F4
Yerbogachen • Russian Fed. **27** G4
Yercaud • India **106** D7
Yerçpótamos • Crete, Greece **93** E7
Yerevan • Armenia **17** H3
Yermak • Kazakhstan **26** M7
Yermasóyia **Beach** • Cyprus .... **69** [193]
Yermasóyia • Cyprus **93** J3
Yermolayevo • Russian Fed. **26** I7
Yeroskipos • Cyprus **93** J3
Yerupaja • Peru **5** G6
Yerupaja • Peru **43** B6
Yerwa • Nigeria **22** H2
Yesa, Embalse de • Spain **11** J2
Yesilbag • Turkey **93** G2
Yesilköy • Turkey **15** J3
Yesilova • Turkey **93** G1
Yessey • Russian Fed. **26** R4
Yeste • Spain **11** I6
Yeu, I. d' • France **10** C7
Yevreyskaya • Russian Fed. **27** L7
Yeysk • Russian Fed. **17** F5
Yi • Uruguay **127** D2
Yi Xian • China **107** J3
Yi'an • China **27** K7
Yialoúsa • Cyprus **93** J2
Yibin • China **29** C5
Yibug Caka • China **28** E2
Yichang • China **29** E4
Yichun • China **27** K7
Yidu • China **29** E4
Yilan • China **27** K7
Yildiz Daglari • Turkey **93** G2
Yildiz Daglari • Turkey **15** I2
Yinchuan • China **29** D3
Yingde • China **29** E6
Yingkou • China **29** G2
Yining • China **26** N9
Yirshi • China **29** F1
Yishun New Town • Singapore **108** E2
Yixing • China **107** J1
Yiyang • China **29** E5
Ylane • Finland **95** E3
Ylikitka • Finland **16** O3
Ylitornio • Finland **16** L3
Ylivieska • Finland **16** M4
Yliöjärvi • Finland **95** D3
Yngaren • Sweden **95** D3
Yoakum • TX, United States **119** N5
Yogan, Cerro • Chile **45** C6
Yogyakarta • Java, Indonesia **110** D7
Yogyakarta [Adm] •
Java, Indonesia **110** D7
Yoho Nat. Park • BC, Canada **122** C4
Yoju • Rep. of Korea **30** D6
Yokadouma • Cameroon **22** H4
Yokkaichi • Japan **30** I7
Yoko • Cameroon **22** H3
Yokohama • Japan **30** J7
Yokosuka • Japan **30** J7
Yokote • Japan **30** K5
Yola • Nigeria **22** G3
Yom • Thailand **109** G2
Yonago • Japan **30** G7
Yongan • D.P.R. of Korea **30** E4
Yongdeng • China **29** C3
Yongdok • Rep. of Korea **30** E6
Yonghung • D.P.R. of Korea **30** D5
Yongju • Rep. of Korea **30** E6
Yonne • France **10** I5
Yonne • France **10** I5
York • United Kingdom **74** E2
York • WA, Australia **34** B6
York • PA, United States **118** H1
York [Adm] • United Kingdom **75** A4
York, Cape • QL, Australia **34** H2
York, Cape, Peninsula •
QL, Australia **34** H2
York I. • Antigua & Barbuda **125** F4
Yorke Peninsula • SA, Australia **34** G6
Yorkshire • United Kingdom **7** K7
Yorkshire Dales Nat. Park **Park** •
United Kingdom .... **72** [44]
Yorkshire Dales Nat. Park •
United Kingdom **75** A4

Yorkshire, North •
United Kingdom **75** A4
Yorkshire Wolds •
United Kingdom **7** L7
Yorktown • VA, United States **118** H3
Yorton • SA, Canada **38** K6
Yosemite Nat. Park **Heritage N** •
CA, United States .... **60** [11]
Yosemite Nat. Park •
CA, United States **117** F3
Yosemite Nat. Park **Park** •
CA, United States .... **120** [51]
Yoshkar Ola • Russian Fed. **17** H3
Yosu • Rep. of Korea **29** B1
You Jiang • China **29** D6
Youghal • Ireland **7** E10
Youghal **Beach** • Ireland .... **68** [40]
Youngstown • NU, Canada **39** N4
Youngstown • OH, United States **41** J3
Youshaoshan • China **26** P10
Youyang • China **29** D5
Yow Beach • Ko Samui, Thailand **109** J2
Ypres • Belgium **80** A13
Yquem, Château • France **85** G3
Ystad **Beach** • Sweden .... **69** [6]
Ystad • Sweden **95** F15
Ytre Arna • Norway **95** A3
Ytre Sula • Norway **94** C3
Yuan Jiang • China **29** C6
Yuanling • China **29** E5
Yuantouzhu • China **107** J1
Yuba City • CA, United States **40** B4
Yubari • Japan **30** K3
Yucatán [Adm] • Mexico **37** D3
Yucatán Channel • Mexico **37** D3
Yucatán, Peninsula de • Mexico **37** D4
Yucca House Nat. Mon. **Park** •
CO, United States .... **120** [95]
Yudoma • Russian Fed. **27** M5
Yuen Long • Hong Kong, China **107** H5
Yuendumu • NT, Australia **112** H1
Yuendumu Aboriginal Land •
NT, Australia **112** H1
Yulara • NT, Australia **112** H3
Yulin • Shaanxi, China **29** D3
Yulin • Guangxi, China **31** E2
Yulin Jiao • China **25** M8
Yulongxue Shan • China **29** C4
Yuma • AZ, United States **118** J3
Yumari • Venezuela **43** D3
Yumen • China **29** B3
Yun-Gun-Gui Gaoyuian • China **31** C1
Yunak • Turkey **15** M5
Yunan • China **107** G6
Yungas • Bolivia **44** D2
Yunkai Dashan • China **31** E2
Yunkanjini Aboriginal Land •
NT, Australia **112** H1
Yunzhong Shan • China **29** E3
Yurga • Russian Fed. **26** N6
Yurimaguas • Peru **43** B5
Yurungkax He • China **28** C1
Yushan • Taiwan **29** G6
Yushkozero • Russian Fed. **17** E2
Yushu • China **29** B4
Yuxi • China **31** C2
Yuxikou • China **107** J1
Yuyao • China **107** J4
Yuzawa • Japan **30** K5
Yuzhno-Kuril'sk • Russian Fed. **27** O8
Yuzhnyy Bug • Ukraine **17** D5
Yuzhno-Sakhalinsk •
Russian Fed. **27** N7
Yvelines • France **85** E3
Yverdon-les-Bains • Switzerland **89** G1
Yvetot • France **10** F4
Yvoir • Belgium **80** A15

Za Qu • China **28** G2
Zaanse Schans • Netherlands **80** C2
Zaanstad • Netherlands **80** C2
Zabarjad • Egypt **21** G3
Zabid • Yemen **18** D7
Zabid **Heritage C** • Yemen .... **63** [102]
Zabkowice Slaskie • Poland **13** F7
Zablotiv • Ukraine **14** M1
Zabrze • Poland **13** H7
Zacatecas **Heritage C** • Mexico .... **62** [14]
Zacatecas • Mexico **123** E1
Zacatecas [Adm] • Mexico **37** (1) B1
Zadar • Croatia **14** C5
Zadetkyi Kyun • Myanmar **31** B5
Zadi • Angola **23** B5
Zadoi • China **28** F2
Zafra • Spain **11** E6
Zagan • Poland **13** E6
Zagazig, El • Egypt **101** F2
Zaghouan • Tunisia **101** E2
Zagora • Croatia **14** D5
Zagorá **Beach** • Greece .... **69** [165]
Zagorá • Greece **92** C4
Zagorá • Greece **92** D4
Zagora • Morocco **101** D6
Zagreb • Croatia **15** B4
Zagreb • Croatia **14** C4
Zagros, Kuhha-ye • Iran **18** F3
Zagvya • Hungary **13** J10
Zaháro • Greece **15** C6
Zaháro **Beach** • Greece .... **69** [157]
Zahedan • Iran **18** H4
Záhrada Cech • Czech Rep. **96** C2
Zajecar • F.R. of Yugoslavia **14** J2
Zakamensk • Russian Fed. **27** G6
Zakatały • Azerbaijan **17** H2
Zakinthos **Beach** • Greece .... **69** [151]
Zákinthos • Greece **92** C3
Zákinthos • Greece **92** C3
Zákinthos [I.] • Greece **92** C3
Zákinthos [I.] • Greece **92** C3
Zakopane • Poland **13** I8
Zákros • Crete, Greece **93** E8
Zala • Hungary **13** G1
Zala • Romania **14** H4
Zalaegerszeg • Hungary **13** F11
Zalau • Romania **14** J4
Zalalovo • Russian Fed. **26** H6
Zalim • Saudi Arabia **18** D5
Zalingei • Sudan **23** J3
Zallaca • Spain **71** A16
Zaltan • Libya **21** C2

Zhob • Pakistan **28** A2
Zhongba • China **28** D3
Zhongdian • China **29** B5
Zhongning • China **29** D3
Zhongsha Qundao •
South China Sea **107** G8
Zhongshan • China **107** H1
Zhongye Qundao •
South China Sea **31** E4
Zhoukoudian **Heritage C** • China .... **63** [147]
Zhoukouzhen • China **29** E4
Zhoushan • China **107** J4
Zhoushan Dao • China **107** J4
Zhoushan Qundao • China **107** J4
Zhu Jiang • China **107** H2
Zhuanghe • China **30** B5
Zhuhai Holiday Resort •
Zhuhai, China **107** H1
Zhuhai Special Economic Zone •
China **107** H1
Zhuji • China **107** J4
Zhujing • China **107** J4
Zhuzhou • China **29** E5
Ziar • Slovak Rep. **13** H9
Zibo • China **29** F3
Zicavo • Corsica, France **85** L4
Ziegenhals • Germany **81** F4
Zielona Góra • Poland **13** E6
Zierikzee • Netherlands **5** G3
Zigong • China **29** C5
Ziguinchor • Senegal **22** A2
Zihuatanejo • Mexico **123** E3
Zijin Shan • China **29** E3
Zijpe **Beach** • Netherlands .... **68** [48]
Zilina • Slovak Rep. **13** H8
Zillah • Libya **21** C2
Zillertal • Austria **89** H7
Zillertaler Alpen •
Austria/Italy **89** H7
Zima • China **27** F6
Zimba • Zambia **24** D3
Zimbabwe • Africa .... **102** J
Zimnicea • Romania **97** D1
Zinal • Switzerland **89** G6
Zinder • Niger **20** G6
Zingst • Germany **8** H2
Zingst **Beach** • Germany .... **69** [273]
Zingst **Spa** • Germany .... **83** [277]
Zinnowitz **Spa** • Germany .... **83** [283]
Zion • St Kitts & Nevis **125** G4
Zion Nat. Park •
UT, United States **118** J1
Zion Nat. Park **Park** •
UT, United States .... **120** [80]
Zipaquirá • Colombia **43** C3
Zippori • Israel **98** A4
Zirje • Croatia **14** C6
Zirndorf • Germany **9** F7
Zittau • Germany **9** J6
Ziway, Lake • Ethiopia **23** F2
Ziyaragiriyushi • Maldives **106** E2
Zlatá Koruna • Czech Rep. **96** C4
Zlaté Moravce • Slovak Rep. **13** H9
Zlatibor • Bulgaria **14** K6
Zlatni Pyasurtsi • Bulgaria **97** D4
Zlatograd • Bulgaria **15** G2
Zlatoust • Russian Fed. **26** I6
Zleby • Czech Rep. **96** C2
Zlin • Czech Rep. **13** G8
Zlocieniec • Poland **13** F4
Zlotów • Poland **13** G4
Zloten • Poland **13** G5
Zmerovce • Czech Rep. **96** C4
Zoetemeer • Netherlands **80** C3
Zoldo Alto **Ski** • Italy .... **70** [225]
Zoldo Alto • Italy **90** B4
Zomba • Malawi **24** E3
Zonári, Akra • Rhodes, Greece **93** F2
Zongo • Dem. Rep. of Congo **22** H4
Zongsan Hot Springs • China **107** H1
Zonguldak • Turkey **15** M2
Zonhoven **Beach** • Belgium .... **68** [53]
Zonhoven • Belgium **80** A15
Zonnebeke [Battlefield] •
Belgium **80** A13
Zons • Germany **81** E3
Zoologischer Garten Berlin •
Germany **81** F2
Zoomarine **Park** • Portugal .... **73** [80]
Zoorama • France **85** G1
Zorzor • Liberia **22** C3
Zossen • Germany **81** F4
Zouar • Chad **20** I4
Zouérat • Mauritania **20** C4
Zrenjanin • F.R. of Yugoslavia **14** H4
Zrinska Gora • Croatia **14** D4
Zuancheng • China **107** J3
Zuari Estuary • Goa, India **105** B1
Zufar • Oman **25** G8
Zug **Ski** • Austria .... **70** [130]
Zug • Switzerland **89** G3
Zuger See • Switzerland **89** G3
Zugspitze • Austria/Germany **82** J6
Zuid-Beveland • Netherlands **80** A10
Zuid-Holland • Netherlands **80** A6
Zújar, Embalse del • Spain **11** F6
Zújar • Spain **82** C1
Zumaia **Beach** • Spain .... **68** [68]
Zumbo • Mozambique **24** E3
Zuni • NM, United States **118** J2
Zunyi • China **29** D5
Zuoz • Switzerland **89** G4
Zuqar, Jabal • Yemen **21** H5
Zürich • Switzerland **89** D9
Zürichsee • Switzerland **89** G3
Zurmi • Nigeria **20** G6
Zurrieq • Malta **93** H4
Zürs **Ski** • Austria .... **70** [131]
Zürs • Austria **89** H5
Zuru • Nigeria **22** E2
Zusmarshausen • Germany **82** J2
Zut • Croatia **14** C6
Zutphen • Netherlands **80** A8
Zuwarah • Libya **100** C8
Zuwarah • Libya **21** B1
Zvikov • Czech Rep. **96** B3
Zvishavane • Zimbabwe **102** J4
Zvishtov • Bulgaria **14** M4
Zvolen • Slovak Rep. **13** I9
Zweibrücken • Germany **9** I7
Zweisel • Germany **9** H6
Zweisimmen **Ski** • Switzerland .... **70** [87]
Zweisimmen • Switzerland **89** G2
Zwettl • Austria **13** E9
Zwickau • Germany **9** H6
Zwickauer Mulde • Germany **80** C3
Zwijndrecht • Netherlands **80** C3
Zwolle • Netherlands **80** C8
Zyrardów • Poland **13** J5
Zyryan • Kazakhstan **26** N8
Zyryanka • Russian Fed. **27** P3
Zywiec • Poland **13** I8

WORLD

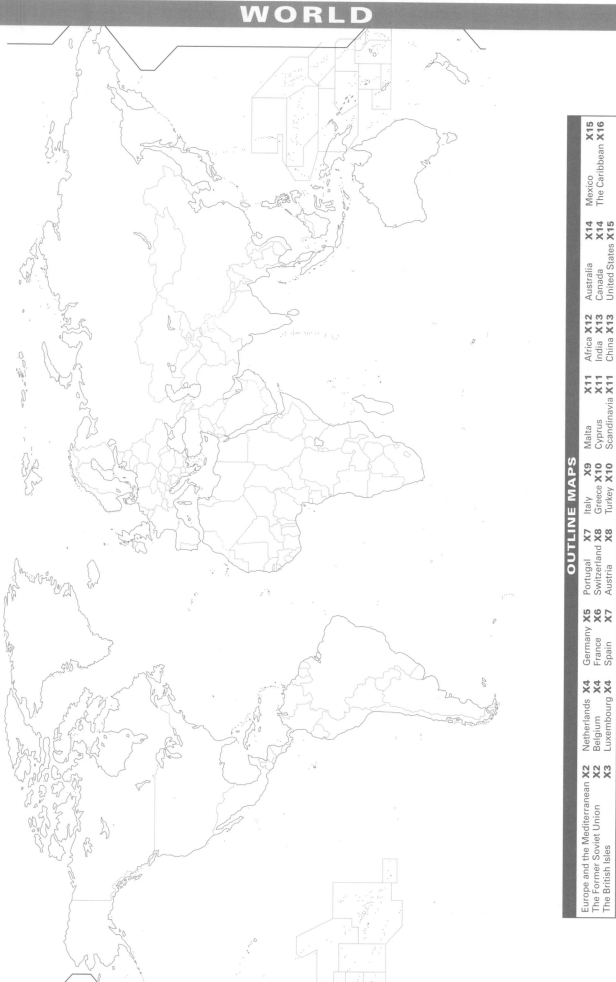

OUTLINE MAPS

EUROPE AND THE MEDITERRANEAN

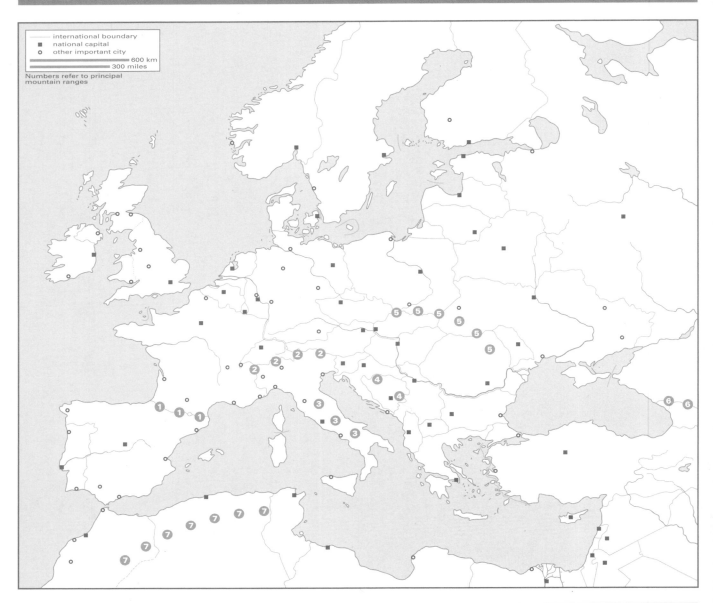

THE FORMER SOVIET UNION

BRITISH ISLES

international boundary
county/unitary authority boundary (UK),
regional boundary (Ireland)
national capital
capital of constituent parts of UK
other important city/town
100 kilometres
50 miles

Groups of very small unitary authorities are
shaded in light blue
Letters refer to English Tourist Board regions

CHANNEL IS.

NETHERLANDS

international boundary
provincial boundary
national capital
provincial capital
other important city/town

80 km
40 miles

BELGIUM AND LUXEMBOURG

international boundary
provincial boundary
national capital
provincial capital
other important city/town

80 km
40 miles

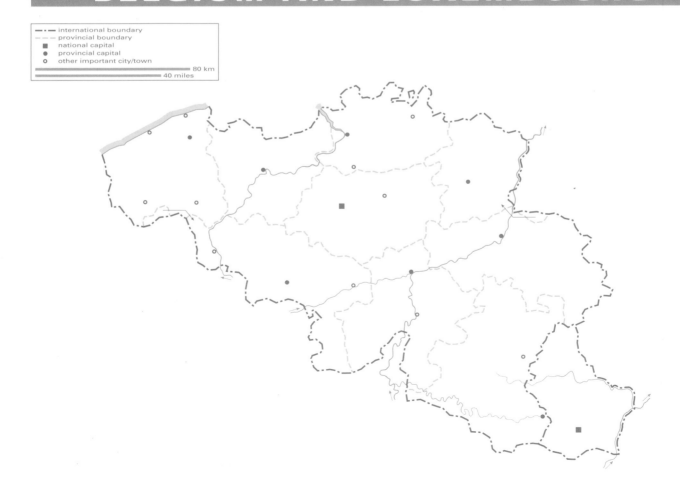

GERMANY

international boundary
Land boundary
national capital
Land capital
other important city/town
100 km
50 miles

FRANCE

- —·—·— international boundary
- — — — regional boundary
- ■ national capital
- ● regional capital
- ○ other important city/town

200 km
100 miles

60 kilometres
30 miles

SPAIN AND PORTUGAL

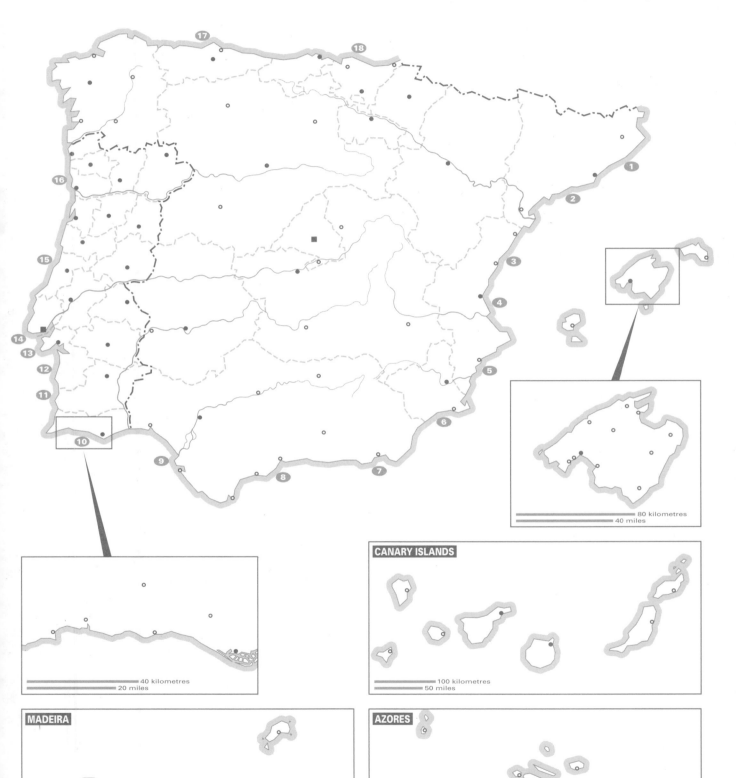

----- international boundary
----- autonomous community boundary (Spain)
district boundary (Portugal)
■ national capital
● autonomous community capital (Spain)
district capital (Portugal)
○ other important city/town

200 km
100 miles

Numbers refer to Spanish and Portuguese 'Costas'

80 kilometres
40 miles

40 kilometres
20 miles

CANARY ISLANDS

100 kilometres
50 miles

MADEIRA

40 km
20 miles

AZORES

200 kilometres
100 miles

SWITZERLAND

international boundary
■ national capital
○ other important city/town

80 km
40 miles

Numbers indicate principal Alpine ranges

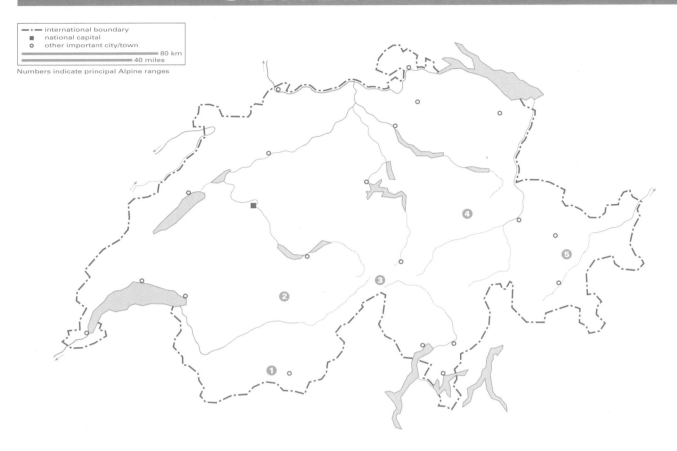

AUSTRIA

international boundary   ·
Land boundary
■ national capital
● Land capital
○ other important city/town

100 km
50 miles

Numbers indicate principal Alpine ranges

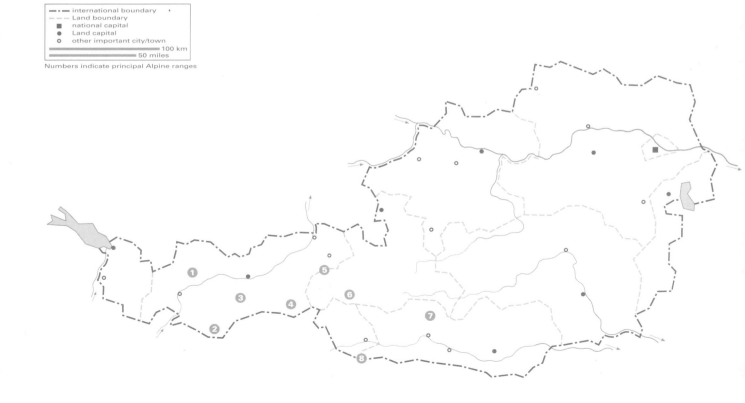

ITALY

international boundary
regional boundary
■ national capital
● regional capital
○ other important city/town

200 km
100 miles

GREECE AND WESTERN TURKEY

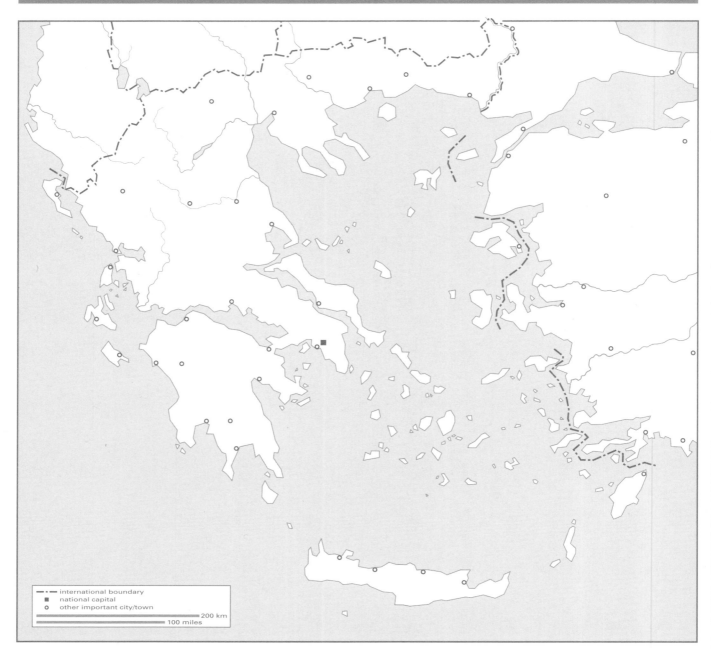

international boundary
■ national capital
○ other important city/town

200 km
100 miles

TURKEY

international boundary
■ national capital
○ other important city/town

400 km
200 miles

SCANDINAVIA

international boundary
regional boundary
■ national capital
○ other important city/town

400 km
200 miles

MALTA

CYPRUS

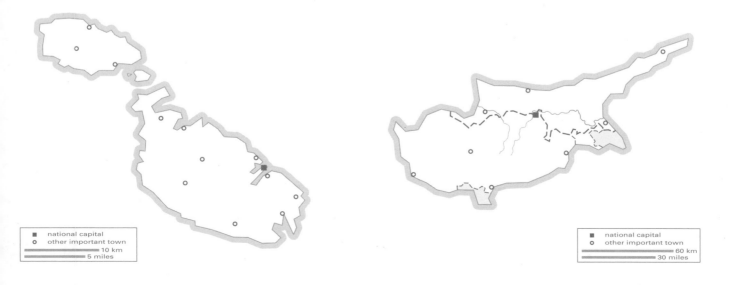

■ national capital
○ other important town

10 km
5 miles

■ national capital
○ other important town

60 km
30 miles

AFRICA

international boundary
national capital
other important city

SOUTH AFRICA

international boundary
provincial boundary
national capital
provincial capital
other important city/town

600 km
300 miles

INDIA

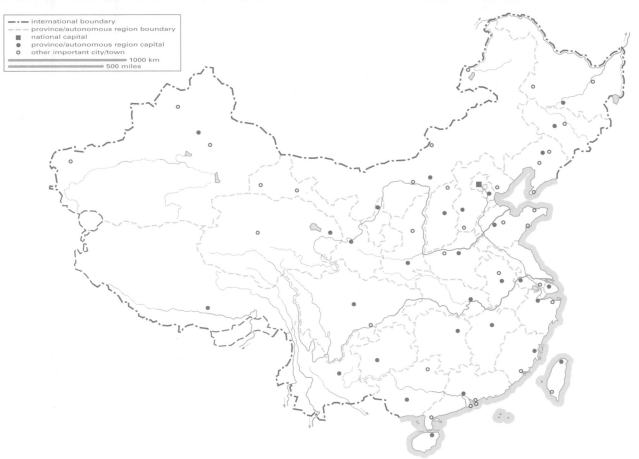

international boundary
state/union territory boundary
■ national capital
● state/union territory capital
○ other important city/town

800 km
400 miles

CHINA

international boundary
province/autonomous region boundary
■ national capital
● province/autonomous region capital
○ other important city/town

1000 km
500 miles

AUSTRALIA

state/territory boundary
■ national capital
● state/territory capital
○ other important city/town
—— 1000 km
—— 500 miles

CANADA

international boundary
province/territory boundary
■ national capital
● province/territory capital
○ other important city/town
—— 1000 km
—— 500 miles

UNITED STATES

international boundary
state boundary
■ national capital
● state capital
○ other important city/town

800 km
400 miles

1000 km
500 miles

300 km
150 miles

MEXICO

international boundary
state boundary
■ national capital
● state capital
○ other important city/town

500 km
250 miles

THE CARIBBEAN

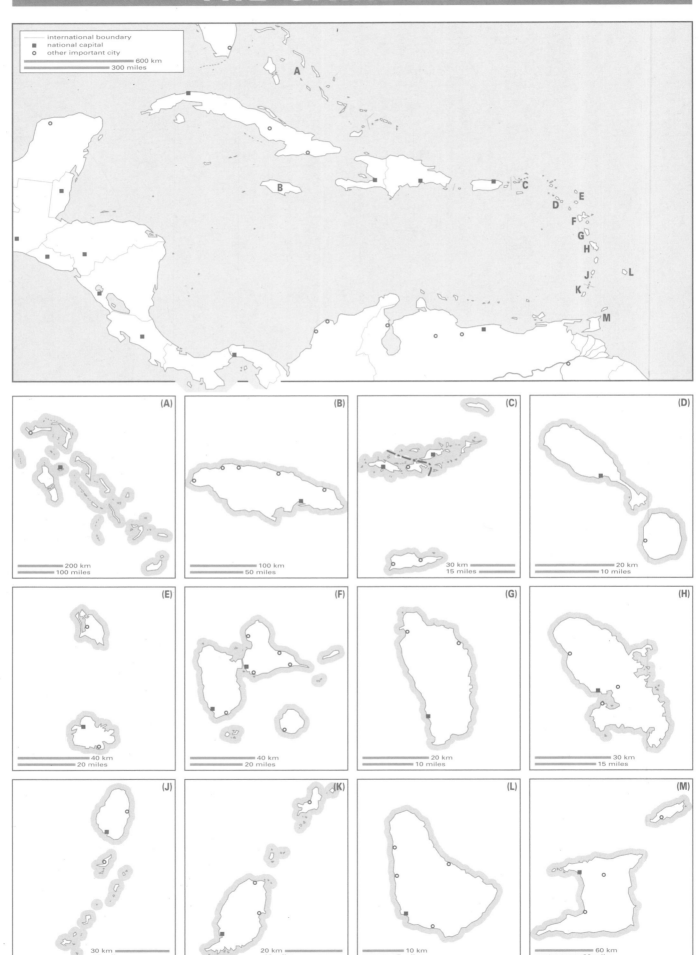